BUTTERWORTHS ROAD TRAFFIC HANDBOOK

Second Edition
1993

Edited by

MALCOLM MARSH

LLB, Solicitor

BUTTERWORTHS
LONDON, DUBLIN & EDINBURGH
1993

United Kingdom	Butterworth & Co (Publishers) Ltd, 88 Kingsway, LONDON WC2B 6AB and 4 Hill Street, EDINBURGH EH2 3JZ
Australia	Butterworths, SYDNEY, MELBOURNE, BRISBANE, ADELAIDE, PERTH, CANBERRA and HOBART
Belgium	Butterworth & Co (Publishers) Ltd, BRUSSELS
Canada	Butterworths Canada Ltd, TORONTO and VANCOUVER
Ireland	Butterworth (Ireland) Ltd, DUBLIN
Malaysia	Malayan Law Journal Sdn Bhd, KUALA LUMPUR
New Zealand	Butterworths of New Zealand Ltd, WELLINGTON and AUCKLAND
Puerto Rico	Equity de Puerto Rico, Inc, HATO REY
Singapore	Butterworths Asia, SINGAPORE
USA	Butterworths Legal Publishers, AUSTIN, Texas; BOSTON, Massachusetts; CLEARWATER, Florida (D & S Publishers); ORFORD, New Hampshire (Equity Publishing); ST PAUL, Minnesota; and SEATTLE, Washington

A CIP Catalogue record for this book is available from the British Library.

ISBN 0 406 02348 4

Typeset, printed and bound in Great Britain by
William Clowes Limited, Beccles and London

PREFACE

This is the second edition of this handbook. It contains the most important enactments relating to road traffic law in England, Wales and Scotland. It is also designed as the accompanying handbook for the Butterworths Road Traffic Service. Butterworths Road Traffic Service is in a looseleaf format and provides commentary on the main traffic offences created by the legislation. In this handbook the statutes are in chronological order and they are followed by statutory instruments in the same order. The main addition to the legislation since the first edition has been the Road Traffic Act 1991.

The remainder of the Preface provides an overview of the law as it stands at 31 December 1992. Chronological order does not provide a suitable basis for the overview and, consequently, the following headings will be used:

    i. the driver and driving standards;
    ii. vehicle construction and use;
    iii. driver licensing and vehicle registration;
    iv. traffic regulation;
    v. Scotland.

The driver and driving standards

For most drivers the Highway Code is a guide which will govern their behaviour behind the wheel of a car or the handlebars of a motor cycle; the new Code as published in January 1993 is contained in the appendices to the statutory instrument section of this work, as is fitting given that the Road Traffic Act 1988, s 38 establishes that the Code may be used in court when assessing driver behaviour.

Part I of the Road Traffic Act 1988 deals with the most serious lapses in driving behaviour, including offences relating to the impairment of driving by drink and drugs together with careless and dangerous driving. Offences relating to reckless driving have been replaced by similar offences relating to dangerous driving by the Road Traffic Act 1991 upon the recommendations contained in the North Committee Report on Road Traffic. A new offence of causing death through drunken driving has been introduced.

So much has been written about the drugs and alcohol provisions that the sections resist any reasonably concise summary. One small annoyance to persons researching the law for drink and driving offences is that evidential rules are separated from the substantive provisions and placed in the Road Traffic Offenders Act 1988, ss 16 and 17. Indeed for nearly all offences reference needs to be made to the Road Traffic Offenders Act 1988 for penalties and procedures.

The procedural provisions of the law relating to drink driving have led to much case law and some technical defences still remain. In addition there has been a great deal of case law relating to the consequences following conviction— in particular obligatory disqualification.

The prescribed limit for alcohol has remained constant since the introduction of breath-testing procedures in 1967, this despite recommendations that a lower level should be used. It seems likely that a Europe-wide prescribed limit, a limit much lower than that of Great Britain, will soon have to be considered.

Following the drink-drive provisions the Road Traffic Act 1988 deals with motor-racing on the highway and then protective measures relating to the wearing of seat belts and helmets. The safety theme is continued with provisions on parking and the use of bicycles.

Traffic directions, that is signals given by police and traffic wardens, and traffic signs, that is the prescribed diagrams and light signals we all learn for our driving tests, both trace their existence to the Road Traffic Regulation Act 1984 or its predecessor which deals with traffic control. However, the motorist's failure to comply with a direction or sign is penalised in ss 35 and 36 within Part I of the 1988 Act; the pedestrian failing to comply with a direction commits an offence under s 38.

One important, although specialised, aspect of driver behaviour is the hours driven by heavy goods vehicle drivers. Part VI of the Transport Act 1968 provides the framework for both domestic and EEC controls to operate.

Vehicle construction and use

Part II of the Road Traffic Act 1988 deals with vehicle construction and use in a manner which, compared to the complexity of the subject, appears quite concise; it does so by leaving the substance of the controls to regulations. The penalties for offences under the regulations are provided for in the Road Traffic Offenders Act 1988. The vehicle construction and use requirements are set out in the Pedal Cycles (Construction and Use) Regulations 1983, the Road Vehicle (Construction and Use) Regulations 1986 as amended and the Road Vehicle Lighting Regulations 1989. Compliance is ensured by the constructional requirements of the regulations (which may be satisfied by domestic or EEC-type approval arrangements), by periodic testing provided for in the Motor Vehicle (Test) Regulations 1981 (not printed in this work) and by penal provision under the Road Traffic Act 1988, s 42. There are some qualifications to this general pattern.

Certain loads and special purpose vehicles cannot be brought within the main requirement setting regulations even though those regulations make a range of provision and rarely set absolute standards for all vehicles. These "special types" vehicles are dealt with by rules which balance relaxation of many normal controls, such as weight and size, by imposing limitations by way of prescribed routes, a requirement for notice of route and special speed limits. The Motor Vehicles (Authorisation of Special Types) General Order 1979 as amended sets out the modifications; failure to comply with the Order robs the individual of the relaxation granted under the Order and renders the individual liable under the construction and use regulations.

Separate regulations cater for goods and public passenger vehicles. While the requirements for construction and use of goods vehicles are dealt with in the main regulations, testing is dealt with separately in the Goods Vehicles (Plating and Testing) Regulations 1988, as amended. Plating, it should be noted, is the process of marking maximum weights on goods vehicles; mostly these will be a manufacturer's plate issued pursuant to a type approval arrangement (goods vehicles have separate type approval regulations too) but if no manufacturer's plate is affixed a Ministry plate will be issued following tests under the 1988 regulations.

All the regulations cited above are contained in this handbook; they form the substance of construction and use control. Type approval regulations are principally of use to manufacturers and have not been included in this handbook. An equally small readership could be anticipated for the separate regulations relating to the construction and use of public passenger vehicles, community buses and minibuses; they have not been included.

Although the technical requirements of construction and use are amended many times each year the changes are usually minor and often, because of arrangements with the motor manufacturing industry, not operative for many months or even years. The basic scheme of the statute and statutory instruments is well established and unlikely to change.

Driver licensing and vehicle registration

The idea of driving as a licensed activity is probably quite alien to many people today who see freedom to drive as their right once they have passed a test; regrettably some people do not acknowledge the need for a test of competence either! In fact the Road Traffic Act 1988 Part III sets out the need to be licensed, the framework of the driving test system, the requirements as to fitness to drive and the minimum ages for different categories of motor vehicles. The Road Traffic Offenders Act 1988 completes the scheme by providing the main ways in which offending motorists can have their driving entitlements withdrawn by disqualification or placed at risk by endorsement.

The Motor Vehicles (Driving Licences) Regulations 1987, as amended, provide much of the detail of licensing and have recently been amended more closely to agree with the licensing arrangements of other EEC states. Among the more important regulations are reg 4 which provides for minimum ages, reg 9 which sets out the conditions attached to provisional licences and reg 25 which confers certain entitlements on persons taking up residence in Great Britain. Recognition of other driving entitlements is provided for in Part III of the Road Traffic Act 1988 and in the Motor Vehicles (International Circulation) Order 1975, as amended.

Vehicle registration enables the vehicle excise licensing system to function and provides a reference point for the programme of periodic vehicle testing; increasingly vehicle registration is being used to detect offences and to support the administration of the fixed penalty system. The Vehicles (Excise) Act 1971 is regularly amended in detail by Finance Acts but remains substantially unaltered since its introduction, a state of affairs which preserves much of the Act in a transitional state. The Act and the Road Vehicle (Registration and Licensing) Regulations 1971 establish the principle of taxing vehicles using or being kept on the public road and deal with the duty payable for different classes of vehicle, the periods for which it must be paid and provide for exemption.

Traffic regulation

The Road Traffic Regulation Act 1984 or one of its predecessors provides the legal basis for nearly all the features of our modern roads: speed limits, zebra crossings, traffic wardens, parking controls, one-way streets, motorways, etc. A number of major regulations need to be considered.

The Motorways Traffic (England and Wales) Regulations 1982 and the Motorway Traffic (Scotland) Regulations 1964 are almost identical but both are included in the handbook. Despite a significant increase in the mileage of motorway available in recent years there has been no change in these regulations since 1984. The same applies to the "Zebra" Pedestrian Crossings Regulations 1971 and the "Pelican" Pedestrian Crossings Regulations 1987 apart from amendments to the markings required; the obligations imposed on drivers and pedestrians are a seemingly permanent part of our way of life.

The Traffic Signs Regulations and General Directions 1981 are one of the more colourful statutory instruments as printed by Her Majesty's Stationery Office; consideration of cost and size has kept the large number of diagrams in these regulations beyond the scope of the handbook. However, the regulations and directions are themselves included, with reg 7 being particularly important as it lists the signs which, if disobeyed, may lead to prosecution and those which may lead to endorsement.

Traffic regulation of a rather different kind is effected by the control of transport operators contained in the Transport Act 1968 and public transport operators contained in the Public Passenger Vehicles Act 1981.

Scotland

All the statutory material printed applies to Scotland. Awaiting commencement in Scotland is the Road Traffic Offenders Act 1988, ss 27(4), 30 (except so far as it relates to ss 75–77), and Part III except ss 51, 52(1)–(3), 53, 62–78, 80, 81 and 83–90.

Certain parts of the Roads (Scotland) Act 1984 have been included for England and Wales.

All statutory instruments apart from the Motorway Traffic (England and Wales) Regulations 1982 extend to Scotland.

The contents of this handbook take into account materials available as at 31 December 1992, although some later material has been included where possible.

Malcolm Marsh
December 1992

CONTENTS

APPENDICES

Index

PART I
STATUTES

TRANSPORT ACT 1968
(c 73)

ARRANGEMENT OF SECTIONS

PART V
REGULATION OF CARRIAGE OF GOODS BY ROAD

The licensing authority

An Act to make further provision with respect to transport and related matters
[25 October 1968]

PART V

REGULATION OF CARRIAGE OF GOODS BY ROAD

The licensing authority

59. The licensing authority for Part V

[(1) The traffic commissioner for any traffic area constituted for the purposes of the Public Passenger Vehicles Act 1981 shall exercise the functions conferred on him by this Part of this Act and is in this Part of this Act referred to as "the licensing authority."]

(2) In the exercise of his functions under this Part of this Act ... the licensing authority shall act under the general directions of the Minister.

(3), (4) ...   **[1]**

NOTES
Commencement: 6 January 1986 (sub-s (1)); before 1 January 1970 (remainder).
Commencement order: SI 1985 No 1887.
Sub-s (1): substituted by the Transport Act 1985, s 3(4).
Sub-s (2): words omitted repealed by the Transport Act 1982, s 74, Sch 6.
Sub-s (3): repealed by the Transport Act 1985, s 139(3), Sch 8.
Sub-s (4): repealed by the Transport (London) Act 1969, s 47(2), Sch 6.

Operators' licences

60. Users of certain goods vehicles to hold operators' licences

(1) Subject to subsection (2) of this section and to the other provisions of this Part of this Act, no person shall, after the appointed day for the purposes of this section, use a goods vehicle on a road for the carriage of goods—

    (a) for hire or reward; or
    (b) for or in connection with any trade or business carried on by him,

except under a licence granted under this Part of this Act (hereafter in this Part of this Act referred to as an "operator's licence").

(2) Subsection (1) of this section shall not apply—

    (a) to the use of a small goods vehicle as defined in subsection (4) of this section; or

    (b) to the use of a vehicle of any class specified in regulations [; or

    (c) to the use of a goods vehicle for international carriage by a haulier established in a member State other than the United Kingdom and not established in the United Kingdom; or

    (d) to the use of a goods vehicle for international carriage by a haulier established in Northern Ireland and not established in Great Britain.]

(3) It is hereby declared that, for the purposes of this Part of this Act, the performance by a local or public authority of their functions constitutes the carrying on of a business.

(4) For the purposes of subsection (2)(a) of this section a small goods vehicle is a goods vehicle which—

    (a) does not form part of a vehicle combination and has a relevant plated weight not exceeding [3.5 tonnes] or (not having a relevant plated weight) has an unladen weight not exceeding [1525 kilograms]; or

    (b) forms part of a vehicle combination (not being an articulated combination) which is such that—

        (i) if all the vehicles comprised in the combination (or all of them except any small trailer) have relevant plated weights, the aggregate of the relevant plated weights of the vehicles comprised in the combination (exclusive of any such trailer) does not exceed [3.5 tonnes];

        (ii) in any other case, the aggregate of the unladen weights of those vehicles (exclusive of any such trailer) does not exceed [1525 kilograms]; or

    (c) forms part of an articulated combination which is such that—

        (i) if the trailer comprised in the combination has a relevant plated weight, the aggregate of the unladen weight of the motor vehicle comprised in the combination and the relevant plated weight of that trailer does not exceed [3.5 tonnes];

        (ii) in any other case, the aggregate of the unladen weights of the motor vehicle and the trailer comprised in the combination does not exceed [1525 kilograms].

In any provision of this subsection "relevant plated weight" means a plated weight of the description specified in relation to that provision by regulations; and in paragraph (b) of this subsection "small trailer" means a trailer having an unladen weight not exceeding [1020 kilograms].

[(4A) In subsection (2)(c) and (d) of this section "established", "haulier" and "international carriage" have the same meaning as in Council Regulation (EEC) No 881/92 of 26th March 1992 on access to the market in the carriage of goods by road within the Community to or from the territory of a member State or passing across the territory of one or more member States;]

(5) A person who uses a vehicle in contravention of this section shall be liable on summary conviction to a fine not exceeding [level 4 on the standard scale]. **[2]**

NOTES

    Commencement: Before 1 January 1970-1 March 1971 (except sub-s (4A)): 1 January 1993 (sub-s (4A)).

    Commencement orders: SI 1969 No 1613, 1970 No 1631.

    Sub-s (2): words in square brackets inserted by the Goods Vehicles (Community Authorisations) Regulations 1992, SI 1992 No 3077, reg 14(1), (2).

Sub-s (4): regulations, see the Goods Vehicles (Operators' Licences, Qualifications and Fees) Regulations 1984, post.

Sub-s 4: amended by the Goods Vehicles (Operators Licences) Regulations 1977, SI 1977 No 1737, and the Road Traffic Acts 1960 and 1972, Road Traffic Regulation Act 1967, and Transport Act 1968 (Metrication) Regulations 1981, SI 1981 No 1373 and Transport Act 1968 (Metrication) (Amendment) Regulations 1984, SI 1984 No 177.

Sub-s (4A): inserted by the Goods Vehicles (Community Authorisations) Regulations 1992, SI 1992 No 3077, reg 14(1), (3).

Sub-s (5): maximum fine increased and converted to a level on the standard scale by the Criminal Justice Act 1982, ss 37, 38, 46, as amended.

61. Authorised vehicles

(1) Subject to subsection (2) of this section, the vehicles authorised to be used under an operator's licence shall be—

(a) such motor vehicles, being vehicles belonging to the holder of the licence or in his possession under an agreement for hire-purchase, hire or loan, as are specified in the licence;

(b) trailers from time to time belonging to the holder of the licence or in his possession under an agreement for hire-purchase, hire or loan, not exceeding at any time such maximum number as is specified in the licence;

(c) unless the licence does not permit the addition of authorised vehicles under this paragraph and subject to subsection (3) of this section, motor vehicles not exceeding such maximum number as is specified in the licence, being vehicles belonging to the holder of the licence or in his possession under an agreement for hire-purchase, hire or loan, but acquired by him, or coming into his possession, under such an agreement, only after the grant of the licence.

For the purposes of paragraphs (b) and (c) of this subsection different types of trailers or different types of motor vehicles, as the case may be, may be distinguished in a licence and a maximum number may be specified in the licence for trailers or vehicles of each type.

(2) An operator's licence shall not authorise the use of any vehicle unless the place which is for the time being its operating centre—

(a) is in the area of the licensing authority by whom the licence was granted; or

(b) is outside that area and has not been the operating centre of that vehicle for a period of more than three months.

For the purposes of paragraph (b) of this subsection, two or more successive periods which are not separated from each other by an interval of at least three months shall be treated as a single period having a duration equal to the total duration of those periods.

(3) A motor vehicle which, after the grant of an operator's licence, is acquired by the holder of the licence, or comes into his possession under an agreement for hire-purchase, hire or loan, and thereupon becomes an authorised vehicle by virtue of subsection (1)(c) of this section, shall cease to be an authorised vehicle on the expiration of one month from the date on which it was acquired by him or came into his possession unless before the expiration of that period he delivers to the licensing authority a notice in such form as the authority may require to the effect that the vehicle has been acquired by him, or has come into his possession, as the case may be.

(4) Where the licensing authority by whom a licence was granted receives a notice under subsection (3) of this section to the effect that the holder of the

licence has acquired, or come into possession of, a vehicle as mentioned in that subsection, he shall, if the vehicle has become an authorised vehicle by virtue of subsection (1)(c) of this section, vary the licence by directing that the vehicle be specified therein.

(5) A motor vehicle specified in an operator's licence shall not, while it remains so specified, be capable of being effectively specified in any other operator's licence.

(6) Where it comes to the knowledge of the licensing authority by whom an operator's licence was granted that a vehicle specified therein—

(a) has ceased to be used under the licence (otherwise than because of a fluctuation in business or because it is undergoing repair or maintenance); or

(b) is specified in another operator's licence,

he may vary the licence by directing that the vehicle be removed therefrom. [3]

62. Applications for operators' licences

(1) A person may apply for an operator's licence to the licensing authority for each area in which, if the licence is granted, the applicant will have an operating centre or operating centres; and a person may hold separate operators' licences in respect of different areas but shall not at any time hold more than one such licence in respect of the same area.

(2) A person applying for an operator's licence shall give to the licensing authority a statement giving such particulars as the authority may require of the motor vehicles proposed to be used under the licence which—

(a) belong to the applicant, or

(b) are in his possession under an agreement for hire-purchase, hire or loan, or

(c) he intends, if the application is granted, to acquire, or to obtain possession of under such an agreement,

and also stating the number and type of any trailers proposed to be so used.

(3) . . .

(4) A person applying for an operator's licence shall give to the licensing authority any further information which he may reasonably require for the discharge of his duties in relation to the application, and in particular shall, if he is required by the licensing authority so to do, give to him—

(a) such particulars as he may require with respect to the purposes for which the vehicles referred to in the statement under subsection (2) of this section are proposed to be used;

(b) particulars of the arrangements for securing that Part VI of this Act (or, so long as those sections remain in force, sections 73 and 186 of the Act of 1960) will be complied with in the case of those vehicles, and for securing that those vehicles are not overloaded;

(c) particulars of the facilities and arrangements for securing that those vehicles will be maintained in a fit and serviceable condition;

(d) particulars of any activities carried on, at any time before the making of the application, by—

(i) the applicant,

(ii) any company of which the applicant is or has been a director;

(iii) where the applicant is a company, any person who is a director of the company;

(iv) where the applicant proposes to operate the said vehicles in partnership with other persons, any of those other persons;

(v) any company of which any such person as is mentioned in sub-paragraph (iii) or (iv) of this paragraph is or has been a director;

(vi) any company of which the applicant is a subsidiary,

being activities in carrying on any trade or business in the course of which vehicles of any description are operated, or as a person employed for the purposes of any such trade or business, or as a director of a company carrying on any such trade or business;

(e) particulars of any convictions during the five years preceding the making of the application—

(i) of the applicant; and

(ii) of any other person as to whose activities particulars may be required to be given under paragraph (d) of this subsection,

being convictions such as are mentioned in subsection (4) of section 69 of this Act (taking references in that subsection to the holder of the licence as references to the applicant or, as the case may be, to that other person);

(f) particulars of the financial resources which are or are likely to be available to the applicant;

(g) where the applicant is a company, the names of the directors and officers of the company, and of any company of which the first-mentioned company is a subsidiary, and where the authorised vehicles are proposed to be operated by the applicant in partnership with other persons, the names of those other persons.

[(4A) A person who has applied for an operator's licence shall forthwith notify the licensing authority if, in the interval between the making of the application and the date on which it is disposed of, a conviction occurs which, if the period of five years specified in paragraph (e) of subsection (4) of this section had not expired, would be a conviction falling within that paragraph; and for the purposes of this subsection an application shall be taken to be disposed of,—

(a) if the licensing authority is required, by virtue of regulations under section 91 of this Act, to cause a statement containing his decision on the application to be issued, on the date on which that statement is issued, and

(b) in any other case, on the date on which the applicant receives notice from the licensing authority of his decision on the application.

(4B) A person who knowingly fails to comply with subsection (4A) of this section shall be liable on summary conviction to a fine not exceeding [level 4 on the standard scale], and [section 6 of the Road Traffic Offenders Act 1988] (time for bringing summary proceedings for certain offences) shall apply in relation to an offence under this subsection as it applies in relation to the offences [under the Road Traffic Act 1988 or the Road Traffic Offenders Act 1988] to which it is applied by virtue of [Schedule 1 to the Road Traffic Offenders Act 1988]].

(5) Any statement or information to be given to a licensing authority under this section shall be given in such form as the authority may require.   **[4]**

NOTES

Commencement: 1 January 1975 (sub-ss (4A), (4B)); before 1 January 1970–1 March 1971 (remainder).

Commencement orders: SI 1969 No 1613, 1970 No 1631.

Sub-s (3): repealed by the Transport Act 1982, s 74(2), Sch 6.

Sub-s (4A): added by the Road Traffic Act 1974, s 16, Sch 4, para 1.

Sub-s (4B): added by the Road Traffic Act 1974, s 16, Sch 4, para 1; maximum fine increased and converted to a level on the standard scale by the Criminal Justice Act 1982, ss 37, 38, 46, as amended; other words in square brackets substituted by the Road Traffic (Consequential Provisions) Act 1988, s 4, Sch 3, para 6(1).
Act of 1960: Road Traffic Act 1960.

63. Objections to grant of operators' licences

(1) ... the licensing authority shall publish in the prescribed manner notice of any application to the authority for an operators' licence.

(2) ...

(3) Any of the following persons, that is to say—

    (a) a prescribed trade union or association, being a trade union or association whose members consist of or include—

        (i) persons holding operators' licences or carriers' licences; or
        (ii) employees of any such persons;

    (b) a chief officer of police;
    (c) a local authority,
    [(d) a planning authority,]

may object to the grant of any application [for an operator's licence] on the ground that any of the requirements mentioned in section 64(2) of this Act are not satisfied in the case of the application.

(4) Any objection under this section shall be made within the prescribed time and in the prescribed manner (which shall be stated in the notice published under subsection (1) of this section) and shall contain particulars of the ground on which it is made.

(5) The onus of proof of the existence of the ground on which an objection is made shall lie on the objector.

(6) In this section—

"local authority" means—
    (a) as respects England and Wales, the council of a county, ..., county district or London borough, ... and the Common Council of the City of London;
    (b) ...
["planning authority" means any body other than a local authority which by virtue of any statutory provision for the time being in force is—
    (a) in England and Wales, the local planning authority for any area for the purpose of determining applications for planning permission under [Part III of the Town and Country Planning Act 1990] (general planning control); and
    (b) in Scotland, the planning authority for any area for the purpose of determining applications for planning permission under Part III of the Town and Country Planning (Scotland) Act 1972 (general planning control):
"statutory provision" means a provision contained in an Act or in subordinate legislation within the meaning of the Interpretation Act 1978; and]
"trade union" has the same meaning as in [the Trade Union and Labour Relations (Consolidation) Act 1992].   **[5]**

NOTES
Commencement: Before 1 January 1970-1 March 1971.
Commencement orders: SI 1969 No 1613, SI 1970 No 1631.
Sub-ss (1), (2): words omitted repealed by the Transport Act 1982, ss 52, 74, Sch 4, Part II, Sch 6.

Sub-s (3): amended by the Transport Act 1982, s 52, Sch 4, Part II.

Sub-s (6): first words omitted in definition "local authority" repealed by the Local Government Act 1972, s 272(1), Sch 30, second words omitted repealed by the Local Government Act 1985, s 102, Sch 17; third words omitted apply to Scotland only; definition "planning authority" added by the Transport Act 1982, s 52, Sch 4, Part II, para 8, words in square brackets therein substituted with savings by the Planning (Consequential Provisions) Act 1990, s 4, Sch 2, para 22(1), for savings see s 5, Sch 3, para 3 thereof; definition "statutory provision" added by the Transport Act 1982, s 52, Sch 4, Part II, para 8; words in square brackets in definition "trade union" substituted by the Trade Union and Labour Relations (Consolidation) Act 1992, s 300(2), Sch 2, para 2.

64. Decision on applications for operators' licences

(1) [Subject to section 69E of this Act] on an application for an operator's licence, the licensing authority shall in every case consider whether the requirements mentioned in paragraphs (a) to (d) of subsection (2) of this section, and, if the licensing authority in any case thinks fit, paragraph (e) of that subsection, are satisfied, and in doing so shall have regard to any objection duly made under section 63 of this Act.

(2) The said requirements are as follows—

    (a) that the applicant is a fit person to hold an operator's licence, having regard to the matters of which particulars may be required to be given under section 62(4)(d) and (e) of this Act [and to any conviction required to be notified in accordance with section 62(4A) thereof];

    (b) . . .

    (c) that there will be satisfactory arrangements for securing that Part VI of this Act (or, so long as those sections remain in force, sections 73 and 186 of the Act of 1960) will be complied with in the case of the authorised vehicles, and for securing that those vehicles are not overloaded;

    (d) that there will be satisfactory facilities and arrangements for maintaining the authorised vehicles in a fit and serviceable condition [and that the place which is to be the operating centre for those vehicles is suitable for that purpose];

    (e) that the provision of such facilities and arrangements as are mentioned in paragraph (d) of this subsection [and of a suitable operating centre] will not be prejudiced by reason of the applicant's having insufficient financial resources for that purpose.

(3) If the licensing authority determines that any requirement which he has taken into consideration in accordance with subsection (1) of this section is not satisfied, he shall refuse the application but, in any other case, he shall, subject to subsection (4) of this section, [and section 69B of this Act] grant the application.

(4) In any case in which the licensing authority grants an application for an operator's licence, the licensing authority may issue that licence in the terms applied for or, if the authority thinks fit, subject to either or both of the following modifications or limitations, that is to say—

    (a) so that the licence is in respect of motor vehicles other than those of which particulars were contained in the application, or in respect of motor vehicles or trailers greater or less in number than, or differing in type from, those for the use of which authorisation was applied for;

    (b) so that the licence does not permit the addition of authorised vehicles under section 61(1)(c) of this Act.

(5) In exercising his functions under this section in relation to the requirement mentioned in subsection (2)(e) thereof, a licensing authority may be assisted by an assessor drawn from a panel of persons appointed by the

Minister for that purpose; and there shall be paid by the licensing authority to any such assessor in respect of his services remuneration on a scale prescribed by the Minister with the approval of the Treasury.   [6]

NOTES
 Commencement: Before 1 January 1970-1 March 1971.
 Commencement orders: SI 1969 No 1613, 1970 No 259, 1970 No 1631.
 Sub-ss (1), (3): amended by the Transport Act 1982, s 52, Sch 4, Part II, para 2.
 Sub-s (2): amendments in square brackets made by the Road Traffic Act 1974, s 16, Sch 4, para 2; words omitted repealed by the Transport Act 1982, s 74, Sch 6.
 Act of 1960: Road Traffic Act 1960.

65. (*Repealed by the Transport Act 1982, s 74, Sch 5, para (6), Sch 6.*)

66. Conditions as to matters required to be notified to licensing authority

(1) A licensing authority, in granting an operator's licence, may attach thereto such conditions as he thinks fit for requiring the holder to inform him—

(a) of any change, of a kind specified in the conditions, in the organisation, management or ownership of the trade or business in the course of which the authorised vehicles are used;

(b) where the holder of the licence is a company, of any change, or of any change of a kind so specified, in the persons holding shares in the company;

(c) of any other event of a kind so specified affecting the holder of the licence which is relevant to the exercise of any powers of the authority in relation to the licence.

(2) Any person who contravenes any condition attached under this section to a licence of which he is the holder shall be liable on summary conviction to a fine not exceeding [level 4 on the standard scale].   [7]

NOTES
 Commencement: Before 1 January 1970-1 March 1971.
 Commencement orders: SI 1969 No 1613, 1970 No 1631.
 Sub-s (2): maximum fine increased and converted to a level on the standard scale by the Criminal Justice Act 1982, ss 37, 38, 46 as amended.

67. Duration of operators' licences and grant of interim licences

(1) There shall be specified in every operator's licence the date on which the licence is to come into force.

(2) Regulations may specify the dates in the year on which operators' licences shall expire, and, subject to subsections (4) and (5) of this section, an operator's licence shall, unless previously revoked, [or prematurely terminated under s 69 of this Act] continue in force up till and including that one of the specified dates which occurs next before the expiration of the period of five years beginning with the date on which the licence came into force, or of such other period beginning with that date as the licensing authority may in accordance with the next following subsection direct.

(3) The licensing authority may, on granting an operator's licence, direct that in the case of that licence the period relevant for the purposes of subsection (2) of this section—

(a) shall be a period shorter than five years [if it appears to the licensing authority to be appropriate in the case of any applicant];

(b) shall be a period longer or shorter than five years if the licensing authority is of opinion that it is desirable so to direct in order to arrange a suitable and convenient programme of work for the licensing authority.

(4) If, at the date on which an operator's licence is due to expire, proceedings are pending before the licensing authority on an application by the holder of that licence for the grant to him of a new licence in substitution therefor, the existing licence shall continue in force until—

(a) the application; and

(b) any appeal under section 70 of this Act arising out of the application,

are disposed of, without prejudice, however, to the exercise in the meantime of the powers conferred by section 69 of this Act.

(5) If an applicant for an operator's licence so requests, a licensing authority may, if the applicant does not hold an operator's licence granted by that authority, grant to him, pending the determination of the application, an operator's licence expressed to continue in force until the date on which any licence granted on the application or on an appeal arising out of it is expressed to come into force or, if no licence is granted as aforesaid, until the application is refused; and a request for the grant of a licence under this subsection shall not for the purposes of section 63 or [subsections (1) to (3) of section] 64 of this Act be treated as an application for an operator's licence [but shall be so treated for the purposes of section 64(4) of this Act], ... **[8]**

NOTES

Commencement: Before 1 January 1970-1 March 1971.
Commencement orders: SI 1969 No 1613, 1970 No 1631.
Sub-ss (2), (3): amended by the Road Traffic Act 1974, s 16, Sch 4, para 3.
Sub-s (5): amendments in square brackets made by the Road Traffic Act 1974, s 16, Sch 4, para 3; words omitted repealed by the Transport Act 1982, s 74, Sch 6.

68. Variation of operators' licences

(1) [Subject to section 69E of this Act] on the application of the holder of an operator's licence, the licensing authority by whom the licence was granted may at any time while it is in force vary the licence by directing—

(a) that additional vehicles be specified therein, that the maximum number of trailers or of motor vehicles specified therein under paragraph (b) or (c) of section 61(1) of this Act be increased, or, if the licence does not permit the addition of authorised vehicles under the said paragraph (c), that it shall so permit and that a maximum be specified under that paragraph accordingly; or

(b) that vehicles specified therein be removed therefrom or that any such maximum as is mentioned in paragraph (a) of this subsection be reduced; or

[(c) that an alteration or addition be made in or to any of the matters specified for the purposes of the Goods Vehicles (Operators' Licences, Qualifications and Fees) Regulations 1984 in a standard licence as defined in Regulation 3(2) of those Regulations]

(d) that an alteration be made in any condition attached to the licence under section 66 of this Act or that any such condition be removed;

[or (e) that a restricted licence as defined in Regulation 3(2) of the said Regulations of 1984 be converted into a standard licence as defined in that Regulation, or vice versa].

(2) A person applying for a direction under this section shall give to the licensing authority such information as he may reasonably require for the discharge of his duties in relation to the application.

(3) Any information or particulars to be given to a licensing authority under subsection (2) of this section shall be given in such form as the authority may require.

(4) Except in the following cases, that is to say—

(a) ...

(b) where the application is for a direction under subsection (1)(b) of this section; or

[(*bb*) where an application is for a direction as referred to in subsection (1)(c) or (e) of this section; or]

(c) where the licensing authority is satisfied that the application is of so trivial a nature that it is not necessary that an opportunity should be given for objecting to it,

the licensing authority shall publish notice of any application under this section in the manner provided for the publication of notices under subsection (1) of [section 63 of this Act]; and where notice of the application is published in pursuance of this subsection the other provisions of the said section 63 and the provisions of section 64 of this Act shall, so far as applicable and subject to any necessary modifications, apply to that application as they apply to an application for the grant of an operator's licence of which notice is published under subsection (1) of the said section 63.

(5) If an applicant under this section so requests, the licensing authority may, pending the determination of the application, give an interim direction under this section, that is to say, a direction expressed to continue in force only until the application, and any appeal arising out of it, have been disposed of; and a request for such a direction shall not for the purposes of subsection (4) of this section be treated as an application under this section.   **[9]**

NOTES
  Commencement: Before 1 January 1970-1 March 1971.
  Commencement orders: SI 1969 No 1613, 1969 No 1631.
  Sub-s (1): first amendment in square brackets made by the Transport Act 1982, s 52, Sch 4, Part II, para 3; para (c) substituted by the Goods Vehicles (Operators' Licences, Qualifications and Fees) Regulations 1984, SI 1984 No 176, reg 36(2); para (e) added by SI 1977 No 1462, repealed and new para (e) substituted by SI 1984 No 176, regs 2, 36(2), Sch 2.
  Sub-s (4): sub-para (*bb*) added by SI 1984 No 176, reg 36(2A); other amendments made by the Transport Act 1982, ss 52, 74, Sch 4, Part II, para 3, Sch 6.

69. Revocation, suspension and curtailment of operators' licences

(1) Subject to the provisions of this section, the licensing authority by whom an operator's licence was granted may direct that it be revoked, suspended, [terminated on a date earlier than that on which it would otherwise expire under section 67 of this Act] or curtailed on any of the following grounds—

(a) that the holder of the licence has contravened ... any condition attached to his licence under section 66 of this Act;

(b) that during the five years ending with the date on which the direction is given there has been (whether before or after the day on which this section comes into force)—

  (i) any such conviction as is mentioned in [paragraphs (a) to (*ffff*)] of subsection (4) of this section or any such prohibition as is mentioned in paragraph (h) of that subsection; or

  (ii) any such conviction as is mentioned in paragraph (g) of that subsection on occasions appearing to the licensing authority to be sufficiently numerous to justify the giving of a direction under this subsection;

(c) that the holder of the licence made or procured to be made for the purposes of his application for the licence, or for the purposes of an application for the variation of the licence, a statement of fact which (whether to his knowledge or not) was false, or a statement of intention or expectation which has not been fulfilled;

(d) that the holder of the licence has been adjudicated bankrupt or, where the holder is a company, has gone into liquidation (not being a voluntary liquidation for the purpose of reconstruction);

(e) that there has been since the licence was granted or varied a material change in any of the circumstances of the holder of the licence which were relevant to the grant or variation of his licence;

(f) that the licence is liable to revocation, suspension, [premature termination] or curtailment by virtue of a direction under subsection (6) of this section;

and during any time of suspension the licence shall be of no effect.

(2) In any case in which a licensing authority has power to give a direction under the foregoing subsection in respect of any licence, the authority shall also have power to direct that there be attached to the licence any, or any additional, condition such as is mentioned in section 66 of this Act.

(3) Where the existence of any of the grounds mentioned in subsection (1) of this section is brought to the notice of the licensing authority in the case of the holder of any licence granted by him, the authority shall consider whether or not to give a direction under this section in respect of that licence.

[(3A) Where the ground mentioned in subsection (1) of this section consists of a conviction mentioned in paragraph (*ff*) of subsection (4) of this section and there has been, within the 5 years preceding that conviction a previous conviction of the holder of the licence of the offence referred to in that paragraph, the licensing authority shall give a direction under this section to revoke the licence.]

(4) The convictions and prohibitions mentioned in subsection (1)(b) of this section are as follows—

(a) a conviction, in relation to a goods vehicle, of the holder of the licence, or a servant or agent of his [of an offence under section 46 of the Road Traffic Act 1972 [or section 53 of the Road Traffic Act 1988] (plating certificates and goods vehicle test certificates) or], of contravening any provision (however expressed) contained in or having effect under any enactment (including any enactment passed after this Act) relating to—

(i) the maintenance of vehicles in a fit and serviceable condition;

(ii) limits of speed and weight laden and unladen, and the loading of goods vehicles;

(iii) the licensing of drivers;

(b) a conviction of the holder of the licence under—

(i) this Part of this Act . . . ;

(ii) section 233 or 235 of the Act of 1960 so far as applicable (by virtue of Schedule 10 to this Act) to licences, authorisations or means of identification under this Part of this Act . . . ;

(iii) any regulation made under this Act which is prescribed for the purposes of this subsection;

(c) a conviction, in relation to a goods vehicle, of the holder of the licence or a servant or agent of his under, or of conspiracy to contravene, Part VI of this Act or section 73 or 186 of the Act of 1960;

(d) . . . ;

(e) a conviction, in relation to a goods vehicle, of the holder of the licence under, or of conspiracy to contravene, section 200 of the Customs and Excise Act 1952, [section 11 of the Hydrocarbon Oil (Customs and

Excise) Act 1971 or section 13 of the Hydrocarbon Oil Duties Act 1979] (unlawful use of rebated fuel oil);

[(*ee*) a conviction of the holder of the licence or a servant or agent of his of a contravention, in relation to an international road haulage permit, within the meaning of [the Road Traffic Act 1988, of section 169 or 170 of the Road Traffic Act 1972 or of section 173 or 174 of the Road Traffic Act 1988];

(*eee*) a conviction of the holder of the licence or a servant or agent of his under section 2 of the International Road Haulage Permits Act 1975];

(f) a conviction of the holder of the licence under section 18 of the Road Safety Act 1967 [or section 59 of the Road Traffic Act 1972] [or section 74 of the Road Traffic Act 1988] (operator's duty to inspect, and keep records of inspection of, goods vehicles);

[(*ff*) a conviction of the holder of a licence of an offence under Regulation 33(2) of the Goods Vehicles (Operators' Licences, Qualifications and Fees) Regulations 1984;

(*fff*) a conviction of the holder of the licence of an offence under Regulation 33(3) of the said Regulations of 1984;]

[(*ffff*) a conviction of the holder of the licence or a servant or agent of his under—

    (i) section 3 of the Control of Pollution Act 1974;
    (ii) section 2 of the Refuse Disposal (Amenity) Act 1978;
    (iii) section 1 of the Control of Pollution (Amendment) Act 1989, and
    (iv) section 33 of the Environmental Protection Act 1990.]

(g) a conviction, in relation to a goods vehicle, of the holder of the licence, or a servant or agent of his, of contravening

    [(i)] any provision (however expressed) which prohibits or restricts the waiting of vehicles, being a provision contained in an order made under section 1, 6, 9 or [12 of the Road Traffic Regulation Act 1984 (including any such order made by virtue of paragraph 3 of Schedule 9 to that Act) or under any enactment repealed by that Act and re-enacted by virtue of section 84A (2) of the Road Traffic Regulation Act 1967);] [or

    (ii) any provision included in a traffic regulation order, within the meaning of section 1 of that Act, by virtue of [section 2(4) of the Road Traffic Regulation Act 1984 (lorry routes) or section 1(3AA) of the Road Traffic Regulation Act 1967]].

(h) a prohibition of the use of a vehicle under section 184 of the Act of 1960 or of the driving of a vehicle under section 16 of the Road Safety Act 1967 [or section 57 of the Road Traffic Act 1972] [or section 69 or 70 of the Road Traffic Act 1988], being a vehicle of which the holder of the licence was the owner when the prohibition was imposed.

(5) Where the licensing authority directs that an operator's licence be revoked, the authority may order the person who was the holder thereof to be disqualified, indefinitely or for such period as the authority thinks fit, from holding or obtaining an operator's licence, and so long as the disqualification is in force—

(a) notwithstanding anything in section 64 of this Act, no operator's licence shall be granted to him and any operator's licence obtained by him shall be of no effect; and

(b) if he applies for or obtains an operator's licence he shall be liable on summary conviction to a fine not exceeding [level 4 on the standard scale].

An order under this subsection may be limited so as to apply only to the holding or obtaining of an operator's licence in respect of the area of one or more specified licensing authorities and, if the order is so limited, paragraphs (a) and (b) of this subsection shall apply only to any operator's licence to which the order applies; but, notwithstanding section 61(2)(b) of this Act, no other operator's licence held by the person in question shall authorise the use by him of any vehicle at a time when its operating centre is in an area in respect of which he is disqualified by virtue of the order.

(6) Where the licensing authority makes an order under subsection (5) of this section in respect of any person, the authority may direct that if that person, at any time or during such period as the authority may specify—

    (a) is a director of, or holds a controlling interest in—

        (i) a company which holds a licence of the kind to which the order in question applies; or

        (ii) a company of which such a company as aforesaid is a subsidiary; or

    (b) operates any goods vehicles in partnership with a person who holds such a licence,

that licence of that company, or, as the case may be, of that person, shall be liable to revocation, suspension, [premature termination] or curtailment under this section.

(7) The powers conferred by subsections (5) and (6) of this section in relation to the person who was the holder of a licence shall be exercisable also, where that person was a company, in relation to any director of that company, and, where that person operated the authorised vehicles in partnership with other persons, in relation to any of those other persons.

[(7A) Where a licensing authority directs that an operator's licence be suspended or curtailed, the authority may order that—

    (a) in the case of a suspension, any motor vehicle specified in the licence may not be used under any other operator's licence, notwithstanding any authorisation under section 61(1)(c) of this Act, or

    (b) in the case of a curtailment having the effect of removing any motor vehicle from the licence, the motor vehicle may not be used as mentioned in paragraph (a) above and shall not be capable of being effectively specified in any other operator's licence,

and an order made under this subsection shall cease to have effect on such date, not being more than 6 months after the order is made, as may be specified therein or, if it is earlier, on the date on which the licence which is directed to be suspended or curtailed ceases to be in force.]

(8) A licensing authority who has made an order or given a direction under subsection (5), (6), [(7) or (7A)] of this section may, in such circumstances as may be prescribed, cancel that order or direction.

(9) A licensing authority shall not—

    (a) give a direction under subsection (1) or (2) of this section in respect of any licence; or

    (b) make an order or give a direction under subsection (5), (6) or (7) of this section in respect of any person, [or

    (c) make an order under subsection (7A) of this section in respect of any vehicle] without first holding an inquiry if the holder of the licence or that person, as the case may be, requests him to do so.

(10) The licensing authority may direct that any direction or order given or made by him under subsection (1), (2), (5), (6), [(7) or (7A)] of this section shall not take effect until the expiration of the time within which an appeal may be made to the Transport Tribunal against the direction or order and, if such an appeal is made, until the appeal has been disposed of; and if the licensing authority refuses to give a direction under this subsection the holder of the licence, or, as the case may be, the person in respect of whom the direction or order was given or made under any of those subsections, may apply to the tribunal for such a direction, and the tribunal shall give its decision on the application within fourteen days.

(11) For the purposes of this section a person holds a controlling interest in a company if he is the beneficial owner of more than half its equity share capital as defined in [section 744 of the Companies Act 1985].   **[10]**

NOTES
Commencement: 1 June 1984 (para (3A)); 1 January 1975 (sub-s (7A)); before 1 January 1970-1 March 1971 (remainder).
Commencement orders: SI 1969 No 1613, 1970 No 1631.
Sub-s (1): first and final amendments in square brackets made by the Road Traffic Act 1974, s 16, Sch 4, para 4; words omitted in para (a) repealed by the Transport Act 1982, s 74, Sch 6; words in square brackets in para (b) substituted by the Environmental Protection Act 1990, s 162(1), Sch 15, para 10(1), (2)(a) ; para (f) amended by the Road Traffic Act 1974, s 16, Sch 4, para 4.
Sub-s (3A): added by SI 1984 No 176, regs 2, 36(3), Sch 2.
Sub-s (4): para (a), amended by the Road Traffic Act 1974, s 16, Sch 4, para 4, further amended by the Road Traffic (Consequential Provisions) Act 1988, s 4, Sch 3, para 6(2); words omitted in para (b) repealed by the Transport Act 1982, s 74, Sch 6; para (d) repealed by the Employment Act 1980, s 20(3), Sch 2; para (e) amended by the Hydrocarbon Oil Duties Act 1979, s 28(1), Sch 6, para 2; paras (ee), (eee) added by the International Road Haulage Permits Act 1975, s 3(1), in para (ee) words in square brackets substituted by the Road Traffic (Consequential Provisions) Act 1988, s 4, Sch 3, para 6(2); in paras (f), (h), first amendment in square brackets made by the Road Traffic Act 1972, s 203(1), Sch 7, second amendment in square brackets made by the Road Traffic (Consequential Provisions) Act 1988, s 4, Sch 3, para 6(2); paras (ff), (fff) added by SI 1977 No 1462, reg 3(9), repealed, and new paras (ff), (fff) substituted by SI 1984 No 176, regs 2, 36(3), Sch 2; para (ffff) inserted by the Environmental Protection Act 1990, s 162(1), Sch 15, para 10(1), (2)(b); in para (g) first and third amendments made by the Road Traffic Act 1974 s 16, Sch 4, other amendments made by the Road Traffic Regulation Act 1984, s 146, Sch 13.
Sub-s (5): maximum fine in para (b) increased and converted to a level on the standard scale by the Criminal Justice Act 1982, ss 37, 38, 46 as amended.
Sub-ss (6), (8)-(10): amended by the Road Traffic Act 1974, s 16, Sch 4, para 4.
Sub-s (7A): added by the Road Traffic Act 1974, s 16, Sch 4, para 4.
Sub-s (11): amended by the Companies Consolidation (Consequential Provisions) Act 1985, s 30, Sch 2.
Modified by the Goods Vehicles (Operators' Licences, Qualifications and Fees) Regulations 1984, SI 1984 No 176, reg 32, Sch 4.
Act of 1960: Road Traffic Act 1960.

Control of operating centres for goods vehicles on environmental grounds

[69A. Operating centres for authorised vehicles to be specified in operators' licences

(1) A person may not use a place in the area of any licensing authority as an operating centre for authorised vehicles under any operator's licence granted to him by that authority unless it is specified in that licence.

(2) A person applying for an operator's licence shall give to the licensing authority a statement giving such particulars as the authority may require of each place in the area of the authority which will be an operating centre of the applicant in the licence is granted.

(3) Without prejudice to section 62(4) of this Act, a person applying for an operator's licence shall also, if he is required by the licensing authority so to do, give to him such particulars as he may require with respect to the use which the applicant proposes to make, for authorised vehicles under the licence, of any place referred to in the statement under subsection (2) of this section.

(4) Any person who contravenes subsection (1) of this section shall be liable on summary conviction to a fine not exceeding [level 4 on the standard scale].]

[11]

NOTES

Commencement: 1 June 1984.
Commencement order: SI 1984 No 175.
Added by the Transport Act 1982, s 52(2), Sch 4, Part I.
Sub-s (4): maximum fine converted to a level on the standard scale by the Criminal Justice Act 1982, ss 37, 46 as amended.

[69B. Objection to, and refusal or modification of applications for operators' licences on environmental grounds

(1) Any person entitled by virtue of section 63(3) of this Act to object to the grant of any application for an operator's licence on the ground there mentioned may also object to the grant of any such application on the ground that any place which, if the licence is granted, will be an operating centre of the holder of the licence is unsuitable on environmental grounds for use as such.

(2) In the case of any such application, any person who is the owner or occupier of land in the vicinity of any place which, if the licence is granted, will be an operating centre of the holder of the licence may make representations against the grant of the application on the ground that that place is unsuitable on environmental grounds for use as such, provided that any adverse effects on environmental conditions arising from that use would be capable of prejudicially affecting the use or enjoyment of the land.

(3) Where any objection or representations are duly made under this section in respect of any application for an operator's licence, the licensing authority may in any case refuse the application on the ground that the parking of authorised vehicles under the licence at or in the vicinity of any place which, if the licence were granted, would be an operating centre of the holder of the licence would cause adverse effects on environmental conditions in the vicinity of that place.

(4) Where any objection or representations are duly so made in respect of any such application, the licensing authority may refuse the application, subject to subsection (5) of this section, on the ground that any place which, if the licence were granted, would be an operating centre of the holder of the licence is unsuitable for use as such on environmental grounds other than the ground mentioned in subsection (3) of this section.

(5) A licensing authority may not refuse an application for an operator's licence under subsection (4) of this section if the applicant satisfies the authority that the grant of the application will not result in any material change as regards—

    (a) the places in the area of the authority used or to be used as operating centres for authorised vehicles under any operator's licence previously granted by the authority or under the licence applied for; or

    (b) the use of any such place already in use as an operating centre under an existing licence so granted.

(6) Without prejuduce to the power of a licensing authority to issue an operator's licence subject to either or both of the modifications or limitations mentioned in section 64(4) of this Act, in any case where—

    (a) the authority has power to refuse an application for any such licence under subsection (3) or (4) of this section; and

    (b) any place other than a place unsuitable for use as an operating centre is referred to in the statement under section 69A(2) of this Act as a proposed operating centre of the applicant;

the authority may, instead of refusing the application, issue the licence specifying in it only such place or places referred to in that statement as are not unsuitable for use as an operating centre.

For the purposes of this subsection, a place referred to in any such statement given to a licensing authority by an applicant for an operator's licence is unsuitable for use as an operating centre if the licensing authority has power to refuse the application under subsection (3) or (4) of this section in consequence of the proposed use of that place as an operating centre.

(7) A request for the grant of a licence under section 67(5) of this Act pending the determination of a current application shall not be treated as an application for an operator's licence for the purposes of this section, but in granting a licence under section 67(5) a licensing authority may specify in the licence such place or places referred to in the statement given to the authority by the applicant under section 69A(2) of this Act as the authority thinks fit.]

[12]

NOTES
    Commencement: 1 June 1984.
    Commencement order: SI 1984 No 175.
    Added by the Transport Act 1982, s 52(2), Sch 4, Part I.
    See further: the Companies Act 1989, s 144(4), Sch 18, para 7.

[69C. Conditions as to the use of operating centres

(1) Subject to the following provisions of this section, a licensing authority may attach such conditions to an operator's licence as appear to him to be appropriate for the purpose of preventing or minimising any adverse effects on environmental conditions arising from the use for authorised vehicles under the licence of any operating centre of the holder of the licence in the area of authority.

(2) The conditions which may be attached to a licence under this section shall be of such description as may be prescribed; and, without prejudice to the generality of the preceding provision, the descriptions which may be prescribed include conditions regulating—

    (a) the number, type and size of motor vehicles or trailers which may at any one time be at any operating centre of the holder of the licence in the area of the authority for any prescribed purpose;

    (b) the parking arrangements to be provided at or in the vicinity of any such centre; and

    (c) the hours at which operations of any prescribed description may be carried on at any such centre.

(3) Subject to subsection (4) of this section, the licensing authority by whom an operator's licence was granted may at any time vary or remove any condition attached to the licence under this section.

(4) The power to attach a condition to an operator's licence under this

section shall be exercisable by a licensing authority on granting the licence; and that power, and the power to vary or remove any condition so attached, shall also be exercisable in accordance with section 69D of this Act on an application by the holder for variation of the licence.

(5) Where a licensing authority is precluded by section 69B(5) of this Act from refusing an application for an operator's licence the authority may not attach any condition to the licence under this section without first giving the applicant for the licence an opportunity to make representations to the authority with respect to the effect on his business of any condition the authority proposes to attach; and where the applicant makes any such representations the authority shall give special consideration to those representations in determining whether to attach the proposed condition on granting the licence.

(6) Any person who contravenes any condition attached under this section to a licence of which he is the holder shall be liable on summary conviction to a fine not exceeding [level 4 on the standard scale].] **[13]**

NOTES
Commencement: 1 June 1984.
Commencement order: SI 1984 No 175.
Added by the Transport Act 1982, s 52(2), Sch 4, Part I.
Sub-s (6): maximum fine converted to a level on the standard scale by the Criminal Justice Act 1982, ss 37, 46 as amended.

[69D. Variation of operators' licences with respect to operating centres and conditions affecting their use, etc.

(1) Subject to section 69E of this Act, on the application of the holder of an operator's licence, the licensing authority by whom the licence was granted may at any time while it is in force vary the licence by directing—

    (a) that a new place shall be specified in the licence as an operating centre of the holder of the licence, or that any place so specified shall cease to be so specified; or

    (b) that any condition attached to the licence under section 69C of this Act shall be varied or removed.

(2) A person applying for the variation of an operator's licence under this section shall give to the licensing authority such information as he may reasonably require for the discharge of his duties in relation to the application.

(3) The licensing authority shall publish in the prescribed manner notice of any application for a variation under this section, unless the licensing authority is satisfied that the application is of so trivial a nature that it is not necessary that an opportunity should be given for objecting to it or making representations against it.

(4) Any person entitled to object to the grant of any application for a variation of which notice has been published under section 68(4) of this Act may object to the grant of any application for a variation of which notice has been published under section 68(4) or under subsection (3) of this section on either of the following grounds, that is to say—

    (a) that any place which, if the application for variation is granted, will be an operating centre of the holder of the licence is unsuitable on environmental grounds for use as such; or

    (b) that the use in any manner which will be permitted if the application for variation is granted of any operating centre of the holder of the licence will have adverse effects on environmental conditions in the vicinity of that centre.

(5) Subject to subsection (6) of this section, any person who is the owner or occupier of land in the vicinity of—

(a) any place which, if the application for variation is granted, will be an operating centre of the holder of the licence; or

(b) any existing operating centre of the holder of the licence to which the application relates;

may make representations against the grant of any application for a variation of which notice has been published under section 68(4) of this Act or under subsection (3) of this section on either of the grounds mentioned in subsection (4) of this section, but so far only as relates to that place or operating centre.

(6) A person may not by virtue of subsection (5) of this section make representations against the grant of an application for variation of an operator's licence unless any adverse effects on environmental conditions arising from the use of the place or operating centre in question would be capable of prejudicially affecting the use or enjoyment of the land there mentioned.

(7) Where any objection or representations are duly made under this section in respect of any application for a variation of an operator's licence, the licensing authority may refuse the application in any case where it appears to him that the application ought to be refused on either of the gounds mentioned in subsection (4) of this section.

(8) In any case in which the licensing authority grants an application for a variation of an operator's licence of which notice has been published under section 68(4) of this Act or under subsection (3) of this section, the licensing authority may direct that any condition attached to the licence under section 69C of this Act shall be varied or removed or that a condition shall be attached to the licence under that section.

(9) If an applicant under this section so requests, the licensing authority may, pending the determination of the application, give an interim direction under subsection (1) or (8) of this section, that is to say, a direction expressed to continue in force only until the application, and any appeal arising out of it, have been disposed of; and a request for such a direction shall not for the purposes of subsections (3) to (7) of this section be treated as an application for a variation under this section.] **[14]**

NOTES

    Commencement: 1 June 1984.
    Commencement order: SI 1984 No 175.
    Added by the Transport Act 1982, s 52(2), Sch 4, Part I.

[69E. Publication of notice of application for licences and variations in localities affected

(1) The licensing authority for any area shall refuse—

(a) any application to the authority for an operator's licence; and

(b) any application to the authority for the variation of an operator's licence of which notice has been published under section 68(4) or 69(D)(3) of this Act;

without considering the merits of the application unless he is satisfied that notice of the application in such form and containing such information as may be prescribed has been published within the period mentioned in subsection (2) of this section in a local newspaper or newspapers circulating in each locality affected by the application.

(2) The period referred to in subsection (1) of this section is the period beginning twenty-one days before the date on which the application is made and ending twenty-one days after that date.

(3) For the purposes of this section a locality shall be taken to be affected by an application to a licensing authority for, or for the variation of, an operator's licence if it contains any place in the area of the authority which will be an operating centre of the holder of the licence if the application is granted, or (in the case of an application for variation) any existing operating centre of the holder of the licence to which the application relates.]   **[15]**

NOTES
 Commencement: 1 June 1984.
 Commencement order: SI 1984 No 175.
 Added by the Transport Act 1982, s 52(2), Sch 4, Part I.

[69F. Revocation, etc of operators' licences for breach of provisions controlling use of operating centres

(1) Subject to subsection (2) of this section, the licensing authority by whom an operator's licence was granted may direct that it be revoked, suspended, terminated on a date earlier than that on which it would otherwise expire under section 67 of this Act, or curtailed on the ground that the holder of the licence has contravened section 69A of this Act or any condition attached to his licence under section 69C of this Act; and during any time of suspension the licence shall be of no effect.

(2) Section 69 of this Act shall apply as if the power to give a direction under subsection (1) of this section and the ground there mentioned were respectively conferred by and mentioned in subsection (1) of that section.] **[16]**

NOTES
 Commencement: 1 June 1984.
 Commencement order: SI 1984 No 175.
 Added by the Transport Act 1982, s 52(2), Sch 4, Part I.

[69G. Provisions supplementary to sections 69A to 69F operators' licences

(1) Any objection or representations under section 69B or 69D of this Act shall contain particulars of any matters alleged by the person making the objection or representations to be relevant to the determination of the licensing authority to which the objections or representations relate; and the onus of proof of any matters so alleged shall lie on the person making the objection or representations.

(2) Any objection or representations under either of those sections with respect to any application for, or for the variation of, an operator's licence shall be made within the prescribed time and in the prescribed manner, which—

 (a) may differ for representations from that prescribed for objections; and
 (b) shall in either case be stated in the notice of the application published under section 63(1) of this Act of (as the case may be) under section 68(4) or 69(D) of this Act.

(3) In making any of the following determinations, that is to say—

(a) any determination with respect to the suitability of any place on environmental grounds for use as an operating centre for authorised vehicles under an operator's licence;

(b) any determination with respect to attaching any condition under section 69C of this Act to an operator's licence or varying or removing any condition so attached;

(c) any determination with respect to the effect on environmental conditions in any locality of the use in any particular manner of any operating centre of the holder of an operator's licence,

the licensing authority shall have regard to such considerations as may be prescribed as relevant to determinations of that description.

(4) In making any such determination for the purposes of exercising any of his powers under sections 69B to 69D of this Act in relation to an application for, or for the variation of, an operator's licence, the licensing authority shall also have regard to—

(a) any information supplied by the applicant in accordance with section 68, 69A or 69D of this Act; and

(b) any objections or representations duly made under section 69B or 69D.

(5) Any statement or information given to a licensing authority under section 69A or 69D of this Act shall be given in such form as the authority may require.

(6) For the purposes of sections 69D(5)(b) and 69E(3) of this Act an application for a variation of an operator's licence shall be taken to relate to an operating centre of the holder of the licence if any condition attached to the licence which the application seeks to have varied or removed relates to that centre.] **[17]**

NOTES
  Commencement: 1 June 1984.
  Commencement order: SI 1984 No 175.
  Added by the Transport Act 1982, s 52(2), Sch 4, Part I.

70. Rights of appeal in connection with operators' licences

(1) Subject to subsection (2) of this section, a person who—

(a) being an applicant for, or for the variation of, an operator's licence, is aggrieved by the refusal of the application or, as the case may be, by the terms or conditions of the licence or of the variation; or

(b) being the holder of an operator's licence in respect of which, or a person in respect of whom, [or the holder of an operator's licence which specifies a motor vehicle in respect of which] a direction or order has been given or made under section 61(6) or 69(1) to [(7A)] [or 69F(1)] of this Act, is aggrieved by that direction or order; or

(c) having duly made an objection to an application for, or for the variation of, an operator's licence, is aggrieved by the grant of the application,

may appeal to the Transport Tribunal.

(2) No appeal shall lie under the foregoing subsection on the ground that a direction has been given under subsection (3) of section 67 of this Act if it has been given by virtue of paragraph (b) of the said subsection (3). **[18]**

NOTES
Commencement: Before 1 January 1970-1 March 1971.
Commencement orders SI 1969 No 1613, 1970 No 1631.
Sub-s (1): first and second amendments made by the Road Traffic Act 1974, s 16, Sch 4, para 5; third amendment made by the Transport Act 1982, s 52(3), Sch 4, Part II, para 4.

Special authorisations for use of large goods vehicles

71. Control of the use of large goods vehicles

(1)-(5) . . .

(6) For the purposes of . . . the subsequent provisions of this Part of this Act, a large goods vehicle is a goods vehicle (other than a hauling vehicle) which—

(a) has a relevant plated weight exceeding [16260 kilograms] or (not having a relevant plated weight) has an unladen weight exceeding [5080 kilograms]; or

(b) forms part of a vehicle combination (not being an articulated combination) which is such that—

   (i) if all the vehicles comprised in the combination (or all of them except any small trailer) have relevant plated weights, the aggregate of the relevant plated weights of the vehicles comprised in the combination (exclusive of any such trailer) exceeds [16260 kilograms];

   (ii) in any other case, the aggregate of the unladen weights of those vehicles (exclusive of any such trailer) exceeds [5080 kilograms]; or

(c) forms part of an articulated combination which is such that—

   (i) if the trailer comprised in the combination has a relevant plated weight, the aggregate of the unladen weight of the motor vehicle comprised in the combination and the relevant plated weight of that trailer exceeds [16260 kilograms];

   (ii) in any other case, the aggregate of the unladen weights of the motor vehicle and the trailer comprised in the combination exceeds [5080 kilograms].

In any provision of this subsection "relevant plated weight" means a plated weight of the description specified in relation to that provision by regulations; and in paragraph (b) of this subsection "small trailer" means a trailer having an unladen weight not exceeding [1020 kilograms].

(7) . . .

(8) In this section—

"hauling vehicle" means a motor tractor, a light locomotive, a heavy locomotive or the motor vehicle comprised in an articulated combination; . . .

(9), (10) . . . **[19]**

NOTES
Commencement: Before 1 January 1970-1 December 1970 (certain purposes); to be appointed (remainder).
Commencement orders: SI 1969 No 1613, 1970 No 259.
Sub-ss (1)-(5), (7), (9), (10): repealed by the Transport Act 1980, s 69, Sch 9, Part II.
Sub-s (6): words omitted repealed by the Transport Act 1980, s 69, Sch 9, Part II; amendments in square brackets made by SI 1981 No 1373.

Sub-s (8): words omitted repealed by the Transport Act 1980, s 69, Sch 9, Part II.

72–80 (*Repealed by the Transport Act 1980, s 69, Sch 9, Pt II.*)

Enforcement

81. Consignment notes

(1) Subject to subsection (2) of this section, no goods shall be carried on a large goods vehicle unless a document (in this section referred to as a "consignment note") in the prescribed form and containing the prescribed particulars has been completed and signed in the prescribed manner and is carried by the driver of the vehicle.

(2) Subsection (1) of this section shall not apply—

    (a) to the carriage of goods on any journey or in a vehicle of any class exempted from that subsection by regulations; or

    (b) to any carriage of goods which is lawful without the authority of an operator's licence;

and, subject to the provisions of regulations, a licensing authority may dispense with the observance, as respects the carriage of goods under an operator's licence granted by him, of any requirement of that subsection, and may grant such a dispensation either generally, or as respects a particular vehicle, or as respects the use of vehicles for a particular purpose, but he shall not grant such a dispensation unless satisfied that it is not reasonably practicable for the requirement dispensed with to be observed.

(3) The consignment note relating to the goods carried by a vehicle on any journey shall, at the conclusion of that journey, be preserved for the prescribed period by the person who used the vehicle . . . for carrying the goods on that journey.

(4) Any person who uses or drives a vehicle in contravention of subsection (1) of this section or who fails to comply with subsection (3) thereof shall be liable on summary conviction to a fine not exceeding [level 4 on the standard scale].   **[20]**

NOTES
Commencement: To be appointed.
Sub-s (3): words omitted repealed by the Transport Act 1980, s 69, Sch 9, Part II.
Sub-s (4): maximum fine increased and converted to a level on the standard scale by the Criminal Justice Act 1982, ss 37, 38, 46 as amended.

82. Powers of entry and inspection

(1) An officer may, on production if so required of his authority, require any person to produce and permit him to inspect and copy—

    (a) any . . . document which is required by or under section . . . 81 of this Act to be carried by that person as driver of a vehicle;

    (b) any . . . document which that person is required by or under [that section] to preserve;

and that . . . document shall, if the officer so requires by notice in writing served on that person, be produced at the office of the licensing authority specified in the notice within such time (not being less than ten days) from the service of the notice as may be so specified.

(2) An officer may, on production if so required of his authority—

(a) at any time, enter any large goods vehicle and inspect that vehicle and any goods carried by it;

(b) at any time which is reasonable having regard to the circumstances of the case, enter any premises on which he has reason to believe that such a vehicle is kept or that any such ... documents as are mentioned in subsection (1) of this section are to be found, and inspect any such vehicle, and inspect and copy any such ... document, which he finds there.

(3) For the purpose of exercising his powers under subsection (1)(a) or (2)(a) of this section, an officer may detain the vehicle in question during such time as is required for the exercise of that power.

(4) An officer may, at any time which is reasonable having regard to the circumstances of the case, enter any premises of an applicant for an operator's licence or of the holder of such a licence and inspect any facilities on those premises for maintaining the authorised vehicles in a fit and serviceable condition.

(5) Any person who—

(a) fails to comply with any requirement under subsection (1) of this section; or

(b) obstructs an officer in the exercise of his powers under subsection (2), (3) or (4) of this section,

shall be liable on summary conviction to a fine not exceeding [level 3 on the standard scale].

(6) If an officer has reason to believe that a document or article carried on or by the driver of a vehicle, or a document produced to him in pursuance of this Part of this Act ..., is a document or article in relation to which an offence has been committed under—

(a) section 83 of this Act; or

(b) section 233 or 235 of the Act of 1960 as amended by Schedule 10 to this Act,

he may seize that document or article; and where a document or article is seized as aforesaid and within six months of the date on which it was seized no person has been charged since that date with an offence in relation to that document or article under any of those sections and that document or article is still detained, a magistrates' court shall, on an application made for the purpose by the driver or owner of the vehicle, by the person from whom the document was seized or by an officer, make such order respecting the disposal of the document or article and award such costs as the justice of the case may require.

(7) Any proceedings in Scotland under the last foregoing subsection shall be taken by way of summary application in the sheriff court; and in the application of that subsection to Scotland references to costs shall be construed as references to expenses.

(8) In this section "officer" means an examiner appointed under [section 66A of the Road Traffic Act 1988] and any person authorised for the purposes of this section by the licensing authority for any area.

(9) The powers conferred by this section on an officer as defined in subsection (8) of this section shall be exercisable also by a police constable who shall not, if wearing uniform, be required to produce any authority. **[21]**

NOTES
　　Commencement: Before 1 January 1970-1 March 1971 (in part); to be appointed (remainder).
　　Commencement orders: SI 1969 No 1613, 1970 No 259, 1970 No 1631.
　　Sub-ss (1), (2): amended by the Transport Act 1980, ss 66(2)(a), 69, Sch 9, Part II.
　　Sub-s (5): maximum fine increased and converted to a level on the standard scale by the Criminal
Justice Act 1982, ss 37, 38, 46.
　　Sub-s (6): words omitted repealed by the Transport Act 1982, s 74, Sch 6.
　　Sub-s (8): words in square brackets substituted by the Road Traffic Act 1991, s 48, Sch 4, para 1.
　　Act of 1960: Road Traffic Act 1960.

83. Falsification of consignment notes and records

Any person who makes, or causes to be made, any . . . document required to be
made under section . . . 81 of this Act which he knows to be false or, with intent
to deceive, alters or causes to be altered any such . . . document shall be liable—

　　(a) on summary conviction, to a fine not exceeding [the prescribed sum];
　　(b) on conviction on indictment, to imprisonment for a term not exceeding
　　　　two years. **[22]**

NOTES
　　Commencement: To be appointed.
　　Words omitted repealed by the Transport Act 1980, s 69, Sch 9, Part II; amendment in square
brackets made by the Magistrates' Courts Act 1980, s 32(2) as amended.

84. Evidence by certificate

In any proceedings for an offence under this Part of this Act or Schedule 9
thereto a certificate signed by or on behalf of a licensing authority and stating—

　　(a) that, on any date, a person was or was not the holder of an operator's
　　　　licence, . . . granted by the authority;
　　(b) the dates of the coming into force and expiration of any such licence
　　　　. . . granted by the authority;
　　(c) the terms and conditions of any operator's licence . . . granted by the
　　　　authority;
　　(d) that a person is by virtue of an order of the authority disqualified from
　　　　holding or obtaining an operator's licence, . . . indefinitely or for a
　　　　specified period;
　　(e) that a direction, having effect indefinitely or for a specified period,
　　　　has been given by the licensing authority under section 69(6) of this
　　　　Act in relation to any person;
　　(f) that, on any date or during any specified period, any such licence . . .
　　　　granted by the authority was of no effect by reason of a direction that
　　　　it be suspended,

shall be evidence, and in Scotland sufficient evidence, of the facts stated; and a
certificate stating any of the matters aforesaid and purporting to be signed by or
on behalf of a licensing authority shall be deemed to be so signed unless the
contrary is proved. **[23]**

NOTES
　　Commencement: 1 March 1970-1 March 1971.
　　Commencement orders: SI 1969 No 1613, 1970 No 1631.
　　Words omitted repealed by the Transport Act 1980, s 69, Sch 9, Part II, and the Transport Act
1982, s 74(2), Sch 6.

Supplementary

85. Holding companies and subsidiaries

(1) The Minister may by regulations make provision for the purpose of enabling any company, or other body corporate, which has one or more subsidiaries to hold—

(a) an operator's licence under which the authorised vehicles consist of or include vehicles belonging to or in the possession of any of its subsidiaries;

(b) ...

(2) Regulations under this section may modify or supplement any of the provisions of this Part of this Act or [Schedule 10] thereto so far as appears to the Minister to be necessary or expedient for the purpose mentioned in subsection (1) of this section or in connection therewith, and may contain such other supplementary and incidental provisions as appear to the Minister to be requisite. **[24]**

NOTES
Commencement: 20 November 1969.
Commencement order: SI 1969 No 1613.
Sub-s (1): words omitted repealed by the Transport Act 1980, s 69, Sch 9, Part II.
Sub-s (2): amended by the Transport Act 1982, s 74(1), Sch 5, para 6.
Regulations: see the Goods Vehicles (Operators' Licences, Qualifications and Fees) Regulations 1984, post.

86. Operators' licences and special authorisations not to be transferable

Subject to any provision made by regulations under section 85 of this Act, an operator's licence ... shall not be capable of being transferred or assigned, but provision may be made by regulations for treating a person carrying on the trade or business of the holder of an operator's licence ... as if he were the holder thereof (for such purposes, for such period and to such extent as may be specified in the regulations), in the event of the death, incapacity, [or bankruptcy of the holder or, in the case of a company, of the holder going into liquidation, of an administration order being made in relation to] the holder, or of the appointment of a receiver or manager in relation to the trade or business. **[25–28]**

NOTES
Commencement: Before 1 January 1970-1 March 1971.
Commencement orders: SI 1969 No 1613, 1970 No 1631.
Words omitted repealed by the Transport Act 1980, s 69, Sch 9, Part II; words in square brackets substituted by the Insolvency Act 1985, s 235(1), Sch 8, para 16.

91. Regulations and orders for purposes of Part V

(1) The Minister may make regulations for any purpose for which regulations may be made under this Part of this Act and for prescribing anything which may be prescribed under this Part of this Act and generally for the purpose of carrying this Part of this Act into effect and, in particular, but without prejudice to the generality of the foregoing provisions of this subsection, may make regulations with respect to the following matters—

(a) the procedure on applications for, and the determination of questions in connection with, the grant and variation of operators' licences ..., and the procedure under, and the determination of questions for the purposes of, [sections 69 and 69F] of this Act;

    (b) the issue of operators' licences ... and the issue on payment of the prescribed fee of copies of such licences ... in the case of licences ... lost or defaced;

    (c) the means by which vehicles may be identified, whether by plates, marks or otherwise, as being authorised vehicles ... ;

    (d) the custody of operators' licences ... , the production, return and cancellation of such licences ... on expiration or on the giving of a direction under section 69 [or 69F] ... of this Act, and the custody, production and return of documents and plates;

    (e) the notification to the licensing authority of vehicles which have ceased to be used under an operator's licence ... ;

    (f) the repayment in the prescribed circumstances of fees paid under this Part of this Act;

    (g) the circumstances in which goods are to be treated for the purposes of this Part of this Act as carried for hire or reward and the circumstances in which goods are to be treated for those purposes as carried by any person for or in connection with a trade or business carried on by him;

and different regulations may be made as respects different classes of vehicles.

    (2) The power conferred by subsection (1) of this section to make regulations with respect to the means by which vehicles are to be identified as being authorised vehicles ... shall include power to require that any such means of identification prescribed for a vehicle shall be carried notwithstanding that for the time being the vehicle is not being used for a purpose for which an operator's licence ... is required.

    (3) The Minister may by regulations substitute for any weight, distance, volume or area specified by or under this Part of this Act a weight, distance, volume or area expressed in terms of the metric system, being a weight, distance, volume or area which is equivalent to that for which it is substituted or does not differ from it by more than five per cent. thereof.

    (4) The Minister may make regulations—

    (a) for providing that any provision of this Part of this Act shall, in relation to vehicles brought temporarily into Great Britain, have effect subject to such modifications as may be prescribed;

    (b) ...

and different provision may be made by the regulations for different classes of case.

    (5) A definition or description of a class of vehicles for the purposes of any regulation under this Part of this Act may be framed by reference to any characteristic of the vehicles or to any other circumstances whatsoever.

    (6) Any person who contravenes a provision of regulations under this section, a contravention of which is declared by the regulations to be an offence, shall be liable on summary conviction to a fine not exceeding [level 1 on the standard scale].

    (7) Any order or regulations made by the Minister under this Part of this Act ... shall be subject to annulment in pursuance of a resolution of either House of Parliament.

    (8) Before making any regulations under this Part of this Act ... the Minister shall consult with such representative organisations as he thinks fit.

NOTES
    Commencement: Before 1 January 1970 (certain purposes); to be appointed (remainder).
    Commencement order: SI 1969 No 1613.
    Sub-s (1): in para (a) first words omitted repealed by the Transport Act 1980, ss 66(2)(b), 69, Sch
9, Part II, second amendment in square brackets made by the Transport Act 1982, s 52, Sch 4, Part
II, para 6; in paras (b), (c), (e) words omitted repealed by the Transport Act 1980, s 69, Sch 9, Part
II; in para (d) words omitted repealed by the Transport Act 1980, s 69, Sch 9, Part II, amendment
in square brackets made by the Transport Act 1982, s 52, Sch 4, Part II, para 6.
    Sub-ss (2), (4): words omitted repealed by the Transport Act 1980, s 69, Sch 9 Part II.
    Sub-s (6): maximum fine increased and converted to a level on the standard scale by the Criminal
Justice Act 1982, ss 37, 38, 46.
    Sub-ss (7), (8): words omitted repealed by the Transport Act 1982, s 74, Sch 6.
    See further: the Companies Act 1989, s 144(4), Sch 18, para 7.
    Regulations: see the Goods Vehicles (Operators' Licences, Qualifications and Fees) Regulations
1984, post.

92. Interpretation of Part V

(1) In this Part of this Act . . . , unless the context otherwise requires—

"articulated combination" means a combination made up of—
  (a) a motor vehicle which is so constructed that a trailer may by partial
       superimposition be attached to the vehicle in such a manner as to
       cause a substantial part of the weight of the trailer to be borne by the
       vehicle, and
  (b) a trailer attached to it as aforesaid;
"authorised vehicle" means, in relation to an operator's licence, a vehicle
  authorised to be used thereunder, whether or not it is for the time being
  in use for a purpose for which an operator's licence is required and
  whether it is specified therein as so authorised or, being of a type so
  authorised subject to a maximum number, belongs to the holder of the
  licence or is in his possession under an agreement for hire-purchase, hire
  or loan;
"carriage of goods" includes haulage of goods;
"carrier's licence" means a licence granted under Part IV of the Act of
  1960;
"contravention", in relation to any condition or provision, includes a
  failure to comply with the condition or provision, and "contravenes"
  shall be construed accordingly;
"driver" means, in relation to a trailer, the driver of the vehicle by which
  the trailer is drawn and "drive" shall be construed accordingly;
"goods" includes goods or burden of any description;
"goods vehicle" means, subject to subsection (5) of this section, a motor
  vehicle constructed or adapted for use for the carriage of goods, or a
  trailer so constructed or adapted;
"large goods vehicle" shall be construed in accordance with section 71 of
  this Act;
["operating centre', in relation to any vehicle, means the base or centre at
  which the vehicle is normally kept, and references to an operating centre
  of the holder of an operator's licence are references to any place which is
  an operating centre for authorised vehicles under the licence;]
["owner", in relation to any land in England and Wales, means a person,
  other than a mortgagee not in possession, who, whether in his own right
  or as trustee for any other person, is entitled to receive the rack rent of
  the land or, where the land is not let at a rack rent, would be so entitled
  if it were so let];
"prescribed" means prescribed by regulations;

"regulations" means regulations made by the Minister under this Part of
this Act;

"subsidiary" means a subsidiary as defined by [section 736 of the
Companies Act 1985];

"vehicle combination" means a combination of goods vehicles made up
of one or more motor vehicles and one or more trailers all of which are
linked together when travelling;

and any expression not defined above which is also used in the Act of 1960 has
the same meaning as in that Act.

(2) For the purposes of this Part of this Act, the driver of a vehicle, if it
belongs to him or is in his possession under an agreement for hire, hire-purchase
or loan, and in any other case the person whose servant or agent the driver is,
shall be deemed to be the person using the vehicle; and references to using a
vehicle shall be construed accordingly.

(3) In this Part of this Act references to directing that an operator's licence
be curtailed are references to directing (with effect for the remainder of the
duration of the licence or for any shorter period) all or any of the following, that
is to say—

(a) that any one or more of the vehicles specified in the licence be removed
therefrom;

(b) that the maximum number of trailers or of motor vehicles specified in
the licence in pursuance of section 61(1)(b) or (c) of this Act be
reduced;

(c) that the addition of authorised vehicles under the said section 61(1)(c)
be no longer permitted.

[(d) that any one or more of the places specified in the licence as operating
centres be removed therefrom.]

(4) In this Part of this Act, references to the bankruptcy of a person shall,
as respects Scotland, be construed as references to an award of sequestration
having been made of his estate.

(5) In this Part of this Act ..., references to goods vehicles do not include
references to tramcars or trolley vehicles operated under statutory powers within
the meaning of [Schedule 4 to the Road Traffic Act 1988].

(6) Anything required or authorised by this Part of this Act to be done to or
by a licensing authority by whom a licence ... was granted may be done to or
by any person for the time being acting as licensing authority for the area for
which the first-mentioned authority was acting at the time of the granting of the
licence ...   **[30]**

NOTES

Commencement: Before 1 January 1970 (certain purposes); to be appointed (remainder).
Commencement order: SI 1969 No 1613.

Sub-s (1): definition "subsidiary" amended by the Companies Consolidation (Consequential
Provisions) Act 1985, s 30, Sch 2; other amendments made by the Transport Act 1982, ss 52(1), (3),
74(2), Sch 4, Part II, para 7, Sch 6.

Sub-s (3): amended by the Transport Act 1982, s 52(1), (3), Sch 4, Part II, para 7.

Sub-s (5): words omitted repealed by the Transport Act 1982, s 74(2), Sch 6; words in square
brackets substituted by the Road Traffic (Consequential Provisions) Act 1988, s 4, Sch 3, para 6(4).

Sub-s (6): amended by the Transport Act 1980, s 69, Sch 9, Part II.

Act of 1960: Road Traffic Act 1960.

Abolition of carriers' licensing for certain vehicles

93. Carriers' licences not to be required for small vehicles or for medium vehicles covered by operators' licences

(1) Section 164 of the Act of 1960 (users of goods vehicles to hold carriers' licences) shall cease to apply to the use of any vehicle the unladen weight of which does not exceed [1525 kilograms], and any carrier's licence so far as it authorises the use of such a vehicle shall cease to have effect.

(2) The said section 164 shall not apply to the use of any vehicle for the use of which an operator's licence is required, unless that vehicle is a large goods vehicle.   [31–32]

NOTES
    Sub-s (1): amended by SI 1981 No 1373.
    Act of 1960: Road Traffic Act 1960.

PART VI

DRIVERS' HOURS

95. Vehicles and drivers subject to control under Part VI

(1) This Part of this Act shall have effect with a view to securing the observance of proper hours [or periods] of work by persons engaged in the carriage of passengers or goods by road and thereby protecting the public against the risks which arise in cases where the drivers of motor vehicles are suffering from fatigue [but the Secretary of State may by regulations make such provision by way of substitution for or adaptation of the provisions of this Part, or supplemental or incidental to this Part, as he considers necessary or expedient to take account of the operation of any relevant Community provision.

(1A) Regulations under subsection (1) above may in particular—

  (a) substitute different requirements for the requirements of the domestic drivers' hours code or add to, make exceptions from or otherwise modify any of the requirements of that code;

  (b) apply to journeys and work to which no relevant Community provision applies;

  (c) include provision as to the circumstances in which a period of driving or duty to which a relevant Community provision or the domestic drivers' hours code applies is to be included or excluded in reckoning any period for purposes of the domestic drivers' hours code or any relevant Community provision respectively; and

  (d) may contain such transitional, supplemental or consequential provisions as the Secretary of State thinks necessary or expedient.]

(2) This Part of this Act applies to—

  (a) passenger vehicles, that is to say—

    (i) public service vehicles; and

    (ii) motor vehicles (other than public service vehicles) constructed or adapted to carry more than twelve passengers;

  (b) goods vehicles, that is to say—

    (i) heavy locomotives, light locomotives, motor tractors and any motor vehicle so constructed that a trailer may by partial superimposition be attached to the vehicle in such a manner as

to cause a substantial part of the weight of the trailer to be borne
by the vehicle; and

 (ii) motor vehicles (except those mentioned in paragraph (a) of this
subsection) constructed or adapted to carry goods other than the
effects of passengers.

(3) This Part of this Act applies to any such person as follows (in this Part
of this Act referred to as "a driver"), that is to say—

 (a) a person who drives a vehicle to which this Part of this Act applies in
the course of his employment (in this Part of this Act referred to as
"an employee-driver"); and

 (b) a person who drives such a vehicle for the purposes of a trade or
business carried on by him (in this Part of this Act referred to as "an
owner-driver");

and in this Part of this Act references to driving by any person are references to
his driving as aforesaid.   **[33]**

NOTES
 Commencement: 4 January 1978 (sub-s 1A); 20 November 1969 (remainder).
 Commencement order: SI 1969 No 1613.
 Amended by the Road Traffic (Drivers' Ages and Hours of Work) Act 1976, s 2(1)(d), (5).
 Sub-s (1): Regulations, see the Community Drivers' Hours and Recording Equipment
(Exemptions and Supplementary Provisions) Regulations 1986, SI 1986 No 1456, as amended.

96. Permitted driving time and periods of duty

(1) Subject to the provisions of this section, a driver shall not on any working
day drive a vehicle or vehicles to which this Part of this Act applies for periods
amounting in the aggregate to more than ten hours.

(2) Subject to the provisions of this section, if on any working day a driver
has been on duty for a period of, or for periods amounting in the aggregate to,
five and a half hours and—

 (a) there has not been during that period, or during or between any of
those periods, an interval of not less than half an hour in which he
was able to obtain rest and refreshment; and

 (b) the end of that period, or of the last of those periods, does not mark
the end of that working day,

there shall at the end of that period, or of the last of those periods, be such an
interval as aforesaid.

(3) Subject to the provisions of this section, the working day of a driver—

 (a) except where paragraph (b) or (c) of this subsection applies, shall not
exceed eleven hours;

 (b) if during that day he is off duty for a period which is, or periods which
taken together are, not less than the time by which his working day
exceeds eleven hours, shall not exceed twelve and a half hours;

 (c) if during that day—

  (i) all the time when he is driving vehicles to which this Part of this
Act applies is spent in driving one or more express carriages or
contract carriages; and

  (ii) he is able for a period of not less than four hours to obtain rest
and refreshment,

shall not exceed fourteen hours.

(4) Subject to the provisions of this section, there shall be, between any two successive working days of a driver, an interval for rest which—

(a) subject to paragraph (b) of this subsection, shall not be of less than eleven hours;

(b) if during both those days all or the greater part of the time when he is driving vehicles to which this Part of this Act applies is spent in driving one or more passenger vehicles, may, on one occasion in each working week, be of less than eleven hours but not of less than nine and a half hours;

and for the purposes of this Part of this Act a period of time shall not be treated, in the case of an employee-driver, as not being an interval for rest by reason only that he may be called upon to report for duty if required.

(5) Subject to the provisions of this section a driver shall not be on duty in any working week for periods amounting in the aggregate to more than sixty hours.

(6) Subject to the provisions of this section, there shall be, in the case of each working week of a driver, a period of not less than twenty-four hours for which he is off duty, being a period either falling wholly in that week or beginning in that week and ending in the next week; but—

(a) where the requirements of the foregoing provisions of this subsection have been satisfied in the case of any week by reference to a period ending in the next week, no part of that period (except any part after the expiration of the first twenty-four hours of it) shall be taken into account for the purpose of satisfying those requirements in the case of the next week; and

(b) those requirements need not be satisfied in the case of any working week of a driver who on each working day falling wholly or partly in that week drives one or more stage carriages if that week is immediately preceded by a week in the case of which those requirements have been satisfied as respects that driver or during which he has not at any time been on duty.

(7) If in the case of the working week of any driver the following requirement is satisfied, that is to say, that, in each of the periods of twenty-four hours beginning at midnight which make up that week, the driver does not drive a vehicle to which this Part of this Act applies for a period of, or periods amounting in the aggregate to, more than four hours, the foregoing provisions of this section shall not apply to him in that week, except that the provisions of subsections (1), (2) and (3) shall nevertheless have effect in relation to the whole of any working day falling partly in that week and partly in a working week in the case of which that requirement is not satisfied.

(8) If on any working day a driver does not drive any vehicle to which this Part of this Act applies—

(a) subsections (2) and (3) of this section shall not apply to that day, and

(b) the period or periods of duty attributable to that day for the purposes of subsection (5) of this section shall, if amounting to more than eleven hours, be treated as amounting to eleven hours only.

(9) For the purposes of subsections (1) and (7) of this section no account shall be taken of any time spent driving a vehicle elsewhere than on a road if the vehicle is being so driven in the course of operations of agriculture or forestry.

(10) For the purpose of enabling drivers to deal with cases of emergency or otherwise to meet a special need, the Minister may by regulations—

(a) create exemptions from all or any of the requirements of subsections (1) to (6) of this section in such cases and subject to such conditions as may be specified in the regulations;

(b) empower the traffic [commissioner] for any area, subject to the provisions of the regulations—

(i) to dispense with the observance of all or any of those requirements (either generally or in such circumstances or to such extent as the [commissioner thinks] fit) in any particular case for which provision is not made under paragraph (a) of this subsection;

(ii) to grant a certificate (which, for the purposes of any proceedings under this Part of this Act, shall be conclusive evidence of the facts therein stated) that any particular case falls or fell within any exemption created under the said paragraph (a);

and regulations under this subsection may enable any dispensation under paragraph (b)(i) of this subsection to be granted retrospectively and provide for a document purporting to be a certificate granted by virtue of paragraph (b)(ii) of this subsection to be accepted in evidence without further proof.

(11) If any of the requirements of [the domestic driver's hours code], is contravened in the case of any driver—

(a) that driver; and

(b) any other person (being that driver's employer or a person to whose orders that driver was subject) who caused or permitted the contravention,

shall be liable on summary conviction to a fine not exceeding [level 4 on the standard scale]; but a person shall not be liable to be convicted under this subsection if he proves to the court—

(i) that the contravention was due to unavoidable delay in the completion of a journey arising out of circumstances which he could not reasonably have foreseen; or

(ii) in the case of a person charged under paragraph (b) of this subsection, that the contravention was due to the fact that the driver had for any particular period or periods driven or been on duty otherwise than in the employment of that person or, as the case may be, otherwise than in the employment in which he is subject to the orders of that person, and that the person charged was not, and could not reasonably have become, aware of that fact.

[(11A) Where, in the case of a driver . . . of a motor vehicle, there is in Great Britain a contravention of any requirement of the international rules as to periods of driving, or distance driven, or periods on or off duty, then the offender and any other person (being the offender's employer or a person to whose orders the offender was subject) who caused or permitted the contravention shall be liable on summary conviction to a fine not exceeding [level 4 on the standard scale].]

[(11B) But a person shall not be liable to be convicted under subsection (11A) if—

(a) he proves the matters specified in paragraph (i) of subsection (11); or

(b) being charged as the offender's employer or a person to whose orders the offender was subject, he proves the matters specified in paragraph (ii) of that subsection.]

(12) The Minister may by order—

(a) direct that subsection (1) of this section shall have effect with the substitution for the reference to ten hours of a reference to nine hours, either generally or with such exceptions as may be specified in the order;

(b) direct that paragraph (a) of subsection (3) of this section shall have effect with the substitution for the reference to eleven hours of a reference to any shorter period, or remove, modify or add to the provisions of that subsection containing exceptions to the said paragraph (a);

(c) remove, modify or add to any of the requirements of subsections (2), (4), (5) or (6) of this section or any of the exemptions provided for by subsections (7), (8) and (9) thereof;

and any order under this subsection may contain such transitional and supplementary provisions as the Minister thinks necessary or expedient, including provisions amending any definition in section 103 of this Act which is relevant to any of the provisions affected by the order.

[(13) In this Part of this Act "the domestic driver's hours code" means the provisions of subsections (1) to (6) of this section as for the time being in force (and, in particular, as modified, added to or substituted by or under any instrument in force under section 95(1) of this Act or subsection (10) or (12) of this section).]   **[34]**

NOTES

Commencement: 1 September 1978 (sub-s (11B)); 4 January 1978 (sub-s (13)); 17 October 1972 (sub-s (11A)); 22 January 1970 (sub-ss (10), (12)); 1 March 1970-15 March 1970 (sub-ss (1)-(9), (11)).

Commencement orders: SI 1970 No 41, 1970 No 259, 1970 No 385.

Sub-s (10): para (b) amended by the Transport Act 1985, s 3(5), Sch 2, Part II.

Sub-s (10): Regulations, see the Drivers' Hours (Goods Vehicles) (Exemption) Regulations 1986, SI 1986 No 1492.

Sub-s (11): amended by the Road Traffic (Drivers' Ages and Hours of Work) Act 1976, s 2(1)(e), (f); maximum fine increased and converted to a level on the standard scale by the Criminal Justice Act 1982, ss 37, 38, 46 as amended; words omitted repealed by the Community Drivers' Hours and Recording Equipment Regulations 1986, SI 1986 No 1457, reg 2.

Sub-s (11A): added by the European Communities Act 1972, s 4, Sch 4, para 9(2)(a); maximum fine increased and converted to a level on the standard scale by the Criminal Justice Act 1982, ss 37, 38, 46 as amended; words omitted repealed by the Community Drivers' Hours and Recording Equipment Regulations 1986, SI 1986 No 1457, reg 2.

Sub-s (11B): inserted by the Transport Act 1978, s 10.

Sub-s (13): added by the Road Traffic (Drivers' Ages and Hours of Work) Act 1976, s 2(1)(e), (f).

Section modified by the Drivers' Hours (Goods Vehicles) (Modifications) Order 1970, SI 1970 No 257, the Drivers' Hours (Passenger and Goods Vehicles) (Modifications) Order 1971, SI 1971 No 818, the Drivers' Hours (Harmonisation with Community Rules) Regulations 1986, SI 1986 No 1458, the Drivers' Hours (Goods Vehicles) (Modifications) Order 1986, SI 1986 No 1459 and the Drivers' Hours (Goods Vehicles) (Exemptions) Regulations 1986, SI 1986 No 1492.

97. Installation and use of recording equipment

[(1) No person shall use, or cause or permit to be used, a vehicle to which this section applies

[(a) unless there is in the vehicle recording equipment which—

[(i)] has been installed in accordance with the Community Recording Equipment Regulation;

[(ii)] complies with Annexes I and II to that Regulation; and

[(iii)] is being used as provided by [Articles 13 to 15] of that Regulation;
[or

(b) in which there is recording equipment which has been repaired (whether before or after installation) otherwise than in accordance with the Community Recording Equipment Regulation;]

and any person who contravenes this subsection shall be liable on summary conviction to a fine not exceeding [level 5 on the standard scale.]

[(1A) A person shall not be liable to be convicted under subsection [(1) of this section if he proves to the court that he neither knew nor ought to have known that the recording equipment had not been installed or repaired, as the case may be, in accordance with the Community Recording Equipment Regulation.]

(2) A person shall not be liable to be convicted under subsection (1)[(a)] of this section if he proves to the court that the vehicle in question was proceeding to a place where recording equipment which would comply with the requirements of Annexes I and II of the Community Recording Equipment Regulation was to be installed in the vehicle in accordance with that Regulation.

(3) A person shall not be liable to be convicted under subsection (1)[(a)] of this section by reason of the recording equipment installed in the vehicle in question not being in working order if he proves to the court that—

(a) it had not become reasonably practicable for the equipment to be repaired by an approved fitter or workshop; and

(b) the requirements of [Article 16(2)] of the Community Recording Equipment Regulation were being complied with.

(4) A person shall not be liable to be convicted under subsection (1)[(a)] of this section by reason of any seal on the recording equipment installed in the vehicle in question not being intact if he proves to the court that—

(a) the breaking or removal of the seal could not have been avoided;

(b) it had not become reasonably practicable for the seal to be replaced by an approved fitter or workshop; and

(c) in all other respects the equipment was being used as provided by [Articles 13 to 15] of the Community Recording Equipment Regulation.

(5) For the purposes of this section recording equipment is used as provided by [Articles 13 to 15] of the Community Recording Equipment Regulation if, and only if, the circumstances of its use are such that each requirement of those Articles is complied with.

(6) This section applies at any time to any vehicle to which this Part of this Act applies if, at that time, Article 3 of the Community Recording Equipment Regulation requires recording equipment to be installed and used in that vehicle; and in this section and sections 97A and 97B of this Act any expression which is also used in that Regulation has the same meaning as in that Regulation.

(7) In this Part of this Act—

["the Community Recording Equipment Regulation" means Council Regulation (EEC) No. 3821/85 of 20th December 1985 on recording equipment in road transport as read with the Community Drivers' Hours and Recording Equipment (Exemptions and Supplementary Provisions) Regulations 1986;]   **[35]**

NOTES
Commencement: 23 November 1989 (sub-s (1A)); 13 March 1984 (sub-s (1)); 14 January 1980-31 December 1981 (remainder).
Substituted by SI 1979 No 1746, reg 2(1).
Sub-s (1): substituted by SI 1984 No 144, reg 1; fifth amendment in square brackets therein made by SI 1986 No 1457, reg 3(3); other amendments in square brackets made by SI 1989 No 2121, reg 2(2).
Sub-s (1A): added by SI 1989 No 2121, reg 2(3).
Sub-s (2): amended by SI 1989 No 2121, reg 2(4).
Sub-ss (3), (4): first amendment in square brackets made by SI 1989 No 2121, reg 2(4); second words in square brackets substituted by SI 1986 No 1457, reg 3(3).
Sub-s (5): words in square brackets substituted by SI 1986 No 1457, reg 3(3).
Sub-s (7): the regulations are contained post.

97A. Provisions supplementary to section 97

[(1) If an employed [driver] of a vehicle to which section 97 of this Act applies fails—

(a) without reasonable excuse to return any record sheet which relates to him to his employer within twenty-one days of completing it; or

(b) where he has two or more employers by whom he is employed as a [driver] of such a vehicle, to notify each of them of the name and address of the other or others of them,

he shall be liable on summary conviction to a fine not exceeding [level 4 on the standard scale].

(2) If the employer of [drivers] of a vehicle to which section 97 of this Act applies fails without reasonable excuse to secure that they comply with subsection (1)(a) of this section, he shall be liable on summary conviction to a fine not exceeding [level 4 on the standard scale].

(3) Where a [driver] of a vehicle to which section 97 of this Act applies has two or more employers by whom he is employed as a [driver] of such a vehicle, subsection (1)(a) and subsection (2) of this section shall apply as if any reference to his employer, or any reference which is to be construed as such a reference, were a reference to such of those employers as was the first to employ him in that capacity.]   **[36]**

NOTES
Commencement: 14 January 1980 (certain purposes); 31 December 1981 (remainder).
Substituted by the Passenger and Goods Vehicles (Recording Equipment) Regulations 1979, SI 1979 No 1746, reg 2(1).
Sub-s (1), (2): maximum fines increased and converted to the standard scale by the Criminal Justice Act 1982, ss 37, 39(2), 46, Sch 3; other amendments made by the Community Drivers' Hours and Recording Equipment Regulations 1986, SI 1986 No 1457, reg 3(3).
Sub-s (3): amended by the Community Drivers' Hours and Recording Equipment Regulations 1986, SI 1986 No 1457, reg 3(3).

[97AA. Forgery, etc of seals on recording equipment

(1) A person who, with intent to deceive, forges, alters, or uses any seal on recording equipment installed in, or designed for installation in, a vehicle to which section 97 of this Act applies, shall be guilty of an offence.

(2) A person guilty of an offence under subsection (1) above shall be liable—

(a) on conviction on indictment, to imprisonment for a term not exceeding two years, or

(b) on summary conviction, to a fine not exceeding the statutory maximum.

(3) In the application of this section in England and Wales a person "forges" a seal if he makes a false seal in order that it may be used as a genuine.]   **[36A]**

NOTES
Commencement: 23 November 1989.
Inserted by the Passenger and Goods Vehicles (Recording Equipment) Regulations 1989, SI 1989/2121, reg 3.

97B. Records etc produced by equipment may be used in evidence

[(1) Where recording equipment is installed in a vehicle to which this Part of this Act applies, any record produced by means of the equipment shall, in any proceedings under this Part of this Act, be evidence, and in Scotland sufficient evidence, of the matters appearing from the record.

(2) Any entry made on a record sheet by a [driver] for the purposes of [Article 15(2) or (5) or 16(2)] of the Community Recording Equipment Regulation shall, in any proceedings under this Part of this Act, be evidence, and in Scotland sufficient evidence, of the matters appearing from that entry.]

[37–38]

NOTES
Commencement: 14 January 1980.
Substituted by the Passenger and Goods Vehicles (Recording Equipment) Regulations 1979, SI 1979 No 1746, reg 2(1).
Sub-s (2): amended by the Community Drivers' Hours and Recording Equipment Regulations 1986, SI 1986 No 1457, reg 3(3).

98. Written records

(1) The Minister may make regulations—

(a) for requiring drivers to keep, and employers of employee-drivers to cause to be kept, in such books as may be specified in the regulations records with respect to such matter relevant to the enforcement of this Part of this Act as may be so specified; and

(b) for requiring owner-drivers and the employers of employee-drivers to maintain such registers as may be so specified with respect to any such books as aforesaid which are in their possession or in that of any employee-drivers in their employment.

(2) Regulations under this section may contain such supplementary and incidental provisions [including provisions supplementary and incidental to the requirements of [the applicable Community rules] as to [books, records or documents]] as the Minister thinks necessary or expedient, including in particular provisions—

(a) specifying the person or persons from whom books and registers required for the purposes of the regulations [or of [the applicable Community rules]] are to be obtained and, if provision is made for them to be obtained from the Minister, charging a fee for their issue by him (which shall be payable into the Consolidated Fund);

(b) as to the form and manner of making of entries in such books and registers;

(c) as to the issue by and return to the employers of employee-drivers of books required to be kept by the latter for the purposes of the regulations;

(d) requiring any book in current use for the purposes of the regulations to be carried on, or by the driver of, any vehicle, as to the preservation of any books and registers used for those purposes, and otherwise as to the manner in which those books and registers are to be dealt with;

(e) for exemptions from all or any of the requirements of the regulations in respect of drivers of small goods vehicles as defined in section 103(6) of this Act and for other exemptions from all or any of those requirements.

[(2A) The requirements of regulations made under this section shall not apply as respects the driving of a vehicle to which section 97 of this Act applies and in relation to which subsection (1)(b) of that section has come into force.]

(3) Subject to the provisions of any regulations made by the Minister, the traffic [commissioner] for any area may dispense with the observance by any employee-driver or his employer, or by any owner-driver, of any requirement imposed under this section, either generally or in such circumstances or to such extent as the [commissioner thinks] fit, but the traffic [commissioner] shall not grant such a dispensation unless satisfied that it is not reasonably practicable for the requirement dispensed with to be observed.

(4) Any person who contravenes any regulations made under this section [or any requirement as to [books, records or documents] of [the applicable Community rules]] shall be liable on summary conviction to a fine not exceeding [level 4 on the standard scale]; but the employer of an employee-driver shall not be liable to be convicted under this subsection by reason of contravening any such regulation whereby he is required to cause any records to be kept if he proves to the court that he has given proper instructions to his employees with respect to the keeping of the records and has from time to time taken reasonable steps to secure that those instructions are being carried out.

[(4A) A person shall not be liable to be convicted under subsection (4) of this section by reason of contravening any regulation made under this section if he proves to the court that, if the vehicle in question had been such a vehicle as is mentioned in subsection (2A) of this section, there would have been no contravention of the provisions of this Part of this Act so far as they relate to the use of such vehicles.]

(5) Any entry made by an employee-driver for the purposes of regulations under this section [or of [the applicable community rules]] shall, in any proceedings under this Part of this Act, be admissible in evidence against his employer.   **[39]**

NOTES
Commencement: 14 January 1980 (sub-ss (2A), (4A); 20 November 1969 (remainder).
Commencement order: SI 1969 No 1613.
Sub-s (1): Regulations, see the Drivers Hours (Keeping of Records) Regulations 1987, SI 1987 No 1421.
Sub-ss (2), (5): amended by the European Communities Act 1972, s 4, Sch 4, para 9(2)(a), (c), further amended by the Road Traffic (Drivers' Ages and Hours of Work) Act 1976, s 2(1)(c), (g).
Sub-ss (2A), (4A): added by the Passenger and Goods Vehicles (Recording Equipment) Regulations 1979, SI 1979 No 1746, reg 3(1), (2).
Sub-s (3): amended by the Transport Act 1985, s 3, Sch 2, Part II.
Sub-s (4): first amendment made by the European Communities Act 1972, s 4, Sch 4, para 9(2), further amended by the Road Traffic (Drivers' Ages and Hours of Work) Act 1976, s 2(1); maximum fine increased and converted to a level on the standard scale by the Criminal Justice Act 1982, ss 37, 38, 46, as amended.

99. Inspection of records and other documents

(1) An officer may, on production if so required of his authority, require any person to produce, and permit him to inspect and copy—

(a) any book or register which that person is required by regulations under section 98 of this Act to carry or have in his possession for the purpose of making in it any entry required by those regulations or which is required under those regulations to be carried on any vehicle of which that person is the driver;

(b) any ..., book or register which that person is required by regulations under section ... 98 of this Act to preserve;

[(bb) any record sheet which that person is required by [Article 14(2)] of the Community Recording Equipment Regulation to retain or by [Article 15(7)] of that Regulation to be able to produce];

(c) if that person is the owner of a vehicle to which this Part of this Act applies, any other document of that person which the officer may reasonably require to inspect for the purpose of ascertaining whether the provisions of this Part of this Act or of regulations made thereunder have been complied with;

[(d) any ... book, register or document required by [the applicable Community rules] or which the officer may reasonably require to inspect for the purpose of ascertaining whether the requirements of [the applicable Community rules] have been complied with];

and that record [sheet], book, register or document shall, if the officer so requires by notice in writing served on that person, be produced at the office of the traffic [commissioner] specified in the notice within such time (not being less than ten days) from the service of the notice as may be so specified.

(2) An officer may, on production if so required of his authority—

[(a) at any time, enter any vehicle to which this Part of this Act applies and inspect that vehicle and any recording equipment installed in it and inspect and copy any record sheet on the vehicle on which a record has been produced by means of the equipment or an entry has been made];

(b) at any time which is reasonable having regard to the circumstances of the case, enter any premises on which he has reason to believe that such a vehicle is kept or that any such [record sheets], books, registers or other documents as are mentioned in subsection (1) of this section are to be found, and inspect any such vehicle, and inspect and copy any such record [sheet], book, register or document, which he finds there.

(3) For the purpose of exercising his powers under subsection (2)(a) and, in respect of a document carried on, or by the driver of, a vehicle, under subsection (1)(a) [or (d)] of this section, an officer may detain the vehicle in question during such time as is required for the exercise of that power.

(4) Any person who—

(a) fails to comply with any requirement under subsection (1) of this section; or

(b) obstructs an officer in the exercise of his powers under subsection (2) or (3) of this section,

shall be liable on summary conviction to a fine not exceeding [level 3 on the standard scale].

[4A] A person shall not be liable to be convicted under subsection (4) of this section by reason of failing to comply with any requirement under subsection (1)(a) or (b) of this section if he proves to the court that, if the vehicle in question had been such a vehicle as is mentioned in section 98(2A) of this Act, there would have been no contravention of the provisions of this Part of this Act so far as they relate to the use of such vehicles.]

(5) Any person who makes, or causes to be made, [any record or entry on a record sheet kept or carried for the purposes of the Community Recording Equipment Regulation or] section 97 of this Act or any entry in a [book, register or document kept or carried] for the purposes of regulations under section 98 thereof [or [the applicable Community rules]] which he knows to be false or, with intent to deceive, alters or causes to be altered any such record or entry shall be liable—

    (a) on summary conviction, to a fine not exceeding [the prescribed sum];
    (b) on conviction on indictment, to imprisonment for a term not exceeding two years.

(6) If an officer has reason to believe that an offence under subsection (5) of this section has been committed in respect of any record or document inspected by him under this section, he may seize that record or document; and where a record or document is seized as aforesaid and within six months of the date on which it was seized no person has been charged since that date with an offence in relation to that record or document under that subsection and the record or document has not been returned to the person from whom it was taken, a magistrate's court shall, on an application made for the purpose by that person or by an officer, make such order respecting the disposal of the record or document and award such costs as the justice of the case may require.

(7) Any proceedings in Scotland under subsection (6) of this section shall be taken by way of summary application in the sheriff court; and in the application of that subsection to Scotland references to costs shall be construed as references to expenses.

(8) In this section "officer" means [an examiner appointed under section 66A of the Road Traffic Act 1988] and any person authorised for the purposes of this section by the traffic [commissioner] for any area.

(9) The powers conferred by this section on an officer as defined in subsection (8) of this section shall be exercisable also by a police constable, who shall not, if wearing uniform, be required to produce any authority.

(10) In this section references to the inspection and copying of any record produced by means of equipment installed for the purposes of section 97 of this Act in a vehicle include references to the application to the record of any process for eliciting the information recorded thereby and to taking down the information elicited from it.   [40]

NOTES
    Commencement: 14 January 1980 (sub-s (4A)); 1 March 1970 (sub-ss (1)-(9) certain purposes); to be appointed (remainder).
    Commencement order: SI 1970 No 259.
    Sub-s (1): words omitted from para (b) repealed by the Passenger and Goods Vehicles (Recording Equipment) Regulations 1979, SI 1979 No 1746, reg 3; para (bb) added by SI 1979 No 1746, reg 3, amended by the Community Drivers' Hours and Recording Equipment Regulations 1986, SI 1986 No 1457, reg 3(3); para (d) added by the European Communities Act, s 4, Sch 4, para 9(2), amended by the Road Traffic (Drivers' Ages and Hours of Work) Act 1976, s 2(1); fifth amendment in square brackets made by SI 1979 No 1746, reg 3; final amendment in square brackets made by the Transport Act 1985, s 3(5), Sch 2, Part II, para 1(4).

Sub-s (2): amended by SI 1979 No 1746, reg 3.
Sub-s (3): amended by the European Communities Act, s 4, Sch 4, para 9(2).
Sub-s (4): maximum fine increased and converted to a level on the standard scale by the Criminal Justice Act 1982, ss 37, 38, 46 as amended.
Sub-s (4A): added by SI 1979 No 1746, reg 3.
Sub-s (5): first amendment made by SI 1979 No 1746, reg 3; second amendment made by the Road Traffic (Drivers' Ages and Hours of Work) Act 1976, s 2(1); third amendment made by the European Communities Act, s 4, Sch 4, para 9(2), further amended by the Road Traffic (Drivers' Ages and Hours of Work) Act 1976, s 2(1); final amendment made by the Magistrates' Courts Act 1980, s 32(2) as amended.
Sub-s (8): first words in square brackets substituted by the Road Traffic Act 1991, s 48, Sch 4, para 2; second amendment in square brackets made by the Transport Act 1985, s 3(5), Sch 2, Part II, para 1(4).
Act of 1960: Road Traffic Act 1960.

100. Power to give effect to international agreements

(1) The Minister may by order make, in relation to Great Britain such provision as appears to him to be requisite for enabling the United Kingdom to become a party to any international agreement relating to the drivers or crews of vehicles used on international journeys, and, without prejudice to the generality of the foregoing provisions of this subsection, an order under this subsection may—

    (a) modify or exclude any of the provisions contained in or having effect under this Part of this Act or contained in or having effect under any other enactment passed before or after this Act;

    (b) provide for exemptions from all or any of the provisions of the order;

    (c) provide for the punishment of contraventions of any provision of the order;

    (d) contain such supplementary, incidental or consequential provisions as appear to the Minister to be necessary or expedient.

(2) The Governor of Northern Ireland may, by Order in the Privy Council of Northern Ireland, make provision in relation to Northern Ireland for any purpose for which provision may be made in relation to Great Britain under subsection (1) of this section, and in relation to any such Order the provisions of that subsection shall apply accordingly as if for references to the Minister there were substituted references to the Governor of Northern Ireland and such Order may authorise the Ministry of Home Affairs for Northern Ireland to make regulations for any of the purposes of the Order.   **[41]**

NOTES
    Commencement: 1 March 1970.
    Commencement order: SI 1970 No 259.

101. Orders and regulations under Part VI

(1) In relation to orders or regulations made under this Part of this Act, the provisions of this section shall have effect in addition to the provisions of section 157 of this Act.

(2) Any order or regulations under this Part of this Act may make different provision for different classes of case.

(3) No order shall be made under section 96(12) or 100(1) of this Act unless a draft of the order has been laid before, and approved by a resolution of, each House of Parliament; and any regulations made under this Part of this Act (except regulations made [under section 95(1) or] by virtue of an Order under section 100(2)) shall be subject to annulment in pursuance of a resolution of either House of Parliament.

[(3A) No regulations shall be made under section 95(1) of this Act unless a draft of the regulations has been laid before, and approved by a resolution of, each House of Parliament.]

(4) No recommendation shall be made to the Governor of Northern Ireland in Council to make an Order under subsection (2) of section 100 of this Act unless a draft thereof has been laid before the Parliament of Northern Ireland and has been approved by resolution of each House of Parliament of Northern Ireland; and an Order under that subsection which authorises the making of regulations may make provision for the laying of such regulations before the Parliament of Northern Ireland and for their annulment in such circumstances as may be specified in the Order.

(5) A definition or description of a class of vehicles for the purposes of any order or regulation under this Part of this Act may be framed by reference to any characteristic of the vehicles or to any other circumstances whatsoever.

(6) Before making any order or regulations under this Part of this Act the Minister shall consult with such representative organisations as he thinks fit.
[42]

NOTES
    Commencement: 4 January 1978 (sub-s (3A)); 20 November 1969 (remainder).
    Commencement order: SI 1969 No 1613.
    Sub-s (3): amended by the Road Traffic (Drivers' Ages and Hours of Work) Act 1976, s 2(1)(i).
    Sub-s (3A): added by the Road Traffic (Drivers' Ages and Hours of Work) Act 1976, s 2(1)(i).

102. Application to the Crown and exemption for police and fire brigade

(1) Subject to subsection (2) of this section, this Part of this Act shall apply to vehicles and persons in the public service of the Crown.

(2) This Part of this Act shall not apply in the case of motor vehicles owned by the Secretary of State for Defence and used for naval, military or air force purposes or in the case of vehicles so used while being driven by persons for the time being subject to the orders of a member of the armed forces of the Crown.

[(3) Where an offence under this Part of this Act is alleged to have been committed in connection with a vehicle in the public service of the Crown, proceedings may be brought in respect of the offence against a person nominated for the purpose on behalf of the Crown; and, subject to subsection (3A) below, where any such offence is committed any person so nominated shall also be guilty of the offence as well as any person actually responsible for the offence (but without prejudice to proceedings against any person so responsible).

(3A) Where a person is convicted of an offence by virtue of subsection (3) above—

    (a) no order may be made on his conviction save an order imposing a fine,

    (b) payment of any fine imposed on him in respect of that offence may not be enforced against him, and

    (c) apart from the imposition of any such fine, the conviction shall be disregarded for all purposes other than any appeal (whether by way of case stated or otherwise).]

(4) This Part of this Act shall not apply in the case of motor vehicles while being used for police or fire brigade purposes.   [43]

NOTES
  Commencement: 15 May 1989 (sub-ss (3), (3A)); before 1 January 1970 (remainder).
  Commencement order: SI 1969 No 1613.
  Sub-s (3): substituted by the Road Traffic (Consequential Provisions) Act 1988, s 4, Sch 3, para
6(6).
  Sub-s (3A): added by the Transport Act 1982, s 64; substituted by the Road Traffic (Consequential
Provisions) Act 1988, s 4, Sch 3, para 6(6).

102A. Exclusion of application to tramcars and trolley vehicles

[(1) This Part of this Act and section 255 of the Road Traffic Act 1960 in its
application thereto shall not apply to tramcars or trolley vehicles operated under
statutory powers.

(2) In this section "operated under statutory powers' means, in relation to
tramcars or trolley vehicles, that their use is authorised or regulated by special
Act of Parliament or by an order having the force of an Act.

(3) Subsection (1) above shall have effect subject to any such Act or order as
is mentioned in subsection (2) above, and any such Act or order may apply to
the tramcars or trolley vehicles to which it relates any of the provisions excluded
by the said subsection (1).]   **[44]**

NOTES
  Commencement: 15 May 1989.
  Added by the Road Traffic (Consequential Provisions) Act 1988, s 4, Sch 3, para 6(7).

103. Interpretation, supplementary provisions, etc, for Part VI

(1) In this Part of this Act—
  "agriculture" has the meaning assigned by section 109(3) of the Agriculture
    Act 1947 or, in relation to Scotland, section 86(3) of the Agriculture
    (Scotland) Act 1948;
  ["the Community Recording Equipment Regulation" has the meaning
    given by section 97(7) of this Act];
  "driver", "employee-driver" and "owner-driver" have the meaning
    assigned by section 95(3) of this Act;
  "employer", in relation to an employee-driver, means the employer of
    that driver in the employment by virtue of which that driver is an
    employee-driver;
  ["the applicable Community rules" means any directly applicable
    Community provision for the time being in force about the driving of
    road vehicles];
  ["the domestic drivers' hours code" has the meaning given by section
    96(13) of this Act];
  "prescribed" means prescribed by regulations made by the Minister;
  ["recording equipment" has the meaning given by section 97(7) of this
    Act];
  ["record sheet" includes a temporary sheet attached to a record sheet in
    accordance with [Article 16(2)] of the Community Recording Equipment
    Regulation];
  ["relevant Community provision" means any Community provision for
    the time being in force about the driving of road vehicles, whether
    directly applicable or not]
  "working day", in relation to any driver, means—
  (a) any period during which he is on duty and which does not fall to be
    aggregated with any other such period by virtue of paragraph (b) of
    this definition; and

(b) where a period during which he is on duty is not followed by an interval for rest of not less than eleven hours or (where permitted by virtue of section 96(4)(b) of this Act) of not less than nine and a half hours, the aggregate of that period and each successive such period until there is such an interval as aforesaid, together with any interval or intervals between periods so aggregated;

["working week" means, subject to subsection (5) of this section, a week beginning at midnight between Sunday and Monday;]

and any expression not defined above which is also used in the Act of 1960 has the same meaning as in that Act.

(2) For the purposes of this Part of this Act a director of a company shall be deemed to be employed by it.

(3) In this Part of this Act references to a person driving a vehicle are references to his being at the driving controls of the vehicle for the purpose of controlling its movements, whether it is in motion or is stationary with the engine running.

(4) In this Part of this Act references to a driver being on duty are references—

(a) in the case of an employee-driver, to his being on duty (whether for the purpose of driving a vehicle to which this Part of this Act applies or for other purposes) in the employment by virtue of which he is an employee-driver, or in any other employment under the person who is his employer in the first-mentioned employment; and

(b) in the case of an owner-driver, to his driving a vehicle to which this Part of this Act applies for the purposes of a trade or business carried on by him or being otherwise engaged in work for the purposes of that trade or business, being work in connection with such a vehicle or the load carried thereby.

(5) The traffic [commissioner] for any area may, on the application of an owner-driver or of the employer of an employee-driver, from time to time direct that a week beginning at midnight between two days other than [Sunday and Monday] shall be, or be deemed to have been, a working week in relation to that owner-driver or employee-driver; but where by virtue of any such direction a new working week begins before the expiration of a previous working week then, without prejudice to the application of the provisions of this Part of this Act in relation to the new working week, those provisions shall continue to apply in relation to the previous working week until its expiration.

(6) In [section] 98(2)(e) of this Act "a small goods vehicle" means a goods vehicle which has a plated weight of the prescribed description not exceeding [3500 kilograms] or (not having a plated weight) has an unladen weight not exceeding [1525 kilograms]; but the Minister may by regulations direct that the foregoing provisions of this subsection shall have effect, in relation to either or both of those sections—

(a) with the substitution for either of the weights there specified of such other weight as may be specified in the regulations;

(b) with the substitution for either of those weights or for any other weight for the time being specified as aforesaid of a weight expressed in terms of the metric system, being a weight which is equivalent to that for which it is substituted or does not differ from it by more than five per cent. thereof.

[(7) An offence under this Part of this Act may be treated for the purpose of conferring jurisdiction on a court (but without prejudice to any jurisdiction it may have apart from this subsection) as having been committed in any of the following places, that is to say—

(a) the place where the person charged with the offence was driving when evidence of the offence first came to the attention of a constable or vehicle examiner;

(b) the place where that person resides or is or is believed to reside or be at the time when the proceedings are commenced: or

(c) the place where at that time that person or, in the case of an employee-driver, that person's employer or, in the case of an owner-driver, the person for whom he was driving, has his place or principal place of business or his operating centre for the vehicle in question.

In this subsection "vehicle examiner" means an officer within the meaning of section 99 of this Act.]

(8) The enactments specified in Schedule 11 to this Act shall have effect subject to the amendments there specified.

(9) Any order made under section 166(2) of this Act appointing a day for the purposes of any of the provisions of this Part of this Act may contain such transitional provision as the Minister thinks necessary or expedient as respects the application of any particular provision of this Part of this Act to a working week or working day falling partly before and partly after the date on which that provision comes into operation. **[45]**

NOTES

Commencement: Before 1 January 1970 (sub-ss (1)-(7), (9)); 1 March 1970 (sub-s (8)).
Commencement orders: SI 1969 No 1613, 1970 No 259.

Sub-s (1): definitions "the Community Recording Equipment Regulation" and "recording equipment" added by the Passenger and Goods Vehicles (Recording Equipment) Regulations 1979, SI 1979 No 1746, reg 3(7); definition "record sheet" added by the Passenger and Goods Vehicles (Recording Equipment) Regulations 1979, SI 1979 No 1746, reg 3(7), amended by the Community Drivers' Hours and Recording Equipment Regulations 1986, SI 1986 No 1457, reg 3(3)(g); definition "the applicable Community rules" substituted and definitions "the domestic drivers' hours code", and "relevant Community provision" added by the Road Traffic (Drivers' Ages and Hours of Work) Act 1976, s 2(1)(a), (b); definition "working week" substituted by the Drivers' Hours (Harmonisation with Community Rules) Regulations 1986, SI 1986 No 1458, reg 3; words omitted repealed by the Transport Act 1985, s 139(3), Sch 8.

Sub-s (5): first amendment made by Transport Act 1985, s 3(5), Sch 2, Part II; second amendment made by the Drivers' Hours (Harmonisation with Community Rules) Regulations 1986, SI 1986 No 1458, reg 3.

Sub-s (6): first amendment made by SI 1979 No 1746, reg 3(8); second and third amendments made by SI 1981 No 1373, reg 4(2), Schedule, Part IIIB.

Sub-s (7): substituted by the Road Traffic (Drivers' Ages and Hours of Work) Act 1976, s 3.

Act of 1960: Road Traffic Act 1960.

VEHICLES (EXCISE) ACT 1971

(c 10)

ARRANGEMENT OF SECTIONS

EXCISE DUTY ON, AND LICENSING OF, MECHANICALLY PROPELLED VEHICLES

An Act to consolidate certain enactments relating to excise duties on mechanically propelled vehicles, and to the licensing and registration of such vehicles with amendments to give effect to recommendations of the Law Commission and the Scottish Law Commission   [16 March 1971]

EXCISE DUTY ON, AND LICENSING OF, MECHANICALLY PROPELLED VEHICLES

1. Charge of duty

(1) Subject to the provisions of this Act, a duty of excise shall be charged in respect of every mechanically propelled vehicle used or kept on any public road in [the United Kingdom] and shall be paid upon a licence to be taken out by the person keeping the vehicle.

(2) The duty chargeable under this section in respect of a vehicle of any description shall be chargeable by reference to the annual rate applicable in accordance with the provisions of that one of [Schedules 1 to 5] to this Act which relates to vehicles of that description.

(3) For the purposes of the said duty, in so far as chargeable in respect of the keeping of a vehicle on a road, a vehicle shall be deemed—

    (a) to be chargeable with the like duty as on the occasion of the issue of the vehicle licence or last vehicle licence issued for the vehicle under this Act, and to be so chargeable by reference to the rate specified in the same Schedule to this Act as on that occasion, or

    (b) if no vehicle licence has been issued for the vehicle under this Act, to be chargeable by reference to the rate applicable to it under Schedule 5 to this Act.

(4) Nothing in this section shall operate so as to render lawful the keeping of a vehicle for any period, in any manner or at any place, if to do so would be unlawful apart from this section.   **[46]**

NOTES
     Commencement: 1 April 1971.
     This section derived from the Vehicles (Excise) Act 1962, ss 1, 4.
     Sub-s (1): words in square brackets substituted by the Finance Act 1991, s 10(2)(a), Sch 3, Part I, paras 1, 2.
     Sub-s (2): words in square brackets substituted by the Finance Act 1988, s 4(1), (7), (9), Sch 2, Part II, paras 1, 2.

2. Commencement and duration of licences, and rate of duty

(1) A vehicle licence may be taken out—

    (a) in the case of any vehicle, for any period of twelve months;

(b) in the case of any vehicle the annual rate of duty applicable to which exceeds [£35] for any period of [six months],

(c) ...

and shall, subject to the provisions of section 13 of this Act, first have effect on the day specified by the applicant in the application for the licence.

(2) A licence for a period of four months shall expire with such day in the fourth month after that in which the licence first has effect as corresponds to the day preceding that on which it first has effect, so however that a licence for that period shall—

(a) if it first has effect on the first day of a month, expire with the last day of the third month after that month; and

(b) if it first has effect on 30th or 31st October, expire with the last day of the following February.

(3) A licence which first has effect before the day on which it is issued shall not affect any criminal liability incurred before that day.

(4) The duty payable on a vehicle licence for a vehicle of any description shall—

(a) if the licence is taken out for a period of twelve months, be paid at the annual rate of duty applicable to vehicles of that description;

(b) if the licence is taken out for a period of [six months, be paid at a rate equal to one half of the said annual rate plus ten per cent of that amount;]

(c) ...

and in computing the rate of duty in accordance with paragraph (b) ... above, any fraction of 5p shall be treated as 5p if it exceeds 2.5p and shall otherwise be disregarded.

(5) Notwithstanding anything in this Act, the Secretary of State may, during the period of two years beginning with the day when this subsection first takes effect, provide by regulations that, in such cases as may be determined by or under the regulations, the duration of a licence taken out after the coming into force of the regulations shall be longer or shorter, by such period not exceeding thirty days as may be so determined, than its duration would have been apart from the regulations; and where the duration of a licence is altered by virtue of this subsection the duty payable upon the licence shall be increased or reduced proportionately.

(6) At the expiration of the period of two years mentioned in subsection (5) above that subsection shall cease to have effect, but without prejudice to any licence issued, or any payment made or falling to be made, by virtue of any regulations in force under that subsection immediately before the expiration of that period.   **[47]**

NOTES

Commencement: 1 April 1971.

Sub-s (1) derived from the Vehicles (Excise) Act 1962, s 2(1), the Vehicle and Driving Licences Act 1969, s 4(1), and SI 1968 No 439; sub-ss (2), (3) derived from the Vehicle and Driving Licences Act 1969, s 4(3), (7); sub-s (4) derived from the Vehicles (Excise) Act 1962, s 2(2); sub-ss (5), (6) derived from the Vehicle and Driving Licences Act 1969, s 4(8), (9), and SI 1970 No 1681.

Sub-s (1): in para (b) first amendment made by the Finance Act 1985, s 4(4), (8) in respect of licences taken out after 19 March 1985; second amendment made by the Vehicle Licences (Duration and Rate of Duty) Order 1980, SI 1980 No 1183; para (c) repealed by the Finance Act 1988, ss 4, 148, Sch 14, Part II.

Sub-s (4): amendment in square brackets made by SI 1980 No 1183; words omitted repealed by the Finance Act 1988, s 148, Sch 14, Part II.

3. Collection of duty, etc

(1) The duty chargeable under this Act shall be levied by the Secretary of State.

(2) Subject to the provisions of this Act the Secretary of State and his officers (including any body or person authorised by the Secretary of State to act as his agent for the purposes of this Act) shall have for the purpose of levying the duty aforesaid the same powers, duties and liabilities as the Commissioners of Customs and Excise and their officers have with respect to duties of excise [(other than duties on imported goods) and to the issue and cancellation of licences on which duties of excise are imposed and to other matters (not being matters relating only to duties on imported goods) under the Acts relating to duties of excise and excise licences; and, subject to those provisions and in particular to section 28 or 29 and to section 35(3) of this Act, all enactments relating to those duties and to punishments and penalties in connection therewith (other than enactments relating only to duties on imported goods) shall apply accordingly.]

(3) Without prejudice to subsection (2) above, the Secretary of State shall, with respect to the duty of excise chargeable under this Act and the excise licences provided for thereby, have the powers given to the said Commissioners by the Acts relating to duties of excise and excise licences for the restoration of any forfeiture and the mitigation or remission of any penalty or part thereof.

(4) The duty levied by the Secretary of State under this Act shall be paid into the Consolidated Fund.

(5) Any sums received by the Secretary of State by virtue of this Act by way of fees shall be paid into the Consolidated Fund.   **[48]**

NOTES
     Commencement: 1 April 1971.
     Sub-ss (1)–(4) derived from the Vehicles (Excise) Act 1962, s 5, the National Loans Act 1968, s 1(8), and SI 1970 No 1681; sub-s (5) derived from the Vehicle and Driving Licences Act 1969, s 36(2).
     Sub-s (2): amended by the Customs and Excise Management Act 1979, s 177(1), Sch 4, para 12, Table, Part I.

EXEMPTIONS FROM DUTY

4. Exemptions from duty of certain descriptions of vehicle

(1) No duty shall be chargeable under this Act in respect of mechanically propelled vehicles of any of the following descriptions, that is to say—

     [(*aa*) electrically propelled vehicles]
     (a) fire engines;
     (b) vehicles kept by a local authority while they are used or kept on a road for the purposes of their fire brigade service;
     (c) ambulances;
     [(*ca*) veterinary ambulances;]
     [(*cb*) vehicles used solely as mine rescue vehicles or for the purpose of conveying or drawing emergency winding-gear at mines;]
     (d) road rollers;
     (e) vehicles used on tram lines, . . .
     (f) vehicles used or kept on a road for no purpose other than the haulage of lifeboats and the conveyance of the necessary gear of the lifeboats which are being hauled;

(g) vehicles (including cycles with an attachment for propelling them by mechanical power) which do not exceed [ten] hundredweight in weight unladen and are adapted, and used or kept on a road, for invalids;

(h) road construction vehicles used or kept on a road solely for the conveyance of built-in road construction machinery (with or without articles or material used for the purposes of that machinery);

(i) vehicles constructed or adapted, and used, solely for the conveyance of machinery for spreading material on roads to deal with frost, ice or snow or for the conveyance of such machinery and articles and material used for the purposes of that machinery;

(j) local authority's watering vehicles;

(k) tower wagons used solely by a street lighting authority, or by any person acting in pursuance of a contract with such an authority, for the purpose of installing or maintaining materials or apparatus for lighting streets, roads or public places;

[(*ka*) vehicles . . . neither constructed nor adapted for use nor used for the carriage of a driver or passenger;

(*kb*) vehicles (other than ambulances) used for the carriage of disabled persons by bodies for the time being recognised for the purposes of this paragraph by the Secretary of State;]

[(*l*) vehicles which are made available by the Secretary of State to any person, body or local authority in pursuance of section 11 or section 13 of the National Health Service Reorganisation Act 1973 and which are used in accordance with the terms on which they are so made available.]

[(1A) The Secretary of State shall recognise a body for the purposes of subsection (1)(*kb*) above if, on application made to him in such manner as he may specify, it appears to him that the body is concerned with the care of disabled persons.

(1B) The issue by the Secretary of State of a nil licence in respect of a mechanically propelled vehicle shall be treated, where the document is issued by virtue of paragraph (*kb*) of subsection (1) above, as recognition by him for the purposes of that paragraph of the body by reference to whose use of the vehicle the document is issued.

(1C) The Secretary of State may withdraw recognition of a body for the purposes of subsection (1)(*kb*) above if it appears to him that the body is no longer concerned with the care of disabled persons.

(1D) The reference in subsection (1B) above to the issue by the Secretary of State of a nil licence is a reference to the issue by him in accordance with regulations under this Act of a document which—

(a) is in the form of a vehicle licence, and

(b) has the word "NIL" marked in the space provided for indicating the amount of duty payable.]

(2) In this section—

["fire engine" means a vehicle—

(a) constructed or adapted for use for the purpose of fire fighting, salvage or both, and

(b) used solely for the purposes of a fire brigade (whether or not one maintained under the Fire Services Act 1947);]

["ambulance" means a vehicle which—

(a) is constructed or adapted for, and used for no other purpose than, the carriage of sick, injured or disabled persons to or from welfare centres or places where medical or dental treatment is given; and

(b) is readily identifiable as a vehicle used for the carriage of such persons by virtue of being marked "Ambulance" on both sides;

"disabled person" means a person suffering from a physical or mental defect or disability;

"veterinary ambulance" means a vehicle which—

(a) is used for no other purpose than the carriage of sick or injured animals to or from places where veterinary treatment is given; and

(b) is readily identifiable as a vehicle used for the carriage of such animals by virtue of being marked "Veterinary Ambulance" on both sides;]

["weight unladen" shall be construed in accordance with the Road Traffic Act 1988;]

"road construction vehicle" means a vehicle constructed or adapted for use for the conveyance of built-in road construction machinery and not constructed or adapted for the conveyance of any other load except articles and material used for the purposes of that machinery;

"road construction machinery" means a machine or contrivance suitable for use for the construction or repair of roads and used for no purpose other than the construction or repair of roads at the public expense;

"built-in road construction machinery", in relation to a vehicle, means road construction machinery built in as part of the vehicle or permanently attached thereto;

"local authority's watering vehicle" means a vehicle used solely within the area of a local authority by that local authority, or by any person acting in pursuance of a contract with that local authority, for the purpose of cleansing or watering roads or cleansing gulleys;

["tower wagon" means a goods vehicle—

(a) into which there is built, as part of the vehicle, any expanding or extensible contrivance designed for facilitating the erection, inspection, repair or maintenance of overhead structures or equipment, and

(b) which is neither constructed nor adapted for use nor used for the conveyance of any load other than—

(i) such a contrivance and articles used in connection therewith, and

(ii) articles used in connection with the installation or maintenance, by means of such a contrivance, of materials or apparatus for lighting streets, roads or public places.]

"street lighting authority" means any local authority or Minister having power under any enactment to provide or maintain materials or apparatus for lighting streets, roads or public places.

[(3) In its application to Northern Ireland, this section shall have effect as if—

(a) in paragraph (b) of subsection (1) for "a local authority" there were substituted "the Fire Authority for Northern Ireland" and for "their" there were substituted "its";

(b) in paragraph (j) of that subsection for "local authority's" there were substituted "district council's";

(c) in subsection (2)—

(i) in the definition of "fire engine", for "the Fire Services Act 1947" there were substituted "the Fire Services (Northern Ireland) Order 1984";

      (ii) in the definition of "weight unladen" for "section 190(2) of the Road Traffic Act 1988" there were substituted "Article 2(3) of the Road Traffic (Northern Ireland) Order 1981";

     (iii) in the definition of "local authority's watering vehicle", for "local authority's" there were substituted "district council's" and for the words "local authority", in each place where they occur, there were substituted "district council"; and

     (iv) in the definition of "street lighting authority", for "local authority or Minister" there were substituted "Northern Ireland department"].   **[49]**

NOTES

Commencement: 1 October 1991 (sub-s (3)); 21 March 1990 (sub-ss (1A)-(1D)); 1 April 1971 (remainder).

This section derived from the Vehicles (Excise) Act 1962, s 6(1), (8).

Sub-s (1): para (*aa*) added by the Finance Act 1980, s 4(4); paras (*ca*), (*ka*), (*kb*) added by the Finance Act 1990, s 6(1), (2), (3), (6); para (*cb*) inserted by the Finance Act 1991, s 8(1), (2); words omitted from para (e) repealed by the Finance (No 2) Act 1975, s 5(5), (6); para (g) amended by the Finance Act 1972, s 128(3); words omitted from para (*ka*) repealed by the Finance Act 1991, ss 8(1), (3), (7), 123, Sch 17, Part III; para (l) added by the National Health Service (Vehicles) Order 1974, SI 1974 No 168, art 3.

Sub-ss (1A)-(1D): added by the Finance Act 1990, s 6(4), (6).

Sub-s (2): definitions "fire engine" and "weight unladen" inserted by the Finance Act 1991, s 8(1), (4), (5), (7), (8); definitions "ambulance", "disabled person" and "veterinary ambulance" added by the Finance Act 1990, s 6(5), (6); definition "tower wagon" substituted by the Finance Act 1986, s 3(7), Sch 2, Part I, para 2.

Sub-s (3): added by the Finance Act 1991, s 10(2)(a), Sch 3, Part I, paras 1, 3.

---

5. Exemptions from duty in connection with vehicle testing, etc

(1) A mechanically propelled vehicle shall not be chargeable with any duty under this Act by reason of its use on public roads—

   (a) solely for the purpose of submitting it by previous arrangement for a specified time on a specified date for, or bringing it away from, a compulsory test; or

   (b) in the course of a compulsory test, solely for the purpose of taking it to, or bringing it away from, any place where a part of the test is to be or, as the case may be, has been carried out, or of carrying out any part of the test, the person so using it being an authorised person; or

   (c) where the relevant certificate is refused on a compulsory test, solely for the purpose of delivering it by previous arrangement for a specified time on a specified date at a place where work is to be done on it to remedy the defects on the ground of which the certificate was refused, or bringing it away from a place where work has been done on it to remedy such defects.

(2) In paragraph (c) above the reference to work done or to be done on the vehicle to remedy the defects there mentioned is, in a case where the relevant certificate which is refused is a test certificate, a reference to work done or to be done to remedy those defects for a further compulsory test and includes, in a case where the relevant certificate which is refused is a goods vehicle test certificate, type approval certificate or Minister's approval certificate, a reference to work done or to be done to alter the vehicle in some aspect of design, construction, equipment or marking on account of which the certificate was refused.

(3) In this section—

   "compulsory test" means an examination under [section 45 of the Road Traffic Act 1988] with a view to obtaining a test certificate without which a vehicle licence cannot be granted for the vehicle under this Act or, in the case of a goods vehicle for which by virtue of [section 66(3) of that Act] a vehicle licence cannot be so granted, an examination under regulations under [section 49 or for the purposes of sections 54 to 58] of that Act (examinations as to a goods vehicle's compliance with construction and use or type approval requirements respectively) or an examination under regulations under [section 61(2)(a)] of that Act (in connection with alterations to goods vehicles subject to type approval requirements) or for the purposes of [section 60] of that Act (appeals);

"the relevant certificate" means a test certificate as defined in subsection (2) of the said [section 45], a goods vehicle test certificate as defined in the said [section 49], a type approval certificate or a Minister's approval certificate as defined in the said [sections 54 to 58];

"authorised person" in the case of a compulsory test under the said [section 45] means a [person who is, or is acting on behalf of, an examiner or inspector entitled to carry out examinations for the purposes of that section], or a person acting under the personal direction of such a person as aforesaid; and in the case of any other compulsory test means a [vehicle examiner] or a person carrying out the test under his direction or a person driving the vehicle in pursuance of a requirement to do so under regulations under which the compulsory test is carried out;

["vehicle examiner"] means an examiner appointed under section 66A of the Road Traffic Act 1988.]

[(4) In its application to Northern Ireland, this section shall have effect as if—

(a) in subsection (2) for the word "Minister's" there were substituted "Department's"; and

(b) for subsection (3) there were substituted the following subsection—

"(3) In this section—

"authorised person" means an inspector of vehicles within the meaning of Article 2(2) of the Road Traffic (Northern Ireland) Order 1981;

"compulsory test" means an examination to obtain a vehicle test certificate under Article 33 of the Road Traffic (Northern Ireland) Order 1981 without which a vehicle licence cannot be obtained for the vehicle under this Act, or an examination to obtain a goods vehicle certificate, public service vehicle licence or certificate of inspection under Article 53, 60(1) or 67 respectively of that Order;

"the relevant certificate" means a vehicle test certificate, a goods vehicle certificate, a public service vehicle licence (those expressions having the same meanings as they have in the Road Traffic (Northern Ireland) Order 1981) a certificate of inspection within the meaning of Article 67(2) of that Order, a type approval certificate within the meaning of Article 31A of that Order or a Department's approval certificate within the meaning of that Article.]

[50]

NOTES

Commencement: 1 October 1991 (sub-s (4)); 1 April 1971.

This section derived from the Vehicles Excise Act 1962, s 6(5), the Road Safety Act 1967, s 27, and the Vehicle and Driving Licences Act 1969, s 10.

Sub-s (3): words in square brackets in definitions "compulsory test" and "the relevant certificate" and first words in square brackets in definition "authorised person" substituted by the Road Traffic

(Consequential Provisions) Act 1988, s 4, Sch 3, para 8(2); remaining words in square brackets in definition "authorised person" and whole of definition "vehicle examiner" substituted by the Road Traffic Act 1991, s 48, Sch 4, para 4.
    Sub-s (4): added by the Finance Act 1991, ss 10(2)(a), 123, Sch 3, Part I, paras 1, 4.

6. Exemptions from duty in respect of vehicles acquired by overseas residents

[(1) A mechanically propelled vehicle shall not be chargeable with any duty under this Act if it has been supplied to the person keeping it by a taxable person within the meaning of [*section 2(2) of the Value Added Tax Act 1983*] [section 2C of the Value Added Tax Act 1983] and the supply has been zero-rated in pursuance of [subsection (7) of section 16] of that Act; but if, at any time, the value added tax that would have been chargeable on the supply but for the zero-rating becomes payable under [subsection (9)] of that section, or would have become so payable but for any authorisation or waiver under that subsection, then the provisions of subsection (3) below shall apply in relation to that vehicle.]

    (2) ...

    (3) Where under subsection (1) ... above the provisions of this subsection are to apply in relation to a vehicle, the vehicle shall be deemed never to have been exempted from duty under the said subsection (1) ... and, without prejudice to the provisions of section 9 of this Act, unless, or except to the extent that, the Secretary of State sees fit to waive payment of the whole or part of the duty, there shall be recoverable by the Secretary of State as a debt due to him—

(a) from the person by whom the vehicle was acquired from its manufacturer, the duty in respect of the whole period since the registration of the vehicle; or

(b) from any other person who is for the time being the keeper of the vehicle, the duty in respect of the period since the vehicle was first kept by that other person,

other than any part of that period by reference to which there was calculated an amount ordered to be paid by the person in question in respect of the vehicle in pursuance of section 9(1) of this Act.   [51]

NOTES
    Commencement: 1 April 1971 (sub-s (3)); 1 April 1973 (sub-s (1)).
    This section derived from the Finance Act 1969, s 6(1), and SI 1970 No 1681.
    Sub-s (1): substituted with savings by the Finance Act 1972, s 55(6), (7); amended by the Value Added Tax Act 1983, s 50(1), Sch 9, para 2; words in italics prospectively repealed, and subsequent words in square brackets prospectively substituted, by the Finance (No 2) Act 1992, s 14, Sch 3, Part III, para 91, as from a day to be appointed.
    Sub-ss (2), (3): words omitted repealed by the Finance Act 1972, ss 54(8), 134, Sch 28, Part II.

7. Miscellaneous exemptions from duty

(1) If an applicant for a vehicle licence satisfies the Secretary of State that the vehicle is intended to be used on public roads—

(a) only in passing from land in his occupation to other land in his occupation, and

(b) for distances not exceeding in the aggregate six miles in any calendar week,

then, with the consent of the Treasury, the Secretary of State may exempt the vehicle from the duty chargeable under this Act in respect of the use of the vehicle on roads; but if a vehicle so exempted is used on public roads otherwise than for the purpose or to the extent specified above, the vehicle shall cease to be exempted.

[(2) A mechanically propelled vehicle shall not be chargeable with any duty under this Act by reason of its use by or for the purposes of a person ('a disabled person') suffering from a physical defect or disability or by reason of its being kept for such use if—

(a) it is registered under this Act in the name of that person; and

(b) he has obtained, or is eligible for, a grant under paragraph 2 of Schedule 2 to the National Health Service Act 1977 [or section 46 of the National Health Service (Scotland) Act 1978] [or Article 30(3) of the Health and Personal Social Services (Northern Ireland) Order 1972] in relation to that vehicle or is in receipt of a [disability living allowance by virtue of entitlement to the mobility component at the higher rate or] [a mobility supplement]; and

(c) no other vehicle registered in his name under this Act is exempted from duty under this subsection [*subsection (2C) below*] or section 7 of the Finance Act 1971;

and for the purposes of this subsection a vehicle shall be deemed to be registered in the name of a disabled person in receipt of [disability living allowance by virtue of such entitlement or of] [a mobility supplement] if it is registered in the name of [an appointee] or in the name of a person nominated for the purposes of this subsection by the disabled person or by [an appointee].]

[(2A) In subsection (2) above—

'mobility supplement' means a mobility supplement under—

(*a*) a scheme made under the Personal Injuries (Emergency Provisions) Act 1939, or

(*b*) an Order in Council made under section 12 of the Social Security (Miscellaneous Provisions) Act 1977,

or any payment appearing to the Secretary of State to be of a similar kind and specified by him by order made by statutory instrument; and

'appointee' means—

(i) a person appointed pursuant to regulations under the Social Security Act 1975 [or the Social Security (Northern Ireland) Act 1975] to exercise any of the rights or powers of a person in receipt of a mobility allowance, or

(ii) a person to whom a mobility supplement is paid for application for the benefit of another person in receipt of the supplement.

(2B) An order under subsection (2A) above may provide that it shall be deemed to have come into force on any date after 20th November 1983.]

[*(2C) A mechanically propelled vehicle suitable for use by persons having a particular disability that so incapacitates them in the use of their limbs that they have to be driven and cared for by a full-time constant attendant and registered in the name of such a disabled person under this Act shall not be chargeable with any duty under this Act by reason of its use by or for the purposes of that disabled person or by reason of its being kept for such use where—*

(*a*) *the disabled person is sufficiently disabled to be eligible under the Health and Personal Social Services (Northern Ireland) Order 1972 for an invalid tricycle but too disabled to drive it; and*

(b) no vehicle exempted from duty under subsection (2) above is (or by virtue of that subsection is deemed to be) registered in his name under this Act.

(2D) Subsection (2C) above applies only in relation to Northern Ireland.]

(3) A mechanically propelled vehicle shall not be chargeable with any duty under this Act by reason of its use for clearing snow from public roads by means of a snow plough or similar contrivance, whether forming part of the vehicle or not, or by reason of its being kept for such use or by reason of its use for the purpose of going to or from the place where it is to be used for clearing snow from public roads by those means.

[(3A) Regulations under this Act may provide that, in such cases, subject to such conditions and for such period as may be prescribed, a mechanically propelled vehicle shall not be chargeable with any duty under this Act if it has been imported by—

(a) a person for the time being appointed to serve with any body, contingent or detachment of the forces of any prescribed country, being a body, contingent or detachment which is for the time being present in the United Kingdom on the invitation of Her Majesty's Government in the United Kingdom, or

(b) a member of any country's military forces, except Her Majesty's United Kingdom forces, who is for the time being appointed to serve in the United Kingdom under the orders of any prescribed organisation, or

(c) a person for the time being recognised by the Secretary of State as a member of a civilian component of such a force as is mentioned in paragraph (a) above or as a civilian member of such an organisation as is mentioned in paragraph (b) above, or

(d) any prescribed dependant of a person falling within paragraph (a), paragraph (b) or paragraph (c) above.]

(4) ...

[(4A) A mechanically propelled vehicle shall not be chargeable with any duty under this Act at a time when it is used or kept on a road by a health service body, as defined in section 60(7) of the National Health Service and Community Care Act 1990 or a National Health Service trust established under Part I of that Act or the National Health Service (Scotland) Act 1978 [or a health and social services body, as defined in Article 7(b) of the Health and Personal Social Services (Northern Ireland) Order 1991 or a Health and Social Services Trust established under that Order].]

(5) ...   [52]

NOTES
Commencement: 1 October 1991 (sub-ss (2C), (2D); 1 April 1991 (sub-s (4A)); 25 July 1986 (sub-s (3A); 21 November 1983 (sub-ss (2A), (2B)); 1 December 1978 (sub-s (2)); 1 April 1971–25 July 1986 (remainder).
Sub-ss (1), (3), (4), (5) derived from the Vehicles (Excise) Act 1962, s 6(2)-(4), (6), 7; sub-s (2) derived from the Finance Act 1964, s 11, and SI 1968 No 1699.
Sub-s (2): substituted by the Finance Act 1978, s 8(1); words in first pair of square brackets inserted by Finance Act 1980, s 4(6), (7); words in second pair of square brackets inserted by Finance Act 1991, s 10(2)(a), Sch 3, Part I, paras 1, 5; words in third and sixth pairs of square brackets substituted by the Disability Living Allowance and Disability Working Allowance Act 1991, s 4(2), Sch 2, para 1; amendments in fourth, seventh, eighth and ninth pairs of square brackets made by Finance Act 1984, s 5(1), (2), (5); words printed in italics in fifth pair of square brackets inserted by the Finance Act 1991, s 10(2)(a), Sch 3, Part I, paras 1, 5 and prospectively repealed by the Finance (No 2) Act 1992, ss 12(1)(b), (2), 82, Sch 18, Pt IV, as from a day to be appointed;

remaining words printed in italics prospectively repealed by the Finance (No 2) Act 1992, ss 12(1)(b), (2), 82, Sch 18, Part IV.

Sub-ss (2A), (2B): added by the Finance Act 1984, s 5; words in square brackets therein added by Finance Act 1991, s 10(2)(a), Sch 3, Pt I, paras 1, 5.

Sub-ss (2C), (2D) inserted by the Finance Act 1991, s 10(2)(a), Sch 3, Pt I, paras 1, 5; and both prospectively repealed by the Finance (No 2) Act 1992, ss 12(1)(b), (2), 82, Sch 18, Part IV, as from a day to be appointed.

Sub-s (2A): Order, see the Motor Vehicles (Exemption from Vehicles Excise Duty) Order 1985, SI 1985 No 722.

Sub-s (3A): added by the Finance Act 1986, s 3(7), Sch 2, Part I, para 3.

Sub-s (3A): Regulations, see the Road Vehicles (Exemption from Duty) Regulations 1986, SI 1986 No 1467.

Sub-s (4): repealed by the Finance Act 1991, ss 8(1), (6), (9), 123, Sch 19, Pt III.

Sub-s (4A): added by the National Health Service and Community Care Act 1990, s 60, Sch 8, Part I, para 2; words in square brackets therein added by the Finance Act 1991, s 10(2)(a), Sch 3, Part I, paras 1, 5.

Sub-s (5): repealed by the Finance Act 1991, ss 10(2)(a), 123, Sch 3, Part I, paras 1, 5, Sch 19, Part IV.

LIABILITY TO PAY DUTY AND CONSEQUENCES OF NON-PAYMENT THEREOF

8. Using and keeping vehicles without a licence

(1) If any person uses or keeps on a public road any mechanically propelled vehicle for which a licence is not in force, not being a vehicle exempted from duty under this Act by virtue of any enactment (including any provision of this Act), he shall be liable to the greater of the following penalties, namely—

(a) an excise penalty of [level 3 on the standard scale]; or

(b) an excise penalty equal to five times the amount of the duty chargeable in respect of the vehicle.

(2) In any proceedings for an offence under this section it shall be a defence to prove that—

(a) while an expired vehicle licence for the vehicle was in force an application was duly made for a further vehicle licence for the vehicle to take effect from or before the expiration of the expired licence and for a period including the time in question; and

(b) the expired licence was at that time fixed to and exhibited on the vehicle in the manner prescribed in pursuance of section 12(4) of this Act; and

(c) the period between the expiration of the expired licence and that time did not exceed fourteen days.

For the purposes of paragraph (a) above an application for a further licence is made when the application is received by the Secretary of State.

(3) For the purposes of this section—

(a) where a vehicle for which a vehicle licence is in force is transferred by the holder of the licence to another person, the licence shall be treated as no longer in force unless it is delivered to that other person with the vehicle;

(b) the amount of the duty chargeable in respect of a vehicle shall be taken to be an amount equal to the annual rate of duty applicable to the vehicle at the date on which the offence was committed or, where in the case of a vehicle kept on a public road that rate differs from the annual rate by reference to which the vehicle was at that date chargeable under section 1 of this Act in respect of the keeping thereof, equal to the last mentioned rate.

For the purposes of paragraph (b) above the offence shall, in the case of a conviction for a continuing offence, be taken to have been committed on the date or latest date to which the conviction relates.   [53]

NOTES
Commencement: 1 April 1971.
Sub-s (1) derived from the Vehicles (Excise) Act 1962, s 7; sub-s (2) derived from the Vehicle and Driving Licences Act 1969, s 29(1), (2), and SI 1970 No 1681; sub-s (3) derived from the Finance Act 1967, s 11(2) and the Finance Act 1962, s 5(1).
Sub-s (1): £50 penalty increased and converted to the standard scale by the Criminal Justice Act 1982, ss 37, 38, 46, as amended.

9. Additional liability for keeping unlicensed vehicle

(1) Where a person convicted of an offence under section 8 of this Act is the person by whom the vehicle in respect of which the offence was committed was kept at the time it was committed, the court shall, in addition to any penalty which it may impose under that section, order him to pay an amount calculated in accordance with subsections (2) to (4) below.

(2) The said amount shall, subject to subsection (3) below, be an amount equal to one three-hundred-and-sixty-fifth of the annual rate of duty appropriate to the vehicle in question for each day in the relevant period, and the relevant period shall be one ending with the date of the offence and beginning—

    (a) if the person convicted has before that date notified the Secretary of State of his acquisition of the vehicle in accordance with regulations under this Act, with the date on which the notification was received by the Secretary of State or, if later, with the expiry of the vehicle licence last in force for the vehicle, or

    (b) in any other case, with the expiry of the vehicle licence last in force for the vehicle before the date of the offence or, if there has not at any time before that date been a vehicle licence in force for the vehicle, with the date on which the vehicle was first kept by that person:

Provided that, where the person convicted has been ordered to pay an amount under this section on the occasion of a previous conviction in respect of the same vehicle, and the offence then charged was committed after the date specified above for the beginning of the relevant period, that period shall begin instead with the day following that on which the former offence was committed.

(3) Where the person convicted proves—

    (a) that throughout any day comprised in the relevant period the vehicle in question was not kept by him, or

    (b), (c) . . .

    (d) that he has paid duty in respect of the vehicle for any such day, whether or not on a licence,

the said amount shall be calculated as if that day were not comprised in the relevant period.

[(3A) Where an order has previously been made against a person under section 26A of this Act to pay an amount for a month or part of a month in the case of a vehicle, the amount which he is ordered to pay under this section in the case of the vehicle shall be calculated as if no part of that month were comprised in the relevant period.]

(4) In relation to any day comprised in the relevant period, the reference in subsection (2) above to the annual rate of duty appropriate to the vehicle in question is a reference to the annual rate applicable to it on that day; and,

except so far as it is proved to have fallen within some other description for the whole of any such day, a vehicle shall be taken for the purposes of this section to have belonged throughout the relevant period to that description of vehicle to which it belonged for the purposes of duty at the date of the offence or, if the prosecution so elect, the date when a vehicle licence for it was last issued.

(5) Where, on a person's conviction of an offence under section 8 of this Act, an order is made under [section 1C of the Powers of Criminal Courts Act 1973] [or the Probation Act (Northern Ireland) 1950] ... discharging him absolutely or conditionally, the foregoing provisions of this section shall apply as if the conviction were deemed to be a conviction for all purposes.

(6) In the foregoing provisions of this section any reference to the expiry of a vehicle licence includes a reference to its surrender, and to its being treated as no longer in force for the purposes of section 8 of this Act by virtue of subsection (3)(a) of that section; and in the case of a conviction for a continuing offence, the offence shall be taken for the purposes of those provisions to have been committed on the date or latest date to which the conviction relates.

(7) The foregoing provisions of this section shall have effect subject to the provisions (applying with the necessary modifications) of any enactment relating to the imposition of fines by magistrates' courts, other than one conferring a discretion as to their amount; and any sum payable by virtue of an order under this section shall be treated as a fine, and the order as a conviction, for the purposes of Part III of the Magistrates' Courts Act 1952 (including any enactment having effect as if contained in that Part) and of any other enactment relating to the recovery or application of sums ordered to be paid by magistrates' courts.

(8) In its application to Scotland, this section shall have effect as if for subsections (5) and (7) there were substituted the following subsections respectively—

"(5) Where a person is convicted on indictment of, or is charged before a court of summary jurisdiction with, an offence under section 8 of this Act, and an order is made under Part I of the Criminal Justice (Scotland) Act 1949 discharging him absolutely or placing him on probation, the foregoing provisions of this section shall apply as if the conviction on indictment were a conviction for all purposes, or, as the case may be, the making of the order by the court of summary jurisdiction were a conviction."

"(7) The foregoing provisions of this section shall have effect subject to the provisions (applying with the necessary modifications) of any enactment relating to the imposition of fines by courts of summary jurisdiction, other than one conferring a discretion as to their amount; and any sum payable by virtue of an order under this section shall be treated as a fine, and the order as a conviction, for the purposes of any enactment relating to the recovery or application of sums ordered to be paid by courts of summary jurisdiction."

[(9) In its application to Northern Ireland, this section shall have effect as if for subsection (7) there were substituted the following subsection—

"(7) A sum payable by virtue of any order made under this section by a court shall be recoverable as a sum adjudged to be paid by a conviction and treated for all purposes as a fine within the meaning of section 20 of the Administration of Justice Act (Northern Ireland) 1954."]   **[54]**

NOTES
Commencement: 27 July 1989 (sub-s (3A)); 1 April 1971 (remainder).
This section derived from the Finance Act 1967, s 12(1)–(7), (10), the Vehicle and Driving Licences Act 1969, ss 2(8), 4(4), 12(4), Sch I, paras 11, 16–18, and SI 1970 No 1681.
Sub-s (2): Regulations, see the Road Vehicles (Registration and Licensing) Regulations 1971, post.
Sub-s (3): paras (b) and (c) repealed, except in relation to any amount payable in respect of any day before the day on which this Act is passed, by the Finance Act 1987, ss 2, 72, Sch 1, Part III, para 8, Sch 16, Part I.
Sub-s (3A): added, in relation to licences taken out on or after 27 July 1989, by the Finance Act 1989, s 14(3), (7).
Sub-s (5): words in first pair of square brackets substituted, and words omitted repealed, by the Criminal Justice Act 1991, ss 100, 101(2), Sch 11, para 9, Sch 13; words in second pair of square brackets inserted by the Finance Act 1991, s 10(2)(a), Sch 3, Part I, paras 1, 6(1).
Sub-s (9): added by the Finance Act 1991, s 10(2)(a), Sch 3, paras 1, 6(2).

10. Continuous liability for duty

(1) Subject to the provisions of this section and of section 11 of this Act, a person who for any period keeps a vehicle in respect of which duty under this Act has at any time become chargeable shall, whether or not it is still a mechanically propelled vehicle, be liable to pay duty under this Act in respect of the vehicle for that period.

(2) Subject as aforesaid, a person shall not be liable by virtue of subsection (1) above to pay duty under this Act in respect of a vehicle—

    (a) for any period for which duty under this Act in respect of the vehicle has been paid and has not been repaid in consequence of the surrender of a licence;

    (b) for any period in respect of which he has, in accordance with regulations under section 11 of this Act, given notice to the Secretary of State that the vehicle will not be used or kept on a public road;

    (c) for any period when the vehicle is not a mechanically propelled vehicle and a notice stating that it has ceased to be such a vehicle has, in accordance with regulations under section 11 of this Act, been given to the Secretary of State and not revoked in pursuance of subsection (2) of that section;

    (d) for any period when the vehicle is exempt from duty by virtue of section 4 or 6 or section 7 (except subsection (3)) of this Act;

    (e) for any period when he keeps the vehicle solely for the purpose of selling or supplying it in the course of his business as a motor dealer or using it under the authority of a trade licence in the course of his business as a motor trader within the meaning of section 16 of this Act;

    (f) . . .

    (g) for any period by reference to which there was calculated an amount ordered to be paid by him in respect of the vehicle in pursuance of section 9(1) of this Act.

(3) A person shall not by virtue of subsection (2)(b) above be exempt from his liability for any period under subsection (1) above in respect of a vehicle if—

    (a) at any time during that period he or any other person with his consent uses or keeps the vehicle on a public road and no vehicle licence is in force for the vehicle at that time; or

    (b) after he has given notice under the said subsection (2)(b) in relation to the vehicle in respect of that period he applies for a vehicle licence for the vehicle to have effect on any day included in the first thirty days of that period;

and for the purposes of paragraph (a) above the consent there mentioned shall be presumed to have been given unless the contrary is shown, but any use or keeping of the vehicle in question as respects which the vehicle is exempt by virtue of any enactment for the time being in force from duty under this Act shall be disregarded.

(4) Sums payable in pursuance of this section by way of duty in respect of a vehicle shall accrue due from day to day at one three-hundred-and-sixty-fifth of the annual rate of duty applicable to the vehicle on that day.

(5) Without prejudice to any other mode of recovering sums payable by virtue of this section, where an application for a vehicle licence for twelve months or four months for a vehicle is made by a person by whom such sums are payable in respect of the vehicle and a vehicle licence other than a temporary licence is to be issued in pursuance of the application, the licence shall, if the Secretary of State so directs but subject to subsection (6) below, be made to have effect for a shorter period specified in the direction, being a period which is not less than thirty days and is such that the difference between the amount tendered in connection with the application and the amount chargeable upon the licence for the specified period does not exceed the aggregate amount of the sums aforesaid; and the amount so chargeable shall be equal to the number of days in the specified period multiplied by—

(a) where the application is for a licence for twelve months, one three-hundred-and-sixty-fifth of the annual rate of duty under this Act payable in respect of the vehicle on the date of the application; and

(b) where the application is for a licence for four months, eleven three-thousand-six-hundred-and-fiftieths of that rate;

and where a licence is made to have effect for a specified period in pursuance of this subsection the aggregate amount of the sums aforesaid shall be treated as reduced by the difference aforesaid.

(6) A person to whom a licence is issued for a period specified in a direction under subsection (5) above may appeal to the county court, or in Scotland by way of summary application to the sheriff, on the ground that the Secretary of State was not authorised by that subsection to give the direction.   **[55]**

NOTES
   Commencement: 1 April 1971.
   This section derived from the Vehicle and Driving Licences Act 1969, ss 11, 24, and SI 1970 No 1681.
   Section 2: para (f) repealed by the Finance Act 1988, s 148, Sch 14, Part II.

11. Provisions supplementary to s 10

(1) For the purposes of section 10 of this Act a vehicle in respect of which a vehicle licence has been issued and sums are payable by virtue of that section for any period shall, except so far as it is shown to have been a mechanically propelled vehicle of some other description during that period, be deemed to have belonged throughout that period to the description to which it belonged on the date when the last such licence was issued in respect of it.

(2) When a vehicle in respect of which a notice has been given in pursuance of subsection (2)(c) of section 10 of this Act becomes a mechanically propelled vehicle, its keeper for the time being shall forthwith give to the Secretary of State a further notice revoking the first-mentioned notice; and where a person required to give such a further notice does not do so, then—

    (a) if he knowingly fails to give it he shall be liable on summary conviction to a fine not exceeding [level 3 on the standard scale]; and

    (b) in a case where he became the keeper of the vehicle after the first-mentioned notice was given it shall be deemed to have been revoked on the date when he became the keeper of the vehicle, and in any other case the first-mentioned notice shall be deemed not to have been given.

(3) The Secretary of State may by regulations make such provision as he considers appropriate for the purposes of section 10(2)(b) or (c) of this Act or subsection (2) above including, without prejudice to the generality of the power conferred by this subsection, provision—

    (a) as to the form of and particulars to be included in a notice under those provisions, the manner of giving such a notice and the time at which it is to be treated as being given;

    (b) for securing that notice under the said paragraph (b) is not given in respect of a period of less than thirty days or more than twelve months;

    (c) as to the mode of calculating the period in respect of which notice under the said paragraph (b) is to be treated as given;

    (d) with respect to the mode of proving the giving of notice;

    (e) for deeming notice to have been given in relation to a vehicle in respect of any period or at any time if in the circumstances of any particular case the Secretary of State considers it reasonable to do so.

                                                      [56]

NOTES

    Commencement: 1 April 1971.

    This section derived from the Vehicle and Driving Licences Act 1969, ss 12(1)–(3), 32, and SI 1970 No 1681.

    Sub-s (2): maximum fine increased and converted to a level on the standard scale by the Criminal Justice Act 1982, ss 37, 38, 46, as amended.

ISSUE, EXHIBITION, EXCHANGE, SURRENDER, ETC OF LICENCES

12. Issue and exhibition of licences

(1) Every person applying for a vehicle licence shall make such a declaration and furnish such particulars with respect to the vehicle for which the licence is to be taken out or otherwise as may be prescribed.

(2) Every vehicle licence shall be issued for the vehicle specified in the application for the licence and shall not entitle the person to whom it is issued to use or keep any other vehicle.

(3) The Secretary of State shall not be required to issue any vehicle licence for which application is made unless he is satisfied—

    (i) that the licence applied for is the appropriate licence for the vehicle specified in the application; and

    (ii) in the case of an application for a licence for a vehicle purporting to be the first application for a licence for the vehicle, that a licence has not previously been issued for that vehicle.

(4) Subject to the provisions of regulations under this Act, and without prejudice to section 8 thereof, any person who uses or keeps on a public road any mechanically propelled vehicle on which duty under this Act is chargeable without there being fixed to and exhibited on that vehicle in the prescribed

manner a licence for, or in respect of the use of, that vehicle issued under this Act and for the time being in force shall be liable on summary conviction to a fine not exceeding [level 1 on the standard scale].

(5) In any proceedings for an offence under subsection (4) above it shall be a defence to prove that—

    (a) while an expired vehicle licence for the vehicle was in force an application was duly made for a further vehicle licence for the vehicle to take effect from or before the expiration of the expired licence and for a period including the time in question; and

    (b) the expired licence was at that time fixed to and exhibited on the vehicle in the manner prescribed in pursuance of subsection (4) above; and

    (c) the period between the expiration of the expired licence and that time did not exceed fourteen days.

For the purposes of paragraph (a) above an application for a further licence is made when the application is received by the Secretary of State.

(6) Regulations under this Act may provide for the issue of new licences in the place of licences which may be lost or destroyed, and for the fee to be paid on the issue of a new licence.

(7) Any vehicle licence may be transferred in the prescribed manner.   **[57]**

NOTES
   Commencement: 1 April 1971.
   Sub-ss (1), (2), (4), (6), (7) derived from the Vehicles (Excise) Act 1962, s 8(1), (2), (a), (3), (4), (5); sub-s (3) derived from the Vehicles (Excise) Act 1962, s 8(2)(b), the Vehicle and Driving Licences Act 1969, s 2(8), Sch I, para 4, and SI 1970 No 1681; sub-s (5) derived from the Vehicle and Driving Licences Act 1969, s 29(1), (2), and SI 1970 No 1681.
   Sub-s (4): maximum fine increased and converted to the standard scale by the Criminal Justice Act 1982, ss 37, 38, 46, as amended.
   Sub-s (4): regulations, see the Road Vehicles (Registration and Licensing) Regulations 1971, post.

13. Temporary licences

(1) Where an application is made for a vehicle licence for any period . . . , the Secretary of State may, if he thinks fit, instead of issuing forthwith a vehicle licence for that period—

    (a) issue a vehicle licence (in this Act referred to as a "temporary licence") for fourteen days or such other period as may be prescribed and having effect from such day as may be prescribed; and

    (b) issue from time to time a further temporary licence in respect of the vehicle to which a previous temporary licence relates.

(2) Nothing in this section shall affect the amount of any duty payable in connection with an application for a vehicle licence.

[(2A) Where an application for a vehicle licence is made to a body [(other than a Northern Ireland department)] authorised by the Secretary of State to act as his agent for the purpose of issuing licences, then, before the body issues a licence under subsection (1)(a) above, it may require the applicant to pay to it in connection with the issue a fee of £2 or such other sum as may be prescribed.]

(3) Where an application is made for a vehicle licence for any period and a temporary licence is issued in pursuance of the application, subsection (3)(a) of

section 8 of this Act shall not apply to the first-mentioned licence if on a transfer of the relevant vehicle during the currency of the temporary licence the temporary licence is delivered with the vehicle to the transferee.   **[58]**

NOTES
    Commencement: 25 July 1985 (sub-s (2A)); 1 April 1971 (remainder).
    This section derived from the Vehicle and Driving Licences Act 1969, s 5, and SI 1970 No 1681.
    Sub-s (1): words omitted repealed by the Finance Act 1988, s 148, Sch 14, Part II.
    Sub-s (2A): added by the Finance Act 1985, s 9(1); words in square brackets inserted by Finance Act 1991, s 10(2)(a), Sch 3, Part I, paras 1, 7.

14. Issue, etc of temporary licences by motor dealers

(1) The Secretary of State may by regulations make such provisions as he considers appropriate with respect to the allocation of temporary licences to motor dealers who apply for such allocations and appear to the Secretary of State suitable to receive them and with respect to the issue of the licences by motor dealers.

(2) Without prejudice to the generality of subsection (1) above, regulations under this section may include provision—

    (a) as to the mode of application for the allocation of licences and as to the fees payable in respect of allocations;

    (b) specifying the categories of vehicles for which allocations of licences may be made;

    (c) prohibiting the issue of temporary licences in pursuance of applications for trade licences . . . ;

    (d) for requiring a motor dealer to pay to the Secretary of State, in respect of each licence allocated to the dealer, the excise duty chargeable in respect of the licence which will be specified in the application in consequence of which the allocated licence can be issued;

    (e) as to the replacement of allocated licences which are lost, damaged or destroyed and as to the fees payable in connection with their replacement; and

    (f) as to the transfer of licences allocated to a motor dealer in cases where the dealer dies or becomes incapacitated or bankrupt and in such other cases as may be prescribed.

(3) Without prejudice to the generality of subsection (1) above, regulations under this section may also include provision for—

    (a) requiring a motor dealer to whom an allocation of licences is made to keep a record in the prescribed form of the licences allocated to him and of the licences issued by him, and to permit the record to be inspected at all reasonable times by any officer of the Secretary of State and any constable;

    (b) restricting the circumstances in which a motor dealer may issue licences;

    (c) requiring a motor dealer, before he issues a temporary licence in respect of a vehicle—

        (i) to obtain from the proposed holder of the licence an application for a vehicle licence in the prescribed form,

        (ii) to ascertain that the prescribed requirements as to test certificates and insurance are satisfied in respect of the vehicle,

        (iii) to ensure that the temporary licence is appropriate for the vehicle and takes effect on the prescribed date, and

(iv) to make on the temporary licence, and on any copy of it specified in the regulations, such entries as the Secretary of State may determine;

(d) requiring a motor dealer by whom a temporary licence is issued to deliver or despatch to the Secretary of State, within the prescribed period beginning with the day on which the dealer issues the licence, the prescribed particulars and documents relating to the licence and the vehicle for which it is issued; and

(e) securing that after any change takes effect in the rate of excise duty chargeable in respect of a vehicle licence of any description, a temporary licence previously allocated to a dealer is not issued by him in consequence of an application for a vehicle licence of that description, but that a temporary licence issued in contravention of regulations made in pursuance of the foregoing provisions of this paragraph shall not be invalid by reason only of the contravention.

[59]

NOTES
Commencement: 1 April 1971.
This section derived from the Vehicle and Driving Licences Act 1969, s 6(1), (2), (3)(a)–(e), and SI 1970 No 1681.
Sub-s (2): words omitted repealed by the Finance Act 1988, s 148, Sch 14, Part II.

15. Provisions supplementary to s 14

(1) Any unissued licence allocated to a motor dealer in pursuance of section 14 of this Act may at any time be surrendered in the prescribed manner to the Secretary of State by the dealer or by any person to whom the licence has been transferred under regulations made in pursuance of subsection (2)(f) of that section.

(2) A motor dealer and any other person having the custody of any unissued licence allocated to the dealer in pursuance of section 14 of this Act shall, if required to do so by the Secretary of State and subject to section 25(2) of this Act, forthwith surrender any such licence to the Secretary of State in such manner as the Secretary of State may direct; and a person who knowingly fails to comply with a requirement made by the Secretary of State under this subsection shall be liable on summary conviction to a fine of [level 3 on the standard scale].

(3) On the surrender of a licence in pursuance of this section the dealer or other person in question shall be entitled to be paid by the Secretary of State the amount paid by the dealer in respect of the licence under regulations made in pursuance of section 14(2)(d) of this Act.

(4) Where a licence is issued by a motor dealer in contravention of regulations made in pursuance of section 14(3)(e) of this Act, the dealer shall be liable to pay to the Secretary of State a sum equal to the amount (if any) by which the amount paid by the dealer as mentioned in subsection (3) above is exceeded by the amount which would have been so paid if the allocation of the licence to the dealer had taken place at the time when the licence was issued.

[60]

NOTES
Commencement: 1 April 1971.
This section derived from the Vehicle and Driving Licences Act 1969, ss 7(1)–(4), 32, and SI 1970 No 1681.
Sub-s (2): fine increased and converted to the standard scale by the Criminal Justice Act 1982, ss 37, 38, 46, as amended.

16. Trade licences

(1) If a motor trader or a vehicle tester applies in the prescribed manner to the Secretary of State to take out a licence under this section (in this Act referred to as a "trade licence")—

> (i) in the case of a motor trader, for all mechanically propelled vehicles which are from time to time temporarily in his possession in the course of his business as a motor trader . . .; or
>
> (ii) in the case of a vehicle tester, for all mechanically propelled vehicles which are from time to time submitted to him for testing in the course of his business as a vehicle tester; or
>
> (iii) in the case of a motor trader who is a manufacturer of mechanically propelled vehicles, for all vehicles kept and used by him solely for purposes of conducting research and development in the course of his business as such a manufacturer [and all vehicles which are from time to time submitted to him by other manufacturers for testing on roads in the course of that business],

the Secretary of State may, subject to the prescribed conditions, issue to him a trade licence on payment of duty at the rate applicable to the licence in accordance with the following provisions of this section:

Provided that the holder of a trade licence shall not be entitled by virtue of that licence—

> (a) to use more than one mechanically propelled vehicle at any one time, . . .; or
>
> (b) to use any vehicle for any purpose other than such purposes as may be prescribed; or
>
> (c) [except in such circumstances as may be prescribed] to keep any vehicle on a road if it is not being used thereon.

[(1A) Subsection (1) above has effect in relation to an application made by a person who satisfies the Secretary of State that he intends to commence business as a motor trader or vehicle tester as it has effect in relation to an application made by a motor trader or vehicle tester.]

(2) Regulations shall be made under this section prescribing the conditions subject to which trade licences are to be issued and the purposes for which the holder of a trade licence may use a vehicle under the licence.

(3) The purposes which may be prescribed as those for which the holder of a trade licence may use a vehicle under the licence shall not include the conveyance of goods or burden of any description other than—

> (a) a load which is carried solely for the purpose of testing or demonstrating the vehicle or any of its accessories or equipment and which is returned to the place of loading without having been removed from the vehicle except for such purpose or in the case of accident; or
>
> (b) . . .
>
> [(bb) in the case of a vehicle which is being delivered or collected, a load consisting of another vehicle used or to be used for travel from or to the place of delivery or collection; or]
>
> (c) any load built in as part of the vehicle or permanently attached thereto; or
>
> (d) a load consisting of parts, accessories or equipment designed to be fitted to the vehicle and of tools for so fitting them; or

(e) a load consisting of a trailer [other than a trailer which is for the time being a disabled vehicle];

and, for the purposes of this subsection, where a vehicle is so constructed that a trailer may by partial superimposition be attached to the vehicle in such a manner as to cause a substantial part of the weight of the trailer to be borne by the vehicle, the vehicle and the trailer shall be deemed to constitute a single vehicle.

(4) [Subject to subsections (4A) and (4B) below, a trade licence] may be taken out—

(a) for a period of twelve months; or
[(b) for a period of six months]

and shall first have effect on the day specified by the applicant in the application for the licence.

[(4A) A trade licence taken out by a person who is not a motor trader or vehicle tester (having satisfied the Secretary of State as mentioned in subsection (1A) above) shall be for a period of six months only.

(4B) The Secretary of State may require that a trade licence taken out by a motor trader or vehicle tester who does not hold any existing trade licence shall be for a period of six months only.]

(5) The rate of duty applicable to a trade licence taken out for a period of twelve months shall be [£100] or, if the licence is to be used only for vehicles to which Schedule 1 to this Act relates, [£20]; and the rate of duty applicable to a licence taken out for a period of [six months] shall be [eleven twentieths] of the rate applicable to the corresponding trade licence taken out for a period of twelve months, any fraction of 5p being treated as 5p if it exceeds 2.5p but otherwise being disregarded.

(6) Nothing in this section shall operate to prevent a person entitled to take out a trade licence from holding two or more trade licences.

(7) If any person holding a trade licence or trade licences issued under this section uses on a public road by virtue of that licence or those licences—

(i) a greater number of vehicles at any one time than he is authorised to use by virtue of that licence or those licences; or
(ii) any vehicle for any purpose other than such purposes as may have been prescribed under subsection (2) above;

or if that person uses that licence or any of those licences for the purpose of keeping on a road [in any circumstances other than such circumstances as may have been prescribed under paragraph (c) of the proviso to subsection (1) above] a vehicle which is not being used on that road, he shall be liable to the greater of the following penalties, namely—

(a) an excise penalty of [level 3 on the standard scale]; or
(b) an excise penalty equal to five times the amount of the duty chargeable in respect of the vehicle or vehicles.

The amount of the duty chargeable in respect of a vehicle shall be calculated for the purposes of this subsection in the same manner as it is calculated for the purposes of section 8 of this Act by virtue of subsection (3) thereof.

(8) In this section—

["disabled vehicle" includes a vehicle which has been abandoned or is scrap;]

"motor trader" [means—

(a) a manufacturer or repairer of, or dealer in, mechanically propelled vehicles, or

(b) any person not falling within paragraph (a) above who carries on a business of such description as may be prescribed;
and a person shall be treated for the purposes of paragraph (a) above] as a dealer in such vehicles if he carries on a business consisting wholly or mainly of collecting and delivering mechanically propelled vehicles, and not including any other activities except activities as a manufacturer or repairer of, or dealer in, such vehicles;

"vehicle tester" means a person, other than a motor trader, who regularly in the course of his business engages in the testing on roads of mechanically propelled vehicles belonging to other persons; and

. . .   **[61]**

NOTES

Commencement: 1 January 1987 (sub-ss (1A), (4A), (4B)); 1 April 1971 (remainder).

Sub-ss (1)–(3), (5)–(8) derived from the Vehicles (Excise) Act 1962, s 12(1)–(3), (5), (6), (9), (10); sub-s (4) derived from the Vehicle and Driving Licences Act 1969, s 4(1)(2).

Sub-s (1): words omitted repealed, in relation to licences taken out after 31 December 1987, by the Finance Act 1987, ss 2, 72, Sch 1, Part II, para 5, Sch 16, Part I; amendments in square brackets made by the Finance Act 1986, s 3(1), (7), (8), Sch 2, Part I, para 4.

Sub-ss (1A), (4A), (4B): added by the Finance Act 1986, s 3(1), (7), (8), Sch 2, Part I, para 4.

Sub-s (3): words omitted repealed, in relation to licences taken out after 31 December 1987, and final amendment in square brackets made by the Finance Act 1987, ss 2, 72, Sch 1, Part II, para 5, Sch 16, Part I; other amendment in square brackets made by the Finance Act 1986, s 3(7), (8), Sch 2, part I, para 4.

Sub-s (4): amended by the Finance Act 1986, s 3(7), (8), Sch 2, Part I, para 4.

Sub-s (5): sums in square brackets substituted, in relation to licences taken out after 31 December 1987, by the Finance Act 1987, s 2, further substituted, in relation to licences taken out after 14 March 1989, by the Finance Act 1989, s 6(6), (7); other amendments made by the Finance Act 1986, s 3(6), (7), (8), Sch 2, Part I, para 4.

Sub-s (7): first amendment in square brackets made by the Finance Act 1987, s 2, Sch 1, Part III, para 14; £50 penalty increased and converted to the standard scale by the Criminal Justice Act 1982, ss 37, 38, 46, as amended.

Sub-s (8): definition "disabled vehicle" amended by the Finance Act 1984, s 4(4), (6); definition "motor trader" amended by the Finance Act 1986, s 3(7), (8), Sch 2, Part I, para (8); definition omitted repealed, in relation to licences taken out after 31 December 1987, by the Finance Act 1987, s 72(7), Sch 16, Part I.

17. Surrender of licences

(1) The holder of a licence (other than a licence for a tramcar)—

(a) may at any time surrender the licence to the Secretary of State in the prescribed manner; and

(b) shall on so surrendering the licence be entitled, if he satisfies the prescribed requirements and subject to the following provisions of this section, to receive from the Secretary of State, by way of rebate of duty paid upon the surrendered licence, a sum equal to the relevant amount multiplied by the number of days in the relevant period:

Provided that no sum shall be payable under this subsection in a case where the relevant period is less than thirty days.

(2) In this section "the relevant amount", in relation to a surrendered licence, means one three-hundred-and-sixty-fifth of the annual rate by reference to which duty was charged upon the licence and "the relevant period", in relation to a surrendered licence, means the period beginning with the day following that on which the licence is received by the Secretary of State in

pursuance of paragraph (a) of subsection (1) above and ending with the day on which the licence would have expired by the effluxion of time.

The Secretary of State may, for the purposes of this subsection, treat a surrendered licence delivered to him by post as received by him on the day on which it was posted.

(3) If during the currency of a temporary licence issued in pursuance of an application for a vehicle licence for any period, the temporary licence is surrendered under this section, it shall be treated for the purposes of this section as issued for that period or, if the Secretary of State so directs but subject to subsection (4) below, for any other period specified in the direction being a period for which by virtue of section 10(5) of this Act a vehicle licence could be issued in pursuance of the application; and where a further vehicle licence issued in pursuance of the application is held by any person at the time of the surrender of the temporary licence or is received by him thereafter—

    (a) the further licence shall cease to be in force and he shall forthwith return it to the Secretary of State and shall, if he knowingly fails to do so, be liable on summary conviction to a fine not exceeding [level 3 on the standard scale]; and

    (b) if the Secretary of State considers that there has been undue delay in complying with paragraph (a) above he may, without prejudice to any liability under that paragraph, reduce the relevant period by such number of days as he thinks fit for the purpose of calculating the sum payable in pursuance of subsection (1) above in respect of the surrendered temporary licence.

(4) A person who in pursuance of this section is paid a sum which was calculated by reference to a period specified in a direction under subsection (3) above may appeal to the county court, or in Scotland by way of summary application to the sheriff, on the ground that the Secretary of State was not authorised by that subsection to give the direction. **[62]**

NOTES

    Commencement: 1 April 1971.

    This section derived from the Vehicle and Driving Licences Act 1969, ss 8(1)–(4), 24, 32, and SI 1970 No 1681.

    Sub-s (3): maximum fine in para (a) increased and converted to the standard scale by the Criminal Justice Act 1982, ss 37, 38, 46, as amended.

18. Alteration of vehicle or of its use

(1) Subject to the provisions of this section, where a vehicle licence has been taken out for a vehicle at any rate under this Act and the vehicle is at any time while the licence is in force used in an altered condition or in a manner or for a purpose which brings it within, or which if it was used solely in that condition or in that manner or for that purpose would bring it within, a description of vehicle to which a higher rate of duty is applicable under this Act, duty at that higher rate shall become chargeable in respect of the licence for the vehicle.

(2) Where duty at a higher rate becomes chargeable under subsection (1) above in respect of any vehicle licence, the licence may be exchanged for a new vehicle licence, for the period beginning with the date on which the higher rate of duty becomes chargeable and expiring at the end of the period for which the original vehicle licence was issued, on payment of the appropriate proportion of the difference between—

(a) the amount payable under this Act on the original vehicle licence; and

(b) the amount payable under this Act on a vehicle licence taken out for the period for which the original licence was issued but at the higher rate of duty, that amount being calculated, if that rate has been changed since the issue of the original licence, as if that rate had been in force at all material times at the level at which it is in force when it becomes chargeable.

(3) For the purposes of subsection (2) above the appropriate proportion is the proportion which the number of days in the period beginning when the higher rate of duty becomes chargeable and ending with the end of the period for which the original licence was issued bears to the number of days in the whole of the last-mentioned period, that period being treated as 365 days in the case of a licence for twelve months and 120 days in the case of a licence for four months.

(4) Where a vehicle licence has been taken out for a vehicle, and by reason of the vehicle being used as mentioned in subsection (1) above, a higher rate of duty becomes chargeable and duty at the higher rate was not paid before the vehicle was so used, the person so using the vehicle shall be liable to the greater of the following penalties, namely—

(a) an excise penalty of [level 3 on the standard scale]; or

(b) an excise penalty of an amount equal to five times the difference between the duty actually paid on the licence and the amount of the duty at that higher rate.

(5) Where a vehicle licence has been taken out for a vehicle of a certain description, duty at a higher rate applicable to vehicles of some other description shall not become chargeable in respect of the vehicle by reason of the vehicle being used as mentioned in subsection (1) above, unless the vehicle as used while the said licence is in force satisfies all the conditions which must be satisfied in order to bring the vehicle for the purposes of the charge of duty under this Act into the said other description of vehicles.

(6) Where duty has been paid in respect of a vehicle at a rate applicable under Schedule 4 to this Act, then, so long as the vehicle is to a substantial extent being used for the conveyance of goods or burden belonging to a particular person (whether the person keeping the vehicle or not), duty at a higher rate shall not become chargeable in respect of the vehicle by reason only that it is used for the conveyance without charge in the course of their employment of employees of the person aforesaid.

(7) Where duty has been paid in respect of a vehicle at a rate applicable to farmers' goods vehicles under Schedule 4 to this Act, duty at a higher rate shall not become chargeable in respect of the vehicle by reason only that, on an occasion when the vehicle is being used by the person in whose name it is registered under this Act for the purpose of the conveyance of the produce of, or of articles required for the purposes of, the agricultural land which he occupies, it is also used for the conveyance for some other person engaged in agriculture of the produce of, or of articles required for the purposes of, the agricultural land occupied by that other person, if it is shown—

(a) that the vehicle is so used only occasionally;

(b) that the goods conveyed for that other person represent only a small proportion of the total amount of goods which the vehicle is conveying on that occasion; and

(c) that no payment or reward of any kind is, or is agreed to be, made or given for the conveyance of the goods of that other person.

(8) Where duty has been paid in respect of a vehicle at a rate applicable to farmers' goods vehicles under Schedule 4 to this Act, duty at a higher rate shall not become chargeable in respect of the vehicle by reason only that, during such periods and in such areas as may be specified by order of the Treasury made by statutory instrument, it is used, whether or not by the person in whose name it is registered under this Act, for any such purpose as is specified in the order.

An order under this subsection may be revoked or varied by a subsequent order of the Treasury.

(9) Subsection (8) above shall continue in force until such date as Her Majesty may by Order in Council determine.

(10) In its application to Northern Ireland, this section shall have effect as if—

(a) for subsection (8) there were substituted the following subsection—

"(8) Where duty has been paid under this Act in respect of a vehicle either—

(a) as an agricultural tractor under Schedule 3, or
(b) as a farmer's goods vehicle under Schedule 4,

duty at a higher rate shall not become chargeable in respect of that vehicle by reason only that it is used by the person in whose name it is registered for conveying to or from any agricultural land in his occupation livestock owned by him in connection with the agricultural activities carried on by him on that land; but this subsection shall not have effect in relation to a vehicle used for conveying any livestock which for the time being is part of the stock in trade of a dealer in cattle and is conveyed in the course of his business as such dealer."; and

(b) subsection (9) were omitted.]　　　　　　**[63]**

NOTES

Commencement: 1 April 1971.

This section derived from the Vehicles (Excise) Act 1962, s 10.

Sub-s (4): £50 penalty increased and converted to the standard scale by the Criminal Justice Act 1982, ss 37, 38, 46, as amended.

Sub-s (10): added by the Finance Act 1991, s 10(2)(a), Sch 3, Part I, paras 1, 8.

18A. Additional liability in relation to alteration of vehicle or its use

[(1) Where a person convicted of an offence under section 18 of this Act is the person by whom the vehicle in respect of which the offence was committed was kept at the time it was committed, the court shall, in addition to any penalty which it may impose under that section, order him to pay an amount (the "additional duty") calculated in accordance with this section.

(2) The additional duty shall, subject to subsections (7) and (8) below, be an amount equal to one three-hundred-and-sixty-fifth of the appropriate annual rate of duty for each day in the relevant period.

(3) The following Cases are referred to in subsections (5) and (6) below—

CASE A

Where—

(a) at the time of the offence the vehicle in question had a plated weight (the "higher plated weight") which exceeds the plated weight (the "previous plated weight") which it had when the current licence was taken out; and

(b) the current licence was taken out at the rate of duty applicable to the previous plated weight.

CASE B

Where—

(a) the vehicle in question is a tractor unit (within the meaning of paragraph 15 of Schedule 4 to this Act);

(b) the current licence was taken out at a rate of duty applicable to the use of the vehicle only with semi-trailers having not less than two axles or, as the case may be, only with semi-trailers having not less than three axles; and

(c) the offence consisted in using the vehicle with a semi-trailer with a smaller number of axles than that mentioned in paragraph (b) above, *in circumstances in which it was not treated by virtue of paragraph 14(2) of Schedule 4 to this Act as being licensed in accordance with the requirements of this Act.*

CASE C

Where—

(a) the current licence was taken out at the rate of duty applicable, by virtue of paragraph 8 of Schedule 4 to this Act, to a weight lower than the plated weight of the vehicle in question; and

(b) the offence consisted in using the vehicle in contravention of a condition imposed by virtue of paragraph 8(3) of Schedule 4.

CASE D

Where the current licence was taken out at a rate of duty lower than that applicable to the vehicle in question by reference to its plated weight and the circumstances of the case do not bring it within Case A, B or C.

CASE E

Where the current licence was taken out at a rate of duty lower than that at which duty was chargeable in respect of that condition or manner of use of the vehicle which constituted the offence and the circumstances of the case do not bring it within Case A, B, C or D.

(4) In this section "current licence" means the licence in relation to which the offence was committed.

(5) In this section "appropriate annual rate of duty" means the difference between the rate of duty at which the current licence was taken out and—

(a) in Case A, the rate which would have been applicable had the current licence been taken out by reference to the higher plated weight;

(b) in Case B, the rate which would have been applicable had the current licence been taken out by reference to that use of the vehicle which constituted the offence;

(c) in Case C, the rate which would have been applicable had the current licence been taken out by reference to the plated weight of the vehicle;

(d) in Case D, the rate which would have been applicable had the current licence been taken out by reference to the plated weight of the vehicle; and

(e) in Case E, the rate which would have been applicable had the current licence been taken out by reference to that condition or use of the vehicle which constituted the offence.

(6) In this section "relevant period" means the period ending with the day on which the offence was committed and beginning—

(a) in relation to Case A, with the day on which the vehicle in question was plated with the higher plated weight; and

(b) in relation to each of the other Cases, with the day on which the current licence first took effect.

(7) Where the person convicted proves—

(a) that throughout any day comprised in the relevant period he was not the keeper of the vehicle in question;

(b) [or]

(c) that he had, before his conviction, paid the higher of the two rates of duty referred to in the relevant paragraph of subsection (5) above in respect of the vehicle for any such day, whether or not on a licence;
. . .

(d) . . .

the additional duty shall be calculated as if that day were not comprised in the relevant period.

(8) Where a person is convicted of more than one contravention of section 18 of this Act in respect of the same vehicle (whether or not in the same proceedings) the court shall, in calculating the additional duty payable in respect of any one of those offences, reduce the amount calculated in accordance with the preceding provisions of this section in relation to a particular period by the amount of the additional duty ordered to be paid under this section in relation to that period in respect of the other offence or, as the case may be, offences.

(9) Except so far as it is proved to have fallen within some other description for the whole of any day comprised in the relevant period, the vehicle in question shall be taken for the purposes of this section to have belonged throughout the relevant period to that description of vehicle to which it belonged for the purposes of duty at the date of the offence.

(10) Where, on a person's conviction of an offence under section 18 of this Act, an order is made under Part I of the Powers of Criminal Courts Act 1973 [or the Probation Act (Northern Ireland) 1950] placing him on probation or discharging him absolutely or conditionally, this section shall apply as if the conviction were deemed to be a conviction for all purposes.

(11) This section shall have effect subject to the provisions (applying with the necessary modifications) of any enactment relating to the imposition of fines by magistrates' courts, other than one conferring a discretion as to their amount; and any sum payable by virtue of an order under this section shall be treated as a fine, and the order as a conviction, for the purposes of Part III of the Magistrates' Courts Act 1980 (including any enactment having effect as if contained in that Part) and of any other enactment relating to the recovery or application of sums ordered to be paid by magistrates' courts.

(12) In its application to Scotland, this section shall have effect as if for subsections (10) and (11) there were substituted the following subsections—

"(10) Where a person is convicted on indictment of, or is charged before a court of summary jurisdiction with, an offence under section 18 of this Act, and an order is made under section 182 or 383 of the Criminal Procedure (Scotland) Act 1975 discharging him absolutely, or under section 183 or 384 of that Act placing him on probation, this section shall apply as if the making of the order were a conviction for all purposes.

(11) Any sum payable by virtue of an order under this section shall be treated as a fine imposed by a court of summary jurisdiction."

[(12A) In its application to Northern Ireland, this section shall have effect as if—

(a) in subsections (3) and (5) for "plated weight", in each place, there were substituted "relevant maximum weight or, as the case may be, relevant maximum train weight";

(b) in subsection (6) for "plated with the higher plated weight" there were substituted "rated at the higher relevant maximum weight or, as the case may be, the higher relevant maximum train weight"; and

(c) for subsection (11) there were substituted the following subsections—

"(11) A sum payable by virtue of any order made under this section by a court shall be recoverable as a sum adjudged to be paid by a conviction and treated for all purposes as a fine within the meaning of section 20 of the Administration of Justice Act (Northern Ireland) 1954.

(11A) In this section "relevant maximum weight" and "relevant maximum train weight" have the same meaning as in Schedule 4 to this Act.]

(13) This section is subject to Schedule 7 to this Act.] **[64]**

NOTES
Commencement: 30 July 1982.
Added by the Finance Act 1982, s 7.
Sub-s (3): words in italics repealed in relation to licences taken out on or after 1 January 1993 by the Finance (No 2) Act 1992, ss 11(1), (10), (11), 82, Sch 18, Part III.
Sub-s (7): amended by the Finance Act 1987, ss 2, 72, Sch 16, Part I.
Sub-s (10): words in square brackets inserted by the Finance Act 1991, s 10(2)(a), Sch 3, Part I, paras 1, 9(1).
Sub-s (12A): added by the Finance Act 1991, s 9(2)(a), Sch 3, Part I, paras 1, 9(2).

[Rebate of duty

18B. Combined transport of goods

(1) This section applies to any goods vehicle which—

(a) has a plated gross weight or a plated train weight which exceeds 3,500 kilograms, or

(b) has neither a plated gross weight nor a plated train weight, but has a design weight which exceeds 3,500 kilograms.

(2) Where in the course of the transport of goods between member States by means of combined transport a goods vehicle to which this section applies is transported by rail in *Great Britain* [the United Kingdom] at a time when a vehicle licence for it is in force, the holder of the licence shall, on making a claim, be entitled to receive from the Secretary of State, by way of rebate of the

duty paid upon the licence, a sum of an amount calculated in accordance with the method prescribed for the purpose by the Secretary of State.

(3) The Secretary of State may by regulations prescribe when and how a claim for a rebate under this section is to be made and the evidence to be provided in support of such a claim.

(4) For the purposes of this section —

(a) goods are transported by means of combined transport where they are loaded on a goods vehicle which is transported by rail between the following points, namely the nearest suitable rail loading station to the point of loading and the nearest suitable rail unloading station to the point of unloading;

(b) "design weight" and "goods vehicle" have the same meanings as in Schedule 4 to this Act; and

(c) references to the plated gross weight or plated train weight of a goods vehicle shall be construed in accordance with paragraph 9 of that Schedule.]

[(5) In its application to Northern Ireland, this section shall have effect as if—

(a) for "plated gross weight", in each place, there were substituted "relevant maximum weight"; and

(b) for "plated train weight", in each place, there were substituted "relevant maximum train weight".]　　　　　　　　　**[64A]**

NOTES

Prospectively added by the Finance Act 1991, s 9(1), (2).

Sub-s (2): words in square brackets prospectively substituted for words "Great Britain" by the Finance Act 1991, s 10(2)(a), Sch 3, Part I, paras 1, 10.

Sub-s (5): added by the Finance Act 1991, s 10(2)(a), Sch 3, Part I, paras 1, 10.

REGISTRATION AND REGISTRATION MARKS, ETC

19. Registration and registration marks

(1) It shall be the duty of the Secretary of State—

(a) on the first issue by him of a vehicle licence for a vehicle; or

(b) where particulars in respect of the vehicle are furnished to him by a motor dealer in pursuance of section 20 of this Act before the Secretary of State first issues a vehicle licence for the vehicle, on receiving the said particulars,

to register the vehicle in such manner as the Secretary of State thinks fit without any further application in that behalf by the person taking out the licence and, except where the Secretary of State registers the vehicle on receiving the said particulars, to assign to the vehicle a registration mark indicating the registered number of the vehicle.

[(1A) The Secretary of State may, in such circumstances as he may determine—

(a) assign a registration mark to a vehicle to which another registration mark has been previously assigned;

(b) assign to a vehicle (whether on its first registration or not) a registration mark previously assigned to another vehicle;

(c) (whether in connection with an assignment falling within either of the preceding paragraphs or not) withdraw any registration mark for the time being assigned to a vehicle;

(d) re-assign to a vehicle a registration mark previously assigned to it but subsequently withdrawn.]

(2) The registration mark [for the time being] assigned to a vehicle under this section shall be fixed in the prescribed manner on the vehicle, or on any other vehicle drawn by that vehicle, or on both.　　　　　　**[65]**

NOTES

Commencement: 27 July 1989 (sub-s (1A)); 1 April 1971 (remainder).

This section derived from the Vehicles (Excise) Act 1962, s 3, and the Vehicle and Driving Licences Act 1969, s 20(5).

Sub-s (1A): added, with savings, by the Finance Act 1989, s 10.

Sub-s (2): words in square brackets added, with savings, by the Finance Act 1989, s 10.

20. Issue etc of vehicle registration marks by motor dealers

(1) The Secretary of State may by regulations make such provision as he considers appropriate with respect to the allocation of registration marks for vehicles to motor dealers who apply for such allocations and appear to the Secretary of State suitable to receive them and with respect to the assigning of the marks to vehicles by motor dealers.

(2) Without prejudice to the generality of subsection (1) above, regulations under this section may include provision—

(a) as to the mode of application for the allocation of registration marks;

(b) as to the transfer of registration marks allocated to a motor dealer in cases where the dealer dies or becomes incapacitated or bankrupt and in such other cases as may be prescribed; and

(c) subject to section 25(2) of this Act, as to the cancellation of allocations of registration marks.

(3) Without prejudice to the generality of subsection (1) above, regulations under this section may also include provision for—

(a) restricting the circumstances in which a motor dealer may assign a registration mark to a vehicle;

(b) securing that registration marks allocated to a dealer are assigned by him in such sequence as the Secretary of State considers appropriate and that no registration mark is assigned to a vehicle to which such a mark has already been assigned; and

(c) requiring a motor dealer to furnish the Secretary of State within the prescribed period with the prescribed particulars in respect of each vehicle to which the dealer assigns a registration mark.

(4) A registration mark assigned to a vehicle in pursuance of this section shall be deemed to be assigned to it under section 19 of this Act.　　　　**[66]**

NOTES

Commencement: 1 April 1971.

This section derived from the Vehicle and Driving Licences Act 1969, s 20(1)–(4), and SI 1970 No 1681.

21. Distinctive signs for hackney carriages

On every mechanically propelled vehicle which is chargeable with duty as a hackney carriage there shall, subject to the prescribed exceptions, be exhibited, in conjunction with the mark required under section 19 of this Act to be fixed on the vehicle, a distinctive sign indicating—

    (a) that the vehicle is a hackney carriage; and

    (b) the number of persons for which the vehicle has seating capacity;

and regulations under this Act shall provide for such signs to be exhibited as aforesaid. **[67]**

NOTES
    Commencement: 1 April 1971.
    This section derived from the Vehicles (Excise) Act 1962, s 14.

22. Failure to fix, and obscuration of, marks and signs

(1) If any mark to be fixed or sign to be exhibited on a vehicle in accordance with section 19 or 21 of this Act is not so fixed or exhibited, the person driving the vehile, or, where the vehicle is not being driven, the person keeping the vehicle, shall be guilty of an offence:

    Provided that it shall be a defence for a person charged under this subsection with failing to fix a mark on a vehicle to prove—

    (a) that he had no reasonable opportunity of registering the vehicle under this Act and that the vehicle was being driven on a public road for the purpose of being so registered; or

    (b) in a case where the charge relates to a vehicle to which [section 47 of the Road Traffic Act 1988 applies by virtue of subsection (2)(b) thereof (vehicles manufactured before the prescribed period and used before registration)] that he had no reasonable opportunity of so registering the vehicle and that the vehicle was being driven on a road for the purposes of or in connection with its examination under [section 45 of the said Act of 1988 (examinations for test certificates) in circumstances in which its use is exempted from the said section 47(1) by regulations under section 47(6) thereof].

(2) If any mark fixed or sign exhibited on a vehicle as aforesaid is in any way obscured or rendered or allowed to become not easily distinguishable, the person driving the vehicle, or, where the vehicle is not being driven, the person keeping the vehicle, shall be guilty of an offence:

    Provided that it shall be a defence for a person charged with such an offence to prove that he took all steps reasonably practicable to prevent the mark or sign being obscured or rendered not easily distinguishable.

(3) Any person guilty of an offence under this section shall be liable on summary conviction to a fine not exceeding [level 3 on the standard scale].

[(4) In its application to Northern Ireland, subsection (1) above shall have effect as if for paragraph (b) of the proviso there were substituted the following paragraph—

    "(b) in a case where the charge relates to a vehicle to which Article 34 of the Road Traffic (Northern Ireland) Order 1981 applies by virtue of paragraph (2)(b) thereof, that he had no opportunity of so registering the vehicle and that the vehicle was being driven on a road for the purposes of or in connection with its examination under Article 33 of the said Order of 1981 in circumstances in which its use is exempted from paragraph (1) of the said Article 34 by regulations under paragraph (5) thereof.] **[68]**

NOTES
Commencement: 1 April 1971 (except sub-s (4)); 1 October 1991 (sub-s (4)).
Sub-s (1) derived from the Vehicles (Excise) Act 1962, s 15(1), and the Road Traffic (Amendment) Act 1967, s 4(4); sub-ss (2), (3) derived from the Vehicles (Excise) Act 1962, s 15(2), (3).
Sub-s (1): words in square brackets substituted by the Road Traffic (Consequential Provisions) Act 1988, s 54, Sch 3, para 8(3).
Sub-s (3): enhanced penalty on a subsequent conviction now abolished, maximum fine on any conviction increased and converted to the standard scale by the Criminal Justice Act 1982, ss 35, 37, 38, 46, as amended.
Sub-s (4): added by the Finance Act 1991, s 10(2)(b), Sch 3, Part I, paras 1, 11.

23. Regulations with respect to the transfer and identification of vehicles

Regulations under this Act may—

  (a) require a person who becomes or ceases to be the keeper of a mechanically propelled vehicle, or who acts as the auctioneer at the sale of such a vehicle by auction; to furnish the prescribed information to the Secretary of State in the prescribed manner;

  (b) specify the size, shape and character of the registration marks or the signs to be affixed to any such vehicle (including a vehicle used by virtue of a trade licence) and the manner in which the marks or signs are to be displayed and rendered easily distinguishable by day and by night;

  (c) make provision for the issue of trade plates to holders of trade licences and for the charging of a fee for the replacement of such plates by reason of damage to them or of their loss or destruction;

  (d) make provision with respect to the furnishing of information and production of certificates of insurance or security and test certificates relating to mechanically propelled vehicles in respect of which duty is not chargeable under this Act and with respect to the registration and identification of such vehicles (including vehicles belonging to the Crown);

  (e) make provision with respect to the inspection [, transfer] and surrender of any registration document issued in respect of a vehicle and provide that, in a case where the surrender of such a document is required in connection with an application for a licence under this Act, the licence shall not be issued if the document is not surrendered;

  (f) make provision with respect to the replacement of any such document . . . ; and

  (g) provide for information contained in any records maintained by the Secretary of State with respect to the marking, registration or keeping of vehicles to be made public or to be made available, either without payment or on payment of the prescribed fee, to such persons as may be determined by or under the regulations.

Regulations under this section which require a person to furnish information relating to vehicles exempted from duty by virtue of section 7(2) of this Act may require him to furnish in addition such evidence of the facts giving rise to the exemption as is prescribed by the regulations. **[69]**

NOTES
Commencement: 1 April 1971.
This section derived from the Vehicles (Excise) Act 1962, s 16, the Finance Act 1964, s 11(1), the Finance Act 1969, s 6, Sch 12, Part II, para 6, and SI 1970 No 1681.
Para (e): amended by the Finance Act 1987, s 2(1), Sch 1, Part III, para 16.
Para (f): words omitted repealed by the Finance Act 1986, ss 3(1), (7), 114(6), Sch 2, Part I, para 6(a), Sch 23, Part II.

MISCELLANEOUS

24. Marking of engines and bodies

(1) The Secretary of State may by regulations make such provision as he thinks appropriate with respect to the marking of the engines and bodies of mechanically propelled vehicles.

(2) Without prejudice to the generality of subsection (1) above regulations under this section may include provision—

    (a) as to the persons by whom and the times at which engines and bodies of vehicles are to be marked;

    (b) as to the form of any mark and the manner and position in which it is to be made; and

    (c) for requiring particulars of marks made in pursuance of the regulations to be furnished to the Secretary of State.   **[70]**

NOTES
    Commencement: 1 April 1971.
    This section derived from the Vehicle and Driving Licences Act 1969, s 19 (except sub-s (2)(d)) and SI 1970 No 1681.

25. Review of Secretary of State's decisions relating to motor traders, etc

(1) If the Secretary of State—

    (a) rejects an application by a motor dealer for an allocation of temporary licences or registration marks in pursuance of this Act; or

    (b) requires a motor dealer or any other person to surrender any unissued temporary licences allocated to the dealer in pursuance of this Act or cancels an allocation of registration marks made to a dealer in pursuance of this Act; or

    (c) refuses an application for a trade licence made by a motor trader or vehicle tester within the meaning of section 16 of this Act,

and the dealer, trader, tester or other person in question requests the Secretary of State within the prescribed period to review his decision, it shall be the duty of the Secretary of State to comply with the request and, in doing so, to consider any representations made to him in writing within the period aforesaid by the person who made the request.

(2) Such a requirement or cancellation as is mentioned in subsection (1)(b) above shall not take effect before the expiration of the period aforesaid and, where during that period a request is made in pursuance of that subsection in respect of the requirement or cancellation, shall not take effect before the Secretary of State gives notice in writing of the result of the review to the person who made the request.

For the purposes of this subsection a notice may be given to any person by delivering it to him or by leaving it at his proper address or by sending it to him by post; and for the purposes of this subsection and section 26 of the Interpretation Act 1889 in its application to this subsection the proper address of any person shall be his latest address as known to the person giving the notice.   **[71]**

NOTES
    Commencement: 1 April 1971.
    This section derived from the Vehicle and Driving Licences Act 1969, ss 21(1), (2), 35, and SI 1970 No 1681.

26. Forgery and false information

(1) If any person forges or fraudulently alters or uses, or fraudulently lends or allows to be used by any other person—

    (a) any mark to be fixed or sign to be exhibited on a mechanically propelled vehicle in accordance with section 19 or 21 of this Act; or

    (b) any trade plates or replacements such as are mentioned in section 23(c) of this Act; or

    (c) any licence or registration document under this Act,

he shall be liable on summary conviction to a fine not exceeding [the prescribed sum] or on conviction on indictment to imprisonment for a term not exceeding two years.

    (2) Any person who—

    (a) in connection with an application for a licence or for the allocation of temporary licences or registration marks makes a declaration which to his knowledge is false or in any material respect misleading; or

    (b) being required by virtue of this Act to furnish particulars relating to, or to the keeper of, any vehicle, furnishes any particulars which to his knowledge are false or in any material respect misleading,

shall be liable on summary conviction to a fine not exceeding [the prescribed sum] or on conviction on indictment to imprisonment for a term not exceeding two years. **[72]**

NOTES

    Commencement: 1 April 1971.

    Sub-s (1) derived from the Vehicles (Excise) Act 1962, s 17(1), the Vehicle and Driving Licences Act 1969, s 28(1), (2), and the Finance Act 1969, s 6(2)(b); sub-s (2) derived from the Vehicles (Excise) Act 1962, s 17(2), and the Vehicle and Driving Licences Act 1969, s 28(1), (2).

    References to the "prescribed sum" were substituted by the Magistrates' Courts Act 1980, s 32(2), as amended.

[26A. Dishonoured cheques: additional liability in certain cases

(1) Where a person has been convicted of an offence under section 102 of the Customs and Excise Management Act 1979 (payment for licence by dishonoured cheque) in relation to a licence issued under this Act, the court shall, in addition to any penalty which it may impose under that section, order him to pay an amount equal to one twelfth of the appropriate annual rate of duty for each month or part of a month in the relevant period.

    (2) The relevant period for the purposes of this section is the period which—

    (a) begins with the first day of the period for which the licence was applied for or, if it is later, the day on which the licence first was to have effect, and

    (b) ends with whichever is the earliest of the following, namely—

        (i) the end of the month in which the order is made;

        (ii) the date on which the licence was due to expire;

        (iii) the end of the month during which the licence was delivered up; and

        (iv) the end of the month preceding that in which a new licence for the licensed vehicle first had effect.

    (3) The appropriate annual rate of duty for the purposes of this section is the annual rate of duty which, at the beginning of the relevant period, was appropriate to a vehicle of the description specified in the application.

(4) Where an order has previously been made against a person under section 9 of this Act to pay an amount for a month or part of a month in the case of a vehicle, the amount which he is ordered to pay under this section in the case of the vehicle shall be calculated as if no part of that month were comprised in the relevant period.]　　　　　　　　　　　　　　　　　　　　　　　**[73]**

NOTES
　Commencement: 27 July 1989.
　Added, in relation to licences taken out on or after 27 July 1989, by the Finance Act 1989, s 14(1), (7).

27. Duty to give information

(1) Where it is alleged that a mechanically propelled vehicle has been used or kept in contravention of section 8, 16(7) or 18(4) of this Act—

　　(a) the person keeping the vehicle shall give such information as he may be required by or on behalf of a chief officer of police or the Secretary of State to give as to the identity of the person or persons concerned and, if he fails to do so, shall be guilty of an offence unless he shows to the satisfaction of the court that he did not know and could not with reasonable diligence have ascertained the identity of the person or persons concerned;

　　(b) any other person shall, if required as aforesaid, give such information as it is in his power to give and which may lead to the identification of any of the persons concerned and, if he fails to do so, shall be guilty of an offence; and

　　(c) in a case where it is alleged that the vehicle has been used at any time in contravention of the said section 8, the person who is alleged to have so used the vehicle shall, if required as aforesaid, give such information as it is in his power to give as to the identity of the person by whom the vehicle was kept at that time and, if he fails to do so, shall be guilty of an offence.

(2) The following persons shall be treated for the purposes of subsection (1)(a) and (b) above as persons concerned, that is to say—

　　(a) in relation to an alleged offence of using a vehicle in contravention of section 8, 16(7) or 18(4) of this Act, both the driver and any person using the vehicle;

　　(b) in relation to an alleged offence of keeping the vehicle in contravention of the said section 8, the person keeping the vehicle.

(3) A person guilty of an offence under subsection (1) of this section shall be liable on summary conviction to a fine not exceeding [level 3 on the standard scale].

[(4) In its application to Northern Ireland, subsection (1)(a) above shall have effect as if for "a chief officer of police" there were substituted "the Chief Constable of the Royal Ulster Constabulary".]　　　　　　　　　　**[74]**

NOTES
　Commencement: 1 April 1971 (except sub-s (4)); 1 October 1991 (sub-s (4)).
　Sub-s (1) derived from the Vehicles (Excise) Act 1962, s 18(1), the Finance Act 1967, s 12(8), and the Vehicle and Driving Licences Act 1969, ss 2(8), 28(4); sub-ss (2), (3) derived from the Vehicles (Excise) Act 1962, s 18(2), (3), and Vehicle and Driving Licences Act 1969, s 28(4).
　Sub-s (3): maximum fine increased and converted to the standard scale by the Criminal Justice Act 1982, ss 37, 38, 46, as amended.
　Sub-s (4): added by the Finance Act 1991, s 10(2)(a), Sch 3, Part I, paras 1, 12.

LEGAL PROCEEDINGS ETC

28. Institution and conduct of proceedings in England and Wales

(1) Subject to the provisions of this section, summary proceedings for an offence under section 8, 11(2), 16(7), 18(4) or 26(1) or (2) of this Act or under regulations made in pursuance of this Act may be instituted in England and Wales by the Secretary of State or a constable (in this section severally referred to as "the authorised prosecutor") at any time within six months from the date on which evidence sufficient in the opinion of the authorised prosecutor to warrant the proceedings came to his knowledge; but no proceedings for any offence shall be instituted by virtue of this subsection more than three years after the commission of the offence.

(2) No proceedings for an offence under section 8, 16(7) or 18(4) of this Act shall be instituted in England and Wales except by the authorised prosecutor; and no proceedings for such an offence shall be so instituted by a constable except with the approval of the Secretary of State.

(3) A certificate stating—

(a) the date on which such evidence as is mentioned in subsection (1) above came to the knowledge of the authorised prosecutor; or

(b) that the Secretary of State's approval is given for the institution by a constable of any proceedings specified in the certificate,

and signed by or on behalf of the authorised prosecutor or, as the case may be, the Secretary of State shall for the purposes of this section be conclusive evidence of the date or approval in question; and a certificate purporting to be given in pursuance of this subsection and to be signed as aforesaid shall be deemed to be so signed unless the contrary is proved.

(4) In a magistrates' court or before the registrar of a county court any proceedings by or against the Secretary of State under this Act may be conducted on behalf of the Secretary of State by a person authorised by him for the purposes of this subsection.

(5) [Section 145 of the Customs and Excise Management Act 1979] (which restricts the bringing of proceedings under that Act) and *[section 147(1)]* [section 146A] of that Act (which extends the time for bringing such proceedings) shall not apply to proceedings in England or Wales for offences under this Act.

[75]

NOTES

Commencement: 1 April 1971.

Sub-ss (1)–(4) derived from the Vehicle and Driving Licences Act 1969, s 25(2)–(4), (6), and SI 1970 No 1681; sub-s 5 derived from the Vehicles (Excise) Act 1962, s 19(2).

Sub-s (5): words in italics substituted by the Customs and Excise Management Act 1979, s 177(1), Sch 4, para 12, Table, Part I, further substituted, in relation to offences committed on or after 27 July 1989, by the Finance Act 1989, s 16(3), (4).

[28A Institution of proceedings in Northern Ireland

Section 28 of this Act shall also apply in relation to the institution of proceedings in Northern Ireland, but as if—

(a) for any reference in that section to England and Wales there were substituted a reference to Northern Ireland; and

(b) in subsection (4) of that section for the words from the beginning to
"county court" there were substituted "In a court of summary
jurisdiction or before a county court".]   **[75A]**

NOTES
Commencement: 1 October 1991.
Inserted by the Finance Act 1991, s 10(2)(a), Sch 3, Pt I, paras 1, 13.

29. (*Applies to Scotland only.*)

30. Limitation on the bringing of proceedings for recovery of underpayments and overpayments of duty

(1) Where the amount of the duty which has been paid on a vehicle licence for
a vehicle is less than the amount payable on the licence appropriate to that
vehicle, the Secretary of State may take proceedings for the recovery of that
amount at any time before the expiration of the twelve months beginning with
the end of the period in respect of which the licence was taken out.

(2) No proceedings shall be brought for enforcing any repayment of duty to
which a person may be entitled in respect of any overpayment of duty made on
a vehicle licence taken out by him, unless the proceedings are brought before
the expiration of the twelve months beginning with the end of the period in
respect of which the licence was taken out.   **[76]**

NOTES
Commencement: 1 April 1971.
This section derived from the Vehicles (Excise) Act, s 11, and SI 1970 No 1681.

31. Admissibility of records as evidence

(1) A statement contained in a document purporting to be—

(a) a part of the records maintained by the Secretary of State in connection
with any functions exercisable by the Secretary of State by virtue of
this Act; or

(b) a copy of a document forming part of those records; or

(c) a note of any information contained in those records,

and to be authenticated by a person authorised in that behalf by the Secretary
of State shall be admissible in any proceedings as evidence of any fact stated
therein to the same extent as oral evidence of that fact is admissible in those
proceedings.

(2) In subsection (1) above "document" and "statement" have the same
meanings as in subsection (1) of section 10 of the Civil Evidence Act 1968, and
the reference to a copy of a document shall be construed in accordance with
subsection (2) of that section; but nothing in this subsection shall be construed
as limiting to civil proceedings the references to proceedings in subsection (1)
above.

(3) Nothing in the foregoing provisions of this section shall enable evidence
to be given with respect to any matter other than a matter of the prescribed
description.

(4) In its application to Scotland this section shall have effect as if—

(a) in subsection (1), for the words from "as evidence" onwards there
were substituted the words "as sufficient evidence of any fact stated
therein, so however that nothing in this subsection shall be deemed to

make such a statement evidence in any proceedings except where oral evidence to the like effect would have been admissible in those proceedings"; and

(b) in subsection (2), for the references to subsections (1) and (2) of section 10 of the Civil Evidence Act 1968 there were substituted references to subsections (3) and (4) respectively of section 17 of the Law Reform (Miscellaneous Provisions) (Scotland) Act 1968.

[(5) In its application to Northern Ireland, this section shall have effect as if in subsection (2) for "subsection (1) of section 10 of the Civil Evidence Act 1968" there were substituted "subsection (1) of section 6 of the Civil Evidence Act (Northern Ireland 1971".]   [77]

NOTES
Commencement: 1 April 1971 (except sub-s (5)); 1 October 1991 (sub-s (5)).
This section derived from the Vehicle and Driving Licences Act 1969, s 27, and SI 1970 No 1681.
Sub-s (5): added by the Finance Act 1991, s 10(2)(a), Sch 3, Part I, paras 1, 14.

32. Evidence of admissions in certain proceedings

[(1)] Where in any proceedings in England and Wales for an offence under section 8 or section 16(7) of this Act—

(a) it is proved to the satisfaction of the court, on oath or in manner prescribed by rules made under section 15 of the Justices of the Peace Act 1949, that a requirement under section 27(1)(a) or (b) of this Act to give information as to the identity of the driver of, or the person using or keeping, a particular vehicle on the particular occasion on which the offence is alleged to have been committed has been served on the accused by post; and

(b) a statement in writing is produced to the court purporting to be signed by the accused that the accused was the driver of, or the person using or keeping, that vehicle on that occasion,

the court may accept the statement as evidence that the accused was the driver of, or the person using or keeping, that vehicle on that occasion.

[(2) Subsection (1) above shall apply in Northern Ireland as if—

(a) for the words "England and Wales" there were substituted "Northern Ireland"; and

(b) for the words from "rules" to "1949" there were substituted "magistrates' courts rules as defined in Article 2(3) of the Magistrates' Courts (Northern Ireland) Order 1981."]   [78]

NOTES
Commencement: 1 April 1971 (sub-s (1)); 1 October 1991 (sub-s (2)).
This section derived from the Finance Act 1965, s 7.
Sub-s (1): numbered by the Finance Act 1991, s 10(2)(a), Sch 3, Part I, paras 1, 15.
Sub-s (2): added by the Finance Act 1991, s 10(2)(a), Sch 3, Part I, paras 1, 15.

33. Burden of proof in certain proceedings

If in any proceedings under section 8, 16(7) or 26(2) of this Act any question arises—

(a) as to the number of mechanically propelled vehicles used, or

(b) as to the character, weight, horse-power or cylinder capacity of any mechanically propelled vehicle, or

    (c) as to the number of persons for which a mechanically propelled vehicle has seating capacity, or

    (d) as to the purpose for which any mechanically propelled vehicle has been used,

the burden of proof in respect of the matter in question shall lie on the defendant.   **[79]**

NOTES

Commencement: 1 April 1971.

This section derived from the Vehicles (Excise) Act 1962, s 20.

34. Fixing of amount payable under s 9 on plea of guilty by absent accused

[(1)] Where in pursuance of [section 12(2) of the Magistrates' Courts Act 1980] a person is convicted in his absence of an offence under section 8 of this Act [, or under section 102 of the Customs and Excise Management Act 1979 in relation to a licence issued under this Act,] and it is proved to the satisfaction of the court, on oath or in the manner prescribed by rules made under [section 144 of the Magistrates' Courts Act 1980] that there was served on the accused with the summons a notice stating that, in the event of his being convicted of the offence, it will be alleged that an order requiring him to pay an amount specified in the notice falls to be made by the court in pursuance of section 9(1) [or, as the case may be, 26A(1)] of this Act then, unless in the notification purporting to be given by or on behalf of the accused in pursuance of [the said section 12(2)] it is stated that the amount so specified is inappropriate, the court shall proceed in pursuance of the said section 9(1) [or, as the case may be, 26A(1)] as if that amount had been calculated as required by that subsection.

[(2) In its application to Northern Ireland, subsection (1) above shall have effect as if—

    (a) for "section 12(2) of the Magistrates' Courts Act 1980" and "the said section 12(2)" there were substituted "Article 24(2) of the Magistrates' Courts (Northern Ireland) Order 1981" and "the said Article 24(2)" respectively; and

    (b) for the words from "or in" to "1980" there were substituted "or by affidavit or in the manner prescribed by magistrates' courts rules as defined by Article 2(3) of the Magistrates' Courts (Northern Ireland) Order 1981".]   **[80–82]**

NOTES

Commencement: 1 April 1971 (sub-s (1)); 1 October 1991 (sub-s (2)).

This section derived from the Vehicle and Driving Licences Act 1969, s 30.

Sub-s (1): numbered by the Finance Act 1991, s 10(2)(a), Sch 3, Part I, paras 1, 16; first, third and fifth amendments in square brackets made by the Magistrates' Courts Act 1980, s 154, Sch 7, para 93; other words in square brackets added, in relation to licences taken out on or after 27 July 1989, by the Finance Act 1989, s 14(5), (7).

Sub-s (2): added by the Finance Act 1991, s 10(2)(a), Sch 3, Part I, paras 1, 16.

SUPPLEMENTARY

37. Regulations

(1) Regulations under this Act may be made generally for the purpose of carrying this Act (except section 31) into effect and may—

    (a) make different provision for different circumstances;

    (b) provide for exemptions from any provisions of the regulations; and

(c) contain such incidental and supplemental provisions as the Secretary of State considers expedient for the purposes of the regulations;

and nothing in any other provision of this Act shall be construed as prejudicing the generality of the foregoing provisions of this subsection.

(2) Regulations under this Act may contain provisions prescribing any matter which is to be prescribed under this Act, but any fee prescribed under this Act, except a fee for which provision is made by [section 13(2A) or] section 23(c) thereof, shall be of an amount approved by the Treasury.

(3) Regulations under this Act except regulations under section 2(5) or 11(3) may provide that a person who contravenes or fails to comply with any specified provision of the regulations shall be guilty of an offence and a person guilty of such an offence shall be liable on summary conviction to a fine of an amount not exceeding—

   [(a) in the case of regulations prescribed for the purposes of this paragraph, of regulations made under section 24 or of a contravention or failure to comply with requirements imposed in pursuance of section 23(a) above, level 3 on the standard scale;]
   (b) in any other case, [level 1 on the standard scale].

[(3A) The prescribing of regulations for the purposes of subsection (3)(a) above shall not affect the punishment for a contravention of or a failure to comply with those regulations before they were so prescribed.]

(4) Any power to make regulations which is exercisable by the Secretary of State by virtue of section 11(3), 14, 15(1), 17(1), 20, 23 or 24 of this Act includes power to provide by the regulations that any document for which provision is made by the regulations shall be in such form and contain such particulars as may be specified by a person specified in the regulations.

(5) Any power to make regulations conferred on the Secretary of State by this Act shall be exercisable by statutory instrument which, except in the case of a statutory instrument containing only regulations made under section 7(4) or (5) or 38(5) of this Act, shall be subject to annulment in pursuance of a resolution of either House of Parliament.   [83]

NOTES

Commencement: 15 May 1987 (sub-s (3A)); 1 April 1971 (remainder).

Sub-ss (1), (5) derived from the Vehicles (Excise) Act 1962, s 23(1), (3), the Vehicle and Driving Licences Act 1969, s 34(1), (2), (5), and SI 1970 No 1681; sub-ss (2), (3) derived from the Vehicles (Excise) Act 1962, ss 17(3), 23(2), and the Vehicle and Driving Licences Act 1969, ss 6(3)(f), 19(2)(d), 20(3)(d), 23(2), 32; sub-s (4) derived from the Vehicle and Driving Licences Act 1969, s 34(3), and SI 1970 No 1681.

Regulations, see the Road Vehicles (Registration and Licensing) Regulations 1971, post, the Road Vehicles (Excise) (Prescribed Particulars) Regulations 1981, SI 1981 No 931 as amended, the Motor Vehicles (International Circulation) Regulations 1975, SI 1975 No 1208 and the Recovery of Vehicles (Prescribed Purposes) Regulations 1989, SI 1989 No 1376.

Sub-s (2): amended by the Finance Act 1985, s 9(2).

Sub-s (3): sub-para (a) substituted by the Finance Act 1987, s 2(1), (6), Sch 1, Part III, paras 7, 18; maximum fines increased and converted to levels on the standard scale by the Criminal Justice Act 1982, ss 37, 38, 46, as amended.

Sub-s (3A): added by the Finance Act 1987, s 2(1), (6), Sch 1, Part III, para 18.

38. Interpretation

(1) In this Act, unless the context otherwise requires—

   ["community bus" means a vehicle used on public roads solely in accordance with a community bus permit (within the meaning of section

22 of the Transport Act 1985), and not used for providing a service under an agreement providing for service subsidies (within the meaning of section 63(10)(b) of that Act;]

['conditional sale agreement' means an agreement for the sale of a vehicle under which the purchase price or part of it is payable by instalments, and the property in the vehicle is to remain in the seller (notwithstanding that the buyer is to be in possession of the vehicle) until such conditions as may be specified in the agreement are fulfilled;]

"gas" means any fuel which is wholly gaseous at a temperature of 60 degrees Fahrenheit under a pressure of 30 inches of mercury;

["hackney carriage" means a mechanically propelled vehicle standing or plying for hire and includes any mechanically propelled vehicle bailed or (in Scotland) hired under a hire agreement by a person whose trade it is to sell such vehicles or bail or hire them under hire agreements [but does not include a community bus];]

["hire agreement" means an agreement for the bailment or (in Scotland) the hiring of a vehicle which is not a hire-purchase agreement;

"hire-purchase agreement" means an agreement, other than a conditional sale agreement, under which—

(a) a vehicle is bailed or (in Scotland) hired in return for periodical payments by the person to whom it is bailed or hired, and

(b) the property in the vehicle will pass to that person if the terms of the agreement are complied with and one or more of the following occurs—

    (i) the exercise of an option to purchase by that person,

    (ii) the doing of any other specified act by any party to the agreement,

    (iii) the happening of any other specified event;]

"licence" means a vehicle licence or a trade licence;

"motor dealer" means a person carrying on the business of selling or supplying mechanically propelled vehicles;

"prescribed" means prescribed by regulations made by the Secretary of State;

"public road" means a road which is repairable at the public expense;

. . .

"temporary licence" has the meaning assigned to it by section 13(1) of this Act;

"trade licence" means a licence issued under section 16(1) of this Act; and

"transfer date" has the same meaning as in the Vehicle and Driving Licences Act 1969, that is to say, such date as the Secretary of State may by order appoint for the purposes of section 1(1) of that Act;

"vehicle licence" means a licence under this Act for a mechanically propelled vehicle.

(2) For the purposes of any provision of this Act and any subsequent enactment relating to the keeping of mechanically propelled vehicles on public roads, a person keeps such a vehicle on a public road if he causes it to be on such a road for any period, however short, when it is not in use there.

(3) A mechanically propelled vehicle shall not be treated as an electrically propelled vehicle for the purposes of this Act unless the electrical motive power is derived either from a source external to the vehicle or from any electrical storage battery which is not connected to any source of power when the vehicle is in motion.

(4) . . .

(5) The unit of horse-power or cylinder capacity for the purposes of any rate

of duty under this Act shall be calculated in accordance with regulations under this Act.

(6) References in this Act to any enactment shall be construed, unless the context otherwise requires, as references to that enactment as amended by or under any other enactment.   **[84]**

NOTES

Commencement: 1 April 1971.

Sub-s (1) derived from the Vehicles (Excise) Act 1962, s 24(1), the Vehicle and Driving Licences Act 1969, s 33(1), and SI 1970 No 1681; sub-s (2) derived from the Vehicle and Driving Licences Act 1969, s 9; sub-ss (3)–(5) derived from the Vehicles (Excise) Act 1962, s 24(2)–(4); sub-s (6) derived from the Vehicles (Excise) Act 1962, s 24(6), and the Vehicle and Driving Licences Act 1969, s 33(2).

Sub-s (1): definition "community bus" added by the Finance Act 1989, s 7(2); definitions "conditional sale agreement", "hire agreement" and "hire-purchase agreement" added by the Consumer Credit Act 1974, s 192(3)(a), Sch 4, para 32; definition "hackney carriage" substituted by the Consumer Credit Act 1974, s 192(3)(a), Sch 4, para 32, words in square brackets therein added by the Finance Act 1989, s 7(3); definition "seven day licence" repealed by the Finance Act 1988, s 148, Sch 14, Part II.

Sub-s (4): repealed by the Finance Act 1991, s 123, Sch 19, Pt III, in relation to licences taken out after 20 March 1991.

---

39. Transitional provisions, savings, repeals and revocation

(1) This Act shall have effect subject to the modifications specified in Part I of Schedule 7 thereto (being modifications required during the transition to the provisions of this Act from the law in force at the passing of this Act relating to the system of vehicle licensing and registration).

(2) The modifications of this Act so specified shall cease to have effect on such day as the Secretary of State may appoint by order made by statutory instrument which shall be subject to annulment in pursuance of a resolution of either House of Parliament; and different days may be appointed under this subsection for different modifications so specified or for different modifications so far as they apply to such cases only as may be specified in the order.

(3) Where during the period between the passing and the commencement of this Act any provision of the Vehicle and Driving Licences Act 1969 is brought into force and either—

    (a) this Act or any provision thereof is by virtue of subsection (1) above and any modifications specified in Part I of Schedule 7 thereto directed to have effect as if the corresponding provision of this Act were omitted; or

    (b) there would be at the commencement of this Act, if the power given by this subsection were not exercised, any other inconsistency in effect between the provision of any enactment repealed by this Act and the corresponding provision of this Act,

the Secretary of State may, without prejudice to section 37 of the Interpretation Act 1889 (exercise of statutory powers before commencement of Acts), exercise the power given him by subsection (2) above at any time after the passing of this Act.

(4) The other transitional provisions and savings contained in Part II of Schedule 7 to this Act shall have effect.

(5) The enactments specified in Part I of Schedule 8 to this Act are hereby repealed to the extent specified in the third column of that Schedule; and the order specified in Part II of that Schedule is hereby revoked.

(6) The provisions of Part II of Schedule 7 to this Act shall not be taken as prejudicing the operation of section 38 of the Interpretation Act 1889 (which relates to the effect of repeals). **[85–87]**

NOTES
Commencement: 16 March 1971 (sub-ss (2), (3)); 1 April 1971 (remainder).

SCHEDULES

(*Schedule 6: repealed by the Finance Act 1991, s 123, Sch 19, Pt III, in relation to licences taken out after 20 March 1991.*)

SCHEDULE 7

Section 39

TRANSITIONAL PROVISIONS

PART I

MODIFICATIONS OF THIS ACT RELATING TO THE SYSTEM OF VEHICLE LICENSING AND REGISTRATION ETC

Excise duty on, and licensing of, mechanically propelled vehicles

1. Section 2(1) shall have effect as if—
   (a) there were inserted at the beginning the words "Subject to the provisions of section 2A of this Act";
   (b) in paragraph (a) and in paragraph (b) there were added at the end the words "running from the beginning of the month in which the licence first has effect";
   (c) there were inserted after paragraph (a) the following paragraph—

   "(aa) in the case of any vehicle, for one calendar year;";

   (d) the words following paragraph (c) were omitted.

2. Section 2 shall have effect as if subsections (2) and (3) were omitted.

3. Section 2(4) shall have effect as if—
   (a) there were inserted at the beginning the words "Subject to the provisions of section 2A of this Act";
   (b) in paragraph (a) for the words "a period of twelve months" there were substituted the words "one calendar year or any other period of twelve months".

4. Section 2 shall have effect as if subsections (5) and (6) were omitted.

5. After section 2 there shall be inserted the following section—

"2A. Power to modify duration of licences and rates of duty

(1) Subject to the following provisions of this section, the Secretary of State may by order provide that vehicle licences (other than licences for one calendar year) may be taken out for such periods as may be specified in the order, being—
   (a) periods of a fixed number of months (not exceeding fifteen) running from the beginning of the month in which the licence first has effect; or
   [(*aa*) in the case of licences taken out on the first registration of vehicles of such description as may be so specified, periods exceeding by such number of days (not exceeding thirty) as may be determined by or under the order the periods for which the licence would otherwise have effect by virtue of section 2(1) above or any provision made under paragraph (a) above; or]
   (b) in the case of vehicles of such description, or of such description and used in such circumstances, as may be so specified, periods of less than a month.

(2) A licence for any period specified in an order under this section shall be taken out on payment of duty at such rate as may be so specified:

Provided that—

(a) the rate of duty on any licence taken out for a vehicle for a period [of a fixed number of months other than twelve or for a period of less than a month] shall be such as to bear to the annual rate of duty applicable to that vehicle no less proportion than the period for which the licence is taken out bears to a year; and

(b) the rate of duty on any licence taken out for a vehicle for a period of three months or for a period of four months shall not exceed for each month of the period ten per cent. of the annual rate of duty applicable to the vehicle.

(3) Any order made by the Secretary of State under this section may be made so as to apply only to vehicles of specified descriptions and may make different provision for vehicles of different descriptions or for different circumstances.

(4) The power to make orders under this section shall be exercisable by statutory instrument [subject to annulment in pursuance of a resolution of either House of Parliament] and shall include power [to make transitional provisions] to vary or revoke any such order and to amend or repeal the following provisions of section 2 of this Act, that is to say, in subsection (1), paragraphs (a), (b) and (c) and, in subsection (4), paragraphs (b) and (c) and so much of the remainder of the subsection as relates to those two paragraphs.".

Liability to pay duty and consequences of non-payment thereof

6. Section 8 shall have effect as if subsection (2) were omitted.

7. Section 9 shall have effect as if—

(a) in subsection (2) for the words "one-three-hundred and sixty-fifth" there were substituted the words "one twelfth", for the words "day in the relevant period" there were substituted the words "calendar month or part of a calendar month in the relevant period" and, in the proviso, for the words "day following that on which" there were substituted the words "calendar month immediately following that in which";

(b) in subsection (3)—

(i) in paragraph (a), for the word "day" there were substituted the words "month or part of a month";

(ii) ...

(iii) in [paragraph (d)] and in the words following paragraph (d), for the word "day" there were in each case substituted the words "month or part";

(c) in subsection (4), for the words "In relation to any day" there were substituted the words "In relation to any month or part of a month", for the words "on that day" there were substituted the words "at the beginning of that month or part" and for the words "such day" there shall be substituted the words "such month or part".

8. Sections 10 and 11 shall be omitted.

Issue, exhibition, exchange, surrender, etc. of licences

9. Section 12 shall have effect as if subsection (5) were omitted.

10. ...

11. Sections 14 and 15 shall be omitted.

12. Section 16 shall have effect as if for subsections (4) and (5) there were substituted the following subsections—

"(4) [Subject to subsections (4A) and (4B) below, a trade licence] may be taken out either for one calendar year or, [for a period of six months beginning with the first day of January or July].

(5) The rate of duty applicable to a trade licence taken out for a calendar year shall be *[£85]* [£100] or, if the licence is to be used only for vehicles to which Schedule 1 to this Act relates, *[£17]* [£20]; and the rate of duty applicable to a licence taken out for a period of [six months] shall be [eleven twentieths] of the rate applicable to the corresponding trade licence taken out for a calendar year,

any fraction of 5p being treated as 5p if it exceeds 2.5p but otherwise being disregarded."

13. Section 17 shall have effect as if there were substituted for subsections (1) and (2) the following subsections—

"(1) The holder of a licence (other than a licence for a tramcar) may at any time surrender the licence to the Secretary of State.

(2) Where a licence is surrendered to the Secretary of State under subsection (1) above, the holder shall be entitled to be repaid by the Secretary of State by way of rebate of duty paid for the licence the following amount in respect of each complete month of the period of the currency of the licence which is unexpired at the date of the surrender, that is to say—

(a) . . .

(b) . . . , an amount equal to one twelfth of the annual rate of duty chargeable on the licence."

14. Until the date appointed for the cesser of paragraph 10 above section 17 shall have effect as if subsection (3) were omitted.

15. On and after the said date section 17(3) shall have effect until the date appointed for the cesser of paragraph 13 above as if paragraph (b) were omitted together with the words from "or, if the Secretary of State so directs" to "application" in the second place where it occurs.

16. Section 17 shall have effect as if subsection (4) were omitted.

17. Section 18(3) shall have effect as if for the words "number of days" there were substituted in each place where they occur the words "number of months" and for the words from "that period being treated" to the end there were substituted the words "any incomplete month being treated as a whole month".

[17A. Section 18A shall have effect as if—

(a) in subsection (2) for the words "one three-hundred-and-sixty-fifth" there were substituted the words "one twelfth" and for the words "day in the relevant period" there were substituted the words "calendar month or part of a calendar month in the relevant period";

(b) in subsection (7)—

(i) in paragraph (a), for the words "day" there were substituted the words 'month or part of a month';

(ii) . . .

(iii) in . . . [paragraph (c)] and in the words following [that paragraph] , for the word "day" there were in each case substituted the words "month or part";

(c) in subsection (9), for the words "any day comprised in the relevant period" there were substituted the words "any month or part of a month comprised in the relevant period.]

Registration and registration marks, etc.

18. Section 19(1) shall have effect as if paragraph (b) together with the preceding "or" and the words "except where the Secretary of State registers the vehicle on receiving the said particulars" were omitted.

19. Section 20 shall be omitted.

20. For section 23 there shall be substituted the following—

"23.—(1) Regulations under this Act may—

(a) make provision with respect to the registration of mechanically propelled vehicles;

(b) require the Secretary of State to make the prescribed returns with respect to mechanically propelled vehicles registered with him, and provide for making any particulars contained in the register available for use by the prescribed persons on payment, in the prescribed cases, of the prescribed fee;

(c) require any person [by whom or] to whom any mechanically propelled vehicle is sold or disposed of to furnish the prescribed particulars in the prescribed manner;

(d) provide for the issue of registration [documents] in respect of the registration of any mechanically propelled vehicle, and for the [transfer] surrender and production, and the inspection by the prescribed persons, of any [documents] so issued;

(e) provide for the issue of new registration [documents] in the place of any such books which may be lost or destroyed, . . . ; and

(f) prescribe the size, shape and character of the registration marks or the signs to be fixed on any vehicle and the manner in which those marks or signs are to be displayed and rendered easily distinguishable whether by night or by day.

(2) Regulations under this Act may—

(a) prescribe the form of, and the particulars to be included in, the register of trade licences;

(b) make provision for assigning general registration marks to persons holding trade licences and, without prejudice to the foregoing, prescribe the registration marks to be carried by vehicles the use of which is authorised by virtue of such licences; and

(c) make provision for the issue of trade plates to holders of trade licences and for the charging of a fee for the replacement of such plates by reason of damage to them or of their loss or destruction.

(3) Regulations under this Act may—

(a) extend any of the provisions as to registration, and provisions incidental to any such provisions, to any mechanically propelled vehicles in respect of which duty is not chargeable under this Act (including vehicles belonging to the Crown); and

(b) provide for the identification of any such vehicles.

(4) Regulations under subsection (3) above which require a person to furnish information relating to vehicles exempted from duty by virtue of section 7(2) of this Act may require him to furnish in addition such evidence of the facts giving rise to the exemption as is prescribed by the regulations.

Miscellaneous

21. Section 24 shall be omitted.

22. Section 25 shall have effect as if—

(a) in subsection (1), paragraph (a) together with the last reference in that subsection to a motor dealer so far as it relates to that paragraph were omitted;

(b) in subsection (1), paragraph (b) together with the last reference in that subsection to a motor dealer so far as it relates to that paragraph and the reference therein to any other person in question and subsection (2) were omitted.

23. Section 26 shall have effect as if in subsection (1) there were substituted for the reference to section 23(c) of this Act a reference to section 23(2)(c) thereof; and as if in subsection (2) there were omitted therefrom the words "or for the allocation of temporary licences or registration marks".

Supplementary

24. For section 37(3) there shall be substituted the following subsection—

[(3) Any person who contravenes or fails to comply with any regulations under this Act (other than regulations under section 2(5), 11(3), 14, 20 or 24) shall be guilty of an offence and liable on summary conviction—

(a) in the case of regulations prescribed for the purposes of this paragraph, to a fine not exceeding level 3 on the standard scale; and

(b) in any other case, to a fine not exceeding level 2 on the standard scale.

(3A) Regulations under section 14, 20 or 24 above may provide that a person who contravenes or fails to comply with any specified provision of the regulations shall be guilty of an offence and a person guilty of such an offence shall be liable on summary conviction—

    (a) in the case of regulations under section 14 or 20, to a fine not exceeding level 1 on the standard scale; and

    (b) in the case of regulations under section 24, to a fine not exceeding level 3 on the standard scale.

(3B) The prescribing of regulations for the purposes of subsection (3)(a) above shall not affect the punishment for a contravention of or failure to comply with those regulations before they were so prescribed.] **[88]**

NOTES

Commencement: 30 July 1982 (para 17A); 1 April 1971 (remainder).

Paras 1, 3, 5, 12, 13, 17, 18, 20, 24 derived from the Vehicles (Excise) Act 1962, ss 2(2), (4), (5), 3, 9, 10(3), 13(1), 16, 17(3); paras 2, 4, 6, 9–11, 14–16, 19, 21–23 derived from the Vehicle and Driving Licences Act 1969, ss 4(3), (7)–(9), 5–7, 8(4), (5), 11, 12, 19, 20(1)–(4), 21(1)(a), (b), (2), 24 28(2)(b), 29, 32; para 7 derived from the Finance Act 1967, s 12(2)–(4).

Para 5: first and second amendments made by the Finance Act 1986, s 3(7), Sch 2, Part I, para 1; third and final amendments made by the Finance Act 1980, s 4(5), (7).

Para 7: words omitted repealed and words in square brackets substituted by the Finance Act 1987, ss 2(1), (6), (8), 72(7), Sch 1, Part III, para 12, Sch 16, Part I.

Para 10: repealed by virtue of SI 1984 No 1619.

Para 12: sums in italics substituted, in relation to licences taken out after 31 December 1987, by the Finance Act 1987, s 2, further substituted by subsequent sums in square brackets, in relation to licences taken out after 14 March 1989, by the Finance Act 1989, s 6(6), (7); other amendments in square brackets made by the Finance Act 1986, s 3, (6)-(8) Sch 2, Part I, para 4.

Para 13: words omitted repealed by the Finance Act 1986, ss 3(1), (7), (8), 114(6), Sch 2, Part I, para 5, Sch 23, Part II.

Para 17A: added by the Finance Act 1982, s 7(3); words omitted repealed and words in square brackets substituted by the Finance Act 1987, ss 2(1), (6), (8)(b), 72(7), Sch 1, Part III, paras 7, 12, Sch 16, Part I.

Para 20: words omitted repealed by the Finance Act 1986, ss 3(7), 114, Sch 2, Part II, para 6, Sch 23, Part II; first and third amendments in square brackets made by the Finance Act 1987, s 2, Sch 1, Part III, para 16; other words in square brackets substituted by the Finance Act 1989, s 13.

Para 24: amended by the Finance Act 1987, s 2(1), (6), Sch 1, Part III, para 18.

PART II

OTHER TRANSITIONAL PROVISIONS AND SAVINGS

1. In so far as any regulation, order, licence or other instrument made or issued, or having effect as if made or issued, under any enactment repealed by this Act or any other thing done or deemed to have been done under any such enactment, could have been made, issued or done under a corresponding provision of this Act it shall not be invalidated by the repeals effected by section 39(5) of this Act, but shall have effect as if made, issued or done under that corresponding provision.

Provided that this paragraph shall not be construed as saving the order specified in Part II of Schedule 8 to this Act.

2. Without prejudice to paragraph 1 above, any provision of this Act relating to anything done or required or authorised to be done under, or by reference to, that provision, this Act or any other provision of this Act shall have effect as if any reference to that provision, to this Act or to that other provision, as the case may be, included a reference to the corresponding provision of the enactments repealed by this Act or to the Act containing the corresponding provision so repealed.

3. No licence or other instrument issued or made or having effect as if issued or made by a local authority under any enactment repealed by this Act and nothing done or deemed to have been done by or in relation to a local authority under any such enactment shall be prevented from being treated for the purposes of the foregoing paragraphs as a licence or other instrument or other thing which could have been issued, made or done under a corresponding provision of this Act by reason only that it could have been issued, made or done under that corresponding provision by or in relation to the Secretary of State and not by or in relation to a local authority.

In this paragraph "local authority" has the same meaning as it has in the Vehicle and Driving Licences Act 1969.

4. No licence issued under this Act and in force when any of the following modifications of this Act contained in Part I of this Schedule ceases to have effect under section 39(2) of this Act shall be affected by reason of any such modification so ceasing to have effect; nor shall any right to be repaid by way of rebate of duty any such amount as is referred to in section 17(2) accruing on a surrender of a licence before the modification contained in paragraph 13 of the said Part I ceases to have effect under the said section 39(2) be affected by reason of that modification so ceasing to have effect.

The modifications of this Act referred to above are those contained in paragraphs 1, 2, 3, 5, 12 and 17 of the said Part I.

5. Nothing in this Act shall affect the enactments repealed thereby in their operation in relation to offences committed before the commencement of this Act.

6. In relation to a vehicle for which a licence was issued before and is in force after the commencement of this Act, or the last licence was issued between the commencement of the Vehicles (Excise) Act 1949 and the commencement of this Act, section 1(3) of this Act shall have effect as if for the reference in paragraph (a) to the same Schedule to this Act there were substituted a reference to the Schedule to this Act corresponding to the enactment under which duty was chargeable for the licence.

7. In relation to a vehicle exempted from duty under the Vehicles (Excise) Act 1962 by virtue of section 6(2A) or (2B) thereof to which the provisions of section 6(3) of this Act apply, the reference in the said section 6(3) to the vehicle being deemed never to have been exempted from duty under subsection (1) or (2) of that section shall include a reference to the vehicle being deemed never to have been exempted from duty under the said section 6(2A) or (2B).

8. In relation to a vehicle for which a licence was taken out before and is in force at the commencement of this Act, section 18 of this Act shall have effect as if—

    (a) any reference to any rate of duty or amount payable under this Act included a reference to a rate of duty or an amount payable under the Vehicles (Excise) Act 1962;

    (b) for any reference to duty paid in respect of a vehicle at a rate applicable under Schedule 4 to this Act, there were substituted a reference to duty paid at a rate applicable under Schedule 4 to the said Act of 1962.

9. For the purposes of section 22 of this Act a person shall be treated as having been previously convicted of an offence under that section if he has been convicted of an offence under the corresponding enactment in the Vehicles (Excise) Act 1949 or the Vehicles (Excise) Act 1962.

10. Where in pursuance of section 12(7) of the Vehicles (Excise) Act 1962 (which relates to appeals to the Secretary of State from refusals of local authorities to issue trade licences) an appeal is pending at the transfer date, the making of the appeal shall be treated as a request in pursuance of subsection (1) of section 25 of this Act in respect of such a refusal as is mentioned in paragraph (c) of that subsection.

11. Any enactment passed before the commencement of this Act referring, whether specifically or by means of a general description, to an enactment repealed by this Act shall, unless the contrary intention appears, be construed as referring to the corresponding provision of this Act, and any document made or issued (whether before or after the commencement of this Act) referring, whether specifically or by means of a general description, to an enactment repealed by this Act shall, unless the contrary intention appears, be similarly construed.

12. Nothing in this Act shall require any charge or fee to be paid which would not have been payable if this Act had not been passed.

13. Unless the context otherwise requires, references in this Schedule to enactments repealed by this Act include references to the order revoked by this Act. **[89]**

NOTES

    Commencement: 1 April 1971.
    Paras 4, 10 derived from the Vehicle and Driving Licences Act 1969, ss 21(3), 46.

MAGISTRATES' COURTS ACT 1980
(c 43)

An Act to consolidate certain enactments relating to the jurisdiction of, and the practice and procedure before, magistrates' courts and the functions of justices' clerks, and to matters connected therewith, with amendments to give effect to recommendations of the Law Commission   [1 August 1980]

PART I
CRIMINAL JURISDICTION AND PROCEDURE
Summary trial of information

12. Non-appearance of accused: plea of guilty

(1) Subject to subsection (7) below, this section shall apply where a summons has been issued requiring a person to appear before a magistrates' court, other than a [youth court], to answer to an information for a summary offence, not being an offence for which the accused is liable to be sentenced to be imprisoned for a term exceeding 3 months, and the clerk of the court is notified by or on behalf of the prosecutor that the following documents have been served upon the accused with the summons, that is to say—

(a) a notice containing such statement of the effect of this section [and section 18 of the Criminal Justice Act 1991 (unit fines)] as may be prescribed; and;

(b) a concise statement in the prescribed form of such facts relating to the charge as will be placed before the court by or on behalf of the prosecutor if the accused pleads guilty without appearing before the court.

[(1A) The reference in subsection (1) above to the issue of a summons requiring a person to appear before a magistrates' court other than a youth court includes a reference to the issue of a summons requiring a person who has attained the age of 16 at the time when it is issued to appear before a youth court.]

(2) Subject to subsections (3) to (5) below, where the clerk of the court receives a notification in writing purporting to be given by the accused or by a [legal representative] acting on his behalf that the accused desires to plead guilty without appearing before the court, the clerk of the court shall inform the prosecutor of the receipt of the notification and if at the time and place appointed for the trial or adjourned trial of the information the accused does not appear and it is proved to the satisfaction of the court, on oath or in such other manner as may be prescribed, that the notice and statement of facts referred to in subsection (1) above have been served upon the accused with the summons, then—

(a) subject to section 11(3) and (4) above, the court may proceed to hear and dispose of the case in the absence of the accused, whether or not the prosecutor is also absent, in like manner as if both parties had appeared and the accused had pleaded guilty; or

(b) if the court decides not to proceed as aforesaid, the court shall adjourn or further adjourn the trial for the purpose of dealing with the information as if the notification aforesaid had not been given.

(3) If at any time before the hearing the clerk of the court receives an intimation in writing purporting to be given by or on behalf of the accused that he wishes to withdraw the notification aforesaid, the clerk of the court shall inform the prosecutor thereof and the court shall deal with the information as if this section had not been passed.

(4) Before accepting the plea of guilty and convicting the accused in his absence under sub-section (2) above, the court shall cause the notification and statement of facts aforesaid, including any submission received with the notification which the accused wishes to be brought to the attention of the court with a view to mitigation of sentence, to be read out before the court [by the clerk of the court].

(5) If the court proceeds under subsection (2) above to hear and dispose of the case in the absence of the accused, the court shall not permit any statement to be made by or on behalf of the prosecutor with respect to any facts relating to the offence charged other than the statement of facts aforesaid except on a resumption of the trial after an adjournment under section 10(3) above.

(6) In relation to an adjournment by reason of the requirements of paragraph (b) of subsection (2) above or to an adjournment on the occasion of the accused's conviction in his absence under that subsection, the notice required by section 10(2) above shall include notice of the reason for the adjournment.

(7) The Secretary of State may by order made by statutory instrument provide that this section shall not apply in relation to such offences (in addition to an offence for which the accused is liable to be sentenced to be imprisoned for a term exceeding 3 months) as may be specified in the order, and any order under this subsection—

    (a) may vary or revoke any previous order thereunder; and
    (b) shall not be made unless a draft thereof has been approved by
        resolution of each House of Parliament.

(8) Any such notice or statement as is mentioned in subsection (1) above may be served in Scotland with a summons which is so served under the Summary Jurisdiction (Process) Act 1881.

[(9) Where the clerk of the court has received such a notification as is mentioned in subsection (2) above but the accused nevertheless appears before the court at the time and place appointed for the trial or adjourned trial the court may, if the accused consents, proceed under this section as if he were absent.]   [89A]

NOTES
    Commencement: 6 July 1981 (except sub-s (9)); 1 April 1986 (sub-s (9)).
    Commencement order: SI 1981 No 457; SI 1985 No 1849.
    Sub-s (1): words in square brackets substituted or inserted by the Criminal Justice Act 1991, ss 70, 100, Sch 11, paras 24, 40(1); (2)(n).
    Sub-s (1A): inserted by the Criminal Justice Act 1991, s 69.
    Sub-s (2): words in square brackets substituted by the Courts and Legal Services Act 1990, s 125(3), Sch 18, para 25(1), (4)(a).
    Sub-s (4): words in square brackets added by the Prosecution of Offences Act 1985, s 31(5), Sch 1, Pt I, para 1.
    Sub-s (9): added by the Prosecution of Offences Act 1985, s 31(5), Sch 1, Pt I, para 1.

PUBLIC PASSENGER VEHICLES ACT 1981
(c 14)

ARRANGEMENT OF SECTIONS

PART II

GENERAL PROVISIONS RELATING TO PUBLIC SERVICE VEHICLES

Fitness of public service vehicles

An Act to consolidate certain enactments relating to public passenger vehicles
[15 April 1981]

PART II

GENERAL PROVISIONS RELATING TO PUBLIC SERVICE VEHICLES
Fitness of public service vehicles

6. Certificate of initial fitness (or equivalent) required for use as public service vehicles

(1) A public service vehicle adapted to carry more than eight passengers shall not be used on a road unless—

    (a) [an examiner appointed under section 66A of the Road Traffic Act 1988] [or an authorised inspector] has issued a certificate (in this Act referred to as a "certificate of initial fitness") that the prescribed conditions as to fitness are fulfilled in respect of the vehicle; or

    (b) a certificate under section 10 of this Act has been issued in respect of the vehicle; or

(c) there has been issued in respect of the vehicle a certificate under section 47 of the Road Traffic Act 1972 [or sections 55 to 58 of the Road Traffic Act 1988] (type approval) of a kind which by virtue of regulations is to be treated as the equivalent of a certificate of initial fitness.

[(1A) ..., regulations may make provision with respect to the examination of vehicles for the purposes of subsection (1)(a) above by or under the direction of authorised inspectors and the issue or refusal of certificates of initial fitness by such inspectors on any such examinations.]

(2) Subject to section 68(3) of this Act, if a vehicle is used in contravention of subsection (1) above, the operator of the vehicle shall be liable on summary conviction to a fine not exceeding [level 4 on the standard scale].   **[90–91]**

NOTES
Commencement: 30 October 1981.
Commencement order: SI 1981 No 1387.
This section derived from the Transport Act 1980, s 17(1), (3).
Sub-s (1): words in first pair of square brackets substituted by the Road Traffic Act 1991, s 48, Sch 4, para 14; words in second pair of square brackets prospectively inserted by the Transport Act 1982, s 10(3)(b), as from a day to be appointed, as amended by the Road Traffic Act 1991, s 48, Sch 4, para 19(1), (2); words in third pair of square brackets added by the Road Traffic (Consequential Provisions) Act 1988, s 4, Sch 3, para 22.
Sub-s (1): "prescribed conditions as to fitness", see the Public Service Vehicles (Conditions of Fitness, Use and Certification) Regulations 1981, SI 1981 No 257.
Sub-s (1A): prospectively added by the Transport Act 1982, s 10(8), as from a day to be appointed; words omitted repealed by the Road Traffic Act 1991, s 83, Sch 8.
Sub-s (2): maximum fine converted to the standard scale by the Criminal Justice Act 1982, ss 37, 46, as amended.
Modified by the Transport Act 1985, s 23.

7. (*Repealed by the Road Traffic Act 1991, ss 9(1), 83, Sch 8.*)

8. Powers of, and facilities for, inspection of public service vehicles

(1), (1A), (2) ...

(3) The Secretary of State may—
  (a) provide and maintain stations where inspections of public service vehicles ... may be carried out;
  (b) designate premises as stations where such inspections may be carried out; and
  (c) provide and maintain apparatus for the carrying out of such inspections;

and in this Act "official PSV testing station" means a station provided, or any premises for the time being designated, under this subsection.   **[92–93]**

NOTES
Commencement: 1 August 1986 (sub-s (1A)); 30 October 1981 (remainder).
Commencement orders: SI 1981 No 1387, SI 1986 No 1088.
This section derived from the Transport Act 1980, s 16.
Sub-s (1): repealed by the Road Traffic Act 1991, ss 11, 83, Sch 8.
Sub-s (1A): added by the Transport Act 1985, s 139(2), Sch 7, and repeled by the Road Traffic Act 1991, ss 11, 83, Sch 8.
Sub-s (2): repealed by the Road Traffic Act 1991, ss 11, 83, Sch 8.
Sub-s (3): words omitted repealed by the Road Traffic Act 1991, ss 11, 83, Sch 8.
Sub-s (1A): modified for a transitional period by the Transport Act 1985 (Commencement No 4) Order 1986, SI 1986 No 1088, art 3.

9. (*Repealed by the Road Traffic Act 1991, ss 12, 83, Sch 8.*)

9A. Extension of sections 8 and 9 to certain passenger vehicles other than public service vehicles

[(1) Section 8 of this Act shall apply, ... , to any motor vehicle (other than a tramcar) which is adapted to carry more than eight passengers but is not a public service vehicle as it applies to a public service vehicle.

(2) ...　　　　　　　　　　　　　　　　　　　　　　　　　　　　　　　　**[94]**

NOTES
　Commencement: 1 August 1986.
　Commencement order: SI 1986 No 1088.
　Added by the Transport Act 1985, s 33.
　Sub-s (1): words omitted repealed by the Road Traffic Act 1991, s 83, Sch 8.
　Sub-s (2): repealed by the Road Traffic Act 1991, s 83, Sch 8.

Public service vehicle operators' licences

12. PSV operators' licences

[(1) A public service vehicle shall not be used on a road for carrying passengers for hire or reward except under a PSV operators' licence granted in accordance with the following provisions of this Part of this Act.]

(2) The authority having power to grant a PSV operator's licence is the traffic [commissioner] for any traffic area in which, if the licence is granted, there will be one or more operating centres of vehicles used under the licence; and, subject to the provisions of this Part of this Act, a PSV operator's licence authorises the holder to use anywhere in Great Britain vehicles which have their operating centre in the area of the traffic [commissioner] by whom the licence was granted.

(3) A person may hold two or more PSV operators' licences each granted by the traffic [commissioner] for [a different area], but shall not at the same time hold more than one such licence granted by the [commissioner] for the same area.

(4) An application for a PSV operator's licence shall be made in such form as the traffic [commissioner] may require, and an applicant shall give the [commissioner] such information as [he] may reasonably require for disposing of the application.

(5) Subject to section 68(3) of this Act, if a vehicle is used in contravention of subsection (1) above, the operator of the vehicle shall be liable on summary conviction to a fine not exceeding [level 4 on the standard scale].　　　　**[95]**

NOTES
　Commencement: 30 October 1981.
　Commencement order: SI 1981 No 1387.
　This section derived from the Transport Act 1980, s 19.
　Sub-s (1): substituted by the Transport Act 1985, s 1(3), Sch 1, para 4.
　Sub-ss (2)-(4): amended by the Transport Act 1985, s 3(5), Sch 2, Part II, para 4(4).
　Sub-s (5): maximum fine converted to the standard scale by the Criminal Justice Act 1982, ss 37, 46, as amended.
　Modified by the Transport Act 1985, s 12 and prospectively by the Transport Act 1985, s 18, as from a day to be appointed.
　Sub-s (3): modified by SI 1986 No 1628, reg 5(1), Sch Pt I.

13. Classification of licences

(1) A PSV operator's licence may be either a standard licence or a restricted licence.

(2) A standard licence authorises the use of any description of public service vehicle and may authorise use either—

(a) on both national and international operations; or

(b) on national operations only.

(3) A restricted licence authorises the use (whether on national or international operations) of—

(a) public service vehicles not adapted to carry more than eight passengers; and

(b) public service vehicles not adapted to carry more than sixteen passengers when used—

(i) otherwise than in the course of a business of carrying passengers; or

(ii) by a person whose main occupation is not the operation of public service vehicles adapted to carry more than eight passengers.

(4) For the purposes of subsection (3)(b)(i) above, a vehicle used for carrying passengers by a local or public authority shall not be regarded as used in the course of a business of carrying passengers unless it is used by the public service vehicle undertaking of that authority.   **[96]**

NOTES
Commencement: 30 October 1981.
Commencement order: SI 1981 No 1387.
This section derived from the Transport Act 1980, s 20.

18. Duty to exhibit operator's disc

(1) Where a vehicle is being used in circumstances such that a PSV operator's licence is required, there shall be fixed and exhibited on the vehicle in the prescribed manner an operator's disc issued under this section showing particulars of the operator of the vehicle and of the PSV operator's licence under which the vehicle is being used.

(2) [A traffic commissioner] on granting a PSV operator's licence shall supply the person to whom the licence is granted with a number of operators' discs equal to the maximum number of vehicles which he may use under the licence in accordance with the condition or conditions attached to the licence under section 16(1) [or (1A)] of this Act; and if [(in the case of any condition or conditions attached under section 16(1))] that maximum number is later increased on the variation of one or more of those conditions, the traffic [commissioner] on making the variation shall supply him with further operators' discs accordingly.

(3) Regulations may make provision—

(a) as to the form of operators' discs and the particulars to be shown on them;

(b) with respect to the custody and production of operators' discs;

(c) for the issue of new operators' discs in place of those lost, destroyed or defaced;

(d) for the return of operators' discs on the revocation or expiration of a PSV operator's licence or in the event of a variation of one or more conditions attached to a licence under section 16(1) of this Act having the effect of reducing the maximum number of vehicles which may be used under the licence.

(4) Subject to section 68(3) of this Act, if a vehicle is used in contravention of subsection (1) above, the operator of the vehicle shall be liable on summary conviction to a fine not exceeding [level 3 on the standard scale].   [97]

NOTES
    Commencement: 30 October 1981.
    Commencement order: SI 1981 No 1387.
    This section derived from the Transport Act 1980, s 24.
    Sub-s (1): "prescribed", see the Public Service Vehicles (Operator's Licences) Regulations 1981, post.
    Sub-s (2): first and final words in square brackets substituted by the Transport Act 1985, s 3(5), Sch 2, Part II, para 4(9); other words in square brackets added by the Transport Act 1985, s 24(2).
    Sub-s (4): maximum fine converted to the standard scale by the Criminal Justice Act 1982, ss 37, 46, as amended.
    Modified by the Transport Act 1985, s 12.
    Sub-s (1): modified by SI 1986 No 1628, reg 5(1), Sch Pt I.

19. Duty to inform traffic commissioners of relevant convictions etc

(1) A person who has applied for a PSV operator's licence shall forthwith notify the traffic [commissioner] to whom the application was made if, in the interval between the making of the application and the date on which it is disposed of, a relevant conviction occurs of the applicant, or any employee or agent of his, or of any person proposed to be engaged as transport manager whose repute and competence are relied on in connection with the application.

(2) It shall be the duty of the holder of a PSV operator's licence to give notice in writing to the traffic [commissioner] by whom the licence was granted of—

(a) any relevant conviction of the holder; and
(b) any relevant conviction of any officer, employee or agent of the holder for an offence committed in the course of the holder's road passenger transport business,

and to do so within 28 days of the conviction in the case of a conviction of the holder or his transport manager and within 28 days of the conviction coming to the holder's knowledge in any other case.

(3) It shall be the duty of the holder of a PSV operator's licence within 28 days of the occurrence of—

(a) the bankruptcy or liquidation of the holder, or the sequestration of his estate [or the making of an administration order under [Part II of the Insolvency Act 1986] in relation to the holder] or the appointment of a receiver, manager or trustee of his road passenger transport business; or
(b) any change in the identity of the transport manager of the holder's road passenger transport business,

to give notice in writing of that event to the traffic [commissioner] by whom the licence was granted.

(4) [A traffic commissioner] on granting or varying a PSV operator's licence, or at any time thereafter, may require the holder of the licence to inform [him] forthwith or within a time specified by [him] of any material change specified by [him] in any of [the holder's] circumstances which were relevant to the grant or variation of the licence.

(5) Subject to section 68(1) of this Act, a person who fails to comply with subsection (1), (2) or (3) above or with any requirement under subsection (4) above shall be liable on summary conviction to a fine not exceeding [level 3 on the standard scale]. **[98]**

NOTES
 Commencement: 30 October 1981.
 Commencement order: SI 1981 No 1387.
 This section derived from the Transport Act 1980, s 25.
 Sub-ss (1)-(4): amended by the Transport Act 1985, s 3(5), Sch 2, Part II, para 4(10).
 Sub-s (3): first words in square brackets added with savings by the Insolvency Act 1985, s 235(1), Sch 8, para 34, and the Insolvency Act 1986, s 437, Sch 11; second words in square brackets therein substituted by the Insolvency Act 1986, s 439(2), Sch 11.
 Sub-s (5): maximum fine converted to the standard scale by the Criminal Justice Act 1982, ss 37, 46, as amended.
 Modified by the Transport Act 1985, s 12.
 Sub-ss (1)-(3): modified by SI 1986 No 1628, reg 5(1), Sch Pt I.

20. Duty to give traffic commissioners information about vehicles

(1) It shall be the duty of the holder of a PSV operator's licence, on the happening to any public service vehicle owned by him of any failure or damage of a nature calculated to affect the safety of occupants of the public service vehicle or of persons using the road, to report the matter as soon as is practicable *to the* [*Secretary of State*] [in accordance with regulations made by virtue of subsection (2A) below].

(2) It shall be the duty of the holder of a PSV operator's licence, on any alteration otherwise than by replacement of parts being made in the structure or fixed equipment of any public service vehicle owned by him, to give notice of the alteration as soon as is practicable *to the* [*Secretary of State*] [in accordance with regulations made by virtue of subsection (2A) below].

[(2A) Regulations may make provision—

  (a) for any report or notice required under subsection (1) or (2) above to be made or given to the Secretary of State or to the prescribed testing authority;
  (b) for requiring a public service vehicle to be submitted for examination in the event of any such failure or damage as is mentioned in subsection (1) above or any such alteration as is mentioned in subsection (2) above; and
  (c) for the examinations to be carried out under the regulations and, in particular, for authorising any such examination to be carried out by or under the direction of [an examiner appointed under section 66A of the Road Traffic Act 1988] or an authorised inspector.]

(3) The traffic [commissioner] by whom a PSV operator's licence was granted may—

  (a) require the holder of the licence to supply [him] forthwith or within a specified time with such information as [he] may reasonably require about the public service vehicles owned by [the holder] and normally kept at an operating centre within the area of [that commissioner], and to keep up to date information supplied by [the holder] under this paragraph; or
  (b) require the holder or former holder of the licence to supply [him] forthwith or within a specified time with such information as [he] may reasonably require about the public service vehicles owned by [the holder or former holder] at any material time specified by [him] which

were at that time normally kept at an operating centre within the area of [that commissioner].

In this subsection "material time" means a time when the PSV operator's licence in question was in force.

(4) Subject to section 68(1) of this Act, a person who fails to comply with the provisions of subsection (1) or (2) above or with any requirement under subsection (3) above shall be liable on summary conviction to a fine not exceeding [level 3 on the standard scale].

(5) A person who in purporting to comply with any requirement under subsection (3) above supplies any information which he knows to be false or does not believe to be true shall be liable on summary conviction to a fine not exceeding [level 4 on the standard scale].

(6) . . .   **[99–103]**

NOTES
   Commencement: 30 October 1981.
   Commencement order: SI 1981 No 1387.
   This section derived from the Transport Act 1980, s 26.
   Sub-ss (1), (2): words in first pair of square brackets substituted by the Transport Act 1985, s 29; for the words in italics there are prospectively substituted the words in the second pair of square brackets by the Transport Act 1982, s 10(9), as from a day to be appointed.
   Sub-s (2A): prospectively added by the Transport Act 1982, s 10(9), as from a day to be appointed: words in square brackets therein substituted by the Road Traffic Act 1991, s 48, Sch 4, para 19(4).
   Sub-s (3): amended by the Transport Act 1985, s 3, Sch 2, Part II.
   Sub-ss (4), (5): maximum fines converted to the standard scale by the Criminal Justice Act 1982, ss 37, 46, as amended.
   Sub-s (6): repealed by the Road Traffic Act 1991, s 83, Sch 8.
   Modified by the Transport Act 1985, s 12.

Drivers' licences

22, 23, 23A. (*Repealed by the Road Traffic (Driver Licensing and Information Systems) Act 1989, ss 1(1), 16, Sch 6.*)

Regulation of conduct etc. of drivers, inspectors, conductors and passengers

24. Regulation of conduct of drivers, inspectors and conductors

(1) Regulations may make provision for regulating the conduct, when acting as such, of—

   (a) . . . drivers of public service vehicles,
   (b) inspectors and conductors of such vehicles, [and
   (c) drivers, inspectors and conductors of tramcars.]

(2) Subject to section 68(1) of this Act, if a person to whom regulations having effect by virtue of this section apply contravenes, or fails to comply with, any of the provisions of the regulations, he shall be liable on summary conviction to a fine not exceeding [level 2 on the standard scale] and, in the case of an offence by a person acting as driver [of a public service vehicle], the court by which he is convicted may, if it thinks fit, cause particulars of the conviction to be endorsed upon [the counterpart of] the licence granted to that person under [Part III of the Road Traffic Act 1988].

(3) The person who has the custody of the licence [and its counterpart] shall, if so required by the convicting court, produce [them] within a reasonable time for the purpose of endorsement, and, subject to section 68(1) of this Act, if he

fails to do so, shall be liable on summary conviction to a fine not exceeding [level 3 on the standard scale].

(4) In this section and in section 25 of this Act "inspector", in relation to a public service vehicle, means a person authorised to act as an inspector by the holder of the PSV operator's licence under which the vehicle is being used.

[(5) Notwithstanding section 1(1) of this Act, in this section and in sections 25 and 26 of this Act "public service vehicle" shall be construed as meaning a public service vehicle being used on a road for carrying passengers for hire or reward.]   **[104]**

NOTES

Commencement: 30 October 1981 (sub-ss (1)(a), (b), (2)–(4)); 1 April 1991 (sub-s (5)); to be appointed (remainder).

Commencement order: SI 1981 No 1387.

Sub-ss (1)–(3) derived from the Road Traffic Act 1960, s 146; sub-s (4) derived from the Transport Act 1980, Sch 5, Part I, para 6(2).

Sub-s (1): words omitted repealed by the Road Traffic (Driver Licensing and Information Systems) Act 1989, ss 7, 16, Sch 3, para 2(a), Sch 6; sub-s (1)(c) and the word "and" immediately preceding it, prospectively added by the Transport and Works Act 1992, s 61(1), (2), as from a day to be appointed.

"Regulations", see the Public Service Vehicles (Conduct of Drivers, Inspectors, Conductors and Passengers) Regulations 1990, SI 1990 No 1020.

Sub-s (2): maximum fine converted to the standard scale by the Criminal Justice Act 1982, ss 37, 46, as amended; words in the second pair of square brackets prospectively inserted by the Transport and Works Act 1992, s 61(1), (2)(b), as from a day to be appointed; words in third and fourth pairs of square brackets substituted or added with savings by the Road Traffic (Driver Licensing and Information Systems) Act 1989, s 7, Sch 3, para 2.

Sub-s (3): first words in square brackets added with savings, words in square brackets substituted with savings by the Road Traffic (Driver Licensing and Information Systems) Act 1989, s 7, Sch 3, para 2 (as amended with savings by SI 1990 No 144, reg 2(3), Sch 3, para 3(2), for savings see reg 3 thereof); maximum fine converted to the standard scale by the Criminal Justice Act 1982, ss 37, 46, as amended.

Sub-s (5): added by the Road Traffic (Driver Licensing and Information Systems) Act 1989, s 7, Sch 3, para 2(c).

25. Regulation of conduct of passengers

(1) Regulations may make provision generally as to the conduct of passengers on public service vehicles [or tramcars] and in particular (but without prejudice to the generality of the foregoing provision) for—

> (a) authorising the removal from a public service vehicle [or tramcar] of a person infringing the regulations by the driver, inspector or conductor of the vehicle or on the request of the driver, inspector or conductor by a police constable;
>
> (b) requiring a passenger in a public service vehicle [or tramcar] who is reasonably suspected by the driver, inspector or conductor thereof of contravening the regulations to give his name and address to the driver, inspector or conductor on demand;
>
> (c) requiring a passenger to declare, if so requested by the driver, inspector or conductor, the journey he intends to take or has taken in the vehicle, and to pay the fare for the whole of that journey and to accept any ticket provided therefor;
>
> (d) requiring, on demand being made for the purpose by the driver, inspector or conductor, production during the journey and surrender at the end of the journey by the holder thereof of any ticket issued to him;
>
> (e) requiring a passenger, if so requested by the driver, inspector or conductor, to leave the vehicle on the completion of the journey the fare for which he has paid;

(f) requiring the surrender by the holder thereof on the expiry of the period for which it is issued of a ticket issued to him.

(2) ...

(3) Subject to section 68(1) of this Act, if a person contravenes, or fails to comply with, a provision of regulations having effect by virtue of this section, he shall be liable on summary conviction to a fine not exceeding [level 3 on the standard scale].

(4) In the application of this section to Scotland, subsection (1)(b) shall have effect as if after the word "address" there were inserted the words "to a police constable or". **[105]**

NOTES

Commencement: 30 October 1981.

Commencement order: SI 1981 No 1387.

Sub-s (1): words in square brackets prospectively inserted by the Transport and Works Act 1992, s 61(1), (3), as from a day to be appointed; "Regulations", see the Public Service Vehicles (Conduct of Drivers, Inspectors, Conductors and Passengers) Regulations 1990, post.

Sub-s (2): repealed with savings by the Police and Criminal Evidence Act 1984, s 119, Sch 7, Part I, SI 1985 No 1934, arts 2, 3(a), Schedule.

Sub-ss (1), (3) derived from the Road Traffic Act 1960, s 147; sub-s (2) derived from the Public Service Vehicles (Arrest of Offenders) Act 1975, s 1.

Sub-s (3): maximum fine converted to the standard scale by the Criminal Justice Act 1982, ss 37, 46, as amended.

26. Control of number of passengers

(1) Regulations may make provision with respect to public service vehicles for—

    (a) the determination by or under the regulations of the number of the seated passengers and standing passengers respectively for whom a vehicle is constructed or adapted and fit to carry;

    (b) the determination by or under the regulations of the number of such passengers respectively who may be carried in a vehicle;

    (c) the marks to be carried on a vehicle showing those numbers and the manner in which those marks are to be carried.

(2) Subject to section 68(1) and (3) of this Act, if a person contravenes, or fails to comply with, a provision of regulations having effect by virtue of this section, he shall be liable on summary conviction to a fine not exceeding [level 2 on the standard scale]. **[106]**

NOTES

Commencement: 30 October 1981.

Commencement order: SI 1981 No 1387.

This section derived from the Road Traffic Act 1960, s 148.

Sub-s (2): existing maximum fine retained and converted to the standard scale by the Criminal Justice Act 1982, ss 37, 39(1), 46, Sch 2, as amended.

Modified by the Transport Act 1985, s 12.

Supplementary provisions

27. Returns to be provided by persons operating public service vehicles

(1) It shall be the duty of a person carrying on the business of operating public service vehicles [or tramcars] to keep such accounts and records in relation thereto and to make to the Secretary of State such financial and statistical returns, and in such manner and at such times, as the Secretary of State may from time to time require.

(2) Subject to section 68(3) of this Act, if a person fails to comply with the requirements of subsection (1) above, he shall be liable on summary conviction to a fine not exceeding [level 3 on the standard scale].

(3) This section shall not apply to the British Railways Board or [London Regional Transport or to any subsidiary of London Regional Transport (within the meaning of the London Regional Transport Act 1984)]. **[107]**

NOTES

Commencement: 30 October 1981.
Commencement order: SI 1981 No 1387.
This section derived from the Road Traffic Act 1960, s 157.
Sub-s (1): words in square brackets prospectively inserted by the Transport and Works Act 1992, s 61(1), (4), as from a day to be appointed.
Sub-s (2): maximum fine converted to the standard scale by the Criminal Justice Act 1982, ss 37, 46, as amended.
Sub-s (3): amended by the London Regional Transport Act 1984, s 71(3)(a), Sch 6, para 22.

ROAD TRAFFIC REGULATION ACT 1984

(c 27)

ARRANGEMENT OF SECTIONS

PART I

GENERAL PROVISIONS FOR TRAFFIC REGULATION

Outside Greater London

PART II

TRAFFIC REGULATION IN SPECIAL CASES

PART III

CROSSINGS AND PLAYGROUNDS

Pedestrian Crossings

School Crossings

An Act to consolidate the Road Traffic Regulation Act 1967 and certain related enactments, with amendments to give effect to recommendations of the Law Commission and the Scottish Law Commission. [26 June 1984]

PART I

GENERAL PROVISIONS FOR TRAFFIC REGULATION

Outside Greater London

1. Traffic regulation orders outside Greater London

(1) [The traffic authority for a road outside Greater London may move an order under this section (referred to in this Act as a "traffic regulation order") in respect of the road] where it appears to the authority making the order that it is expedient to make it—

(a) for avoiding danger to persons or other traffic using the road or any other road or for preventing the likelihood of any such danger arising, or

(b) for preventing damage to the road or to any building on or near the road, or

(c) for facilitating the passage on the road or any other road of any class of traffic (including pedestrians), or

(d) for preventing the use of the road by vehicular traffic of a kind which, or its use by vehicular traffic in a manner which, is unsuitable having regard to the existing character of the road or adjoining property, or

(e) (without prejudice to the generality of paragraph (d) above) for preserving the character of the road in a case where it is specially suitable for use by persons on horseback or on foot, or

(f) for preserving or improving the amenities of the area through which the road runs.

(2) ...

[(3) A traffic regulation order made by a local traffic authority may, with the consent of the Secretary of State, extend to a road in relation to which he is the traffic authority if the order forms part of a scheme of general traffic control relating to roads of which at least one has a junction with the length of road in question.]

(4), (5) ...   **[108]**

NOTES

Commencement: 26 September 1984 (except sub-s (3)); 1 November 1991 (sub-s (3)).

Sub-s (1) derived from the Road Traffic Regulation Act 1967, s 1(1), and the Transport Act 1968, s 126(1), Sch 14, Part VI, paras 1, 2; sub-ss (2), (3) derived from the Road Traffic Regulation Act 1967, s 1(2), (2A), (2B) and the Local Government, Planning and Land Act 1980 Sch 7, para 9(1); sub-ss (4), (5) derived from the Road Traffic Regulation Act 1967, s 1(7).

Sub-s (1): amended by the New Roads and Street Works Act 1991, s 168(1), Sch 8, Part II, para 17, Sch 9.

Sub-s (2): repealed by the New Roads and Street Works Act 1991, s 168(1), Sch 8, Part II, para 17, Sch 9.

Sub-s (3): substituted by the New Roads and Street Works Act 1991, s 168(1), Sch 8, Part II, para 17.

Sub-ss (4), (5): repealed by the New Roads and Street Works Act 1991, s 168(1), Sch 8, Part II, para 17, Sch 9.

See further: SI 1986 No 179, SI 1986 No 180.

Extended with modifications to the Isles of Scilly by SI 1990 No 714.

2. What a traffic regulation order may provide

(1) [A traffic regulation order may move] any provision prohibiting, restricting or regulating the use of a road, or of any part of the width of a road, by vehicular traffic, or by vehicular traffic of any class specified in the order,—

(a) either generally or subject to such exceptions as may be specified in the order or determined in a manner provided for by it, and

(b) subject to such exceptions as may be so specified or determined, either at all times or at times, on days or during periods so specified.

(2) [The provision that may be made by a regulation order] includes any provision—

(a) requiring vehicular traffic, or vehicular traffic of any class specified in the order, to proceed in a specified direction or prohibiting its so proceeding;

(b) specifying the part of the carriageway to be used by such traffic proceeding in a specified direction;

(c) prohibiting or restricting the waiting of vehicles or the loading and unloading of vehicles;

(d) prohibiting the use of roads by through traffic; or

(e) prohibiting or restricting overtaking.

(3) The provision that may be made by a traffic regulation order also includes provision prohibiting, restricting or regulating the use of a road, or of any part of the width of a road, by, or by any specified class of, pedestrians—

(a) either generally or subject to exceptions specified in the order, and

(b) either at all times or at times, on days or during periods so specified.

(4) [A local traffic authority may include] in a traffic regulation order any such provision—

(a) specifying through routes for heavy commercial vehicles, or

(b) prohibiting or restricting the use of heavy commercial vehicles (except in such cases, if any, as may be specified in the order) in such zones or on such roads as may be so specified,

as they consider expedient for preserving or improving the amenities of their area or of some part or parts of their area.

(5) Nothing in subsection (4) above shall be construed as limiting the scope of any power or duty to control vehicles conferred or imposed on any local authority or the Secretary of State otherwise than by virtue of that subsection.

[109]

NOTES

Commencement: 26 September 1984.

Sub-s (1) derived from the Road Traffic Regulation Act 1967, s 1(3), the Transport Act 1968, Sch 14, Part VI, para 3, and the Road Traffic Act 1974, Sch 6, para 4; sub-s (2) derived from the Road Traffic Regulation Act 1967, s 1(3), and the Transport Act 1968, Sch 14, Part VI, para 3; sub-s (3) derived from the Road Traffic Act 1967, s 1(3A), and the Transport Act 1968, s 126(2); sub-ss (4), (5) derived from the Road Traffic Regulation Act 1967, s 1(3AA), (3AB) and the Heavy Commercial Vehicles (Controls and Regulations) Act 1973, s 1.

Sub-ss (1)–(3): amended by the New Roads and Street Works Act 1991, s 168(1), Sch 8, Part II, para 18.

See further: SI 1986 No 179, SI 1986 No 180.

Extended with modifications to the Isles of Scilly by SI 1990 No 714.

3. Restrictions on traffic regulation orders

(1) . . . , a traffic regulation order shall not be made with respect to any road which would have the effect—

(a) of preventing at any time access for pedestrians, or

(b) of preventing for more than 8 hours in any period of 24 hours access for vehicles of any class,

to any premises situated on or adjacent to the road, or to any other premises accessible for pedestrians, or (as the case may be) for vehicles of that class, from, and only from, the road.

(2) Subsection (1) above, so far as it relates to vehicles, shall not have effect in so far as the authority making the order are satisfied, and it is stated in the order that they are satisfied, that—

(a) for avoiding danger to persons or other traffic using the road to which the order relates or any other road, or

(b) for preventing the likelihood of any such danger arising, or

(c) for preventing damage to the road or buildings on or near it, or

(d) for facilitating the passage of vehicular traffic on the road, or

(e) for preserving or improving the amentities of an area by prohibiting or restricting the use on a road or roads in that area of heavy commercial vehicles,

it is requisite that subsection (1) above should not apply to the order.

(3) Provision for regulating the speed of vehicles on roads shall not be made by a traffic regulation order.

(4) Subject to section 39(3) of the Public Passenger Vehicles Act 1981 (which excepts trial areas from the operation of this subsection), no prohibition or restriction on waiting imposed by a traffic regulation order shall apply to a stage carriage. **[110]**

NOTES

Commencement: 26 September 1984.

Sub-ss (1), (2) derived from the Road Traffic Regulation Act 1967, s 1(5), (6), the Transport Act 1968, s 126(4), and the Heavy Commercial Vehicles (Controls and Regulations) Act 1973, s 1(2); sub-s (3) derived from the Road Traffic Regulation Act 1967, s 1(4); sub-s (4) derived from the Road Traffic Regulation Act 1967, s 1(3) and the Public Passenger Vehicles Act 1981, s 39(3).

Sub-s (1): words omitted repealed by the New Roads and Street Works Act 1991, s 168(1), Sch 8, Part II, para 19.

Sub-s (4): repealed with savings by the Transport Act 1985, s 139(3), Sch 8, SI 1986 No 1794, art 3.

See further: SI 1986 No 179, SI 1986 No 180.

Extended with modifications to the Isles of Scilly by SI 1990 No 714.

4. Provisions supplementary to ss 2 and 3

(1) A traffic regulation order may make provision for identifying any part of any road to which, or any time at which or period during which, any provision contained in the order is for the time being to apply by means of a traffic sign of a type or character specified in the order (being a type prescribed or character authorised under section 64 of this Act) and for the time being lawfully in place; and for the purposes of any such order so made any such traffic sign placed on and near a road shall be deemed to be lawfully in place unless the contrary is proved.

(2) A traffic regulation order which imposes any restriction on the use by vehicles of a road, or the waiting of vehicles in a road, may include provision with respect to the issue and display of certificates or other means of identification of vehicles which are excepted from the restriction, whether generally or in particular circumstances or at particular times.

(3) A traffic regulation order may also include provision with respect to the issue, display and operation of devices (to be approved either generally or specially by the Secretary of State) for indicating the time at which a vehicle arrived at, and the time at which it ought to leave, any place in a road in which waiting is restricted by the order, or one or other of those times, and for treating the indications given by any such device as evidence of such facts and for such purposes as may be prescribed by the order.   **[111]**

NOTES

Commencement: 26 September 1984.

This section derived from the Road Traffic Regulation Act 1967, s 1(3B)-(3D) and the Transport Act 1968, Sch 14, Part I.

Extended with modifications to the Isles of Scilly by SI 1990 No 714.

5. Contravention of traffic regulation order

(1) A person who contravenes a traffic regulation order, or who uses a vehicle, or causes or permits a vehicle to be used in contravention of a traffic regulation order, shall be guilty of an offence.

(2) ... **[112]**

NOTES
Commencement: 26 September 1984.
Sub-s (1) derived from the Road Traffic Regulation Act 1967, s 1(8), and the Transport Act 1968, s 126(2); sub-s (2) derived from the Road Traffic Regulation Act 1967, s 1(7).
Sub-s (2): repealed by the New Roads and Street Works Act 1991, s 168(1), (2), Sch 8, Part II, para 20, Sch 9.
Extended with modifications to the Isles of Scilly by SI 1990 No 714.

PART II
TRAFFIC REGULATION IN SPECIAL CASES

17. Traffic regulation on special roads

[(1) A special road shall not be used except by traffic of a class authorised to do so—

    (a) in England and Wales, by a scheme made, or having effect as if made, under section 16 of the Highways Act 1980 or by virtue of paragraph 3 of Schedule 23 to that Act, or

    (b) *(applies to Scotland only.)*

(2) The Secretary of State may make regulations with respect to the use of special roads, [such regulations may, in particular—

    (a) regulate the manner in which and the conditions subject to which special roads may be used by traffic authorised to do so;]

    (b) authorise, or enable such authority as may be specified in the regulations to authorise, the use of special roads on occasion or in an emergency or for the purpose of crossing, or for the purpose of securing access to premises abutting on or adjacent to the roads, by traffic other than that described in paragraph (a) above; ...

    (c) relax, or enable any authority so specified to relax, any prohibition or restriction imposed by the regulations.

    [(d) include provisions having effect in such places, at such times, in such manner or in such circumstances as may for the time being be indicated by traffic signs in accordance with the regulations.]

(3) Regulations made under subsection (2) above may make provision with respect to special roads generally, or may make different provision with respect to special roads provided for the use of different classes of traffic, or may make provision with respect to any particular special road.

(4) If a person uses a special road in contravention of this section or of regulations under subsection (2) above, he shall be guilty of an offence.

[(5) The provisions of this section and of any regulations under subsection (2) above do not apply in relation to a road, or part of a road, until the date declared by the traffic authority, by notice published in the prescribed manner, to be the date on which the road or part is open for use as a special road.
This does not prevent the making of regulations under subsection (2) above before that date, so as to come into force in relation to that road or part on that date.]

(6) In this section "use", in relation to a road, includes crossing, ... **[113]**

NOTES
Commencement: 26 September 1984 (sub-ss (2)–(4), (6)); 1 November 1991 (sub-ss (1), (5)).
Sub-ss (1)-(3) derived from the Road Traffic Regulation Act 1967, s 13(1)-(3), and the Highways

Act 1980, Sch 24, para 16; sub-ss (4)-(6) derived from the Road Traffic Regulation Act 1967, s 13(4)-(6).

Sub-s (1): substituted by the New Roads and Street Works Act 1991, s 168(1), Sch 8, Part II, para 28(1), (2).

Sub-s (2): words in square brackets substituted by the New Roads and Street Works Act 1991, s 168(1), Sch 8, Part II, para 28(1), (3); words omitted repealed, and para (d) added, by the Road Traffic Act 1991, ss 48, 83, Sch 4, para 25, Sch 8.

Sub-s (5): substituted by the New Roads and Street Works Act 1991, s 168(1), Sch 8, Part II, para 28(1), (4).

Sub-s (6): words omitted repealed by the New Roads and Street Works Act 1991, s 168(1), Sch 8, Part II, para 28(1), (5).

Extended with modifications to the Isles of Scilly by SI 1990 No 714.

[17A. Further provisions as to special roads

(1) On the date declared by the traffic authority, by notice published in the prescribed manner, to the date on which a special road, or a part of a special road, is open for use as a special road, any existing order under section 1, 6, 9 or 84 of this Act relating to that road or part shall cease to have effect.

(2) This is without prejudice to any power to make orders under those provisions in relation to the road or part as a special road; and any such power may be exercised before the date referred to above, so as to take effect on that date.

(3) The procedure for making an order applies in such a case with such modifications as may be prescribed.]   **[113A]**

NOTES

Commencement: 1 November 1991.

Inserted by the New Roads and Street Works Act 1991, s 168(1), Sch 8, Pt II, para 29.

18. One-way traffic on trunk roads

(1) Where the Secretary of State proposes to make [an order under section 10 of the Highways Act 1980 or section 5 of the Roads (Scotland) Act 1984 directing] that a road shall become a trunk road, and considers it expedient—

(a) that the road, when it becomes a trunk road, should be used only for traffic passing in one direction, and

(b) that any other road which is a trunk road, or is to become a trunk road by virtue of the order, should be used only for traffic passing in the other direction,

the order may make provision for restricting the use of those roads accordingly as from such date as may be specified in the order.

(2) Subsection (1) above shall have effect without prejudice to the powers of the Secretary of State under section 1 of this Act.

(3) A person who uses a vehicle, or causes or permits a vehicle to be used, in contravention of any provision made by virtue of subsection (1) above shall be guilty of an offence.   **[114]**

NOTES

Commencement: 26 September 1984.

Sub-ss (1), (2) derived from the Road Traffic Regulation Act 1967, s 14(1), and the Highways Act 1980, Sch 24, para 16; sub-s (3) derived from the Road Traffic Regulation Act 1967, s 14(2).

Sub-s (1): words in square brackets substituted by the New Roads and Street Works Act 1991, s 168(1), Sch 8, Part II, para 30.

Extended with modifications to the Isles of Scilly by SI 1990 No 714.

PART III

CROSSINGS AND PLAYGROUNDS

Pedestrian Crossings

25. Pedestrian crossing regulations

(1) The Secretary of State may make regulations with respect to the precedence of vehicles and pedestrians respectively, and generally with respect to the movement of traffic (including pedestrians), at and in the vicinity of crossings.

(2) Without prejudice to the generality of subsection (1) above, regulations under that subsection may be made—

    (a) prohibiting pedestrian traffic on the carriageway within 100 yards of a crossing, and

    (b) with respect to the indication of the limits of a crossing, or of any other matter whatsoever relating to the crossing, by marks or devices on or near the roadway or otherwise, and generally with respect to the erection of traffic signs in connection with a crossing.

(3) Different regulations may be made under this section in relation to different traffic conditions, and in particular (but without prejudice to the generality of the foregoing words) different regulations may be made in relation to crossings in the vicinity of, and at a distance from, a junction of roads, and in relation to traffic which is controlled by the police, and by traffic signals, and by different kinds of traffic signals, and traffic which is not controlled.

(4) Regulations may be made under this section applying only to a particular crossing or particular crossings specified in the regulations.

(5) A person who contravenes any regulations made under this section shall be guilty of an offence.

(6) In this section "crossing" means a crossing for pedestrians established—

    (a) by a local authority under section 23 of this Act, or

    (b) by the Secretary of State in the discharge of the duty imposed on him by section 24 of this Act,

and (in either case) indicated in accordance with the regulations having effect as respects that crossing; and, for the purposes of a prosecution for a contravention of the provisions of a regulation having effect as respects a crossing, the crossing shall be deemed to be so established and indicated unless the contrary is proved.   **[115]**

NOTES

    Commencement: 26 September 1984.

    This section derived from the Road Traffic Regulation Act 1967, s 23.

    See the "Zebra" Pedestrian Crossings Regulations 1971 and the "Pelican" Pedestrian Crossing Regulations 1987, post.

    Extended with modifications to the Isles of Scilly by SI 1990 No 714.

School Crossings

28. Stopping of vehicles at school crossings

(1) When between the hours of eight in the morning and half-past five in the afternoon a vehicle is approaching a place in a road where children on their way to or from school, or from one part of a school to another, are crossing or seeking to cross the road, a school crossing patrol wearing a uniform approved

by the Secretary of State shall have power, by exhibiting a prescribed sign, to require the person driving or propelling the vehicle to stop it.

(2) When a person has been required under subsection (1) above to stop a vehicle—

    (a) he shall cause the vehicle to stop before reaching the place where the children are crossing or seeking to cross and so as not to stop or impede their crossing, and

    (b) the vehicle shall not be put in motion again so as to reach the place in question so long as the sign continues to be exhibited.

(3) A person who fails to comply with paragraph (a) of subsection (2) above, or who causes a vehicle to be put in motion in contravention of paragraph (b) of that subsection, shall be guilty of an offence.

(4) In this section—

    (a) "prescribed sign" means a sign of a size, colour and type prescribed by regulations made by the Secretary of State or, if authorisation is given by the Secretary of State for the use of signs of a description not so prescribed, a sign of that description;

    (b) "school crossing patrol" means a person authorised to patrol in accordance with arrangements under section 26 of this Act;

and regulations under paragraph (a) above may provide for the attachment of reflectors to signs or for the illumination of signs.

(5) For the purposes of this section—

    (a) where it is proved that a sign was exibited by a school crossing patrol, it shall be presumed, unless the contrary is proved, to be of a size, colour and type prescribed, or of a description authorised, under subsection (4)(b) above, and, if it was exhibited in circumstances in which it was required by the regulations to be illuminated, to have been illuminated in the prescribed manner;

    (b) where it is proved that a school crossing patrol was wearing a uniform, the uniform shall be presumed, unless the contrary is proved, to be a uniform approved by the Secretary of State; and

    (c) where it is proved that a prescribed sign was exhibited by a school crossing patrol at a place in a road where children were crossing or seeking to cross the road, it shall be presumed, unless the contrary is proved, that those children were on their way to or from school or from one part of a school to another.   **[116]**

NOTES

    Commencement: 26 September 1984.

    This section derived from the Road Traffic Regulation Act 1967, s 25, and the Road Traffic Act 1974, Sch 6, para 7.

    Sub-s (1): "prescribed", see the Traffic Signs Regulations and General Directions 1981, post.

    Extended with modifications to the Isles of Scilly by SI 1990 No 714.

PART IV

PARKING PLACES

Provision of off-street parking, and parking on roads without payment

35. Provisions as to use of parking places provided under s 32 or 33

(1) As respects any parking place—

    (a) provided by a local authority under section 32 of this Act, or
    (b) provided under any letting or arrangements made by a local authority
        under section 33(4) of this Act,

the local authority, subject to Parts I and III of Schedule 9 to this Act, may by order make provision as to—

    (i) the use of the parking place, and in particular the vehicles or class of vehicles which may be entitled to use it,
    (ii) the conditions on which it may be used,
    (iii) the charges to be paid in connection with its use (where it is an off-street one), and
    (iv) the removal from it of a vehicle left there in contravention of the order and the safe custody of the vehicle

[and the power under paragraph (iii) to make provision as to the payment of charges shall include power to make provision requiring those charges, or any part of them, to be paid by means of the hire or purchase in advance, or the use, of parking devices in accordance with the order.]

(2) Where under section 34 of this Act a means of access to any premises has been provided by a local authority through an off-street parking place, then, subject to Parts I to III of Schedule 9 to this Act and to the provisions of any agreement made by the local authority under subsection (3) of section 34 and to any rights granted by them under that subsection, the authority may by an order under subsection (1) above make provision as to the use of the parking place as the means of access and, in particular, as to the vehicles or class of vehicles which may be entitled to use the means of access and as to the conditions on which the means of access may be used.

(3) An order under subsection (1) above may provide for a specified apparatus or device to be used—

    (a) as a means to indicate—

        (i) the time at which a vehicle arrived at, and the time at which it ought to leave, a parking place, or one or other of those times, or
        (ii) the charges paid or payable in respect of a vehicle in an off-street parking place; or

    (b) as a means to collect any such charges,

and may make provision regulating the use of any such apparatus or device; but an order shall not provide for the use of any apparatus or device not generally or specially approved for the purpose by the Secretary of State.

[(3A) An order under subsection (1) above may also provide—

    (a) for regulating the issue, use and surrender of parking devices;
    (b) for requiring vehicles to display parking devices when left in any parking place in respect of which the parking devices may be used;
    (c) without prejudice to the generality of paragraph (b) above, for regulating the manner in which parking devices are to be displayed or operated;
    (d) for prescribing the use, and the manner of use, of apparatus, of such type as may be approved by the Secretary of State either generally or specially, designed to be used in connection with parking devices;
    (e) for treating—

        (i) the indications given by a parking device, or
        (ii) the display or the failure to display a parking device on or in any vehicle left in any parking place,

as evidence (and, in Scotland, as sufficient evidence) of such facts as may be provided by the order;

(f) for the refund, in such circumstances and in such manner as may be prescribed in the order, of the whole or part of the amount of any charge paid in advance in respect of a parking device;

(g) for the payment of a deposit in respect of the issue of a parking device and for the repayment of the whole or any part of any such deposit.

(3B) In this section and in section 35A below "parking device" means either a card, disc, token, meter, permit, stamp or other similar device, whether used in a vehicle or not, of such type or design as may be approved by the Secretary of State either generally or specially, which, being used either by itself, or in conjunction with any such apparatus as is referred to in subsection (3A)(d) above—

(a) indicates, or causes to be indicated, the payment of a charge, and—

(i) the period in respect of which it has been paid and the time of the beginning or end of the period, or

(ii) whether or not the period for which it has been paid or any further period has elapsed, or

(iii) the period for which the vehicle in relation to which the parking device is used is permitted to park in the parking place, and the time of the beginning or end of the period, or

(iv) whether or not the period for which the vehicle in relation to which the parking device is used is permitted to park in the parking place or any further period has elapsed; or

(b) operates apparatus controlling the entry of vehicles to or their exit from the parking place, or enables that apparatus to be operated;

or any other device of any such description as may from time to time be prescribed for the purposes of this section and section 35A below by order made by the Secretary of State either generally or specially.

(3C) An order under subsection (3B) above which revokes or amends a previous order under that subsection may make such saving and transitional provision as appears to the Secretary of State to be necessary or expedient.

(3D) The power to make orders under subsection (3B) above is exercisable by statutory instrument which shall be subject to annulment in pursuance of a resolution of either House of Parliament.]

(4)–(9) ... **[117]**

NOTES

Commencement: 16 May 1990 (sub-ss (3A)-(3D)); 26 September 1984 (remainder).

Sub-s (1) derived from the Road Traffic Regulation Act 1967, s 31(1), and the Transport Act 1968, Sch 14, Part VI, para 1; sub-s (2) derived from the Road Traffic Regulation Act 1967, s 31(1A), and the Highways Act 1971, s 9(3); sub-ss (3), (4)-(9) derived from the Road Traffic Regulation Act 1967, s 31(2)-(7).

Sub-s (1): words in square brackets added with savings by the Parking Act 1989, s 1(1), (2).

Sub-ss (3A), (3B), (3C), (3D): added with savings by the Parking Act 1989, s 1(1), (3).

Sub-ss (4)-(7): repealed with savings by the Parking Act 1989, s 1(1), (4).

Sub-s (8): repealed by the Road Traffic (Consequential Provisions) Act 1988, s 3(1), Sch 1, Part I.

Sub-s (9): repealed by the Road Traffic Act 1991, s 44(2), 83, Sch 8.

See further: SI 1986 No 259, SI 1986 No 179.

Extended with modifications to the Isles of Scilly by SI 1990 No 714.

[35A. Offences and proceedings in connection with parking places provided under s 32 or 33

(1) In the event of any contravention of, or non-compliance with, a provision of an order under section 35(1) above, the person responsible shall be guilty of an offence.

(2) A person who, with intent to defraud—

(a) interferes with any such apparatus or device mentioned in section 35(3) above as is by an order under section 35(1) above to be used for the collection of charges at an off-street parking place, or operates or attempts to operate it by the insertion of objects other than current coins or bank notes of the appropriate denomination, or the appropriate credit or debit cards, or

(b) interferes with any such apparatus as is mentioned in section 35(3A)(d) above or with a parking device, or operates or attempts to operate any such apparatus or any parking device otherwise than in the manner prescribed, or

(c) displays a parking device otherwise than in the manner prescribed,

shall be guilty of an offence.

(3) An order under section 35(1) above may include provision—

(a) for determining the person responsible for any contravention of or non-compliance with the order;

(b) for treating—

(i) the indications given by any such apparatus or device as is mentioned in section 35(3) above used in pursuance of the order, or

(ii) the indications given by any such apparatus as is mentioned in section 35(3A)(d) above used in pursuance of the order, or any tickets issued by it, or the absence of any such ticket from a vehicle left in a parking place,

as evidence (and, in Scotland, as sufficient evidence) of such facts and for such purposes as may be provided by the order;

(c) for applying with any appropriate adaptations any of the provisions of subsections (4) to (6) of section 47 of this Act.

(4) The reference in subsection (5) of section 47 of this Act to apparatus provided for the purposes of a parking place and operated by the insertion of coins or bank notes or by means of credit or debit cards shall, where that subsection is applied by virtue of subsection (3)(c) above, include references to—

(a) any such apparatus as is referred to in section 35(3A)(d) above, and

(b) any such device as is referred to in section 35(3B) above;

and the said subsection (5) of section 47 of this Act (as modified by this subsection) shall apply to an offence under subsection (2)(b) or (c) above as it applies to an offence under that section.

(5) While a vehicle is within a parking place, it shall not be lawful for the driver or conductor of the vehicle, or for any person employed in connection with it, to ply for hire or accept passengers for hire; and if a person acts in contravention of this subsection he shall be guilty of an offence.

(6) In this section—

"credit card" means a card or similar thing issued by any person, use of which enables the holder to defer the payment by him of the charge for parking a vehicle; and

"debit card" means a card or similar thing issued by any person, use of which by the holder causes the charge for parking a vehicle to be paid by the electronic transfer of funds from any current account of his at a bank or other institution providing banking services.]   **[117A]**

NOTES
Commencement: 16 May 1990.
Added by the Parking Act 1989, s 2.

[35B. Display of information

(1) The Secretary of State may make regulations requiring local authorities to display at off-street parking places provided by them under section 32 above such information about parking there as is specified in the regulations.

(2) Regulations under this section may also—

(a) require the display of any orders under section 35(1) above relating to the parking place;

(b) specify the manner in which the information and orders are to be displayed;

(c) exempt local authorities, in specified circumstances or subject to specified conditions, from the requirement to display information and orders, or to display them in the specified manner; and

(d) provide, in relation to a parking place at which a local authority fails to comply with the regulations or with any specified provision of the regulations, that, except in any specified circumstances, any order under section 35(1) above shall be of no effect in its application to that parking place in so far as it requires the payment of any charge in connection with use of the parking place—

(i) while the failure to comply continues, and

(ii) as respects vehicles parked there when the failure to comply was remedied, during a specified period thereafter.

(3) Regulations under this section may make different provision for different circumstances and for different descriptions of parking place, and may exempt specified descriptions of parking place from any provision of the regulations.

(4) In any proceedings for contravention of, or non-compliance with, an order under section 35(1) above relating to an off-street parking place, it shall be assumed, unless the contrary is shown, that any relevant regulations under this section were complied with at all material times.]   **[117B]**

NOTES
Commencement: 16 May 1990.
Added by the Parking Act 1989, s 2.

[35C. Variation of charges at off-street parking places

(1) Where an order under section 35(1)(iii) of this Act makes provision as to the charges to be paid in connection with the use of off-street parking places, the authority making that order may vary those charges by notice given under this section.

(2) The variation of any such charges by notice is not to be taken to prejudice any power to vary those charges by order under section 35 of this Act.

(3) The Secretary of State may by regulations make provision as to the procedure to be followed by any local authority giving notice under this section.

(4) The regulations may, in particular, make provision with respect to—

(a) the publication, where an authority propose to give notice, of details of their proposal;

(b) the form and manner in which notice is to be given; and

(c) the publication of notices.

(5) In giving any notice under this section a local authority shall comply with the regulations.] **[117C]**

NOTES

Prospectively added by the Road Traffic Act 1991, s 41, as from a day to be appointed.

PART V

TRAFFIC SIGNS

General provisions

64. General provisions as to traffic signs

(1) In this Act "traffic sign" means any object or device (whether fixed or portable) for conveying, to traffic on roads or any specified class of traffic, warnings, information, requirements, restrictions or prohibitions of any description—

(a) specified by regulations made by the Ministers acting jointly, or

(b) authorised by the Secretary of State,

and any line or mark on a road for so conveying such warnings, information, requirements, restrictions or prohibitions.

(2) Traffic signs shall be of the size, colour and type prescribed by regulations made as mentioned in subsection (1)(a) above except where the Secretary of State authorises the erection or retention of a sign of another character; and for the purposes of this subsection illumination, whether by lighting or by the use of reflectors or reflecting material, or the absence of such illumination, shall be part of the type or character of a sign.

(3) Regulations under this section may be made so as to apply either generally or in such circumstances only as may be specified in the regulations.

(4) Except as provided by this Act, no traffic sign shall be placed on or near a road except—

(a) a notice in respect of the use of a bridge;

(b) a traffic sign placed, in pursuance of powers conferred by a special Act of Parliament or order having the force of an Act, by the owners or operators of a tramway, light railway or trolley vehicle undertaking, a dock undertaking or a harbour undertaking; or

(c) a traffic sign placed on any land—

(i) by a person authorised under the following provisions of this Act to place the sign on a [road], and

(ii) for a purpose for which he is authorised to place it on a [road].

(5) Regulations under this section, or any authorisation under subsection (2) above, may provide that [section 36 of the Road Traffic Act 1988] (drivers to comply with traffic directions) shall apply to signs of a type specified in that

behalf by the regulations or, as the case may be, to the sign to which the authorisation relates.

(6) References in any enactment (including any enactment contained in this Act) to the erection or placing of traffic signs shall include references to the display of traffic signs in any manner, whether or not involving fixing or placing.   **[118]**

NOTES
   Commencement: 26 September 1984.
   This section derived from the Road Traffic Regulation Act 1967, s 54, and the Road Traffic Act 1972, Sch 7.
   Sub-s (4): words in square brackets substituted by the New Roads and Street Works Act 1991, s 168(1), Sch 8, Part II, para 47.
   Sub-s (5): words in square brackets substituted by the Road Traffic (Consequential Provisions) Act 1988, s 4, Sch 3, para 25(3).
   Extended with modifications to the Isles of Scilly by SI 1990 No 714.

65. Powers and duties of highway authorities as to placing of traffic signs

[(1) The traffic authority may cause or permit traffic signs to be placed on or near a road, subject to and in conformity with such general directions as may be given by the Ministers acting jointly or such other directions as may be given by the Secretary of State.]

[(1A) The power to give general directions under subsection (1) above includes power to require equipment used in connection with traffic signs to be of a type approved in accordance with the directions.]

[(2) The Secretary of State may give directions to a local traffic authority—]
  (a) for the placing of a traffic sign of any prescribed type or authorised character specified in the directions, or
  (b) for replacing a sign so specified by, or converting it into, a sign of another prescribed type or authorised character so specified.

(3) The power to give general directions under subsection (1) above shall be exercisable by statutory instrument.

[(3A) No charge may be made—
  (a) in England and Wales, by a highway authority which is the council of a county, metropolitan district or London borough or the Common Council of the City of London, or
  (b) in Scotland, by a local roads authority,
with respect to the exercise of their power under subsection (1) above to permit a traffic sign to be placed on or near any road in their area if—
  (i) the sign conveys information of a temporary nature or is otherwise intended to be placed only temporarily; and
  (ii) the sign is to be placed by a body which is prescribed for the purposes of this subsection as being a body appearing to the Secretary of State to be representative of the interests of road users or any class of road users.]

(4) In this section—
  "authorised character" means a character authorised by the Secretary of State; and
  "prescribed type" means a type prescribed by regulations made under section 64(1)(a) of this Act.   **[119]**

NOTES
Commencement: 26 September 1984 (sub-ss (3), (4)); 16 November 1989 (sub-s (3A));
1 November 1991 (sub-ss (1), (1A), (2)).
Sub-ss (1)-(3), (4) derived from the Road Traffic Regulation Act 1967, s 55(1)-(3).
Sub-s (1): substituted by the New Roads and Street Works Act 1991, s 168(1), Sch 8, Part II,
para 48.
Sub-s (1A): inserted by the Road Traffic Act 1991, s 48, Sch 4, para 29.
Sub-s (2): amended by the New Roads and Street Works Act 1991, s 168(1), Sch 8, Part II,
para 48.
Sub-s (3A): added with savings by the Local Government and Housing Act 1989, s 153.
Functions conferred on highway authorities which are London authorities transferred for certain
purposes to the Secretary of State by the London Traffic Control System (Transfer) Order 1986, SI
1986 No 315, art 3.
Extended with modifications to the Isles of Scilly by SI 1990 No 714.

66. Traffic signs for giving effect to local traffic regulations

(1) A constable, or a person acting under the instructions (whether general or specific) of the chief officer of police, may place on a [road], or on any structure on a highway, traffic signs (of any size, colour and type prescribed or authorised under section 64 of this Act) indicating prohibitions, restrictions or requirements relating to vehicular traffic, as may be requisite—

(a) for giving effect to regulations, orders or directions under any enactment mentioned in subsection (2) below, or

(b) for giving effect to directions given under [section 31(4) of the Road Traffic Act 1988] (which enables directions to be given in consequence of the holding of an authorised race or trial of speed).

(2) The enactments referred to in subsection (1) above are—

(a) section 52 of the Metropolitan Police Act 1839 (which relates to prevention of obstruction on public occasions or in the neighbourhood of public buildings in the metropolitan police district);

(b) section 22 of the local Act of the second and third year of the reign of Queen Victoria, chapter 94 (which makes similar provision in relation to the City of London);

(c) section 21 of the Town Police Clauses Act 1847 (which likewise makes similar provision for areas to which that Act is applied); and

(d) section 385 of the Burgh Police (Scotland) Act 1892 and any corresponding provision contained in a local Act relating to any part of Scotland.

(3) In this section "prescribed" means prescribed by regulations under section 64(1)(a) of this Act. **[120]**

NOTES
Commencement: 26 September 1984.
This section derived from the Road Traffic Regulation Act 1967, s 57, and the Road Traffic Act
1972, Sch 7.
Sub-s (1): word in first square brackets substituted by the New Roads and Street Works Act
1991, s 168(1), Sch 8, Part II, para 49; in para (b) words in second square brackets substituted by
the Road Traffic (Consequential Provisions) Act 1988, s 4, Sch 3, para 25(4).
Extended with modifications to the Isles of Scilly by SI 1990 No 714.

67. Emergencies and temporary obstructions

(1) A constable, or a person acting under the instructions (whether general or specific) of the chief officer of police, may place on a [road], or on any structure on a [road], traffic signs (of any size, colour and type prescribed or authorised under section 64 of this Act), indicating prohibitions, restrictions or requirements relating to vehicular traffic, as may be necessary or expedient to prevent or

mitigate congestion or obstruction of traffic, or danger to or from traffic, in consequence of extraordinary circumstances; and the power to place signs conferred by this subsection shall include power to maintain a sign for a period of 7 days or less from the time when it was placed, but no longer.

(2) [Section 36 of the Road Traffic Act 1988] (drivers to comply with traffic directions) shall apply to signs placed in the exercise of the powers conferred by subsection (1) above.

(3) Regulations under section 64 of this Act prescribing any type of object or device for warning traffic of a temporary obstruction may include provisions for authorising (subject to such conditions as may be specified in the regulations) persons not otherwise authorised to do so to place an object or device of that type on or near roads, or on or near any description of road so specified, in such circumstances and for such periods as may be so specified.   **[121]**

NOTES

Commencement: 26 September 1984.

Sub-ss (1), (2) derived from the Road Traffic Regulation Act 1967, s 58(1), (2), and the Road Traffic Act 1972, Sch 7; sub-s (3) derived from the Road Traffic Regulation Act 1967, s 59.

Sub-s (1): amended by the New Roads and Street Works Act 1991, s 168(1), Sch 8, Part II, para 50.

Sub-s (2): words in square brackets substituted by the Road Traffic (Consequential Provisions) Act 1988, s 4, Sch 3, para 25(5).

Extended with modifications to the Isles of Scilly by SI 1990 No 714.

68. Placing of traffic signs in connection with exercise of other powers

(1) This section applies to any authority having power to make—

(a) an order under or by virtue of any of the following provisions of this Act, namely, sections 1 to 4, sections 14, 19, 29, . . . 32, 35, 37, 38, 45 and 46 and subsections (2) and (4) of section 49, or

(b) an order as respects a road outside Greater London under section 9 of this Act, or

(c) an order to which this paragraph applies by virtue of any provision of Part VI of this Act.

(2) Without prejudice to any powers conferred by or under any other provision of this Act, but subject to subsection (3) below, an authority to whom this section applies may place and maintain, or cause to be placed and maintained, such traffic signs, of any type prescribed or character authorised under section 64 of this Act, as the authority may consider necessary in connection with any order made by the authority as respects any road and falling within any of paragraphs (a) to (c) of subsection (1) above [or, in the case of a traffic authority having power to make an order under section 14 of this Act, as the authority may consider necessary in connection with any order made or notice issued by them under that section]; but, if the order is made [or, as the case may be, the notice is issued] by an authority other than the [traffic authority] for the road, the authority by whom the order is made [or, as the case may be, the notice is issued]—

(a) shall consult with the [traffic authority] as to the placing of the signs, and

(b) unless the [traffic authority] are unwilling to do so, shall enter into arrangements with the [traffic authority] for the signs to be placed and maintained by the [traffic authority].

(3) The power conferred by subsection (2) above on an authority to whom this section applies shall be exercisable subject to and in conformity with any

general directions given under section 65(1) of this Act, whether that authority is a [traffic authority] or not; and any other power conferred by section 65 to give directions to a [traffic authority] shall include power to give the like directions to an authority to whom this section applies.   **[122]**

NOTES
Commencement: 26 September 1984.
This section derived from the Road Traffic Regulation Act 1967, s 56A(1)-(3), and the Transport Act 1968, Sch 14, Part III.
Sub-s (1): figure omitted repealed by the New Roads and Street Works Act 1991, s 168(2), Sch 9.
Sub-s (2): words in second, fifth, sixth, seventh and eighth pairs of square brackets substituted by the New Roads and Street Works Act 1991, s 168(1), Sch 8, Part II, para 51(1), (3); words in first, third and fourth pairs of square brackets inserted by the Road Traffic (Temporary Restrictions) Act 1991, s 1(3).
Sub-s (3): amended by the New Roads and Street Works Act 1991, s 168(1), Sch 8, Part II, para 51(1), (3).
Extended with modifications to the Isles of Scilly by SI 1990 No 714.

PART VI

SPEED LIMITS

81. General speed limit for restricted roads

(1) It shall not be lawful for a person to drive a motor vehicle on a restricted road at a speed exceeding 30 miles per hour.

(2) The Ministers acting jointly may by order made by statutory instrument and approved by a resolution of each House of Parliament increase or reduce the rate of speed fixed by subsection (1) above, either as originally enacted or as varied under this subsection.   **[123]**

NOTES
Commencement: 26 September 1984.
This section derived from the Road Traffic Regulation Act 1967, s 71.
Extended with modifications to the Isles of Scilly by SI 1990 No 714.

82. What roads are restricted roads

(1) Subject to the provisions of this section and of section 84(3) of this Act, a road is a restricted road for the purposes of section 81 of this Act [if—

    (a) in England and Wales, there is provided on it a system of street lighting furnished by means of lamps placed not more than 200 yards apart;

    (b) in Scotland, there is provided on it a system of carriageway lighting furnished by means of lamps placed not more than 185 metres apart and the road is of a classification or type specified for the purposes of this subsection in regulations made by the Secretary of State.]

(2) [The traffic authority for a road may direct]—

    (a) that [the road] which is a restricted road for the purposes of section 81 of this Act shall cease to be a restricted road for those purposes, or

    (b) that [the road] which is not a restricted road for those purposes shall become a restricted road for those purposes.

[(3) A special road is not a restricted road for the purposes of section 81 on or after the date declared by the traffic authority, by notice published in the prescribed manner, to be the date on which the special road, or the relevant part of the special road, is open for use as a special road.]   **[124]**

NOTES

Commencement: 26 September 1984 (sub-ss (1), (2)); 1 November 1991 (sub-s (3)).

This section derived from the Road Traffic Regulation Act 1967, s 72(1), (3), (5).

Sub-s (1): amended by the New Roads and Street Works Act 1991, s 168(1), Sch 8, Part II, para 59(1), (2).

Sub-s (2): words in square brackets substituted by the New Roads and Street Works Act 1991, s 168(1), Sch 8, Part II, para 59(1), (3).

Sub-s (3): substituted by the New Roads and Street Works Act 1991, s 168(1), Sch 8, Part II, para 59(1), (4).

Extended with modifications to the Isles of Scilly by SI 1990 No 714.

83. Provisions as to directions under s 82(2)

(1) [A direction under section 82(2) by the Secretary of State shall be given] by means of an order made by the Secretary of State after giving public notice of his intention to make an order.

[(2) A direction under section 82(2) by a local traffic authority shall be given by means of an order made by the authority.]

(3) Section 68(1)(c) of this Act shall apply to any order made under subsection (2) above. **[125]**

NOTES

Commencement: 26 September 1984 (sub-ss (1), (3)); 1 November 1991 (sub-s (2)).

Sub-ss (1)–(3) derived from the Road Traffic Regulation Act 1967, ss 56A(1), 73(1)-(3), and the Transport Act 1968, Sch 14, Part III, Part VI, para 1.

Sub-s (1): amended by the New Roads and Street Works Act 1991, s 168(1), Sch 8, Part II, para 60(1), (2).

Sub-s (2): substituted by the New Roads and Street Works Act 1991, Sch 8, Part II, para 60(1), (3).

See further: SI 1986 No 259; SI 1986 No 179; SI 1986 No 180.

Extended with modifications to the Isles of Scilly by SI 1990 No 714.

84. Speed limits on roads other than restricted roads

[(1) An order made under this subsection as respects any road may prohibit—

   (a) the driving of motor vehicles on that road at a speed exceeding that specified in the order,

   (b) the driving of motor vehicles on that road at a speed exceeding that specified in the order during periods specified in the order, or

   (c) the driving of motor vehicles on that road at a speed exceeding the speed for the time being indicated by traffic signs in accordance with the order.

(1A) An order made by virtue of subsection (1)(c) above may—

   (a) make provision restricting the speeds that may be indicated by traffic signs or the periods during which the indications may be given, and

   (b) provide for the indications to be given only in such circumstances as may be determined by or under the order;

but any such order must comply with regulations made under subsection (1B) below, except where the Secretary of State authorises otherwise in a particular case.

(1B) The Secretary of State may make regulations governing the provision which may be made by orders of local authorities under subsection (1)(c) above, and any such regulations may in particular—

   (*a*) prescribe the circumstances in which speed limits may have effect by virtue of an order,

   (*b*) prescribe the speed limits which may be specified in an order, and

(c) make transitional provision and different provision for different
cases.]

[(2) The power to make an order under subsection (1) is exercisable by the
traffic authority, who shall before exercising it in any case give public notice of
their intention to do so.]

(3) While an order [made by virtue of subsection (1)(a)] above is in force as
respects a road, that road shall not be a restricted road for the purposes of
section 81 of this Act.

(4) This section does not apply to any part of a special road which is open
for use as a special road.

(5) Section 68(1)(c) of this Act shall apply to any order made under
subsection (1) above.

[(6) Any reference in a local Act to roads subject to a speed limit shall,
unless the contrary intention appears, be treated as not including a reference to
roads subject to a speed limit imposed only by virtue of subsection (1)(b) or (c)
above.]   **[126]**

NOTES
Commencement: 26 September 1984 (sub-ss (3)–(5)); 1 July 1992 (remainder).
This section derived from the Road Traffic Regulation Act 1967, ss 56A(1), 74(1), (2), (7), and
the Transport Act 1968, Sch 14, Part III, Part VI, para 1.
Sub-s (1): substituted by the Road Traffic Act 1991, s 45.
Sub-ss (1A), (1B): added by the Road Traffic Act 1991, s 45.
Sub-s (2): substituted by the New Roads and Street Works Act 1991, s 168(1), Sch 8, Part II,
para 61.
Sub-s (3): amended by the Road Traffic Act 1991, s 45.
Sub-s (6): added by the Road Traffic Act 1991, s 45.
See further: SI 1986 No 259; SI 1986 No 179; SI 1986 No 180.
Extended with modifications to the Isles of Scilly by SI 1990 No 714.

85. Traffic signs for indicating speed restrictions

(1) For the purpose of securing that adequate guidance is given to drivers of
motor vehicles as to whether any, and if so what, limit of speed is to be observed
on any road, it shall be the duty of the Secretary of State, [in the case of a road
for which he is the traffic authority, to] erect and maintain . . . traffic signs in
such positions as may be requisite for that purpose.

(2) [In the case of any road, it is the duty of the local traffic authority]—

(a) to erect and maintain . . . traffic signs in such positions as may be
requisite in order to give effect to general or other directions given by
the Secretary of State for the purpose mentioned in subsection (1)
above, and
(b) to alter or remove traffic signs as may be requisite in order to give
effect to such directions, either in consequence of the making of an
order by the Secretary of State or otherwise.

(3) If a local authority makes default in executing any works required for
the performance of the duty imposed on them by subsection (2) above, the
Secretary of State may himself execute the works; and the expense incurred by
him in doing so shall be recoverable by him from the [local traffic authority]
and, in England or Wales, shall be so recoverable summarily as a civil debt.

(4) [Where no such system of street or carriageway lighting as is mentioned
in section 82(1) is provided on a road,] but a limit of speed is to be observed on

the road, a person shall not be convicted of driving a motor vehicle on the road at a speed exceeding the limit unless the limit is indicated by means of such traffic signs as are mentioned in subsection (1) or subsection (2) above.

(5) In any proceedings for a contravention of section 81 of this Act, where the proceedings relate to driving on a road provided with [such a system of street or carriageway lighting], evidence of the absence of traffic signs displayed in pursuance of this section to indicate that the road is not a restricted road for the purposes of that section shall be evidence that the road is a restricted road for those purposes.

(6) Where by regulations made under section 17(2) of this Act a limit of speed is to be observed, then, if it is to be observed—

(a) on all special roads, or
(b) on all special roads provided for the use of particular classes of traffic, or
(c) on all special roads other than special roads of such description as may be specified in the regulations, or
(d) as mentioned in paragraph (a), (b) or (c) above except for such lengths of special road as may be so specified,

this section shall not apply in relation to that limit (but without prejudice to its application in relation to any lower limit of maximum speed or, as the case may be, any higher limit of minimum speed, required by any such regulations to be observed on any specified length of any specified special road).

(7) The power to give general directions under subsection (2) above shall be exercisable by statutory instrument.   **[127]**

NOTES
Commencement: 26 September 1984.
Sub-ss (1)-(5), (7) derived from the Road Traffic Regulation Act 1967, s 75(1)-(6); sub-s (6) derived from the Road Traffic Regulation Act 1967, s 13(3A), and the Transport Act 1968, s 129(1).
Sub-s (1): words omitted repealed by the Road Traffic Act 1991, ss 48, 83, Sch 4, para 30, Sch 8; and amended by the New Roads and Street Works Act 1991, s 168(1), Sch 8, Part II, para 62(1), (2); "prescribed", see Traffic Signs (Speed Limits) Regulations and General Directions 1969, post.
Sub-s (2): words omitted repealed by the Road Traffic Act 1991, ss 48, 83, Sch 4, para 30, Sch 8; and amended by the New Roads and Street Works Act 1991, s 168(1), Sch 8, Part II, para 62(1), (3).
Sub-s (3): words in square brackets substituted by the New Roads and Street Works Act 1991, s 168(1), Sch 8, Part II, para 62(1), (4).
Sub-s (4): amended by the New Roads and Street Works Act 1991, s 168(1), Sch 8, Part II, para 62(1), (5).
Sub-s (5): amended by the New Roads and Street Works Act 1991, s 168(1), Sch 8, Part II, para 62(1), (6).
Extended with modifications to the Isles of Scilly by SI 1990 No 714.

---

86. Speed limits for particular classes of vehicles

(1) It shall not be lawful for a person to drive a motor vehicle of any class on a road at a speed greater than the speed specified in Schedule 6 to this Act as the maximum speed in relation to a vehicle of that class.

(2) Subject to subsections (4) and (5) below, the Secretary of State may by regulations vary subject to such conditions as may be specified in the regulations, the provisions of that Schedule.

(3) Regulations under this section may make different provision as respects the same class of vehicles in different circumstances.

(4) . . .

(5) The Secretary of State shall not have power under this section to vary the speed limit imposed by section 81 of this Act.

(6) The Secretary of State shall not have power under this section to impose a speed limit, as respects driving on roads which are not restricted roads for the purposes of section 81 of this Act, on a vehicle which—

    (a) is constructed solely for the carriage of passengers and their effects;
    (b) is not adapted to carry more than 8 passengers exclusive of the driver;
    (c) is neither a heavy motor car nor an invalid carriage;
    (d) is not drawing a trailer; and
    (e) is fitted with pneumatic tyres on all its wheels.   **[128]**

NOTES
Commencement: 26 September 1984.
This section derived from the Road Traffic Regulation Act 1967, s 78(1)-(6).
Sub-s (4): repealed by the New Roads and Street Works Act 1991, s 168(1), Sch 8, Part II, para 63, Sch 9.
Extended with modifications to the Isles of Scilly by SI 1990 No 714.

87. Exemption of fire brigade, ambulance and police vehicles from speed limits

No statutory provision imposing a speed limit on motor vehicles shall apply to any vehicle on an occasion when it is being used for fire brigade, ambulance or police purposes, if the observance of that provision would be likely to hinder the use of the vehicle for the purpose for which it is being used on that occasion.   **[129]**

NOTES
Commencement: 26 September 1984.
This section derived from the Road Traffic Regulation Act 1967, s 79.
Extended with modifications to the Isles of Scilly by SI 1990 No 714.

88. Temporary speed limits

(1) Where it appears to the Secretary of State desirable to do so in the interests of safety or for the purpose of facilitating the movement of traffic, he may, after giving public notice of his intention to do so, by order prohibit, for a period not exceeding 18 months, the driving of motor vehicles—

    (a) on all roads, or on all roads in any area specified in the order, or on all roads of any class so specified, or on all roads other than roads of any class so specified, or on any road so specified, at a speed greater than that specified in the order, or
    (b) on any road specified in the order, at a speed less than the speed specified in the order, subject to such exceptions as may be so specified.

(2) Any prohibition imposed by an order under subsection (1) above may be so imposed either generally, or at times, on days or during periods specified in the order; but the provisions of any such order shall not, except in so far as may be provided by the order, affect the provisions of sections 81 to 84 of this Act.

(3) For the purposes of an order under subsection (1)(a) above, roads may be classified by reference to any circumstances appearing to the Secretary of State to be suitable for the purpose, including their character, the nature of the traffic to which they are suited or the traffic signs provided on them.

(4) The provisions of any order under subsection (1) above may be continued, either indefinitely or for a specified period, by an order of the

Secretary of State made by statutory instrument, which shall be subject to annulment in pursuance of a resolution of either House of Parliament.

(5) Where by virtue of an order under this section a speed limit is to be observed, then—

    (a) if it is to be observed on all roads, on all roads of any class specified in the order or on all roads other than roads of any class so specified, section 85 of this Act shall not apply in relation to that limit;

    (b) if it is to be observed on all roads in any area and, at all points where roads lead into the area, is indicated as respects the area as a whole by means of such traffic signs as are mentioned in subsection (1) or subsection (2) of section 85 of this Act, the limit shall, for the purposes of subsection (4) of that section, be taken as so indicated with respect to all roads in the area.

(6) This section does not apply to any part of a special road which is open for use as a special road.

(7) If a person drives a motor vehicle on a road in contravention of an order under subsection (1)(b) above, he shall be guilty of an offence; but a person shall not be liable to be convicted of so driving solely on the evidence of one witness to the effect that, in the opinion of the witness, he was driving the vehicle at a speed less than that specified in the order.

(8) The first order to be made under subsection (1)(b) shall not be made until a draft of the order has been laid before Parliament and approved by a resolution of each House of Parliament.   **[130]**

NOTES

    Commencement: 26 September 1984.

    Sub-ss (1)-(5) derived from the Road Traffic Regulation Act 1967, s 77(1)-(3), (5), and the Transport Act 1968, s 126(11)(a), sub-ss (6)-(8) derived from the Road Traffic Regulation Act 1967, s 77(6), (7), (9).

    Extended with modifications to the Isles of Scilly by SI 1990 No 714.

89. Speeding offences generally

(1) A person who drives a motor vehicle on a road at a speed exceeding a limit imposed by or under any enactment to which this section applies shall be guilty of an offence.

(2) A person prosecuted for such an offence shall not be liable to be convicted solely on the evidence of one witness to the effect that, in the opinion of the witness, the person prosecuted was driving the vehicle at a speed exceeding a specified limit.

(3) The enactments to which this section applies are—

    (a) any enactment contained in this Act except section 17(2);

    (b) section 2 of the Parks Regulation (Amendment) Act 1926; and

    (c) any enactment not contained in this Act, but passed after 1st September 1960, whether before or after the passing of this Act.

(4) If a person who employs other persons to drive motor vehicles on roads publishes or issues any time-table or schedule, or gives any directions, under which any journey, or any stage or part of any journey, is to be completed within some specified time, and it is not practicable in the circumstances of the case for that journey (or that stage or part of it) to be completed in the specified time without the commission of such an offence as is mentioned in subsection (1) above, the publication or issue of the time-table or schedule, or the giving of the

directions may be produced as prima facie evidence that the employer procured or (as the case may be) incited the persons employed by him to drive the vehicles to commit such an offence.   **[131–133]**

NOTES
  Commencement: 26 September 1984.
  This section derived from the Road Traffic Regulation Act 1967, s 78A, the Road Traffic Act 1972, s 203(2), and the Criminal Act Law 1977, Sch 12.
  Extended with modifications to the Isles of Scilly by SI 1990 No 714.

90, 91. *(Repealed by the Road Traffic (Consequential Provisions) Act 1988, s 3(1), Sch 1, Part I; s 91 repealed by the New Roads and Street Works Act 1991, s 168(1), (2), Sch 8, Part II, para 64, Sch 9.)*

PART VIII

CONTROL AND ENFORCEMENT

Traffic Wardens

96. Additional powers of traffic wardens

(1) An order under section 95(5) of this Act may provide that, for the purposes of any functions which traffic wardens are authorised by the order to discharge, but subject to the provisions of subsection (3) below, references to a constable or police constable in all or any of the enactments specified in subsection (2) below shall include references to a traffic warden.

(2) The enactments referred to in subsection (1) above are—

    (a) section 52 of the Metropolitan Police Act 1839, so far as it relates to the giving by the commissioner of directions to constables for preventing obstructions;

    (b) section 22 of the local Act of the second and third year of the reign of Queen Victoria, chapter 94, so far as it makes similar provision with respect to the City of London;

    [(bb) in this Act—

        (i) section 100(3) (which relates to the interim disposal of vehicles removed under section 99); and

        (ii) sections 104 and 105 (which relate to the immobilisation of illegally parked vehicles);]

    (c) in [the Road Traffic Act 1988]—

        (i) [sections 35(1), 36 and 37] (which relate to compliance with traffic directions given by police constables);

        (ii) [section 163] (which relates to the power of a constable to stop vehicles);

        (iii) [section 164(1), (2) and (6)] (which relate to the power of a constable to require the production of a driving licence in certain circumstances);

        (iv) [sections 165 and 169] (which relate to the powers of constables to obtain names and addresses of drivers and others and to require production of evidence of insurance or security and test certificates); and

        (v) . . .

    [(d) section 11 of the Road Traffic Offenders Act 1988].

(3) Any power of a constable for the purposes of the following provisions of

[the Road Traffic Act 1988, namely, sections 163, 164(1), (2) and (6) and 165], shall be exercisable by a traffic warden under an order made by virtue of subsection (1) above only where—

    (a) the traffic warden is assisting a constable, or

    (b) the traffic warden has reasonable cause to believe that an offence has been committed of a description specified in relation to the section in question for the purposes of this paragraph by the order, and, in the case of a power for the purposes of [section 165 of the Road Traffic Act 1988], the order authorises the use of that power in relation to that offence, or

    (c) in the case of a power for the purposes of [section 163 of the Road Traffic Act 1988], the traffic warden is exercising functions in connection with the control and regulation of traffic (including pedestrians) or stationary vehicles.

[(4) Where an order has been made pursuant to subsection (2)(bb)(i) above, in section 100(3) of this Act the words "chief officer of the police force to which the constable belongs" shall be deemed to include a reference to a chief officer of police under whose direction a traffic warden acts.

(5) Any order made under section 95(5) of this Act may make different provision for different cases or classes of case, or in respect of different areas.]

[134–136]

NOTES

    Commencement: 26 September 1984 (except sub-ss (4), (5)); 1 October 1991 (sub-ss (4), (5)).

    This section derived from the Road Traffic Regulation Act 1967, s 81(4A), (4B), the Transport Act 1968, s 131(6), and the Road Traffic Act 1972, Sch 7.

    Sub-s (1): para (bb) added by the Road Traffic Act 1991, s 48, Sch 4, para 31.

    Sub-ss (2), (3): words omitted repealed and words in square brackets substituted, by the Road Traffic (Consequential Provisions) Act 1988, s 4, Sch 3, para 25.

    Sub-ss (4), (5): added by the Road Traffic Act 1991, s 48, Sch 4, para 31.

    Extended with modifications to the Isles of Scilly by SI 1990 No 714.

Removal or immobilisation of vehicles

99. Removal of vehicles illegally, obstructively or dangerously parked, or abandoned or broken down

(1) The Secretary of State may by regulations make provision for the removal of vehicles which have been permitted to remain at rest—

    (a) on a road in contravention of any statutory prohibition or restriction, or

    (b) on a road in such a position or in such condition or in such circumstances as to cause obstruction to other persons using the road or as to be likely to cause danger to such persons, or

    (c) on a road, or on any land in the open air, in such a position or in such condition or in such circumstances as to appear, to an authority empowered by the regulations to remove such vehicles, to have been abandoned without lawful authority,

or which have broken down on a road.

(2) Regulations under this section—

    (a) may provide, in the case of a vehicle which may be removed from a road, for the moving of the vehicle from one position on a road to another position on that or another road;

(b) may provide for repealing byelaws dealing with the same subject-matter as the regulations, and for suspending, while the regulations remain in force, any power of making such byelaws;

...

(3) Where it appears to an authority which (apart from this subsection) is empowered to remove a vehicle in pursuance of regulations under this section that the vehicle is on land which is occupied by any person, the authority shall give him notice in the prescribed manner that they propose to remove the vehicle in pursuance of the regulations, and shall not be entitled to remove it if he objects to the proposal in the prescribed manner and within the prescribed period.

(4) Where in pursuance of regulations under this section an authority proposes to remove a vehicle which appears to the authority to be abandoned and in their opinion is in such a condition that it ought to be destroyed, then (except where they are empowered by the regulations to remove the vehicle from a road in a case falling within paragraph (a) or paragraph (b) of subsection (1) above) they shall, not less than the prescribed period before removing it, cause to be affixed to the vehicle a notice stating that they propose to remove it for destruction when that period expires.

(5) In this section "vehicle" means any vehicle, whether or not it is in a fit state for use on roads, and includes any chassis or body, with or without wheels, appearing to have formed part of such a vehicle, and any load carried by, and anything attached to, such a vehicle.

[(6) For the purposes of this section, the suspension under section 13A or 49 of this Act of the use of a parking place is a restriction imposed under this Act.]

[137]

NOTES

Commencement: 26 September 1984 (except sub-s (6)); 1 October 1991 (sub-s (6)).

Sub-ss (1)-(4) derived from the Road Traffic Regulation Act 1967, s 20(1)-(3), (7)(a)-(c), and SI 1967/1900, art 2, sch 1; sub-s (5) derived from the Road Traffic Regulation Act 1967, s 20(8), SI 1967/1900, art 2, sch 1, the Local Government Act 1972, sch 19, para 10(2), and the Local Government (Scotland) Act 1973, sch 14, para 62.

Sub-s (1): "Regulations", see the Removal and Disposal of Vehicles Regulations 1986, SI 1986 No 183 and the Removal and Disposal of Vehicles (Loading Areas) Regulations 1986, SI 1986 No 184.

Sub-s (2): para (c) and the word "and" immediately preceding it repealed by the Road Traffic Act 1991, s 83, Sch 8.

Sub-s (6): added by the Road Traffic Act 1991, s 48, Sch 4, para 32.

Extended with modifications to the Isles of Scilly by SI 1990 No 714.

100. Interim disposal of vehicles removed under s 99

(1) ...

(2) Any vehicle removed by the council of a [non-metropolitan] district in England under regulations made under section 99 of this Act shall be delivered by them to the council of the county comprising the district in accordance with such arrangements (including arrangements as to the sharing of any expenses incurred or sums received by the two councils under section 99 of this Act or this section or under section 101 or 102 of this Act) as may be agreed between the two councils or, in default of agreement, as may be determined by the Secretary of State.

(3) Any vehicle removed by a constable in pursuance of any such regulations and appearing to him to have been abandoned may be delivered by the chief

officer of the police force to which the constable belongs to a local authority, with the consent of that authority.

(4) While a vehicle is in the custody of an authority in pursuance of this section or of regulations under section 99 of this Act, other than a vehicle which in the opinion of that authority is in such a condition that it ought to be destroyed, it shall be the duty of that authority to take such steps as are reasonably necessary for the safe custody of the vehicle.

(5) in this section "local authority"—

   (a) in relation to England, means [the council of a county, metropolitan district or London borough or the Common Council of the City of London];

   (b) in relation to Wales, means the council of a county or of a district; and

   (c) in relation to Scotland, means the local highway authority,

and "vehicle" has the meaning assigned to it by section 99(5) of this Act.   **[138]**

NOTES
   Commencement: 26 September 1984.
   Sub-ss (1), (3), (4) derived from the Road Traffic Regulation Act 1967, s 20(4)-(6), and SI 1967/1900, art 2, Sch 1; sub-s (2) derived from the Road Traffic Regulation Act 1967, s 20(4A), and the Local Government Act 1972, Sch 19, para 10(1); sub-s (5) derived from the Road Traffic Regulation Act 1967, s 20(8), SI 1967/1900, art 2, Sch 1, the Local Government Act 1972, Sch 19, para 10(2), and the Local Government (Scotland) Act 1973, Sch 14, para 62.
   Sub-s (1): repealed by the Local Government Act 1985, s 102(2), Sch 17.
   Sub-ss (2), (5): amended by the Local Government Act 1985, s 8(1), Sch 5, para 4(31).
   Extended with modifications to the Isles of Scilly by SI 1990 No 714.

101. Ultimate disposal of vehicles abandoned and removable under this Act

(1) Subject to subsections (3) to *(5)* [(5A)] below, a competent authority may, in such manner as they think fit, dispose of a vehicle which appears to them to be abandoned and which has been, or could at any time be, removed in pursuance of—

   (a) an order to which this section applies, or

   (b) regulations under section 99 of this Act.

(2) This section applies to the following orders, that is to say—

   (a) any order under section 35 of this Act;

   (b) any order relating to a parking place designated under section 45 of this Act; and

   (c) any order containing a provision having effect by virtue of section 53(3) of this Act.

(3) The time at which a competent authority may dispose of a vehicle under subsection (1) above is as follows, that is to say—

   (a) in the case of a vehicle which in their opinion is in such a condition that it ought to be destroyed and on which no current licence was displayed at the time of its removal, any time after its removal;

   (b) in the case of a vehicle which in their opinion is in such condition that it ought to be destroyed and on which a current licence was so displayed, any time after the licence expires;

   (c) in any other case, any time after such steps as may be prescribed have been taken by a competent authority (or partly by one competent authority and partly by the other) to find a person appearing to the authority taking such steps to be the owner of the vehicle and either—

      (i) they have failed to find such a person, or

      (ii) he has failed to comply with a notice served on him in the prescribed manner by a competent authority requiring him to remove the vehicle from their custody within the prescribed period.

but, in a case where it appears to the authority proposing to dispose of the vehicle that a licence is in force in respect of the vehicle, not a time earlier than the expiry of the licence.

(4) If, before a vehicle [found outside Greater London] is disposed of by an authority in pursuance of subsections (1) to (3) above, the vehicle is claimed by a person who satisfies the authority that he is its owner and pays such sums in respect of its removal and storage as may be prescribed to the authority entitled to those sums, the authority shall permit him to remove the vehicle from their custody within such period as may be prescribed.

[(4A) If, before a vehicle found in Greater London is disposed of by an authority in pursuance of subsections (1) to (3) above, the vehicle is claimed by a person who satisfies the authority that he is its owner and pays—

    (a) any penalty charge payable in respect of the parking of the vehicle in the place from which it was removed; and

    (b) such sums in respect of the removal and storage of the vehicle—

      (i) as the authority may require; or

      (ii) in the case of sums payable to a competent authority which is not a local authority, as may be prescribed,

the authority shall permit him to remove the vehicle from their custody within such period as they may specify or, where paragraph (b)(ii) applies, as may be prescribed.]

(5) If, before the end of the period of one year beginning with the date on which a vehicle [found outside Greater London] is sold by an authority in pursuance of this section, any person satisfies that authority that at the time of the sale he was the owner of the vehicle, that authority shall pay him any sum by which the proceeds of sale exceed the aggregate of such sums in respect of the removal, storage and disposal of the vehicle as may be prescribed.

[(5A) If, before the end of the period of one year beginning with the date on which a vehicle found in Greater London is sold by an authority in pursuance of this section, any person satisfies that authority that at the time of the sale he was the owner of the vehicle, that authority shall pay him any sum by which the proceeds of sale exceed the aggregate of—

    (a) any penalty charge payable in respect of the parking of the vehicle in the place from which it was removed; and

    (b) such sums in respect of the removal, storage and disposal of the vehicle—

      (i) as the authority may require; or

      (ii) in the case of sums payable to a competent authority which is not a local authority, as may be prescribed.]

(6) If in the case of any vehicle it appears to the authority in question that more than one person is or was its owner at the relevant time, such one of them as the authority think fit shall be treated as its owner for the purposes of subsections (4) *and (5)* [to (5A)] above.

(7) The Secretary of State may by regulations require an authority by whom

a vehicle is disposed of in pursuance of this section to give such information relating to the disposal as may be prescribed to such persons as may be prescribed.

(8) In this section—

"competent authority", in relation to a vehicle, means—

(a) the chief officer of the police force in whose area is the place from which the vehicle has been removed or could at any time be removed, or

(b) the local authority in whose area that place is or to whom the vehicle has been delivered by the chief officer of a police force;

"licence", in relation to a vehicle, means a licence issued for the vehicle under the Vehicles (Excise) Act 1971;

"owner", in relation to a vehicle which is the subject of a hiring agreement or hire-purchase agreement, includes the person entitled to possession of the vehicle under the agreement; and

"local authority" has the meaning assigned to it by section 100(5) and "vehicle" has the meaning assigned to it by section 99(5) of this Act.   **[139]**

NOTES
Commencement: 26 September 1984.
This section derived from the Road Traffic Regulation Act 1967, s 53(1)-(5), and SI 1967/1900, art 2, Sch 1.
Sub-s (1): reference in square brackets prospectively substituted by the Road Traffic Act 1991, s 67(1), (2), as from a day to be appointed.
Sub-s (4): words in square brackets prospectively inserted by the Road Traffic Act 1991, s 67(1), (3), as from a day to be appointed.
Sub-s (4A): prospectively inserted by the Road Traffic Act 1991, s 67(1), (4), as from a day to be appointed.
Sub-s (5): words in square brackets prospectively inserted by the Road Traffic Act 1991, s 67(1), (5), as from a day to be appointed.
Sub-s (5A): prospectively inserted by the Road Traffic Act 1991, s 67(1), (6), as from a day to be appointed.
Sub-s (6): words in square brackets prospectively substituted by the Road Traffic Act 1991, s 67(1), (7), as from a day to be appointed.
Extended with modifications to the Isles of Scilly by SI 1990 No 714.

102. Charges for removal, storage and disposal of vehicles

(1) The provisions of this section shall have effect where a vehicle—

(a) is removed from a parking place in pursuance of an order to which section 101 of this Act applies, or

(b) is removed from a road, or from land in the open air, in pursuance of regulations under section 99 of this Act.

(2) In any such case—

(a) the appropriate authority shall be entitled to recover from any person responsible such charges as may be prescribed in respect of the removal of the vehicle;

(b) the chief officer of a police force or a local authority [other than a London authority] in whose custody any such vehicle is during any period shall be entitled to recover from any person responsible charges ascertained by reference to a prescribed scale in respect of that period; and

(c) the chief officer of a police force or a local authority [other than a London authority] who dispose of any such vehicle in pursuance of section 101 of this Act shall be entitled to recover from any person responsible charges determined in the prescribed manner in respect of its disposal.

[and

(d) a London authority shall be entitled to recover from any person responsible, such charges in respect of the removal, storage and disposal of a vehicle removed from a parking place designated under section 6, 9 or 45 of this Act or otherwise provided or controlled by that authority as they may require.]

(3) Any sum recoverable by virtue of this section shall, in England or Wales, be recoverable as a simple contract debt in any court of competent jurisdiction or, in the case of a sum not exceeding £20, summarily as a civil debt.

(4) Without prejudice to subsection (3) above, where by virtue of paragraph (a) or (b) of subsection (2) above any sum is recoverable in respect of a vehicle by the chief officer of a police force or a local authority in whose custody the vehicle is, the chief officer or local authority shall be entitled to retain custody of it until that sum has been paid.

(5) The court by which a person is convicted of an offence under section 2(1) of the Refuse Disposal (Amenity) Act 1978 in respect of a motor vehicle may, on the application of an authority and in addition to any other order made by the court in relation to that person, order him to pay to the authority any sum which, in the opinion of the court, the authority are entitled to recover from him under this section in respect of the vehicle.

(6) For the purposes of this section a vehicle removed, as mentioned in subsection (1) above, [by the council of a non-metropolitan district] in England shall be treated as in the custody of the council of the county comprising that district while it is in the custody of the district council by whom it was so removed.

(7) Any sum recovered under this section by the chief officer of a police force shall be paid into the police fund.

(8) In this section—

"appropriate authority"—

(a) in relation to a vehicle removed by a constable or a person acting in aid of a police force, means the chief officer of the police force to which the constable belongs or in whose aid that person was acting, and

[(b) in relation to a vehicle removed (by a person other than a constable or person acting in aid of a police force) from a place outside Greater London, which is a parking place provided or controlled by a local authority, or from a place (not being a parking place) on a road or land in the open air, means the local authority in whose area that place is,]

and for the purposes of paragraph (b) above a parking place provided under a letting or arrangements made by a local authority in pursuance of section 33(4) of this Act shall be treated as provided by the local authority;

"person responsible", in relation to a vehicle, means—

(a) the owner of the vehicle at the time when it was put in the place from which it was removed as mentioned in subsection (1) above, unless he shows that he was not concerned in, and did not know of, its being put there;

(b) any person by whom the vehicle was put in that place;

(c) any person convicted of an offence under section 2(1) of the Refuse Disposal (Amenity) Act 1978 in consequence of the putting of the vehicle in that place; and

"local authority" has the meaning assigned to it by section 100(5) and "vehicle" has the meaning assigned to it by section 99(5) of this Act.

[and

"London authority" means any council of a London borough or the Common Council of the City of London.]

[(9) For the purposes of—

(a) subsection (2)(d) above, and

(b) paragraph (b) in the definition of "appropriate authority" in subsection (8) above,

a parking place provided under a letting or arrangements made by a local authority in pursuance of section 33(4) of this Act shall be treated as provided by that authority.]   **[140]**

NOTES

Commencement: 26 September 1984.

Sub-ss (1)–(3) derived from the Road Traffic Regulation Act 1967, s 52(1), (2), (7), and SI 1967/1900, art 2, Sch 1; sub-s (4) derived from the Road Traffic Regulation Act 1967, s 52(2A), and the Road Traffic Act 1974, s 19; sub-ss (5), (8) derived from the Road Traffic Regulation Act 1967, s 52(2), (3), SI 1967/1900, art 2, Sch 1, and the Refuse Disposal (Amenity) Act 1978, s 12(4); sub-ss (6), (7) derived from the Road Traffic Regulation Act 1967, s 52(4), (5), SI 1967/1900, art 2, Sch 1, and the Local Government Act 1972, Sch 19, para 23.

Sub-s (2): paras (b), (c) prospectively amended, para (d) prospectively added by the Road Traffic Act 1991, s 68(1), (2), as from a day to be appointed.

Sub-s (8): words in square brackets prospectively substituted or added, and words in italics prospectively repealed by the Road Traffic Act 1991, ss 68(1), (3), 83, Sch 8, as from a day to be appointed.

Sub-s (9): prospectively added by the Road Traffic Act 1991, s 68(1), (4), as from a day to be appointed.

Sub-s (6): amended by the Local Government Act 1985, s 8, Sch 5, para 4.

Extended with modifications to the Isles of Scilly by SI 1990 No 714.

103. Supplementary provisions as to removal of vehicles

(1) The Secretary of State may by regulations provide that, in relation to any vehicle which is or was in any part of a loading area while the parking of it in that area is or was prohibited by virtue of section 61 of this Act, sections 99 to 102 of this Act shall have effect with such additions, omissions and amendments as are prescribed by the regulations.

(2) In this section "loading area" has the same meaning as in section 61 of this Act.

[(3) Regulations made under sections 99 to 102 of this Act may make different provision for different cases or classes of case or in respect of different areas.]   **[141]**

NOTES

Commencement: 26 September 1984.

Sub-ss (1), (2) derived from the Local Government (Miscellaneous Provisions) Act 1976, s 37(1)(c), (7); sub-s (3) derived from the Road Traffic Regulation Act 1967, ss 20(7)(d), 52(6), 53(6), and SI 1967/1900, art 2, Sch 1.

Sub-s (1): "regulations", see the Removal and Disposal of Vehicles (Loading Areas) Regulations 1986, SI 1986 No 184.
Sub-s (3): substituted by the Road Traffic Act 1991, s 48, Sch 4, para 33.
Extended with modifications to the Isles of Scilly by SI 1990 No 714.

104. Immobilisation of vehicles illegally parked

(1) Subject to sections 105 and 106 of this Act, where a constable finds on a road a vehicle which has been permitted to remain at rest there in contravention of any prohibition or restriction imposed by or under any enactment, he may—

    (a) fix an immobilisation device to the vehicle while it remains in the place in which he finds it; or

    (b) move it from that place to another place on the same or another road and fix an immobilisation device to it in that other place;

or authorise another person to take under his direction any action he could himself take by virtue of paragraph (a) or (b) above.

(2) On any occasion when an immobilisation device is fixed to a vehicle in accordance with this section the constable or other person fixing the device shall also affix to the vehicle a notice—

    (a) indicating that such a device has been fixed to the vehicle and warning that no attempt should be made to drive it or otherwise put it in motion until it has been released from that device;

    (b) specifying the steps to be taken in order to secure its release; and

    (c) giving such other information as may be prescribed.

(3) A vehicle to which an immobilisation device has been fixed in accordance with this section may only be released from that device by or under the direction of a [person authorised to give such a direction by the chief officer of police within whose area the vehicle in question was found].

(4) Subject to subsection (3) above, a vehicle to which an immobilisation device has been fixed in accordance with this section shall be released from that device on payment in any manner specified in the notice affixed to the vehicle under subsection (2) above of such charge in respect of the release as may be prescribed.

(5) A notice affixed to a vehicle under this section shall not be removed or interfered with except by or under the authority of the person in charge of the vehicle or the person by whom it was put in the place where it was found by the constable; and any person contravening this subsection shall be guilty of an offence.

(6) Any person who, without being authorised to do so in accordance with this section, removes or attempts to remove an immobilisation device fixed to a vehicle in accordance with this section shall be guilty of an offence.

(7) Where a vehicle is moved in accordance with this section before an immobilisation device is fixed to it, any power of removal under regulations for the time being in force under section 99 of this Act which was exercisable in relation to that vehicle immediately before it was so moved shall continue to be exercisable in relation to that vehicle while it remains in the place to which it was so moved.

(8) In relation to any vehicle which is removed in pursuance of any such regulations or under section 3 of the Refuse Disposal (Amenity) Act 1978 (duty of local authority to remove abandoned vehicles) from a place to which it was moved in accordance with this section, references in the definition of "person

responsible" in section 102(8) of this Act and section 5 of the said Act of 1978 mentioned above (recovery from person responsible of charges and expenses in respect of vehicles removed) to the place from which the vehicle was removed shall be read as references to the place in which it was immediately before it was moved in accordance with this section.

(9) In this section "immobilisation device" means any device or appliance designed or adapted to be fixed to a vehicle for the purpose of preventing it from being driven or otherwise put in motion, being a device or appliance of a type approved by the Secretary of State for use for that purpose in accordance with this section.

(10) . . .

(11) Any sum received by virtue of subsection (4) above shall be paid into the police fund.

(12) Regulations under subsection (2) or (4) above may make different provision for different cases [or classes of case or in respect of different areas].

[(12A) For the purposes of this section, the suspension under section 13A or 49 of this Act of the use of a parking place is a restriction imposed under this Act.]   **[142]**

NOTES
    Commencement: 26 September 1984.
    This section derived from the Transport Act 1982, ss 53(1)-(10), 73(2), (5)(a).
    See the Vehicles (Charges for Release from Immobilisation Devices) Regulations 1989, SI 1989 No 745.
    Sub-s (3): amended by the Road Traffic Act 1991, s 48, Sch 4, para 34.
    Sub-s (10): repealed by the Road Traffic Act 1991, s 83, Sch 8.
    Sub-s (12): words in square brackets added by the Road Traffic Act 1991, s 48, Sch 4, para 34.
    Sub-s (12A): added by the Road Traffic Act 1991, s 48, Sch 4, para 35.
    Extended with modifications to the Isles of Scilly by SI 1990 No 714.

105. Exemptions from s 104

(1) Subject to the following provisions of this section, section 104(1) of this Act shall not apply in relation to a vehicle found by a constable in the circumstances mentioned in that subsection if either—

    (a) a current disabled person's badge is displayed on the vehicle; or
    (b) the vehicle is in a meter bay within a parking place designated by a designation order.

(2) The exemption under subsection (1)(b) above shall not apply in the case of any vehicle [found otherwise than in Greater London] if—

    (a) the meter bay in which it was found was not authorised for use as such at the time when it was left there (referred to below in this section as the time of parking); or
    (b) an initial charge was not duly paid at the time of parking; or
    (c) there has been since that time any contravention in relation to the relevant parking meter of any provision made by virtue of section 46(2)(c) of this Act; or
    (d) more than two hours have elapsed since the end of any period for which an initial charge was duly paid at the time of parking or (as the case may be) since the end of any unexpired time in respect of another vehicle available on the relevant parking meter at the time of parking.

[(2A) The exemption under subsection (1)(b) above shall not apply in the case of any vehicle found in Greater London if the meter bay in which it was found was not authorised for use as such at the time when it was left there.]

(3) For the purposes of *subsection (2)(a)* [subsections (2)(a) and (2A)] above, a meter bay in a parking place designated by a designation order is not authorised for use as such at any time when—

    (a) by virtue of section 49(1)(a) of this Act the parking place is treated for the purposes of sections 46 and 47 of this Act as if it were not designated by that order; or

    (b) the use of the parking place or of any part of it that consists of or includes that particular meter bay is suspended . . .

(4) In relation to any vehicle found in a meter bay within a parking place designated by a designation order, references in subsection (2) above to an initial charge are references to an initial charge payable in respect of that vehicle under section 45 or 50 of this Act.

(5) In any case where section 104(1) of this Act would apply in relation to a vehicle but for subsection (1)(a) above, the person guilty of contravening the prohibition or restriction mentioned in section 104(1) is also guilty of an offence under this subsection if the conditions mentioned in subsection (6) below are met.

(6) Those conditons are that at the time when the contravention occurred—

    (a) the vehicle was not being used [in accordance with regulations under] section 21 of the Chronically Sick and Disabled Persons Act 1970 (badges for display on motor vehicles used by disabled persons); and

    (b) he was not using the vehicle in circumstances falling within section [117(1)(b)] of this Act.

(7) In this section, "meter bay" means a parking space equipped with a parking meter; and the references in subsection (2) above to the relevant parking meter are references to the parking meter relating to the meter bay in which the vehicle in question was found.   **[143–144]**

NOTES

   Commencement: 26 September 1984.

   This section derived from the Transport Act 1982, s 54(1)-(6), (8).

   Sub-s (2): words in square brackets prospectively inserted by the Road Traffic Act 1991, s 81, Sch 7, para 6, as from a day to be appointed.

   Sub-s (2A): prospectively inserted by the Road Traffic Act 1991, s 81, Sch 7, para 6, as from a day to be appointed.

   Sub-s (3): words in square brackets prospectively substituted by the Road Traffic Act 1991, s 81, Sch 7, para 6, as from a day to be appointed; words omitted repealed by s 83 of, Sch 8 to, the 1991 Act.

   Sub-s (6): amended by the Road Traffic Act 1991, s 48, Sch 4, para 36.

   Extended with modifications to the Isles of Scilly by SI 1990 No 714.

Enforcement of excess parking charges

107. Liability of vehicle owner in respect of excess parking charge

(1) This section applies where—

    (a) an excess charge has been incurred in pursuance of an order under sections 45 and 46 of this Act;

    (b) notice of the incurring of the excess charge has been given or affixed as provided in the order; and

(c) the excess charge has not been duly paid in accordance with the order;

and in the following provisions of this Part of this Act "the excess charge offence" means the offence under section 47 of this Act of failing duly to pay the excess charge.

(2) Subject to the following provisions of this section—

(a) for the purposes of the institution of proceedings in respect of the excess charge offence against any person as being the owner of the vehicle at the relevant time, and

(b) in any proceedings in respect of the excess charge offence brought against any person as being the owner of the vehicle at the relevant time,

it shall be conclusively presumed (notwithstanding that that person may not be an individual) that he was the driver of the vehicle at that time and, accordingly, that acts or omissions of the driver of the vehicle at that time were his acts or omissions.

(3) Subsection (2) above shall not apply in relation to any person unless, within the period of 6 months beginning on the day on which the notice of the incurring of the excess charge was given or affixed as mentioned in subsection (1)(b) above, a notice under section 108 of this Act has been served on him—

(a) by or on behalf of the authority which is the local authority for the purposes of sections 45 and 46 of this Act in relation to the parking place concerned, or

(b) by or on behalf of the chief officer of police.

(4) If the person on whom a notice under section 108 of this Act is served in accordance with subsection (3) above was not the owner of the vehicle at the relevant time, subsection (2) above shall not apply in relation to him if he furnishes a statutory statement of ownership to that effect in compliance with the notice.

(5) The presumption in subsection (2) above shall not apply in any proceedings brought against any person as being the owner of the vehicle at the relevant time if, in those proceedings, it is proved—

(a) that at the relevant time the vehicle was in the possession of some other person without the consent of the accused, or

(b) that the accused was not the owner of the vehicle at the relevant time and that he has a reasonable excuse for failing to comply with the notice under section 108 of this Act served on him in accordance with subsection (3) above.   **[145]**

NOTES

Commencement: 26 September 1984.
This section derived from the Road Traffic Act 1974, s 2(1)-(5).
Extended with modifications to the Isles of Scilly by SI 1990 No 714.

108. Notice in respect of excess parking charge

(1) A notice under this section shall be in the prescribed form, shall give particulars of the excess charge and shall provide that, unless the excess charge is paid before the expiry of the appropriate period, the person on whom the notice is served—

(a) is required, before the expiry of that period, to furnish to the authority or chief officer of police by or on behalf of whom the notice was served a statutory statement of ownership (as defined in Part I of Schedule 8 to this Act), and

(b) is invited, before the expiry of that period, to furnish to that authority or chief officer of police a statutory statement of facts (as defined in Part II of that Schedule).

(2) If, in any case where—

(a) a notice under this section has been served on any person, and

(b) the excess charge specified in the notice is not paid within the appropriate period,

the person so served fails without reasonable excuse to comply with the notice by furnishing a statutory statement of ownership he shall be guilty of an offence.

(3) If, in compliance with or in response to a notice under this section any person furnishes a statement which is false in a material particular, and does so recklessly or knowing it to be false in that particular, he shall be guilty of an offence.

(4) Where a notice under this section has been served on any person in respect of any excess charge—

(a) payment of the charge by any person before the date on which proceedings are begun for the excess charge offence, or, as the case may be, for an offence under subsection (2) above in respect of a failure to comply with the notice, shall discharge the liability of that or any other person (under this or any other enactment) for the excess charge offence or, as the case may be, for the offence under subsection (2) above;

(b) conviction of any person of the excess charge offence shall discharge the liability of any other person (under this or any other enactment) for that offence and the liability of any person for an offence under subsection (2) above in respect of a failure to comply with the notice; and

(c) conviction of the person so served of an offence under subsection (2) above in respect of a failure to comply with the notice shall discharge the liability of any person for the excess charge offence;

but, except as provided by this subsection, nothing in section 107 of this Act or this section shall affect the liability of any person for the excess charge offence.

[146]

NOTES
Commencement: 26 September 1984.
This section derived from the Road Traffic Act 1974, s 2(6)-(9).
Extended with modifications to the Isles of Scilly by SI 1990 No 714.

109. Modifications of ss 107 and 108 in relation to hired vehicles

(1) This section shall apply where—

(a) a notice under section 108 of this Act has been served on a vehicle-hire firm, and

(b) at the relevant time the vehicle in respect of which the notice was served was let to another person by the vehicle-hire firm under a hiring agreement to which this section applies.

(2) Where this section applies, it shall be a sufficient compliance with the notice served on the vehicle-hire firm if the firm furnishes to the chief officer of police or local authority by or on behalf of whom the notice was served a

statement in the prescribed form, signed by or on behalf of the vehicle-hire firm, stating that at the relevant time the vehicle concerned was hired under a hiring agreement to which this section applies, together with—

   (a) a copy of that hiring agreement, and

   (b) a copy of a statement of liability in the prescribed form, signed by the hirer under that hiring agreement;

and accordingly, in relation to the vehicle-hire firm on whom the notice was served, the reference in section 108(2) of this Act to a statutory statement of ownership shall be construed as a reference to a statement under this subsection together with the documents specified in paragraphs (a) and (b) above.

(3) If, in a case where this section applies, the vehicle-hire firm has complied with the notice served on the firm by furnishing the statement and copies of the documents specified in subsection (2) above, then sections 107 and 108 of this Act shall have effect as if in those provisions—

   (a) any reference to the owner of the vehicle were a reference to the hirer under the hiring agreement, and

   (b) any reference to a statutory statement of ownership were a reference to a statutory statement of hiring.

(4) Where, in compliance with a notice under section 108 of this Act, a vehicle-hire firm has furnished copies of a hiring agreement and statement of liability as mentioned in subsection (2) above, a person authorised in that behalf by the chief officer of police or local authority to whom the documents are furnished may, at any reasonable time within 6 months after service of that notice, and on production of his authority, require the production by the firm of the originals of those documents; and if, without reasonable excuse, a vehicle-hire firm fails to produce the original of a document when required to do so under this subsection, the firm shall be treated as not having complied with the notice under section 108 of this Act.

(5) This section applies to a hiring agreement, under the terms of which the vehicle concerned is let to the hirer for a fixed period of less than 6 months (whether or not that period is capable of extension by agreement between the parties or otherwise); and any reference in this section to the currency of the hiring agreement includes a reference to any period during which, with the consent of the vehicle-hire firm, the hirer continues in possession of the vehicle as hirer, after the expiry of the fixed period specified in the agreement, but otherwise on terms and conditions specified in it.

(6) In this section "statement of liability" means a statement made by the hirer under a hiring agreement to which this section applies to the effect that the hirer acknowledges that he will be liable, as the owner of the vehicle, in respect of any excess charge which, during the currency of the hiring agreement, may be incurred with respect to the vehicle in pursuance of an order under sections 45 and 46 of this Act.

(7) In this section—

   "hiring agreement" refers only to an agreement which contains such particulars as may be prescribed and does not include a hire-purchase agreement within the meaning of the Consumer Credit Act 1974, and

   "vehicle-hire firm" means any person engaged in hiring vehicles in the course of a business.   **[147]**

NOTES
Commencement: 26 September 1984.
This section derived from the Road Traffic Act 1974, s 3.
Extended with modifications to the Isles of Scilly by SI 1990 No 714.
Sub-s (7): "prescribed", see the Road Traffic (Owner Liability) Regulations 1975, SI 1975 No 324.

110. Time for bringing, and evidence in, proceedings for certain offences

(1) Proceedings in England or Wales for an offence under section 108(3) of this Act may be brought within a period of six months from the date on which evidence sufficient in the opinion of the prosecutor to warrant the proceedings came to his knowledge; but no such proceedings shall be brought by virtue of this section more than 3 years after the commission of the offence.

(2) Proceedings in Scotland for an offence to which subsection (1) above applies shall not be commenced after the expiry of the period of 3 years from the commission of the offence; but, subject to the foregoing limitation, and notwithstanding anything in section 331 of the Criminal Procedure (Scotland) Act 1975, any such proceedings may be commenced at any time within 6 months after the date on which evidence sufficient in the opinion of the Lord Advocate to justify the proceedings came to his knowledge or, where such evidence was reported to him by a local authority, within 6 months after the date on which it came to their knowledge, and subsection (3) of the said section 331 shall apply for the purposes of this subsection as it applies for the purposes of that section.

(3) For the purposes of subsections (1) and (2) above a certificate signed by or on behalf of the prosecutor or, as the case may be, the Lord Advocate or the local authority, and stating the date on which evidence such as is mentioned in the subsection in question came to his or their knowledge, shall be conclusive evidence of that fact; and a certificate stating that matter and purporting to be so signed shall be deemed to be so signed unless the contrary is proved.

(4) Where any person is charged with the offence of failing to pay an excess charge, and the prosecutor produces to the court any of the statutory statements in Schedule 8 to this Act or a copy of a statement of liability (within the meaning of section 109 of this Act) purporting—

    (a) to have been furnished in compliance with or in response to a notice under section 108 of this Act, and

    (b) to have been signed by the accused,

the statement shall be presumed, unless the contrary is proved, to have been signed by the accused and shall be evidence (and, in Scotland, sufficient evidence) in the proceedings of any facts stated in it tending to show that the accused was the owner, the hirer or the driver of the vehicle concerned at a particular time.   **[148]**

NOTES
Commencement: 26 September 1984.
This section derived from the Road Traffic Act 1974, s 4.
Extended with modifications to the Isles of Scilly by SI 1990 No 714.

111. Supplementary provisions as to excess charges

(1) The provisions of Schedule 8 to this Act shall have effect for the purposes of sections 107 to 109 of this Act (in this section referred to as "the specified sections").

(2) In the specified sections—

"appropriate period", in relation to a notice under section 108 of this Act, means the period of 14 days from the date on which the notice is served, or such longer period as may be specified in the notice or as may be allowed by the chief officer of police or authority by or on behalf of whom the notice is served;

"driver", in relation to an excess charge and in relation to an offence of failing duly to pay such a charge, means the person driving the vehicle at the time when it is alleged to have been left in the parking place concerned;

"relevant time", in relation to an excess charge, means the time when the vehicle was left in the parking place concerned, notwithstanding that the period in respect of which the excess charge was incurred did not begin at that time.

(3) For the purposes of the specified sections the owner of a vehicle shall be taken to be the person by whom the vehicle is kept; and for the purpose of determining, in the course of any proceedings brought by virtue of the specified sections, who was the owner of the vehicle at any time, it shall be presumed that the owner was the person who was the registered keeper of the vehicle at that time.

(4) Notwithstanding the presumption in subsection (3) above, it shall be open to the defence in any proceedings to prove that the person who was the registered keeper of a vehicle at a particular time was not the person by whom the vehicle was kept at that time, and it shall be open to the prosecution to prove that the vehicle was kept by some other person at that time.

(5) A notice under section 108 of this Act may be served on any person—

    (a) by delivering it to him or by leaving it at his proper address, or

    (b) by sending it to him by post;

and, where the person on whom such a notice is to be served is a body corporate, it shall be duly served if it is served on the secretary or clerk of that body.

(6) For the purposes of subsection (5) above and of section 7 of the Interpretation Act 1978 (references to service by post) in its application to that subsection, the proper address of any person on whom such a notice is to be served—

    (a) shall, in the case of the secretary or clerk of a body corporate, be that of the registered or principal office of that body or the registered address of the person who is the registered keeper of the vehicle concerned at the time of service, and

    (b) shall in any other case be the last known address of the person to be served.

(7) References in this section to the person who was or is the registered keeper of a vehicle at any time are references to the person in whose name the vehicle was or is at that time registered under the Vehicles (Excise) Act 1971; and, in relation to any such person the reference in subsection (6)(a) above to that person's registered address is a reference to the address recorded in the record kept under that Act with respect to that vehicle as being that person's address.

(8) For the purposes of sections 1(2) and 2(1) of the Magistrates' Courts Act 1980 (power to issue summons or warrant and jurisdiction to try offences), any offence under subsection (2) of section 108 of this Act shall be treated as committed at any address which at the time of service of the notice under that

section to which the offence relates was the accused's proper address (in accordance with subsection (6) above) for the service of any such notice as well as at the address to which any statutory statement furnished in response to that notice is required to be returned in accordance with the notice. **[149]**

NOTES
Commencement: 26 September 1984.
This section derived from the Road Traffic Act 1974, s 5, and the Transport Act 1982, sch 5, para 18.
Extended with modifications to the Isles of Scilly by SI 1990 No 714.

PART IX

FURTHER PROVISIONS AS TO ENFORCEMENT

General Provisions

112. Information as to identity of driver or rider

(1) This section applies to any offence under any of the foregoing provisions of this Act except—

> (a) sections 43, 52, 88(7), 104, 105 and 108;
> (b) the provisions of subsection (2) or (3) of section 108 as modified by subsections (2) and (3) of section 109; and
> (c) section [35A(5)] in its application to England and Wales.

(2) Where the driver of a vehicle is alleged to be guilty of an offence to which this section applies—

> (a) the person keeping the vehicle shall give such information as to the identity of the driver as he may be required to give—
>> (i) by or on behalf of a chief officer of police, or
>> (ii) in the case of an offence under section [35A(1)] or against section 47 of this Act, by or on behalf of a chief officer of police or, in writing, by or on behalf of the local authority for the parking place in question; and
> (b) any other person shall, if required as mentioned in paragraph (a) above, give any information which it is in his power to give and which may lead to the identification of the driver.

(3) In subsection (2) above, references to the driver of a vehicle include references to the person riding a bicycle or tricycle (not being a motor vehicle); and—

> (a) ...
> (b) in relation to an offence under section 61(5) of this Act, subsection (2)(a) above shall have effect as if, for sub-paragraphs (i) and (ii), there were substituted the words "by a notice in writing given to him by a local authority in whose area the loading area in question is situated",

and in subsection (2)(a) above, as modified by paragraph (b) of this subsection, "local authority" means any of the following, that is to say, a county council, ... a district council, a London borough council and the Common Council of the City of London.

(4) Except as provided by subsection (5) below, a person who fails to comply with the requirements of subsection (2)(a) above shall be guilty of an offence unless he shows to the satisfaction of the court that he did not know, and could not with reasonable diligence have ascertained, who was the driver of the

vehicle or, as the case may be, the rider of the bicycle or tricycle; and a person who fails to comply with the requirements of subsection (2)(b) above shall be guilty of an offence.

(5) As regards Scotland, subsection (4) above shall not apply where the offence of which the driver of the vehicle is alleged to be guilty is an offence under section 61(5) of this Act.   **[150]**

NOTES

Commencement: 26 September 1984.

Sub-ss (1), (4) derived from the Road Traffic Regulation Act 1967, s 85(1), (3); sub-s (2) derived from the Road Traffic Regulation Act 1967, s 85(2), the Transport Act 1968, s 127(8), and the Vehicle and Driving Licences Act 1969, s 16(6); sub-s (3) derived from the Road Traffic Regulation Act 1967, s 85(2), and the Local Government (Miscellaneous Provisions) Act 1976, ss 37(6), 44(1).

Sub-ss (1), (2): figures in square brackets substituted by the Parking Act 1989, s 4, Schedule, para 6.

Sub-s (3): words omitted repealed by the Local Government Act 1985, s 102(2), Sch 17.

Extended with modifications to the Isles of Scilly by SI 1990 No 714.

113, 114. (*Repealed by the Road Traffic (Consequential Provisions) Act 1988, s 3(1), Sch 1, Part I.*)

115. Mishandling of parking documents and related offences

[(1) A person shall be guilty of an offence who, with intent to deceive—

    (a) uses, or lends to, or allows to be used by, any other person,—

        (i) any parking device or apparatus designed to be used in connection with parking devices;

        (ii) any ticket isued by a parking meter, parking device or apparatus designed to be used in connection with parking devices;

        (iii) any authorisation by way of such a certificate, other means of identification or device as is referred to in any of sections 4(2), 4(3), 7(2) and 7(3) of this Act; or

        (iv) any such permit or token as is referred to in section 46(2)(i) of this Act;

    (b) makes or has in his possession anything so closely resembling any such thing as is mentioned in paragraph (a) above as to be calculated to deceive; or

    (c) in Scotland, forges or alters any such thing as is mentioned in that paragraph.]

(2) A person who knowingly makes a false statement for the purpose of procuring the grant or issue to himself or any other person of any such authorisation as is mentioned in subsection (1) above shall be guilty of an offence.

[(2A) In any proceedings for an offence under this section it shall be assumed, unless the contrary is shown, that any such device as is referred to in section 35(3B) or, as the case may be, section 51(4) of this Act, or any apparatus designed to be used in connection with parking devices, is of a type and design approved by the Secretary of State.]

(3) Summary proceedings in Scotland for an offence under this section may be brought—

    (a) within a period of 6 months from the date of the commission of the alleged offence, or

(b) within a period which exceeds neither 3 months from the date in which it came to the knowledge of the procurator fiscal that the offence had been committed nor one year from the date of the commission of the offence,

whichever period is the longer.   **[151]**

NOTES
  Commencement: 16 May 1990 (sub-s (2A)); 8 September 1986 (sub-s (1)); 26 September 1984 (remainder).
  Sub-ss (1), (2) derived from the Road Traffic Regulation Act 1967, s 86(1), (3), and the Transport Act 1968, s 127(9), (10); sub-s (3) derived from the Road Traffic Regulation Act 1967, s 91.
  Sub-s (1): substituted by the Road Traffic Regulation (Parking) Act 1986, s 2(2).
  Sub-s (2A): added by the Parking Act 1989, s 4, Schedule, para 7.
  Extended with modifications to the Isles of Scilly by SI 1990 No 714.

116. Provisions supplementary to s 115

(1) If any person authorised in that behalf by or under a designation order has reasonable cause to believe that a document or article carried on a vehicle, or by the driver or person in charge of a vehicle, is a document or article in relation to which an offence has been committed under subsection (1) of section 115 of this Act (so far as that subsection relates to such authorisations as are referred to in it) or under subsection (2) of that section, he may detain that document or article, and may for that purpose require the driver or person in charge of the vehicle to deliver up the document or article; and if the driver or person in charge of the vehicle fails to comply with that requirement, he shall be guilty of an offence.

(2) When a document or article has been detained under subsection (1) above and—

(a) at any time after the expiry of 6 months from the date when that detention began no person has been charged since that date with an offence in relation to the document or article under subsection (1) or (2) of section 115 of this Act, and

(b) the document or article has not been returned to the person to whom the authorisation in question was issued or to the person who at the date was the driver or person in charge of the vehicle,

then, on an application made for the purpose to a magistrates' court (or, in Scotland, on a summary application made for the purpose to the sheriff court), the court shall make such order respecting disposal of the document or article and award such costs (or, in Scotland, expenses) as the justice of the case may require.

(3) Any of the following, but no other, persons shall be entitled to make an application under subsection (2) above with respect to a document or article, that is to say—

(a) the person to whom the authorisation was issued;

(b) the person who, at the date when the detention of the document or article began, was the driver or person in charge of the vehicle; and

(c) the person for the time being having possession of the document or article.   **[152]**

NOTES
  Commencement: 26 September 1984.
  This section derived from the Road Traffic Regulation Act 1967, s 86(4), (5), and the Transport Act 1968, s 127(10).
  Extended with modifications to the Isles of Scilly by SI 1990 No 714.

117. Wrongful use of disabled person's badge

[(1) A person who at any time acts in contravention of, or fails to comply with, any provision of an order under this Act relating to the parking of motor vehicles is also guilty of an offence under this section if at that time—

    (a) there was displayed on the motor vehicle in question a badge of a form prescribed under section 21 of the Chronically Sick and Disabled Persons Act 1970, and

    (b) he was using the vehicle in circumstances where a disabled person's concession would be available to a disabled person's vehicle,

but he shall not be guilty of an offence under this section if the badge was issued under that section and displayed in accordance with regulations made under it.]

  (3) In this section—

. . .

"disabled person's concession" means—

    (a) an exemption from an order under this Act given by reference to disabled persons' vehicles; or

    (b) a provision made in any order under this Act for the use of a parking place by disabled persons' vehicles.   **[153]**

NOTES

Commencement: 26 September 1984.

This section derived from the Road Traffic Regulation Act 1967, s 86A, and the Disabled Persons Act 1981, s 2.

Sub-s (1): substituted for original sub-ss (1), (2) by the Road Traffic Act 1991, s 35(6).

Sub-s (3): definition omitted repealed by the Road Traffic Act 1991, s 83, Sch 8.

Extended with modifications to the Isles of Scilly by SI 1990 No 714.

118. (*Repealed by the Road Traffic (Consequential Provisions) Act 1988, s 3(1), Sch 1, Part I.*)

Special Provisions relating to Scotland

119. Aiding and abetting

As respects Scotland, a person who aids, abets, counsels, procures or incites any other person to commit an offence against the provisions of this Act or any regulations made under it shall be guilty of an offence and shall be liable on conviction to the same punishment as might be imposed on conviction of the first-mentioned offence.   **[154]**

NOTES

Commencement: 26 September 1984.

This section derived from the Road Traffic Regulation Act 1967, s 88.

Extended with modifications to the Isles of Scilly by SI 1990 No 714.

PART X

GENERAL AND SUPPLEMENTARY PROVISIONS

130. Application of Act to Crown

(1) Subject to the provisions of this section and section 132 of this Act, the provisions of this Act specified in subsection (2) below shall apply to vehicles and persons in the public service of the Crown.

(2) The provisions referred to in subsection (1) above are

(a) sections 1 to 5, 9 to 16, 21 to 26, 38, 42, 45 to 51, 52(2) and (3), 58 to 60, 62 to 67, 69 to 71, [76 to 90], 99, 100, 104, 105, 125 and 126;
(b) except in relation to vehicles and persons in the armed forces of the Crown when on duty, sections 6 to 8; and
(c) ...

(3) In relation to vehicles used for naval, military or air force purposes, while being driven by persons for the time being subject to the orders of a member of the armed forces of the Crown, the Secretary of State may by regulations vary the provisions of any statutory provision imposing a speed limit on motor vehicles; but regulations under this subsection may provide that any variation made by the regulations shall have effect subject to such conditions as may be specified in the regulations.

(4), (5) ...   [155]

NOTES
Commencement: 26 September 1984.
    This section derived from the Road Traffic Regulation Act 1967, s 97, the Transport Act 1968, s 126(12), and the Transport Act 1982, ss 67, 72(b).
    Words omitted repealed by the Road Traffic (Consequential Provisions) Act 1988, s 3(1), Sch 1, Part I.
    Sub-s (2): words in square brackets substituted by the New Roads and Street Works Act 1991, s 168(1), Sch 8, Pt II, para 74.
    Extended with modifications to the Isles of Scilly by SI 1990 No 714.

136. Meaning of "motor vehicle" and other expressions relating to vehicles

(1) In this Act, subject to section 20 of the Chronically Sick and Disabled Persons Act 1970 (which makes special provision with respect to invalid carriages), "motor vehicle" means a mechanically propelled vehicle intended or adapted for use on roads, and "trailer" means a vehicle drawn by a motor vehicle.

(2) In this Act "motor car" means a mechanically propelled vehicle, not being a motor cycle or an invalid carriage, which is constructed itself to carry a load or passengers and of which the weight unladen—

(a) if it is constructed solely for the carriage of passengers and their effects, is adapted to carry not more than 7 passengers exclusive of the driver, and is fitted with tyres of such type as may be specified in regulations made by the Secretary of State, does not exceed 3050 kilograms;
(b) if it is constructed or adapted for use for the conveyance of goods or burden of any description, does not exceed 3050 kilograms (or 3500 kilograms if the vehicle carries a container or containers for holding, for the purposes of its propulsion, any fuel which is wholly gaseous at 17.5 degrees Celsius under a pressure of 1.013 bar or plant and materials for producing such fuel); or
(c) in a case falling within neither of the foregoing paragraphs, does not exceed 2540 kilograms.

(3) In this Act "heavy motor car" means a mechanically propelled vehicle, not being a motor car, which is constructed itself to carry a load or passengers and of which the weight unladen exceeds 2540 kilograms.

(4) In this Act (except for the purposes of section 57) "motor cycle" means

a mechanically propelled vehicle (not being an invalid carriage) with fewer than 4 wheels, of which the weight unladen does not exceed 410 kilograms.

(5) In this Act "invalid carriage" means a mechanically propelled vehicle of which the weight unladen does not exceed 254 kilograms and which is specially designed and constructed, and not merely adapted, for the use of a person suffering from some physical defect or disability and is used solely by such a person.

(6) In this Act "motor tractor" means a mechanically propelled vehicle which is not constructed itself to carry a load, other than excepted articles, and of which the weight unladen does not exceed 7370 kilograms.

(7) In this Act "light locomotive" and "heavy locomotive" mean a mechanically propelled vehicle which is not constructed itself to carry a load, other than excepted articles, and of which the weight unladen—

(a) in the case of a light locomotive, exceeds 7370 but does not exceed 11690 kilograms, and

(b) in the case of a heavy locomotive, exceeds 11690 kilograms.

(8) In subsections (6) and (7) above "excepted articles" means any of the following, that is to say, water, fuel, accumulators and other equipment used for the purpose of propulsion, loose tools and loose equipment.   **[156]**

NOTES
Commencement: 26 September 1984.
This section derived from the Road Traffic Regulation Act 1967, s 99(1)-(8), SI 1981/1373, Sch, Part II, and SI 1981/1374, Sch.
Extended with modifications to the Isles of Scilly by SI 1990 No 714.

137. Supplementary provisions relating to s 136

(1) A sidecar attached to a motor vehicle shall, if it complies with such conditions as may be specified in regulations made by the Secretary of State, be regarded as forming part of the vehicle to which it is attached and not as being a trailer.

(2) For the purposes of section 136 of this Act, in a case where a motor vehicle is so constructed that a trailer may by partial superimposition be attached to the vehicle in such a manner as to cause a substantial part of the weight of the trailer to be borne by the vehicle, that vehicle shall be deemed to be a vehicle itself constructed to carry a load.

(3) For the purposes of that section, in the case of a motor vehicle fitted with a crane, dynamo, welding plant or other special appliance or apparatus which is a permanent or essentially permanent fixture, the appliance or apparatus shall not be deemed to constitute a load or goods or burden of any description, but shall be deemed to form part of the vehicle.

(4) The Secretary of State may by regulations vary any of the maximum or minimum weights specified in section 136 of this Act; and such regulations may have effect—

(a) either generally or in the case of vehicles of any class specified in the regulations, and

(b) either for the purposes of this Act and of all regulations made under it or for such of those purposes as may be so specified.

(5) Nothing in section 86 of this Act shall be construed as limiting the powers conferred by subsection (4) above.　　　**[157]**

NOTES

Commencement: 26 September 1984.

138. Meaning of "heavy commercial vehicle"

(1) Subject to subsections (4) to (7) below, in this Act "heavy commercial vehicle" means any goods vehicle which has an operating weight exceeding 7.5 tonnes.

(2) The operating weight of a goods vehicle for the purposes of this section is—

(a) in the case of a motor vehicle not drawing a trailer, or in the case of a trailer, its maximum laden weight;

(b) in the case of an articulated vehicle, its maximum laden weight (if it has one) and otherwise the aggregate maximum laden weight of all the individual vehicles forming part of that articulated vehicle; and

(c) in the case of a motor vehicle (other than an articulated vehicle) drawing one or more trailers, the aggregate maximum laden weight of the motor vehicle and the trailer or trailers attached to it.

(3) In this section—

"articulated vehicle" means a motor vehicle with a trailer so attached to it as to be partially superimposed upon it;

"goods vehicle" means a motor vehicle constructed or adapted for use for the carriage of goods or burden of any description, or a trailer so constructed or adapted;

"trailer" means any vehicle other than a motor vehicle;

and references to the maximum laden weight of a vehicle are references to the total laden weight which must not be exceeded in the case of that vehicle if it is to be used in Great Britain without contravening any regulations for the time being in force under [section 41 of the Road Traffic Act 1988] (construction and use regulations).

(4) The Secretary of State may by regulations amend subsections (1) and (2) above (whether as originally enacted or as previously amended under this subsection)—

(a) by substituting weights of a different description for any of the weights there mentioned, or

(b) in the case of subsection (1) above, by substituting a weight of a different description or amount, or a weight different both in description and amount, for the weight there mentioned.

(5) Different regulations may be made under subsection (4) above for the purposes of different provisions of this Act and as respects different classes of vehicles or as respects the same class of vehicles in different circumstances and as respects different times of the day or night and as respects roads in different localities.

(6) Regulations made under subsection (4) above shall not so amend subsection (1) above that there is any case in which a goods vehicle whose operating weight (ascertained in accordance with subsection (2) above as

originally enacted) does not exceed 7.5 tonnes is a heavy commercial vehicle for any of the purposes of this Act.

(7) For the purpose of determining whether or not any vehicle is a heavy commercial vehicle for the purposes of a traffic regulation order or experimental traffic order—

(a) made before 13th August 1981 (whether or not varied or, in the case of an experimental traffic order, continued after that date); and

(b) including any such provision as is referred to in section 2(4) of this Act;

the provisions contained in paragraph 8 of Schedule 10 to this Act shall, during the transitional period specified in that paragraph, have effect in substitution for the provisions of subsections (1) to (6) above.

(8) In subsection (7) above, "experimental traffic order" does not include an order made in respect of traffic on roads in Greater London.   **[158]**

NOTES
Commencement: 26 September 1984.
This section derived from the Road Traffic Regulation Act 1967, s 104(1A)-(1G), and the Transport Act 1982, s 56(1), (3), (4).
Sub-s (3): words in square brackets substituted by the Road Traffic (Consequential Provisions) Act 1988, s 4, Sch 3, para 25(8).
Extended with modifications to the Isles of Scilly by SI 1990 No 714.

139. Hovercraft

(1) For the purposes of this Act, a hovercraft—

(a) shall be a motor vehicle, whether or not it is intended or adapted for use on roads; but

(b) shall be treated, subject to subsection (2) below, as not being a vehicle of any of the classes defined in subsections (2) to (7) of section 136 of this Act.

(2) The Secretary of State may by regulations provide—

(a) that any provision of this Act, which would otherwise apply to hovercraft, shall not apply to them or shall apply to them subject to such modifications as may be specified in the regulations, or

(b) that any such provision, which would not otherwise apply to hovercraft, shall apply to them subject to such modifications (if any) as may be so specified.

(3) In this section "hovercraft" has the same meaning as in the Hovercraft Act 1968.   **[159]**

NOTES
Commencement: 26 September 1984.
This section derived from the Road Traffic Regulation Act 1967, s 101, and the Hovercraft Act 1968, Sch, para 4.
Extended with modifications to the Isles of Scilly by SI 1990 No 714.

140. Certain vehicles not to be treated as motor vehicles

(1) For the purposes of this Act—

(a) a mechanically propelled vehicle which is an implement for cutting grass, is controlled by a pedestrian and is not capable of being used or adapted for any other purpose;

(b) any other mechanically propelled vehicle controlled by a pedestrian which may be specified by regulations made by the Secretary of State for the purposes of this section and of [section 189 of the Road Traffic Act 1988]; and

(c) an electrically assisted pedal cycle of such class as may be prescribed by regulations so made,

shall be treated as not being a motor vehicle.

(2) In this section "controlled by a pedestrian" means that the vehicle either—

(a) is constructed or adapted for use only under such control, or

(b) is constructed or adapted for use either under such control or under the control of a person carried on it, but is not for the time being in use under, or proceeding under, the control of a person carried on it.

[160]

NOTES

Commencement: 26 September 1984.

This section derived from the Road Traffic Regulation Act 1967, s 103, the Road Traffic Act 1972, Sch 7, and the Transport Act 1981, s 24(1).

Sub-s (1): in para (b) words in square brackets substituted by the Road Traffic (Consequential Provisions) Act 1988, s 4, Sch 3, para 25(9).

Extended with modifications to the Isles of Scilly by SI 1990 No 714.

141. (*Repealed by the Road Traffic Act 1991, s 83, Sch 8.*)

[141A. Tramcars and trolley vehicles: regulations

(1) The Secretary of State may by regulations provide that such of the provisions mentioned in subsection (2) below as are specified in the regulations shall not apply, or shall apply with modifications—

(a) to all tramcars or to tramcars of any specified class, or

(b) to all trolley vehicles or to trolley vehicles of any specified class.

(2) The provisions referred to in subsection (1) above are the provisions of sections 1 to 14, 18 and 81 to 89 of this Act.

(3) Regulations under this section—

(a) may make different provision for different cases,

(b) may include such transitional provisions as appear to the Secretary of State to be necessary or expedient, and

(c) may make such amendments to any special Act as appear to the Secretary of State to be necessary or expedient in consequence of the regulations or in consequence of the application to any tramcars or trolley vehicles of any of the provisions mentioned in subsection (2) above.

(4) In this section—

"special Act" means a local Act of Parliament passed before the commencement of this section which authorises or regulates the use of tramcars or trolley vehicles;

"tramcar" includes any carriage used on any road by virtue of an order under the Light Railways Act 1896; and "trolley vehicle" means a mechanically propelled vehicle adapted for use on roads without rails under power transmitted to it from some external source (whether or not there is in addition a source of power on board the vehicle).] **[161]**

NOTES
Commencement: 1 July 1992.
Inserted by the Road Traffic Act 1991, s 46(1).

142. General interpretation of Act

(1) In this Act, except where the context otherwise requires, the following expressions have the meanings hereby assigned to them respectively, that is to say—

"bridge authority" means the authority or person responsible for the maintenance of a bridge;

"bridleway" means a way over which the public have the following, but no other, rights of way, that is to say, a right of way on foot and a right of way on horseback or leading a horse, with or without a right to drive animals of any description along the way;

["credit card" and "debit card" have the meanings given by section 35A(6) of this Act;]

"designation order" means an order under section 45 of this Act (including any order so made by virtue of section 50(1) of this Act) and "designated parking place" means a parking place designated by a designation order;

"disabled person's badge" means any badge issued, or having effect as if issued, under any regulations for the time being in force under section 21 of the Chronically Sick and Disabled Persons Act 1970;

"disabled person's vehicle" means a vehicle lawfully displaying a disabled person's badge;

"driver", where a separate person acts as steersman of a motor vehicle, includes that person as well as any other person engaged in the driving of the vehicle, and "drive" and "driving" shall be construed accordingly;

"excess charge" has the meaning assigned to it by section 46(1) of this Act;

"experimental traffic order" has the meaning assigned to it by section 9(1) of this Act;

"except in section 71(2) of this Act, "footpath" means a way over which the public has a right of way on foot only;

. . .

"initial charge" has the meaning assigned to it by section 46(1) of this Act;

. . .

"magistrates' court" and "petty sessions area" have the same meanings as in the Magistrates' Courts Act 1980;

"the Ministers" means the Secretaries of State charged with general responsibility under this Act in relation to England, Wales and Scotland respectively;

["off-street parking accommodation" means parking accommodation for vehicles off the highway, or in Scotland, off the road;]

subject to section 111(3) and (4) of, and paragraph 11(2) and (3) of Schedule 12 to, this Act, "owner", in relation to a vehicle which is subject to a hiring agreement or hire-purchase agreement, means the person in possession of the vehicle under that agreement;

"parking device" has the meaning assigned to it by [section 35(3B) or, as the case may be,] section 51(4) of this Act;

"parking meter" has the meaning assigned to it by section 46(2)(a) of this Act;

"prescribed" means prescribed by regulations made by the Secretary of State;

"public service vehicle" [has the same meaning] as in the Public Passenger Vehicles Act 1981;

["road"—

    (a) in England and Wales, means any length of highway or of any other road to which the public has access, and includes bridges over which a road passes, and

    (b) in Scotland, has the same meaning as in the Roads (Scotland) Act 1984;

"special road", in England and Wales, has the same meaning as in the Highways Act 1980, and in Scotland has the same meaning as in the Roads (Scotland) Act 1984;]

"statutory", in relation to any prohibition, restriction, requirement or provision, means contained in, or having effect under, any enactment (including any enactment contained in this Act);

"street parking place" and "off-street parking place" refer respectively to parking places on land which does, and on land which does not, form part of a road;

["traffic authority" and "local traffic authority" have the meaning given by s 121A of this Act;]

"traffic sign" has the meaning assigned to it by section 64(1) of this Act; and

"traffic regulation order" has the meaning assigned to it by section 1 of this Act.

(2) Any reference in this Act to a tricycle shall be construed as including a reference to a cycle which is not a motor vehicle and has 4 or more wheels.

(3) References in this Act to a class of vehicles or traffic (other than the references in section 17) shall be construed as references to a class defined or described by reference to any characteristics of the vehicles or traffic or to any other circumstances whatsoever.   **[162]**

NOTES

Commencement: 26 September 1984.

Sub-s (1) derived from the Road Traffic Regulation Act 1967, ss 20(8), 52(3), 53(5), 102, 104(1), the Transport (London) Act 1969, s 34(5), the Local Government (Scotland) Act 1973, Sch 14, para 72, the Road Traffic Act 1974, s 5(1), the Transport Act 1980, Sch 5, Part II, the Magistrates' Courts Act 1980, Sch 8, para 5, the Highways Act 1980, Sch 24, para 16(h), the Public Passenger Vehicles Act 1981, Sch 7, para 7, and the Disabed Persons Act 1981, s 2(c); sub-s (2) derived from the Road Traffic Regulation Act 1967, s 102; sub-s (3) derived from the Road Traffic Regulation Act 1967, s 104(2), and the Road Traffic (Drivers' Ages and Hours of Work) Act 1976, Sch 1, para 16.

Sub-s (1): definitions "credit card" and "debit card" added, and in definition "parking device" words in square brackets added, by the Parking Act 1989, s 4, Schedule, para 8; definitions omitted repealed, and definition "off-street parking accommodation" inserted, by the New Roads and Street Works Act 1991, s 168(1), Sch 8, Part II, para 78(1)–(3); definition "public service vehicle" amended by the Transport Act 1985, s 1, Sch 1, para 15; definitions "road" and "special road" substituted, and definitions "traffic authority" and "local traffic authority" inserted, by the New Roads and Street Works Act 1991, s 168(1), Sch 8, Part II, para 78(1), (4)–(6).

Extended with modifications to the Isles of Scilly by SI 1990 No 714.

SCHEDULES

SCHEDULE 6

Section 86

SPEED LIMITS FOR VEHICLES OF CERTAIN CLASSES

PART I

VEHICLES FITTED WITH PNEUMATIC TYRES ON ALL WHEELS (SEE APPLICATION PROVISIONS BELOW THE FOLLOWING TABLE)

TABLE

1	2	3		
Item No	Class of Vehicle	Maximum speed (in miles per hour) while vehicle is being driven on:		
		(a) Motorway	(b) Dual carriageway road not being a motorway	(c) Other road
1.	A passenger vehicle, motor caravan or dual-purpose vehicle not drawing a trailer being a vehicle with an unladen weight exceeding 3·05 tonnes or adapted to carry more than 8 passengers—			
	(i) if not exceeding 12 metres in overall length	70	60	50
	(ii) if exceeding 12 metres in overall length	60	60	50
2.	An invalid carriage	not applicable	20	20
3.	A passenger vehicle, motor caravan, car-derived van or dual-purpose vehicle drawing one trailer	[60]	[60]	50
4.	A passenger vehicle, motor caravan, car-derived van or dual-purpose vehicle drawing more than one trailer	40	20	20
5.	(1) A goods vehicle having a maximum laden weight not exceeding 7·5 tonnes and which is not— (a) an articulated vehicle, or (b) drawing a trailer, or (c) a car-derived van	70	60	50
	(2) A goods vehicle which is—			

1	2	3		
Item No	Class of Vehicle	Maximum speed (in miles per hour) while vehicle is being driven on:		
		(a) Motorway	(b) Dual carriage-way road not being a motorway	(c) Other road
	(a)(i) an articulated vehicle having a maximum laden weight not exceeding 7·5 tonnes, or (ii) a motor vehicle, other than a car-derived van, which is drawing one trailer where the aggregate maximum laden weight of the motor vehicle and the trailer does not exceed 7·5 tonnes	60	[60]	50
	(b)(i) an articulated vehicle having a maximum laden weight exceeding 7·5 tonnes, (ii) a motor vehicle having a maximum laden weight exceeding 7·5 tonnes and not drawing a trailer, or (iii) a motor vehicle drawing one trailer where the aggregate maximum laden weight of the motor vehicle and the trailer exceeds 7·5 tonnes	60	50	40
	(c) a motor vehicle, other than a car-derived van, drawing more than one trailer	40	20	20
6.	A motor tractor (other than an industrial tractor), a light locomotive or a heavy locomotive—			
	(a) if the provisions about springs and wings as specified in paragraph 3 of Part IV of this Schedule are complied with and the vehicle is not drawing a trailer, or if those provisions are complied with and the vehicle is drawing one trailer which also complies with those provisions	40	30	30
	(b) in any other case	20	20	20
7.	A works truck	18	18	18
8.	An industrial tractor	not applicable	18	18
[9.	An agricultural motor vehicle	40	40	40]

Application

This Part applies only to motor vehicles, not being track-laying vehicles, every wheel of which is fitted with a pneumatic tyre and to such vehicles drawing one or more trailers,

not being track-laying vehicles, every wheel of which is fitted with a pneumatic tyre.
[163]

NOTES
Commencement: 26 September 1984.
This Schedule derived from the Road Traffic Regulation Act 1967, Sch 5, and SI 1984 No 325.
Items 3, 5 amended and item 9 added by SI 1986 No 1175, reg 2.
Extended with modifications to the Isles of Scilly by SI 1990 No 714.

PART II

**VEHICLES (OTHER THAN TRACK-LAYING VEHICLES) NOT FITTED WITH
PNEUMATIC TYRES ON ALL WHEELS (SEE APPLICATION PROVISIONS
BELOW THE FOLLOWING TABLE)**

TABLE

1	2	3
Item No	Class of Vehicle	Maximum Speed (in miles per hour) while vehicle is being driven on a road
1.	A motor vehicle, or in the case of motor vehicle drawing one or more trailers, the combination, where— (a) every wheel is fitted with a resilient tyre, or (b) at least one wheel is fitted with a resilient tyre and every wheel which is not fitted with a resilient tyre is fitted with a pneumatic tyre	20
2.	A motor vehicle, or in the case of a motor vehicle drawing one or more trailers, the combination, where any wheel is not fitted with either a pneumatic tyre or a resilient tyre	5

Application

This Part does not apply to—

    (a) a motor vehicle which is a track-laying vehicle; or
    (b) a motor vehicle which is not a track-laying vehicle but which is drawing one or more trailers any one of which is a track-laying vehicle.   **[164]**

NOTES
Commencement: 26 September 1984.
This Schedule derived from the Road Traffic Regulation Act 1967, Sch 5, and SI 1984 No 325.
Extended with modifications to the Isles of Scilly by SI 1990 No 714.

PART III
TRACK-LAYING VEHICLES (SEE APPLICATION PROVISIONS BELOW THE FOLLOWING TABLE)

TABLE

1	2	3
Item No	Class of Vehicle	Maximum Speed (in miles per hour) while vehicle is being driven on a road
1.	A motor vehicle being a track-laying vehicle which is fitted with— (a) springs between its frame and its weight-carrying rollers, and (b) resilient material between the rims of its weight-carrying rollers and the surface of the road, and which is not drawing a trailer	20
2.	A vehicle specified in item 1 above drawing one or more trailers each of which is either— (a) a track-laying vehicle fitted with springs and resilient material as mentioned in that item, or (b) not a track-laying vehicle and each wheel of which is fitted with either a pneumatic tyre or a resilient tyre	20
3.	A vehicle specified in item 1 above drawing one or more trailers any one of which is either— (a) a track-laying vehicle not fitted with springs and resilient material as mentioned in that item, or (b) not a track-laying vehicle and at least one wheel of which is not fitted with either a pneumatic tyre or a resilient tyre	5
4.	A motor vehicle being a track-laying vehicle which is not fitted with springs and resilient material as mentioned in item 1 above, whether drawing a trailer or not	5
5.	A motor vehicle not being a track-laying vehicle, which is drawing one or more trailers any one or more of which is a track-laying vehicle— (a) if every wheel of the motor vehicle and of any non-track-laying trailer is fitted with a pneumatic tyre or with a resilient tyre, and every trailer which is a track-laying vehicle is fitted with springs and resilient material as mentioned in item 1 (b) in any other case	20 5

Application

This Part applies to—

(a) a motor vehicle which is a track-laying vehicle, and
(b) a motor vehicle of any description which is drawing one or more trailers any one or more of which is a track-laying vehicle. **[165]**

NOTES
Commencement: 26 September 1984.
This Schedule derived from the Road Traffic Regulation Act 1967, Sch 5, and SI 1984 No 325.
Extended with modifications to the Isles of Scilly by SI 1990 No 714.

PART IV

APPLICATION AND INTERPRETATION

1. This Schedule does not apply to a vehicle which is being used for the purpose of experiments or trials under section 6 of the Road Improvements Act 1925 or section 283 of the Highways Act 1980.

2. In this Schedule—

["agricultural motor vehicle"] "articulated vehicle", "dual-purpose vehicle", "industrial tractor", "passenger vehicle", "pneumatic tyre", track-laying", "wheel" and "works truck" have the same meanings as are respectively given to those expressions in Regulation 3(1) of the Motor Vehicles (Construction and Use) Regulations 1978;

"car-derived van" means a goods vehicle which is constructed or adapted as a derivative of a passenger vehicle and which has a maximum laden weight not exceeding 2 tonnes;

"construction and use requirements" has the same meaning as in [section 41(7) of the Road Traffic Act 1988];

"dual-carriageway road" means a road part of which consists of a central reservation to separate a carriageway to be used by vehicles proceeding in one direction from a carriageway to be used by vehicles proceeding in the opposite direction;

"goods vehicle" has the same meaning as in [section 192(1) of the Road Traffic Act 1988];

"maximum laden weight" in relation to a vehicle or a combination of vehicles means—

(a) in the case of a vehicle, or combination of vehicles, in respect of which a gross weight not to be exceeded in Great Britain is specified in construction and use requirements, that weight;

(b) in the case of any vehicle, or combination of vehicles, in respect of which no such weight is specified in construction and use requirements, the weight which the vehicle, or combination of vehicles, is designed or adapted not to exceed when in normal use and travelling on a road laden;

"motor caravan" has the same meaning as in Regulation 2(1) of the Motor Vehicles (Type Approval) (Great Britain) Regulations 1979;

"motorway" has the same meaning as in Regulation 3(1) of the Motorways Traffic (England and Wales) Regulations 1982, as regards England and Wales, and Regulation 2(2) of the Motorways Traffic (Scotland) Regulations 1964, as regards Scotland: and

"resilient tyre" means a tyre, not being a pneumatic tyre, which is soft or elastic.

3. The specification as regards springs and wings mentioned in item 6 of Part I of this Schedule is that the vehicle—

(i) is equipped with suitable and sufficient springs between each wheel and the frame of the vehicle, and

(ii) unless adequate protection is afforded by the body of the vehicle, is provided with wings or other similar fittings to catch, so far as practicable, mud or water thrown up by the rotation of the wheels.

4. A vehicle falling in two or more classes specified in Part I, II or III of this Schedule shall be treated as falling within the class for which the lower or lowest speed limit is specified.   **[166]**

NOTES
Commencement: 26 September 1984.
This Schedule derived from the Road Traffic Regulation Act 1967, Sch 5, and SI 1984 No 325.
Para 2: first amendment in square brackets made by SI 1986 No 1175, reg 2; in definitions

"construction and use requirements" and "goods vehicle" words in square brackets substituted by the Road Traffic (Consequential Provisions) Act 1988, s 4, Sch 3, para 25(10).
Extended with modifications to the Isles of Scilly by SI 1990 No 714.

SCHEDULE 8

Section 111

STATUTORY STATEMENTS (EXCESS CHARGES)

PART I

STATUTORY STATEMENT OF OWNERSHIP OR HIRING

1. For the purposes of the specified sections, a statutory statement of ownership is a statement in the prescribed form, signed by the person furnishing it and stating—

   (a) whether he was the owner of the vehicle at the relevant time; and
   (b) if he was not the owner of the vehicle at the relevant time, whether he ceased to be the owner before, or became the owner after, the relevant time, and, if the information is in his possession, the name and address of the person to whom, and the date on which, he disposed of the vehicle or, as the case may be, the name and address of the person from whom, and the date on which, he acquired it.

2. For the purposes of the specified sections, a statutory statement of hiring is a statement in the prescribed form, signed by the person furnishing it, being the person by whom a statement of liability was signed and stating—

   (a) whether at the relevant time the vehicle was let to him under the hiring agreement to which the statement of liability refers; and
   (b) if it was not, the date on which he returned the vehicle to the possession of the vehicle-hire firm concerned.   **[167]**

NOTES
Commencement: 26 September 1984.
This Schedule derived from the Road Traffic Act 1974, s 5, Sch 1, and the Transport Act 1982, Sch 5, para 19.
Extended with modifications to the Isles of Scilly by SI 1990 No 714.

PART II

STATUTORY STATEMENT OF FACTS

3. For the purposes of the specified sections, a statutory statement of facts is a statement which is in the prescribed form and which—

   (a) states that the person furnishing it was not the driver of the vehicle at the relevant time;
   (b) states the name and address at the time when the statement is furnished of the person who was the driver of the vehicle at the relevant time; and
   (c) is signed both by the person furnishing it and by the person stated to be the driver of the vehicle at the relevant time.   **[168]**

NOTES
Commencement: To be appointed.
This Schedule derived from the Road Traffic Act 1974, s 5, Sch 1, and the Transport Act 1982, Sch 5, para 19.
Extended with modifications to the Isles of Scilly by SI 1990 No 714.

PART III

INTERPRETATION

4. In this Schedule "the specified sections" has the meaning assigned to it by subsection (1) of section III of this Act.

5. Subsections (2) to (4) of that section shall have effect for the purposes of Parts I and II of this Schedule as they have effect for the purposes of the specified sections.

6. In paragraph 2 above "statement of liability", "hiring agreement" and "vehicle-hire firm" have the same meanings as in section 109 of this Act. **[169]**

NOTES

Commencement: 26 September 1984.

This Schedule derived from the Road Traffic Act 1974, s 5, Sch 1, and the Transport Act 1982, Sch 5, para 19.

Extended with modifications to the Isles of Scilly by SI 1990 No 714.

ROADS (SCOTLAND) ACT 1984
(c 54)

ARRANGEMENT OF SECTIONS

PART I
PUBLIC ROADS

Special roads

PART V
ROADS AND BUILDING CONTROL

Works and excavations

Control of traffic

Footways, footpaths and verges

Horse traffic etc

Miscellaneous

Section   Para

PART VIII
INTERFERENCE AND DAMAGE

Obstruction of view

General obstruction

Roadside dangers

Miscellaneous

Offences

PART XI
OFFENCES

PART XIII
GENERAL

Interpretation

SCHEDULES

An Act to make provision as regards roads in Scotland; and for connected purposes.   [31 October 1984]

PART I

PUBLIC ROADS

Special roads

7. General provision as to special roads

(1) Subject to the provisions of this Act, all such roads as immediately before the commencement of this Act were special roads, being roads provided in pursuance of a scheme made under section 1 of the Special Roads Act 1949, shall continue to be, and to be known as, special roads.

(2) Roads which continue to be special roads by virtue of subsection (1) above shall continue, subject to the provisions of this Act, to be special roads for the use of traffic of the classes for the use of which they were special roads immediately before the commencement of this Act.

(3) A roads authority may be authorised by means of a scheme under this section to provide, along a route prescribed by the scheme, a special road for the use of traffic of any class so prescribed.

(4) Subject to subsection (10) below, a roads authority authorised by a scheme under this section, or by any such scheme as is referred to in subsection (1) above, to provide a special road are in this Act referred to in relation to that road as the "special road authority".

(5) A special road authorised by a scheme under this section may be provided by means of—

    (a) the construction by the special road authority of a new road along the route prescribed by the scheme or along any part of that route;

    (b) the appropriation under this Act of any road (or proposed road in course of construction) comprised in that route for which the special road authority are the roads authority;

    (c) the transfer to that authority under this Act of any road (or proposed road in course of construction) comprised in that route for which they are not the roads authority.

(6) A scheme under this section authorising the provision of a special road shall—

    (a) in the case of a road to be provided by the Secretary of State, be made by the Secretary of State, and

    (b) in the case of a road to be provided by a local roads authority, be made by that authority and confirmed by the Secretary of State,

in accordance with the provisions of Parts II and III of Schedule 1 to this Act.

(7) Before making or confirming a scheme under this section, the Secretary of State shall give due consideration to the requirements of local and national planning, and to the requirements of agriculture and industry.

(8) If objection to a scheme under this section is duly made in accordance with Schedule 1 to this Act—

    (a) by the roads authority for any road (or proposed road) comprised in the route of the special road authorised by the scheme;

    (b) by any navigation authority or water authority on whom notice is required to be served under paragraph 3 of that Schedule on the ground that any bridge or tunnel over or under navigable waters for which provision is made by the scheme is likely to obstruct or impede the performance of their functions under any enactment or to interfere with the reasonable requirements of navigation over the waters affected by the scheme,

and is not withdrawn, the scheme shall be subject to special parliamentary procedure.

(9) Part IV of Schedule 1 to this Act shall have effect for the purposes of the application to schemes under this section of the Statutory Orders (Special Procedure) Act 1945; and Schedule 2 to this Act shall have effect with respect to the validity and date of operation of such schemes.

(10) A scheme under this section may be submitted to the Secretary of State jointly by any two or more local roads authorities, and any such scheme may determine which of those authorities shall be the special road authority for the special road and may provide—

    (a) for the performance by the special road authority, in relation to the road, of any roads functions of another authority who are party to the submission; and

    (b) for the making of contributions by that other authority to the special road authority in respect of expenditure incurred in the performance of those functions. **[170]**

NOTES
Commencement: 1 January 1985.

8. Further provision as regards classification of traffic for purposes of special roads

(1) Different classes of traffic may be prescribed by a scheme under section 7 of this Act in relation to different parts of the special road to which the scheme relates.

(2) The classes of traffic prescribed by any such scheme shall be prescribed by reference to the classes set out in Schedule 3 to this Act.

(3) The Secretary of State may by order vary the classes of traffic specified in the said Schedule 3 and the composition of any such class; and where any such order has come into operation, any reference in a scheme in force under the said section 7, whether that scheme was made or confirmed before or after the date on which the order comes into operation, to any class of traffic to which the order relates shall be construed as a reference to that class as varied by the order.

[(4) A variation order may contain provision applying the variations made by the order to existing schemes (whether made by the Secretary of State or a local roads authority); and in the absence of such provision a variation order does not affect the classes of traffic prescribed in an existing scheme.

(5) In subsection (4) above an "existing scheme" means a scheme under section 7 made before the order comes into operation.] **[171]**

NOTES
Commencement: 1 January 1985.
Sub-ss (4), (5): added by the New Roads and Street Works Act 1991, s 45.

9. Supplementary orders relating to special roads

(1) Subject to section 113 of this Act, provision in relation to a special road may be made by an order under this section—

(a) for appropriating as part of the special road, as from such date as may be specified in the order, any road (or proposed road in course of construction) comprised in the route prescribed by the scheme authorising the special road and which is a road (or proposed road) for which the special road authority are the roads authority;

(b) for transferring to the special road authority, as from such date as may be specified in the order, any road (or proposed road in course of construction) comprised in that route and for which they are not the roads authority;

(c) for authorising the special road authority—

(i) to stop up, divert, improve or otherwise alter any road which crosses or enters the route of the special road or is or will be otherwise affected by the construction or improvement of the special road;

(ii) to construct any new road for purposes connected with any such alterations as aforesaid or for any other purpose connected with the special road or its construction and to close after such period as may be specified in the order any new road temporarily so constructed;

(d) for transferring to such roads authority as may be specified in the order, as from such date as may be so specified, any road constructed by the special road authority in pursuance of the order or any previous order made under this section;

(e) for authorising or requiring the special road authority to exercise, either concurrently with or to the exclusion of any regional council, any functions which, apart from the order, would be exercisable by that regional council in relation to the special road or any part thereof other than functions of that authority as regional or general planning authority within the meaning of the Town and Country Planning (Scotland) Act 1972; or

(f) for any other purpose incidental to the purposes aforesaid or otherwise incidental to the construction or maintenance of, or other dealing with, the special road.

(2) An order under this section shall—

(a) in the case of a special road provided or to be provided by the Secretary of State, be made by the Secretary of State;

(b) in the case of a special road provided or to be provided by a local roads authority, be made by that authority and confirmed by the Secretary of State;

in accordance with Parts I and III of Schedule 1 to this Act; and Schedule 2 to this Act shall have effect with respect to the validity and date of operation of any such order.

(3) No order authorising the stopping up of a road shall be made or confirmed by the Secretary of State under this section unless he is satisfied that another reasonably convenient route is available or will be provided in pursuance of an order under this section before the road is stopped up.

(4) No order providing for the appropriation by or transfer to a special road authority of an existing road comprised in the route prescribed by the scheme

authorising the special road shall be made or confirmed by the Secretary of State under this section unless he is satisfied—

    (a) that another reasonably convenient route is available for traffic other than traffic of the class authorised by the scheme, or will be provided in pursuance of an order under this section before the date on which the appropriation or transfer takes effect, or

    (b) that no such other route is reasonably required for any such other traffic.

    (5) An order under this section may provide for the payment of contributions—

    (a) by the special road authority to any other roads authority in respect of any additional liabilities imposed on that other authority in consequence of the provisions of the order or of any previous order made under this section;

    (b) to the special road authority by any other authority in respect of any liabilities so imposed on the special road authority, being liabilities which would otherwise have fallen to be discharged by the other authority;

and may also provide for the determination by arbitration of disputes as to the payment of such contributions.   **[172]**

NOTES
Commencement: 1 January 1985.

10. Certain special roads to be trunk roads

(1) A special road to be provided by the Secretary of State in accordance with a scheme under section 7 of this Act shall, except in so far as it is provided by means of the appropriation or transfer of any existing road, become a trunk road on such date as may be specified in the scheme.

    (2) A road (not being a trunk road) which, by means of an order under section 9 of this Act, is appropriated as a special road to be provided by the Secretary of State, and a road which, by means of such an order, is transferred to the Secretary of State, shall become a trunk road on the date on which it is so appropriated or is so transferred, as the case may be.   **[173]**

NOTES
Commencement: 1 January 1985.

PART V

ROADS AND BUILDING CONTROL

Works and excavations

56. Control of works and excavations

(1) Subject to section 61 of this Act and without prejudice to any requirement imposed by, under or by virtue of any other enactment, no works shall be executed in, or excavation made under, a public road except with the roads authority's consent in writing and in accordance with any reasonable conditions which they think fit to attach to the consent.

    (2) An application for the consent of a roads authority under subsection (1) above shall be in writing. On receipt of the application they shall give the applicant notice of all statutory undertakers whose apparatus is, in the opinion

of the authority, likely to be affected by the works or excavation and the applicant shall then forthwith in writing intimate the application to those undertakers of whom he has received such notice.

(3) This section does not apply to works or excavations to which the *street works code, as contained in the Public Utilities Street Works Act 1950, applies* [provisions of Part IV of the New Roads and Street Works Act 1991 apply].

(4) A person shall, as soon as reasonably practicable after he—

    (a) executes such works as are, or
    (b) makes such excavation as is,

mentioned in subsection (1) above, make good any damage to the road occasioned by the works or excavation and shall immediately thereafter give notice to the authority that the damage is made good; and without prejudice to section 66 of this Act, until twelve months have elapsed from the authority certifying that the damage has been made good to their satisfaction (which certificate shall not be withheld unreasonably) the person shall maintain so much of the road as is made good.

(5) At the completion of the works or excavation mentioned in subsection (1) above any opening left in the road shall be provided with a door or cover by the person executing the works or making the excavation; and such door or cover shall be constructed in such manner, and of such materials, as may be specified by the roads authority.

(6) A person who contravenes—

    (a) subsection (1) above; or
    (b) subsection (5) above,

commits an offence.

(7) Works executed, or an excavation made, in contravention of subsection (1) above may be removed, or as the case may be filled in, by the roads authority; and the authority may recover such expenses as are reasonably incurred in so doing, or in maintaining an excavation which has under this subsection been filled in, from the person who executed those works or made that excavation.

(8) The roads authority shall, where practicable, notify the person mentioned in subsection (7) above about anything removed under that subsection; but if the person cannot be traced, or if he has not recovered the thing within a reasonable period of time after being so notified, the authority may dispose of the thing.

(9) Any proceeds of a disposal under subsection (8) above shall be used to meet any such expenses in relation to the removal or filling in as are mentioned in subsection (7) above. Thereafter any surplus shall be given to the person so mentioned if he can be traced and if he cannot may be retained by the roads authority.

(10) Where a person contravenes subsection (4) (other than by a failure duly to give information) or (5) above, the roads authority may make good the damage to the road, or as the case may be provide a door or cover for the opening, and recover from him such expenses as are reasonably incurred in so doing.   **[174]**

NOTES
Commencement: 1 January 1985.
Sub-s (3): words in italics prospectively substituted by the New Roads and Street Works Act 1991, s 168(1), Sch 8, Part III, para 83, as from a day to be appointed.

57. Dangerous works

(1) Where, in the opinion of the roads authority, works which a person is executing in, or excavations which he is making under, a road are causing, or are likely to cause, a danger the authority may by notice to him require him within such period as may be specified in the notice to take such steps as will ensure that such danger is brought to an end or as the case may be does not arise.

(2) Notwithstanding any consent granted under section 56 or 61 of this Act and without prejudice to the generality of subsection (1) above, steps specified in the notice under that subsection may include the removal of the works or filling in of the excavations.

(3) Subsections (1) and (2) above do not apply to works or excavations which are in contravention of section 56(1) or 61(1) of this Act.

(4) Without prejudice to sections 56 and 61 of this Act, but notwithstanding any consent granted under either of those sections, a person executing works, or making excavations—

(a) which constitute a danger; or
(b) who permits them to become a danger,

commits an offence.

(5) This section does not apply to works or excavations to which the *street works code, as contained in the Public Utilities Street Works Act 1950, applies* [provisions of Part IV of the New Roads and Street Works Act 1991 apply].

(6) A person upon whom a notice has been served under subsection (1) above may within 28 days of such service refer the matter by summary application to the sheriff; and the decision of the sheriff on the matter shall be final. **[175]**

NOTES
Commencement: 1 January 1985.
Sub-s (5): words in italics prospectively substituted by the New Roads and Street Works Act 1991, s 168(1), Sch 8, Part III, para 84, as from a day to be appointed.

58. Occupation of parts of road for deposit of building materials etc

(1) Subject to subsection (7) below, a person who without, or otherwise than in accordance with, the written permission of the roads authority, in conducting operations for the construction, repair, maintenance or demolition of any building, occupies, for the purpose of depositing materials or otherwise in connection with those operations, a part of a road, whether public or private, or erects staging or scaffolding which projects over a part of a road, commits an offence.

(2) Such permission as is mentioned in subsection (1) above may be granted either unconditionally or subject to such conditions, including conditions as to the duration of the permission, as may be specified therein; and notwithstanding anything in any enactment or in any rule of law, a person who complies with the permission (including the conditions) does not by the occupation or erection in respect of which the permission is granted commit an offence:

Provided that the foregoing provisions of this subsection shall not constitute a defence as regards any such contravention as is mentioned in section 128(1) of this Act.

(3) Subject to subsection (7) below, where a person by such occupation as is mentioned in subsection (1) above commits an offence under that subsection, any other person who, in connection with the operations, either by himself or by his servant or agent, deposits materials on the part of the road so occupied commits an offence.

(4) Where a person is charged with an offence under subsection (1) above it shall be a defence for him to prove that he took all reasonable precautions and exercised all due diligence to avoid the commission of the offence.

(5) Where a person is charged with an offence under subsection (3) above, it shall be a defence for him to prove that the offence—

    (a) took place on the instructions, or by the authority, of his employer or of the person conducting the operations, or
    (b) was due to a mistake, or
    (c) was due to reliance on information supplied to him,

and that he was unaware that he was depositing the materials otherwise than under and in accordance with a permission granted under subsection (1) above.

(6) If in any case the defence provided by subsection (5) above involves the allegation that the offence took place on the instructions, or by the authority, of another person, or was due to reliance on information supplied by another person, the person charged shall not, without leave of the court, be entitled to rely on that defence unless, within a period ending seven days before the hearing, he has served on the prosecutor notice giving such information identifying or assisting in the identification of that other person as is then in his possession.

(7) The occupation mentioned in the foregoing provisions of this section does not include occupation with a builder's skip (within the meaning of section 85 of this Act).   **[176]**

NOTE
    Commencement: 1 January 1985.

59. Control of obstructions in roads

(1) Subject to subsection (6) below, nothing shall be placed or deposited in a road so as to cause an obstruction except with the roads authority's consent in writing and in accordance with any reasonable conditions which they think fit to attach to the consent.

(2) A person who contravenes subsection (1) above commits an offence.

(3) Without prejudice to subsection (2) above, a person who contravenes subsection (1) above may be required by the roads authority or by a constable in uniform to remove the obstruction forthwith, and commits an offence if he fails to do so.

(4) Where—

    (a) a requirement under subsection (3) above is not complied with;
    (b) the person who placed or deposited the obstruction cannot be readily traced; or

(c) the case is one of emergency,

the roads authority or a constable may remove the obstruction (or cause it to be removed) and recover such expenses as are reasonably incurred in so doing from the said person.

(5) Subsections (8) and (9) of section 56 of this Act shall apply in relation to anything removed under subsection (4) above as they apply in relation to anything removed under subsection (7) of that section, except that where the removal is by a constable the said subsections (8) and (9) shall be read as if any reference therein to the roads authority were a reference to the police authority.

(6) The foregoing provisions of this section do not apply—

(a) where section 58, 85 or 86 of this Act or section 2 of the Refuse Disposal (Amenity) Act 1978 (penalty for unauthorised dumping of motor vehicles etc) applies;

(b) to works to which the *street works code, as contained in the Public Utilities Street Works Act 1950, applies* [provisions of Part IV of the New Roads and Street Works Act 1991 apply].   **[177]**

NOTES

Commencement: 1 January 1985.

Sub-s (6): words in italics prospectively substituted by the New Roads and Street Works Act 1991, s 168(1), Sch 8, Part III, para 85, as from a day to be appointed.

60. Fencing and lighting of obstructions and excavations

(1) Without prejudice to *section 8 of the Public Utilities Street Works Act 1950 (which sets out requirements as to safety, obstruction and other matters to be observed during and in conjunction with the execution of certain works by statutory undertakers),* or to sections 57 to 59 or section 85 of this Act, where any person places or deposits anything on a road so as to cause an obstruction, or executes works in a road, he shall, whether or not the obstruction is, or works are, on or in the road with the consent of the roads authority—

(a) cause the obstruction or works to be marked in such manner and with such materials as may, for the purpose of making it or them immediately visible to oncoming traffic, be specified;

(b) provide such lighting of the obstruction or works during the hours of darkness as is necessary for preventing danger to traffic and for warning traffic of danger;

(c) erect such fences, barriers and traffic signs for preventing danger to traffic, for regulating traffic, and for warning traffic of danger, as may be necessary and remove them as soon as they cease to be necessary therefor; and

(d) in the case of an obstruction or works whose nature so requires, cause any building adjoining the road to be shored up or otherwise protected.

(2) If the person referred to in subsection (1) above fails to fulfil a requirement imposed on him by that subsection, the roads authority may fulfil the requirement and recover the expenses reasonably incurred by them in so doing from that person.

(3) A person who fails to fulfil a requirement imposed on him by subsection (1) above commits an offence.

(4) A person who, without lawful authority or reasonable excuse, takes down, alters or removes any fence, barrier, shoring or other support or protection, or any traffic sign erected in pursuance of subsection (1) and (2)

above, or removes, interferes with or extinguishes any light placed in pursuance of either of those subsections to indicate an obstruction or works on or in any road commits an offence.

(5) In this section—
"hours of darkness" means the time between half an hour after sunset and half an hour before sunrise; and
"specified" means specified by the Secretary of State in regulations.

[(6) This section shall not apply to an undertaker executing road works, within the meaning of Part IV of the New Roads and Street Works Act 1991.]

[178]

NOTES
Commencement: 1 January 1985.
Sub-s (1): words in italics prospectively repealed by the New Roads and Street Works Act 1991, s 168(1), Sch 8, Part III, para 86(a), as from a day to be appointed.
Sub-s (6): prospectively added by the New Roads and Street Works Act 1991, s 168(1), Sch 8, Part III, para 86(b), as from a day to be appointed.

61. Granting of permission to place and maintain etc apparatus under a road

(1) Subject to subsections (3) and (5) below, the roads authority may permit, subject to such reasonable conditions as they consider appropriate (including, without prejudice to the generality of this subsection, conditions as to future cessation or withdrawal of the permission and indemnification of the authority against claims arising out of what is so permitted), a person to place and leave, or to retain, and thereafter (in either case) to maintain, repair and reinstate, apparatus in or under a public road or proposed public road and to break open, and to have access to, the road or proposed road, for those purposes[; and such permission shall be in writing].

(2) In subsection (1) above, "proposed public road" means a new road in course of construction by or on behalf of the roads authority.

(3) Before giving permission under subsection (1) above, the roads authority shall give not less than 28 days notice of their intention so to do to any other person whose apparatus is, or plans for the installation of apparatus are, likely to be affected by the works which would thereby be authorised.

(4) [Works carried out by a person in pursuance of permission under subsection (1) above are not] *undertakers' works within the meaning of section 1 of the Public Utilities Street Works Act 1950* [road works within the meaning of section 107 of the New Roads and Street Works Act 1991].

(5) Subsection (1) above does not apply to the apparatus of statutory undertakers or of local authorities [nor does it apply to apparatus in respect of which permission has been granted under section 109 of the New Roads and Street Works Act 1991 to execute road works].   **[179]**

NOTES
Commencement: 1 January 1985.
Sub-s (1): words in square brackets prospectively added by the New Roads and Street Works Act 1991, s 168(1), Sch 8, Part III, para 87(a), as from a day to be appointed.
Sub-s (4): first words in square brackets substituted by Electricity Act 1989, Sch 16, para 30; words in italics prospectively substituted by the New Roads and Street Works Act 1991, s 168(1), Sch 8, Part III, para 87(b), as from a day to be appointed.
Sub-s (5): words in square brackets prospectively added by the New Roads and Street Works Act 1991, s 168(1), Sch 8, Part III, para 87(c), as from a day to be appointed.

[61A. Charge for occupation of road

(1) The Secretary of State may make provision by regulations requiring a person who occupies a public road by doing anything to which this section applies to pay a charge to the roads authority if the duration of the occupation exceeds the longer of the following periods—

   (a) such period as may be prescribed; or
   (b) such period as is agreed by the authority and the person to be reasonable or, in default of such agreement, is determined by arbitration to be reasonable in the circumstances.

(2) This section applies to the occupation of a public road by doing anything which would require the consent or permission of a roads authority under any of the following provisions of this Act—

   section 56 (works executed in or excavations under a public road);
   section 58 (occupation of road for deposit of building materials and erection of scaffolding);
   section 59 (placing or depositing anything in a road);
   section 61 (placing, leaving, retaining, maintaining, repairing and reinstating apparatus in or under a public road); or
   section 85 (depositing a builder's skip).

(3) For the purposes of paragraph (b) of subsection (1) above, in default of agreement, the roads authority's view as to what is a reasonable period shall be acted upon pending the decision of the arbiter.

(4) The regulations may provide that if a person applying to the roads authority for consent or permission under any of the provisions of this Act specified in subsection (2) above submits together with his application an estimate of the likely duration of the occupation, the period stated in the estimate shall be taken to be agreed by the authority to be reasonable unless they give notice, in such manner and within such period as may be prescribed, objecting to the estimate.

(5) The regulations may provide that if it appears to the person occupying the road that by reason of matters not previously foreseen or reasonably foreseeable the duration of the occupation—

   (a) is likely to exceed the prescribed period,
   (b) is likely to exceed the period stated in the previous estimate, or
   (c) is likely to exceed the period previously agreed or determined to be a reasonable period,

he may submit an estimate or revised estimate accordingly, and that if he does so any previous estimate, agreement or determination shall cease to have effect and the period stated in the new estimate shall be taken to be agreed by the roads authority to be reasonable unless they give notice, in such manner and within such period as may be prescribed, objecting to the estimate.

(6) The amount of the charge shall be determined in such manner as may be prescribed by reference to the duration and extent of the occupation and different rates of charge may be prescribed according to the purpose of the occupation and such other factors as appear to the Secretary of State to be relevant.

(7) The regulations may make provision as to the time and manner of making payment of any charge.

(8) The regulations shall provide that a roads authority may reduce the

amount, or waive payment, of a charge in any particular case, in such classes of case as they may decide or as may be prescribed, or generally.

(9) In this section "prescribed" means prescribed by the Secretary of State by regulations.]   **[179A]**

NOTES
Prospectively inserted by the New Roads and Street Works Act 1991, s 168(1), Sch 8, Part III, para 88, as from a day to be appointed.

Control of traffic

62. Temporary prohibition or restriction of traffic etc on roads for reasons of public safety or convenience

(1) Where, as regards any road, an order under section 14 of the Road Traffic Regulation Act 1984 (which makes provision for the temporary prohibition or restriction of traffic and foot passage on roads in certain circumstances) cannot be made but in the opinion of the roads authority considerations of public safety or convenience require, or make it desirable that there should be, a temporary restriction on, or temporary prohibition of, traffic or foot passage on the road, the authority may make an order imposing such restriction or prohibition and (where practicable) specifying an alternative route or alternative routes.

(2) An order under subsection (1) above—
(a) shall not have the effect of preventing at any time access for foot passengers to any premises situated on or adjacent to the road or to any other premises accessible for foot passengers only from the road;
(b) may relate to vehicles, or persons, in general or to a class thereof; and
(c) without prejudice to paragraph (a) above may be subject to such conditions or exceptions as are considered necessary by the roads authority.

(3) In subsection (1) above "temporary" means for a period not exceeding seven days.

(4) Notice of an order under subsection (1) above shall be given by the authority by advertisement in a newspaper circulating in the area to which the order relates; and the order shall not come into effect before the date of the advertisement.

(5) A person who contravenes a restriction or prohibition imposed by virtue of subsection (1) above commits an offence.   **[180]**

NOTE
Commencement: 1 January 1985.

Footpaths, footways and verges

63. New access over verges and footways

(1) Where, in the opinion of the roads authority, vehicles when driven to or from premises adjacent to a public road are habitually being taken across that road's verge or footway other than by way of a satisfactory vehicular crossing they may serve a notice on the owner or occupier of the premises requiring that—
(a) by such date as is specified in the notice he shall have commenced; and

(b) within such period thereafter as is, and to such detailed specifications as are, so specified he shall have completed,

the construction of such a crossing over the affected part of the verge or footway.

(2) A vehicular crossing constructed under or by virtue of this section shall on completion be part of the public road.

(3) A person upon whom a notice has been served under subsection (1) above may within 28 days of such service refer the matter by summary application to the sheriff; and the decision of the sheriff on the matter shall be final. **[181]**

NOTE
Commencement: 1 January 1985.

64. Use of appliances etc on footways, footpaths and cycle tracks

(1) No enactment prohibiting or restricting the use of footways, footpaths or cycle tracks shall affect the use of appliances or vehicles—

(a) for the construction, maintenance, improvement or cleansing of a road;
(b) subject to subsection (2) below, by statutory undertakers for works on footways, footpaths or cycle tracks maintainable by a roads authority, in connection with apparatus belonging to the statutory undertakers.

(2) Statutory undertakers may exercise rights enjoyed by them by virtue of subsection (1)(b) above only if they have obtained the consent of the roads authority; and such consent may be subject to such reasonable conditions as the authority think fit.

(3) In this section "statutory undertakers" includes an authority responsible for sewerage. **[182]**

NOTE
Commencement: 1 January 1985.

Horse traffic etc

65. Regulation of drivers of horsedrawn carts etc

(1) The driver of a drawn vehicle commits an offence if he conveys on it on any road anything which is not adequately secured and which, were it to fall off, might be expected to endanger other road users.

(2) The owner of a drawn vehicle commits an offence if he permits a child of under—

(a) 14 years of age to drive that vehicle on a road; or
(b) 16 years of age (not being such child as is mentioned in paragraph (a) above) to drive that vehicle on a road other than under the immediate supervision of a person of 18 years of age or more.

(3) In subsections (1) and (2) above, "drawn vehicle" means a vehicle pulled by one or more draught animals. **[183]**

NOTE
Commencement: 1 January 1985.

Miscellaneous

66. Maintenance of vaults and cellars etc

(1) As regards any road, the following things shall be kept in good condition and repair by their owners or occupiers or by occupiers of the premises to which the things belong—

    (a) every vault, arch, cellar and tunnel under the road;

    (b) every opening into any such vault, arch, cellar or tunnel from the surface of the road;

    (c) every door or cover (whether fixed or removable) to any such opening;

    (d) every pavement light in the surface of the road; and

    (e) every wall or other structure supporting any such vault, arch, cellar, tunnel, door or cover.

(2) Where an owner or occupier is in contravention of subsection (1) above the roads authority may by notice to him require him within 28 days of the date of service of the notice to replace, repair or put into good condition the thing in respect of which the contravention arises.

(3) A person upon whom a notice has been served under subsection (2) above may, within the 28 days mentioned in that subsection, refer the matter by summary application to the sheriff; and the decision of the sheriff on the matter shall be final.

(4) A local roads authority may, if they think fit, pay the whole or any part of any expenditure incurred by a person in complying with subsection (1) or (2) above.   **[184]**

NOTE
    Commencement: 1 January 1985.

67. Power to direct that doors etc should not open outward into road

Where a door, gate, window, window shutter or bar opens outward into a road so as to interfere with the safety or convenience of road users the roads authority may by notice to the owner or occupier of the premises to which the thing belongs require him within such period as may be specified in the notice to take such steps as will ensure that such interference no longer occurs.   **[185]**

NOTE
    Commencement: 1 January 1985.

PART VIII

INTERFERENCE AND DAMAGE

Obstruction of view

83. Prevention of obstruction of view at corners, bends and junctions

(1) Where the roads authority are of the opinion that it is necessary, for the prevention of danger arising from obstruction of the view of road users, to impose restrictions with respect to land at or near a corner, bend or junction in a road they may serve a notice (in this section referred to as an "obstruction notice")—

    (a) upon the owner or occupier of the land directing him, within such period (being not less than 28 days) as may be specified in the notice, to alter the height or character of any wall (not being a wall forming part of the structure of any other permanent building), fence, advertising hoarding, hedge, tree or shrub thereon so as to cause it to conform with any requirements specified in the notice;

(b) upon the owner, occupier and any lessee of the land restraining him, either absolutely or subject to such conditions as may be specified in the notice, from permitting any building, wall, fence or advertising hoarding to be erected or hedge, tree or shrub to be planted, on the land:

Provided that an obstruction notice shall not inhibit reconstruction, or repair, which does not create any new obstruction of the view of road users.

(2) In subsection (1) above "advertising hoarding" means a hoarding or similar structure used, or adapted for use, for the display of advertisements.

(3) Restrictions imposed by an obstruction notice shall come into force upon its service and shall remain in force until it is withdrawn by the roads authority; and such restrictions shall, while in force, be binding upon any successor in title to the owner or occupier of the land to which they relate unless that successor proves that when he became the owner or occupier of the land he had, after making due inquiries, no reasonable cause to suspect that any such restrictions were in force.

(4) A person may, within 28 days of the receipt of an obstruction notice, object in writing (specifying the grounds of objection) to the roads authority; and the question whether the notice shall be withdrawn as respects any requirement or restriction objected to shall then be determined in the manner provided by section 84 of this Act.

(5) A person upon whom an obstruction notice is served shall have power, notwithstanding anything in any conveyance or in any lease or other agreement, to do all such things as may be necessary for complying with the requirements of the notice.

(6) Without prejudice to section 141 of this Act, where an obstruction notice has been served upon a person the roads authority may, with the consent of that person, do on his behalf anything necessary for complying with the requirements of the notice.

(7) Subject to subsections (4) and (6) above, and without prejudice to any other proceedings which may be instituted against him, a person who fails to comply with the requirements of, or acts in contravention of, an obstruction notice served on him commits an offence.

(8) A person upon whom an obstruction notice is served shall be entitled to recover from the roads authority any expenses reasonably incurred by him in carrying out any directions contained in the notice; and a person sustaining loss in direct consequence of any requirement of such a notice or a person who proves that his property is injuriously affected by restrictions imposed by such a notice shall, if he makes a claim within six months after its service, be entitled to recover from the roads authority compensation for the injury sustained.

(9) Nothing in this section shall authorise the service by a local roads authority of an obstruction notice with respect to—

(a) any wall—

      (i) forming part of an ancient monument or other object of archaeological interest, except with the consent in writing of the Secretary of State; or

      (ii) forming part of, or necessary for the maintenance of, a railway, canal, inland waterway, dock or harbour;

   (b) a protected tree; or

   (c) a listed building.

(10) In subsection (9) above—

"protected tree" means a tree which is subject to a tree preservation order under section 58(1) of the Town and Country Planning (Scotland) Act 1972; and

"listed building" has the meaning assigned to it by section 52(7) of that Act.   **[186]**

NOTE

Commencement: 1 January 1985.

84. Determination of questions arising out of section 83

(1) A question as to whether—

   (a) a notice served under subsection (1) of section 83 of this Act shall be withdrawn as respects any requirement or restriction objected to under subsection (4) of that section; or

   (b) any expenses were reasonably incurred by any person in carrying out directions contained in a notice served under that section,

shall be decided—

      (i) if the parties so agree, by a single arbiter appointed by them; or

      (ii) in default of such agreement, by the sheriff.

(2) In determining any such question as is mentioned in paragraph (a) of subsection (1) above, the arbiter or sheriff shall have power to order that the requirement or restriction shall have effect subject to such modifications, if any, as he may direct.   **[187]**

NOTE

Commencement: 1 January 1985.

General obstruction

85. Control of builders' skips on road

(1) A builder's skip shall not be deposited on a road without—

   (a) the [written] permission of the roads authority; and

   (b) its being clearly and indelibly marked with its owner's name and with his telephone number or address.

(2) Such permission as is mentioned in subsection (1)(a) above may be granted either unconditionally or subject to such conditions as may be specified in the permission; and the conditions may in particular relate to the siting and lighting of the skip, the care of the contents of the skip and the removal of the skip at the end of the period of permission.

(3) An owner of a skip who uses it, or causes or permits it to be used, on a road in contravention of this section commits an offence.

(4) In proceedings for an offence under subsection (3) above it shall be a

defence, except in relation to a contravention of subsection (1)(b) above, to prove that some other person undertook the responsibility of complying with the permission or condition contravened, and that the offence was committed without the consent or connivance of the owner; and that other person may be charged with and convicted of the contravention as if he were the owner.

(5) In this section and in section 86 of this Act, "builders' skip" means a container designed to be carried on a road vehicle and to be placed on a road for the removal and disposal of builders' materials, rubble, waste, household and other rubbish or earth. **[188]**

NOTES
Commencement: 1 January 1985.
Sub-s (1): words in square brackets prospectively inserted by the New Roads and Street Works Act 1991, s 168(1), Sch 8, Part III, para 89, as from a day to be appointed.

86. Removal of builders' skips causing danger or obstruction

(1) Notwithstanding that there is in force a permission granted under section 85 of this Act for the depositing of a builders' skip on a road, a constable in uniform may require the removal or repositioning of, or himself cause to be removed or repositioned, any builders' skip which, in his opinion, is causing, or is likely to cause, a danger or obstruction.

(2) The roads authority may require the removal or repositioning of a builders' skip where there is a contravention of section 85 of this Act, and failing removal or repositioning within a reasonable period of time after so requiring, may remove or reposition it themselves.

(3) Subsections (1) and (2) above are without prejudice to section 129(2) of this Act.

(4) Any expenses reasonably incurred by the police authority under subsection (1), or the roads authority under subsection (2), above in the removal or repositioning of a builders' skip may be recovered from its owner.

(5) The police authority or, as the case may be, the roads authority shall, where practicable, notify the owner of the skip of its removal under subsection (1) or (2) above; but if the owner cannot be traced or if a reasonable period of time after his being so notified has elapsed and he has not recovered the skip, the police authority or roads authority may dispose of the skip and its contents.

(6) Any proceeds of a disposal under subsection (5) above shall be used in the first place to meet the expenses reasonably incurred in the said removal and thereafter any surplus shall be given to the owner if he can be traced and if he cannot may be retained by the police authority, or roads authority, as the case may be. **[189]**

NOTE
Commencement: 1 January 1985.

87. Power to remove structures from roads

(1) Without prejudice to sections 59 and 129(2) of this Act, where a structure has been erected, deposited or placed on a road otherwise than under or by virtue of an enactment the roads authority may, by notice, require that within such period as may be specified in the notice the person having control or possession of the structure—

(a) shall remove it; and

(b) if the authority consider reinstatement of the road to be requisite, shall carry out such reinstatement.

(2) In subsection (1) above, "structure" includes any machine, pump, post or other object of such a nature as to be capable of causing obstruction; and a structure may be treated for the purposes of that subsection as having been erected notwithstanding that it is on wheels.   **[190]**

NOTE
Commencement: 1 January 1985.

88. Removal of projections which impede or endanger road users

(1) Without prejudice to section 129(8) of this Act, the roads authority may, after giving 28 days notice to the owner and occupier of any building, remove or alter any such projection therefrom as interferes with safe or convenient passage along a road and is specified in the notice.

(2) Subject to subsection (3) below, the roads authority shall pay compensation to any person who sustains damage by reason of the removal or alteration of a projection in pursuance of subsection (1) above.

(3) No compensation shall be payable under subsection (2) above in respect of a projection made without any consent which was, by or under any enactment, required for it.   **[191]**

NOTE
Commencement: 1 January 1985.

89. Removal of accidental obstructions from roads

(1) Where an object has fallen onto a road so as to cause an obstruction, the roads authority shall, where practicable, intimate to the owner of the object that he must remove it forthwith; and if the owner cannot be traced or if he fails to remove the object within a reasonable period of time after being so notified or if the case is one of emergency, the roads authority shall remove it themselves.

(2) Pending the removal of such an object by the owner or by the roads authority, the authority may take all reasonable steps (including the placing of lights, signs and fences on the road) for the purpose of warning road users of the obstruction.

(3) Any expenses reasonably incurred by the roads authority under this section may be recovered from the owner; but not such expenses shall be recoverable if the owner proves that he took reasonable care to secure that the object did not cause or contribute to an obstruction.

(4) The roads authority shall, where practicable, give notice to the owner of an object of its removal by them under subsection (1) above; but if the owner cannot be traced or if after a reasonable period of time after being so notified he has not recovered the object, the roads authority may dispose of it.

(5) Any proceeds of a disposal under subsection (4) above shall be used in the first place to meet the expenses reasonably incurred by the roads authority under this section and thereafter any surplus shall be given to the owner if he can be traced and if he cannot may be retained by the roads authority.   **[192]**

NOTE
Commencement: 1 January 1985.

90. Restriction on placing bridges, beams, rails etc over roads

(1) No overhead bridge, beam, rail, pipe, cable, wire or other similar apparatus shall be fixed or placed over, along or across a road without the consent of the roads authority; and that authority may attach to their consent such reasonable terms and conditions as they think fit.

(2) A person who contravenes subsection (1) above or the terms or conditions of any consent given thereunder commits an offence.

(3) Subsection (1) above does not apply to any works or apparatus of statutory undertakers.

(4) A person aggrieved by the refusal of a consent required by this section, or by any terms or conditions attached to any such consent, may, within 28 days of the refusal or consent, refer the matter by summary application to the sheriff; and the decision of the sheriff on the matter shall be final. **[193]**

NOTE
Commencement: 1 January 1985.

91. Prevention of danger to road from nearby vegetation and fences etc or from retaining walls being inadequate

(1) Where a hedge, tree or shrub overhangs a road so as to—

    (a) endanger or obstruct the passage of vehicles or pedestrians;
    (b) obstruct or interfere with—

        (i) road users' view of the road;
        (ii) the light from a public lamp; or
        (iii) a traffic sign; or

    (c) increase the likelihood of obstruction of the road by drifting snow,

the roads authority may, by notice served either on the owner of the hedge, tree or shrub, or on the occupier of the land on which it is growing, require him within 28 days from the date of service of the notice to carry out such work on the hedge, tree or shrub as is necessary to remove the cause of danger, obstruction or interference.

(2) Subject to subsections (3) and (4) below, where it appears to the roads authority that a hedge, tree, shrub, fence or wall on or near a road is in such condition that it, or part of it, is likely to cause danger by falling on the road, or that a retaining wall (whether or not near the road) is in such condition that there is constituted a danger to the road or to road users, they may, by notice served either on the owner of the hedge, tree, shrub, fence or wall, or on the occupier of the land on which it is situated, require him within 28 days from the date of the service of the notice to carry out such work as will obviate the danger.

(3) Subject to subsection (4) below, if in the opinion of the roads authority the danger referred to in subsection (2) above is imminent they may dispense with the service of the notice required by that subsection, may themselves carry out the work forthwith, and may recover the expenses reasonably incurred in so doing from the owner or occupier.

(4) Subsection (3) above does not apply, and subsection (2) above does not except in any case with the consent of the Secretary of State apply, as regards a wall (or retaining wall) forming part of an ancient monument or other object of archaeological interest; and any such consent may direct that the said subsection

(2) shall apply in that case with such modifications as may be specified in the consent:

Provided that where in the opinion of the roads authority the danger referred to in the said subsection (2) is imminent, they may before obtaining such consent (and without service of the notice required by that subsection) carry out such work, or take such other steps, as will for the time being safeguard road users.

(5) The roads authority may make such contribution as they think fit towards any expenses reasonably incurred by a person in carrying out necessary work in pursuance of subsection (1) or (2) above.

(6) As soon as may be after the necessity for work under this section on a protected tree or on a wall (or retaining wall) forming part of a listed building arises and before any such work is commenced, the roads authority shall give notice of the proposed work to the planning authority:

Provided that, if in the opinion of the roads authority there is imminent danger of the tree or wall falling on the road, they may dispense with the giving of such notice.

(7) Nothing in this section shall impose on the roads authority any liability in respect of injury to persons or damage to property.

(8) In—
  (a) subsection (2) above, "retaining wall" means a wall which serves, or is intended to serve, as a support for earth or other material on only one side; and
  (b) subsection (6) above—
    (i) "planning authority" has the meaning assigned by section 172 of the Local Government (Scotland) Act 1973; and
    (ii) "protected tree" means a tree which is subject to a tree preservation order under section 58(1) of the Town and Country Planning (Scotland) Act 1972.

(9) A person upon whom a notice has been served under subsection (1) or (2) above may within 28 days of such service refer the matter by summary application to the sheriff; and the decision of the sheriff on the matter shall be final.   **[194]**

NOTE
Commencement: 1 January 1985.

---

92. Restriction on planting of trees etc near carriageway

(1) No tree or shrub planted in accordance with section 51 of this Act shall be planted within 5 metres of the edge of a made-up carriageway without the roads authority's consent which shall not be unreasonably withheld.

(2) If a tree or shrub is planted in contravention of this section, the roads authority may, by notice served either on the owner or on the occupier of the land in which the tree or shrub is planted, require him to remove it within 28 days from the date of the service of the notice.

(3) A person who fails to comply with a notice given under subsection (2) above commits an offence.

(4) In this section, "made-up carriageway" means a carriageway, or a part thereof, which has been metalled or in any way provided with a surface suitable for the passage of vehicles. **[195]**

NOTE

Commencement: 1 January 1985.

Roadside dangers

93. Protection of road users from dangers near a road

(1) If, in the opinion of the roads authority, anything which is on land beside or near to a road—

    (a) but is not itself a building constitutes a danger to road users and there is no other provision of this Act under or by virtue of which they may take steps to obviate the danger, they shall, under this subsection, take such steps;

    (b) and is a building constitutes a danger to road users and there is no other such provision as aforesaid, they shall under this subsection take such steps by way of enclosure or screening,

as they consider appropriate to afford protection from the danger or to ensure that the danger is not so constituted; and they may, subject to subsection (6)(a) below, recover the expenses reasonably incurred in so doing from the owner of the land.

(2) Where there is on land adjoining a road—

    (a) a fence made with barbed wire, or in or on which barbed wire has been laid;

    (b) an electrified fence; or

    (c) a wall or window-sill incorporating spikes, broken glass, barbed wire or a similar device,

and such wire, electrified fence, spikes, glass or device is in the opinion of the roads authority likely to be injurious to persons or animals lawfully using the road, the roads authority may serve a notice on the occupier of the land requiring him, within such period as may be specified in the notice, to take such steps as may be so specified to remove the risk of injury.

(3) Where the roads authority are occupiers of land adjoining a road, and there is on that land any such thing as is described in paragraphs (a) to (c) of subsection (2) above, then—

    (a) in the case of a local roads authority, any ratepayer within the region or islands area; and

    (b) in the case of the Secretary of State, any person,

may, if of the opinion required of a roads authority by the said subsection, serve a notice on the authority requiring them to take such steps as may be specified in the notice to remove the risk of injury.

(4) If the period specified in a notice served under subsection (3) above expires without the steps so specified having been taken, the person who served the notice may apply to the sheriff who may, if he is satisfied that the steps specified in the notice are necessary, order the roads authority to take those steps.

(5) In subsection (2) above "barbed wire" means any wire or strip metal with spikes or jagged projections.

(6) A person who considers that in all the circumstances he should not be required—

    (a) to pay such expenses as are mentioned in subsection (1) above, may within 28 days of the first written intimation to him by the roads authority of their intention to recover those expenses from him; or

    (b) to take such steps as are specified in a notice served on him under subsection (2) above, may within 28 days of such notice,

refer the matter by summary application to the sheriff; and the decision of the sheriff on the matter shall be final.   **[196]**

NOTE
    Commencement: 1 January 1985.

98. Control of stray and other animals on roads

(1) An animal which is left on, or allowed to stray onto, a road other than at a place where that road is running through unenclosed *countryside* [land] may be seized and detained by the roads authority or by a constable; and the person so leaving an animal or allowing it so to stray commits an offence.

(2) Subject to subsection (3) below, the owner of an animal seized or detained under subsection (1) above may recover it from the roads authority, or as the case may be from the police authority, on payment to them of their reasonable expenses in acting under the said subsection (1):

Provided that no such payment shall be exigible where the owner took all reasonable steps to ensure that the animal was not so left as is mentioned in subsection (1) above or, as the case may be, did not so stray as is there mentioned.

(3) Subject to the proviso to subsection (2) above, the roads authority, or as the case may be police authority, may sell, or otherwise dispose of, an animal so detained by them if, within three days of their giving intimation, in a newspaper circulating in their area, of the seizure, detention and prospective sale or disposal, the said expenses are not paid.

(4) Any proceeds of a sale or disposal under subsection (2) above shall be used to meet the said expenses. Thereafter any surplus shall be given to the owner of the animal if he can be traced and if he cannot may be retained by the roads authority or as the case may be police authority.

(5) In proceedings for an offence under subsection (1) above, it shall be a defence for a person accused of allowing an animal to stray onto a road to prove that he took all reasonable steps to prevent such straying.

(6) In subsection (1) above, "countryside" has the meaning assigned to it by section 2 of the Countryside (Scotland) Act 1967.   **[197]**

NOTES
    Commencement: 1 January 1985.
    Sub-s (1): prospectively amended by the Natural Heritage (Scotland) Act 1991, s 27(1), Sch 10, para 11(3), as from a day to be appointed.

Offences

100. Damage to roads etc

A person who without lawful authority or reasonable excuse—

    (a) deposits anything whatsoever on a road so as to damage the road;

    (b) paints or otherwise inscribes or affixes upon the surface of a road or upon a tree, traffic sign, milestone, structure or works on or in a road, a picture, letter, sign or other mark; or

    (c) by lighting a fire within, or by permitting a fire for which he is responsible to spread to within, 30 metres of a road, damages the road or endangers traffic on it,

commits an offence. [197A]

NOTE

   Commencement: 1 January 1985.

101. Placing rope, wire or other apparatus in road without adequate warning

A person who, for any purpose, places or causes to be placed in a road rope, wire or other apparatus in such manner as endangers road users and who fails to take all necessary steps to give adequate warning of the danger, commits an offence. [197B]

NOTE

   Commencement: 1 January 1985.

102. Ploughing of unenclosed land

A person who, in ploughing unenclosed land adjoining a public road, fails to make side ridges at least 3 metres in breadth along the sides of the road, commits an offence. [197C]

NOTE

   Commencement: 1 January 1985.

PART XI
OFFENCES

129. Miscellaneous summary offences

(1) A person who in or beside any road leaves open and unfenced, or insufficiently covered or insufficiently fenced, an opening into a vault or cellar commits an offence:

    Provided that the foregoing provisions of this subsection do not apply in relation to the duty under section 56(5) of this Act first to provide a door or cover.

(2) A person who, without lawful authority or reasonable excuse, places or deposits anything in a road so as to obstruct the passage of, or to endanger, road users commits an offence:

    Provided that no person shall, in respect of the same actings, be convicted both under the foregoing provisions of this subsection and under section 59(2), 90, 95, 100(a) or 101 of this Act, or subsection (9) of this section, of an offence.

(3) A person who, in a road, as the case may be drives, leads or propels a vehicle or animal commits an offence if any load which is thereby being carried projects beyond the vehicle or animal so as in any way to obstruct other road users.

(4) Without prejudice to subsection (2) above, a person who, in a road, pitches a tent or encamps commits an offence.

(5) Subject to section 64 of this Act, a person who, in a footway, footpath or cycle track, as the case may be drives, rides, leads or propels a vehicle or horse, or any swine or cattle, commits an offence:

Provided that the foregoing provisions of this subsection do not apply—

(a) where and in so far as the vehicle or animal is being taken across the footway, footpath or cycle track;

(b) in relation to a pedal cycle which is either not being ridden or is being ridden on a cycle track;

(c) except on a cycle track where there is no public right of passage on foot, in relation to—

(i) a perambulator, push-chair or other form of baby carriage; or

(ii) an invalid carriage whose motive power is provided solely by its rider or some other person, or by an electric motor, or by a combination of these sources; or

(d) where there is a specific right so to drive, ride, lead or propel.

(6) A person who parks a motor vehicle ("motor vehicle" having the same meaning as in the Road Traffic Act 1972) wholly or partly on a cycle track commits an offence.

(7) A person who in a road rides or drives furiously, recklessly or carelessly a horse or other animal (whether or not that horse or animal is attached to a cart or a carriage) commits an offence.

(8) Without prejudice to subsection (2) above, a person who, over or along a footway, places a shade, awning or other projection less than either or both—

(a) 2·25 metres above the level of the footway;

(b) 50 centimetres inwards from a carriageway,

commits an offence.

(9) A person who displays goods for sale by placing them in, or hanging them over, a footway or footpath commits an offence:

Provided that the foregoing provisions of this subsection do not apply to—

(a) the offer or exposure for sale of newspapers;

(b) the display of goods for sale by a street trader trading under and in accordance with a street trader's licence;

(c) the display of goods for sale in connection with the carrying on of a private market under and in accordance with a market operator's licence; or

(d) any activity in respect of which a certificate under the Pedlars Act 1871 has been granted,

and in the foregoing paragraphs of this proviso "street trader's licence", "private market" and "market operator's licence" shall be construed in accordance with section 97(6) of this Act.

(10) Where materials, tools, machinery or other equipment—

(a) have been deposited in any place for use by the roads authority in constructing or maintaining a road; or

(b) are in a quarry which has been opened by the authority for the purpose of their obtaining such materials for that use,

a person who without reasonable excuse takes away, or displaces, the materials, tools, machinery or equipment commits an offence.   **[197D]**

NOTE
Commencement: 1 January 1985.

130. Offences by bodies corporate

(1) Where an offence under or by virtue of this Act has been committed by a body corporate and is proved to have been committed with the consent or connivance of, or to be attributable to neglect on the part of, a director, manager, secretary or other similar officer of the body corporate, or a person purporting to act in such capacity, he as well as the body corporate is guilty of that offence and shall be liable to be proceeded against and punished accordingly.

(2) Where the affairs of a body corporate are managed by its members, subsection (1) above applies in relation to the acts and defaults of a member in connection with his functions of management as if he were a director of the body corporate. **[197E]**

NOTE
Commencement: 1 January 1985.

131. Penalties and mode of trial

(1) An offence under this Act shall, unless there is express provision to the contrary, be triable only summarily.

(2) The penalty on conviction of any offence under this Act shall be determined in accordance with Schedule 8 thereto; and in that Schedule—

- (a) column 1 specifies the provision of this Act creating the offence and column 2 the maximum penalty which may be imposed in respect of that offence;
- (b) references to a level on the standard scale are references to the standard scale as defined in section 75 of the Criminal Justice Act 1982; and
- (c) "the statutory maximum" has the meaning ascribed to it by section 74 of that Act. **[197F]**

NOTE
Commencement: 1 January 1985.

Interpretation

151. Interpretation

(1) In this Act, unless the context otherwise requires—

"approaches", in relation to a bridge or tunnel, includes the facings of any embankment or cutting adjacent to the bridge or tunnel;
"building" includes any erection, however, and with whatever material, it is constructed and any part of a building;
"carriageway" shall be construed in accordance with subsection (2) below;
"cattle-grid" has the meaning given by section 41(6) of this Act;
"classified road" shall be construed in accordance with section 11 of this Act;
"common" has the same meaning as in the Acquisition of Land (Authorisation Procedure) (Scotland) Act 1947;
"cycle track" shall be construed in accordance with subsection (2) below;
"days" means clear days;

"enactment" includes an enactment in this Act or in a local or private Act and a provision of an order, a scheme, regulations or any other instrument made under or confirmed by a public general, local or private Act;

"footpath" shall be construed in accordance with subsections (2) and (3)(a) and (b), and "footway" in accordance with subsection (2), below;

"frontager", in relation to a road or proposed road, means the owner of any land fronting or abutting it;

"improvement", in relation to a road, means the doing of anything for the benefit of road users, or any class of road users, beyond that which is essential to placing the road in a proper state of repair, and includes the improvement of the amenity—

    (a) of the road; and

    (b) of land abutting on, or adjacent to, the road;

"local authority" means a regional or islands council;

"local roads authority" has the meaning given by paragraph (a) of the definition of "roads authority" in this subsection;

"maintenance" includes—

    (a) repair; and

    (b) watering to allay dust but, without prejudice to subsection (1) of section 25 of the Local Government and Planning (Scotland) Act 1982 (restriction of powers of local authorities as regards street cleansing), not such cleansing as an islands or district council are required by subsections (1) and (3) of that section to undertake;

"navigation authority" means persons authorised by any enactment to work, maintain, conserve, improve or control any canal or other inland navigation, navigable river, estuary, harbour or dock;

"notice" means notice in writing;

"obstruction" includes obstruction of view;

"occupier" means the person in occupation or having the charge, management or control of land, either on his own account or as the agent of another person;

"open space" has the same meaning as in the Acquisition of Land (Authorisation Procedure) (Scotland) Act 1947;

"operator", in relation to a telecommunications code system, has the same meaning as in paragraph 1 of Schedule 4 to the Telecommunications Act 1984;

"owner"—

    (a) in relation to land means, subject to paragraph (b) below, the person for the time being entitled to receive, or who would, if the same were let, be entitled to receive, the rents of the land, and includes a trustee, factor, tutor or curator, and in the case of public or municipal property applies to the persons to whom the management thereof is entrusted; and

    (b) in relation to special roads (whether existing or proposed) includes any person who under the Lands Clauses Acts would be entitled to sell and convey the land to promoters of an undertaking and also includes a lessee under a lease the unexpired portion of which exceeds three years;

"pedal cycle" means a cycle whose motive power is provided solely by the legs of its rider or riders or which complies with the requirements specified in Regulation 4 of the Electrically Assisted Pedal Cycles Regulations 1983;

"private road" means any road other than a public road;

"proposed road" means (without prejudice to the definition in this subsection of "proposed public road") a new road in course of construction, or proposed to be constructed, by or on behalf of any person;

"proposed public road" means either—

(a) a new road in course of construction, or proposed to be constructed, by or on behalf of a roads authority; or

(b) an existing road which is a prospective public road within the meaning of [Part IV of the New Roads and Street Works Act 1991];

"public road" means a road which a roads authority have a duty to maintain;

"railway undertakers" means persons authorised by any enactment to carry on a railway undertaking;

"road" means, subject to subsection (3) below, any way (other than a waterway) over which there is a public right of passage (by whatever means [and whether subject to a toll or not]) and includes the road's verge, and any bridge (whether permanent or temporary) over which, or tunnel through which, the road passes; and any reference to a road includes a part thereof;

"roads authority" means—

(a) in relation to a road or proposed road other than any such as is mentioned in paragraph (b) of this definition, the regional or islands council within whose area the road is (such council being in this Act referred to as a "local roads authority"); and

(b) in relation to a trunk road (whether existing or in course of construction) or, without prejudice to section 4 of this Act, to a special road provided by him under section 7(5) (or to be provided by him under section 7(5)(a) or (b)) or to any other road constructed (or to be constructed) by him under section 19(1) of this Act, the Secretary of State; and references to "they" in relation to a roads authority shall be taken to relate also to the Secretary of State;

"special road authority" has the meaning given by section 7(4) of this Act;

"special road" means a road provided or to be provided in accordance with a scheme under section 7 of this act;

"statutory undertakers" has the same meaning as in section 275 of the Town and Country Planning (Scotland) Act 1972 except that it includes the Post Office and, except in sections 133 and 140(4) of this Act, the operator of any telecommunications code system;

"swing bridge" includes any opening bridge operated by mechanical means;

"telecommunications apparatus", "the telecommunications code" and "telecommunications code system" have the same meanings as in paragraph 1 of Schedule 4 to the Telecommunications Act 1984;

"tidal waters" has the same meaning as in section 35(1) of the Rivers (Prevention of Pollution) (Scotland) Act 1951;

"traffic" includes pedestrians and animals;

"traffic sign" has the same meaning as in section 64(1) of the Road Traffic Regulation Act 1984;

"trunk road" means a road which is a trunk road by virtue of section 5 of this Act or of an order or direction under that section or section 198(2) of the Town and Country Planning (Scotland) Act 1972;

"use", in relation to a road, includes crossing;

"vehicle" means a vehicle of any description and includes a machine or implement of any kind drawn or propelled along roads (whether or not by mechanical power);

"water authority" shall be construed in accordance with section 3 of the Water (Scotland) Act 1980; and

"works", as regards any road, includes—

    (a) making an alteration to it;
    (b) breaking up or opening it;
    (c) constructing or laying anything under it;
    (d) building anything into it; and
    (e) carrying out any other operations of a like nature;

and cognate expressions shall be construed accordingly.

(2) For the purpose of this Act, where over a road the public right of passage referred to in the definition of "road" in subsection (1) above—

    (a) is by foot only, the road is—

        (i) where it is associated with a carriageway, a "footway"; and
        (ii) where it is not so associated, a "footpath";

    (b) is by pedal cycle only, or by pedal cycle and foot only, the road is a "cycle track";

    (c) includes such a right by vehicle, other than a right by pedal cycle only, the road is a "carriageway".

(3) This Act does not confer any power or impose any duty as regards a road or proposed road which—

    (a) being a footpath only, is a public path created under section 30 of the Countryside (Scotland) Act 1967 (power of planning authority to create public paths by agreement);

    (b) being a footpath only, forms part of a long-distance route the proposals for which have been approved by the Secretary of State under section 40(1) of that Act (approval of proposals relating to a long-distance route); or

    (c) forms part of land owned or managed by an islands or district council and used by them for the provision of facilities for recreational, sporting, cultural or social activities in the discharge of their duties under section 14 of the Local Government and Planning (Scotland) Act 1982.

(4) Any reference in this Act to apparatus belonging to statutory undertakers shall, in relation to the operator of a telecommunications code system, have effect as a reference to telecommunications apparatus kept installed for the purposes of that system.   **[197G]**

NOTES

Commencement: 1 January 1985.

Sub-s (1): definition "proposed public road" prospectively amended by the New Roads and Street Works Act 1991, s 168(1), Sch 8, Part III, para 94(a), as from a day to be appointed; definition "road" amended by s 168(1) of, and Sch 8, Part III, para 94(b) to, the 1991 Act.

SCHEDULE 3

Section 8(2)

CLASSES OF TRAFFIC FOR PURPOSES OF SPECIAL ROADS

CLASS I:

Heavy and light locomotives,

motor tractors,

heavy motor cars,

motor cars,

motor cycles whereof the cylinder capacity of the engine is not less than 50 cubic centimetres, and

trailers drawn thereby,

which comply with general regulations as to construction and use made under section 40 of the Road Traffic Act 1972 and in the case of which—:

(i) the whole weight of the vehicle is transmitted to the road surface by means of wheels;

(ii) all wheels of the vehicle are equipped with pneumatic tyres;

(iii) the vehicle is not controlled by a pedestrian;

(iv) the vehicle is not a vehicle chargeable with duty under paragraph 2 of Part I of Schedule 3 to the Vehicles (Excise) Act 1971; and

(v) it is so constructed, being a motor vehicle, as to be capable of attaining a speed of 25 miles per hour on the level under its own power, when unladen and not drawing a trailer.

CLASS II:

Motor vehicles and trailers the use of which for or in connection with the conveyance of abnormal indivisible loads is authorised by order made by the Secretary of State under section 42(1) of the Road Traffic Act 1972.

Motor vehicles and trailers constructed for naval, military, air force or other defence purposes, the use of which is authorised by order made by the Secretary of State under section 42(1) of the Road Traffic Act 1972.

Motor vehicles and trailers, to which Articles 16 (which relates to vehicles for moving excavated material), 17 (which relates among other things to vehicles constructed for use outside the United Kingdom) and 21 (which relates to engineering plant) of the Motor Vehicles (Authorisation of Special Types) General Order 1973 relate and which are authorised to be used by those Articles or by any other Order under section 42(1) of the Road Traffic Act 1972, the said motor vehicles being so constructed as to be capable of attaining a speed of 25 miles per hour on the level under their own power, when unladen and not drawing a trailer.

CLASS III:	Motor vehicles controlled by pedestrians.
CLASS IV:	All motor vehicles (other than invalid carriages and motor cycles whereof the cylinder capacity of the engine is less than 50 cubic centimetres) not comprised in Class I, Class II or Class III.
CLASS V:	Vehicles drawn by animals.
CLASS VI:	Vehicles (other than pedal cycles, perambulators, push-chairs and other forms of baby carriages) drawn or propelled by pedestrians.
CLASS VII:	Pedal cycles, motor cycles whereof the cylinder capacity of the engine is less than 50 cubic centimetres and invalid carriages.
CLASS VIII:	Animals ridden, led or driven (other than dogs held on a lead).
CLASS IX:	Pedestrian, perambulators, push-chairs and other forms of baby carriages, and dogs held on a lead.

In this Schedule any expression defined for the purposes of the Road Traffic Act 1972 has the same meaning as in that Act and the expression "abnormal indivisible load" has the same meaning as in the Motor Vehicles (Authorisation of Special Types) General Order 1973.   **[197H]**

NOTE
    Commencement: 1 January 1985.

SCHEDULE 7
Section 126

RESTRICTED ROADS

AMENDMENT OF ROAD TRAFFIC REGULATION ACT 1984 (C 27)

(Paras 1–3 amend the Road Traffic Regulation Act 1984, ss 82(1), 85, respectively.)

4. In section 134(2) (provisions as to regulations), after the word "sections" there shall be inserted the words "82(1),".

Transitional provision

5. Where, immediately prior to the commencement of this Schedule—

(a) a road is or is deemed to be a restricted road for the purposes of section 81 of the Road Traffic Regulation Act 1984, and that road would, apart from this paragraph, cease to be a restricted road in consequence of the first regulations made by the Secretary of State under section 82(1) of that Act as amended by paragraph 2 above; or

(b) a road is not and is not deemed to be a restricted road for those purposes and that road would, apart from this paragraph, become a restricted road in consequence of those regulations,

the roads authority may, prior to the commencement of the regulations, make an order specifying the road, and the road shall, notwithstanding the commencement of the regulations, continue to be, or to be deemed to be, a restricted road or as the case may be, a road which is not a restricted road until such time as the order is superseded, in relation to that road, by a direction under section 82(2) of that Act (directions making specified roads restricted or not restricted) or an order under section 84(1) of that Act (power to fix speed limits).   **[197I]**

NOTE
    Commencement: 1 January 1985.

ROAD TRAFFIC ACT 1988
(c 52)

ARRANGEMENT OF SECTIONS

PART I

PRINCIPAL ROAD SAFETY PROVISIONS

Driving offences

PART II

CONSTRUCTION AND USE OF VEHICLES AND EQUIPMENT

Using vehicle in dangerous condition

General regulation of construction, use etc

Tests of vehicles other than goods vehicles to which section 49 applies

Tests of certain classes of goods vehicles

Approval of design, construction, equipment and marking of vehicles

Conditions for grant of excise licence

PART III

LICENSING OF DRIVERS OF VEHICLES

PART VI

THIRD-PARTY LIABILITIES

PART VII

MISCELLANEOUS AND GENERAL

An Act to consolidate certain enactments relating to road traffic with amendments to give effect to recommendations of the Law Commission and the Scottish Law Commission   [15 November 1988]

PART I

PRINCIPAL ROAD SAFETY PROVISIONS

Driving offences

[1. Causing death by dangerous driving

A person who causes the death of another person by driving a mechanically propelled vehicle dangerously on a road or other public place is guilty of an offence.]   **[198]**

NOTES
  Commencement: 1 July 1992.
  This section and ss 2, 2A post were substituted for the original ss 1, 2 by the Road Traffic Act 1991, s 1

[2. Dangerous driving

A person who drives a mechanically propelled vehicle dangerously on a road or other public place is guilty of an offence.]   **[199]**

NOTES
  Commencement: 1 July 1992.
  See the note to s 1 ante.

[2A. Meaning of dangerous driving

(1) For the purposes of sections 1 and 2 above a person is to be regarded as driving dangerously if (and, subject to subsection (2) below, only if)—

  (a) the way he drives falls far below what would be expected of a competent and careful driver, and
  (b) it would be obvious to a competent and careful driver that driving in that way would be dangerous.

(2) A person is also to be regarded as driving dangerously for the purposes of sections 1 and 2 above if it would be obvious to a competent and careful driver that driving the vehicle in its current state would be dangerous.

(3) In subsections (1) and (2) above "dangerous" refers to danger either of injury to any person or of serious damage to property; and in determining for the purposes of those subsections what would be expected of, or obvious to, a competent and careful driver in a particular case, regard shall be had not only to the circumstances of which he could be expected to be aware but also to any circumstances shown to have been within the knowledge of the accused.

(4) In determining for the purposes of subsection (2) above the state of a vehicle, regard may be had to anything attached to or carried on or in it and to the manner in which it is attached or carried.]   **[199A]**

NOTES
  Commencement: 1 July 1992.
  See the note to s 1 ante.

[3. Careless, and inconsiderate, driving

If a person drives a mechanically propelled vehicle on a road or other public place without due care and attention, or without reasonable consideration for other persons using the road or place, he is guilty of an offence.]   **[200]**

NOTES
 Commencement: 1 July 1992.
 Substituted by the Road Traffic Act 1991, s 2.

3A. Causing death by careless driving when under influence of drink or drugs

(1) If a person causes the death of another person by driving a mechanically propelled vehicle on a road or other public place without due care and attention, or without reasonable consideration for other persons using the road or place, and—

  (a) he is, at the time when he is driving, unfit to drive through drink or drugs, or
  (b) he has consumed so much alcohol that the proportion of it in his breath, blood or urine at that time exceeds the prescribed limit, or
  (c) he is, within 18 hours after that time, required to provide a specimen in pursuance of section 7 of this Act, but without reasonable excuse fails to provide it,

he is guilty of an offence.

  (2) For the purposes of this section a person shall be taken to be unfit to drive at any time when his ability to drive properly is impaired.

  (3) Subsection (1)(b) and (c) above shall not apply in relation to a person driving a mechanically propelled vehicle other than a motor vehicle.]   **[200A]**

NOTES
 Commencement: 1 July 1992.
 Inserted by the Road Traffic Act 1991, s 3.

PRINCIPAL ROAD SAFETY PROVISIONS: MOTOR VEHICLES

Drink and drugs

4. Driving, or being in charge, when under influence of drink or drugs

(1) A person who, when driving or attempting to drive a [mechanically propelled vehicle] on a road or other public place, is unfit to drive through drink or drugs is guilty of an offence.

  (2) Without prejudice to subsection (1) above, a person who, when in charge of a [mechanically propelled vehicle] which is on a road or other public place, is unfit to drive through drink or drugs is guilty of an offence.

  (3) For the purposes of subsection (2) above, a person shall be deemed not to have been in charge of a [mechanically propelled vehicle] if he proves that at the material time the circumstances were such that there was no likelihood of his driving it so long as he remained unfit to drive through drink or drugs.

  (4) The court may, in determining whether there was such a likelihood as is mentioned in subsection (3) above, disregard any injury to him and any damage to the vehicle.

(5) For the purposes of this section, a person shall be taken to be unfit to drive if his ability to drive properly is for the time being impaired.

(6) A constable may arrest a person without warrant if he has reasonable cause to suspect that that person is or has been committing an offence under this section.

(7) For the purpose of arresting a person under the power conferred by subsection (6) above, a constable may enter (if need be by force) any place where that person is or where the constable, with reasonable cause, suspects him to be.

(8) Subsection (7) above does not extend to Scotland, and nothing in that subsection affects any rule of law in Scotland concerning the right of a constable to enter any premises for any purpose. **[201]**

NOTES
Commencement: 15 May 1989.
This section derived from the Road Traffic Act 1972, s 5, and the Transport Act 1981, s 25(1), (2).
Sub-ss (1)–(3): words in square brackets substituted by the Road Traffic Act 1991, s 4.

5. Driving or being in charge of a motor vehicle with alcohol concentration above prescribed limit

(1) If a person—

(a) drives or attempts to drive a motor vehicle on a road or other public place, or
(b) is in charge of a motor vehicle on a road or other public place,

after consuming so much alcohol that the proportion of it in his breath, blood or urine exceeds the prescribed limit he is guilty of an offence.

(2) It is a defence for a person charged with an offence under subsection (1)(b) above to prove that at the time he is alleged to have committed the offence the circumstances were such that there was no likelihood of his driving the vehicle whilst the proportion of alcohol in his breath, blood or urine remained likely to exceed the prescribed limit.

(3) The court may, in determining whether there was such a likelihood as is mentioned in subsection (2) above, disregard any injury to him and any damage to the vehicle. **[202]**

NOTES
Commencement: 15 May 1989.
This section derived from the Road Traffic Act 1972, s 6, and the Transport Act 1981, s 25(3), Sch 8.

6. Breath tests

(1) Where a constable in uniform has reasonable cause to suspect—

(a) that a person driving or attempting to drive or in charge of a motor vehicle on a road or other public place has alcohol in his body or has committed a traffic offence whilst the vehicle was in motion, or
(b) that a person has been driving or attempting to drive or been in charge of a motor vehicle on a road or other public place with alcohol in his body and that that person still has alcohol in his body, or

    (c) that a person has been driving or attempting to drive or been in charge of a motor vehicle on a road or other public place and has committed a traffic offence whilst the vehicle was in motion,

he may, subject to section 9 of this Act, require him to provide a specimen of breath for a breath test.

(2) If an accident occurs owing to the presence of a motor vehicle on a road or other public place, a constable may, subject to section 9 of this Act, require any person who he has reasonable cause to believe was driving or attempting to drive or in charge of the vehicle at the time of the accident to provide a specimen of breath for a breath test.

(3) A person may be required under subsection (1) or subsection (2) above to provide a specimen either at or near the place where the requirement is made or, if the requirement is made under subsection (2) above and the constable making the requirement thinks fit, at a police station specified by the constable.

(4) A person who, without reasonable excuse, fails to provide a specimen of breath when required to do so in pursuance of this section is guilty of an offence.

(5) A constable may arrest a person without warrant if—

    (a) as a result of a breath test he has reasonable cause to suspect that the proportion of alcohol in that person's breath or blood exceeds the prescribed limit, or

    (b) that person has failed to provide a specimen of breath for a breath test when required to do so in pursuance of this section and the constable has reasonable cause to suspect that he has alcohol in his body,

but a person shall not be arrested by virtue of this subsection when he is at a hospital as a patient.

(6) A constable may, for the purpose of requiring a person to provide a specimen of breath under subsection (2) above in a case where he has reasonable cause to suspect that the accident involved injury to another person or of arresting him in such a case under subsection (5) above, enter (if need be by force) any place where that person is or where the constable, with reasonable cause, suspects him to be.

(7) Subsection (6) above does not extend to Scotland, and nothing in that subsection shall affect any rule of law in Scotland concerning the right of a constable to enter any premises for any purpose.

(8) In this section "traffic offence" means an offence under—

    (a) any provision of Part II of the Public Passenger Vehicles Act 1981,
    (b) any provision of the Road Traffic Regulation Act 1984,
    (c) any provision of the Road Traffic Offenders Act 1988 except Part III, or
    (d) any provision of this Act except Part V.   **[203]**

NOTES

    Commencement: 15 May 1989.

    This section derived from the Road Traffic Act 1972, s 7, the Transport Act 1981, s 25(3), Sch 8, and the Road Traffic Regulation Act 1984, Sch 13, para 13.

7. Provision of specimens for analysis

(1) In the course of an investigation into whether a person has committed an offence under [section 3A, 4] or 5 of this Act a constable may, subject to the following provisions of this section and section 9 of this Act, require him—

    (a) to provide two specimens of breath for analysis by means of a device of a type approved by the Secretary of State, or

    (b) to provide a specimen of blood or urine for a laboratory test.

(2) A requirement under this section to provide specimens of breath can only be made at a police station.

(3) A requirement under this section to provide a specimen of blood or urine can only be made at a police station or at a hospital; and it cannot be made at a police station unless—

    (a) the constable making the requirement has reasonable cause to believe that for medical reasons a specimen of breath cannot be provided or should not be required, or

    (b) at the time the requirement is made a device or a reliable device of the type mentioned in subsection (1)(a) above is not available at the police station or it is then for any other reason not practicable to use such a device there, or

    (c) the suspected offence is one under [section 3A or 4] of this Act and the constable making the requirement has been advised by a medical practitioner that the condition of the person required to provide the specimen might be due to some drug;

but may then be made notwithstanding that the person required to provide the specimen has already provided or been required to provide two specimens of breath.

(4) If the provision of a specimen other than a specimen of breath may be required in pursuance of this section the question whether it is to be a specimen of blood or a specimen of urine shall be decided by the constable making the requirement, but if a medical practitioner is of the opinion that for medical reasons a specimen of blood cannot or should not be taken the specimen shall be a specimen of urine.

(5) A specimen of urine shall be provided within one hour of the requirement for its provision being made and after the provision of a previous specimen of urine.

(6) A person who, without reasonable excuse, fails to provide a specimen when required to do so in pursuance of this section is guilty of an offence.

(7) A constable must, on requiring any person to provide a specimen in pursuance of this section, warn him that a failure to provide it may render him liable to prosecution.   **[204]**

NOTES

    Commencement: 15 May 1989.

    This section derived from the Road Traffic Act 1972, s 8(1)-(5), (7), (8), and the Transport Act 1981, s 25(3), Sch 8.

    Sub-ss (1), (3)(c): words in square brackets substituted by the Road Traffic Act 1991, s 48, Sch 4, para 42.

8. Choice of specimens of breath

(1) Subject to subsection (2) below, of any two specimens of breath provided by any person in pursuance of section 7 of this Act that with the lower proportion of alcohol in the breath shall be used and the other shall be disregarded.

(2) If the specimen with the lower proportion of alcohol contains no more than 50 microgrammes of alcohol in 100 millilitres of breath, the person who provided it may claim that it should be replaced by such specimen as may be required under section 7(4) of this Act and, if he then provides such a specimen, neither specimen of breath shall be used.

(3) The Secretary of State may by regulations substitute another proportion of alcohol in the breath for that specified in subsection (2) above. **[205]**

NOTES
Commencement: 15 May 1989.
This section derived from the Road Traffic Act 1972, s 8(6), (9), and the Transport Act 1981, s 25(3), Sch 8.

9. Protection for hospital patients

(1) While a person is at a hospital as a patient he shall not be required to provide a specimen of breath for a breath test or to provide a specimen for a laboratory test unless the medical practitioner in immediate charge of his case has been notified of the proposal to make the requirement; and—

    (a) if the requirement is then made, it shall be for the provision of a specimen at the hospital, but

    (b) if the medical practitioner objects on the ground specified in subsection (2) below, the requirement shall not be made.

(2) The ground on which the medical practitioner may object is that the requirement or the provision of a specimen or, in the case of a specimen of blood or urine, the warning required under section 7(7) of this Act, would be prejudicial to the proper care and treatment of the patient. **[206]**

NOTES
Commencement: 15 May 1989.
This section derived from the Road Traffic Act 1972, s 9, and the Transport Act 1982, s 25(3), Sch 8.

10. Detention of persons affected by alcohol or a drug

(1) Subject to subsections (2) and (3) below, a person required to provide a specimen of breath, blood or urine may afterwards be detained at a police station until it appears to the constable that, were that person then driving or attempting to drive a [mechanically propelled vehicle] on a road, he would not be committing an offence under section 4 or 5 of this Act.

(2) A person shall not be detained in pursuance of this section if it appears to a constable that there is no likelihood of his driving or attempting to drive a [mechanically propelled vehicle] whilst his ability to drive properly is impaired or whilst the proportion of alcohol in his breath, blood or urine exceeds the prescribed limit.

(3) A constable must consult a medical practitioner on any question arising under this section whether a person's ability to drive properly is or might be impaired through drugs and must act on the medical practitioner's advice. **[207]**

NOTES

Commencement: 15 May 1989.

This section derived from the Road Traffic Act 1972, s 11, and the Transport Act 1981, s 25(3), Sch 8.

Sub-ss (1), (2): words in square brackets substituted by the Road Traffic Act 1991, s 48, Sch 4, para 43.

11. Interpretation of sections 4 to 10

(1) The following provisions apply for the interpretation of sections [3A] to 10 of this Act.

(2) In those sections—

"breath test" means a preliminary test for the purpose of obtaining, by means of a device of a type approved by the Secretary of State, an indication whether the proportion of alcohol in a person's breath or blood is likely to exceed the prescribed limit,

"drug" includes any intoxicant other than alcohol,

"fail" includes refuse;

"hospital" means an institution which provides medical or surgical treatment for in-patients or out-patients,

"the prescribed limit" means, as the case may require—
    (a) 35 microgrammes of alcohol in 100 millilitres of breath,
    (b) 80 milligrammes of alcohol in 100 millilitres of blood, or
    (c) 107 milligrammes of alcohol in 100 millilitres of urine,
        or such other proportion as may be prescribed by regulations made by
        the Secretary of State.

(3) A person does not provide a specimen of breath for a breath test or for analysis unless the specimen—
    (a) is sufficient to enable the test or the analysis to be carried out, and
    (b) is provided in such a way as to enable the objective of the test or
        analysis to be satisfactorily achieved.

(4) A person provides a specimen of blood if and only if he consents to its being taken by a medical practitioner and it is so taken.   **[208]**

NOTES

Commencement: 15 May 1989.

This section derived from the Road Traffic Act 1972, s 12, the Transport Act 1981, s 25(3), Sch 8, and the Transport Act 1982, s 59.

Sub-s (1): amended by the Road Traffic Act 1991, s 48, Sch 4, para 44.

Motor racing and motoring events on public ways

12. Motor racing on public ways

(1) A person who promotes or takes part in a race or trial of speed between motor vehicles on a public way is guilty of an offence.

(2) In this section "public way" means, in England and Wales, a [highway] and, in Scotland, a public road.   **[209]**

NOTES

Commencement: 15 May 1989.

This section derived from the Road Traffic Act 1972, s 14, and the Roads (Scotland) Act 1984, Sch 9, para 68(2).

Sub-s (2): word in square brackets substituted by the Road Traffic Act 1991, s 48, Sch 4, para 45.

13. Regulation of motoring events on public ways

(1) A person who promotes or takes part in a competition or trial (other than a race or trial of speed) involving the use of motor vehicles on a public way is guilty of an offence unless the competition or trial—

    (a) is authorised, and

    (b) is conducted in accordance with any conditions imposed,

by or under regulations under this section.

(2) The Secretary of State may by regulations authorise, or provide for authorising, the holding of competitions or trials (other than races or trials of speed) involving the use of motor vehicles on public ways either—

    (a) generally, or

    (b) as regards any area, or as regards any class or description of competition or trial or any particular competition or trial,

subject to such conditions, including conditions requiring the payment of fees, as may be imposed by or under the regulations.

(3) Regulations under this section may—

    (a) prescribe the procedure to be followed, and the particulars to be given, in connection with applications for authorisation under the regulations, and

    (b) make different provision for different classes or descriptions of competition or trial.

(4) In this section "public way" means, in England and Wales, a [highway] and, in Scotland, a public road. **[210]**

NOTES

Commencement: 15 May 1989.

This section derived from the Road Traffic Act 1972, s 15, and the Roads (Scotland) Act 1984, Sch 9, para 68(3).

Sub-s (1): "regulations", see the Motor Vehicles (Competitions and Trials) Regulations 1969, SI 1969 No 414 as amended.

Sub-s (4): word in square brackets substituted by the Road Traffic Act 1991, s 48, Sch 4, para 46.

[13A. Disapplication of sections 1 to 3 for authorised motoring events

(1) A person shall not be guilty of an offence under sections 1, 2 or 3 of this Act by virtue of driving a vehicle in a public place other than a road if he shows that he was driving in accordance with an authorisation for a motoring event given under regulations made by the Secretary of State.

(2) Regulations under this section may in particular—

    (a) prescribe the persons by whom, and limit the circumstances in which and the places in respect of which, authorisations my be given under the regulations;

    (b) specify conditions which must be included among those incorporated in authorisations;

    (c) provide for authorisations to cease to have effect in prescribed circumstances;

    (d) provide for the procedure to be followed, the particulars to be given, and the amount (or the persons who are to determine the amount) of any fees to be paid, in connection with applications for authorisations;

(e) make different provisions for different cases.] **[210A]**

NOTES
Commencement: 1 July 1992.
Inserted by the Road Traffic Act 1991, s 5.
Regulations: see the Motor Vehicles (Off Road Events) Regulations 1992, SI 1992 No 1370, as amended.

PRINCIPAL ROAD SAFETY PROVISIONS: PROTECTIVE MEASURES

Seat belts, helmets, etc

14. Seat belts: adults

(1) The Secretary of State may make regulations requiring, subject to such exceptions as may be prescribed, persons who are driving or riding in motor vehicles on a road to wear seat belts of such description as may be prescribed.

(2) Regulations under this section—

(a) may make different provision in relation to different classes of vehicles, different descriptions of persons and different circumstances,

(b) shall include exceptions for—

(i) the users of vehicles constructed or adapted for the delivery of goods or mail to consumers or [addressees], as the case may be, while engaged in making local rounds of deliveries,

(ii) the drivers of vehicles while performing a manoeuvre which includes reversing,

(iii) any person holding a valid certificate signed by a medical practitioner to the effect that it is inadvisable on medical grounds for him to wear a seat belt,

(c) may make any prescribed exceptions subject to such conditions as may be prescribed, and

(d) may prescribe cases in which a fee of a prescribed amount may be charged on an application for any certificate required as a condition of any prescribed exception.

(3) A person who drives or rides in a motor vehicle in contravention of regulations under this section is guilty of an offence; but, notwithstanding any enactment or rule of law, no person other than the person actually committing the contravention is guilty of an offence by reason of the contravention.

(4) If the holder of any such certificate as is referred to in subsection (2)(b) above is informed by a constable that he may be prosecuted for an offence under subsection (3) above, he is not in proceedings for that offence entitled to rely on the exception afforded to him by the certificate unless—

(a) it is produced to the constable at the time he is so informed, or

(b) it is produced—

(i) within seven days after the date on which he is so informed, or

(ii) as soon as is reasonably practicable,

at such police station as he may have specified to the constable, or

(c) where it is not produced at such police station, it is not reasonably practicable for it to be produced there before the day on which the proceedings are commenced.

(5) For the purposes of subsection (4) above, the laying of the information

or, in Scotland, the service of the complaint on the accused shall be treated as the commencement of the proceedings.

(6) Regulations under this section requiring the wearing of seat belts by persons riding in motor vehicles shall not apply to children under the age of fourteen years.   **[211]**

NOTES
Commencement: 15 May 1989.
This section derived from the Road Traffic Act 1972, s 33A, the Transport Act 1981, s 27(1), and the Road Traffic (Production of Documents) Act 1985, s 1(1), (2).
Sub-s (2): word in square brackets in para (b)(i) substituted by the Road Traffic Act 1991, s 48, Sch 4, para 47.
See the Motor Vehicles (Wearing of Seat Belts) Regulations 1982, post, and the Motor Vehicles (Wearing of Seat Belts in Rear Seats by Adults) Regulations 1991, post.

15. Restriction on carrying children not wearing seat belts in motor vehicles

(1) Except as provided by regulations, where a child under the age of fourteen years is in the front of a motor vehicle, a person must not without reasonable excuse drive the vehicle on a road unless the child is wearing a seat belt in conformity with regulations.

(2) It is an offence for a person to drive a motor vehicle in contravention of subsection (1) above.

(3) Except as provided by regulations, where a child under the age of fourteen years is in the rear of a motor vehicle and any seat belt is fitted in the rear of that vehicle, a person must not without reasonable excuse drive the vehicle on a road unless the child is wearing a seat belt in conformity with regulations.

(4) It is an offence for a person to drive a motor vehicle in contravention of subsection (3) above.

(5) Provision may be made by regulations—
    (a) excepting from the prohibition in subsection (1) or (3) above children of any prescribed description, vehicles of a prescribed class or the driving of vehicles in such circumstances as may be prescribed,
    (b) defining in relation to any class of vehicle what part of the vehicle is to be regarded as the front of the vehicle for the purposes of subsection (1) above or as the rear of the vehicle for the purposes of subsection (3) above,
    (c) prescribing for the purposes of subsection (1) or (3) above the descriptions of seat belt to be worn by children of any prescribed description and the manner in which such seat belt is to be fixed and used.

(6) Regulations made for the purposes of subsection (3) above shall include an exemption for any child holding a valid certificate signed by a medical practitioner to the effect that it is inadvisable on medical grounds for him to wear a seat belt.

(7) If the driver of a motor vehicle is informed by a constable that he may be prosecuted for an offence under subsection (4) above, he is not in proceedings for that offence entitled to rely on an exception afforded to a child by a certificate referred to in subsection (6) above unless—
    (a) it is produced to the constable at the time he is so informed, or
    (b) it is produced—

(i) within seven days after the date on which he is so informed, or
(ii) as soon as is reasonable practicable,

at such police station as he may have specified to the constable, or
(c) where it is not produced at such police station, it is not reasonably practicable for it to be produced there before the day on which the proceedings are commenced.

(8) For the purposes of subsection (7) above, the laying of the information or, in Scotland, the service of the complaint on the accused shall be treated as the commencement of the proceedings.

(9) In this section—

"regulations" means regulations made by the Secretary of State under this section, and
"seat belt" includes any description of restraining device for a child and any reference to wearing a seat belt is to be construed accordingly.

(10) ...   **[212]**

NOTES
Commencement: 15 May 1989.
This section derived from the Road Traffic Act 1972, s 33B, 33C, the Transport Act 1981, s 28(1), and the Motor Vehicles (Wearing of Rear Seat Belts by Children) Act 1988, s 1(1).
Sub-s (10): repealed by the Road Traffic Act 1991, s 83, Sch 8.
See the Motor Vehicles (Wearing of Seat Belts by Children) Regulations 1982, SI 1982 No 1342, and the Motor Vehicles (Wearing of Seat Belts by Children in Rear Seats) Regulations 1989, post.

[15A. Safety equipment for children in motor vehicles

(1) The Secretary of State may make regulations prescribing (by reference to shape, construction or any other quality) types of equipment of any description to which this section applies that are recommended as conducive to the safety in the event of accident of prescribed classes of children in prescribed classes of motor vehicles.

(2) Regulations under this section may make provision for securing that when equipment of a type prescribed by the regulations is sold or offered for sale as equipment which is so conducive—

(a) appropriate information is provided in relation to it in such manner as may be prescribed, and
(b) inappropriate information is not provided in relation to it.

(3) Except in such circumstances as may be prescribed, if a person sells, or offers for sale, equipment of any description for which a type is prescribed under this section as equipment which is so conducive and that equipment—

(a) is not of a type so prescribed, or
(b) is sold or offered for sale in contravention of regulations under this section,

he is, subject to subsection (5) below, guilty of an offence.

(4) Except in such circumstances as may be prescribed, if a person sells, or offers for sale, equipment of any description for which a type is prescribed under this section as equipment conducive to the safety in the event of accident—

(a) of children not of a class prescribed in relation to equipment of that type, or

(b) of children in motor vehicles not of a class prescribed in relation to equipment of that type,

he is, subject to subsection (5) below, guilty of an offence.

(5) A person shall not be convicted of an offence under this section in respect of the sale or offer for sale of equipment if he proves that it was sold or, as the case may be, offered for sale for export from Great Britain.

(6) The provisions of Schedule 1 to this Act shall have effect in relation to contraventions of this section.

(7) Regulations under this section may make different provision in relation to different circumstances.

(8) This section applies to equipment of any description for use in a motor vehicle consisting of—

(a) a restraining device for a child or for a carry-cot, or
(b) equipment designed for use by a child in conjunction with any description of restraining device.

(9) References in this section to selling or offering for sale include respectively references to letting on hire and offering to let on hire.]   **[212A]**

NOTES
Commencement: 27 June 1991.
Inserted by the Motor Vehicles (Safety Equipment for Children) Act 1991, s 1.

16. Wearing of protective headgear

(1) The Secretary of State may make regulations requiring, subject to such exceptions as may be specified in the regulations, persons driving or riding (otherwise than in side-cars) on motor cycles of any class specified in the regulations to wear protective headgear of such description as may be so specified.

(2) A requirement imposed by regulations under this section shall not apply to any follower of the Sikh religion while he is wearing a turban.

(3) Regulations under this section may make different provision in relation to different circumstances.

(4) A person who drives or rides on a motor cycle in contravention of regulations under this section is guilty of an offence; but notwithstanding any enactment or rule of law no person other than the person actually committing the contravention is guilty of an offence by reason of the contravention unless the person actually committing the contravention is a child under the age of sixteen years.   **[213]**

NOTES
Commencement: 15 May 1989.
This section derived from the Road Traffic Act 1972, s 32, the Motor-Cycle Crash-Helmets (Religious Exemption) Act 1976, s 1, and the Motor-Cycle Crash-Helmets (Restriction of Liability) Act 1985, s 1(1), (2).
See the Motor Cycles (Protective Helmets) Regulations 1980, post.

17. Protective helmets for motor cyclists

(1) The Secretary of State may make regulations prescribing (by reference to shape, construction or any other quality) types of helmet recommended as

affording protection to persons on or in motor cycles, or motor cycles of different classes, from injury in the event of accident.

(2) If a person sells, or offers for sale, a helmet as a helmet for affording such protection and the helmet is neither—

    (a) of a type prescribed under this section, nor

    (b) of a type authorised under regulations made under this section and sold or offered for sale subject to any conditions specified in the authorisation,

subject to subsection (3) below, he is guilty of an offence.

(3) A person shall not be convicted of an offence under this section in respect of the sale or offer for sale of a helmet if he proves that it was sold or, as the case may be, offered for sale for export from Great Britain.

(4) The provisions of Schedule 1 to this Act shall have effect in relation to contraventions of this section.

(5) In this section and that Schedule "helmet" includes any head-dress, and references in this section to selling or offering for sale include respectively references to letting on hire and offering to let on hire.   **[214]**

NOTES

Commencement: 15 May 1989.

This section derived from the Road Traffic Act 1972, s 33, and the Local Government Act 1985, Sch 5, para 2(3).

See the Motor Cycles (Protective Helmets) Regulations 1980, post.

18. Authorisation of head-worn appliances for use on motor cycles

(1) The Secretary of State may make regulations prescribing (by reference to shape, construction or any other quality) types of appliance of any description to which this section applies as authorised for use by persons driving or riding (otherwise than in sidecars) on motor cycles of any class specified in the regulations.

(2) Regulations under this section—

    (a) may impose restrictions or requirements with respect to the circumstances in which appliances of any type prescribed by the regulations may be used, and

    (b) may make different provision in relation to different circumstances.

(3) If a person driving or riding on a motor cycle on a road uses an appliance of any description for which a type is prescribed under this section and that appliance—

    (a) is not of a type so prescribed, or

    (b) is otherwise used in contravention of regulations under this section,

he is guilty of an offence.

(4) If a person sells, or offers for sale, an appliance of any such description as authorised for use by persons on or in motor cycles, or motor cycles of any class, and that appliance is not of a type prescribed under this section as authorised for such use, he is, subject to subsection (5) below, guilty of an offence.

(5) A person shall not be convicted of an offence under this section in respect of the sale or offer for sale of an appliance if he proves that it was sold or, as the case may be, offered for sale for export from Great Britain.

(6) The provisions of Schedule 1 to this Act shall have effect in relation to contraventions of subsection (4) above.

(7) This section applies to appliances of any description designed or adapted for use—

(a) with any headgear, or

(b) by being attached to or placed upon the head,

(as, for example, eye protectors or earphones).

(8) References in this section to selling or offering for sale include respectively references to letting on hire and offering to let on hire.   **[215]**

NOTES

    Commencement: 15 May 1989.

    This section derived from the Road Traffic Act 1972, s 33AA, the Transport Act 1982, s 57(1), and the Local Government Act 1985, Sch 5, para 2(3).

    See the Motor Cycles (Eye Protectors) Regulations 1985, post.

Stopping on verges, etc, or in dangerous positions, etc

19. Prohibition of parking of HGVs on verges, central reservations and footways

(1) Subject to subsection (2) below, a person who parks a heavy commercial vehicle (as defined in section 20 of this Act) wholly or partly—

(a) on the verge of a road, or

(b) on any land situated between two carriageways and which is not a footway, or

(c) on a footway,

is guilty of an offence.

(2) A person shall not be convicted of an offence under this section in respect of a vehicle if he proves to the satisfaction of the court—

(a) that it was parked in accordance with permission given by a constable in uniform, or

(b) that it was parked in contravention of this section for the purpose of saving life or extinguishing fire or meeting any other like emergency, or

(c) that it was parked in contravention of this section but the conditions specified in subsection (3) below were satisfied.

(3) The conditions mentioned in subsection (2)(c) above are—

(a) that the vehicle was parked on the verge of a road or on a footway for the purpose of loading or unloading, and

(b) that the loading or unloading of the vehicle could not have been satisfactorily performed if it had not been parked on the footway or verge, and

(c) that the vehicle was not left unattended at any time while it was so parked.

(4) In this section "carriageway" and "footway", in relation to England and Wales, have the same meanings as in the Highways Act 1980.   **[216]**

NOTES

    Commencement: 15 May 1989.

    This section derived from the Road Traffic Act 1972, s 36A(1)-(3), (4), the Heavy Commercial Vehicles (Controls and Regulations) Act 1973, s 2(1), and the Highways Act 1980, Sch 24, para 21.

19A. (*This section, as inserted by the Road Traffic (Consequential Provisions) Act 1988, s 4, Sch 2, Part II, para 22(1), repealed by the Road Traffic Act 1991, s 83, Sch 8.*)

20. Definition of "heavy commercial vehicle" for the purposes of sections 19

(1) In section 19 of this Act, "heavy commercial vehicle" means any goods vehicle which has an operating weight exceeding 7.5 tonnes.

(2) The operating weight of a goods vehicle for the purposes of this section is—

    (a) in the case of a motor vehicle not drawing a trailer or in the case of a trailer, its maximum laden weight,

    (b) in the case of an articulated vehicle, its maximum laden weight (if it has one) and otherwise the aggregate maximum laden weight of all the individual vehicles forming part of that articulated vehicle, and

    (c) in the case of a motor vehicle (other than an articulated vehicle) drawing one or more trailers, the aggregate maximum laden weight of the motor vehicle and the trailer or trailers attached to it.

(3) In this section "articulated vehicle" means a motor vehicle with a trailer so attached to it as to be partially superimposed upon it; and references to the maximum laden weight of a vehicle are references to the total laden weight which must not be exceeded in the case of that vehicle if it is to be used in Great Britain without contravening any regulations for the time being in force under section 41 of this Act.

(4) In this section, and in the definition of "goods vehicle" in section 192 of this Act as it applies for the purposes of this section, "trailer" means any vehicle other than a motor vehicle.

(5) The Secretary of State may by regulations amend subsections (1) and (2) above (whether as originally enacted or as previously amended under this subsection)—

    (a) by substituting weights of a different description for any of the weights there mentioned, or

    (b) in the case of subsection (1) above, by substituting a weight of a different description or amount, or a weight different both in description and amount, for the weight there mentioned.

(6) Different regulations may be made under subsection (5) above as respects different classes of vehicles or as respects the same class of vehicles in different circumstances and as respects different times of the day or night and as respects different localities.

(7) Regulations under subsection (5) above shall not so amend subsection (1) above that there is any case in which a goods vehicle whose operating weight (ascertained in accordance with subsection (2) above as originally enacted) does not exceed 7.5 tonnes is a heavy commercial vehicle for any of the purposes of section 19 of this Act. **[217]**

NOTES

    Commencement: 15 May 1989.

    This section derived from the Road Traffic Act 1972, s 36A(5)-(11), the Heavy Commercial Vehicles (Controls and Regulations) Act 1973, and the Transport Act 1982, s 56(2).

21. Prohibition of driving or parking on cycle tracks

(1) Subject to the provisions of this section, any person who, without lawful authority, drives or parks a motor vehicle wholly or partly on a cycle track is guilty of an offence.

(2) A person shall not be convicted of an offence under subsection (1) above with respect to a vehicle if he proves to the satisfaction of the court—

    (a) that the vehicle was driven or (as the case may be) parked in contravention of that subsection for the purpose of saving life, or extinguishing fire or meeting any other like emergency, or

    (b) that the vehicle was owned or operated by a highway authority or by a person discharging functions on behalf of a highway authority and was driven or (as the case may be) parked in contravention of that subsection in connection with the carrying out by or on behalf of that authority of any of the following, that is, the cleansing, maintenance or improvement of, or the maintenance or alteration of any structure or other work situated in, the cycle track or its verges, or

    (c) that the vehicle was owned or operated by statutory undertakers and was driven or (as the case may be) parked in contravention of that subsection in connection with the carrying out by those undertakers of any works in relation to any apparatus belonging to or used by them for the purpose of their undertaking.

(3) In this section—

    (a) "cycle track" and other expressions used in this section and in the Highways Act 1980 have the same meaning as in that Act,

    (b) in subsection (2)(c) above "statutory undertakers" means any body who are statutory undertakers within the meaning of the Highways Act 1980, any sewerage authority within the meaning of that Act or the operator of a telecommunications code system (as defined by paragraph 1(1) of Schedule 4 to the Telecommunications Act 1984), and in relation to any such sewerage authority "apparatus" includes sewers or sewerage disposal works.

(4) This section does not extend to Scotland.   **[218]**

NOTES
Commencement: 15 May 1989.
This section derived from the Cycle Tracks Act 1972, ss 2, 8, 9(3).

22. Leaving vehicles in dangerous positions

If a person in charge of a vehicle causes or permits the vehicle or a trailer drawn by it to remain at rest on a road in such a position or in such condition or in such circumstances as to [involve a danger of injury] to other persons using the road, he is guilty of an offence.   **[219]**

NOTES
Commencement: 15 May 1989.
This section derived from the Road Traffic Act 1972, s 24.
Words in square brackets substituted by the Road Traffic Act 1991, s 48, Sch 4, para 48.

Other restrictions in interests of safety

[22A. Causing danger to road-users

(1) A person is guilty of an offence if he intentionally and without lawful authority or reasonable cause—

(a) causes anything to be on or over a road, or

(b) interferes with a motor vehicle, trailer or cycle, or

(c) interferes (directly or indirectly) with traffic equipment,

in such circumstances that it would be obvious to a reasonable person that to do so would be dangerous.

(2) In subsection (1) above "dangerous" refers to danger either of injury to any person while on or near a road, or of serious damage to property on or near a road; and in determining for the purposes of that subsection what would be obvious to a reasonable person in a particular case, regard shall be had not only to the circumstances of which he could be expected to be aware but also to any circumstances shown to have been within the knowledge of the accused.

(3) In subsection (1) above "traffic equipment" means—

(a) anything lawfully placed on or near a road by a highway authority;

(b) a traffic sign lawfully placed on or near a road by a person other than a highway authority;

(c) any fence, barrier or light lawfully placed on or near a road—

    (i) in pursuance of section 174 of the Highways Act 1980, *section 8 of the Public Utilities Street Works Act 1950* or section 65 of the New Roads and Street Works Act 1991 (which provide for guarding, lighting and signing in streets where works are undertaken), or

    (ii) by a constable or a person acting under the instructions (whether general or specific) of a chief officer of police.

(4) For the purposes of subsection (3) above anything placed on or near a road shall unless the contrary is proved be deemed to have been lawfully placed there.

(5) In this section "road" does not include a footpath or bridleway.

(6) This section does not extend to Scotland.] **[219A]**

NOTES

Commencement: 1 July 1992.

Inserted by the Road Traffic Act 1991, s 6.

Sub-s (3)(c)(i): words in italics prospectively repealed by the New Roads and Street Works Act 1991, s 168(1), (2), Sch 8, Part IV, para 121(1), (2), Sch 9, partly as from a day to be appointed.

23. Restriction of carriage of persons on motor cycles

(1) Not more than one person in addition to the driver may be carried on a [motor bicycle].

(2) No person in addition to the driver may be carried on a [motor bicycle] otherwise than sitting astride the motor cycle and on a proper seat securely fixed to the motor cycle behind the driver's seat.

(3) If a person is carried on a motor cycle in contravention of this section, the driver of the motor cycle is guilty of an offence. **[220]**

NOTES

Commencement: 15 May 1989.

This section derived from the Road Traffic Act 1972, s 16.

Sub-ss (1), (2): words in square brackets substituted by the Road Traffic (Driver Licensing and Information Systems) Act 1989, s 7, Sch 3, para 6.

24. Restriction of carriage of persons on bicycles

(1) Not more than one person may be carried on a road on a bicycle not propelled by mechanical power unless it is constructed or adapted for the carriage of more than one person.

(2) In this section—

    (a) references to a person carried on a bicycle include references to a person riding the bicycle, and

    (b) "road" includes bridleway.

(3) If a person is carried on a bicycle in contravention of subsection (1) above, each of the persons carried is guilty of an offence.   **[221]**

NOTES
    Commencement: 15 May 1989.
    This section derived from the Road Traffic Act 1972, s 21.

25. Tampering with motor vehicles

If, while a motor vehicle is on a road or on a parking place provided by a local authority, a person—

    (a) gets on to the vehicle, or

    (b) tampers with the brake or other part of its mechanism,

without lawful authority or reasonable cause he is guilty of an offence.   **[222]**

NOTES
    Commencement: 15 May 1989.
    This section derived from the Road Traffic Act 1972, s 29.

26. Holding or getting on to vehicle in order to be towed or carried

(1) If, for the purpose of being carried, a person without lawful authority or reasonable cause takes or retains hold of, or gets on to, a motor vehicle or trailer while in motion on a road he is guilty of an offence.

(2) If, for the purpose of being drawn, a person takes or retains hold of a motor vehicle or trailer while in motion on a road he is guilty of an offence.

[223]

NOTES
    Commencement: 15 May 1989.
    This section derived from the Road Traffic Act 1972, s 30.

27. Control of dogs on roads

(1) A person who causes or permits a dog to be on a designated road without the dog being held on a lead is guilty of an offence.

(2) In this section "designated road" means a length of road specified by an order in that behalf of the local authority in whose area the length of road is situated.

(3) The powers which under subsection (2) above are exercisable by a local authority in England and Wales are, in the case of a road part of the width of which is in the area of one local authority and part in the area of another, exercisable by either authority with the consent of the other.

(4) An order under this section may provide that subsection (1) above shall apply subject to such limitations or exceptions as may be specified in the order,

and (without prejudice to the generality of this subsection) subsection (1) above does not apply to dogs proved—

(a) to be kept for driving or tending sheep or cattle in the course of a trade or business, or

(b) to have been at the material time in use under proper control for sporting purposes.

(5) An order under this section shall not be made except after consultation with the chief officer of police.

(6) The Secretary of State may make regulations—

(a) prescribing the procedure to be followed in connection with the making of orders under this section, and

(b) requiring the authority making such an order to publish in such manner as may be prescribed by the regulations notice of the making and effect of the order.

(6) In this section "local authority" means—

(a) in relation to England and Wales, the council of a county, metropolitan district or London borough or the Common Council of the City of London, and

(b) in relation to Scotland, a regional or islands council.

(7) The power conferred by this section to make an order includes power, exercisable in like manner and subject to the like conditions, to vary or revoke it.

(8) The power conferred by this section to make an order includes power, exercisable in like manner and subject to the like conditions, to vary or revoke it.   [224]

NOTES
Commencement: 15 May 1989.

This section derived from the Road Traffic Act 1972, s 31, the Local Government Act 1972, Sch 19, para 1, the Local Government (Scotland) Act 1973, Sch 14, para 82, and the Local Government Act 1985, Sch 5, para 2(2).

See the Control of Dogs on Roads Order (Procedure) (England and Wales) Regulations 1962, SI 1962 No 2340 as amended and local orders.

Cycling offences and cycle racing

[28. Dangerous cycling

(1) A person who rides a cycle on a road dangerously is guilty of an offence.

(2) For the purposes of subsection (1) above a person is to be regarded as riding dangerously if (and only if)—

(a) the way he rides falls far below what would be expected of a competent and careful cyclist, and

(b) it would be obvious to a competent and careful cyclist that riding in that way would be dangerous.

(3) In subsection (2) above "dangerous" refers to danger either of injury to any person or of serious damage to property; and in determining for the purposes of that subsection what would be obvious to a competent and careful

cyclist in a particular case, regard shall be had not only to the circumstances of which he could be expected to be aware but also to any circumstances shown to have been within the knowledge of the accused.]   **[225]**

NOTES
Commencement: 1 July 1992.
Substituted by the Road Traffic Act 1991, s 7.

29. Careless, and inconsiderate, cycling

If a person rides a cycle on a road without due care and attention, or without reasonable consideration, for other persons using the road, he is guilty of an offence.

                                                                                [226]

NOTES
Commencement: 15 May 1989.
This section derived from the Road Traffic Act 1972, s 18.
Words omitted repealed by the Road Traffic Act 1991, s 83, Sch 8.

30. Cycling when under influence of drink or drugs

(1) A person who, when riding a cycle on a road or other public place, is unfit to ride through drink or drugs (that is to say, is under the influence of drink or a drug to such an extent as to be incapable of having proper control of the cycle) is guilty of an offence.

(2) In Scotland a constable may arrest without warrant a person committing an offence under this section.

(3) . . .   **[227]**

NOTES
Commencement: 15 May 1989.
This section derived from the Road Traffic Act 1972, s 19(1), (3)-(5), and the Police and Criminal Evidence Act 1984, Sch 7, Part I.
Sub-s (3): repealed by the Road Traffic Act 1991, s 83, Sch 8.

31. Regulation of cycle racing on public ways

(1) A person who promotes or takes part in a race or trial of speed on a public way between cycles is guilty of an offence, unless the race or trial—

    (a) is authorised, and
    (b) is conducted in accordance with any conditions imposed,

by or under regulations under this section.

(2) The Secretary of State may by regulations authorise, or provide for authorising, for the purposes of subsection (1) above, the holding on a public way other than a bridleway—

    (a) of races or trials of speed of any class or description, or
    (b) of a particular race or trial of speed,

in such cases as may be prescribed and subject to such conditions as may be imposed by or under the regulations.

(3) Regulations under this section may—

    (a) prescribe the procedure to be followed, and the particulars to be given, in connection with applications for authorisation under the regulations, and

(b) make different provision for different classes or descriptions of race or trial.

(4) Without prejudice to any other powers exercisable in that behalf, the chief officer of police may give directions with respect to the movement of, or the route to be followed by, vehicular traffic during any period, being directions which it is necessary or expedient to give in relation to that period to prevent or mitigate—

(a) congesting or obstruction of traffic, or
(b) danger to or from traffic,

in consequence of the holding of a race or trial of speed authorised by or under regulations under this section.

(5) Directions under subsection (4) above may include a direction that any road or part of a road specified in the direction shall be closed during the period to vehicles or to vehicles of a class so specified.

[(6) In this section "public way" means, in England and Wales, a highway, and in Scotland, a public road but does not include a footpath.] **[228]**

NOTES
Commencement: 1 July 1992 (sub-s (6)); 15 May 1989 (remainder).
This section derived from the Road Traffic Act 1972, s 20, and the Roads (Scotland) Act 1984, Sch 9, para 68(8).
Sub-s (6): substituted by the Road Traffic Act 1991, s 48, Sch 4, para 49.
See the Cycle Racing on Highways Regulations 1960, SI 1960 No 250 as amended.

32. Electrically assisted pedal cycles

(1) An electrically assisted pedal cycle of a class specified in regulations made for the purposes of section 189 of this Act and section 140 of the Road Traffic Regulation Act 1984 shall not be driven on a road by a person under the age of fourteen.

(2) A person who—

(a) drives such a pedal cycle, or
(b) knowing or suspecting that another person is under the age of fourteen, causes or permits him to drive such a pedal cycle,

in contravention of subsection (1) above is guilty of an offence. **[229]**

NOTES
Commencement: 15 May 1989.
This section derived from the Road Traffic Act 1972, s 24(2), and the Road Traffic Regulation Act 1984, Sch 13, para 50.
See the Electrically Assisted Pedal Cycles Regulations 1983, SI 1983 No 1168.

Use of motor vehicles away from roads

33. Control of use of footpaths and bridleways for motor vehicle trials

(1) A person must not promote or take part in a trial of any description between motor vehicles on a footpath or bridleway unless the holding of the trial has been authorised under this section by the local authority.

(2) A local authority shall not give an authorisation under this section unless satisfied that consent in writing to the use of any length of footpath or bridleway for the purposes of the trial has been given by the owner and by the occupier of the land over which that length of footpath or bridleway runs, and any such

authorisation may be given subject to compliance with such conditions as the authority think fit.

(3) A person who—

    (a) contravenes subsection (1) above, or

    (b) fails to comply with any conditions subject to which an authorisation under this section has been granted,

is guilty of an offence.

(4) The holding of a trial authorised under this section is not affected by any statutory provision prohibiting or restricting the use of footpaths or bridleways or a specified footpath or bridleway; but this section does not prejudice any right or remedy of a person as having any interest in land.

(5) In this section "local authority"—

    (a) in relation to England and Wales, means the council of a county, metropolitan district or London borough, and

    (b) in relation to Scotland, means a regional or islands council.   **[230]**

NOTES

Commencement: 15 May 1989.

This section derived from the Road Traffic Act 1972, s 35, the Local Government Act 1972, Sch 19, para 3, the Local Government (Scotland) Act 1973, Sch 14, para 83, and the Local Government Act 1985, Sch 5, para 2(4).

34. Prohibition of driving motor vehicles elsewhere than on roads

(1) Subject to the provisions of this section, if without lawful authority a person drives a motor vehicle—

    (a) on to or upon any common land, moorland or land of any other description, not being land forming part of a road, or

    (b) on any road being a footpath or bridleway,

he is guilty of an offence.

(2) It is not an offence under this section to drive a motor vehicle on any land within fifteen yards of a road, being a road on which a motor vehicle may lawfully be driven, for the purpose only of parking the vehicle on that land.

(3) A person shall not be convicted of an offence under this section with respect to a vehicle if he proves to the satisfaction of the court that it was driven in contravention of this section for the purpose of saving life or extinguishing fire or meeting any other like emergency.

(4) It is hereby declared that nothing in this section prejudices the operation of—

    (a) section 193 of the Law of Property Act 1925 (rights of the public over commons and waste lands), or

    (b) any byelaws applying to any land,

or affects the law of trespass to land or any right or remedy to which a person may by law be entitled in respect of any such trespass or in particular confers a right to park a vehicle on any land.   **[231]**

NOTES

Commencement: 15 May 1989.

This section derived from the Road Traffic Act 1972, s 36.

Directions to traffic and to pedestrians and traffic signs

35. Drivers to comply with traffic directions

(1) Where a constable is for the time being engaged in the regulation of traffic in a road, a person driving or propelling a vehicle who neglects or refuses—

    (a) to stop the vehicle, or
    (b) to make it proceed in, or keep to, a particular line of traffic,

when directed to do so by the constable in the execution of his duty is guilty of an offence.

    (2) Where—

    (a) a traffic survey of any description is being carried out on or in the vicinity of a road, and
    (b) a constable gives to a person driving or propelling a vehicle a direction—

        (i) to stop the vehicle,
        (ii) to make it proceed in, or keep to, a particular line of traffic, or
        (iii) to proceed to a particular point on or near the road on which the vehicle is being driven or propelled,

    being a direction given for the purposes of the survey (but not a direction requiring any person to provide any information for the purposes of a traffic survey),

the person is guilty of an offence if he neglects or refuses to comply with the direction.

    (3) The power to give such a direction as is referred to in subsection (2) above for the purposes of a traffic survey shall be so exercised as not to cause any unreasonable delay to a person who indicates that he is unwilling to provide any information for the purposes of the survey.   **[232]**

NOTES
    Commencement: 15 May 1989.
    This section derived from the Road Traffic Act 1972, ss 22(1), 22A, and the Road Traffic Act 1974, s 6.

36. Drivers to comply with traffic signs

(1) Where a traffic sign, being a sign—

    (a) of the prescribed size, colour and type, or
    (b) of another character authorised by the Secretary of State under the provisions in that behalf of the Road Traffic Regulation Act 1984,

has been lawfully placed on or near a road, a person driving or propelling a vehicle who fails to comply with the indication given by the sign is guilty of an offence.

    (2) A traffic sign shall not be treated for the purposes of this section as having been lawfully placed unless either—

    (a) the indication given by the sign is an indication of a statutory prohibition, restriction or requirement, or
    (b) it is expressly provided by or under any provision of the Traffic Acts that this section shall apply to the sign or to signs of a type of which the sign is one;

and, where the indication mentioned in paragraph (a) of this subsection is of the general nature only of the prohibition, restriction or requirement to which the sign relates, a person shall not be convicted of failure to comply with the indication unless he has failed to comply with the prohibition, restriction or requirement to which the sign relates.

(3) For the purposes of this section a traffic sign placed on or near a road shall be deemed—

    (a) to be of the prescribed size, colour and type, or of another character authorised by the Secretary of State under the provisions in that behalf of the Road Traffic Regulation Act 1984, and

    (b) (subject to subsection (2) above) to have been lawfully so placed,

unless the contrary is proved.

(4) Where a traffic survey of any description is being carried out on or in the vicinity of a road, this section applies to a traffic sign by which a direction is given—

    (a) to stop a vehicle,

    (b) to make it proceed in, or keep to, a particular line of traffic, or

    (c) to proceed to a particular point on or near the road on which the vehicle is being driven or propelled,

being a direction given for the purposes of the survey (but not a direction requiring any person to provide any information for the purposes of the survey).

(5) Regulations made by the Secretary of State for Transport, the Secretary of State for Wales and the Secretary of State for Scotland acting jointly may specify any traffic sign for the purposes of column 5 of the entry in Schedule 2 to the Road Traffic Offenders Act 1988 relating to offences under this section (offences committed by failing to comply with certain signs involve discretionary disqualification). **[233]**

NOTES

    Commencement: 15 May 1989.

    This section derived from the Road Traffic Act 1972, ss 22, 22A(1), (2), Sch 4, Part I, column 5, the Road Traffic Act 1974, s 6, and the Road Traffic Regulation Act 1984, Sch 13, para 14.

    Traffic Acts: Road Traffic Regulation Act 1984, Road Traffic Offenders Act 1988, Road Traffic (Consequential Provisions) Act 1988 (so far as it reproduces the effect of provisions repealed by that Act), Road Traffic Act 1988.

    See the Traffic Signs Regulations and General Directions 1981, post, and the Traffic Signs (Welsh and English Language Provisions) Regulations and General Directions 1985, SI 1985 No 713.

37. Directions to pedestrians

Where a constable in uniform is for the time being engaged in the regulation of vehicular traffic in a road, a person on foot who proceeds across or along the carriageway in contravention of a direction to stop given by the constable in the execution of his duty, either to persons on foot or to persons on foot and other traffic, is guilty of an offence. **[234]**

NOTES

    Commencement: 15 May 1989.

    This section derived from the Road Traffic Act 1972, s 23.

Promotion of road safety

38. The Highway Code

(1) The Highway Code shall continue to have effect, subject however to revision in accordance with the following provisions of this section.

(2) Subject to the following provisions of this section, the Secretary of State may from time to time revise the Highway Code by revoking, varying, amending or adding to the provisions of the Code in such manner as he thinks fit.

(3) Where the Secretary of State proposes to revise the Highway Code by making any alterations in the provisions of the Code (other than alterations merely consequential on the passing, amendment or repeal of any statutory provision) he must lay the proposed alterations before both Houses of Parliament and must not make the proposed revision until after the end of a period of forty days beginning with the day on which the alterations were so laid.

(4) If within the period mentioned in subsection (3) above either House resolves that the proposed alterations be not made, the Secretary of State must not make the proposed revision (but without prejudice to the laying before Parliament of further proposals for alteration in accordance with that subsection).

(5) Before revising the Highway Code by making any alterations in its provisions which are required by subsection (3) above to be laid before Parliament, the Secretary of State must consult with such representative organisations as he thinks fit.

(6) The Secretary of State must cause the Highway Code to be printed and may cause copies of it to be sold to the public at such price as he may determine.

(7) A failure on the part of a person to observe a provision of the Highway Code shall not of itself render that person liable to criminal proceedings of any kind but any such failure may in any proceedings (whether civil or criminal, and including proceedings for an offence under the Traffic Acts, the Public Passenger Vehicles Act 1981 or sections 18 to 23 of the Transport Act 1985) be relied upon by any party to the proceedings as tending to establish or negative any liability which is in question in those proceedings.

(8) In this section "the Highway Code" means the code comprising directions for the guidance of persons using roads issued under section 45 of the Road Traffic Act 1930, as from time to time revised under this section or under any previous enactment.

(9) For the purposes of subsection (3) above—

(a) "statutory provision" means a provision contained in an Act or in subordinate legislation within the meaning of the Interpretation Act 1978 (and the reference to the passing or repeal of any such provision accordingly includes the making or revocation of any such provision),
(b) where the proposed alterations are laid before each House of Parliament on different days, the later day shall be taken to be the day on which they were laid before both Houses, and
(c) in reckoning any period of forty days, no account shall be taken of any time during which Parliament is dissolved or prorogued or during which both Houses are adjourned for more than four days.   **[235]**

NOTES

   Commencement: 15 May 1989.
   This section derived from the Road Traffic Act 1972, s 37, the Transport Act 1982, s 60, and the Road Traffic Regulation Act 1984, Sch 13, para 16.
   Traffic Acts: Road Traffic Regulation Act 1984, Road Traffic Offenders Act 1988, Road Traffic (Consequential Provisions) Act 1988 (so far as it reproduces the effect of provisions repealed by that Act), Road Traffic Act 1988.

39. Powers of Secretary of State and local authorities as to giving road safety information and training

(1) The Secretary of State may, with the approval of the Treasury, provide for promoting road safety by disseminating information or advice relating to the use of roads.

(2) Each local authority must prepare and carry out a programme of measures designed to promote road safety and may make contributions towards the cost of measures for promoting road safety taken by other authorities or bodies.

(3) Without prejudice to the generality of subsection (2) above, in pursuance of their duty under that subsection each local authority—

   (a) must carry out studies into accidents arising out of the use of vehicles on roads or parts of roads, other than [roads for which the Secretary of State is the highway authority (in Scotland, roads authority)], within their area,

   (b) must, in the light of those studies, take such measures as appear to the authority to be appropriate to prevent such accidents, including the dissemination of information and advice relating to the use of roads, the giving of practical training to road users or any class or description of road users, the construction, improvement, maintenance or repair of [roads for the maintenance of which they are responsible] and other measures taken in the exercise of their powers for controlling, protecting or assisting the movement of traffic on roads, and

   (c) in constructing new roads, must take such measures as appear to the authority to be appropriate to reduce the possibilities of such accidents when the roads come into use.

(4) In this section "local authority" means—

   (a) in relation to England and Wales, the council of a county, metropolitan district or London borough or the Common Council of the City of London,

   (b) in relation to Scotland, a regional or islands council.   **[236]**

NOTES
Commencement: 15 May 1989.
   This section derived from the Road Traffic Act 1972, s 38(1)–(2A), (5), the Road Traffic Act 1974, s 8(1), the Roads (Scotland) Act 1984, Sch 9, para 68(7), the Local Government Act 1972, Sch 18, para 4, the Local Government (Scotland) Act 1973, Sch 14, para 84, and the Local Government Act 1985, Sch 5, Part I, para 2(5).
   Sub-s (3): words in square brackets substituted by the New Roads and Street Works Act 1991, s 168(1), Sch 8, Part IV, para 121(1), (3).

40. Powers of Secretary of State to subsidise bodies other than local authorities for giving road safety information and training

The Secretary of State may, with the approval of the Treasury, make out of monies provided by Parliament contributions towards the cost of measures for promoting road safety, being measures taken by authorities or bodies other than local authorities (within the meaning of section 39 of this Act).   **[237]**

NOTES
Commencement: 15 May 1989.
   This section derived from the Road Traffic Act 1972, s 39, and the Road Traffic Act 1974, s 8(2).

PART II

CONSTRUCTION AND USE OF VEHICLES AND EQUIPMENT

[Using vehicle in dangerous condition

40A. Using vehicle in dangerous condition etc

A person is guilty of an offence if he uses, or causes or permits another to use, a motor vehicle or trailer on a road when—

    (a) the condition of the motor vehicle or trailer, or of its accessories or equipment, or

    (b) the purpose for which it is used, or

    (c) the number of passengers carried by it, or the manner in which they are carried, or

    (d) the weight, position or distribution of its load, or the manner in which it is secured,

is such that the use of the motor vehicle or trailer involves a danger of injury to any person.] **[237A]**

NOTES
Commencement: 1 July 1992.
This section, and the cross-heading preceding it, inserted by the Road Traffic Act 1991, s 8(1).

General regulation of construction, use etc

41. Regulation of construction, weight, equipment and use of vehicles

(1) The Secretary of State may make regulations generally as to the use of motor vehicles and trailers on roads, their construction and equipment and the conditions under which they may be so used.

Subsections (2) to (4) below do not affect the generality of this subsection.

(2) In particular, the regulations may make provision with respect to any of the following matters—

    (a) the width, height and length of motor vehicles and trailers and the load carried by them, the diameter of wheels, and the width, nature and condition of tyres, of motor vehicles and trailers,

    (b) the emission or consumption of smoke, fumes or vapour and the emission of sparks, ashes and grit,

    (c) noise,

    (d) the maximum weight unladen of heavy locomotives and heavy motor cars, and the maximum weight laden of motor vehicles and trailers, and the maximum weight to be transmitted to the road or any specified area of the road by a motor vehicle or trailer of any class or by any part or parts of such a vehicle or trailer in contact with the road, and the conditions under which the weights may be required to be tested,

    (e) the particulars to be marked on motor vehicles and trailers, [(by means of the fixing of plates or otherwise) and the circumstances in which they are to be marked,]

    (f) the towing of or drawing of vehicles by motor vehicles,

    (g) the number and nature of brakes, and for securing that brakes, silencers and steering gear are efficient and kept in proper working order,

    (h) lighting equipment and reflectors,

(j) the testing and inspection, by persons authorised by or under the regulations, of the brakes, silencers, steering gear, tyres, lighting equipment and reflectors of motor vehicles and trailers on any premises where they are (if the owner of the premises consents),

[(jj) speed limiters,]

(k) the appliances to be fitted for—

    (i) signalling the approach of a motor vehicle, or

    (ii) enabling the driver of a motor vehicle to become aware of the approach of another vehicle from the rear, or

    (iii) intimating any intended change of speed or direction of a motor vehicle,

and the use of any such appliance, and for securing that any such appliance is efficient and kept in proper working order,

(l) for prohibiting the use of appliances fitted to motor vehicles for signalling their approach, being appliances for signalling by sound, at any times, or on or in any roads or localities, specified in the regulations.

(3) The Secretary of State may, as respects goods vehicles, make regulations under this section—

(a) prescribing other descriptions of weight which are not to be exceeded in the case of such vehicles,

(b), (c) . . .

(d) providing that weights of any description or other particulars which are to be marked on particular goods vehicles may be determined in accordance with regulations under section 49 of this Act.

(4) Regulations under this section with respect to lighting equipment and reflectors—

(a) may require that lamps be kept lit at such times and in such circumstances as may be specified in the regulations, and

(b) may extend, in like manner as to motor vehicles and trailers, to vehicles of any description used on roads, whether or not they are mechanically propelled.

[(4A) Regulations under this section with respect to speed limiters may include provision—

(a) as to the checking and sealing of speed limiters by persons authorised in accordance with the regulations and the making of charges by them,

(b) imposing or providing for the imposition of conditions to be complied with by authorised persons,

(c) as to the withdrawal of authorisations.]

(5) Different regulations may be made under this section as respects different classes of vehicles or as respects the same class of vehicles in different circumstances and as respects different times of the day or night and as respects roads in different localities.

(6) In framing regulations under this section prescribing a weight of any description which is not to be exceeded in the case of goods vehicles of a class for which a certificate of conformity or Minister's approval certificate may be issued under section 57 or 58 of this Act the Secretary of State must have regard to the design weight of the like description determined by virtue of section 54

of this Act for vehicles of that class and must secure that the first-mentioned weight does not exceed the design weight.

(7) In this Part of this Act—

"construction and use requirements" means requirements, whether applicable generally or at specified times or in specified circumstances, imposed under this section,

"plated particulars" means such particulars as are required to be marked on a goods vehicle in pursuance of regulations under this section by means of a plate,

"plated weights" means such weights as are required to be so marked.

[238]

NOTES

Commencement: 1 April 1992 (sub-ss (2)(jj), 4A); 15 May 1989 (remainder).

This section derived from the Road Traffic Act 1972, s 40(1)-(4), (7), and the Road Traffic Act 1974, s 9(1), (2), Sch 2, para 6, Sch 7.

Sub-s (2): words in square brackets in para (e) added, para (jj) inserted, by the Road Traffic Act 1991, s 48, Sch 4, para 50(1)-(3).

Sub-s (3): paras (b), (c) repealed by the Road Traffic Act 1991, s 83, Sch 8.

Sub-s (4A): inserted by the Road Traffic Act 1991, s 48, Sch 4, para 50(1), (4).

See the Road Vehicles (Registration and Licensing) Regulations 1971, SI 1971 No 450, Sch 2, Part II, paras 5A–5D, 6–8, 8A–8C post; the International Carriage of Dangerous Goods (Rear Marking of Motor Vehicles) Regulations 1975, SI 1975 No 2111; the Public Service Vehicles (Conditions of Fitness, Equipment, Use and Certification) Regulations 1981, SI 1981 No 257 as amended; the Road Transport (International Passenger Services) Regulations 1984, SI 1984 No 748 as amended; the Road Vehicles (Construction and Use) Regulations 1986, post; the Road Vehicles Lighting Regulations 1989, post.

[41A. Breach of requirement as to brakes, steering-gear or tyres

A person who—

(a) contravenes or fails to comply with a construction and use requirement as to brakes, steering-gear or tyres, or

(b) uses on a road a motor vehicle or trailer which does not comply with such a requirement, or causes or permits a motor vehicle or trailer to be so used,

is guilty of an offence.] **[238A]**

NOTES

Commencment: 1 July 1992.

This section and ss 41B, 42 post, substituted for the original s 42 by the Road Traffic Act 1991, s 8(2).

[41B Breach of requirement as to weight: goods and passenger vehicles

(1) A person who—

(a) contravenes or fails to comply with a construction and use requirement as to any description of weight applicable to—

(i) a goods vehicle, or

(ii) a motor vehicle or trailer adapted to carry more than eight passengers, or

(b) uses on a road a vehicle which does not comply with such a requirement, or causes or permits a vehicle to be so used,

is guilty of an offence.

(2) In any proceedings for an offence under this section in which there is alleged a contravention of or failure to comply with a construction and use

requirement as to any description of weight applicable to a goods vehicle, it shall be a defence to prove either—

(a) that at the time when the vehicle was being used on the road—

(i) it was proceeding to a weighbridge which was the nearest available one to the place where the loading of the vehicle was completed for the purpose of being weighed, or

(ii) it was proceeding from a weighbridge after being weighed to the nearest point at which it was reasonably practicable to reduce the weight to the relevant limit, without causing an obstruction on any road, or

(b) in a case where the limit of that weight was not exceeded by more than 5 per cent—

(i) that that limit was not exceeded at the time when the loading of the vehicle was originally completed, and

(ii) that since that time no person has made any addition to the load.]   **[238B]**

NOTES
Commencement: 1 July 1992.
See the note to s 41A ante.

[42. Breach of other construction and use requirements

A person who—

(a) contravenes or fails to comply with any construction or use requirement other than one within section 41A(a) or 41B(1)(a) of this Act, or

(b) uses on a road a motor vehicle or trailer which does not comply with such a requirement, or causes or permits a motor vehicle or trailer to be so used,

is guilty of an offence.]   **[239]**

NOTES
Commencement: 1 July 1992.
See the note to s 41A ante.

43. Temporary exemption from application of regulations under section 41

(1) Subject to subsections (2) to (4) below, where any regulations under section 41 of this Act contain provisions varying the requirements as regards the construction or weight of any class of vehicles, provision shall be made by the regulations for exempting from those provisions for such period, not being less than five years, as may be specified in the regulations any vehicle of that class registered under the Vehicles (Excise) Act 1971 before the expiration of one year from the making of the regulations.

(2) No such provision contained in regulations under section 41 as imposes or varies requirements with respect to the braking systems with which motor vehicles must be equipped shall be taken, for the purposes of subsection (1) above or of any other provision of the regulations, to be one relating to the construction of vehicles.

(3) Where regulations under section 41 contain provisions varying the requirements as regards the construction or weight of any class of vehicle, and the Secretary of State is satisfied—

(a) that it is requisite that those provisions shall apply at a date specified in the regulations to vehicles registered before the expiration of one year from the making of the regulations, or to such of them as are specified in the regulations, and

(b) that no undue hardship or inconvenience will be caused by their application then to those vehicles,

then, if the regulations state that the Secretary of State is so satisfied, subsection (1) above shall not apply in relation to those provisions.

(4) Subsection (1) above shall not apply in relation to—

(a) regulations made with respect to any description of weight of goods vehicles, other than their maximum unladen weight, or

(b) regulations made by virtue of section 41(3) of this Act. **[240]**

NOTES
Commencement: 15 May 1989.
This section derived from the Road Traffic Act 1972, s 41.

44. Authorisation of use on roads of special vehicles not complying with regulations under section 41

(1) The Secretary of State may by order authorise, subject to such restrictions and conditions as may be specified by or under the order, the use on roads—

(a) of special motor vehicles or trailers, or special types of motor vehicles or trailers, which are constructed either for special purposes or for tests or trials,

(b) of vehicles or trailers, or types of vehicles or trailers, constructed for use outside the United Kingdom,

(c) of new or improved types of motor vehicles or trailers, whether wheeled or wheelless, or of motor vehicles or trailers equipped with new or improved equipment or types of equipment, and

(d) of vehicles or trailers carrying loads of exceptional dimensions,

[and sections 40A to 42 of this Act shall not apply in relation to] the use of such vehicles, trailers, or types in accordance with the order.

(2) The Secretary of State may by order make provision for securing that, subject to such restrictions and conditions as may be specified by or under the order, regulations under section 41 of this Act shall have effect in their application to such vehicles, trailers and types of vehicles and trailers as are mentioned in subsection (1) above subject to such modifications or exceptions as may be specified in the order.

(3) The powers conferred by this section on the Secretary of State to make orders shall be exercisable by statutory instrument except in the case of orders applying only to specified vehicles or to vehicles of specified persons, but in that excepted case (as in others) the order may be varied or revoked by subsequent order of the Secretary of State. **[241]**

NOTES
Commencement: 15 May 1989.
This section derived from the Road Traffic Act 1972, s 42.
Sub-s (1): words in square brackets substituted by the Road Traffic Act 1991, s 48, Sch 4, para 51.
See the Motor Vehicles (Authorisation of Special Types) (No 2) Order 1951, SI 1951 No 1963, and Motor Vehicles (Authorisation of Special Types) General Order 1979, post.

Tests of vehicles other than goods vehicles to which section 49 applies

45. Tests of satisfactory condition of vehicles

(1) This section applies to motor vehicles other than goods vehicles which are required by regulations under section 49 of this Act to be submitted for a vehicle test under that section and has effect for the purpose of ascertaining whether the [following requirements are complied with, namely—

(a) the prescribed statutory requirements relating to the construction and condition of motor vehicles or their accessories or equipment, and

(b) the requirement that the condition of motor vehicles should not be such that their use on a road would involve a danger of injury to any person.]

(2) The Secretary of State may by regulations make provision—

(a) for the examination of vehicles submitted for examination under this section, and

(b) for the issue, where it is found on such an examination that the requirements mentioned in subsection (1) above are complied with, of a certificate (in this Act referred to as a "test certificate") that at the date of the examination the requirements were complied with in relation to the vehicle.

(3) Examinations for the purposes of this section shall be carried out by—

(a) persons, not being officers of the Secretary of State, authorised for those purposes by the Secretary of State (in this section and section 46 of this Act referred to as "authorised examiners"),

[(aa) any authorised inspector]

[(b) examiners appointed under section 66A of this Act], or

(c) inspectors appointed by any council designated by the Secretary of State for the purposes of this section and section 46 of this Act, being the council of a county, district or London borough or the Common Council of the City of London or the council of a region or islands area.

(4) Where a test certificate is refused, the examiner or inspector must issue a notification of the refusal stating the grounds of the refusal, and a person aggrieved by the refusal or the grounds of the refusal may appeal to the Secretary of State.

(5) On any such appeal the Secretary of State must cause a further examination to be made [by an officer of the Secretary of State appointed by him for the purpose] and either issue a test certificate or issue a notification of the refusal stating the grounds of the refusal.

(6) For the purposes of their functions under this section the Secretary of State or a council designated for the purposes of this section may provide and maintain—

(a) stations where examinations under this section may be carried out, and

(b) apparatus for carrying out such examinations.

(7) The Secretary of State may make regulations under this section for the purpose of giving effect to this section and for prescribing anything authorised by this section and section 46 of this Act to be prescribed.

(8) In its application to vehicles in which recording equipment is required

by Article 3 of the Community Recording Equipment Regulation to be installed
and used, this section shall have effect as if any reference to prescribed statutory
requirements relating to the construction and condition of motor vehicles or
their accessories or equipment included a reference to the prescribed
requirements of so much of that Regulation as relates to the installation of
recording equipment and the seals to be fixed to such equipment.   **[242]**

NOTES
   Commencement: 15 May 1989.
   This section derived from the Road Traffic Act 1972, s 43, the Local Government Act 1972, Sch
19, para 5, the Local Government (Scotland) Act 1973, Sch 14, para 85, the Local Government Act
1985, Sch 17, and the Passenger and Goods Vehicles (Recording Equipment) Regulations 1981, SI
1981 No 1692, reg 2(1).
   Sub-s (1): words in square brackets substituted by the Road Traffic Act 1991, s 48, Sch 4, para
52(1), (2).
   Sub-s (3): para (aa) prospectively inserted by the Transport Act 1982, s 10(2)(a), (as amended by
the Road Traffic (Consequential Provisions) Act 1988, s 4, Sch 2, Part I), as from a day to be
appointed; para (b) substituted by the Road Traffic Act 1991, s 48, Sch 4, para 52(1), (3).
   Sub-s (5): words in square brackets prospectively inserted by the Transport Act 1982, s 21(1) (as
amended by the Road Traffic (Consequential Provisions) Act 1988, s 4, Sch 2, Part I), as from a day
to be appointed.
   See the Motor Vehicles (Tests) Regulations 1981, post.

46. Particular aspects of regulations under section 45

Regulations under section 45 of this Act may, in particular, make provision as
to—

   (a) the authorisation of examiners [in accordance with subsection (3)(a)
       of that section], the imposition of conditions to be complied with by
       authorised examiners and the withdrawal of authorisations,
   (b) the manner in which, conditions under which and apparatus with
       which examinations are carried out, the maintenance of that apparatus
       in an efficient state, and the inspection of premises at which and
       apparatus with which examinations are being, or are to be, carried
       out,
   (c) the manner in which applications may be made for the examination
       of vehicles under section 45 of this Act, the manner in which and time
       within which appeals may be brought under subsection (4) of that
       section, the information to be supplied and documents to be produced
       on such an application, examination or appeal, the fees to be paid on
       such an application or appeal, and the repayment of the whole or part
       of the fee paid on such an appeal where it appears to the Secretary of
       State that there were substantial grounds for contesting the whole or
       part of the decision appealed against,
   (d) the form of, and particulars to be contained in, test certificates and
       notifications of the refusal of test certificates, and the supply by the
       Secretary of State of forms for such certificates and notifications and
       the charges to be made for the supply of such forms,
   (e) the issue of duplicates of test certificates lost or defaced and the fee to
       be paid for the issue of such duplicates,
   (f) the issue of copies of test certificates and the fees to be paid for the
       issue of such copies,
   (g) the keeping by designated councils and authorised examiners [and, in
       the case of examinations carried out by authorised inspectors, by
       approved testing authorities] of registers of test certificates in the
       prescribed form and containing the prescribed particulars, and the
       inspection of such registers by such persons and in such circumstances
       as may be prescribed,

(h) the keeping of records by designated councils *and authorised examiners* [authorised examiners and approved testing authorities] and the providing by them of returns and information to the Secretary of State,

and regulations under that section may make different provision in relation to different cases or classes of cases. **[243]**

NOTES
  Commencement: 15 May 1989.
  This section derived from the Road Traffic Act 1972, s 43(6).
  Words in square brackets in para (a) inserted by the Road Traffic Act 1991, s 48, Sch 4, para 53.
  Paras (g), (h) prospectively amended by the Transport Act 1982, s 10(2), (as amended by the Road Traffic (Consequential Provisions) Act 1988, s 4, Sch 2, Part I), as from a day to be appointed.

47. Obligatory test certificates

(1) A person who uses on a road at any time, or causes or permits to be so used, a motor vehicle to which this section applies, and as respects which no test certificate has been issued within the appropriate period before that time, is guilty of an offence.

In this section and section 48 of this Act, the "appropriate period" means a period of twelve months or such shorter period as may be prescribed.

(2) Subject to subsections (3) and (5) below, the motor vehicles to which this section applies at any time are—

(a) those first registered under the Vehicles (Excise) Act 1971, the Vehicles (Excise) Act 1962, the Vehicles (Excise) Act 1949 or the Roads Act 1920, not less than three years before that time, and

(b) those which, having a date of manufacture not less than three years before that time, have been used on roads (whether in Great Britain or elsewhere) before being registered under the Vehicles (Excise) Act 1971 or the Vehicles (Excise) Act 1962,

being, in either case, motor vehicles other than goods vehicles which are required by regulations under section 49 of this Act to be submitted for a goods vehicle test.

(3) As respects a vehicle being—

(a) a motor vehicle used for the carriage of passengers and with more than eight seats, excluding the driver's seat, or

(b) a taxi (as defined in section 64(3) of the Transport Act 1980), being a vehicle licensed to ply for hire, or

(c) an ambulance, that is to say, a motor vehicle which is constructed or adapted, and primarily used, for the carriage of persons to a place where they will receive, or from a place where they have received, medical or dental treatment, and which, by reason of design, marking or equipment is readily identifiable as a vehicle so constructed or adapted,

subsection (2)(a) above shall have effect as if for the period there mentioned there were substituted a period of one year.

(4) For the purposes of subsection (2)(b) above, there shall be disregarded the use of a vehicle before it is sold or supplied by retail.

(5) This section does not apply to vehicles of such classes as may be prescribed.

(6) The Secretary of State may by regulations exempt from subsection (1) above the use of vehicles for such purposes as may be prescribed.

(7) The Secretary of State may by regulations exempt from subsection (1) above the use of vehicles in any such area as may be prescribed.

(8) For the purposes of this section the date of manufacture of a vehicle shall be taken to be the last day of the year during which its final assembly is completed, except where after that day modifications are made to the vehicle before it is sold or supplied by retail, and in that excepted case shall be taken to be the last day of the year during which the modifications are completed.

(9) The Secretary of State may by order made by statutory instrument direct that subsection (2) above shall have effect with the substitution, for three years (in both places), of such other period (not being more than ten years) as may be specified in the order.

An order under this subsection shall not have effect unless approved by resolution of each House of Parliament. **[244]**

NOTES
Commencement: 15 May 1989.
This section derived from the Road Traffic Act 1972, s 44(1)-(7), (11), (13), the Transport Act 1980, Sch 9, Part I, and the Motor Vehicles (Tests) (Extension) Order 1982, SI 1982 No 1550.

48. Supplementary provisions about test certificates

(1) For the purpose of spreading the work of issuing certificates in contemplation of a change in—
    (a) the length of the appropriate period, or
    (b) the length of the period specified in section 47(2)(a) and (b) of this Act,

(and whether for the purposes of that section or section 66 of this Act), the order or, as the case may be, regulations changing the length of that period may be made so as to come into operation on different days as respects vehicles first registered under any of the enactments mentioned in setion 47(2) of this Act at different times.

(2) Where—
    (a) within the appropriate period after a test certificate is issued or treated for the purposes of section 47 of this Act as issued, but
    (b) not earlier than one month before the end of that period,

a further test certificate is issued as respects the same vehicle, the further certificate shall be treated for the purposes of that section as if issued at the end of the appropriate period.

(3) Where the particulars contained in a test certificate in accordance with regulations made under section 45 of this Act include a date of expiry falling later, but not more than one month later, than the end of the appropriate period after the date on which it is issued—
    (a) the certificate shall be deemed to have been issued in respect of the same vehicle as an earlier test certificate, and
    (b) the date on which it was issued shall be deemed to have been a date falling within the last month of the appropriate period after the date on which that earlier certificate was issued or treated for the purposes of section 47 of this Act as issued;

and any date of expiry contained in a test certificate shall be deemed to have been entered in accordance with regulations under section 45 of this Act unless the contrary is proved.

(4) The Secretary of State may by regulations make provision for the issue, in such circumstances as may be prescribed, of a certificate of temporary exemption in respect of a public service vehicle adapted to carry more than eight passengers, exempting that vehicle from the provisions of section 47(1) of this Act for such period as may be specified in the certificate.

(5) In relation to any public service vehicle so adapted—

    (a) subsections (2) and (3) above shall have effect as if for "one month" (in both places) there were substituted "two months", and

    (b) subsection (3) above shall have effect as if for "last month" there were substituted "last two months".

(6) ... **[245]**

NOTES
    Commencement: 15 May 1989.
    This section derived from the Road Traffic Act 1972, s 44(8)-(10A), and the Transport Act 1982, s 16.
    Sub-s (6): repealed by the Road Traffic Act 1991, s 83, Sch 8.

Tests of certain classes of goods vehicles

49. Tests of satisfactory condition of goods vehicles and determination of plated weights, etc

(1) The Secretary of State may by regulations make provision for the examination of goods vehicles of any prescribed class—

    (a) for the purpose of selecting or otherwise determining plated weights or other plated particulars for goods vehicles of that class, or

    (b) for the purpose of ascertaining whether any prescribed construction and use requirements (whether relating to plated particulars or not) are complied with in the case of goods vehicles of that class,

[or

    (c) for the purpose of ascertaining whether the condition of the vehicle is such that its use on a road would involve a danger of injury to any person,

or for any of those purposes.]

(2) In particular the regulations may make provision—

    (a) for the determination, according to criteria or by methods prescribed by or determined under the regulations, of the plated particulars for a goods vehicle (including its plated weights), on an examination of the vehicle for the purpose, and for the issue on such an examination, except as provided by regulations made by virtue of paragraph (c) of this subsection, of a certificate (in this Act referred to as a "plating certificate") specifying those particulars,

    (b) for the issue, for a goods vehicle which has been found on examination for the purpose to comply with the prescribed construction and use requirements [and the requirement that the condition of the vehicle is not such that its use on a road would involve a danger of injury to any person], of a certificate (in this Act referred to as a "goods vehicle test certificate") stating that the vehicle has been found so to comply, and

    (c) for the refusal of a goods vehicle test certificate for a goods vehicle which is so found not to comply with those requirements and for requiring a written notification to be given—

(i) of any such refusal, and

(ii) of the grounds of the refusal,

and for the refusal of a plating certificate where a goods vehicle test certificate is refused.

(3) References in subsections (1) and (2) above to construction and use requirements shall be construed—

(a) in relation to an examination of a vehicle solely for the purpose of ascertaining whether it complies with any such requirements, as references to such of those requirements as are applicable to the vehicle at the time of the test, and

(b) in relation to an examination of a vehicle both for that purpose and for the purpose of determining its plated particulars, as references to such of those requirements as will be applicable to the vehicle if a plating certificate is issued for it.

(4) In this Part of this Act—

"examination for plating" means an examination under regulations under this section for the purpose of determining plated particulars for a goods vehicle, and

"goods vehicle test" means an examination under regulations under this section for the purpose of ascertaining whether any prescribed construction and use requirements [, or the requirement that the condition of the vehicle is not such that its use on a road would involve a danger of injury to any person,] are complied with in the case of a goods vehicle.

(5) In its application to vehicles in which recording equipment is required by Article 3 of the Community Recording Equipment Regulation to be installed and used, this section shall have effect as if any reference to prescribed construction and use requirements included a reference to prescribed requirements of so much of that Regulation as relates to the installation of recording equipment and the seals to be fixed to such equipment.   **[246]**

NOTES

Commencement: 15 May 1989.

This section derived from the Road Traffic Act 1972, s 45(1), (2), (9A), the Passenger and Goods Vehicles (Recording Equipment) Regulations 1981, SI 1981 No 1692, reg 2(2), and the Community Drivers' Hours and Recording Equipment Regulations 1986, SI 1986 No 1457, art 3.

Sub-ss (1), (2), (4): amended by the Road Traffic Act 1991, s 48, Sch 4, para 54.

See the Goods Vehicles (Plating and Testing) Regulations 1988, post.

---

50. Appeals against determinations

(1) Any person aggrieved by a determination made on an examination under regulations under section 49 of this Act by the person in charge of the examination may appeal to [the Secretary of State].

(2), (3) . . .

(4) On the appeal the Secretary of State must cause the vehicle to be re-examined by an officer appointed by him for the purpose and must make such determination on the basis of the re-examination as he thinks fit.

(5) Regulations under section 49 of this Act may make the like provision in relation to a determination on an appeal under this section as they make in relation to a determination on an examination under the regulations.   **[247]**

NOTES
　Commencement: 15 May 1989.
　This section derived from the Road Traffic Act 1972, s 45(3)-(5).
　Sub-ss (1)–(3): words in square brackets in sub-s (1) substituted, and sub-ss (2), (3) repealed, by the Road Traffic Act 1991, ss 48, 83, Sch 4, para 55, Sch 8.

51. Particular aspects of regulations under section 49

(1) Without prejudice to the generality of subsection (1) of section 49 of this Act, regulations under that section may—

    (a) require or authorise goods vehicles to which the regulations apply to be submitted for examination under the regulations and, in particular—

        (i) require any such vehicle to be submitted for a goods vehicle test at periodic intervals, and

        (ii) require or authorise any such vehicle to be submitted for re-examination on the making of any prescribed alteration to it or its equipment and, for the purpose of determining whether any such re-examination is necessary, require any such alteration to be notified to the Secretary of State [or the prescribed testing authority], and

        (iii) require any such vehicle to be submitted for examination or re-examination for any purpose of plating or certification,

    [(*aa*) require the payment of a fee on any notification of any alteration to a vehicle or its equipment which is required by the regulations to be notified to the Secretary of State or the prescribed testing authority;]

    (b) authorise any examination under the regulations to be carried out by or under the direction of a . . . vehicle examiner [or an authorised inspector],

    (c) prescribe the conditions subject to which vehicles will be accepted for such examination and without prejudice to that—

        (i) authorise any person by whom an examination of the vehicle under the regulations or section 50 of this Act is carried out to drive the vehicle, whether on a road or elsewhere, and

        (ii) require that a driver of a vehicle examined under those regulations or that section is, except so far as permitted to be absent by the person carrying out the examination, present throughout the whole of the examination and drives the vehicle when directed to do so and operates the controls in accordance with any directions given to him, by that person,

    (d) require the plating certificate for any vehicle to which the regulations apply to specify any alteration to the vehicle or its equipment which is required by the regulations to be notified to the Secretary of State [or the prescribed testing authority],

    (e) authorise the amendment of a plating certificate or the issue of a different plating certificate on the re-examination of any vehicle,

    (f) provide for the period of validity of goods vehicle test certificates,

    (g) specify the manner in which, and the time before or within which, applications may be made for the examination of vehicles under the regulations or appeals may be brought under section 50 of this Act and the information to be supplied and documents to be produced on any such application, examination or appeal,

    (h) make provision as to the fees to be paid on any such application or appeal and as to the repayment of the whole or part of any fee paid on such an appeal where it appears to the Secretary of State that there were substantial grounds for contesting the whole or part of the determination appealed from,

(j) make provision as to the form of, and particulars to be contained in, plating certificates and goods vehicle test certificates and notifications of the refusal of the latter certificates,

(k) provide for the issue of replacements for plates marked with plated particulars, plating certificates and goods vehicle test certificates which have been lost or defaced and for the payment of a fee for their issue,

(l) exempt prescribed classes of vehicles from all or any of the provisions of the regulations either generally or in prescribed circumstances,

(m) make different provision for different cases.

(2) Regulations under section 49 of this Act may provide that a person who contravenes or fails to comply with a requirement of regulations imposed by virtue of subsection (1)(c)(ii) above is guilty of an offence.

(3) In this section any reference to the driving of a vehicle is, in relation to a trailer, a reference to the driving of the vehicle by which the trailer is drawn.

[248]

NOTES

Commencement: 15 May 1989.

This section derived from the Road Traffic Act 1972, s 45(6), (7), (10), and the Transport Act 1978, s 9(2).

Sub-s (1): paras (a), (b), (d) amended and para (*aa*) prospectively added by the Transport Act 1982, ss 10(3), (7), 22(1) (as amended by the Road Traffic (Consequential Provisions) Act 1988, s 4, Sch 2, Part I and by the Road Traffic Act 1991, s 48, Sch 4, para 19(1), (2), as from a day to be appointed); word omitted from para (b) repealed by s 83 of, and Sch 8 to, the 1991 Act.

52. Supplementary provisions about tests, etc, of goods vehicles

(1) Without prejudice to any regulations made under section 49 of this Act by virtue of section 51(1)(c) of this Act, the Secretary of State may give directions with respect to the manner in which examinations under regulations under section 49 or under section 50 of this Act are to be carried out.

(2) The Secretary of State may provide and maintain stations where examinations of goods vehicles under regulations under section 49 or under section 50 of this Act may be carried out and may provide and maintain the apparatus for carrying out such examinations. **[249]**

NOTES

Commencement: 15 May 1989.

This section derived from the Road Traffic Act 1972, s 45(8), (9).

53. Obligatory goods vehicle test certificates

(1) If any person at any time on or after the relevant date—

(a) uses on a road a goods vehicle of a class required by regulations under section 49 of this Act to have been submitted for examination for plating, or

(b) causes or permits to be used on a road a goods vehicle of such a class,

and at that time there is no plating certificate in force for the vehicle, he is guilty of an offence.

In this subsection "relevant date", in relation to any goods vehicle, means the date by which it is required by the regulations to be submitted for examination for plating.

(2) If any person at any time on or after the relevant date—

(a) uses on a road a goods vehicle of a class required by regulations under section 49 of this Act to have been submitted for a goods vehicle test, or

(b) causes or permits to be used on a road a goods vehicle of such a class,

and at that time there is no goods vehicle test certificate in force for the vehicle, he is guilty of an offence.

In this subsection "relevant date", in relation to any goods vehicle, means the date by which it is required by the regulations to be submitted for its first goods vehicle test.

(3) Any person who—

(a) uses a goods vehicle on a road, or

(b) causes or permits a goods vehicle to be so used,

when an alteration has been made to the vehicle or its equipment which is required by regulations under section 49 of this Act to be, but has not been, notified to the Secretary of State [or the prescribed testing authority] is guilty of an offence.

(4) In any proceedings for an offence under subsection (3) above, it shall be a defence to prove that the alteration was not specified in the relevant plating certificate in accordance with regulations under section 49 of this Act.

(5) The Secretary of State may by regulations—

(a) exempt from all or any of the preceding provisions of this section the use of goods vehicles for such purposes or in such an area as may be prescribed, and

(b) make provision for the issue in respect of a vehicle in such circumstances as may be prescribed of a certificate of temporary exemption exempting that vehicle from the provisions of subsection (1) or (2) above for such period as may be specified in the certificate.

[250]

NOTES

Commencement: 15 May 1989.

This section derived from the Road Traffic Act 1972, s 46.

Sub-s (3): words in square brackets prospectively added by the Transport Act 1982, s 10(7) (as amended by the Road Traffic (Consequential Provisions) Act 1988, s 4, Sch 2, Part I), as from a day to be appointed.

See the Goods Vehicles (Plating and Testing) Regulations 1988 post.

Approval of design, construction, equipment and marking of vehicles

54. Type approval requirements

(1) Without prejudice to section 41 of this Act, the Secretary of State may by regulations prescribe requirements (in this Part of this Act referred to as "type approval requirements")—

(a) with respect to the design, construction, equipment and marking of vehicles of any class, being requirements which are applicable before, whether or not they are applicable after, vehicles of that class are used on a road,

(b) with respect to the design, construction, equipment and marking of vehicle parts of any class, being requirements which are applicable before, whether or not they are applicable after, vehicle parts of that class are fitted to a vehicle used on a road.

(2) Regulations under this section may provide for the determination, according to criteria or by methods prescribed by or determined under the regulations, of weights of any description which in the opinion of the Secretary of State should not be exceeded in the case of vehicles of any class.

(3) In this Part of this Act references to design weights shall be construed as references to weights determined by virtue of subsection (2) above.

(4) Subject to subsection (5) below, the following provisions of this Act to the end of section 60 apply in relation to parts of vehicles as they apply in relation to vehicles and, accordingly, any reference in those provisions to a vehicle, other than a reference to a goods vehicle, is to be read as including a reference to a vehicle part.

(5) Any provision which relates solely to goods vehicles or design weights does not apply in relation to parts of vehicles, but particular exclusions in those provisions do not affect the generality of this exclusion.

(6) In this Part of this Act, "the relevant aspects of design, construction, equipment and marking", in relation to any vehicle, means those aspects of design, construction, equipment and marking which are subject to the type approval requirements or which were used as criteria in determining design weights for that vehicle. **[251]**

NOTES

Commencement: 15 May 1989.

This section derived from the Road Traffic Act 1972, ss 47(1)-(3), 49A(1), (2), and the Road Traffic Act 1974, s 10(1)(a), (3), Sch 7.

See the Motor Vehicles (Type Approval for Goods Vehicles) (Great Britain) Regulations 1982, SI 1982 No 1271 as amended, and the Motor Vehicles (Type Approval) (Great Britain) Regulations 1984, SI 1984 No 981, as amended.

55. Type approval certificates

(1) Where the Secretary of State is satisfied on application made to him by the manufacturer of a vehicle of a class to which regulations under section 54 of this Act apply and after examination of the vehicle—

(a) that the vehicle complies with the relevant type approval requirements, and

(b) that adequate arrangements have been made to secure that other vehicles purporting to conform with that vehicle in the relevant aspects of design, construction, equipment and marking will so conform in all respects or with such variations as may be permitted,

he may approve that vehicle as a type vehicle.

(2) Where the Secretary of State approves a vehicle as a type vehicle he must issue a certificate (in this Part of this Act referred to as a "type approval certificate") stating that the vehicle complies with the relevant type approval requirements and specifying—

(a) the permitted variations from the type vehicle, and

(b) the design weights for vehicles so conforming in all respects and for vehicles so conforming with any such variations.

(3) In the following provisions of this section and in sections 56 to 59 of this Act "conform" means conform in all respects or with any permitted variation.

(4) Subject to subsection (6) below, a type approval certificate may be issued for a type vehicle where the Secretary of State is satisfied that one or more, but not all, of the relevant type approval requirements are complied with in the case of that vehicle.

(5) A further type approval certificate may be issued by virtue of subsection (4) above on the application of any person—

    (a) who manufactures any part of the vehicle, or
    (b) by whom the vehicle is finally assembled;

and references in the following provisions of this section and in sections 56 to 59 of this Act to a manufacturer shall be construed accordingly.

(6) The first type approval certificate issued for a type vehicle by virtue of subsection (4) above must specify the design weights for conforming vehicles, and accordingly—

    (a) so much of subsection (2) above or section 57(1) to (3) of this Act as requires the Secretary of State [or the prescribed testing authority] or a manufacturer to specify in any certificate under this or that section the design weights or plated weights for a vehicle or as requires the Secretary of State or a manufacturer to mark or secure the marking of the plated weights on a vehicle does not apply to a subsequent type approval certificate issued by virtue of subsection (4) above or to the certificates of conformity issued in consequence of such a type approval certificate, and

    (b) so much of section 58(2) of this Act as requires the Secretary of State to specify in any certificate issued by him the design weights and plated weights for a vehicle or to secure that the plated weights are marked on a vehicle does not apply to a Minister's approval certificate issued by virtue of subsection (4) above.

(7) Subsection (6) above does not apply in relation to vehicle parts.

(8) Where the Secretary of State determines on an application under this section not to issue a type approval certificate in respect of a vehicle, he must give to the applicant a written notification of the determination, stating the grounds on which it is based. **[252]**

NOTES
    Commencement: 15 May 1989.
    This section derived from the Road Traffic Act 1972, ss 47(4), (9)(a), (10), (13), 49A(2)(a), and the Road Traffic Act 1974, s 10(1)(a), (b), (3), Sch 7.
    Sub-s (6): words in square brackets in para (a) prospectively added by the Transport Act 1982, s 17(1)(a) (as amended by the Road Traffic (Consequential Provisions) Act 1988, s 4, Sch 2, Part I), as from a day to be appointed.

56. Conditions of, and cancellation or suspension of, type approval certificates

(1) A type approval certificate may be issued subject to conditions with respect to—

    (a) the inspection by officers of the Secretary of State of vehicles purporting to conform with the type vehicle in the relevant aspects of design, construction, equipment and marking and of parts of such vehicles and their equipment, and the entry of premises where they are manufactured, and

(b) the notification by the manufacturer of differences of design, construction, equipment or marking (other than permitted variations) between any such vehicles and the type vehicle which might affect the type approval requirements or the criteria for determining the design weights of those vehicles.

(2) If—

(a) it appears to the Secretary of State that there has been a breach of a condition subject to which a type approval certificate has been granted, or

(b) the Secretary of State ceases to be satisfied as to any other matter relevant to a type approval certificate,

he may cancel or suspend the certificate, but the cancellation or suspension shall not affect the validity of any certificate of conformity previously issued in consequence of the type approval certificate.

(3) Where the Secretary of State cancels or suspends a certificate in pursuance of this section, he shall give a written notification of that fact to the holder of the certificate stating the grounds for the cancellation or suspension.

[253]

NOTES
   Commencement: 15 May 1989.
   This section derived from the Road Traffic Act 1972, s 48(1), (6), (7), and the Road Traffic Act 1974, s 10(1)(b).

57. Certificates of conformity

(1) The manufacturer of a type vehicle in respect of which a type approval certificate is in force may issue, in respect of each vehicle manufactured by him which conforms with the type vehicle in such of the relevant aspects of design, construction, equipment and marking as are mentioned in the type approval certificate, a certificate (in this Part of this Act referred to as a "certificate of conformity")—

(a) stating that it does so conform, and
(b) specifying the design weights for the vehicle,

and must in the case of goods vehicles of such classes as may be prescribed specify in the certificate one or more of the plated weights for the vehicle.

(2) Where a manufacturer issues a certificate of conformity for a goods vehicle, the Secretary of State [or the prescribed testing authority] must—

(a) on an application made by any person containing such information as *he* [the Secretary of State or that authority] may require with respect to the proposed circumstances of operation of the goods vehicle, and
(b) on production of that certificate,

specify in the certificate any plated weights for the goods vehicle not so specified by the manufacturer.

(3) Where a manufacturer issues a certificate of conformity for a goods vehicle then—

(a) if he is required by subsection (1) above to specify any plated weights for the goods vehicle in the certificate, he must mark those weights on the goods vehicle by means of a plate fixed to it, and

(b) in any other case the Secretary of State [or the prescribed testing authority] must on an application for the purpose secure that those weights are so marked.

(4) Any certificate of conformity issued in consequence of any type approval certificate issued by virtue of section 55(4) of this Act shall relate only to the requirement or requirements to which that type approval certificate relates.

(5) Subsections (2) and (3) above do not apply in relation to vehicle parts.

[254]

NOTES

Commencement: 15 May 1989.

This section derived from the Road Traffic Act 1972, ss 47(5)-(7), (9)(b), 49A(2)(a), and the Road Traffic Act 1974, s 10(1)(a), (b), (c), (d), (3), Sch 7.

Sub-s (2): first words in square brackets prospectively added, word in italics prospectively repealed and second words in square brackets prospectively substituted by the Transport Act 1982, s 17(1) (as amended by the Road Traffic (Consequential Provisions) Act 1988, s 4, Sch 2, Part I), as from a day to be appointed.

Sub-s (3): words in square brackets prospectively added by the Transport Act 1982, s 17(1) (as amended by the Road Traffic (Consequential Provisions) Act 1988, s 4, Sch 2, Part I), as from a day to be appointed.

---

58. Minister's approval certificates

(1) Where the Secretary of State is satisfied, on application made to him by any person in respect of a vehicle of a class to which regulations under section 54 of this Act apply and after examination of the vehicle, that—

(a) the vehicle complies with the relevant type approval requirements, and

(b) in the case of a goods vehicle, the Secretary of State has sufficient information to enable the plated weights to be ascertained for the vehicle,

he may issue a certificate (in this Part of this Act referred to as a "Minister's approval certificate").

(2) The certificate must state that the vehicle complies with those requirements and specify—

(a) its design weights, and

(b) in the case of a goods vehicle, its plated weights,

and, where the Secretary of State issues such a certificate in respect of a goods vehicle, he must secure that the plated weights are marked on the vehicle by means of a plate fixed to it.

(3) Where by virtue of section 57(4) of this Act a certificate of conformity issued in respect of a vehicle relates to one or more, but not all, of the relevant type approval requirements, the Secretary of State may issue in respect of that vehicle a Minister's approval certificate relating to one or more of the other relevant type approval requirements.

(4) Where—

(a) a Minister's approval certificate is given as respects a vehicle, and

(b) the Secretary of State is satisfied—

(i) on the application of the manufacturer of the vehicle or, in the case of an imported vehicle, the importer of the vehicle, and

(ii) after the consideration of such evidence as he thinks necessary, that another vehicle manufactured by that manufacturer or, as the case may be, imported by that importer conforms with the first mentioned vehicle as respects the relevant aspects of design, construction, equipment and marking,

the Secretary of State may issue a Minister's approval certificate in respect of that other vehicle without examining it.

(5) Where the Secretary of State issues such a certificate by virtue of subsection (4) above, he must specify the plated weights which are to be marked on the other vehicle.

(6) Subsection (4) above shall apply in relation to vehicles brought into Great Britain from Northern Ireland as it applies in relation to imported vehicles, and references in that subsection to the importer shall be construed accordingly.

(7) Where the Secretary of State determines on an application under this section not to issue a Minister's approval certificate in respect of a vehicle, he must give to the applicant a written notification of the determination, stating the grounds on which it is based.   [255]

NOTES
   Commencement: 15 May 1989.
   This section derived from the Road Traffic Act 1972, s 47(8), (9)(c), (11)-(13), and the Road Traffic Act 1974, s 10(1)(a), (e), (2), Sch 7.

59. Supplementary provisions as to certificates of conformity and Minister's approval certificates

(1) The Secretary of State may by regulations require that prescribed alterations—

   (a) in any of the relevant aspects of design, construction, equipment or marking, or
   (b) in any such aspect which affects the plated weight,

made to any vehicle for which a certificate of conformity or a Minister's approval certificate is issued shall, subject to any exemption granted under subsection (2) below, be notified to the Secretary of State [or the prescribed testing authority].

(2) The Secretary of State may by notice in writing given to the manufacturer of vehicles or to the owner of a vehicle for which a Minister's approval certificate is issued—

   (a) direct that any specified alteration in any of the aspects mentioned in subsection (1) above to a vehicle to which the direction relates shall be notified to the Secretary of State [or the prescribed testing authority],
   (b) exempt a vehicle to which the notice relates from all or any of the requirements of regulations under subsection (1) above, subject to compliance with any conditions specified in the notice.

(3) Without prejudice to the provisions of section 61 of this Act, the Secretary of State may by regulations require that a certificate of conformity or Minister's approval certificate issued for any vehicle shall specify—

   (a) the regulations, if any, applicable to the vehicle under subsection (1) above at the time of the issue of the certificate,
   (b) any additional alteration to that vehicle required by any direction under subsection (2) above to be notified to the Secretary of State [or the prescribed testing authority], and

(c) any exemption applicable to that vehicle under that subsection.

(4) A certificate of conformity or a Minister's approval certificate specifying any plated weights shall be treated for the purposes of the provisions of this Part of this Act and any regulations made under them relating to plating certificates (except section 50(1) and (2) of this Act) as a plating certificate.

This subsection does not apply in relation to vehicle parts.   **[256]**

NOTES
    Commencement: 15 May 1989.
    This section derived from the Road Traffic Act 1972, ss 48(2)-(5), 49A(2)(b), and the Road Traffic Act 1974, s 10(1)(a), (b), (3), Sch 7.
    Sub-ss (1)-(3): words in square brackets prospectively added by the Transport Act 1982, s 10(7) (as amended by the Road Traffic (Consequential Provisions) Act 1988, s 4, Sch 2, Part I), as from a day to be appointed.
    See the Motor Vehicles (Type Approval for Goods Vehicles) (Great Britain) Regulations 1982, SI 1982 No 1271 as amended.

60. Appeals

(1) A person aggrieved by the determination made on behalf of the Secretary of State with respect to a type approval certificate, a certificate of conformity or a Minister's approval certificate under sections 54 to 59 of this Act, including any determination with respect to design weights or plated weights, may within the prescribed time and in the prescribed mannner appeal to the Secretary of State.

(2) On the appeal the Secretary of State—

(a) shall have the like powers and duties as he has on an original application for a type approval or a Minister's approval certificate or in respect of the plated weights to be included in a certificate of conformity,

(b) may hold an inquiry in connection with it, and

(c) may appoint an assessor for the purpose of assisting him with the appeal or any such inquiry.

[(1) A person aggrieved by a determination made on behalf of the Secretary of State with respect to a type approval certificate, a certificate of conformity or Minister's approval certificate under [sections 54 to 59] of this Act, including any determination with respect to design weights or plated weights, may appeal to the Secretary of State.

(2) A person aggrieved by a determination made by the prescribed testing authority with respect to the plated weights for any goods vehicle may appeal to the Secretary of State.

[This subsection does not apply in relation to vehicle parts.]

(3) Any appeal under this section must be made within the prescribed time and in the prescribed manner; and on any such appeal the Secretary of State shall have—

(a) in a case within subsection (1) above, the like powers and duties as he has on an original application for a type approval or Minister's approval certificate or in respect of the plated weights to be included in a certificate of conformity; and

(b) in a case within subsection (2) above, the like powers and duties as he would have had if the application in respect of the plated weights for the goods vehicle concerned had been made to him.

(4) The Secretary of State may hold an inquiry in connection with any appeal under this section and may appoint an assessor for the purposes of assisting him with the appeal or any such inquiry.] **[257]**

NOTES
Commencement: 15 May 1989.
This section derived from the Road Traffic Act 1972, s 49.
Prospectively substituted by the Transport Act 1982, s 17(2) (as amended by the Road Traffic (Consequential Provisions) Act 1988, s 4, Sch 2, Pt I), as from a day to be appointed.

61. Regulations for the purposes of sections 54 to 60

(1) The Secretary of State may make regulations for the purposes of sections 54 to 60 of this Act.

[(1A) Without prejudice to the generality of subsection (1) above, regulations made under this section for the purposes of [sections 54 to 60] of this Act may provide—

(a) for the fees to be payable on any application for a determination by the prescribed testing authority of any plated weights for a goods vehicle; and

(b) for the issue by the prescribed testing authority of plates for marking on goods vehicles any plated weights, whether determined by that authority or not (including in particular the issue of such plates on behalf of the Secretary of State for the purposes of [section 58(2)] and for the fees to be payable to that authority for the issue of any such plates.]

(2) Without prejudice to the generality of subsection (1) above, such regulations—

(a) may provide for the examination of any vehicle in respect of which a certificate of conformity or a Minister's approval certificate is in force in the event of an alteration being made to the vehicle which is notifiable by virtue of section 59(1) or (2) of this Act and, in particular, may empower a . . . vehicle examiner [or an authorised inspector] to require the vehicle to be examined at a testing station provided under section 52, 62 or 72 of this Act [or designated under section 10(12) of the Transport Act 1982],

(b) may authorise the cancellation, suspension or amendment of a certificate of conformity or a Minister's approval certificate on an examination of any vehicle in pursuance of regulations made by virtue of paragraph (a) above,

(c) shall give a right of appeal to any person aggrieved by a determination on any such examination and for that purpose may apply section 50(1) to (4) of this Act,

(d) may contain the like provisions with respect to any such examination and any appeal brought by virtue of paragraph (c) above as may be contained in regulations made by virtue of paragraphs (b), (c), (g) and (h) of [section 51(1)] of this Act in relation to the examinations and appeals there mentioned,

[(d) may contain the like provisions with respect to any notification of any such alteration as is mentioned in paragraph (a) above, with respect to any examination of any vehicle in pursuance of regulations made by virtue of that paragraph and with respect to any appeal brought by virtue of paragraph (c) above as may be contained in regulations made by virtue of paragraphs (*aa*), (b), (c), (g) and (h) of section 51(1) of this Act in relation to the notifications, examinations and appeals there mentioned.]

(e) may require the payment of fees or other charges in connection with the provision by the Secretary of State of services or facilities or the issue by him of certificates and other documents,

(f) may provide—

    (i) for the authorisation of persons to carry out examinations, in connection with the issue of type approval certificates, of vehicles or vehicle parts of such classes as may be specified in the regulations,

    (ii) for the imposition of conditions to be complied with by persons so authorised, and

    (iii) for the withdrawal of authorisations,

(g) may make provision as to the form of, and particulars to be contained in, certificates of conformity and provide for the supply by the Secretary of State of forms for such certificates,

(h) may provide for the issue of replacements for plates fixed to vehicles under sections 54 to 58 of this Act, certificates of conformity and Minister's approval certificates which have been lost or defaced and provide for the payment of a fee for their issue,

(j) may require persons empowered by sections 54 to 58 of this Act to issue certificates of conformity to keep records—

    (i) of certificates of conformity issued by them, and

    (ii) of the vehicles or vehicle parts in respect of which such certificates are issued,

and may authorise the inspection of such records by such persons and in such circumstances as may be prescribed, and

(k) may make different provisions for different cases.

(3) Without prejudice to any regulations made by virtue of section 51(1)(c) of this Act, as applied by this section, the Secretary of State may give directions with respect to the manner in which examinations to which such regulations apply are to be carried out.

(4) Where regulations under this section impose the like requirement as may be imposed by regulations made by virtue of section 51(1)(c)(ii) of this Act, the regulations may provide that a person who contravenes or fails to comply with a requirement so imposed is guilty of an offence.

(5) ...   **[258]**

NOTES

Commencement: 15 May 1989 (sub-ss (1), (2)-(5)); to be appointed (sub-s (1A)).

This section derived from the Road Traffic Act 1972, s 50(1), (2), (5), (6), the Road Traffic Act 1974, s 10(4), Sch 2, paras 7, 8(1), (4), the Public Passenger Vehicles Act 1981, Sch 7, para 15, and the Transport Act 1982, Sch 5, para 10(b).

Sub-s (1A): prospectively added by the Transport Act 1982, s 17(4) (as amended by the Road Traffic (Consequential Provisions) Act 1988, s 4, Sch 2, Part I), as from a day to be appointed.

Sub-s (2): first words in square brackets in para (a) prospectively added and para (d) prospectively substituted by the Transport Act 1982, ss 10(3)(a), 22(2) (as amended by the Road Traffic (Consequential Provisions) Act 1988, s 4, Sch 2, Part I, and by the Road Traffic Act 1991, s 48, Sch 4, para 19(1), (2)), as from a day to be appointed; second words in square brackets in para (a) prospectively added by the Road Traffic (Consequential Provisions) Act 1988, s 4, Sch 2, Part I, as from a day to be appointed. Words omitted from para (a) repealed by the Road Traffic Act 1991, s 83, Sch 8.

Sub-s (5): repealed by the Road Traffic Act 1991, s 83, Sch 8.

See the Motor Vehicles (Type Approval) (Great Britain) Regulations 1984, SI 1984 No 981 as amended, the Motor Vehicles (Type Approval for Goods Vehicles) (Great Britain) Regulations 1982, SI 1982 No 1271 as amended, and the Motor Vehicles (Type Approval and Approval Marks) (Fees) Regulations 1992, SI 1992 No 489.

62. Other supplementary provisions

(1) The Secretary of State may provide and maintain stations where examinations of vehicles under sections 54 to 61 of this Act or regulations under those sections may be carried out and may provide and maintain the apparatus for carrying out such examinations.

(2) Where an agreement entered into between Her Majesty's Government and the Government of a country outside Great Britain provides for the recognition in Great Britain of arrangements under the law of that country with respect to the approval of the design, construction, equipment or marking of vehicles of any description manufactured in that country, the Secretary of State may make regulations—

    (a) applying, with such adaptations and modifications as he thinks fit, all or any of the provisions of sections 54 to 60 of this Act and of regulations under section 61 of this Act, so far as relating to type approval certificates and certificates of conformity, to vehicles of that description manufactured in that country,

    (b) providing that a certificate issued under any such provision as so applied shall be treated for the purposes of any other provisions of this Part of this Act prescribed by the regulations as a type approval certificate or as a certificate of conformity,

    (c) providing for the cancellation or suspension (subject to any savings prescribed by the regulations) of any such certificate in the event of the agreement ceasing to be in force or being modified.

(3) Except in the case of vehicles of such class as may be prescribed, in sections 57, 58 and 61 of this Act "goods vehicle" includes a vehicle which is a chassis for, or will otherwise form part of, a vehicle which when completed will be a goods vehicle. **[259]**

NOTES
    Commencement: 15 May 1989.
    This section derived from the Road Traffic Act 1972, s 50(3), (4), (6), the Road Traffic Act 1974, Sch 2, para 8(2), (3), (4), Sch 7, and the Public Passenger Vehicles Act 1981, Sch 7, para 15.

63. Obligatory type approval certificates, certificates of conformity and Minister's approval certificates

(1) If—

    (a) any person at any time on or after the day appointed by regulations made by the Secretary of State in relation to vehicles or vehicle parts to which type approval requirements prescribed by those regulations apply—

        (i) uses on a road, or
        (ii) causes or permits to be so used,
    a vehicle of that class or a vehicle to which is fitted a vehicle part of that class, and

    (b) it does not appear from one or more certificates then in force under sections 54 to 58 of this Act that the vehicle or vehicle part complies with those requirements,

he is guilty of an offence.

Different days may be appointed under this subsection in relation to different classes of vehicles or vehicle parts.

(2) If a plating certificate—

- (a) has been issued for a goods vehicle to which section 53(1) of this Act or subsection (1) above applies, but
- (b) does not specify a maximum laden weight for the vehicle together with any trailer which may be drawn by it,

any person who on or after the relevant date within the meaning of section 53(1) of this Act or, as the case may be, the day appointed under subsection (1) above uses the vehicle on a road for drawing a trailer, or causes or permits it to be so used, is guilty of an offence.

(3) Any person who—

- (a) uses a vehicle on a road, or
- (b) causes or permits a vehicle to be so used,

when an alteration has been made to the vehicle or its equipment which is required by regulations or directions under section 59 of this Act to be, but has not been, notified to the Secretary of State [or the prescribed testing authority] is guilty of an offence.

(4) In any proceedings for an offence under subsection (3) above, it shall be a defence to prove that the regulations were not or, as the case may be, the alteration was not, specified in the relevant certificate of conformity or Minister's approval certificate in accordance with regulations under section 59(3) of this Act.

(5) The Secretary of State may by regulations—

- (a) exempt from all or any of the preceding provisions of this section the use of vehicles for such purposes or in such an area as may be prescribed,
- (b) except any class of goods vehicles from the provisions of subsection (2) above, and
- (c) make provision for the issue in respect of a vehicle or vehicle part in such circumstances as may be prescribed of a certificate of temporary exemption exempting that vehicle or vehicle part from the provisions of subsection (1) above for such period as may be specified in the certificate.   **[260]**

NOTES

Commencement: 15 May 1989.

This section derived from the Road Traffic Act 1972, s 51, and the Road Traffic Act 1974, Sch 2, para 7, 9, Sch 7.

Sub-s (3): words in square brackets prospectively added by the Transport Act 1982, s 10(7) (as amended by the Road Traffic (Consequential Provisions) Act 1988, s 4, Sch 2, Part I), as from a day to be appointed.

See the Motor Vehicles (Type Approval) (Great Britain) Regulations 1984, SI 1984 No 981 as amended, and the Goods Vehicles (Plating and Testing) Regulations 1988, Part VIII, reg 45 post.

63A. Alteration of plated weights for goods vehicles without examination

[(1) The Secretary of State may by regulations make provision—

- (a) for the determination, in such circumstances as may be prescribed, of the plated weights (or any of the plated weights) for goods vehicles of any prescribed class otherwise than on an examination under regulations made under section 49 or 61 of this Act; and

(b) for the amendment of any approval certificate in force in respect of a vehicle of any such class so as to specify the weights determined for that vehicle under the regulations in place of any weights superseded by those weights or the cancellation of any such certificate and the issue in place of it of a different certificate specifying the weights so determined in place of any weights so superseded.

(2) Any person aggrieved by a determination of plated weights for a goods vehicle under regulations made under this section may appeal to the Secretary of State and on the appeal the Secretary of State shall cause the vehicle to be examined by an officer of the Secretary of State appointed by him for the purpose and shall make such determination on the basis of the examination as he thinks fit.

(3) Without prejudice to the generality of subsection (1) above, regulations under this section—

(a) may provide for the determination of any plated weights for a goods vehicle under the regulations to be made by the Secretary of State or by the prescribed testing authority;
(b) may contain the like provisions with respect to any appeal brought by virtue of subsection (2) above and any examination on any such appeal as may be contained in any regulations made by virtue of paragraphs (c), (g) and (h) of section 51(1) of this Act in relation to an appeal under section 50(1) and any examination on any such appeal;
(c) may specify the manner in which, and the time before or within which, applications may be made for the determination of plated weights of vehicles under the regulations, and the information to be supplied and documents to be produced on any such application;
(d) may make provision as to the fees to be paid on any such application;
(e) may provide for the issue of replacements for any plates fixed to a vehicle specifying weights superseded by weights specified in an approval certificate amended under the regulations or in any certificate issued under the regulations in place of an approval certificate, and for the payment of a fee for their issue; and
(f) may make different provision for different cases.

(4) In this section "approval certificate" means a plating certificate and any certificate of conformity or Minister's approval certificate specifying any plated weights.

(5) Any certificate issued in respect of a goods vehicle under regulations made under this section in replacement of an approval certificate of any description mentioned in subsection (4) above—

(a) shall be in the form appropriate for an approval certificate of that description;
(b) shall be identical in content with the certificate it replaces, save for any alterations in the plated weights authorised by the regulations; and
(c) shall be treated for the purposes of this Part of this Act (including this section) and any regulations made under any provision of this Part of this Act as if it were the same certificate as the certificate it replaces;

and any plate so issued in replacement of a plate fixed to the vehicle under section 57 or 58 of this Act shall, when fixed to the vehicle, be treated as so fixed under that section.] **[261]**

NOTES
Commencement: To be appointed.
Prospectively added by the Transport Act 1982, s 18 as amended by the Road Traffic (Consequential Provisions) Act 1988, s 4, Sch 2, Part I), as from a day to be appointed.

64. Using goods vehicle with unauthorised weights as well as authorised weights marked on it

(1) If there is fixed to a goods vehicle a plate containing plated weights of any description—

    (a) determined for that vehicle by virtue of sections 49 to 52 of this Act, or

    (b) specified in a certificate for that vehicle under section 57(1) or (2) or 58(2) or (5) of this Act,

the vehicle shall not, while it is used on a road, be marked with any other weights, except other plated weights, other weights required or authorised to be marked on the vehicle by regulations under section 41 of this Act or weights so authorised for the purposes of this section by regulations made by the Secretary of State and marked in the prescribed manner.

(2) In the event of a contravention of or failure to comply with this section the owner of the vehicle is guilty of an offence.   **[262]**

NOTES
Commencement: 15 May 1989.
This section derived from the Road Traffic Act 1972, s 172.
See the Road Vehicles (Marking of Special Weights) Regulations 1983, SI 1983 No 910 as amended.

65. Vehicles and parts not to be sold without required certificate of conformity or Minister's approval certificate

(1) If—

    (a) any person at any time on or after the day appointed by regulations under section 63(1) of this Act supplies a vehicle or vehicle part of a class to which those regulations apply, and

    (b) it does not appear from one or more certificates in force at that time under sections 54 to 58 of this Act that the vehicle or vehicle part complies with all the relevant type approval requirements prescribed by those regulations,

he is guilty of an offence.

(2) In this section references to supply include—

    (a) sell,

    (b) offer to sell or supply, and

    (c) expose for sale.

(3) A person shall not be convicted of an offence under this section in respect of the supply of a vehicle or vehicle part if he proves—

    (a) that it was supplied for export from Great Britain,

    (b) that he had reasonable cause to believe that it would not be used on a road in Great Britain or, in the case of a vehicle part, that it would not be fitted to a vehicle used on a road in Great Britain or would not be so used or fitted until it had been certified under sections 54 to 58 of this Act, or

    (c) that he had reasonable cause to believe that it would only be used for purposes or in any area prescribed by the Secretary of State under section 63(5) of this Act or, in the case of a goods vehicle, under section 53(5) of this Act.

(4) Nothing in subsection (1) above shall affect the validity of a contract or any rights arising under or in relation to a contract. **[263]**

NOTES
Commencement: 15 May 1989.
This section derived from the Road Traffic Act 1972, s 62, and the Road Traffic Act 1974, Sch 2, para 11.

Conditions for grant of excise licence

66. Regulations prohibiting the grant of excise licences for certain vehicles except on compliance with certain conditions

(1) The Secretary of State may by regulations provide that where—

    (a) application is made for a licence under the Vehicles (Excise) Act 1971 for a vehicle to which section 47 of this Act applies, and

    (b) in the case of an application relating to a vehicle to which that section applies by virtue of subsection (2)(b) of that section, it appears from the application that the vehicle has been used on roads (whether in Great Britain or elsewhere) before the date of the application,

the licence shall not be granted unless one of the following conditions is satisfied.

(2) Those conditions are that—

    (a) there is produced such evidence as may be prescribed of the granting of an effective test certificate or (if it is so prescribed) there is produced such a certificate or the Secretary of State is provided with a copy of it, or

    (b) there is made such a declaration as may be prescribed that the vehicle is not intended to be used during the period for which the licence is to be in force except for a purpose prescribed under subsection (6), or in an area prescribed under subsection (7), of section 47, or

    (c) in the case of an application relating to a vehicle to which section 47 applies by virtue of subsection (2)(b) of that section, the owner of the vehicle declares in writing the year in which the vehicle was manufactured, and the specified period from the date of manufacture has not expired.

(3) The Secretary of State may by regulations provide that where application is made for a licence under the Vehicles (Excise) Act 1971 for a goods vehicle to which section 53(2) of this Act applies or for a vehicle of any class to which section 63(1) of this Act applies, the licence shall not be granted unless the requirements of subsection (4), subsection (5) or subsection (6) below are satisfied.

(4) The requirements of this subsection are that—

    (a) on any application, after the relevant date within the meaning of section 53(2), for a licence for a vehicle to which section 53(2) applies, there is produced evidence that an effective goods vehicle test certificate is in force for the vehicle,

    (b) on the first application, after the day appointed by regulations made by virtue of section 63(1), for a licence for a vehicle of any class to which those regulations apply, there is produced evidence that there is or are one or more certificates in force for the vehicle under sections

54 to 58 of this Act from which it appears that the vehicle complies with all the relevant type approval requirements prescribed by those regulations.

(5) The requirements of this subsection are that there is made such a declaration as may be prescribed that the vehicle is not intended to be used during the period for which the licence is to be in force except for a purpose or in an area prescribed under paragraph (a) of section 53(5) or 63(5) of this Act.

(6) The requirements of this subsection are that there is produced in respect of the vehicle a certificate of temporary exemption issued by virtue of paragraph (b) of section 53(5) or paragraph (c) of section 63(5) which exempts that vehicle from the provisions of section 53(2) or 63(1) of this Act, as the case may be, for a period which includes the date on which the licence is to come into force.

(7) Regulations under subsection (3) above may be made so as to apply to such classes only of vehicles as may be specified in the regulations.

(8) For the purposes of this section the date of manufacture of a vehicle shall be taken to be the last day of the year during which its final assembly is completed, except where after that day modifications are made to the vehicle before it is sold or supplied by retail, and in that excepted case shall be taken to be the last day of the year during which the modifications are completed.

(9) In this section—

"appropriate period" has the same meaning as in section 47 of this Act,
"effective goods vehicle test certificate" means, in relation to an application for a licence for a vehicle, a goods vehicle test certificate relating to the vehicle which will be in force on the date on which the licence is to come into force,
"effective test certificate" means, in relation to an application for a licence for a vehicle, a test certificate relating to the vehicle and issued within the appropriate period before the date on which the licence is to come into force,
"specified period" means the period for the time being specified in section 47(2)(a) and (b) of this Act. **[264]**

NOTES
Commencement: 15 May 1989.
 This section derived from the Road Traffic Act 1972, s 52, and the Road Traffic Act 1974, Sch 2, para 10.

[Vehicle examiners

66A. Appointment of examiners

(1) The Secretary of State shall appoint such examiners as he considers necessary for the purpose of carrying out the functions conferred on them by this Part of this Act, the Public Passenger Vehicles Act 1981, the Transport Act 1968 and any other enactment.

(2) An examiner appointed under this section shall act under the general directions of the Secretary of State.

(3) In this Part of this Act "vehicle examiner" means an examiner appointed under this section.] **[264A]**

NOTES

Commencement: 1 July 1992

This section and the cross-heading preceding it inserted by the Road Traffic Act 1991, s 9(1).

Testing vehicles on roads

67. Testing of condition of vehicles on roads

(1) An authorised examiner may test a motor vehicle on a road for the purpose of—

[(a) ascertaining whether the following requirements, namely—

(i) the construction and use requirements, and

(ii) the requirement that the condition of the vehicle is not such that its use on a road would involve a danger of injury to any person,

are complied with as respects the vehicle;]

(b) bringing to the notice of the driver any failure to comply with those requirements.

[(2) For the purpose of testing a vehicle under this section the examiner—

(a) may require the driver to comply with his reasonable instructions, and

(b) may drive the vehicle.]

(3) A vehicle shall not be required to stop for a test except by a constable in uniform.

(4) The following persons may act as authorised examiners for the purposes of this section—

(a) . . .

(b) a person appointed as an examiner under section [66A] of this Act,

(c) a person appointed to examine and inspect public carriages for the purposes of the Metropolitan Public Carriage Act 1869,

(d) a person appointed to act for the purposes of this section by the Secretary of State,

(e) a constable authorised so to act by or [on behalf of a] chief officer of police, and

(f) a person appointed by the police authority for a police area to act, under the directions of the chief officer of police, for the purposes of this section.

(5) A person mentioned in subsection (4)(a) to (d) and (f) must produce his authority to act for the purposes of this section if required to do so.

(6) On the examiner proceeding to test a vehicle under this section, the driver may, unless the test is required under subsection (7) or (8) below to be carried out forthwith, elect that the test shall be deferred to a time, and carried out at a place, fixed in accordance with Schedule 2 to this Act, and the provisions of that Schedule shall apply accordingly.

(7) Where it appears to a constable that, by reason of an accident having occurred owing to the presence of the vehicle on a road, it is requisite that a test should be carried out forthwith, he may require it to be so carried out and, if he is not to carry it out himself, may require that the vehicle shall not be taken away until the test has been carried out.

(8) Where in the opinion of a constable the vehicle is apparently so defective

that it ought not to be allowed to proceed without a test being carried out, he may require the test to be carried out forthwith.

(9) If a person obstructs an authorised examiner acting under this section, or fails to comply with a requirement of this section or Schedule 2 to this Act, he is guilty of an offence.

(10) In this section and in Schedule 2 to this Act—

    (a) "test" includes "inspect" or "inspection", as the case may require, and

    (b) references to a vehicle include references to a trailer drawn by it.**[265]**

NOTES
    Commencement: 15 May 1989.
    This section derived from the Road Traffic Act 1972, s 53, the Road Traffic Act 1974, Sch 6, para 14, Sch 7, and the Public Passenger Vehicles Act 1981, Sch 7, para 14.
    Sub-ss (1), (2), (4): amended by the Road Traffic Act 1991, ss 10, 83, Sch 8.

Inspection of public passenger vehicles and goods vehicles

68. Inspection of public passenger vehicles and goods vehicles

(1) A vehicle examiner—

    (a) may at any time, on production if so required of his authority, inspect any vehicle to which this section applies and for that purpose detain the vehicle during such time as is required for the inspection, and

    (b) may at any time which is reasonable having regard to the circumstances of the case enter any premises on which he has reason to believe that such a vehicle is kept [and an authorised inspector may excerise the powers given by paragraph (a) above in relation to any vehicle brought to the place of inspection in pursuance of a direction under subsection (3) below].

(2) The power conferred by subsection (1) above to inspect a vehicle includes power to test it and to drive it for the purpose of testing it.

(3) A person who intentionally obstructs an examiner in the exercise of his powers and under subsection (1) above is guilty of an offence.

(4) A vehicle examiner or a constable in uniform may at any time require any person in charge of a vehicle to which this section applies and which is stationary on a road to proceed with the vehicle for the vehicle for the purpose of having it inspected under this section to any place where an inspection can be suitably carried out (not being more than five miles from the place where the requirement is made).

(5) A person in charge of a vehicle who refuses or neglects to comply with a requirement made under subsection (4) above is guilty of an offence.

(6) This section applies to—

    (a) goods vehicles,
    (b) public service vehicles, and
    (c) motor vehicles which are not public service vehicles but are adapted to carry more than eight passengers;

but subsection (1)(b) above shall not apply in relation to vehicles within paragraph (c) above or in relation to vehicles used to carry passengers for hire or reward only under permits granted under section 19 or 22 of the Transport Act 1985 (use of vehicles by educational and other bodies or in providing community bus services).]   **[266]**

NOTES
Commencement: 1 July 1992.
Commencement order: SI 1992 No 1286.
Whole section, and cross-heading preceding it, substituted by the Road Traffic Act 1991, s 11.
Sub-s (1): words in square brackets prospectively added by the Transport Act 1982, s 10(b) (as amended by the Road Traffic (Consequential Provisions) Act 1988, s 4, Sch 2, Part I, and by the Road Traffic Act 1991, s 48, Sch 4, para 19(1), (3)) as from a day to be appointed. It is thought that the reference to "subsection (3)" in those words as prospectively added by the 1982 Act (and as amended by the 1991 Act) should be a reference to "subsection (4)"

[*Prohibition of unfit vehicles*

69. Power to prohibit driving of unfit vehicles

(1) If on any inspection of a vehicle under section 41, 45, 49, 61, 67, 68 or 77 of this Act it appears to a vehicle examiner [or authorised inspector] that owing to any defects in the vehicle it is, or is likely to become, unfit for service, he may prohibit the driving of the vehicle on a road—

    (a) absolutely, or
    (b) for one or more specified purposes, or
    (c) except for one or more specified purposes.

(2) If on any inspection of a vehicle under any of the enactments mentioned in subsection (1) above it appears to an authorised constable that owing to any defects in the vehicle driving it (or driving it for any particular purpose or purposes or for any except one or more particular purposes) would involve a danger of injury to any person, he may prohibit the driving of the vehicle on a road—

    (a) absolutely, or
    (b) for one or more specified purposes, or
    (c) except for one or more specified purposes.

(3) A prohibition under this section shall come into force as soon as the notice under subsection (6) below has been given if—

    (a) it is imposed by an authorised constable, or
    (b) in the opinion of the vehicle examiner [or authorised inspector] imposing it the defects in the vehicle in question are such that driving it, or driving it for any purpose within the prohibition, would involve a danger of injury to any person.

(4) Except where subsection (3) applies, a prohibition under this section shall (unless previously removed under section 72 of this Act) come into force at such time not later than ten days from the date of the inspection as seems appropriate to the vehicle examiner [or authorised inspector] imposing the prohibition, having regard to all the circumstances.

(5) A prohibition under this section shall continue in force until it is removed under section 72 of this Act.

(6) A person imposing a prohibition under this section shall forthwith give notice in writing of the prohibition to the person in charge of the vehicle at the time of the inspection—

    (a) specifying the defects which occasioned the prohibition;
    (b) stating whether the prohibition is on all driving of the vehicle or driving it for one or more specified purposes or driving it except for one or more specified purposes (and, where applicable, specifying the purpose or purposes in question); and
    (c) stating whether the prohibition is to come into force immediately or at the end of a specified period.

(7) Where a notice has been given under subsection (6) above, any vehicle examiner [or authorised inspector] or authorised constable may grant an exemption in writing for the use of the vehicle in such manner, subject to such conditions and for such purposes as may be specified in the exemption.

(8) Where such a notice has been given, any vehicle examiner [or authorised inspector] or authorised constable may by endorsement on the notice vary its terms and, in particular, alter the time at which the prohibition is to come into force or suspend it if it has come into force.

(9) In this section "authorised constable" means a constable authorised to act for the purposes of this section by or on behalf of a chief officer of police.]

[267]

NOTES

Commencement: 1 July 1992.

This section, the cross-heading preceeding it and s 69A post substituted for the original s 69 by the Road Traffic Act 1991, s 12.

Sub-ss (1), (3), (4), (7), (8): words in square brackets prospectively inserted by the Transport Act 1982, s 10(3) (as amended by the Road Traffic Act 1991, s 48, Sch 4, para 19(1), (2)), as from a day to be appointed.

[69A. Prohibitions conditional on inspection etc

(1) Where it appears to the person imposing a prohibition under section 69 of this Act that the vehicle is adapted to carry more than eight passengers, or is a public service vehicle not so adapted, the prohibition may be imposed with a direction making it irremovable unless and until the vehicle has been inpsected to an official PSV testing station within the meaning of the Public Passenger Vehicles Act 1981.

(2) Where it appears to that person that the vehicle is of a class to which regulations under section 49 of this Act apply, the prohibition may be imposed with a direction making it irremovable unless and until the vehicle has been inspected at an official testing station.

(3) Where it appears to that person that the vehicle is one to which section 47 of this Act applies, or would apply if the vehicle had been registered under the Vehicles (Excise) Act 1971 more than three years earlier, the prohibition may be imposed with a direction making it irremovable unless and until the vehicle has been inspected, and a test certificate issued, under section 45 of this Act.

(4) In any other case, the prohibition may be imposed with a direction making it irremovable unless and until the vehicle has been inspected in accordance with regulations under section 72 of this Act by a vehicle examiner or authorised constable (within the meaning of section 69 of this Act).] **[267A]**

NOTES

Commencement; 1 July 1992.

Subsituted as noted to s 69 ante.

70. Power to prohibit driving of overloaded goods vehicles

(1) Subsections (2) and (3) below apply where a goods vehicle [, or, a motor vehicle adapted to carry more than eight passengers,] has been weighed in pursuance of a requirement imposed under section 78 of this Act and it appears to—

(a) [a vehicle examiner],

(b) a person authorised with the consent of the Secretary of State to act for the purposes of this subsection by—

    (i) a highway authority other than the Secretary of State, or

    (ii) a local roads authority in Scotland, or

(c) a constable authorised to act for those purposes by or on behalf of a chief officer of police,

that the limit imposed by construction and use requirements with respect to any description of weight which is applicable to that vehicle has been exceeded or would be exceeded if it were used on a road [or that by reason of excessive overall weight or, excessive axle weight on any axle driving the vehicle would involve a danger of injury to any person].

(2) The person to whom it so appears may, whether or not a notice is given under section 69(6) of this Act, give notice in writing to the person in charge of the vehicle prohibiting the driving of the vehicle on a road until—

(a) that weight is reduced to that limit [or, as the case may be, so that it is no longer excessive], and

(b) official notification has been given to whoever is for the time being in charge of the vehicle that it is permitted to proceed.

(3) The person to whom it so appears may also by direction in writing require the person in charge of the vehicle to remove it (and, if it is a motor vehicle drawing a trailer, also to remove the trailer) to such place and subject to such conditions as are specified in the direction; and the prohibition shall not apply to the removal of the vehicle or trailer in accordance with that direction.

(4) Official notification for the purposes of subsection (2) above—

(a) must be in writing and be given by [a vehicle examiner], a person authorised as mentioned in subsection (1) above or a constable authorised as so mentioned, and

(b) may be withheld until the vehicle has been weighed or reweighed in order to satisfy the person giving the notification that the weight has been sufficiently reduced.

(5) Nothing in this section shall be construed as limiting the power of the Secretary of State to make regulations under section 71(2) of this Act. **[268]**

NOTES

Commencement: 15 May 1989.

This section derived from the Road Traffic Act 1972, s 57(7)-(7B), the Heavy Commercial Vehicles (Controls and Regulations) Act 1973, s 3(1), the Road Traffic Act 1974, Sch 6, para 15, the Transport Act 1978, Sch 3, para 2(2)(b), (c), Sch 4, and the Roads (Scotland) Act 1984, Sch 9, para 68(8).

Sub-ss (1), (2), (4): amended by the Road Traffic Act 1991, s 13.

[71. Unfit and overloaded vehicles: offences

(1) A person who—

(a) drives a vehicle in contravention of a prohibition under section 69 or 70 of this Act, or

(b) causes or permits a vehicle to be driven in contravention of such a prohibition, or

    (c) fails to comply within a reasonable time with a direction under section 70(3) of this Act,

is guilty of an offence.

    (2) The Secretary of State may by regulations provide for exceptions from subsection (1) above.]   **[269]**

NOTES
    Commencement: 1 July 1992.
    Substituted by the Road Traffic Act 1991, s 14.

[72. Removal of prohibitions

    (1) Subject to the following provisions of this section, a prohibition under section 69 or 70 of this Act may be removed by any vehicle examiner or authorised constable [or authorised inspectors] if he is satisfied that the vehicle is fit for service.

    (2) If the prohibition has been imposed with a direction under section 69A(1) or (2) of this Act, the prohibition shall not be removed unless and until the vehicle has been inspected in accordance with the direction.

    (3) If the prohibition has been imposed with a direction under section 69A(3) of this Act, subsection (1) above shall not apply; but the prohibition shall be removed, by such person as may be prescribed, if (and only if) any prescribed requirements relating to the inspection of the vehicle and the issue and production of a test certificate have been complied with.

    (4) If the prohibition has been imposed with a direction under section 69A(4) of this Act, the prohibition shall not be removed unless and until any prescribed requirements relating to the inspection of the vehicle have been complied with.

    (5) A person aggrieved by the refusal of a vehicle examiner or authorised constable [or authorised inspector] to remove a prohibition may, within the prescribed time and in the prescribed manner, appeal to the Secretary of State.

    (6) The Secretary of State may make such order on the appeal as he thinks fit.

    (7) Where a vehicle examiner or authorised constable [or authorised inspector] removes a prohibition, he must forthwith give notice of the removal to the owner of the vehicle.

    (8) The Secretary of State may require the payment of fees, in accordance with prescribed scales and rates, for the inspection of a vehicle with a view to the removal of a prohibition; and—

    (a) payment of fees may be required to be made in advance, and
    (b) the Secretary of State must ensure that all the scales and rates prescribed for the purposes of this subsection are reasonably comparable with—

       (i) in the case of goods vehicles, the fees charged by virtue of section 51(1)(h) in respect of periodic examination, and
       (ii) in the case of other vehicles, the fees charged by virtue of section 46(c).

    (9) The Secretary of State may make regulations for prescribing anything which may be prescribed under this section and for regulating the procedure, and fees payable, on appeals to him under subsection (5) above.

(10) In this section "authorised constable" means a constable authorised to act for the purposes of this section by or on behalf of a chief officer of police.

[270]

NOTES
  Commencement: 1 July 1992.
  This section, and s 72A post, substituted for the original s 72 by the Road Traffic Act 1991, s 15.
  Sub-ss (1), (5), (7): words in square brackets prospectively inserted by the Transport Act 1982, s 20 (as substituted by the Road Traffic Act 1991, s 48, Sch 4, para 20), as from a day to be appointed.

[72A. Official testing stations

The Secretary of State may provide and maintain stations (in this Part of this Act referred to as "official testing stations") where inspections of goods vehicles for the purposes of section 72 may be carried out and may provide and maintain the apparatus for carrying out such inspections.]   [270A]

NOTES
  Commencement: 1 July 1992.
  Substituted as noted to s 72 ante.

73. Provisions supplementary to sections 69 to 72

[(1) Where it appears to a person giving a notice under section 69(6) or 70(2) of this Act that the vehicle concerned is an authorised vehicle, he must as soon as practicable take steps to bring the contents of the notice to the attention of—

(a) the traffic commissioner by whom the operator's licence was granted for the vehicle, and

(b) the holder of the licence if he is not in charge of the vehicle at the time when the notice is given.

(1A) Where it appears to a person giving a notice under section 69(6) or 70(2) of this Act that the vehicle concerned is used under a PSV operator's licence, he must as soon as practicable take steps to bring the contents of the notice to the attention of—

(a) the traffic commissioner by whom the PSV operator's licence was granted for the vehicle, and

(b) the holder of the licence if he is not in charge of the vehicle at the time when the notice is given.

(1B) in a case not within subsection (1) or subsection (1A) above, a person giving a notice under section 69(6) or 70(2) of this must Act as soon as practicable take steps to bring the contents of the notice to the attention of the owner of the vehicle if he is not in charge of it at the time when the notice is given.

(1C) A person giving a notice to the owner of a vehicle under section 72(7) of this Act must as soon as practicable take steps to bring the contents of the notice to the attention of any other person—

(a) who was the person to whom the previous notice under section 69(6) or 70(2) was given and was then the owner of the vehicle, or

(b) to whose attention the contents of the previous notice were brought under this section.]

(2) . . .

(3) Any reference in sections 69 to 72 of this Act to the driving of a vehicle

is, in relation to a trailer, a reference to the driving of the vehicle by which the trailer is drawn.

(4) In this section and section 72 of this Act "authorised vehicle" and "operator's licence" have the same meaning as in Part V of the Transport Act 1968 [; and "PSV operator's licence" has the same meaning as in the Public Passenger Vehicles Act 1981]. **[271]**

NOTES
Commencement: 1 July 1992 (sub-ss (1)–(1C)); 15 May 1989 (remainder).
This section derived from the Road Traffic Act 1972, ss 57(8), (11), (12), 58(4).
Sub-ss (1)–(1C): substituted for the original sub-s (1) by the Road Traffic Act 1991, s 48, Sch 4, para 56(1), (2).
Sub-s (2): repealed by the Road Traffic Act 1991, s 48, Sch 4, para 56(1), (3).
Sub-s (4): words in square brackets added by the Road Traffic Act 1991, s 48, Sch 4, para 56(1), (4).

Miscellaneous provisions about vehicles and vehicle parts

74. Operators' duty to inspect, and keep records of inspections of, goods vehicles

(1) The Secretary of State may make regulations requiring the operator for the time being of a goods vehicle to which the regulations apply to secure—

    (a) the carrying out by a suitably qualified person (including the operator if so qualified) of an inspection of the vehicle for the purpose of ascertaining whether [the following requirements are complied with, namely—

        (i)] the construction and use requirements with respect to any prescribed matters, being requirements applicable to the vehicle, [and

        (ii) the requirement that the condition of the vehicle is not such that its use on a road would involve a danger of injury to any person], and

    (b) the making and authentication of records of such matters relating to any such inspection as may be prescribed, including records of the action taken to remedy any defects discovered on the inspection,

and providing for the preservation of such records for a prescribed period not exceeding fifteen months and their custody and production during that period.

(2) Regulations under this section may—

    (a) apply to all goods vehicles or to goods vehicles of such classes as may be prescribed,

    (b) require the inspection of goods vehicles under the regulations to be carried out at such times, or before the happening of such events, as may be prescribed, and

    (c) make different provision for different cases.

(3) Any person who contravenes or fails to comply with any provision of regulations under this section is guilty of an offence.

(4) In this section "the operator", in relation to a goods vehicle, means the person to whom it belongs or the hirer of it under a hire purchase agreement; but, if he has let it on hire (otherwise than by way of hire-purchase) or lent it to any other person, it means a person of a class prescribed by regulations under this section in relation to any particular class of goods vehicles or, subject to any such regulations, that other person. **[272]**

NOTES
Commencement: 15 May 1989.
This section derived from the Road Traffic Act 1972, s 59(1)-(4).
Sub-s (1): words in square brackets substituted or inserted by the Road Traffic Act 1991, s 48,
Sch 4, para 57.

75. Vehicles not to be sold in unroadworthy condition or altered so as to be unroadworthy

(1) Subject to the provisions of this section no person shall supply a motor vehicle or trailer in an unroadworthy condition.

(2) In this section references to supply include—

    (a) sell,
    (b) offer to sell or supply, and
    (c) expose for sale.

(3) For the purposes of subsection (1) above a motor vehicle or trailer is in an unroadworthy condition if—

    (a) it is in such a condition that the use of it on a road in that condition would be unlawful by virtue of any provision made by regulations under section 41 of this Act as respects—

        (i) brakes, steering gear or tyres, or
        (ii) the construction, weight or equipment of vehicles, or
        (iii) . . .

    [(b) it is in such a condition that its use on a road would involve a danger of injury to any person].

(4) Subject to the provisions of this section no person shall alter a motor vehicle or trailer so as to render its condition such that the use of it on a road in that condition

    [(a)] would be unlawful by virtue of any provision made as respects the construction, weight or equipment of vehicles by regulations under section 41.
[or
    (b) would involve a danger of injury to any person.]

(5) A person who supplies or alters a motor vehicle or trailer in contravention of this section, or causes or permits it to be so supplied or altered, is guilty of an offence.

(6) A person shall not be convicted of an offence under this section in respect of the supply or alteration of a motor vehicle or trailer if he proves—

    (a) that it was supplied or altered, as the case may be, for export from Great Britain, or
    (b) that he had reasonable cause to believe that the vehicle or trailer would not be used on a road in Great Britain, or would not be so used until it had been put into a condition in which it might lawfully be so used, . . .

[(6A) Paragraph (b) of subsection (6) above shall not apply in relation to a person who, in the course of a trade or business—

    (a) exposes a vehicle or trailer for sale, unless he also proves that he took all reasonable steps to ensure that any prospective purchaser would be aware that its use in its current condition on a road in Great Britain would be unlawful, or

(b) offers to sell a vehicle or trailer, unless he also proves that he took all reasonable steps to ensure that the person to whom the offer was made was aware of that fact.]

(7) Nothing in the preceding provisions of this section shall affect the validity of a contract or any rights arising under a contract.

(8) . . .

[273]

NOTES

Commencement: 1 July 1992 (sub-s (6A)); 15 May 1989 (remainder).

This section derived from the Road Traffic Act 1972, s 60, and the Road Traffic Act 1974, s 11(1)-(4).

Sub-ss (3), (4), (6): amended by the Road Traffic Act 1991, ss 16(1)-(4), 83, Sch 8.

Sub-s (6A): inserted by the Road Traffic Act 1991, s 16(1), (5).

Sub-s (8): repealed by the Road Traffic Act 1991, s 83, Sch 8.

76. Fitting and supply of defective or unsuitable vehicle parts

(1) If any person—

(a) fits a vehicle part to a vehicle, or
(b) causes or permits a vehicle part to be fitted to a vehicle,

in such circumstances that the use of the vehicle on a road would, by reason of that part being fitted to the vehicle, [involve a danger of injury to any person or], constitute a contravention of or failure to comply with any of the construction and use requirements, he is guilty of an offence.

(2) A person shall not be convicted of an offence under subsection (1) above if he proves—

(a) that the vehicle to which the part was fitted was to be exported from Great Britain, or
(b) that he had reasonable cause to believe that that vehicle—

(i) would not be used on a road in Great Britain, or
(ii) that it would not be so used until it had been put into a condition in which its use [on a road] would not constitute a contravention of or a failure to comply with any of the construction and use requirements [and would not involve a danger of injury to any person.]

(3) If a person—

(a) supplies a vehicle part or causes or permits a vehicle part to be supplied, and
(b) has reasonable cause to believe that the part is to be fitted to a motor vehicle, or to a vehicle of a particular class, or to a particular vehicle,

he is guilty of an offence if that part could not be fitted to a motor vehicle or, as the case may require, to a vehicle of that class or of a class to which the particular vehicle belongs, except in such circumstances that the use of the vehicle on a road would, by reason of that part being fitted to the vehicle, constitute a contravention of or failure to comply with any of the construction and use requirements [or involve a danger of injury to any person].

(4) In this section references to supply include—

(a) sell, and

(b) offer to sell or supply.

(5) A person shall not be convicted of an offence under subsection (3) above in respect of the supply of a vehicle part if he proves—

(a) that the part was supplied for export from Great Britain, or
(b) that he had reasonable cause to believe that—
    (i) it would not be fitted to a vehicle used on a road in Great Britain, or
    (ii) it would not be so fitted until it had been put into such a condition that it could be fitted otherwise than in such circumstances that the use of the vehicle on a road would, by reason of that part being fitted to the vehicle, constitute a contravention of or failure to comply with any of the construction and use requirements [or involve a danger of injury to any person].

(6) An authorised examiner may at any reasonable hour enter premises where, in the course of a business, vehicle parts are fitted to vehicles or are supplied and test and inspect any vehicle or vehicle part found on those premises for the purpose of ascertaining whether—

(a) a vehicle part has been fitted to the vehicle in such circumstances that the use of the vehicle on a road would, by reason of that part being fitted to the vehicle, constitute a contravention of or failure to comply with any of the construction and use requirements [or involve a danger of injury to any person], or
(b) the vehicle part could not be supplied for fitting to a vehicle used on roads in Great Britain without the commission of an offence under subsection (3) above.

(7) For the purpose of testing a motor vehicle and any trailer drawn by it the authorised examiner may drive it and for the purpose of testing a trailer may draw it with a motor vehicle.

(8) Any person who obstructs an authorised examiner acting under subsection (6) or (7) above is guilty of an offence.

(9) In subsections (6) to (8) above "authorised examiner" means a person who may act as an authorised examiner for the purposes of section 67 of this Act; and any such person, other than a constable in uniform, shall produce his authority to act for the purpose of subsections (6) and (7) above if required to do so.

(10) Nothing in this section shall affect the validity of a contract or of any rights arising under a contract.   [274]

NOTES

Commencement: 15 May 1989.

This section derived from the Road Traffic Act 1972, s 60A, and the Road Traffic Act 1974, s 12(1).

Sub-ss (1)–(3), (5), (6): words in sqaure brackets inserted or added by the Road Traffic Act 1991, s 48, Sch 4, para 58.

77. Testing condition of used vehicles at sale rooms, etc

(1) An authorised examiner may at any reasonable hour enter premises where used motor vehicles or trailers are supplied in the course of a business and test and inspect any used motor vehicle or trailer found on the premises for the purpose of ascertaining whether it is in an unroadworthy condition for the purposes of section 75(1) of this Act.

(2) In this section (except paragraph (d) below) references to supply include—

(a) sell,
(b) offer for sale or supply,
(c) expose for sale, and
(d) otherwise keep for sale or supply.

(3) An authorised examiner may at any reasonable hour enter premises where vehicles or vehicle parts of a class prescribed for the purposes of section 63 of this Act are supplied in the course of a business and test and inspect any such vehicle or vehicle part for the purpose of ascertaining whether the vehicle or vehicle part complies with the type approval requirements applicable to a vehicle or vehicle part of that class.

(4) For the purpose of testing a motor vehicle and any trailer drawn by it the authorised examiner may drive it and for the purpose of testing a trailer may draw it with a motor vehicle.

(5) A person who obstructs an authorised examiner acting under this section is guilty of an offence.

(6) In this section "authorised examiner" means a person who may act as an authorised examiner for the purposes of section 67 of this Act; and any such person, other than a constable in uniform, shall produce his authority to act for the purposes of that section if required to do so.

(7) A motor vehicle or trailer shall be treated for the purposes of this section as used if, but only if, it has previously been sold or supplied by retail.   **[275]**

NOTES
Commencement: 15 May 1989.
This section derived from the Road Traffic Act 1972, s 61, and the Road Traffic Act 1974, ss 10(5), 11(5).

78. Weighing of motor vehicles

(1) Subject to any regulations made by the Secretary of State, an authorised person may, on production of his authority, require the person in charge of a motor vehicle—

(a) to allow the vehicle or any trailer drawn by it to be weighed, either laden or unladen, and the weight transmitted to the road by any parts of the vehicle or trailer in contact with the road to be tested, and
(b) for that purpose, to proceed to a weighbridge or other machine for weighing vehicles.

(2) For the purpose of enabling a vehicle or a trailer drawn by it to be weighed or a weight to be tested in accordance with regulations under subsection (1) above, an authorised person may require the person in charge of the vehicle to drive the vehicle or to do any other thing in relation to the vehicle or its load or the trailer or its load which is reasonably required to be done for that purpose.

(3) If a person in charge of a motor vehicle—

(a) refuses or neglects to comply with any requirement under subsection (1) or (2) above, or
(b) obstructs an authorised person in the exercise of his functions under this section,

he is guilty of an offence.

(4) An authorised person may not require the person in charge of the motor vehicle to unload the vehicle or trailer, or to cause or allow it to be unloaded, for the purpose of its being weighed unladen.

(5) Regulations under subsection (1) above may make provision with respect to—

(a) the manner in which a vehicle or trailer is to be weighed or a weight is to be tested as mentioned in subsection (1) above, and

(b) the limits within which, unless the contrary is proved, any weight determined by a weighbridge or other machine for weighing vehicles is to be presumed to be accurate for the purposes of any provision made by or under this Act or by or under any other enactment relating to motor vehicles or trailers,

and the regulations may make different provision in relation to vehicles of different classes, in relation to different types of weighbridges and other machines and in relation to different circumstances.

(6) If—

(a) at the time when the requirement is made the vehicle is more than five miles from the weighbridge or other machine, and

(b) the weight is found to be within the limits authorised by law,

the highway authority (in Scotland, roads authority) on whose behalf the requirement is made must pay, in respect of loss occasioned, such amount as in default of agreement may be determined by a single arbitrator (in Scotland, arbiter) agreed upon by the parties or, in default of agreement, appointed by the Secretary of State.

(7) The Secretary of State may by order designate areas in Great Britain where subsection (6) above is to have effect, in such cases as may be specified by the order, with the substitution for five miles of a greater distance so specified.

An order under this subsection shall be made by statutory instrument subject to annulment by a resolution of either House of Parliament.

(8) In this section—

(a) "road" includes any land which forms part of a harbour or which is adjacent to a harbour and is occupied wholly or partly for the purposes of harbour operations,

(b) "authorised person" means a person authorised by a highway authority (in Scotland, a road authority) or a constable authorised on behalf of such an authority by a police authority or a chief officer of police,

and in this subsection "harbour" and "harbour operations" have the meanings given to them by section 57(1) of the Harbours Act 1964. **[276]**

NOTES
   Commencement: 15 May 1989.
   This section derived from the Road Traffic Act 1972, s 160(1)-(2A), (7), the Road Traffic Act 1974, s 14(1)-(3), (5), the Transport Act 1978, Sch 3, para 6, and the Roads (Scotland) Act 1984, Sch 9, para 68(9)(a), (b).
   See the Road Vehicle (Construction and Use) Regulations 1986, post and the Weighing of Motor Vehicles (Use of Dynamic Axle Weighing Machines) Regulations 1978, SI 1978 No 1180.

79. Further provisions relating to weighing of motor vehicles

(1) Where a motor vehicle or trailer is weighed under section 78 of this Act, a certificate of weight must be given to the person in charge of the vehicle, and the certificate so given shall exempt the motor vehicle and the trailer, if any,

from being weighed so long as it is during the continuance of the same journey carrying the same load.

(2) On production of his authority—

(a) ...
(b) an examiner appointed under section [66A] of this Act, or
(c) any of the Secretary of State's officers authorised by him in that behalf,

may at any time exercise with respect to the weighing of [goods vehicles, public service vehicles, and vehicles which are not public service vehicles but are adapted to carry more than eight passengers,] all such powers with respect to the weighing of motor vehicles and trailers as are exercisable under section 78 of this Act by a constable authorised as mentioned in subsection (8) of that section.

(3) The provisions of section 78 of this Act shall apply accordingly in relation to [such vehicles]—

(a) as if references to a constable so authorised included references to such [an] examiner or officer of the Secretary of State, and
(b) as if the reference in subsection (6) to the authority on whose behalf the requirement is made were a reference to the Secretary of State, and
(c) as if the reference in that subsection to the Secretary of State were a reference, in relation to England and Wales, to the Lord Chief Justice of England and, in relation to Scotland, to the Lord President of the Court of Session.

(4) A certificate in the prescribed form which—

(a) purports to be signed by an authorised person (within the meaning of section 78 of this Act) or by a person exercising powers by virtue of subsection (2) above, and
(b) states, in relation to a vehicle identified in the certificate, any weight determined in relation to that vehicle on the occasion of its being brought to a weighbridge or other machine in pursuance of a requirement under section 78(1) of this Act,

shall be evidence (in Scotland, sufficient evidence) of the matter so stated.

(5) If, for the purposes of or in connection with the determination of any weight in relation to a vehicle which is brought to a weighbridge or other machine as mentioned in section 78(1) of this Act, an authorised person (within the meaning of that section) or a person exercising powers by virtue of subsection (2) above—

(a) drives a vehicle or does any other thing in relation to a vehicle or its load or a trailer or its load, or
(b) requires the driver of a vehicle to drive it in a particular manner or to a particular place or to do any other thing in relation to a vehicle or its load or a trailer or its load,

neither he nor any person complying with such a requirement shall be liable for any damage to or loss in respect of the vehicle or its load or the trailer or its load unless it is shown that he acted without reasonable care.   **[277]**

NOTES

Commencement: 15 May 1989.

This section derived from the Road Traffic Act 1972, s 160(3)-(6), the Road Traffic Act 1974, s 14(1), (4), (5), the Public Passenger Vehicles Act 1981, Sch 7, para 14, and the Roads (Scotland) Act 1984, Sch 9, para 68(9)(c).

Sub-ss (2), (3): amended by the Road Traffic Act 1988, ss 48, 83, Sch 4, para 59, Sch 8.

80. Approval marks

(1) Where any international agreement to which the United Kingdom is a party or a Community obligation provides—

    (a) for markings to be applied—

        (i) to motor vehicle parts of any description to indicate conformity with a type approved by any country, or

        (ii) to a motor vehicle to indicate that the vehicle is fitted with motor vehicle parts of any description and either that the parts conform with a type approved by any country or that the vehicle is such that as so fitted it conforms with a type so approved, and

    (b) for motor vehicle parts or, as the case may be, motor vehicles, bearing those markings to be recognised as complying with the requirements imposed by the law of another country,

the Secretary of State may by regulations designate the markings as approval marks, and any markings so designated shall be deemed for the purposes of the Trade Descriptions Act 1968 to be a trade description, whether or not the markings fall within the definition of the expression in section 2 of that Act.

(2) Any person who, without being authorised by the competent authority to apply any approval mark, applies that mark or a mark so nearly resembling it as to be calculated to deceive is guilty of an offence under the Trade Descriptions Act 1968, whether or not he would be guilty of such an offence apart from this subsection.

(3) The conditions subject to which approval of any type may be given on behalf of the United Kingdom or the use of approval marks indicating conformity with a type approved by the United Kingdom may be authorised may include such conditions as to testing or inspection and the payment of fees as the Secretary of State may impose.

(4) In this section—

"motor vehicle" means a mechanically propelled vehicle or a vehicle designed or adapted for towing by a mechanically propelled vehicle,

"motor vehicle part" means any article made or adapted for use as part of a mechanically propelled vehicle or a vehicle drawn by a mechanically propelled vehicle, or for use as part of the equipment of any such vehicle, and shall be treated as including any equipment for the protection of drivers or passengers in or on a motor vehicle notwithstanding that it does not form part of, or of the equipment of, that vehicle, and

"the competent authority" means—

    (a) as respects any approval marks indicating conformity with a type approved by the United Kingdom, the Secretary of State, and

    (b) as respects any approval marks indicating conformity with a type approved by any other country, the authority having power under the law of that country to authorise the use of that mark. **[278]**

NOTES
Commencement: 15 May 1989.
This section derived from the Road Traffic Act 1972, s 63, and the Designation of Approval Marks (European Communities) Regulations 1973, SI 1973 No 1193.
See the Motor Vehicles (Designation of Approval Marks) Regulations 1979, SI 1979 No 1088 as amended.

Pedal cycles and horse-drawn vehicles

81. Regulation of brakes, bells etc, on pedal cycles

(1) The Secretary of State may make regulations as to the use on roads of cycles, their construction and equipment and the conditions under which they may be so used.

(2) In particular, but without prejudice to the generality of subsection (1) above, the regulations may make provision as to—

(a) the number, nature and efficiency of brakes and their maintenance in proper working order,

(b) the appliances to be fitted for signalling approach and their maintenance in proper working order, and

(c) the testing and inspection, by persons authorised under the regulations, of any equipment prescribed under this section and of lighting equipment and reflectors.

(3) Regulations under this section may provide for repealing byelaws dealing with the same subject-matter as the regulations, and for suspending while the regulations remain in force any power of making such byelaws.

(4) Regulations under this section may be made so as to apply either generally or in such circumstances only as may be specified in the regulations.

(5) Regulations under this section as to the use on roads of cycles may prohibit the sale or supply, or the offer of a sale or supply, of a cycle for delivery in such a condition that the use of it on a road in that condition would be a contravention of the regulations, but no provision made by virtue of this subsection shall affect the validity of any contract or any rights arising under a contract.

(6) If a person sells or supplies or offers to sell or supply a cycle in contravention of any prohibition imposed by regulations made by virtue of subsection (5) above, he is guilty of an offence, unless he proves—

(a) that it was sold, supplied or offered for export from Great Britain, or

(b) that he had reasonable cause to believe that it would not be used on a road in Great Britain, or would not be so used until it had been put into a condition in which it might lawfully be so used. **[279]**

NOTES
Commencement: 15 May 1989.
This section derived from the Road Traffic Act 1972, s 66.
See the Pedal Cycle (Construction and Use) Regulations 1983, post and the Road Vehicles Lighting Regulations 1989, post.

82. Regulation of brakes on horse-drawn vehicles

(1) The Secretary of State may make regulations for regulating the number, nature and use of brakes, including skid pans and locking-chains, in the case of vehicles drawn by horses or other animals, or any class of such vehicles, when used on roads.

(2) Regulations under this section may be made for securing that such brakes are efficient and kept in proper working order, and for empowering persons authorised by or under the regulations to test and inspect any such brakes, whether on a road or elsewhere.

(3) Regulations under this section may provide for repealing byelaws dealing with the same subject matter as the regulations, and for suspending while the regulations remain in force any power of making such byelaws.

(4) Regulations under this section may be made so as to apply either generally or in such circumstances only as may be specified in the regulations.
[280]

NOTES
Commencement: 15 May 1989.
This section derived from the Road Traffic Act 1972, s 67.

Miscellaneous

83. Offences to do with reflectors and tail lamps

A person who sells, or offers or exposes for sale, any appliance adapted for use as a reflector or tail lamp to be carried on a vehicle in accordance with the provisions of this Act or of any regulations made under it, not being an appliance which complies with the construction and use requirements applicable to a class of vehicles for which the appliance is adapted, is guilty of an offence. **[281]**

NOTES
Commencement: 15 May 1989.
This section derived from the Road Traffic Act 1972, s 81(2), and the Road Traffic Act 1974, s 9(3).

84. Appointment of officials and destination of fees

(1) Subject to the consent of the Treasury as to number, the Secretary of State may appoint such officers and servants as he considers necessary for the operation of the provisions of sections 68 to 73 of this Act.

(2) There shall be paid to [examiners appointed under section 66A] of this Act such remuneration or salaries and such allowances (if any) as the Secretary of State may, with the consent of the Treasury, determine.

(3) In every year there shall be paid out of monies provided by Parliament such sums as the Secretary of State may, with the consent of the Treasury, direct in respect of the remuneration, salaries and allowances under subsection (2) above and the other expenses of examiners.

(4) Any sum received by the Secretary of State in pursuance of sections 45, 46, 49 to 51, 54 to 62, 72(9) and 80 of this Act shall be paid into the Consolidated Fund. **[282]**

NOTES
Commencement: 15 May 1989.
This section derived from the Road Traffic Act 1972, s 83(2)–(5) and the Transport Act 1978, Sch 3, para 5.
Sub-s (2): words in square brackets substituted by the Road Traffic Act 1991, s 48, Sch 4, para 60.

85. Interpretation of Part II

[(1)] In this Part of this Act—

"the Community Recording Equipment Regulation" means Council Regulation (EEC) No. 3821/85 of 20th December 1985 on recording equipment in road transport, as read with the Community Drivers' Hours and Recording Equipment (Exemptions and Supplementary Provisions) Regulations 1986, the Community Drivers' Hours and Recording Equipment (Exemptions and Supplementary Provisions) (Amendment) Regulations 1986 and the Community Drivers' Hours and Recording Equipment (Exemptions and Supplementary Provisions) (Amendment) Regulations 1987,

"licensing authority" means a licensing authority for the purposes of Part V of the Transport Act 1968,

"official testing station" means a testing station maintained by the Secretary of State under section [72A] of this Act [or premises designated by him under section 10(2) of the Transport Act 1982],

"prescribed" means prescribed by regulations made by the Secretary of State,

["prescribed testing authority" means such approved testing authority as may be prescribed,]

["public service vehicle" has the same meaning as in the Public Passenger Vehicles Act 1981,]

"sold or supplied by retail" means sold or supplied otherwise than to a person acquiring solely for the purpose of release or of re-supply for a valuable consideration,

"tail lamp" means, in relation to a vehicle, any lamp carried attached to the vehicle for the purpose of showing a red light to the rear in accordance with regulations under section 41 of this Act,

"traffic area" has the same meaning as in the Public Passenger Vehicles Act 1981, and

"vehicle part" means any article which is a motor vehicle part, within the meaning of section 80 of this Act, and any other article which is made or adapted for use as part of, or as part of the equipment of, a vehicle which is intended or adapted to be used on roads but which is not a motor vehicle within the meaning of that section.

[(2) References in any provision of this Part of this Act to an authorised inspector are references to a person authorised by the Secretary of State under section 8 of the Transport Act 1982 to exercise the function to which that provision relates.]   **[283]**

NOTES

Commencement: 15 May 1989.

This section as originally enacted derived from the Road Traffic Act 1972, s 82, the Road Traffic Act 1974, Sch 2, para 13, Sch 7, the Interpretation Act 1978, s 17(2), the Transport Act 1978, Sch 3, para 4, the Public Passenger Vehicles Act 1981, Sch 7, para 14, and the Community Drivers' Hours and Recording Equipment Regulations 1986, SI 1986 No 1457, art 3(1), (2)(b).

Sub-s (1): first words in square brackets in definition "official testing station" and definition "public service vehicle", substituted or inserted by the Road Traffic Act 1991, s 48, Sch 4, para 61;

remaining words in square brackets prospectively added by the Road Traffic (Consequential Provisions) Act 1988, s 4, Sch 2, Part I, as from a day to be appointed.

Sub-s (2): prospectively added by the Road Traffic (Consequential Provisions) Act 1988, s 4, Sch 2, Part I, as from a day to be appointed.

86. Index to Part II

The expressions listed in the left-hand column below are respectively defined or (as the case may be) fall to be construed in accordance with the provisions of this Part of this Act listed in the right-hand column in relation to those expressions.

Expression	Relevant provision
Certificate of conformity	Section 57(1)
Community Recording Equipment Regulation	Section 85
Construction and use requirements	Section 41(7)
Design weights	Section 54(3)
Examination for plating	Section 49(4)
Goods vehicle test	Section 49(4)
Goods vehicle test certificate	Section 49(2)(b)
Licensing authority	Section 85
Minister's approval certificate	Section 58(1)
Official testing station	Section 85
Plating certificate	Section 49(2)(a)
Plated particulars	Section 41(7)
Plated weights	Section 41(7)
Prescribed	Section 85
[Public service vehicle]	[Section 85]
Relevant aspects of design, construction, equipment and marking	Section 54(6)
Sold or supplied by retail	Section 85
Tail lamp	Section 85
Test certificate	Section 45(2)
Traffic area	Section 85
Type approval certificate	Section 55(2)
Type approval requirements	Section 54(1)
[Vehicle examiner]	[Section 66A]
Vehicle part	Section 85

NOTES

Commencement: 15 May 1989.

Words in square brackets inserted, and words omitted repealed, by the Road Traffic Act 1991, ss 48, 83, Sch 4, para 62, Sch 8.

PART III

LICENSING OF DRIVERS OF VEHICLES

Requirement to hold licence

87. Drivers of a motor vehicles to have driving licences

(1) It is an offence for a person to drive on a road a motor vehicle of any class [otherwise than in accordance with] a licence authorising him to drive a motor vehicle of that class.

(2) It is an offence for a person to cause or permit another person to drive on a road a motor vehicle of any class [otherwise than in accordance with a licence authorising that other person] to drive a motor vehicle of that class.

[(3) . . .]　　　　　　　　　　　　　　　　　　　　　　　　　　　**[285]**

NOTES

Commencement: 15 May 1989.

This section derived from the Road Traffic Act 1972, s 84(1), (2), and the Road Traffic (Drivers' Ages and Hours of Work) Act 1976, Sch 1, para 1(a).

Sub-ss (1), (2): words in square brackets substituted by the Road Traffic Act 1991, s 17(1), (2).

Sub-s (3): added by the Road Traffic (Driver Licensing and Information Systems) Act 1989, s 7, Sch 3, para 7; and repealed by s 16 of, Sch 6 to, that Act.

88. Exceptions

(1) Notwithstanding section 87 of this Act, a person may drive or cause or permit another person to drive a vehicle of any class if—

　[(*a*) the driver has held—

　　　(i) a licence under this Part of this Act to drive vehicles of that or a corresponding class, or
　　　(ii) a Northern Ireland licence to drive vehicles of that or a corresponding class, or
　　　(iii) a British external licence or British Forces licence to drive vehicles of that or a corresponding class, or
　　　(iv) an exchangeable licence to drive vehicles of that or a corresponding class, and

　(b) either—

　　　(i) a qualifying application by the driver for the grant of a licence to drive vehicles of that class for a period which includes that time has been received by the Secretary of State, or
　　　(ii) a licence to drive vehicles of that class granted to him has been revoked or surrendered in pursuance of section 99(3) or (4) of this Act otherwise than by reason of a current disqualification or of its having been granted in error, and]

　(c) any conditions which by virtue of section 97(3) or 98(2) of this Act apply to the driving under the authority of the licence of vehicles of that class are complied with.

[(1A) An application for the grant of a licence to drive vehicles of any class is a qualifying application for the purposes of subsection (1)(b)(i) above if—

　(a) the requirements of paragraphs (a), (b) so far as it relates to initial evidence and (c) of section 97(1) of this Act have been satisfied;
　(b) the applicant—

　　　(i) is not subject to a current disqualification which is relevant to the licence he applies for, and
　　　(ii) is not prevented from obtaining it by section 89 of this Act; and

　(c) the declaration made in pursuance of section 92(1) of this Act indicates that he is not suffering from a relevant disability.

(1B) A disqualification is relevant to a licence for which a person makes an application if—

　(a) in the case of an application made by virtue of any provision of subsection (1)(a) above, the disqualification subsists under or by virtue of any provision of the Road Traffic Acts and relates to vehicles of the class to which his application relates;

(b) in the case of an application made by virtue of subsection (1)(a)(ii) above, the disqualification subsists under or by virtue of any provision of the law of Northern Ireland and relates to vehicles of the class, or of a class corresponding to the class, to which his application relates;

(c) in the case of an application made by virtue of subsection (1)(a)(iii) above, the disqualification subsists under or by virtue of any provision of the relevant external law or, as the case may be, is a disqualification for holding or obtaining a British Forces licence and relates to vehicles of the class, or of a class corresponding to the class, to which his application relates; and

(d) in the case of an application made by virtue of subsection (1)(a)(iv) above, the disqualification subsists under or by virtue of any provision of the law of the member State or country or territory under which the licence which he held was granted and relates to vehicles of the class, or of a class corresponding to the class, to which his application relates;

but a disqualification which does not prevent the person disqualified from obtaining a provisional licence or, as the case may be, a licence corresponding to a provisional licence is relevant to a full licence but not to a provisional licence.]

(2) The benefit of subsection (1) above does not extend—

(a) beyond the date when a licence is granted in pursuance of the application mentioned in subsection (1)(b) above or (as the case may be) in pursuance of section 99(7) of this Act in consequence of the revocation or surrender so mentioned, or

(b) in a case where a licence is not in fact so granted, beyond the expiration of the period of one year or such shorter period as may be prescribed, beginning on the date of the application or (as the case may be) the revocation or surrender mentioned in subsection (1)(b) above [, or

(c) in a case where a licence is refused under section 92(3) of this Act, beyond the day on which the applicant receives notice of the refusal.]

(3) The Secretary of State may by regulations provide that subsection (1) above shall also apply (where the requirements of that subsection are otherwise met) in the case of a person who has not previously held a licence to drive vehicles of the relevant class.

(4) Regulations made by virtue of subsection (3) above shall, if not previously revoked, expire at the end of the period of one year beginning with the day on which they came into operation.

(5) Regulations may provide that a person who becomes resident in Great Britain shall, during the prescribed period after he becomes so resident, be treated for the purposes of section 87 of this Act as the holder of a licence authorising him to drive motor vehicles of the prescribed classes if—

(a) he satisfies the prescribed conditions, and

(b) he is the holder of a permit of the prescribed description authorising him to drive vehicles under the law of a country outside the United Kingdom.

(6) Regulations made by virtue of subsection (5) above may provide for the application of any enactment relating to licences [, counterparts of licences] or

licence holders, with or without modifications, in relation to any such permit and its holder respectively.

(7) Notwithstanding section 87 of this Act—

 (a) a person who is not the holder of a licence may act as steersman of a motor vehicle, being a vehicle on which a speed limit of five miles per hour or less is imposed by or under section 86 of the Road Traffic Regulation Act 1984, under the orders of another person engaged in the driving of the vehicle who is licensed in that behalf in accordance with the requirements of this Part and Part IV of this Act, and

 (b) a person may cause or permit another person who is not the holder of a licence so to act.

[(8) In this Part of this Act—

 "British external licence" means a licence granted in the Isle of Man or any of the Channel Islands under the relevant external law;

 "British Forces licence" means a licence granted in the Federal Republic of Germany by the British authorities to members of the British Forces or of the civilian components of those Forces or their dependants; and

 "relevant external law" means the law for the time being in force in the Isle of Man or any of the Channel Islands which corresponds to this Part of this Act.]   **[286]**

NOTES

Commencement: 1 June 1990 (sub-ss (1A), (1B), (8)); 15 May 1989 (remainder).

This section derived from the Road Traffic Act 1972, s 84(3)-(5), the Road Traffic Act 1974, Sch 3, para 1, the Road Traffic (Drivers' Ages and Hours of Work) Act 1976, Sch 1, para 1(b), (c), the Transport Act 1981, s 29(1), the Driving Licences (Community Driving Licence) Regulations 1982, SI 1982 No 1555, reg 3(1), the Road Traffic (Driving Licences) Act 1983, s 1(3)(a), and the Road Traffic Regulation Act 1984, Sch 13, para 18.

Sub-s (1): words in square brackets substituted by the Road Traffic (Driver Licensing and Information Systems) Act 1989, s 3.

Sub-ss (1A), (1B), (8): added by the Road Traffic (Driver Licensing and Information Systems) Act 1989, s 3.

Sub-s (2): words in square brackets added by the Road Traffic (Driver Licensing and Information Systems) Act 1989, s 3.

Sub-s s (6): words in square brackets added with savings, by SI 1990 No 144, reg 2(1), Sch 1, para 1; for savings see reg 3 thereof.

See the Motor Vehicles (Driving Licences) Regulations 1987, and the Motor Vehicles (Driving Licences) (Large Goods and Passenger-Carrying Vehicles) Regulations 1990, post.

Tests

89. Tests of competence to drive

(1) A licence authorising the driving of motor vehicles of any class shall not be granted to any person unless he satisfies the Secretary of State—

 [(a) that at some time during the period of two years ending with the date the application is made but not earlier than the appointed day he has passed—

  (i) the test of competence to drive prescribed by virtue of subsection (3) below, or

  (ii) a Northern Ireland test of competence to drive which corresponds to such a test, or

  (iii) a test of competence which under subsection (6) below is a sufficient test;

  or that, if it is available to him, he satisfies the alternative requirement of section 89A of this Act; or

(b) that at some time not earlier than the appointed day he has held—

    (i) a full licence authorising the driving of vehicles of that class, or

    (ii) a full Northern Ireland licence authorising the driving of vehicles of that or a corresponding class;

or that, if it is available to him, he satisfies the alternative requirement of section 89A of this Act; or

(c) that at some time during the period of two years ending with the date the application is made he has passed a test of competence to drive vehicles of that or a corresponding class conducted under any relevant external law or for the purpose of obtaining a British Forces licence; or

(d) that at some time not earlier than the appointed day he has held a full British external licence or a full British Forces licence to drive vehicles of that or a corresponding class or that, if it is available to him, he satisfies the alternative requirement of section 89A of this Act; or

(e) that at some time during the period of two years ending with the date the application is made he has passed a test of competence to drive vehicles of that or a corresponding class conducted under the law of another member State or of Gibraltar or a designated country or territory; or

(f) that, at the time of the application for the licence—

    (i) he holds an exchangeable licence authorising the driving of vehicles of that or a corresponding class, and

    (ii) he is normally resident in Great Britain or (where the exchangeable licence is a Community licence) the United Kingdom but has not been so resident for more than the prescribed period.]

This subsection is subject to the provisions of this Part of this Act as to provisional licences and to the provisions of any regulations made by virtue of section 105(2)(f) of this Act.

[(2) For the purposes of subsection (1) above—

(a) a licence which has been revoked under section 99(3) of this Act or any corresponding provision of the law of Northern Ireland or under any corresponding provision of the relevant external law as a licence granted in error shall be disregarded for the purposes of paragraph (b) or, as the case may be, paragraph (d) of that subsection;

(b) a test of competence to drive any class of goods vehicle or any class of passenger-carrying vehicle conducted under a relevant external law is to be disregarded for the purposes of paragraph (c) of that subsection unless the Secretary of State, by order made by statutory instrument, designates that law as one which makes satisfactory provision for tests of competence to drive such vehicles;

(c) a British external licence to drive any class of goods vehicle or any class of passenger-carrying vehicle is to be disregarded for the purposes of paragraph (d) of that subsection unless the Secretary of State, by order made by statutory instrument, designates the relevant external law under which it is granted as one which makes satisfactory provision for the granting of such licences.]

[(2A) Except as provided under subsection (5A) below, no person submitting himself for a test of competence to drive a motor bicycle shall be permitted to take the test unless he furnishes the prescribed certificate of completion by him of an approved training course for motor cyclists either with his application for an appointment for a test or to the person who is to conduct the test.]

(3) Regulations may make provision with respect to—

    (a) the nature of tests of competence to drive for the purposes of this section [and section 36 of the Road Traffic Offenders Act 1988 (disqualification),],

    (b) the qualifications, selection and appointment of persons by whom they may be conducted and the revocation of any appointment,

    (c) evidence of the results of such tests,

and generally with respect to such tests.

(4) In particular, regulations may, without prejudice to the generality of subsection (3) above, provide—

    (a) for requiring a person submitting himself for a test to provide a vehicle for the purposes of the test [, in the case of prescribed classes of goods vehicle, loaded or unloaded as may be prescribed and, if requirements as respects loading are prescribed, loaded in accordance with the requirements],

    (b) for requiring a fee, of such amount as may be specified in the regulations or, in such cases as may be prescribed, specified by such person as may be prescribed, to be paid by a person who submits himself for a test or applies for an appointment for a test,

    (c) for ensuring that a person submitting himself for a test and failing to pass that test shall not be eligible to submit himself for another test by the same or any other person before the expiration of a period specified in the regulations, except under an order made by a court or sheriff under the power conferred by section 90 of this Act,

and different regulations may be made with respect to tests of competence to drive different classes of vehicles.

(5) If regulations make provision for a test of competence to drive to consist of separate parts, they may make for each part—

    (a) any provision that could be made for a test not consisting of separate parts, and

    (b) provision for the supply by the Secretary of State of forms for certificates evidencing the results and for charges to be made for the supply.

[(5A) Regulations may prescribe cases in which persons are exempt from the requirement imposed by subsection (2A) above; and the regulations may—

    (a) limit the exemption to persons in prescribed circumstances;

    (b) limit the exemption to a prescribed period;

    (c) attach conditions to the exemption; and

    (d) regulate applications for, and the issue and form of, certificates evidencing a person's exemption from that requirement.]

(6) For the purposes of subsection [(1)(a)(iii) above or section 89A(2)(b)(iii) below], a test of competence shall be sufficient for the granting of a licence authorising the driving of—

    (a) vehicles of any class, if at the time the test was passed it authorised the granting of a licence to drive vehicles of that class,

    (b) vehicles of [all] classes which are designated by regulations as a group for the purposes of subsection (1)(a) above, if at the time the test was passed it authorised the granting of a licence to drive vehicles of any class included in the group [, and

(c) vehicles of all classes included in another such group, if a person passing the test is treated by virtue of regulations made for the purposes of this paragraph as competent also to drive vehicles of a class included in that other group.]

(7) If vehicles of any classes are designated by regulations as a group for the purposes of subsection (1)(b) above, a licence authorising the driving of vehicles of a class included in the group shall be deemed for the purposes of subsection [(1)(b)(i) above or section 89A(4)(a) below to authorise the driving of—

    (a) vehicles of all classes included in the group, and

    (b) vehicles of all classes included in another such group, if a person holding the licence is treated by virtue of regulations as competent also to drive vehicles of a class included in that other group].

The reference in this subsection to a licence does not include a licence which has been revoked in pursuance of section 99(3) of this Act.

(8) For the purposes of this section and section 88(1) of this Act, an exchangeable licence issued in respect of a member State, country or territory shall not be treated as authorising a person to drive a vehicle of any [class] if—

    (a) the licence is not for the time being valid for that purpose, or

    (b) it was issued in respect of that [class] for a purpose corresponding to that mentioned in section 97(2) of this Act.

[(9) A test of competence falling within paragraphs (a)(ii), (c) or (e) of subsection (1) above shall be sufficient for the granting of a licence authorising the driving of—

    (a) vehicles of all classes designated by regulations as a group for the purposes of subsection (1)(a) above, if at the time the test was passed it authorised the granting of a licence to drive vehicles of any class included in the group, or of any class corresponding to a class included in the group, and

    (b) vehicles of all classes included in another such group, if a person passing a test of competence authorising the granting of a licence to drive vehicles of a class included in the group mentioned in paragraph (a) above is treated by virtue of regulations as competent also to drive vehicles of a class included in that other group.

(10) A full Northern Ireland licence, a full British external licence, a full British Forces licence or an exchangeable licence shall be treated for the purposes of paragraphs (b)(ii), (d) or (f) (as the case may be) of subsection (1) above as authorising the driving of—

    (a) vehicles of all classes designated by regulations as a group for the purposes of subsection (1)(b) above, if the licence authorises the driving of vehicles of any class included in the group, or any class corresponding to a class included in the group, and

    (b) vehicles of all classes included in another such group, if by virtue of regulations a person holding a licence authorising him to drive vehicles of any class included in the group mentioned in paragraph (a) above is treated as competent also to drive vehicles of a class included in that other group.

(11) In this section "designated country or territory" means a country or territory designated under section 108(2) of this Act for the purposes of the definition of exchangeable licence and in this section and section 89A "the appointed day" means the day appointed for the coming into force of section 1

of the Road Traffic (Driver Licensing and Information Systems) Act 1989.]

[287]

NOTES

    Commencement: 1 April 1991 (sub-ss (2), (9)-(11)); 1 December 1990 (sub-ss (2A), (5A); 15 May 1989 (remainder).

    This section, as originally enacted, derived from the Road Traffic Act 1972, s 85(1), (2), (4)-(7), the Road Traffic (Drivers' Ages and Hours of Work) Act 1976, Sch 1, para 2, the Transport Act 1981, s 23(6)(a), (7), the Driving Licences (Community Driving Licence) Regulations 1982, SI 1982 No 1555, reg 2(1), (2), and the Road Traffic Act 1983, s 1(3)(a), (b), (c).

    Sub-s (1): words in square brackets substituted by the Road Traffic (Driver Licensing and Information Systems) Act 1989, s 4(2).

    Sub-s (2): substituted by the Road Traffic (Driver Licensing and Information Systems) Act 1989, s 4(3).

    Sub-ss (2A), (5A): added by the Road Traffic (Driver Licensing and Information Systems) Act 1989, s 6(1).

    Sub-s (3): words in square brackets in para (a) added by the Road Traffic Act 1991, s 48, Sch 4, para 63.

    Sub-s (4): words in square brackets added by the Road Traffic (Driver Licensing and Information Systems) Act 1989, s 7, Sch 3, para 8(a).

    Sub-s (6): first word in square brackets substituted and final words in square brackets added, by the Road Traffic (Driver Licensing and Information Systems) Act 1989, s 7, Sch 3, para 8(b).

    Sub-ss (7), (8): words in square brackets substituted by the Road Traffic (Driver Licensing and Information Systems) Act 1989, s 7, Sch 3, para 8(c), (d).

    Sub-ss (9)–(11): substituted for the original sub-s (9) by the Road Traffic (Driver Licensing and Information Systems) Act 1989, s 7, Sch 3, para 8(e).

89A. The alternative requirements to those in section 89

[(1) The alternative requirements referred to in section 89(1) of this Act are the following.

    (2) The requirement which is alternative to that specified in section 89(1)(a) on an application by a person for a licence authorising the driving of motor vehicles of any class other than any class of goods vehicle or passenger-carrying vehicle prescribed for the purposes of subsection (3) below—

      (a) is available to that person if the application is made within the period of ten years beginning with the appointed day, and

      (b) is that at some time before the appointed day and during the period of ten years ending with the date the application is made he has passed—

        (i) the test of competence to drive prescribed by virtue of section 89(3) of this Act or a test of competence to drive which corresponds to such a test, or

        (ii) a Northern Ireland test of competence to drive which corresponds to any test falling within (i) above, or

        (iii) a test of competence which under section 89(6) of this Act is a sufficient test or a test of competence to drive which corresponds to such a test.

    (3) The requirement which is alternative to that specified in section 89(1)(a) on an application by a person for a licence authorising the driving of any class of goods vehicle or passenger-carrying vehicle prescribed for the purposes of this subsection—

      (a) is available to that person if the application is made within the period of five years beginning with the appointed day, and

      (b) is that at some time before the appointed day and during the period of five years ending with the date the application is made he has passed—

(i) a test of competence to drive a heavy goods vehicle or public service vehicle of a class corresponding to the class of vehicle to which his application relates, or

(ii) a corresponding Northern Ireland test of competence to drive a heavy goods vehicle or public service vehicle of a class which corresponds to the class of goods vehicle or passenger-carrying vehicle to which his application relates.

(4) The requirement which is alternative to that specified in section 89(1)(b) on an application by a person for a licence authorising the driving of motor vehicles of any class other than any class of goods vehicle or passenger-carrying vehicle prescribed for the purposes of subsection (5) below is that at some time before the appointed day but not earlier than 1st January 1976 he has held—

(a) a full licence authorising the driving of vehicles of a class corresponding to the class of motor vehicle to which his application relates, or

(b) a full Northern Ireland licence authorising the driving of vehicles of a class corresponding to the class of motor vehicle to which his application relates.

(5) The requirement which is alternative to that specified in section 89(1)(b) on an application by a person for a licence authorising the driving of any class of goods vehicle or passenger-carrying vehicle prescribed for the purposes of this subsection is that at some time before the appointed day but not earlier than the beginning of the period of five years ending with the appointed day he has held—

(a) a full heavy goods vehicle or a public service vehicle driver's licence authorising the driving of vehicles of a class corresponding to the class of vehicle to which his application relates, or

(b) a full Northern Ireland licence to drive heavy goods vehicles of a class corresponding to the class of vehicle to which his application relates or a Northern Ireland licence to drive public service vehicles of a class corresponding to the class of vehicle to which his application relates.

(6) The requirement which is alternative to that specified in section 89(1)(d) on an application by a person for a licence authorising the driving of motor vehicles of any class—

(a) is available to that person if the application is made within the period of ten years beginning with the appointed day, and

(b) is that at some time before the appointed day and during the period of ten years ending with the date the application is made he has held a full British external licence or a full British Forces licence to drive vehicles of that or a corresponding class.

(7) In this section "heavy goods vehicle" and "public service vehicle" have the same meaning as they had for the purposes of Part IV of this Act or section 22 of the Public Passenger Vehicles Act 1981 before their repeal by section 1 of the Road Traffic (Driver Licensing and Information Systems) Act 1989.] **[288]**

NOTES
    Commencement: To be appointed.
    Added by the Road Traffic (Driver Licensing and Information Systems) Act 1989, s 4(4).
    See the Motor Vehicles (Driving Licences) (Large Goods and Passenger-Carrying Vehicles) Regulations 1990, post.

90. Review of conduct of test

(1) On the application of a person who has submitted himself for a test of competence to drive—

    (a) a magistrates' court acting for the petty sessions area in which he resides, or

    (b) in Scotland, the sheriff within whose jurisdiction he resides,

may determine whether the test was properly conducted in accordance with regulations.

    (2) The court or, as the case may be, sheriff may, if it appears that the test was not so conducted—

    (a) order that the applicant shall be eligible to submit himself for another test before the expiration of the period specified for the purposes of section 89(4)(c) of this Act, and

    (b) order that any fee payable by the applicant in respect of the test shall not be paid or, if it has been paid, shall be repaid.

    (3) If regulations make provision for a test of competence to drive to consist of separate parts, this section applies in relation to each part as well as in relation to the whole of the test. **[289]**

NOTES
Commencement: 15 May 1989.
This section derived from the Road Traffic Act 1972, s 85(3), and the Transport Act 1981, s 23(6).

91. Repayment of test fees

A fee paid in pursuance of regulations made by virtue of section 89(4) of this Act on application for an appointment for a test may be repaid in the following cases and not otherwise—

    (a) if no such appointment is made, or an appointment made is subsequently cancelled by or on behalf of the Secretary of State,

    (b) if the person for whom the appointment is made gives such notice cancelling the appointment as may be prescribed for the purposes of this paragraph by regulations,

    (c) if the person for whom the appointment is made keeps the appointment, but the test does not take place, or is not completed, for reasons attributable neither to him nor to any vehicle provided by him for the purposes of the test, or

    (d) if an order for the repayment of the fee is made by the court or, as the case may be, sheriff under section 90 of this Act pursuant to a finding that the test was not properly conducted in accordance with the regulations. **[290]**

NOTES
Commencement: 15 May 1989.
This section derived from the Road Traffic Act 1972, s 86.

Physical fitness

92. Requirements as to physical fitness of drivers

(1) An application for the grant of a licence must include a declaration by the applicant, in such form as the Secretary of State may require, stating whether he is suffering or has at any time (or, if a period is prescribed for the purposes of this subsection, has during that period) suffered from any relevant disability or any prospective disability.

    (2) In this Part of this Act—

"disability" includes disease,

"relevant disability" in relation to any person means—

(a) any prescribed disability, and

(b) any other disability likely to cause the driving of a vehicle by him in pursuance of a licence to be a source of danger to the public, and

"prospective disability" in relation to any person means any other disability which—

(a) at the time of the application for the grant of a licence or, as the case may be, the material time for the purposes of the provision in which the expression is used, is not of such a kind that it is a relevant disability, but

(b) by virtue of the intermittent or progressive nature of the disability or otherwise, may become a relevant disability in course of time.

(3) If it appears from the applicant's declaration, or if on inquiry the Secretary of State is satisfied from other information, that the applicant is suffering from a relevant disability, the Secretary of State must, subject to the following provisions of this section, refuse to grant the licence.

(4) The Secretary of State must not by virtue of subsection (3) above refuse to grant a licence—

(a) on account of any relevant disability which is prescribed for the purposes of this paragraph, if the applicant has at any time passed a relevant test and it does not appear to the Secretary of State that the disability has arisen or become more acute since that time or was, for whatever reason, not disclosed to the Secretary of State at that time,

(b) on account of any relevant disability which is prescribed for the purposes of this paragraph, if the applicant satisfies such conditions as may be prescribed with a view to authorising the grant of a licence to a person in whose case the disability is appropriately controlled,

(c) on account of any relevant disability which is prescribed for the purposes of this paragraph, if the application is for a provisional licence.

(5) Where as a result of a test of competence to drive [or of information obtained under the relevant powers] the Secretary of State is satisfied that the person who took the test [or in relation to whom the information was obtained] is suffering from a disability such that there is likely to be a danger to the public—

(a) if he drives any vehicle, or

(b) if he drives a vehicle other than a vehicle of a particular [class],

the Secretary of State must serve notice in writing to that effect on that person and must include in the notice a description of the disability.

(6) Where a notice is served in pursuance of subsection (5)(a) above, then—

(a) if the disability is not prescribed under subsection (2) above, it shall be deemed to be so prescribed in relation to the person who took the test, and

(b) if the disability is prescribed for the purposes of subsection (4)(c) above it shall be deemed not to be so prescribed in relation to him.

(7) Where a notice is served in pursuance of subsection (5)(b) above, any licence granted to the person who took the test shall be limited to vehicles of the particular [class] specified in the notice [and, if the Secretary of State so directs in the notice, his entitlement to drive other classes of vehicles by virtue of section 98(2) of this Act shall be limited as specified in the notice.]

[(7A) If he considers it appropriate to do so the Secretary of State may, after serving a notice in pursuance of subsection (5)(a) above, serve a notice in pursuance of subsection (5)(b) above or, after serving a notice in pursuance of subsection (5)(b) above, serve a notice in pursuance of subsection (5)(a) above or a further notice in pursuance of subsection (5)(b) above; and on his serving a further notice under any of those provisions the notice previously served shall cease to have effect and any limited licence previously granted shall be revoked by the subsequent notice.

(7B) In subsection (5) above the references to a test of competence to drive and to information obtained under the relevant powers are references respectively to a test of competence prescribed for the purposes of section 89 or so much of such a test as is required to be taken in pursuance of section 94(5)(c) of this Act and to information obtained in pursuance of section 94(5)(a) or (b) of this Act.

(7C) A person whose licence is revoked by virtue of subsection (7A) above must deliver the licence [and its counterpart] to the Secretary of State forthwith after the revocation and a person who, without reasonable excuse, fails to do so is guilty of an offence.]

(8) In this section "relevant test", in relation to an application for a licence, means any such test of competence as is mentioned in section 89 of this Act or a test as to fitness or ability in pursuance of section 100 of the Road Traffic Act 1960 as originally enacted, being a test authorising the grant of a licence in respect of vehicles of the classes to which the application relates.

(9) Without prejudice to subsection (8) above, for the purposes of subsection (4)(a) above—
    [(a) an applicant shall be treated as having passed a relevant test if, and on the day on which, he passed a test of competence to drive which—

        (i) under a provision of the law of Northern Ireland or a relevant external law corresponding to subsections (3) and (4) or (6) of section 89 of this Act, either is prescribed in relation to vehicles of classes corresponding to the classes to which the application relates or is sufficient under that law for the granting of a licence authorising the driving of vehicles of those classes, or
        (ii) is sufficient for the granting of a British Forces licence authorising the driving of vehicles of those classes, and]

    (b) in the case of an applicant who is treated as having passed a relevant test by virtue of paragraph (a) above, disclosure of a disability to [his licensing authority] shall be treated as disclosure to the Secretary of State.

. . . . .

[(10) A person who holds a licence authorising him to drive a motor vehicle of any class and who drives a motor vehicle of that class on a road is guilty of an offence if the declaration included in accordance with subsection (1) above in the application on which the licence was granted was one which he knew to be false.] **[291]**

NOTES
    Commencement: 1 July 1992 (sub-s (10)); 1 June 1990 (sub-ss (7A)-(7C)); 15 May 1989 (remainder).
    This section, as originally enacted, derived from the Road Traffic Act 1972, s 87(1)-(4), (6), (7), and the Road Traffic Act 1974, Sch 3, para 2(1)-(3), (6).
    Sub-s (5): first and second words in square brackets added, and final words in square brackets substituted, by the Road Traffic (Driver Licensing and Information Systems) Act 1989, s 5(2).

Sub-s (7): first word in square brackets substituted, and second words in square brackets added, by the Road Traffic (Driver Licensing and Information Systems) Act 1989, s 5(3).

Sub-ss (7A)-(7C): inserted by the Road Traffic (Driver Licensing and Information Systems) Act 1989, s 5(4) (as amended, in the case of sub-s (7C), with savings by SI 1990 No 144, reg 2(3), Sch 3, para 1(a); for savings see reg 3 thereof).

Sub-s (9): words in square brackets substituted by the Road Traffic (Driver Licensing and Information Systems) Act 1989, s 5(5), and words omitted repealed by s 16 of, and Sch 6 to, that Act.

Sub-s (10); added by the Road Traffic Act 1991, s 18(1).

93. Revocation of licence because of disability or prospective disability

(1) If the Secretary of State is at any time satisfied on inquiry—

    (a) that a licence holder is suffering from a relevant disability, and

    (b) that the Secretary of State would be required by virtue of section 92(3) or (7) of this Act to refuse an application for the licence made by him at that time,

the Secretary of State may serve notice in writing on the licence holder revoking the licence with effect from such date as may be specified in the notice, not being earlier than the date of service of the notice.

(2) If the Secretary of State is at any time satisfied on inquiry that a licence holder is suffering from a prospective disability, the Secretary of State may—

    (a) serve notice in writing on the licence holder revoking the licence with effect from such date as may be specified in the notice, not being earlier than the date of service of the notice, and

    (b) on receipt of the licence so revoked [and its counterpart] and of an application made for the purposes of this subsection, grant to the licence holder, free of charge, a new licence for a period determined by the Secretary of State under section 99(1)(b) of this Act.

(3) A person whose licence is revoked under subsection (1) or (2) above must deliver up the licence [and its counterpart] to the Secretary of State forthwith after the revocation [and a person who, without reasonable excuse, fails to do so is guilty of an offence].

(4) Where a person whose licence is revoked under subsection (1) or (2) above—

    (a) is not in possession of his licence [or its counterpart] in consequence of the fact that he has surrendered [them] to a constable or authorised person (within the meaning of Part III of the Road Traffic Offenders Act 1988) on receiving a fixed penalty notice given to him under section 54 of that Act but

    (b) delivers [them] to the Secretary of State immediately on [their] return,

he is not in breach of the duty under subsection (3) above. [292]

NOTES

    Commencement: 15 May 1989.

    This section derived from the Road Traffic Act 1972, s 87(5), (5A), the Road Traffic Act 1974, Sch 3, para 2(4), (5), and the Transport Act 1982, s 35(7).

    Sub-s (2): words in square brackets in para (b) inserted with savings, by SI 1990 No 144, reg 2(1), Sch 1, para 2(a); for savings see reg 3 thereof.

    Sub-s (3): first words in square brackets added with savings, by SI 1990 No 144, reg 2(1), Sch 1, para 2(b); for savings see reg 3 thereof; second words in square brackets added by the Road Traffic (Driver Licensing and Information Systems) Act 1989, s 5(6).

    Sub-s (4): words in square brackets added or substituted with savings, by SI 1990 No 144, reg 2(1), Sch 1, para 2(c); for savings see reg 3 thereof.

94. Provision of information, etc relating to disabilities

(1) If at any time during the period for which his licence remains in force, a licence holder becomes aware—

    (a) that he is suffering from a relevant or prospective disability which he has not previously disclosed to the Secretary of State, or

    (b) that a relevant or prospective disability from which he has at any time suffered (and which has been previously so disclosed) has become more acute since the licence was granted,

the licence holder must forthwith notify the Secretary of State in writing of the nature and extent of his disability.

(2) The licence holder is not required to notify the Secretary of State under subsection (1) above if—

    (a) the disability is one from which he has not previously suffered, and

    (b) he has reasonable grounds for believing that the duration of the disability will not extend beyond the period of three months beginning with the date on which he first becomes aware that he suffers from it.

(3) A person who fails without reasonable excuse to notify the Secretary of State as required by subsection (1) above is guilty of an offence.

[(3A) A person who holds a licence authorising him to drive a motor vehicle of any class and who drives a motor vehicle of that class on a road is guilty of an offence if at any earlier time while the licence was in force he was required by subsection (1) above to notify the Secretary of State but has failed without reasonable excuse to do so.]

(4) If [the prescribed circumstances obtain in relation to a person who is an applicant for, or the holder of, a licence or if] the Secretary of State has reasonable grounds for believing that a person who is an applicant for, or the holder of, a licence may be suffering from a relevant or prospective disability, subsection (5) below applies for the purpose of enabling the Secretary of State to satisfy himself whether or not [that person may be suffering from that or any other relevant or prospective disability].

(5) The Secretary of State may by notice in writing served on the applicant or holder—

    (a) require him to provide the Secretary of State, within such reasonable time as may be specified in the notice, with such an authorisation as is mentioned in subsection (6) below, or

    (b) require him, as soon as practicable, to arrange to submit himself for examination—

        (i) by such registered medical practitioner or practitioners as may be nominated by the Secretary of State, or

        (ii) with respect to a disability of a prescribed description, by such officer of the Secretary of State as may be so nominated,

    for the purpose of determining whether or not he suffers or has at any time suffered from a relevant or prospective disability, or

    (c) except where the application is for, or the licence held is, a provisional licence, require him to submit himself for [such a test of competence to drive as the Secretary of State directs in the notice.]

(6) The authorisation referred to in subsection (5)(a) above—

    (a) shall be in such form and contain such particulars as may be specified in the notice by which it is required to be provided, and

(b) shall authorise any registered medical practitioner who may at any time have given medical advice or attention to the applicant or licence holder concerned to release to the Secretary of State any information which he may have, or which may be available to him, with respect to the question whether, and if so to what extent, the applicant or licence holder concerned may be suffering, or may at any time have suffered, from a relevant or prospective disability.

(7) If he considers it appropriate to do so in the case of any applicant or licence holder, the Secretary of State—

(a) may include in a single notice under subsection (5) above requirements under more than one paragraph of that subsection, and

(b) may at any time after the service of a notice under that subsection serve a further notice or notices under that subsection.

(8) If any person on whom a notice is served under subsection (5) above—

(a) fails without reasonable excuse to comply with a requirement contained in the notice, or

(b) fails any test of competence which he is required to take as mentioned in paragraph (c) of that subsection,

the Secretary of State may exercise his powers under sections 92 and 93 of this Act as if he were satisfied that the applicant or licence holder concerned is suffering from a relevant disability which is not prescribed for the purposes of any paragraph of section 92(4) of this Act or, if the Secretary of State so determines, as if he were satisfied that the applicant or licence holder concerned is suffering from a prospective disability.

(9) [Except where the requirement is made in the circumstances prescribed for the purposes of subsection (5) above, it shall be for the Secretary of State (and not for any other person) to] defray any fees or other reasonable expenses of a registered medical practitioner in connection with—

(a) the provision of information in pursuance of an authorisation required to be provided under subsection (5)(a) above, or

(b) any examination which a person is required to undergo as mentioned in subsection (5)(b) above.   **[293]**

NOTES

Commencement: 1 July 1992 (sub-s (3A)); 15 May 1989 (remainder).

This section derived from the Road Traffic Act 1972, ss 87A, 170(5A), and the Road Traffic Act 1974, s 13(2), Sch 3, para 3.

Sub-s (3A): inserted by the Road Traffic Act 1991, s 18(2).

Sub-s (4): first words in square brackets added, and second words in square brackets substituted, by the Road Traffic (Driver Licensing and Information Systems) Act 1989, s 5(7).

Sub-ss (5), (9): words in square brackets substituted by the Road Traffic (Driver Licensing and Information Systems) Act 1989, s 5(8), (9).

[94A.   Driving after refusal or revocation of licence

(1) A person who drives a motor vehicle of any class on a road otherwise than in accordance with a licence authorising him to drive a motor vehicle of that class is guilty of an offence if—

(a) at any earlier time the Secretary of State has in accordance with section 92(3) of this Act refused to grant such a licence, or has under section 93(1) or (2) revoked such a licence, and

(b) he has not since that earlier time held such a licence.

(2) Section 88 of this Act shall apply in relation to subsection (1) above as it applies in relation to section 87.]   **[293A]**

NOTES
    Commencement: 1 July 1992.
    Inserted by the Road Traffic Act 1991, s 18(3).

95. Notification of refusal of insurance on grounds of health

(1) If an authorised insurer refuses to issue to any person such a policy of insurance as complies with the requirements of Part VI of this Act on the ground that the state of health of that person is not satisfactory, or on grounds which include that ground, the insurer shall as soon as practicable notify the Secretary of State of that refusal and of the full name, address, sex and date of birth of that person as disclosed by him to the insurer.

(2) In subsection (1) above "authorised insurer" means a person or body of persons carrying on insurance business within Group 2 in Part II of Schedule 2 to the Insurance Companies Act 1982 and being a member of the Motor Insurers' Bureau (a company limited by guarantee and incorporated under the Companies Act 1929 on 14th June 1946).   **[294]**

NOTES
    Commencement: 15 May 1989.
    This section derived from the Road Traffic Act 1972, ss 92(2), (3), 145(2), the Road Traffic Act 1974, s 20(1), Sch 3, para 7(2), the Insurance Companies Act 1981, Sch 4, para 22, and the Insurance Companies Act 1982, Sch 5, para 12.

96. Driving with uncorrected defective eyesight

(1) If a person drives a motor vehicle on a road while his eyesight is such (whether through a defect which cannot be or one which is not for the time being sufficiently corrected) that he cannot comply with any requirement as to eyesight prescribed under this Part of this Act for the purposes of tests of competence to drive, he is guilty of an offence.

(2) A constable having reason to suspect that a person driving a motor vehicle may be guilty of an offence under subsection (1) above may require him to submit to a test for the purpose of ascertaining whether, using no other means of correction than he used at the time of driving, he can comply with the requirement concerned.

(3) If that person refuses to submit to the test he is guilty of an offence. **[295]**

NOTES
    Commencement: 15 May 1989.
    This section derived from the Road Traffic Act 1972, s 91.

Granting of licences, their form and duration

97. Grant of licences

(1) Subject to [the following provisions of this section] and section 92 of this Act [and, in the case of licences to drive large goods vehicles or passenger-carrying vehicles, to Part IV of this Act], the Secretary of State must . . . grant a licence to a person who—

(a) makes an application for it in such manner and containing such
particulars as the Secretary of State may specify [and pays the fee (if
any) which is prescribed],

(b) provides the Secretary of State with such evidence or further evidence
in support of the application as the Secretary of State may require,

(c) surrenders to the Secretary of State any previous licence granted to
him after [1st January 1976] [and its counterpart] or provides the
Secretary of State with an explanation for not surrendering [them]
which the Secretary of State considers adequate and, where the
application is made by virtue of section [89(1)(d) or (f) of this Act,
surrenders to the Secretary of State his British external licence, his
British Forces licence or his exchangeable licence, as the case may be,
and]

(d) is not [, in accordance with section 88(1B) of this Act, subject to a
current disqualification which is relevant to the licence he applies for]
and is not prevented from obtaining it by the provisions of section 89
of this Act.

(2) If the application for the licence states that it is made for the purpose of
enabling the applicant to drive a motor vehicle with a view to passing a test of
competence to drive, any licence granted in pursuance of the application shall
be a provisional licence for that purpose, and nothing in section 89 of this Act
shall apply to such a licence.

(3) A provisional licence—

(a) shall be granted subject to prescribed conditions,

(b) shall, in any cases prescribed for the purposes of this paragraph, be
restricted so as to authorise only the driving of vehicles of the classes
so prescribed,

(c) may, in the case of a person appearing to the Secretary of State to be
suffering from a relevant disability or a prospective disability, be
restricted so as to authorise only the driving of vehicles of a particular
construction or design specified in the licence, . . .

(d) shall not authorise a person, before he has passed a test of competence
to drive, to drive a [motor bicycle without a side-car], unless it is a
learner motor cycle (as defined in subsection (5) below) or its first use
(as defined in regulations) occurred before 1st January 1982 and the
cylinder capacity of its engine does not exceed 125 cubic centimetres
[, and

(e) except as provided under subsection (3B) below, shall not authorise a
person, before he has passed a test of competence to drive, to drive on
a road a motor bicycle except where he has successfully completed an
approved training course for motor cyclists or is undergoing training
on such a course and is driving the motor cycle on the road as part of
the training.]

[(3A) Regulations may make provision as respects the training in the driving
of motor bicycles of persons wishing to obtain licences authorising the driving
of such motor cycles by means of courses of training provided in accordance
with the regulations; and the regulations may in particular make provision with
respect to—

(a) the nature of the courses of training;

(b) the approval by the Secretary of State of the persons providing the
courses and the withdrawal of his approval;

   (c) the maximum amount of any charges payable by persons undergoing
the training;

   (d) certificates evidencing the successful completion by persons of a
course of training and the supply by the Secretary of State of the forms
which are to be used for such certificates; and

   (e) the making, in connection with the supply of forms of certificates, of
reasonable charges for the discharge of the functions of the Secretary
of State under the regulations;

and different provision may be made for training in different classes of motor
cycles.

   (3B) Regulations may prescribe cases in which persons holding a provisional
licence are exempt from the restriction imposed by subsection (3)(e) above on
their driving under the licence; and the regulations may—

   (a) limit the exemption to persons in prescribed circumstances;

   (b) limit the exemption to a prescribed period or in respect of driving in
a prescribed area;

   (c) attach conditions to the exemption; and

   (d) regulate applications for, and the issue and form of, certificates
evidencing the holder's exemption from the restriction.]

   (4) Regulations may authorise or require the Secretary of State to refuse a
provisional licence authorising the driving of a motor cycle of a prescribed class
if the applicant has held such a provisional licence and the licence applied for
would come into force within the prescribed period—

   (a) beginning at the end of the period for which the previous licence
authorised (or would, if not surrendered or revoked, have authorised)
the driving of such a motor cycle, or

   (b) beginning at such other time as may be prescribed.

   (5) A learner motor cycle is a motor cycle which either is propelled by
electric power or has the following characteristics—

   (a) the cylinder capacity of its engine does not exceed 125 cubic
centimetres,

   (b) the maximum power output of its engine does not exceed nine
kilowatts (as measured in accordance with International Standards
Organisation standard 4106-1978.09.01), and

   (c) its power to weight ratio does not exceed 100 kilowatts per metric
tonne, the power being the maximum power output mentioned in
paragraph (b) above and the weight that mentioned in subsection (6)
below.

   (6) The weight referred to in subsection (5) above is the weight of the motor
cycle with a full supply of fuel in its tank, an adequate supply of other liquids
needed for its propulsion and no load other than its normal equipment, including
loose tools.

   (7) ...   **[296]**

NOTES

   Commencement: 1 December 1990 (sub-ss 3A, 3B); 15 May 1989 (remainder).

   This section derived from the Road Traffic Act 1972, s 88(1)-(2B), (6), the Road Traffic Act 1974,
Sch 3, para 4(1), (2), the Transport Act 1981, s 23(1), (2), the Driving Licences (Community Driving
Licence) Regulations 1982, SI 1982 No 1555, reg 3(2), and the Road Traffic (Driving Licences) Act
1983, s 1(3)(d).

   Sub-s (1): first words in square brackets substituted by the Road Traffic (Driver Licensing and
Information Systems) Act 1989, s 6(2); second words in square brackets substituted, words omitted
repealed, paras (a), (d) amended, and first and fourth words in square brackets in para (c) substituted,

by the Road Traffic (Driver Licensing and Information Systems) Act 1989, ss 7, 16, Sch 3, para 9, Sch 6; remaining words in square brackets in para (c) substituted or inserted, with savings, by SI 1990 No 144, reg 2(1), Sch 1, para 3, for savings see reg 3 thereof.

Sub-s (3): words in square brackets substituted or added, and words omitted repealed, by the Road Traffic (Driver Licensing and Information Systems) Act 1989, ss 6(2), 7, 16, Sch 3, para 10, Sch 6, as from a day to be appointed.

Sub-ss (3A), (3B): added by the Road Traffic (Driver Licensing and Information Systems) Act 1989, s 6(2)(c)

Sub-s (7): repealed by the Road Traffic Act 1991, ss 17(3), 83, Sch 8.

98. Form of licence

(1) A licence shall be in such form as the Secretary of State may determine and shall—

   (a) state whether, apart from subsection (2) below, it authorises its holder to drive motor vehicles of all classes or of certain classes only and, in the latter case, specify those classes,

   (b) specify the restrictions on the driving of vehicles of any class in pursuance of the licence to which its holder is subject by virtue of the provisions of section 101 of this Act, [and]

   (c) in the case of a provisional licence, specify the conditions subject to which it is granted, . . .

   (d) . . .

(2) Subject to subsections (3) [, (4) and (4A)] below, a [person who holds a licence which] authorises its holder to drive motor vehicles of certain classes only (not being—

   [(a) a provisional licence, or

   (b) any other prescribed description of licence)]

[may] drive motor vehicles of all other classes subject to the same conditions as if he were authorised by a provisional licence to drive motor vehicles of those other classes.

(3) [Subsection (2) above does not] authorise a person to drive—

   (a) a vehicle of a class for the driving of which he could not, by reason of the provisions of section 101 of this Act, lawfully hold a licence, or

   (b) unless he has passed a test of competence to drive, a [motor bicycle without a side-car] which, by virtue of section 97(3)(d) of this Act, a provisional licence would not authorise him to drive before he had passed that test [, or

   (c) unless he has passed a test of competence to drive, a motor bicycle on a road in circumstances in which, by virtue of section 97(3)(e) of this Act, a provisional licence would not authorise him to drive it before he had passed that test.]

(4) In such cases [or as respects such classes of vehicles] as the Secretary of State may prescribe, the provisions of subsections (2) and (3) above shall not apply or shall apply subject to such limitations as he may prescribe.

[(4A) [Subsection (2) above does not] authorise a person on whom a notice under section 92(5)(b) of this Act has been served to drive motor vehicles otherwise than in accordance with the limits specified in the notice.]

(5) . . .   [297]

NOTES

   Commencement: 1 June 1990 (sub-ss (4A)); 15 May 1989 (remainder).

   This section derived from the Road Traffic Act 1972, s 88(3)-(6), the Road Traffic Act 1974, Sch

3, para 4(3), (4), the Road Traffic (Drivers' Ages and Hours of Work) Act 1976, Sch 1, para 3, and the Transport Act 1981, s 23(3).

    Sub-s (1): first word in square brackets added with savings, para (d) and the word "and" preceding it, repealed with savings, by SI 1990 No 144, reg 2(1), Sch 1, para 4(a), for savings see reg 3 thereof.

    Sub-s (2): first words in square brackets substituted, and paras (a), (b) substituted for paras (a)-(c) as originally enacted, by the Road Traffic (Driver Licensing and Information Systems) Act 1989, ss 5(1)(a), 7, Sch 3, para 11(b); second and final words in square brackets substituted with savings by SI 1990 No 144, reg 2(1), Sch 1, para 4(b), for savings see reg 3 thereof.

    Sub-s (3): first words in square brackets substituted with savings, by SI 1990 No 144, reg 2(1), Sch 1, para 4(c), for savings see reg 3 thereof; other words in square brackets substituted or added, by the Road Traffic (Driver Licensing and Information Systems) Act 1989, s 7, Sch 3, para 11(c).

    Sub-s (4): words in square brackets added, by the Road Traffic (Driver Licensing and Information Systems) Act 1989, s 7, Sch 3, para 11(d).

    Sub-s (4A): added by the Road Traffic (Driver Licensing and Information Systems) Act 1989, s 5(10)(b) (as amended with savings by SI 1990 No 144, reg 2(3), Sch 3, para 1(b), for savings see reg 3 thereof).

    Sub-s (5): repealed by the Road Traffic Act 1991, ss 17(3), 83, Sch 8.

99. Duration of licences

(1) [In so far as a licence authorises its holder to drive motor vehicles of classes other than any prescribed class of goods vehicle or any prescribed class of passenger-carrying vehicle, it] shall, unless previously revoked or surrendered, remain in force, subject to subsection (2) below—

    (a) except in a case falling within paragraph (b) or (c) of this subsection, for the period ending on the seventieth anniversary of the applicant's date of birth or for a period of three years, whichever is the longer,

    (b) except in a case falling within paragraph (c) of this subsection, if the Secretary of State so determines in the case of a licence to be granted to a person appearing to him to be suffering from a relevant or prospective disability, for such period of not more than three years and not less than one year as the Secretary of State may determine, and

    (c) in the case of a licence granted in exchange for a subsisting licence and in pursuance of an application requesting a licence for the period authorised by this paragraph, for a period equal to the remainder of that for which the subsisting licence was granted,

and any such period shall begin with the date on which the licence in question is expressed to come into force.

[(1A) In so far as a licence authorises its holder to drive any prescribed class of goods vehicle or passenger-carrying vehicle, it shall, unless previously revoked, suspended or surrendered, remain in force—

    (a) except in a case falling within paragraph (c) or (d) of this subsection—

        (i) for the period ending on the forty-fifth anniversary of the applicant's date of birth or for a period of five years, whichever is the longer, or

        (ii) where the applicant's age at the date on which the licence is to come into force will exceed forty-five but not sixty-five years, for the period ending on the sixty-sixth anniversary of the applicant's date of birth or for a period of five years, whichever is the shorter,

    (b) except in a case falling within paragraph (d) of this subsection, where the applicant's age at that date will exceed sixty-five years, for a period of one year,

    (c) except in a case falling within paragraph (b) or (d) of this subsection, if the Secretary of State so determines in the case of a licence to be granted to a person appearing to him to be suffering from a relevant or prospective disability, for such period of not more than three years and not less than one year as the Secretary of State may determine, and

(d) in the case of a licence granted in exchange for a subsisting licence and in pursuance of an application requesting a licence for the period authorised by this paragraph, for a period equal to the remainder of that for which the subsisting licence was granted,

and any such period shall begin with the date on which the licence in question is expressed to come into force.]

(2) To the extent that a provisional licence authorises the driving of a motor cycle of a prescribed class it shall, unless previously surrendered or revoked, remain in force—

(a) for such period as may be prescribed, or
(b) if the licence is granted to the holder of a previous licence which was surrendered, revoked or treated as being revoked—

   (i) for the remainder of the period for which the previous licence would have authorised the driving of such a motor cycle, or
   (ii) in such circumstances as may be prescribed, for a period equal to that remainder at the time of surrender or revocation.

(3) Where it appears to the Secretary of State—

[(a) that a licence granted by him to any person was granted in error or with an error or omission in the particulars specified in the licence, or
(aa) that the counterpart of a licence granted by him to any person is required to be endorsed in pursuance of any enactment or was issued with an error or omission in the particulars specified in the counterpart or required to be so endorsed on it, or]
(b) that the particulars specified in a licence granted by him to any person [or in its counterpart] do not comply with any requirement imposed since the licence was granted by any provision made by or having effect under any enactment,

the Secretary of State may serve notice in writing on that person revoking the licence and requiring him to surrender the licence [and its counterpart] forthwith to the Secretary of State [and it shall be the duty of that person to comply with the requirement].

(4) Where the name or address of the licence holder as specified in a licence ceases to be correct, its holder must forthwith surrender the licence [and its counterpart] to the Secretary of State and provide him with particulars of the alterations falling to be made in the name or address and, in the case of a provisional licence as respects which the prescribed conditions are satisfied, with a statement of his sex and date of birth.

(5) A person who [without reasonable excuse] fails to comply with the duty under subsection [(3) or] (4) above is guilty of an offence.

(6) Where a person who has a duty under this section to surrender his licence [and its counterpart] is not in possession of [them] in consequence of the fact that he has surrendered [them] to a constable or authorised person (within the meaning of Part III of the Road Traffic Offenders Act 1988) on receiving a fixed penalty notice given to him under section 54 of that Act, he does not fail to comply with the duty if he surrenders the licence [and its counterpart] to the Secretary of State immediately on [their] return.

(7) On the surrender of a licence [and its counterpart] by any person in pursuance of subsection (3) or (4) above, the Secretary of State—

(a) must, except where the licence was granted in error [or the licence and its counterpart are] surrendered in pursuance of subsection (3) above in consequence of an error or omission appearing to the Secretary of State to be attributable to that person's fault or in consequence of a current disqualification, and

(b) may in such an excepted case which does not involve a current disqualification,

grant to that person free of charge a new licence for such period (subject to subsection (8) below) that it expires on the date on which the surrendered licence would have expired had it not been surrendered.

(8) Where the period for which the surrendered licence was granted was based on an error with respect to the licence holder's date of birth such that, if that error had not been made, that licence would have been expressed to expire on a different date, the period of the new licence shall be such that it expires on that different date.   **[298]**

NOTES

Commencement: 1 April 1991 (sub-s (1A)); 15 May 1989 (remainder).

This section derived from the Road Traffic Act 1972, s 89, the Road Traffic Act 1974, Sch 3, para 5, the Transport Act 1981, s 23(4), (5), the Transport Act 1982, s 35(7), and the Criminal Justice Act 1988, Sch 14, para 77.

Sub-s (1): words in square brackets substituted by the Road Traffic (Driver Licensing and Information Systems) Act 1989, s 7, Sch 3, para 12(a).

Sub-s (1A): prospectively added by the Road Traffic (Driver Licensing and Information Systems) Act 1989, s 2(2).

Sub-s (3): first words in square brackets substituted with savings, and second and third words in square brackets added with savings, by SI 1990 No 144, reg 2(1), Sch 1, para 5(a), for savings see reg 3 thereof; final words in square brackets added by the Road Traffic (Driver Licensing and Information Systems) Act 1989, s 7, Sch 3, para 12(b).

Sub-s (4): words in square brackets added with savings by SI 1990 No 144, reg 2(1), Sch 1, para 5(b); for savings see reg 3 thereof.

Sub-s (5): words in square brackets added by the Road Traffic (Driver Licensing and Information Systems) Act 1989, s 7, Sch 3, para 12(c).

Sub-ss (6), (7): words in square brackets substituted or inserted with savings SI 1990 No 144, reg 2(1), Sch 1, para 5(c), (d); for savings see reg 3 thereof.

Appeals

100. Appeals relating to licences

(1) A person who is aggrieved by the Secretary of State's—

(a) refusal to grant or revocation of a licence in pursuance of section 92 or 93 of this Act, or

(b) determination under section 99(1)(b) of this Act to grant a licence for three years or less, or

(c) revocation of a licence in pursuance of section 99(3) of this Act,

or by a notice served on him in pursuance of section 92(5) of this Act may, after giving to the Secretary of State notice of his intention to do so, appeal to a magistrates' court acting for the petty sessions area in which he resides or, in Scotland, to the sheriff within whose jurisdiction he resides.

(2) On any such appeal the court or sheriff may make such order as it or he thinks fit and the order shall be binding on the Secretary of State.

(3) It is hereby declared that, without prejudice to section 90 of this Act, in

any proceedings under this section the court or sheriff is not entitled to entertain any question as to whether the appellant passed a test of competence to drive if he was declared by the person who conducted it to have failed it. **[299]**

NOTES
 Commencement: 15 May 1989.
 This section derived from the Road Traffic Act 1972, s 90, the Road Traffic Act 1974, Sch 3, para 6, and the Transport Act 1981, Sch 12, Part III.

Disqualification (otherwise than on conviction)

101. Disqualification of persons under age

(1) A person is disqualified for holding or obtaining a licence to drive a motor vehicle of a class specified in the following Table if he is under the age specified in relation to it in the second column of the Table.

TABLE

Class of motor vehicle	Age (in years)
1. Invalid carriage	16
2. Motor cycle	16
3. Small passenger vehicle or small goods vehicle	17
4. Agricultural tractor	17
5. Medium-sized goods vehicle	18
6. Other motor vehicles	21

(2) The Secretary of State may by regulations provide that subsection (1) above shall have effect as if for the classes of vehicles and the ages specified in the Table in that subsection there were substituted different classes of vehicles and ages or different classes of vehicles or different ages.

(3) Subject to subsection (4) below, the regulations may—
  (a) apply to persons of a class specified in or under the regulations,
  (b) apply in circumstances so specified,
  (c) impose conditions or create exemptions or provide for the imposition of conditions or the creation of exemptions,
  (d) contain such transitional and supplemental provisions (including provisions amending section 108, 120 or 183(5) of this Act) as the Secretary of State considers necessary or expedient.

(4) For the purpose of defining the class of persons to whom, the class of vehicles to which, the circumstances in which or the conditions subject to which regulations made by virtue of subsection (2) above are to apply where an approved training scheme for drivers is in force, it is sufficient for the regulations to refer to a document which embodies the terms (or any of the terms) of the scheme or to a document which is in force in pursuance of the scheme.

(5) In subsection (4) above—
  "approved" means approved for the time being by the Secretary of State for the purpose of the regulations,
  "training scheme for drivers" means a scheme for training persons to drive vehicles of a class in relation to which the age which is in force under this section (but apart from any such scheme) is 21 years,
but no approved training scheme for drivers shall be amended without the approval of the Secretary of State. **[300]**

NOTES
 Commencement: 15 May 1989.
 This section derived from the Road Traffic Act 1972, s 96, and the Road Traffic (Drivers' Ages and Hours of Work) Act 1976, s 1(1).

102. Disqualification to prevent duplication of licences

A person is disqualified for obtaining a licence authorising him to drive a motor vehicle of any class so long as he is the holder of another licence authorising him to drive a motor vehicle of that class, whether the licence is suspended or not.   **[301]**

NOTES

     Commencement: 15 May 1989.
     This section derived from the Road Traffic Act 1972, s 97.

[Effects of disqualification

103. Obtaining licence, or driving, while disqualified

(1) A person is guilty of an offence if, while disqualified for holding or obtaining a licence, he—

     (a) obtains a licence, or
     (b) drives a motor vehicle on a road.

(2) A licence obtained by any person who is disqualified is of no effect (or, where the disqualification relates only to vehicles of a particular class, is of no effect in relation to vehicles of that class).

(3) A constable in uniform may arrest without warrant any person driving a motor vehicle on a road whom he has reasonable cause to suspect of being disqualified.

(4) Subsections (1) and (3) above do not apply in relation to disqualification by virtue of section 101 of this Act.

(5) Subsections (1)(b) and (3) above do not apply in relation to disqualification by virtue of secton 102 of this Act.

(6) In the application of subsections (1) and (3) above to a person whose disqualification is limited to the driving of motor vehicles of a particular class by virtue of—

     (a) section 102 or 117 of this Act, or
     (b) subsection (9) of section 36 of the Road Traffic Offenders Act 1988 (disqualification until test is passed),

the references to disqualification for holding or obtaining a licence and driving motor vehicles are references to disqualification for holding or obtaining a licence to drive and driving motor vehicles of that class.]   **[302]**

NOTES

     Commencement: 1 July 1992.
     This section, and the cross-heading preceding it, substituted by the Road Traffic Act 1991, s 19.

Miscellaneous

104. Conduct of proceedings in certain courts by or against the Secretary of State

(1) Any proceedings by or against the Secretary of State in a magistrates' court or before the registrar of a county court under this Part of this Act or Part II of the Road Traffic Offenders Act 1988 may be conducted on behalf of the Secretary of State by a person authorised by him for the purposes of this subsection.

(2) Any proceedings in any court in Scotland, other than the High Court of Justiciary or the Court of Session, against the Secretary of State under this Part of this Act or Part II of the Road Traffic Offenders Act 1988 may be conducted on behalf of the Secretary of State by any person authorised by him for the purposes of this subsection.   **[303]**

NOTES

Commencement: 15 May 1989.

This section derived from the Road Traffic Act 1972, s 106.

105. Regulations

(1) The Secretary of State may make regulations for any purpose for which regulations may be made under the provisions of this Part of this Act and the relevant provisions of the Road Traffic Offenders Act 1988 and for prescribing anything which may be prescribed under any of those provisions, and otherwise for the purpose of carrying any of those provisions into effect.

(2) In particular, but without prejudice to the generality of subsection (1) above, the regulations may make provision with respect to—

    (a) licences [and counterparts of licences],

    (b) making any particulars with respect to any persons who are disqualified or whose licences are suspended or [whose counterparts of licences are] endorsed available for use by the police,

    (c) preventing a person holding more than one licence,

    (d) facilitating identification of holders of licences,

    (e) providing for the issue of a [new licences and counterparts of licences in the place of licences or counterparts of licences] lost or defaced on payment of such fee as may be prescribed,

    [(*ee*) the correspondence . . . of one class of motor vehicle with another class of motor vehicle or of one test of competence to drive with another (whatever the law under which the classification is made or the test conducted),]

    (f) the effect of a change in the classification of motor vehicles . . . on licences then in force or issued or on the right to or the subsequent granting of licences, and

    (g) enabling a person—

        (i) whose entitlement to the grant of a licence to drive a class of motor vehicle is preserved by regulations made by virtue of paragraph (f) above, and

        (ii) who satisfies such conditions as may be prescribed, to drive (and be employed in driving) that class of motor vehicle while he applies for the licence to be granted to him,

and different regulations may be made as respects different classes of vehicles or as respects the same class of vehicles in different circumstances.

(3) The regulations may—

    (a) make different provision for different circumstances,

    (b) provide for exemptions from any provision of the regulations, and

    (c) contain such incidental and supplemental provisions as the Secretary of State considers expedient for the purposes of the regulations,

and nothing in the other provisions of this Part of this Act shall be construed as prejudicing the generality of the preceding provisions of this subsection.

(4) Any fee prescribed under this Part of this Act shall be of an amount

approved by the Treasury, and different fees may be prescribed for different circumstances.

(5) In subsection (1) above "the relevant provisions of the Road Traffic Offenders Act 1988" means the following provisions of that Act: sections 2, 7, 8, 23 to 26, 27, 31 and 34 to 48.   **[304]**

NOTES
Commencement: 15 May 1989.
This section derived from the Road Traffic Act 1972, s 107, and the Road Traffic (Drivers' Ages and Hours of Work) Act 1976, Sch 1, para 4.
Sub-s (2): words in square brackets in paras (a), (b) added with savings, and in para (e) words in square brackets substituted with savings, by SI 1990 No 144, reg 2(1), Sch 1, para 6, for savings see reg 3 thereof; para (*ee*) added by the Road Traffic (Driver Licensing and Information Systems) Act 1989, s 7, Sch 3, para 14, and amended by the Road Traffic Act 1991, s 83, Sch 8; words omitted from para (f) repealed by the Road Traffic Act 1991, s 83, Sch 8.
See the Motor Vehicles (Driving Licences) Regulations 1971, post.

106. Destination of fees for licences, etc

(1) All fees received by the Secretary of State for licences under this Part of this Act shall be paid into the Consolidated Fund.

(2) Fees in respect of tests of competence to drive payable by virtue of regulations made by virtue of section 89(4) of this Act shall be paid to such person as may be prescribed by the regulations, and any such fees received by a person so prescribed (other than any as to which the regulations provide that they are to be paid to the person conducting the test and retained by him as remuneration) shall be paid into the Consolidated Fund.   **[305]**

NOTES
Commencement: 15 May 1989.
This section derived from the Road Traffic Act 1972, s 108.

107. Service of notices

A notice authorised to be served on any person by section 92, 93 or 99(3) of this Act may be served on him by delivering it to him or by leaving it at his proper address or by sending it to him by post; and for the purposes of this section and section 7 of the Interpretation Act 1978 in its application to this section the proper address of any person shall be his latest address as known to the person serving the notice.   **[306]**

NOTES
Commencement: 15 May 1989.
This section derived from the Road Traffic Act 1972, s 109.

108. Interpretation

(1) In this Part of this Act—

"agricultural tractor" means a tractor used primarily for work on land in connection with agriculture,

"articulated goods vehicle" means a motor vehicle which is so constructed that a trailer designed to carry goods may by partial superimposition be attached to it in such manner as to cause a substantial part of the weight of the trailer to be borne by the motor vehicle, and "articulated goods vehicle combination" means an articulated goods vehicle with a trailer so attached,

["British external licence" and "British Forces licence" have the meanings given by section 88(8) of this Act,]

"Community licence" means a document issued in respect of a member State other than the United Kingdom by an authority of that or another member State (including the United Kingdom) authorising the holder to drive a motor vehicle, not being—

  (a) a document containing a statement to the effect that that or a previous document was issued in exchange for a document issued in respect of a State other than a member State, or
  (b) a document in any of the forms for an international driving permit annexed to the Paris Convention on Motor Traffic of 1926, the Geneva Convention on Road Traffic of 1949 or the Vienna Convention on Road Traffic of 1968,

"disability" has the meaning given by section 92 of this Act,

"disqualified" means disqualified for holding or obtaining a licence [(or, in cases where the disqualification is limited, a licence to drive motor vehicles of the class to which the disqualification relates)], and "disqualification" is to be interpreted accordingly,

"exchangeable licence" means a Community licence or a document which would be a Community licence if—

  (a) Gibraltar, and
  (b) each country or territory within this paragraph by virtue of an order under subsection (2) below,
      were or formed part of a member State other than the United Kingdom,

["full licence" means a licence other than a provisional licence,]

"licence" [(except where the context otherwise requires)] means a licence to drive a motor vehicle granted under this Part of this Act [and "counterpart", in relation to a licence, means a document in such form as the Secretary of State may determine, issued with the licence, containing such information as he determines and designed for the endorsement of particulars relating to the licence],

"maximum gross weight", in relation to a motor vehicle or trailer, means the weight of the vehicle laden with the heaviest load which it is constructed or adapted to carry,

"maximum train weight", in relation to an articulated goods vehicle combination, means the weight of the combination laden with the heaviest load which it is constructed or adapted to carry,

"medium-sized goods vehicle" means a motor vehicle which is constructed or adapted to carry or to haul goods and is not adapted to carry more than nine persons inclusive of the driver and the permissible maximum weight of which exceeds 3.5 but not 7.5 tonnes,

["Northern Ireland driving licence" or "Northern Ireland licence" means a licence to drive a motor vehicle granted under the law of Northern Ireland,

"passenger-carrying vehicle" has the meaning given by section 121(1) of this Act,] "permissible maximum weight", in relation to a goods vehicle (of whatever description), means—

    (a) in the case of a motor vehicle which neither is an articulated goods vehicle nor is drawing a trailer, the relevant maximum weight of the vehicle,

    (b) in the case of an articulated goods vehicle—

        (i) when drawing only a semi-trailer, the relevant maximum train weight of the articulated goods vehicle combination,

        (ii) when drawing a trailer as well as a semi-trailer, the aggregate of the relevant maximum train weight of the articulated goods vehicle combination and the relevant maximum weight of the trailer,

        (iii) when drawing a trailer but not a semi-trailer, the aggregate of the relevant maximum weight of the articulated goods vehicle and the relevant maximum weight of the trailer,

        (iv) when drawing neither a semi-trailer nor a trailer, the relevant maximum weight of the vehicle,

    (c) in the case of a motor vehicle (not being an articulated goods vehicle) which is drawing a trailer, the aggregate of the relevant maximum weight of the motor vehicle and the relevant maximum weight of the trailer,

"prescribed" means prescribed by regulations,

"prospective disability" has the meaning given by section 92 of this Act,

"provisional licence" means a licence granted by virtue of section 97(2) of this Act,

"regulations" means regulations made under section 105 of this Act,

"relevant disability" has the meaning given by section 92 of this Act,

["relevant external law" has the meaning given by section 88(8) of this Act,]

"relevant maximum weight", in relation to a motor vehicle or trailer, means—

    (a) in the case of a vehicle to which regulations under section 49 of this Act apply which is required by regulations under section 41 of this Act to have a maximum gross weight for the vehicle marked on a plate issued by the Secretary of State under regulations under section 41, the maximum gross weight so marked on the vehicle,

    (b) in the case of a vehicle which is required by regulations under section 41 of this Act to have a maximum gross weight for the vehicle marked on the vehicle and does not also have a maximum gross weight marked on it as mentioned in paragraph (a) above, the maximum gross weight marked on the vehicle,

    (c) in the case of a vehicle on which a maximum gross weight is marked by the same means as would be required by regulations under section 41 of this Act if those regulations applied to the vehicle, the maximum gross weight so marked on the vehicle,

    (d) in the case of a vehicle on which a maximum gross weight is not marked as mentioned in paragraph (a), (b) or (c) above, the notional maximum gross weight of the vehicle, that is to say, such weight as is produced by multiplying the unladen weight of the vehicle by the number prescribed by the Secretary of State for the class of vehicle into which that vehicle falls,

"relevant maximum train weight", in relation to an articulated goods vehicle combination, means—

(a) in the case of an articulated goods vehicle to which regulations under section 49 of this Act apply which is required by regulations under section 41 of this Act to have a maximum train weight for the combination marked on a plate issued by the Secretary of State under regulations under section 41, the maximum train weight so marked on the motor vehicle,

(b) in the case of an articulated goods vehicle which is required by regulations under section 41 of this Act to have a maximum train weight for the combination marked on the vehicle and does not also have a maximum train weight marked on it as mentioned in paragraph (a) above, the maximum train weight marked on the motor vehicle,

(c) in the case of an articulated goods vehicle on which a maximum train weight is marked by the same means as would be required by regulations under section 41 of this Act if those regulations applied to the vehicle, the maximum train weight so marked on the motor vehicle,

(d) in the case of an articulated goods vehicle on which a maximum train weight is not marked as mentioned in paragraph (a), (b) or (c) above, the notional maximum gross weight of the combination, that is to say, such weight as is produced by multiplying the sum of the unladen weights of the motor vehicle and the semi-trailer by the number prescribed by the Secretary of State for the class of articulated goods vehicle combination into which that combination falls,

"semi-trailer", in relation to an articulated goods vehicle, means a trailer attached to it in the manner described in the definition of articulated goods vehicle,

"small goods vehicle" means a motor vehicle (other than a motor cycle or invalid carriage) which is constructed or adapted to carry or to haul goods and is not adapted to carry more than nine persons inclusive of the driver and the permissible maximum weight of which does not exceed 3.5 tonnes,

"small passenger vehicle" means a motor vehicle (other than a motor cycle or invalid carriage) which is constructed solely to carry passengers and their effects and is adapted to carry not more than nine persons inclusive of the driver, and

"test of competence to drive" means such a test conducted under section 89 of this Act.

["approved training course for motor cyclists" and, in relation to such a course, "prescribed certificate of completion" mean respectively any course of training approved under, and the certificate of completion prescribed in, regulations under section 97(3A) of this Act.]

(2) If the Secretary of State is satisfied that satisfactory provision for the granting of licences to drive motor vehicles is made by the law of a country or territory which neither is nor forms part of a member State, he may by order made by statutory instrument designate that country or territory as a country or

territory within paragraph (b) of the definition of exchangeable licence in subsection (1) above.

(3) Before making any order under subsection (2) above, the Secretary of State shall consult with such representative organisations as he thinks fit. **[307]**

NOTES
Commencement: 15 May 1989.
This section derived from the Road Traffic Act 1972, s 110, the Road Traffic (Drivers' Ages and Hours of Work) Act 1976, Sch 1, para 5, Sch 3, Part I, the Transport Act 1981, s 30(2), the Driving Licences (Community Driving Licence) Regulations 1982, SI 1982 No 1555, reg 3(3), and the Road Traffic (Driving Licences) Act 1983, s 1(1), (2).
Sub-s (1): definitions "British external licence" and "British Forces Licence", "full licence", "Northern Ireland driving licence" or "Northern Ireland licence", "passenger-carrying vehicle", "relevant external law", "approved training course for motor cyclists" and "prescribed certificate of completion" added by the Road Traffic (Driver Licensing and Information Systems) Act 1989, s 7, Sch 3, para 15; words in square brackets in definition "disqualified" added, by the Road Traffic (Driver Licensing and Information Systems) Act 1989, s 7, Sch 3, para 15; in definition "licence" first words in square brackets added by the Road Traffic (Driver Licensing and Information Systems) Act 1989, s 7, Sch 3, para 15, second words in square brackets added with savings by SI 1990 No 144, reg 2(1), Sch 1, para 7, for savings see reg 3 thereof.

109. Provisions as to Northern Ireland drivers' licences

(1) The holder of a [Northern Ireland driving licence] may drive, and a person may cause or permit the holder of such a licence to drive, in Great Britain, a motor vehicle of any class which he is authorised by that licence to drive, and which he is not disqualified from driving under this Part [or Part IV] of this Act, notwithstanding that he is not the holder of a licence under this Part of this Act.

(2) Any driver holding a [Northern Ireland driving licence] shall be under the like obligation to produce such a licence [and its counterpart as if they had respectively been a licence granted under this part of this Act and the counterpart to such a licence], and the provisions—

(a) of this Act, and
(b) of the Road Traffic Offenders Act 1988, being the provisions connected with the licensing of drivers within the meaning of that Act,

as to the production of licences [and counterparts of licences] granted under this Part of this Act shall apply accordingly.

(3) The holder of any such licence who by an order of the court is disqualified for holding or obtaining a licence under this Part of this Act must produce the licence so held by him [and its counterpart] to the court within such time as the court may determine, and the court must, on production of the licence [and its counterpart], forward [them] to the Secretary of State.

(4) If the holder fails to produce the licence [and its counterpart] within that time, he is guilty of an offence.

(5) If the holder of any such licence is convicted of an offence and the court orders particulars of the conviction to be endorsed in accordance with section 44 of the Road Traffic Offenders Act 1988, the court shall send those particulars to the Secretary of State.   **[308]**

NOTES
Commencement: 15 May 1989.
This section derived from the Road Traffic Act 1972, s 111, and the Road Traffic (Drivers' Ages and Hours of Work) Act 1976, Sch 1, para 6.
Sub-s (1): first words in square brackets substituted, and final words in square brackets inserted by the Road Traffic (Driver Licensing and Information Systems) Act 1989, s 7, Sch 3, para 16(a).
Sub-s (2): first words in square brackets substituted by the Road Traffic (Driver Licensing and

Information Systems) Act 1989, s 7, Sch 3, para 16(b); second words in square brackets substituted with savings and final words in square brackets inserted with savings by SI 1990 No 144, reg 2(1), Sch 1, para 8(a), for savings see reg 3 thereof.

Sub-s (3): words in square brackets inserted or substituted with savings by SI 1990 No 144, reg 2(1), Sch 1, para 8(b); for savings see reg 3 thereof.

Sub-s (4): words in square brackets inserted with savings by SI 1990 No 144, reg 2(1), Sch 1, para 8(c); for savings see reg 3 thereof.

[PART IV

LICENSING OF DRIVERS OF LARGE GOODS VEHICLES AND PASSENGER-CARRYING VEHICLES

[110. Licensing of drivers of large goods vehicles and passenger-carrying vehicles

(1) Licences under Part III of this Act to drive motor vehicles of classes which include large goods vehicles or passenger-carrying vehicles or large goods vehicles or passenger-carrying vehicles of any class shall be granted by the Secretary of State in accordance with this Part of this Act and shall, in so far as they authorise the driving of large goods vehicles or passenger-carrying vehicles, be otherwise subject to this Part of this Act in addition to Part III of this Act.

(2) In this Part of this Act—

"large goods vehicle driver's licence" means a licence under Part III of this Act in so far as it authorises a person to drive large goods vehicles of any class; and

"passenger-carrying vehicle driver's licence" means a licence under Part III of this Act in so far as it authorises a person to drive passenger-carrying vehicles of any class.] **[309]**

NOTES
Commencement: 1 April 1991.
This Part of this Act (ss 110–122) repealed and re-enacted by the Road Traffic (Driver Licensing and Information Systems) Act 1989, ss 1(1), 2(1), 16, Schs 2, 6.

[111. Functions of traffic commissioners

(1) The traffic commissioner for any area constituted for the purposes of the Public Passenger Vehicles Act 1981 shall exercise the functions conferred by the following provisions of this Part of this Act relating to the conduct of applicants for and holders of large goods vehicle and passenger-carrying vehicle drivers' licences.

(2) Traffic commissioners shall, in the exercise of those functions, act in accordance with directions given by the Secretary of State; but such directions shall be general directions not relating to the exercise of functions in a particular case.] **[310]**

NOTES
Commencement: 1 April 1991.
Commencement order: SI 1990 No 2610.
See the note to s 110 ante.

[112. Grant of licences: fitness as regards conduct

The Secretary of State shall not grant to an applicant a large goods vehicle driver's licence or a passenger-carrying vehicle driver's licence unless he is satisfied, having regard to his conduct, that he is a fit person to hold the licence applied for.] **[311]**

NOTES
    Commencement: 1 April 1991.
    See the note to s 110 ante.

[113. Grant of licences: referral of matters of conduct to traffic commissioners

(1) Any question arising under section 112 of this Act relating to the conduct of an applicant for a licence may be referred by the Secretary of State to the traffic commissioner for the area in which the applicant resides.

(2) On any reference under subsection (1) above, the traffic commissioner shall determine whether the applicant for the licence is or is not, having regard to his conduct, a fit person to hold a licence to drive large goods vehicles or passenger-carrying vehicles, as the case may be.

(3) A traffic commissioner to whom a reference has been made under this section may require the applicant for the licence to furnish the commissioner with such information as he may require and may, by notice to the applicant, require him to attend before the commissioner at the time and place specified by the commissioner to furnish the information and to answer such questions (if any) relating to his application as the commissioner may put to him.

(4) If the applicant fails without reasonable excuse to furnish information to or attend before or answer questions properly put by a commissioner when required to do so under subsection (3) above, the commissioner may decline to proceed further with the application and, if he does so, the commissioner shall notify the Secretary of State of that fact and the Secretary of State shall refuse to grant the licence.

(5) The traffic commissioner to whom a reference has been made under this section shall, unless he has declined to proceed further with the application, notify the Secretary of State and the applicant of his determination in the matter and the decision of the commissioner shall be binding on the Secretary of State.]   **[312]**

NOTES
    Commencement: 1 April 1991.
    See the note to s 110 ante.

[114. Conditions of certain licences

(1) A large goods vehicle or passenger-carrying vehicle driver's licence issued as a provisional licence, or a full large goods vehicle or passenger-carrying vehicle driver's licence issued to a person under the age of 21, shall be subject to the prescribed conditions, and if the holder of the licence fails, without reasonable excuse, to comply with any of the conditions he is guilty of an offence.

(2) It is an offence for a person knowingly to cause or permit another person who is under the age of 21 to drive a large goods vehicle of any class or a passenger-carrying vehicle of any class in contravention of the prescribed conditions to which that other person's licence is subject.]   **[313]**

NOTES
    Commencement: 1 April 1991.
    See the note to s 110 ante

[115. Revocation or suspension of licences

(1) A large goods vehicle or passenger-carrying vehicle driver's licence—

(a) must be revoked if there come into existence, in relation to its holder, such circumstances relating to his conduct as may be prescribed;

(b) must be revoked or suspended if his conduct is such as to make him unfit to hold such a licence;

and where the licence is suspended under paragraph (b) above it shall during the time of suspension be of no effect.

(2) Where it appears that the conduct of the holder of a licence falls within both paragraph (a) and paragraph (b) of subsection (1) above, proceedings shall be taken or continued under paragraph (a) and not under paragraph (b) and accordingly the power to suspend the licence, rather than revoke it, shall not be available.

(3) Regulations made for the purposes of [this section or section 117 of this Act]—

(a) may make different provision for large goods vehicles and for passenger-carrying vehicles and for different descriptions of persons; and

(b) shall provide for the determination of the cases in which, under section 117 of this Act, a person whose licence has been revoked is to be disqualified indefinitely or for a period and, if for a period, for the determination of the period.]   [314]

NOTES

Commencement: 1 April 1991.

See the note to s 110 ante.

Sub-s (3): words in square brackets substituted by the Road Traffic Act 1991, s 48, Sch 4, para 64.

[116. Revocation or suspension of licences: referral of matters of conduct to traffic commissioners

(1) Any question arising under section 115(1)(b) of this Act as to whether a person is or is not, by reason of his conduct, fit to hold a large goods vehicle or passenger-carrying vehicle driver's licence, as the case may be, may be referred by the Secretary of State to the traffic commissioner for the area in which the holder of the licence resides.

(2) Where, on any reference under subsection (1) above, the traffic commissioner determines that the holder of the licence is not fit to hold a large goods vehicle or passenger-carrying vehicle driver's licence, as the case may be, he shall also determine whether the conduct of the holder of the licence is such as to require the revocation of his licence or only its suspension; and, if the former, whether the holder of the licence should be disqualified under section 117(2)(a) of this Act (and, if so, for what period) or under section 117(2)(b) of this Act.

(3) A traffic commissioner to whom a reference has been made under subsection (1) above may require the holder of the licence to furnish the commissioner with such information as he may require and may, by notice to the holder, require him to attend before the commissioner at the time and place specified by the commissioner to furnish the information and to answer such questions (if any) relating to the subject matter of the reference as the commissioner may put to him.

(4) If the holder of the licence fails without reasonable excuse to furnish information to or to attend before or answer questions properly put by a commissioner when required to do so under subsection (3) above, the

commissioner may notify the failure to the Secretary of State and, if the commissioner does so, the Secretary of State may, as he thinks fit, revoke the licence or suspend it for such period as he thinks fit.

(5) Except where he has given such a notification as is mentioned in subsection (4) above, the traffic commissioner to whom a reference has been made under subsection (1) above shall notify his determination in the matter to the Secretary of State and the holder of the licence and the decision of the commissioner shall be binding on the Secretary of State.

(6) Where the Secretary of State, without making such a reference, determines to revoke or suspend a person's licence under section 115(1) of this Act he shall notify his determination in the matter to the holder of the licence and, where he suspends it, to the traffic commissioner for the area in which the holder of the licence resides.]   **[315]**

NOTES
> Commencement: 1 April 1991.
> See the note to s 110 ante.

[117. Disqualification on revocation of licence

(1) Where in pursuance of section 115(1)(a) of this Act the Secretary of State revokes a person's large goods vehicle or passenger-carrying vehicle driver's licence, the Secretary of State must, in accordance with the regulations made [in pursuance of section 115(3)], order that person to be disqualified indefinitely or for the period determined in accordance with the regulations.

(2) Where in pursuance of section 115(1)(b) of this Act the Secretary of State revokes a person's large goods vehicle or passenger-carrying vehicle driver's licence, the Secretary of State may—

(a) order the holder to be disqualified indefinitely or for such period as the Secretary of State thinks fit, or

(b) except where the licence is a provisional licence, if it appears to the Secretary of State that, owing to the conduct of the holder of the licence, it is expedient to require him to comply with the prescribed conditions applicable to provisional licences under Part III of this Act until he passes the prescribed test of competence to drive large goods vehicles or passenger-carrying vehicles of any class, order him to be disqualified for holding or obtaining a full licence until he passes such a test.

[(2A) Regulations may make provision for the application of subsections (1) and (2) above, in such circumstances and with such modifications as may be prescribed, where a person's large goods vehicle or passenger-carrying vehicle driver's licence is treated as revoked by virtue of section 37(1) of the Road Traffic Offenders Act 1988 (effect of disqualification by order or a court).]

(3) If, while the holder of a large goods vehicle or passenger-carrying vehicle driver's licence is disqualified under subsection (1) above, the circumstances prescribed for the purposes of section 115(1)(a) of this Act cease to exist in his case, the Secretary of State must, on an application made to him for the purpose, remove the disqualification.

(4) Where the holder of a large goods vehicle or passenger-carrying vehicle driver's licence is disqualified under subsection (2)(a) above, the Secretary of

State may, in such circumstances as may be prescribed, remove the disqualification.

(5) Where the holder of a full licence is disqualified under subsection (2)(b) above, the Secretary of State must not afterwards grant him a full licence to drive a large goods vehicle or passenger-carrying vehicle of any class unless satisfied that he has since the disqualification passed the prescribed test of competence to drive vehicles of that class, and until he passes that test any full licence obtained by him shall be of no effect.

(6) So long as the disqualification under subsection (1) or (2)(a) above of the holder of a large goods vehicle or passenger-carrying vehicle driver's licence continues in force, a large goods vehicle or passenger-carrying vehicle driver's licence must not be granted to him and any such licence obtained by him shall be of no effect.

(7) In this section "disqualified"—

  (a) in a case of revocation on the ground of the conduct of the holder of the licence as a driver, means disqualified for holding or obtaining a licence under Part III of this Act to drive large goods vehicles of the prescribed classes and passenger-carrying vehicles of the prescribed classes; and

  (b) in a case of revocation of a passenger-carrying vehicle driver's licence on the ground of the conduct of the holder otherwise than as a driver, means disqualified for holding or obtaining a licence under Part III of this Act to drive passenger-carrying vehicles of the prescribed classes.] **[316]**

NOTES
  Commencement: 1 July 1992 (sub-s (2A)); 1 April 1991 (remainder).
  See the note to s 110 ante.
  Sub-s (1): words in square brackets substituted by the Road Traffic Act 1991, s 48, Sch 4, para 65(1), (2).
  Sub-s (2A): inserted by the Road Traffic Act 1991, s 48, Sch 4, para 65(1), (3).
  See the Motor Vehicles (Driving Licences) (Large Goods and Passenger-Carrying Vehicles) Regulations 1990, post.

[118. Revoked or suspended licences: surrender, return and endorsement

(1) Where, in pursuance of section 115 of this Act, the Secretary of State revokes a licence, he must serve notice on the holder of the licence requiring him to deliver the licence [and its counterpart] forthwith to the Secretary of State, and it shall be the duty of the holder of the licence to comply with the requirement.

(2) Where, in pursuance of section 115 of this Act, the Secretary of State suspends a licence, then—

  (a) where he does so without making any reference under section 116 of this Act to a traffic commissioner, the Secretary of State must serve notice on the holder of the licence requiring him to deliver the licence [and its counterpart] forthwith to the traffic commissioner for the area in which the holder of the licence resides;

  (b) where he does so in pursuance of a determination of a traffic commissioner on such a reference, the traffic commissioner must, if the [licence and its counterpart have] not previously been delivered to him, serve notice on the holder of the licence requiring him to deliver [them] forthwith to the commissioner;

and it shall be the duty of the holder of the licence to comply with the requirement.

(3) Any holder of a licence who fails without reasonable excuse to comply with his duty under subsection (1) or (2) above is guilty of an offence.

(4) On the delivery of a licence [and its counterpart] by a person to the Secretary of State in pursuance of subsection (1) above, the Secretary of State must issue to him, on payment of such fee (if any) as may be prescribed, a licence authorising the driving of the classes of vehicles which are unaffected by the revocation.

[(5) On the delivery of a suspended licence and its counterpart to a traffic commissioner, the traffic commissioner must endorse the counterpart of the licence with particulars of the suspension and return the licence and its counterpart to the holder.]   **[317]**

NOTES
Commencement: 1 April 1991.
See the note to s 110 ante.
Sub-ss (1), (4): words in square brackets added with savings by virtue of SI 1990 No 144, reg 2(3), Sch 3, para 2(2); for savings see reg 3 thereof.
Sub-s (2): words in square brackets substituted with savings and other words in square brackets added with savings by virtue of SI 1990 No 144, reg 2(3), Sch 3, para 2(2); for savings see reg 3 thereof.
Sub-s (5): substituted with savings by virtue of SI 1990 No 144, reg 2(3), Sch 3, para 2(2); for savings see reg 3 thereof.

[119. Appeal to magistrates' court or sheriff

(1) A person who, being the holder of, or an applicant for, a large goods vehicle or passenger-carrying vehicle driver's licence, is aggrieved by the Secretary of State's—

    (a) refusal or failure to grant such a licence in pursuance of section 112 or 113(4) of this Act,

    (b) suspension or revocation of such a licence in pursuance of section 115 or 116(4) of this Act, or

    (c) ordering of disqualification under section 117(2) of this Act,

may, after giving to the Secretary of State and any traffic commissioner to whom the matter was referred notice of his intention to do so, appeal to a magistrates' court acting for the petty sessions area in which the holder of or applicant for the licence resides or, in Scotland, to the sheriff within whose jurisdiction he resides.

(2) On any appeal under subsection (1)(a) or (b) above the Secretary of State and, if the matter was referred to a traffic commissioner, the commissioner shall be respondent.

(3) On any appeal under subsection (1) above the court or sheriff may make such order as it or he thinks fit and the order shall be binding on the Secretary of State.]   **[318]**

NOTES
Commencement: 1 April 1991.
See the note to s 110 ante.

[120. Regulations

(1) The Secretary of State may make regulations for any purpose for which regulations may be made under this Part of this Act and for prescribing anything

which may be prescribed under this Part of this Act and generally for the purpose of carrying the provisions of this Part of this Act into effect.

(2) Regulations under this section may in particular require applicants for tests of competence under Part III of this Act to drive large goods vehicles or passenger-carrying vehicles or for large goods vehicle or passenger-carrying vehicle driver's licences (whether full or provisional) to have such qualifications, experience and knowledge as may be prescribed and, in particular, where they are to be authorised to drive large goods vehicles or passenger-carrying vehicles of any class at an age below the normal minimum age for driving vehicles of that class, to fulfil such requirements with respect to participation in an approved training scheme for drivers as may be prescribed.

(3) In subsection (2) above—

"approved training scheme for drivers" means a training scheme for drivers (as defined in section 101(5) of this Act) approved for the time being by the Secretary of State for the purposes of regulations under that section; and

"normal minimum age for driving", in relation to the driving of vehicles of any class, means the age which is in force under section 101 of this Act (but apart from any approved training scheme for drivers) in relation to that class of vehicle.

(4) Regulations under this section may make different provision as respects different classes of vehicles or as respects the same class of vehicles in different circumstances.

(5) Regulations under this section may provide that a person who contravenes or fails to comply with any specified provision of the regulations is guilty of an offence.

(6) The Secretary of State may by regulations provide that this Part of this Act shall not apply to large goods vehicles or passenger-carrying vehicles of such classes as may be prescribed either generally or in such circumstances as may be prescribed.] **[319]**

NOTES
Commencement: 1 April 1991.
See the note to s 110 ante.

[121. Interpretation

(1) In this Part of this Act—

"conduct" means—

(*a*) in relation to an applicant for or the holder of a large goods vehicle driver's licence, his conduct as a driver of a motor vehicle, and

(*b*) in relation to an applicant for or the holder of a passenger-carrying vehicle driver's licence, his conduct both as a driver of a motor vehicle and in any other respect relevant to his holding a passenger-carrying vehicle driver's licence,

including, in either case, such conduct in Northern Ireland;

["counterpart", in relation to a licence to drive under Part III of this Act, has the same meaning as in that Part;]

"full licence" means a large goods vehicle or passenger-carrying vehicle driver's licence other than a provisional licence;

"large goods vehicle" means—

(*a*) an articulated goods vehicle, or

(*b*) a motor vehicle (not being an articulated goods vehicle) which is constructed or adapted to carry or to haul goods and the permissible maximum weight of which exceeds 7.5 tonnes;

"passenger-carrying vehicle" means—

(*a*) a large passenger-carrying vehicle, that is to say, a vehicle used for carrying passengers which is constructed or adapted to carry more than 16 passengers, or

(*b*) a small passenger-carrying vehicle, that is to say, a vehicle used for carrying passengers for hire or reward which is constructed or adapted to carry more than 8 but not more than 16 passengers;

"notice" means notice in writing and "notify" shall be construed accordingly;

"prescribed" means, unless the context requires otherwise, prescribed by regulations under section 120 of this Act;

"provisional licence" means a licence granted by virtue of section 97(2) of this Act;

and "articulated goods vehicle" and "permissible maximum weight" have the same meanings as in Part III of this Act.]　　　　　　　　　**[320]**

NOTES

Commencement: 1 April 1991.

See the note to s 110 ante.

Sub-s (1): words in square brackets added with savings by virtue of SI 1990 No 144, reg 2(3), Sch 3, para 2(3); for savings see reg 3 thereof.

[122. Provisions as to Northern Ireland licences

(1) In this section "Northern Ireland driving licence" has the same meaning as in Part III of this Act.

(2) The Secretary of State may exercise as respects Great Britain the like power of revoking or suspending any Northern Ireland driving licence and of making an order under section 117(2) of this Act as is conferred on him in relation to a large goods vehicle or passenger-carrying vehicle driver's licence by sections 115(1)(b) and 117(2) of this Act, and the provisions of sections 115(1), 116, 117 and (with the exception of subsection (3)) 118 shall have effect accordingly subject to the modification that references to the traffic commissioner for the area in which the holder of the licence resides shall be construed as references to the prescribed traffic commissioner.

(3) Where a revoked Northern Ireland driving licence [and its counterpart are] surrendered to the Secretary of State in pursuance of section 118 of this Act, the Secretary of State shall send [them] to the licensing authority in Northern Ireland together with particulars of the revocation.

(4) A holder of a Northern Ireland driving licence who is aggrieved by the revocation or suspension of the licence or the ordering of disqualification by virtue of subsection (2) above shall have the like right of appeal as is conferred by section 119 of this Act except that an appeal brought by virtue of this subsection shall, if the appellant is not resident in Great Britain, lie to a prescribed magistrates' court or a prescribed sheriff.]　　　　　　　　　**[321]**

NOTES
Commencement: 1 April 1991.
See the note to s 110 ante.
Sub-s (3): words in square brackets substituted with savings by virtue of SI 1990 No 144, reg 2(3), Sch 3, para 2(4); for savings see reg 3 thereof.

PART V

DRIVING INSTRUCTION

Instructors to be registered or licensed

123. Driving instruction for payment to be given only by registered or licensed persons

(1) No paid instruction in the driving of a motor car shall be given unless—

(a) the name of the person giving the instruction is in the register of approved instructors established in pursuance of section 23 of the Road Traffic Act 1962 (in this Part of this Act referred to as "the register"), or

(b) the person giving the instruction is the holder of a current licence granted under this Part of this Act authorising him to give such instruction.

(2) No paid instruction in the driving of a motor car shall be given unless there is fixed to and exhibited on that motor car in such manner as may be prescribed by regulations either—

(a) a certificate in such form as may be so prescribed that the name of the person giving the instruction is in the register, or

(b) a current licence granted under this Part of this Act authorising the person giving the instruction to give such instruction.

(3) For the purposes of subsections (1) and (2) above, instruction is paid instruction if payment of money or money's worth is, or is to be, made by or in respect of the person to whom the instruction is given for the giving of the instruction and for the purposes of this subsection instruction which is given—

(a) free of charge to a person who is not the holder of a current licence to drive a motor vehicle granted under Part III of this Act (other than a provisional licence),

(b) by, or in pursuance of arrangements made by, a person carrying on business in the supply of motor cars, and

(c) in connection with the supply of a motor car in the course of that business,

shall be deemed to be given for payment of money by the person to whom the instruction is given.

(4) Where instruction is given in contravention of subsection (1) above—

(a) the person by whom it is given, and

(b) if that person is employed by another to give that instruction, that other, as well as that person,

is guilty of an offence.

(5) In proceedings against a person for an offence under subsection (4) above it shall be a defence for him to prove that he did not know, and had no reasonable cause to believe, that his name or, as the case may be, that of the person employed by him, was not in the register at the material time.

(6) If instruction is given in contravention of subsection (2) above, the person by whom it is given is guilty of an offence.

(7) Any reference in this Part of this Act to a current licence is a reference to a licence which has not expired and has not been cancelled, revoked or suspended.

(8) In this section "provisional licence" has the same meaning as in Part III of this Act. **[322]**

NOTES
Commencement: 15 May 1989.
This section derived from the Road Traffic Act 1972, s 126, and the Road Traffic (Driving Instruction) Act 1984, s 1(1)-(3).

124. Exemption of police instructors from prohibition imposed by section 123

(1) Section 123(1) and (2) of this Act does not apply to the giving of instruction by a police instructor in pursuance of arrangements made by a chief officer of police or, under the authority of a chief officer of police, in pursuance of arrangements made by a local authority.

(2) In this section—

"police instructor" means a person who is—
  (a) a member of a police force whose duties consist of or include, or have consisted of or included, the giving of instruction in the driving of motor cars to persons being members of a police force, or
  (b) a civilian employed by a police authority for the purpose of giving such instruction to such persons, and

"local authority" means—
  (a) in relation to England and Wales, the council of a county, metropolitan district, or London borough or the Common Council of the City of London,
  (b) in relation to Scotland, a regional or islands council.

(3) In the application of subsection (2) above to the metropolitan police, the reference to a civilian employed by a police authority is to be read as a reference to a civilian employed under the Commissioner of Police of the Metropolis or the Receiver for the Metropolitan Police District. **[323]**

NOTES
Commencement: 15 May 1989.
This section derived from the Road Traffic Act 1972, s 127, the Local Government Act 1970, Sch 30, the Road Traffic (Driving Instruction) Act 1984, s 1(4), and the Local Government Act 1985, Sch 5, para 2(6).

Registration

125. The register of approved instructors

(1) The compilation and maintenance of the register shall continue by virtue of this Act.

(2) An application for the entry of a person's name in the register must be made, in manner determined by the Secretary of State, accompanied by particulars so determined, to the officer of the Secretary of State (in this Part of this Act referred to as "the Registrar") by whom the register is, on behalf of the Secretary of State, compiled and maintained.

(3) Where a person duly applies for the entry of his name in the register, the Registrar must, on payment of such fee, if any, as may be prescribed by regulations, enter his name in the register if he satisfies the Registrar that the following conditions are fulfilled in his case—

    (a) he has passed such examination of ability to give instruction in the driving of motor cars (consisting of a written examination, a practical test of ability and fitness to drive and a practical test of ability and fitness to instruct) as may be so prescribed,

    (b) he is the holder of a current licence of one of the following kinds—

        (i) a licence to drive a motor car granted under Part III of this Act (not being a provisional licence), and

        (ii) a licence to drive a motor car (not being a licence corresponding to a provisional licence) granted under the law in force in Northern Ireland,

    (c) during the period of six years ending with the day on which the application is made, the periods (if any) for which he did not hold one or more of the following licences, that is—

        (i) a current licence of one of the kinds mentioned in paragraph (b) above, and

        (ii) a current foreign licence, that is to say, a document issued under the law of a country outside the United Kingdom authorising the holder to drive a motor car in that country,

    did not amount in aggregate to more than two years,

    (d) he has not, during any part of the period of four years ending with the day on which the application is made, been disqualified under section 34 or 36 of the Road Traffic Offenders Act 1988 for holding or obtaining a licence to drive a motor vehicle granted under Part III of this Act, and

    (e) apart from fulfilment of the preceding conditions, he is a fit and proper person to have his name entered in the register.

(4) At any time when a person who held a current licence of one of the following kinds, that is—

    (a) a licence to drive a motor car granted under Part III of this Act, being a provisional licence, and

    (b) a licence to drive a motor car (being a licence corresponding to a provisional licence) granted under the law in force in Northern Ireland,

had passed the test of competence to drive a motor car prescribed by virtue of section 89(3) of this Act or the corresponding law in force in Northern Ireland, he shall be regarded for the purposes of paragraph (c) of subsection (3) above as having held a current licence of one of the kinds mentioned in paragraph (b) of that subsection.

(5) The entry of a person's name in the register shall be subject to the condition that, so long as his name is in the register, he will, if at any time required to do so by the Registrar, undergo the test prescribed by regulations of continued ability and fitness to give instruction in the driving of motor cars.

(6) Regulations may provide that persons of such class as may be specified in the regulations shall be exempt from the condition mentioned in subsection (3)(a) above as regards such part of the examination mentioned in that paragraph as may be so specified.

(7) If the Secretary of State is satisfied that satisfactory provision is made by the law of Northern Ireland for the establishment of a register containing the names of persons qualified under that law to give instruction in the driving of motor cars, a person who satisfies the Registrar—

(a) that his name is in the register established under that law, and

(b) that he is resident in Great Britain,

shall be exempt from the condition mentioned in subsection (3)(a) above.

(8) The Registrar must, on making a decision on an application under subsection (2) above, give notice in writing of the decision to the applicant which, in the case of a decision to refuse the application, must state the grounds for the refusal.

(9) In this section "provisional licence" has the same meaning as in Part III of this Act.   **[324]**

NOTES
    Commencement: 15 May 1989.
    This section derived from the Road Traffic Act 1972, s 128(1)-(5), the Motor Cars (Driving Instruction) Regulations 1977, SI 1977 No 1043, reg 4(a), and the Road Traffic (Driving Instruction) Act 1984, s 2(1), (2).

126. Duration of registration

(1) Unless previously removed under the following provisions of this Part of this Act, the name of a person shall, subject to subsection (2) below, be removed from the register at the end of the period of four years beginning with—

(a) the first day of the month next after that in which the entry of his name was made, or

(b) where his name has been retained in the register under section 127 of this Act, the day with which the last further period for which his name was so retained began.

(2) If an application for the retention of his name in the register is made under section 127 of this Act before the end of that period, the name must not be removed except in pursuance of a decision of the Registrar having effect under that section.

(3) Where a person whose name has been removed from the register under subsection (1) above applies under section 125(2) of this Act for his name to be entered again in the register, he shall be required again to pass the examination mentioned in section 125(3)(a) of this Act unless the application is made before the end of the period of one year beginning with the end of the period of four years mentioned in subsection (1) above.   **[325]**

NOTES
    Commencement: 15 May 1989.
    This section derived from the Road Traffic Act 1972, ss 128(6), (7), 129(5).

127. Extension of duration of registration

(1) A person may, before the time when his name is required under section 126(1) of this Act to be removed from the register, apply to the Registrar, in manner determined by the Secretary of State, accompanied by particulars so determined, for the retention of his name in the register for a further period of four years.

(2) On an application under subsection (1) above, he shall be entitled, on

payment of such fee, if any, as may be prescribed by regulations, to have his name retained in the register for that further period, if he satisfies the Registrar that the following conditions are fulfilled in his case.

(3) Those conditions are—

(a) that he has not refused to undergo any such test as is mentioned in section 125(5) of this Act which he has been required to undergo during the period of four years ending with the time when his name is required under section 126(1) of this Act to be removed from the register,

(b) that his ability and fitness to give instruction in the driving of motor cars continue, having regard to any such test or tests which he has undergone during that period, to be of a satisfactory standard,

(c) that he is the holder of a current licence of one of the kinds mentioned in section 125(3)(b) of this Act,

(d) that he has not during any part of that period been disqualified under section 34 or 36 of the Road Traffic Offenders Act 1988 for holding or obtaining a licence to drive a motor vehicle granted under Part III of this Act, and

(e) that, apart from fulfilment of the preceding conditions, he continues to be a fit and proper person to have his name entered in the register.

(4) The retention of a person's name under this section shall be subject to the condition mentioned in section 125(5) of this Act.

(5) Before refusing an application under subsection (1) above the Registrar must give to the applicant written notice stating that he is considering the refusal of the application and giving particulars of the grounds on which he is considering it.

(6) Where the Registrar gives notice under subsection (5) above—

(a) the applicant may, within the period of twenty-eight days beginning with the day on which the notice is given, make representations with respect to the proposal refusal,

(b) the Registrar must not decide to refuse the application until after the expiration of that period, and

(c) before deciding whether or not to refuse the application, the Registrar must take into consideration any such representations made by the applicant within that period.

(7) On deciding to grant or refuse an application the Registrar must give notice in writing of the decision to the person concerned.

(8) A decision to refuse an application shall take effect—

(a) where no appeal under the following provisions of this Part of this Act is brought against the decision within the time limited for the appeal, on the expiration of that time,

(b) where such an appeal is brought and is withdrawn or struck out for want of prosecution, on the withdrawal or striking out of the appeal,

(c) where such an appeal is brought and not withdrawn or struck out for want of prosecution, if and when the appeal is dismissed, and not otherwise. **[326]**

NOTES
Commencement: 15 May 1989.
This section derived from the Road Traffic Act 1972, s 129(1)-(5), and the Motor Cars (Driving Instruction) Regulations 1977, SI 1977 No 1043, reg 4(b).

128. Removal of names from register

(1) The Registrar may remove the name of a person from the register if he is satisfied that—

    (a) in a case where his name has not been retained in the register under section 127 of this Act, at any time since the entry of his name was made, and

    (b) in a case where his name has been so retained under that section, at any time since it was last retained,

any of the following conditions was fulfilled in his case.

(2) Those conditions are—

    (a) that he held neither of the kinds of current licence mentioned in section 125(3)(b) of this Act,

    (b) that he was disqualified under section 34 or 36 of the Road Traffic Offenders Act 1988 for holding or obtaining a licence to drive a motor vehicle under Part III of this Act,

    (c) that he refused to undergo a test such as is mentioned in section 125(5) of this Act,

    (d) that he failed to pass such a test,

    (e) that he ceased, apart from fulfilment of any of the preceding conditions, to be a fit and proper person to have his name included in the register.

(3) The Registrar may remove the name of a person from the register if the entry of his name in the register, or the retention of his name in the register, was made by mistake or procured by fraud.

(4) Before removing the name of a person from the register under this section, the Registrar must give him written notice stating that he is considering the removal and giving particulars of the grounds on which he is considering it.

(5) Where the Registrar gives notice to a person under subsection (4) above—

    (a) that person may, within the period of twenty-eight days beginning with the day on which the notice is given, make representations with respect to the proposed removal,

    (b) the Registrar must not decide to remove his name from the register until after the expiration of that period, and

    (c) before deciding whether or not to remove his name from the register, the Registrar must take into consideration any such representations made by him within that period,

(6) The Registrar must, on making a decision to remove a name from the register, give notice in writing of the decision to the person concerned.

(7) A decision to remove a name from the register shall take effect—

    (a) where no appeal under the following provisions of this Part of this Act is brought against the decision within the time limited for the appeal, on the expiration of that time,

    (b) where such an appeal is brought and is withdrawn or struck out for want of prosecution, on the withdrawal or striking out of the appeal,

    (c) where such an appeal is brought and not withdrawn or struck out for want of prosecution, if and when the appeal is dismissed, and not otherwise.

[(8) Where a person whose name has been removed from the register under this section applies under subsection (2) of section 125 of this Act for his name to be entered again in the register and either—

    (a) the application is made after the end of the period of one year beginning with the date on which his name was removed; or

    (b) his name was removed on the grounds that he has failed to pass such a test as is mentioned in subsection (5) of that section,

the Registrar shall not regard the condition specified in paragraph (a) of subsection (3) of that section as fulfilled unless he is satisfied that that person has again passed the examination mentioned in that paragraph since the date on which his name was removed from the register.] **[327]**

NOTES
    Commencement: 15 May 1989.
    This section derived from the Road Traffic Act 1972, s 130.
    Sub-s (8): added by the Motor Cars (Driving Instruction) (Amendment) Regulations 1991, SI 1991 No 1129.

Licences

129. Licences for giving instruction so as to obtain practical experience

(1) A licence under this section is granted for the purpose of enabling a person to acquire practical experience in giving instruction in driving motor cars with a view to undergoing such part of the examination referred to in section 125(3)(a) of this Act as consists of a practical test of ability and fitness to instruct.

    (2) Subject to subsection (3) below, where—

    (a) a person applies to the Registrar in manner determined by the Secretary of State, accompanied by particulars so determined, and

    (b) the Registrar is satisfied—

        (i) that the applicant has passed the other parts of that examination, and

        (ii) that the conditions set out in section 125(3)(b) to (e) of this Act are fulfilled in his case,

the Registrar must, on payment of such fee, if any, as may be prescribed by regulations, grant to the applicant a licence to give paid instruction (within the meaning of section 123(1) and (2) of this Act) in the driving of a motor car.

    (3) The Registrar may refuse to grant a licence under this section to an applicant to whom such a licence has previously been issued.

    (4) The Registrar must, on making a decision on an application under subsection (2) above, give notice in writing of the decision to the applicant which, in the case of a decision to refuse the application, must state the grounds of the refusal.

    (5) A licence under this section shall be in such form, shall be in force for such period, and shall be granted subject to such conditions, as may be prescribed by regulations.

    (6) Notwithstanding any provision of regulations made by virtue of subsection (5) above prescribing the period for which a licence is to be in force, where a person applies for a new licence in substitution for a licence held by him and current at the date of the application, the previous licence shall not expire—

(a) until the commencement of the new licence, or

(b) if the Registrar decides to refuse the application, until the time limited for an appeal under the following provisions of this Part of this Act against the decision has expired and, if such an appeal is duly brought, it is finally disposed of.

(7) Before deciding to refuse an application for a new licence in substitution for a licence current at the date of the application, the Registrar must give to the applicant written notice stating that he is considering the refusal and giving particulars of the grounds on which he is considering it.

(8) Where the Registrar gives notice under subsection (7) above—

(a) the applicant may, within the period of fourteen days beginning with the day on which the notice is given, make representations with respect to the proposed refusal, and

(b) the Registrar must not decide to refuse the application until after the expiration of that period, and

(c) before deciding whether or not to refuse the application, the Registrar must take into consideration any such representations made within that period. **[328]**

NOTES

Commencement: 15 May 1989.

This section derived from the Road Traffic Act 1972, s 131(1)-(6), the Motor Cars (Driving Instruction) Regulations 1977, SI 1977 No 1043, reg 4(c), and the Road Traffic (Driving Instruction) Act 1984, s 3(1), (2).

130. Revocation of licences

(1) The registrar may revoke a licence granted under section 129 of this Act—

(a) if the person to whom the licence was granted fails to comply with any of the conditions subject to which it was granted, or

(b) if the Registrar is satisfied that, at any time since the licence was granted, any of the conditions mentioned in subsection (2) below was fulfilled in his case, or

(c) if the licence was granted by mistake or procured by fraud.

(2) The conditions referred to in subsection (1)(b) above are—

(a) that he held neither of the kinds of current licence mentioned in section 125(3)(b) of this Act, or

(b) that he was disqualified under section 34 or 36 of the Road Traffic Offenders Act 1988 for holding or obtaining a licence to drive a motor vehicle under Part III of this Act, or

(c) that he ceased, apart from fulfilment of either of the preceding conditions, to be a fit and proper person to have his name in the register.

(3) Before revoking a licence granted to a person under this section the Registrar must give him written notice stating that he is considering the revocation and giving particulars of the grounds on which he is considering it.

(4) Where the Registrar gives notice to a person under subsection (3) above—

(a) that person may, within the period of fourteen days beginning with the day on which the notice is given, make representation with respect to the proposed revocation, and

(b) the Registrar must not decide to revoke the licence until after the expiration of that period, and

(c) before deciding whether or not to revoke the licence, the Registrar must take into consideration any such representations made within that period.

(5) The Registrar must, on making a decision to revoke a licence granted under this section, give notice in writing of the decision to the person concerned.

(6) A decision to revoke a licence granted under this section shall take effect—

(a) where no appeal under the following provisions of this Part of this Act is brought against the decision within the time limited for the appeal, on the expiration of that time,

(b) where such an appeal is brought and is withdrawn or struck out for want of prosecution, on the withdrawal or striking out of the appeal,

(c) where such an appeal is brought and not withdrawn or struck out for want of prosecution, if and when the appeal is dismissed, and not otherwise. **[329]**

NOTES
Commencement: 15 May 1989.
This section derived from the Road Traffic Act 1972, s 131(7), (8).

Appeals

131. Appeals

(1) A person who is aggrieved by a decision of the Registrar—

(a) to refuse an application for the entry of his name in the register, or

(b) to refuse an application for the retention of his name in the register, or

(c) to remove his name from the register,

may by notice in writing appeal to the Secretary of State within the period of twenty-eight days beginning with the day on which notice of the decision was given in accordance with this Part of this Act.

(2) A person who is aggrieved by a decision of the Registrar—

(a) to refuse an application for the grant of a licence under this Part of this Act, or

(b) to revoke such a licence,

may by notice in writing appeal to the Secretary of State within the period of fourteen days beginning with the day on which notice of the decision was given in accordance with this Part of this Act.

(3) On the appeal the Secretary of State may make such order—

(a) for the grant or refusal of the application or,

(b) for the removal or the retention of the name in the register, or the revocation or continuation of the licence,

(as the case may be) as he thinks fit.

(4) An order for such refusal, removal or revocation may direct that an application by the appellant—

(a) for the grant of a licence under this Part of this Act, or

(b) for his name to be entered in the register,

shall not be entertained before the expiration of such period, not exceeding four years beginning with the day on which the order is made, as may be specified in the order.

(5) Schedule 3 to this Act has effect in relation to an appeal under this section. **[330]**

NOTES
Commencement: 15 May 1989.
This section derived from the Road Traffic Act 1972, s 132.

Examinations and tests

132. Examinations and tests of ability to give driving instruction

(1) Regulations may make provision with respect to—

  (a) the nature of examinations of the ability of persons to give instruction in the driving of motor cars and tests of continued ability and fitness to give such instruction, and
  (b) evidence of the results of such tests and examinations,

and generally with respect to such tests and examinations.

(2) In particular, but without prejudice to the generality of subsection (1) above, the regulations may make provision—

  (a) for requiring a person submitting himself to any part of such an examination which consists of a practical test, or to such a test of continued ability and fitness, to provide a vehicle for the purposes of the test, being a vehicle in respect of which such conditions as may be specified in regulations are complied with,
  (b) for requiring a person applying to submit himself for any part of such an examination to pay to the Registrar such fee as may be specified in the regulations in relation to that part, and
  (c) for requiring a person who desires to submit himself for any part of such an examination to supply the Registrar with such particulars as the Secretary of State may determine. **[331]**

NOTES
Commencement: 15 May 1989.
This section derived from the Road Traffic Act 1972, s 133(1), and the Road Traffic (Driving Instruction) Act 1984, s 4(1).

133. Review of examinations

(1) On the application of a person who has submitted himself for any part of an examination of ability to give instruction in the driving of motor cars—

  (a) the magistrates' court acting for the petty sessions area in which he resides, or
  (b) in Scotland, the sheriff within whose jurisdiction he resides,

may determine whether that part of the examination was properly conducted in accordance with regulations.

(2) If it appears to the court or sheriff that that part of the examination was not so conducted, the court or sheriff may order that any fee payable by the applicant in respect of that part shall not be paid or, if it has been paid, shall be repaid.

(3) No appeal shall lie under section 131 of this Act in respect of any matter in respect of which an application may be made to a magistrates' court or a sheriff under subsection (1) above. **[332]**

NOTES
Commencement: 15 May 1989.
This section derived from the Road Traffic Act 1972, s 133(2), (3), and the Road Traffic (Driving Instruction) Act 1984, s 4(2).

General and supplemental

134. Power to alter conditions for entry or retention in, and removal from, register and for grant or revocation of licences

Regulations may—

    (a) alter or add to the conditions as to which the Registrar is required by this Part of this Act to be satisfied for the entry of a name in the register, the retention of a name in the register, the removal of a name from the register, the grant of a licence and the revocation of a licence, or omit any of those conditions,

    (b) alter the period at the expiration of which a person's name which is entered or retained in the register after the coming into force of the regulation must, unless retained or further retained, be removed from the register. **[333]**

NOTES
Commencement: 15 May 1989.
This section derived from the Road Traffic Act 1972, s 134.

135. Power to prescribe form of certificate of registration, etc

(1) Regulations may prescribe all or any of the following—

    (a) a form of certificate for issue to persons whose names are in the register as evidence of their names' being in the register,

    (b) a form of badge for use by such persons, and

    (c) an official title for such use.

(2) If a person whose name is not in the register—

    (a) takes or uses a title prescribed under this section, or

    (b) wears or displays a badge or certificate so prescribed, or

    (c) takes or uses any name, title, addition or description implying that his name is in the register,

he is guilty of an offence unless he proves that he did not know, and had no reasonable cause to believe, that his name was not in the register at the material time.

(3) If a person carrying on business in the provision of instruction in the driving of motor vehicles—

    (a) uses a title or description so prescribed in relation to any person employed by him whose name is not in the register, or

    (b) issues any advertisement or invitation calculated to mislead with respect to the extent to which persons whose names are in the register are employed by him, he is guilty of an offence unless he proves that he did not know, and had no reasonable cause to believe, that the name or names in question were not in the register at the material time.   **[334]**

NOTES
Commencement: 15 May 1989.
This section derived from the Road Traffic Act 1972, s 135.

136. Surrender of certificates and licences

Where—

    (a) the name of a person to whom a certificate prescribed under section 135 of this Act has been issued is removed from the register in pursuance of this Part of this Act, or

    (b) a licence granted under this Part of this Act to a person expires or is revoked,

that person must, if so required by the Registrar by notice in writing, surrender the certificate or licence, as the case may be, to the Registrar within the period of fourteen days beginning with that on which the notice is given and, if he fails to do so, he is guilty of an offence.   **[335]**

NOTES
Commencement: 15 May 1989.
This section derived from the Road Traffic Act 1972, s 136.

137. Production of certificates and licences to constables and authorised persons

(1) A person to whom a certificate prescribed under section 135 of this Act is issued, or to whom a licence under this Part of this Act is granted, must, on being so required by a constable or any person authorised in writing by the Secretary of State in that behalf, produce the certificate or licence for examination.

    (2) Where—

    (a) the name of a person is removed from the register, or

    (b) a licence granted under this Part of this Act to a person expires or is revoked,

then, if that person fails to satisfy an obligation imposed on him by section 136 of this Act, a constable or a person authorised in writing by the Secretary of State in that behalf may require him to produce any such certificate issued to him or the licence, and upon its being produced may seize it and deliver it to the Registrar.

    (3) A person who is required under subsection (1) or (2) above to produce a document and fails to do so is, subject to subsection (4) below, guilty of an offence.

    (4) In proceedings against any person for an offence under subsection (3) above, it shall be a defence for him to show that—

    (a) within seven days beginning with the day following that on which the production of the document was so required, it was produced—

        (i) where the requirement was made by a constable, at a police station specified at the time the production was required by the person required to produce the document,

        (ii) where the requirement was made by a person other than a constable, at a place specified at that time by that person, or

(b) the document was produced at that police station or, as the case may be, place as soon as was reasonably practicable, or

(c) it was not reasonably practicable for it to be produced at that police station or, as the case may be, place before the day on which the proceedings were commenced,

and for the purposes of this subsection the laying of the information or, in Scotland, the service of the complaint on the accused shall be treated as the commencement of the proceedings.   **[336]**

NOTES

Commencement: 15 May 1989.

This section derived from the Road Traffic Act 1972, s 137, and the Road Traffic (Production of Documents) Act 1985, s 1(1), (3).

138. Offences by corporations

Where a body corporate is guilty of an offence under this Part of this Act and the offence is proved to have been committed with the consent or connivance of, or to be attributable to neglect on the part of, a director, manager, secretary or other similar officer of the body corporate, or a person who was purporting to act in any such capacity, he, as well as the body corporate, is guilty of that offence and liable to be proceeded against and punished accordingly.   **[337]**

NOTES

Commencement: 15 May 1989.

This section derived from the Road Traffic Act 1972, s 139.

139. Service of notices

(1) A notice authorised or required to be given by this Part of this Act to a person may be given by delivering it to him, or by leaving it at his proper address, or by sending it to him by post.

(2) For the purposes of this section and of section 7 of the Interpretation Act 1978 in its application to this section, the proper address of a person shall be, in the case of a person whose name is included in the register, his address on the register, and in any other case, his usual or last known address.   **[338]**

NOTES

Commencement: 15 May 1989.

This section derived from the Road Traffic Act 1972, s 140, and the Interpretation Act 1978, s 17(2).

140. Receipts

Any sums received on account of fees payable by virtue of any provision of this Part of this Act shall be paid into the Consolidated Fund.   **[339]**

NOTES

Commencement: 15 May 1989.

This section derived from the Road Traffic Act 1972, s 141(2).

141. Regulations

The Secretary of State may make regulations for any purpose for which provision is by this Part of this Act authorised to be made by regulations, and in this Part of this Act "regulations" means regulations made under this section.   **[340]**

NOTES
Commencement: 15 May 1989.
This section derived from the Road Traffic Act 1972, s 142.
See the Motor Cars (Driving Instruction) Regulations 1989, SI 1989 No 2057, as amended.

142. Index to Part V

The expressions listed in the left-hand column below are respectively defined or (as the case may be) fall to be construed in accordance with the provisions of this Part of this Act listed in the right-hand column in relation to those expressions.

Expression	*Relevant provision*
Current licence	Section 123(7)
The register	Section 123
The Registrar	Section 125(2)
Regulations	Section 141

[341]

NOTE
Commencement: 15 May 1989.

PART VI

THIRD-PARTY LIABILITIES

Compulsory insurance or security against third-party risks

143. Users of motor vehicles to be insured or secured against third-party risks

(1) Subject to the provisions of this Part of this Act—

    (a) a person must not use a motor vehicle on a road unless there is in force in relation to the use of the vehicle by that person such a policy of insurance or such a security in respect of third party risks as complies with the requirements of this Part of this Act, and

    (b) a person must not cause or permit any other person to use a motor vehicle on a road unless there is in force in relation to the use of the vehicle by that other person such a policy of insurance or such a security in respect of third party risks as complies with the requirements of this Part of this Act.

(2) If a person acts in contravention of subsection (1) above he is guilty of an offence.

(3) A person charged with using a motor vehicle in contravention of this section shall not be convicted if he proves—

    (a) that the vehicle did not belong to him and was not in his possession under a contract of hiring or of loan,

    (b) that he was using the vehicle in the course of his employment, and

    (c) that he neither knew nor had reason to believe that there was not in force in relation to the vehicle such a policy of insurance or security as is mentioned in subsection (1) above.

(4) This Part of this Act does not apply to invalid carriages.   **[342]**

NOTES
Commencement: 15 May 1989.

This section derived from the Road Traffic Act 1972, s 143.

144. Exceptions from requirement of third party insurance or security

(1) Section 143 of this Act does not apply to a vehicle owned by a person who has deposited and keeps deposited with the Accountant General of the Supreme Court the sum of [£500,000], at a time when the vehicle is being driven under the owner's control.

[(1A) The Secretary of State may by order made by statutory instrument substitute a greater sum for the sum for the time being specified in subsection (1) above.

(1B) No order shall be made under subsection (1A) above unless a draft of it has been laid before and approved by resolution of each House of Parliament.]

(2) Section 143 does not apply—

(a) to a vehicle owned—

(i) by the council of a county or county district in England and Wales, the Common Council of the City of London, the council of a London borough, the Inner London Education Authority, or a joint authority (other than a police authority) established by Part IV of the Local Government Act 1985,

(ii) by a regional, islands or district council in Scotland, or

(iii) by a joint board or committee in England or Wales, or joint committee in Scotland, which is so constituted as to include among its members representatives of any such council, at a time when the vehicle is being driven under the owner's control,

(b) to a vehicle owned by a police authority or the Receiver for the Metropolitan Police district, at a time when it is being driven under the owner's control, or to a vehicle at a time when it is being driven for police purposes by or under the direction of a constable, or by a person employed by a police authority, or employed by the Receiver, or

(c) to a vehicle at a time when it is being driven on a journey to or from any place undertaken for salvage purposes pursuant to Part IX of the Merchant Shipping Act 1894,

(d) to the use of a vehicle for the purpose of its being provided in pursuance of a direction under section 166(2)(b) of the Army Act 1955 or under the corresponding provision of the Air Force Act 1955,

[(da) to a vehicle owned by a health service body, as defined in section 60(7) of the National Health Service and Community Care Act 1990, at a time when the vehicle is being driven under the owner's control,

(db) to an ambulance owned by a National Health Service trust established under Part I of the National Health Service and Community Care Act 1990 or the National Health Service (Scotland) Act 1978, at a time when a vehicle is being driven under the owner's control,]

(e) to a vehicle which is made available by the Secretary of State to any person, body or local authority in pursuance of section 23 or 26 of the National Health Service Act 1977 at a time when it is being used in accordance with the terms on which it is so made available,

(f) to a vehicle which is made available by the Secretary of State to any local authority, education authority or voluntary organisation in

Scotland in pursuance of section 15 or 16 of the National Health Service (Scotland) Act 1978 at a time when it is being used in accordance with the terms on which it is so made available.   **[343]**

NOTES

Commencement: 1 July 1992 (sub-ss (1A), (1B)); 15 May 1989 (remainder).

This section derived from the Road Traffic Act 1972, s 144, the Local Government Act 1972, Sch 30, the National Health Service (Vehicles) Order 1974, SI 1974 No 168, the National Health Service (Vehicles) (Scotland) Order 1974, SI 1974 No 1491, the Interpretation Act 1978, s 17(2), the London Regional Transport Act 1984, Sch 6, para 10, and the Local Government Act 1985, Sch 14, para 49, Sch 17.

Sub-s (1): figure in square brackets substituted by the Road Traffic Act 1991, s 20(1), (2).

Sub-ss (1A), (1B): inserted by Road Traffic Act 1991, s 20(1), (3).

Sub-s (2): paras (*da*), (*db*) added by the National Health Service and Community Care Act 1990, s 60, Sch 8, Part I, para 4.

145. Requirements in respect of policies of insurance

(1) In order to comply with the requirements of this Part of this Act, a policy of insurance must satisfy the following conditions.

(2) The policy must be issued by an authorised insurer.

(3) Subject to subsection (4) below, the policy—

(a) must insure such person, persons or classes of persons as may be specified in the policy in respect of any liability which may be incurred by him or them in respect of the death of or bodily injury to any person or damage to property caused by, or arising out of, the use of the vehicle on a road in Great Britain, and

(b) must insure him or them in respect of any liability which may be incurred by him or them in respect of the use of the vehicle and of any trailer, whether or not coupled, in the territory other than Great Britain and Gibraltar of each of the member States of the Communities according to the law on compulsory insurance against civil liability in respect of the use of vehicles of the State where the liability may be incurred, and

(c) must also insure him or them in respect of any liability which may be incurred by him or them under the provisions of this Part of this Act relating to payment for emergency treatment.

(4) The policy shall not, by virtue of subsection (3)(a) above, be required—

(a) to cover liability in respect of the death, arising out of and in the course of his employment, of a person in the employment of a person insured by the policy or of bodily injury sustained by such a person arising out of and in the course of his employment, or

(b) to provide insurance of more than £250,000 in respect of all such liabilities as may be insured in respect of damage to property caused by, or arising out of, any one accident involving the vehicle, or

(c) to cover liability in respect of damage to the vehicle, or

(d) to cover liability in respect of damage to goods carried for hire or reward in or on the vehicle or in or on any trailer (whether or not coupled) drawn by the vehicle, or

(e) to cover any liability of a person in respect of damage to property in his custody or under his control, or

(f) to cover any contractual liability.

(5) In this Part of this Act "authorised insurer" means a person or body of persons carrying on insurance business within Group 2 in Part II of Schedule 2

to the Insurance Companies Act 1982 and being a member of the Motor Insurers' Bureau (a company limited by guarantee and incorporated under the Companies Act 1929 on 14th June 1946).

(6) If any person or body of persons ceases to be a member of the Motor Insurers' Bureau, that person or body shall not by virtue of that cease to be treated as an authorised insurer for the purposes of this Part of this Act—

    (a) in relation to any policy issued by the insurer before ceasing to be such a member, or

    (b) in relation to any obligation (whether arising before or after the insurer ceased to be such a member) which the insurer may be called upon to meet under or in consequence of any such policy or under section 157 of this Act by virtue of making a payment in pursuance of such an obligation.   **[344]**

NOTES

Commencement: 15 May 1989.

This section derived from the Road Traffic Act 1972, s 145, the Motor Vehicles (Compulsory Insurance) (No 2) Regulations 1973, SI 1973 No 2143, reg 3, the Road Traffic Act 1974, s 20(1), (3), the Insurance Companies Act 1981, Sch 4, para 22, the Insurance Companies Act 1982, Sch 5, para 12, and the Motor Vehicles (Compulsory Insurance) Regulations 1987, SI 1987 No 2171, reg 2.

146. Requirements in respect of securities

(1) In order to comply with the requirements of this Part of this Act, a security must satisfy the following conditions.

(2) The security must be given either by an authorised insurer or by some body of persons which carries on in the United Kingdom the business of giving securities of a like kind and has deposited and keeps deposited with the Accountant General of the Supreme Court the sum of £15,000 in respect of that business.

(3) Subject to subsection (4) below, the security must consist of an undertaking by the giver of the security to make good, subject to any conditions specified in it, any failure by the owner of the vehicle or such other persons or classes of persons as may be specified in the security duly to discharge any liability which may be incurred by him or them, being a liability required under section 145 of this Act to be covered by a policy of insurance.

(4) In the case of liabilities arising out of the use of a motor vehicle on a road in Great Britain the amount secured need not exceed—

    (a) in the case of an undertaking relating to the use of public service vehicles (within the meaning of the Public Passenger Vehicles Act 1981), £25,000,

    (b) in any other case, £5,000.   **[345]**

NOTES

Commencement: 15 May 1989.

This section derived from the Road Traffic Act 1972, s 146, and the Motor Vehicles (Compulsory Insurance) (No 2) Regulations 1973, SI 1973 No 2143.

147. Issue and surrender of certificates of insurance and of security

(1) A policy of insurance shall be of no effect for the purposes of this Part of this Act unless and until there is delivered by the insurer to the person by whom the policy is effected a certificate (in this Part of this Act referred to as a "certificate of insurance") in the prescribed form and containing such particulars

of any conditions subject to which the policy is issued and of any other matters as may be prescribed.

(2) A security shall be of no effect for the purposes of this Part of this Act unless and until there is delivered by the person giving the security to the person to whom it is given a certificate (in this Part of this Act referred to as a "certificate of security") in the prescribed form and containing such particulars of any conditions subject to which the security is issued and of any other matters as may be prescribed.

(3) Different forms and different particulars may be prescribed for the purposes of subsection (1) or (2) above in relation to different cases or circumstances.

(4) Where a certificate has been delivered under this section and the policy or security to which it relates is cancelled by mutual consent or by virtue of any provision in the policy or security, the person to whom the certificate was delivered must, within seven days from the taking effect of the cancellation—

    (a) surrender the certificate to the person by whom the policy was issued or the security was given, or

    (b) if the certificate has been lost or destroyed, make a statutory declaration to that effect.

(5) A person who fails to comply with subsection (4) above is guilty of an offence. **[346]**

NOTES
    Commencement: 15 May 1989.
    This section derived from the Road Traffic Act 1972, s 147.

148. Avoidance of certain exceptions to policies or securities

(1) Where a certificate of insurance or certificate of security has been delivered under section 147 of this Act to the person by whom a policy has been effected or to whom a security has been given, so much of the policy or security as purports to restrict—

    (a) the insurance of the persons insured by the policy, or

    (b) the operation of the security,

(as the case may be) by reference to any of the matters mentioned in subsection (2) below shall, as respects such liabilities as are required to be covered by a policy under section 145 of this Act, be of no effect.

(2) Those matters are—

    (a) the age or physical or mental condition of persons driving the vehicle,

    (b) the condition of the vehicle,

    (c) the number of persons that the vehicle carries,

    (d) the weight or physical characteristics of the goods that the vehicle carries,

    (e) the time at which or the areas within which the vehicle is used,

    (f) the horsepower or cylinder capacity or value of the vehicle,

    (g) the carrying on the vehicle of any particular apparatus, or

    (h) the carrying on the vehicle of any particular means of identification other than any means of identification required to be carried by or under the Vehicles (Excise) Act 1971.

(3) Nothing in subsection (1) above requires an insurer or the giver of a

security to pay any sum in respect of the liability of any person otherwise than in or towards the discharge of that liability.

(4) Any sum paid by an insurer or the giver of a security in or towards the discharge of any liability of any person which is covered by the policy or security by virtue only of subsection (1) above is recoverable by the insurer or giver of the security from that person.

(5) A condition in a policy or security issued or given for the purposes of this Part of this Act providing—

    (a) that no liability shall arise under the policy or security, or
    (b) that any liability so arising shall cease,

in the event of some specified thing being done or omitted to be done after the happening of the event giving rise to a claim under the policy or security, shall be of no effect in connection with such liabilities as are required to be covered by a policy under section 145 of this Act.

(6) Nothing in subsection (5) above shall be taken to render void any provision in a policy or security requiring the person insured or secured to pay to the insurer or the giver of the security any sums which the latter may have become liable to pay under the policy or security and which have been applied to the satisfaction of the claims of third parties.

(7) Notwithstanding anything in any enactment, a person issuing a policy of insurance under section 145 of this Act shall be liable to indemnify the persons or classes of persons specified in the policy in respect of any liability which the policy purports to cover in the case of those persons or classes of persons.   [347]

NOTES
    Commencement: 15 May 1989.
    This section derived from the Road Traffic Act 1972, s 148(1), (2), (4).

149. Avoidance of certain agreements as to liability towards passengers

(1) This section applies where a person uses a motor vehicle in circumstances such that under section 143 of this Act there is required to be in force in relation to his use of it such a policy of insurance or such a security in respect of third-party risks as complies with the requirements of this Part of this Act.

(2) If any other person is carried in or upon the vehicle while the user is so using it, any antecedent agreement or understanding between them (whether intended to be legally binding or not) shall be of no effect so far as it purports or might be held—

    (a) to negative or restrict any such liability of the user in respect of persons carried in or upon the vehicle as is required by section 145 of this Act to be covered by a policy of insurance, or
    (b) to impose any conditions with respect to the enforcement of any such liability of the user.

(3) The fact that a person so carried has willingly accepted as his the risk of negligence on the part of the user shall not be treated as negativing any such liability of the user.

(4) For the purposes of this section—

(a) references to a person being carried in or upon a vehicle include references to a person entering or getting on to, or alighting from, the vehicle, and

(b) the reference to an antecedent agreement is to one made at any time before the liability arose. **[348]**

NOTES
Commencement: 15 May 1989.
This section derived from the Road Traffic Act 1972, s 148(3).

150. Insurance or security in respect of private use of vehicle to cover use under car-sharing arrangements

(1) To the extent that a policy or security issued or given for the purposes of this Part of this Act—

(a) restricts the insurance of the persons insured by the policy or the operation of the security (as the case may be) to use of the vehicle for specified purposes (for example, social, domestic and pleasure purposes) of a non-commercial character, or

(b) excludes from that insurance or the operation of the security (as the case may be)—

(i) use of the vehicle for hire or reward, or

(ii) business or commercial use of the vehicle, or

(iii) use of the vehicle for specified purposes of a business or commercial character,

then, for the purposes of that policy or security so far as it relates to such liabilities as are required to be covered by a policy under section 145 of this Act, the use of a vehicle on a journey in the course of which one or more passengers are carried at separate fares shall, if the conditions specified in subsection (2) below are satisfied, be treated as falling within that restriction or as not falling within that exclusion (as the case may be).

(2) The conditions referred to in subsection (1) above are—

(a) the vehicle is not adapted to carry more than eight passengers and is not a motor cycle,

(b) the fare or aggregate of the fares paid in respect of the journey does not exceed the amount of the running costs of the vehicle for the journey (which for the purposes of this paragraph shall be taken to include an appropriate amount in respect of depreciation and general wear), and

(c) the arrangements for the payment of fares by the passenger or passengers carried at separate fares were made before the journey began.

(3) Subsections (1) and (2) above apply however the restrictions or exclusions described in subsection (1) are framed or worded.

(4) In subsections (1) and (2) above "fare" and "separate fares" have the same meaning as in section 1(4) of the Public Passenger Vehicles Act 1981. **[349]**

NOTES
Commencement: 15 May 1989.
This section derived from the Road Traffic Act 1972, s 148(5)-(7), the Interpretation Act 1978, s 17, and the Transport Act 1980, s 61.

151. Duty of insurers or persons giving security to satisfy judgment against persons insured or secured against third-party risks

(1) This section applies where, after a certificate of insurance or certificate of security has been delivered under section 147 of this Act to the person by whom a policy has been effected or to whom a security has been given, a judgment to which this subsection applies is obtained.

(2) Subsection (1) above applies to judgments relating to a liability with respect to any matter where liability with respect to that matter is required to be covered by a policy of insurance under section 145 of this Act and either—

(a) it is a liability covered by the terms of the policy or security to which the certificate relates, and the judgment is obtained against any person who is insured by the policy or whose liability is covered by the security, as the case may be, or

(b) it is a liability, other than an excluded liability, which would be so covered if the policy insured all persons or, as the case may be, the security covered the liability of all persons, and the judgment is obtained against any person other than one who is insured by the policy or, as the case may be, whose liability is covered by the security.

(3) In deciding for the purposes of subsection (2) above whether a liability is or would be covered by the terms of a policy or security, so much of the policy or security as purports to restrict, as the case may be, the insurance of the persons insured by the policy or the operation of the security by reference to the holding by the driver of the vehicle of a licence authorising him to drive it shall be treated as of no effect.

(4) In subsection (2)(b) above "excluded liability" means a liability in respect of the death of, or bodily injury to, or damage to the property of any person who, at the time of the use which gave rise to the liability, was allowing himself to be carried in or upon the vehicle and knew or had reason to believe that the vehicle had been stolen or unlawfully taken, not being a person who—

(a) did not know and had no reason to believe that the vehicle had been stolen or unlawfully taken until after the commencement of his journey, and

(b) could not reasonably have been expected to have alighted from the vehicle.

In this subsection the reference to a person being carried in or upon a vehicle includes a reference to a person entering or getting on to, or alighting from, the vehicle.

(5) Notwithstanding that the insurer may be entitled to avoid or cancel, or may have avoided or cancelled, the policy or security, he must, subject to the provisions of this section, pay to the persons entitled to the benefit of the judgment—

(a) as regards liability in respect of death or bodily injury, any sum payable under the judgment in respect of the liability, together with any sum which, by virtue of any enactment relating to interest on judgments, is payable in respect of interest on that sum,

(b) as regards liability in respect of damage to property, any sum required to be paid under subsection (6) below, and

(c) any amount payable in respect of costs.

(6) This subsection requires—

(a) where the total of any amount paid, payable or likely to be payable under the policy or security in respect of damage to property caused by, or arising out of, the accident in question does not exceed £250,000, the payment of any sum payable under the judgment in respect of the liability, together with any sum which, by virtue of any enactment relating to interest on judgments, is payable in respect of interest on that sum,

(b) where that total exceeds £250,000, the payment of either—

    (i) such proportion of any sum payable under the judgment in respect of the liability as £250,000 bears to that total, together with the same proportion of any sum which, by virtue of any enactment relating to interest on judgments, is payable in respect of interest on that sum, or

    (ii) the difference between the total of any amounts already paid under the policy or security in respect of such damage and £250,000, together with such proportion of any sum which, by virtue of any enactment relating to interest on judgments is payable in respect of interest on any sum payable under the judgment in respect of the liability as the difference bears to that sum,

whichever is the less, unless not less than £250,000 has already been paid under the policy or security in respect of such damage (in which case nothing is payable).

(7) Where an insurer becomes liable under this section to pay an amount in respect of a liability of a person who is insured by a policy or whose liability is covered by a security, he is entitled to recover from that person—

(a) that amount, in a case where he became liable to pay it by virtue only of subsection (3) above, or

(b) in a case where that amount exceeds the amount for which he would, apart from the provisions of this section, be liable under the policy or security in respect of that liability, the excess.

(8) Where an insurer becomes liable under this section to pay an amount in respect of a liability of a person who is not insured by a policy or whose liability is not covered by a security, he is entitled to recover the amount from that person or from any person who—

(a) is insured by the policy, or whose liability is covered by the security, by the terms of which the liability would be covered if the policy insured all persons or, as the case may be, the security covered the liability of all persons, and

(b) caused or permitted the use of the vehicle which gave rise to the liability.

(9) In this section—

(a) "insurer" includes a person giving a security,

(b) . . .

(c) "liability covered by the terms of the policy or security" means a liability which is covered by the policy or security or which would be so covered but for the fact that the insurer is entitled to avoid or cancel, or has avoided or cancelled, the policy or security.

(10) In the application of this section to Scotland, the words "by virtue of any enactment relating to interest on judgments" in subsections (5) and (6) (in each place where they appear) shall be omitted.   **[350]**

NOTES

Commencement: 15 May 1989.

This section derived from the Road Traffic Act 1972, s 149(1)-(1E), (4)-(6), and the Motor Vehicles (Compulsory Insurance) Regulations 1987, SI 1987 No 2171, reg 3.

Sub-s (9): para (6) repealed by the Road Traffic Act 1991, s 83, Sch 8.

152. Exceptions to section 151

(1) No sum is payable by an insurer under section 151 of this Act—

   (a) in respect of any judgment unless, before or within seven days after the commencement of the proceedings in which the judgment was given, the insurer had notice of the bringing of the proceedings, or

   (b) in respect of any judgment so long as execution on the judgment is stayed pending an appeal, or

   (c) in connection with any liability if, before the happening of the event which was the cause of the death or bodily injury or damage to property giving rise to the liability, the policy or security was cancelled by mutual consent or by virtue of any provision contained in it, and also—

   (i) before the happening of that event the certificate was surrendered to the insurer, or the person to whom the certificate was delivered made a statutory declaration stating that the certificate had been lost or destroyed, or

   (ii) after the happening of that event, but before the expiration of a period of fourteen days from the taking effect of the cancellation of the policy or security, the certificate was surrendered to the insurer, or the person to whom it was delivered made a statutory declaration stating that the certificate had been lost or destroyed, or

   (iii) either before or after the happening of that event, but within that period of fourteen days, the insurer has commenced proceedings under this Act in respect of the failure to surrender the certificate.

(2) Subject to subsection (3) below, no sum is payable by an insurer under section 151 of this Act if, in an action commenced before, or within three months after, the commencement of the proceedings in which the judgment was given, he has obtained a declaration—

   (a) that, apart from any provision contained in the policy or security, he is entitled to avoid it on the ground that it was obtained—

   (i) by the non-disclosure of a material fact, or

   (ii) by a representation of fact which was false in some material particular, or

   (b) if he has avoided the policy or security on that ground, that he was entitled so to do apart from any provision contained in it

[and, for the purposes of this section, "material" means of such a nature as to influence the judgment of a present insurer in determining whether he will take the risk and, if so, at what premium and on what conditions.]

(3) An insurer who has obtained such a declaration as is mentioned in subsection (2) above in an action does not by reason of that become entitled to the benefit of that subsection as respects any judgment obtained in proceedings commenced before the commencement of that action unless before, or within seven days after, the commencement of that action he has given notice of it to the person who is the plaintiff (or in Scotland pursuer) in those proceedings

specifying the non-disclosure or false representation on which he proposes to rely.

(4) A person to whom notice of such an action is so given is entitled, if he thinks fit, to be made a party to it.   **[351]**

NOTES

Commencement: 15 May 1989.

This section derived from the Road Traffic Act 1972, s 149(2), (3), (6).

Sub-s (2): words in square brackets added by the Road Traffic Act 1991, s 48, Sch 4, para 66.

153. Bankruptcy, etc, of insured or secured persons not to affect claims by third parties

(1) Where, after a certificate of insurance or certificate of security has been delivered under section 147 of this Act to the person by whom a policy has been effected or to whom a security has been given, any of the events mentioned in subsection (2) below happens, the happening of that event shall, notwithstanding anything in the Third Parties (Rights Against Insurers) Act 1930, not affect any such liability of that person as is required to be covered by a policy of insurance under section 145 of this Act.

(2) In the case of the person by whom the policy was effected or to whom the security was given, the events referred to in subsection (1) above are—

    (a) that he becomes bankrupt or makes a composition or arrangement with his creditors or that his estate is sequestrated or he grants a trust deed for his creditors,

    (b) that he dies and—

        (i) his estate falls to be administered in accordance with an order under section 421 of the Insolvency Act 1986,

        (ii) an award of sequestration of his estate is made, or

        (iii) a judicial factor is appointed to administer his estate under section 11A of the Judicial Factors (Scotland) Act 1889,

    (c) that if that person is a company—

        (i) a winding-up order or an administration order is made with respect to the company,

        (ii) a resolution for a voluntary winding-up is passed with respect to the company,

        (iii) a receiver or manager of the company's business or undertaking is duly appointed, or

        (iv) possession is taken, by or on behalf of the holders of any debentures secured by a floating charge, of any property comprised in or subject to the charge.

(3) Nothing in subsection (1) above affects any rights conferred by the Third Parties (Rights Against Insurers) Act 1930 on the person to whom the liability was incurred, being rights so conferred against the person by whom the policy was issued or the security was given.   **[352]**

NOTES

Commencement: 15 May 1989.

This section derived from the Road Traffic Act 1972, s 150, the Insolvency Act 1985, Sch 8, para 20(a)-(c), the Bankruptcy (Scotland) Act 1985, Sch 7, para 10(a), (b), and the Insolvency Act 1986, Sch 14.

154. Duty to give information as to insurance or security where claim made

(1) A person against whom a claim is made in respect of any such liability as is required to be covered by a policy of insurance under section 145 of this Act must, on demand by or on behalf of the person making the claim—

(a) state whether or not, in respect of that liability—

    (i) he was insured by a policy having effect for the purposes of this Part of this Act or had in force a security having effect for those purposes, or

    (ii) he would have been so insured or would have had in force such a security if the insurer or, as the case may be, the giver of the security had not avoided or cancelled the policy or security, and

(b) if he was or would have been so insured, or had or would have had in force such a security—

    (i) give such particulars with respect to that policy or security as were specified in any certificate of insurance or security delivered in respect of that policy or security, as the case may be, under section 147 of this Act, or

    (ii) where no such certificate was delivered under that section, give the following particulars, that is to say, the registration mark or other identifying particulars of the vehicle concerned, the number or other identifying particulars of the insurance policy issued in respect of the vehicle, the name of the insurer and the period of the insurance cover.

(2) If without reasonable excuse, a person fails to comply with the provisions of subsection (1) above, or wilfully makes a false statement in reply to any such demand as is referred to in that subsection, he is guilty of an offence.   [353]

NOTES
Commencement: 15 May 1989.
This section derived from the Road Traffic Act 1972, s 151, and the Motor Vehicles (Compulsory Insurance) (No 2) Regulations 1973, SI 1973 No 2143, reg 9(1).

155. Deposits

(1) Where a person has deposited a sum with the Accountant General of the Supreme Court under section 144 or 146 of this Act, then, so long as any liabilities incurred by him, being such liabilities as are required to be covered by a policy of insurance under section 145 of this Act, have not been discharged or otherwise provided for, no part of that sum shall be applicable in discharge of any other liabilities incurred by him.

(2) Any regulations made, or having effect as if made, by the Secretary of State or the Board of Trade under section 20 of the Insurance Companies Act 1958 which apply to deposits made by insurers carrying on motor vehicle insurance business shall, with such necessary modifications and adaptations as, after consultation with the Lord Chancellor, may be prescribed, apply to deposits made with the Accountant General under section 144 or 146 of this Act.

(3) Such provision as might be made by the Secretary of State or the Board of Trade under section 20 of the Insurance Companies Act 1958 with respect to deposits under that Act may, after consultation with the Lord Chancellor, be made by regulations with respect to deposits made with the Accountant General under section 144 or 146 of this Act.   [354]

NOTES
  Commencement: 15 May 1989.
  This section derived from the Road Traffic Act 1972, s 152.

156. Power to require evidence of insurance or security on application for vehicle excise licence

Provision may be made by regulations under section 37 of the Vehicles (Excise) Act 1971 for requiring a person applying for a licence under that Act in respect of a motor vehicle to produce such evidence as may be prescribed that either—

  (a) on the date when the licence comes into operation there will be in force the necessary policy of insurance or the necessary security in relation to the use of the vehicle by the applicant or by other persons on his order or with his permission, or

  (b) the vehicle is a vehicle to which section 143 of this Act does not apply at a time when it is being driven under the owner's control.   **[355]**

NOTES
  Commencement: 15 May 1989.
  This section derived from the Road Traffic Act 1972, s 153.

Payments for treatment of traffic casualties

157. Payment for hospital treatment of traffic casualties

(1) Subject to subsection (2) below, where—

  (a) a payment, other than a payment under section 158 of this Act, is made (whether or not with an admission of liability) in respect of the death of, or bodily injury to, any person arising out of the use of a motor vehicle on a road or in a place to which the public have a right of access, and

  (b) the payment is made—

    (i) by an authorised insurer, the payment being made under or in consequence of a policy issued under section 145 of this Act, or

    (ii) by this owner of a vehicle in relation to the use of which a security under this Part of this Act is in force, or

    (iii) by the owner of a vehicle who has made a deposit under this Part of this Act, and

  (c) the person who has so died or been bodily injured has to the knowledge of the insurer or owner, as the case may be, received treatment at a hospital, whether as an in-patient or as an out-patient, in respect of the injury so arising,

the insurer or owner must pay the expenses reasonably incurred by the hospital in affording the treatment, after deducting from the expenses any moneys actually received in payment of a specific charge for the treatment, not being moneys received under any contributory scheme.

(2) The amount to be paid shall not exceed [£2,780.00] for each person treated as an in-patient or [£278.00] for each person as an out-patient.

(3) For the purposes of this section "expenses reasonably incurred" means—

  (a) in relation to a person who receives treatment at a hospital as an in-patient, an amount for each day he is maintained in the hospital representing the average daily cost, for each in-patient, of the maintenance of the hospital and the staff of the hospital and the maintenance and treatment of the in-patients in the hospital, and

(b) in relation to a person who receives treatment at a hospital as an out-patient, reasonable expenses actually incurred. **[356]**

NOTES

Commencement: 15 May 1989.

This section derived from the Road Traffic Act 1972, s 154.

Sub-s (2): figures in square brackets substituted by the Road Traffic Accidents (Payments for Treatment) Order 1992, SI 1992 No 2402, reg 2.

158. Payment for emergency treatment of traffic casualties

(1) Subsection (2) below applies where—

(a) medical or surgical treatment or examination is immediately required as a result of bodily injury (including fatal injury) to a person caused by, or arising out of, the use of a motor vehicle on a road, and

(b) the treatment or examination so required (in this Part of this Act referred to as "emergency treatment") is effected by a legally qualified medical practitioner.

(2) The person who was using the vehicle at the time of the event out of which the bodily injury arose must, on a claim being made in accordance with the provisions of section 159 of this Act, pay to the practitioner (or, where emergency treatment is effected by more than one practitioner, to the practitioner by whom it is first effected)—

(a) a fee of [£20.10] in respect of each person in whose case the emergency treatment is effected by him, and

(b) a sum, in respect of any distance in excess of two miles which he must cover in order—

(i) to proceed from the place from which he is summoned to the place where the emergency treatment is carried out by him, and

(ii) to return to the first mentioned place,

equal to [39] pence for every complete mile and additional part of a mile of that distance.

(3) Where emergency treatment is first effected in a hospital, the provisions of subsections (1) and (2) above with respect to payment of a fee shall, so far as applicable, but subject (as regards the recipient of a payment) to the provisions of section 159 of this Act, have effect with the substitution of references to the hospital for references to a legally qualified medical practitioner.

(4) Liability incurred under this section by the person using a vehicle shall, where the event out of which it arose was caused by the wrongful act of another person, be treated for the purposes of any claim to recover damage by reason of that wrongful act as damage sustained by the person using the vehicle. **[357]**

NOTES

Commencement: 15 May 1989.

This section derived from the Road Traffic Act 1972, s 155.

Sub-s (2): figures in square brackets substituted by the Road Traffic Accidents (Payments for Treatment) Order 1992, SI 1992 No 2402, reg 3.

159. Supplementary provisions as to payments for treatment

(1) A payment falling to be made under section 157 or 158 of this Act in respect of treatment in a hospital must be made—

(a) in England and Wales, in the case of a hospital vested in the Secretary of State for the purposes of the National Health Service Act 1977, to the Area Health Authority, District Health Authority or special health authority responsible for the administration of the hospital or the Secretary of State if no such authority is so responsible,

(b) in Scotland, in the case of a hospital vested in the Secretary of State, to the Secretary of State or on his behalf to any Health Board authorised by him for the purpose, and

(c) in the case of any other hospital, to the hospital.

(2) A claim for a payment under section 158 of this Act may be made at the time when the emergency treatment is effected, by oral request to the person who was using the vehicle, and if not so made must be made by request in writing served on him within seven days from the day on which the emergency treatment was effected.

(3) Any such request in writing—

(a) must be signed by the claimant or, in the case of a hospital, by an executive officer of the Authority (in Scotland, Board) or hospital claiming the payment or by an officer of the Secretary of State,

(b) must state the name and address of the claimant, the circumstances in which the emergency treatment was effected, and that it was first effected by the claimant or, in the case of a hospital, in the hospital, and

(c) may be served by delivering it to the person who was using the vehicle or by sending it in a prepaid registered letter, or the recorded delivery service, addressed to him at his usual or last known address.

(4) A payment made under section 158 of this Act shall operate as a discharge, to the extent of the amount paid, of any liability of the person who was using the vehicle, or of any other person, to pay any sum in respect of the expenses or remuneration of the practitioner or hospital concerned of or for effecting the emergency treatment.

(5) A chief officer of police must, if so requested by a person who alleges that he is entitled to claim a payment under section 158 of this Act, provide that person with any information at the disposal of the chief officer—

(a) as to the identification marks of any motor vehicle which that person alleges to be a vehicle out of the use of which the bodily injury arose, and

(b) as to the identity and address of the person who was using the vehicle at the time of the event out of which it arose.   **[358]**

NOTES

Commencement: 15 May 1989.

This section derived from the Road Traffic Act 1972, s 156; the National Health Service (Scotland) Act 1972, s 64, Sch 6, para 156A; the National Health Service Reorganisation Act 1973, s 57, Sch 4, paras 136, 150; the National Health Act 1977, s 129, Sch 15, para 56; the Health Services Act 1980, Sch 1, Part I, para 21.

General

160. Regulations

(1) The Secretary of State may make regulations for any purpose for which regulations may be made under this Part of this Act and for prescribing anything which may be prescribed under this Part of this Act and generally for the purpose of carrying this Part of this Act into effect.

In this Part of this Act "regulations" means regulations under this section and "prescribed" means prescribed by regulations.

(2) In particular, but without prejudice to the generality of subsection (1) above, the regulations may make provision—

(a) as to forms to be used for the purposes of this Part of this Act,

(b) as to applications for and the issue of certificates of insurance and certificates of security and any other documents which may be prescribed, and as to the keeping of records of documents and the providing of particulars of them or the giving of information with respect to them to the Secretary of State or a chief officer of police,

(c) as to the issue of copies of any such certificates or other documents which are lost or destroyed,

(d) as to the custody, production, cancellation and surrender of any such certificates or other documents, and

(e) for providing that any provisions of this Part of this Act shall, in relation to vehicles brought into Great Britain by persons making only a temporary stay in Great Britain, have effect subject to such modifications and adaptations as may be prescribed. **[359]**

NOTES
Commencement: 15 May 1989.
This section derived from the Road Traffic Act 1972, ss 157, 158(1).
See the Motor Vehicles (Third Party Risks) Regulations 1972, post.

161. Interpretation

(1) In this Part of this Act—

"hospital" means [any health service hospital, within the meaning of the National Health Service Act 1977 or the National Health Service (Scotland) Act 1978 and any other] institution, not being an institution carried on for profit, which provides medical or surgical treatment for in-patients,

"policy of insurance" includes a covering note,

"salvage" means the preservation of a vessel which is wrecked, stranded or in distress, or the lives of persons belonging to, or the cargo or apparel of, such a vessel, and

"under the owner's control" means, in relation to a vehicle, that it is being driven by the owner or by a servant of the owner in the course of his employment or is otherwise subject to the control of the owner.

(2) In any provision of this Part of this Act relating to the surrender, or the loss or destruction, of a certificate of insurance or certificate of security, references to such a certificate—

(a) shall, in relation to policies or securities under which more than one certificate is issued, be construed as references to all certificates, and

(b) shall, where any copy has been issued of any certificate, be construed as including a reference to that copy.

(3) In this Part of this Act, any reference to an accident includes a reference to two or more causally related accidents. **[360]**

NOTES
Commencement: 15 May 1989.
This section derived from the Road Traffic Act 1972, s 158, and the Motor Vehicles (Compulsory Insurance) Regulations 1987, SI 1987 No 2171, reg 4.
Sub-s (1): in definition "hospital" words in square brackets substituted by the National Health Service and Community Care Act 1990, s 66(1), Sch 9, para 35.

162. Index to Part VI

The expressions listed in the left-hand column below are respectively defined or (as the case may be) fall to be construed in accordance with the provisions of this Part of this Act listed in the right-hand column in relation to those expressions.

Expression	Relevant provision
Accident	Section 161(3)
Authorised insurer	Section 145(2)
Certificate of insurance	Sections 147(1) and 161(2)
Certificate of security	Sections 147(2) and 161(2)
Hospital	Section 161(1)
Policy of insurance	Section 161(1)
Prescribed	Section 160(1)
Regulations	Section 160(1)
Salvage	Section 161(1)
Under the owner's control	Section 161(1)

[361]

NOTES
    Commencement: 15 May 1989.

PART VII

MISCELLANEOUS AND GENERAL

Powers of constables and other authorised persons

163. Power of police to stop vehicles

(1) A person driving a [mechanically propelled vehicle] on a road must stop the vehicle on being required to do so by a constable in uniform.

(2) A person riding a cycle on a road must stop the cycle on being required to do so by a constable in uniform.

(3) If a person fails to comply with this section he is guilty of an offence.

[362]

NOTES
    Commencement: 15 May 1989.
    This section derived from the Road Traffic Act 1972, s 159.
    Sub-s (1): words in square brackets substituted by the Road Traffic Act 1991, s 48, Sch 4, para 67.

164. Power of constables to require production of driving licence and in certain cases statement of date of birth

(1) Any of the following persons—

    (a) a person driving a motor vehicle on a road,

    (b) a person whom a constable [or vehicle examiner] has reasonable cause to believe to have been the driver of a motor vehicle at a time when an accident occurred owing to its presence on a road,

    (c) a person whom a constable [or vehicle examiner] has reasonable cause to believe to have committed an offence in relation to the use of a motor vehicle on a road, or

    (d) a person—

      (i) who supervises the holder of a provisional licence while the holder is driving a motor vehicle on a road, or

      (ii) whom a constable [or vehicle examiner] has reasonable cause to believe was supervising the holder of a provisional licence while driving, at a time when an accident occurred owing to the presence of the vehicle on a road or at a time when an offence is suspected of having been committed by the holder of the provisional licence in relation to the use of the vehicle on a road,

must, on being so required by a constable [or vehicle examiner], produce his licence [and its counterpart] for examination, so as to enable the constable [or vehicle examiner] to ascertain the name and address of the holder of the licence, the date of issue, and the authority by which [they were] issued.

(2) [A person required by a constable under subsection (1) above to produce his licence] must in prescribed circumstances, on being so required by the constable, state his date of birth.

(3) If—

    [(*a*) the Secretary of State has—

      (i) revoked a licence under section 93 or 99 of this Act, or

      (ii) revoked or suspended a large goods vehicle driver's licence or a passenger-carrying vehicle driver's licence under section 115 of this Act, and]

    (b) the holder of the licence fails to deliver it [and its counterpart] to the Secretary of State [or the traffic commissioner, as the case may be] in pursuance of [section 93, 99 or 118 (as the case may be)],

a constable [or vehicle examiner] may require him to [produce the licence and its counterpart], and upon [their] being produced may seize [them] and deliver [them] to the Secretary of State.

(4) Where a constable has reasonable cause to believe that the holder of a licence, or any other person, has knowingly made a false statement for the purpose of obtaining the grant of the licence, the constable may require the holder of the licence to produce it [and its counterpart] to him.

[(4A) Where a constable to whom a provisional licence has been produced by a person driving a motor bicycle has reasonable cause to believe that the holder was not driving it as part of the training being provided on a training course for motor cyclists, the constable may require him to produce the prescribed certificate of completion of a training course for motor cyclists.]

(5) Where a person has been required under [section 26 or 27 of the Road Traffic Offenders Act 1988 or section 44 of the Powers of Criminal Courts Act 1973 or section 223A or 436A of the Criminal Procedure (Scotland) Act 1975] to produce a licence [and its counterpart] to the court and fails to do so, a constable may require him to produce [them] and, upon [their] being produced, may seize [them] and deliver [them] to the court.

(6) If a person required under the preceding provisions of this section to produce a licence [and its counterpart] or state his date of birth [or to produce his certificate of completion of a training course for motor cyclists] . . . fails to do so he is, subject to subsections (7) [to (8A)] below, guilty of an offence.

(7) Subsection (6) above does not apply where a person required on any occasion under the preceding provisions of this section to produce a licence [and its counterpart]—

    (a) produces on that occasion a current receipt for the licence [and its counterpart] issued under section 56 of the Road Traffic Offenders Act 1988 and, if required to do so, produces the licence [and its counterpart] in person immediately on [their] return at a police station that was specified on that occasion, or

    (b) within seven days after that occasion produces such a receipt in person at a police station that was specified by him on that occasion and, if required to do so, produces the licence [and its counterpart] in person immediately on [their] return at that police station.

(8) In proceedings against any person for the offence of failing to produce a licence [and its counterpart] it shall be a defence for him to show that—

    (a) within seven days after the production of his licence [and its counterpart] was required he produced [them] in person at a police station that was specified by him at the time [their] production was required, or

    (b) he produced [them] in person there as soon as was reasonably practicable, or

    (c) it was not reasonably practicable for him to produce [them] there before the day on which the proceedings were commenced,

and for the purposes of this subsection the laying of the information or, in Scotland, the service of the complaint on the accused shall be treated as the commencement of the proceedings.

[(8A) Subsection (8) above shall apply in relation to a certificate of completion of a training course for motor cyclists as it applies in relation to a licence.]

(9) Where in accordance with this section a person has stated his date of birth to a constable, the Secretary of State may serve on that person a notice in writing requiring him to provide the Secretary of State—

    (a) with such evidence in that person's possession or obtainable by him as the Secretary of State may specify for the purpose of verifying that date, and

    (b) if his name differs from his name at the time of his birth, with a statement in writing specifying his name at that time,

and a person who knowingly fails to comply with a notice under this subsection is guilty of an offence.

(10) A notice authorised to be served on any person by subsection (9) above may be served on him by delivering it to him or by leaving it at his proper address or by sending it to him by post; and for the purposes of this subsection and section 7 of the Interpretation Act 1978 in its application to this subsection the proper address of any person shall be his latest address as known to the person giving the notice.

(11) In this section "licence" [, "counterpart"] and "provisional licence" [and "training course for motor cyclists" and, in relation to such a course, "the prescribed certificate of completion"] have the same meanings as in Part III of this Act [and "vehicle examiner" means an examiner appointed under section 66A of this Act.]   **[363]**

NOTES

    Commencement: 1 July 1992 (sub-s (8A)); 1 December 1990 (sub-s (4A)); 15 May 1989 (remainder).

    This section derived from the Road Traffic Act 1972, s 161, the Transport Act 1981, s 22, the

Transport Act 1982, s 35(6), and the Road Traffic (Production of Documents) Act 1985, s 1(1), (4), (7).

Sub-s (1): words in first, second, third, fourth and sixth pair of square brackets substituted by the Road Traffic Act 1991, s 48, Sch 4, para 68(1), (2); remaining words in square brackets substituted by SI 1990 No 144, reg 2(1), Sch 1, para 9; for saving see reg 3 thereof.

Sub-s (2): words in square brackets substituted by the Road Traffic Act 1991, s 48, Sch 4, para 68(1), (3).

Sub-s (3): para (a) and second and third words in square brackets in para (b) substituted by the Road Traffic (Driver Licensing and Information Systems) Act 1989, s 7, Sch 3, para 18; first words in square brackets in para (b), and second, third, fourth and fifth words in square brackets after para (b) substituted with savings by SI 1990 No 144, reg 2(1), Sch 1, para 9 (for savings, see reg 3 thereof); remaining words in square brackets inserted by the Road Traffic Act 1991, s 48, Sch 4, para 68(1), (4).

Sub-s (4): words in square brackets added with savings by SI 1990 No 144, reg 2(1), Sch 1, para 9; for savings see reg 3 thereof.

Sub-s (4A): added by the Road Traffic (Driver Licensing and Information Systems) Act 1989, s 7, Sch 3, para 18.

Sub-s (5): first, words in square brackets substituted by the Road Traffic Act 1991, s 48, Sch 4, para 68(1), (5); remaining words in square brackets substituted or inserted with savings by SI 1990 No 144, reg 2(1), Sch 1, para 9; for savings, see reg 3 thereof).

Sub-s (6): first words in square brackets substituted by SI 1990 No 144, reg 2(1), Sch 1, para 9 (for savings, see reg 3 thereof); second words in square brackets substituted by the Road Traffic (Driver Licensing and Information Systems) Act 1989, s 7, Sch 3, para 18; remaining words in square brackets substituted, and words omitted repealed, by the Road Traffic Act 1991, ss 48, 83, Sch 4, para 68(1), (6), Sch 8.

Sub-ss (7), (8): words in square brackets substituted or inserted by SI 1990 No 144, reg 2(1), Sch 1, para 9 (for savings, see reg 3 thereof).

Sub-s (8A): inserted by the Road Traffic Act 1991, s 48, Sch 4, para 68(1), (7).

Sub-s (11): first words in square brackets inserted with savings by SI 1990 No 144, reg 2(1), Sch 1, para 9 (for savings, see reg 3 thereof); second words in square brackets inserted by the Road Traffic (Driver Licensing and Information Systems) Act 1989, s 7, Sch 3, para 18; remaining words in square brackets added by the Road Traffic Act 1991, s 48, Sch 4, para 68(1), (8).

165. Power of constables to obtain names and addresses of drivers and others, and to require production of evidence of insurance or security and test certificates

(1) Any of the following persons—

    (a) a person driving a motor vehicle (other than an invalid carriage) on a road, or

    (b) a person whom a constable [or vehicle examiner] has reasonable cause to believe to have been the driver of a motor vehicle (other than an invalid carriage) at a time when an accident occurred owing to its presence on a road, or

    (c) a person whom a constable [or vehicle examiner] has reasonable cause to believe to have committed an offence in relation to the use on a road of a motor vehicle (other than an invalid carriage),

must, on being so required by a constable [or vehicle examiner], give his name and address and the name and address of the owner of the vehicle and produce the following documents for examination.

(2) Those documents are—

    (a) the relevant certificate of insurance or certificate of security (within the meaning of Part VI of this Act), or such other evidence that the vehicle is not or was not being driven in contravention of section 143 of this Act as may be prescribed by regulations made by the Secretary of State,

    (b) in relation to a vehicle to which section 47 of this Act applies, a test certificate issued in respect of the vehicle as mentioned in subsection (1) of that section, and

    (c) in relation to a goods vehicle the use of which on a road without a plating certificate or goods vehicle test certificate is an offence under section 53(1) or (2) of this Act, any such certificate issued in respect of that vehicle or any trailer drawn by it.

(3) Subject to subsection (4) below, a person who fails to comply with a requirement under subsection (1) above is guilty of an offence.

(4) A person shall not be convicted of an offence under [subsection (3)] above by reason only of failure to produce any certificate or other evidence . . . if in proceedings against him for the offence he shows that—

(a) within seven days after the date on which the production of the certificate or other evidence was required it was produced at a police station that was specified by him at the time when its production was required, or
(b) it was produced there as soon as was reasonably practicable, or
(c) it was not reasonably practicable for it to be produced there before the day on which the proceedings were commenced,

and for the purposes of this subsection the laying of the information or, in Scotland, the service of the complaint on the accused shall be treated as the commencement of the proceedings.

(5) A person—

(a) who supervises the holder of a provisional licence granted under Part III of this Act while the holder is driving on a road a motor vehicle (other than an invalid carriage), or
(b) whom a constable [or vehicle examiner] has reasonable cause to believe was supervising the holder of such a licence while driving, at a time when an accident occurred owing to the presence of the vehicle on a road or at a time when an offence is suspected of having been committed by the holder of the provisional licence in relation to the use of the vehicle on a road,

must, on being so required by a constable [or vehicle examiner], give his name and address and the name and address of the owner of the vehicle.

(6) A person who fails to comply with a requirement under subsection (5) above is guilty of an offence.

(7) In this section "owner", in relation to a vehicle which is the subject of a hiring agreement, includes each party to the agreement [and "vehicle examiner" means an examiner appointed under section 66A of this Act.] **[364]**

NOTES
Commencement: 15 May 1989.
This section derived from the Road Traffic Act 1972, s 162, the Road Traffic Act 1974, s 10(6), Sch 7, and the Road Traffic (Production of Documents) Act 1985, s 1(1), (5).
Sub-ss (1), (5), (7): words in square brackets inserted or added by the Road Traffic Act 1991, s 48, Sch 4, para 69.
Sub-s (4): words in square brackets substituted by the Road Traffic (Driver Licensing and Information Systems) Act 1989, s 7, Sch 3, para 19; words omitted repealed by the Road Traffic Act 1991, s 83, Sch 8.

[166. Powers of certain officers as respects goods vehicles and passenger-carrying vehicles

[A person authorised for the purpose by a traffic commissioner appointed under the Public Passenger Vehicles Act 1981,] may, on production if so required of his authority, exercise in the case of goods vehicles or passenger-carrying vehicles of any prescribed class all such powers as are, under section 164(1) or (3) or 165 of this Act, exercisable by a constable.]   **[365]**

NOTES

Commencement: 1 April 1991.

Substituted by the Road Traffic (Driver Licensing and Information Systems) Act 1989, s 7, Sch 3, para 20.

Words in square brackets substituted by the Road Traffic Act 1991, s 48, Sch 4, para 70.

167. Power of arrest in Scotland for reckless or careless driving or cycling

A constable—

    (a) may arrest without warrant the driver of a motor vehicle who within his view commits an offence under section 2 or 3 of this Act unless the driver either gives his name and address or produces for examination his licence to drive a motor vehicle granted under Part III of this Act [and the counterpart of the licence], and

    (b) may arrest without warrant the rider of a cycle who within his view commits an offence under section 28 or 29 of this Act unless the rider gives his name and address.

This section extends only to Scotland.   **[366]**

NOTES

Commencement: 15 May 1989.

This section derived from the Road Traffic Act 1972, s 164(2), and the Police and Criminal Evidence Act 1984, Sch 7, Part I.

Words in square brackets added with savings by SI 1990 No 144, reg 2(1), Sch 1, para 10; for savings see reg 3 thereof.

Duty to give name and address

168. Failure to give, or giving false, name and address in case of reckless or careless or inconsiderate driving or cycling

Any of the following persons—

    (a) the driver of a [mechanically propelled vehicle] who is alleged to have committed an offence under section 2 or 3 of this Act, or

    (b) the rider of a cycle who is alleged to have committed an offence under section 28 or 29 of this Act,

who refuses, on being so required by any person having reasonable ground for so requiring, to give his name or address, or gives a false name or address, is guilty of an offence.   **[367]**

NOTES

Commencement: 15 May 1989.

This section derived from the Road Traffic Act 1972, s 164(1).

Words in square brackets substituted by the Road Traffic Act 1991, s 48, Sch 4, para 71.

169. Pedestrian contravening constable's direction to stop to give name and address

A constable may require a person committing an offence under section 37 of this Act to give his name and address, and if that person fails to do so he is guilty of an offence.   **[368]**

NOTES

Commencement: 15 May 1989.

This section derived from the Road Traffic Act 1972, s 165.

Duties in case of accident

170. Duty of driver to stop, report accident and give information or documents

(1) This section applies in a case where, owing to the presence of a [mechanically propelled vehicle] on a road, an accident occurs by which—

(a) personal injury is caused to a person other than the driver of that [mechanically propelled vehicle], or

(b) damage is caused—

(i) to a vehicle other than that [mechanically propelled vehicle] or a trailer drawn by that [mechanically propelled vehicle], or

(ii) to an animal other than an animal in or on that [mechanically propelled vehicle] or a trailer drawn by that [mechanically propelled vehicle], or

(iii) to any other property constructed on, fixed to, growing in or otherwise forming part of the land on which the road in question is situated or land adjacent to such land.

(2) The driver of the [mechanically propelled vehicle] must stop and, if required to do so by any person having reasonable grounds for so requiring, give his name and address and also the name and address of the owner and the identification marks of the vehicle.

(3) If for any reason the driver of the [mechanically propelled vehicle] does not give his name and address under subsection (2) above, he must report the accident.

(4) A person who fails to comply with subsection (2) or (3) above is guilty of an offence.

(5) If, in a case where this section applies by virtue of subsection (1)(a) above, the driver of [a motor vehicle] does not at the time of the accident produce such a certificate of insurance or security, or other evidence, as is mentioned in section 165(2)(a) of this Act—

(a) to a constable, or

(b) to some person who, having reasonable grounds for so doing, has required him to produce it,

the driver must report the accident and produce such a certificate or other evidence.

This subsection does not apply to the driver of an invalid carriage.

(6) To comply with a duty under this section to report an accident or to produce such a certificate of insurance or security, or other evidence, as is mentioned in section 165(2)(a) of this Act, the driver—

(a) must do so at a police station or to a constable, and

(b) must do so as soon as is reasonably practicable and, in any case, within twenty-four hours of the occurrence of the accident.

(7) A person who fails to comply with a duty under subsection (5) above is guilty of an offence, but he shall not be convicted by reason only of a failure to produce a certificate or other evidence if, within [seven] days after the occurrence

of the accident, the certificate or other evidence is produced at a police station that was specified by him at the time when the accident was reported.

(8) In this section "animal" means horse, cattle, ass, mule, sheep, pig, goat or dog. **[369]**

NOTES
Commencement: 15 May 1989.
This section derived from the Road Traffic Act 1972, ss 25, 166, and the Road Traffic Act 1974, Sch 6, paras 12, 20.
Sub-ss (1)–(3), (5), (7): words in square brackets substituted by the Road Traffic Act 1991, s 48, Sch 4, para 72.

Other duties to give information or documents

171. Duty of owner of motor vehicle to give information for verifying compliance with requirement of compulsory insurance or security

(1) For the purpose of determining whether a motor vehicle was or was not being driven in contravention of section 143 of this Act on any occasion when the driver was required under section 165(1) or 170 of this Act to produce such a certificate of insurance or security, or other evidence, as is mentioned in section 165(2)(a) of this Act, the owner of the vehicle must give such information as he may be required, by or on behalf of a chief officer of police, to give.

(2) A person who fails to comply with the requirement of subsection (1) above is guilty of an offence.

(3) In this section "owner", in relation to a vehicle which is the subject of a hiring agreement, includes each party to the agreement. **[370]**

NOTES
Commencement: 15 May 1989.
This section derived from the Road Traffic Act 1972, s 167.

[172. Duty to give information as to identity of driver etc in certain circumstances

(1) This section applies—
(a) to any offence under the preceding provisions of this Act except—
(i) an offence under Part V, or
(ii) an offence under section 13, 16, 51(2), 61(4), 67(9), 68(4), 96 or 120,
and to an offence under section 178 of this Act,
(b) to any offence under sections 25, 26 or 27 of the Road Traffic Offenders Act 1988,
(c) to any offence against any other enactment relating to the use of vehicles on roads, except an offence under paragraph 8 of Schedule 1 to the Road Traffic (Driver Licensing and Information Systems) Act 1989, and
(d) to manslaughter, or in Scotland culpable homicide, by the driver of a motor vehicle.

(2) Where the driver of a vehicle is alleged to be guilty of an offence to which this section applies—
(a) the person keeping the vehicle shall give such information as to the identity of the driver as he may be required to give by or on behalf of a chief officer of police, and

(b) any other person shall if required as stated above give any information which it is in his power to give and may lead to identification of the driver.

(3) Subject to the following provisions, a person who fails to comply with a requirement under subsection (2) above shall be guilty of an offence.

(4) A person shall not be guilty of an offence by virtue of paragraph (a) of subsection (2) above if he shows that he did not know and could not with reasonable diligence have ascertained who the driver of the vehicle was.

(5) Where a body corporate is guilty of an offence under this section and the offence is proved to have been committed with the consent or connivance of, or to be attributable to neglect on the part of, a director, manager, secretary or other similar officer of the body corporate, or a person who was purporting to act in any such capacity, he, as well as the body corporate, is guilty of that offence and liable to be proceeded against and punished accordingly.

(6) Where the alleged offender is a body corporate, or in Scotland a partnership or an unincorporated association, or the proceedings are brought against him by virtue of subsection (5) above or subsection (11) below, subsection (4) above shall not apply unless, in addition to the matters there mentioned, the alleged offender shows that no record was kept of the persons who drove the vehicle and that the failure to keep a record was reasonable.

(7) A requirement under subsection (2) may be made by written notice served by post; and where it is so made—

(a) it shall have effect as a requirement to give the information within the period of 28 days beginning with the day on which the notice is served, and
(b) the person on whom the notice is served shall not be guilty of an offence under this section if he shows either that he gave the information as soon as reasonably practicable after the end of that period or that it has not been reasonably practicable for him to give it.

(8) Where the person on whom a notice under subsection (7) above is to be served is a body corporate, the notice is duly served if it is served on the secretary or clerk of that body.

(9) For the purposes of section 7 of the Interpretation Act 1978 as it applies for the purposes of this section the proper address of any person in relation to the service on him of a notice under subsection (7) above is—

(a) in the case of the secretary or clerk of a body corporate, that of the registered or principal office of that body or (if the body corporate is the registered keeper of the vehicle concerned) the registered address, and
(b) in any other case, his last known address at the time of service.

(10) In this section—

"registered address", in relation to the registered keeper of a vehicle, means the address recorded in the record kept under the Vehicles (Excise) Act 1971 with respect to that vehicle as being that person's address, and "registered keeper", in relation to a vehicle, means the person in whose name the vehicle is registered under that Act;

and references to the driver of a vehicle include references to the rider of a cycle.

(11) Where, in Scotland, an offence under this section is committed by a partnership or by an unincorporated association other than a partnership and is proved to have been committed with the consent or connivance or in consequence of the negligence of a partner in the partnership or, as the case may be, a person concerned in the management or control of the association, he (as well as the partnership or association) shall be guilty of the offence.] **[371]**

NOTES
Commencement: 1 July 1992.
Substituted by the Road Traffic Act 1991, s 21.

Forgery, false statements, etc

173. Forgery of documents, etc

(1) A person who, with intent to deceive—

(a) forges, alters or uses a document or other thing to which this section applies, or
(b) lends to, or allows to be used by, any other person a document or other thing to which this section applies, or
(c) makes or has in his possession any document or other thing so closely resembling a document or other thing to which this section applies as to be calculated to deceive,

is guilty of an offence.

(2) This section applies to the following documents and other things—

(a) any licence under any Part of this Act [or, in the case of a licence to drive, any counterpart of such a licence],
(b) any test certificate, goods vehicle test certificate, plating certificate, certificate of conformity or Minister's approval certificate (within the meaning of Part II of this Act),
(c) any certificate required as a condition of any exception prescribed under section 14 of this Act,
[(cc) any seal required by regulations made under section 41 of this Act with respect to speed limiters.]
[cc) any notice removing a prohibition under [section 69 or 70] of this Act;]
(d) [any plate containing particulars required to be marked on a vehicle by regulations under section 41 of this Act] or containing other particulars required to be marked on a goods vehicle by sections 54 to 58 of this Act or regulations under those sections,
[(dd) any document evidencing the appointment of an examiner under section 66A of this Act,]
(e) any records required to be kept by virtue of section 74 of this Act,
(f) any document which, in pursuance of section 89(3) ... of this Act, is issued as evidence of the result of a test of competence to drive,
[(ff) any certificate provided for by regulations under section 97(3A) of this Act relating to the completion of a training course for motor cyclists,]

(g) any badge or certificate prescribed by regulations made by virtue of section 135 of this Act,

(h) any certificate of insurance or certificate of security under Part VI of this Act,

(j) any document produced as evidence of insurance in pursuance of Regulation 6 of the Motor Vehicles (Compulsory Insurance) (No. 2) Regulations 1973,

(k) any document issued under regulations made by the Secretary of State in pursuance of his power under section 165(2)(a) of this Act to prescribe evidence which may be produced in lieu of a certificate of insurance or a certificate of security, . . .

(l) any international road haulage permit, [and

(m) a certificate of the kind referred to in section 34B(1) of the Road Traffic Offenders Act 1988.]

(3) In the application of this section to England and Wales "forges" means makes a false document or other thing in order that it may be used as genuine.

[(4) In this section "counterpart", in relation to a licence to drive under Part III of this Act, has the same meaning as in that Part.]   [372]

NOTES

Commencement: 1 April 1990 (sub-s (4)); 15 May 1989 (remainder).

This section derived from the Road Traffic Act 1972, s 169, the Motor Vehicles (Compulsory Insurance) (No 2) Regulations 1973, SI 1973 No 2143, reg 9, the Road Traffic Act 1974, Sch 2, para 14, the International Road Haulage Permits Act 1975, s 3(2), the Forgery and Counterfeiting Act 1981, s 12, and the Transport Act 1981, s 27(2).

Sub-s (2): in para (a) words in square brackets added with savings by SI 1990 No 144, reg 2(1), Sch 1, para 11(a), for savings see reg 3 thereof; first para (cc) and paras (dd), (ff), (m) inserted or added, words in para (d) substituted, and words omitted from para (k) repealed, by the Road Traffic Act 1991, ss 48, 83, Sch 4, para 73, Sch 8; second para (cc) prospectively inserted by the Transport Act 1982, s 23(3) (as amended by the Road Traffic (Consequential Provisions) Act 1988, s 4, Sch 2, Part I); words omitted from para (f) repealed by the Road Traffic (Driver Licensing and Information Systems) Act 1989, ss 7, 16, Sch 3, para 22, Sch 6.

Sub-s (4): added with savings by SI 1990 No 144, reg 2(1), Sch 1, para 11(b); for savings see reg 3 thereof.

174. False statements and withholding material information

(1) A person who knowingly makes a false statement for the purpose—

(a) of obtaining the grant of a licence under any Part of this Act to himself or any other person, or

(b) of preventing the grant of any such licence, or

(c) of procuring the imposition of a condition or limitation in relation to any such licence, or

(d) of securing the entry or retention of the name of any person in the register of approved instructors maintained under Part V of this Act, or

(e) of obtaining the grant of an international road haulage permit to himself or any other person,

is guilty of an offence.

(2) A person who, in supplying information or producing documents for the purposes either of sections 53 to 60 and 63 of this Act or of regulations made under sections 49 to 51, 61, 62 and 66(3) of this Act—

(a) makes a statement which he knows to be false in a material particular or recklessly makes a statement which is false in a material particular, or

(b) produces, provides, sends or otherwise makes use of a document which he knows to be false in a material particular or recklessly produces, provides, sends or otherwise makes use of a document which is false in a material particular,

is guilty of an offence.

(3) A person who—

(a) knowingly produces false evidence for the purposes of regulations under section 66(1) of this Act, or

(b) knowingly makes a false statement in a declaration required to be made by the regulations,

is guilty of an offence.

(4) A person who—

(a) wilfully makes a false entry in any record required to be made or kept by regulations under section 74 of this Act, or

(b) with intent to deceive, makes use of any such entry which he knows to be false,

is guilty of an offence.

(5) A person who makes a false statement or withholds any material information for the purpose of obtaining the issue—

(a) of a certificate of insurance or certificate of security under Part VI of this Act, or

(b) of any document issued under regulations made by the Secretary of State in pursuance of his power under section 165(2)(a) of this Act to prescribe evidence which may be produced in lieu of a certificate of insurance or a certificate of security,

is guilty of an offence. **[373]**

NOTES
Commencement: 15 May 1989.
This section derived from the Road Traffic Act 1972, s 170(1)-(3), (5), (6), the Road Traffic Act 1974, Sch 2, para 15, and the International Road Haulage Permits Act 1975, s 3(3).

175. *Issue of false documents* **[Falsification of documents]**

If a person issues—

(a) any such document as is referred to in section 174(5)(a) or (b) of this Act, or

(b) a test certificate or certificate of conformity (within the meaning of Part II of this Act),

and the document or certificate so issued is to his knowledge false in a material particular, he is guilty of an offence.

[(1) A person shall be guilty of an offence who issues—

(a) any such document as is referred to in paragraph (a) or (b) of section 174(5) of this Act;

(b) a test certificate, plating certificate, goods vehicle test certificate or certificate of conformity;

(c) a certificate of temporary exemption under regulations made under section 48(4) or 53(5)(b) of this Act; or

(d) a notice removing a prohibition under section 69 or 70 of this Act;

if the document or certificate so issued is to his knowledge false in a material particular.

(2) A person who amends a certificate of conformity shall be guilty of an offence if the certificate as amended is to his knowledge false in a material particular.

(3) Expressions used in subsections (1)(b) and (2) above have the same meanings as they respectively have for the purposes of Part II of this Act.] [374]

NOTES
Commencement: 15 May 1989.
This section derived from the Road Traffic Act 1972, s 171, and the Road Traffic Act 1974, Sch 2, para 16.
Prospectively substituted by the Transport Act 1982, s 24(1) (as amended by the Road Traffic (Consequential Provisions) Act 1988, s 4, Sch 2, Part I), as from a day to be appointed.

176. Power to seize articles in respect of which offences under sections 173 to 175 may have been committed

(1) If a constable has reasonable cause to believe that a document produced to him—

(a) in pursuance of section 137 of this Act, or
(b) in pursuance of any of the preceding provisions of this Part of this Act,

is a document in relation to which an offence has been committed under section 173, 174 or 175 of this Act or under section 115 of the Road Traffic Regulation Act 1984, he may seize the document.

[(1A) Where a licence to drive or a counterpart of a licence may be seized by a constable under subsection (1) above, he may also seize the counterpart or the licence, as the case may be, produced with it.]

(2) When a document is seized under subsection (1) above, the person from whom it was taken shall, unless—

(a) the document has been previously returned to him, or
(b) he has been previously charged with an offence under any of those sections,

be summoned before a magistrates' court or, in Scotland, the sheriff to account for his possession of the document.

(3) The court or sheriff must make such order respecting the disposal of the document and award such costs as the justice of the case may require.

[(3A) An order under subsection (3) above respecting the disposal of a licence to drive or a counterpart of a licence may include an order respecting the disposal of any document seized under subsection (1A) above.]

(4) If a constable, [an examiner appointed under section 66A] of this Act [or an authorised inspector appointed under section 8 of the Transport Act 1982] has reasonable cause to believe that a document or plate carried on a motor vehicle or by the driver of the vehicle is a document or plate to which this subsection applies, he may seize it.

For the purposes of this subsection the power to seize includes power to detach from a vehicle.

(5) Subsection (4) above applies to a document or plate in relation to which an offence has been committed under sections 173, 174 or 175 of this Act in so far as they apply—

(a) to documents evidencing the appointment of examiners [under section 66A] of this Act, or

(b) to goods vehicle test certificates, plating certificates [notices removing prohibitions under section 69 or 70 of this Act], certificates of conformity or Minister's approval certificates (within the meaning of Part II of this Act), or

(c) to plates containing plated particulars (within the meaning of that Part) or containing other particulars required to be marked on goods vehicles by sections 54 to 58 of this Act or regulations made under them, or

(d) to records required to be kept by virtue of section 74 of this Act, or

(e) to international road haulage permits.

(6) When a document or plate is seized under subsection (4) above, either the driver or owner of the vehicle shall, if the document or plate is still detained and neither of them has previously been charged with an offence in relation to the document or plate under section 173, 174 or 175 of this Act, be summoned before a magistrates' court or, in Scotland, the sheriff to account for his possession of, or the presence on the vehicle of, the document or plate.

(7) The court or sheriff must make such order respecting the disposal of the document or plate and award such costs as the justice of the case may require.

[(8) In this section "counterpart", in relation to a licence to drive under Part III of this Act, has the same meaning as in that Part.] **[375]**

NOTES

Commencement: 1 April 1990 (sub-ss (1A), (3A), (8)); 15 May 1989 (remainder).

This section derived from the Road Traffic Act 1972, s 173, the Road Traffic Act 1974, Sch 2, para 17, the International Road Haulage Permits Act 1975, s 3(4), the Public Passenger Vehicles Act 1981, Sch 7, para 14, and the Road Traffic Regulation Act 1984, Sch 13, para 22.

Sub-ss (1A), (3A), (8): added with savings by SI 1990 No 144, reg 2(1), Sch 1, para 11; for savings see reg 3 thereof.

Sub-s (4): first words in square brackets substituted by the Road Traffic Act 1991, s 48, Sch 4, para 74, second words in square brackets prospectively inserted by the Transport Act 1982, s 24(2)(a) (as amended by the Road Traffic (Consequential Provisions) Act 1988, s 4, Sch 2, Part I, and by the Road Traffic Act 1991, s 48, Sch 4, para 22(1), (2)), as from a day to be appointed.

Sub-s (5): first words in square brackets substituted by the Road Traffic Act 1991, s 48, Sch 4, para 74, and second words in square brackets prospectively added by the Transport Act 1982, s 24(2)(b) (as amended by the Road Traffic (Consequential Provisions) Act 1988, s 4, Sch 2, Part I), as from a day to be appointed.

177. Impersonation of, or of person employed by, authorised examiner

If a person, with intent to deceive, falsely represents himself to be, or to be employed by, a person authorised [in accordance with regulations made under section 41 of this Act with respect to the checking and sealing of speed limiters or a person authorised] by the Secretary of State for the purposes of section 45 of this Act, he is guilty of an offence. **[376]**

NOTES

Commencement: 15 May 1989.

This section derived from the Road Traffic Act 1972, s 174.

Words in square brackets inserted by the Road Traffic Act 1991, s 48, Sch 4, para 75.

Offences in Scotland

178. Taking motor vehicle without authority, etc

(1) A person who in Scotland—

    (a) takes and drives away a motor vehicle without having either the consent of the owner of the vehicle or other lawful authority, or

    (b) knowing that a motor vehicle has been so taken, drives it or allows himself to be carried in or on it without such consent or authority,

is, subject to subsection (2) below, guilty of an offence.

  (2) If—

    (a) the jury, on proceedings under this section on indictment, or

    (b) the court, on summary proceedings under this section,

is satisfied that the accused acted in the reasonable belief that he had lawful authority, or in the reasonable belief that the owner would, in the circumstances of the case, have given consent if he had been asked for it, the accused shall not be liable to be convicted of the offence.

  (3) A constable may arrest without warrant a person reasonably suspected by him of having committed or of attempting to commit an offence under this section.   **[377]**

NOTES

Commencement: 15 May 1989.

This section derived from the Road Traffic Act 1972, s 175.

Inquiries

179. General power to hold enquiries

Without prejudice to any other provision of this Act, the Secretary of State may hold inquiries for the purposes of this Act.   **[378]**

NOTES

Commencement: 15 May 1989.

This section derived from the Road Traffic Act 1972, s 186.

180. General provisions as to inquiries

(1) Where under any of the provisions of this Act an inquiry is held by the Secretary of State—

    (a) notice of the inquiry may be given and published in accordance with such general or special directions as the Secretary of State may give,

    (b) the Secretary of State and, if authorised by him, the person appointed to hold the inquiry may by order require any person, subject to the payment or tender of the reasonable expenses of his attendance, to attend as a witness and give evidence or to produce any documents in his possession or power which relate to any matter in question at the inquiry and are such as would be subject to production in a court of law,

    (c) the person holding the inquiry shall have power to take evidence on oath and for that purpose to administer oaths, and

    (d) the Secretary of State may make such order as to the payment of the costs incurred by him in connection with the inquiry (including such reasonable sum not exceeding £30 a day as he may determine for the services of any officer engaged in the inquiry) by such party to the inquiry as he thinks fit, and may certify the amount of the costs so incurred.

(2) Any amount certified as mentioned in subsection (1)(d) above and

directed by the Secretary of State to be paid by any person shall be recoverable from that person—

    (a) in England or Wales, by the Secretary of State summarily as a civil debt (without prejudice to any other means of recovering it), or

    (b) *(applies to Scotland only)*.

(3) A person who fails without reasonable excuse to comply with any of the provisions of an order under subsection (1)(b) above is guilty of an offence.

[379]

NOTES
    Commencement: 15 May 1989.
    This section derived from the Road Traffic Act 1972, s 187.

181. General provisions as to accident inquiries

(1) Where an accident arises out of the presence of a [mechanically propelled vehicle] on a road, the Secretary of State may direct inquiry to be made into the cause of the accident.

(2) Where any accident arising out of the presence of a [mechanically propelled vehicle] on a road has occurred, a person authorised by the Secretary of State in that behalf may, on production if so required of his authority, inspect any vehicle in connection with which the accident arose, and for that purpose may enter at any reasonable time any premises where the vehicle is.

(3) If a person obstructs a person so authorised in the performance of his duty under subsection (2) above, he is guilty of an offence.

(4) If in any case the Secretary of State considers that an inquiry to be made by him under this section should be made by means of the holding of a public inquiry, he may direct a public inquiry to be held.

(5) A report made by or to the Secretary of State as the result of an inquiry under this section shall not be used in evidence by or on behalf of a person by or against whom any legal proceedings are instituted in consequence of the accident to which the inquiry relates. **[380]**

NOTES
    Commencement: 15 May 1989.
    This section derived from the Road Traffic Act 1972, s 26.
    Sub-ss (1), (2): words in square brackets substituted by the Road Traffic Act 1991, s 48, Sch 4, para 76.

182. Special provisions as to accident inquiries in Greater London

(1) Where, owing to the presence of a vehicle on a road, an accident occurs within Greater London and it appears to the Secretary of State that the sole or a contributory cause of the accident was—

    (a) the nature or character of the road or of the road surface, or

    (b) a defect in the design or construction of the vehicle or in the materials used in the construction of the road or vehicle,

he may, if he thinks fit, cause an inquiry to be held into the cause of the accident.

(2) In this section "road" includes a highway and a bridge carrying a highway and any lane, mews, footway, square, court, alley or passage whether a thoroughfare or not. **[381]**

NOTES
Commencement: 15 May 1989.
This section derived from the Road Traffic Act 1972, s 27.

Application to the Crown

183. Application to the Crown

(1) Subject to the provisions of this section—

    (a) Part I of this Act,

    (b) Part II of this Act, except sections 68 to 74 and 77,

    (c) Part III of this Act, except section 103(3),

    (d) Part IV of this Act, and

    (e) in this Part, sections 163, 164, 168, 169, 170(1) to (4), 177, 178, 181 and 182,

apply to vehicles and persons in the public service of the Crown.

(2) Sections 49 to 63 [63A] and section 65 of this Act apply—

    (a) to vehicles in the public service of the Crown only if they are registered or liable to be registered under the Vehicles (Excise) Act 1971, and

    (b) to trailers in the public service of the Crown only while drawn by vehicles (whether or not in the public service of the Crown) which are required to be so registered.

(3) Where those sections so apply they do so subject to the following modifications—

    (a) examinations of such vehicles in pursuance of regulations under section 49 or 61(2)(a) of this Act may be made by or under the directions of examiners authorised by the Secretary of State for the purpose instead of by or under the directions of examiners appointed under section [66A of this Act] [or of authorised inspectors under section 8 of the Transport Act 1982 . . .

(4) Neither section 97(3) nor section 98(3) of this Act, in so far as they prevent such a licence as is there mentioned from authorising a person to drive certain motor cycles, applies—

    (a) in the case of motor cycles owned by the Secretary of State for Defence and used for naval, military or air force purposes, or

    (b) in the case of motor cycles so used while being ridden by persons for the time being subject to the orders of a member of the armed forces of the Crown.

(5) Subject to regulations made under subsection (2) of section 101 of this Act, that section (in so far as it prohibits persons under 21 from holding or obtaining a licence to drive motor vehicles or persons under 18 from holding or obtaining a licence to drive medium-sized goods vehicles) does not apply—

    (a) in the case of motor vehicles owned by the Secretary of State for Defence and used for naval, military or air force purposes, or

    (b) in the case of vehicles so used while being driven by persons for the time being subject to the orders of a member of the armed forces of the Crown.

[(6) The functions under Part IV of this Act of traffic commissioners in relation to licences issued to persons subject to the Naval Discipline Act 1957, to military law or to air force law to drive large goods vehicles or passenger-carrying vehicles in the public service of the Crown shall be exercised by the prescribed authority.]

(7) Section 165 of this Act, in so far as it provides for the production of test certificates and the giving of names and addresses, applies to a person in connection with a vehicle to which section 47 of this Act applies notwithstanding that he or the driver is or was at any material time in the public service of the Crown.

(8) Subsection (1) of section 165 of this Act, in so far as it provides for the production of any certificate mentioned in subsection (2)(c) of that section, applies to a person in connection with a goods vehicle so mentioned notwithstanding that he or the driver is or was at any material time in the public service of the Crown.   **[382]**

NOTES
Commencement: 15 May 1989.
This section derived from the Road Traffic Act 1972, s 188(1)-(4), (6), (7), the Road Traffic Act 1974, Sch 2, para 18, Sch 7, the Road Traffic (Drivers' Ages and Hours of Work) Act 1976, Sch 1, para 12, the Public Passenger Vehicles Act 1981, Sch 7, para 14, and the Transport Act 1981, Sch 9, para 16.
Sub-s (2): figure in italics prospectively repealed and figure in square brackets prospectively substituted by the Road Traffic (Consequential Provisions) Act 1988, s 4, Sch 2, Part I, as from a day to be appointed.
Sub-s (3): first words in square brackets substituted, and words omitted repealed, by the Road Traffic Act 1991, s 48, Sch 4, para 77, and second words in square brackets prospectively added and words in italics prospectively repealed by the Road Traffic (Consequential Provisions) Act 1988, s 4, Sch 2, Part I, as from a day to be appointed.
Sub-s (6): substituted by the Road Traffic (Driver Licensing and Information Systems) Act 1989, s 7, Sch 3, para 23.

184. Application of sections 5 to 10 to persons subject to service discipline

(1) Sections 5 to 10 of this Act, in their application to persons subject to service discipline, apply outside as well as within Great Britain and have effect as if—

    (a) references to proceedings for an offence under any enactment included references to proceedings for the corresponding service offence,

    (b) references to the court included a reference to any naval, military or air force authority before whom the proceedings take place,

    (c) references to a constable included references to a member of the provost staff,

    (d) references to a police station included references to a naval, military or air force unit or establishment,

    (e) references to a hospital included references to a naval, military or air force unit or establishment at which medical or surgical treatment is provided for persons subject to service discipline, and

    (f) in section 6(1) the reference to a traffic offence included a reference to the corresponding service offence.

(2) In relation to persons for the time being subject to service discipline, the power to arrest conferred on a constable by section 4(6) of this Act is also exercisable by a member of the provost staff and is so exercisable outside as well as within Great Britain.

(3) In this section—

"corresponding service offence", in relation to an offence under any enactment, means an offence under section 42 of the Naval Discipline Act 1957 or an offence against section 70 of the Army Act 1955 or section 70 of the Air Force Act 1955 committed by an act or omission which is punishable under that enactment or would be so punishable if committed in Great Britain,

"member of the provost staff" means a provost officer or any person legally exercising authority under or on behalf of a provost officer,

"persons subject to service discipline" means persons subject to that Act of 1957, to military law or to air force law and other persons to whom section 42 of that Act of 1957 or section 70 of either of those Acts of 1955 for the time being applies,

"provost officer" means a person who is a provost officer within the meaning of that Act of 1957 or either of those Acts of 1955.   **[383]**

NOTES

Commencement: 15 May 1989.

This section derived from the Road Traffic Act 1972, s 189(1)(a)-(f), (2), (3), and the Transport Act 1981, Sch 9, para 17.

Interpretation

185. Meaning of "motor vehicle" and other expressions relating to vehicles

(1) In this Act—

"heavy locomotive" means a mechanically propelled vehicle which is not constructed itself to carry a load other than any of the excepted articles and the weight of which unladen exceeds 11690 kilograms,

"heavy motor car" means a mechanically propelled vehicle, not being a motor car, which is constructed itself to carry a load or passengers and the weight of which unladen exceeds 2540 kilograms,

"invalid carriage" means a mechanically propelled vehicle the weight of which unladen does not exceed 254 kilograms and which is specially designed and constructed, and not merely adapted, for the use of a person suffering from some physical defect or disability and is used solely by such a person,

"light locomotive" means a mechanically propelled vehicle which is not constructed itself to carry a load other than any of the excepted articles and the weight of which unladen does not exceed 11690 kilograms but does exceed 7370 kilograms,

"motor car" means a mechanically propelled vehicle, not being a motor cycle or an invalid carriage, which is constructed itself to carry a load or passengers and the weight of which unladen—

    (a) if it is constructed solely for the carriage of passengers and their effects, is adapted to carry not more than seven passengers exclusive of the driver and is fitted with tyres of such type as may be specified in regulations made by the Secretary of State, does not exceed 3050 kilograms,

    (b) if it is constructed or adapted for use for the conveyance of goods or burden of any description, does not exceed 3050 kilograms, or 3500 kilograms if the vehicle carries a container or containers for holding for the purposes of its propulsion any fuel which is wholly gaseous at 17.5 degrees Celsius under a pressure of 1.013 bar or plant and materials for producing such fuel,

    (c) does not exceed 2540 kilograms in a case not falling within subparagraph (a) or (b) above,

"motor cycle" means a mechanically propelled vehicle, not being an invalid carriage, with less than four wheels and the weight of which unladen does not exceed 410 kilograms,

"motor tractor" means a mechanically propelled vehicle which is not constructed itself to carry a load, other than the excepted articles, and the weight of which unladen does not exceed 7370 kilograms,

"motor vehicle" means, subject to section 20 of the Chronically Sick and Disabled Persons Act 1970 (which makes special provision about invalid carriages, within the meaning of that Act), a mechanically propelled vehicle intended or adapted for use on roads, and

"trailer" means a vehicle drawn by a motor vehicle.

(2) In subsection (1) above "excepted articles" means any of the following: water, fuel, accumulators and other equipment used for the purpose of propulsion, loose tools and loose equipment. **[384]**

NOTES
Commencement: 15 May 1989.
This section derived from the Road Traffic Act 1972, s 190(1)-(8), SI 1981 No 1373, and SI 1981 No 1374.

186. Supplementary provisions about those expressions

(1) For the purposes of section 185 of this Act, a side car attached to a motor vehicle, if it complies with such conditions as may be specified in regulations made by the Secretary of State, is to be regarded as forming part of the vehicle to which it is attached and as not being a trailer.

(2) For the purposes of section 185 of this Act, in a case where a motor vehicle is so constructed that a trailer may by partial super-imposition be attached to the vehicle in such a manner as to cause a substantial part of the weight of the trailer to be borne by the vehicle, that vehicle is to be deemed to be a vehicle itself constructed to carry a load.

(3) For the purposes of section 185 of this Act, in the case of a motor vehicle fitted with a crane, dynamo, welding plant or other special appliance or apparatus which is a permanent or essentially permanent fixture, the appliance or apparatus is not to be deemed to constitute a load or goods or burden of any description, but is to be deemed to form part of the vehicle.

(4) The Secretary of State may by regulations vary any of the maximum or minimum weights specified in section 185 of this Act.

(5) Regulations under subsection (4) above may have effect—
  (a) either generally or in the case of vehicles of any class specified in the regulations, and
  (b) either for the purposes of the provisions of the Road Traffic Acts and of all regulations made under those provisions or for such of those purposes as may be so specified.

(6) Nothing in section 86 of the Road Traffic Regulation Act 1984 limits the powers conferred by subsection (4) above. **[385]**

NOTES
Commencement: 15 May 1989.
This section derived from the Road Traffic Act 1972, s 190(9)-(11), and the Road Traffic Regulation Act 1984, Sch 13, para 24.
Road Traffic Acts: Road Traffic Offenders Act 1988, Road Traffic (Consequential Provisions)

Act 1988 (so far as it reproduces the effect of provisions repealed by that Act), Road Traffic Act 1988.

187. Articulated vehicles

(1) Unless it falls within subsection (2) below, a vehicle so constructed that it can be divided into two parts both of which are vehicles and one of which is a motor vehicle shall (when not so divided) be treated for the purposes of the enactments mentioned in subsection (3) below as that motor vehicle with the other part attached as a trailer.

(2) A passenger vehicle so constructed that—

    (a) it can be divided into two parts, both of which are vehicles and one of which is a motor vehicle, but cannot be so divided without the use of facilities normally available only at a workshop, and

    (b) passengers carried by it when not so divided can at all times pass from either part to the other,

shall (when not so divided) be treated for the purposes of the enactments mentioned in subsection (3) below as a single motor vehicle.

(3) The enactments referred to in subsections (1) and (2) above are the Road Traffic Act 1960, Parts I and II of the Public Passenger Vehicles Act 1981, and the Traffic Acts.

(4) In this section "passenger vehicle" means a vehicle constructed or adapted for use solely or principally for the carriage of passengers.   **[386]**

NOTES
    Commencement: 15 May 1989.
    This section derived from the Road Traffic Act 1972, s 191, the Interpretation Act 1978, s 17, the Transport Act 1980, s 63, and the Road Traffic Regulation Act 1984, Sch 13, para 25.
    Road Traffic Acts: Road Traffic Regulation Act 1984, Road Traffic Offenders Act 1988, Road Traffic (Consequential Provisions) Act 1988 (so far as it reproduces the effect of provisions repealed by that Act), Road Traffic Act 1988.

188. Hover vehicles

(1) For the purposes of the Road Traffic Acts, a hovercraft within the meaning of the Hovercraft Act 1968 (in this section referred to as a hover vehicle)—

    (a) is a motor vehicle, whether or not it is intended or adapted for use on roads, but

    (b) apart from that is to be treated, subject to subsection (2) below, as not being a vehicle of any of the classes defined in section 185 of this Act.

(2) The Secretary of State may by regulations provide—

    (a) that any provisions of this Act which would otherwise apply to hover vehicles shall not apply to them or shall apply to them subject to such modifications as may be specified in the regulations, or

    (b) that any such provision which would not otherwise apply to hover vehicles shall apply to them subject to such modifications (if any) as may be specified in the regulations.   **[387]**

NOTES
    Commencement: 15 May 1989.
    This section derived from the Road Traffic Act 1972, s 192(1), (2).
    Road Traffic Acts: Road Traffic Offenders Act 1988, Road Traffic (Consequential Provisions) Act 1988 (so far as it reproduces the effect of provisions repealed by that Act), Road Traffic Act 1988.

189. Certain vehicles not to be treated as motor vehicles

(1) For the purposes of the Road Traffic Acts—

(a) a mechanically propelled vehicle being an implement for cutting grass which is controlled by a pedestrian and is not capable of being used or adapted for any other purpose,

(b) any other mechanically propelled vehicle controlled by a pedestrian which may be specified by regulations made by the Secretary of State for the purposes of this section and section 140 of the Road Traffic Regulation Act 1984, and

(c) an electrically assisted pedal cycle of such a class as may be prescribed by regulations so made,

is to be treated as not being a motor vehicle.

(2) In subsection (1) above "controlled by a pedestrian" means that the vehicle either—

(a) is constructed or adapted for use only under such control, or

(b) is constructed or adapted for use either under such control or under the control of a person carried on it, but is not for the time being in use under, or proceeding under, the control of a person carried on it.

         [388]

NOTES

Commencement: 15 May 1989.

This section derived from the Road Traffic Act 1972, s 193, the Transport Act 1981, s 24(1), and the Road Traffic Regulation Act 1984, Sch 13, para 26.

Road Traffic Acts: Road Traffic Offenders Act 1988, Road Traffic (Consequential Provisions) Act 1988 (so far as it reproduces the effect of provisions repealed by that Act), Road Traffic Act 1988.

190. Method of calculating weight of motor vehicles and trailers

(1) This section applies for the purposes of the Traffic Acts and of any other enactments relating to the use of motor vehicles or trailers on roads.

(2) The weight unladen of a vehicle or trailer shall be taken to be the weight of the vehicle or trailer—

(a) inclusive of the body and all parts (the heavier being taken where alternative bodies or parts are used) which are necessary to or ordinarily used with the vehicle or trailer when working on a road, but

(b) exclusive of the weight of water, fuel or accumulators used for the purpose of the supply of power for the propulsion of the vehicle or, as the case may be, of any vehicle by which the trailer is drawn, and of loose tools and loose equipment.   **[389]**

NOTES

Commencement: 15 May 1989.

This section derived from the Road Traffic Act 1972, s 194, and the Road Traffic Regulation Act 1984, Sch 13, para 27.

Traffic Acts: Road Traffic Regulations Act 1984, Road Traffic Offenders Act 1988, Road Traffic (Consequential Provisions) Act 1988 (so far as it reproduces the effect of provisions repealed by that Act), Road Traffic Act 1988.

191. Interpretation of statutory references to carriages

A motor vehicle or trailer—

(a) is to be deemed to be a carriage within the meaning of any Act of Parliament, whether a public general Act or a local Act, and of any rule, regulation or byelaw made under any Act of Parliament, and

(b) if used as a carriage of any particular class shall for the purpose of any enactment relating to carriages of any particular class be deemed to be a carriage of that class. **[390]**

NOTES
Commencement: 15 May 1989.
This section derived from the Road Traffic Act 1972, s 195.

192. General interpretation of Act

(1) In this Act—

["approved testing authority" means a person authorised by the Secretary of State under section 8 of the Transport Act 1982 to carry on a vehicle testing business within the meaning of Part II of that Act]

"bridleway" means a way over which the public have the following, but no other, rights of way: a right of way on foot and a right of way on horseback or leading a horse, with or without a right to drive animals of any description along the way,

"carriage of goods" includes the haulage of goods,

"cycle" means a bicycle, a tricycle, or a cycle having four or more wheels, not being in any case a motor vehicle,

"driver", where a separate person acts as a steersman of a motor vehicle, includes (except for the purposes of section 1 of this Act) that person as well as any other person engaged in the driving of the vehicle, and "drive" is to be interpreted accordingly,

"footpath", in relation to England and Wales, means a way over which the public have a right of way on foot only,

"goods" includes goods or burden of any description,

"goods vehicle" means a motor vehicle constructed or adapted for use for the carriage of goods, or a trailer so constructed or adapted,

["highway authority", in England and Wales, means—

(a) in relation to a road for which he is the highway authority within the meaning of the Highways Act 1980, the Secretary of State, and

(b) in relation to any other road, the council of the county, metropolitan district or London borough, or the Common Council of the City of London, as the case may be;]

"international road haulage permit" means a licence, permit, authorisation or other document issued in pursuance of a Community instrument relating to the carriage of goods by road between member States or an international agreement to which the United Kingdom is a party and which relates to the international carriage of goods by road,

"owner", in relation to a vehicle which is the subject of a hiring agreement or hire-purchase agreement, means the person in possession of the vehicle under that agreement, "petty sessions area" has the same meaning as in the Magistrates' Courts Act 1980,

"prescribed" means prescribed by regulations made by the Secretary of State,

"road",

[(a)] in relation to England and Wales, means any highway and any other road to which the public has access, and includes bridges over which a road passes,
[and

(b) in relation to Scotland, means any road within the meaning of the Roads (Scotland) Act 1984 and any other way to which the public has access, and includes bridges over which a road passes,]

"the Road Traffic Acts" means the Road Traffic Offenders Act 1988, the Road Traffic (Consequential Provisions) Act 1988 (so far as it reproduces the effect of provisions repealed by that Act) and this Act,

"statutory", in relation to any prohibition, restriction, requirement or provision, means contained in, or having effect under, any enactment (including any enactment contained in this Act),

"the Traffic Acts" means the Road Traffic Acts and the Road Traffic Regulation Act 1984,

"traffic sign" has the meaning given by section 64(1) of the Road Traffic Regulation Act 1984,

"tramcar" includes any carriage used on any road by virtue of an order under the Light Railways Act 1896, and

"trolley vehicle" means a mechanically propelled vehicle adapted for use on roads without rails [under] power transmitted to it from some external source [(whether or not there is in addition a source of power on board the vehicle)].

(2) In this Act—

"carriageway"
"footway"
"local roads authority"
"public road"
. . .
"roads authority"
"special road" and
"trunk road",

in relation to Scotland, have the same meanings as in the Roads (Scotland) Act 1984, and "footpath", in relation to Scotland, means a way over which the public have a right of way on foot only (whether or not associated with a carriageway).

(3) References in this Act to a class of vehicles are to be interpreted as references to a class defined or described by reference to any characteristics of the vehicles or to any other circumstances whatsoever [and accordingly as

authorising the use of "category" to indicate a class of vehicles, however defined or described].   **[391]**

NOTES
Commencement: 15 May 1989.
This section derived from the Road Traffic Act 1972, s 196(1), (2), the Local Government Act 1972, Sch 19, para 6, the International Road Haulage Permits Act 1975, s 3(5), the Road Traffic (Drivers' Ages and Hours of Work) Act 1976, Sch 1, para 13, the Road Traffic Regulation Act 1984, Sch 13, para 28, the Roads (Scotland) Act 1984, Sch 9, para 68(6), (10), and the Local Government Act 1985, Sch 5, para 2(7).
Sub-s (1): definition "approved testing authority" prospectively added by the Road Traffic (Consequential Provisions) Act 1988, s 4, Sch 2, Part I, as from a day to be appointed; definition "highway authority" substituted by the New Roads and Street Works Act 1991, s 168(1), Sch 8, Part IV, para 121(1), (4); definitions "road" and "trolley vehicle" amended by the Road Traffic Act 1991, s 48, Sch 4, para 78(1)–(3).
Sub-s (2): words omitted repealed by the Road Traffic Act 1991, ss 48, 83 Sch 4, para 78(4), Sch 8.
Sub-s (3): words in square brackets added by the Road Traffic (Driver Licensing and Information Systems) Act 1989, s 7, Sch 3, para 24.

[192A. Tramcars and other guided vehicles: drink and drugs

(1) Sections 4 to 11 of this Act shall not apply (to the extent that apart from this subsection they would) to vehicles on any transport system to which Chapter I of Part II of the Transport and Works Act 1992 (offences involving drink or drugs on railways, tramways and certain other guided transport systems) applies.

(2) Subject to subsection (1) above, the Secretary of State may by regulations provide that sections 4 to 11 of this Act shall apply to vehicles on a system of guided transport specified in the regulations with such modifications as he considers necessary or expedient.

(3) Regulations under subsection (2) above may make different provision for different cases.

(4) In this section—

"guided transport" means transport by vehicles guided by means external to the vehicles (whether or not the vehicles are also capable of being operated in some other way), and
"vehicle" includes mobile traction unit.]   **[391A]**

NOTES
Commencement: 7 December 1992.
Inserted by the Transport and Works Act 1992, s 39.

193. (*Repealed by the Road Traffic Act 1991, s 83, Sch 8.*)

[193A. Tramcars and trolley vehicles

(1) The Secretary of State may by regulations provide that such of the provisions mentioned in subsection (2) below as are specified in the regulations shall not apply, or shall with modifications—

(a) to all tramcars or to tramcars of any specified class, or

(b) to all trolley vehicles or to trolley vehciles of any specified class.

(2) The provisions referred to in subsection (1) above are the provisions of—

(a) sections 12, 40A to 42, 47, 48, 66, 68 to 73, 75 to 79, 83, 87 to 109, 143 to 165, 168, 170, 171, 178, 190 and 191 of this Act, and

(b) sections 1, 2, 7, 8, 22, 25 to 29, 31, 32, 34 to 48, 96 and 97 of the Road Traffic Offenders Act 1988 (provisions requiring warning of prosecution etc and provisions connected with the licensing of drivers).

(3) Regulations under this section—

(a) may make different provision for different cases,

(b) may include such transitional provisions as appear to the Secretary of State to be necessary or expedient, and

(c) may make such amendments to any special Act as appear to the Secretary of State to be necessary or expedient in consequence of the regulations or in consequence of the application to any tramcars or trolley vehicles of any of the provisions mentioned in subsection (2) above.

(4) In this section "special Act" means a local Act of Parliament passed before the commencement of this section which authorises or regulates the use of tramcars or trolley vehicles.] **[392]**

NOTES

Commencement: 1 July 1992.

Inserted by the Road Traffic Act 1991, s 46(2).

194. General index

The expressions listed in the left-hand column below are respectively defined or (as the case may be) fall to be construed in accordance with the provisions of this Act listed in the right-hand column in relation to those expressions.

Expression	Relevant provision
Bridleway	Section 192
Carriage of goods	Section 192
Carriageway	Section 192
Cycle	Section 192
Drive	Section 192
Driver	Section 192
Footpath	Section 192
Footway	Section 192
Goods	Section 192
Goods vehicle	Section 192
Goods vehicle test certificate	Section 49(2)(b)
Heavy locomotive	Section 185
Heavy motor car	Section 185
Highway authority	Section 192
International road haulage permit	Section 192
Invalid carriage	Section 185
Light locomotive	Section 185
Local roads authority	Section 192

Expression	Relevant provision
Motor car	Section 185
Motor cycle	Section 185
Motor tractor	Section 185
Motor vehicle	Sections 185, 186(1), 187, 188, 189
Owner	Section 192
Plating certificate	Section 49(2)(a)
Prescribed	Section 192
Public road	Section 192
Road	Section 192
Roads authority	Section 192
Road Traffic Acts	Section 192
Special road	Section 192
Statutory	Section 192
Test certificate	Section 45(2)
Traffic Acts	Section 192
Traffic sign	Section 192
Trailer	Section 185
Tramcar	Section 192
Trolley vehicle	Section 192
Trunk road	Section 192
Unladen weight	Section 190

[393]

NOTE
  Commencement: 15 May 1989.

Supplementary

195. Provisions as to regulations

(1) Any power conferred by this Act upon the Secretary of State to make regulations shall be exercisable by statutory instrument.

(2) Before making any regulations under this Act (other than regulations under section 88(3) or Part V) the Secretary of State must consult with such representative organisations as he thinks fit.

(3) A statutory instrument whereby any power conferred by this Act upon the Secretary of State to make regulations is exercised (other than the power conferred by sections 8(3), 11(2), 14, 15 (where exercisable for the purposes of subsection (3) of that section) or 189) shall be subject to annulment in pursuance of a resolution of either House of Parliament.

(4) The Secretary of State must not make any regulations under section 8(3), 11(2), 14 or (where made for the purposes of subsection (3) of that section) 15 of this Act unless a draft of the regulations has been approved by both Houses of Parliament.

(5) Regulations under section 189 of this Act shall not have effect unless approved by resolution of each house of Parliament.   **[394]**

NOTES
Commencement: 15 May 1989.
This section derived from the Road Traffic Act 1972, s 199(1), (2), (3)-(5), and the Transport Act 1981, s 29(2), Sch 9, para 18.

196. Provision, etc, of weighbridges

(1) A highway authority may—

    (a) provide, erect, maintain and operate, or join with another highway authority in providing, erecting, maintaining and operating, weighbridges or other machines for weighing vehicles, or

    (b) contribute towards the cost of the provision, erection, maintenance and operation of any such weighbridge or other machine by any other authority or person.

(2) The Secretary of State may exercise the powers conferred by subsection (1) above whether or not in his capacity as highway authority, but may provide, erect, maintain and operate any such machine on a road for which he is not the the highway authority only with the consent of the highway authority.

(3) Accordingly the presence of any such machine on a road in consequence of the exercise of those powers by virtue of subsection (2) above (as in any other case) shall not be taken to be an obstruction of the road.

(4) The provision or erection, or the making of a contribution towards the provision or erection, of any such weighbridge or other machine shall be a purpose for which the highway authority may borrow.

(5) In relation to Scotland, references in this section to a highway authority are to be read as references to a roads authority. **[395]**

NOTES
Commencement: 15 May 1989.
This section derived from the Road Traffic Act 1972, s 200, and the Roads (Scotland) Act 1984, Sch 9, para 68(11).

197. Short title, commencement and extent

(1) . . .

(3) This Act, except section 80 and except as provided by section 184, does not extend to Northern Ireland. **[396]**

NOTE
Commencement: 15 May 1989.

SCHEDULES

SCHEDULE 1

Sections 17, 18

SUPPLEMENTARY PROVISIONS IN CONNECTION WITH PROCEEDINGS FOR OFFENCES UNDER SECTIONS [15A,] 17 AND 18(4)

Proceedings in England and Wales

1.—(1) A person against whom proceedings are brought in England and Wales for an offence under section [15A,] 17 or 18(4) of this Act is, upon information duly laid by him and on giving the prosecution not less than three clear days' notice of his intention, entitled to have any person to whose act or default he alleges that the contravention of that section was due brought before the court in the proceedings.

(2) If, after the contravention has been proved, the original accused proves that the contravention was due to the act or default of that other person—

    (a) that other person may be convicted of the offence, and

    (b) if the original accused further proves that he has used all due diligence to secure that section [15A,] 17 or, as the case may be, 18(4) was complied with, he shall be acquitted of the offence.

(3) Where an accused seeks to avail himself of the provisions of sub-paragraphs (1) and (2) above—

    (a) the prosecution, as well as the person whom the accused charges with the offence, has the right to cross-examine him, if he gives evidence, and any witness called by him in support of his pleas, and to call rebutting evidence, and

    (b) the court may make such order as it thinks fit for the payment of costs by any party to the proceedings to any other party to the proceedings.

2.—(1) Where—

    (a) it appears that an offence under section [15A,] 17 or 18(4) of this Act has been committed in respect of which proceedings might be taken in England and Wales against some person (referred to below in this paragraph as "the original offender"), and

    (b) a person proposing to take proceedings in respect of the offence is reasonably satisfied—

        (i) that the offence of which complaint is made was due to an act or default of some other person, being an act or default which took place in England and Wales, and

        (ii) that the original offender could establish a defence under paragraph 1 of this Schedule,

the proceedings may be taken against that other person without proceedings first being taken against the original offender.

(2) In any such proceedings the accused may be charged with, and on proof that the contravention was due to his act or default be convicted of, the offence with which the original offender might have been charged.

3.—(1) Where proceedings are brought in England and Wales against a person (referred to below in this paragraph as "the accused") in respect of a contravention of section [15A,] 17 or 18(4) of this Act and it is proved—

    (a) that the contravention was due to the act or default of some other person, being an act or default which took place in Scotland, and

    (b) that the accused used all due diligence to secure compliance with that section,

the accused shall, subject to the provisions of this paragraph, be acquitted of the offence.

(2) The accused is not entitled to be acquitted under this paragraph unless within seven days from the date of the service of the summons on him—

    (a) he has given notice in writing to the prosecution of his intention to rely upon the provisions of this paragraph, specifying the name and address of the person to whose act or default he alleges that the contravention was due, and

    (b) he has sent a like notice to that person.

(3) The person specified in a notice served under this paragraph is entitled to appear at the hearing and to give evidence and the court may, if it thinks fit, adjourn the hearing to enable him to do so.

(4) Where it is proved that the contravention of section [15A,] 17 or 18(4) of this Act was due to the act or default of some person other than the accused, being an act or default which took place in Scotland, the court must (whether or not the accused is acquitted) cause notice of the proceedings to be sent to the Secretary of State.

Proceedings in Scotland

4.—(1) Where a contravention of section [15A,] 17 or 18(4) of this Act committed by a person in Scotland (referred to in this sub-paragraph as "the original offender") was due to the act or default of any other person, being an act or default which took place in Scotland then, whether or not proceedings are taken against the original offender, that other person may be charged with and convicted of the contravention and shall be liable on conviction to the same punishment as might have been inflicted on the original offender if he had been convicted of the contravention.

(2) Where a person (referred to in this sub-paragraph as "the accused") who is charged in Scotland with a contravention of section [15A,] 17 or 18(4) of this Act proves to the satisfaction of the court—

    (a) that he used all due diligence to secure that the provision in question was complied with, and

    (b) that the contravention was due to the act or default of some other person,

the accused shall be acquitted of the contravention.

Proceedings in Great Britain

5.—[(1A) Subject to the provisions of this paragraph, in any proceedings (whether in England and Wales or Scotland) for an offence under section 15A of this Act it shall be a defence for the accused to prove—

    (a) if the offence is under subsection (3)(a) of that section—

        (i) that he purchased the equipment in question as being of a type which could be lawfully sold or offered for sale as conducive to the safety in the event of accident of prescribed classes of children in prescribed classes of motor vehicles and with a written warranty to that effect;

        (ii) that he had no reason to believe at the time of the commission of the alleged offence that it was not of such a type; and

        (iii) that it was then in the same state as when he purchased it;

    (b) if the offence is under subsection (3)(b) of that section, he provided information in relation to the equipment and it is alleged that it did not include appropriate information or included or consisted of inappropriate information—

        (i) that the information provided by him was information which had been provided to him with a written warranty to the effect that it was the information required to be provided by him under section 15A of this Act; and

        (ii) that he had no reason to believe at the time of the commission of the alleged offence that the information provided by him was not the information required to be provided under that section; or

    (c) if the offence is under subsection (3)(b) of that section, he provided information in relation to the equipment and it is alleged that it was not provided in the manner required under that section—

        (i) that the information provided by him had been provided to him either with a written warranty to the effect that it was provided to him in the manner in which it was required to be provided by him under that section or with instructions as to the manner in which the information should be provided by him and with a written warranty to the effect that provision in that manner would comply with regulations under that section;

        (ii) that he had no reason to believe at the time of the commission of the alleged offence that he was not providing the information in the manner required under that section; and

        (iii) that the information was then in the same state as when it was provided to him or, as the case may be, that it was provided by him in accordance with the instructions given to him.]

(1) Subject to the provisions of this paragraph, in any proceedings (whether in England and Wales or Scotland) for an offence under section 17 or 18(4) of this Act it shall be a defence for the accused to prove—

    (a) that he purchased the helmet or appliance in question as being of a type which—

        (i) in the case of section 17, could be lawfully sold or offered for sale under that section, and

        (ii) in the case of section 18(4), could be lawfully sold or offered for sale under section 18 as authorised for use in the manner in question,
and with a written warranty to that effect, and

    (b) that he had no reason to believe at the time of the commission of the alleged offence that it was not of such a type, and

    (c) that it was then in the same state as when he purchased it.

(2) A warranty is only a defence in any such proceedings if—

    (a) the accused—

        (i) has, not later than three clear days before the date of the hearing, sent to the prosecutor a copy of the warranty with a notice stating that he intends to rely on it and specifying the name and address of the person from whom he received it, and

        (ii) has also sent a like notice of his intention to that person, and

    (b) in the case of a warranty given by a person outside the United Kingdom, the accused proves that he had taken reasonable steps to ascertain, and did in fact believe in, the accuracy of the statement contained in the warranty.

(3) Where the accused is a servant of the person who purchased the [equipment, helmet or appliance in question under a warranty, or to whom the information in question was provided] under a warranty, he is entitled to rely on the provisions of this paragraph in the same way as his employer would have been entitled to do if he had been the accused.

(4) The person by whom the warranty is alleged to have been given is entitled to appear at the hearing and to give evidence and the court may, if it thinks fit, adjourn the hearing to enable him to do so.

[6.—(1) An accused who in any proceedings for an offence under section 15A, 17 or 18(4) of this Act wilfully applies to equipment, information, a helmet or, as the case may be, an appliance a warranty not given in relation to it is guilty of an offence.

(2) A person who, in respect of equipment, a helmet or appliance sold by him, or information provided by him, being equipment, a helmet, an appliance or information in respect of which a warranty might be pleaded under paragraph 5 of this Schedule, gives to the purchaser a false warranty in writing, is guilty of an offence, unless he proves

that when he gave the warranty he had reason to believe that the statements or description contained in it were accurate.

(3) Where the accused in a prosecution for an offence under section 15A, 17 or 18(4) of this Act relies successfully on a warranty given to him or his employer, any proceedings under sub-paragraph (2) above in respect of the warranty may, at the option of the prosecutor, be taken before a court having jurisdiction in the place—

(a) where the equipment, helmet or appliance, or any of the equipment, helmets or appliances, to which the warranty relates was procured;
(b) where the information, or any of it, to which the warranty relates was provided; or
(c) where the warranty was given.

7. In this Schedule, "equipment" means equipment to which section 15A of this Act applies and "appliance" means an appliance to which section 18 of this Act applies.]

[397]

NOTES
Commencement: 15 May 1989.
This Schedule derived from the Road Traffic Act 1972, s 33AA(7), Sch 1, and the Transport Act 1982, s 57(1).
This Schedule amended by the Motor Vehicles (Safety Equipment for Children) Act 1991, s 2.

SCHEDULE 2

Section 67

DEFERRED TESTS OF CONDITIONS OF VEHICLES

1. Where the driver is the owner of the vehicle, he may at the time of electing that the test shall be deferred—

(a) specify a period of seven days within which the deferred test is to take place, being a period falling within the next thirty days, disregarding any day on which the vehicle is outside Great Britain, and
(b) require that the deferred test shall take place on premises then specified by him where the test can conveniently be carried out or that it shall take place in such area in England and Wales, being a county district or Greater London, or such area in Scotland, being an islands area or district, as he may specify at that time.

2. When the driver is not the owner of the vehicle he shall inform the examiner of the name and address of the owner of the vehicle and the owner shall be afforded an opportunity of specifying such a period, and such premises or area.

3.—(1) Where under the preceding provisions of this Schedule a period has been specified within which the deferred test is to be carried out, the time for carrying it out shall be such time within that period as may be notified, being a time not earlier than two days after the giving of the notification.

(2) Where no such period has been specified, the time for the carrying out of the deferred test shall be such time as may be notified, being a time not earlier than seven days after the giving of the notification.

(3) Where premises have been specified under the preceding provisions of this Schedule for the carrying out of the deferred test, and the test can conveniently be carried out on those premises, it must be carried out there.

(4) Where sub-paragraph (3) above does not apply, the place for carrying out the deferred test shall be such place as may be notified with the notification of the time for the carrying out of the test, and where an area has been so specified the place shall be a place in that area.

(5) Notwithstanding the preceding provisions of this paragraph, the time and place for the carrying out of the deferred test may be varied by agreement between an authorised examiner and the owner of the vehicle.

(6) In this paragraph—

"notified" means notified in writing to the owner of the vehicle on behalf of the Secretary of State, and

"notification" shall be construed accordingly,

and any notification under this paragraph may be given by post.

4. The owner of the vehicle must produce it, or secure its production, at the time and place fixed for the carrying out of the deferred test.

5.—(1) References in this Schedule to the owner of a vehicle are references to the owner of the vehicle at the time at which the election is made under section 67(6) of this Act that the test should be deferred.

(2) For the purposes of this Schedule—

(a) subject to sub-paragraph (b) below, if at the time at which that election is made the vehicle is in the possession of a person under a hire-purchase agreement or hiring agreement, that person shall be deemed to be the owner of the vehicle to the exclusion of any other person,

(b) if at that time the vehicle is being used under an international circulation permit, the person to whom the permit was issued shall be deemed to be the owner of the vehicle to the exclusion of any other person. **[398]**

NOTES

Commencement: 15 May 1989.

This Schedule derived from the Road Traffic Act 1972, Sch 3, and the Local Government Act 1972, Sch 30.

SCHEDULE 3

Section 131

APPEALS UNDER SECTION 131 AGAINST DECISIONS OF THE REGISTRAR

1. On an appeal under section 131 of this Act, the Registrar shall be made respondent.

2.—(1) The Secretary of State shall refer every such appeal to a person, or two or three persons, appointed by him to hold an inquiry and report to him.

(2) The person or persons so appointed may be appointed either for the purposes of one particular inquiry, or of inquiries into any such appeal that may be made to the Secretary of State during such period as the Secretary of State may determine.

(3) No person so appointed shall be an officer of the Secretary of State.

(4) The Secretary of State may, for the purpose of any such inquiry, appoint up to three assessors to advise the person or persons holding it on matters arising out of it.

(5) The Secretary of State shall, before making an order under section 131 of this Act, consider any report made to him under this paragraph.

(6) The Secretary of State shall pay to any person or persons holding inquiries under this paragraph and to any assessors appointed under this paragraph such fees and such expenses, if any, incurred by them as he may, with the approval of the Treasury, determine.

3.—(1) The Secretary of State may by rules made by statutory instrument make provision as to the procedure on an appeal under section 131 of this Act.

(2) In particular, but without prejudice to the generality of sub-paragraph (1) above, the rules may make provision—

(a) prescribing the form and contents of the notice of appeal,

(b) enabling the party to an appeal to appear at an inquiry held under this Schedule by counsel or a solicitor or any person of such other description, if any, as may be specified by the rules,

(c) requiring proceedings on any such inquiry to be held in public, except in so far as may otherwise be provided by the rules,

(d) defining the functions of any assessors appointed by the Secretary of State.

4.—(1) The Secretary of State may on an appeal under section 131 of this Act—

(a) order the appellant to pay the whole or part of the costs incurred by the Secretary of State in connection with the appeal, or
(b) direct that the whole or part of the costs of the appellant incurred in connection with the appeal shall be treated as part of the administrative expenses of the Secretary of State.

(2) The Secretary of State may certify the amount of any such costs, and any amount so certified and ordered to be paid by the appellant shall be recoverable from him.

5. Section 180 of this Act, in its application to an inquiry caused by the Secretary of State to be held under paragraph 2 above, shall have effect as if subsection (1)(d) were omitted. **[399–400]**

NOTES
Commencement: 15 May 1989.
This Schedule derived from the Road Traffic Act 1972, Sch 6.

(Schedule 4 repealed by the Road Traffic Act 1991, s 83, Sch 8.)

ROAD TRAFFIC OFFENDERS ACT 1988
(c 53)

ARRANGEMENT OF SECTIONS

PART I
TRIAL

Introductory

Trial

An Act to consolidate certain enactments relating to the prosecution and punishment (including the punishment without conviction) of road traffic offences with amendments to give effect to recommendations of the Law Commission and the Scottish Law Commission   **[15 November 1988]**

PART I

TRIAL

Introductory

1. Requirement of warning etc of prosecutions for certain offences

(1) Subject to section 2 of this Act, [a person shall not be convicted of an offence to which this section applies unless]—

     (a) he was warned at the time the offence was committed that the question of prosecuting him for some one or other of the offences to which this section applies would be taken into consideration, or

     (b) within fourteen days of the commission of the offence a summons (or, in Scotland, a complaint) for the offence was served on him, or

     (c) within fourteen days of the commission of the offence a notice of the intended prosecution specifying the nature of the alleged offence and the time and place where it is alleged to have been committed, was—

         (i) in the case of an offence under section 28 or 29 of the Road Traffic Act 1988 (cycling offences), served on him,

         (ii) in the case of any other offence, served on him or on the person, if any, registered as the keeper of the vehicle at the time of the commission of the offence.

(2) A notice shall be deemed for the purposes of subsection (1)(c) above to have been served on a person if it was sent by registered post or recorded delivery service addressed to him at his last known address, notwithstanding that the notice was returned as undelivered or was for any other reason not received by him.

(3) The requirement of subsection (1) above shall in every case be deemed to have been complied with unless and until the contrary is proved.

(4) Schedule 1 to this Act shows the offences to which this section applies.

[401]

NOTES

     Commencement: 15 May 1989.

     This section derived from the Road Traffic Act 1972, s 179(1)-(3), the Road Traffic Act 1974, Sch 6, para 22, the Criminal Law Act 1977, Sch 12, para 1, and the Road Traffic Regulation Act 1984, Sch 13, para 23.

     Sub-s (1): words in square brackets substituted by the Road Traffic Act 1991, s 48, Sch 4, para 80.

2. Requirement of warning etc: supplementary

(1) The requirement of section 1(1) of this Act does not apply in relation to an offence if, at the time of the offence or immediately after it, an accident occurs owing to the presence on a road of the vehicle in respect of which the offence was committed.

(2) The requirement of section 1(1) of this Act does not apply in relation to an offence in respect of which—

(a) a fixed penalty notice (within the meaning of Part III of this Act) has been given or fixed under any provision of that Part, or
(b) a notice has been given under section 54(4) of this Act.

(3) Failure to comply with the requirement of section 1(1) of this Act is not a bar to the conviction of the accused in a case where the court is satisfied—

(a) that neither the name and address of the accused nor the name and address of the registered keeper, if any, could with reasonable diligence have been ascertained in time for a summons or, as the case may be, a complaint to be served or for a notice to be served or sent in compliance with the requirement, or
(b) that the accused by his own conduct contributed to the failure.

[(4) Failure to comply with the requirement of section 1(1) of this Act in relation to an offence is not a bar to the conviction of a person of that offence by virtue of the provisions of—

(a) section 24 of this Act, or
(b) any of the enactments mentioned in section 24(6);

but a person is not to be convicted of an offence by virtue of any of those provisions if section 1 applies to the offence with which he was charged and the requirement of section 1(1) was not satisfied in relation to the offence charged.]

[402]

NOTES
Commencement: 15 May 1989.
This section derived from the Road Traffic Act 1972, ss 177(4), 179(3A), (4), Sch 4, Part IV, paras 5-7, the Road Traffic Act 1974, Sch 6, para 22, the Criminal Law Act 1977, Sch 12, paras 2, 3, and the Transport Act 1982, s 49(12).
Sub-s (4): substituted for the original sub-ss (4)–(6) by the Road Traffic Act 1991, s 48, Sch 4, para 81.

3. Restriction on institution of proceedings for certain offences

(1) . . .

(2) In England and Wales, proceedings for an offence under section 94(3) of the Road Traffic Act 1988 (notice about relevant or prospective disability) shall not be instituted except by the Secretary of State or by a constable acting with the approval of the Secretary of State.

[403]

NOTES
Commencement: 15 May 1989.
This section derived from the Road Traffic Act 1972, ss 170(5A), 123, the Local Government Act 1972, Sch 30, the Road Traffic Act 1974, s 13(2), and the Transport Act 1985, Sch 2, para 3(2).
Sub-s (1): repealed by the Road Traffic (Driver Licensing and Information Systems) Act 1989, s 16, Sch 6.

4. Offences for which local authorities in England and Wales may institute proceedings

(1) The council of a county, metropolitan district or London Borough or the Common Council of the City of London may institute proceedings for an offence under section [15A of the Road Traffic Act 1988 (safety equipment for children in motor vehicles) or under section 17 or 18 of that Act] (helmets and other head-worn appliances for motor cyclists).

(2) The council of a county, metropolitan district or London Borough or the Common Council of the City of London may institute proceedings for an offence under section 27 of that Act (dogs on roads) relating to a road in their area.

(3) The council of a county, district or London borough or the Common Council of the City of London may institute proceedings for offences under section [35A(1), (2) or (5)] of the Road Traffic Regulation Act 1984 which are committed in connection with parking places provided by the council, or provided under any letting arrangements made by the council under section 33(4) of that Act.

(4) The council of a county, metropolitan district or London borough or the Common Council of the City of London may institute proceedings for an offence under section 47 or 52 of the Road Traffic Regulation Act 1984 in connection with a designated parking place controlled by the council.

(5) In England, the council of a county or metropolitan district and, in Wales, the council of a country or district may institute proceedings for an offence under section 53 of the Road Traffic Regulation Act 1984 in connection with a designated parking place in the council's area except, in Wales, any parking place for which another council has responsibility.

(6) In this section "parking place" means a place where vehicles, or vehicles of any class, may wait and "designated parking place" has the same meaning as in the Road Traffic Regulation Act 1984.

(7) This section extends to England and Wales only.　　　　　　　**[404]**

NOTES
Commencement: 15 May 1989.
This section derived from the Road Traffic Act 1972, ss 31(6), (7), 33(4), 33AA(6), the Local Government Act 1972, Sch 19, paras 1, 2, the Road Traffic Regulation Act 1984, ss 32(4), 35(8), 47(7), 52(2), and the Local Government Act 1985, Sch 5, para 2(2), (3).
Sub-s (1): words in square brackets substituted by the Motor Vehicles (Safety Equipment for Children) Act 1991, s 3(1).
Sub-s (3): figures in square brackets substituted by the Parking Act 1989, s 4, Schedule, para 10.

5. Exemption from Licensing Act offence

A person liable to be charged with an offence under [section 3A, 4], 5, 7 or 30 of the Road Traffic Act 1988 (drink and drugs) is not liable to be charged under section 12 of the Licensing Act 1872 with the offence of being drunk while in charge, on a highway or other public place, of a carriage.　　　　　　　**[405]**

NOTES
Commencement: 15 May 1989.
This section derived from the Road Traffic Act 1972, ss 13, 19(2), the Transport Act 1981, Sch 9, para 1, and the Roads (Scotland) Act 1984, Sch 11.
Words in square brackets substituted by the Road Traffic Act 1991, s 48, Sch 4, para 82.

6. Time within which summary proceedings for certain offences must be commenced

(1) Subject to subsection (2) below, summary proceedings for an offence to which this section applies may be brought within a period of six months from the date on which evidence sufficient in the opinion of the prosecutor to warrant the proceedings came to his knowledge.

(2) No such proceedings shall be brought by virtue of this section more than three years after the commission of the offence.

(3) For the purposes of this section, a certificate signed by or on behalf of the prosecutor and stating the date on which evidence sufficient in his opinion to warrant the proceedings came to his knowledge shall be conclusive evidence of that fact.

(4) A certificate stating that matter and purporting to be so signed shall be deemed to be so signed unless the contrary is proved.

(5) In relation to proceedings in Scotland, subsection (3) of section 331 of the Criminal Procedure (Scotland) Act 1975 (date of commencement of proceedings) shall apply for the purposes of this section as it applies for the purposes of that.

(6) Schedule 1 to this Act shows the offences to which this section applies.

[406]

NOTES

Commencement: 15 May 1989.

This section derived from the Road Traffic Act 1972, s 180, and the Transport Act 1982, s 46(2)–(5).

7. Duty of accused to provide licence

A person who is prosecuted for an offence involving [obligatory or discretionary disqualification] and who is the holder of a licence must—

    (a) cause it to be delivered to the clerk of the court not later than the day before the date appointed for the hearing, or

    (b) post it, at such a time that in the ordinary course of post it would be delivered not later than that day, in a letter duly addressed to the clerk and either registered or sent by the recorded delivery service, or

    (c) have it with him at the hearing

[and the foregoing obligations imposed on him as respects the licence also apply as respects the counterpart to the licence.] **[407]**

NOTES

Commencement: 15 May 1989.

This section derived from the Road Traffic Act 1972, s 101(4).

First words in square brackets substituted by the Road Traffic Act 1991, s 48, Sch 4, para 83, and second words in square brackets added with savings by SI 1990 No 144, reg 2(2), Sch 2, para 1; for savings see reg 3 thereof.

8. Duty to include date of birth and sex in written plea of guilty

A person who—

    (a) gives a notification to the clerk of a court in pursuance of section 12(2) of the Magistrates' Courts Act 1980 (written pleas of guilty), or

    (b) gives a written intimation of a plea of guilty in pursuance of section 334(3) of the Criminal Procedure (Scotland) Act 1975, in respect of an offence involving obligatory or discretionary disqualification or of such other offence as may be prescribed by regulations under section 105 of the Road Traffic Act 1988, must include in the notification or intimation a statement of the date of birth and sex of the accused.   **[408]**

NOTES
    Commencement: 15 May 1989.
    This section derived from the Road Traffic Act 1972, s 104(2), (6)(a), the Road Traffic Act 1974, Sch 3, para 11, and the Magistrates' Courts Act 1980, Sch 7, para 111.

Trial

9. Mode of trial

An offence against a provision of the Traffic Acts specified in column 1 of Part I of Schedule 2 to this Act or regulations made under such a provision (the general nature of which offence is indicated in column 2) shall be punishable as shown against the offence in column 3 (that is, on summary conviction or on indictment or in either one way or the other).   **[409–410]**

NOTES
    Commencement: 15 May 1989.
    This section derived from the Road Traffic Act 1972, s 177(1), (2)(a), and the Road Traffic Regulation Act 1984, s 98(1), (2)(a).
    Traffic Acts: Road Traffic Regulation Act 1984, Road Traffic Act 1988, Road Traffic (Consequential Provisions) Act 1988 (so far as it reproduces the effect of provisions repealed by that Act), Road Traffic Offenders Act 1988.

10. (*Applies to Scotland only.*)

11. Evidence by certificate as to driver, user or owner

(1) In any proceedings in England and Wales for an offence to which this section applies, a certificate in the prescribed form, purporting to be signed by a constable and certifying that a person specified in the certificate stated to the constable—

 (a) that a particular [mechanically propelled vehicle] was being driven or used by, or belonged to, that person on a particular occasion, or
 (b) that a particular [mechanically propelled vehicle] on a particular occasion was used by, or belonged to, a firm and that he was, at the time of the statement, a partner in that firm, or
 (c) that a particular [mechanically propelled vehicle] on a particular occasion was used by, or belonged to, a corporation and that he was, at the time of the statement, a director, officer or employee of that corporation,

shall be admissible as evidence for the purpose of determining by whom the vehicle was being driven or used, or to whom it belonged, as the case may be, on that occasion.

(2) Nothing in subsection (1) above makes a certificate admissible as evidence in proceedings for an offence except in a case where and to the like extent to which oral evidence to the like effect would have been admissible in those proceedings.

(3) Nothing in subsection (1) above makes a certificate admissible as evidence in proceedings for an offence—

(a) unless a copy of it has, not less than seven days before the hearing or trial, been served in the prescribed manner on the person charged with the offence, or

(b) if that person, not later than three days before the hearing or trial or within such further time as the court may in special circumstances allow, serves a notice in the prescribed form and manner on the prosecutor requiring attendance at the trial of the person who signed the certificate.

(4) In this section "prescribed" means prescribed by rules made by the Secretary of State by statutory instrument.

(5) Schedule 1 to this Act shows the offences to which this section applies.

[411]

NOTES

Commencement: 15 May 1989.

This section derived from the Road Traffic Act 1972, s 181, and the Road Traffic Regulations Act 1984, s 113.

Sub-s (1): words in square brackets substituted by the Road Traffic Act 1991, s 48, Sch 4, para 84.

12. Proof, in summary proceedings, of identity of driver of vehicle

(1) Where on the summary trial in England and Wales of an information for an offence to which this subsection applies—

(a) it is proved to the satisfaction of the court, on oath or in manner prescribed by rules made under section 144 of the Magistrates' Courts Act 1980, that a requirement under section 172(2) of the Road Traffic Act 1988 to give information as to the identity of the driver of a particular vehicle on the particular occasion to which the information relates has been served on the accused by post, and

(b) a statement in writing is produced to the court purporting to be signed by the accused that the accused was the driver of that vehicle on that occasion,

the court may accept that statement as evidence that the accused was the driver of that vehicle on that occasion.

(2) Schedule 1 to this Act shows the offences to which subsection (1) above applies.

(3) Where on the summary trial in England and Wales of an information for an offence to which section 112 of the Road Traffic Regulation Act 1984 applies—

(a) it is proved to the satisfaction of the court, on oath or in manner prescribed by rules made under section 144 of the Magistrates' Courts Act 1980, that a requirement under section 112(2) of the Road Traffic Regulation Act 1984 to give information as to the identity of the driver of a particular vehicle on the particular occasion to which the information relates has been served on the accused by post, and

(b) a statement in writing is produced to the court purporting to be signed by the accused that the accused was the driver of that vehicle on that occasion,

the court may accept that statement as evidence that the accused was the driver of that vehicle on that occasion.

[(4) In summary proceedings in Scotland for an offence to which section 20(2) of the Road Traffic Act 1988 applies, where—

(a) it is proved to the satisfaction of the court that a requirement under section 172(2) of the Road Traffic Act 1988 to give information as to the identity of a driver on a particular occasion to which the complaint relates has been served on the accused by post, and

(b) a statement in writing is produced to the court, purporting to be signed by the accused, that the accused was the driver of that vehicle on that occasion,

that statement shall be sufficient evidence that the accused was the driver of the vehicle on that occasion.]   **[412]**

NOTES

Commencement: 15 May 1989.

This section derived from the Road Traffic Act 1972, s 183, and the Road Traffic Regulations Act 1984, s 114.

Sub-s (4): prospectively added by the Road Traffic Act 1991, s 48, Sch 4, para 85, as from a day to be appointed.

13. Admissibility of records as evidence

(1) This section applies to a statement contained in a document purporting to be—

(a) a part of the records maintained by the Secretary of State in connection with any functions exercisable by him by virtue of Part III of the Road Traffic Act 1988 or a part of any other records maintained by the Secretary of State with respect to vehicles [or of any records maintained with respect to vehicles by an approved testing authority in connection with the exercise by that authority of any functions conferred on such authorities, or on that authority as such an authority, by or under any enactment], or

(b) a copy of a document forming part of those records, or

(c) a note of any information contained in those records,

and to be authenticated by a person authorised in that behalf by the Secretary of State [or (as the case may be) the approved testing authority].

(2) A statement to which this section applies shall be admissible in any proceedings as evidence (in Scotland, sufficient evidence) of any fact stated in it to the same extent as oral evidence of that fact is admissible in those proceedings.

(3) In the preceding subsections—

(a) "document" and "statement" have the same meanings as in section 10(1) of the Civil Evidence Act 1968 or, in Scotland, section 17(3) of the Law Reform (Miscellaneous Provisions) (Scotland) Act 1968, and

(b) the reference to a copy of a document shall be construed in accordance with section 10(2) of the Civil Evidence Act 1968 or, in Scotland, section 17(4) of the Law Reform (Miscellaneous Provisions) (Scotland) Act 1968.

Nothing in this subsection shall be construed as limiting to civil proceedings the references to proceedings in the preceding provisions of this section.

(4) In any case where—

(a) a statement to which this section applies is produced to a magistrates' court in any proceedings for an offence involving obligatory or discretionary disqualification,

(b) the statement specifies an alleged previous conviction of an accused person of any such offence or any order made on the conviction,

(c) it is proved to the satisfaction of the court, on oath or in such manner as may be prescribed by rules under section 144 of the Magistrates' Courts Act 1980, that not less than seven days before the statement is so produced a notice was served on the accused, in such form and manner as may be so prescribed, specifying the previous conviction or order and stating that it is proposed to bring it to the notice of the court in the event of or, as the case may be, in view of his conviction, and

(d) the accused is not present in person before the court when the statement is so produced,

the court may take account of the previous conviction or order as if the accused had appeared and admitted it.

(5) Nothing in the preceding provisions of this section enables evidence to be given in respect of any matter other than a matter of a description prescribed by regulations made by the Secretary of State.

(6) The power to make regulations under this section shall be exercisable by statutory instrument, which shall be subject to annulment in pursuance of a resolution of either House of Parliament. **[413]**

NOTES
Commencement: 15 May 1989.
This section derived from the Road Traffic Act 1972, ss 182, 196(1), 199(1), (3), the Road Traffic Act 1974, s 13(3), and the Transport Act 1981, Sch 9, para 15.
Sub-s (1): words in square brackets prospectively added by the Road Traffic (Consequential Provisions) Act 1988, s 4, Sch 2, Part I, as from a day to be appointed.

14. Use of records kept by operators of goods vehicles

In any proceedings [for an offence under section 40A of the Road Traffic Act 1988 or] for a contravention of or failure to comply with construction and use requirements (within the meaning of Part II of the Road Traffic Act 1988) or regulations under section 74 of that Act, any record purporting to be made and authenticated in accordance with regulations under that section shall be evidence (and in Scotland sufficient evidence) of the matters stated in the record and of its due authentication. **[414]**

NOTES
Commencement: 15 May 1989.
This section derived from the Road Traffic Act 1972, s 59(5).
Words in square brackets substituted by the Road Traffic Act 1991, s 48, Sch 4, para 86.

15. Use of specimens in proceedings for an offence under section 4 or 5 of the Road Traffic Act

(1) This section and section 16 of this Act apply in respect of proceedings for an offence under [section 3A, 4 or 5 of the Road Traffic Act 1988 (driving offences connected with drink or drugs)]; and expressions used in this section and section 16 of this Act have the same meaning as in [sections 3A to 10] of that Act.

(2) Evidence of the proportion of alcohol or any drug in a specimen of breath, blood or urine provided by the accused shall, in all cases [(including cases where the specimen was not provided in connection with the alleged offence)], be taken into account and, subject to subsection (3) below, it shall be assumed that the proportion of alcohol in the accused's breath, blood or urine at the time of the alleged offence was not less than in the specimen.

[(3) That assumption shall not be made if the accused proves—

    (a) that he consumed alcohol before he provided the specimen and—

        (i) in relation to an offence under section 3A, after the time of the alleged offence, and

        (ii) otherwise, after he had ceased to drive, attempt to drive or be in charge of a vehicle on a road or other public place, and

    (b) that had he not done so the proportion of alcohol in his breath, blood or urine would not have exceeded the prescribed limit and, if it is alleged that he was unfit to drive through drink, would not have been such as to impair his ability to drive properly.]

(4) A specimen of blood shall be disregarded unless it was taken from the accused with his consent by a medical practitioner.

(5) Where, at the time a specimen of blood or urine was provided by the accused, he asked to be provided with such a specimen, evidence of the proportion of alcohol or any drug found in the specimen is not admissible on behalf of the prosecution unless—

    (a) the specimen in which the alcohol or drug was found is one of two parts into which the specimen provided by the accused was divided at the time it was provided, and

    (b) the other part was supplied to the accused. **[415]**

NOTES

Commencement: 1 July 1992 (sub-s (3)); 15 May 1989 (remainder).

This section derived from the Road Traffic Act 1972, s 10(1), (2), (4), (6), and the Transport Act 1981, s 25(3), Sch 8.

Sub-ss (1)–(3): words in square brackets substituted by the Road Traffic Act 1991, s 48, Sch 4, para 87.

---

16. Documentary evidence as to specimens in such proceedings

(1) Evidence of the proportion of alcohol or a drug in a specimen of breath, blood or urine may, subject to subsections (3) and (4) below and to section 15(5) of this Act, be given by the production of a document or documents purporting to be whichever of the following is appropriate, that is to say—

    (a) a statement automatically produced by the device by which the proportion of alcohol in a specimen of breath was measured and a certificate signed by a constable (which may but need not be contained in the same document as the statement) that the statement relates to a specimen provided by the accused at the date and time shown in the statement, and

    (b) a certificate signed by an authorised analyst as to the proportion of alcohol or any drug found in a specimen of blood or urine identified in the certificate.

(2) Subject to subsections (3) and (4) below, evidence that a specimen of blood was taken from the accused with his consent by a medical practitioner may be given by the production of a document purporting to certify that fact and to be signed by a medical practitioner.

(3) Subject to subsection (4) below—

    (a) a document purporting to be such a statement or such a certificate (or both such a statement and such a certificate) as is mentioned in subsection (1)(a) above is admissible in evidence on behalf of the prosecution in pursuance of this section only if a copy of it either has been handed to the accused when the document was produced or has been served on him not later than seven days before the hearing, and

(b) any other document is so admissible only if a copy of it has been served on the accused not later than seven days before the hearing.

(4) A document purporting to be a certificate (or so much of a document as purports to be a certificate) is not so admissible if the accused, not later than three days before the hearing or within such further time as the court may in special circumstances allow, has served notice on the prosecutor requiring the attendance at the hearing of the person by whom the document purports to be signed.

(5) (*Applies to Scotland only*.)

(6) A copy of a certificate required by this section to be served on the accused or a notice required by this section to be served on the prosecutor may be served personally or sent by registered post or recorded delivery service.

(7) In this section "authorised analyst" means—

(a) any person possessing the qualifications prescribed by regulations made under [section 27 of the Food Safety Act 1990] as qualifying persons for appointment as public analysts under those Acts, and

(b) any other person authorised by the Secretary of State to make analyses for the purposes of this section. **[416]**

NOTES

Commencement: 15 May 1989.

This section derived from the Road Traffic Act 1972, s 10(3)-(5), (7)-(9), the Interpretation Act 1978, s 17, and the Transport Act 1981, s 25(3), Sch 8.

Sub-s (7): words in square brackets substituted by the Food Safety Act 1990, s 59(1) Sch 3, para 38.

---

17. Provisions as to proceedings for certain offences in connection with the construction and use of vehicles and equipment

(1) If in any proceedings for an offence under [section 40A, 41A, 41B or 42 of the Road Traffic Act 1988 (using vehicle in dangerous condition or contravention] of construction and use regulations)—

(a) any question arises as to a weight of any description specified in the plating certificate for a goods vehicle, and

(b) a weight of that description is marked on the vehicle,

it shall be assumed, unless the contrary is proved, that the weight marked on the vehicle is the weight so specified.

(2) If, in any proceedings for an offence—

(a) under Part II of the Road Traffic Act 1988, except sections 47 and 75, or

(b) under section 174(2) or (5) (false statements and deception) of that Act,

any question arises as to the date of manufacture of a vehicle, a date purporting to be such a date and marked on the vehicle in pursuance of regulations under that Part of that Act shall be evidence (and in Scotland sufficient evidence) that the vehicle was manufactured on the date so marked.

(3) If in any proceedings for the offence of driving a . . . vehicle on a road, or causing or permitting a . . . vehicle to be so driven, in contravention of a prohibition under section 70(2) of the Road Traffic Act 1988 any question arises

whether a weight of any description has been reduced to a limit imposed by construction and use requirements, [, or so that it has ceased to be excessive,] the burden of proof shall lie on the accused.

(4) (*Applies to Scotland only.*)   **[417]**

NOTES
  Commencement: 15 May 1989.
  This section derived from the Road Traffic Act 1972, ss 64, 170(7), the Road Traffic Act 1974, Sch 2, para 12, Sch 7, and the Road Traffic Regulation Act 1984, Sch 13, para 17.
  Sub-ss (1), (3): words in square brackets substituted or inserted, and words omitted repealed, by the Road Traffic Act 1991, ss 48, 83, Sch 4, para 88, Sch 8.
  Traffic Acts: Road Traffic Regulation Act 1984, Road Traffic Act 1988, Road Traffic (Consequential Provisions) Act 1988 (so far as it reproduces the effect of provisions repealed by that Act), Road Traffic Offenders Act 1988.

18. Evidence by certificate as to registration of driving instructors and licences to give instruction

(1) A certificate signed by the Registrar and stating that, on any date—

  (a) a person's name was, or was not, in the register,
  (b) the entry of a person's name was made in the register or a person's name was removed from it,
  (c) a person was, or was not, the holder of a current licence under section 129 of the Road Traffic Act 1988, or
  (d) a licence under that section granted to a person came into force or ceased to be in force,

shall be evidence, and in Scotland sufficient evidence, of the facts stated in the certificate in pursuance of this section.

(2) A certificate so stating and purporting to be signed by the Registrar shall be deemed to be so signed unless the contrary is proved.

(3) In this section "current licence", "Registrar" and "register" have the same meanings as in Part V of the Road Traffic Act 1988.   **[418–419]**

NOTES
  Commencement: 15 May 1989.
  This section derived from the Road Traffic Act 1972, s 138.

19. (*Applies to Scotland only.*)

[20. Speeding offences etc: admissibility of certain evidence

(1) Evidence (which in Scotland shall be sufficient evidence) of a fact relevant to proceedings for an offence to which this section applies may be given by the production of—

  (a) a record produced by a prescribed device, and
  (b) (in the same or another document) a certificate as to the circumstances in which the record was produced signed by a constable or by a person authorised by or on behalf of the chief officer of police for the police area in which the offence is alleged to have been committed;

but subject to the following provisions of this section.

(2) This section applies to—

(a) an offence under section 16 of the Road Traffic Regulation Act 1984 consisting in the contravention of a restriction on the speed of vehicles imposed under section 14 of that Act;

(b) an offence under subsection (4) of section 17 of that Act consisting in the contravention of a restriction on the speed of vehicles imposed under that section;

(c) an offence under section 88(7) of that Act (temporary minimum speed limits);

(d) an offence under section 89(1) of that Act (speeding offences generally);

(e) an offence under section 36(1) of the Road Traffic Act 1988 consisting in the failure to comply with an indication given by a light signal that vehicular traffic is not to proceed.

(3) The Secretary of State may by order amend subsection (2) above by making additions to or deletions from the list of offences for the time being set out there; and an order under this subsection may make such transitional provision as appears to him to be necessary or expedient.

(4) A record produced or measurement made by a prescribed device shall not be admissible as evidence of a fact relevant to proceedings for an offence to which this section applies unless—

(a) the device is of a type approved by the Secretary of State, and

(b) any conditions subject to which the approval was given are satisfied.

(5) Any approval given by the Secretary of State for the purposes of this section may be given subject to conditions as to the purposes for which, and the manner and other circumstances in which, any device of the type concerned is to be used.

(6) In proceedings for an offence to which this section applies, evidence (which in Scotland shall be sufficient evidence)—

(a) of a measurement made by a device, or of the circumstances in which it was made, or

(b) that a device was of a type approved for the purposes of this section, or that any conditions subject to which an approval was given were satisfied,

may be given by the production of a document which is signed as mentioned in subsection (1) above and which, as the case may be, gives particulars of the measurement or of the circumstances in which it was made, or states that the device was of such a type or that, to the best of the knowledge and belief of the person making the statement, all such conditions were satisfied.

(7) For the purposes of this section a document purporting to be a record of the kind mentioned in subsection (1) above, or to be a certificate or other document signed as mentioned in that subsection or in subsection (6) above, shall be deemed to be such a record, or to be so signed, unless the contrary is proved.

(8) Nothing in subsection (1) or (6) above makes a document admissible as evidence in proceedings for an offence unless a copy of it has, not less than seven days before the hearing or trial, been served on the person charged with the offence; and nothing in those subsections makes a document admissible as evidence of anything other than the matters shown on a record produced by a prescribed device if that person, not less than three days before the hearing or trial or within such further time as the court may in special circumstances allow,

serves a notice on the prosecutor requiring attendance at the hearing or trial of the person who signed the document.

(9) In this section "prescribed device" means device of a description specified in an order made by the Secretary of State.

(10) The powers to make orders under subsections (3) and (9) above shall be exercisable by statutory instrument, which shall be subject to annulment in pursuance of a resolution of either House of Parliament.]   **[420–421]**

NOTES
Commencement: 1 July 1992.
Commencement order: SI 1992 No 1286.
Substituted by the Road Traffic Act 1991, s 23.
See the Road Traffic Offenders (Prescribed Devices) Order 1992, SI 1992 No 1209, and the Road Trafic Offenders (Prescribed Devices) (No 2) Order 1992, SI 1992 No 2843.

21. (*Applies to Scotland only.*)

22. Notification of disability

(1) If in any proceedings for an offence committed in respect of a motor vehicle it appears to the court that the accused may be suffering from any relevant disability or prospective disability (within the meaning of Part III of the Road Traffic Act 1988) the court must notify the Secretary of State.

(2) A notice sent by a court to the Secretary of State in pursuance of this section must be sent in such manner and to such address and contain such particulars as the Secretary of State may determine.   **[422–423]**

NOTES
Commencement: 15 May 1989.
This section derived from the Road Traffic Act 1972, s 92(1), and the Road Traffic Act 1974, Sch 3, para 7(1).

VERDICT

23. (*Applies to Scotland only.*)

[24. Alternative verdicts: general

(1) Where—
    (a) a person charged with an offence under a provision of the Road Traffic Act 1988 specified in the first column of the Table below (where the general nature of the offences is also indicated) is found not guilty of that offence, but
    (b) the allegations in the indictment or information (or in Scotland complaint) amount to or include an allegation of an offence under one or more of the provisions specified in the corresponding entry in the second column,

he may be convicted of that offence or of one or more of those offences.

Offence charged	*Alternative*
Section 1 (causing death by dangerous driving)	Section 2 (dangerous driving) Section 3 (careless, and inconsiderate, driving)

Offence charged	Alternative
Section 2 (dangerous driving)	Section 3 (careless, and inconsiderate, driving)
Section 3A (causing death by careless driving when under influence of drink or drugs)	Section 3 (careless, and inconsiderate, driving)
	Section 4(1) (driving when unfit to drive through drink or drugs)
	Section 5(1)(a) (driving with excess alcohol in breath, blood or urine)
	Section 7(6) (failing to provide specimen)
Section 4(1) (driving or attempting to drive when unfit to drive through drink or drugs)	Section 4(2) (being in charge of a vehicle when unfit to drive through drink or drugs)
Section 5(1)(a) (driving or attempting to drive with excess alcohol in breath, blood or urine)	Section 5(1)(b) (being in charge of a vehicle with excess alcohol in breath, blood or urine)
Section 28 (dangerous cycling)	Section 29 (careless, and inconsiderate, cycling)

(2) Where the offence with which a person is charged is an offence under section 3A of the Road Traffic Act 1988, subsection (1) above shall not authorise his conviction of any offence of attempting to drive.

(3) Where a person is charged with having committed an offence under section 4(1) or 5(1)(a) of the Road Traffic Act 1988 by driving a vehicle, he may be convicted of having committed an offence under the provision in question by attempting to drive.

(4) Where by virtue of this section a person is convicted before the Crown Court of an offence triable only summarily, the court shall have the same powers and duties as a magistrates' court would have had on convicting him of that offence.

(5) Where, in Scotland, by virtue of this section a person is convicted under solemn procedure of an offence triable only summarily, the penalty imposed shall not exceed that which would have been competent on a conviction under summary procedure.

(6) This section has effect without prejudice to section 6(3) of the Criminal Law Act 1967 (alternative verdicts on trial on indictment), sections 61, 63, 64, 312 and 457A of the Criminal Procedure (Scotland) Act 1975 and section 23 of this Act.]   **[424]**

NOTES

  Commencement: 1 July 1992.
  Commencement order: SI 1992 No 1286.
  Substituted by the Road Traffic Act 1991, s 24.

AFTER CONVICTION

25. Information as to date of birth and sex

(1) If on convicting a person of an offence involving obligatory or discretionary disqualification or of such other offence as may be prescribed by regulations

under section 105 of the Road Traffic Act 1988 the court does not know his date of birth, the court must order him to give that date to the court in writing.

(2) If a court convicting a person of such an offence in a case where—

(a) notification has been given to the clerk of a court in pursuance of section 12(2) of the Magistrates' Courts Act 1980 (written pleas of guilty), or written intimation of a plea of guilty has been given in pursuance of section 334(3) of the Criminal Procedure (Scotland) Act 1975, and

(b) the notification or intimation did not include a statement of the person's sex,

does not know the person's sex, the court must order the person to give that information to the court in writing.

(3) A person who knowingly fails to comply with an order under subsection (1) or (2) above is guilty of an offence.

(4) Nothing in section 56(5) of the Criminal Justice Act 1967 (where a magistrates' court commits a person to the Crown Court to be dealt with, certain powers and duties transferred to that court) applies to any duty imposed upon a magistrates' court by subsection (1) or (2) above.

(5) Where a person has given his date of birth in accordance with this section or section 8 of this Act, the Secretary of State may serve on that person a notice in writing requiring him to provide the Secretary of State—

(a) with such evidence in that person's possession or obtainable by him as the Secretary of State may specify for the purpose of verifying that date, and

(b) if his name differs from his name at the time of his birth, with a statement in writing specifying his name at that time.

(6) A person who knowingly fails to comply with a notice under subsection (5) above is guilty of an offence.

(7) A notice to be served on any person under subsection (5) above may be served on him by delivering it to him or by leaving it at his proper address or by sending it to him by post; and for the purposes of this subsection and section 7 of the Interpretation Act 1978 in its application to this subsection the proper address of any person shall be his latest address as known to the person serving the notice.   **[425]**

NOTES

Commencement: 15 May 1989.

This section derived from the Road Traffic Act 1972, ss 104, 109, the Road Traffic Act 1974, Sch 3, para 11, and the Magistrates' Courts Act 1980, Sch 7, para 111.

[26. Interim disqualification]

(1) Where a magistrates' court—

(a) commits an offender to the Crown Court under subsection (1) of section 56 of the Criminal Justice Act 1967, or any enactment to which that section applies, or

(b) remits an offender to another magistrates' court under section 39 of the Magistrates' Courts Act 1980,

to be dealt with for an offence involving obligatory or discretionary disqualification, it may order him to be disqualified until he has been dealt with in respect of the offence.

(2) Where a court in England and Wales—

(a) defers passing sentence on an offender under section 1 of the Powers of Criminal Courts Act 1973 in respect of an offence involving obligatory or discretionary disqualification, or

(b) adjourns after convicting an offender of such an offence but before dealing with him for the offence,

it may order the offender to be disqualified until he has been dealt with in respect of the offence.

(3) Where a court in Scotland—

(a) adjourns a case under section 179 or section 380 of the Criminal Procedure (Scotland) Act 1975 (for inquiries to be made or to determine the most suitable method of dealing with the offender);

(b) remands a person in custody or on bail under section 180 or section 381 of the Criminal Procedure (Scotland) Act 1975 (to enable a medical examination and report to be made);

(c) defers sentence under section 219 or section 432 of the Criminal Procedure (Scotland) Act 1975;

(d) remits a convicted person to the High Court for sentence under section 104 of the Criminal Procedure (Scotland) Act 1975,

in respect of an offence involving obligatory or discretionary disqualification, it may order the accused to be disqualified until he has been dealt with in respect of the offence.

(4) Subject to subsection (5) below, an order under this section shall cease to have effect at the end of the period of six months beginning with the day on which it is made, if it has not ceased to have effect before that time.

(5) In Scotland, where a person is disqualified under this section where section 219 or section 432 of the Criminal Procedure (Scotland) Act 1975 (deferred sentence) applies and the period of deferral exceeds 6 months, subsection (4) above shall not prevent the imposition under this section of any period of disqualification which does not exceed the period of deferral.

(6) Where a court orders a person to be disqualified under this section ("the first order"), no court shall make a further order under this section in respect of the same offence or any offence in respect of which an order could have been made under this section at the time the first order was made.

(7) Where a court makes an order under this section in respect of any person it must—

(a) require him to produce to the court any licence held by him and its counterpart, and

(b) retain the licence and counterpart until it deals with him or (as the case may be) cause them to be sent to the clerk of the court which is to deal with him.

(8) If the holder of the licence has not caused it and its counterpart to be delivered, or has not posted them, in accordance with section 7 of this Act and does not produce the licence and counterpart as required under subsection (7) above, then he is guilty of an offence.

(9) Subsection (8) above does not apply to a person who—

(a) satisfies the court that he has applied for a new licence and has not received it, or

(b) surrenders to the court a current receipt for his licence and its counterpart issued under section 56 of this Act, and produces the licence and counterpart to the court immediately on their return.

(10) Where a court makes an order under this section in respect of any person, sections 44(1) and 47(2) of this Act and section 109(3) of the Road Traffic Act 1988 (Northern Ireland drivers' licences) shall not apply in relation to the order, but—

(a) the court must send notice of the order to the Secretary of State, and

(b) if the court which deals with the offender determines not to order him to be disqualified under section 34 or 35 of this Act, it must send notice of the determination to the Secretary of State.

(11) A notice sent by a court to the Secretary of State in pursuance of subsection (10) above must be sent in such manner and to such address and contain such particulars as the Secretary of State may determine.

(12) Where on any occasion a court deals with an offender—

(a) for an offence in respect of which an order was made under this section, or

(b) for two or more offences in respect of any of which such an order was made,

any period of disqualification which is on that occasion imposed under section 34 or 35 of this Act shall be treated as reduced by any period during which he was disqualified by reason only of an order made under this section in respect of any of those offences.

(13) Any reference in this or any other Act (including any Act passed after this Act) to the length of a period of disqualification shall, unless the context otherwise requires, be construed as a reference to its length before any reduction under this section.

(14) In relation to licences which came into force before 1st June 1990, the references in this section to counterparts of licences shall be disregarded.] **[426]**

NOTES
   Commencement: 1 July 1992.
   Commencement order: SI 1992 No 1286.
   Substituted by the Road Traffic Act 1991, s 25.

PART II

SENTENCE

Introductory

27. Production of licence

(1) Where a person who is the holder of a licence is convicted of an offence involving obligatory [or discretionary disqualification, and a court proposes to make an order disqualifying him or an order under section 44 of this Act, the court must, unless it has already received them,] require the licence [and its counterpart] to be produced to it.

(2) . . .

(3) If the holder of the licence has not caused it [and its counterpart] to be

delivered, or posted it [and its counterpart], in accordance with section 7 of this Act and does not produce it [and its counterpart] as required [under this section or section 44 of the Powers of Criminal Courts Act 1973, or section 223A or 436A of the Criminal Procedure (Scotland) Act 1975] then, unless he satisfies the court that he has applied for a new licence and has not received it—

(a) he is guilty of an offence, and
(b) the licence shall be suspended from the time when its production was required until [it and its counterpart are] produced to the court and shall, while suspended, be of no effect.

(4) Subsection (3) above does not apply where the holder of the licence—

(a) has caused a current receipt for the licence [and its counterpart] issued under section 56 of this Act to be delivered to the clerk of the court not later than the day before the date appointed for the hearing, or
(b) has posted such a receipt, at such time that in the ordinary course of post it would be delivered not later than that day, in a letter duly addressed to the clerk and either registered or sent by the recorded delivery service, or
(c) surrenders such a receipt to the court at the hearing,

and produces the licence [and its counterpart] to the court immediately on [their] return.   **[427]**

NOTES
Commencement: 15 May 1989 (sub-ss (1)-(3), sub-s (4) in relation to England and Wales); to be appointed (sub-s (4) in relation to Scotland).
This section derived from the Road Traffic Act 1972, ss 101(4), 103(4), the Road Traffic Act 1974, Sch 3, para 10, and the Transport Act 1982, s 35(4).
Sub-s (1): first words in square brackets substituted by the Road Traffic Act 1991, s 48, Sch 4, para 91(1), (2); second words in square brackets added with savings by SI 1990 No 144, reg 2(2), Sch 2, para 3(a); for savings see reg 3 thereof.
Sub-s (2): repealed by the Road Traffic Act 1991, ss 48, 83, Sch 4, para 91(1), (3), Sch 8.
Sub-s (3): first three and final words in square brackets substituted or inserted with savings by SI 1990 No 144, reg 2(2), Sch 2, para 3(6) (for savings see reg 3 thereof); remaining words in square brackets inserted by the Road Traffic Act 1991, s 48, Sch 4, para 91(1), (4).
Sub-s (4): words in square brackets substituted or inserted with savings by SI 1990 No 144, reg 2(2), Sch 2, para 3(c); for savings, see reg 3 thereof.

[28. Penalty points to be attributed to an offence

(1) Where a person is convicted of an offence involving obligatory endorsement, then, subject to the following provisions of this section, the number of penalty points to be attributed to the offence is—

(a) the number shown in relation to the offence in the last column of Part I or Part II of Schedule 2 to this Act, or
(b) where a range of numbers is shown, a number within that range.

(2) Where a person is convicted of an offence committed by aiding, abetting, counselling or procuring, or inciting to the commission of, an offence involving obligatory disqualification, then, subject to the following provisions of this section, the number of penalty points to be attributed to the offence is ten.

(3) Where both a range of numbers and a number followed by the words "(fixed penalty)" is shown in the last column of Part I of Schedule 2 to this Act in relation to an offence, that number is the number of penalty points to be attributed to the offence for the purposes of sections 57(5) and 77(5) of this Act; and, where only a range of numbers is shown there, the lowest number in the

range is the number of penalty points to be attributed to the offence for those purposes.

(4) Where a person is convicted (whether on the same occasion or not) of two or more offences committed on the same occasion and involving obligatory endorsement, the total number of penalty points to be attributed to them is the number or highest number that would be attributed on a conviction of one of them (so that if the convictions are on different occasions the number of penalty points to be attributed to the offences on the later occasion or occasions shall be restricted accordingly).

(5) In a case where (apart from this subsection) subsection (4) above would apply to two or more offences, the court may if it thinks fit determine that that subsection shall not apply to the offences (or, where three or more offences are concerned, to any one or more of them).

(6) Where a court makes such a determination it shall state its reasons in open court and, if it is a magistrates' court, or in Scotland a court of summary jurisdiction, shall cause them to be entered in the register (in Scotland, record) of its proceedings.

(7) The Secretary of State may by order made by statutory instrument—

    (a) alter a number or range of numbers shown in relation to an offence in the last column of Part I or Part II of Schedule 2 to this Act (by substituting one number or range for another, a number for a range, or a range for a number),

    (b) where a range of numbers is shown in relation to an offence in the last column of Part I, add or delete a number together with the words "(fixed penalty)", and

    (c) alter the number of penalty points shown in subsection (2) above;

and an order under this subsection may provide for different numbers or ranges of numbers to be shown in relation to the same offence committed in different circumstances.

(8) Where the Secretary of State exercises his power under subsection (7) above by substituting or adding a number which appears together with the words "(fixed penalty)", that number shall not exceed the lowest number in the range shown in the same entry.

(9) No order shall be made under subsection (7) above unless a draft of it has been laid before and approved by resolution of each House of Parliament.]
[428]

NOTES
    Commencement: 1 July 1992.
    Commencement order: SI 1992 No 1286.
    Substituted by the Road Traffic Act 1991, s 27.

[29. Penalty points to be taken into account on conviction

(1) Where a person is convicted of an offence involving obligatory endorsement, the penalty points to be taken into account on that occasion are (subject to subsection (2) below)—

    (a) any that are to be attributed to the offence or offences of which he is convicted, disregarding any offence in respect of which an order under section 34 of this Act is made, and

(b) any that were on a previous occasion ordered to be endorsed on the counterpart of any licence held by him, unless the offender has since that occasion and before the conviction been disqualified under section 35 of this Act.

(2) If any of the offences was committed more than three years before another, the penalty points in respect of that offence shall not be added to those in respect of the other.

(3) In relation to licences which came into force before 1st June 1990, the reference in subsection (1) above to the counterpart of a licence shall be construed as a reference to the licence itself.]   **[429]**

NOTES
Commencement: 1 July 1992.
Commencement order: SI 1992 No 1286.
Substituted by the Road Traffic Act 1991, s 28.

30. Penalty points: modification where fixed penalty also in question

(1) Sections 28 and 29 of this Act shall have effect subject to this section in any case where—

(a) a person is convicted of an offence involving [obligatory endorsement], and
(b) the court is satisfied that [the counterpart of] his licence has been or is liable to be endorsed under section 57 or 77 of this Act in respect of an offence (referred to in this section as the "connected offence") committed on the same occasion as the offence of which he is convicted.

(2) ... the number of penalty points to be attributed to the offence of which he is convicted is—

(a) the number of penalty points to be attributed to that offence under section [28] of this Act apart from this section, less
(b) the number of penalty points required to be endorsed on [the counterpart of] his licence under section 57 or 77 of this Act in respect of the connected offence [(except so far as they have already been deducted by virtue of this paragraph)].

(3) ...   **[430]**

NOTES
Commencement: 15 May 1989 (certain purposes); to be appointed (remaining purposes).
This section derived from the Transport Act 1982, s 44.
Sub-s (1): first words in square brackets substituted by the Road Traffic Act 1991, s 48, Sch 4, para 92(1), (2); remaining words in square brackets added with savings by SI 1990 No 144, reg 2(2), Sch 2, para 5; for savings see reg 3 thereof.
Sub-s (2): first and final words in square brackets substituted or inserted, and words omitted repealed, by the Road Traffic Act 1991, ss 48, 83, Sch 4, para 92(1), (3), Sch 8; remaining words in square brackets added with savings by SI 1990 No 144, reg 2(2), Sch 2, para 5; for savings see reg 3 thereof.
Sub-s (3): repealed by the Road Traffic Act 1991, ss 48, 83, Sch 4, para 92(1), (4), Sch 8.

31. Court may take particulars endorsed on licence into consideration

(1) Where a person is convicted of an offence involving [obligatory or discretionary disqualification] and his licence [and its counterpart are] produced to the court—

(a) any existing endorsement on [the counterpart of] his licence is prima facie evidence of the matters endorsed, and

(b) the court may, in determining what order to make in pursuance of the conviction, take those matters into consideration.

(2) (*Applies to Scotland only.*)   [431–432]

NOTES

Commencement: 15 May 1989.

This section derived from the Road Traffic Act 1972, s 101(1), (4A), (8), the Road Traffic Act 1974, Sch 3, para 10, the Transport Act 1981, Sch 9, paras 6, 9, and the Criminal Justice (Scotland) Act 1987, Sch 1, para 3.

Sub-s (1): first words in square brackets substituted by the Road Traffic Act 1991, s 48, Sch 4, para 93; remaining words in square brackets substituted or inserted with savings by SI 1990 No 144, reg 2(2), Sch 2, para 6; for savings see reg 3 thereof.

32. (*Applies to Scotland only.*)

Fine and imprisonment

33. Fine and imprisonment

(1) Where a person is convicted of an offence against a provision of the Traffic Acts specified in column 1 of Part I of Schedule 2 to this Act or regulations made under any such provision, the maximum punishment by way of fine or imprisonment which may be imposed on him is that shown in column 4 against the offence and (where appropriate) the circumstances or the mode of trial there specified.

(2) Any reference in column 4 of that Part to a period of years or months is to be construed as a reference to a term of imprisonment of that duration. [433]

NOTES

Commencement: 15 May 1989.

This section derived from the Road Traffic Act 1972, s 177(1), (2)(b), and the Road Traffic Regulation Act 1984, s 98(1), (2)(b).

Traffic Acts: Road Traffic Regulation Act 1984, Road Traffic Act 1988, Road Traffic (Consequential Provisions) Act 1988 (so far as it reproduces the effect of provisions repealed by that Act), Road Traffic Offenders Act 1988.

Disqualification

34. Disqualification for certain offences

(1) Where a person is convicted of an offence involving obligatory disqualification, the court must order him to be disqualified for such period not less than twelve months as the court thinks fit unless the court for special reasons thinks fit to order him to be disqualified for a shorter period or not to order him to be disqualified.

[(1A) Where a person is convicted of an offence under section 12A of the Theft Act 1968 (aggravated vehicle-taking), the fact that he did not drive the vehicle in question at any particular time or at all shall not be regarded as a special reason for the purposes of subsection (1) above.]

[(2) Where a person is convicted of an offence involving discretionary disqualification, and either—

(a) the penalty points to be taken into account on that occasion number fewer than twelve, or

(b) the offence is not one involving obligatory endorsement,

the court may order him to be disqualified for such period as the court thinks fit.]

(3) Where a person convicted of an offence under any of the following provisions of the Road Traffic Act 1988, that is—

[(aa) section 3A (causing death by careless driving when under the influence of drink or drugs),]
(a) section 4(1) (driving or attempting to drive while unfit),
(b) section 5(1)(a) (driving or attempting to drive with excess alcohol), and
(c) section 7(6) (failing to provide a specimen) where that is an offence involving obligatory disqualification,

has within the ten years immediately preceding the commission of the offence been convicted of any such offence, subsection (1) above shall apply in relation to him as if the reference to twelve months were a reference to three years.

[(4) Subject to subsection (3) above, subsection (1) above shall apply as if the reference to twelve months were a reference to two years—

(a) in relation to a person convicted of—

(i) manslaughter, or in Scotland culpable homicide, or
(ii) an offence under section 1 of the Road Traffic Act 1988 (causing death by dangerous driving), or
(iii) an offence under section 3A of that Act (causing death by careless driving while under the influence of drink or drugs), and

(b) in relation to a person on whom more than one disqualification for a fixed period of 56 days or more has been imposed within the three years immediately preceding the commission of the offence.

(4A) For the purposes of subsection (4)(b) above there shall be disregarded any disqualification imposed under section 26 of this Act or section 44 of the Powers of Criminal Courts Act 1973 or section 223A or 436A of the Criminal Procedure (Scotland) Act 1975 (offences committed by using vehicles) and any disqualification imposed in respect of an offence of stealing a motor vehicle, an offence under section 12 or 25 of the Theft Act 1968, an offence under section 178 of the Road Traffic Act 1988, or an attempt to commit such an offence.]

(5) The preceding provisions of this section shall apply in relation to a conviction of an offence committed by aiding, abetting, counselling or procuring, or inciting to the commission of, an offence involving obligatory disqualification as if the offence were an offence involving discretionary disqualification.

(6) This section is subject to section 48 of this Act.   **[434]**

NOTES
   Commencement: 1 July 1992 (sub-ss (2), (4), (4A); 1 April 1992 (sub-s (1A)); 15 May 1989 (remainder).
   This section derived from the Road Traffic Act 1972, s 93(1), (2), (4), (6), Sch 4, Part I, column 5, the Transport Act 1981, Sch 9, para 3, the Transport Act 1982, Sch 5, para 13, the Road Traffic Regulation Act 1984, s 98(1), (2)(c), and the Criminal Justice Act 1988, s 67.
   Sub-s (1A): inserted by the Aggravated Vehicle-Taking Act 1992, s 3(2).
   Sub-s (2): substituted by the Road Traffic Act 1991, s 29(1), (2).
   Sub-s (3): para (aa) inserted by the Road Traffic Act 1991, s 29(1), (3).
   Sub-ss (4), (4A): substituted for the original sub-s (4) by the Road Traffic Act 1991, s 29(1), (4).

[34A. Reduced disqualification period for attendance on courses

(1) This section applies where—

  (a) a person is convicted of an offence under section 3A (causing death by careless driving when under influence of drink or drugs), 4 (driving or being in charge when under influence of drink or drugs), 5 (driving or being in charge with excess alcohol) or 7 (failing to provide a specimen) of the Road Traffic Act 1988, and

  (b) the court makes an order under section 34 of this Act disqualifying him for a period of not less than twelve months.

(2) Where this section applies, the court may make an order that the period of disqualification imposed under section 34 shall be reduced if, by a date specified in the order under this section, the offender satisfactorily completes a course approved by the Secretary of State for the purposes of this section and specified in the order.

(3) The reduction made by an order under this section in a period of disqualification imposed under section 34 shall be a period specified in the order of not less than three months and not more than one quarter of the unreduced period (and accordingly where the period imposed under section 34 is twelve months, the reduced period shall be nine months).

(4) The court shall not make an order under this section unless—

  (a) it is satisfied that a place on the course specified in the order will be available for the offender,

  (b) the offender appears to the court to be of or over the age of 17,

  (c) the court has explained the effect of the order to the offender in ordinary language, and has informed him of the amount of the fees for the course and of the requirement that he must pay them before beginning the course, and

  (d) the offender has agreed that the order should be made.

(5) The date specified in an order under this section as the latest date for completion of a course must be at least two months before the last day of the period of disqualification as reduced by the order.

(6) An order under this section shall name the petty sessions area (or in Scotland the sheriff court district or, where an order has been made under this section by a stipendiary magistrate, the commission area) in which the offender resides or will reside.]   **[434A]**

NOTES
Commencement: 1 July 1992.
Commencement order: SI 1992 No 1286.
This section, and ss 34B, 34C post, inserted by the Road Traffic Act 1991, s 30.

[34B. Certificates of completion of courses

(1) An offender shall be regarded for the purposes of section 34A of this Act as having completed a course satisfactorily if (and only if) a certificate that he has done so is received by the clerk of the supervising court before the end of the period of disqualification imposed under section 34.

(2) If the certificate referred to in subsection (1) above is received by the clerk of the supervising court before the end of the period of disqualification imposed under section 34 but after the end of the period as it would have been

reduced by the order, the order shall have effect as if the reduced period ended with the day on which the certificate is received by the clerk.

(3) The certificate referred to in subsection (1) above shall be a certificate in such form, containing such particulars, and given by such person, as may be prescribed by, or determined in accordance with, regulations made by the Secretary of State.

(4) A course organiser shall give the certificate mentioned in subsection (1) above to the offender not later than fourteen days after the date specified in the order as the latest date for completion of the course, unless the offender fails to make due payment of the fees for the course, fails to attend the course in accordance with the organiser's reasonable instructions, or fails to comply with any other reasonable requirements of the organiser.

(5) Where a course organiser decides not to give the certificate mentioned in subsection (1) above, he shall give written notice of his decision to the offender as soon as possible, and in any event not later than fourteen days after the date specified in the order as the latest date for completion of the course.

(6) An offender to whom a notice is given under subsection (5) above may, within such period as may be prescribed by rules of court, apply to the supervising court for a declaration that the course organiser's decision not to give a certificate was contrary to subsection (4) above; and if the court grants the application section 34A of this Act shall have effect as if the certificate had been duly received by the clerk of the court.

(7) If fourteen days after the date specified in the order as the latest date for completion of the course the course organiser has given neither the certificate mentioned in subsection (1) above nor a notice under subsection (5) above, the offender may, within such period as may be prescribed by rules of court, apply to the supervising court for a declaration that the course organiser is in default; and if the court grants the application section 34A of this Act shall have effect as if the certificate had been duly received by the clerk of the court.

(8) A notice under subsection (5) above shall specify the ground on which it is given, and the Secretary of State may by regulations make provision as to the form of notices under that subsection and as to the circumstances in which they are to be treated as given.

(9) Where the clerk of a court receives a certificate of the kind referred to in subsection (1) above, or a court grants an application under subsection (6) or (7) above, the clerk or court must send notice of that fact to the Secretary of State; and the notice must be sent in such manner and to such address, and must contain such particulars, as the Secretary of State may determine.] **[434B]**

NOTES

Commencement: 1 July 1992.
Commencement order: SI 1992 No 1286.
See the note to s 34A ante.

[34C. Provisions supplementary to sections 34A and 34B

(1) The Secretary of State may issue guidance to course organisers, or to any category of course organiser as to the conduct of courses approved for the purposes of section 34A of this Act; and—

(a) course organisers shall have regard to any guidance given to them under this subsection, and

(b) in determining for the purposes of section 34B(6) whether any instructions or requirements of an organiser were reasonable, a court shall have regard to any guidance given to him under this subsection.

(2) In sections 34A and 34B and this section—

"course organiser", in relation to a course, means the person who, in accordance with regulations made by the Secretary of State, is responsible for giving the certificates mentioned in section 34B(1) in respect of the completion of the course;

"petty sessions area" has the same meaning as in the Magistrates' Courts Act 1980;

"supervising court", in relation to an order under section 34A, means—

(a) in England and Wales, a magistrates' court acting for the petty sessions area named in the order as the area where the offender resides or will reside;

(b) in Scotland, the sheriff court for the district where the offender resides or will reside or, where the order is made by a stipendiary magistrate and the offender resides or will reside within his commission area, the district court for that area,

and any reference to the clerk of a magistrates' court is a reference to the clerk to the justices for the petty sessions area for which the court acts.

(3) Any power to make regulations under section 34B or this section—

(a) includes power to make different provision for different cases, and to make such incidental or supplemental provision as appears to the Secretary of State to be necessary or expedient;

(b) shall be exercisable by statutory instrument, which shall be subject to annulment in pursuance of a resolution of either House of Parliament.]   **[434C]**

NOTES
Commencement: 1 July 1992.
Commencement order: SI 1992 No 1286.
See the note to s 34A ante.

35. Disqualification for repeated offences

(1) Where—

(a) a person is convicted of an offence [to which this subsection applies], and

(b) the penalty points to be taken into account on the occasion number twelve or more,

the court must order him to be disqualified for not less than the minimum period unless the court is satisfied, having regard to all the circumstances, that there are grounds for mitigating the normal consequences of the conviction and thinks fit to order him to be disqualified for a shorter period or not to order him to be disqualified.

[(1A) Subsection (1) above applies to—

(a) an offence involving discretionary disqualification and obligatory endorsement, and

(b) an offence involving obligatory disqualification in respect of which no order is made under section 34 of this Act.]

(2) The minimum period referred to in subsection (1) above is—

(a) six months if no previous disqualification imposed on the offender is to be taken into account, and

(b) one year if one, and two years if more than one, such disqualification is to be taken into account;

and a previous disqualification imposed on an offender is to be taken into account if it [was for a fixed period of 56 days or more and was imposed] within the three years immediately preceding the commission of the latest offence in respect of which penalty points are taken into account under section 29 of this Act.

(3) Where an offender is convicted on the same occasion of more than one offence [to which subsection (1) above applies]—

(a) not more than one disqualification shall be imposed on him under subsection (1) above,

(b) in determining the period of the disqualification the court must take into account all the offences, and

(c) for the purposes of any appeal any disqualification imposed under subsection (1) above shall be treated as an order made on the conviction of each of the offences.

(4) No account is to be taken under subsection (1) above of any of the following circumstances—

(a) any circumstances that are alleged to make the offence or any of the offences not a serious one,

(b) hardship, other than exceptional hardship, or

(c) any circumstances which, within the three years immediately preceding the conviction, have been taken into account under that subsection in ordering the offender to be disqualified for a shorter period or not ordering him to be disqualified.

(5) References in this section to disqualification do not include a disqualification imposed under section 26 of this Act or section 44 of the Powers of Criminal Courts Act 1973 [or section 223A or 436A of the Criminal Procedure (Scotland) Act 1975 (offences committed by using vehicles) or a disqualification imposed in respect of an offence of stealing a motor vehicle, an offence under section 12 or 25 of the Theft Act 1968, an offence under section 178 of the Road Traffic Act 1988, or an attempt to commit such an offence].

[(5A) The preceding provisions of this section shall apply in relation to a conviction of an offence committed by aiding, abetting, counselling, procuring, or inciting to the commission of, an offence involving obligatory disqualification as if the offence were an offence involving discretionary disqualification.]

(6) *(Applies to Scotland only.)*

(7) This section is subject to section 48 of this Act.   **[435]**

NOTES

Commencement: 1 July 1992 (sub-ss (1A), (5A)); 15 May 1989 (remainder).

This section derived from the Road Traffic Act 1972, Sch 4, Part I, column 5, the Transport Act 1981, s 19(2), (4)-(6), (9), and the Transport Act 1982, s 48(3).

Sub-ss (1), (2), (3), (5): words in square brackets substituted by the Road Traffic Act 1991, s 48, Sch 4, para 95(1), (2), (4)-(6).

Sub-ss (1A), (5A): inserted by the Road Traffic Act 1991, s 48, Sch 4, para 95(1), (3), (7).

[36. Disqualification until test is passed

(1) Where this subsection applies to a person the court must order him to be disqualified until he passes the appropriate driving test.

(2) Subsection (1) above applies to a person who is disqualified under section 34 of this Act on conviction of—

    (a) manslaughter, or in Scotland culpable homicide, by the driver of a motor vehicle, or

    (b) an offence under section 1 (causing death by dangerous driving) or section 2 (dangerous driving) of the Road Traffic Act 1988.

(3) Subsection (1) above also applies—

    (a) to a person who is disqualified under section 34 or 35 of this Act in such circumstances or for such period as the Secretary of State may by order prescribe, or

    (b) to such other persons convicted of such offences involving obligatory endorsement as may be so prescribed.

(4) Where a person to whom subsection (1) above does not apply is convicted of an offence involving obligatory endorsement, the court may order him to be disqualified until he passes the appropriate driving test (whether or not he has previously passed any test).

(5) In this section—

    "appropriate driving test" means—

        (a) an extended driving test, where a person is convicted of an offence involving obligatory disqualification or is disqualified under section 35 of this Act,

        (b) a test of competence to drive, other than an extended driving test, in any other case,

    "extended driving test" means a test of competence to drive prescribed for the purposes of this section, and

    "test of competence to drive" means a test prescribed by virtue of section 89(3) of the Road Traffic Act 1988.

(6) In determining whether to make an order under subsection (4) above, the court shall have regard to the safety of road users.

(7) Where a person is disqualified until he passes the extended driving test—

    (a) any earlier order under this section shall cease to have effect, and

    (b) a court shall not make a further order under this section while he is so disqualified.

(8) Subject to subsection (9) below, a disqualification by virtue of an order under this section shall be deemed to have expired on production to the Secretary of State of evidence, in such form as may be prescribed by regulations

under section 105 of the Road Traffic Act 1988, that the person disqualified has passed the test in question since the order was made.

(9) A disqualification shall be deemed to have expired only in relation to vehicles of such classes as may be prescribed in relation to the test passed by regulations under that section.

(10) Where there is issued to a person a licence on the counterpart of which are endorsed particulars of a disqualification under this section, there shall also be endorsed the particulars of any test of competence to drive that he has passed since the order of disqualification was made.

(11) For the purposes of an order under this section, a person shall be treated as having passed a test of competence to drive other than an extended driving test if he passes a corresponding test conducted—

   (a) under the law of Northern Ireland, the Isle of Man, any of the Channel Islands, another member State, Gibraltar or a designated country or territory (as defined by section 89(11) of the Road Traffic Act 1988), or
   (b) for the purposes of obtaining a British Forces licence (as defined by section 88(8) of that Act);

and accordingly subsections (8) to (10) above shall apply in relation to such a test as they apply in relation to a test prescribed by virtue of section 89(3) of that Act.

(12) This section is subject to section 48 of this Act.

(13) The power to make an order under subsection (3) above shall be exercisable by statutory instrument; and no such order shall be made unless a draft of it has been laid before and approved by resolution of each House of Parliament.

(14) The Secretary of State shall not make an order under subsection (3) above after the end of 2001 if he has not previously made such an order.] **[436]**

NOTES
   Commencement: 1 July 1992.
   Commencement order: SI 1992 No 1286.
   Substituted by the Road Traffic Act 1991, s 32.

37. Effect of order of disqualification

(1) Where the holder of a licence is disqualified by an order of a court, the licence shall be treated as being revoked with effect from the beginning of the period of disqualification.

   [(1A) Where—

   (a) the disqualification is for a fixed period shorter than 56 days in respect of an offence involving obligatory endorsement, or
   (b) the order is made under section 26 of this Act,

subsection (1) above shall not prevent the licence from again having effect at the end of the period of disqualification.]

(2) Where the holder of the licence appeals against the order and the disqualification is suspended under section 39 of this Act, the period of disqualification shall be treated for the purpose of subsection (1) above as beginning on the day on which the disqualification ceases to be suspended.

(3) Notwithstanding anything in Part III of the Road Traffic Act 1988, a person disqualified by an order of a court under section [36] of this Act is (unless he is also disqualified otherwise than by virtue of such an order) entitled to obtain and to hold a provisional licence and to drive a motor vehicle in accordance with the conditions subject to which the provisional licence is granted.   **[437]**

NOTES

Commencement: 1 July 1992 (sub-s (1A)); 15 May 1989 (remainder).

This section derived from the Road Traffic Act 1972, s 98(1), (3), and the Road Traffic Act 1974, Sch 3, para 9.

Sub-s (1A): inserted by the Road Traffic Act 1991, s 33.

Sub-s (3): figures in square brackets substituted by the Road Traffic Act 1991, s 48, Sch 4, para 96.

38. Appeal against disqualification

(1) A person disqualified by an order of a magistrates' court under section 34 or 35 of this Act may appeal against the order in the same manner as against a conviction.

(2) (*Applies to Scotland only.*)   **[438]**

NOTES

Commencement: 15 May 1989.

This section derived from the Road Traffic Act 1972, s 94(1), (3), the Criminal Justice (Scotland) Act 1980, Sch 7, para 23, and the Transport Act 1981, Sch 9, para 5.

39. Suspension of disqualification pending appeal

(1) Any court in England and Wales (whether a magistrates' court or another) which makes an order disqualifying a person may, if it thinks fit, suspend the disqualification pending an appeal against the order.

(2) (*Applies to Scotland only.*)

(3) Where a court exercises its power under subsection (1) or (2) above, it must send notice of the suspension to the Secretary of State.

(4) The notice must be sent in such manner and to such address and must contain such particulars as the Secretary of State may determine.   **[439]**

NOTES

Commencement: 15 May 1989.

This section derived from the Road Traffic Act 1972, s 94(2), (3), (3A), the Road Traffic Act 1974, Sch 6, para 17, and the Criminal Justice (Scotland) Act 1980, Sch 7, para 23.

40. Power of appellate courts in England and Wales to suspend disqualification

(1) This section applies where a person has been convicted by or before a court in England and Wales of an offence involving obligatory or discretionary disqualification and has been ordered to be disqualified; and in the following provisions of this section—

(a) any reference to a person ordered to be disqualified is to be construed as a reference to a person so convicted and so ordered to be disqualified, and

(b) any reference to his sentence includes a reference to the order of disqualification and to any other order made on his conviction and, accordingly, any reference to an appeal against his sentence includes a reference to an appeal against any order forming part of his sentence.

(2) Where a person ordered to be disqualified—

(a) appeals to the Crown Court, or
(b) appeals or applies for leave to appeal to the Court of Appeal,

against his conviction or his sentence, the Crown Court or, as the case may require, the Court of Appeal may, if it thinks fit, suspend the disqualification.

(3) Where a person ordered to be disqualified has appealed or applied for leave to appeal to the House of Lords—

(a) under section 1 of the Administration of Justice Act 1960 from any decision of a Divisional Court of the Queen's Bench Division which is material to his conviction or sentence, or
(b) under section 33 of the Criminal Appeal Act 1968 from any decision of the Court of Appeal which is material to his conviction or sentence,

the Divisional Court or, as the case may require, the Court of Appeal may, if it thinks fit, suspend the disqualification.

(4) Where a person ordered to be disqualified makes an application in respect of the decision of the court in question under section 111 of the Magistrates' Courts Act 1980 (statement of case by magistrates' court) or section 28 of the Supreme Court Act 1981 (statement of case by Crown Court) the High Court may, if it thinks fit, suspend the disqualification.

(5) Where a person ordered to be disqualified—

(a) applies to the High Court for an order of certiorari to remove into the High Court any proceedings of a magistrates' court or of the Crown Court, being proceedings in or in consequence of which he was convicted or his sentence was passed, or
(b) applies to the High Court for leave to make such an application,

the High Court may, if it thinks fit, suspend the disqualification.

(6) Any power of a court under the preceding provisions of this section to suspend the disqualification of any person is a power to do so on such terms as the court thinks fit.

(7) Where, by virtue of this section, a court suspends the disqualification of any person, it must send notice of the suspension to the Secretary of State.

(8) The notice must be sent in such manner and to such address and must contain such particulars as the Secretary of State may determine. **[440–441]**

NOTES

Commencement: 15 May 1989.

This section derived from the Road Traffic Act 1972, s 94A, and the Road Traffic Act 1974, Sch 3, para 8.

---

41. (*Applies to Scotland only.*)

[41A. Suspension of disqualification pending determination of applications under section 34B

(1) Where a person makes an application to a court under section 34B of this Act, the court may suspend the disqualification to which the application relates pending the determination of the application.

(2) Where a court exercises its power under subsection (1) above it must send notice of the suspension to the Secretary of State.

(3) The notice must be sent in such manner and to such address, and must contain such particulars, as the Secretary of State may determine.] **[441A]**

NOTES
  Commencement: 1 July 1992.
  Commencement order: SI 1992 No 1286.
  Inserted by the Road Traffic Act 1991, s 48, Sch 4, para 97.

42. Removal of disqualification

(1) Subject to the provisions of this section, a person who by an order of a court is disqualified may apply to the court by which the order was made to remove the disqualification.

(2) On any such application the court may, as it thinks proper having regard to—

> (a) the character of the person disqualified and his conduct subsequent to the order,
> (b) the nature of the offence, and
> (c) any other circumstances of the case,

either by order remove the disqualification as from such date as may be specified in the order or refuse the application.

(3) No application shall be made under subsection (1) above for the removal of a disqualification before the expiration of whichever is relevant of the following periods from the date of the order by which the disqualification was imposed, that is—

> (a) two years, if the disqualification is for less than four years,
> (b) one half of the period of disqualification, if it is for less than ten years but not less than four years,
> (c) five years in any other case;

and in determining the expiration of the period after which under this subsection a person may apply for the removal of a disqualification, any time after the conviction during which the disqualification was suspended or he was not disqualified shall be disregarded.

(4) Where an application under subsection (1) above is refused, a further application under that subsection shall not be entertained if made within three months after the date of the refusal.

(5) If under this section a court orders a disqualification to be removed, the court—

> (a) must cause particulars of the order to be endorsed on [the counterpart of] the licence, if any, previously held by the applicant, and
> (b) may in any case order the applicant to pay the whole or any part of the costs of the application.

[(5A) Subsection (5)(a) above shall apply only where the disqualification was imposed in respect of an offence involving obligatory endorsement; and in any other case the court must send notice of the order made under this section to the Secretary of State.

(5B) A notice under subsection (5A) above must be sent in such manner and to such address, and must contain such particulars, as the Secretary of State may determine.]

(6) The preceding provisions of this section shall not apply where the disqualification was imposed by order under section 36(1) of this Act. **[442]**

NOTES
Commencement: 1 July 1992 (sub-ss (5A), (5B)); 15 May 1989 (remainder).
This section derived from the Road Traffic Act 1972, s 95.
Sub-s (5): words in square brackets added with savings by SI 1990 No 144, reg 2(2), Sch 2, para 9; for savings see reg 3 thereof.
Sub-ss (5A), (5B): inserted by the Road Traffic Act 1991, s 48, Sch 4, para 98.

43. Rule for determining end of period of disqualification

In determining the expiration of the period for which a person is disqualified by an order of a court made in consequence of a conviction, any time after the conviction during which the disqualification was suspended or he was not disqualified shall be disregarded. **[443]**

NOTES
Commencement: 15 May 1989.
This section derived from the Road Traffic Act 172, s 94(4).

Endorsement

44. Endorsement of licences

(1) Where a person is convicted of an offence involving obligatory endorsement, the court must order there to be endorsed on [the counterpart of] any licence held by him particulars of the conviction and also—

(a) if the court orders him to be disqualified, particulars of the disqualification, or

(b) if the court does not order him to be disqualified—

(i) particulars of the offence, including the date when it was committed, and

(ii) the penalty points to be attributed to the offence.

(2) Where the court does not order the person convicted to be disqualified, it need not make an order under subsection (1) above if for special reasons it thinks fit not to do so.

(3) (*Applies to Scotland only.*)

(4) This section is subject to section 48 of this Act. **[444]**

NOTES
Commencement: 15 May 1989.
This section derived from the Road Traffic Act 1972, s 101(1), (2), Sch 4, Part I, column 5, the Transport Act 1981, s 19(1), Sch 9, paras 6, 7, the Transport Act 1982, s 48(3), and the Road Traffic Regulation Act 1984, s 98(1), (2)(d), Sch 13, para 20.
Sub-s (1): words in square brackets added with savings by SI 1990 No 144, reg 2(2), Sch 2, para 10; for savings see reg 3 thereof.

45. Effect of endorsement

(1) An order that any particulars or penalty points are to be endorsed on [the counterpart of] any licence held by the person convicted shall, whether he is at the time the holder of a licence or not, operate as an order that [the counterpart of] any licence he may then hold or may subsequently obtain is to be so endorsed

until he becomes entitled under subsection (4) below to have a licence issued to him [with its counterpart] free from the particulars or penalty points.

(2) On the issue of a new licence to a person, any particulars or penalty points ordered to be endorsed on [the counterpart of] any licence held by him shall be entered on [the counterpart of] the licence unless he has become entitled under subsection (4) below to have a licence issued to him [with its counterpart] free from those particulars or penalty points.

(3) . . .

(4) [A person the counterpart of whose licence has been ordered to be endorsed is entitled to have issued to him with effect from the end of the period for which the endorsement remains effective a new licence with a counterpart free from the endorsement if] he applies for a new licence in pursuance of section 97(1) of the Road Traffic Act 1988, surrenders any subsisting licence [and its counterpart], pays the fee prescribed by regulations under Part III of that Act and satisfies the other requirements of section 97(1).

(5) An endorsement ordered on a person's conviction of an offence remains effective (subject to subsections (6) and (7) below)—

    (a) if an order is made for the disqualification of the offender, until four years have elapsed since the conviction, and

    (b) if no such order is made, until either—

        (i) four years have elapsed since the commission of the offence, or

        [(ii) an order is made for the disqualification of the offender under section 35 of this Act].

(6) Where the offence was one under section 1 or 2 of that Act (causing death by dangerous driving and dangerous driving), the endorsement remains in any case effective until four years have elapsed since the conviction.

(7) Where the offence was one—

    [(a) section 3A, 4(1) or 5(1)(a) of that Act (driving offences connected with drink or drugs), or]

    (b) under section 7(6) of that Act (failing to provide specimen) involving obligatory disqualification,

the endorsement remains effective until eleven years have elapsed since the conviction.   **[445]**

NOTES

    Commencement: 15 May 1989.

    This section derived from the Road Traffic Act 1972, s 101(1), (3), (5)-(7A), and the Transport Act 1981, Sch 9, paras 6-12.

    Sub-ss (1), (2): words in square brackets added with savings by SI 1990 No 144, reg 2(2), Sch 2, para 11(a), (b); for savings see reg 3 thereof.

    Sub-s (3): repealed by the Road Traffic (Driver Licensing and Information Systems) Act 1989, ss 7, 16, Sch 3, para 25, Sch 6.

    Sub-s (4): words in square brackets substituted or inserted with savings by SI 1990 No 144, reg 2(2), Sch 2, para 11(d); for savings see reg 3 thereof.

    Sub-ss (5)–(7): words in square brackets substituted by the Road Traffic Act 1991, s 48, Sch 4, para 99.

General

46. Combination of disqualification and endorsement with probation orders and orders for discharge

(1) Notwithstanding anything in [section 1C(3)] of the Powers of Criminal Courts Act 1973 (conviction of offender . . . discharged to be disregarded for the

purposes of enactments relating to disqualification), a court in England and Wales which on convicting a person of an offence involving obligatory or discretionary disqualification makes—

(a) a probation order, or

(b) an order discharging him absolutely or conditionally,

may on that occasion also exercise any power conferred, and must also discharge any duty imposed, on the court by sections 34, 35, 36 or 44 of this Act.

(2) A conviction—

(a) in respect of which a court in England and Wales has ordered a person to be disqualified, or

(b) of which particulars have been endorsed on [the counterpart of] any licence held by him,

is to be taken into account, notwithstanding anything in [section 1C(1)] of the Powers of Criminal Courts Act 1973 (conviction of offender . . . discharged to be disregarded for the purpose of subsequent proceedings), in determining his liability to punishment or disqualification for any offence involving obligatory or discretionary disqualification committed subsequently.

(3) *(Applies to Scotland only.)*   **[446]**

NOTES

Commencement: 15 May 1989.

This section derived from the Road Traffic Act 1972, ss 93(8), 101(9), 102, the Powers of Criminal Courts Act 1973, Sch 5, para 43, the Criminal Justice (Scotland) Act 1980, s 55, the Transport Act 1981, Sch 9, para 13, and the Criminal Justice Act 1982, Sch 15, para 16.

Sub-s (1): words in square brackets substituted, and words omitted repealed, by the Criminal Justice Act 1991, ss 100, 101(2), Sch 11, para 38(1), Sch 13.

Sub-s (2): first words in square brackets inserted with savings by SI 1990 No 144, reg 2(2), Sch 2, para 12; for savings see reg 3 thereof; second words in square brackets substituted, and words omitted repealed, by the Criminal Justice Act 1991, ss 100, 101(2), Sch 11, para 38(2), Sch 13.

47. Supplementary provisions as to disqualifications and endorsements

(1) In any case where a court exercises its power under section 34, 35 or 44 of this Act not to order any disqualification or endorsement or to order disqualification for a shorter period than would otherwise be required, it must state the grounds for doing so in open court and, if it is a magistrates' court or, in Scotland, a court of summary jurisdiction, must cause them to be entered in the register (in Scotland, record) of its proceedings.

(2) Where a court orders the endorsement of [the counterpart of] any licence held by a person it may [, and where a court orders the holder of a licence to be disqualified for a period of 56 days or more it must,] send the [licence and its counterpart, on their] being produced to the court, to the Secretary of State; and if the court orders the endorsement but does not send the licence [and its counterpart] to the Secretary of State it must send him notice of the endorsement.

(3) Where on an appeal against [an order for the endorsement of a licence or the disqualification of a person] the appeal is allowed, the court by which the appeal is allowed must send notice of that fact to the Secretary of State.

(4) A notice sent by a court to the Secretary of State in pursuance of this section must be sent in such manner and to such address and contain such particulars as the Secretary of State may determine, and a licence [and the counterpart of a licence] so sent in pursuance of this section must be sent to such address as the Secretary of State may determine.   **[447]**

NOTES

Commencement: 15 May 1989.

This section derived from the Road Traffic Act 1972, s 105, and the Transport Act 1981, Sch 9, para 14.

Sub-s (2): first, third and fourth words in square backets substituted or inserted with savings by SI 1990 No 144, reg 2(2), Sch 2, para 13(a); for savings see reg 3 thereof; second words in square brackets substituted by the Road Traffic Act 1991, s 48, Sch 4, para 100(1), (2).

Sub-s (3): words in square brackets substituted by the Road Traffic Act 1991, s 48, Sch 4, para 100(1), (3).

Sub-s (4): words in square brackets added with savings by SI 1990 No 144, reg 2(2), Sch 2, para 13(b); for savings see reg 3 thereof.

[48. Exemption from disqualification and endorsement for certain construction and use offences

(1) Where a person is convicted of an offence under section 40A of the Road Traffic Act 1988 (using vehicle in dangerous condition etc) the court must not—

    (a) order him to be disqualified, or

    (b) order any particulars or penalty points to be endorsed on the counterpart of any licence held by him,

if he proves that he did not know, and had no reasonable cause to suspect, that the use of the vehicle involved a danger of injury to any person.

(2) Where a person is convicted of an offence under section 41A of the Road Traffic Act 1988 (breach of requirement as to brakes, steering-gear or tyres) the court must not—

    (a) order him to be disqualified, or

    (b) order any particulars or penalty points to be endorsed on the counterpart of any licence held by him,

if he proves that he did not know, and had no reasonable cause to suspect, that the facts of the case were such that the offence would be committed.

(3) In relation to licences which came into force before 1st June 1990, the references in subsections (1) and (2) above to the counterpart of a licence shall be construed as references to the licence itself.]   **[448]**

NOTES

Commencement: 1 July 1992.

Commencement order: SI 1992 No 1286.

Substituted by the Road Traffic Act 1991, s 48, Sch 4, para 101.

49. Offender escaping consequences of endorseable offence by deception

(1) This section applies where in dealing with a person convicted of an offence involving obligatory endorsement a court was deceived regarding any circumstances that were or might have been taken into account in deciding whether or for how long to disqualify him.

(2) If—

    (a) the deception constituted or was due to an offence committed by that person, and

    (b) he is convicted of that offence,

the court by or before which he is convicted shall have the same powers and duties regarding an order for disqualification as had the court which dealt with him for the offence involving obligatory endorsement but must, in dealing with him, take into account any order made on his conviction of the offence involving obligatory endorsement.   **[449]**

NOTES
Commencement: 15 May 1989.
This section derived from the Transport Act 1981, s 21.

50. (*Applies to Scotland only*.)

PART III

FIXED PENALTIES

Introductory

51. Fixed penalty offences

(1) Any offence in respect of a vehicle under an enactment specified in column 1 of Schedule 3 to this Act is a fixed penalty offence for the purposes of this Part of this Act, but subject to subsection (2) below and to any limitation or exception shown against the enactment in column 2 (where the general nature of the offence is also indicated).

(2) An offence under an enactment so specified is not a fixed penalty offence for those purposes if it is committed by causing or permitting a vehicle to be used by another person in contravention of any provision made or restriction or prohibition imposed by or under any enactment.

(3) The Secretary of State may by order provide for offences to become or (as the case may be) to cease to be fixed penalty offences for the purposes of this Part of this Act, and may make such modifications of the provisions of this Part of this Act as appear to him to be necessary for the purpose. **[450]**

NOTES
Commencement: 15 May 1989.
This section derived from the Transport Act 1982, ss 27(5), (6), 29(2).

52. Fixed penalty notices.

(1) In this Part of this Act "fixed penalty notice" means a notice offering the opportunity of the discharge of any liability to conviction of the offence to which the notice relates by payment of a fixed penalty in accordance with this Part of this Act.

(2) A fixed penalty notice must give such particulars of the circumstances alleged to constitute the offence to which it relates as are necessary for giving reasonable information about the alleged offence.

(3) A fixed penalty notice must state—

    (a) the period during which, by virtue of section 78(1) of this Act, proceedings cannot be brought against any person for the offence to which the notice relates, being the period of twenty-one days following the date of the notice or such longer period (if any) as may be specified in the notice (referred to in this Part of this Act as the "suspended enforcement period"),

    (b) the amount of the fixed penalty, and

    (c) the justices' clerk or, in Scotland, the clerk of court to whom and the address at which the fixed penalty may be paid.

(4) (*Applies to Scotland only*.) **[450A]**

NOTES
    Commencement: 15 May 1989 (sub-ss (1)–(3), sub-s (4) in relation to England and Wales); to be appointed (sub-s (4) in relation to Scotland).
    This section derived from the Transport Act 1982, ss 27(8), 29(6)(a), (b).

[53. Amount of fixed penalty

(1) The fixed penalty for an offence is—

    (a) such amount as the Secretary of State may by order prescribe, or

    (b) one half of the maximum amount of the fine to which a person committing that offence would be liable on summary conviction,

whichever is the less.

    (2) Any order made under subsection (1)(a) may make different provision for different cases or classes of case or in respect of different areas.]   **[450B]**

NOTES
    Commencement: 1 April 1992.
    Substituted by the Road Traffic Act 1991, s 48, Sch 4, para 102.

Giving notices to suspected offenders

54. Notices on-the-spot or at a police station

(1) This section applies where [in England and Wales] on any occasion a constable in uniform has reason to believe that a person he finds is committing or has on that occasion committed a fixed penalty offence.

    (2) Subject to subsection (3) below, the constable may give him a fixed penalty notice in respect of the offence.

    (3) Where the offence appears to the constable to involve obligatory endorsement, the constable may only give him a fixed penalty notice under subsection (2) above in respect of the offence if—

    (a) he produces his licence [and its counterpart] for inspection by the constable,

    (b) the constable is satisfied, on inspecting the licence [and its counterpart], that he would not be liable to be disqualified under section 35 of this Act if he were convicted of that offence, and

    (c) he surrenders his licence [and its counterpart] to the constable to be retained and dealt with in accordance with this Part of this Act.

    (4) Where—

    (a) the offence appears to the constable to involve obligatory endorsement, and

    (b) the person concerned does not produce his licence [and its counterpart] for inspection by the constable,

the constable may give him a notice stating that if, within seven days after the notice is given, he produces the notice together with his licence [and its counterpart] in person to a constable or authorised person at the police station specified in the notice (being a police station chosen by the person concerned) and the requirements of subsection (5)(a) and (b) below are met he will then be given a fixed penalty notice in respect of the offence.

    (5) If a person to whom a notice has been given under subsection (4) above produces the notice together with his licence [and its counterpart] in person to a constable or authorised person at the police station specified in the notice within

seven days after the notice was so given to him and the following requirements are met, that is—

   (a) the authorised person is satisfied, on inspecting the licence [and its counterpart], that he would not be liable to be disqualified under section 35 of this Act if he were convicted of the offence, and

   (b) he surrenders his licence [and its counterpart] to the constable or authorised person to be retained and dealt with in accordance with this Part of this Act,

the constable or authorised person must give him a fixed penalty notice in respect of the offence to which the notice under subsection (4) above relates.

(6) A notice under subsection (4) above shall give such particulars of the circumstances alleged to constitute the offence to which it relates as are necessary for giving reasonable information about the alleged offence.

(7) A licence [and a counterpart of a licence] surrendered in accordance with this section must be sent to the fixed penalty clerk.

(8) ...

(9) In this Part of this Act "authorised person", in relation to a fixed penalty notice given at a police station, means a person authorised for the purposes of this section by or on behalf of the chief officer of police for the area in which the police station is situated.

[(10) In determining for the purposes of subsections (3)(b) and (5)(a) above whether a person convicted of an offence would be liable to disqualification under section 35, it shall be assumed, in the case of an offence in relation to which a range of numbers is shown in the last column of Part I of Schedule 2 to this Act, that the number of penalty points to be attributed to the offence would be the lowest in the range.] **[450C]**

NOTES

Commencement: 1 July 1992 (sub-s (10)) (in relation to England and Wales); 15 May 1989 (except sub-s (10)) (in relation to England and Wales); to be appointed (in relation to Scotland).

This section derived from the Transport Act 1982, ss 27(1), (3), 28(1), (1)(a), (2), (3), (5), 34(3).

Sub-s (1): words in square brackets inserted by the Road Traffic Act 1991, s 48, Sch 4, para 103.

Sub-s (3): words in square brackets inserted by SI 1990 No 144, reg 2(2), Sch 2, para 15.

Sub-s (4): words in square brackets inserted by SI 1990 No 144, reg 2(2), Sch 2, para 15.

Sub-s (5): words in square brackets inserted by SI 1990 No 144, reg 2(2), Sch 2, para 15.

Sub-s (7): words in square brackets inserted by SI 1990 No 144, reg 2(2), Sch 2, para 15.

Sub-s (8): repealed by the Road Traffic Act 1991, s 83, Sch 8.

Sub-s (10): added by the Road Traffic Act 1991, s 48, Sch 4, para 103.

55.. Effect of fixed penalty notice given under section 54

(1) This section applies where a fixed penalty notice relating to an offence has been given to any person under section 54 of this Act, and references in this section to the recipient are to the person to whom the notice was given.

(2) No proceedings shall be brought against the recipient for the offence to which the fixed penalty notice relates unless before the end of the suspended enforcement period he has given notice requesting a hearing in respect of that offence in the manner specified in the fixed penalty notice.

(3) Where—

   (a) the recipient has not given notice requesting a hearing in respect of the offence to which the fixed penalty notice relates in the manner so specified, and

(b) the fixed penalty has not been paid in accordance with this Part of this Act before the end of the suspended enforcement period,

a sum equal to the fixed penalty plus one-half of the amount of that penalty may be registered under section 71 of this Act for enforcement against the recipient as a fine. **[450D]**

NOTES

    Commencement: 15 May 1989 (in relation to England and Wales); to be appointed (in relation to Scotland).

    This section derived from the Transport Act 1982, s 30.

56.. Licence receipts

(1) A constable or authorised person to whom a person surrenders his licence [and its counterpart] on receiving a fixed penalty notice given to him under section 54 of this Act must issue a receipt for the licence [and its counterpart] under this section.

    (2) The fixed penalty clerk may, on the application of a person who has surrendered his licence [and its counterpart] in those circumstances, issue a new receipt for [them].

    (3) A receipt issued under this section ceases to have effect—

      (a) if issued by a constable or authorised person, on the expiration of the period of one month beginning with the date of issue or such longer period as may be prescribed, and

      (b) if issued by the fixed penalty clerk, on such date as he may specify in the receipt,

or, if earlier, on the return of the licence [and its counterpart] to the licence holder. **[450E]**

NOTES

    Commencement: 15 May 1989 (in relation to England and Wales); to be appointed (in relation to Scotland).

    This section derived from the Transport Act 1982, s 35(1)–(3).

    Words in square brackets inserted by SI 1990 No 144, reg 2(2), Sch 2, para 16.

57.. Endorsement of licences without hearings

(1) Subject to subsection (2) below, where a person (referred to in this section as "the licence holder") has surrendered his licence [and its counterpart] to a constable or authorised person on the occasion when he was given a fixed penalty notice under section 54 of this Act, [the counterpart of] his licence may be endorsed in accordance with this section without any order of a court.

    (2) [The counterpart of] a person's licence may not be endorsed under this section if at the end of the suspended enforcement period—

      (a) he has given notice, in the manner specified in the fixed penalty notice, requesting a hearing in respect of the offence to which the fixed penalty notice relates, and

      (b) the fixed penalty has not been paid in accordance with this Part of this Act.

    (3) On the payment of the fixed penalty before the end of the suspended enforcement period, the fixed penalty clerk must endorse the relevant particulars on the [counterpart of the] licence and return it [together with the licence] to the licence holder.

(4) Where any sum determined by reference to the fixed penalty is registered under section 71 of this Act for enforcement against the licence holder as a fine, the fixed penalty clerk must endorse the relevant particulars on the [counterpart of the] licence and return it [together with the licence] to the licence holder—

(a) if he is himself the clerk who registers that sum, on the registration of that sum, and

(b) in any other case, on being notified of the registration by the clerk who registers that sum.

(5) References in this section to the relevant particulars are to—

(a) particulars of the offence, including the date when it was committed, and

(b) the number of penalty points to be attributed to the offence.

(6) On endorsing [the counterpart of] a person's licence under this section the fixed penalty clerk must send notice of the endorsement and of the particulars endorsed to the Secretary of State. **[450F]**

NOTES

Commencement: 15 May 1989 (in relation to England and Wales); to be appointed (in relation to Scotland).

This section derived from the Transport Act 1982, s 34(1), (2), (4)–(6), (10).

Words in square brackets inserted by SI 1990 No 144, reg 2(2), Sch 2, para 17.

58.. Effect of endorsement without hearing

(1) Where [the counterpart of] a person's licence is endorsed under section 57 of this Act he shall be treated for the purposes of sections 13(4), 28, 29 and 45 of this Act and of the Rehabilitation of Offenders Act 1974 as if—

(a) he had been convicted of the offence,

(b) the endorsement had been made in pursuance of an order made on his conviction by a court under section 44 of this Act, and

(c) the particulars of the offence endorsed by virtue of section 57(5)(a) of this Act were particulars of his conviction of that offence.

(2) In relation to any endorsement of [the counterpart of] a person's licence under section 57 of this Act—

(a) the reference in section 45(4) of this Act to the order for endorsement, and

(b) the references in section 13(4) of this Act to any order made on a person's conviction,

are to be read as references to the endorsement itself. **[450G]**

NOTES

Commencement: 15 May 1989 (in relation to England and Wales); to be appointed (in relation to Scotland).

This section derived from the Transport Act 1982, s 34(7), (8).

Words in square brackets inserted by SI 1990 No 144, reg 2(2), Sch 2, para 18.

59.. Notification of court and date of trial in England and Wales

(1) On an occasion when a person is given a fixed penalty notice under section 54 of this Act in respect of an offence, he may be given written notification specifying the magistrates' court by which and the date on which the offence will be tried if he gives notice requesting a hearing in respect of the offence as permitted by the fixed penalty notice.

(2) Subject to subsections (4) and (5) below, where—

    (a) a person has been notified in accordance with this section of the court and date of trial of an offence in respect of which he has been given a fixed penalty notice, and

    (b) he has given notice requesting a hearing in respect of the offence as permitted by the fixed penalty notice,

the provisions of the Magistrates' Courts Act 1980 shall apply as mentioned in subsection (3) below.

(3) Those provisions are to have effect for the purpose of any proceedings in respect of that offence as if—

    (a) the allegation in the fixed penalty notice with respect to that offence were an information duly laid in accordance with section 1 of that Act, and

    (b) the notification of the court and date of trial were a summons duly issued on that information by a justice of the peace for the area for which the magistrates' court notified as the court of trial acts, requiring the person notified to appear before that court to answer to that information and duly served on him on the date on which the notification was given.

(4) If, in a case within subsection (2) above, notice is served by or on behalf of the chief officer of police on the person who gave notice requesting a hearing stating that no proceedings are to be brought in respect of the offence concerned, that subsection does not apply and no such proceedings are to be brought against the person who gave notice requesting a hearing.

(5) Section 14 of that Act (proceedings invalid where accused did not know of them) is not applied by subsection (2) above in a case where a person has been notified in accordance with this section of the court and date of trial of an offence.

(6) ...   **[450H]**

NOTES

    Commencement: to be appointed. Note, however, that the repeal of sub-s (6) was brought into force on 1 July 1992.

    This section derived from the Transport Act 1982, s 39.

    Sub-s (6): repealed by the Road Traffic Act 1991, s 83, Sch 8.

60.. (*Repealed by the Road Traffic Act 1991, s 83, Sch 8.*)

61.. **Fixed penalty notice mistakenly given: exclusion of fixed penalty procedures**

(1) This section applies where, on inspection of a licence [and its counterpart] sent to him under section 54(7) of this Act, it appears to the fixed penalty clerk that the person whose licence it is would be liable to be disqualified under section 35 of this Act if he were convicted of the offence in respect of which the fixed penalty notice was given.

(2) The fixed penalty clerk must not endorse the [counterpart of the] licence under section 57 of this Act but must instead send it [together with the licence] to the chief officer of police.

(3) Nothing in this Part of this Act prevents proceedings being brought in respect of the offence in respect of which the fixed penalty notice was given where those proceedings are commenced before the end of the period of six months beginning with the date on which that notice was given.

(4) Where proceedings in respect of that offence are commenced before the end of that period, the case is from then on to be treated in all respects as if no fixed penalty notice had been given in respect of the offence.

(5) Accordingly, where proceedings in respect of that offence are so commenced, any action taken in pursuance of any provision of this Part of this Act by reference to that fixed penalty notice shall be void (including, but without prejudice to the generality of the preceding provision—

(a) the registration under section 71 of this Act of any sum, determined by reference to the fixed penalty for that offence, for enforcement against the person whose licence it is as a fine, and

(b) any proceedings for enforcing payment of any such sum within the meaning of sections 73 and 74 of this Act (defined in section 74(5))).

[(6) In determining for the purposes of subsection (1) above whether a person convicted of an offence would be liable to disqualification under section 35, it shall be assumed, in the case of an offence in relation to which a range of numbers is shown in the last column of Part I of Schedule 2 to this Act, that the number of penalty points to be attributed to the offence would be the lowest in the range.] **[450J]**

NOTES

Commencement: 1 July 1992 (sub-s (6)) (in relation to England and Wales); 15 May 1989 (except sub-s (6)) (in relation to England and Wales); to be appointed (in relation to Scotland).

This section derived from the Transport Act 1982, s 41(1)–(4).

Sub-s (1), (2): words in square brackets inserted by SI 1990 No 144, reg 2(2), Sch 2, para 19.

Sub-s (6): added by the Road Traffic Act 1991, s 48, Sch 4, para 104.

Notices fixed to vehicles

62.. Fixing notices to vehicles

(1) Where on any occasion a constable has reason to believe in the case of any stationary vehicle that a fixed penalty offence is being or has on that occasion been committed in respect of it, he may fix a fixed penalty notice in respect of the offence to the vehicle unless the offence appears to him to involve obligatory endorsement.

(2) A person is guilty of an offence if he removes or interferes with any notice fixed to a vehicle under this section, unless he does so by or under the authority of the driver or person in charge of the vehicle or the person liable for the fixed penalty offence in question. **[450K]**

NOTES

Commencement: 15 May 1989.

This section derived from the Transport Act 1982, ss 27(2), (4), 29(7).

63.. Service of notice to owner if penalty not paid

(1) This section applies where a fixed penalty notice relating to an offence has been fixed to a vehicle under section 62 of this Act.

(2) Subject to subsection (3) below, if at the end of the suspended enforcement period the fixed penalty has not been paid in accordance with this Part of this Act, a notice under this section may be served by or on behalf of the chief officer of police on any person who appears to him (or to any person authorised to act on his behalf for the purposes of this section) to be the owner of the vehicle.

Such a notice is referred to in this Part of this Act as a "notice to owner".

(3) Subsection (2) above does not apply where before the end of the suspended enforcement period—

(a) any person has given notice requesting a hearing in respect of the offence in the manner specified in the fixed penalty notice, and

(b) the notice so given contains a statement by that person to the effect that he was the driver of the vehicle at the time when the offence is alleged to have been committed.

That time is referred to in this Part of this Act as the "time of the alleged offence".

(4) A notice to owner—

(a) must give particulars of the alleged offence and of the fixed penalty concerned,

(b) must state the period allowed for response to the notice, and

(c) must indicate that, if the fixed penalty is not paid before the end of that period, the person on whom the notice is served is asked to provide before the end of that period to the chief officer of police by or on whose behalf the notice was served a statutory statement of ownership (as defined in Part I of Schedule 4 to this Act).

(5) For the purposes of this Part of this Act, the period allowed for response to a notice to owner is the period of twenty-one days from the date on which the notice is served, or such longer period (if any) as may be specified in the notice.

(6) A notice to owner relating to any offence must indicate that the person on whom it is served may, before the end of the period allowed for response to the notice, either—

(a) give notice requesting a hearing in respect of the offence in the manner indicated by the notice, or

(b) if—

   (i) he was not the driver of the vehicle at the time of the alleged offence, and

   (ii) a person purporting to be the driver wishes to give notice requesting a hearing in respect of the offence,

provide, together with a statutory statement of ownership provided as requested in that notice, a statutory statement of facts (as defined by Part II of Schedule 4 to this Act) having the effect referred to in paragraph 3(2) of that Schedule (that is, as a notice requesting a hearing in respect of the offence given by the driver).

(7) In any case where a person on whom a notice to owner relating to any offence has been served provides a statutory statement of facts in pursuance of subsection (6)(b) above—

(a) any notice requesting a hearing in respect of the offence that he purports to give on his own account shall be of no effect, and

(b) no sum may be registered for enforcement against him as a fine in respect of the offence unless, within the period of two months immediately following the period allowed for response to the notice to owner, no summons or, in Scotland, complaint in respect of the offence in question is served on the person identified in the statement as the driver.   **[450L]**

NOTES

Commencement: 15 May 1989.

This section derived from the Transport Act 1982, ss 31(1)–(4), (9), 32(3), (5).

64. Enforcement or proceedings against owner

(1) This section applies where—

   (a) a fixed penalty notice relating to an offence has been fixed to a vehicle under section 62 of this Act,

   (b) a notice to owner relating to the offence has been served on any person under section 63(2) of this Act before the end of the period of six months beginning with the day on which the fixed penalty notice was fixed to the vehicle, and

   (c) the fixed penalty has not been paid in accordance with this Part of this Act before the end of the period allowed for response to the notice to owner.

(2) Subject to subsection (4) below and to section 63(7)(b) of this Act, a sum equal to the fixed penalty plus one-half of the amount of that penalty may be registered under section 71 of this Act for enforcement against the person on whom the notice to owner was served as a fine.

(3) Subject to subsection (4) below and to section 65 of this Act, proceedings may be brought in respect of the offence against the person on whom the notice to owner was served.

(4) If the person on whom the notice to owner was served—

   (a) was not the owner of the vehicle at the time of the alleged offence, and

   (b) provides a statutory statement of ownership to that effect in response to the notice before the end of the period allowed for response to the notice,

he shall not be liable in respect of the offence by virtue of this section nor shall any sum determined by reference to the fixed penalty for the offence be so registered by virtue of this section for enforcement against him as a fine.

(5) Subject to subsection (6) below—

   (a) for the purposes of the institution of proceedings by virtue of subsection (3) above against any person on whom a notice to owner has been served, and

   (b) in any proceedings brought by virtue of that subsection against any such person,

it shall be conclusively presumed (notwithstanding that that person may not be an individual) that he was the driver of the vehicle at the time of the alleged offence and, accordingly, that acts or omissions of the driver of the vehicle at that time were his acts or omissions.

(6) That presumption does not apply in any proceedings brought against any person by virtue of subsection (3) above if, in those proceedings, it is proved that at the time of the alleged offence the vehicle was in the possession of some other person without the consent of the accused.

(7) Where—

   (a) by virtue of subsection (3) above proceedings may be brought in respect of an offence against a person on whom a notice to owner was served, and

   (b) section 74(1) of this Act does not apply,

section 127(1) of the Magistrates' Courts Act 1980 (information must be laid within six months of time offence committed) and section 331(1) of the Criminal

Procedure (Scotland) Act 1975 (proceedings must be commenced within six months of that time) shall have effect as if for the reference to six months there were substituted a reference to twelve months.   **[450M]**

NOTES
Commencement: 15 May 1989.
This section derived from the Transport Act 1982, ss 31(5)–(8), 32(2), 49(13).

65. Restrictions on proceedings against owner and others

(1) In any case where a notice to owner relating to an offence may be served under section 63 of this Act, no proceedings shall be brought in respect of the offence against any person other than a person on whom such a notice has been served unless he is identified as the driver of the vehicle at the time of the alleged offence in a statutory statement of facts provided in pursuance of section 63(6)(b) of this Act by a person on whom such a notice has been served.

(2) Proceedings in respect of an offence to which a notice to owner relates shall not be brought against the person on whom the notice was served unless, before the end of the period allowed for response to the notice, he has given notice, in the manner indicated by the notice to owner, requesting a hearing in respect of the offence.

(3) Proceedings in respect of an offence to which a notice to owner relates may not be brought against any person identified as the driver of the vehicle in a statutory statement of facts provided in response to the notice if the fixed penalty is paid in accordance with this Part of this Act before the end of the period allowed for response to the notice.

(4) Once any sum determined by reference to the fixed penalty for an offence has been registered by virtue of section 64 of this Act under section 71 for enforcement as a fine against a person on whom a notice to owner relating to that offence has been served, no proceedings shall be brought against any other person in respect of that offence.   **[450N]**

NOTES
Commencement: 15 May 1989.
This section derived from the Transport Act 1982, ss 32(1), (4), (6), 33(6).

66. Hired vehicles

(1) This section applies where—
  (a) a notice to owner has been served on a vehicle-hire firm,
  (b) at the time of the alleged offence the vehicle in respect of which the notice was served was let to another person by the vehicle-hire firm under a hiring agreement to which this section applies, and
  (c) within the period allowed for response to the notice the firm provides the chief officer of police by or on whose behalf the notice was served with the documents mentioned in subsection (2) below.

(2) Those documents are a statement on an official form, signed by or on behalf of the firm, stating that at the time of the alleged offence the vehicle concerned was hired under a hiring agreement to which this section applies, together with—
  (a) a copy of that hiring agreement, and
  (b) a copy of a statement of liability signed by the hirer under that hiring agreement.

(3) In this section a "statement of liability" means a statement made by the hirer under a hiring agreement to which this section applies to the effect that the hirer acknowledges that he will be liable, as the owner of the vehicle, in respect of any fixed penalty offence which may be committed with respect to the vehicle during the currency of the hiring agreement and giving such information as may be prescribed.

(4) In any case where this section applies, sections 63, 64 and 65 of this Act shall have effect as if—

(a) any reference to the owner of the vehicle were a reference to the hirer under the hiring agreement, and

(b) any reference to a statutory statement of ownership were a reference to a statutory statement of hiring,

and accordingly references in this Part of this Act (with the exceptions mentioned below) to a notice to owner include references to a notice served under section 63 of this Act as it applies by virtue of this section.

This subsection does not apply to references to a notice to owner in this section or in section 81(2)(b) of or Part I of Schedule 4 to this Act.

(5) In any case where this section applies, a person authorised in that behalf by the chief officer of police to whom the documents mentioned in subsection (2) above are provided may, at any reasonable time within six months after service of the notice to owner (and on the production of his authority) require the firm to produce the originals of the hiring agreement and statement of liability in question.

(6) If a vehicle-hire firm fails to produce the original of a document when required to do so under subsection (5) above, this section shall thereupon cease to apply (and section 64 of this Act shall apply accordingly in any such case after that time as it applies in a case where the person on whom the notice to owner was served has failed to provide a statutory statement of ownership in response to the notice within the period allowed).

(7) This section applies to a hiring agreement under the terms of which the vehicle concerned is let to the hirer for a fixed period of less than six months (whether or not that period is capable of extension by agreement between the parties or otherwise); and any reference in this section to the currency of the hiring agreement includes a reference to any period during which, with the consent of the vehicle-hire firm, the hirer continues in possession of the vehicle as hirer, after the expiry of the fixed period specified in the agreement, but otherwise on the terms and conditions so specified.

(8) In this section—

"hiring agreement" refers only to an agreement which contains such particulars as may be prescribed and does not include a hire-purchase agreement within the meaning of the Consumer Credit Act 1974, and

"vehicle-hire firm" means any person engaged in hiring vehicles in the course of a business.   **[450P]**

NOTES

Commencement: 15 May 1989.

This section derived from the Transport Act 1982, s 45.

67. False statements in response to notices to owner

A person who, in response to a notice to owner, provides a statement which is false in a material particular and does so recklessly or knowing it to be false in that particular is guilty of an offence.   **[450Q]**

NOTES
> Commencement: 15 May 1989.
> This section derived from the Transport Act 1982, s 46(1).

68. "Owner", "statutory statement" and "official form"

(1) For the purposes of this Part of this Act, the owner of a vehicle shall be taken to be the person by whom the vehicle is kept; and for the purposes of determining, in the course of any proceedings brought by virtue of section 64(3) of this Act, who was the owner of a vehicle at any time, it shall be presumed that the owner was the person who was the registered keeper of the vehicle at that time.

(2) Notwithstanding the presumption in subsection (1) above, it is open to the defence in any proceedings to prove that the person who was the registered keeper of a vehicle at a particular time was not the person by whom the vehicle was kept at that time and to the prosecution to prove that the vehicle was kept by some other person at that time.

(3) References in this Part of this Act to statutory statements of any description are references to the statutory statement of that description defined in Schedule 4 to this Act; and that Schedule shall also have effect for the purpose of requiring certain information to be provided in official forms for the statutory statements so defined to assist persons in completing those forms and generally in determining what action to take in response to a notice to owner.

(4) In this Part of this Act "official form", in relation to a statutory statement mentioned in Schedule 4 to this Act or a statement under section 66(2) of this Act, means a document supplied by or on behalf of a chief officer of police for use in making that statement.   **[450R]**

NOTES
> Commencement: 15 May 1989.
> This section derived from the Transport Act 1982, s 49(2), (3), (9), (10).

The fixed penalty procedure

69. Payment of penalty

(1) Payment of a fixed penalty under this Part of this Act must be made to such justices' clerk or, in Scotland, clerk of court as may be specified in the fixed penalty notice relating to that penalty.

(2) Without prejudice to payment by any other method, payment of a fixed penalty under this Part of this Act may be made by properly addressing, pre-paying and posting a letter containing the amount of the penalty (in cash or otherwise) and, unless the contrary is proved, shall be regarded as having been made at the time at which that letter would be delivered in the ordinary course of post.

(3) A letter is properly addressed for the purposes of subsection (2) above if it is addressed to the fixed penalty clerk at the address specified in the fixed penalty notice relating to the fixed penalty as the address at which the fixed penalty may be paid.

(4) References in this Part of this Act [(except in sections 75 to 77)], in relation to any fixed penalty or fixed penalty notice, to the fixed penalty clerk are references to the clerk specified in accordance with subsection (1) above in the fixed penalty notice relating to that penalty or (as the case may be) in that fixed penalty notice.   **[450S]**

NOTES
Commencement: 15 May 1989.
This section derived from the Transport Act 1982, s 33(1)–(3).
Words in square brackets inserted by the Road Traffic Act 1991, s 48, Sch 4, para 105.

70. Registration certificates

(1) This section and section 71 of this Act apply where by virtue of section 55(3) or 64(2) of this Act a sum determined by reference to the fixed penalty for any offence may be registered under section 71 of this Act for enforcement against any person as a fine.

In this section and section 71 of this Act—
   (a) that sum is referred to as a "sum payable in default", and
   (b) the person against whom that sum may be so registered is referred to as the "defaulter".

(2) Subject to subsection (3) below, the chief officer of police may in respect of any sum payable in default issue a certificate (referred to in this section and section 71 as a "registration certificate") stating that the sum is registrable under section 71 for enforcement against the defaulter as a fine.

(3) (*Applies to offences committed in Scotland.*)

(4) Where the chief officer of police or the fixed penalty clerk issues a registration certificate under this section, he must—
   (a) if the defaulter appears to him to reside in England and Wales, cause it to be sent to the clerk to the justices for the petty sessions area in which the defaulter appears to him to reside, and
   (b) if the defaulter appears to him to reside in Scotland, cause it to be sent to the clerk of a court of summary jurisdiction for the area in which the defaulter appears to him to reside.

(5) A registration certificate issued under this section in respect of any sum payable in default must—
   (a) give particulars of the offence to which the fixed penalty notice relates,
   (b) indicate whether registration is authorised under section 55(3) or 64(2) of this Act, and
   (c) state the name and last known address of the defaulter and the amount of the sum payable in default.   **[450T]**

NOTES
Commencement: 15 May 1989.
This section derived from the Transport Act 1982, s 36(1), (2), (4), (5).

71. Registration of sums payable in default

(1) Where the clerk to the justices for a petty sessions area receives a registration certificate issued under section 70 of this Act in respect of any sum payable in default, he must, subject to subsection (4) below, register that sum for enforcement as a fine in that area by entering it in the register of a magistrates' court acting for that area.

(2), (3) (*Sub-s (2) applies to Scotland only; sub-s (3) applies to offences committed in Scotland.*)

(4) Where it appears to the clerk receiving a registration certificate issued under section 70 of this Act in respect of any sum payable in default that the defaulter does not reside in the petty sessions area or (as the case may be) within the jurisdiction of the court of summary jurisdiction in question—

    (a) he is not required by subsection (1) or (2) above to register that sum, but

    (b) he must cause the certificate to be sent to the appropriate clerk,

and subsection (1) or, as the case may be, (2) above shall apply accordingly on receipt by the appropriate clerk of the certificate as it applies on receipt by the clerk to whom it was originally sent.

(5) For the purposes of subsection (4) above, the appropriate clerk—

    (a) if the defaulter appears to the clerk receiving the registration certificate to reside in England and Wales, is the clerk to the justices for the petty sessions area in which the defaulter appears to him to reside, and

    (b) if the defaulter appears to the clerk receiving the registration certificate to reside in Scotland, is the clerk of a court of summary jurisdiction for the area in which the defaulter appears to him to reside.

(6) On registering any sum under this section for enforcement as a fine, the clerk to the justices for a petty sessions area or, as the case may be, the clerk of a court of summary jurisdiction must give to the defaulter notice of registration—

    (a) specifying the amount of that sum, and

    (b) giving the information with respect to the offence and the authority for registration included in the registration certificate by virtue of section 70(5)(a) and (b) of this Act or (in a case within subsection (3) above) the corresponding information.

(7) On the registration of any sum in a magistrates' court or a court of summary jurisdiction by virtue of this section any enactment referring (in whatever terms) to a fine imposed or other sum adjudged to be paid on the conviction of such a court shall have effect in the case in question as if the sum so registered were a fine imposed by that court on the conviction of the defaulter on the date of the registration.

(8) Accordingly, in the application by virtue of this section of the provisions of the Magistrates' Courts Act 1980 relating to the satisfaction and enforcement of sums adjudged to be paid on the conviction of a magistrates' court, section 85 of that Act (power to remit a fine in whole or in part) is not excluded by subsection (2) of that section (references in that section to a fine not to include any other sum adjudged to be paid on a conviction) from applying to a sum registered in a magistrates' court by virtue of this section.

(9) For the purposes of this section, where the defaulter is a body corporate, the place where that body resides and the address of that body are either of the following—

    (a) the registered or principal office of that body, and

    (b) the address which, with respect to the vehicle concerned, is the address recorded in the record kept under the Vehicles (Excise) Act 1971 as being that body's address.   **[450U]**

NOTES
Commencement: 15 May 1989.
This section derived from the Transport Act 1982, s 36(6)(a), (7)–(11).

72. Notices on-the-spot or at a police station: when registration and endorsement invalid

(1) This section applies where—

(a) a person who has received notice of the registration, by virtue of section 55(3) of this Act, of a sum under section 71 of this Act for enforcement against him as a fine makes a statutory declaration to the effect mentioned in subsection (2) below, and

(b) that declaration is, within twenty-one days of the date on which the person making it received notice of the registration, served on the clerk of the relevant court.

(2) The statutory declaration must state—

(a) that the person making the declaration was not the person to whom the relevant fixed penalty notice was given, or

(b) that he gave notice requesting a hearing in respect of the alleged offence as permitted by the fixed penalty notice before the end of the suspended enforcement period.

(3) In any case within subsection (2)(a) above, the relevant fixed penalty notice, the registration and any proceedings taken before the declaration was served for enforcing payment of the sum registered shall be void.

(4) Where in any case within subsection (2)(a) above the person to whom the relevant fixed penalty notice was given surrendered a licence [and its counterpart] held by the person making the declaration, any endorsement of [that counterpart] made under section 57 of this Act in respect of the offence in respect of which that notice was given shall be void.

(5) In any case within subsection (2)(b) above—

(a) the registration, any proceedings taken before the declaration was served for enforcing payment of the sum registered, and any endorsement, in respect of the offence in respect of which the relevant fixed penalty notice was given, made under section 57 of this Act before the declaration was served, shall be void, and

(b) the case shall be treated after the declaration is served as if the person making the declaration had given notice requesting a hearing in respect of the alleged offence as stated in the declaration.

(6) The clerk of the relevant court must—

(a) cancel an endorsement of [the counterpart of] a licence under section 57 of this Act that is void by virtue of this section on production of the licence [and its counterpart] to him for that purpose, and

(b) send notice of the cancellation to the Secretary of State.

(7) References in this section to the relevant fixed penalty notice are to the fixed penalty notice relating to the fixed penalty concerned.   **[450V]**

NOTES
Commencement: 15 May 1989.
This section derived from the Transport Act 1982, ss 37(1), (2), (4)–(6), 38(1), (6).
Words in square brackets inserted or substituted by SI 1990 No 144, reg 2(2), Sch 2, para 20.

73.. Notices fixed to vehicles: when registration invalid

(1) This section applies where—

    (a) a person who has received notice of the registration, by virtue of section 64(2) of this Act, of a sum under section 71 of this Act for enforcement against him as a fine makes a statutory declaration to the effect mentioned in subsection (2) below, and

    (b) that declaration is, within twenty-one days of the date on which the person making it received notice of the registration, served on the clerk of the relevant court.

(2) The statutory declaration must state either—

    (a) that the person making the declaration did not know of the fixed penalty concerned or of any fixed penalty notice or notice to owner relating to that penalty until he received notice of the registration, or

    (b) that he was not the owner of the vehicle at the time of the alleged offence of which particulars are given in the relevant notice to owner and that he has a reasonable excuse for failing to comply with that notice, or

    (c) that he gave notice requesting a hearing in respect of that offence as permitted by the relevant notice to owner before the end of the period allowed for response to that notice.

(3) In any case within subsection (2)(a) or (b) above—

    (a) the relevant notice to owner,

    (b) the registration, and

    (c) any proceedings taken before the declaration was served for enforcing payment of the sum registered,

shall be void but without prejudice, in a case within subsection (2)(a) above, to the service of a further notice to owner under section 63 of this Act on the person making the declaration.

This subsection applies whether or not the relevant notice to owner was duly served in accordance with that section on the person making the declaration.

(4) In any case within subsection (2)(c) above—

    (a) no proceedings shall be taken, after the statutory declaration is served until the end of the period of twenty-one days following the date of that declaration, for enforcing payment of the sum registered, and

    (b) where before the end of that period a notice is served by or on behalf of the chief officer of police on the person making the declaration asking him to provide a new statutory statement of ownership to that chief officer of police before the end of the period of twenty-one days from the date on which the notice is served, no such proceedings shall be taken until the end of the period allowed for response to that notice.

(5) Where in any case within subsection (2)(c) above—

    (a) no notice is served by or on behalf of the chief officer of police in accordance with subsection (4) above, or

    (b) such a notice is so served and the person making the declaration provides a new statutory statement of ownership in accordance with the notice, then—

        (i) the registration and any proceedings taken before the declaration was served for enforcing payment of the sum registered shall be void, and

(ii) the case shall be treated after the time mentioned in subsection (6) below as if the person making the declaration had given notice requesting a hearing in respect of the alleged offence as stated in the declaration.

(6) The time referred to in subsection (5) above is—

(a) in a case within paragraph (a) of that subsection, the end of the period of twenty-one days following the date of the statutory declaration,

(b) in a case within paragraph (b) of that subsection, the time when the statement is provided.

(7) In any case where notice is served by or on behalf of the chief officer of police in accordance with subsection (4) above, he must cause the clerk of the relevant court to be notified of that fact immediately on service of the notice.

(8) References in this section to the relevant notice to owner are to the notice to owner relating to the fixed penalty concerned.   **[450W]**

NOTES
Commencement: 15 May 1989.
This section derived from the Transport Act 1982, ss 37(1), (3), (7)–(10), 38(2), (6).

74.. Provisions supplementary to sections 72 and 73

(1) In any case within section 72(2)(b) or 73(2) of this Act—

(a) section 127(1) of the Magistrates' Courts Act 1980 (limitation of time), and

(b) section 331(1) of the Criminal Procedure (Scotland) Act 1975 (statutory offences time limit),

shall have effect as if for the reference to the time when the offence was committed or (as the case may be) the time when the contravention occurred there were substituted a reference to the date of the statutory declaration made for the purposes of section 72(1) or, as the case may be, 73(1).

(2) Where, on the application of a person who has received notice of the registration of a sum under section 71 of this Act for enforcement against him as a fine, it appears to the relevant court (which for this purpose may be composed of a single justice) that it was not reasonable to expect him to serve, within twenty-one days of the date on which he received the notice, a statutory declaration to the effect mentioned in section 72(2) or, as the case may be, 73(2) of this Act, the court may accept service of such a declaration by that person after that period has expired.

(3) A statutory declaration accepted under subsection (2) above shall be taken to have been served as required by section 72(1) or, as the case may be, section 73(1) of this Act.

(4) For the purposes of sections 72(1) and 73(1) of this Act, a statutory declaration shall be taken to be duly served on the clerk of the relevant court if it is delivered to him, left at his office, or sent in a registered letter or by the recorded delivery service addressed to him at his office.

(5) In sections 72, 73 and this section—

(a) references to the relevant court are—

(i) in the case of a sum registered under section 71 of this Act for enforcement as a fine in a petty sessions area in England and

Wales, references to any magistrates' court acting for that area, and

  (ii) (*applies to Scotland only*),

 (b) references to the clerk of the relevant court, where that court is a magistrates' court, are references to a clerk to the justices for the petty sessions area for which that court is acting, and

 (c) references to proceedings for enforcing payment of the sum registered are references to any process issued or other proceedings taken for or in connection with enforcing payment of that sum.

(6) For the purposes of sections 72, 73 and this section, a person shall be taken to receive notice of the registration of a sum under section 71 of this Act for enforcement against him as a fine when he receives notice either of the registration as such or of any proceedings for enforcing payment of the sum registered.

(7) Nothing in the provisions of sections 72 or 73 or this section is to be read as prejudicing any rights a person may have apart from those provisions by virtue of the invalidity of any action purportedly taken in pursuance of this Part of this Act which is not in fact authorised by this Part of this Act in the circumstances of the case; and, accordingly, references in those provisions to the registration of any sum or to any other action taken under or by virtue of any provision of this Part of this Act are not to be read as implying that the registration or action was validly made or taken in accordance with that provision.   **[450X]**

NOTES
  Commencement: 15 May 1989.
  This section derived from the Transport Act 1982, s 38(3)–(5), (7), (8).

[Conditional offer of fixed penalty]

75–77.. (*Apply to offences committed in Scotland.*)

Proceedings in fixed penalty cases

78.. General restriction on proceedings

(1) Proceedings shall not be brought against any person for the offence to which a fixed penalty notice relates until the end of the suspended enforcement period.

(2) Proceedings shall not be brought against any person for the offence to which a fixed penalty notice relates if the fixed penalty is paid in accordance with this Part of this Act before the end of the suspended enforcement period.
                                                                                          [450Y]

NOTES
  Commencement: 15 May 1989.
  This section derived from the Transport Act 1982, ss 29(1), 33(5).

79.. Statements by constables

(1) In any proceedings a certificate that a copy of a statement by a constable with respect to the alleged offence (referred to in this section as a "constable's witness statement") was included in or given with a fixed penalty notice or a notice under section 54(3) of this Act given to the accused on a date specified in the certificate shall, if the certificate purports to be signed by the constable or authorised person who gave the accused the notice, be evidence of service of a copy of that statement by delivery to the accused on that date.

(2) In any proceedings a certificate that a copy of a constable's witness statement was included in or served with a notice to owner served on the accused in the manner and on a date specified in the certificate shall, if the certificate purports to be signed by any person employed by the police authority for the police area in which the offence to which the proceedings relate is alleged to have been committed, be evidence of service in the manner and on the date so specified both of a copy of that statement and of the notice to owner.

(3) Any address specified in any such certificate as is mentioned in subsection (2) above as being the address at which service of the notice to owner was effected shall be taken for the purposes of any proceedings in which the certificate is tendered in evidence to be the accused's proper address, unless the contrary is proved.

(4) Where a copy of a constable's witness statement is included in or served with a notice to owner served in any manner in which the notice is authorised to be served under this Part of this Act, the statement shall be treated as duly served for the purposes of section 9 of the Criminal Justice Act 1967 (proof by written statement) notwithstanding that the manner of service is not authorised by subsection (8) of that section.

(5) In relation to any proceedings in which service of a constable's witness statement is proved by certificate under this section—

    (a) that service shall be taken for the purposes of subsection (2)(c) of that section (copy of statement to be tendered in evidence to be served before hearing on other parties to the proceedings by or on behalf of the party proposing to tender it) to have been effected by or on behalf of the prosecutor, and

    (b) subsection (2)(d) of that section (time for objection) shall have effect with the substitution, for the reference to seven days from the service of the copy of the statement, of a reference to seven days from the relevant date.

(6) In subsection (5)(b) above "relevant date" means—

    (a) where the accused gives notice requesting a hearing in respect of the offence in accordance with any provision of this Part of this Act, the date on which he gives that notice, and

    (b) where a notice in respect of the offence was given to the accused under section 54(4) of this Act but no fixed penalty notice is given in respect of it, the last day for production of the notice under section 54(5) at a police station in accordance with that section.

(7) This section does not extend to Scotland. **[450Z]**

NOTES
    Commencement: 15 May 1989 (in relation to England and Wales); to be appointed (in relation to Scotland).
    This section derived from the Transport Act 1982, s 47(1)–(5), (8).

80. Certificates about payment

In any proceedings a certificate—

    (a) that payment of a fixed penalty was or was not received, by a date specified in the certificate, by the fixed penalty clerk, or

    (b) that a letter containing an amount sent by post in payment of a fixed penalty was marked as posted on a date so specified,

shall, if the certificate purports to be signed by the fixed penalty clerk, be evidence (and, in Scotland, sufficient evidence) of the facts stated. **[450AA]**

NOTES
Commencement: 15 May 1989.
This section derived from the Transport Act 1982, s 33(4).

81. Documents signed by the accused

(1) Where—

    (a) any person is charged with a fixed penalty offence, and

    (b) the prosecutor produces to the court a document to which this subsection applies purporting to have been signed by the accused,

the document shall be presumed, unless the contrary is proved, to have been signed by the accused and shall be evidence (and, in Scotland, sufficient evidence) in the proceedings of any facts stated in it tending to show that the accused was the owner, the hirer or the driver of the vehicle concerned at a particular time.

(2) Subsection (1) above applies to any document purporting to be—

    (a) a notice requesting a hearing in respect of the offence charged given in accordance with a fixed penalty notice relating to that offence, or

    (b) a statutory statement of any description defined in Schedule 4 to this Act or a copy of a statement of liability within the meaning of section 66 of this Act provided in response to a notice to owner.   **[450BB]**

NOTES
Commencement: 15 May 1989.
This section derived from the Transport Act 1982, s 47(6), (7).

Miscellaneous

82. Accounting for fixed penalties: England and Wales

(1) In England and Wales, sums paid by way of fixed penalty for an offence shall be treated for the purposes of section 61 (application of fines and fees) of the Justices of the Peace Act 1979 as if they were fines imposed on summary conviction for that offence.

(2) Where, in England and Wales, a justices' clerk for a petty sessions area comprised in the area of one responsible authority (within the meaning of section 59 of that Act) discharges functions in connection with a fixed penalty for an offence alleged to have been committed in a petty sessions area comprised in the area of another such authority—

    (a) that other authority must make to the first-mentioned authority such payment in connection with the discharge of those functions as may be agreed between them or, in default of such agreement, as may be determined by the Secretary of State, and

    (b) any such payment between responsible authorities shall be taken into account in determining for the purposes of subsection (4) of that section the net cost to those authorities respectively of the functions referred to in subsection (1) of that section.

(3) Subsection (2) above does not apply to functions discharged in connection with a fixed penalty on or after the registration of a sum determined by reference to the penalty under section 71 of this Act.   **[450CC]**

NOTES
Commencement: 15 May 1989 (in relation to England and Wales); to be appointed (in relation to Scotland).
This section derived from the Transport Act 1982, s 33(1), (7), (8).

83.. Powers of court where clerk deceived

(1) This section applies where—

(a) in endorsing [the counterpart of] any person's licence under section 57 of this Act, the fixed penalty clerk is deceived as to whether endorsement under that section is excluded by section 61(2) of this Act by virtue of the fact that the licence holder would be liable to be disqualified under section 35 of this Act if he were convicted of the offence, or

(b) *(applies to offences committed in Scotland)*.

(2) If—

(a) the deception constituted or was due to an offence committed by the licence holder, and

(b) the licence holder is convicted of that offence,

the court by or before which he is convicted shall have the same powers and duties as it would have had if he had also been convicted by or before it of the offence of which particulars were endorsed under section 57 or, as the case may be, 77 of this Act. **[450DD]**

NOTES

Commencement: 15 May 1989.

This section derived from the Transport Act 1982, s 34(9).

Words in square brackets inserted by SI 1990 No 144, reg 2(2), Sch 2, para 24.

84.. Regulations

The Secretary of State may by regulations make provision as to any matter incidental to the operation of this Part of this Act, and in particular—

(a) for prescribing any information or further information to be provided in any notice, notification, certificate or receipt under section 52(1), 54(4), 56, 59(1), 60(1), 63(2), 70(2) and (3)(b), 73(4)(b), 75(2) and (3) or 76(5) and (6) of this Act or in any official form for a statutory statement mentioned in Schedule 4 to, or a statement under section 66(2) of, this Act,

(b) for requiring any such official form to be served with any notice served under section 63 or 73(4) of this Act, and

(c) for prescribing the duties of justices' clerks or (as the case may be) clerks of courts of summary jurisdiction and the information to be supplied to them. **[450EE]**

NOTES

Commencement: 15 May 1989.

This section derived from the Transport Act 1982, s 49(1).

85.. Service of documents

(1) Subject to any requirement of this Part of this Act with respect to the manner in which a person may be provided with any such document, he may be provided with the following documents by post (but without prejudice to any other method of providing him with them), that is to say—

(a) any of the statutory statements mentioned in Schedule 4 to this Act, and

(b) any of the documents mentioned in section 66(2) of this Act.

(2) Where a notice requesting a hearing in respect of an offence is permitted by a fixed penalty notice or notice to owner relating to that offence to be given

by post, section 7 of the Interpretation Act 1978 (service of documents by post) shall apply as if that notice were permitted to be so given by this Act.

(3) A notice to owner may be served on any person—

    (a) by delivering it to him or by leaving it at his proper address, or

    (b) by sending it to him by post,

and where the person on whom such a notice is to be served is a body corporate it is duly served if it is served on the secretary or clerk of that body.

(4) For the purposes of this Part of this Act and of section 7 of the Interpretation Act 1978 as it applies for the purposes of subsection (3) above the proper address of any person in relation to the service on him of a notice to owner is—

    (a) in the case of the secretary or clerk of a body corporate, that of the registered or principal office of that body or the registered address of the person who is or was the registered keeper of the vehicle concerned at the time of service, and

    (b) in any other case, his last known address at the time of service.

(5) In subsection (4) above, "registered address", in relation to the registered keeper of a vehicle, means the address recorded in the record kept under the Vehicles (Excise) Act 1971 with respect to that vehicle as being that person's address.   **[450FF]**

NOTES
    Commencement: 15 May 1989.
    This section derived from the Transport Act 1982, s 49(4)–(7), (8).

86.. Functions of traffic wardens

(1) An order under section 95(5) of the Road Traffic Regulation Act 1984 may not authorise the employment of a traffic warden to discharge any function under this Part of this Act in respect of an offence if the offence appears to the traffic warden to be an offence involving obligatory endorsement [unless that offence was committed whilst the vehicle concerned was stationary].

(2) In so far as an order under that section authorises the employment of traffic wardens for the purposes of this Part of this Act, references in this Part of this Act to a constable or, as the case may be, to a constable in uniform include a traffic warden.   **[450GG]**

NOTES
    Commencement: 15 May 1989.
    This section derived from the Transport Act 1982, ss 49(11), 50(3).
    Words in square brackets added by the Road Traffic Act 1991, s 48, Sch 4, para 106.

87.. Guidance on application of Part III

The Secretary of State must issue guidance to chief officers of police for police areas in respect of the operation of this Part of this Act with the objective so far as possible of working towards uniformity.   **[450HH]**

NOTES
    Commencement: 15 May 1989.
    This section derived from the Transport Act 1982, s 51.

88.. Procedure for regulations and orders

(1) Any power conferred by this Part of this Act on the Secretary of State to make any order or regulations shall be exercisable by statutory instrument.

(2) Before making—

(a) an order under section 51, 53 or 75 of this Act, or
(b) regulations under section 84 of this Act,

the Secretary of State must consult with such representative organisations as he thinks fit.

(3) A statutory instrument containing regulations or an order under any provision of this Part of this Act shall be subject to annulment in pursuance of a resolution of either House of Parliament.

(4) Regulations under this Part of this Act may—

(a) make different provision for different cases, and
(b) contain such incidental and supplemental provisions as the Secretary of State considers expedient for the purposes of the regulations.

[450JJ]

NOTES
Commencement: 15 May 1989.
This section derived from the Transport Act 1982, s 73(1), (3)–(5).

89.. Interpretation

(1) In this Part of this Act—

"authorised person" has the meaning given by section 54(9) of this Act;
["chief constable" means, in Scotland in relation to any conditional offer, the chief constable for the area in which the conditional offer has been issued.]
"chief officer of police" (except in the definition of "authorised person") means, in relation to any fixed penalty notice[, notice to owner or conditional offer] the chief officer of police for the police area in which the fixed penalty offence in question is alleged to have been committed,
"court of summary jurisdiction" has the same meaning as in section 462(1) of the Criminal Procedure (Scotland) Act 1975,
"driver" except in section 62 of this Act means, in relation to an alleged fixed penalty offence, the person by whom, assuming the offence to have been committed, it was committed,
"justices' clerk" means the clerk to the justices for a petty sessions area,
"petty sessions area" has the same meaning as in the Magistrates' Courts Act 1980, and
"proceedings", except in relation to proceedings for enforcing payment of a sum registered under section 71 of this Act, means criminal proceedings.

(2) In this Part of this Act—

(a) references to a notice requesting a hearing in respect of an offence are references to a notice indicating that the person giving the notice wishes to contest liability for the offence or seeks a determination by a court with respect to the appropriate punishment for the offence,
(b) references to an offence include an alleged offence; and

(c) references to the person who is or was at any time the registered
keeper of a vehicle are references to the person in whose name the
vehicle is or was at that time registered under the Vehicles (Excise)
Act 1971.   **[450KK]**

NOTES
    Commencement: 15 May 1989.
    This section derived from the Transport Act 1982, ss 34(11), 47(1A), 49(8), 50(1), (2), (4).
    Definition "chief constable" inserted, and the words in square brackets in the definition "chief
officer of police" substituted, by the Road Traffic Act 1991, s 48, Sch 4, para 107.

90. Index to Part III

The expressions listed in the left hand column below are respectively defined or
(as the case may be) fall to be construed in accordance with the provisions of
this Part of this Act listed in the right-hand column in relation to those
expressions.

Expression	*Relevant provision*
Authorised person	Section 54(9)
Conditional offer	[Section 75(3)]
Fixed penalty	Section 53
Fixed penalty clerk	Section 69(4) [and 75(4)]
Fixed penalty notice	Section 52
Fixed penalty offence	Section 51
Notice to owner	Sections 63(2) and 66(4)
Notice requesting a hearing in respect of an offence	Section 89(2)
Offence	Section 89(2)
Official form	Section 68(4)
Owner	Section 68(1)
Period allowed for response to a notice to owner	Section 63(5)
Proper address, in relation to the service of a notice to owner	Section 85(4)
Registered keeper	Section 89(2)
Statutory statement of facts	Part II of Schedule 4
Statutory statement of hiring	Part I of Schedule 4
Statutory statement of ownership	Part I of Schedule 4
Suspended enforcement period	Section 52(3)(a)
Time of the alleged offence	Section 63(3)

[450LL]

NOTES
    Commencement: 15 May 1989.
    This section derived from the Transport Act 1982, s 50(6).
    Words in square brackets inserted by the Road Traffic Act 1991, s 48, Sch 4, para 108

PART IV

MISCELLANEOUS AND GENERAL

91. Penalty for breach of regulations

If a person acts in contravention of or fails to comply with—

(a) any regulations made by the Secretary of State under the Road Traffic
Act 1988 other than regulations made under section 31, 45 or 132,

(b) any regulations made by the Secretary of State under the Road Traffic Regulation Act 1984, other than regulations made under section 28, Schedule 4, Part III of Schedule 9 or Schedule 12,

and the contravention or failure to comply is not made an offence under any other provision of the Traffic Acts, he shall for each offence be liable on summary conviction to a fine not exceeding level 3 on the standard scale. **[451]**

NOTES
Commencement: 15 May 1989.
This section derived from the Road Traffic Act 1972, s 178, the Road Traffic Act 1974, s 21(2), the Criminal Procedure (Scotland) Act 1975, ss 289F, 289G, the Criminal Justice Act 1982, ss 38, 46, 54, and the Road Traffic Regulation Act 1984, s 118, Sch 7.
Traffic Acts: Road Traffic Regulation Act 1984, Road Traffic Act 1988, Road Traffic (Consequential Provisions) Act 1988 (so far as it reproduces the effect of provisions repealed by that Act), Road Traffic Offenders Act 1988.

92. Application to Crown

The following provisions of this Act apply to vehicles and persons in the public service of the Crown: sections 1, 2, 3, 15, 16 [20] and 49 and the provisions connected with the licensing of drivers. **[452]**

NOTES
Commencement: 15 May 1989.
This section derived from the Road Traffic Act 1972, s 188(1), and the Transport Act 1982, Sch 5, para 25.
Figure in square brackets substituted by the Road Traffic Act 1991, s 48, Sch 4, para 109.

93. Application of sections 15 and 16 to persons subject to service discipline

(1) Sections 15 and 16, in their application to persons subject to service discipline, apply outside as well as within Great Britain and have effect as if—

(a) references to proceedings for an offence under any enactment included references to proceedings for the corresponding service offence,

(b) references to the court included a reference to any naval, military, or air force authority before whom the proceedings take place,

(c) references to a constable included references to a member of the provost staff, and

(d) in section 15, subsection (4) were omitted.

(2) Expressions used in this section have the same meaning as in sections [3A] to 10 of the Road Traffic Act 1988. **[453]**

NOTES
Commencement: 15 May 1989.
This section derived from the Road Traffic Act 1972, s 189(1)(a)-(c), (h), and the Transport Act 1981, Sch 9, para 17(c).
Sub-s (2): figure in square brackets substituted by the Road Traffic Act 1991, s 48, Sch 4, para 110.

94. Proceedings in respect of offences in connection with Crown vehicles

(1) Where an offence under the Traffic Acts is alleged to have been committed in connection with a vehicle in the public service of the Crown, proceedings may be brought in respect of the offence against a person nominated for the purpose on behalf of the Crown.

(2) Subject to subsection (3) below, where any such offence is committed any person so nominated shall also be guilty of the offence as well as any person

actually responsible for the offence (but without prejudice to proceedings against any person so responsible).

(3) Where any person is convicted of an offence by virtue of this section—

    (a) no order is to be made on his conviction save an order imposing a fine,

    (b) payment of any fine imposed on him in respect of that offence is not to be enforced against him, and

    (c) apart from the imposition of any such fine, the conviction is to be disregarded for all purposes other than any appeal (whether by way of case stated or otherwise). **[454–455]**

NOTES
Commencement: 15 May 1989.
This section derived from the Road Traffic Act 1972, s 188(8), (9), the Transport Act 1982, s 64, and the Road Traffic Regulation Act 1984, s 130(4), (5).
Traffic Acts: Road Traffic Regulation Act 1984, Road Traffic Act 1988, Road Traffic (Consequential Provisions) Act 1988 (so far as it reproduces the effect of provisions repealed by that Act), Road Traffic Offenders Act 1988.

95. (*Applies to Scotland only.*)

96. Meaning of "offence involving obligatory endorsement"

For the purposes of this Act, an offence involves obligatory endorsement if it is an offence under a provision of the Traffic Acts specified in column 1 of Part I of Schedule 2 to this Act or an offence specified in column 1 of Part II of that Schedule and either—

    (a) the word "obligatory" (without qualification) appears in column 6 (in the case of Part I) or column 3 (in the case of Part II) against the offence, or

    (b) that word appears there qualified by conditions relating to the offence which are satisfied. **[456]**

NOTES
Commencement: 15 May 1989.
This section derived from the Road Traffic Act 1972, ss 101(1), 177(1), (2)(d), the Transport Act 1982, s 27(9), and the Road Traffic Regulation Act 1984, Sch 13, para 20.
Traffic Acts: Road Traffic Regulation Act 1984, Road Traffic Act 1988, Road Traffic (Consequential Provisions) Act 1988 (so far as it reproduces the effect of provisions repealed by that Act), Road Traffic Offenders Act 1988.

97. Meaning of "offence involving obligatory disqualification" and "offence involving discretionary disqualification"

(1) For the purposes of this Act, an offence involves obligatory disqualification if it is an offence under a provision of the Traffic Acts specified in column 1 of Part I of Schedule 2 to this Act or an offence specified in column 1 of Part II of that Schedule and either—

    (a) the word "obligatory" (without qualification) appears in column 5 (in the case of Part I) or column 2 (in the case of Part II) against the offence, or

    (b) that word appears there qualified by conditions or circumstances relating to the offence which are satisfied or obtain.

(2) For the purposes of this Act, an offence involves discretionary disqualification if it is an offence under a provision of the Traffic Acts specified

in column 1 of Part I of Schedule 2 to this Act or an offence specified in column 1 of Part II of that Schedule and either—

(a) the word "discretionary" (without qualification) appears in column 5 (in the case of Part I) or column 2 (in the case of Part II) against the offence, or

(b) that word appears there qualified by conditions or circumstances relating to the offence which are satisfied or obtain.   **[457]**

NOTES
Commencement: 15 May 1989.
This section derived from the Road Traffic Act 1972, ss 93(1), (2), 177(1), (2)(c), and the Road Traffic Regulation Act 1984, Sch 13, para 19.
Traffic Acts: Road Traffic Regulation Act 1984, Road Traffic Act 1988, Road Traffic (Consequential Provisions) Act 1988 (so far as it reproduces the effect of provisions repealed by that Act), Road Traffic Offenders Act 1988.

98. General interpretation

(1) In this Act—

"disqualified" means disqualified for holding or obtaining a licence and "disqualification" is to be construed accordingly,

"driver" has the same meaning as in the Road Traffic Act 1988,

"licence" means a licence to drive a motor vehicle granted under Part III of that Act [and "counterpart", in relation to such a licence, has the same meaning as in that part of that Act],

"provisional licence" means a licence granted by virtue of section 97(2) of that Act,

"the provisions connected with the licensing of drivers" means sections 7, 8, 22, 25 to 29, 31, 32, 34 to 48, 96 and 97 of this Act,

"road"—

(a) in relation to England and Wales, means any highway and any other road to which the public has access, and includes bridges over which a road passes, and

(b) (*Applies to Scotland only.*)

"the Road Traffic Acts" means the Road Traffic Act 1988, the Road Traffic (Consequential Provisions) Act 1988 (so far as it reproduces the effect of provisions repealed by that Act) and this Act, and

"the Traffic Acts" means the Road Traffic Acts and the Road Traffic Regulation Act 1984.

(2) Sections 185 and 186 of the Road Traffic Act 1988 (meaning of "motor vehicle" and other expressions relating to vehicles) apply for the purposes of this Act as they apply for the purposes of that [Act].

(3) In the Schedules to this Act—

"RTRA" is used as an abbreviation for the Road Traffic Regulation Act 1984, and
"RTA" is used as an abbreviation for the Road Traffic Act 1988 [or, if followed by "1989", the Road Traffic Driver Licensing and Information Systems) Act 1989].

(4) Subject to any express exception, references in this Act to any Part of this Act include a reference to any Schedule to this Act so far as relating to that Part.   **[458]**

NOTES
Commencement: 15 May 1989.
This section derived from the Road Traffic Act 1972, ss 110, 190, 196, and the Transport Act 1982, s 50(5).
Sub-s (1): in definition "licence" words in square brackets added with savings by SI 1990 No 144, reg 2(2), Sch 2, para 25; for savings see reg 3 thereof; in definition "licence", words in square brackets substituted by the Road Traffic Act 1991, s 48, Sch 4, para 111(1).
Sub-s (2): word in square brackets added by the Road Traffic Act 1991, s 48, Sch 4, para 111(2).
Sub-s (3): words in square brackets added by the Road Traffic (Driver Licensing and Information Systems) Act 1989, s 7, Sch 3, para 26.

99. Short title, commencement and extent

(1) This Act may be cited as the Road Traffic Offenders Act 1988.

(2) This Act, except so far as it may be brought into force under subsection (3) or (5) below, shall come into force at the end of the period of six months beginning with the day on which it is passed.

(3), (4) (*Apply to Scotland only.*)

(5) Section 59 of this Act shall come into force on such day or days as the Secretary of State may by order made by statutory instrument appoint.

(6) An order under subsection (3) or (5) above may contain such transitional provisions and savings (whether or not involving the modification of any provisions contained in an Act or in subordinate legislation (within the meaning of the Interpretation Act 1978)) as appear to the Secretary of State necessary or expedient in connection with the provisions brought (wholly or partly) into force by the order, and different days may be appointed for different purposes.

(7) This Act, except as provided by section 93, does not extend to Northern Ireland.   **[459]**

NOTES
Commencement: 15 May 1989.
This section derived from the Road Traffic Act 1972, s 209(2), and the Transport Act 1982, ss 73(1), 76(2), (4), (6), (8).

SCHEDULES
SCHEDULE 1
Sections 1 etc

OFFENCES TO WHICH SECTIONS 1, 6, 11 AND 12(1) APPLY

1. (1) Where section 1, 6, 11 or 12(1) of this Act is shown in column 3 of this Schedule against a provision of the Road Traffic Act 1988 specified in column 1, the section in question applies to an offence under that provision.

(2) The general nature of the offence is indicated in column 2.

[1A. Section 1 also applies to—

    (a) an offence under section 16 of the Road Traffic Regulation Act 1984 consisting in the contravention of a restriction on the speed of vehicles imposed under section 14 of that Act,

    (b) an offence under subsection (4) of section 17 of that Act consisting in the contravention of a restriction on the speed of vehicles imposed under that section, and

(c) an offence under section 88(7) or 89(1) of that Act (speeding offences).]

2. Section 6 also applies—

(a) to an offence under section 67 of this Act, . . .
(b) *(applies to Scotland only.)* [, and
(c) [to] an offence under section 1(5) of the Road Traffic (Driver Licensing and Information Systems) Act 1989.]

3. Section 11 also applies to—

(a) any offence to which section 112 of the Road Traffic Regulation Act 1984 (information as to identity of driver or rider) applies except an offence under section 61(5) of that Act,
(b) any offence which is punishable under section 91 of this Act,
[(bb) an offence under paragraph 3 of Schedule 1 to the Road Traffic (Driver Licensing and Information Systems) Act 1989, and]
(c) any offence against any other enactment relating to the use of vehicles on roads.

4. Section 12(1) also applies to—

(a) any offence which is punishable under section 91 of this Act,
[(aa) an offence under paragraph 3(1) of Schedule 1 to the Road Traffic (Driver Licensing and Information Systems) Act 1989, and]
(b) any offence against any other enactment relating to the use of vehicles on roads.

(1) Provision creating offence	(2) General nature of offence	(3) Applicable provisions of this Act
RTA section 1	Causing death by [dangerous] driving	Section 11 of this Act.
RTA section 2	[Dangerous] driving	Sections 1, 11 and 12(1) of this Act.
RTA section 3	Careless, and inconsiderate, driving	Sections 1, 11 and 12(1) of this Act.
[RTA section 3A	Causing death by careless driving when under influence of drink or drugs	Section 11 of this Act.]
RTA section 4	Driving or attempting to drive, or being in charge of a [mechanically propelled vehicle], when unfit to drive through drink or drugs	Sections 11 and 12(1) of this Act.
RTA section 5	Driving or attempting to drive, or being in charge of a motor vehicle, with excess alcohol in breath, blood or urine	Sections 11 and 12(1) of this Act.
RTA section 6	Failing to provide a specimen of breath for a breath test	Sections 11 and 12(1) of this Act.
RTA section 7	Failing to provide specimen for analysis or laboratory test	Sections 11 and 12(1) of this Act.
RTA section 12	Motor racing and speed trials	Sections 11 and 12(1) of this Act.
RTA section 14	Driving or riding in a motor vehicle in contravention of regulations requiring the wearing of seat belts	Sections 11 and 12(1) of this Act.
RTA section 15	Driving motor vehicle with child not wearing seat belt	Sections 11 and 12(1) of this Act.

(1) Provision creating offence	(2) General nature of offence	(3) Applicable provisions of this Act
RTA section 19	Prohibition of parking of heavy commercial vehicles on verges and footways	Sections 11 and 12(1) of this Act.
RTA section 22	Leaving vehicles in dangerous positions	Sections 1, 11 and 12(1) of this Act.
RTA section 23	Carrying passenger on motor-cycle contrary to section 23	Sections 11 and 12(1) of this Act.
RTA section 24	Carrying passenger on bicycle contrary to section 24	Sections 11 and 12(1) of this Act.
RTA section 25	Tampering with motor vehicles	Section 11 of this Act.
RTA section 26(1)	Holding or getting onto vehicle in order to be carried	Section 11 of this Act.
RTA section 26(2)	Holding onto vehicle in order to be towed	Sections 11 and 12(1) of this Act.
RTA section 28	[Dangerous] cycling	Sections 1, 11 and 12(1) of this Act.
RTA section 29	Careless, and inconsiderate, cycling	Sections 1, 11 and 12(1) of this Act.
RTA section 30	Cycling when unfit through drink or drugs	Sections 11 and 12(1) of this Act.
RTA section 31	Unauthorised or irregular cycle racing, or trials of speed	Sections 11 and 12(1) of this Act.
RTA section 33	Unauthorised motor vehicle trial on footpaths or bridleways	Sections 11 and 12(1) of this Act.
RTA section 34	Driving motor vehicles elsewhere than on roads	Sections 11 and 12(1) of this Act.
RTA section 35	Failing to comply with traffic directions	Sections 1, 11 and 12(1) of this Act.
RTA section 36	Failing to comply with traffic signs	Sections 1, 11 and 12(1) of this Act.
[RTA section 40A	Using vehicle in dangerous condition etc	Sections 11 and 12(1) of this Act.
RTA section 41A	Breach of requirement as to brakes, steering-gear or tyres	Sections 11 and 12(1) of this Act.
RTA section 41B	Breach of requirement as to weight: goods and passenger vehicles	Sections 11 and 12(1) of this Act.]
RTA section 42	[Breach or other construction and use requirements]	Sections 11 and 12(1) of this Act.
RTA section 47	Using, etc, vehicle without required test certificate being in force	Sections 11 and 12(1) of this Act.
RTA section 53	Using, etc, goods vehicle without required plating certificate or goods vehicle test certificate being in force, or where Secretary of State is required by regulations under section 49 to be notified of an alteration to the vehicle or its equipment but has not been notified	Sections 11 and 12(1) of this Act.
RTA section 63	Using, etc, vehicle without required certificate being in force showing that it, or a	Sections 11 and 12(1) of this Act.

(1) Provision creating offence	(2) General nature of offence	(3) Applicable provisions of this Act
	part fitted to it, complies with type approval requirements applicable to it, or using, etc, certain goods vehicles for drawing trailer when plating certificate does not specify maximum laden weight for vehicle and trailer, or using, etc, goods vehicle where Secretary of State has not been but is required to be notified under section 48 of alteration to it or its equipment	
RTA section 71	Driving, etc, . . . vehicle in contravention of prohibition on driving it as being unfit for service or overloaded, or refusing, neglecting or otherwise failing to comply with a direction to remove a . . . vehicle found overloaded	Sections 11 and 12(1) of this Act.
RTA section 78	Failing to comply with requirement about weighing motor vehicle or obstructing authorised person	Sections 11 and 12(1) of this Act.
RTA section 87(1)	Driving [otherwise than in accordance with] a licence	Sections 11 and 12(1) of this Act.
RTA section 87(2)	Causing or permitting a person to drive [otherwise than in accordance with] a licence	Section 11 of this Act.
[RTA section 92(10)	Driving after making false declaration as to physical fitness	Sections 6, 11 and 12(1) of this Act.]
RTA [section 94(3)]	Failure to notify the Secretary of State of onset of, or deterioration in, relevant or prospective disability	Section 6 of this Act.
[RTA section 94(3A)	Driving after such a failure	Sections 6, 11 and 12(1) of this Act.
RTA section 94A	Driving after refusal of licence under section 92(3) or revocation under section 93	Sections 6, 11 and 12(1) of this Act.]
RTA section 99	Driving licence holder failing [when his licence is revoked, to surrender it or], when his particulars become incorrect, to surrender licence [and counterpart] and give particulars	Section 6 of this Act.
RTA section 103(1)(a)	Obtaining driving licence while disqualified	Section 6 of this Act.
RTA section 103(1)(b)	Driving while disqualified	Sections 6, 11 and 12(1) of this Act.

(1) Provision creating offence	(2) General nature of offence	(3) Applicable provisions of this Act
[RTA section 114(1)	Failing to comply with conditions of LGV or PCV driver's licence	Sections 11 and 12(1) of this Act.
RTA section 114(2)	Causing or permitting a person under 21 to drive LGV or PCV in contravention of conditions of that person's licence	Section 11 of this Act.]
. . . . .	. . . . .	. . . . .
RTA section 143	Using motor vehicle, or causing or permitting it to be used, while uninsured or unsecured against third party risks	Sections 6, 11 and 12(1) of this Act.
RTA section 163	Failing to stop vehicle when required by constable	Sections 11 and 12(1) of this Act.
RTA section 164(6)	Failing to produce driving licence [and counterpart] [etc] or to state date of birth	Sections 11 and 12(1) of this Act.
RTA section 165(3)	Failing to give constable certain names and addresses or to produce certificate of insurance or certain test and other like certificates	Sections 11 and 12(1) of this Act.
RTA section 165(6)	Supervisor of learner driver failing to give constable certain names and addresses	Section 11 of this Act.
RTA section 168	Refusing to give, or giving false, name and address in case of reckless, careless or inconsiderate driving or cycling	Sections 11 and 12(1) of this Act.
RTA section 170	Failure by driver to stop, report accident or give information or documents	Sections 11 and 12(1) of this Act.
RTA section 171	Failure by owner of motor vehicle to give police information for verifying compliance with requirement of compulsory insurance or security	Sections 11 and 12(1) of this Act.
RTA section 174(1) or [5]	Making false statements in connection with licences under this Act and with registration as an approved driving instructor; or making false statement or withholding material information in order to obtain the issue of insurance certificates, etc	Section 6 of this Act.
RTA section 175	Issuing false documents	Section 6 of this Act.

[460]

NOTES
   Commencement: 1 July 1992 [para 1A]; 15 May 1989 (remainder).
   This Schedule derived from the Road Traffic Act 1972, s 177(1), (2)(e), Sch 4, Part I, column 7,

the Heavy Commercial Vehicles (Controls and Regulations) Act 1973, s 2(2), the Road Traffic Act 1974, ss 13(4), 15(5), Sch 6, para 24, the Criminal Law Act 1977, s 18, the Transport Act 1981, ss 27(4), 28(2), the Transport Act 1982, s 46(2)-(5), the Road Traffic Regulation Act 1984, ss 98(1), (2)(e), 113(1), the Criminal Justice Act 1988, s 36(2), and the Motor Vehicles (Wearing of Rear Seat Belts by Children) Act 1988, s 1(2).

Para 1A: inserted by the Road Traffic Act 1991, s 22, Sch 1, paras 1, 2.

Para 2: words omitted repealed, and first words in (outer) square brackets inserted, by the Road Traffic (Driver Licensing and Information Systems) Act 1989, ss 7, 16, Sch 3, para 27(a), Sch 6; remaining words in square brackets inserted by the Road Traffic Act 1991, s 22, Sch 1, paras 1, 3.

Paras 3, 4: amended by the Road Traffic (Driver Licensing and Information Systems) Act 1989, ss 7, 16, Sch 3, para 27(b), (c), Sch 6.

Table: the entries relating to RTA ss 1, 2, 4, 28, 42, 71, 87(1), (2), 94, 164(6) (second amendment), 174(1) or (6) were amended, those relating to RTA ss 3A, 40A, 41A, 41B, 92(10), 94(3A), 94A were inserted, and those relating to RTA ss 97, 98 were repealed, by the Road Traffic Act 1991, ss 22, 83, Sch 1, paras 1, 4–17, Sch 8.

In the entry for RTA section 99, first words in square brackets added by the Road Traffic (Driver Licensing and Information Systems) Act 1989, s 7, Sch 3, para 27(d), other words in square brackets added with savings by, or by virtue of, SI 1990 No 144, regs 2(2), (3), 3, Sch 2, para 26, Sch 3, para 3(4); entries for RTA sections 110(1), (2), 112(6), (7) repealed, and entries for RTA s 114(1), (2), added, by the Road Traffic (Driver Licensing and Information Systems) Act 1989, ss 4, 7, Sch 3, para 27, Sch 6; in entry for RTA section 164(6), first words in square brackets added with savings by SI 1990 No 144, regs 2(2), 3, Sch 2, para 26.

RTA: Road Traffic Act 1988.

Section 9 etc

SCHEDULE 2

PROSECUTION AND PUNISHMENT OF OFFENCES

PART I

OFFENCES UNDER THE TRAFFIC ACTS

(1) Provision creating offence	(2) General nature of offence	(3) Mode of prosecution	(4) Punishment	(5) Disqualification	(6) Endorsement	(7) Penalty points
Offences under the Road Traffic Regulation Act 1984						
RTRA section 5	Contravention of traffic regulation order	Summarily	Level 3 on the standard scale			
RTRA section 8	Contravention of order regulating traffic in Greater London	Summarily	Level 3 on the standard scale			
RTRA section 11	Contravention of experimental traffic order	Summarily	Level 3 on the standard scale			
RTRA section 13	Contravention of experimental traffic scheme in Greater London	Summarily	Level 3 on the standard scale			
RTRA section 16(1)	Contravention of temporary prohibition or restriction	Summarily	Level 3 on the standard scale	[Discretionary if committed in respect of a speed restriction	[Obligatory if committed in respect of a speed restriction]	[3–6 or 3 (fixed penalty)]
RTRA section 17(4)	Use of special road contrary to scheme or regulations	Summarily	Level 4 on the standard scale	Discretionary if committed in respect of a motor vehicle otherwise than by unlawfully stopping or allowing the vehicle to remain at	Obligatory if committed as mentioned in the entry in column 5	[3–6 or 3 (fixed penalty) if committed in respect of a speed restriction, 3 in any other case]

Offences under the Road Traffic Regulation Act 1984 (continued)

(1) Provision creating offence	(2) General nature of offence	(3) Mode of prosecution	(4) Punishment	(5) Disqualification	(6) Endorsement	(7) Penalty points
				rest on a part of a special road on which vehicles are in certain circumstances permitted to remain at rest		
RTRA section 18(3)	One-way traffic on trunk road	Summarily	Level 3 on the standard scale			
RTRA section 20(5)	Contravention of prohibition or restriction for roads of certain classes	Summarily	Level 3 on the standard scale			
RTRA section 25(5)	Contravention of pedestrian crossing regulations	Summarily	Level 3 on the standard scale	Discretionary if committed in respect of a motor vehicle	Obligatory if committed in respect of a motor vehicle	3
RTRA section 28(3)	Not stopping at school crossing	Summarily	Level 3 on the standard scale	Discretionary if committed in respect of a motor vehicle	Obligatory if committed in respect of a motor vehicle	3
RTRA section 29(3)	Contravention of order relating to street playground	Summarily	Level 3 on the standard scale	Discretionary if committed in respect of a motor vehicle	Obligatory if committed in respect of a motor vehicle	2
RTRA section [35A(1)]	Contravention of order as to use of parking place	Summarily	(a) Level 3 on the standard scale in the case of an offence committed by a person in a street parking place	......	......	......

Offences under the Road Traffic Regulation Act 1984 (continued)

(1) Provision creating offence	(2) General nature of offence	(3) Mode of prosecution	(4) Punishment	(5) Disqualification	(6) Endorsement	(7) Penalty points
			reserved for disabled persons' vehicles or in an off-street parking place reserved for such vehicles, where that person would not have been guilty of that offence if the motor vehicle in respect of which it was committed had been a disabled person's vehicle (b) Level 2 on the standard scale in any other case			
RTRA section [35A(2)]	[Misuse of apparatus for collecting charges or of parking device or connected apparatus]	Summarily	Level 3 on the standard scale			
RTRA section [35A(5)]	Plying for hire in parking place	Summarily	Level 2 on the standard scale			
RTRA section 43(5)	Unauthorised disclosure of information in respect of licensed parking place	Summarily	Level 3 on the standard scale			
RTRA section 43(10)	Failure to comply with term or conditions of licence to operate parking place	Summarily	Level 3 on the standard scale			

Offences under the Road Traffic Regulation Act 1984 (continued)

(1) Provision creating offence	(2) General nature of offence	(3) Mode of prosecution	(4) Punishment	(5) Disqualification	(6) Endorsement	(7) Penalty points
RTRA section 43(12)	Operation of public off-street parking place without licence	Summarily	Level 3 on the standard scale			
RTRA section 47(1)	Contraventions relating to designated parking places	Summarily	(a) Level 3 on the standard scale in the case of an offence committed by a person in a street parking place reserved for disabled persons' vehicles where that person would not have been guilty of that offence if the motor vehicle in respect of which it was committed had been a disabled person's vehicle (b) Level 2 in any other case			
RTRA section 47(3)	Tampering with parking meter	Summarily	Level 3 on the standard scale			
RTRA section 52(1)	Misuse of parking device	Summarily	Level 2 on the standard scale			
RTRA section 53(5)	Contravention of certain provisions of designation orders	Summarily	Level 3 on the standard scale			
RTRA section 53(6)	Other contraventions of designation orders	Summarily	Level 2 on the standard scale			

Offences under the Road Traffic Regulation Act 1984 (continued)

(1) Provision creating offence	(2) General nature of offence	(3) Mode of prosecution	(4) Punishment	(5) Disqualification	(6) Endorsement	(7) Penalty points
RTRA section 61(5)	Unauthorised use of loading area	Summarily	Level 3 on the standard scale			
RTRA section 88(7)	Contravention of minimum speed limit	Summarily	Level 3 on the standard scale			
RTRA section 89(1)	Exceeding speed limit	Summarily	Level 3 on the standard scale	Discretionary	Obligatory	[3–6 or 3 (fixed penalty)]
RTRA section 104(5)	Interference with notice as to immobilisation device	Summarily	Level 2 on the standard scale			
RTRA section 104(6)	Interference with immobilisation device	Summarily	Level 3 on the standard scale			
RTRA section 105(5)	Misuse of disabled person's badge (immobilisation devices)	Summarily	Level 3 on the standard scale			
RTRA section 108(2) (or that subsection as modified by section 109(2) and (3))	Non-compliance with notice (excess charge)	Summarily	Level 3 on the standard scale			
RTRA section 108(3) (or that subsection as modified by section 109(2) and (3))	False response to notice (excess charge)	Summarily	Level 5 on the standard scale			
RTRA section 112(4)	Failure to give information as to identity of driver	Summarily	Level 3 on the standard scale			

Offences under the Road Traffic Regulation Act 1984 (continued)

(1) Provision creating offence	(2) General nature of offence	(3) Mode of prosecution	(4) Punishment	(5) Disqualification	(6) Endorsement	(7) Penalty points
RTRA section 115(1)	Mishandling or faking parking documents	(a) Summarily (b) On indictment	(a) The statutory maximum (b) 2 years			
RTRA section 115(2)	False statement for procuring authorisation	Summarily	Level 4 on the standard scale			
RTRA section 116(1)	Non-delivery of suspect document or article	Summarily	Level 3 on the standard scale			
RTRA section 117	Wrongful use of disabled person's badge	Summarily	Level 3 on the standard scale			
RTRA section 129(3)	Failure to give evidence at inquiry	Summarily	Level 3 on the standard scale			

Offences under the Road Traffic Act 1988

(1) Provision creating offence	(2) General nature of offence	(3) Mode of prosecution	(4) Punishment	(5) Disqualification	(6) Endorsement	(7) Penalty points
RTA section 1	Causing death by [dangerous] driving	On indictment	5 years	Obligatory	Obligatory	[3–11]
RTA section 2	[dangerous] driving	(a) Summarily (b) On indictment	(a) 6 months or the statutory maximum or both (b) 2 years or a fine or both	[Obligatory]	Obligatory	[3–11]
RTA section 3	Careless, and inconsiderate, driving	Summarily	Level 4 on the standard scale	Discretionary	Obligatory	3–9
[RTA section 3A]	Causing death by careless driving when under the influence of drink or drugs	On indictment	5 years or a fine or both	Obligatory	Obligatory	3–11
RTA section 4(1)	Driving or attempting to drive when unfit to drive through drink or drugs	Summarily	6 months or level 5 on the standard scale or both	Obligatory	Obligatory	[3–11]

Offences under the Road Traffic Act 1988 (continued)

(1) Provision creating offence	(2) General nature of offence	(3) Mode of prosecution	(4) Punishment	(5) Disqualification	(6) Endorsement	(7) Penalty points
RTA section 4(2)	Being in charge of a [mechanically propelled vehicle] when unfit to drive through drink or drugs	Summarily	3 months or level 4 on the standard scale or both	Discretionary	Obligatory	10
RTA section 5(1)(a)	Driving or attempting to drive with excess alcohol in breath, blood or urine	Summarily	6 months or level 5 on the standard scale or both	Obligatory	Obligatory	[3–11]
RTA section 5(1)(b)	Being in charge of a motor vehicle with excess alcohol in breath, blood or urine	Summarily	3 months or level 4 on the standard scale or both	Discretionary	Obligatory	10
RTA section 6	Failing to provide a specimen of breath for a breath test	Summarily	Level 3 on the standard scale	Discretionary	Obligatory	4
RTA section 7	Failing to provide specimen for analysis or laboratory test	Summarily	(a) Where the specimen was required to ascertain ability to drive or proportion of alcohol at the time offender was driving or attempting to drive, 6 months or level 5 on the standard scale or both (b) In any other case, 3 months or level 4 on the standard scale or both	(a) Obligatory in case mentioned in column 4(a) (b) Discretionary in any other case	Obligatory	(a) [3–11 in case] mentioned in column 4(a) (b) 10 in any other case

Offences under the Road Traffic Act 1988 (continued)

(1) Provision creating offence	(2) General nature of offence	(3) Mode of prosecution	(4) Punishment	(5) Disqualification	(6) Endorsement	(7) Penalty points
RTA section 12	Motor racing and speed trials on public ways	Summarily	Level 4 on the standard scale	Obligatory	Obligatory	[3–11]
RTA section 13	Other unauthorised or irregular competitions or trials on public ways	Summarily	Level 3 on the standard scale			
RTA section 14	Driving or riding in a motor vehicle in contravention of regulations requiring wearing of seat belts	Summarily	Level 2 on the standard scale			
RTA section 15(2)	Driving motor vehicle with child in front not wearing seat belt	Summarily	Level 2 on the standard scale			
RTA section 15(4)	Driving motor vehicle with child in rear not wearing seat belt	Summarily	Level 1 on the standard scale			
[RTA section 15A(3) or (4)	Selling etc, in certain circumstances equipment as conducive to the safety of children in motor vehicles.	Summarily	Level 3 on the standard scale]			
RTA section 16	Driving or riding motor cycles in contravention of regulations requiring wearing of protective headgear	Summarily	Level 2 on the standard scale			
RTA section 17	Selling, etc, helmet not of the prescribed type as helmet for affording protection for motor cyclists	Summarily	Level 3 on the standard scale			

Offences under the Road Traffic Act 1988 (continued)

(1) Provision creating offence	(2) General nature of offence	(3) Mode of prosecution	(4) Punishment	(5) Disqualification	(6) Endorsement	(7) Penalty points
RTA section 18(3)	Contravention of regulations with respect to use of head-worn appliances on motor cycles	Summarily	Level 2 on the standard scale			
RTA section 18(4)	Selling, etc, appliance not of prescribed type as approved for use on motor cycles	Summarily	Level 3 on the standard scale			
RTA section 19	Prohibition of parking of heavy commercial vehicles on verges, etc	Summarily	Level 3 on the standard scale			
RTA section 21	Driving or parking on cycle track	Summarily	Level 3 on the standard scale			
RTA section 22	Leaving vehicles in dangerous positions	Summarily	Level 3 on the standard scale	Discretionary if committed in respect of a motor vehicle	Obligatory if committed in respect of a motor vehicle	3
[RTA section 22A	Causing danger to road-users	(a) Summarily (b) On indictment	(a) 6 months or the statutory maximum or both (b) 7 years or a fine or both]			
RTA section 23	Carrying passenger on motor-cycle contrary to section 23	Summarily	Level 3 on the standard scale	Discretionary	Obligatory	[7]
RTA section 24	Carrying passenger on bicycle contrary to section 24	Summarily	Level 1 on the standard scale			

Offences under the Road Traffic Act 1988 (continued)

(1) Provision creating offence	(2) General nature of offence	(3) Mode of prosecution	(4) Punishment	(5) Disqualification	(6) Endorsement	(7) Penalty points
RTA section 25	Tampering with motor vehicles	Summarily	Level 3 on the standard scale			
RTA section 26	Holding or getting on to vehicle, etc, in order to be towed or carried	Summarily	Level 1 on the standard scale			
RTA section 27	Dogs on designated roads without being held on lead	Summarily	Level 1 on the standard scale			
RTA section 28	[Dangerous] cycling	Summarily	[Level 4] on the standard scale			
RTA section 29	Careless, and inconsiderate, cycling	Summarily	[Level 3] on the standard scale			
RTA section 30	Cycling when unfit through drink or drugs	Summarily	Level 3 on the standard scale			
RTA section 31	Unauthorised or irregular cycle racing or trials of speed on public ways	Summarily	Level 1 on the standard scale			
RTA section 32	Contravening prohibition on persons under 14 driving electrically assisted pedal cycles	Summarily	Level 2 on the standard scale			
RTA section 33	Unauthorised motor vehicle trial on footpaths or bridleways	Summarily	Level 3 on the standard scale			
RTA section 34	Driving motor vehicles elsewhere than on roads	Summarily	Level 3 on the standard scale			

Offences under the Road Traffic Act 1988 (continued)

(1) Provision creating offence	(2) General nature of offence	(3) Mode of prosecution	(4) Punishment	(5) Disqualification	(6) Endorsement	(7) Penalty points
RTA section 35	Failing to comply with traffic directions	Summarily	Level 3 on the standard scale	Discretionary, if committed in respect of a motor vehicle by failure to comply with a direction of a constable or traffic warden	Obligatory if committed as described in column 5	3
RTA section 36	Failing to comply with traffic signs	Summarily	Level 3 on the standard scale	Discretionary, if committed in respect of a motor vehicle by failure to comply with an indication given by a sign specified for the purposes of this paragraph in regulations under RTA section 36	Obligatory if committed as described in column 5	3
RTA section 37	Pedestrian failing to stop when directed by constable regulating traffic	Summarily	Level 3 on the standard scale			
RTA section 40A	Using vehicle in dangerous condition etc	Summarily	(a) Level 5 on the standard scale if committed in respect of a goods vehicle or a vehicle adapted to carry more than eight passengers	Discretionary	Obligatory	3

Offences under the Road Traffic Act 1988 (continued)

(1) Provision creating offence	(2) General nature of offence	(3) Mode of prosecution	(4) Punishment	(5) Disqualification	(6) Endorsement	(7) Penalty points
			(b) Level 4 on the standard scale in any other case			
RTA section 41A	Breach of requirement as to brakes, steering-gear or tyres	Summarily	(a) Level 5 on the standard scale if committed in respect of a goods vehicle or a vehicle adapted to carry more than eight passengers (b) Level 4 on the standard scale in any other case	Discretionary	Obligatory	3
RTA section 41B	Breach of requirement as to weight: goods and passenger vehicles	Summarily	Level 5 on the standard scale			
RTA section 42	Breach of other construction and use requirements	Summarily	(a) Level 4 on the standard scale if committed in respect of a goods vehicle or a vehicle adapted to carry more then eight passengers (b) Level 3 on the standard scale in any other case			
RTA section 47	Using, etc, vehicle without required test certificate being in force	Summarily	(a) Level 4 on the standard scale in the case of a vehicle adapted to carry more than eight passengers			

Offences under the Road Traffic Act 1988 (continued)

(1) Provision creating offence	(2) General nature of offence	(3) Mode of prosecution	(4) Punishment	(5) Disqualification	(6) Endorsement	(7) Penalty points
Regulations under RTA section 49 made by virtue of section 51(2)	Contravention of requirement of regulations (which is declared by regulations to be an offence) that driver of goods vehicle being tested be present throughout test or drive, etc, vehicle as and when directed	Summarily	(b) Level 3 on the standard scale in any other case Level 3 on the standard scale			
RTA section 53(1)	Using, etc, goods vehicle without required plating certificate being in force	Summarily	Level 3 on the standard scale			
RTA section 53(2)	Using, etc, goods vehicle without required goods vehicle test certificate being in force	Summarily	Level 4 on the standard scale			
RTA section 53(3)	Using, etc, goods vehicle where Secretary of State is required by regulations under section 49 to be notified of an alteration to the vehicle or its equipment but has not been notified	Summarily	Level 3 on the standard scale			

Offences under the Road Traffic Act 1988 (continued)

(1) Provision creating offence	(2) General nature of offence	(3) Mode of prosecution	(4) Punishment	(5) Disqualification	(6) Endorsement	(7) Penalty points
Regulations under RTA section 61 made by virtue of subsection (4)	Contravention of requirement of regulations (which is declared by regulations to be an offence) that driver of goods vehicle being tested after notifiable alteration be present throughout test and drive, etc, vehicle as and when directed	Summarily	Level 3 on the standard scale			
RTA section 63(1)	Using, etc, goods vehicle without required certificate being in force showing that it complies with type approval requirements applicable to it	Summarily	Level 4 on the standard scale			
RTA section 63(2)	Using, etc, certain goods vehicles for drawing trailer when plating certificate does not specify maximum laden weight for vehicle and trailer	Summarily	Level 3 on the standard scale			
RTA section 63(3)	Using, etc, goods vehicle where Secretary of State is required to be notified under section 59 of alteration to it or its equipment but has not been notified	Summarily	Level 3 on the standard scale			

Offences under the Road Traffic Act 1988 (continued)

(1) Provision creating offence	(2) General nature of offence	(3) Mode of prosecution	(4) Punishment	(5) Disqualification	(6) Endorsement	(7) Penalty points
RTA section 64	Using goods vehicle with unauthorised weights as well as authorised weights marked on it	Summarily	Level 3 on the standard scale			
RTA section 65	Supplying vehicle or vehicle part without required certificate being in force showing that it complies with type approval requirements applicable to it	Summarily	Level 5 on the standard scale			
RTA section 67	Obstructing testing of vehicle by examiner on road or failing to comply with requirements of RTA section 67 or Schedule 2	Summarily	Level 3 on the standard scale			
RTA section 68	Obstructing inspection, etc, of . . . vehicle by examiner or failing to comply with requirement to take . . . vehicle for inspection	Summarily	Level 3 on the standard scale			
RTA section 71	Driving, etc, . . . vehicle in contravention of prohibition on driving it as being unfit for service, or refusing, neglecting or otherwise failing to comply with direction to remove a . . . vehicle found overloaded	Summarily	Level 5 on the standard scale			

Offences under the Road Traffic Act 1988 (continued)

(1) Provision creating offence	(2) General nature of offence	(3) Mode of prosecution	(4) Punishment	(5) Disqualification	(6) Endorsement	(7) Penalty points
RTA section 74	Contravention of regulations requiring goods vehicle operator to inspect, and keep records of inspection of, goods vehicles	Summarily	Level 3 on the standard scale			
RTA section 75	Selling, etc, unroadworthy vehicle or trailer or altering vehicle or trailer so as to make it unroadworthy	Summarily	Level 5 on the standard scale			
RTA section 76(1)	Fitting of defective or unsuitable vehicle parts	Summarily	Level 5 on the standard scale			
RTA section 76(3)	Supplying defective or unsuitable vehicle parts	Summarily	Level 4 on the standard scale			
RTA section 76(8)	Obstructing examiner testing vehicles to ascertain whether defective or unsuitable part has been fitted, etc	Summarily	Level 3 on the standard scale			
RTA section 77	Obstructing examiner testing condition of used vehicles at sale rooms, etc	Summarily	Level 3 on the standard scale			
RTA section 78	Failing to comply with requirement about weighing motor vehicle or obstructing authorised person	Summarily	Level 5 on the standard scale			

Offences under the Road Traffic Act 1988 (continued)

(1) Provision creating offence	(2) General nature of offence	(3) Mode of prosecution	(4) Punishment	(5) Disqualification	(6) Endorsement	(7) Penalty points
RTA section 81	Selling, etc, pedal cycle in contravention of regulations as to brakes, bells, etc	Summarily	Level 3 on the standard scale			
RTA section 83	Selling, etc, wrongly made tail lamps or reflectors	Summarily	Level 5 on the standard scale			
[RTA section 87(1)	Driving otherwise than in accordance with a licence	Summarily	Level 3 on the standard scale	Discretionary in a case where the offender's driving would not have been in accordance with any licence that could have been granted to him.	Obligatory in the case mentioned in column 5	3–6]
RTA section 87(2)	Causing or permitting a person to drive [otherwise than in accordance with] a licence	Summarily	Level 3 on the standard scale			
[RTA section 92(7C)	Failure to deliver licence revoked by virtue of section 92(7A) to Secretary of State	Summarily	Level 3 on the standard scale			
[RTA section 92(10)	Driving after making false declaration as to physical fitness	Summarily	Level 4 on the standard scale	Discretionary	Obligatory	3–6]
RTA section 93(3)	Failure to deliver licence revoked to Secretary of State	Summarily	Level 3 on the standard scale]			

Offences under the Road Traffic Act 1988 (continued)

(1) Provision creating offence	(2) General nature of offence	(3) Mode of prosecution	(4) Punishment	(5) Disqualification	(6) Endorsement	(7) Penalty points
RTA [section 94(3)]	Failure to notify Secretary of State of onset of, or deterioration in, relevant or prospective disability	Summarily	Level 3 on the standard scale			
[RTA section 94(3A)	Driving after such a failure	Summarily	Level 3 on the standard scale	Discretionary	Obligatory	3–6
RTA section 94A	Driving after refusal of licence under section 92(3) or revocation under section 93	Summarily	6 months or level 5 on the standard scale or both	Discretionary	Obligatory	3–6]
RTA section 96	Driving with uncorrected defective eyesight, or refusing to submit to test of eyesight	Summarily	Level 3 on the standard scale	Discretionary	Obligatory	[3]
...... RTA section 99[(5)]	Driving licence holder failing [when his licence is revoked, to surrender it or], when his particulars become incorrect, to surrender licence [and counterpart] and give particulars	Summarily	Level 3 on the standard scale	......	......	......
RTA section 103(1)(a)	Obtaining driving licence while disqualified	Summarily	Level 3 on the standard scale			

Offences under the Road Traffic Act 1988 (continued)

(1) Provision creating offence	(2) General nature of offence	(3) Mode of prosecution	(4) Punishment	(5) Disqualification	(6) Endorsement	(7) Penalty points
RTA section 103(1)(b)	Driving while disqualified	(a) Summarily, in England and Wales (b) Summarily, in Scotland (c) On indictment, in Scotland	(a) 6 months or level 5 on the standard scale or both (b) 6 months or the statutory maximum or both (c) 12 months or a fine or both	Discretionary	Obligatory	[6]
RTA section 109	Failing to produce to court Northern Ireland driving licence [and counterpart]	Summarily	Level 3 on the standard scale			
[RTA section 114]	Failing to comply with conditions of LGV or PCV licence, or causing or permitting person under 21 to drive LGV or PCV in contravention of such conditions	Summarily	Level 3 on the standard scale			
RTA section 118	Failing to surrender revoked or suspended LGV or PCV licence	Summarily	Level 3 on the standard scale]			
Regulations made by virtue of RTA section [120(5)]	Contravention of provision of regulations (which is declared by regulations to be an offence) about [LGV or PCV] driver's licence	Summarily	Level 3 on the standard scale			

Offences under the Road Traffic Act 1988 (continued)

(1) Provision creating offence	(2) General nature of offence	(3) Mode of prosecution	(4) Punishment	(5) Disqualification	(6) Endorsement	(7) Penalty points
RTA section 123(4)	Giving of paid driving instruction by unregistered and unlicensed persons or their employers	Summarily	Level 4 on the standard scale			
RTA section 123(6)	Giving of paid instruction without there being exhibited on the motor car a certificate of registration or a licence under RTA Part V	Summarily	Level 3 on the standard scale			
RTA section 135	Unregistered instructor using title or displaying badge, etc, prescribed for registered instructor, or employer using such title, etc, in relation to his unregistered instructor or issuing misleading advertisement, etc	Summarily	Level 4 on the standard scale			
RTA section 136	Failure of instructor to surrender to Registrar certificate or licence	Summarily	Level 3 on the standard scale			
RTA section 137	Failing to produce certificate of registration or licence as driving instructor	Summarily	Level 3 on the standard scale			

Offences under the Road Traffic Act 1988 (continued)

(1) Provision creating offence	(2) General nature of offence	(3) Mode of prosecution	(4) Punishment	(5) Disqualification	(6) Endorsement	(7) Penalty points
RTA section 143	Using motor vehicle while uninsured or unsecured against third party risks	Summarily	[Level 5] on the standard scale	Discretionary	Obligatory	6–8
RTA section 147	Failing to surrender certificate of insurance or security to insurer on cancellation or to make statutory declaration of loss or destruction	Summarily	Level 3 on the standard scale			
RTA section 154	Failing to give information, or wilfully making a false statement, as to insurance or security when claim made	Summarily	Level 4 on the standard scale			
RTA section 163	Failing to stop motor vehicle or cycle when required by constable	Summarily	Level 3 on the standard scale			
RTA section 164	Failing to produce driving licence [and counterpart] [etc] or to state date of birth, or failing to provide the Secretary of State with evidence of date of birth, etc	Summarily	Level 3 on the standard scale			
RTA section 165	Failing to give … certain names and addresses or to produce certain documents	Summarily	Level 3 on the standard scale			

Offences under the Road Traffic Act 1988 (continued)

(1) Provision creating offence	(2) General nature of offence	(3) Mode of prosecution	(4) Punishment	(5) Disqualification	(6) Endorsement	(7) Penalty points
RTA section 168	Refusing to give, or giving false, name and address in case of reckless, careless or inconsiderate driving or cycling	Summarily	Level 3 on the standard scale			
RTA section 169	Pedestrian failing to give constable his name and address after failing to stop when directed by constable controlling traffic	Summarily	Level 1 on the standard scale			
RTA section 170(4)	Failing to stop after accident and give particulars or report accident	Summarily	[Six months or level 5 on the standard scale or both]	Discretionary	Obligatory	[5–10]
RTA section 170(7)	Failure by driver, in case of accident involving injury to another, to produce evidence of insurance or security or to report accident	Summarily	Level 3 on the standard scale			
RTA section 171	Failure by owner of motor vehicle to give police information for verifying compliance with requirement of compulsory insurance or security	Summarily	Level 4 on the standard scale			
RTA section 172	Failure of person keeping vehicle and others to give police informa-	Summarily	Level 3 on the standard scale	[Discretionary, if committed otherwise than by	Obligatory, if committed otherwise	3]

Offences under the Road Traffic Act 1988 (continued)

(1) Provision creating offence	(2) General nature of offence	(3) Mode of prosecution	(4) Punishment	(5) Disqualification	(6) Endorsement	(7) Penalty points
	tion as to identity of driver, etc, in the case of certain offences			virtue of subsection (5) or (11)	then by virtue of subsection (5) or (11)	
RTA section 173	Forgery, etc, of licences, test certificates, certificates of insurance and other documents and things	(a) Summarily (b) On indictment	(a) The statutory maximum (b) 2 years			
RTA section 174	Making certain false statements, etc, and withholding certain material information	Summarily	Level 4 on the standard scale			
RTA section 175 [175(1)] [RTA section 175(2)]	Issuing false documents False amending certificate of conformity	Summarily Summarily	Level 4 on the standard scale level 4 on the standard scale]			
RTA section 177	Impersonation of, or of person employed by, authorised examiner	Summarily	Level 3 on the standard scale			
RTA section 178	Taking, etc, in Scotland a motor vehicle without authority or, knowing that it has been so taken, driving it or allowing oneself to be carried in it without authority	(a) Summarily (b) On indictment	(a) 3 months or the statutory maximum or both (b) 12 months or a fine or both	Discretionary	. . . . .	. . . . .
RTA section 180	Failing to attend, give evidence or produce documents to, inquiry held by Secretary of State, etc	Summarily	Level 3 on the standard scale			

Offences under the Road Traffic Act 1988 (continued)

(1) Provision creating offence	(2) General nature of offence	(3) Mode of prosecution	(4) Punishment	(5) Disqualification	(6) Endorsement	(7) Penalty points
RTA section 181	Obstructing inspection of vehicles after accident	Summarily	Level 3 on the standard scale			
RTA Schedule 1 paragraph 6	Applying warranty to [equipment, protective helmet, appliance or information in defending proceedings under RTA section 15A,] 17 or 18(4) where no warranty given, or applying false warranty	Summarily	Level 3 on the standard scale			

Offences under this Act

(1) Provision creating offence	(2) General nature of offence	(3) Mode of prosecution	(4) Punishment	(5) Disqualification	(6) Endorsement	(7) Penalty points
Section 25 of this Act	Failing to give information as to date of birth or sex to court or to provide Secretary of State with evidence of date of birth, etc	Summarily	Level 3 on the standard scale			
Section 26 of this Act	Failing to produce driving licence [and counterpart] to court making order for interim disqualification	Summarily	Level 3 on the standard scale			

Offences under this Act (continued)

(1) Provision creating offence	(2) General nature of offence	(3) Mode of prosecution	(4) Punishment	(5) Disqualification	(6) Endorsement	(7) Penalty points
Section 27 of this Act	Failing to produce licence [and counterpart] to court for endorsement on conviction of offence involving obligatory endorsement or on committal for sentence, etc, for offence involving obligatory or discretionary disqualification when no interim disqualification ordered	Summarily	Level 3 on the standard scale			
Section 62 of this Act	Removing fixed penalty notice fixed to vehicle	Summarily	Level 2 on the standard scale			
Section 67 of this Act	False statement in response to notice to owner	Summarily	Level 5 on the standard scale			

[*Offences under the Road Traffic (Driver Licensing and Information Systems) Act 1989*

(1) Provision creating offence	(2) General nature of offence	(3) Mode of prosecution	(4) Punishment	(5) Disqualification	(6) Endorsement	(7) Penalty points
RTA 1989 s 1(5)	Failure of holder of existing HGV or PSV driver's licence to surrender it upon revocation or surrender of his existing licence under Part III of RTA	Summarily	Level 3 on the standard scale			

Offences under the Road Traffic (Driver Licensing and Information Systems) Act 1989 (continued)

(1) Provision creating offence	(2) General nature of offence	(3) Mode of prosecution	(4) Punishment	(5) Disqualification	(6) Endorsement	(7) Penalty points
RTA 1989, Schedule 1, para 3	Failing to comply with conditions of existing HGV driver's licence, or causing or permitting person under 21 to drive HGV in contravention of such conditions	Summarily	Level 3 on the standard scale			
RTA 1989, Schedule 1, para 8(2)	Contravention of provision of regulations (which is declared by regulations to be an offence) about existing HGV or PSV driver's licences	Summarily	Level 3 on the standard scale			
RTA 1989, Schedule 1, para 10(4)	Taking PSV test before applying for licence or within prescribed period afterwards	Summarily	Level 3 on the standard scale			
RTA 1989, Schedule 1, para 10(5)	Taking PSV test after refusal of licence	Summarily	Level 3 on the standard scale			

NOTES
Commencement: 15 May 1989.

This Schedule derived from the Road Traffic Act 1972, s 177(3), (5), Sch 4, Parts I, II, III, the Heavy Commercial Vehicles (Controls and Regulations) Act 1973, ss 2(2), 3(2), the Road Traffic Act 1974, ss 11(2), 13(4), 15(5), 21(2)-(4), Sch 5, Part III, Part IV, para 4(4)(b), (5), (6), Sch 7, the Road Traffic (Drivers' Ages and Hours of Work) Act 1976, Sch 1, para 15, Sch 3, Part I, the Criminal Law Act 1977, s 28(2), Sch 1, Sch 5, para 2, Sch 6, Sch 11, paras 5, 11-13, Sch 13, the Transport Act 1978, Sch 3, para 7, the Magistrates' Courts Act 1980, Sch 7, para 112, the Transport Act 1981, ss 24(3), 25(4), 26(1), 27(4), 28(2), Sch 7, Sch 9, paras 19-22, the Criminal Justice Act 1982, ss 38, 39, 46, 54, Sch 2, Sch 3, Sch 6, the Transport Act 1982, ss 29(7), 46(1), 57(2), 58, 63(1), (2), the Road Traffic (Driving Instruction) Act 1984, s 1(5), the Road Traffic Regulation Act 1984, Sch 7, columns 1-6, Sch 13, para 51, the Cycle Tracks Act 1984, s 2(1), the Roads (Scotland) Act 1984, Sch 9, para 68(12), the Criminal Justice (Scotland) Act 1987, Sch 2, the Criminal Justice Act 1988, s 36(2), Sch 14, para 52, and the Motor Vehicles (Wearing of Rear Seat Belts by Children) Act 1988, s 1(2).

Entries relating to the Road Traffic Regulation Act 1984: in the entries relating to ss 16(1), 17(4), 89(1), figures and words in square brackets substituted by the Road Traffic Act 1991, s 26, Sch 2, paras 1-4; entry relating to s 30(5) repealed by the New Roads and Street Works Act 1991, s 168(2), Sch 9; in the entries relating to s 35A(1), (2), (5), figures and words in square brackets substituted by the Parking Act 1989, s 4, Schedule, para 11.

Entries relating to the Road Traffic Act 1988: entries relating to ss 1-3, 4(1), (2), 5(1)(a), 7, 12, 23, 28, 29, 87(1), (2), 94, 96, 103(1)(b), 143, 164 (second amendment), 165, 170(4), 172, 178 are amended, the entries relating to ss 40A, 41A, 41B, 42 are substituted (for the original entry relating to s 42), the entries relating to ss 22A, 92(10), 94(3A), 94A, are inserted, and the entries to ss 97, 98 are repealed, by the Road Traffic Act 1991, ss 26, 83, Sch 2, paras 1, 5-31, Sch 8; entry relating to s 15A(3) or (4) inserted, and entry relating to Sch 1, para 6 amended, by the Motor Vehicles (Safety Equipment for Children) Act 1991, s 3(2), (3); entries relating to ss 92(7C), 93(3), 114, 118 added by the Road Traffic (Driver Licensing and Information Systems Act) 1989, s 7, Sch 3, para 28 (as amended with savings by SI 1990 No 144, regs 2(3), 3, Sch 3, para 3(5)); in entry relating to s 99, first and second words in square brackets added by the Road Traffic (Driver Licensing and Information Systems) Act 1989, s 7, Sch 3, para 28 (as amended with savings by SI 1990 No 144, regs 2(3), 3, Sch 3, para 3(5)), final words in square brackets added with savings by SI 1990 No 144, regs 2(2), 3, Sch 2, para 27; in entries relating to ss 109, 164, words in square brackets added with savings by SI 1990 No 144, regs 2(2), 3, Sch 2, para 27; entries relating to ss 110, 112 repealed and entry relating to s 117(4) amended, by the Road Traffic (Driver Licensing and Information Systems) Act 1989, ss 7, 16, Sch 3, para 28, Sch 6; entry relating to s 175, words in italics prospectively repealed, and words in square brackets prospectively added, by the Transport Act 1982, s 24(3) (as amended by the Road Traffic (Consequential Provisions) Act 1988, s 4, Sch 2, Part I), as from a day to be appointed.

Entries relating to this Act: words in square brackets in entries relating to ss 26, 27 added with savings by SI 1990 No 144, reg 2(2), Sch 2, para 27(d), (e), for savings see reg 3 thereof; entry relating to s 45 repealed by the Road Traffic (Driver Licensing and Information Systems) Act 1989, s 16, Sch 6.

Entries relating to the Road Traffic (Driver Licensing and Information Systems) Act 1989: added by the Road Traffic (Driver Licensing and Information Systems) Act 1989, s 7, Sch 3, para 29.

PART II
OTHER OFFENCES

(1) Offence	(2) Disqualification	(3) Endorsement	(4) Penalty points
Manslaughter or, in Scotland, culpable homicide by the driver of a motor vehicle	Obligatory	Obligatory	[3–11]
[An offence under section 12A of the Theft Act 1968 (aggravated vehicle-taking)	Obligatory	Obligatory	3–11]
Stealing or attempting to steal a motor vehicle	Discretionary	......	......
An offence or attempt to commit an offence in respect of a motor vehicle under section 12 of the Theft Act 1968 (taking conveyance without consent of owner etc or, knowing it has been so taken, driving it or allowing oneself to be carried in it)	Discretionary	......	......
An offence under section 25 of the Theft Act 1968 (going equipped for stealing, etc) committed with reference to the theft or taking of motor vehicles	Discretionary	......	......

NOTES
   Commencement: 15 May 1989.
   This Schedule derived from the Road Traffic Act 1972, s 177(3), (5), Sch 4, Parts I, II, III, the
Heavy Commercial Vehicles (Controls and Regulations) Act 1973, ss 2(2), 3(2), the Road Traffic
Act 1974, ss 11(2), 13(4), 15(5), 21(2)-(4), Sch 5, Part III, Part IV, para 4(4)(b), (5), (6), Sch 7, the
Road Traffic (Drivers' Ages and Hours of Work) Act 1976, Sch 1, para 15, Sch 3, Part I, the
Criminal Law Act 1977, s 28(2), Sch 1, Sch 5, para 2, Sch 6, Sch 11, paras 5, 11-13, Sch 13, the
Transport Act 1978, Sch 3, para 7, the Magistrates' Courts Act 1980, Sch 7, para 112, the Transport
Act 1981, ss 24(3), 25(4), 26(1), 27(4), 28(2), Sch 7, Sch 9, paras 19-22, the Criminal Justice Act 1982,
ss 38, 39, 46, 54, Sch 2, Sch 3, Sch 6, the Transport Act 1982, ss 29(7), 46(1), 57(2), 58, 63(1), (2), the
Road Traffic (Driving Instruction) Act 1984, s 1(5), the Road Traffic Regulation Act 1984, Sch 7,
columns 1-6, Sch 13, para 51, the Cycle Tracks Act 1984, s 2(1), the Roads (Scotland) Act 1984, Sch
9, para 68(12), the Criminal Justice (Scotland) Act 1987, Sch 2, the Criminal Justice Act 1988, s
36(2), Sch 14, para 52, and the Motor Vehicles (Wearing of Rear Seat Belts by Children) Act 1988,
s 1(2).
   First figures in square brackets substituted, and words omitted repealed, by the Road Traffic Act
1991, ss 26, 83, Sch 2, para 32, Sch 8; second words and figures in square brackets inserted by the
Aggravated Vehicle Taxing Act 1992, s 3(1).

SCHEDULE 3
Section 51

FIXED PENALTY OFFENCES

(1) Provision creating offence	(2) General nature of offence
Offences under the Vehicles (Excise) Act 1971	
Section 12(4) of the Vehicles (Excise) Act 1971	Using or keeping a vehicle on a public road without licence being exhibited in the prescribed manner.
Section 22(1) of that Act	Driving or keeping a vehicle without required registration mark or hackney carriage sign.
Section 22(2) of that Act	Driving or keeping a vehicle with registration mark or hackney carriage sign obscured, etc.
Offence under the Greater London Council (General Powers) Act 1974	
Section 15 of the Greater London Council (General Powers) Act 1974	Parking vehicles on footways, verges, etc.
Offence under the Highways Act 1980	
Section 137 of the Highways Act 1980	Obstructing a highway, but only where the offence is committed in respect of a vehicle.
Offences under the Road Traffic Regulation Act 1984	
RTRA section 5(1)	Using a vehicle in contravention of a traffic regulation order outside Greater London.
RTRA section 8(1)	Breach of traffic regulation order in Greater London.
RTRA section 11	Breach of experimental traffic order.
RTRA section 13	Breach of experimental traffic scheme regulations in Greater London.
RTRA section 16(1)	Using a vehicle in contravention of temporary prohibition or restriction of traffic in case of execution of works, etc.
RTRA section 17(4)	Wrongful use of special road.

(1) Provision creating offence	(2) General nature of offence
Offences under the Road Traffic Regulation Act 1984—cont	
RTRA section 18(3)	Using a vehicle in contravention of provision for one-way traffic on trunk road.
RTRA section 20(5)	Driving a vehicle in contravention of order prohibiting or restricting driving vehicles on certain classes of roads.
RTRA section 25(5)	Breach of pedestrian crossing regulations, except an offence in respect of a moving motor vehicle [other than a contravention of regulation 8 of the "Zebra" Pedestrian Crossings Regulations 1971 or of regulations 16 or 17 of the "Pelican" Pedestrian Crossings Regulations and General Directions 1987].
RTRA section 29(3)	Using a vehicle in contravention of a street playground order . . .
RTRA section [35A(1)]	Breach of an order regulating the use, etc, of a parking place provided by a local authority, but only where the offence is committed in relation to a parking place provided on a road.
RTRA section 47(1)	Breach of a provision of a parking place designation order and other offences committed in relation to a parking place designated by such an order, except any offence of failing to pay an excess charge within the meaning of section 46.
RTRA section 53(5)	Using vehicle in contravention of any provision of a parking place designation order having effect by virtue of section 53(1)(a) (inclusion of certain traffic regulation provisions).
RTRA section 53(6)	Breach of a provision of a parking place designation order having effect by virtue of section 53(1)(b) (use of any part of a road for parking without charge).
RTRA section 88(7)	Driving a motor vehicle in contravention of an order imposing a minimum speed limit under section 88(1)(b).
RTRA section 89(1)	Speeding offences under RTRA and other Acts.
Offences under the Road Traffic Act 1988	
RTA section 14	Breach of regulations requiring wearing of seat belts.
RTA section 15(2)	Breach of restriction on carrying children in front of vehicles.
RTA section 16	Breach of regulations relating to protective headgear for motor cycle drivers and passengers.
RTA section 19	Parking a heavy commercial vehicle on verge or footway.

(1) Provision creating offence	(2) General nature of offence
Offences under the Road Traffic Act 1988—cont	
[RTA section 19A	Parking a vehicle other than a heavy commercial vehicle on verge, etc.]
RTA section 22	Leaving vehicle in dangerous position.
RTA section 23	Unlawful carrying of passengers on motor cycles.
RTA section 34	Driving motor vehicle elsewhere than on a road.
RTA section 35	Failure to comply with traffic directions.
RTA section 36	Failure to comply with traffic signs.
[RTA section 40A	Using vehicle in dangerous condition etc.
RTA section 41A	Breach of requirement as to brakes, steering gear or tyres.
RTA section 41B	Breach of requirement as to weight: goods and passenger vehicles.]
RTA section 42	[Breach of other construction and use requirements.]
RTA section 87(1)	Driving vehicle [otherwise than in accordance with] requisite licence.
. . . . .	. . . . .
RTA section 163	Failure to stop vehicle on being so required by constable in uniform.

[463]

NOTES

Commencement: 15 May 1989.

This Schedule derived from the Transport Act 1982, Sch 1, and the Road Traffic Regulation Act 1984, Sch 13, para 55.

Words in square brackets in entry relating to the Road Traffic Regulation Act 1984, s 25(5) added, in relation to England and Wales by SI 1990 No 335, art 3, and in relation to Scotland by SI 1990 No 466, art 3; words omitted from entry relating to s 29(3) of the 1984 Act, and whole of entry relating to s 30(5) of that Act, repealed by the New Roads and Street Works Act 1991, s 168(2), Sch 9; figures in square brackets in entry relating to the Road Traffic Regulation Act 1984, s 35A(1) substituted by the Parking Act 1989, s 4, Schedule, para 11; entries relating to the Road Traffic Act 1988, ss 40A, 41A, 41B inserted, and entry relating to s 97 thereof repealed, by the Road Traffic Act 1991, ss 48, 83, Sch 4, para 112, Sch 8.

SCHEDULE 4

Section 68

STATUTORY STATEMENTS

PART I

STATUTORY STATEMENT OF OWNERSHIP OR HIRING

1.—(1) For the purposes of Part III of this Act, a statutory statement of ownership is a statement on an official form signed by the person providing it and stating whether he was the owner of the vehicle at the time of the alleged offence and, if he was not the owner of the vehicle at that time, whether—

(a) he was never the owner, or

(b) he ceased to be the owner before, or became the owner after, that time,

and in a case within paragraph (b) above, stating, if the information is in his possession, the name and address of the person to whom, and the date on which, he disposed of the vehicle or (as the case may be) the name and address of the person from whom, and the date on which, he acquired it.

(2) An official form for a statutory statement of ownership shall—

(a) indicate that the person providing the statement in response to a notice to owner relating to an offence may give notice requesting a hearing in respect of the offence in the manner specified in the form, and

(b) direct the attention of any person proposing to complete the form to the information provided in accordance with paragraph 3(3) below in any official form for a statutory statement of facts.

2.—(1) For the purposes of Part III of this Act, a statutory statement of hiring is a statement on an official form, signed by the person providing it, being a person by whom a statement of liability was signed, and stating—

(a) whether at the time of the alleged offence the vehicle was let to him under the hiring agreement to which the statement of liability refers, and

(b) if it was not, the date on which he returned the vehicle to the possession of the vehicle-hire firm concerned.

(2) An official form for a statutory statement of hiring shall—

(a) indicate that the person providing the statement in pursuance of a notice relating to an offence served under section 63 of this Act by virtue of section 66 of this Act may give notice requesting a hearing in respect of the offence in the manner specified in the form, and

(b) direct the attention of any person proposing to complete the form to the information provided in accordance with paragraph 3(3) below in any official form for a statutory statement of facts.

(3) In sub-paragraph (1) above "statement of liability", "hiring agreement" and "vehicle-hire firm" have the same meanings as in section 66 of this Act. **[464]**

NOTES

Commencement: 15 May 1989.

This Schedule derived from the Transport Act 1982, Sch 3.

PART II

STATUTORY STATEMENT OF FACTS

3.—(1) For the purposes of Part III of this Act, a statutory statement of facts is a statement on an official form, signed by the person providing it, which—

(a) states that the person providing it was not the driver of the vehicle at the time of the alleged offence, and

(b) states the name and address at the time when the statement is provided of the person who was the driver of the vehicle at the time of the alleged offence.

(2) A statutory statement of facts has effect as a notice given by the driver requesting a hearing in respect of the offence if it is signed by the person identified in the statement as the driver of the vehicle at the time of the alleged offence.

(3) An official form for a statutory statement of facts shall indicate—

(a) that if a person identified in the statement as the driver of the vehicle at the time of the alleged offence signs the statement he will be regarded as having given notice requesting a hearing in respect of the offence,

(b) that the person on whom the notice to owner relating to the offence is served may not give notice requesting a hearing in respect of the offence on his own account if he provides a statutory statement of facts signed by a person so identified, and

(c) that if the fixed penalty is not paid before the end of the period stated in the notice to owner as the period for response to the notice, a sum determined by reference to that fixed penalty may be registered without any court hearing for enforcement as a fine against the person on whom the notice to owner is served, unless he has given notice requesting a hearing in respect of the offence,

but that, in a case within paragraph (c) above, the sum in question may not be so registered if the person on whom the notice to owner is served provides a statutory statement of facts as mentioned in paragraph (b) above until two months have elapsed from the end of the period so stated without service of a summons or, in Scotland, complaint in respect of the offence on the person identified in that statement as the driver of the vehicle. **[465–466]**

(Schedule 5 applies to Scotland only.)

ROAD TRAFFIC (CONSEQUENTIAL PROVISIONS) ACT 1988
(c 54)

ARRANGEMENT OF SECTIONS

An Act to make provision for repeals (including a repeal to give effect to a recommendation of the Law Commission and the Scottish Law Commission), consequential amendments, transitional and transitory matters and savings in connection with the consolidation of enactments in the Road Traffic Act 1988 and the Road Traffic Offenders Act 1988.   [15 November 1988]

1. Meaning of "the Road Traffic Acts", "the repealed enactments", etc

(1) In this Act—

"the Road Traffic Acts" means the Road Traffic Act 1988, the Road Traffic Offenders Act 1988 and, so far as it reproduces the effect of the repealed enactments, this Act, and

"the repealed enactments" means the enactments repealed or revoked by this Act.

(2) Expressions used in this Act and in the Road Traffic Act 1988 have the same meaning as in that Act.   **[467]**

2. Continuity, and construction of references to old and new law

(1) The substitution of the Road Traffic Acts for the repealed enactments does not affect the continuity of the law.

(2) Anything done or having effect as if done under or for the purposes of a provision of the repealed enactments has effect, if it could have been done under or for the purposes of the corresponding provision of the Road Traffic Acts, as if done under or for the purposes of that corresponding provision.

(3) Any reference, whether express or implied, in the Road Traffic Acts or any other enactment, instrument or document to a provision of the Road Traffic Acts is to be read, in relation to the times, circumstances or purposes in relation to which the corresponding provision of the repealed enactments had effect and so far as the nature of the reference permits, as including a reference to that corresponding provision.

(4) Any reference, whether express or implied, in any enactment, instrument or document to a provision of the repealed enactments is to be read, in relation to the times, circumstances or purposes in relation to which the corresponding provision of the Road Traffic Acts has effect and so far as the nature of the reference permits, as including a reference to that corresponding provision.   **[468]**

NOTES
    Commencement: 15 February 1989.
    Road Traffic Acts: Road Traffic Act 1988, Road Traffic Offenders Act 1988, Road Traffic (Consequential Provisions) Act 1988 (so far as it reproduces the effect of enactments repealed by that Act).

3. Repeals

(1) The enactments specified in Part I of Schedule 1 to this Act are repealed to the extent specified in the third column.

(2) Those repeals include the repeal, in accordance with Recommendations of the Law Commission and the Scottish Law Commission, of section 34 of the Road Traffic Act 1972 (requirements as to employment of persons to attend to locomotives and trailers) as no longer of practical utility.

(3) The subordinate legislation specified in Part II of that Schedule is revoked to the extent specified in the third column.   **[469]**

NOTE
    Commencement: 15 February 1989.

4. Prospective and consequential amendments

Schedule 2 to this Act (which re-enacts or makes consequential amendments of provisions which made prospective amendments of the repealed and other enactments, so that the re-enacted or amended provisions prospectively amend the Road Traffic Acts and other enactments) and Schedule 3 to this Act (which makes other consequential amendments) shall have effect.   **[470]**

NOTES
    Commencement: 15 May 1989 (certain purposes); to be appointed (remaining purposes).
    Road Traffic Acts: Road Traffic Act 1988, Road Traffic Offenders Act 1988, Road Traffic (Consequential Provisions) Act 1988 (so far as it reproduces the effect of enactments repealed by that Act).

5. Transitional provisions and savings

(1) Schedule 4 to this Act (which makes certain transitional provisions and contains savings in connection with the repeals made by this Act) shall have effect.

(2) Nothing in that Schedule affects the general operation of section 16 of the Interpretation Act 1978 (general savings implied on a repeal).   **[471–472]**

NOTES
　Commencement: 15 February 1989.

6. (*Repealed by the Road Traffic Act 1991, s 83, Sch 8.*)

7. Saving for law of nuisance

Nothing in the Road Traffic Acts authorises a person to use on a road a vehicle so constructed or used as to cause a public or private nuisance, or in Scotland a nuisance, or affects the liability, whether under statute or common law, of the driver or owner so using such a vehicle.   **[473]**

NOTES
　Commencement: 15 February 1989.
　This section derived from the Road Traffic Act 1972, s 207.
　Road Traffic Acts: Road Traffic Act 1988, Road Traffic Offenders Act 1988, Road Traffic (Consequential Provisions) Act 1988 (so far as it reproduces the effect of enactments repealed by that Act).

8. Short title, commencement and extent

(1) This Act may be cited as the Road Traffic (Consequential Provisions) Act 1988.

(2) This Act, except those provisions that may be brought into force in accordance with subsection (3) below, shall come into force at the end of the period of three months beginning with the day on which it is passed.

(3) The following provisions of Schedule 2 to this Act—

    (a) in Part I, paragraphs 1 and 15 to 20,
    (b) Part II (except paragraph 22 so far as relates to subsections (5) to (8) of the new section inserted by that paragraph, which therefore come into force in accordance with subsection (2) above), and
    (c) [Paragraphs 15 to 20 of Schedule 2 to this Act],

shall come into force on such day as the Secretary of State may by order made by statutory instrument appoint, and different days may be so appointed for different provisions and for different purposes.

(4) An order under subsection (3) above bringing any provision of Part I of Schedule 2 to this Act (wholly or partly) into force may contain such transitional provisions and savings (whether or not involving the modification of any provision contained in an Act or in subordinate legislation within the meaning of the Interpretation Act 1978) as appear to the Secretary of State necessary or expedient in connection with that provision.

(5) This Act does not extend to Northern Ireland except so far as it affects other enactments extending to Northern Ireland.   **[474]**

NOTES
Commencement: 15 February 1989.
Sub-ss (3), (4) dervied from the Road Traffic Act 1972, s 204(2), the Road Traffic Act 1974, s 24(4), and the Transport Act 1982, ss 73(1), 76(2), (4), (8).
Sub-s (3): words in square brackets substituted by the Road Traffic Act 1991, s 48, Sch 4, para 114.

SCHEDULES
SCHEDULE 1

Section 3

REPEALS AND REVOCATIONS
PART I
ENACTMENTS REPEALED

Chapter	Short title	Extent of repeal
1968 c 73	Transport Act 1968	In Schedule 11, the entry for section 244 of the Road Traffic Act 1960.
1972 c 20	Road Traffic Act 1972	The whole Act.
1972 c 27	Road Traffic (Foreign Vehicles) Act 1972	Section 1(6)(a)(ii). In Schedule 2, the entry relating to sections 68 to 73 and 76 to 79 of the Road Traffic Act 1972 and regulations made under those sections.
1972 c 70	Local Government Act 1972	In section 186(1), the words from the beginning to first "and". Schedule 19.
1973 c 44	Heavy Commercial Vehicles (Controls and Regulations) Act 1973	The whole Act.
1973 c 62	Powers of Criminal Courts Act 1973	In Schedule 5, paragraph 43.
1973 c 65	Local Government (Scotland) Act 1973	In Schedule 14, paragraphs 82 to 86.
1974 c 50	Road Traffic Act 1974	Sections 6 to 15. Sections 20 to 22. Schedule 2. Schedule 3. Schedule 5. In Schedule 6, paragraphs 12 to 24.
1975 c 21	Criminal Procedure (Scotland) Act 1975	In Schedule 7D, the entries relating to the Road Traffic Act 1972.
1975 c 46	International Road Haulage Permits Act 1975	In section 3, subsections (2) to (5).
1976 c 3	Road Traffic (Drivers' Ages and Hours of Work) Act 1976	Section 1. Section 4(2)(b). Schedules 1 and 2.
1976 c 57	Local Government (Miscellaneous Provisions) Act 1976	In section 80(1), the definition of "the Act of 1972".

Chapter	Short title	Extent of repeal
1976 c 62	Motor-Cycle Crash Helmets (Religious Exemption) Act 1976	The whole Act.
1977 c 45	Criminal Law Act 1977	Section 50. In Schedule 1, the entries relating to the Road Traffic Act 1972. In Schedule 5, paragraph 2. In Schedule 6, the entry relating to the Road Traffic Act 1972. In Schedule 12, the amendments of the Road Traffic Act 1972.
1977 c 49	National Health Service Act 1977	In Schedule 15, paragraph 56.
1978 c 55	Transport Act 1978	In section 9, in subsection (1) the words from the beginning to third "and" and subsection (2). In section 24(2), the definition of "the 1972 Act". In Schedule 3, Part A.
1980 c 34	Transport Act 1980	Section 37(4). Section 61. Section 63.
1980 c 43	Magistrates' Courts Act 1980	In Schedule 7, paragraphs 111 and 112.
1980 c 53	Health Services Act 1980	In Schedule 1, paragraph 21.
1980 c 62	Criminal Justice (Scotland) Act 1980	Section 7(2). Section 26(8). Section 55. In Schedule 7, paragraph 23.
1980 c 66	Highways Act 1980	In Schedule 24, paragraph 21.
1981 c 14	Public Passenger Vehicles Act 1981	In Schedule 7, paragraphs 12 to 15.
1981 c 31	Insurance Companies Act 1981	In Schedule 4, paragraph 22.
1981 c 45	Forgery and Counterfeiting Act 1981	In section 12, the words "section 169(3) of the Road Traffic Act 1972".
1981 c 56	Transport Act 1981	Part IV. Schedules 7 and 8. In Schedule 9, Part I.
1982 c 48	Criminal Justice Act 1982	In section 39, subsection (1)(b)(i). In Schedule 2, the entry relating to the Road Traffic Act 1972. In Schedule 3, the entries relating to the Road Traffic Act 1972. In Schedule 6, the entries relating to the Road Traffic Act 1972. In Schedule 15, paragraph 16.
1982 c 49	Transport Act 1982	Section 16. In section 17, subsection (3) and, in subsection (4), the

Chapter	Short title	Extent of repeal
1982 c 49—*cont*	Transport Act 1982—*cont*	words from "and in subsection (4)(a) of that section" to the end.
		In section 24, the last column of the entries made by subsection (3)(b).
		Part III.
		Sections 56 to 60.
		Sections 63 and 64.
		Section 73(3).
		Schedules 1, 2, and 3.
		In Schedule 5, paragraphs 7 to 16, 17(1), 25 and 26.
1982 c 50	Insurance Companies Act 1982	In Schedule 5, paragraph 12.
1983 c 43	Road Traffic (Driving Licences) Act 1983	Section 1.
		In section 2, subsections (1) and (2).
1984 c 13	Road Traffic (Driving Instruction) Act 1984	The whole Act.
1984 c 27	Road Traffic Regulation Act 1984	Section 35(8).
		Section 47(7).
		In section 52(2), the words "and subsection (7)".
		Section 53(7).
		Section 78.
		Section 90.
		Section 98.
		Sections 113 and 114.
		Section 118.
		Sections 120 and 121.
		Section 130(2)(c), (4) and (5).
		In section 145(2), the words "Section 90 and".
		Schedule 7.
		In Schedule 10, paragraph 12.
		In Schedule 13, paragraphs 13 to 28, 50, 51 and 54 to 56.
1984 c 32	London Regional Transport Act 1984	In Schedule 6, paragraph 10.
1984 c 38	Cycle Tracks Act 1984	Section 2.
1984 c 54	Roads (Scotland) Act 1984	In Schedule 9, paragraphs 68, 88(2) and 93(39).
1984 c 60	Police and Criminal Evidence Act 1984	In Schedule 2, the entry relating to the Road Traffic Act 1972.
		In Schedule 5, in Part II the entry relating to the Road Traffic Act 1972.
1985 c 28	Motor-Cycle Crash-Helmets (Restriction of Liability) Act 1985	The whole Act.
1985 c 34	Road Traffic (Production of Documents) Act 1985	The whole Act.
1985 c 51	Local Government Act 1985	In Schedule 5, paragraphs 2 and 4(21).
		In Schedule 14, paragraph 49.
1985 c 66	Bankruptcy (Scotland) Act 1985	In Schedule 7, paragraph 10.

Chapter	Short title	Extent of repeal
1985 c 67	Transport Act 1985	In Schedule 2, in Part II paragraph 3.
1985 c 73	Law Reform (Miscellaneous Provisions) (Scotland) Act 1985	Section 38. In Schedule 2, paragraphs 26 and 27. In Schedule 3, paragraph 2.
1986 c 45	Insolvency Act 1986	In Schedule 14, the entry relating to the Road Traffic Act 1972.
1987 c 41	Criminal Justice (Scotland) Act 1987	In Schedule 1, paragraph 3.
1988 c 23	Motor Vehicles (Wearing of Rear Seat Belts by Children) Act 1988	Section 1. Section 3(2) and (3).
1988 c 33	Criminal Justice Act 1988	Section 37(2). Section 63. Section 68. In Schedule 15, paragraphs 92 to 94.

[475]

NOTES
    Commencement: 15 February 1989.

PART II
SUBORDINATE LEGISLATION REVOKED

Year and Number	Title	Extent of Revocation
SI 1973/2143	Motor Vehicles (Compulsory Insurance) (No 2) Regulations 1973	Regulations 3, 4 and 9.
SI 1977/1043	Motor Cars (Driving Instruction) Regulations 1977	Regulation 4.
SI 1981/160	Road Traffic (Northern Ireland Consequential Amendments) Order 1981	Article 2.
SI 1981/1692	Passenger and Goods Vehicles (Recording Equipment) Regulations 1981	All the Regulations.
SI 1982/1550	Motor Vehicles (Tests) (Extension) Order 1982	The whole Order.
SI 1982/1555	Driving Licences (Community Driving Licence) Regulations 1982	Regulations 2, 3 and 5.
SI 1986/368	Road Traffic Accidents (Payments for Treatment) (England and Wales) Order 1986	The whole Order.

Year and Number	Title	Extent of Revocation
SI 1986/408	Road Traffic Accidents (Payments for Treatment) (Scotland) Order 1986	The whole Order.
SI 1986/555	Fixed Penalty (Increase) (Scotland) (No 2) Order 1986	The whole Order.
SI 1986/1078	Road Vehicles (Construction and Use) Regulations 1986	Regulation 91.
SI 1986/1327	Fixed Penalty (Increase) Order 1986	The whole Order.
SI 1987/353	Road Traffic Accidents (Payments for Treatment) Order 1987	The whole Order.
SI 1987/2171	Motor Vehicles (Compulsory Insurance) Regulations 1987	Regulations 2 to 4.

[476–480]

NOTES
Commencement: 15 February 1989.

(Sch 2, Part I: paras 1, 4(2), 8, 9, 10(b), 13(b)(ii), 15(b) repealed by the Road Traffic Act 1991, s 83, Sch 8; paras 2, 3, 4(1), (3)–(6), 5–7, 10(a), 11, 12, 13(a), (b)(i), (iii), 14 amend the Transport Act 1982, ss 9, 10, 13, 17, 18, 21–24, 26; paras 15–19 amend the Road Traffic Act 1988, ss 61, 84, 85, 183, 192; para 20 amends the Road Traffic Offenders Act 1988, s 13(1); Sch 2, Parts II–IV repealed by the Road Traffic Act 1991, ss 49, 83, Sch 8.)

SCHEDULE 3

Section 4

CONSEQUENTIAL AMENDMENTS

The Thames Embankment Act 1862 (c. 93.)

1. Section 41 of the Thames Embankment Act 1862 does not apply to motor tractors, heavy motor cars, motor cars, motor cycles or invalid carriages but, subject to that, nothing in the Traffic Acts affects the provisions of that section.

2-39   . . .   **[481]**

NOTES
Commencement: 15 February 1989.
Paras 1–5, 6(1), (2), (4) (6)–(8), 7, 8(2)(a)–(c), (3), (4), 9(1)(a), (b), (2), (3)(a), (c), (4), (5), 10, 11(a), 12–36, 37(3), 38, 39 contain amendments only; paras 6(3), (5), 8(1), (2)(d), 9(1)(c), (3)(b), 11(b), (c), 37(1), (2) repealed by the Road Traffic Act 1991, s 83, Sch 8.
Traffic Acts: Road Traffic Regulation Act 1984, Road Traffic Act 1988, Road Traffic Offenders Act 1988, Road Traffic (Consequential Provisions) Act 1988 (so far as it reproduces the effect of enactments repealed by that Act).

SCHEDULE 4

Section 5

TRANSITIONAL PROVISIONS AND SAVINGS

General rules for old savings and transitional provisions

1.—(1) The repeal by this Act of an enactment previously repealed subject to savings does not affect the continued operation of those savings.

(2) The repeal by this Act of a saving made on the previous repeal of an enactment

does not affect the operation of the saving in so far as it is not specifically reproduced in the Road Traffic Acts but remains capable of having effect.

(3) Where the purpose of a repealed enactment was to secure that the substitution of the provisions of the Act containing that enactment for provisions repealed by that Act did not affect the continuity of the law, the repealed enactment, so far as it is not specifically reproduced in the Road Traffic Acts, shall continue to have effect, so far as it is capable of doing so, for the purposes of the Road Traffic Acts.

Old offences

2. The Road Traffic Acts (including this Act so far as not included in that expression) do not affect the operation of the repealed enactments in relation to offences committed before the commencement of those Acts or to appeals against or suspension of disqualification by virtue of convictions for offences so committed or against orders made in consequence of such convictions.

Road Traffic Act 1974 (c. 3.)

3.—(1) Any provision contained in an enactment passed or instrument made before 31 July 1974 which was not repealed by the Road Traffic Act 1974 and in which any expression was given the same meaning as in, or was otherwise to be construed by reference to, any provision of sections 68 to 82 of the Road Traffic Act 1972 which was repealed by that Act shall continue to be construed as if that provision had not been so repealed.

(2) The Secretary of State may by regulations made by statutory instrument make such amendments as he considers appropriate to take account of section 9 of the Road Traffic Act 1974—

    (a) in any enactment passed or instrument made before 31 July 1974 which refers (whether directly or by virtue of the Interpretation Act 1978 or otherwise) to any provision of sections 68 to 82 of the Road Traffic Act 1972 which was repealed by the Road Traffic Act 1974,

    (b) in the reference in paragraph 4 of Schedule 4 to the Road Traffic Act 1988, to section 83 of that Act, and

    (c) in the definition of "hours of darkness" in paragraph 2(2)(a) of Schedule 12 to the Road Traffic Regulation Act 1984.

(3) A statutory instrument containing regulations under sub-paragraph (2) above shall be subject to annulment in pursuance of a resolution of either House of Parliament.

Road Traffic (Drivers' Ages and Hours of Work) Act 1976 (c. 3.)

4.—(1) Subject to sub-paragraph (2) below, a person who, immediately before 1st January 1976, fulfilled any of the conditions in paragraph 2(1) of Schedule 2 to the Road Traffic (Drivers' Ages and Hours of Work) Act 1976 shall not, by reason only of the provisions of section 101 of the Road Traffic Act 1988, be disqualified for holding or obtaining a licence authorising him to drive motor vehicles falling within the class described in paragraph 5 or 6 of the Table set out in section 101(1) of that Act.

(2) A person shall not be treated, by virtue of sub-paragraph (1) above, as entitled to the grant of a licence authorising him to drive a goods vehicle the permissible maximum weight of which exceeds 10 tonnes or a motor vehicle constructed solely for the carriage of passengers and their effects which is adapted to carry more than fifteen passengers inclusive of the driver.

Road Traffic Regulation Act 1984 (c. 27.)

5.—(1) Notwithstanding the repeal by this Act of the provisions of section 98 of and Schedule 7 to the Road Traffic Regulation Act 1984 (prosecution of offences), those provisions shall, in relation to the interim period (within the meaning of Schedule 12 to that Act), continue to have effect in relation to offences under Schedule 12 to that Act.

(2) To the extent that section 135 of that Act (application to Isles of Scilly) applied to

the repealed enactments, it shall continue to apply to the corresponding provisions of the Road Traffic Acts.

Payments for traffic casualties

6. Where an accident giving rise to death or bodily injury in respect of which a payment is made under section 157 of the Road Traffic Act 1988, or claimed under section 158 of that Act, occurred before 1st April 1987, the amount payable shall not exceed the amount that would have been payable under the corresponding repealed enactment.

Licences, disqualification and endorsement

7.—(1) For the purposes of section 92(4)(a) of the Road Traffic Act 1988, a person to whom a licence was granted after the making of a declaration under paragraph (c) of the proviso to section 5(2) of the Road Traffic Act 1930 (which contained transitional provisions with respect to certain disabilities) shall be treated as having passed, at the time of the declaration, a relevant test in respect of vehicles of the classes to which the licence related.

(2) The references in sections 125(3)(d), 127(3)(d), 128(2)(b) and 130(b) of the Road Traffic Act 1988 to section 34 or 36 of the Road Traffic Offenders Act 1988 and to Part III of the Road Traffic Act 1988 include a reference—

(a) to section 93 of the Road Traffic Act 1972 and to Part III of that Act, and
(b) to section 5 of the Road Traffic Act 1962 and Part II of the Road Traffic Act 1960, (but not to section 104 of the 1960 Act).

(3) For the purposes of section 29 of the Road Traffic Offenders Act 1988, an order for endorsement which was made before the commencement of section 19 of the Transport Act 1981 counts as an order made in pursuance of section 44 of the Road Traffic Offenders Act 1988 for the endorsement of three penalty points, unless a disqualification was imposed on the offender on that or any subsequent occasion.

(4) For the purposes of section 2 of this Act as it has effect for the purposes of section 34(3) of the Road Traffic Offenders Act 1988—

(a) a previous conviction of an offence under section 6(1) of the Road Traffic Act 1972, as it had effect immediately before the substitution of a new section 6(1) by the Transport Act 1981, shall be treated as a conviction of an offence under section 5(1)(a) of the Road Traffic Act 1988, and
(b) a previous conviction of an offence under section 9(3) of the 1972 Act, as it had effect immediately before the substitution of a new section 8(7) by the 1981 Act, shall be treated as a conviction of an offence under section 7(6) of the Road Traffic Act 1988.

(5) The references in sections 36(4), 37(3) and 42(6) of the Road Traffic Offenders Act 1988 to an order under subsection (1) of section 36 include a reference to an order under section 93(7) of the Road Traffic Act 1972, section 5(7) of the Road Traffic Act 1962 or section 104(3) of the Road Traffic Act 1960.

(6) Where, in pursuance of section 93(5) of the Road Traffic Act 1972, a period of disqualification was imposed on an offender in addition to any other period or periods then, for the purpose of determining whether an application may be made under section 42 of the Road Traffic Offenders Act 1988 for the removal of either or any of the disqualifications the periods shall be treated as one continuous period of disqualification.

Hovercraft

8. For the purposes of the Hovercraft Act 1968 (under which enactments and instruments relating, amongst other things, to motor vehicles may, if passed before the commencement of that Act, be applied to hovercraft) any enactment contained in the Road Traffic Acts, being an enactment derived from an enactment so passed, and any instrument made or having effect as if made under such an enactment, shall be treated

as included among the enactments and instruments which can be so applied.   **[482–483]**

(*Sch 5: repealed by the Road Traffic Act 1991, s 83, Sch 8.*)

ROAD TRAFFIC (DRIVER LICENSING AND INFORMA-TION SYSTEMS) ACT 1989
(c 22)

*An Act to amend the law relating to driving licences and to regulate the operation of
systems providing drivers of motor vehicles with guidance and information
derived from automatically processed data or collecting, storing and processing
the data*   [21 July 1989]

PART I
DRIVING LICENCES

1. Abolition of special licences for driving HGVs and PSVs

(1) On the appointed day Part IV of the Road Traffic Act 1988 and section 22
of the Public Passenger Vehicles Act 1981 (which require special driving
licences to be held for driving heavy goods vehicles and public service vehicles)
shall cease to have effect but the repeal of those provisions does not imply that
it is lawful for a person to drive a heavy goods vehicle or a public service vehicle
of any class on or after that day on the authority of an existing licence under
Part III of the 1988 Act (ordinary licences) and, for the purposes of section 87
of that Act (offence of driving without Part III licence), his licence shall not be
taken to authorise him to drive vehicles of those classes.

(2) Subsection (1) above shall not, however, invalidate existing licences for
driving heavy goods vehicles or public service vehicles and the holder of such a
licence may, during the currency of that licence and his existing licence under
Part III of the 1988 Act, continue to drive any heavy goods vehicle or public
service vehicle which the first-mentioned licence authorises him to drive or a
goods vehicle of any class or, as the case may be, a passenger-carrying vehicle
of any class prescribed for the purposes of this subsection without obtaining a
new licence under the said Part III.

(3) Any of the following proceedings pending at the appointed day, that is
to say—

(a) any application questioning the conduct of a test of competence to
drive under section 115 of the 1988 Act, and

(b) any reconsideration by, or appeal from, a licensing authority under
section 116 of the 1988 Act or section 23 of the 1981 Act,

may be continued and, as the case may be, any order relative to the test (or fees)
made or licence issued notwithstanding the repeals made by this Act and any

order of eligibility to take a test so made shall be treated as relating to a corresponding test and any heavy goods vehicle or public service vehicle driver's licence so issued shall be treated as an existing licence.

(4) Where, during the currency of a person's existing licence for driving heavy goods vehicles or public service vehicles, his existing licence under Part III of the 1988 Act is revoked or surrendered, it shall be his duty to surrender his first-mentioned licence to the traffic commissioner for the traffic area in which he resides.

(5) A person who without reasonable excuse fails to comply with the duty under subsection (4) above is guilty of an offence.

(6) The provisions of Part I of Schedule 1 to this Act have effect for the purpose of re-enacting with modifications and assimilating the provisions of Part IV of the 1988 Act and the 1981 Act for the purposes of licences under those Acts continued in force by subsection (2) above and the transitory provisions of Part II of that Schedule shall also have effect.

(7) In this Part of this Act—

"the appointed day" means the day appointed for the coming into force of this section;

"existing", in relation to a licence, means in force immediately before the appointed day;

"traffic area" means a traffic area constituted for the purposes of the 1981 Act;

"traffic commissioner" means a traffic commissioner appointed for the purposes of the 1981 Act;

"the 1981 Act" means the Public Passenger Vehicles Act 1981;

"the 1988 Act" means the Road Traffic Act 1988;

and in subsection (2) above the reference to the vehicles which the holder of a heavy goods vehicle driver's licence is authorised to drive includes a reference to the vehicles which he is authorised to drive by virtue of regulations under paragraph 8(2)(a) of Schedule 1 to this Act and the reference to prescribed classes of goods vehicles or passenger-carrying vehicles is a reference to classes of goods vehicles or passenger-carrying vehicles (within the meaning of the 1988 Act) prescribed under that paragraph.   **[484]**

NOTES

Commencement: 1 April 1991 (sub-ss (1)–(5); sub-s (7), certain purposes); 1 June 1990 (sub-ss (6) and (7), certain purposes); 8 November 1989 (sub-s (6), certain purposes).

Commencement orders: SI 1989 No 1843, SI 1990 No 802, SI 1990/2610.

SCHEDULES

SCHEDULE 1

Section 1

EXISTING HGV AND PSV DRIVERS' LICENCES

PART I

EXISTING HGV AND PSV DRIVERS' LICENCES

Preliminary

1. In this Part of this Schedule—

"conduct" means—

(a) in relation to the holder of an existing heavy goods vehicle licence, his conduct as a driver of a motor vehicle, and

(b) in relation to the holder of an existing public service vehicle licence, his conduct both as a driver of a motor vehicle and in any other respect relevant to his holding a public service vehicle licence,
including, in either case, such conduct in Northern Ireland;

"existing licence" means a licence to drive heavy goods vehicles or public service vehicles (as the case may be) continued in force by section 1(2) of this Act, and "existing heavy goods vehicle licence" and "existing public service vehicle licence" shall be construed accordingly;

"full", in relation to an existing heavy goods vehicle licence, indicates a licence other than a provisional licence;

"heavy goods vehicle" has the same meaning as it had for the purposes of Part IV of the 1988 Act before its repeal by section 1 of this Act and "large goods vehicle"has the same meaning;

"notice" means notice in writing and "notify" shall be construed accordingly;

"passenger-carrying vehicle" has the same meaning as it has in Part IV of the 1988 Act;

"prescribed", unless the context requires otherwise, means prescribed by regulations made under paragraph 8 below; and

"public service vehicle" has the same meaning as it had for the purposes of section 22 of the 1981 Act before its repeal by section 1 of this Act.

Functions of Secretary of State and Traffic Commissioners

2.—(1) The functions conferred by the following provisions of this Part of this Schedule in relation to existing licences shall be functions of the Secretary of State except where, by any provision, the function is conferred on a traffic commissioner or any court.

(2) Traffic commissioners shall, in the exercise of those functions, act in accordance with directions given by the Secretary of State; but such directions shall be general directions not relating to the exercise of functions in a particular case.

Conditions of existing HGV licences

3.—(1) An existing heavy goods vehicle licence issued as a provisional licence, or an existing full heavy goods vehicle licence held by a person under the age of 21, is subject to the prescribed conditions, and if the holder of the licence fails, without reasonable excuse, to comply with any of the conditions he is guilty of an offence.

(2) It is an offence for a person knowingly to cause or permit another person who is under the age of 21 to drive a heavy goods vehicle of any class in contravention of any prescribed conditions to which that other person's licence is subject.

Duration of existing licences

4.—(1) An existing heavy goods vehicle licence shall, unless previously revoked, suspended or surrendered, continue in force for 3 years from the date on which it is expressed to take effect.

(2) Subject to sub-paragraph (3) below, a provisional heavy goods vehicle licence shall, unless previously revoked, suspended or surrendered, continue in force for 6 months from the date on which it is expressed to take effect.

(3) Sub-paragraph (2) above does not apply to a heavy goods vehicle licence treated as a provisional licence by virtue of regulations under paragraph 8 below.

(4) An existing public service vehicle licence shall, unless previously revoked, suspended or surrendered, continue in force for 5 years from the date on which it is expressed to take effect.

(5) If on the date on which an application is made under Part III of the 1988 Act for a licence to drive large goods vehicles or passenger-carrying vehicles, the applicant is the holder of an existing heavy goods vehicle licence or an existing public service vehicle licence, as the case may be, his existing licence shall not expire in accordance with the foregoing provisions before the application is disposed of.

Revocation or suspension of existing licences

5.—(1) An existing heavy goods vehicle licence or public service vehicle licence—

(a) must be revoked—

(i) if its holder develops such physical disability as may be prescribed, or
(ii) if there come into existence, in relation to its holder, such circumstances relating to his conduct as may be prescribed;

(b) must be revoked or suspended if his conduct or physical disability is such as to make him unfit to hold such a licence;

and where the licence is suspended under paragraph (b) above it shall during the time of suspension be of no effect.

(2) Where it appears that the conduct or physical disability of the holder of an existing licence falls within both sub-paragraph (1)(a) above and sub-paragraph (1)(b) above, proceedings shall be taken or continued under sub-paragraph (1)(a) and not sub-paragraph (1)(b) and accordingly the power to suspend the licence, rather than revoke it, shall not be available.

(3) Regulations made for the purposes of sub-paragraph (1)(a) above—

(a) may make different provision for heavy goods vehicles and for public service vehicles and for different descriptions of persons; and
(b) shall provide for the determination of the cases in which, under paragraph 6 below, a person whose licence has been revoked is to be disqualified indefinitely or for a period and, if for a period, for the determination of the period.

(4) Any question arising under sub-paragraph (1)(b) above as to whether a person is or is not, by reason of his conduct, fit to hold a heavy goods vehicle licence or a public service vehicle licence, as the case may be, may be referred by the Secretary of State to the traffic commissioner for the area in which the holder of the licence resides.

(5) Where, on any reference under sub-paragraph (4) above, the traffic commissioner determines that the holder of the licence is not fit to hold a heavy goods vehicle licence or a public service vehicle licence, as the case may be, he shall also determine whether the conduct of the holder of the licence is such as to require the revocation of his licence or only its suspension; and, if the former, whether the holder of the licence should be disqualified under paragraph 6(2)(a) below (and, if so, for what period) or under paragraph 6(2)(b) below.

(6) A traffic commissioner to whom a reference has been made under sub-paragraph (4) above may require the holder of the licence to furnish the commissioner with such information as he may require and may, by notice to the holder, require him to attend before the commissioner at the time and place specified by the commissioner to furnish the information and to answer such questions (if any) relating to the subject matter of the reference as the commissioner may put to him.

(7) If the holder of the licence fails without reasonable excuse to furnish information to or to attend before or answer questions properly put by a commissioner when required to do so under sub-paragraph (6) above, the commissioner may notify the failure to the Secretary of State and, if the commissioner does so, the Secretary of State may, as he thinks fit, revoke the licence or suspend it for such period as he thinks fit.

(8) Except where he has given such a notification as is mentioned in sub-paragraph (7) above, the traffic commissioner to whom a reference has been made under sub-paragraph (4) above shall notify the Secretary of State and the holder of the licence of his determination in the matter and the decision of the commissioner shall be binding on the Secretary of State.

(9) Where the Secretary of State, without making such a reference, determines to revoke or suspend a person's licence under sub-paragraph (1) above he shall notify his determination in the matter to the holder of the licence and, where he suspends it, to the traffic commissioner for the area in which the holder of the licence resides.

Disqualification on revocation of existing licences

6.—(1) Where in purusance of paragraph 5(1)(a) above the Secretary of State revokes a person's existing licence, the Secretary of State must, in accordance with the regulations made for the purposes of that paragraph, order that person to be disqualified indefinitely or for the period determined in accordance with the regulations.

(2) Where in pursuance of paragraph 5(1)(b) above the Secretary of State revokes an existing licence, he may—

    (a) order the holder to be disqualified indefinitely or for such period as the Secretary of State thinks fit, or

    (b) except where the licence is a provisional licence, if it appears to the Secretary of State that, owing to the conduct or physical disability of the holder of the licence it is expedient to require him to comply with the prescribed conditions applicable to provisional licences under Part III of the 1988 Act until he passes the prescribed test of competence under that Part to drive large goods vehicles or passenger-carrying vehicles of any class, order him to be disqualified for holding or obtaining a full licence to drive until he passes such a test.

(3) If, while the holder of an existing licence is disqualified under sub-paragraph (1) above, the circumstances prescribed for the purposes of paragraph 5(1)(a)(ii) above cease to exist in his case, the Secretary of State must, on an application made to him for the purpose, remove the disqualification.

(4) Where the holder of an existing licence is disqualified under sub-paragraph (2)(a) above, the Secretary of State may, in such circumstances as may be prescribed, remove the disqualification.

(5) Where the holder of an existing full licence is disqualified under sub-paragraph (2)(b) above, the Secretary of State must not afterwards grant him a full licence under Part III of the 1988 Act to drive large goods vehicles or passenger-carrying vehicles of any class unless satisfied that he has since the disqualification passed the prescribed test of competence under that Part to drive vehicles of that class, and until he passes that test any such full Part III licence obtained by him shall be of no effect.

(6) So long as the disqualification under sub-paragraph (1) or (2)(a) above of the holder of an existing licence continues in force, no licence under Part III of the 1988 Act to drive large goods vehicles or passenger-carrying vehicles (as the case may be) shall be granted to him and any such licence obtained by him shall be of no effect.

(7) In this paragraph "disqualified"—

    (a) in a case of revocation on the ground of the conduct of the holder of the licence as a driver, means disqualified for holding or obtaining a licence under Part III of the 1988 Act to drive large goods vehicles of the prescribed classes and passenger-carrying vehicles of the prescribed classes; and

    (b) in a case of revocation of a public service vehicle licence on the ground of the conduct of the holder otherwise than as a driver, means disqualified for holding or obtaining a licence under Part III of the 1988 Act to drive passenger-carrying vehicles of the prescribed classes.

Appeals relating to existing licences

7.—(1) The holder of an existing licence who is aggrieved by the Secretary of State's—

    (a) suspension or revocation of his licence under paragraph 5 above, or

    (b) ordering of disqualification under paragraph 6 above,

may, after giving to the Secretary of State and any traffic commissioner to whom the matter was referred notice of his intention to do so, appeal to a magistrates' court acting for the petty sessions area in which the holder of the licence resides, or, in Scotland, to the sheriff within whose jurisdiction he resides.

(2) On an appeal under sub-paragraph (1)(a) above the Secretary of State and, if the matter was referred to a traffic commissioner, the commissioner shall be respondent.

(3) On any appeal under sub-paragraph (1) above the court or sheriff may make such order as it or he thinks fit and the order shall be binding on the Secretary of State.

Regulations

8.—(1) The Secretary of State may make regulations for prescribing anything which may be prescribed under this Part of this Schedule and generally for the purpose of carrying its provisions into effect.

(2) Regulations under this paragraph may make different provision for different cases and circumstances and may in particular—

(a) provide that a full licence to drive heavy goods vehicles of a particular class shall also be treated for the purposes of this Part of this Schedule as a provisional licence to drive heavy goods vehicles of another prescribed class;

(b) make provision with respect to the custody and production of existing licences and requiring, and regulating the procedure on, the surrender or production to the Secretary of State, a traffic commissioner or any constable or officer of existing licences which have been revoked or suspended or have expired;

(c) provide for the issue by traffic commissioners of duplicate licences in place of existing licences lost or defaced on payment of the prescribed fee;

(d) provide that a person who contravenes or fails to comply with any specified provision is guilty of an offence; and

(e) provide that this Part of this Schedule shall not apply to prescribed classes of heavy goods vehicle or of public service vehicle either generally or in such circumstances as may be prescribed.

(3) The power to make regulations under this paragraph is exercisable by statutory instrument which shall be subject to annulment in pursuance of a resolution of either House of Parliament.

(4) Before making any regulations under this paragraph the Secretary of State must consult with such representative organisations as he thinks fit.

Provisions as to existing Northern Ireland licences

9.—(1) In this paragraph "existing Northern Ireland licence" means a licence specifically to drive heavy goods vehicles or public service vehicles granted under the law of Northern Ireland.

(2) The Secretary of State may exercise as respects Great Britain the like power of revoking or suspending any existing Northern Ireland licence and of making an order under paragraph 6(2) above as is conferred on him in relation to an existing heavy goods vehicle licence or public service vehicle licence by paragraphs 5(1)(b) and 6(2) above, and the provisions of paragraphs 5(1) and (4) to (9) and 6(2), (4), (5), (6) and (7) and the power to make regulations under paragraph 8(2)(b) shall have effect accordingly subject to the modification that references to the traffic commissioner for the area in which the holder of the licence resides shall be construed as references to the prescribed traffic commissioner.

(3) Where an existing Northern Ireland licence which has been revoked is surrendered to the Secretary of State in pursuance of regulations made under paragraph 8(2)(b), the Secretary of State shall send it to the licensing authority in Northern Ireland together with particulars of the revocation.

(4) A holder of an existing Northern Ireland licence who is aggrieved by the revocation or suspension of the licence or the ordering of disqualification by virtue of sub-paragraph (2) above shall have the like right of appeal as is conferred by paragraph

7 above except that an appeal brought by virtue of this sub-paragraph shall, if the appellant is not resident in Great Britain, lie to a prescribed magistrates' court or a prescribed sheriff.   **[485]**

NOTES
   Commencement: 1 April 1991.
   Commencement order: SI 1990 No 2610.
   See also the Motor Vehicles (Driving Licences) (Heavy Goods and Public Service Vehicles) Regulations 1990, SI 1990 No 2611 post.
   The 1988 Act: Road Traffic Act 1988.

PART II
TRANSITORY PROVISIONS

10. ...

   11. Notwithstanding section 87 of the 1988 Act, a person who is the holder of a licence to drive motor vehicles granted under Part III of that Act and coming into force on or after 1st June 1990 and is also the holder of—

   (a) a licence under Part IV of that Act to drive heavy goods vehicles of any class, or
   (b) a licence under section 22 of the 1981 Act to drive public service vehicles of any class,

may drive, or be caused or permitted to drive, a heavy goods vehicle or (as the case may be) a public service vehicle of that class notwithstanding that his licence under Part III of the 1988 Act does not authorise him to drive such a vehicle.

   12. The power to make regulations under paragraph 8 above includes power to prescribe the classes of goods vehicle or passenger-carrying vehicle which, by virtue of section 1(2) of this Act, the holder of an existing licence is authorised to drive during the currency of his existing licence.   **[486]**

NOTES
   Commencement: 1 April 1991 (para 12); 1 June 1990 (para 11).
   Commencement orders: SI 1989 No 1843, SI 1990 No 802, SI 1990 No 2610.
   Para 10: repealed by theRoad Traffic (Driver Licensing and Information Systems) Act 1989, s 16, Sch 6.
   Para 11: prospectively repealed by the Road Traffic (Driver Licensing and Information Systems) Act 1989, s 16, Sch 6, as from a day to be appointed.
   The 1981 Act: Public Passenger Vehicles Act 1981.
   The 1988 Act: Road Traffic Act 1988.

RADIOACTIVE MATERIAL (ROAD TRANSPORT) ACT
1991
(c 27)

ARRANGEMENT OF SECTIONS

An Act to make new provision with respect to the transport of radioactive material by road; to repeal section 5(2) of the Radioactive Substances Act 1948; and for connected purposes [27 June 1991]

1. Preliminary

(1) In this Act "radioactive material" means any material having a specific activity in excess of—

    (a) 70 kilobecquerels per kilogram; or

    (b) such lesser specific activity as may be specified in an order made by the Secretary of State;

and the power to make an order under this subsection shall be exercisable by statutory instrument which shall be subject to annulment in pursuance of a resolution of either House of Parliament.

(2) In this Act—

"examiner" means any examiner appointed under section 68(1) of the Road Traffic Act 1988;

"inspector" means any inspector appointed under subsection (3) below;

"packaging", in relation to radioactive material which has been consigned for transport, means an assembly of packaging components which encloses the material completely;

"packaging components" means components intended for use as part of the packaging of such material, and includes—

    (a) receptacles, absorbent materials, spacing structures and radiation shielding; and

    (b) devices for cooling, for absorbing mechanical shocks and for thermal insulation;

"radioactive package" means a package comprising radioactive material which has been consigned for transport and its packaging;

"transport" means transport by road.

(3) The Secretary of State may—

    (a) appoint as inspectors, to assist him in the execution of this Act and regulations made under it, such number of persons appearing to him to be qualified for the purpose as he may consider necessary; and

    (b) make to or in respect of any person so appointed such payments by way of remuneration, allowances or otherwise as he may with the approval of the Treasury determine. **[487]**

NOTE

Commencement: 27 August 1991.

2. Regulations

(1) The Secretary of State may make such regulations as appear to him to be necessary or expedient—

    (a) to prevent any injury to health, or any damage to property or to the environment, being caused by, or by any incident arising out of, the transport of radioactive material; and

(b) to give effect to such international regulations for the safe transport of radioactive material as may from time to time be published by the International Atomic Energy Agency.

(2) Without prejudice to the generality of subsection (1) above, regulations under this section may make provision with respect to—

(a) the design of packaging for radioactive material and the manufacture and maintenance of packaging components;

(b) the preparation, labelling, consignment, handling, transport, storage in transit and delivery of radioactive packages;

(c) the placarding of vehicles used to transport such packages; and

(d) the keeping of records and the furnishing of information.

(3) Regulations under this section may also—

(a) impose requirements by reference to the approval of the Secretary of State or of any person or body specified in the regulations;

(b) make different provision for different cases or different circumstances; and

(c) provide for such exceptions, limitations and conditions, and make such supplementary, incidental, consequential or transitional provisions, as the Secretary of State considers necessary or expedient.

(4) Any person who contravenes or fails to comply with any regulations under this section shall be guilty of an offence.

(5) The power to make regulations under this section shall be exercisable by statutory instrument which shall be subject to annulment in pursuance of a resolution of either House of Parliament.

(6) Subsection (2) of section 5 of the Radioactive Substances Act 1948 shall cease to have effect; and any regulations under that subsection which are in force at the commencement of this Act shall have effect as if made under this section.   **[488]**

NOTES

Commencement: 27 August 1991.

See the Radioactive Substances (Carriage by Road) (Great Britain) Regulations 1974, SI 1974 No 1735, as amended.

3. Prohibitions and directions

(1) If it appears to an inspector or examiner, as respects any vehicle used to transport radioactive packages—

(a) that the vehicle, or any radioactive package which is being transported by it, fails to comply with any regulations under section 2 above;

(b) that the vehicle, or any radioactive package which is or was being transported by it, has been involved in an accident;

(c) that any radioactive package which was being transported by the vehicle, or any radioactive material which was contained in such a package, has been lost or stolen,

he may prohibit the driving of the vehicle.

(2) If it appears to an inspector that any radioactive package or packaging component fails to comply with any regulations under section 2 above, he may prohibit the transport of that package or, as the case may require, the use of that component as part of the packaging of radioactive materials.

(3) A prohibition imposed under this section may apply either absolutely or

for a specified purpose and either without any limitation of time or for a specified period.

(4) Where an inspector or examiner imposes a prohibition under subsection (1) above, he may also by a direction in writing require the person in charge of the vehicle to remove it (and, if it is motor vehicle drawing a trailer, also to remove the trailer) to such place and subject to such conditions as are specified in the direction; and the prohibition shall not apply to the removal of the vehicle or trailer in accordance with the direction.

(5) Where an inspector or examiner imposes a prohibition under this section, he shall forthwith give notice of the prohibition to the person in charge of the vehicle, package or packaging component, specifying the failure to comply or, as the case may be, the accident or other incident in consequence of which the prohibition is imposed and—

    (a) stating whether the prohibition applies absolutely or for a specified purpose (and if the latter specifying the purpose); and

    (b) stating whether the prohibition applies without limitation of time or for a specified period;

and any direction under subsection (4) above may be given either in such a notice or in a separate notice given to the person in charge of the vehicle.

(6) A prohibition under this section shall come into force as soon as notice of it has been given in accordance with subsection (5) above and shall continue in force—

    (a) until it is removed under subsection (7) below; or

    (b) in the case of a prohibition imposed only for a specified period, until either it is removed or that period expires, whichever first occurs.

(7) A prohibition under subsection (1) above may be removed by any inspector or examiner, and a prohibition under subsection (2) above may be removed by any inspector, if he is satisfied—

    (a) in the case of a prohibition imposed in consequence of a failure to comply with any regulations under section 2 above, that appropriate action has been taken to remedy that failure;

    (b) in the case of a prohibition imposed in consequence of an accident or other incident, either that no failure so to comply was occasioned by that accident or incident or that appropriate action has been taken to remedy any such failure which was so occasioned;

and on doing so, the inspector or examiner shall forthwith give notice of the removal of the prohibition to the person in charge of the vehicle, package or packaging component.

(8) Any person who contravenes a prohibition under this section, or fails to comply with a direction under subsection (4) above, shall be guilty of an offence.   **[489]**

NOTE
    Commencement: 27 August 1991.

4. Enforcement notices

(1) If an inspector is of the opinion that any person is failing or is likely to fail to comply with any regulations under section 2 above which make provision for regulating the manufacture, or requiring the maintenance, of packaging components, he may serve a notice under this section on that person.

(2) A notice under this section shall—

(a) state that the inspector is of the said opinion;

(b) specify the matters constituting the failure to comply with the regulations in question or the matters making it likely that such a failure will occur, as the case may be;

(c) specify the steps that must be taken in order to remedy those matters and the period within which those steps must be taken.

(3) Any person who fails to comply with a notice under this section shall be guilty of an offence.   **[490]**

NOTE
Commencement: 27 August 1991.

5. Powers of entry

(1) An inspector or examiner shall, on producing, if so required, some duly authenticated document showing his authority, have a right at all reasonable hours—

(a) to enter any vehicle used to transport radioactive packages for the purpose of ascertaining—

(i) whether the vehicle, or any radioactive package which is being transported by it, fails to comply with any regulations under section 2 above;

(ii) whether the vehicle, or any radioactive package which is or was being transported by it, has been involved in an accident; and

(iii) whether any radioactive package which was being transported by the vehicle, or any radioactive material which was contained in such a package, has been lost or stolen; and

(b) in the case of an inspector, to enter any premises for the purpose of ascertaining whether there is on the premises any vehicle used for transporting radioactive packages, or any radioactive package or packaging component which fails to comply with regulations under section 2 above.

(2) If a justice of the peace, on sworn information in writing or, in Scotland, on evidence on oath, is satisfied that there are reasonable grounds for entering any vehicle or premises for any such purpose as is mentioned in subsection (1) above and either—

(a) that admission to the vehicle or premises has been refused, or a refusal is apprehended, and (in the case of premises) that notice of the intention to apply for the warrant has been given to the occupier; or

(b) that an application for admission, or the giving of such a notice, would defeat the object of the entry, or that the case is one of urgency, or (in the case of premises) that they are unoccupied or the occupier temporarily absent,

he may by warrant signed by him authorise the inspector or examiner to enter and search the vehicle or premises, using reasonable force if need be.

(3) A warrant granted under this section shall continue in force until executed.

(4) An inspector or examiner who enters any vehicle or premises by virtue of this section, or of a warrant issued under it, may seize anything which he has

reasonable grounds for believing is evidence in relation to an offence under section 2(4) above.

(5) Any person who intentionally obstructs any person exercising any power conferred by this section, or by a warrant issued under it, shall be guilty of an offence.

(6) If any person who enters any vehicle or premises by virtue of this section, or of a warrant issued under it, discloses any information thereby obtained with respect to any manufacturing process or trade secret, he shall, unless the disclosure was made in the performance of his duty, be guilty of an offence.

(7) *(Applies to Scotland only.)*

[491]

NOTE
Commencement: 27 August 1991.

6. Offences and penalties

(1) Where an offence under this Act which has been committed by a body corporate is proved to have been committed with the consent or connivance of, or to be attributable to any neglect on the part of—

 (a) any director, manager, secretary or other similar officer of the body corporate; or
 (b) any person who was purporting to act in any such capacity,

he as well as the body corporate shall be deemed to be guilty of that offence and shall be liable to be proceeded against and punished accordingly.

(2) Any person guilty of an offence under section 5(5) above shall be liable on summary conviction to a fine not exceeding level 3 on the standard scale.

(3) Any person guilty of any other offence under this Act shall be liable—

 (a) on conviction on indictment, to a fine or to imprisonment for a term not exceeding two years or to both;
 (b) on summary conviction, to a fine not exceeding the statutory maximum or to imprisonment for a term not exceeding two months or to both.

(4) The court by or before which any person is convicted of an offence under section 2(4) or 3(8) above in respect of any radioactive material may order the material to be destroyed or disposed of and any expenses reasonably incurred in connection with the destruction or disposal to be defrayed by that person. **[492]**

NOTE
Commencement: 27 August 1991.

7. Expenses

Any expenses incurred by the Secretary of State in consequence of the provisions of this Act shall be payable out of money provided by Parliament. **[493]**

NOTE
Commencement: 27 August 1991.

8. Corresponding provision for Northern Ireland

An Order in Council under paragraph 1(1)(b) of Schedule 1 to the Northern Ireland Act 1974 (legislation for Northern Ireland in the interim period) which contains a statement that it is made only for purposes corresponding to the purposes of this Act—

(a) shall not be subject to paragraph 1(4) and (5) of that Schedule (affirmative resolution of both Houses of Parliament); but

(b) shall be subject to annulment in pursuance of a resolution of either House of Parliament.   **[494]**

NOTE
  Commencement: 27 June 1991.

9. Short title, repeals, commencement and extent

(1) This Act may be cited as the Radioactive Material (Road Transport) Act 1991.

(2) The enactments mentioned in the Schedule to this Act are hereby repealed to the extent specified in the third column of that Schedule.

(3) Except for section 8 above, this Act shall not come into force until the end of the period of two months beginning with the day on which it is passed.

(4) Except for section 8 above, this Act does not extend to Northern Ireland.   **[495]**

NOTE
  Commencement: 27 August 1991.

SCHEDULE

Section 9(2)

REPEALS

Chapter	Short title	Extent of Repeal
1948 c. 37.	The Radioactive Substances Act 1948.	In section 5, subsection (2) and in subsection (6) the words from "and for the purposes of subsection (2)" to the end. In section 7, in subsection (1), the words "or any vehicle, vessel or aircraft", and the words "vehicle, vessel or aircraft", and in subsection (2) the words "vehicle, vessel or aircraft" in both places where they occur.

[496]

NOTE
  Commencement: 27 August 1991.

ROAD TRAFFIC ACT 1991

(c 40)

ARRANGEMENT OF SECTIONS

PART I

GENERAL

PART II

TRAFFIC IN LONDON

PART III

SUPPLEMENTARY

An Act to amend the law about road traffic   [25 July 1991]

PART I

GENERAL

Construction and use

9. Vehicle examiners

(1) ...

(2) Any reference in any Act, or in any instrument made under any Act, to a certifying officer or public service vehicle examiner appointed under the Public Passenger Vehicles Act 1981 or to an examiner appointed under section 68(1) of the Road Traffic Act 1988 shall, so far as may be appropriate in consequence of the preceding provisions of this section, be construed as a reference to an examiner appointed under section 66A of the Road Traffic Act 1988.   **[497]**

NOTES

Commencement: 1 July 1992.

Sub-s (1): repeals the Public Passenger Vehicles Act 1981, s 7, and the Road Traffic Act 1988, s 68(1), (2), and inserts s 66A of the 1988 Act.

Penalties

31. Experimental period for section 30

(1) Subject to the following provisions, no order shall be made under section 34A of the Road Traffic Offenders Act 1988 after the end of 1997 or such later time as may be specified in an order made by the Secretary of State.

(2) At any time before the restriction imposed by subsection (1) above has taken effect, the Secretary of State may by order provide that it shall not do so.

(3) In this section "the experimental period" means the period beginning when section 30 above comes into force and ending—

     (a) when the restriction imposed by subsection (1) above takes effect, or

     (b) if the Secretary of State makes an order under subsection (2) above, on a date specified in the order (being a date falling before the time when the restriction imposed by subsection (1) above would otherwise have taken effect).

(4) During the experimental period—

    (a) no order shall be made under section 34A of the Road Traffic Offenders Act 1988 by virtue of a person's conviction under section 3A of the Road Traffic Act 1988, and

    (b) no order shall be made under section 34A of the Road Traffic Offenders Act 1988 except by a magistrates' court acting for a petty sessions area (or in Scotland, a sheriff court for a district or a stipendiary magistrate for a commission area) which is for the time being designated for the purposes of this section.

(5) In relation to orders made under section 34A during the experimental period, that section shall have effect with the omission of subsection (6) and section 34B shall have effect as if references to the supervising court were references to the court which made the order.

(6) The power to designate an area or district for the purposes of this section shall be exercisable by the Secretary of State by order, and includes power to revoke any designation previously made.

(7) An order under subsection (6) above shall specify the period for which an area or district is designated, and may—

    (a) specify different periods for different areas or districts, and

    (b) extend or abridge any period previously specified.

(8) The power to make an order under subsection (1) above shall not be exercisable after the end of 1997, and no more than one order may be made under that subsection.

(9) Any power of the Secretary of State to make orders under this section shall be exercisable by statutory instrument, and—

    (a) no order shall be made under subsection (1) or (2) above unless a draft of it has been laid before and approved by resolution of each House of Parliament, and

    (b) any statutory instrument containing an order under subsection (6) above shall be subject to annulment in pursuance of a resolution of either House. **[498]**

NOTE
Commencement: 1 July 1992.

PART II

TRAFFIC IN LONDON

Priority routes

50. Designation of priority routes

(1) The Secretary of State may by order ("a priority route order") designate any road in London as a priority route.

(2) The Secretary of State shall exercise his powers under subsection (1) above so as to provide for a network of priority routes in London ("the priority route network") with a view to improving the movement of traffic.

(3) Before making a priority route order, the Secretary of State shall consult—

    (a) the London authority within whose area the proposed priority route is;

(b) the relevant Commissioner or, if appropriate, both Commissioners; and

(c) London Regional Transport.

(4) Where it appears to the Secretary of State that the designation of any road as a priority route is likely to affect a road within the area of—

(a) a London authority other than that consulted under subsection (3)(a) above; or

(b) a county council,

he shall also consult that other London authority, or that county council, before making the proposed priority route order. **[499]**

NOTE
Commencement: 1 October 1991.

51. The Secretary of State's traffic management guidance

(1) The Secretary of State shall issue to the London authorities and the Director guidance ("the Secretary of State's traffic management guidance") with respect to the management of traffic in London, and in particular with respect to priority routes and the priority route network.

(2) Any such guidance may—

(a) include provision—

(i) setting out the Secretary of State's objectives in designating priority routes; and

(ii) with respect to the role of the Director; and

(b) be varied at any time by the Secretary of State.

(3) Before issuing or varying any such guidance, the Secretary of State shall consult—

(a) such associations of London authorities (if any) as he thinks appropriate;

(b) the two Commissioners;

(c) the Disabled Persons Transport Advisory Committee; and

(d) London Regional Transport.

(4) In preparing any such guidance, the Secretary of State shall have regard to the needs of people with a disability. **[500]**

NOTE
Commencement: 1 October 1991.

52. The Traffic Director for London

(1) The Secretary of State shall appoint a person to be known as the Traffic Director for London (in this Act referred to as "the Director").

(2) Schedule 5 to this Act shall have effect with respect to the Director.

(3) In addition to the specific duties imposed on him by this or any other enactment, the Director shall have the general duty—

(a) of co-ordinating the introduction and maintenance of traffic management measures taken by highway authorities in relation to priority routes established under this Part of this Act; and

(b) of monitoring the operation of those measures.

(4) The Director shall keep under review the manner in which the London authorities exercise their functions under Part III of the New Roads and Street Works Act 1991 in relation to priority routes or roads which, in his opinion, are likely to affect traffic using any priority route.

(5) The Secretary of State shall set objectives which he expects the Director to meet in exercising his functions.

(6) The Secretary of State shall publish, in such manner as he considers appropriate, any objectives which he sets under subsection (5) above.

(7) The Director shall exercise his functions—

(a) so as to meet any such objectives, so far as it is reasonably practicable for him to do so; and
(b) in accordance with any directions which the Secretary of State may from time to time see fit to give him.

(8) Any objectives set for the Director under subsection (5) above and any directions given to him under subsection (7) above may be specific or general.

(9) The Secretary of State shall publish, in such manner as he considers appropriate, any directions which he gives to the Director under subsection (7) above.   **[501]**

NOTE
  Commencement: 1 October 1991.

53. The Director's network plan

(1) As soon as is reasonably practicable after first receiving a copy of the Secretary of State's traffic management guidance, the Director shall prepare and submit to him, and to each of the London authorities, his plans for the design and operation of the priority route network ("the network plan").

(2) The Director may divide the network plan into such parts as he considers appropriate and prepare and submit those parts separately.

(3) In preparing the network plan, or any part of it, the Director shall have regard to the Secretary of State's traffic management guidance and to the needs of people with a disability.

(4) Before submitting the network plan, or any part of it, the Director shall consult—

(a) the Secretary of State;
(b) the relevant Commissioner or, if appropriate, both Commissioners;
(c) any London authority within whose area there is any road which, in the opinion of the Director, is likely to be affected;
(d) such county councils (if any) as he thinks appropriate;
(e) such associations of London authorities (if any) as he thinks appropriate; and
(f) London Regional Transport.

(5) The network plan shall, in particular, include provision with respect to—

(a) the Director's overall objectives for particular priority routes;
(b) the traffic management measures which he expects to see taken in relation to priority routes in general or particular priority routes;

(c) the Director's requirements as to the timetable for the phased introduction of the priority route network; and

(d) the operation and maintenance of traffic management measures taken in respect of priority routes.

(6) The Director may from time to time vary the network plan, but before doing so he shall consult the persons mentioned in subsection (4) above.

(7) In preparing any variation, the Director shall have regard to the Secretary of State's traffic management guidance and to the needs of people with a disability.

(8) After varying the network plan, the Director shall submit it to the Secretary of State and to each of the London authorities.

(9) The Director shall—

(a) keep the network plan under review; and

(b) have regard to the desirability of varying it, particularly in the light of any further guidance issued by the Secretary of State under section 51 of this Act. **[502]**

NOTE

Commencement: 1 October 1991.

Local plans and trunk road local plans

54. Duty of London authorities to prepare local plans

(1) Each London authority shall, after first receiving a copy of—

(a) the Secretary of State's traffic management guidance; and

(b) the network plan,

prepare a statement ("the local plan") of their proposals with respect to the operation of those priority routes which are within their area and with respect to which they are the highway authority.

(2) A local plan shall be in such form as may be specified by the Director.

(3) Where the Director prepares and submits the network plan in parts, subsection (1) above applies separately with respect to each part of the network plan.

(4) A local plan shall be prepared in accordance with the timetable set out in the network plan by virtue of section 53(5)(c) of this Act.

(5) Where the Secretary of State asks a London authority to make provision in their local plan with respect to a trunk road within their area which is a priority route, that authority may make, or (as the case may be) vary, their local plan so that it also has effect in relation to that trunk road.

(6) In preparing their local plan, a London authority shall have regard to—

(a) the Secretary of State's traffic management guidance; and

(b) the network plan.

(7) A London authority's local plan shall, in particular—

(a) indicate which of their powers under the Highways Act 1980 or the Road Traffic Regulation Act 1984 they propose to exercise in relation to the priority routes to which their plan relates and the manner in which they propose to exercise them;

(b) identify any orders made under the Act of 1984 which are, in their opinion, inconsistent with their plan and indicate their proposals for varying or revoking them;

(c) indicate—

   (i) which of their powers under the Act of 1980 or the Act of 1984 they propose to exercise in relation to those other roads in their area which are (or would otherwise be) likely to affect, or be affected by, traffic using any of the priority routes to which their plan relates; and

   (ii) the manner in which they propose to exercise them;

(d) indicate how the proposals referred to in paragraphs (a), (b) and (c) relate, in particular, to the needs of people with a disability;

(e) specify—

   (i) the period which they consider will be required to implement their plan, on the assumption that it is approved by the Director; and

   (ii) a timetable ("the local plan timetable") for implementing the different elements of their plan;

(f) specify a programme of maintenance of those traffic management measures which are derived from the exercise, on or in relation to the priority routes to which their plan relates, of powers under the Acts of 1980 and 1984;

(g) specify the amount of the expenditure which, in the opinion of the authority, they will incur as a direct result of implementing their plan; and

(h) deal with any other matter which they consider relevant to the proper and effective implementation of their plan.

(8) In preparing their local plan, a London authority shall consult—

(a) the relevant Commissioner or, if appropriate, both Commissioners;

(b) London Regional Transport;

(c) such organisations representing the interests of people with a disability who may be affected by the plan as appear to the authority to be appropriate; and

(d) any other London authority within whose area there is situated any road which is not a priority route but which is, in the authority's opinion, likely to be affected by any of the priority routes to which their plan relates.

(9) A London authority shall submit their local plan to the Director for his approval.

(10) The Director shall not approve a local plan unless he is satisfied—

(a) that it is consistent with the Secretary of State's traffic management guidance and with the network plan;

(b) in the case of any provision which is inconsistent with the network plan or the Secretary of State's traffic management guidance, that that provision is nevertheless appropriate for inclusion in the local plan;

(c) with the costing of the authority's proposals; and

(d) with the local plan timetable.

(11) Every London authority shall—

(a) keep their local plan under review; and

(b) consider whether it needs to be varied, particularly in the light of—

      (i) any further guidance issued by the Secretary of State under section 51 of this Act; and

      (ii) any variation of the network plan made by the Director under section 53(6) of this Act.   **[503]**

NOTE
   Commencement: 1 October 1991.

55. The Director's trunk road local plans

(1) Where any priority route, or part of a priority route, is a trunk road, the Secretary of State may give a direction to the Director requiring him to prepare a statement of the Director's proposals with respect to the operation of that priority route or of such part of it as may be specified in the direction.

(2) Subsection (1) above does not apply in relation to any trunk road in relation to which provision has been made by a London authority (under section 54(5) of this Act) in their local plan.

(3) A statement prepared under subsection (1) above is referred to in this Part of this Act as a "trunk road local plan".

(4) The Director may from time to time vary any trunk road local plan.

(5) In preparing any trunk road local plan or variation, the Director shall have regard to the Secretary of State's traffic management guidance and the network plan and shall consult—

   (a) the Secretary of State;
   (b) the relevant Commissioner or, if appropriate, both Commissioners;
   (c) any London authority within whose area is situated—

      (i) any priority route to which the trunk road local plan will apply; or

      (ii) any road which is not a priority route but which, in the opinion of the Director, is likely to be affected by any priority route to which the trunk road local plan will apply;

   (d) such organisations representing the interests of people with a disability who may be affected by the plan as appear to him to be appropriate; and

   (e) London Regional Transport.

(6) Any trunk road local plan shall—

   (a) indicate which powers under the Highways Act 1980 or the Road Traffic Regulation Act 1984 the Director proposes should be exercised in relation to the priority routes to which the plan relates and the manner in which he proposes they should be exercised;

   (b) identify any orders made under the Act of 1984 which are, in his opinion, inconsistent with the plan and indicate his proposals for their variation or revocation;

   (c) indicate—

      (i) which powers under the Act of 1980 or the Act of 1984 he proposes should be exercised in relation to those other roads within London which are (or would otherwise be) likely to affect, or be affected by, traffic using any of the priority routes to which the plan relates; and

      (ii) the manner in which he proposes they should be exercised;

(d) indicate how the proposals referred to in paragraphs (a), (b) and (c) relate, in particular, to the needs of people with a disability;

(e) specify—

　(i) the period which he considers will be required to implement the plan; and

　(ii) a timetable for implementing the different elements of the plan;

(f) specify a programme of maintenance of those traffic management measures, which are derived from the exercise, on or in relation to the priority routes to which the plan relates, of powers under the Acts of 1980 and 1984; and

(g) deal with any other matter which the Director considers relevant to the proper and effective implementation of the plan.

(7) The Director shall, in relation to each of his trunk road local plans—

(a) keep the plan under review; and

(b) consider whether it needs to be varied, particularly in the light of—

　(i) any further guidance issued by the Secretary of State under section 51 of this Act; and

　(ii) any variation of the network plan which he makes under section 53(6) of this Act. **[504]**

NOTE

Commencement: 1 October 1991.

56. The Minister's trunk road local plans

(1) Where any priority route, or part of a priority route, is a trunk road with respect to which—

(a) no provision has been made in a local plan; and

(b) no direction has been given under section 55(1) of this Act,

the Secretary of State shall prepare a statement of his own proposals ("the Minister's trunk road local plan") with respect to the operation of that priority route or any part of it.

(2) A Minister's trunk road local plan may be varied at any time by the Secretary of State.

(3) In preparing any such plan or variation, the Secretary of State shall consult—

(a) the Director;

(b) any London authority within whose area is situated—

　(i) any priority route to which the plan will apply; or

　(ii) any road which is not a priority route but which, in the opinion of the Secretary of State, is likely to be affected by any priority route to which the plan will apply;

(c) the relevant Commissioner or, if appropriate, both Commissioners;

(d) such organisations representing the interests of people with a disability who may be affected by the plan as appear to him to be appropriate; and

(e) London Regional Transport.

(4) A Minister's trunk road local plan shall, in particular—

(a) indicate which powers under the Highways Act 1980 or the Road Traffic Regulation Act 1984 the Secretary of State proposes should be

exercised in relation to the priority routes to which the plan relates
and the manner in which he proposes they should be exercised;

(b) identify any orders made under the Act of 1984 which are, in his
opinion, inconsistent with the plan and indicate his proposals for
their variation or revocation;

(c) indicate—

(i) which powers under the Act of 1980 or the Act of 1984 he
proposes should be exercised in relation to those other roads
within London which are (or would otherwise be) likely to affect,
or be affected by, traffic using any of the priority routes to which
the plan relates; and

(ii) the manner in which he proposes they should be exercised;

(d) indicate how the proposals referred to in paragraphs (a), (b) and (c)
relate, in particular, to the needs of people with a disability;

(e) specify—

(i) the period which he considers will be required to implement the
plan; and

(ii) a timetable for implementing the different elements of the plan;

(f) specify a programme of maintenance of those traffic management
measures which are derived from the exercise, on or in relation to the
priority routes to which the plan relates, of powers under the Acts of
1980 and 1984; and

(g) deal with any other matter which he considers relevant to the proper
and effective implementation of the plan.

(5) Where the Secretary of State considers that the implementation of any
part of the plan requires a London authority to exercise any of its powers he
may, in writing, ask the authority to exercise such powers as he may specify in
his request.

(6) Where—

(a) the Secretary of State has sent such a request to a London authority;
but

(b) the authority have not, in his opinion, exercised the powers in question
within a reasonable period,

the Secretary of State may direct them to do so.

(7) Where a London authority have failed to comply with a direction under
subsection (6) above within such period as the Secretary of State considers could
reasonably be required by them, he may himself exercise the powers in question.

(8) Anything done by the Secretary of State in the exercise of those powers
shall be treated for all purposes as if it had been done by the authority.

(9) Where the Secretary of State proposes to exercise any of the powers of a
London authority by virtue of subsection (7) above, he may direct that authority
not to exercise those or any other such powers, in such circumstances or in
relation to such matters, as may be specified in the direction.

(10) Where, having intervened under subsection (7) above, the Secretary of
State is satisfied that continued intervention by him is unnecessary—

(a) he shall notify the authority accordingly in writing; and

(b) with effect from the date on which that notice is served by him, any
direction given by him with respect to his intervention shall cease to
have effect.

(11) Any reasonable administrative expenses incurred by the Secretary of State in the exercise of his powers under subsection (7) above shall be recoverable by him from the London authority as a civil debt.   **[505]**

NOTE
Commencement: 1 October 1991.

57. Implementation of local plans

(1) Where the Director has approved a London authority's local plan, or has himself prepared a local plan on behalf of a London authority under section 61 of this Act, it shall be the duty of that authority to—

(a) implement the plan as soon as is reasonably practicable; and
(b) continue to act in a manner which is compatible with it.

(2) Every London authority shall provide the Director with such information, in such form and manner, as he may reasonably require with respect to the implementation or otherwise of their local plan.

(3) Where a London authority's local plan has effect in relation to a trunk road, by virtue of section 54(5) of this Act, the duty imposed by subsection (1) above shall apply in relation to the plan so far as it has that effect only if the Director, with the consent of the Secretary of State, gives a direction to that effect.   **[506]**

NOTE
Commencement: 1 October 1991.

58. Implementation by Director of certain plans

(1) Where the Secretary of State gives a direction to the Director requiring him to implement any trunk road local plan, or Minister's trunk road local plan, or part of any such plan, it shall be the duty of the Director to implement the provisions of the plan or (as the case may be) of that part of the plan, so far as they have effect in relation to any trunk road, as soon as is reasonably practicable.

(2) Any direction given under subsection (1) above may require any provision to which it applies to be implemented to such limited extent as may be specified in the direction.

(3) In so doing, the Director shall have all the powers which the Secretary of State would have in relation to any trunk road with respect to which the plan has effect, so far as may be necessary or expedient for the purpose of implementing the provisions of the plan.

(4) Anything done by the Director in purported exercise of those powers shall be taken to have been done by the Secretary of State.

(5) Where the Director considers that the implementation of any part of the plan requires a London authority to exercise any of its powers he may, in writing, ask the authority to exercise such powers as he may specify in his request.

(6) Where—

(a) the Director has sent such a request to a London authority; but
(b) the authority have not, in his opinion, exercised the powers in question within a reasonable period,

the Director may direct them to do so.

(7) Where a London authority have failed to comply with a direction under subsection (6) above within such period as the Director considers could reasonably be required by them, he may himself exercise the powers in question.

(8) Anything done by the Director in the exercise of those powers shall be treated for all purposes as if it had been done by the London authority.

(9) Where the Director proposes to exercise any of the powers of a London authority by virtue of subsection (7) above, he may direct that authority not to exercise those or any other such powers, in such circumstances or in relation to such matters, as may be specified in the direction.

(10) Where, having intervened under subsection (7) above, the Director is satisfied that continued intervention by him is unnecessary—

    (a) he shall notify the London authority accordingly in writing; and

    (b) with effect from the date on which that notice is served by him, any direction given by him with respect to his intervention shall cease to have effect.

(11) Any reasonable administrative expenses incurred by the Director in the exercise of his powers under subsection (7) above shall be recoverable by him from the London authority as a civil debt.

(12) Where the Secretary of State implements any of the provisions of a trunk road local plan, he shall have in relation to those provisions the powers conferred upon the Director by subsections (5) to (11) above. **[507]**

NOTE
    Commencement: 1 October 1991.

59. Variation of local plans

(1) A London authority may vary their local plan, but only with the written consent of the Director.

(2) The Director may give a direction to any London authority requiring them to vary their local plan in such manner as may be specified in the direction.

(3) In varying their local plan, a London authority shall have regard to the Secretary of State's traffic management guidance and to the network plan.

(4) Before varying their local plan, a London authority shall consult—

    (a) the relevant Commissioner or, if appropriate, both Commissioners;

    (b) London Regional Transport;

    (c) such organisations representing the interests of people with a disability who may be affected by the plan as appear to the authority to be appropriate; and

    (d) any other London authority within whose area there is situated any road which is not a priority route but which is, in the authority's opinion, likely to be affected by the proposed variation.

(5) Where a London authority fail, within a reasonable time, to comply with any direction given under subsection (2) above, the Director may vary the local plan on their behalf.

(6) Before varying a local plan on behalf of a London authority the Director shall consult—

    (a) that authority;

    (b) the relevant Commissioner or, if appropriate, both Commissioners;

    (c) London Regional Transport;

    (d) such organisations representing the interests of people with a disability who may be affected by the plan as appear to the Director to be appropriate; and

    (e) any other London authority within whose area there is situated any road which is not a priority route but which is, in his opinion, likely to be affected by the proposed variation.

(7) Any reasonable administrative expenses incurred by the Director under subsection (5) above shall be recoverable by him from the London authority concerned as a civil debt. **[508]**

NOTE
Commencement: 1 October 1991.

---

60. Proposed action by London authorities likely to affect priority routes

(1) No London authority shall exercise any power under the Highways Act 1980 or the Road Traffic Regulation Act 1984, in a way which will affect, or be likely to affect, a priority route unless the requirements of subsection (3) below have been satisfied.

(2) Subsection (1) above does not apply where the exercise of the power—

    (a) accords with the provisions of the authority's approved local plan; or

    (b) is in response to a request made, or direction given, under this Act by the Director or the Secretary of State.

(3) The requirements mentioned in subsection (1) above are that—

    (a) the authority have given notice to the Director, in such manner as he may require, of their proposal to exercise the power in the way in question; and

    (b) either—

        (i) the Director has approved their proposal; or

        (ii) the period of one month beginning with the date on which he received notice of the proposal has expired without his having objected to it.

(4) The Secretary of State may by an instrument in writing exclude any power from the application of this section to the extent specified in the instrument.

(5) Any such instrument may, in particular, exclude a power as respects—

    (a) all or any of the London authorities;

    (b) all or any of the priority routes; or

    (c) the exercise of the power in such manner or circumstances as may be specified in the instrument.

(6) If a London authority exercise any power in contravention of this section, the Director may take such steps as he considers appropriate to reverse or modify the effect of the exercise of that power.

(7) Any reasonable expenses incurred by the Director in taking any steps under subsection (6) above shall be recoverable by him from the London authority concerned as a civil debt. **[509]**

NOTE
Commencement: 1 October 1991.

61. Intervention powers

(1) Where it appears to the Director that a London authority have failed—

(a) to prepare a local plan in accordance with the requirements of section 54 of this Act; or

(b) to submit their local plan to him in accordance with those requirements,

he may direct the authority to do so within such period as he may specify in the direction.

(2) Where the Director has given such a direction, but the London authority concerned have not complied with it within a reasonable time, he may himself prepare a local plan on their behalf.

(3) Where the Director refuses to approve a local plan under section 54 of this Act, the London authority concerned shall prepare and submit a new local plan under that section unless the Director serves written notice on them of his intention to exercise his powers under subsection (5) below.

(4) In preparing any local plan in compliance with subsection (3) above, the London authority shall comply with any directions given to them by the Director.

(5) If the Director—

(a) has refused to approve a local plan which has been prepared in accordance with the requirements of section 54 of this Act; and

(b) has served on the London authority concerned a notice of the kind mentioned in subsection (3) above,

he may himself prepare a local plan on behalf of that authority.

(6) Where the Director prepares a local plan on behalf of a London authority under this section—

(a) he shall consult—

(i) that authority;

(ii) the relevant Commissioner or, if appropriate, both Commissioners;

(iii) London Regional Transport;

(iv) such organisations representing the interests of people with a disability who may be affected by the plan as appear to the Director to be appropriate; and

(v) any other London authority within whose area there is situated any road which is not a priority route but which is, in his opinion, likely to be affected by any of the priority routes to which the plan relates; and

(b) any reasonable administrative expenses incurred by him in preparing the plan shall be recoverable by him from the authority as a civil debt. **[510]**

NOTE
Commencement: 1 October 1991.

---

62. Failure to implement local plans

(1) Where it appears to the Director that a London authority—

(a) have not implemented, or are unlikely to implement, their local plan in accordance with the local plan timetable; or

(b) have not implemented, or are unlikely to implement, it in a satisfactory manner,

he may direct the authority to take such steps as are required to implement it in accordance with the local plan timetable, or (as the case may be) to implement it in a satisfactory manner, in accordance with such other timetable as he may draw up and specify in the direction.

(2) Where it appears to the Director that a London authority have acted in a manner which is incompatible with their local plan, he may direct them to take such steps as he considers appropriate with a view to securing, so far as is reasonably practicable, that the effects of that action are removed.

(3) Where a London authority have failed to comply with a direction under subsection (1) or (2) above, the Director may (with the consent of the Secretary of State) take any steps which still remain to be taken by the authority in accordance with the terms of the direction.

(4) The Secretary of State may limit his consent to the implementation by the Director of part only of the local plan, and where he does so the Director's powers under subsection (3) above shall be limited to implementing that part.

(5) For the purposes of enabling him to exercise the powers given to him by subsection (3) above, the Director shall have all the powers which the London authority concerned have in connection with the implementation of their local plan.

(6) Anything done by the Director in the exercise of those powers shall be treated for all purposes as if it had been done by the London authority.

(7) Where the Director proposes to exercise any of the powers of a London authority by virtue of subsection (5) above, he may direct that authority not to exercise those or any other powers, in such circumstances or in relation to such matters, as may be specified in the direction.

(8) Where, having intervened under subsection (3) above, the Director is satisfied that continued intervention by him is unnecessary—

(a) he shall notify the London authority accordingly in writing; and
(b) with effect from the date on which that notice is served by him, any direction given by him with respect to his intervention shall cease to have effect.

(9) Any reasonable administrative expenses incurred by the Director in the exercise of his powers under this section shall be recoverable by him from the London authority as a civil debt. **[511]**

NOTE
Commencement: 1 October 1991.

Parking in London

63. The Secretary of State's parking guidance

(1) The Secretary of State shall issue guidance ("the Secretary of State's parking guidance") to the London authorities with a view to those authorities co-ordinating their action with respect to parking in London.

(2) It shall be the duty of the joint planning committee for London established under section 5 of the Local Government Act 1985—

(a) to make proposals to the Secretary of State (if it thinks fit) as to the content of the Secretary of State's parking guidance; and

(b) to keep that guidance under review, with a view to making from time to time such further proposals as it considers appropriate.

(3) Before issuing or varying any guidance under this section, the Secretary of State shall consult—

(a) the two Commissioners;

(b) London Regional Transport;

(c) the Disabled Persons Transport Advisory Committee;

(d) such associations of London authorities (if any) as he thinks appropriate; and

(e) such other persons (if any) as he thinks appropriate.

(4) In connection with the preparation of the Secretary of State's parking guidance regard shall be had to the needs of people with a disability.

(5) The Secretary of State's parking guidance may, in particular, include provision with respect to appropriate levels for—

(a) parking charges;

(b) penalty charges;

(c) charges made by London authorities for the removal, storage and disposal of vehicles; and

(d) charges in respect of the release of vehicles from immobilisation devices fixed under section 69 of this Act.

(6) The Secretary of State's parking guidance may be varied at any time by the Secretary of State.   **[512]**

NOTE
Commencement: 1 October 1991.

64, 65. (*Amend the Road Traffic Regulation Act 1984, ss 8, 11, 46, 47.*)

66. Parking penalties in London

(1) Where, in the case of a stationary vehicle in a designated parking place, a parking attendant has reason to believe that a penalty charge is payable with respect to the vehicle, he may—

(a) fix a penalty charge notice to the vehicle; or

(b) give such a notice to the person appearing to him to be in charge of the vehicle.

(2) For the purposes of this Part of this Act, a penalty charge is payable with respect to a vehicle, by the owner of the vehicle, if—

(a) the vehicle has been left—

    (i) otherwise than as authorised by or under any order relating to the designated parking place; or

    (ii) beyond the period of parking which has been paid for;

(b) no parking charge payable with respect to the vehicle has been paid; or

(c) there has, with respect to the vehicle, been a contravention of, or failure to comply with, any provision made by or under any order relating to the designated parking place.

(3) A penalty charge notice must state—

(a) the grounds on which the parking attendant believes that a penalty charge is payable with respect to the vehicle;

(b) the amount of the penalty charge which is payable;

(c) that the penalty charge must be paid before the end of the period of 28 days beginning with the date of the notice;

(d) that if the penalty charge is paid before the end of the period of 14 days beginning with the date of the notice, the amount of the penalty charge will be reduced by the specified proportion;

(e) that, if the penalty charge is not paid before the end of the 28 day period, a notice to owner may be served by the London authority on the person appearing to them to be the owner of the vehicle;

(f) the address to which payment of the penalty charge must be sent.

(4) In subsection (3)(d) above "specified proportion" means such proportion, applicable to all cases, as may be determined by the London authorities acting through the Joint Committee.

(5) A penalty charge notice fixed to a vehicle in accordance with this section shall not be removed or interfered with except by or under the authority of—

(a) the owner, or person in charge, of the vehicle; or

(b) the London authority for the place in which the vehicle in question was found.

(6) A person contravening subsection (5) above shall be guilty of an offence and liable on summary conviction to a fine not exceeding level 2 on the standard scale.

(7) Schedule 6 to this Act shall have effect with respect to penalty charges, notices to owners and other matters supplementing the provisions of this section.   [513]

NOTE

Commencement: to be appointed.

67, 68. (*Amend the Road Traffic Regulation Act 1984, ss 101, 102 ante, as from a day to be appointed.*)

69. Immobilisation of vehicles in parking places

(1) Where, in the case of a stationary vehicle in a designated parking place, a parking attendant has reason to believe that the vehicle has been permitted to remain at rest there in any of the circumstances specified in section 66(2)(a), (b) or (c) of this Act, he or another person acting under his direction may fix an immobilisation device to the vehicle.

(2) On any occasion when an immobilisation device is fixed to a vehicle in accordance with this section, the person fixing the device shall also fix to the vehicle a notice—

(a) indicating that such a device has been fixed to the vehicle and warning that no attempt should be made to drive it or otherwise put it in motion until it has been released from that device;

(b) specifying the steps to be taken in order to secure its release; and

(c) giving such other information as may be prescribed.

(3) A vehicle to which an immobilisation device has been fixed in accordance with this section may only be released from that device by or under

the direction of a person authorised by the relevant authority to give such a direction.

(4) Subject to subsection (3) above, a vehicle to which an immobilisation device has been fixed in accordance with this section shall be released from that device on payment in any manner specified in the notice fixed to the vehicle under subsection (2) above of—

(a) the penalty charge payable in respect of the parking; and
(b) such charge in respect of the release as may be required by the relevant authority.

(5) A notice fixed to a vehicle in accordance with this section shall not be removed or interfered with except by or under the authority of—

(a) the owner, or person in charge, of the vehicle; or
(b) the relevant authority.

(6) A person contravening subsection (5) above shall be guilty of an offence and liable on summary conviction to a fine not exceeding level 2 on the standard scale.

(7) Any person who, without being authorised to do so in accordance with this section, removes or attempts to remove an immobilisation device fixed to a vehicle in accordance with this section shall be guilty of an offence and shall be liable on summary conviction to a fine not exceeding level 3 on the standard scale.

(8) In this section "relevant authority" means the London authority for the place in which the vehicle in question was found.   **[514]**

NOTE
Commencement: to be appointed.

70. Exemptions from section 69

(1) Section 69(1) of this Act shall not apply in relation to a vehicle if—

(a) a current disabled person's badge is displayed on the vehicle;
(b) not more than 15 minutes have elapsed since the end of any period for which the appropriate charge was duly paid at the time of parking; or
(c) not more than 15 minutes have elapsed since the end of any unexpired time (in respect of another vehicle) which is available at the relevant parking meter at the time of parking.

(2) In any case in which section 69(1) of this Act would apply to a vehicle but for subsection (1)(a) above and the vehicle was not, at the time at which it was parked, being used—

(a) in accordance with regulations under section 21 of the Chronically Sick and Disabled Persons Act 1970; and
(b) in circumstances falling within section 117(1)(b) of the Road Traffic Regulation Act 1984 (use where a disabled person's concession would be available),

the person in charge of the vehicle at that time shall be guilty of an offence and liable on summary conviction to a fine not exceeding level 3 on the standard scale.

(3) In this section "disabled person's badge" has the same meaning as in section 142(1) of the Road Traffic Regulation Act 1984, and "parking meter" has the same meaning as in section 46(2)(a) of that Act.   **[515]**

NOTE
Commencement: to be appointed.

71. Representations in relation to removal or immobilisation of vehicles

(1) The owner or person in charge of a vehicle who—

    (a) removes it from the custody of a London authority in accordance with subsection (4A) of section 101 of the Road Traffic Regulation Act 1984 (ultimate disposal of vehicles abandoned and removable under that Act);

    (b) receives any sum in respect of the vehicle under subsection (5A) of that section;

    (c) is informed that the proceeds of sale of the vehicle did not exceed the aggregate amount mentioned in subsection (5A) of that section; or

    (d) secures its release from an immobilisation device in accordance with section 69(4) of this Act,

shall thereupon be informed of his right under this section to make representations to the relevant authority and of the effect of section 72 of this Act.

(2) The relevant authority shall give that information, or shall cause it to be given, in writing.

(3) Any person to whom subsection (1) above applies may make representations to the relevant authority on one or more of the grounds mentioned in subsection (4) below.

(4) The grounds are—

    (a) that there were no reasonable grounds for the parking attendant concerned to believe that the vehicle had been permitted to remain at rest in the parking place in circumstances specified in section 66(2)(a), (b) or (c) of this Act;

    (b) that the vehicle had been permitted to remain at rest in the parking place by a person who was in control of the vehicle without the consent of the owner;

    (c) that the place in which the vehicle was at rest was not a designated parking place;

    (d) in a case within subsection (1)(d) above, that, by virtue of an exemption given by section 70 of this Act, section 69 of this Act did not apply to the vehicle at the time in question; or

    (e) that the penalty or other charge in question exceeded the amount applicable in the circumstances of the case.

(5) An authority may disregard any representations which are received by them after the end of the period of 28 days beginning with the date on which the person making them is informed, under subsection (1) above, of his right to make representations.

(6) It shall be the duty of an authority to whom representations are duly made under this section, before the end of the period of 56 days beginning with the date on which they receive the representations—

(a) to consider them and any supporting evidence which the person making them provides; and

(b) to serve on that person notice of their decision as to whether they accept that the ground in question has been established.

(7) Where an authority serve notice under subsection (6)(b) above that they accept that a ground has been established they shall (when serving that notice) refund any sums—

(a) paid under subsection (4A) of section 101 of the Act of 1984 when the vehicle was removed from the custody of the authority;

(b) deducted from the proceeds of sale of the vehicle under subsection (5A) of that section; or

(c) paid under section 69(4) of this Act when the vehicle was released,

except to the extent (if any) to which those sums were properly paid or deducted.

(8) Where an authority serve notice under subsection (6)(b) above that they do not accept that a ground has been established, that notice shall—

(a) inform the person on whom it is served of his right to appeal to a parking adjudicator under section 72 of this Act;

(b) indicate the nature of a parking adjudicator's power to award costs against any person appealing to him under that section; and

(c) describe in general terms the form and manner in which such an appeal is required to be made.

(9) Where an authority fail to comply with subsection (6) above before the end of the period of 56 days mentioned there—

(a) they shall be deemed to have accepted that the ground in question has been established and to have served notice to that effect under subsection (7) above; and

(b) subsection (7) above shall have effect as if it required any refund to be made immediately after the end of that period.

(10) A person who makes any representation under this section or section 72 of this Act which is false in a material particular and does so recklessly or knowing it to be false in that particular is guilty of an offence.

(11) Any person convicted of an offence under subsection (10) above shall be liable on summary conviction to a fine not exceeding level 5 on the standard scale.

(12) Any notice required to be served under this section may be served by post.

(13) Where the person on whom any document is required to be served by subsection (6) above is a body corporate, the document is duly served if it is sent by post to the secretary or clerk of that body.

(14) In this section and in section 72 of this Act "relevant authority" has the same meaning as in section 69(8) of this Act. **[516]**

NOTE
Commencement: to be appointed.

72. Appeals to parking adjudicator in relation to decisions under section 71

(1) Where an authority serve notice under subsection (6)(b) of section 71 of this Act that they do not accept that a ground on which representations were made under that section has been established, the person making those representations may, before—

(a) the end of the period of 28 days beginning with the date of service of that notice; or

(b) such longer period as a parking adjudicator may allow,

appeal to a parking adjudicator against the authority's decision.

(2) On an appeal under this section, the parking adjudicator shall consider the representations in question and any additional representations which are made by the appellant on any of the grounds mentioned in section 71(4) of this Act and, if he concludes—

(a) that any of the representations are justified; and

(b) that the relevant authority would have been under the duty imposed by section 71(7) of this Act to refund any sum if they had served notice that they accepted that the ground in question had been established,

he shall direct that authority to make the necessary refund.

(3) It shall be the duty of any authority to whom such a direction is given to comply with it forthwith.   [517]

NOTE
Commencement: to be appointed.

73. Appointment of parking adjudicators by joint committee of the London authorities

(1) The London authorities shall establish a single joint committee under section 101(5) of the Local Government Act 1972 ("the Joint Committee") before the end of the period of two months beginning with the date on which the Secretary of State first issues his guidance under section 63 of this Act.

(2) The functions conferred on the London authorities by this section and section 74 of this Act shall be discharged by the Joint Committee.

(3) The London authorities shall—

(a) with the consent of the Lord Chancellor, appoint persons to act as parking adjudicators for the purposes of this Part of this Act;

(b) provide accommodation and administrative staff for the parking adjudicators; and

(c) determine the places at which parking adjudicators are to sit.

(4) To be qualified for appointment as a parking adjudicator, a person must have a five year general qualification (within the meaning of section 71 of the Courts and Legal Services Act 1990).

(5) Each parking adjudicator shall be appointed for such term, not exceeding 5 years, as the London authorities may specify in relation to his appointment.

(6) On the expiry of his term of appointment, a parking adjudicator shall be eligible for re-appointment.

(7) A parking adjudicator may be removed from office only for misconduct or on the ground that he is unable or unfit to discharge his functions but shall otherwise hold and vacate office in accordance with the terms of his appointment.

(8) The expenses of the Joint Committee incurred in the discharge of functions conferred on the London authorities by this Act shall be defrayed by the London authorities in such proportions as they may decide or, in default of a decision by them, as may be determined by an arbitrator nominated by the Chartered Institute of Arbitrators on the application of the Joint Committee.

(9) The costs of any reference to arbitration under subsection (8) above shall be borne by the London authorities in equal shares.

(10) Where the Secretary of State is satisfied that there has been, or is likely to be, a failure on the part of the London authorities to agree on the proportions in which the expenses of the Joint Committee are to be defrayed by them under subsection (8) above he may give the Joint Committee such directions as he considers appropriate in order to require it to refer the matter to arbitration under that subsection.

(11) The Secretary of State shall by regulations make provision as to the procedure to be followed in relation to proceedings before parking adjudicators.

(12) The regulations may, in particular, include provision—

(a) as to the manner in which appeals to parking adjudicators are to be made or withdrawn;

(b) authorising an appeal to a parking adjudicator to be disposed of on the basis of written representations unless the appellant requests an oral hearing;

(c) prescribing the procedure to be followed before the hearing of an appeal by a parking adjudicator;

(d) requiring any such hearing to be held in public except in prescribed circumstances;

(e) as to the persons entitled to appear and be heard on behalf of the parties;

(f) requiring persons to attend to give evidence and to produce documents;

(g) as to evidence at the hearing;

(h) as to the adjournment of hearings;

(i) for the award of costs in prescribed circumstances;

(j) for the settlement of costs, by taxation (and in particular by taxation in a county court) or by some other prescribed method;

(k) authorising decisions of parking adjudicators to be reserved;

(l) authorising or requiring parking adjudicators—

(i) to revise or set aside decisions;

(ii) to revoke or vary orders made by them;

(m) requiring decisions of, and orders made by, parking adjudicators, to be recorded;

(n) as to the proof of decisions of, and orders made by, parking adjudicators;

(o) authorising the correction of clerical errors in records kept in accordance with the requirements of the regulations;

(p) requiring service of—

(i) notice of decisions of parking adjudicators;

(ii) copies of any orders made by such adjudicators; or

(iii) notice of any corrections made by parking adjudicators in their decisions or orders.

(13) Subject to any provision made by the regulations, a parking adjudicator may regulate his own procedure.

(14) If any person who is required to attend a hearing held by a parking adjudicator, or to produce any document to a parking adjudicator in accordance with any regulations under subsection (11) above, fails without reasonable excuse to do so, he shall be guilty of an offence and liable on summary conviction to a fine not exceeding level 2 on the standard scale.

(15) Any amount which is payable under an adjudication of a parking adjudicator shall, if a county court so orders, be recoverable by the person to whom the amount is payable, as if it were payable under a county court order.

(16) Subsection (15) above does not apply to a penalty charge which remains payable following an adjudication under paragraph 5 of Schedule 6 to this Act.

(17) In accordance with such requirements as may be imposed by the Joint Committee, each parking adjudicator shall make an annual report to the Joint Committee on the discharge of his functions.

(18) The Joint Committee shall make and publish an annual report in writing to the Secretary of State on the discharge by the parking adjudicators of their functions. **[518]**

NOTE
Commencement: 1 October 1991.

74. Fixing of certain parking and other charges for London

(1) It shall be the duty of the London authorities to set the levels of additional parking charges to apply in London.

(2) Different levels may be set for different areas in London and for different cases or classes of case.

(3) In discharging their duties under this section the London authorities shall have regard to the Secretary of State's parking guidance.

(4) The London authorities shall submit to the Secretary of State, for his approval, the levels of additional parking charges which they propose to set under subsection (1) above.

(5) If—

    (a) the London authorities fail to discharge their duty under subsection (1) above; or
    (b) the Secretary of State does not approve the levels of additional parking charges proposed by the London authorities,

the levels of additional parking charges for London shall be set by regulations made by the Secretary of State.

(6) It shall be the duty of the London authorities to impose additional parking charges at the levels set in accordance with the provisions of this section.

(7) The London authorities shall publish, in such manner as the Secretary of State may determine, the levels of additional parking charges which they have set.

(8) In this section "additional parking charges" means penalty charges, charges made by London authorities for the removal, storage and disposal of vehicles and charges in respect of the release of vehicles from immobilisation devices fixed under section 69 of this Act. **[519]**

NOTE
Commencement: 1 October 1991.

75. (*Inserts the Road Traffic Regulation Act 1984, s 106A.*)

76. Special parking areas

(1) Where a London authority apply to the Secretary of State for an order to be made under this section, the Secretary of State may make an order designating the whole, or any part, of that authority's area as a special parking area.

(2) Before making an order under this section, the Secretary of State shall consult the relevant Commissioner or, if appropriate, both Commissioners.

(3) While an order under this section is in force, the following provisions shall cease to apply in relation to the special parking area designated by the order—

  (a) section 8 of the Road Traffic Regulation Act 1984 (contravention of, or failure to comply with, an order under section 6 of that Act to be an offence), so far as it relates to the contravention of, or failure to comply with, any provision of such an order—

    (i) prohibiting or restricting the waiting of vehicles on any road; or
    (ii) relating to any of the matters mentioned in paragraph 7 or 8 of Schedule 1 to that Act (conditions for loading or unloading, or delivery or collecting);

  (b) section 11 of the Act of 1984 (contravention of, or failure to comply with, an experimental traffic order under section 9 of that Act to be an offence), so far as it relates to any contravention of, or failure to comply with, any provision of such an experimental traffic order—

    (i) prohibiting or restricting the waiting of vehicles on any road; or
    (ii) relating to any of the matters mentioned in paragraph 7 or 8 of Schedule 1 to that Act (conditions for loading or unloading, or delivery or collecting);

  (c) section 16 of the Act of 1984 (contravention of a temporary restriction order or notice under section 14 of that Act to be an offence), so far as it relates to the contravention of any provision of an order or notice under section 14 of that Act which suspends any provision of an order made under section 45 or 46 of the Act of 1984;

  (d) section 15 of the Greater London Council (General Powers) Act 1974 (parking of vehicles on verges, central reservations and footpaths etc. to be an offence);

  (e) section 19 of the Road Traffic Act 1988 (parking of heavy vehicles on verges, central reservations and footpaths etc. to be an offence);

  (f) section 21 of the Act of 1988 (prohibition of driving or parking on cycle tracks), so far as it makes it an offence to park a motor vehicle wholly or partly on a cycle track.

(4) The Secretary of State may by order amend subsection (3) above by adding further provisions (but only in so far as they apply in relation to stationary vehicles).

(5) Before making an order under subsection (4) above, the Secretary of State shall consult—

  (a) the two Commissioners; and
  (b) such associations of London authorities (if any) as he thinks appropriate.   **[520]**

NOTE
  Commencement: 1 October 1991.

77. Application of provisions in relation to special parking areas

(1) This section applies in relation to any vehicle which is stationary in a special parking area (but which is not in a designated parking place) in circumstances in which an offence would have been committed with respect to the vehicle but for section 76(3) above.

(2) A penalty charge shall be payable with respect to the vehicle by the owner of the vehicle.

(3) Section 66 of, and Schedule 6 to, this Act shall apply in relation to penalty charges payable by virtue of subsection (2) above, but subject to such modifications (if any) as the Secretary of State considers it appropriate to make in the order designating the special parking area in question.

(4) Where a parking attendant has reason to believe that a penalty charge is payable with respect to the vehicle by virtue of subsection (2) above, he or another person acting under his direction may fix an immobilisation device to the vehicle.

(5) Subsections (2) to (8) of section 69 of this Act shall apply in relation to a device fixed to a vehicle under subsection (4) above, but subject to such modifications (if any) as the Secretary of State considers it appropriate to make in the order designating the special parking area in question.

(6) An order under section 76 designating a special parking area may make such modifications of any provision of, or amended by, this Part of this Act as the Secretary of State considers appropriate in consequence of the provisions of section 76 or this section or of the order.   [521]

NOTE
  Commencement: 1 October 1991.

Miscellaneous

78. Enforcement

(1) In this section—

"certificated bailiff", means any person authorised to act as such under subsection (6) below; and
"a Part II debt" means any sum which is—

(a) payable under, or by virtue of, any provision of this Part of this Act; and
(b) recoverable as if it were payable under a county court order.

(2) The Lord Chancellor may by order make provision—

(a) for warrants of execution in respect of Part II debts, or such class or classes of Part II debts as may be specified in the order, to be executed by certificated bailiffs;
(b) as to the requirements which must be satisfied before any person takes, with a view to enforcing the payment of—

(i) a Part II debt; or
(ii) such class or classes of Part II debts as may be so specified,

any other step of a kind specified by the order.

(3) Any such order may make such incidental and supplemental provision (including modifications of any enactment other than this Act) as the Lord Chancellor considers appropriate in consequence of the provision made by that order under subsection (2) above.

(4) The Lord Chancellor may by regulations make provision in connection with the certification of bailiffs under this section and the execution of warrants of execution by such bailiffs.

(5) The regulations may, in particular, make provision—

(a) as to the security (if any) to be required from certificated bailiffs;
(b) as to the fees and expenses payable with respect to executions by certificated bailiffs; and
(c) for the suspension or cancellation of certificates issued under this section and with respect to the effect of any such suspension or cancellation.

(6) For the purposes of this section, a person is a certificated bailiff if he is authorised to act as such by a certificate signed—

(a) by a judge assigned to a county court district; or
(b) in such circumstances as may be specified in regulations made by the Lord Chancellor, by a district judge.

(7) Any person who is not a certificated bailiff but who purports to levy a distress as such a bailiff, and any person authorising him to levy it, shall be deemed to have committed a trespass. **[522]**

NOTE
Commencement: 1 October 1991.

79. Application to Crown and visiting forces

(1) Nothing in Part II of this Act applies in relation to any vehicle which—

(a) at the relevant time is used or appropriated for use for naval, military or airforce purposes;
(b) belongs to any visiting forces (within the meaning of the Visiting Forces Act 1952); or
(c) at the relevant time is used or appropriated for use, by any such forces.

(2) Sections 66 and 69 to 71 of this Act apply to—

(a) vehicles in the public service of the Crown which are required to be registered under the Vehicles (Excise) Act 1971 (other than those which are exempted by subsection (1)(a) above); and
(b) persons in the public service of the Crown. **[523]**

NOTE
Commencement: to be appointed.

80. Financial provisions

(1) With a view to reimbursing (in whole or in part) reasonable costs incurred by any London authority under sections 54 to 59, 61 and 62 of this Act, the Director may make such payments to the authority as he considers appropriate.

(2) The Secretary of State may, with the consent of the Treasury, make such grants to the Director as he considers appropriate to enable the Director to discharge his functions. **[524]**

NOTE
    Commencement: 1 October 1991.

81. Minor and consequential amendments

The minor and consequential amendments set out in Schedule 7 to this Act shall
have effect.   [525]

NOTE
    Commencement: partly as from 1 October 1991; partly as from 1 July 1992; partly as from 1
September 1992; partly as from a day to be appointed.

82. Interpretation of Part II

(1) In this Part of this Act—

"Commissioner" means the Commissioner of Police of the Metropolis or
the Commissioner of Police for the City of London;

"designated parking place" means a parking place in London which is
designated as a parking place under an order made under section 6, 9
or 45 of the Road Traffic Regulation Act 1984;

"the Director" means the Traffic Director for London appointed under
section 52 of this Act;

"immobilisation device" has the same meaning as in section 104(9) of the
Road Traffic Regulation Act 1984;

"the Joint Committee" has the meaning given by section 73(1) of this
Act;

"local plan" has the meaning given in section 54(1) of this Act;

"local plan timetable" has the meaning given in section 54(7)(e) of this
Act;

"London" means the area comprising the areas of the London boroughs,
the City of London and the Temples;

"London authority" means any council of a London borough or the
Common Council of the City of London;

"Minister's trunk road local plan" has the meaning given in section 56(1);

"network plan" has the meaning given by section 53(1) of this Act;

"parking attendant" has the same meaning as in section 63A of the Road
Traffic Regulation Act 1984 (which is inserted by section 44 of this
Act);

"penalty charge" has the same meaning as in section 66 of this Act;

"prescribed" means prescribed by regulations made by the Secretary of
State;

"priority route" means a road designated by a priority route order;

"priority route order" has the meaning given in section 50(1) of this Act;

"priority route network" has the meaning given in section 50(2) of this
Act;

"road" has the same meaning as in the Road Traffic Regulation Act 1984;

"the Secretary of State's parking guidance" has the meaning given in
section 63(1) of this Act;

"the Secretary of State's traffic management guidance" has the meaning
given in section 51(1) of this Act;

"trunk road" has the same meaning as in section 10 of the Highways Act
1980;

"trunk road local plan" has the meaning given in section 55(3) of this Act;

"vehicle hiring agreement" and "vehicle-hire firm" have the same
meanings as in section 66 of the Road Traffic Offenders Act 1988
(hired vehicles).

(2) For the purposes of this Part of this Act, the owner of a vehicle shall be taken to be the person by whom the vehicle is kept.

(3) In determining, for the purposes of this Part of this Act, who was the owner of a vehicle at any time, it shall be presumed that the owner was the person in whose name the vehicle was at that time registered under the Vehicles (Excise) Act 1971.

(4) Section 28 of the Chronically Sick and Disabled Persons Act 1970 (power to define "disability" and other expressions) shall apply in relation to this Part of this Act as it applies to that Act.

(5) In determining, for the purposes of any provision of this Part of this Act, whether a penalty charge has been paid before the end of a particular period, it shall be taken to be paid when it is received by the London authority concerned.

(6) Any power to make an order or regulations conferred by this Part shall be exercisable by statutory instrument.

(7) Any statutory instrument made under this Part of this Act shall be subject to annulment in pursuance of a resolution of either House of Parliament. **[526]**

NOTE
Commencement: 1 October 1991.

PART III
SUPPLEMENTARY

83. Repeals

The enactments mentioned in Schedule 8 to this Act (which include enactments which are spent) are hereby repealed to the extent specified in the third column of that Schedule. **[527]**

NOTE
Commencement: partly as from 1 October 1991; partly as from 1 April 1992; partly as from 1 July 1992; partly as from a day to be appointed.

84. Commencement

(1) The preceding sections of, and the Schedules to, this Act shall come into force on such day as the Secretary of State may appoint by order made by statutory instrument; and different days may be appointed for different purposes and in respect of different areas.

(2) An order under subsection (1) above may make such transitional provision as appears to the Secretary of State to be necessary or expedient. **[528]**

NOTE
Commencement: 25 July 1991.

85. Expenses

Any expenditure incurred by the Secretary of State under or by virtue of this Act shall be payable out of money provided by Parliament. **[529]**

NOTE
Commencement: 25 July 1991.

86. Extent

Except in so far as it amends any enactment extending there, this Act does not extend to Northern Ireland. **[530]**

NOTE
Commencement: 25 July 1991.

87. Short Title

This Act may be cited as the Road Traffic Act 1991. **[531]**

NOTE
Commencement: 25 July 1991.

(*Schs 1, 2 amend the Road Traffic Offenders Act 1988, Schs 1, 2.*)

SCHEDULE 3
Section 43

PERMITTED AND SPECIAL PARKING AREAS OUTSIDE LONDON

Permitted parking areas

1.—(1) Where an application for an order under this sub-paragraph is made to the Secretary of State—

(a) with respect to the whole, or any part, of their area, by a county council in England and Wales;

(b) with respect to the whole of their area, by a metropolitan district council;

(c) with respect to the whole of their areas, by two or more metropolitan district councils acting jointly;

(d) (*applies to Scotland only.*)

(e) with respect to the whole, or any part, of their area, by a district council in Wales acting with the consent of the county council; or

(f) with respect to the whole, or any part, of the Isles of Scilly, by the Council of the Isles of Scilly,

he may make an order designating the whole, or any part, of the area to which the application relates as a permitted parking area.

(2) Before making any such application, a county council in Wales shall consult the district councils whose areas lie wholly or partly within the area to which the application relates.

(3) Before making an order under sub-paragraph (1) above, the Secretary of State shall consult the appropriate chief officer of police.

(4) While an order under sub-paragraph (1) above is in force, the following provisions shall cease to apply in relation to the permitted parking area designated by the order—

(a) section 35A(1) of the Road Traffic Regulation Act 1984 (offences), so far as it relates to the contravention of, or non-compliance with, any provision of an order made under section 35 of that Act (use of parking places) in relation to parking places provided under section 32(1)(b) of that Act (power of local authorities to provide free parking places on roads); and

(b) section 47(1) of the Act of 1984 (offences) in so far as it applies in relation to any designated parking place.

(5) The Secretary of State may by order amend sub-paragraph (4) above by adding further provisions (but only in so far as they apply in relation to stationary vehicles).

(6) Before making an order under sub-paragraph (5) above, the Secretary of State shall consult—

(a) such representatives of chief officers of police; and

(b) such associations of local authorities (if any),

as he considers appropriate.

Special parking areas

2.—(1) Where an application for an order under this sub-paragraph is made to the Secretary of State—

(a) with respect to the whole, or any part, of their area, by a county council in England and Wales;
(b) with respect to the whole, or any part, of their area, by a metropolitan district council;
(c) with respect to the whole, or any part, of their area, by a regional or islands council in Scotland; or
(d) with respect to the whole, or any part, of the Isles of Scilly, by the Council of the Isles of Scilly,

he may make an order designating the whole, or any part, of the area to which the application relates as a special parking area.

(2) Before making any such application, a county council in Wales shall consult the district councils whose areas lie wholly or partly within the area to which the application relates.

(3) Before making an order under sub-paragraph (1) above, the Secretary of State shall consult the appropriate chief officer of police.

(4) While an order under sub-paragraph (1) above is in force, the following provisions shall cease to apply in relation to the special parking area designated by the order—

(a) section 5 of the Road Traffic Regulation Act 1984 (contravention of a traffic regulation order under section 1 of that Act to be an offence), so far as it relates to the contravention of any provision of such an order prohibiting or restricting the waiting, or the loading and unloading, of vehicles;
(b) section 11 of the Act of 1984 (contravention of, or failure to comply with, experimental traffic order under section 9 of that Act), so far as it relates to the contravention of, or failure to comply with, any provision of such an order prohibiting or restricting the waiting, or the loading and unloading, of vehicles;
(c) section 129(6) of the Roads (Scotland) Act 1984 (parking of a motor vehicle wholly or partly on a cycle track to be an offence);
(d) section 19 of the Road Traffic Act 1988 (parking of heavy vehicles on verges, central reservations and footpaths etc. to be an offence);
(e) section 21 of the Act of 1988 (prohibition of driving or parking on cycle tracks), so far as it makes it an offence to park a motor vehicle wholly or partly on a cycle track.

(5) The Secretary of State may by order amend sub-paragraph (4) above by adding further provisions (but only in so far as they apply in relation to stationary vehicles).

(6) Before making an order under sub-paragraph (5) above, the Secretary of State shall consult—

(a) such representatives of chief officers of police; and
(b) such associations of local authorities (if any);

as he considers appropriate.

Control of parking in permitted and special parking areas

3.—(1) This paragraph applies in relation to any vehicle which is stationary in a permitted parking area, or special parking area, in circumstances in which an offence would have been committed with respect to the vehicle but for paragraph 1 or (as the case may be) paragraph 2 above.

(2) A penalty charge shall be payable with respect to the vehicle, by the owner of the vehicle.

(3) An order under paragraph 1 or 2 above designating a permitted parking area, or special parking area, may—

    (a) provide for such provisions of Part II of this Act as the Secretary of State considers appropriate to apply, with such modifications (if any) as he considers appropriate, in relation to the permitted or special parking area in question; and

    (b) make such modifications of any enactment, including any provision of this Act, as the Secretary of State considers appropriate in consequence of the provisions of paragraph 1 or 2 above, this paragraph or the order.

Orders under this Schedule

4.—(1) Any power to make an order conferred by this Schedule shall be exercisable by statutory instrument.

(2) Any such statutory instrument shall be subject to annulment in pursuance of a resolution of either House of Parliament. **[532]**

NOTE
Commencement: 1 October 1991.

SCHEDULE 5

Section 52

THE TRAFFIC DIRECTOR FOR LONDON

Status

1. The Traffic Director for London shall be a corporation sole.

2. The Director shall not be regarded as the servant or agent of the Crown or as enjoying any status, immunity or privilege of the Crown; and the Director's property shall not be regarded as property of, or held on behalf of, the Crown.

Tenure of office

3.—(1) Subject to the following provisions of this paragraph, the Director shall hold and vacate office in accordance with the terms of his appointment.

(2) The Director shall be appointed for a term not exceeding five years.

(3) At the end of a term of appointment the Director shall be eligible for re-appointment.

(4) The Director may at any time resign his office by notice in writing addressed to the Secretary of State.

(5) The Secretary of State may remove the Director from office—

    (a) if a bankruptcy order has been made against him, or his estate has been sequestrated or he has made a composition or arrangement with, or granted a trust deed for, his creditors; or

    (b) if satisfied that he is otherwise unable or unfit to discharge his functions.

(6) The Director's terms of appointment may provide for his removal from office (without assigning cause) on notice from the Secretary of State of such length as may be specified in those terms, subject, if those terms so provide, to compensation of such amount as the Secretary of State may, with the approval of the Treasury, determine.

Remuneration etc

4.—(1) There shall be paid to the Director such remuneration and such travelling and other allowances as the Secretary of State may determine.

(2) In the case of any such holder of the office of Director as may be determined by the Secretary of State, there shall be paid such pension, allowances or gratuities to or in

respect of him, or such payments towards the provision of a pension, allowances or gratuities to or in respect of him, as may be so determined.

(3) If the Secretary of State determines that there are special circumstances which make it right that a person ceasing to hold office as Director should receive compensation, there may be paid to him a sum by way of compensation of such amount as the Secretary of State may determine.

(4) Sub-paragraph (3) above does not apply in the case of a person who receives compensation by virtue of paragraph 3(6) above.

(5) The approval of the Treasury shall be required for the making of a determination under this paragraph.

Staff

5.—(1) The Director shall act only with the approval of the Secretary of State, given with the approval of the Treasury, in determining—

(a) the number of persons to be employed by him;
(b) the remuneration, allowances and gratuities to be paid to or in respect of such persons; and
(c) any other terms and conditions of their service.

(2) Anything authorised or required by or under any enactment to be done by the Director may be done by any person employed by him who has been authorised by the Director, whether generally or specially, for that purpose.

(3) Employment by the Director shall be included among the kinds of employment to which a scheme under section 1 of the Superannuation Act 1972 may apply; . . .

(4) The Director shall pay to the Treasury, at such times as the Treasury may direct, such sums as the Treasury may determine in respect of the increase in the sums payable out of money provided by Parliament under that Act attributable to sub-paragraph (3) above.

(5) Where an employee of the Director who is (by reference to that employment) a participant in a scheme under section 1 of that Act, becomes a holder of the office of Director, the Treasury may determine that his term of office shall be treated for the purposes of the scheme as employment by the Director (whether or not any benefits are payable to or in respect of him by virtue of paragraph 4(2) above).

Financial provisions

6. The remuneration of the Director and any other payments made under paragraphs 3(6) or 4 above to or in respect of him shall be paid out of grants made by the Secretary of State under section 80(2) of this Act.

Accounts

7.—(1) The Director shall keep accounts and shall prepare a statement of accounts in respect of each financial year.

(2) The accounts shall be kept, and the statement shall be prepared, in such form as the Secretary of State may, with the approval of the Treasury, direct.

(3) The accounts shall be audited by persons appointed in respect of each financial year by the Secretary of State.

(4) No person shall be qualified to be appointed as auditor under this paragraph unless he is—

(a) a member of a body of accountants established in the United Kingdom and for the time being recognised for the purposes of Part II of the Companies Act 1989; or
(b) a member of the Chartered Institute of Public Finance and Accountancy;

but a firm may be appointed as auditor under this paragraph if each of its members is qualified to be so appointed.

(5) In this paragraph, and in paragraph 8 below, "financial year" means—

   (a) the period beginning with the day on which the first person to hold the office of Director takes office and ending with the following 31st March; and

   (b) each subsequent period of twelve months ending with 31st March.

Annual report etc

8.—(1) As soon as possible after the end of each financial year, the Director shall submit to the Secretary of State an annual report on the discharge in that year of his functions.

(2) Each report shall contain a copy of the statement of accounts prepared and audited under paragraph 7 above in respect of that financial year.

(3) The Secretary of State shall lay a copy of the Director's annual report before each House of Parliament.

(4) The Director shall provide the Secretary of State with such information relating to his property and the discharge and proposed discharge of his functions as the Secretary of State may require; and for that purpose shall—

   (a) permit any person authorised in that behalf by the Secretary of State to make copies of any accounts or other documents; and

   (b) give such explanation as may be required of any such accounts or documents.

Evidence

9. A document purporting to be duly executed under the seal of the Director or to be signed on the Director's behalf shall be received in evidence and, unless the contrary is proved, be deemed to be so executed or signed.

Public records

10–12. . . .   **[533]**

NOTES

Commencement: 1 October 1991.

Paras 10–12: amend the Public Records Act 1958, Sch 1, Table, Pt II, para 3, the Parliamentary Commissioner Act 1967, Sch 2, the House of Commons Disqualification Act 1975, Sch 1, Pt III and the Northern Ireland Assembly Disqualification Act 1975, Sch 1, Pt III.

SCHEDULE 6

Section 66(7)

PARKING PENALTIES

The notice to owner

1.—(1) Where—

   (a) a penalty charge notice has been issued with respect to a vehicle under section 66 of this Act; and

   (b) the period of 28 days for payment of the penalty charge has expired without that charge being paid,

the London authority concerned may serve a notice ("a notice to owner") on the person who appears to them to have been the owner of the vehicle when the alleged contravention occurred.

(2) A notice to owner must state—

   (a) the amount of the penalty charge payable;

   (b) the grounds on which the parking attendant who issued the penalty charge notice believed that a parking charge was payable with respect to the vehicle;

   (c) that the penalty charge must be paid before the end of the period of 28 days beginning with the date on which the notice to owner is served;

   (d) that failure to pay the penalty charge may lead to an increased charge being payable;

(e) the amount of that increased charge;
(f) that the person on whom the notice is served ("the recipient") may be entitled to make representations under paragraph 2 below; and
(g) the effect of paragraph 5 below.

(3) The Secretary of State may prescribe additional matters which must be dealt with in any notice to owner.

Representations against notice to owner

2.—(1) Where it appears to the recipient that one or other of the grounds mentioned in sub-paragraph (4) below are satisfied, he may make representations to that effect to the London authority who served the notice on him.

(2) Any representations under this paragraph must be made in such form as may be specified by the London authorities, acting through the Joint Committee.

(3) The authority may disregard any such representations which are received by them after the end of the period of 28 days beginning with the date on which the notice to owner was served.

(4) The grounds are—
  (a) that the recipient—
      (i) never was the owner of the vehicle in question;
      (ii) had ceased to be its owner before the date on which the alleged contravention occurred; or
      (iii) became its owner after that date;
  (b) that the alleged contravention did not occur;
  (c) that the vehicle had been permitted to remain at rest in the parking place by a person who was in control of the vehicle without the consent of the owner;
  (d) that the relevant designation order is invalid;
  (e) that the recipient is a vehicle-hire firm and—
      (i) the vehicle in question was at the material time hired from that firm under a vehicle hiring agreement; and
      (ii) the person hiring it had signed a statement of liability acknowledging his liability in respect of any penalty charge notice fixed to the vehicle during the currency of the hiring agreement;
  (f) that the penalty charge exceeded the amount applicable in the circumstances of the case.

(5) Where the ground mentioned in sub-paragraph (4)(a)(ii) above is relied on in any representations made under this paragraph, those representations must include a statement of the name and address of the person to whom the vehicle was disposed of by the person making the representations (if that information is in his possession).

(6) Where the ground mentioned in sub-paragraph (4)(a)(iii) above is relied on in any representations made under this paragraph, those representations must include a statement of the name and address of the person from whom the vehicle was acquired by the person making the representations (if that information is in his possession).

(7) It shall be the duty of an authority to whom representations are duly made under this paragraph—
  (a) to consider them and any supporting evidence which the person making them provides; and
  (b) to serve on that person notice of their decision as to whether they accept that the ground in question has been established.

Cancellation of notice to owner

3.—(1) Where representations are made under paragraph 2 above and the London authority concerned accept that the ground in question has been established they shall—
  (a) cancel the notice to owner; and

(b) state in the notice served under paragraph 2(7) above that the notice to owner has been cancelled.

(2) The cancellation of a notice to owner under this paragraph shall not be taken to prevent the London authority concerned serving a fresh notice to owner on another person.

(3) Where the ground that is accepted is that mentioned in paragraph 2(4)(e) above, the person hiring the vehicle shall be deemed to be its owner for the purposes of this Schedule.

Rejection of representations against notice to owner

4. Where any representations are made under paragraph 2 above but the London authority concerned do not accept that a ground has been established, the notice served under paragraph 2(7) above ("the notice of rejection") must—

(a) state that a charge certificate may be served under paragraph 6 below unless before the end of the period of 28 days beginning with the date of service of the notice of rejection—

   (i) the penalty charge is paid; or
   (ii) the person on whom the notice is served appeals to a parking adjudicator against the penalty charge;

(b) indicate the nature of a parking adjudicator's power to award costs against any person appealing to him; and

(c) describe in general terms the form and manner in which an appeal to a parking adjudicator must be made,

and may contain such other information as the authority consider appropriate.

Adjudication by parking adjudicator

5.—(1) Where an authority serve notice under sub-paragraph (7) of paragraph 2 above, that they do not accept that a ground on which representations were made under that paragraph has been established, the person making those representations may, before—

(a) the end of the period of 28 days beginning with the date of service of that notice; or

(b) such longer period as a parking adjudicator may allow,

appeal to a parking adjudicator against the authority's decision.

(2) On an appeal under this paragraph, the parking adjudicator shall consider the representations in question and any additional representations which are made by the appellant on any of the grounds mentioned in paragraph 2(4) above and may give the London authority concerned such directions as he considers appropriate.

(3) It shall be the duty of any authority to whom a direction is given under sub-paragraph (2) above to comply with it forthwith.

Charge certificates

6.—(1) Where a notice to owner is served on any person and the penalty charge to which it relates is not paid before the end of the relevant period, the authority serving the notice may serve on that person a statement (a "charge certificate") to the effect that the penalty charge in question is increased by 50 per cent.

(2) The relevant period, in relation to a notice to owner, is the period of 28 days beginning—

(a) where no representations are made under paragraph 2 above, with the date on which the notice to owner is served;

(b) where—

   (i) such representations are made;
   (ii) a notice of rejection is served by the authority concerned; and

(iii) no appeal against the notice of rejection is made,

with the date on which the notice of rejection is served; or

(c) where there has been an unsuccessful appeal against a notice of rejection, with the date on which notice of the adjudicator's decision is served on the appellant.

(3) Where an appeal against a notice of rejection is made but is withdrawn before the adjudicator gives notice of his decision, the relevant period in relation to a notice to owner is the period of 14 days beginning with the date on which the appeal is withdrawn.

Enforcement of charge certificate

7. Where a charge certificate has been served on any person and the increased penalty charge provided for in the certificate is not paid before the end of the period of 14 days beginning with the date on which the certificate is served, the authority concerned may, if a county court so orders, recover the increased charge as if it were payable under a county court order.

Invalid notices

8.—(1) This paragraph applies where—

(a) a county court makes an order under paragraph 7 above;
(b) the person against whom it is made makes a statutory declaration complying with sub-paragraph (2) below; and
(c) that declaration is, before the end of the period of 21 days beginning with the date on which notice of the county court's order is served on him, served on the county court which made the order.

(2) The statutory declaration must state that the person making it—

(a) did not receive the notice to owner in question;
(b) made representations to the London authority concerned under paragraph 2 above but did not receive a rejection notice from that authority; or
(c) appealed to a parking adjudicator under paragraph 5 above against the rejection by that authority of representations made by him under paragraph 2 above but had no response to the appeal.

(3) Sub-paragraph (4) below applies where it appears to a district judge, on the application of a person on whom a charge certificate has been served, that it would be unreasonable in the circumstances of his case to insist on him serving his statutory declaration within the period of 21 days allowed for by sub-paragraph (1) above.

(4) Where this sub-paragraph applies, the district judge may allow such longer period for service of the statutory declaration as he considers appropriate.

(5) Where a statutory declaration is served under sub-paragraph (1)(c) above—

(a) the order of the court shall be deemed to have been revoked;
(b) the charge certificate shall be deemed to have been cancelled;
(c) in the case of a declaration under sub-paragraph (2)(a) above, the notice to owner to which the charge certificate relates shall be deemed to have been cancelled; and
(d) the district judge shall serve written notice of the effect of service of the declaration on the person making it and on the London authority concerned.

(6) Service of a declaration under sub-paragraph (2)(a) above shall not prevent the London authority serving a fresh notice to owner.

(7) Where a declaration has been served under sub-paragraph (2)(b) or (c) above, the London authority shall refer the case to the parking adjudicator who may give such direction as he considers appropriate.

Offence of giving false information

9.—(1) A person who, in response to a notice to owner served under this Schedule, makes any representation under paragraph 2 or 5(2) above which is false in a material particular and does so recklessly or knowing it to be false in that particular is guilty of an offence.

(2) Any person guilty of such an offence shall be liable on summary conviction to a fine not exceeding level 5 on the standard scale.

Service by post

10. Any charge certificate, or notice under this Schedule—

    (a) may be served by post; and
    (b) where the person on whom it is to be served is a body corporate, is duly served if it is sent by post to the secretary or clerk of that body. **[534]**

NOTE

Commencement: to be appointed.

SCHEDULE 8

Section 83

REPEALS

Chapter	Short title	Extent of Repeal
1970 c. 44.	The Chronically Sick and Disabled Persons Act 1970	In section 21(4) the words "and any badge" onwards. In section 21(5) the words "and in the case" onwards.
1972 c. 27.	The Road Traffic (Foreign Vehicles) Act 1972.	In Schedule 1— the entry relating to section 8(1) of the Public Passenger Vehicles Act 1981; in the entry relating to section 68 of the Road Traffic Act 1988, the word "goods".
1972 c. 71.	The Criminal Justice Act 1972.	Section 24(2).
1973 c. 62.	The Powers of Criminal Courts Act 1973.	In section 44(3), paragraphs (a) and (b) and the word "and" immediately preceding them.
1975 c. 46.	The International Road Haulage Permits Act 1975	In section 1(9), the words "section 56(1) of the Road Traffic Act 1972 or".
1981 c. 14.	The Public Passenger Vehicles Act 1981.	Section 7, Section 8(1) to (2). In section 8(3), the words "for the purposes of this Act". Section 9. In section 9A(1), the words "with the omission of subsection (1)(b)". Section 9A(2). Section 20(6). Section 51(2). In section 53(1), the words "certifying officers, public service vehicle examiners" and the words "public service" in the second place where they appear. Section 65(1)(f).

Chapter	Short title	Extent of Repeal
		In section 66A(1), paragraph (b) and the word "or" immediately preceding it.
		In section 68(4), the reference to section 9(9)(b).
		In section 82(1), the definition of "certifying officer".
		In Schedule 7, paragraph 17(a).
1982 c. 49.	The Transport Act 1982.	In section 9, the paragraph beginning "Any functions under section 9".
		Section 10(5).
		In section 10(8), the words from "Without prejudice" to "their functions".
		Section 19.
		Section 21(2) and (3).
		Section 23(4).
		In Schedule 5, paragraph 21.
1984 c. 27.	The Road Traffic Regulation Act 1984.	In section 17(2), the word "or" at the end of paragraph (b).
		Section 35(9).
		In section 51(5), the words "being not less than 2 years".
		In section 55(4)(c), the words from "to the Council" to "City of London".
		In section 85(1), the words "the prescribed".
		In section 85(2)(a), the words "the prescribed".
		In section 99(2), paragraph (c) and the word "and" immediately preceding it.
		In section 102(2), the word "and" at the end of paragraph (b).
		In section 102(8), the words following paragraph (b) in the definition of "appropriate authority", and the word "and" at the end of the definition of "person responsible".
		Section 104(10).
		In section 105(3)(b), the words "under section 49(4) of this Act."
		In section 106—
		subsections (2) to (4), (6) and (10);
		in subsection (5), the words "After the end of the experimental period";

Chapter	Short title	Extent of Repeal
		in subsection (9), the words "except in the case of an order to which subsection (6) above applies
		In section 117(3), the definition of "disabled person's badge".
		Section 141.
		In Schedule 13, in paragraph 40, the words "and for" onwards.
1985 c. 67	The Transport Act 1985.	In Part II of Schedule 2, paragraph 4(3) and (11)(b).
		In Schedule 7, paragraph 21(2) and (3).
1988 c. 52.	The Road Traffic Act 1988.	Section 15(10).
		Section 19A.
		In section 29, the words "In this section" to the end.
		Section 30(3).
		Section 41(3)(b) and (c).
		Section 48(6).
		Section 50(2) and (3).
		In section 51(1)(b), the word "goods".
		In section 61(2)(a), the words from "goods" to "service".
		Section 61(5).
		Section 67(4)(a).
		Section 73(2).
		Section 75(3)(a)(iii).
		In section 75(6), paragraph (c) and the word "or" immediately preceding it.
		Section 75(8).
		Section 79(2)(a).
		In section 86, in the table, the entry for "Goods vehicle examiner".
		Section 97(7).
		Section 98(5).
		In section 105(2)(ee), the words "for any purpose of this Part of this Act.
		In section 105(2)(f), the words "for the purposes of this Part of this Act".
		Section 151(9)(b).
		In section 164(6), the words "to a constable".
		In section 165(4), the words "to a constable".
		In section 173(2), the word "and" at the end of paragraph (k).

Chapter	Short title	Extent of Repeal
		In section 183(3), paragraph (b) and the word "and" immediately preceding it.
		In section,192(2), the word ""road""
		Section 193.
		Schedule 4.
1988 c. 53.	The Road Traffic Offenders Act 1988.	In section 17(3), the word "goods" in each place where it occurs.
		Section 23(2).
		Section 27(2).
		In section 30(2), the words "Subject to section 28(2) of this Act,".
		Section 30(3).
		Section 54(8).
		Section 59(6).
		Section 60.
		In Schedule 1, in the Table— in the entry relating to section 71 of the Road Traffic Act 1988, in column 2 the word "goods" in each place where it occurs;
		the entries relating to sections 97 and 98 of that Act.
		In Part I of Schedule 2— in the entries relating to sections 68 and 71 of the Road Traffic Act 1988, in column 2 the word "goods" in each place where it occurs;
		the entries relating to sections 97 and 98 of that Act;
		in the entry relating to section 165 of that Act, in column 2 the word "constable";
		the entries in columns 6 and 7 relating to section 178 of that Act;
		in the entry relating to section 26 of the Road Traffic Offenders Act, in column 2 the words "on committal for sentence etc."
		In Part II of Schedule 2, the entries in columns 3 and 4 relating to stealing or attempting to steal a motor vehicle or to section 12 or 25 of the Theft Act 1968.
		In Schedule 3, the entry relating to section 97 of the Road Traffic Act 1988.

Chapter	Short title	Extent of Repeal

1988 c. 54.	The Road Traffic (Consequential Provisions) Act 1988.	Section 6.
		
		In Part I of Schedule 2—
		paragraph 1;
		in paragraph 3(1) the entry beginning "for "section 56(2)(a)"".
		paragraph 4(2);
		paragraph 8;
		paragraph 9;
		paragraph 10(b);
		paragraph 13(b)(ii);
		paragraph 15(b) and the word "and" immediately preceding it.
		Parts II, III and IV of Schedule 2.
		In Schedule 3—
		paragraph 6(3) and (5);
		paragraph 8(1);
		paragraph 8(2)(d) and the word "and" immediately preceding it;
		paragraph 9(1)(c) and the word "and" immediately preceding it;
		paragraph 9(3)(b);
		paragraph 11(b) and (c);
		paragraph 37(1) and (2).
		Schedule 5.

1989 c. 22.	The Road Traffic (Driver Licensing and Information Systems) Act 1989.	In Schedule 3, paragraph 21.
1991 c. 40	The Road Traffic Act 1991.	In Schedule 4, paragraph 79.

[535]

NOTE
   Commencement: partly as from 1 October 1991; partly as from 1 April 1992; partly as from 1 July 1992; partly as from a day to be appointed.

PART II
STATUTORY INSTRUMENTS

PART II

STATUTORY INSTRUMENTS

THE MOTORWAYS TRAFFIC (SCOTLAND) REGULATIONS 1964
(SI 1964 No 1002 (S 69))

NOTES

Made: 30 June 1964.

Authority: Road Traffic Act 1960, s 37.

1. Commencement and citation

These regulations may be cited as the Motorways Traffic (Scotland) Regulations 1964 and shall come into operation on 11th July 1964.   **[1001]**

NOTE

Commencement: 11 July 1964.

2. Interpretation

(1) The Interpretation Act 1889 shall apply for the interpretation of these regulations as it applies for the interpretation of an Act of Parliament.

(2) In these regulations, unless the context otherwise requires, the following expressions have the meanings hereby respectively assigned to them, that is to say—

    (a) "carriageway" means that part of a motorway which is constructed with a surface suitable for the regular passage of vehicular motor traffic along the motorway and is distinguishable from the other parts of the motorway by the fact that on each side that part of the motorway either consists of a marginal strip or is contiguous to a raised kerb, but the said expression does not include any part of a central reservation.

    (b) "central reservation" means that part of a motorway which separates two carriageways running along that motorway parallel or approximately parallel to each other and which is contiguous on one side to one of those carriageways and on the other side to the other of those carriageways;

    (c) "excluded traffic" means traffic which is not traffic of Classes I or II;

    (d) "marginal strip" means a continuous narrow strip of the surface of a carriageway which is at the side of that carriageway and is distinguishable from the rest of that surface by having a colour which is different from the colour of the rest of that surface;

    (e) "the Secretary of State" means the Secretary of State for Scotland;

    (f) "motorway" means any road or part of a road to which these regulations apply by virtue of regulation 3;

    (g) "traffic sign" has the meaning assigned thereto by section 51(1) of the Road Traffic Act 1960;

    (h) "verge" means any part of a motorway which is not a carriageway or a central reservation.

(3) A vehicle shall be treated for the purposes of any provision of these regulations as being on any part of a motorway specified in that provision if any part of the vehicle (whether it is at rest or not) is on the part of the motorway so specified.

(4) Any provision of these regulations containing any prohibition or restriction relating to the driving, moving or stopping of a vehicle, or to its

remaining at rest, shall be construed as a provision that no person shall use a motorway by driving, moving or stopping the vehicle or by causing or permitting it to be driven or moved, or to stop or remain at rest, in contravention of that prohibition or restriction.

(5) In these regulations references to numbered classes of traffic are references to the classes of traffic of those numbers set out in Schedule 2 to the Special Roads Act 1949, or, as for the time being varied or amended by virtue of any order made by the Secretary of State under section 2 of that Act.   **[1002]**

NOTE
Commencement: 11 July 1964.

3. Motorways

These regulations apply to every special road or part of a special road provided in pursuance of a scheme made or confirmed by the Secretary of State under section 1 of the Special Roads Act 1949, being a road or, as the case may be, a part of a road which (save as otherwise provided by or under regulations made under section 37 of the Road Traffic Act 1960) can only be used by traffic of Classes I or II:

Provided that these regulations shall not apply to any part of any such road until such date as may be declared in accordance with section 37(5) of the Road Traffic Act 1960, to be the date on which it is open for use as a special road.
[1003]

NOTE
Commencement: 11 July 1964.

4. Vehicles to be driven on the carriageways only

Subject to the following provisions of these regulations, no vehicle shall be driven on any part of a motorway which is not a carriageway.   **[1004]**

5. Direction of driving

(1) Where there is a traffic sign indicating that there is no entry to a carriageway at a particular place, no vehicle shall be driven or moved on to that carriageway at that place.

(2) Where there is a traffic sign indicating that there is no left or right turn into a carriageway at a particular place, no vehicle shall be so driven or moved as to cause it to turn to the left or (as the case may be) to the right into that carriageway at that place.

(3) Every vehicle on a length of carriageway which is contiguous to a central reservation shall be driven in such a direction only that that reservation is at all times on the right-hand or off-side of the vehicle.

(4) Where traffic signs are so placed that there is a length of carriageway (being a length which is not contiguous to a central reservation) which can be entered at one end only by vehicles driven in conformity with paragraph (1) of this regulation, every vehicle on that length of carriageway shall be driven in such a direction only as to cause it to proceed away from that end of that length of carriageway towards the other end thereof.

(5) Without prejudice to the foregoing provisions of this regulation, no vehicle which—

(a) is on a length of carriageway on which vehicles are required by any of the foregoing provisions of this regulation to be driven in one direction only and is proceeding in or facing that direction, or

(b) is on any other length of carriageway and is proceeding in or facing one direction,

shall be driven or moved so as to cause it to turn and proceed in or face the opposite direction.   **[1005]**

NOTE

    Commencement: 11 July 1964.

6. Restrictions on stopping

(1) Subject to the following provisions of this regulation, no vehicle shall stop or remain at rest on a carriageway.

(2) Where it is necessary for a vehicle which is being driven on a carriageway to be stopped while it is on a motorway—

(a) by reason of a breakdown or mechanical defect or lack of fuel, oil or water required for the vehicle; or

(b) by reason of any accident, illness or other emergency; or

(c) to permit any person carried in or on the vehicle to recover or move any object which has fallen on a motorway; or

(d) to permit any person carried in or on the vehicle to give help which is required by any other person in any of the circumstances specified in the foregoing provisions of this paragraph,

the vehicle shall, as soon and in so far as is reasonably practicable, be driven or moved off the carriageway on to, and may stop and remain at rest on, the verge which lies on the left-hand or near side of that vehicle while it is proceeding along that carriageway in accordance with the provisions of regulation 5.

(3) A vehicle which is at rest on a verge in any of the circumstances specified in paragraph (2) of this regulation—

(a) shall so far as is reasonably practicable be allowed to remain at rest on that verge in such a position only that no part of it or of the load carried thereby shall obstruct or be a cause of danger to vehicles using the carriageway, and

(b) shall not remain at rest on that verge for longer than is necessary in those circumstances.

(4) Nothing in the foregoing provisions of this regulation shall preclude a vehicle from stopping or remaining at rest on a carriageway while it is prevented from proceeding along that carriageway by the presence of any other vehicle or any person or object.   **[1006]**

NOTE

    Commencement: 11 July 1964.

7. Restrictions on reversing

No vehicle on a carriageway shall be driven or moved backwards except in so far as it is necessary to back the vehicle to enable it to proceed forwards along the carriageway or to be connected to any other vehicle.   **[1007]**

NOTE

    Commencement: 11 July 1964.

8. Restrictions on use of verges

No vehicle shall be driven or moved or stop or remain at rest on any verge except in accordance with regulation 6(2) and (3). **[1008]**

NOTE
Commencement: 11 July 1964.

9. Vehicles not to use the central reservation

No vehicle shall be driven or moved or stop or remain at rest on a central reservation. **[1009]**

NOTE
Commencement: 11 July 1964.

10. Vehicles not to be driven by learner drivers

No motor vehicle shall be driven on a motorway by a person who is authorised to drive that vehicle on a road by virtue only of his being the holder of a provisional licence granted to him under section 102(1) of the Road Traffic Act 1960:

Provided that this regulation shall not apply to a vehicle which is being driven on a motorway by a person authorised as aforesaid if that person has, since the date of coming into force of the said provisional licence, passed a test prescribed under section 99(2) of the said Act of 1960, sufficient to entitle him to be granted under that Act a licence, other than a provisional licence, authorising him to drive that vehicle on a road. **[1010]**

NOTE
Commencement: 11 July 1964.

[10A. Restriction on use of right-hand or off-side lane

(1) This regulation applies to—

    (a) a motor vehicle other than—

        (i) a motor car with an unladen weight not exceeding 3 tons;

        (ii) a heavy motor car constructed solely for the carriage of passengers and their effects and not adapted or used for any other purpose; or

        (iii) a motorcycle; and

    (b) a motor vehicle drawing a trailer.

(2) No vehicle to which this regulation applies shall be driven or moved, nor shall it stop or remain at rest, on the right-hand or off-side lane of any length of carriageway which has three traffic lanes at any place where all three lanes are open for use by traffic proceeding in the same direction:

Provided that this prohibition shall not apply to any vehicle while it is being driven on the right-hand or off-side lane in order to pass another vehicle which is carrying or drawing a load of such exceptional width that that vehicle can pass it only if it is driven on the right-hand or off-side lane.] **[1011]**

NOTES
Commencement: 1 July 1968.
This regulation added by SI 1968 No 960, reg 3.

11. Restrictions affecting persons on foot on a motorway

No person shall at any time while on foot go or remain on any part of a motorway other than a verge except in so far as it is necessary for him to do so to get to a verge or to secure compliance with any of these regulations or to recover or move any object which has fallen on a motorway or to give help which is required by any other person in any of the circumstances specified in regulation 6(2). **[1012]**

NOTE
Commencement: 11 July 1964.

12. Restrictions affecting animals carried in vehicles

The person in charge of any animal which is carried by a vehicle using a motorway shall, so far as is practicable, secure that—

   (a) the animal shall not be removed from or permitted to leave the vehicle while the vehicle is on the motorway, and
   (b) if it escapes from, or it is necessary for it to be removed from, or permitted to leave, the vehicle—

        (i) it shall not go or remain on any part of a motorway other than a verge, and
        (ii) it shall whilst it is not on or in the vehicle be held on a lead or otherwise kept under proper control.   **[1013]**

NOTE
Commencement: 11 July 1964.

13. Use of motorway by excluded traffic

(1) Excluded traffic is hereby authorised to use a motorway on the occasions or in the emergencies and to the extent specified in the following provisions of this paragraph, that is to say—

   (a) traffic of Classes III or IV may use a motorway for the maintenance, repair, cleaning or clearance of any part of a motorway or for the erection, laying, placing, maintenance, testing, alteration, repair or removal of any structure, works or apparatus in, on, under or over any part of the motorway;
   (b) pedestrians may use a motorway—

        (i) when it is necessary for them to do so as a result of an accident or emergency or of a vehicle being at rest on a motorway in any of the circumstances specified in regulation 6(2), or
        (ii) in any of the circumstances specified in regulation 14(1)(b), (d), (e) or (f).

(2) Without prejudice to the foregoing provisions of this regulation, the Secretary of State may authorise the use of a motorway by any excluded traffic on occasion or in emergency or for the purpose of enabling such traffic to cross a motorway or to secure access to premises abutting on or adjacent to a motorway.

(3) Without prejudice to the foregoing provisions of this regulation, where by reason of any emergency the use of any road (not being a motorway) by any excluded traffic is rendered impossible or unsuitable the Chief Constable of the police area in which a motorway or any part of a motorway is situated, or any

officer of or above the rank of superintendent authorised in that behalf by that Chief Constable, may—

(a) authorise any excluded traffic to use that motorway or that part of a motorway as an alternative road for the period during which the use of the other road by such traffic continues to be impossible or unsuitable, and

(b) relax any prohibition or restriction imposed by these regulations in so far as he considers it necessary to do so in connection with the use of that motorway or that part of a motorway by excluded traffic in pursuance of any such authorisation as aforesaid. **[1014]**

NOTE
Commencement: 11 July 1964.

14. Exceptions and relaxations

(1) Nothing in the foregoing provisions of these regulations shall preclude any person from using a motorway otherwise than in accordance with those provisions in any of the following circumstances, that is to say—

(a) where he does so in accordance with any direction or permission given by a constable in uniform or with the indication given by a traffic sign;

(b) where he does so in accordance with any permission given by a constable and for the purpose of investigating any accident which has occurred on or near a motorway;

(c) where—

(i) it is necessary for him to do so to avoid or prevent an accident or to obtain or give help required as the result of an accident or emergency, and

(ii) he does so in such manner as to cause as little danger or inconvenience as possible to other traffic on a motorway;

(d) where he does so in the exercise of his duty as a constable or as a member of a fire brigade or of an ambulance service;

(e) where it is necessary for him to do so to carry out in an efficient manner—

(i) the maintenance, repair, cleaning, clearance, alteration or improvement of any part of a motorway, or

(ii) the removal of any vehicle from any part of a motorway, or

(iii) the erection, laying, placing, maintenance, testing, alteration, repair or removal of any structure, works or apparatus in, on, under or over any part of a motorway; or

(f) where it is necessary for him to do so in connection with any inspection, survey, investigation or census which relates to a motorway or any part thereof and which is carried out in accordance with any general or special authority granted by the Secretary of State.

(2) Without prejudice to the foregoing provisions of these regulations, the Secretary of State may relax any prohibition or restriction imposed by these regulations. **[1015]**

NOTE
Commencement: 11 July 1964.

TRAFFIC SIGNS (SPEED LIMITS) REGULATIONS AND GENERAL DIRECTIONS 1969
(SI 1969 No 1487)

NOTES
 Made: 17 October 1969
 Authority: Road Traffic Regulation Act 1984, ss 64, 85

ARRANGEMENT OF REGULATIONS

PART I
GENERAL

PART II
TRAFFIC SIGNS (SPEED LIMITS) REGULATIONS

PART III
GENERAL DIRECTIONS

PART I
GENERAL

1. Citation and commencement

This Instrument may be cited as the Traffic Signs (Speed Limits) Regulations and General Directions 1969 and shall come into operation on the 3rd November 1969. **[1016]**

3. Savings

(1) Where, immediately before the coming into operation of this Instrument—

(a) traffic sign shown in any diagram in the Schedule to the Traffic Signs (Speed Limits) Regulations 1962 as amended by the Traffic Signs (Speed Limits) (Amendment) Regulations 1967 and then complying with the provisions thereof relating thereto, is situated on any road in conformity with the provisions of the Traffic Signs (Speed Limits) Directions 1962, or those Directions as modified by the Special Direction of 1st December 1965 (which modified the general directions contained in the said Instrument of 1962 in relation to traffic signs indicating a maximum speed limit of 50 miles per hour on certain roads); or

(b) a traffic sign prescribed by Regulation 3 of the Traffic Signs (Motorways Speed Limits) Regulations 1965 and then complying with the provisions thereof relating thereto, is situated on any road,

the sign shall, so long as it continues to comply with and conform to such of the said provisions as relate thereto as though the same had not been revoked, be treated as prescribed by the Regulations contained in Part II of this Instrument, and placed in conformity with the provisions of the Directions contained in Part III of this Instrument . . . except that it shall not be treated after 31st December 1970 as so prescribed unless the provisions of Regulation 4 of the Regulations contained in Part II of this Instrument (except paragraph (4) thereof) are complied with in relation to it and to the other signs referred to in that Regulation, or as so placed unless it complies with the provisions of paragraph 9 of the Directions contained in Part III of this Instrument.

For the purposes of Regulation 4 of the Regulations contained in Part II of this Instrument in its application to a sign prescribed by the said Regulations of 1962 or by Regulation 3 of the said Regulations of 1965, the signs shown in diagrams 1 and 2 in the Schedule to the said Regulations of 1962, and the signs described in sub-paragraphs (a), (b) and (c) of paragraph (3) of Regulation 3 of the said Regulations of 1965 shall be treated as being signs of sizes 1 or 2 of the sizes shown in the appropriate numbered diagram set out in the Schedule to the Regulations contained in Part II of this Instrument, and the other signs prescribed by the said Regulations of 1962 and 1965 shall be treated as being signs of sizes 3 or 4 of the sizes shown in such diagrams.

(2) Where, immediately before the coming into operation of this Instrument a traffic sign shown in any diagram in the Schedule to the Traffic Signs (Speed Limits) Regulations 1967 and then complying with the provisions thereof relating thereto, is situated on any road in conformity with the provisions of the Traffic Signs (Speed Limits) General Directions 1967, the sign shall, so long as it continues to comply with and conform to such of the said provisions as relate thereto as though the same had not been revoked, be treated as prescribed by the Regulations contained in Part II of this Instrument and placed in conformity with the provisions of the Directions contained in Part III of this Instrument.

(3) In their application to a trunk road, paragraphs (1) and (2) of this Regulation shall have effect as though any reference to a sign being situated or placed in conformity with any Directions, and any requirement for a sign to comply with any Directions, were omitted. **[1017]**

NOTES

Para (1): words omitted revoked by SI 1977 No 952.

4. Interpretation

(1) In this Instrument—

"the 1967 Act" means the Road Traffic Regulation Act 1967 as amended
by Part IX of the Transport Act 1968.
"motorway" means any part of any special road, on and after such date as
may be declared in accordance with section 13 (5) of the 1967 Act to be
the date on which it is open for use as a special road,—

> (*a*) which (save as otherwise provided by or under regulations made
> under section 13 of the 1967 Act) can only be used by traffic of
> Classes I or II of the classes of traffic set out—
>
> > (i) as respects England and Wales, in Schedule 4 to the
> > Highways Act 1959 as amended by the Special Roads
> > (Classes of Traffic) Order 1961 and the Special Roads
> > (Classes of Traffic) (England and Wales) Order 1968; and
> > (ii) as respects Scotland, in Schedule 2 to the Special Roads Act
> > 1949 as amended by the Special Roads (Classes of Traffic)
> > (Scotland) Order 1964 and the Special Roads (Classes of
> > Traffic) (Scotland) Order 1968; and
>
> (*b*) which is or forms part of a route to which the Minister or the
> Secretary of State has allocated a route number which begins
> with the letter "M" or ends with the letter "(M)", or which is a
> slip road which leads to or from a road which is or forms part of
> such a route;

"on" in relation to a traffic sign stated to be situated or erected on a road
or any part thereof, or required to be so situated or erected, means on or
near that road or part thereof;
"road" means any length of road; and
"speed limit" means a maximum or minimum limit of speed on the
driving of motor vehicles on a road—

> (*a*) imposed by an order under section 12 (which relates to temporary
> restrictions for road works) of the 1967 Act;
> (*b*) imposed by regulations under section 13 (which relates to traffic
> regulation on special roads) of the 1967 Act;
> (*c*) arising by virtue of the road being restricted for the purposes of
> section 71 (which relates to the general speed limit for restricted
> roads) of the 1967 Act;
> (*d*) imposed or deemed to have been imposed by an order under
> section 74 (which relates to speed limits on roads other than
> restricted roads) of the 1967 Act;
> (*e*) imposed by an order under section 77 (which relates to temporary
> speed limits and their continuation) of the 1967 Act on a specified
> road; or
> (*f*) imposed by or under any enactment contained in a local Act,

[but does not include—

> (i) any maximum speed limit imposed by an order under section 77
> of the 1967 Act—
>
> > (*A*) on all roads other than special roads,
> > (B) on all roads of a class specified in the order (not being special
> > roads), or
> > (C) on all roads (not being special roads) other than roads of a
> > class specified in the order, or
>
> (ii) any other speed limit imposed by or under any of the enactments
> mentioned above in this definition, or (subject to sub-paragraph
> (4) of this paragraph) imposed by or under any other enactment.]

(2) Any reference in this Instrument to a numbered diagram is a reference to the diagram of that number set out in the Schedule to the Regulations contained in Part II of this Instrument.

(3) Any reference in this Instrument to a traffic sign shown in a numbered diagram is a reference to a sign of one of the sizes, and of the colour and type shown in that diagram, and any reference to a numbered size of traffic sign shown in a numbered diagram is a reference to a sign of that size shown in that diagram.

(4) Any reference in this Instrument to any enactment or instrument shall be construed, unless the context otherwise requires, as a reference to that enactment or instrument as amended by any subsequent enactment or instrument.

(5) The Interpretation Act 1889 shall apply for the interpretation of this Instrument as it applies for the interpretation of an Act of Parliament, and as if for the purposes of section 38 of that Act this Instrument were an Act of Parliament and the Instrument revoked by paragraph 2 of this Part of this Instrument were an Act of Parliament thereby repealed.   **[1018]**

NOTES

Para (1): amendment in square brackets made by SI 1977 No 952.

PART II
TRAFFIC SIGNS (SPEED LIMITS) REGULATIONS

1. Citation

The Regulations contained in this Part of this Instrument may be cited as the Traffic Signs (Speed Limits) Regulations 1969.   **[1019]**

2. Speed limit signs

The following traffic signs are hereby prescribed to inform drivers of motor vehicles whether any, and if so what, speed limit is in force on a road—

  (a) a sign of one of the sizes, and of the colour and type shown in diagram 1 (the numerals being varied, if appropriate, and having the proportion and form shown in diagram 5) shall inform drivers of motor vehicles that a maximum speed limit is in force of the number of miles per hour shown by the numerals;

  (b) a sign of one of the sizes, and of the colour and type shown in diagram 2 (the numerals being varied, if appropriate, and having the proportion and form shown in diagram 6) shall inform drivers of motor vehicles that a minimum speed limit is in force of the number of miles per hour shown by the numerals;

  (c) a sign of one of the sizes, and of the colour and type shown in diagram 3 shall inform drivers of motor vehicles that a maximum speed limit is not in force; and

  (d) a sign of one of the sizes, and of the colour and type shown in diagram 4 (the numerals being varied, if appropriate, and having the proportion and form shown in diagram 6) shall inform drivers of motor vehicles of the end of a minimum speed limit of the number of miles per hour shown by the numerals.   **[1020]**

3. Variations in the dimension of signs

Any dimension of a sign erected in accordance with the provisions of this Instrument which varies from the dimension specified in the diagram set out in the Schedule to these Regulations relating to a sign of that size shall be treated as being the dimension specified in the diagram if the variation does not exceed 2 1/2 per cent of that dimension.   **[1021]**

4. Illumination of signs

(1) Every terminal sign of size 1 or 2 shown in a numbered diagram, when erected on a trunk or principal road within 50 metres of a street lamp lit by electricity—

    (a) shall throughout the hours of darkness be continuously illuminated by means of internal or external lighting, and may also be illuminated by the use of reflecting material, or

    (b) shall throughout the hours of darkness while the street lamp is lit be continuously illuminated by means of external lighting, and shall also be illuminated by the use of reflecting material.

(2) If any sign is required by the foregoing paragraph of this Regulation to be continuously illuminated by lighting throughout the hours of darkness, or throughout such hours while a street lamp is lit, every sign shown in the same diagram as the first-mentioned sign which is erected at or near the same point on the road or the same junction for the same purpose as the first-mentioned sign shall be continuously illuminated throughout the same period by the same means of internal or external lighting as the first-mentioned sign, and, if any of the said signs is illuminated by the use of reflecting material, every other such sign shall be similarly illuminated.

(3) Any sign shown in a numbered diagram which is not required by the foregoing paragraphs of this Regulation to be illuminated by lighting throughout the hours of darkness, or throughout such hours while a street lamp is lit, may be illuminated throughout the hours of darkness by means of external or internal lighting, or throughout any period during the hours of darkness by means of external lighting and the use of reflecting material and if so illuminated paragraph (2) of this Regulation shall apply as if it were a sign required by paragraph (1) of this Regulation to be illuminated by lighting throughout the hours of darkness, or throughout such hours while a street lamp is lit.

(4) Every sign shown in a numbered diagram which is not illuminated throughout the hours of darkness by lighting shall be illuminated by the use of reflecting material.

(5) Where any sign shown in a numbered diagram is illuminated by a means of external lighting, that means shall be either fitted to the sign or to the structure on which it is mounted or otherwise specially provided.

(6) Where reflecting material is used on any sign shown in a numbered diagram it shall be the same colour as, and extend throughout, that part of the sign to which it is applied, except that no reflecting material shall be applied to any part of a sign coloured black.

(7) In this Regulation—

    "principal road" means a road for the time being classified as a principal road—

(*a*) by the Minister in relation to England excluding Monmouthshire, or the Secretary of State in relation to Wales and Monmouthshire, under section 27 (2) of the Local Government Act 1966 for the purposes of advances under section 235 of the Highways Act 1959; or

(*b*) by the Secretary of State in relation to Scotland under section 28(2) of the Local Government (Scotland) Act 1966 for the purposes of advances under section 8 of the Development and Road Improvement Funds Act 1909;

"hours of darkness" means the time between half-an-hour after sunset and half-an-hour before sunrise; and

"terminal sign" means a sign erected in accordance with the provisions of paragraphs 2 (1) and (2), or 4, of the Directions contained in Part III of this Instrument but does not include any sign erected in accordance with paragraphs 2 (3) and (4), 3 or 5 thereof. **[1022]**

SCHEDULE

Diagram 1 Sign Indicating a Maximum Speed Limit

[1023]

Diagram 2 Sign Indicating a Minimum Speed Limit

[1024]

Diagram 3 De-Restriction Sign—(No Maximum Speed Limit as Defined in Paragraph 4(1) of Part I of this Instrument)

[1025]

Diagram 4 Sign Indicating End of a Minimum Speed Limit

[1026]

Diagram 5 Proportion and Form of Numerals for use with Diagram 1

[1027]

Diagram 6 Proportion and Form of Numerals for use with Diagrams 2 and 4

[1028]

NOTE
For these diagrams, reference should be made to the Queen's Printer's copy of this statutory instrument, which can be obtained from HMSO.

PART III
GENERAL DIRECTIONS

1. The Directions contained in this Part of this Instrument may be cited as the Traffic Signs (Speed Limits) General Directions 1969. **[1029]**

2. Speed limit signs at beginning of speed limit

(1) Except as provided by paragraph 8 of these Directions, there shall be erected, at or as near as practicable to the point on a road where a speed limit in

force on that road begins, signs shown in diagrams 1 or 2 which indicate whether that speed limit is a maximum or minimum speed limit and what the speed limit is.

(2) One such sign shall be erected on each side of the carriageway of the road, or, where the road has more than one carriageway, on each side of each carriageway on which the speed limit begins.

(3) Where the point on a road where a speed limit in force on that road begins is a point at which it has a junction with the side of another road, and where the other road is subject either to no speed limit or to a speed limit other than that to which the first-mentioned road is subject, it shall be a sufficient compliance with this paragraph if there is erected on the first-mentioned road, not further than 20 metres from the point on that road where the speed limit in force on that road begins, a sign or signs shown in diagrams 1 or 2 which indicate whether the speed limit in force on the first-mentioned road is a maximum or a minimum speed limit and what the speed limit is.

(4) One such sign shall be erected on the side of the carriageway of the first-mentioned road being the left hand or near side when a vehicle passes from the said other road, or, where the first-mentioned road has more than one carriageway on the left hand or near side of any carriageway into which a vehicle may duly pass from the said other road.   **[1030]**

3. Other speed limit signs at junctions

(1) Where a road has a junction with the side of another road on which a speed limit is in force and either no speed limit is in force on the first-mentioned road or a speed limit is in force on that road which is different from the speed limit in force on the other road, there shall be erected on the first-mentioned road, not further than 20 metres from the said junction, signs shown in diagrams 1 or 2 which indicate whether the speed limit in force on the said other road is a maximum or minimum speed limit and what the speed limit is.

(2) One such sign shall be erected on each side of the carriageway of the said first-mentioned road, or, where that road has more than one carriageway, on each side of each carriageway from which a vehicle may duly pass into the said other road.

(3) Where the said other road is subject to a maximum speed limit greater than that to which the said first-mentioned road is subject, sub-paragraphs (1) and (2) of this paragraph shall not apply if there is erected on any side of that other road, on each side of the junction and not further than 100 metres from the said junction, a sign in accordance with the provisions of paragraph 6 of these Directions which indicates what the maximum speed limit in force on that other road is.   **[1031]**

4. Derestriction signs at end of speed limit

(1) Except as provided by paragraph 8 of these Directions, there shall be erected, at or as near as practicable to the point on a road where a speed limit in force on that road ends, being a point where there is no other speed limit in force on the road, signs shown in diagram 3 where the speed limit in force is a maximum one, and signs shown in diagram 4 where the speed limit in force is a minimum one.

(2) One such sign shall be erected on each side of the carriageway of the road, or, where the road has more than one carriageway, on each side of each carriageway on which the speed limit ends. **[1032]**

5. Derestriction signs at junctions

(1) Where a road has a junction with the side of another road on which a speed limit is in force and there is no speed limit in force on the first-mentioned road, there shall be erected on the first-mentioned road, not further than 20 metres from the junction, a sign or signs shown in diagram 3 where the speed limit in force is a maximum one, and a sign or signs shown in diagram 4 where the speed limit in force is a minimum one.

(2) One such sign shall be erected on the side of the carriageway of the said first-mentioned road, being the left hand or near side when a vehicle passes from the said other road or, where the first-mentioned road has more than one carriageway, on the left hand or near side of any carriageway in to which a vehicle may duly pass from the said other road.

(3) Where the said other road is not subject to any speed limit, and the said first-mentioned road is subject to a speed limit, there shall be erected on the first-mentioned road, not further than 20 metres from the said junction, signs shown in diagram 3 where the speed limit in force on the said first-mentioned road is a maximum one, and signs shown in diagram 4 where that speed limit is a minimum one.

(4) One such sign shall be erected on each side of the carriageway of the said first-mentioned road, or, where that road has more than one carriageway, on each side of each carriageway from which a vehicle may duly pass into the said other road. **[1033]**

6. Repeater signs

(1) There shall be erected on and along a road specified in column 1 of the following Table on which a speed limit is in force signs shown in diagrams 1 or 2 which indicate whether the speed limit is a maximum or minimum speed limit and what the speed limit is:

Provided that:—

(a) this sub-paragraph shall not apply to any motorway which is subject to a general speed limit which is in force on all motorways, or on all motorways other than those which are for the time being subject to a different speed limit; and

(b) signs shown in diagram 1 shall not be erected along a road on which there is a system of street lighting furnished by means of lamps placed not more than 200 yards apart and on which a maximum speed limit of 30 miles per hour is in force.

(2) There shall be erected on and along a road on which there is a system of street lighting furnished by means of lamps placed not more than 200 yards apart and on which a speed limit is not in force, signs shown in diagram 3.

(3) The signs mentioned in the foregoing sub-paragraphs shall be erected along the carriageway of a road so mentioned, or, where the said road has more than one carriageway, along each carriageway, in such a manner that—

(a) they are situated on each side of the carriageway, or, as the case may be, on each side of each carriageway;

(b) the distance between any one sign on one side of a carriageway and any sign next following that sign on that side and facing in the same direction does not exceed the distance specified in column 2 of the said Table in relation to the road specified in the said column 1;

(c) the distance between any one sign on one side of a carriageway and any sign next following that sign on the other side of that carriageway and facing in the same direction does not exceed the distance specified in column 3 of the said Table in relation to the road specified in the said column 1; and

(d) one such sign is situated on the left or near side of the carriageway, or, as the case may be, of each carriageway, not more than the distance specified in column 4 of the said Table in relation to the road specified in the said column 1 from each end of the length of road required to be signed, as the case may be.

TABLE

Column 1	Column 2	Column 3	Column 4
Type of road:	Maximum distance between consecutive signs on the same side of a carriageway:	Maximum distance between consecutive signs on alternate sides of a carriageway:	Maximum distance between end of length of road required to be signed and first repeater sign:
1. Road more than 250 metres in length on which a maximum speed limit of 35 miles per hour or less is in force, being in the case of a road on which a maximum speed limit of 30 miles per hour is in force, a road on which a system of street lighting furnished by lamps placed 200 yards or less apart is not provided.	400 metres	250 metres	200 metres
2. Road more than 350 metres in length— (i) on which a maximum speed limit of more than 35 miles per hour but of 45 miles per hour or less is in force: or (ii) on which a minimum speed limit is in force: or (iii) on which there is a system of street lighting furnished by means of lamps placed not more than 200 yards apart, and on which a speed limit is not in force.	500 metres	350 metres	250 metres
3. Road more than 450 metres in length, on which a maximum speed limit of more than 45 miles per hour but of 55 miles per hour or less is in force.	700 metres	450 metres	350 metres

Column 1	Column 2	Column 3	Column 4
Type of road:	Maximum distance between consecutive signs on the same side of a carriageway:	Maximum distance between consecutive signs on alternate sides of a carriageway:	Maximum distance between end of length of road required to be signed and first repeater sign:
4. Road more than 500 metres in length on which a maximum speed limit of more than 55 miles per hour but of 65 miles per hour or less is in force.	800 metres	500 metres	400 metres
5. Road more than 600 metres in length on which a maximum speed limit of more than 65 miles per hour but of 75 miles per hour or less is in force.	900 metres	600 metres	450 metres
6. Road more than 700 metres in length on which a maximum speed limit of more than 75 miles per hour is in force.	1000 metres	700 metres	500 metres

[1034]

7. Size of signs

The size of any sign erected in accordance with the provisions of these Directions shall not be smaller than the size specified in the following Table for the type of road on which the sign is erected—

TABLE

Type of road:	Signs at beginning and end of speed limit:	Signs at junctions:	Repeater signs:
1. (a) All motorways (b) Dual carriageway roads over 1 kilometre in length where the width of one of the carriageways is 8 metres or more at the point where the speed limit begins.	Size 1	Size 2	Size 3
2. Other dual carriageway roads over 1 kilometre in length.	Size 1	Size 3	Size 4
3. All other roads.	Size 2	Size 3	Size 4

[1035]

8. Exceptions

Where a speed limit in force on a road begins or ends—

> (a) at a point where the road begins or ends, being a point where it has no junction with another road; or

(b) at a point where the road has a junction with another road on which a speed limit is also in force and the maximum or minimum of speed applicable by virtue of both speed limits is the same,

paragraphs 2 or 4 of these Directions shall not apply as respects the erection of a sign at or near to that point. [1036]

9. Colouring of sign post and back of sign

(1) Where a traffic sign in a numbered diagram is mounted on a post specially provided for the purpose that part of the post which extends above ground level shall be coloured grey except—

(a) in a case where the post is constructed of concrete and in this event it shall remain in its natural colour; or
(b) in any other case where the post is not likely to be readily visible to pedestrians and in this case the post shall be coloured grey and have one white band of between 140 millimetres and 160 millimetres in depth, the lower edge of the band being between 1.5 metres and 1.7 metres above the level of the surface of the ground in the immediate vicinity.

(2) The back of any sign shown in a numbered diagram and any fitting provided for the assembly of such a sign, including any container enclosing apparatus for the illumination of the sign, shall be coloured grey. [1037]

10. Special cases

Nothing in these Directions shall limit the power of the Minister or the Secretary of State by any special Direction to dispense with, add to or modify any of the requirements of these Directions in their application to any particular case.

[1038]

ROAD VEHICLES (REGISTRATION AND LICENSING) REGULATIONS 1971
(SI 1971 No 450)

NOTES
　Made: 17 March 1971
　Authority: Vehicles (Excise) Act 1971, ss 7, 12, 16, 19, 21, 23, 37, 38(5), Sch 2, para 2, Sch 4, para 8

ARRANGEMENT OF REGULATIONS

PART I
PRELIMINARY

PART I

PRELIMINARY

1. Commencement and citation

These Regulations shall come into operation on 1st April 1971 and may be cited
as the Road Vehicles (Registration and Licensing) Regulations 1971.   **[1039]**

NOTES
Commencement: 1 April 1971.

2. Revocation, savings and transitional provisions

The Regulations specified in Parts I and II of Schedule 1 to these Regulations
are hereby revoked but—

   (a) in so far as any application or declaration made, particulars furnished,
        notification given, licence, certificate, registration book or other
        document or trade plate issued, record kept, registration mark
        assigned or other thing done under the Regulations specified in the
        said Part I could have been made, furnished, given, issued, kept,
        assigned or done under a corresponding provision of these Regulations,
        it shall not be invalidated by the said revocation, but shall have effect
        as if made, furnished, given, issued, kept, assigned or done under that
        corresponding provision;
   (b) any reference in such application, declaration, particulars, notifica-
        tion, certificate, registration book or other document to any provision
        of the Regulations specified in the said Part I, whether specifically or

by means of a general description, shall, unless the context otherwise requires, be construed as a reference to a corresponding provision of these Regulations. **[1040]**

NOTES

Commencement: 1 April 1971.

3. Interpretation

(1) In these Regulations, unless the context otherwise requires, the following expressions have the meanings hereby respectively assigned to them, that is to say:—

"the Act" means the Vehicles (Excise) Act 1971;

"agricultural machine" has the same meaning as in Schedule 3 to the Act;

"bicycle" means a mechanically propelled bicycle (including a motor scooter, a bicycle with an attachment for propelling it by mechanical power and a mechanically propelled bicycle used for drawing a trailer or sidecar) not exceeding 8 hundredweight in weight unladen;

"hours of darkness" means the time between half-an-hour after sunset and half-an-hour before sunrise;

"invalid vehicle" means a mechanically propelled vehicle (including a cycle with an attachment for propelling it by mechanical power) which does not exceed [ten] hundredweight in weight unladen and is adapted and used or kept on a road for an invalid or invalids;

"owner" in relation to a vehicle means the person by whom the vehicle is kept . . . and the expression "ownership" shall be construed accordingly;

"pedestrian controlled vehicle" means a mechanically propelled vehicle with three or more wheels which does not exceed 8 hundredweight in weight unladen and which is neither constructed nor adapted for use nor used for the carriage of a driver or passenger;

"prescribed" means, in relation to any declaration or particulars, prescribed by the Road Vehicles (Excise) (Prescribed Particulars) Regulations 1966, as amended by the Road Vehicles (Excise) (Prescribed Particulars) (Amendment) Regulations 1969 and by the Road Vehicles (Excise) (Prescribed Particulars) (Amendment) Regulations 1970;

"register" means the record kept by or on behalf of the Secretary of State of the mechanically propelled vehicles registered by him in pursuance of section 19 of the Act or which in accordance with the provisions of these Regulations are required to be registered with him;

"road" had the same meaning as in section 257 of the Road Traffic Act 1960;

"trade licence" has the meaning assigned to it by section 16 of the Act;

"trade plates" has the meaning assigned thereto in Regulation 31 of these Regulations;

"tricycle" means a mechanically propelled tricycle (including a motor scooter and a tricycle with an attachment for propelling it by mechanical power) not exceeding 8 hundredweight in weight unladen and not being a pedestrian controlled vehicle;

["valeting" means the thorough cleaning of a vehicle prior to its first registration by the Secretary of State including removing wax and grease from the exterior, engine and interior, and "valeted" shall be construed accordingly;]

"works truck" means a mechanically propelled vehicle designed for use in private premises and used on a road only in delivering goods from or to such premises to or from a vehicle on a road in the immediate neighbourhood, or in passing from one part of any such premises to another or to other private premises in the immediate neighbourhood or in connection with road works while at or in the immediate neighbourhood of the site of such works.

(2) Any reference in these Regulations to any enactment shall be construed as a reference to that enactment as amended by or under any subsequent enactment.

(3) The Interpretation Act 1889 shall apply for the interpretation of these Regulations as it applies for the interpretation of an Act of Parliament, and as if for the purposes of section 38 of that Act these Regulations were an Act of Parliament and the Regulations revoked by Regulation 2 of these Regulations were Acts of Parliament thereby repealed.   **[1041]**

NOTES
Commencement: 1 April 1971.
Para (1): words omitted from definition "owner" revoked by SI 1975 No 1342; definition "invalid vehicle" amended by SI 1972 No 1865; definition "valeting" added by SI 1986 No 2101, reg 3.
Road Traffic Act 1960, s 257: see now Road Traffic Act 1972, s 196.
Road Vehicles (Excise) (Prescribed Particulars) Regulations 1966: see now SI 1981 No 931.
Interpretation Act 1889: see now Interpretation Act 1978.

[3A. Exclusion for electrically assisted pedal cycles

The provisions of Parts II and III of these Regulations do not apply to an electrically assisted pedal cycle for the time being prescribed for the purposes of section 103 of the Road Traffic Regulation Act 1967 and section 193 of the Road Traffic Act 1972.]   **[1042]**

NOTES
Commencement: 14 September 1983.
This regulation added by SI 1983 No 1248, reg 2.
Road Traffic Regulation Act 1967, s 103: see now the 1984 Act, s 140.
Road Traffic Act 1972, s 193: see now the 1988 Act, s 189.

PART II

LICENSING AND REGISTRATION

4. Application for licences

A person who keeps a mechanically propelled vehicle and who desires to obtain a licence for it under the Act may apply for it to the Secretary of State not more than 14 days before the licence is to have effect, and shall include with his application (comprising the prescribed declaration and prescribed particulars) and such documents as are required to be produced by him on the application by virtue of the Motor Vehicles (Production of Test Certificates) Regulations 1969 or, as the case may require, the Goods Vehicles (Production of Test Certificates) Regulations 1970, Regulation 9 of the Motor Vehicles (Third Party Risks) Regulations 1961, as amended by the Motor Vehicles (Third Party Risks) (Amendment) Regulations 1969, and Regulation 8 of the Motor Vehicles (International Motor Insurance Card) Regulations 1969, the following—

  [(a) where a registration book has been issued in respect of the vehicle, the registration book, or if he is unable to produce the registration book an application in accordance with regulation 6(1A) for the issue of new registration book; and]

(b) the amount of duty payable on the licence under the Act in respect of the vehicle. **[1043]**

NOTES
Commencement: 1 April 1971.
Amended by SI 1986 No 607, reg 2(a).
The Act: Vehicles (Excise) Act 1971.
Motor Vehicles (Third Party Risks) Regulations 1961: see now SI 1972 No 1217.

[4A. Restriction on registration of vehicles chargeable with car tax

(1) The Secretary of State may refuse to register a vehicle under section 19 of the Act unless there is produced to him, at the time when he would otherwise be required by that section to register the vehicle, a document purporting to be issued by, or by authority of, the Commissioners of Customs and Excise which certifies either—

(a) that the vehicle is not a chargeable vehicle; or
(b) that the tax chargeable on it has been or will be paid; or
(c) that tax on it has been remitted.

(2) Paragraph (1) above shall not apply in relation to the registration of a vehicle which is chargeable with duty under the Act by virtue of section 1 thereof and . . . Schedule 3 thereto, but shall otherwise apply without prejudice to any other requirement of these Regulations.

(3) In this Regulation—

(a) "chargeable vehicle" has the same meaning as in section 52 of the Finance Act 1972; and
(b) "the tax" means car tax chargeable under the said section 52.] **[1044]**

NOTES
Commencement: 5 June 1973.
Added by SI 1973 No 870.
Para 2: words omitted revoked by SI 1981 No 366.
The Act: Vehicles (Excise) Act 1971.

5. Surrender of licences

The holder of a licence (other than a licence for a tramcar) who wishes to surrender his licence and claim a rebate in respect of the unexpired term of the licence in accordance with the provisions of section 17 of the Act (as modified by section 39(1) thereof and paragraphs 13 to 16 (inclusive) of Part I of Schedule 7 thereto) shall make an application in writing, signed by the applicant, to the Secretary of State and at the same time he shall deliver up his licence to the Secretary of State and, in the case of a trade licence, return any trade plates issued to him in connection therewith. **[1045]**

NOTES
Commencement: 1 April 1971.
The Act: Vehicle (Excise) Act 1971.

6. Application for duplicate licence or registration book

[(1) If a licence issued in respect of a vehicle under these Regulations has been lost, stolen, destroyed, mutilated or accidentally defaced or the figures and particulars thereon have become illegible or the colour of the licence has become altered by fading or otherwise the owner of the vehicle shall apply to the Secretary of State for the issue of a duplicate licence and upon the Secretary of State being satisfied as to such loss, theft, destruction, mutilation, defacement, illegibility or alteration as aforesaid and, except where the licence has been lost, stolen or destroyed, upon the receipt of the licence the Secretary of State shall issue a duplicate licence so marked upon payment of a fee of £3.50.

Provided that such fee shall not be payable if the Secretary of State is satisfied that—

    (a) the loss of the licence occurred in the course of the transmission of the licence by the office issuing it to the owner of the vehicle, or

    (b) the licence has been stolen with the vehicle to which it relates and has not been recovered, or

    (c) the licence was issued without charge in respect of a vehicle which is exempted from the payment of vehicle excise duty.

(1A) If when applying for a licence for a vehicle [under regulation 4] the applicant is unable to include the registration book issued in respect of the vehicle with his application he shall apply to the Secretary of State for the issue of a new registration book which shall be issued without charge.

(1B) If at any time a registration book issued in respect of a vehicle under these Regulations has been lost, stolen, destroyed, mutilated or otherwise defaced the owner of the vehicle shall apply to the Secretary of State for the issue of a new registration book and upon being satisfied as to such loss, theft, destruction, mutilation or defacement and, where the registration book has been mutilated or defaced, upon the receipt of the registration book the Secretary of State shall issue a new registration book without charge.]

(2) In the case of the loss [or theft] of any licence or registration book, if at any time after the issue of a duplicate licence or [new] registration book the original licence or registration book is found [or recovered], the owner of the vehicle, if it is in his possession, shall return it to the Secretary of State, or if it is not in his possession but he becomes aware that it is found [or recovered], shall take all reasonable steps to obtain possession of it and if successful shall return it to the Secretary of State.   **[1046]**

NOTES
    Commencement: 28 April 1986 (paras (1)-(1B)); 1 April 1971 (remainder).
    Paras (1), (1A), (1B): substituted for existing para (1) by SI 1986 No 607, reg 2(b); para (1A) further amended by SI 1986 No 1177, reg 3.
    Para (2): amended by SI 1986 No 607, reg 2(c).
    See further SI 1985 No 610, reg 6(2).

7. Alteration of licences and similar offences

(1) No person shall alter, deface, mutilate or add anything to any licence for any mechanically propelled vehicle or exhibit upon any mechanically propelled vehicle any licence which has been altered, defaced, mutilated or added to as aforesaid or upon which the figures or particulars have become illegible or the colour has become altered by fading or otherwise.

(2) No person shall exhibit on any mechanically propelled vehicle anything which is intended to be or could be mistaken for a licence.   **[1047]**

NOTES
    Commencement: 1 April 1971.

8. Registration books

(1) The Secretary of State may, before issuing a registration book or a duplicate thereof to the owner of a mechanically propelled vechicle, require the owner to

satisfy him by production of the vehicle for inspection or other sufficient evidence that the vehicle accords with the prescribed particulars furnished in respect of the vehicle.

(2) The owner of a mechanically propelled vehicle in respect of which a registration book has been issued shall produce it for inspection if he is at any reasonable time required to do so by a police officer or by a person acting on behalf of the Secretary of State.

(3) The Secretary of State may require the owner of a mechanically propelled vehicle to surrender to him for correction the registration book issued in respect of the vehicle in any case where he has reason to believe that the registration book contains particulars which are not correct, and upon being so required the owner of the vehicle shall surrender it to the Secretary of State forthwith who shall, after correcting the particulars, return it to the owner.

(4) No person other than a person acting on behalf of the Secretary of State shall deface or mutilate any registration book or alter or obliterate any entry made therein or, except as provided by Regulation 12(2), make any entry in or addition to a registration book.   **[1048]**

NOTES
  Commencement: 1 April 1971.
  See further SI 1985 No 610, reg 6(2).

9. Assignment of registration marks

(1) The registration mark assigned to a vehicle in accordance with section 19 of the Act shall consist of an index mark followed or preceded by the registered number of the vehicle.

(2) The registered number may contain a single letter of the alphabet, which shall, where the registered number follows the index mark, follow the figures in the registered number, and, where the registered number precedes the index mark, precede the figures in the registered number.

(3) The registration mark assigned to a vehicle shall [, save where the mark is assigned to another vehicle, or another mark is assigned to the vehicle, by the Secretary of State,] remain the registration mark of that vehicle until the vehicle is broken up, destroyed or sent permanently out of Great Britain.

(4) The index mark and registration number which are declared to have been the index mark and registration number of any vehicle at the 31st day of December 1920 shall be the registration mark of the vehicle and shall [, save where the mark is assigned to another vehicle, or another mark is assigned to the vehicle, by the Secretary of State,] thereafter remain the registration mark of that vehicle until the same is broken up, destroyed or sent permanently out of Great Britain: . . .

[(4A) Where at the request of the owner of a vehicle a particular registration mark is to be assigned to it, having previously been assigned to another vehicle, that other vehicle shall be made available for inspection by the Secretary of State at a place designated by him, and the owner of the first-mentioned vehicle shall, before the registration mark is so assigned, pay to the Secretary of State a charge of [£80] for the assignment.

(4B) Paragraph (4A) of this Regulation shall not apply where the request of the owner of the vehicle to which the registration mark is to be assigned is made—

(a) before the 1st March 1977, or

(b) after that date in relation to a mark which has been removed from another vehicle (with a view to its being so assigned) at the request of the owner of that other vehicle made before that date.]

(5) For the purposes of this Regulation the expression "index mark" means such a letter of the alphabet or combination of such letters as fall to be assigned to a vehicle in pursuance of arrangements in that behalf made by the Secretary of State.   **[1049]**

NOTES
   Commencement: 1 February 1977 (paras 4A, 4B); 1 April 1971 (remainder).
   Paras (3), (4): amended by SI 1976 No 2089.
   Para (4A): added by SI 1977 No 230; amended by SI 1982 No 1802, reg 2.
   Para (4B): added by SI 1977 No 230.
   The Act: Vehicles (Excise) Act 1971.

Notification of alteration of vehicles

10. (1) If any alteration, other than an alteration of the nature referred to in the next following Regulations, is made to a mechanically propelled vehicle, which renders any of the particulars contained in the registration book issued in respect of the vehicle incorrect, the owner of the vehicle shall notify the alteration in writing forthwith to the Secretary of State and at the same time send the registration book to him for amendment and he shall after recording the alteration in the register return it amended to show the correct particulars of the vehicle.

(2) Where any such alteration renders incorrect any of the particulars shown upon the licence for the vehicle, the owner of the vehicle shall at the same time as he sends the registration book to the Secretary of State send the licence to him, and he shall issue without charge an amended licence showing the correct particulars of the vehicle.   **[1050]**

NOTES
   Commencement: 1 April 1971.

---

11. (1) Where a licence has been taken out for a mechanically propelled vehicle and the vehicle is at any time while the licence is in force used in an altered condition or in a manner or for a purpose so that duty at a higher rate becomes chargeable in respect of the licence for the vehicle in accordance with section 18 of the Act, the owner of the vehicle shall furnish the prescribed particulars and make the prescribed declaration appropriate to the vehicle and send the same to the Secretary of State together with the licence and the registration book issued in respect of the vehicle and the additional duty chargeable calculated in accordance with the provisions of section 18(2) of the Act.

(2) Where the Secretary of State issues a new licence in exchange for another in accordance with the provisions of section 18(2) of the Act, he shall after recording the alteration in the register return the registration book sent to him in accordance with the preceding paragraph amended to show the correct particulars of the vehicle.   **[1051]**

NOTES
   Commencement: 1 April 1971.
   The Act: Vehicles (Excise) Act 1971.

12. Notification of change of ownership

(1) On a change of ownership of a mechanically propelled vehicle the previous owner of the vehicle shall deliver the registration book issued in respect of the vehicle and may deliver any current licence issued in respect of the vehicle to the new owner and shall notify in writing forthwith the change of ownership to the Secretary of State stating the registration mark of the vehicle, its make and class and the name and address of the new owner.

(2) Upon acquiring the vehicle the new owner shall—

(a) if he intends to use or keep the vehicle upon public roads otherwise than under a trade licence, forthwith insert his name and address in the appropriate part of the registration book and deliver it to the Secretary of State;

(b) if he does not intend to use or keep the vehicle upon public roads, forthwith notify the Secretary of State in writing that he is the owner of the vehicle, and he shall state in such notification the registration mark of the vehicle, its make and class, the name and address of the previous owner and the fact that he does not intend to use or keep the vehicle on public roads;

(c) if he intends to use the vehicle upon public roads solely under a trade licence, at the expiration of three months from the date when he became the owner of the vehicle or, if a further change of ownership occurs, on the date of that change, whichever is the sooner, notify the Secretary of State in writing of his name and address and those of the previous owner. **[1052]**

NOTES
Commencement: 1 April 1971.
Modified by the Finance Act 1987, s 2, Sch 1, Pt III, para 16(4).

13. Notification of change of address of owner

If the owner of a mechanically propelled vehicle changes his address he shall forthwith enter particulars of his new address in the space provided in the registration book issued in respect of the vehicle and send the book to the Secretary of State. **[1053]**

NOTES
Commencement: 1 April 1971.

14. Notification of destruction or permanent export

When any vehicle is broken up, destroyed or sent permanently out of Great Britain, the owner shall forthwith notify the Secretary of State of that fact and shall at the same time surrender the registration book to him. **[1054]**

NOTES
Commencement: 1 April 1971.

15. Notification of registration and licensing particulars

(1) The Secretary of State, upon being requested to do so by a local authority for any purpose connected with the investigation of an offence, or by or on behalf of a chief officer of police, shall supply to that person free of charge such particulars contained in the register as may be requested of any vehicle registered with the Secretary of State, and upon being requested to do so by any person who can show to the satisfaction of the Secretary of State that he has

reasonable cause for his request, shall supply to that person on payment of [£3.50] the name and address of the owner of any vehicle registered with the Secretary of State together with a copy of the particulars shown in the last licence issued in respect of the vehicle.

(2) In this Regulation "local authority" means in relation to England and Wales the council of a county, or the council of a county district, the Common Council of the City of London, or the council of a London borough, and in relation to Scotland means a county council or a town council. **[1055]**

NOTES
 Commencement: 1 April 1971.
 Para (1): amended by SI 1986 No 607, reg 2(d).

PART III

EXHIBITION OF LICENCES AND REGISTRATION MARKS

16. Exhibition of licences

(1) Every licence issued under the Act and in force for a mechanically propelled vehicle, excepting a tramcar, shall be fixed to and exhibited on the vehicle in accordance with the provisions of this Regulation at all times while the vehicle is being used or kept on a public road:

Provided that when such a licence is delivered up with an application for a new licence to [any post office authorised for the time being to issue vehicle licences in accordance with arrangements for that purpose made between the Post Office and the Secretary of State], no licence shall be required to be fixed to and exhibited on the vehicle until the new licence is obtained, when that licence shall be deemed to be the licence in force for the vehicle for the purposes of this Regulation.

(2) Each such licence shall be fixed to the vehicle in a holder sufficient to protect the licence from any effects of the weather to which it would otherwise be exposed.

(3) The licence shall be exhibited on the vehicle:—

 (a) in the case of an invalid vehicle, tricycle or bicycle, other than a case specified in sub-paragraph (b) or (c) of this paragraph, on the near side of the vehicle in front of the driving seat so that all the particulars thereon are clearly visible by daylight from the near side of the road;

 (b) in the case of a bicycle drawing a side-car or to which a side-car is attached when the bicycle is being kept on a public road, on the near side of the handlebars of the bicycle or on the near side of the side-car in front of the driving seat so that all the particulars thereon are clearly visible by daylight from the near side of the road;

 (c) in the case of any vehicle fitted with a glass windscreen in front of the driver extending across the vehicle to its near side, on or adjacent to the near side . . . of the windscreen, so that all particulars thereon are clearly visible by daylight from the near side of the road;

 (d) in the case of any other vehicle, if the vehicle is fitted with a driver's cab containing a near side window, on such window, or on the near side of the vehicle in front of the driver's seat or towards the front of the vehicle in the case of a pedestrian controlled vehicle and not less than 2 feet 6 inches and not more than 6 feet above the surface of the road, so that in each case all the particulars thereon are clearly visible by daylight from the near side of the road.   **[1056]**

NOTES
Commencement: 1 April 1971.
Para (1): amended by SI 1972 No 1865.
Para (3): words omitted revoked by SI 1976 No 1680.

17. Form of registration marks

The size, shape and character of any registration mark which is required to be fixed on a vehicle by virtue of the Act shall be in accordance with the provisions of Schedule 2 to these Regulations.   **[1057]**

NOTES
Commencement: 1 April 1971.
See further SI 1985 No 610, reg 8(1).
The Act: Vehicles (Excise) Act 1971.

Vehicles registered on or after 1st October 1938

18. (1) The provisions of this Regulation shall apply to vehicles, other than works trucks and agricultural machines, first registered on or after the 1st October 1938.

(2) In this and the next following Regulation the expression "relevant area" in relation to a registration mark on a vehicle means the area contained in a square described on the ground, in front of the vehicle in the case of a registration mark on the front of the vehicle and behind the vehicle in the case of a registration mark on the back of the vehicle, where one corner of the square is below the middle of the registration mark and the diagonal of the square from that corner is parallel to the longitudinal axis of the vehicle, but excluding any part of the square within ten feet of the vehicle.

(3) The registration mark of the vehicle shall be fixed and displayed

[(a) in the case of a bicycle, on the back of the vehicle;
(b) in the case of any other vehicle, on both the front and the back of the vehicle,

and] so that in normal daylight the letters and figures are easily legible from every part of the relevant area, the diagonal of the square governing the relevant area being 75 feet, except in the case of a bicycle, an invalid vehicle or a pedestrian controlled vehicle, when it shall be 60 feet:

Provided that in the case of [an invalid vehicle (not being a bicycle) or a pedestrian controlled vehicle] the registration mark at the front of the vehicle may instead be displayed either,

(i) on a plate with duplicate faces, fixed to the vehicle so that each faces sideways, or
(ii) on both sides of the front mudguard,

so that the registration mark is clearly legible from both sides of the vehicle.   **[1058]**

NOTES
Commencement: 1 April 1971.
Para (3): amended by SI 1975 No 1089.

[19. (1) Save as provided in paragraph (2) below, no person shall use or cause or permit to be used on a road during the hours of darkness any motor vehicle unless every letter and number of the registration mark displayed on the back of—

    (a) the motor vehicle if it is not drawing a trailer, or
    (b) the trailer if the motor vehicle is drawing one trailer, or
    (c) the rearmost trailer if the motor vehicle is drawing more than one trailer,

is illuminated so as to be easily legible in the absence of fog from every part of the relevant area, the diagonal of the square governing that area being—

       (i) 15 metres in the case of a bicycle, an invalid vehicle and a pedestrian controlled vehicle, and
      (ii) 18 metres in the case of any other vehicle.

  (2) The provisions of paragraph (1) above do not apply in respect of:—

    (a) a works truck; or
    (b) a vehicle which is not required to be fitted with a rear registration plate.]　　　　　　　　　　　　　　　　　　　　　　　**[1059]**

NOTES
  Commencement: 1 August 1984.
  Substitued by SI 1984 No 814.

20. Vehicles registered before 1st October 1938

The provisions of Schedule 3 to these Regulations shall apply to mechanically propelled vehicles, other than works trucks and agricultural machines, first registered before the 1st October 1938 as regards the exhibition of registration marks.　　　　　　　　　　　　　　　　　　　　　　　　　　　**[1060]**

NOTES
  Commencement: 1 April 1971.
  See further SI 1985 No 610, reg 8(1).

21. Works trucks and agricultural machines

The owner of a works truck or an agricultural machine shall ensure that the registration mark of the vehicle is displayed either on both sides of the vehicle so that it is clearly legible from both sides of the vehicle, or on the back of the vehicle so that it is clearly legible from behind the vehicle, and in either case he shall ensure that the registration mark is so fixed to the vehicle that the letters and figures thereon are in the vertical.　　　　　　　　　　　**[1061]**

NOTES
  Commencement: 1 April 1971.

22. Trailers

(1) Subject to paragraph (3) of this Regulation, where one or more trailers are attached to a mechanically propelled vehicle the owner of the vehicle shall ensure that there is displayed on the trailer or rearmost trailer (as the case may be) the registration mark of the mechanically propelled vehicle, and that such registration mark is fixed to and displayed on the trailer as if the trailer were a vehicle of the same class or description as the mechanically propelled vehicle.

  (2) Where the registration mark of a mechanically propelled vehicle is fixed to and displayed on a trailer attached to it in accordance with the foregoing

paragraph, the requirements of these Regulations as to the fixing to and display of a registration mark on the back of a mechanically propelled vehicle shall not apply to the vehicle drawing the trailer.

(3) Where the mechanically propelled vehicle is a restricted vehicle, the registration mark fixed to and displayed on the trailer in accordance with paragraph (1) of this Regulation may, instead of being that of the vehicle to which the trailer is attached, be that of any other restricted vehicle belonging to the owner of the vehicle to which the trailer is attached, and in such a case the duty in the said paragraph (1) as to fixing and display shall apply as if the other restricted vehicle were the vehicle to which the trailer was attached.

(4) In this Regulation "restricted vehicle" means a vehicle mentioned in section 7(1) of the Act or paragraph 2(1) of Schedule 3 thereto. **[1062]**

NOTES
Commencement: 1 April 1971.
See further SI 1985 No 610, reg 8(3).
The Act: Vehicles (Excise) Act 1971.

PART IV
VEHICLES EXEMPT FROM LICENCE DUTY

23. Extension of provisions to registration

The provisions of Parts II and III of these Regulations as to registration and matters incidental thereto shall extend to the mechanically propelled vehicles to which the three next following Regulations apply (being vehicles in respect of which duty is not chargeable under the Act) subject to the modifications specified in those Regulations 1971. **[1063]**

NOTES
Commencement: 1 April 1971.
The Act: Vehicles (Excise) Act 1971.

24. Vehicles belonging to the Crown

(1) A Government Department which keeps or uses on a road a mechanically propelled vehicle belonging to the Crown which has not previously been registered under the Act, the Vehicles (Excise) Act 1962, the Vehicles (Excise) Act 1949, or the Roads Act 1920 shall make the prescribed declaration and furnish the prescribed particulars as if, subject to the provisions of the next following paragraph, the Department desired to obtain a licence for the vehicle.

(2) Such declaration and particulars shall be forwarded to the Secretary of State.

(3) Upon receipt of such declaration and particulars the Secretary of State shall register the vehicle and assign to the vehicle a registration mark, and any registration mark so assigned shall be deemed to be assigned under section 19 of the Act for the purposes of subsection (2) of that section and these Regulations.

(4) No licence or registration book shall be issued by the Secretary of State in respect of the vehicle so registered.

(5) Every mechanically propelled vehicle belonging to the Crown which is kept or used on a road shall for the purposes of identification carry a certificate of Crown ownership signed by a duly authorised officer of the Government

Department by which the vehicle is kept or used as aforesaid, and the provisions of Regulation 7 (which relates to the alteration of licences and similar offences) and Regulation 16 (which relates to the exhibition of licences) of these Regulations shall apply as if each reference in those Regulations to a licence issued under the Act included a reference to a certificate of Crown ownership.

(6) The provisions of Regulation 10 (which relates to notification of alteration of vehicles), Regulation 12 (which relates to notification of change of ownership of vehicles), Regulation 13 (which relates to notification of change of address of owners of vehicles) and Regulation 14 (which relates to notification of destruction or permanent export of vehicles) of these Regulations shall not, except in so far as Regulation 12 places duties on the previous owner of a vehicle acquired by the Crown, apply in the case of vehicles belonging to the Crown.

(7) Upon the acquisition by the Crown of the ownership of a vehicle which has been registered under the Act, or the transfer of such a vehicle from one Government Department to another, a duly authorised officer of the Department which has acquired the vehicle shall notifiy the change in writing to the Secretary of State, and where the registration book has been delivered to the Crown in accordance with the provisions of Regulation 12(1) of these Regulations any such notification shall be accompanied by the registration book of the vehicle.

(8) Upon the receipt of a notification under the preceding paragraph the Secretary of State shall register the vehicle in the name of the Department from which the notification was received unless that Department has certified that the vehicle is used or appropriated for use for naval, military or air force purposes, and shall retain any registration book accompanying the notification.

(9) Where the ownership of a vehicle registered in the name of a Government Department is acquired by a person other than a Government Department, or such a vehicle is broken up, destroyed or sent permanently out of Great Britain, a duly authorised officer of the Department shall forthwith notify the fact to the Secretary of State.

(10) Where the ownership of a vehicle registered in the name of a Government Department is acquired by a person other than a Government Department, a registration book in respect of the vehicle shall be issued to that person by the Secretary of State.

(11) None of the provisions of Parts II and III of these Regulations and of this Regulation except paragraphs (7) and (8) shall apply to any vehicle belonging to the Crown which is used or appropriated for use for naval, military or air force purposes. **[1064]**

NOTES
    Commencement: 1 April 1971.
    The Act: Vehicles (Excise) Act 1971.

25. Vehicles used for special purposes

(1) This Regulation applies to mechanically propelled vehicles, other than those belonging to the Crown, which are used exclusively on roads not repairable at the public expense or which are exempt from duty by virtue of the provisions of [paragraphs (a), (c), (ca), (d) or (e) of section 4(1)] or section 7(1) of the Act.

(2) The owner of a vehicle to which this Regulation applies which has not previously been registered under the Act shall make the prescribed declaration

and furnish the prescribed particulars as if he desired to take out a licence for the vehicle in accordance with Regulation 4 of these Regulations.

(3) Upon receipt of such declaration and particulars the Secretary of State shall—

(a) register the vehicle and assign to the vehicle a registration mark, and any registration mark so assigned shall be deemed to be assigned under section 19 of the Act for the purposes of subsection (2) of that section and these Regulations; and

(b) issue to the owner a registration book with the appropriate particulars of the vehicle in respect of which it is issued entered therein, but no licence shall be issued in respect of the vehicle. **[1065]**

NOTES

Commencement: 1 April 1971.
Para (1): amended by SI 1990 No 2185.
The Act: Vehicles (Excise) Act 1971.

26. Other exempt vehicles

[(1) This regulation applies to mechanically propelled vehicles which are exempt from duty by or under section 4, 6 or 7(2), (3), (4) or (5) of the Act or section 7 of the Finance Act 1971 other than—

(a) vehicles to which regulation 25 above applies;

(b) invalid carriages complying with requirements prescribed under section 20 of the Chronically Sick and Disabled Persons Act 1970; and

(c) vehicles exempt from duty by section 4(1)(ka) of the Act.]

[(2) The owner of a vehicle to which this Regulation applies shall annually make the prescribed declaration and furnish the prescribed particulars as if, subject to paragraph (3) below, he desired to take out a licence for the vehicle, and in the case of a vehicle for which exemption is claimed under section 7(2) of the Act or section 7 of the Finance Act 1971 he shall include with the prescribed declaration and particulars a certificate issued by the Secretary of State for Social Services or the Secretary of State for Scotland stating—

(a) in a case to which section 7(2) of the Act applies, that he has obtained, or is eligible for, a grant under section 33(3) of the Health Services and Public Health Act 1968 in relation to that vehicle [or that he, or the person in respect of whom he has been appointed in pursuance of regulations under section 81(4)(b) of the Social Security Act 1975 or nominated in pursuance of the said section 7(2), is in receipt of a mobility allowance]; and

(b) in a case to which section 7 of the Finance Act 1971 applies, that—

(i) he has a particular disability that so incapacitates him in the use of his limbs that he has to be driven and cared for by a full-time constant attendant, and

(ii) he is sufficiently disabled to be eligible under the said Act of 1968 for an invalid tricycle if he were not too disabled to drive it.

(3) Such declaration and particulars and any certificate shall be forwarded to the Secretary of State.

(3A) Upon receipt of such declaration and particulars and any certificate the Secretary of State shall—

(a) if the vehicle has not previously been registered under the Act, register the vehicle, assign to the vehicle a registration mark and issue to the owner a registration book with the appropriate particulars of the vehicle in respect of which it is issued entered therein, and any registration mark so assigned shall be deemed to be assigned under section 19 of the Act for the purposes of subsection (2) of that section and these Regulations; and

(b) issue to the owner of the vehicle a document in respect thereof in the form of a licence valid for a period of twelve months running from the beginning of the month in which the document first has effect with the word "NIL" marked in the space provided for indicating the amount of duty payable.]

(4) If at any time duty becomes chargeable under the Act in respect of a mechanically propelled vehicle to which this Regulation applies the owner of the vehicle shall forthwith return to the Secretary of State any document issued by him for exhibition on the vehicle which indicates that no duty was payable in respect of it.

(5) The provisions of Regulation 7 (which relates to the alteration of licences and similar offences) and Regulation 16 (which relates to the exhibition of licences) shall apply in relation to a vehicle to which this Regulation applies as if each reference therein to a licence issued under the Act included a reference to any such document issued in respect of the vehicle as is mentioned in the last preceding paragraph of this Regulation. **[1066]**

NOTES
Commencement: 1 April 1971 (paras (4), (5)); 29 December 1972 (paras (2)–(3A); 3 December 1990 (para (1)).
Para (1): substituted by SI 1990 No 2185.
Paras (2)–(3A): substituted by SI 1972 No 1865.
Para (2): amended by SI 1978 No 1536.
The Act: Vehicles (Excise) Act 1971.

27. Civil defence vehicles

(1) A mechanically propelled vehicle shall not be chargeable with duty under the Act by reason only of any use made of it for the purpose of a local or police authority's functions in connection with civil defence as defined in the Civil Defence Act 1948, or by reason of its being kept on a road for such use.

(2) In this Regulation the expression "police authority", as respects England and Wales, has the same meaning as in the Police Act 1964, and, as respects Scotland, as in the Police (Scotland) Act 1967. **[1067]**

NOTES
Commencement: 1 April 1971.
The Act: Vehicles (Excise) Act 1971.

PART V
TRADE LICENCES

[28. Applications for trade licences

(1) For the purposes of section 16 of the Act the prescribed manner for—

(a) a motor trader to make an application to take out a licence under that section for all mechanically propelled vehicles which are from time to time temporarily in his possession in the course of his business as a motor trader ... ;

(b) a vehicle tester to make an application to take out a licence under that section for all mechanically propelled vehicles which are from time to time submitted to him for testing in the course of his business as a vehicle tester; or

(c) a motor trader, who is a manufacturer of mechanically propelled vehicles, to make an application to take out a licence under that section for all vehicles kept and used by him solely for purposes of conducting research and development in the course of his business as such a manufacturer, and all other vehicles which are from time to time submitted to him by other manufacturers for testing on roads in the course of that business,

shall be to furnish the prescribed particulars and to make the prescribed declaration to the Secretary of State.

(2) The references in paragraph (1) of this Regulation to a motor trader or vehicle tester include references to any person who satisfies the Secretary of State that he intends to commence business as respectively a motor trader or vehicle tester.] **[1068]**

NOTES
Commencement: 1 January 1987.
Substituted by SI 1986 No 2101, reg 4.
Words omitted revoked by SI 1987 No 2123, reg 3.
The Act: Vehicles (Excise) Act 1971.

[28A. Descriptions of business]

The prescribed descriptions of businesses for the purposes of the definition of a "motor trader" in section 16(8) of the Act are those of modifying vehicles (whether by fitting accessories or otherwise) prior to their first registration by the Secretary of State and of valeting vehicles.] **[1069]**

NOTES
Commencement: 1 January 1987.
Added by SI 1986 No 2101, reg 5.

29. Period for review of decision refusing an application for a trade licence

For the purposes of section 25(1)(c) of the Act (which relates to the review by the Secretary of State of his decision refusing an application by a motor trader or vehicle tester for a trade licence) the period within which such a trade or tester shall request the Secretary of State for such a review shall be 28 days calculated from the end of the day on which the decision was given. **[1070]**

NOTES
Commencement: 1 April 1971.
The Act: Vehicles (Excise) Act 1971.

30. Notification of change of address etc

If the holder of a trade licence changes the name of his business or his business address he shall notify this fact and the new name or address forthwith to the Secretary of State and shall at the same time send to the Secretary of State the licence for any necessary amendment. **[1071]**

NOTES
Commencement: 1 April 1971.

31. Issue of trade plates and replacements therefor

(1) The Secretary of State shall issue to every holder of a trade licence in respect of that licence two plates (in these Regulations referred to as "trade plates") appropriate to the class of vehicles on which they will be used showing the general registration mark assigned to the holder of the licence, and one of the plates so issued shall contain means whereby the licence may be fixed thereto:

Provided that where the holder of a trade licence satisfies the Secretary of State that the vehicles which he will use by virtue of the licence include vehicles which would otherwise be liable to duty under Schedule 1 to the Act and other vehicles he shall be entitled to be issued free of charge with two additional trade plates in respect of the vehicles first mentioned in this proviso.

(2) Each trade plate shall remain the property of the Secretary of State, and shall be returned forthwith to the Secretary of State if the person to whom it was issued no longer holds a trade licence which is in force or if that person ceases to be a motor trader or a vehicle tester.

(3) If a trade plate issued by the Secretary of State to the holder of a trade licence is lost, destroyed, mutilated or defaced or the figures and particulars thereon have become illegible or the colour of the plate has become altered by fading or otherwise, the holder shall apply to the Secretary of State for the issue to him of a replacement for that plate, and the Secretary of State upon being satisfied as to such loss, destruction, mutilation, defacement, illegibility or alteration as aforesaid, and upon the receipt of the plate except where the plate has been lost or destroyed, shall issue a replacement for the plate on payment of a fee [, where the plate is one of two replaced at the same time, of [£5.50] in respect of each plate, or, where the plate is not one of two replaced—

   [(i) a fee of £6.50 in respect of a plate which contains means whereby the licence may be fixed thereto and which is to be fixed to the front of the vehicle, or
   (ii) a fee of £4.50 in any other case,]],

and the replacement so issued shall have the same effect as the plate which it replaces:

Provided that where the Secretary of State is satisfied that the figures or particulars have become illegible or the colour of the plate has become altered by fading or otherwise without any act or neglect on the part of the holder of the trade licence he shall issue a replacement free of charge.

(4) In the case of the loss of any trade plate, if at any time after the issue of a replacement the original plate is found, the holder of the trade licence, if the plate is in his possession, shall forthwith return it to the Secretary of State, or if it is not in his possession but he becomes aware that it is found, shall take all reasonable steps to obtain possession of it and if successful shall forthwith return it to the Secretary of State, so, however, that if possession is not obtained, such fact shall be notified to the Secretary of State by the holder of the licence.

[1072]

NOTES
   Commencement: 1 April 1971.
   Para (3): first amendment made by SI 1976 No 1860; further amended by SI 1986 No 1177, reg 4.
   The Act: Vehicles (Excise) Act 1971.

32. Alteration of trade plates and similar offences

(1) No person shall alter, deface, mutilate or add anything to any trade plate or exhibit upon any mechanically propelled vehicle any trade plate which has been altered, defaced, mutilated or added to as aforesaid or upon which the figures or particulars have become illegible or the colour has become altered by fading or otherwise.

(2) No person shall exhibit on any mechanically propelled vehicle anything which could be mistaken for a trade plate.   **[1073]**

NOTES
    Commencement: 1 April 1971.

33. Exhibition of trade plates and licences

No person shall use a vehicle on a public road by virtue of a trade licence except in accordance with the following provisions, that is to say—

   (a) there shall be fixed to and displayed on the vehicle the trade plates issued by the Secretary of State in such a manner that, if the trade plates contained a registration mark assigned to the vehicle, the provisions of Regulations 18 and 19 of these Regulations would be complied with, notwithstanding the vehicle may not have been first registered on or after 1st October 1938 or it is a works truck or an agricultural machine; and

   (b) where in accordance with the provisions of the preceding paragraph a trade plate is required to be fixed to the front of a vehicle, the trade plate so fixed shall be that containing means for fixing the licence thereto, and the trade licence shall be fixed to the vehicle by means of that plate and exhibited on that plate so as to be at all times clearly visible by daylight.   **[1074]**

NOTES
    Commencement: 1 April 1971.

34. Restrictions on use of trade plates and licences

No person, not being the holder of a trade licence, shall use on a public road a vehicle on which there is displayed a trade plate or a trade licence, so, however, that nothing in this Regulation shall apply so as to prevent a person with the consent of the holder of the trade licence from driving a vehicle when the vehicle is being used on a public road by virtue of a trade licence [for a purpose prescribed in regulations 35 to 37 of these Regulations] and by the holder thereof.   **[1075]**

NOTES
    Commencement: 1 April 1971.
    Amended by SI 1986 No 2101, reg 6.

Purposes for which a vehicle may be used

35. (1) In this Regulation, "business purpose", in relation to a motor trader, means—

   (a) a purpose connected with his business as a manufacturer or repairer of or dealer in mechanically propelled vehicles, . . .

(b) a purpose connected with his business as a manufacturer or repairer of or dealer in trailers carried on in conjunction with his business as a motor trader [or]

[(c) a purpose connected with his business of modifying vehicles prior to their first registration by the Secretary of State or of valeting vehicles.]

(2) For the purposes of sub-paragraphs (a) to (k) of paragraph (4) of this Regulation, where a mechanically propelled vehicle is used on a public road by virtue of a trade licence and that vehicle is drawing a trailer, the vehicle and trailer shall be deemed to constitute a single vehicle.

(3) Save as provided in Regulation 36 of these Regulations, no person, being a motor trader and the holder of a trade licence, shall use any mechanically propelled vehicle on a public road by virtue of that licence unless it is a vehicle which is temporarily in his possession in the course of his business as a motor trader . . . .

(4) Save as provided in the said Regulation 36 and without derogation from the provisions of the last preceding paragraph of this Regulation, no person, being a motor trader and the holder of a trade licence, shall use any mechanically propelled vehicle on a public road by virtue of that licence for a purpose other than a business purpose and other than one of the following purposes:—

(a) for its test or trial or the test or trial of its accessories or equipment in the ordinary course of construction [modification] or repair or after completion in either such case;

(b) for proceeding to or from a public weighbridge for ascertaining its unladen weight or to or from any place for its registration or inspection by a person acting on behalf of the Secretary of State;

(c) for its test or trial for the benefit of a prospective purchaser, for proceeding at the instance of a prospective purchaser to any place for the purpose of such test or trial, or for returning after such test or trial;

(d) for its test or trial for the benefit of a person interested in promoting publicity in regard to it, for proceeding at the instance of such a person to any place for the purpose of such test or trial, or for returning after such test or trial;

(e) for delivering it to the place where the purchaser intends to keep it;

(f) for demonstrating its operation or the operation of its accessories or equipment when being handed over to the purchaser;

(g) for delivering it from one part of his premises to another part of his premises, or for delivering it from his premises to the premises of, or between parts of premises of, another manufacturer or repairer of or dealer in mechanically propelled vehicles or removing it from the premises of another manufacturer or repairer of or dealer in mechanically propelled vehicles direct to his own premises;

(h) for proceeding to or returning from a workshop in which a body or a special type of equipment or accessory is to be or has been fitted to it or in which it is to be or has been painted [valeted] or repaired;

(i) for proceeding from the premises of a manufacturer or repairer of or dealer in mechanically propelled vehicles to a place from which it is to be transported by train, ship or aircraft or for proceeding to the premises of such a manufacturer, repairer or dealer from a place to which it has been so transported;

(j) for proceeding to or returning from any garage, auction room or other place at which vehicles are usually stored or usually or periodically offered for sale and at which the vehicle is to be or has been stored or is to be or has been offered for sale as the case may be;

(k) for proceeding to or returning from a place where it is to be or has been tested, or for proceeding to a place where it is to be broken up or otherwise dismantled; or

(l) ... **[1076]**

NOTES
Commencement: 1 April 1971.
Para (1): words omitted revoked and words in square brackets added by SI 1986 No 2101, reg 7.
Para (3): words omitted revoked by SI 1987 No 2123, reg 4.
Para (4): sub-paras (a), (h) amended by SI 1986 No 2101, reg 7, sub-para (l) revoked by SI 1987 No 2123, reg 4.

36. No person, being a motor trader and who is a manufacturer of mechanically propelled vehicles and the holder of a trade licence, shall use any mechanically propelled vehicle, kept by him solely for the purposes of conducting research and development in the course of his business as such a manufacturer, on a public road by virtue of that licence except for such a purpose. **[1077]**

NOTES
Commencement: 1 April 1971.

37. No person, being a vehicle tester and the holder of a trade licence, shall use any mechanically propelled vehicle on a public road by virtue of that licence for any purpose other than testing it or any trailer drawn thereby or any of the accessories or equipment on such vehicle or trailer in the course of his business as a vehicle tester. **[1078]**

NOTES
Commencement: 1 April 1971.

Conveyance of goods or burden

38. (1) No person, being a motor trader and the holder of a trade licence, shall use a mechanically propelled vehicle on a public road by virtue of that licence for the conveyance of goods or burden of any description other than—

(a) a load which is carried by a vehicle being used for a relevant purpose and is carried solely for the purpose of testing or demonstrating the vehicle or any of its accessories or equipment and which is returned to the place of loading without having been removed from the vehicle except for such last mentioned purpose or in the case of accident [or when the load consists of water, fertiliser or refuse]:

In this sub-paragraph "relevant purpose" means a purpose mentioned in Regulation 35(4)(a), (c), (d) and (f) of these Regulations; or

(b) ...
(c) any load built in as part of the vehicle or permanently attached thereto; or
(d) a load consisting of parts, accessories or equipment designed to be fitted to the vehicle and of tools for so fitting them, the vehicle being used for a relevant purpose:

In this sub-paragraph "relevant purpose" means a purpose mentioned in Regulation 35(4)(g), (h) or (i) of these Regulations; or

(e) a load consisting of a trailer, the vehicle carrying the trailer being used for a relevant purpose:

In this sub-paragraph "relevant purpose" means a purpose mentioned in Regulation 35(4)(e), (h) or (i) of these Regulations.

(2) No person, being a motor trader and who is a manufacturer of mechanically propelled vehicles and the holder of a trade licence, shall use any mechanically propelled vehicle, kept by him solely for the purposes of conducting research and development in the course of his business as such a manufacturer, on a public road by virtue of that licence for the conveyance of goods or burden of any description other than—

(a) a load which is carried solely for the purpose of testing the vehicle or any of its accessories or equipment and which is returned to the place of loading without having been removed from the vehicle except for such purpose or in the case of accident; or
(b) any load built in as part of the vehicle or permanently attached thereto,

and nothing in the last preceding paragraph of this Regulation shall be taken as applying to a mechanically propelled vehicle the use of which is restricted by this paragraph.

(3) For the purposes of this Regulation and the next succeeding Regulation, where a vehicle is so constructed that a trailer may by partial superimposition be attached to the vehicle in such a manner as to cause a substantial part of the weight of the trailer to be borne by the vehicle, the vehicle and the trailer shall be deemed to constitute a single vehicle.   **[1079]**

NOTES
Commencement: 1 April 1971.
Para (1): sub-para (a) amended by SI 1986 No 2101, reg 8; sub-para (b) revoked by SI 1987 No 2123, reg 5.
The Act: Vehicles (Excise) Act 1971.

39. No person, being a vehicle tester and the holder of a trade licence, shall use a mechanically propelled vehicle on a public road by virtue of that licence for the conveyance of goods or burden of any description other than—

(a) a load which is carried solely for the purpose of testing or demonstrating the vehicle or any of its accessories or equipment and which is returned to the place of loading without having been removed from the vehicle except for such purpose or in the case of accident; or
(b) any load built in as part of the vehicle or permanently attached thereto.   **[1080]**

NOTES
Commencement: 1 April 1971.

[40. Carriage of passengers

No person, being the holder of a trade licence, shall use a mechanically propelled vehicle on a public road by virtue of that licence for carrying any person on the vehicle or on any trailer drawn by it except a person carried in connection with a purpose for which the holder of the trade licence may use the vehicle on the public road by virtue of that licence.]   **[1081]**

NOTES
Commencement: 1 January 1987.

Substituted by SI 1986 No 2101, reg 9.

PART VI
HACKNEY CARRIAGES

41. Distinctive signs for hackney carriage

(1) The distinctive sign, which subject to the exceptions prescribed in paragraph (2) of this Regulation, every mechanically propelled vehicle which is chargeable with duty as a hackney carriage is required to exhibit in accordance with section 21 of the Act, shall comply with the diagram and specification set out in Schedule 4 to these Regulations, and shall be exhibited on the back of the vehicle in an upright position, so as at all times to be clearly visible in daylight from behind the vehicle.

(2) The following vehicles shall be excepted from the said requirement, that is to say—

    (a) tramcars;

    (b) vehicles in respect of which the rate of duty under the Act as a hackney carriage is not less than the rate of duty under Schedule 5 to the Act;

    (c) vehicles licensed to ply for hire which carry in a conspicuous position on the outside of the vehicle a mark in the form prescribed by the authority by whom it is so licensed indicating clearly that the vehicle is a hackney carriage so licensed;

    (d) hackney carriages temporarily adapted for and being used solely for the conveyance of goods in the course of trade; and

    (e) vehicles with a seating capacity for twenty persons or more.   **[1082]**

NOTES
    Commencement: 1 April 1971.
    The Act: Vehicles (Excise) Act 1971.

42. Seating capacity of hackney carriages

(1) For the purposes of the last preceding Regulation and of Schedule 2 to the Act (which prescribes the annual rates of duty on hackney carriages) the seating capacity of a vehicle shall be determined as follows:—

    (a) where separate seats for each person are provided one person shall be counted for each separate seat provided; and

    (b) where the vehicle is fitted with continuous seats one person shall be counted for each complete length of 16 inches measured in a straight line lengthwise on the front of each seat, and where any such continuous seat is fitted with arms for the purpose of separating the seating spaces and such arms are so constructed that they can be folded back or otherwise put out of use such seat shall be measured for the purposes of this Regulation as if it had not been fitted with such arms:

    Provided that in calculating the seating capacity of any vehicle the driver's seat shall be excluded, and where on any vehicle there are seats alongside the driver's seat, whether separate from or continuous with the driver's seat, and the Secretary of State is satisfied that those seats will not during the currency of the licence to be issued be permitted to be used by members of the public travelling on the vehicle, those seats shall be excluded in calculating the seating capacity of the vehicle.

(2) For the purposes of this Regulation the expression "the driver's seat" means any separate seat occupied by the driver of the vehicle, or, where no such separate seat is provided and the driver occupies a portion of a continuous seat, so much of that seat as extends from the right edge of the seat in the case of a vehicle steered from the right-hand side, or from the left edge of the seat in the case of a vehicle steered from the left-hand side, to a point 18 inches left or right, as the case may be, of the point on the seat directly in rear of the centre of the steering column.   **[1083]**

NOTES
   Commencement: 1 April 1971.
   The Act: Vehicles (Excise) Act 1971.

PART VII
MISCELLANEOUS

43. Horse-power

(1) For the purposes of any rate of duty under the Act the horse-power of any mechanically propelled vehicle deriving its motive power wholly from an internal combustion engine worked by a cylinder or cylinders shall be taken to be:—

  (a) in the case of a single-cylinder engine, the horse-power attributable to the cylinder of the engine; and

  (b) in the case of an engine having two or more cylinders, the sum of the horse-powers attributable to the separate cylinders.

(2) The horse-power attributable to any cylinder of an internal combustion engine shall be deemed to be equal to the square of the internal diameter of such cylinder measured in inches divided by, in the case of a cylinder having a single piston, 2.5, and in the case of a cylinder having two pistons, 1.6.

(3) The horse-power of any mechanically propelled vehicle deriving its power wholly from a steam engine shall be taken to be proportional to the effective heating surface of the boiler supplying steam to such engine, at the rate of 1 horse-power for every 3 square feet in such effective heating surface, and the effective heating surface shall be taken to be:—

  (a) in the case of a boiler having horizontal or approximately horizontal tubes, the whole of that surface of the tubes which is exposed to the flame or hot gases; and

  (b) in the case of a boiler having vertical or approximately vertical tubes, half of that surface of the tubes which is exposed to the flame or hot gases.

(4) In measuring cylinders and boilers for the purpose of calculating horse-power, and in calculating horse-power, fractions of inches and feet and fractions of a unit of horse-power are to be taken into account:

Provided that in the final calculation of horse-power a resultant fraction of less than 0.1 of a unit of horse-power shall be omitted.   **[1084]**

NOTES
   Commencement: 1 April 1971.
   The Act: Vehicles (Excise) Act 1971.

44. Cylinder capacity

(1) For the purposes of any rate of duty under the Act the cylinder capacity of any mechanically propelled vehicle deriving its motive power wholly from an internal combustion engine worked by a cylinder or cylinders shall be taken to be:—

    (a) in the case of a single-cylinder engine, the cylinder capacity attributable to the cylinder of the engine; and

    (b) in the case of an engine having two or more cylinders, the sum of the cylinders capacities attributable to the separate cylinders.

(2) The cylinder capacity attributable to any cylinder of an internal combustion engine shall be deemed to be equal to:—

    (a) in the case of a cylinder having a single piston, the product expressed in cubic centimetres of the square of the internal diameter of such cylinder measured in centimetres, and the distance through which the piston associated with that cylinder moves during one half of a revolution of the engine measured in centimetres multiplied by 0.7854; and

    (b) in the case of a cylinder having more than one piston, the sum of the products expressed in cubic centimetres of the square of the internal diameter of each part of the cylinder in which a piston moves measured in centimetres, and the distance through which the piston associated with that diameter moves during one half of a revolution of the engine measured in centimetres multiplied by 0.7854.

(3) In measuring cylinders for the purpose of calculating cylinder capacity, and in calculating cylinder capacity, fractions of centimetres are to be taken into account. **[1085]**

NOTES
    Commencement: 1 April 1971.
    The Act: Vehicles (Excise) Act 1971.

45. Unladen weight

The owner of a vehicle in respect of which duty under the Act is, or may be, payable by reference to its unladen weight, on being required in writing to do so by a person acting on behalf of the Secretary of State, shall—

    (a) furnish the prescribed declaration of weight; or

    (b) produce the vehicle at a specified time and weighbridge (which time shall be not less than seven days after the date of the requirement) together with any alternative bodies or parts which are by virtue of paragraph 1 of Schedule 6 to the Act required to be included in its unladen weight and cause the vehicle to be weighed at that time and place in the presence of a person acting as aforesaid,

in accordance with whichever course the requirement may specify. **[1086]**

NOTES
    Commencement: 1 April 1971.
    The Act: Vehicles (Excise) Act 1971.

46. Exemption of agricultural machines from duty as goods vehicles in certain cases

(1) This Regulation applies to vehicles which are agricultural machines (as defined in Part I of Schedule 3 to the Act) which do not draw trailers and which

are constructed or adapted for use and used for the conveyance in removable appliances fitted to the vehicle of goods or burden the haulage of which is permissible under paragraphs (a) to (e) of paragraph 2(1) of that Part of that Schedule.

(2) An appliance, not being a tined appliance, which has an external width not exceeding 8 feet 2 inches, an external length not exceeding 5 feet 2 inches and an external height not exceeding 2 feet 2 inches and which does not satisfy condition (b) in paragraph 7(2) of Part I of Schedule 4 to the Act, is hereby prescribed for the purposes of sub-paragraphs (2), (3) and (4) of paragraph 8 of that Part of that Schedule.

(3) Paragraph 7(2) of Part I of Schedule 4 to the Act shall not apply to a vehicle to which this Regulation applies which is fitted with an appliance of the description prescribed by paragraph (2) of this Regulation unless the appliance is used in the following circumstances, that is to say—

(a) another appliance with the same dimensions shall be fitted at the opposite end of the vehicle;
(b) each such appliance shall be so fitted to the vehicle that its longitudinal axis lies in the same vertical plane as the longitudinal axis of the vehicle;
(c) the weight of any goods or burden carried in each such appliance shall not exceed 6(1/2) cwt.;
(d) the weight of any goods or burden carried in the two appliances shall be distributed equally between them;
(e) the goods or burden carried in each appliance shall not be above the highest point of that appliance; and
(f) the vehicle shall not proceed on a public road at a speed exceeding 10 miles per hour.

(4) Paragraph 7(2)(b) of Part I of Schedule 4 to the Act shall not have effect in relation to appliances of the description prescribed by paragraph (2) of this Regulation, but in relation thereto paragraph 7(4) of that Part of that Schedule shall have effect with the substitution of the distance of three miles for the distance of fifteen miles specified therein. **[1087]**

NOTES
Commencement: 1 April 1971.
The Act: Vehicles (Excise) Act 1971.

SCHEDULES
SCHEDULE 1

Regulation 2

REGULATIONS REVOKED

. . .

SCHEDULE 2

Regulation 17

FORM OF REGISTRATION MARKS

PART I

DIAGRAMS SHOWING ARRANGEMENTS OF SPECIMEN REGISTRATION MARKS

[For these diagrams, reference should be made to the Queen's Printer's copy of this statutory instrument, which can be obtained from HMSO.] **[1090]**

NOTES
    Commencement: 1 April 1971.

PART II

SIZE, SHAPE AND CHARACTER OF REGISTRATION MARKS

Interpretation

1. For the purposes of this Schedule:—

    (a) any reference to a numbered diagram is a reference to the diagram of that number set out in Part I of this Schedule;

    (b) the expressions "upper margin", "lower margin" and "side margin", in relation to the black surface upon which a registration mark is inscribed or formed in accordance with paragraph 6 or 7 of this Schedule [or the white or, as the case may be, the yellow background upon which a registration mark is formed in accordance with paragraph 5B or, as the case may be, paragraph 5C of this Schedule or the said paragraph 5B as applied by paragraph 8 of this Schedule], mean respectively the space between the upper edge of the said [surface or background] and the nearest part of each letter and figure situated nearest that side; and

    (c) references to a registration mark which is embossed or pressed are references to a registration mark which consists either of a single plate with letters and figures embossed or pressed thereon or with separate letters and figures attached thereto or of separate plates each with a single letter or figure embossed or pressed thereon or attached thereto.

Arrangement of numbers and letters

2. Where a registration mark consists of an index mark followed by a registered number not containing a letter it shall at the option of the owner be arranged in conformity with either diagram No. 1 or diagram No. 2 or, in the case of a registration mark assigned to a bicycle or an agricultural machine and exhibited on the back of the vehicle, being a mark which consists of an index mark comprising two letters followed by a registered number comprising four figures, in conformity with diagram No. 3.

3. Where a registration mark consists of an index mark preceded by a registered number not containing a letter it shall at the option of the owner be arranged in conformity with either diagram No. 4 or diagram No. 5 or, in the case of a registration mark assigned to a bicycle or an agricultural machine and exhibited on the back of the vehicle, being a mark which consists of an index mark comprising two letters preceded by a registered number comprising four figures, in conformity with diagram No. 6.

4. Where a registration mark consists of an index mark followed by a registered number containing a letter it shall at the option of the owner be arranged in conformity with either diagram No. 7 or diagram No. 8 or, in the case of a registration mark assigned to a bicycle or an agricultural machine and exhibited on the back of the vehicle, being a mark which consists of an index mark comprising three letters followed by a registered number comprising three figures and a letter, in conformity with diagram No. 9.

5. Where a registration mark consists of an index mark preceded by a registered number containing a letter it shall at the option of the owner be arranged in conformity with either diagram No. 10 or diagram No. 11 or, in the case of a registration mark assigned to a bicycle or an agricultural machine and exhibited on the back of the vehicle,

being a mark which consists of an index mark comprising three letters preceded by a registered number comprising a letter and three figures, in conformity with diagram No. 12.

[Character of registration marks

5A. Paragraph 5B below shall apply to the registration mark required to be fixed on a vehicle which is first registered on or after 1st January 1973 other than—

    [(*a*) a vehicle on which, or on the load of which, there is fitted a marking as required by the Road Vehicles Lighting Regulations 1984, Regulation 16, and Schedule 1, item 1 or 6 and Schedule 18, Part I; ·

    (b) a stage carriage as defined in section 2(1) of the Public Passenger Vehicles Act 1981]; and

    (c) a bicycle, an invalid vehicle, a pedestrian controlled vehicle, a works truck and an agricultural machine.

5B. A registration mark to which this paragraph applies shall be exhibited on a plate which is constructed of reflex reflecting material, being a plate which complies with the requirements laid down by the British Standard Specification for reflex reflecting number plates published on 11th September 1972 under the number B.S. AU 145a and is of a type in respect of which there has been issued by the Secretary of State a certificate that a plate of that type complies with those requirements, and in such a case—

    (a) the registration mark, where it is displayed on the front of the vehicle, shall be formed of black letters and figures upon a white background and where it is displayed on the back of the vehicle shall be formed of black letters and figures upon a yellow background;

    (b) that part of the plate which comprises the said background shall be constructed of reflex reflecting material which shall at all times be maintained in a clean and efficient condition;

    (c) no reflex reflecting material shall be applied to any part of the said letters or figures; and

    (d) there shall be legibly and permanently marked on the plate the specification number B.S. AU 145a to indicate that it complies with the British Standard Specification mentioned above,

but nothing in this paragraph shall apply to the registration mark required to be fixed on a vehicle when that mark, in accordance with the provisions of Regulation 22, is displayed on the back of a trailer attached to that vehicle.

5C. The registration mark required to be fixed on the back of any of the following vehicles, that is to say, a bicycle, an invalid vehicle or a pedestrian controlled vehicle (being, in any such case, a vehicle first registered on or after 1st January 1973) shall be exhibited on a plate which is constructed of reflex reflecting material, being a plate which complies with the requirements of the British Standard Specification mentioned in paragraph 5B above and is of a type in respect of which a certificate such as is mentioned in that paragraph has been issued by the Secretary of State, and in such a case—

    (a) the registration mark shall be formed of black letters and figures upon a yellow background;

    (b) that part of the plate which comprises the said background shall be constructed of reflex reflecting material which shall at all times be maintained in a clean and efficient condition;

    (c) no reflex reflecting material shall be applied to any part of the said letters or figures; and

    (d) there shall be legibly and permanently marked on the plate the specification number B.S. AU 145a to indicate that it complies with the British Standard Specification mentioned in the said paragraph 5B.

5D. Paragraphs 6, 7 and 8 below shall apply to the registration mark required to be fixed—

    (a) on a vehicle which is first registered before 1st January 1973; and

    (b) on a vehicle, not being a bicycle, an invalid vehicle or a pedestrian controlled vehicle (but subject, in each of those cases, to paragraph 8A below) or a vehicle to which paragraph 5B above applies, which is first registered on or after that date.

6. A registration mark to which this paragraph applies shall, except where it is so designed and constructed that it may be illuminated from behind by means of the translucency of the letters and figures comprised in the mark or is exhibited on a plate in accordance with paragraph 8 below, be formed of white, silver or light grey letters and figures upon a black surface and every letter and figure shall be indelibly inscribed upon that surface or so attached to the surface that it cannot readily be detached therefrom, and in a case where the letters and figures are exhibited on a flat plate the plate may be constructed of cast or pressed metal having raised letters and figures.

7. Where a registration mark to which this paragraph applies is so designed and constructed as to be illuminated from behind in the manner mentioned in paragraph 6 above, the mark shall be formed of white letters and figures upon a black surface and all the letters and figures shall, when the mark is so illuminated during the hours of darkness, appear white against a black background.

8. A registration mark to which this paragraph applies may be exhibited on a plate which is constructed of reflex reflecting material and which—

    (a) in the case of the registration mark of a vehicle first registered before 1st January 1973, either complies with the requirements laid down by the British Standard Specification for Reflex Reflecting Number plates published on 31st October 1967 under the number B.S. AU 145: 1967, the plate being permanently and legibly marked with the specification number B.S. AU 145 to indicate that it complies with the said Specification, or complies with the requirements of the British Standard Specification mentioned in paragraph 5B above and is of a type in respect of which a certificate such as is mentioned in that paragraph has been issued by the Secretary of State, the plate being permanently and legibly marked as mentioned in sub-paragraph (d) of that paragraph; and

    (b) in the case of the registration mark of a vehicle first registered on or after 1st January 1973, complies with the requirements of the British Standard Specification mentioned in the said paragraph 5B and is of a type in respect of which a certificate such as is mentioned in that paragraph has been issued by the Secretary of State, the plate being permanently and legibly marked as mentioned in sub-paragraph (d) of that paragraph,

and, in either such case, the provisions of sub-paragraphs (a) to (c) of the said paragraph 5B shall apply in relation to the mark and to the plate on which it is exhibited as they apply in relation to a registration mark mentioned in that paragraph and to the plate on which that mark is exhibited.

8A. Paragraphs 6, 7 and 8 above shall apply to the registration mark required to be fixed on any of the following vehicles, that is to say, . . . an invalid vehicle [(not being a bicycle)] or a pedestrian controlled vehicle (being, in any such case, a vehicle which is first registered on or after 1st January 1973) but only insofar as relating to the mark required to be fixed on the front of the vehicle, and in their application to such a registration mark for the purposes of this paragraph the provisions of the said paragraphs 6, 7 and 8 shall have effect accordingly.

8B. Where, in accordance with the provisions of regulation 22, the registration mark required to be fixed on a vehicle is displayed on the back of a trailer attached to that vehicle, the mark may be exhibited on a plate which is constructed of reflex reflecting material, but in any such case the plate shall comply in all respects with such of the provisions of paragraph 5B above, or as the case may be, of paragraph 8 above as apply in relation to the plate when (in accordance with the provisions in question) it is exhibited on the back of the vehicle to which the trailer is attached.

8C. Nothing in paragraph 5B, 5C, 8, 8A, or 8B above shall be taken to authorise any person to apply a specification number as mentioned in any of the first three of those paragraphs in contravention of the Trade Descriptions Act 1968.]

Size and shape

9.—(1) Except as is provided in paragraph 13 or 18 of this Schedule the registration marks displayed on a vehicle shall be displayed on a flat rectangular plate or on a rectangular, flat and unbroken area on the surface of the vehicle, and such marks shall at the option of the owner of the vehicle conform either to the group of provisions contained in paragraphs 10 to 13 inclusive of this Schedule or to the group of provisions contained in paragraphs 14 to 18 inclusive of this Schedule.

(2) For the purposes of the following paragraphs of this Schedule any letter contained in the registered number of a vehicle shall be deemed to be a figure contained in that number.

First group of provisions as to size and shape

10. Subject to the provisions of paragraph 13 of this Schedule, each letter and figure shall be 3(1/2) inches high, every part of each letter and figure shall be 5/8 inch broad, and the total width of the space taken by each letter and figure, except in the case of the figure "1", shall be 2(1/2) inches.

11. Subject to the provisions of paragraph 13 of this Schedule, there shall be an upper margin and a lower margin on the [surface or background] upon which the registration mark is inscribed or formed of at least 1/2 inch, there shall be a side margin on each side of the [surface or background] of at least 1 inch and the space between the nearest parts of adjoining letters and between the nearest parts of adjoining figures shall be 1/2 inch, except that where the registration mark is embossed or pressed the space between the nearest parts of two adjoining figures "1" shall be not less than 1/2 inch nor more than 2(3/8) inches and the space between the nearest part of a figure "1" and the nearest part of any other adjoining figure shall be not less than 1/2 inch nor more than 1(7/16) inches.

12. Subject to the provisions of paragraph 13 of this Schedule, where the registration mark is arranged in accordance with diagram No. 1, diagram No. 4, diagram No. 7 or diagram No. 10, the space between the upper and lower lines shall be 3/4 inch, where it is arranged in accordance with diagram No. 3, diagram No. 6, diagram No. 9 or diagram No. 12, the space between the upper and middle lines and the space between the middle and lower lines, shall in each case be 3/4 inch, and where it is arranged in accordance with diagram No. 2, diagram No. 5, diagram No. 8 or diagram No. 11, the space between the letters and the figures shall be 1(1/2) inches, except that where the registration mark is embossed or pressed the said space of 1(1/2) inches may be exceeded by not more than 15/16 inch.

13. As respects the registration mark assigned to a bicycle, an invalid vehicle or a pedestrian controlled vehicle—

(1) where the registration mark is displayed on the front of the vehicle—
(a) the plate or area upon which the mark is inscribed or formed need not be rectangular if the letters and figures comprised in the mark conform as nearly as possible with the arrangements shown in that one of the diagrams set out in this Schedule with which, in accordance with paragraph 2, 3, 4 or 5 of this Schedule, the mark has been selected to conform; and
(b) the following requirements may be complied with instead of the requirements specified in paragraphs 10, 11 and 12 of this Schedule, that is to say:—

(i) each letter and figure shall be 1(3/4) inches high, every part of each letter and figure shall be 5/16 inch broad, and the total width of the space taken by each letter and figure, except in the case of the figure "1", shall be 1(1/4) inches.
(ii) there shall be an upper margin and a lower margin on the [surface or background] upon which the registration mark is inscribed or formed of at least 1/2 inch and there shall be a side margin on each side of the [surface or background] of at least 1/2 inch; the space between the nearest parts of adjoining letters and between the nearest parts of adjoining figures shall be 1/4 inch, and
(iii) where the mark is arranged in accordance with diagram No. 1, diagram No. 4, diagram No. 7 or diagram No. 10, the space between the upper and lower lines shall be 3/8 inch and where it is arranged in accordance with diagram No. 2, diagram No. 5, diagram No. 8 or diagram No. 11, the space between the letters and the figures shall be 3/4 inch; and

(2) where the registration mark is displayed on the back of the vehicle on a plate—

(a) the corners of the plate may be rounded off, the letters comprised in the index mark (if the arrangement shown in diagram No. 1 or diagram No. 7 is selected) or the figures comprised in the registered number (if the arrangement shown in diagram No. 4 or diagram No. 10 is selected) may be placed to the left so, however, that no part of the first of such letters or the first of such figures, as the case may be, is nearer to the left-hand edge of the plate than 1/2 inch; and

(b) the following requirements may be complied with instead of the requirements specified in paragraphs 10, 11 and 12 of this Schedule, that is to say:—

    (i) each letter and figure shall be 2(1/2) inches high, every part of each letter and figure shall be 3/8 inch broad, and the total width of the space taken by each letter and figure, except in the case of the figure "1", shall be 1(3/4) inches,

    (ii) there shall be an upper margin and a lower margin on the [surface or background] upon which the registration mark is inscribed or formed, and a side margin on each side of the [surface or background] of at least 1/2 inch; the space between the nearest parts of adjoining letters and adjoining figures shall be 1/2 inch, and

    (iii) where the mark is arranged in accordance with diagram No. 1, diagram No. 4, diagram No. 7 or diagram No. 10, the space between the upper and lower lines shall be 1/2 inch, where it is arranged in accordance with diagram No. 3, diagram No. 6, diagram No. 9 or diagram No. 12, the space between the upper and middle lines, and the space between the middle and lower lines, shall in each case be 1/2 inch, and where it is arranged in accordance with diagram No. 2, diagram No. 5, diagram No. 8 or diagram No. 11, the space between the letters and the figures shall be 1 inch.

Alternative group of provisions as to size and shape

14. Subject to the provisions of paragraph 18 of this Schedule, each letter and figure shall be 3(1/8) inches high, every part of each letter and figure shall be 9/16 inch broad, and the total width of the space taken by each letter and figure, except in the case of the figure "1", shall be 2(1/4) inches.

15. Without prejudice to the provisions of the foregoing paragraph, part of the visible surface of every letter and figure comprised in a registration mark which is embossed or pressed shall be flat, every part of the width of the said flat part shall be not less than 1/4 inch, and every such letter and figure shall be so arranged that the said flat part is parallel to the surface of the plate on which the letter or figure appears, and no part of any such letter or figure shall project from the surface of the said plate by more than 3/16 inch.

16. Subject to the provisions of paragraph 18 of this Schedule, there shall be an upper margin and a lower margin on the [surface or background] upon which the registration mark is inscribed or formed, and a side margin on each side of the [surface or background], of at least 7/16 inch and the space between the nearest parts of adjoining letters and between the nearest parts of adjoining figures shall be 7/16 inch, except that where the registration mark is embossed or pressed the space between the nearest parts of two adjoining figures "1" shall be not less than 7/16 inch nor more than 2(1/8) inches and the space between the nearest part of a figure "1" and the nearest part of any other adjoining figure shall be not less than 7/16 inch nor more than 1(9/32) inches.

17. Subject to the provisions of paragraph 18 of this Schedule, where the registration mark is arranged in accordance with diagram No. 1, diagram No. 4, diagram No. 7 or diagram No. 10, the space between the upper and lower lines shall be 3/4 inch, where it is arranged in accordance with diagram No. 3, diagram No. 6, diagram No. 9 or diagram No. 12, the space between the upper and middle lines, and the space between the middle and lower lines, shall in each case be 3/4 inch, and where it is arranged in accordance with diagram No. 2, diagram No. 5, diagram No. 8 or diagram No. 11, the space between the letters and the figures shall be 1(5/16) inches, except that where the registration mark is embossed or pressed the said space of 1(5/16) inches may be exceeded by not more than 27/32 inch.

18. As respects the registration mark assigned to a bicycle, an invalid vehicle or a pedestrian controlled vehicle—

(1) where the registration mark is displayed on the front of the vehicle—

    (a) the plate or area upon which the mark is inscribed or formed need not be rectangular if the letters and figures comprised in the mark conform as nearly as possible with the arrangement shown in that one of the diagrams set out in this Schedule with which, in accordance with paragraph 2, 3, 4 or 5 of this Schedule, the mark has been selected to conform; and

    (b) the following requirements may be complied with instead of the requirements specified in paragraphs 14, 16 and 17 of this Schedule, that is to say:—

        (i) each letter and figure shall be 1(3/4) inches high, every part of each letter and figures shall be 5/16 inch broad, and the total width of the space taken by each letter and figure, except in the case of the figure "1", shall be 1(1/4) inches,

        (ii) there shall be an upper margin and a lower margin on the [surface or background] upon which the registration mark is inscribed or formed, and a side margin on each side of the [surface or background], of at least 1/4 inch; the space between the nearest parts of adjoining letters and the nearest parts of adjoining figures shall be 3/16 inch, and

        (iii) where the mark is arranged in accordance with diagram No. 1, diagram No. 4, diagram No. 7 or diagram No. 10, the space between the upper and lower lines shall be 3/8 inch and where it is arranged in accordance with diagram No. 2, diagram No. 5, diagram No. 8 or diagram No. 11, the space between the letters and the figures shall be 9/16 inch; and

(2) where the registration mark is displayed on the back of the vehicle on a plate—

    (a) the corners of the plate may be rounded off, the letters comprised in the index mark (if the arrangement shown in diagram No. 1 or diagram No. 7 is selected) or the figures comprised in the registered number (if the arrangement shown in diagram No. 4 or diagram No. 10 is selected) may be placed to the left so, however, that no part of the first of such letters or the first of such figures, as the case may be, is nearer to the left-hand edge of the plate than 3/8 inch, and

    (b) the following requirements may be complied with instead of the requirements specified in paragraphs 14, 16 and 17 of this Schedule, that is to say—

        (i) each letter and figure shall be 2(1/2) inches high, every part of each letter and figure shall be 3/8 inch broad, and the total width of the space taken by each letter and figure, except in the case of the figure "1", shall be 1(3/4) inches,

        (ii) there shall be an upper margin and a lower margin on the [surface or background] upon which the registration mark is inscribed or formed, and a side margin on each side of the [surface or background] of at least 3/8 inch; the space between the nearest parts of adjoining letters and adjoining figures shall be 3/8 inch, and

        (iii) where the mark is arranged in accordance with diagram No. 1, diagram No. 4, diagram No. 7 or diagram No. 10, the space between the upper and lower lines shall be 1/2 inch, where it is arranged in accordance with diagram No. 3, diagram No. 6, diagram No. 9 or diagram No. 12, the space between the upper and middle lines and, between the middle and lower lines, shall in each case be 1/2 inch, and where it is arranged in accordance with diagram No. 2, diagram No. 5, diagram No. 8 or diagram No. 11, the space between the letters and the figures shall be 1 inch.**[1091]**

NOTES

    Commencement: 29 December 1972 (paras 5A–8C); 1 April 1971 (remainder).
    Paras 1, 10, 13, 16, 18: amended by SI 1972 No 1865.
    Paras 5A—8C: substituted by SI 1972 No 1865; amended by SI 1984 No 814.
    Para 8A: amended by SI 1975 No 1089.
    See further SI 1985 No 610, reg 8(1).

SCHEDULE 3

Regulation 20

EXHIBITION OF REGISTRATION MARKS ON CERTAIN VEHICLES REGISTERED BEFORE 1ST OCTOBER 1938

Interpretation

1. In this Schedule "vehicle" means a mechanically propelled vehicle, other than a works truck or an agricultural machine first registered before 1st October 1938.

Position and visibility of registration marks

2. Subject to the provisions of the next following paragraph the registration mark of any vehicle shall be exhibited

[(a) in the case of a bicycle, on the back of the vehicle;
(b) in the case of any other vehicle, on both the front and back of the vehicle,

and in either case] in a vertical position, so that every letter or figure of the registration mark is vertical and easily distinguishable, in the case of the letters and figures placed on the front of the vehicle, from in front of the vehicle, and in the case of the letters and figures placed on the back of the vehicle, from behind the vehicle.

3. In the case of ... an invalid vehicle [(not being a bicycle)] or a pedestrian controlled vehicle the front registration mark may be displayed either—

(a) on a flat plate having duplicate faces both conforming with Schedule 2 to these Regulations, and fixed on the vehicle in a vertical position, or
(b) on both sides of the vehicle in a vertical position on a flat unbroken surface forming part of the front mudguard,

in such a manner that from whichever side the vehicle is viewed the letters and figures on one or other face of the plate or side of the mudguard, as the case may be, are easily distinguishable although they may not be distinguishable from the front of the vehicle.

Illumination of registration marks

4. ... **[1092]**

NOTES
Commencement: 1 April 1971.
Paras 2, 3: amended by SI 1975 No 1089.
Para 4: revoked by SI 1984 No 814.
See further SI 1985 No 610, reg 8(1).

SCHEDULE 4

Regulation 41

SIGN TO BE EXHIBITED BY HACKNEY CARRIAGES

[*For this diagram, reference should be made to the Queen's Printer's copy for this statutory instrument, which can be obtained from HMSO.*]

Note: The diagram above is a specimen sign drawn approximately to the scale of one-fourth. The number is to be altered to indicate the actual seating capacity of the vehicle.

Specification

1. The hackney carriage sign is to be approximately semi-circular in shape and of the size shown upon the foregoing diagram and is to be exhibited upon a flat plate or upon a flat surface forming part of the vehicle.

2. The border, letters and figures of the sign must be indelibly inscribed in white, silver or light grey upon a black surface and no letter or figure shall be capable of being detached from such surface. If they are inscribed upon a plate the plate may be of cast or pressed aluminium having raised borders, letters and figures.

3. The width of the surrounding border must be 1/4 inch, the height of all letters 1

inch, and the width of face of letters 3/16 inch; the number must be 2(1/4) inches in height of proportional width and 3/8 inch width of face.

4. A number indicating the seating capacity of the vehicle is to be placed in the central position occupied by the figure "4" in the diagram.   **[1093]**

NOTES
    Commencement: 1 April 1971.

"ZEBRA" PEDESTRIAN CROSSINGS REGULATIONS 1971
(SI 1971 No 1524)

NOTES
    Made: 14 September 1971
    Authority: Road Traffic Regulation Act 1984, ss 25, 64

ARRANGEMENT OF REGULATIONS

PART I
GENERAL

PART II
MARKS, SIGNS AND OTHER PARTICULARS AS RESPECTS ZEBRA CROSSINGS

PART III
REGULATIONS GOVERNING USE OF ZEBRA CROSSINGS AND ZEBRA CONTROLLED AREAS

Prohibition against overtaking at zebra crossings

Prohibition on stopping in areas adjacent to zebra crossings

SCHEDULES

PART I

GENERAL

1. Commencement and citation

These Regulations shall come into operation on 29th September 1971 and may be cited as the "Zebra" Pedestrian Crossings Regulations 1971. **[1094]**

NOTES
Commencement: 29 September 1971.

2. Revocation and savings

(1) Subject to the provisions of the next two paragraphs, the Pedestrian Crossings Regulations 1954 and the Regulations amending those Regulations specified in Schedule 1 are hereby revoked and the said Regulations of 1954 as so amended are hereinafter referred to as "the Regulations of 1954".

(2) Where immediately before the coming into operation of these Regulations a crossing within the meaning of the Regulations of 1954 other than a zebra crossing has been indicated in accordance with Part I of Schedule 1 to the Regulations of 1954, then notwithstanding the revocation effected by the last paragraph the Regulations of 1954 shall continue to apply to that crossing until the 30th November 1973.

(3) Where immediately before the coming into operation of these Regulations, the approach for vehicular traffic to a zebra crossing has been indicated by a pattern of studs on a road in accordance with the provisions of paragraph 8 of Part II of Schedule 1 to the Regulations of 1954, then notwithstanding the revocation effected by paragraph (1) of this Regulation or any variation of a speed limit on that road that approach may until the 30th November 1973 continue to be so indicated so long as the said pattern of studs does not lie within a zebra controlled area or in the vicinity of such an area on the same side of the crossing as that pattern. **[1095]**

NOTES
Commencement: 29 September 1971.
Pedestrian Crossings Regulations 1954: SI 1954 No 370

3. Interpretation

(1) In these Regulations, unless the context otherwise requires, the following expressions have the meanings hereby respectively assigned to them:

"the appropriate Secretary of State" means, in relation to a crossing established on a road in England excluding Monmouthshire, the Secretary of State for the Environment, in relation to a crossing established on a road in Scotland, the Secretary of State for Scotland, and, in relation to a crossing established on a road in Wales or Monmouthshire, the Secretary of State for Wales;

"appropriate authority" means, in relation to a crossing on a trunk road, the appropriate Secretary of State, and in relation to any other crossing the local authority in whose scheme submitted and approved under section 21 of the Act of 1967 the crossing is for the time being included;

"carriageway" does not include that part of any road which consists of a street refuge or central reservation, whether within the limits of a crossing or not;

"central reservation" means any provision, not consisting of a street refuge, made in a road for separating one part of the carriageway of that road from another part of that carriageway for the safety or guidance of vehicular traffic using that road;

"crossing" means a crossing for foot passengers established either—

(a) by a local authority in accordance with the provisions for the time being in force of a scheme submitted and approved under section 21 of the Act of 1967, or

(b) in the case of a trunk road, by the appropriate Secretary of State in the discharge of the duty imposed on him by section 22 of the Act of 1967;

but does not include a "Pelican" crossing within the meaning of the "Pelican" Pedestrian Crossings Regulations 1969;

"dual-carriageway road" means a length of road on which a part of the carriageway thereof is separated from another part thereof by a central reservation;

"give-way line" has the meaning assigned to it by paragraph 2 of Schedule 3:

"one-way street" means any road in which the driving of all vehicles otherwise than in one direction is prohibited at all times;

"stud" means a mark or device on the carriageway, whether or not projecting above the surface thereof;

"zebra controlled area" means, in relation to a zebra crossing, the area of the carriageway in the vicinity of the crossing and lying on both sides of the crossing or only one side of the crossing, being an area the presence and limits of which are indicated in accordance with Schedule 3;

"zebra crossing" means a crossing the presence and limits of which are indicated in accordance with the provisions of Schedule 2;

"uncontrolled zebra crossing" means a zebra crossing at which traffic is not for the time being controlled by a police constable in uniform or by a traffic warden.

(2) Any reference in these Regulations to a numbered Regulation or Schedule is a reference to the Regulation or Schedule bearing that number in the Regulations except where otherwise expressly provided.

(3) Any reference in these Regulations to any enactment shall be construed as a reference to that enactment as amended by any subsequent enactment.

(4) The Interpretation Act 1889 shall apply for the interpretation of these Regulations as it applies for the interpretation of an Act of Parliament, and as if for the purposes of section 38 of that Act these Regulations were an Act of Parliament and the Regulations revoked by Regulation 2 were Acts of Parliament thereby repealed.   **[1096]**

NOTES

Commencement: 29 September 1971.

PART II
MARKS, SIGNS AND OTHER PARTICULARS AS RESPECTS ZEBRA CROSSINGS

4. Zebra crossings

(1) The provisions of Part I of Schedule 2 shall have effect for regulating the manner in which the presence and limits of a crossing are to be indicated by marks or studs on the carriageway for the purpose of constituting it a zebra crossing.

(2) The provisions of Part II of Schedule 2 shall have effect as respects the size, colour and type of the traffic signs which are to be placed at or near a crossing for the purpose of constituting it a zebra crossing.   **[1097]**

NOTES
  Commencement: 29 September 1971.

5. Zebra controlled areas and give-way lines

(1) Subject to paragraph (3) of this Regulation, the provisions of Schedule 3 shall have effect as respects the size, colour and type of the traffic signs which shall be placed in the vicinity of a zebra crossing for the purpose of constituting a zebra controlled area in relation to that crossing and of indicating the presence and limits of that area.

(2) A give-way line (included among the said signs) shall, where provided, also convey to vehicular traffic proceeding towards a zebra crossing the position at or before which a driver of a vehicle should stop it for the purpose of complying with Regulation 8.

(3) Where the appropriate authority is satisfied in relation to a particular area of carriageway in the vicinity of a zebra crossing that, by reason of the layout of, or character of, the roads in the vicinity of the crossing, the application of such a prohibition as is mentioned in Regulation 10 or 12 to that particular area or the constitution of that particular area as a zebra controlled area by the placing of traffic signs in accordance with Schedule 3 would be impracticable, it shall not be necessary for that area to be constituted a zebra controlled area but, if by virtue of this paragraph it is proposed that no area, on either side of the limits of a zebra crossing (not on a trunk road), is to be constituted a zebra controlled area by the 30th November 1973, a notice in writing shall be sent by the appropriate authority before that date to the appropriate Secretary of State stating the reasons why it is proposed that no such area should be so constituted.   **[1098]**

NOTES
  Commencement: 29 September 1971.

6. Variations in dimensions shown in Schedule 3

Any variations in a dimension specified in the diagram in Schedule 3 or otherwise specified in that Schedule shall be treated as permitted by these Regulations if the variation—

   (a) in the case of a dimension of 300 millimetres or more, does not exceed 20% of that dimension; or
   (b) in the case of a dimension of less than 300 millimetres, where the actual dimension exceeds the dimension so specified, does not exceed

30% of the dimension so specified, and where the actual dimension is less than the dimension so specified, does not exceed 10% of the dimension so specified.   **[1099]**

NOTES
Commencement: 29 September 1971.

7. Lamps for illumination of pedestrians at crossings

(1) Where the appropriate authority is satisfied that the presence of a foot passenger—

    (a) at the end of a zebra crossing, being an end at or near which a globe has been placed in accordance with paragraph 2 of Part II of Schedule 2, or

    (b) on a street refuge or central reservation on such a crossing, being a refuge or reservation on which a globe has been placed in accordance with the said paragraph 2,

should be better indicated during the hours of darkness as defined in the Road Transport Lighting Act 1957 the authority may provide a lamp (showing a white light) beneath the globe so as to illuminate during the said hours any such foot passenger.

(2) Every such lamp shall be so arranged that the lowest part thereof is not less than 2 metres above the surface of the ground in the immediate vicinity and that the source of the illumination given thereby is not visible to drivers of approaching vehicles.   **[1100]**

NOTES
Commencement: 29 September 1971.

PART III
REGULATIONS GOVERNING USE OF ZEBRA CROSSINGS AND ZEBRA CONTROLLED AREAS

8. Precedence of pedestrians over vehicles

Every foot passenger on the carriageway within the limits of an uncontrolled zebra crossing shall have precedence within those limits over any vehicle and the driver of the vehicle shall accord such precedence to the foot passenger, if the foot passenger is on the carriageway within those limits before the vehicle or any part thereof has come on to the carriageway within those limits.

For the purpose of this Regulation, in the case of such a crossing on which there is a street refuge or central reservation the parts of the crossing which are situated on each side of the street refuge or central reservation as the case may be shall each be treated as a separate crossing.   **[1101]**

NOTES
Commencement: 29 September 1971.

9. Prohibition against the waiting of vehicles and pedestrians on zebra crossings

(1) The driver of a vehicle shall not cause the vehicle or any part thereof to stop within the limits of a zebra crossing unless either he is prevented from

proceeding by circumstances beyond his control or it is necessary for him to stop in order to avoid an accident.

(2) No foot passenger shall remain on the carriageway within the limits of a zebra crossing longer than is necessary for the purpose of passing over the crossing with reasonable despatch. **[1102]**

NOTES
Commencement: 29 September 1971.

Prohibition against overtaking at zebra crossings

10. The driver of a vehicle while it or any part of it is in a zebra controlled area and it is proceeding towards the limits of an uncontrolled zebra crossing in relation to which that area is indicated (which vehicle is in this and the next succeeding Regulation referred to as "the approaching vehicle") shall not cause the vehicle, or any part of it—

    (a) to pass ahead of the foremost part of another moving motor vehicle, being a vehicle proceeding in the same direction wholly or partly within that area, or

    (b) subject to the next succeeding Regulation, to pass ahead of the foremost part of a stationary vehicle on the same side of the crossing as the approaching vehicle, which stationary vehicle is stopped for the purpose of complying with Regulation 8.

For the purposes of this Regulation—

    (i) the reference to another moving motor vehicle is, in a case where only one other motor vehicle is proceeding in the same direction in a zebra controlled area, a reference to that vehicle, and, in a case where more than one other motor vehicle is so proceeding, a reference to such one of those vehicles as is nearest to the limits of the crossing;

    (ii) the reference to a stationary vehicle is, in a case where only one other vehicle is stopped for the purpose of complying with Regulation 8, a reference to that vehicle and, in a case where more than one other vehicle is stopped for the purpose of complying with that Regulation, a reference to such one of those vehicles as is nearest to the limits of the crossing. **[1103]**

NOTES
Commencement: 29 September 1971.

11. (1) For the purpose of this Regulation, in the case of an uncontrolled zebra crossing, which is on a road, being a one-way street, and on which there is a street refuge or central reservation, the parts of the crossing which are situated on each side of the street refuge or central reservation as the case may be shall each be treated as a separate crossing.

(2) Nothing in paragraph (b) of the last preceding Regulation shall apply so as to prevent the approaching vehicle from passing ahead of the foremost part of a stationary vehicle within the meaning of that paragraph, if the stationary vehicle is stopped for the purpose of complying with Regulation 8 in relation to

an uncontrolled zebra crossing which by virtue of this Regulation is treated as a separate crossing from the uncontrolled zebra crossing towards the limits of which the approaching vehicle is proceeding.   **[1104]**

NOTES
Commencement: 29 September 1971.

Prohibition on stopping in areas adjacent to zebra crossings

12. (1) For the purposes of this Regulation and the next two following Regulations, the expression "vehicle" shall not include a pedal bicycle not having a sidecar attached thereto, whether additional means of propulsion by mechanical power are attached to the bicycle or not.

(2) Save as provided in Regulations 14 and 15, the driver of a vehicle shall not cause the vehicle or any part thereof to stop in a zebra controlled area.   **[1105]**

NOTES
Commencement: 29 September 1971.

(*Reg 13 is spent as from 30 November 1973.*)

14. A vehicle shall not by Regulation 12 or 13 be prevented from stopping in any length of road on any side thereof—
  (a) if the driver has stopped for the purpose of complying with Regulation 8 or Regulation 10(b);
  (b) if the driver is prevented from proceeding by circumstances beyond his control or it is necessary for him to stop in order to avoid an accident; or
  (c) for so long as may be necessary to enable the vehicle, if it cannot be used for such purpose without stopping in that length of road, to be used for fire brigade, ambulance or police purposes or in connection with any building operation, demolition or excavation, the removal of any obstruction to traffic, the maintenance, improvement or reconstruction of that length of road, or the laying, erection, alteration, repair or cleaning in or near to that length of road of any traffic sign or sewer or of any main, pipe or apparatus for the supply of gas, water or electricity, or of any telegraph or telephone wires, cables posts or supports.   **[1106]**

NOTES
Commencement: 29 September 1971.

15. A vehicle shall not by Regulation 12 be prevented from stopping in a zebra controlled area—
  (a) if the vehicle is stopped for the purpose of making a left or right turn;
  (b) if the vehicle is a public service vehicle, being a stage carriage or an express carriage being used otherwise than on an excursion or tour within the meaning of section 159(1) of the Transport Act 1968, and the vehicle is waiting, after having proceeded past the zebra crossing in relation to which the zebra controlled area is indicated, for the purpose of enabling persons to board or alight from the vehicle.   **[1107]**

NOTES
Commencement: 29 September 1971.

SCHEDULES
SCHEDULE 1
Regulation 2(1)

REGULATIONS REVOKED

. . .

[1107A]

SCHEDULE 2
Regulation 4

MANNER OF INDICATING PRESENCE AND LIMITS OF ZEBRA CROSSINGS

PART I

STUDS AND MARKS

1.—(1) Every crossing and its limits shall be indicated by two lines of studs placed across the carriageway in accordance with the following provisions of this paragraph.

(2) Each line formed by the outside edges of the studs shall be so separated from the other line so formed that no point on one line shall be less than 2.4 metres nor more than 5 metres or such greater distance (not being more than 10.1 metres) as the appropriate Secretary of State may authorise in writing in the case of any particular crossing from the nearest point on the other line:

Provided that the preceding provisions of this sub-paragraph shall be regarded as having been complied with in the case of any crossing which for the most part complies with those provisions notwithstanding that those provisions may not be so complied with as respects the distance from one or more points on one line to the nearest point on the other line, so long as the general indication of the lines is not thereby materially impaired.

(3) The studs of which each line is constituted shall be so placed that the distance from the centre of any one stud to the centre of the next stud in the line is not less than 250 millimetres nor more than 715 millimetres, and a distance of not more than 1.3 metres is left between the edge of the carriageway at either end of the line and the centre of the stud nearest thereto:

Provided that the preceding provisions of this sub-paragraph shall be regarded as having been complied with in the case of any line where most of the studs constituting it comply with those provisions notwithstanding that those provisions may not be complied with as respects one or more such studs, so long as the general indication of the line is not thereby materially impaired.

(4) Studs shall not be fitted with reflecting lenses and shall be—
    (a) white, silver or light grey in colour;
    (b) square or circular in plan, the sides of a square stud not being less than 95 millimetres nor more than 110 millimetres in length and the diameters of a circular stud not being less than 95 millimetres nor more than 110 millimetres, and
    (c) so fixed that they do not project more than 16 millimetres above the carriageway at their highest points nor more than 7 millimetres at their edges.

2. A crossing or its limits shall not be deemed to have ceased to be indicated in accordance with the preceding provisions of this Part of this Schedule by reason only of the discolouration or temporary removal or displacement of one or more studs in any line so long as the general indication of the line is not thereby materially impaired.

3. Without derogation from the provisions of the preceding paragraphs of this Part of this Schedule, every crossing shall be further indicated in accordance with the following provisions of this Part and of Part II of this Schedule.

4.—(1) The carriageway shall be marked within the limits of every such crossing with a pattern of alternate black and white stripes:

Provided that where the colour of the surface of the carriageway provides a reasonable contrast with the colour of white that surface may itself be utilised for providing stripes which would otherwise be required to be black.

(2)　Every stripe shall—

- (a)　extend along the carriageway from one line formed by the inside edges of the studs or from a part of the crossing which is not more than 155 millimetres from that line to the other line so formed or to a part of the crossing which is not more than 155 millimetres from that line; and
- (b)　be of width of not less than 500 millimetres or of such smaller width not being less than 380 millimetres as in the case of any particular crossing the appropriate authority may consider necessary having regard to the layout of the carriageway and, in the case of the first stripe at each end of the crossing, not more than 1.3 metres, or in the case of any other stripe, not more than 715 millimetres or of such great width not being more than 840 millimetres as in the case of any particular crossing the appropriate authority may consider necessary having regard to the layout of the carriageway.

(3)　The preceding provisions of this paragraph shall be regarded as having been complied with in the case of any crossing which for the most part complies with those provisions notwithstanding that those provisions may not be complied with as respects one or more stripes and a crossing shall not be deemed to have ceased to be indicated in accordance with those provisions by reason only of the imperfection, discolouration or partial displacement of one or more of the stripes so long as the general appearance of the pattern of stripes is not materially impaired.　　　　　　　　**[1108]**

NOTES

Commencement: 29 September 1971.

PART II

TRAFFIC SIGNS

1.　The traffic signs which are to be placed at or near a crossing for the purpose of constituting it and indicating it as a zebra crossing shall consist of globes in relation to which the following provisions in this Part of this Schedule are complied with.

2.—(1)　At or near each end of every crossing there shall be placed, and in the case of a crossing on which there is a street refuge or central reservation there may be placed on the refuge or reservation, in accordance with the following provisions of this paragraph globes mounted on posts or brackets.

(2)　Globes shall be—

- (a)　yellow in colour;
- (b)　not less than 275 millimetres nor more than 335 millimetres in diameter; and
- (c)　so mounted that the height of the lowest part of the globe is not less than 2.1 metres nor more than 3.1 metres above the surface of the ground in the immediate vicinity.

(3)　Globes shall be illuminated by a flashing light, or where the appropriate Secretary of State so authorises in writing in the case of any particular crossing, by a constant light.

(4)　Where globes are mounted on or attached to posts specially provided for the purpose, every such post shall, in so far as it extends above ground level, be coloured black and white in alternate horizontal bands, the lowest band visible to approaching traffic being coloured black and not less than 275 millimetres nor more than 1 metre in width and each other band being not less than 275 millimetres nor more than 335 millimetres in width:

Provided that nothing in this sub-paragraph shall apply to any container fixed on any such post which encloses the apparatus for providing the illumination of a globe.

3.　A crossing shall not be deemed to have ceased to be indicated in accordance with the preceding provisions of this Part of this Schedule by reason only of—

- (a)　the imperfection, discolouration or disfigurement of any of the globes, posts or brackets; or
- (b)　the failure of the illumination of any of the globes:

Provided that this sub-paragraph shall not apply unless at least one globe is illuminated in accordance with the provisions of sub-paragraph (3) of the last preceding paragraph.

[4. Subject to paragraphs 5 and 6, a globe may be fitted with—

(a) a backing board designed to improve the conspicuity of the globe;
(b) a shield designed to prevent or reduce light from the globe shining into adjacent properties; or
(c) such a board and shield.

5. If a backing board or shield is fitted to a globe it shall—

(a) be firmly secured;
(b) not prevent any driver of a vehicle proceeding through the zebra crossing in question from seeing the globe; and
(c) not constitute a danger to any user of the road.

6. Any backing board shall be coloured black and may have a white border.] **[1109]**

NOTES

Commencement: 29 September 1971.
Paragraphs 4 to 6 were added by SI 1990 No 1828.

SCHEDULE 3

Regulation 5

MANNER OF INDICATING ZEBRA CONTROLLED AREA AND PROVISION AS TO PLACING OF GIVE-WAY LINE

PART I

TRAFFIC SIGNS

1. Subject to the provisions of Regulation 5(3), the traffic signs which are to be placed on a road in the vicinity of a zebra crossing for the purpose of constituting a zebra controlled area lying on both sides of the limits of the crossing or on only one side of such limits and indicating the presence and limits of the crossing or on only one side of such limits and indicating the presence and limits of such an area shall consist of a pattern of lines of the size and type shown in the diagram in Part II of this Schedule and so placed as hereinafter provided.

2. A pattern of lines shall, subject as hereinafter provided, consist of:—

(a) a transverse white broken line (hereinafter referred to as a "give-way line") placed in the carriageway 1 metre from and parallel to the nearer line of studs indicating the limits of the crossing and shall extend across the carriageway in the manner indicated in the said diagram; and
(b) two or more longitudinal white broken lines (hereinafter referred to as "zig-zag lines") placed on the carriageway or, where the road is a dual-carriageway road, on each part of the carriageway, each zig-zag line containing not less than 8 nor more than 18 marks and extending away from the crossing at a point 150 millimetres from the nearest part of the give-way line on the same side of the crossing to a point 150 millimetres from the nearest part of a terminal line of the size and type shown in the said diagram (hereinafter referred to as a "terminal line").

3. Where the appropriate authority is satisfied in relation to a particular area of carriageway in the vicinity of a zebra crossing that by reason of the layout of, or character of, the roads in the vicinity of the crossing it would be impracticable to lay the pattern of lines as shown in the diagram in Part II of this Schedule and in accordance with the preceding paragraph any of the following variations as respects the pattern shall be permitted—

(a) the number of marks contained in each zig-zag line may be reduced from 8 to not less than 2;
(b) a mark contained in a zig-zag line may be varied in length so as to extend for a distance not less than 1 metre and less than 2 metres, but where such a variation

is made as respects a mark each other mark in each zig-zag line shall be of the same or substantially the same length as that mark, so however that the number of marks in each zig-zag line shall not be more than 8 nor less than 2.

4. The angle of the give-way line (if any) in relation to and its distance from the nearer line of studs indicating the limits of a crossing may be varied, if the appropriate authority is satisfied that such variation is necessary having regard to the angle of the crossing in relation to the edge of the carriageway at the place where the crossing is situated.

5. Where by reason of Regulation 5(3) an area of carriageway in the vicinity of a zebra crossing is not constituted a zebra controlled area by the placing of a pattern of lines as provided in the foregoing provisions of this Schedule, a give-way line shall nevertheless be placed on the carriageway as previously provided in this Schedule unless the appropriate authority is satisfied that by reason of the position of that crossing it is impracticable so to place the line.

6. Each mark contained in a give-way line or in a zig-zag line and each terminal line may be illuminated by the use of reflecting material.

7. A zebra controlled area or its limits shall not be deemed to have ceased to be indicated in accordance with the provisions of this Schedule by reason only of the imperfection, discolouration or partial displacement of either a terminal line or one or more of the marks comprised in a give-way line or a zig-zag line, so long as the general indication of any such line is not thereby materially impaired.   **[1110]**

NOTES

Commencement: 29 September 1971.

PART II
DIAGRAM

Pattern of lines on one or both sides of a crossing indicating zebra controlled area.

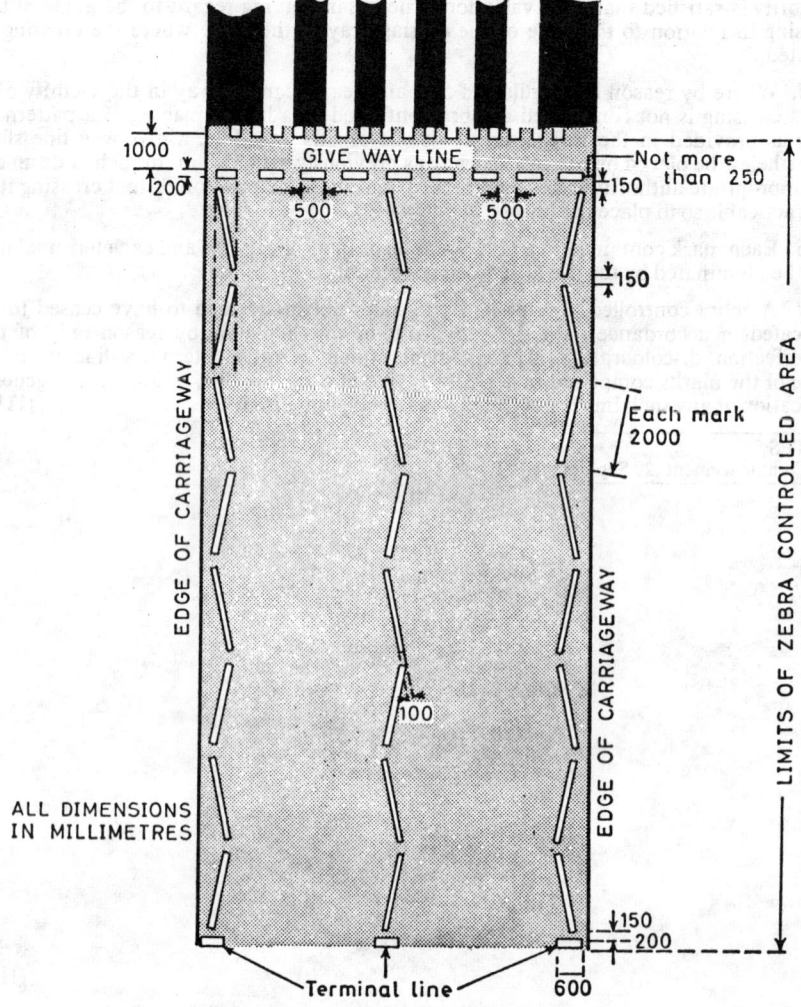

1000

1200

GIVE WAY LINE

500   500

Not more than 250

150

150

Each mark 2000

EDGE OF CARRIAGEWAY

EDGE OF CARRIAGEWAY

LIMITS OF ZEBRA CONTROLLED AREA

100

ALL DIMENSIONS IN MILLIMETRES

150
200

Terminal line   600

Note. Each zig-zag line need not contain the same number of marks

NOTES
Commencement: 29 September 1971.

MOTOR VEHICLES (THIRD PARTY RISKS) REGULATIONS 1972
(SI 1972 No 1217)

NOTES
  Made: 1 August 1972
  Authority: Road Traffic Act 1972, ss 147, 157, 162; Vehicles (Excise) Act 1971, s 37

ARRANGEMENT OF REGULATIONS

COMMENCEMENT AND CITATION

TEMPORARY USE OF EXISTING FORMS

INTERPRETATION

ISSUE OF CERTIFICATES OF INSURANCE OR SECURITY

PRODUCTION OF EVIDENCE AS ALTERNATIVES TO CERTIFICATES

PRODUCTION OF EVIDENCE OR SECURITY ON APPLICATION FOR EXCISE LICENCES

KEEPING OF RECORDS BY COMPANIES

NOTIFICATION TO THE SECRETARY OF STATE OF INEFFECTIVE POLICIES OR SECURITIES

RETURN OF CERTIFICATES TO ISSUING COMPANY

COMMENCEMENT AND CITATION

1. These Regulations shall come into operation on 1st November 1972 and may be cited as the Motor Vehicles (Third Party Risks) Regulations 1972. **[1112]**

NOTES
Commencement: 1 November 1972.

(Reg 2 revokes SI 1961/1465, SI 1969/1733.)

TEMPORARY USE OF EXISTING FORMS

3. Nothing in these Regulations shall affect the validity of any certificate which has been issued before these Regulations came into force in a form prescribed by the Motor Vehicles (Third Party Risks) Regulations 1961, as amended by the Motor Vehicles (Third Party Risks) (Amendment) Regulations 1969, as in force immediately before the coming into operation of these Regulations, and any certificate in such a form may continue to be issued until the expiration of three years from the coming into force of these Regulations. **[1113]**

NOTES
Commencement: 1 November 1972.

INTERPRETATION

4. (1) In these Regulations, unless the context otherwise requires, the following expressions have the meanings hereby respectively assigned to them:—

"the Act" means the Road Traffic Act 1972;

"company" means an authorised insurer within the meaning of Part VI of the Act or a body of persons by whom a security may be given in pursuance of the said Part VI;

"motor vehicle" has the meaning assigned to it by sections 190, 192 and 193 of the Act, but excludes any invalid carriage, tramcar or trolley vehicle to which Part VI of the Act does not apply;

"policy" means a policy of insurance in respect of third party risks arising out of the use of motor vehicles which complies with the requirements of Part VI of the Act and includes a covering note;

"security" means a security in respect of third party risks arising out of the use of motor vehicles which complies with the requirements of Part VI of the Act;

"specified body" means—

(a) any of the local authorities referred to in paragraph (a) of section 144(2) of the Act; or

(b) a Passenger Transport Executive established under an order made under section 9 of the Transport Act 1968, or a subsidiary of that Executive, being an Executive or subsidiary to whose vehicles section 144(2)(a) of the Act has been applied; or

(c) the London Transport Executive or a wholly-owned subsidiary of that Executive referred to in paragraph (e) of section 144(2) of the Act.

(2) Any reference in these Regulations to a certificate in Form A, B, C, D, E or F shall be construed as a reference to a certificate in the form so headed and set out in Part 1 of the Schedule to these Regulations which has been duly made and completed subject to and in accordance with the provisions set out in Part 2 of the said Schedule.

(3) Any reference in these Regulations to any enactment shall be construed as a reference to that enactment as amended by any subsequent enactment.

(4) The Interpretation Act 1889 shall apply for the interpretation of these Regulations as it applies for the interpretation of an Act of Parliament, and as if for the purposes of section 38 of that Act these Regulations were an Act of Parliament and the Regulations revoked by Regulation 2 of these Regulations were Acts of Parliament thereby repealed.   **[1114]**

NOTES
Commencement: 1 November 1972.

ISSUE OF CERTIFICATES OF INSURANCE OR SECURITY

5. (1) A company shall issue to every holder of a security or of a policy other than a covering note issued by the company:—

(a) in the case of a policy or security relating to one or more specified vehicles a certificate of insurance in Form A or a certificate of security in Form D in respect of each such vehicle;

(b) in the case of a policy or security relating to vehicles other than specified vehicles such number of certificates in Form B or Form D as may be necessary for the purpose of complying with the requirements of section 162(1) of the Act and of these Regulations as to the production of evidence that a motor vehicle is not being driven in contravention of section 143 of the Act:

Provided that where a security is intended to cover the use of more than ten motor vehicles at one time the company by whom it was issued may, subject to the consent of the Secretary of State, issue one certificate only, and where such consent has been given the holder of the security may issue duplicate copies of such certificate duly authenticated by him up to such number and subject to such conditions as the Secretary of State may determine.

(2) Notwithstanding the foregoing provisions of this Regulation, where as respects third party risks a policy or security relating to a specified vehicle extends also to the driving by the holder of other motor vehicles, not being specified vehicles, the certificate may be in Form A or Form D, as the case may be, containing a statement in either case that the policy or security extends to such driving of other motor vehicles. Where such a certificate is issued by a company they may, and shall in accordance with a demand made to them by the holder, issue to him a further such certificate or a certificate in Form B.

(3) Every policy in the form of a covering note issued by a company shall have printed thereon or on the back thereof a certificate of insurance in Form C.   **[1115]**

NOTES
Commencement: 1 November 1972.

6. Every certificate of insurance or certificate of security shall be issued not later than four days after the date on which the policy or security to which it relates is issued or renewed. **[1116]**

NOTES

Commencement: 1 November 1972.

PRODUCTION OF EVIDENCE AS ALTERNATIVES TO CERTIFICATES

7. The following evidence that a motor vehicle is not or was not being driven in contravention of section 143 of the Act may be produced in pursuance of section 162 of the Act as an alternative to the production of a certificate of insurance or a certificate of security:—

  (1) a duplicate copy of a certificate of security issued in accordance with the proviso to sub-paragraph (b) of paragraph (1) of Regulation 5 of these Regulations;

  (2) in the case of a motor vehicle of which the owner has for the time being deposited with the Accountant-General of the Supreme Court [the sum for the time being specified in section 144(1) of the Road Traffic Act 1988], a certificate in Form E signed by the owner of the motor vehicle or by some person authorised by him in that behalf that such sum is on deposit;

  (3) in the case of a motor vehicle owned by a specified body, a police authority or the Receiver for the metropolitan police district, a certificate in Form F signed by some person authorised in that behalf by such specified body, police authority or Receiver as the case may be that the said motor vehicle is owned by the said specified body, police authority or Receiver;

  [(4) in the case of a vehicle normally based [in the territory other than the United Kingdom and Gibraltar of a member State of Communities or of [Austria, Czechoslovakia, Finland, the German Democratic Republic, Hungary, Norway, Sweden or Switzerland]], a document issued by the insurer of the vehicle which indicates the name of the insurer, the number or other identifying particulars of the insurance policy issued in respect of the vehicle and the period of the insurance cover. In this paragraph the territory of the state in which a vehicle is normally based is—

  (a) the territory of the state in which the vehicle is registered, or
  (b) in cases where no registration is required for the type of vehicle, but the vehicle bears an insurance plate or distinguishing sign analogous to a registration plate, the territory of the state in which the insurance plate or the sign is issued, or
  (c) in cases where neither registration plate nor insurance plate nor distinguishing sign is required for the type of vehicle, the territory of the state in which the keeper of the vehicle is permanently resident.]
[1117]

NOTES

Commencement: 1 November 1972 (paras (1)-(3)); 1 January 1974 (para (4)).

Para 2: amended by the Motor Vehicles (Third Party Risks) (Amendment) Regulations 1992, SI 1992 No 1283, reg 2(a).

Para (4): added by SI 1973 No 1821; amended by SI 1974 No 792 and SI 1974 No 2187.

8. Any certificate issued in accordance with paragraph (2) or (3) of the preceding Regulation shall be destroyed by the owner of the vehicle to which it relates before the motor vehicle is sold or otherwise disposed of. **[1118]**

NOTES
Commencement: 1 November 1972.

PRODUCTION OF EVIDENCE OR SECURITY ON APPLICATION FOR EXCISE LICENCES

9. (1) Any person applying for a vehicle licence under the Vehicles (Excise) Act 1971 shall, except as hereinafter provided and subject to the provisions of Regulation 8 of the Motor Vehicles (International Motor Insurance Card) Regulations 1971, produce to the Secretary of State either:—

(a) a certificate of insurance, certificate of security or duplicate copy of a certificate of security issued in accordance with these Regulations indicating that on the date when the licence comes into operation there will be in force the necessary policy or the necessary security in relation to the user of the motor vehicle by the applicant or by other persons on his order or with his permission and such further evidence as may be necessary to establish that the certificate relates to such user; or

(b) in the case where the motor vehicle is one of more than ten motor vehicles owned by the same person in respect of which a policy or policies of insurance have been obtained by him from the same authorised insurer, a statement duly authenticated by the authorised insurer to the effect that on the date when the licence becomes operative an insurance policy which complies with Part VI of the Act will be in force in relation to the user of the motor vehicle; or

(c) evidence that section 143 of the Act does not apply to the motor vehicle at a time when it is being driven under the owner's control, in accordance with the following provisions—

(i) in the case of a motor vehicle of which the owner has for the time being deposited with the Accountant-General of the Supreme Court [the aim for the time being specified in section 144(1) of the Road Traffic Act 1988], a certificate in Form E signed by the owner of the motor vehicle or by some person authorised by him in that behalf that such sum is on deposit;

(ii) in the case of a motor vehicle owned by a specified body, a police authority or by the Receiver for the metropolitan police district, a certificate in Form F signed by some person authorised in that behalf by such specified body, police authority or Receiver as the case may be that the vehicle in respect of which the application for a licence is made is owned by the said specified body, police authority or Receiver.

(2) A person engaged in the business of letting motor vehicles on hire shall not, when applying for a licence under the Vehicles (Excise) Act 1971, be required to comply with the provisions of paragraph (1) of this Regulation if the motor vehicle in respect of which the licence is applied for is intended to be used solely for the purpose of being let on hire and driven by the person by whom the motor vehicle is hired or by persons under his control. **[1119]**

NOTES
Commencement: 1 November 1972.
Para (1): amended by the Motor Vehicles (Third Party Risks) (Amendment) Regulations 1992, SI 1992 No 1283, reg 2(a).

KEEPING OF RECORDS BY COMPANIES

10. (1) Every company by whom a policy or a security is issued shall keep a record of the following particulars relative thereto and of any certificates issued in connection therewith:—

    (a) the full name and address of the person to whom the policy, security or certificate is issued;

    (b) in the case of a policy relating to one or more specified motor vehicles the registration mark of each such motor vehicle;

    (c) the date on which the policy or security comes into force and the date on which it expires;

    (d) in the case of a policy the conditions subject to which the persons or classes of persons specified in the policy will be indemnified;

    (e) in the case of a security the conditions subject to which the undertaking given by the company under the security will be implemented;

and every such record shall be preserved for one year from the date of expiry of the policy or security.

(2) Every specified body shall keep a record of the motor vehicles owned by them in respect of which a policy or a security has not been obtained, and of any certificates issued by them under these Regulations in respect of such motor vehicles, and of the withdrawal or destruction of any such certificates.

(3) Any person who has deposited and keeps deposited with the Accountant-General of the Supreme Court [the sum for the time being specified in section 144(1) of the Road Traffic Act 1988] shall keep a record of the motor vehicles owned by him and of any certificates issued by him or on his behalf under these Regulations in respect of such motor vehicles and of the withdrawal or destruction of any such certificates.

(4) Any company, specified body or other person by whom records of documents are required by these Regulations to be kept shall without charge furnish to the Secretary of State or to any chief officer of police on request any particulars thereof. **[1120]**

NOTES
Commencement: 1 November 1972.
Para (3): amended by the Motor Vehicles (Third Party Risks) (Amendment) Regulations 1992, SI 1992 No 1283, reg 2(a).

NOTIFICATION TO THE SECRETARY OF STATE OF INEFFECTIVE POLICIES OR SECURITIES

11. Where to the knowledge of a company a policy or security issued by them ceases to be effective without the consent of the person to whom it was issued, otherwise than by effluxion of time or by reason of his death, the company shall forthwith notify the Secretary of State of the date on which the policy or security ceased to be effective:

Provided that such notification need not be made if the certificate relating to the policy or security has been received by the company from the person to whom the certificate was issued on or before the date on which the policy or security ceases to be effective. **[1121]**

NOTES
Commencement: 1 November 1972.

RETURN OF CERTIFICATES TO ISSUING COMPANY

12. (1) The following provisions shall apply in relation to the transfer of a policy or security with the consent of the holder to any other person:—

(a) the holder shall, before the policy or security is transferred, return any relative certificates issued for the purposes of these Regulations to the company by whom they were issued; and

(b) the policy or security shall not be transferred to any other person unless and until the certificates have been so returned or the company are satisfied that the certificates have been lost or destroyed.

(2) In any case where with the consent of the person to whom it was issued a policy or security is suspended or ceases to be effective, otherwise than by effluxion of time, in circumstances in which the provisions of section 147(4) of the Act (relating to the surrender of certificates) do not apply, the holder of the policy or security shall within seven days from the date when it is suspended or ceases to be effective return any relative certificates issued for the purposes of these Regulations to the company by whom they were issued and the company shall not issue a new policy or security to the said holder in respect of the motor vehicle or vehicles to which the said first mentioned policy or security related unless and until the certificates have been returned to the company or the company are satisfied that they have been lost or destroyed.

(3) Where a policy or security is cancelled by mutual consent or by virtue of any provision in the policy or security, any statutory declaration that a certificate has been lost or destroyed made in pursuance of section 147(4) (which requires any such declaration to be made within a period of seven days from the taking effect of the cancellation) shall be delivered forthwith after it has been made to the company by whom the policy was issued or the security given.

(4) The provisions of the last preceding paragraph shall be without prejudice to the provisions of paragraph (c) of subsection (2) of section 149 of the Act as to the effect for the purposes of that subsection of the making of a statutory declaration within the periods therein stated.   **[1122]**

NOTES
Commencement: 1 November 1972.

ISSUE OF FRESH CERTIFICATES

13. Where any company by whom a certificate of insurance or a certificate of security has been issued are satisfied that the certificate has become defaced or has been lost or destroyed they shall, if they are requested to do so by the person to whom the certificate was issued, issue to him a fresh certificate. In the case of a defaced certificate the company shall not issue a fresh certificate unless the defaced certificate is returned to the company.   **[1123]**

NOTES
Commencement: 1 November 1972.

SCHEDULE

PART I
FORMS OF CERTIFICATES

FORM A
Certificate of Motor Insurance

Certificate No...................   Policy No...................(Optional)

1. Registration mark of vehicle.

2. Name of policy holder.

3. Effective date of the commencement of insurance for the purposes of the relevant law.

4. Date of expiry of insurance.

5. Persons or classes of persons entitled to drive.

6. Limitations as to use.

I/We hereby certify that the policy to which this certificate relates satisfies the requirements of the relevant law applicable in Great Britain.

....
Authorised Insurers

Note: For full details of the insurance cover
     reference should be made to the policy.

FORM B
Certificate of Motor Insurance

Certificate No...................   Policy No...................(Optional)

1. Description of vehicles.

2. Name of policy holder.

3. Effective date of the commencement of insurance for the purposes of the relevant law.

4. Date of expiry of insurance.

5. Persons or classes of persons entitled to drive.

6. Limitations as to use.

I/We hereby certify that the policy to which this certificate relates satisfies the requirements of the relevant law applicable in Great Britain.

....
Authorised Insurers

Note: For full details of the insurance cover
     reference should be made to the policy.

FORM C
Certificate of Motor Insurance

I/We hereby certify that this covering note satisfies the requirements of the relevant law applicable in Great Britain.

....
Authorised Insurers

FORM D

Certificate of Security

Certificate No.................   Security No..................(Optional)

1. Name of policy holder.

2. Effective date of the commencement of insurance for the purposes of the relevant law.

3. Date of expiry of security.

4. Conditions to which security is subject.

I/We hereby certify that the security to which this certificate relates satisfies the requirements of the relevant law applicable in Great Britain.

....
                                              Persons giving authority

Note: For full details of the cover
reference should be made to the security.

FORM E

Certificate of Deposit

I/We hereby certify that I am/we are the owner(s) of the vehicle of which the registration mark is .... and that in pursuance of the relevant law applicable in Great Britain I/we have on deposit with the Accountant-General of the Supreme Court [the sum for the time being specified in section 144(1) of the Road Traffic Act 1988].

Signed ....
on behalf of ....

FORM F

Certificate of Ownership

We hereby certify that the vehicle of which the registration mark is .... is owned by ....

Signed ....
on behalf of ....
                                                              [1124]

_____

NOTES
Commencement: 1 November 1972.
Form E: amended by the Motor Vehicles (Third Party Risks) (Amendment) Regulations 1992, SI 1992 No 1283, reg 2(b)(i).

PART 2

PROVISIONS RELATING TO THE FORMS AND COMPLETION OF CERTIFICATES

[1. Every certificate shall be printed and completed in black [on a white background]. This provision shall not prevent the reproduction of a seal or monogram or similar device referred to in paragraph 2 of this Part of this Schedule, or the presence of a background pattern (of whatever form and whether coloured or not) on the face of the form which does not materially affect the legibility of the certificate.

2. No certificate shall contain any advertising matter, either on the face or on the back thereof:

Provided that the name and address of the company by whom the certificate is issued, or a reproduction of the seal of the company or any monogram or similar device of the company, or the name and address of an insurance broker, shall not be deemed to be advertising matter for the purposes of this paragraph if it is printed or stamped at the foot or on the back of such certificate, or if it forms, or forms part of, any such background pattern as is referred to in the foregoing paragraph.]

3. The whole of each form as set out in Part 1 of this Schedule shall in each case appear on the face of the form, the items being in the order so set out and the certification being set out at the end of the form.

4. The particulars to be inserted on the said forms shall so far as possible appear on the face of the form, but where in the case of any of the numbered headings in Forms A, B, or D, this cannot conveniently be done, any part of such particulars may be inserted on the back of the form, provided that their presence on the back is clearly indicated under the relevant heading.

5. The particulars to be inserted on any of the said forms shall not include particulars relating to any exceptions purporting to restrict the insurance under the relevant policy or the operation of the relevant security which are by subsection (1) of section 148 of the Act rendered of no effect as respects the third party liabilities required by sections 145 and 146 of the Act to be covered by a policy or security.

6.—(1) In any case where it is intended that a certificate of insurance, certificate of security or a covering note shall be effective not only in Great Britain, but also in any of the following territories, that is to say Northern Ireland, the Isle of Man, the Island of Guernsey, the Island of Jersey or the Island of Alderney, Forms A, B, C and D may be modified by the addition thereto, where necessary, of a reference to the relevant legal provisions of such of those territories as may be appropriate.

(2) A certificate of insurance or a certificate of security may contain either on the face or on the back of the certificate a statement as to whether or not the policy or security to which it relates satisfies the requirements of the relevant law in any of the territories referred to in this paragraph.

7. Every certificate of insurance or certificate of security shall be duly authenticated by or on behalf of the company by whom it is issued.

8. A certificate in Form F issued by a subsidiary of a Passenger Transport Executive or by a wholly-owned subsidiary of the London Transport Executive shall indicate under the signature that the issuing body is such a subsidiary of an Executive, which shall there be specified. **[1125]**

NOTES
Commencement: 1 November 1972 (paras 3-8); 1 December 1981 (paras 1, 2).
Paras 1, 2: substituted by SI 1981 No 1567; para 1 amended by the Motor Vehicles (Third Party Risks) (Amendment) Regulations 1992, SI 1992 No 1283, reg 2(b)(ii).
The Act: Road Traffic Act 1972.

MOTOR VEHICLES (COMPULSORY INSURANCE) (NO 2) REGULATIONS 1973
(SI 1973 No 2143)

NOTES
Made: 18 December 1973
Authority: European Communities Act 1972, s 2(2)

ARRANGEMENT OF REGULATIONS

1. (1) These Regulations shall come into operation on 1st January 1974 and may be cited as the Motor Vehicles (Compulsory Insurance) (No. 2) Regulations 1973.

   (2) ...   **[1126]**

NOTES
   Commencement: 1 January 1974.
   Implements Dir 72/166/EEC.
   Para (2): revokes SI 1973 No 1820.

2. (1) In these Regulations "vehicle" means any motor vehicle intended for travel on land and propelled by mechanical power, but not running on rails, and any trailer, whether or not coupled [and references to a relevant foreign state are references to [Austria, Czechoslovakia, Finland, the German Democratic Republic, Hungary, Norway, Sweden or Switzerland]].

   (2) For the purposes of these Regulations the territory in which a vehicle is normally based is—

   (a) the territory of the state [of which the vehicle bears a registration plate] or
   (b) in cases where no registration is required for the type of vehicle, but the vehicle bears an insurance plate or distinguishing sign analogous to a registration plate, the territory of the state in which the insurance plate or the sign is issued, or
   (c) in cases where neither registration plate nor insurance plate nor distinguishing sign is required for the type of vehicle, the territory of the state in which the keeper of the vehicle is permanently resident.

   (3) The Interpretation Act 1889 shall apply for the interpretation of these Regulations as it applies for the interpretation of an Act of Parliament.   **[1127]**

NOTES
   Commencement: 1 January 1974.
   Implements Dir 72/166/EEC.
   Para (1): amended by SI 1974 No 791, further amended by SI 1974 No 2186.
   Para (2): words in square brackets substituted by SI 1987 No 2171, reg 6.

3. 4. (*Revoked by the Road Traffic (Consequential Provisions) Act 1988, s 3, Sch 1, Pt II.*)

5. (1) It shall be an offence for a person to use a specified motor vehicle registered in Great Britain, or any trailer kept by a person permanently resident in Great Britain, whether or not coupled, in the territory other than Great Britain and Gibraltar of any of the member states of the Communities, unless a policy of insurance is in force in relation to the person using that vehicle which insures him in respect of any liability which may be incurred by him in respect of the use of the vehicle in such territory according to the law on compulsory insurance against civil liability in respect of the use of vehicles of the state where the liability may be incurred.

(2) In this Regulation "specified motor vehicle" means a motor vehicle which is exempted from the provisions of section 143 of the Road Traffic Act 1972 (users of motor vehicles to be insured or secured against third-party risks) by virtue of section 144 of that Act.

(3) A person guilty of an offence under this Regulation shall be liable on summary conviction to a fine not exceeding [the statutory maximum] or to imprisonment for a term not exceeding three months, or to both such fine and such imprisonment.

(4) Proceedings for an offence under this Regulation may be taken, and the offence may for all incidental purposes be treated as having been committed in any place in Great Britain.

(5) Sections 180 (time within which summary proceedings for certain offences must be commenced) and 181 (evidence by certificate) of the Road Traffic Act 1972 shall apply for the purposes of an offence under this Regulation as if such an offence were an offence under that Act to which those sections had been applied by column 7 of Part I of Schedule 4 to that Act. **[1128]**

NOTES
Commencement: 1 January 1974.
Implements Dir 72/166/EEC.
Para (3): amended by virtue of the Criminal Justice Act 1988, s 51.

6. (1) Any person appointed by the Secretary of State for the purpose (in this Regulation referred to as an "appointed person") may require a person having custody of any vehicle, being a vehicle which is normally based in the territory of a state [(other than a relevant foreign state)] which is not a member of the Communities or in the non-European territory of a member state or in Gibraltar, when entering Great Britain to produce evidence that any loss or injury which may be caused by such a vehicle is covered throughout the territory in which the treaty establishing the European Economic Community is in force, in accordance with the requirements of the laws of the various member states on compulsory insurance against civil liability in respect of the use of vehicles.

(2) An appointed person may, if no such evidence is produced or if he is not satisfied by such evidence, prohibit the use of the vehicle in Great Britain.

(3) Where an appointed person prohibits the use of a vehicle under this Regulation, he may also direct the driver to remove the vehicle to such place and subject to such conditions as are specified in the direction; and the prohibition shall not apply to the removal of the vehicle in accordance with the direction.

(4) Any person who—

    (a) uses a vehicle or causes or permits a vehicle to be used in contravention of a prohibition imposed under paragraph (2) of this Regulation, or
    (b) refuses, neglects or otherwise fails to comply in a reasonable time with a direction given under paragraph (3) of this Regulation,

shall be guilty of an offence and shall be liable on summary conviction to a fine not exceeding £50.

(5) Section 181 of the Road Traffic Act 1972 shall apply for the purposes of an offence under this Regulation as if such an offence were an offence under that Act to which that section had been applied by column 7 of Part 1 of Schedule 4 to that Act.

(6) A prohibition under paragraph (2) of this Regulation may be removed by an appointed person if he is satisfied that appropriate action has been taken to remove or remedy the circumstances in consequence of which the prohibition was imposed. [1129]

NOTES
Commencement: 1 January 1974.
Implements Dir 72/166/EEC.
Para (1): amended by SI 1974 No 791.

7. (1) Where a constable in uniform has reasonable cause to suspect the driver of a vehicle of having committed an offence under the preceding Regulation, the constable may detain the vehicle, and for that purpose may give a direction, specifying an appropriate person and directing the vehicle to be removed by that person to such place and subject to such conditions as are specified in the direction; and the prohibition shall not apply to the removal of the vehicle in accordance with that direction.

(2) Where under paragraph (1) of this Regulation a constable—
   (a) detains a motor vehicle drawing a trailer, or
   (b) detains a trailer drawn by a motor vehicle,
then, for the purpose of securing the removal of the trailer, he may also (in a case falling within sub-paragraph (a) above) detain the trailer or (in a case falling within sub-paragraph (b) above) detain the motor vehicle; and a direction under paragraph (1) of this Regulation may require both the motor vehicle and the trailer to be removed to the place specified in the direction.

(3) A vehicle which, in accordance with a direction given under paragraph (1) of this Regulation, is removed to a place specified in the direction shall be detained in that place, or in any other place to which it is removed in accordance with a further direction given under that paragraph, until a constable (or, if that place is in the occupation of the Secretary of State, the Secretary of State) authorises the vehicle to be released on being satisfied—
   (a) that the prohibition (if any) imposed in respect of the vehicle under the preceding Regulation has been removed, or that no such prohibition was imposed, or
   (b) that appropriate arrangements have been made for removing or remedying the circumstances in consequence of which any such prohibition was imposed, or
   (c) that the vehicle will be taken forthwith to a place from which it will be taken out of Great Britain to a place not in the European territory other than Gibraltar of a member state of the Communities [and not in the territory of a relevant foreign state].

(4) Any person who—
   (a) drives a vehicle in accordance with a direction given under this Regulation, or
   (b) is in charge of a place at which a vehicle is detained under this Regulation,

shall not be liable for any damage to, or loss in respect of, the vehicle or its load unless it is shown that he did not take reasonable care of the vehicle while driving it or, as the case may be, did not, while the vehicle was detained in that place, take reasonable care of the vehicle or (if the vehicle was detained there with its load) did not take reasonable care of its load.

(5) In this Regulation "appropriate person"—

    (a) in relation to a direction to remove a motor vehicle, other than a motor vehicle drawing a trailer, means a person licensed to drive vehicles of the class to which the vehicle belongs, and

    (b) in relation to a direction to remove a trailer, or to remove a motor vehicle drawing a trailer, means a person licensed to drive vehicles of a class which, when the direction is complied with, will include the motor vehicle drawing the trailer in accordance with that direction.

[1130]

NOTES
    Commencement: 1 January 1974.
    Implements Dir 72/166/EEC.
    Amended by SI 1974 No 791.

8. Nothing in section 145(2) (policies to be issued by authorised insurers) and section 147(1) (policies to be of no effect unless certificates issued) of the Road Traffic Act 1972 shall apply in the case of an insurance policy which is issued elsewhere than in the United Kingdom in respect of a vehicle normally based [in the territory other than the United Kingdom and Gibraltar of a member state of the Communities or of a relevant foreign state]. **[1131]**

NOTES
    Commencement: 1 January 1974.
    Implements Dir 72/166/EEC.
    Amended by SI 1974 No 791.

MOTOR VEHICLES (INTERNATIONAL CIRCULATION) ORDER 1975
(SI 1975 No 1208)

NOTES
    Made: 23 July 1975
    Authority: Motor Vehicles (International Circulation) Act 1952, s 1(1), (4)

ARRANGEMENT OF ARTICLES

DOCUMENTS FOR DRIVERS AND VEHICLES GOING ABROAD

DOCUMENTS FOR DRIVERS AND VEHICLES GOING ABROAD

1. [(1) Subject to the following provisions of this Article, the Minister of Transport may issue to a person resident in the United Kingdom a driving permit in any of the forms A, B and C in Schedule 1 to this Order for use outside the United Kingdom.

(1A) A permit shall be issued to a person only for vehicles of a class or classes in respect of which that person either—

(a) holds a full licence, or has held and is entitled to obtain such a licence and is authorised to drive by virtue of section 84(4) of the Road Traffic Act 1972 or any corresponding Northern Ireland provision (licence applied for or surrendered for correction of particulars, etc.); or

(b) holds a provisional licence, or has held and is entitled to obtain such a licence and is authorised to drive as mentioned in paragraph (a) above, and has passed the test of competence to drive or a test which is a sufficient test;

and in this paragraph 'full licence' means a licence (granted under Part III of the Road Traffic Act 1972 or Part I of the Road Traffic Act (Northern Ireland) 1970) other than a provisional licence, and 'provisional licence' and 'test of competence to drive' have the same meaning as in the said Part III or the said Part I, and 'test of competence which is a sufficient test' has the same meaning as in the said Part III.

(1B) A permit in form A shall not be issued to any person who is under 18 years of age unless the permit is restricted to the driving of motor cycles or invalid carriages, or both.

(1C) A permit in form B shall not be issued to any person who is under 18 years of age.

(1D) A permit in form C shall be limited in its period of validity to three years, or, if shorter—

(a) the unexpired period of the permit holder's current United Kingdom driving licence; or
(b) where the permit holder is authorised to drive by virtue of section 84(4) of the Road Traffic Act 1972 or any corresponding Northern Ireland provision (licence applied for or surrendered for correction of particulars, etc.) the remainder of the period for which he is so authorised together with the period of validity of any licence granted while he is so authorised.]

(2) The Secretary of State may issue for use outside the United Kingdom a document in the form D in Schedule 1 to this Order for any motor vehicle registered under the Vehicles (Excise) Act 1971(c), or in Northern Ireland under the Vehicles (Excise) Act (Northern Ireland) 1972.

(3) The Secretary of State may issue for use outside the United Kingdom with any such motor vehicle or any trailer a document certifying—

(a) the weight of the maximum load which it is to be permitted to carry, and
(b) the permissible maximum weight, that is to say, the weight of the vehicle when ready for the road and carrying the maximum load so specified.

(4) The Secretary of State may assign to any trailer an identification mark to be carried on the trailer outside the United Kingdom.

(5) The Secretary of State may assign to a motor vehicle to which the Decision of 1957 of the Council of the Organisation for European Economic Co-Operation applies, an identification mark in the form of such a trade plate as may be required to be carried on such a vehicle under the provisions of section 1 of the Regulation attached to that Decision.

In this paragraph, "the Decision of 1957 of the Council of the Organisation for European Economic Co-Operation" means the decision of the Council of the Organisation for European Economic Co-Operation concerning the International Circulation of Hired Private Road Motor Vehicles adopted by that Council at its 369th Meeting, in June, 1957.

(6) The Secretary of State may charge a fee for any document issued under this Article or for the assignment of any identification mark under this Article, and the fee shall be of the amount specified in relation thereto in Schedule 2 to this Order.

(7) The Secretary of State may for the purpose of his functions under this Article carry out examinations of vehicles.

(8) The Secretary of State may delegate any of his functions under this Article (including any power of charging fees and the carrying out of *tests or examinations*) to any body concerned with motor vehicles or to any Northern Ireland department.

[(9) Sections 173 of the Road Traffic Act 1988 (forgery of documents, etc., false statements and withholding material information) and Article 174 of the Road Traffic (Northern Ireland) Order 1981 (false statements in connection with forgery of, and fraudulent use of, documents, etc.) shall apply to a Convention driving permit as they apply to licences under that Act or under that Order.

(10) Section 13 of the Road Traffic Offenders Act 1988 and Article 190 of the said Order of 1981 (admissibility of records as evidence) shall apply to records maintained by the Secretary of State in connection with his functions under this Article, or by a body or Northern Ireland department to which in accordance with paragraph (8) of this Article he has delegated the function in connection with which the records are maintained, as that section or that Article apply to records maintained in connection with functions under that Act or under that Order, and the powers conferred by section 13(5) of the said Act of 1988 and Article 190(4) of the said Order of 1981 to prescribe a description of matter which may be admitted as evidence under that section or under that Article shall have effect in relation to the application of that section and that Article by this Article.]   **[1132]**

NOTES
    Commencement: 14 June 1989 (paras (9), (10)); 2 August 1975 (remainder).
    Para (1): (1A)-(1D) in square brackets substituted by SI 1980 No 1095.
    Paras (9), (10): added by SI 1989 No 993, art 3.

VISITORS' DRIVING PERMITS

2. [(1) Subject to the provisions of this Article, it shall be lawful for a person resident outside the United Kingdom who is temporarily in Great Britain and holds—

    (a) a Convention driving permit, or
    (b) a domestic driving permit issued in a country outside the United Kingdom, or
    (c) a British Forces (BFG) driving licence,

during a period of twelve months from the date of his last entry into the United Kingdom to drive, and, except in the case of a holder of a British Forces (BFG) driving licence, for any person to cause or permit such a person to drive, in Great Britain a motor vehicle of any class [other than a large goods vehicle or a passenger-carrying vehicle] which he is authorised by that permit or that licence to drive, notwithstanding that he is not the holder of a driving licence under Part III of the Road Traffic Act 1988.

(2) Subject to the provisions of this Article, it shall be lawful for a person resident outside the United Kingdom who is temporarily in Great Britain and holds—

(a) a Convention driving permit, or

(b) a domestic driving permit issued in a country outside the United Kindgom,

during a period of twelve months from the date of his last entry into the United Kingdom to drive, or for any person to cause or permit such a person to drive, in Great Britain—

(i) in the case of any such person who is resident in a Member State of the European Economic Community, any [large goods vehicle or passenger carrying vehicle]; and

(ii) in the case of any other such person, a [large goods vehicle or passenger carrying vehicle] brought temporarily into Great Britain,

which he is authorised by that permit to drive, notwithstanding that he is not the holder [of a large goods vehicle driver's licence or a passenger-carrying vehicle driver's licence].

(3) Subject to the provisions of this Article, it shall be lawful for a person resident outside the United Kingdom who is temporarily in Great Britain and holds a British Forces (BFG) public service vehicle driving licence during a period of twelve months from the date of his last entry into the United Kingdom to drive, in Great Britain—

(a) in the case of any such person who is resident in a Member State of the European Economic Community, any [passenger-carrying vehi-cle], and

(b) in the case of any other such person, a [passenger-carrying vehicle] brought temporarily into Great Britain,

which he is authorised by that licence to drive, notwithstanding that he is not the holder of [a passenger-carrying vehicle driver's licence].

(4) Nothing in the preceding provisions of this Article shall authorise any person to drive, or any person to cause or permit any person to drive, a vehicle of any class at a time when he is disqualified by virtue of section 101 of the Road Traffic Act 1988 (persons under age) for holding or obtaining a driving licence authorising him to drive vehicles of that class, but in the case of any such person as is mentioned in paragraphs (1), (2) or (3) of this Article, who is driving a vehicle which—

(a) in the case of a person not resident in a Member State of the European Economic Community, is brought temporarily into Great Britain, and
(b) is within the class specified in the first column of paragraph 6 of the Table in subsection (1) of that section, and
(c) is either a vehicle registered in a Convention country or a goods vehicle in respect of which that person holds a certificate of competence which satisfies the international requirements,

the second column of that paragraph, in its application for the purposes of this paragraph, shall have effect as if for '21' there were substituted '18'.

In this paragraph the following expressions have the meanings respectively assigned to them:—

'the international requirements' means—

(i) in relation to a person who is driving a goods vehicle on a journey to which Council Regulation (EEC) No. 3820/85 of 20th December 1985, on the harmonisation of certain social legislation relating to road transport applies, the requirements of Article 5(1)(b) (minimum ages for goods vehicle drivers) of that Regulation;
(ii) in relation to a person who is driving a goods vehicle on a journey to which the European Agreement concerning the work of crews engaged in International Road Transport (AETR) signed at Geneva on 25th March 1971 applies, the requirements of Article 5(1)(b) (conditions to be fulfilled by drivers) of that Agreement;

'Convention country' means a country which is not a Member State of the European Economic Community nor a party to the aforementioned European Agreement nor to [the Convention on Road Traffic concluded at Vienna in the year 1968] the Convention on Road Traffic concluded at Geneva in the year 1949, or the International Convention relative to Motor Traffic concluded at Paris in the year 1926.

(5) This Article shall not authorise a person to drive a motor vehicle of any class if, in consequence of a conviction or of the order of a court, he is disqualified for holding or obtaining a driving licence under Part III of the Road Traffic Act 1988.

(6) The Secretary of State may by order contained in a statutory instrument withdraw the right conferred by paragraph (1)(b), (1)(c), 2(b) or (3) of this Article, or any two or more of those rights either in the case of all domestic driving permits, British Forces (BFG) driving licences or British Forces (BFG) public service vehicle driving licences or in the case of such permits or licences of a description specified in the order or held by persons of a description so specified.

(7) In this Article—

['Convention driving permit' means either—

> (i) a driving permit in the form A in Schedule 1 to this Order issued under the authority of a country outside the United Kingdom, whether or not that country is a party to the Convention on Road Traffic concluded at Geneva in the year 1949 but not so issued as aforesaid after the expiry of a period of five years from the date of the entry into force of the Convention on Road Traffic concluded at Vienna in the year 1968 in accordance with Article 47(1) thereof, if that country is a party to that Convention, or
> (ii) a driving permit in the form B in that Schedule issued under the authority of a country outside the United Kingdom which is a party to the International Convention relative to Motor Traffic concluded at Paris in the year 1926, but not to the Convention of 1949 nor to the Convention of 1968, or
> (iii) a driving permit in the form C in that Schedule issued under the authority of a country outside the United Kingdom which is a party to the Convention of 1968;]

"domestic driving permit" in relation to a country outside the United Kingdom means a document issued under the law of that country and authorising the holder to drive motor vehicles, or a specified class of motor vehicles, in that country, and includes a driving permit issued by the armed forces of any country outside the United Kingdom for use in some other country outside the United Kingdom;

"British Forces (BFG) driving licence" means a driving licence issued in Germany to members of the British Forces or of the civilian component thereof or to the dependants of such members by the British authorities in that country in such a form and in accordance with such licensing system as may from time to time be approved by those authorities; and "British Forces (BFG) public service vehicle driving licence" means any such driving licence authorising the driving of public service vehicles of any class;

"dependants" in relation to such a member of the British Forces or of the civilian component thereof, means any of the following persons, namely—

> (a) the wife or husband of that member; and
> (b) any other person wholly or mainly maintained by him or in his custody, charge or care; and

"public service vehicle" has the same meaning as in the Public Passenger Vehicles Act 1981; and

["large goods vehicle", "passenger-carrying vehicle", "large goods vehicle driver's licence" and "passenger-carrying driver's licence" have the same meaning as in Part IV of the Road Traffic Act 1988].

(8) The provisions of this Article which authorise the holder of a permit or a licence to drive a vehicle during a specified period shall not be construed as authorising the driving of a vehicle at a time when the permit or the licence has ceased to be valid [and, without prejudice to the provisions of paragraph (4) above, a Convention driving permit in the form C in Schedule 1 to this Order shall, if the validity of the permit is by special endorsement thereon made

conditional upon the holder wearing certain devices or upon the vehicle being equipped in a certain manner to take account of his disability, not be valid at a time when any such condition is not satisfied].]   **[1133]**

NOTES
  Commencement: 14 June 1989.
  Substituted by SI 1989 No 993, art 4.
  Paras 1–3: amended by SI 1991 No 771, art 2(a)–(c).
  Para 4: words in square brackets added by SI 1989 No 993, art 6(1).
  Para 7: first words in square brackets substituted by SI 1989 No 993, art 6(2); second words in square brackets added by SI 1991 No 771, art 2(d).
  Para 8: words in square brackets prospectively added by SI 1989 No 993, art 6(3), as from a day to be appointed by notice in the London Gazette.
  Council Regulation (EEC) No. 3820/85: OJ No L370, 31.12.85, p 1.

3. [(1) It shall be lawful—

  (a) for a member of a visiting force of a country to which Part I of the Visiting Forces Act 1952 for the time being applies who holds a driving permit issued under the law of any part of the sending country or issued by the service authorities of the visiting force, or
  (b) for a member of a civilian component of such a visiting force who holds such a driving permit, or
  (c) for a dependant of any such member of a visiting force or of a civilian component thereof who holds such a driving permit,

to drive, or for any person to cause or permit any such person to drive, in Great Britain a motor vehicle of any class [other than a large goods vehicle or a passenger-carrying vehicle] which he is authorised by that permit to drive, notwithstanding that he is not the holder of a driving licence under Part III of the Road Traffic Act 1988.

  (2) This Article shall not authorise a person to drive a motor vehicle of any class if, in consequence of a conviction or of the order of a court, he is disqualified for holding or obtaining a driving licence under Part III of the Road Traffic Act 1988.

  (3) Nothing in this Article shall authorise any person to drive, or any person to cause or permit any other person to drive, a vehicle of any class at a time when he is disqualified by virtue of section 101 of the Road Traffic Act 1988 (persons under age), for holding or obtaining a driving licence authorising him to drive vehicles of that class.

  (4) The interpretative provisions of the Visiting Forces Act 1952 shall apply for the interpretation of this Article and "dependant", in relation to a member of any such visiting force or a civilian component thereof, means any of the following persons namely—

  (a) the wife or husband of that member; and
  (b) any other person wholly or mainly maintained by him or in his custody, charge or care.]   **[1134]**

NOTES
  Commencement: 14 June 1989.
  Substituted by SI 1989 No 993, art 4.
  Para (1): amended by SI 1991 No 771, art 3.

4. Schedule 3 to this Order shall have effect as respects the driving permits referred to in Articles 2 and 3 of this Order. **[1135]**

NOTES
Commencement: 2 August 1975.

EXCISE EXEMPTION AND DOCUMENTS FOR VEHICLES BROUGHT TEMPORARILY INTO
GREAT BRITAIN

5. (1) The next following paragraph shall apply to a vehicle brought temporarily into Great Britain by a person resident outside the United Kingdom if the person bringing that vehicle into Great Britain—

(a) satisfies a registration authority that he is resident outside the United Kingdom and that the vehicle is only temporarily in Great Britain and

(b) complies with any regulations made under paragraph (4) of this Article.

(2) A vehicle to which this paragraph applies shall be exempt from any duty of excise under the Excise Act to the following extent:—

[(a) a vehicle which would, but for this Order, be chargeable with excise duty under section 1 of the Excise Act and Schedule 1, 2 or 5 thereto, and in respect of which relief from customs duty has been afforded by virtue of Parts IV or V of the Customs and Excise Duties (Personal Reliefs for Goods Temporarily Imported) Order 1983, shall be exempted from excise duty for such period as relief from customs duty shall continue to be afforded in respect of that vehicle;]

(b) a vehicle which would, but for this Order, be chargeable with excise duty under section 1 of the Excise Act and Schedule 2 thereto, and which is exempt from customs duty by virtue of the Temporary Importation (Commercial Vehicles and Aircraft) Regulations 1961 shall be exempt from excise duty for such period from the date of importation as that vehicle may remain so exempt from customs duty;

(c) a vehicle [in so far as it is not excluded from the charge of duty under the Excise Act by virtue of Council Regulation (EEC) No 4059/89 of 21st December 1989 and] which, if used for the conveyance of goods or burden, would, but for this Order, be chargeable with excise duty under section 1 of the Excise Act and Schedule 3 or 4 thereto, and which is exempt from customs duty by virtue of the Temporary Importation (Commercial Vehicles and Aircraft) Regulations 1961 shall be exempt from excise duty for such period as that vehicle may remain so exempt from customs duty.

(3) A vehicle registered in the Isle of Man and brought temporarily into Great Britain by a person resident outside the United Kingdom shall be exempt from any duty of excise under the Excise Act for a period not exceeding one year from the date of importation, if the person bringing that vehicle into Great Britain—

(a) satisfies a registration authority that he is resident outside the United Kingdom and that the vehicle is only temporarily in Great Britain, and

(b) complies with any regulations made under paragraph (4) of this Article.

(4) The Secretary of State may by regulations provide—

  (a) for the furnishing to a registration authority by a person who imports a vehicle to which either of the two last preceding paragraphs applies of such particulars as may be prescribed, and

  [(b) for the recording by a registration authority of any particulars which the Secretary of State may by the regulations direct to be recorded, and for the manner of such recording, and for the making of any such particulars available for use by such persons as may be specified in the regulations on payment, in such cases as may be so specified, or such fee as may be prescribed, and]

  (c) for the production to a registration authority of prescribed documents, and

  (d) for the registration of vehicles which by virtue of this Article are exempt from excise duty and for the assignment of registration marks to, and for the issue of registration cards for, such vehicles.

(5) The following provisions of the Excise Act, that is to say:—

  (a) paragraphs (d) and (e) of section 23(1) as substituted by virtue of section 39(1) of, and paragraph 20 of Part I of Schedule 7 to, the Excise Act (which enable the Secretary of State to make regulations as respects registration books for vehicles in respect of which excise licences are issued), and

  (b) paragraph (f) of the said section 23(1) (which enables the Secretary of State to make regulations as to the display on a vehicle of the registration mark assigned to it), and

  (c) section 26(1) (which relates to forgery of licences, registration marks or registration documents),

shall apply in relation to a registration card issued, or a registration mark assigned, in pursuance of this Article as they apply in relation to a registration book or registration document issued, or a registration mark assigned, under the Excise Act.

(6) If regulations under this Article provide for the assignment of a registration mark on production of some document relating to a vehicle which is exempt from excise duty by virtue of this Article, then paragraph (d) of the said section 23(1) shall apply in relation to that document so as to authorise the Secretary of State to make regulations under that section requiring the production of that document for inspection by persons of classes prescribed by regulations made under that section.

(7) Paragraphs (d) and (f) of the said section 23(1), and section 26(1) of the Excise Act shall, in Great Britain, apply in like manner in relation to a registration card issued, or a registration mark assigned, in pursuance of provisions corresponding to paragraph (4) of this Article in Northern Ireland.

(8) In relation to a motor vehicle brought temporarily into Great Britain by a person resident outside the United Kingdom, references in section 19 of the Excise Act and in the said section 23(1) thereof to registration marks shall, where appropriate, include references to nationality signs.

(9) In this Article—

  "the Excise Act" means the Vehicles (Excise) Act 1971;

  "the date of importation", in relation to a vehicle, means the date on which that vehicle was last brought into the United Kingdom;

["registration authority" means the Automobile Association, the Royal Automobile Club, the Royal Scottish Automobile Club, or the Secretary of State;]

and references to registration marks shall, where appropriate, include references to nationality signs. **[1136]**

NOTES
Commencement: 2 August 1975.
Para (2): amended by SI 1985 No 459, art 5, and SI 1991 No 1727, art 3.
Paras (4), (9): amended by SI 1985 No 459, art 5.

EXCISE EXEMPTION AND DOCUMENTS FOR VEHICLES BROUGHT TEMPORARILY INTO
NORTHERN IRELAND

5A. (1) The next following paragraph shall apply to a vehicle brought temporarily into Northern Ireland by a person resident outside the United Kingdom if the person bringing that vehicle into Northern Ireland—

(a) satisfies a registration authority that he is resident outside the United Kingdom and that the vehicle is only temporarily in Northern Ireland, and

(b) complies with any regulations made under paragraph (4) of this Article.

(2) A vehicle to which this paragraph applies shall be exempt from any duty of excise under the Northern Ireland Excise Act to the following extent:—

[(a) a vehicle which would, but for this Order, be chargeable with excise duty under section 1 of the Northern Ireland Excise Act and Schedule 1, 2 or 5 thereto, and in respect of which relief from customs duty has been afforded by virtue of Part IV or V of the Customs and Excise Duties (Personal Reliefs for Goods Temporarily Imported) Order 1983, shall be exempted from excise duty for such period as relief from customs duty shall continue to be afforded in respect of that vehicle;]

(b) a vehicle which would, but for this Order, be chargeable with excise duty under section 1 of the Northern Ireland Excise Act and Schedule 2 thereto, and which is exempt from customs duty by virtue of the Temporary Importation (Commercial Vehicles and Aircraft) Regulations 1961 shall be exempt from excise duty for such period from the date of importation as that vehicle may remain so exempt from customs duty;

(c) a vehicle which, if used for the conveyance of goods or burden, would, but for this Order, be chargeable with excise duty under section 1 of the Northern Ireland Excise Act and Schedule 3 or 4 thereto, and which is exempt from customs duty by virtue of the Temporary Importation (Commercial Vehicles and Aircraft) Regulations 1961 shall be exempt from excise duty for such period as that vehicle may remain so exempt from customs duty.

(3) A vehicle registered in the Isle of Man and brought temporarily into Northern Ireland by a person resident outside the United Kingdom shall be exempt from any duty of excise under the Northern Ireland Excise Act for a period not exceeding one year from the date of importation, if the person bringing that vehicle into Northern Ireland:—

(a) satisfies a registration authority that he is resident outside the United Kingdom and that the vehicle is only temporarily in Northern Ireland, and

(b) complies with any regulations made under paragraph (4) of this Article.

(4) The Secretary of State may by regulations having effect in Northern Ireland provide—

(a) for the furnishing to a registration authority by a person who imports a vehicle to which either of the two last preceding paragraphs applies of such particulars as may be prescribed, and

[(b) for the recording by a registration authority of any particulars which the Secretary of State may by the regulations direct to be recorded, and for the manner of such recording, and for the making of any such particulars available for use by such persons as may be specified in the regulations on payment, in such cases as may be so specified, of such fee as may be prescribed, and]

(c) for the production to a registration authority of prescribed documents, and

(d) for the registration of vehicles which by virtue of this Article are exempt from excise duty and for the assignment of registration marks to, and for the issue of registration cards for, such vehicles.

(5) The following provisions of the Northern Ireland Excise Act, that is to say:—

(a) paragraphs (d) and (e) of section 23(1) as substituted by virtue of section 37(1) of, and paragraph 20 of Part I of Schedule 9 to, the Northern Ireland Excise Act (which enable the Secretary of State to make regulations as respects registration books for vehicles in respect of which excise licences are issued), and

(b) paragraph (f) of the said section 23(1) (which enables the Secretary of State to make regulations as to the display on a vehicle of the registration mark assigned to it), and

(c) section 26(which relates to forgery of licences, registration marks or registration documents),

shall apply in relation to a registration card issued, or a registration mark assigned, in pursuance of this Article as they apply in relation to a registration book or registration document issued, or a registration mark assigned, under the Northern Ireland Excise Act.

(6) If regulations under this Article provide for the assignment of a registration mark on production of some document relating to a vehicle which is exempt from excise duty by virtue of this Article, then paragraph (d) of the said section 23(1) shall apply in relation to that document so as to authorise the Secretary of State to make regulations under that section requiring the production of that document for inspection by persons of classes prescribed by regulations made under that section.

(7) Paragraphs (d) and (f) of the said section 23(1), and section 26 of the Northern Ireland Excise Act shall, in Northern Ireland, apply in like manner in relation to a registration card issued, or a registration mark assigned, in pursuance of provisions corresponding to paragraph (4) of this Article in Great Britain.

(8) In relation to a motor vehicle brought temporarily into Northern Ireland by a person resident outside the United Kingdom, references in section 19 of

the Northern Ireland Excise Act and in the said section 23(1) thereof to
registration marks shall, where appropriate, include references to nationality
signs.

(9) In this Article—

"the Northern Ireland Excise Act" means the Vehicles (Excise) Act
(Northern Ireland) 1972 as that Act has effect subject to the provisions
of Article 2(1) of, and Schedule 1 to, the Northern Ireland (Modification
of Enactments—No. 1) Order 1973;
"the date of importation", in relation to a vehicle, means the date on
which that vehicle was last brought into the United Kingdom;
"registration authority" means the Royal Automobile Club or the
Automobile Association;

and references to registration marks shall, where appropriate, include references
to nationality signs.

(10) Nothing in regulations made or deemed to have been made under this
Article shall apply to any person bringing a motor vehicle into Northern Ireland
from the Republic of Ireland who complies with the provisions of the Motor
Car (Irish Circulation) (Northern Ireland) Regulations 1925.   **[1137]**

NOTES
   Commencement: 2 August 1975.
   Paras (2), (4): amended by SI 1985 No 459, art 5.

6. (1) An application under Part V of the Transport Act 1968 for an operator's
licence for a motor vehicle or trailer brought temporarily into Great Britain by
a person resident outside the United Kingdom shall be made to the licensing
authority for the purpose of the said Part V for the area where the vehicle is
landed.

(2) Regulations made or having effect as if made, under sections 68-82
(provisions as to lighting of vehicles) of the Road Traffic Act 1972, may, either
wholly or partially, and subject to any conditions, vary or grant exemptions
from, the requirements of those sections in the case of motor vehicles or trailers
brought temporarily into Great Britain by persons resident outside the United
Kingdom or in the case of any class of such vehicles.   **[1138]**

NOTES
   Commencement: 2 August 1975.

INTERPRETATION, REPEALS, CITATION AND COMMENCEMENT

7. (1) In this Order—

"the Secretary of State" means the Secretary of State for the Environment;
"prescribed" means prescribed by regulations made by the Secretary of
State.

(2) The Interpretation Act 1889 shall apply for the interpretation of this
Order (except as provided by the next following paragraph of this Article) as it

applies for the interpretation of an Act of Parliament and as if for the purposes of section 38 of that Act this Order (except as aforesaid) was an Act of Parliament and the Orders revoked by Article 8(1) of this Order were Acts of Parliament thereby repealed.

(3) The Interpretation Act (Northern Ireland) 1954 shall apply for the interpretation of Articles 5A and 8(2) of, and Part II of Schedule 4 to, this Order as it applies for the interpretation of a Measure of the Northern Ireland Assembly.

(4) Any reference in this Order to any enactment shall be taken as a reference to that enactment as amended by or under any other enactment; and any reference to an enactment which has effect subject to modifications specified in an enactment shall, when those modifications cease to have effect, then be construed as a reference to the first mentioned enactment as having effect without those modifications.   **[1139]**

NOTES
   Commencement: 2 August 1975.

8. (1) The Orders specified in columns (1) and (2) of Part I of Schedule 4 to this Order are hereby revoked; and notwithstanding the said revocation and without prejudice to the provisions of section 38 of the Interpretation Act 1889 as applied by this Order—

   (a) any permit or document issued, any fee paid or any identification mark assigned under those Orders shall not be invalidated but shall have effect as if issued, paid or assigned under the corresponding provision of this Order;

   (b) any regulations made, or having effect as if made, under these Orders shall have effect as if made under this Order; and

   (c) any period of exemption from excise duty which started to run before this Order comes into operation shall be continued under the corresponding provision of this Order.

(2) The Orders replaced in Northern Ireland by Article 5A of this Order, and specified in columns (1) and (2) of Part II of the said Schedule 4 are hereby revoked; and notwithstanding the said revocation and without prejudice to the provisions of section 28 of the Interpretation Act (Northern Ireland) 1954 as applied by this Order, sub-paragraphs (a) to (c) of the last preceding paragraph shall have effect correspondingly in Northern Ireland.   **[1140]**

NOTES
   Commencement: 2 August 1975.

9. (1) This Order may be cited as the Motor Vehicles (International Circulation) Order 1975.

(2) This Order shall come into operation 10 days after the date on which the Order is made.   **[1141]**

NOTES
   Commencement: 2 August 1975.

SCHEDULES
SCHEDULE 1

Order 1

FORM A FORM OF INTERNATIONAL DRIVING PERMIT UNDER CONVENTION OF 1949

Page 1

United Kingdom of Great Britian and Northern Ireland*

International Motor Traffic

INTERNATIONAL DRIVING PERMIT

Convention on International Road Traffic of 1949.

Issued at ....

Date ....

Signature or seal of issuing authority.

In a permit issued by some other country the name of that country will appear instead and pages 1 and 2 will be drawn up in the language of that country.

Page 2

This permit is valid in the territory of all the Contracting States, with the exception of the territory of the Contracting State where issued, for the period of one year from the date of issue, for the driving of vehicles included in the category or categories mentioned on the last page of this permit.

List of Contracting States (optional)

It is understood that this permit shall in no way affect the obligation of the holder to conform strictly to the laws and regulations relating to residence or to the exercise of a profession which are in force in each country through which he travels.

Form of International Driving Permit under Convention of 1949

PART I	
Particulars concerning the Driver: Surname	1
Other names*	2
Place of birth**	3
Date of birth***	4
Permanent place of residence	5

Vehicles for which the permit is valid:

Motor cycles, with or without a sidecar, invalid carriages and three-wheeled motor vehicles with an unladen weight not exceeding 400 kg (900 lbs).	A

Motor vehicles used for the transport of passengers and comprising, in addition to the driver's seat, at most eight seats, or those used for the transport of goods and having a permissible maximum weight not exceeding 3,500 kg (7,700 lbs.). Vehicles in this category may be coupled with a light trailer.	B

Motor vehicles used for the transport of goods and of which the permissible maximum weight exceeds 3,500 kg (7,700 lbs.). Vehicles in this category may be coupled with a light trailer.	C
Motor vehicles used for the transport of passengers and comprising, in addition to the driver's seat, more than eight seats. Vehicles in this category may be coupled with a light trailer.	D
Motor vehicles of categories B, C or D, as authorised above, with other than a light trailers.	E

"Permissible maximum weight" of a vehicle means the weight of the vehicle and its maximum load when the vehicle is ready for the road.

"Maximum load" means the weight of the load declared permissible by the competent authority of the country of registration of the vehicle.

"Light trailers" shall be those of a permissible maximum weight not exceeding 750 kg (1,650 lbs.).

EXCLUSION

Holder of this permit is deprived of the right to drive in (country) .... by reason ....

Place ....
Date ....
Signature ....

(Seal or stamp of authority)

Exclusions: (countries I-VIII)

Should the above space be already filled, use any other space provided for "Exclusion".

The entire last page (Parts I and II) shall be drawn up in French.

Additional pages shall repeat in other languages the text of Part I of the last page. They shall be drawn up in English, Russian, Chinese and Spanish, and other languages may be added.

PART II

1. ....
2. ....
3. ....
4. ....
5. ....

A   (Seal or stamp of authority)

B   (Seal or stamp of authority)

C   (Seal or stamp of authority)

D   (Seal or stamp of authority)

E   (Seal or stamp of authority)

Photograph

(Seal or stamp of authority)

....
Signature of holder****

EXCLUSIONS
(countries)

I	....	V	....
II	....	VI	....
III	....	VII	....
IV	....	VIII	....

    * Father's or husband's name may be inserted.
   ** If known.
  *** Or approximate age on date of issue.
**** Or thumb impression.

NOTES
    Commencement: 2 August 1975.

FORM B FORM OF INTERNATIONAL DRIVING PERMIT UNDER CONVEN-
TION OF 1926

Page 1

United Kingdom of Great Britian and Northern Ireland*

International Motor Traffic

INTERNATIONAL DRIVING PERMIT

International Convention of April 24th, 1926

ISSUE OF PERMIT

Issued at . . . .

Date . . . .

Seal of
authority

(Signature of issuing authority).

**In a permit issued by some other country the name of that country and its distinguishing
sign and the permit will be drawn up in the language of that country.*

Page 2

The present permit is valid in the territory of all the undermentioned contracting
States for the period of one year from the date of issue for the driving of vehicles included
in the category or categories mentioned on p.   (This should be a reference to the last
page of the permit)

Here insert list of Contracting States

It is understood that this permit in no way diminishes the obligation of the holder to
conform strictly to the laws and regulations relating to residence or to the exercise of a
profession which are in force in each country through which he travels.

Page 3

PARTICULARS CONCERNING THE DRIVER

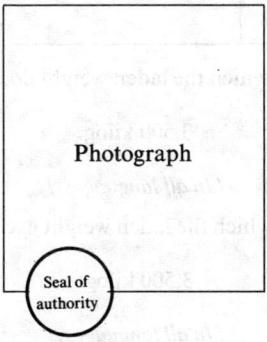

Photograph

Seal of
authority

Surname . . . . (1)
Other names . . . . (2)

Place of birth .... (3)
Date of birth .... (4)
Home address .... (5)

Page 4

(Name of country)

EXCLUSION

M. (surname and other names) ....

authorised as above by the authority of (country) ....

is deprived of the right to drive in (country) ....

by reason of ....

....

....

(Seal of authority)
          Place ....

          Date ....

          Signature ....

Page 5 and the following pages should repeat the particulars given on page 3 translated into as many languages as may be necessary to enable the International Permit to be used in all the Contracting States mentioned on page 2.

Here begin last page

A(1)	B(2)	C(3)
Seal of authority	Seal of authority	Seal of authority

(1) A.—Motor vehicles of which the laden weight does not exceed—

3,500 kilog.

(In all languages.)

(2) B.—Motor vehicles of which the laden weight exceeds—

3,500 kilog.

(In all languages.)

(3) C.—Motor cycles, with or without side-car.

(In all languages.)

(1) . . . .
(2) . . . .
(3) . . . .
(4) . . . .
(5) . . . .   **[1143]**

FORM C FORM OF INTERNATIONAL DRIVING PERMIT UNDER CONVENTION OF 1968

[Page No. 1 *(outside of front cover, coloured grey)*

United Kingdom of Great Britain and Northern Ireland (GB)*

International Motor Traffic

INTERNATIONAL DRIVING PERMIT

No. . . . . . .

Convention on Road Traffic of 8 November, 1968

Valid until . . . .

Issued by . . . .

At . . . .

Date . . . .

Number of domestic driving permit . . . .

Seal
or stamp
of
the issuing
authority
or
association   *Signature of issuing authority or association.*

*In a permit issued by some other country the name of that country and its distinguishing sign will appear instead and pages 1 and 2 will be drawn up in the language of that country.

Page No. 2 *(inside front cover, coloured grey)*

This permit is not valid for the territory of the United Kingdom. It is valid for the territories of all the other Contracting Parties. The categories of vehicles for the driving of which it is valid are stated at the end of the booklet.

List of Contracting States (optional)

This permit shall in no way affect the obligation of the holder to conform to the laws and regulations relating to residence and to the exercise of a profession in each State through which he travels. In particular, it shall cease to be valid in a State if its holder establishes his normal residence there.

Last left-hand page

PARTICULARS CONCERNING THE DRIVER	Surname	1
	Other names[1]	2
	Place of birth[2]	3
	Date of birth[3]	4
	Home address	5

CATEGORIES OF VEHICLES FOR WHICH THE PERMIT IS VALID	
Motor cycles	A
Motor vehicles, other than those in category A, having a permissible maximum weight not exceeding 3,500 kg. (7,700 lb.) and not more than eight seats in addition to the driver's seat	B
Motor vehicles used for the carriage of goods and whose permissible maximum weight exceeds 3,500 kg. (7,700 lb.)	C
Motor vehicles used for the carriage of passengers and having more than eight seats in addition to the driver's seat	D
Combinations of vehicles of which the drawing vehicle is in a category or categories for which the driver is licensed (B and/or C and/or D), but which are not themselves in that category or categories	E

RESTRICTIVE CONDITIONS OF USE[4]

....

....

....

(1) Father's or husband's name may be inserted here.

(2) If the place of birth is unknown, leave blank.

(3) If date of birth is unknown, state approximate age on date of issue of permit.

(4) For example, "Must wear corrective lenses", "Valid only for driving vehicle No. ....", "Vehicle must be equipped to be driven by a one-legged person".

The last two inside pages shall be facing pages printed in French, and the preceding inside pages shall consist of pages repeating the last left-hand page in several other languages which must include English, Russian and Spanish. All inside pages shall be white.

Last right-hand page

1. ....
2. ....
3. ....
4. ....
5. ....

A

$(^5)$

$(^5)$

Photograph

$(^5)$

$(^5)$

$(^5)$

Signature of holder$(^6)$ ....

DISQUALIFICATIONS:

The holder is deprived of the right to drive in the
territory of ....$(^7)$ until ....
    At ....on ....
                       ....$(^8)$ $(^8)$

The holder is deprived of the right to drive in the
territory of ....$(^7)$ until ....
    At ....on ....
                       ....$(^8)$ $(^8)$

    $(^5)$ Seal or stamp of the authority or association issuing the permit. This seal or stamp shall be affixed against categories A, B, C, D and E only if the holder is licensed to drive vehicles in the category in question.

    $(^6)$ Or thumbprint.

    $(^7)$ Name of State.

    $(^8)$ Signature and seal or stamp of the authority which has invalidated the permit in its territory. If the spaces provided for disqualifications on this page have already been used, any further disqualifications should be entered overleaf.]   **[1144]**

NOTES
    Commencement: To be appointed.
    Prospectively added by SI 1980 No 1095, as from a day to be appointed by notice in the London Gazette.

FORM D FORM OF INTERNATIONAL CERTIFICATE FOR MOTOR VEHICLES UNDER CONVENTION OF 1926

Page 1

United Kingdom of Great Britain and Northern Ireland*

International Motor Traffic

INTERNATIONAL CERTIFICATE FOR MOTOR VEHICLES

International Convention of April 24th, 1926

ISSUE OF CERTIFICATE

Place ....
Date ....

Signature of issuing authority.

(Seal of authority)

*In a permit issued by some other country the name of that country will appear instead and the permit will be drawn up in the language of that country.

Page 2

This certificate is valid, in the territory of all the undermentioned contracting States, for the period of one year from the date of issue.

Here insert list of contracting States

Page 3

Owner	Surname	...	1
or	Other names	...	2
Holder	Home address	...	3

Class of vehicle 4
Name of maker of chassis 5
Type of chassis 6
Serial number of type or maker's number of chassis 7

	Number of cylinders	...	8
	Engine number	...	9
Engine	Stroke	...	10
	Bore ...	...	11
	Horse-power...	...	12
	Shape...	...	13
Body	Colour	...	14
	Number of seats	...	15

Weight of car unladen (in kilos)... 16
Weight of car fully laden (in kilos) if exceeding 3,500 kilos 17
Identification mark on the plates 18

Additional pages should repeat the particulars on page 3 translated into as many languages as may be necessary to enable the certificate to be used in all the contracting States mentioned on page 2 and these should be followed by pages for entrance and exit visas.   **[1145]**

NOTES
Commencement: 2 August 1975.

SCHEDULE 2

Order 1(6)

FEES CHARGEABLE FOR DOCUMENTS AND IDENTIFICATION MARKS

The fee for the issue of the following documents shall be as follows:—

Driving permit in Form A or B	£[3]
Certificate in Form D	£[3]
Certificate of maximum load and maximum permissible weight ...	53 new pence
Assignment of identification mark	53 new pence.

[1146]

NOTES
Commencement: 1 August 1980.
Added by SI 1980 No 1095.
Sums in square brackets substituted by SI 1985 No 459, art 6; further *or* substituted by SI 1989 No 993, art 5, as from 1 September 1989.

SCHEDULE 3

Order 4

VISITORS' DRIVING PERMITS

1. In this Schedule "driving permit" means a driving permit which by virtue of this Order authorises a person to drive a motor vehicle without holding a driving licence under Part III of the Road Traffic Act 1972 ['Convention driving permit' has the meaning assigned to it by article 2(7) of this Order]

2.—(1) A court by whom the holder of a driving permit is convicted shall—

   (a) if in consequence of the conviction or of the order of the court he is disqualified for holding or obtaining a driving licence, or

   (b) if the court orders particulars of the conviction to be endorsed on any driving licence held by him,

send particulars of the conviction to the Secretary of State.

   (2) A court shall in no circumstances enter any particulars in a driving permit.

3.—(1) The holder of a driving permit disqualified in consequence of a conviction or of the order of a court for holding or obtaining a driving licence shall, if so required by the court, produce his driving permit within five days, or such longer time as the court may determine, and the court shall forward it to the Secretary of State.

   [(2) The Secretary of State on receiving a permit forwarded under the foregoing sub-paragraph, shall—

   (a) retain the permit until the disqualification ceases to have effect or until the holder leaves Great Britain, whichever is the earlier;

   (b) send the holder's name and address, together with the particulars of the disqualification, to the authority by whom the permit was issued; and

   (c) if the permit is a Convention driving permit, record the particulars of the disqualification on the permit.]

   (3) A person failing to produce a driving permit in compliance with this paragraph shall be guilty of an offence which shall be treated for the purposes of section 177 of the Road Traffic Act 1972 and of Part I of Schedule 4 thereto as an offence against the provision specified in column 1 of that Part as section 101(4) and he shall be liable to be prosecuted and punished accordingly.

4.—(1) A court, on ordering the removal under section 95(1) of the said Act of a disqualification for holding or obtaining a driving licence, shall, if it appears that particulars of the disqualification have been forwarded to the Secretary of State under paragraph 2 of this Schedule, cause particulars of the order also to be forwarded to him.

[(2) The Minister of Transport, on receiving particulars of a court order removing such a disqualification, shall—

(a) in the case of a permit on which particulars of a disqualification were entered in accordance with paragraph 3(2)(c) of this Schedule, enter on the permit particulars of the order removing the disqualification;

(b) send the particulars of the order to the authority by whom the permit was issued; and

(c) return the permit to the holder.]

[(2) The Secretary of State, on receiving particulars of a court order removing such a disqualification, shall—

(a) in the case of a permit on which particulars of a disqualification were recorded in accordance with paragraph 3(2)(c) of this Schedule, enter on the permit particulars of the order removing the disqualification;

(b) send the particulars of the order to the authority by whom the permit was issued; and

(c) return the permit to the holder.]

5.—(1) In the following provisions of the Road Traffic Act 1972, references to a driving licence shall include references to a driving permit.

(2) The said provisions are—

(a) subsections (1) and (4) of section 161 (which, as amended by paragraph 19 of Schedule 6 to the Road Traffic Act 1974, authorises a police constable to require the production of a driving licence and in certain cases statement of date of birth by a person who is, or in certain circumstances has been, driving a vehicle),

(b) subsection (2) of section 164 (which authorises a police constable to arrest a driver committing certain offences unless the driver gives his name and address or produces his driving licence), and

(c) subsections (1) and (2) of section 169 (which relate to the use of a driving licence by a person other than the holder and to forgery of such a licence).

[1147]

NOTES
    Commencement: 2 August 1975.
    Words in italics originally substituted by SI 1980 No 1095, further prospectively revoked and subsequent words in square brackets prospectively substituted by SI 1989 No 993, art 2(3), as from a day to be appointed by notice in the London Gazette.

MOTOR VEHICLES (AUTHORISATION OF SPECIAL TYPES) GENERAL ORDER 1979
(SI 1979 No 1198)

NOTES
    Made: 13 September 1979
    Authority: Road Traffic Act 1988, s 44

ARRANGEMENT OF ARTICLES

PART I

PRELIMINARY

PART I
PRELIMINARY

1. Commencement and citation

This Order shall come into operation on 1st November 1979 and may be cited as the Motor Vehicles (Authorisation of Special Types) General Order 1979.

[1148]

NOTES
Commencement: 1 November 1979.

3. Interpretation

(1) In this Order, unless the context otherwise requires, the following expressions have the following meanings—

"abnormal indivisible load" means a load—
  (a) which cannot without undue expense or risk of damage be divided into two or more loads for the purpose of carriage on roads, and
  (b) which—
    (i) owing to its dimensions, cannot be carried by a heavy motor car or trailer or a combination of a heavy motor car and trailer complying in all respects with the requirements of the Construction and Use Regulations, or
    [(ii) owing to its weight, cannot be carried by a heavy motor car or trailer or a combination of a heavy motor car and trailer having a total laden weight of not more than—
      (A) prior to 1st October 1989, 32,520 kilograms, and
      (B) on or after 1st October 1989, 38,000 kilograms,
and complying in all respect with the requirements of Construction and Use Regulations;]
  ["agricultural motor vehicle", "agricultural trailer" and "agricultural trailed appliance" have the meanings respectively given to those expressions in Regulation 3(1) of the Construction and Use Regulations;]
  "articulated vehicle", ... "locomotive", "overall length", "overall width", "overhang", "registered", "straddle carrier", "track laying", and "wheeled" have the same meanings respectively as in the Construction and Use Regulations;
  "bank holiday" means a day which is a bank holiday under the Banking and Financial Dealings Act 1971;
  "chief officer of police" and "police area", in relation to England and Wales, have respectively the same meanings as in the Police Act 1964, and, in relation to Scotland, have respectively the same meanings as in the Police (Scotland) Act 1967 as amended by the Local Government (Scotland) Act 1973;
  "controlled by a pedestrian" has the same meaning as in section 193(2) of the Road Traffic Act 1972;
  "Construction and Use Regulations" means the Motor Vehicles (Construction and Use) Regulations 1978;
  "day" means any day except a bank holiday, Christmas Day, Good Friday, Sunday or Saturday;
  ["dual carriageway road" has the same meaning as in Schedule 6 to the Road Traffic Regulations Act 1984;]
  "engineering plant" means—

(a) moveable plant or equipment which consists of a motor vehicle or trailer specially designed and constructed for the special purposes of engineering operations, and which cannot, owing to the requirements of those purposes, comply in all respects with the requirements of the Construction and Use Regulations or the Track Laying Regulations and which is not constructed primarily to carry a load other than excavated material raised from the ground by apparatus on the motor vehicle or trailer or materials which the vehicle or trailer is specially designed to treat while carried thereon, or

(b) a mobile crane which does not comply in all respects with the requirements of the Construction and Use Regulations or the Track Laying Regulations;

["hours of darkness" means the time between half an hour after sunset and half an hour before sunrise;]

"lateral projection", "forward projection" and "rearward projection" have the same meanings respectively as in Regulation 139 of the Construction and Use Regulations and references in this Order to a special appliance or apparatus in relation to a vehicle, to a forward projection or a rearward projection in relation to a vehicle, to the distance between vehicles in relation to vehicles carrying a load, and to a combination of vehicles in relation to a motor vehicle which is drawing one or more trailers, shall be construed respectively in the same manner as is provided in the said Regulation 139 for the purposes of Regulation 140 of the said Regulations, and the provisions of sub-paragraph (b), (e), (h), (i) and (j) of the said Regulation 139 shall apply for the purposes of this Order as they apply for the purposes of the said Regulations 139 and 140;

["motorway" has the same meaning as in regulation 3(1) of the Motorways Traffic (England and Wales) Regulations 1982, as regards England and Wales, and regulation 2(2) of the Motorways Traffic (Scotland) Regulations 1964, as regards Scotland;]

"the Minister" means the Minister of Transport;

"Track Laying Regulations" means the Motor Vehicles (Construction and Use) (Track Laying Vehicles) Regulations 1955; and

"tractor" means a motor tractor.

(2) Any reference in this Order to a numbered Article or Schedule is a reference to the Article or Schedule bearing that number in this Order except where otherwise expressly provided. **[1149]**

NOTES
   Commencement: 1 November 1979.
   Para (1): in definition "abnormal indivisible load" words in square brackets substituted by SI 1987 No 2161, art 3; definitions "agricultural motor vehicle", "agricultural trailer", "agricultural trailed appliance" and "hours of darkness" added and words omitted revoked by SI 1984 No 1810, art 3; definition "dual carriageway road" added and definition "motorway" substituted by SI 1987 No 1327, art 3.

4. Speed limits

Nothing in this Order relating to the speed of vehicles shall be taken to authorise any speed which is in excess of any other speed limit imposed by or under any enactment. **[1150]**

NOTES
   Commencement: 1 November 1979.

PART II
MISCELLANEOUS VEHICLES

5. Track laying vehicles (including those used for launching lifeboats)

The Minister authorises the use on roads of track laying motor vehicles and track laying trailers notwithstanding that such vehicles do not comply in all respects with the requirements of the Construction and Use Regulations or the Track Laying Regulations subject to the following conditions:—

(1) (a) the vehicle shall be used only for the purpose of

     (i) demonstration, or

     (ii) enabling it to proceed to the nearest suitable railway station for conveyance to a port for shipment or to proceed to a port for shipment from a place in the immediate vicinity of that port where suitable railway facilities are not available,

  (b) before the vehicle is so used the consent of every highway authority or every person responsible for the maintenance and repair of any road on which it is proposed that the vehicle shall be used shall in each case be obtained in writing, and

  (c) the vehicle shall not be used for the carriage of goods or burden for hire or reward; or

[In condition (b) above, the expression "person responsible for the maintenance and repair of any road" includes any person who is so responsible to a highway authority pursuant to an agreement with that authority.]

(2) the vehicle shall be used only for drawing or in connection with the launching of lifeboats which are the property of the Royal National Lifeboat Institution. **[1151]**

NOTES
    Commencement: 1 November 1979.
    Amended by SI 1986 No 313, art 3.

6. Naval, military, air force and aviation vehicles

The Minister authorises the use on roads of the vehicles specified in Column 1 of Schedule 1 notwithstanding that such vehicles do not comply in all respects with the requirements of the Regulations of the Construction and Use Regulations or the Track Laying Regulations respectively specified opposite thereto in Column 2 of Schedule 1, subject to the vehicles being the property of, or for the time being under the control of, the persons respectively specified opposite thereto in Column 3 of Schedule 1. **[1152]**

NOTES
    Commencement: 1 November 1979.

Grass cutting machines and hedge trimmers

7. The Minister authorises the use on roads of [motor vehicles] constructed or adapted for use as grass cutters or hedge trimmers (not, in either case, being vehicles controlled by a pedestrian) notwithstanding that such vehicles do not comply with [Regulations 53, 57, 62, 79A or 140] of the Construction and Use Regulations subject to the following conditions:—

(a) all other relevant requirements of the Construction and Use Regulations shall be complied with;

(b) the overall width of the vehicle [together with any equipment mounted on it], except when it is actually cutting grass or trimming hedges, shall not exceed 2.5 metres; and

(c) except when the vehicle is actually engaged in such operations, all cutting or trimming blades which form part of the machinery fitted to [or mounted on] the vehicle shall be effectively guarded so that no danger is caused or is likely to be caused to any person.   **[1153]**

NOTES
Commencement: 1 November 1979.
Amended by SI 1984 No 1810, art 4.

9. The Minister authorises the use on roads of trailers constructed or adapted for use as grass cutters or hedge trimmers notwithstanding that such trailers do not comply in all respects with such of the requirements of the Construction and Use Regulations as apply to trailers, subject to the following conditions:—

(a) the requirements of Regulations 107 and 114 of the Construction and Use Regulations, so far as they apply to trailers, shall be complied with;

(b) the unladen weight of the trailer shall not exceed—

    (i) 1020 kilograms if drawn by a locomotive, a motor tractor or a heavy motor car, or

    (ii) 815 kilograms in any other case;

(c) the overall width of the motor vehicle by which the trailer is drawn and, except when it is actually cutting grass or trimming hedges, the overall width of the trailer shall not exceed 2.6 metres;

(d) except when the trailer is actually engaged in such operations, where it is being drawn in such a manner that its longitudinal axis and that of the drawing vehicle are parallel but lie in different vertical planes, the width of road occupied by both vehicles shall not exceed 2.6 metres.

    For the purposes of this paragraph, the said width shall be taken as a distance equivalent to the distance which, if both vehicles were treated as if they were one vehicle at a time when the one is drawing the other in the said manner, would fall to be measured as its overall width;

(e) except when the trailer is actually engaged in such operations, all cutting or trimming blades which form part of the machinery fitted to the trailer shall be effectively guarded so that no danger is caused or is likely to be caused to any person; and

(f) the trailer shall not be driven at a speed exceeding 20 miles per hour.
[1154]

NOTES
Commencement: 1 November 1979.

10. Pedestrian controlled road maintenance vehicles

The Minister authorises the use on roads of motor vehicles constructed or adapted for the gritting of roads, the laying of road markings, the clearing of frost, snow or ice from roads or any other work of maintaining roads, being vehicles controlled by a pedestrian and not constructed or adapted for use or used for the carriage of a driver or passenger, notwithstanding that such vehicles do not comply in all respects with the requirements of Regulations 11, 13, 37, 55 and 67 of the Construction and Use Regulations subject to the following conditions:—

    (a) all other relevant requirements of the Construction and Use Regulations shall be complied with;

    (b) the weight of the vehicle whether laden or unladen, shall not exceed 410 kilograms; and

    (c) the vehicle shall be equipped with an efficient braking system capable of being set or with sufficient other means, not being a braking system, whereby it can be brought to a standstill and held stationary.　**[1155]**

NOTES

    Commencement: 1 November 1979.

11. Vehicle used for experiments or trials

The Minister authorises the use on roads of vehicles in or in connection with the conduct of experiments or trials under section 249 of the Highways Act 1959 notwithstanding that such vehicles do not comply in all respects with the requirements of the Construction and Use Regulations or the Track Laying Regulations.　**[1156]**

NOTES

    Commencement: 1 November 1979.

12. Straddle carriers

The Minister authorises the use on roads of straddle carriers notwithstanding that such vehicles do not comply in all respects with the requirements of Regulations 12, 13(2)(b)(ii), 42, 44, 57, 58, 59(5), (6) and (7) and 101 (except paragraph (1)(a)) of the Construction and Use Regulations, subject to the following conditions:—

    (a) the vehicle shall not be used otherwise than for the purpose of demonstration or in the course of delivery on sale or when proceeding to or returning from a manufacturer or repairer for the purpose of repair or overhaul and, when so used, shall carry no load other than its necessary gear or equipment:

        Provided that a vehicle which does not comply with the said Regulation 58 may, if it complies with the said Regulations 12 and 57, be used whether laden or unladen in passing from one part of any private premises to any other part thereof or to other private premises in the immediate neighbourhood;

    (b) the vehicle shall not travel at a speed exceeding 12 miles per hour;

    (c) the overall width of the vehicle shall not exceed 2.9 metres;

    (d) the vehicle shall not be used if the overall length of the vehicle or, where the vehicle is carrying a load, if the overall length of the vehicle together with the length of any forward projection and of any rearward projection of its load exceeds 9.2 metres except with the consent of the chief officer of police of every police area in which it is proposed that the vehicle will be used;

    (e) save in so far as the chief officer of police of any police area in which it is proposed that the vehicle will be used dispenses, as respects the use of the vehicle in that area, with any of the requirements contained in this paragraph, the [user] of the vehicle shall, not less than two clear days before such use, apply to the chief officer of police of any such area for his consent to the use of the vehicle, and shall, when making the application, furnish to him particulars of the vehicle concerned, of its overall length, of the length of any forward projection or rearward projection of any load proposed to be carried, and of the roads on which it is proposed that the vehicle will be used; and

(f) all the relevant requirements of the Construction and Use Regulations other than those specified above shall be complied with.   **[1157]**

NOTES
Commencement: 1 November 1979.
Para (e): word in square brackets substituted by SI 1987 No 1327, art 6.

13. [Agricultural motor vehicles, agricultural trailers and agricultural trailed appliances]

[(1) Subject to the provisions of paragraph (2), the Secretary of State authorises the use on roads of—

(a) an agricultural motor vehicle,
(b) an agricultural trailer designed to perform functions, other than the carriage of goods, that necessitate an overall width of 2.5 metres being exceeded, or
(c) an agricultural trailed appliance,

notwithstanding that the overall width of the vehicle exceeds 2.5 metres if the relevant conditions specified in Schedule 4 are complied with.

(2) The authorisation specified in paragraph (1) applies only in so far as the width of a vehicle (including an agricultural implement which by virtue of Article 13B is treated as part of the vehicle) cannot, without undue expense or risk of damage, be reduced.]   **[1158]**

NOTES
Commencement: 1 March 1985.
Articles 13—13C substituted for existing article 13 by SI 1984 No 1810, art 6.

13A. Agricultural motor vehicle towing an off-set agricultural trailer or trailed appliance

[(1) The Secretary of State authorises the use on roads of an agricultural motor vehicle towing an agricultural trailer or agricultural trailed appliance in such a manner that the longitudinal axis of the motor vehicle and the longitudinal axis of the trailer are parallel but lie in different vertical planes and the width specified in paragraph (2) below exceeds 2.5 metres provided the relevant conditions specified in Schedule 4 are complied with.

(2) The width referred to in paragraph (1) above is the distance equivalent to the distance which, if both the agricultural motor vehicle and the agricultural trailer or agricultural trailed appliance (when being drawn by the agricultural motor vehicle) are treated as one vehicle, would fall to be measured as its overall width.]   **[1159]**

NOTES
Commencement: 1 March 1985.
Articles 13—13C substituted for existing article 13 by SI 1984 No 1810, art 6.

13B. Provisions supplementary to Articles 13, and 13A

[For the purposes of Articles 13 and 13A and Schedule 4, an agricultural implement rigidly mounted on an agricultural motor vehicle, an agricultural trailer or an agricultural trailed appliance shall be treated as part of that vehicle, trailer or appliance whether or not—

    (a) the implement is permanently attached thereto, and

    (b) part of the weight of the implement is transmitted to the surface of the road otherwise than by the wheels or tracks of the motor vehicle, trailer or appliance.]   **[1160]**

NOTES

    Commencement: 1 March 1985.

    Articles 13—13C substituted for existing article 13 by SI 1984 No 1810, art 6.

13C. Agricultural motor vehicles, agricultural trailers and agricultural trailed appliances with implements projecting rearwards or forwards

[(1) The Secretary of State authorises the use on roads of—

    (a) an agricultural motor vehicle,

    (b) an agricultural trailer, and

    (c) an agricultural trailed appliance,

with an agricultural implement rigidly mounted thereon whether or not—

    (i) the implement is permanently attached thereto, and

    (ii) part of the weight of the implement is transmitted to the surface of the road otherwise than by the wheels or tracks of the motor vehicle, trailer or appliance

provided that the requirements mentioned in paragraph (2) are complied with.

    (2) Those requirements are that:—

    (a) if any part of the implement projects rearwards of the rearmost part of the motor vehicle, trailer or appliance by more than a distance specified in an item in column 2 of Part I of Schedule 5 the conditions specified in that item in column 3 are complied with; and

    (b) if any part of the implement projects forwards of the foremost part of the motor vehicle, trailer or appliance by more than a distance specified in an item in column 2 of Part I of Schedule 5 the conditions specified in that item in column 3 are complied with.]   **[1161]**

NOTES

    Commencement: 1 March 1985.

    Articles 13—13C substituted for existing article 13 by SI 1984 No 1810, art 6.

15. Vehicles for moving excavated material

The Minister authorises the use on roads of moveable plant or equipment (other than engineering plant) being a heavy motor car, trailer or articulated vehicle specially designed and constructed for use in private premises for the primary purpose of moving excavated material and fitted with a tipping body, moving platform or other similar device for discharging its load, and which cannot, owing to the requirements of that purpose, comply in all respects with the requirements of the Construction and Use Regulations, subject to the following conditions:—

    (a) the vehicle shall only be used in proceeding to and from private premises or between private premises and a port in either direction and shall carry no load other than its necessary gear or equipment;

    (b) a heavy motor car not forming part of an articulated vehicle shall not draw any trailer;

(c) where a trailer is drawn by a motor vehicle the motor vehicle shall not draw any other trailer;

(d) in a case where the overall width of the vehicle exceeds [5 metres] the conditions specified in Article 24 shall be complied with;

(e) in the case of a heavy motor car not forming part of an articulated vehicle, and in the case of an articulated vehicle, the sum of the weights transmitted to the road surface by any two wheels in line transversely shall not exceed 22,860 kilograms and the sum of the weights so transmitted by all the wheels shall not exceed 50,800 kilograms;

(f) in the case of a trailer, whether or not forming part of an articulated vehicle, the provisions of Regulation 75(1)(b) and (c) and (2)(b) and (c) of the Construction and Use Regulations shall not apply if the trailer is equipped with an efficient brake or with suitable scotches or similar devices to hold it stationary when necessary;

(g) the overall length of a trailer shall not exceed 8.54 metres and the overall length of an articulated vehicle shall not exceed 13.4 metres;

(h) the vehicle shall not travel on any road, other than a [motorway], at a speed exceeding 12 miles per hour;

(i) every wheel of the vehicle shall be equipped with a pneumatic tyre;

(j) where the overall width of the vehicle exceeds 3.5 metres, at least one person, in addition to the person or persons employed as respects a motor vehicle in driving that vehicle, shall be employed in attending to that vehicle and any load carried thereby and any trailer drawn by that vehicle and any load carried on the trailer and to give warning to the driver of the said motor vehicle and to any other person of any danger likely to be caused to any such other person by reason of the presence of the vehicle or the vehicle and trailer on the road:

Provided that, where three or more vehicles authorised by this Article are travelling together in convoy, it shall be a sufficient compliance with this paragraph if only the foremost and rearmost vehicles in the convoy are attended in the manner prescribed in this paragraph;

(k) save in so far as the chief officer of police of any police area in which it is proposed that the vehicle will be used dispenses, as respects the use of the vehicle in that area, with any of the requirements contained in this paragraph as to length of notice or particulars to be given, the [user] of the vehicle, if its overall width exceeds 2.9 metres, before using it on a road, shall give at least two clear days' notice to the chief officer of police of any such area and such notice shall contain particulars of the vehicle concerned, of its overall width, and of the time, date and route of the proposed journey;

(l) subject to any variation in the time, date or route of the journey which may be directed by any such chief officer of police, the vehicle shall be used only in circumstances which accord with the particulars given in compliance with the foregoing paragraph as to the time, date and route of the journey and only if the overall width of the vehicle does not exceed the width of which particulars have been given as aforesaid;

(m) in the case of the use of a vehicle in respect of which any of the requirements of the Construction and Use Regulations as to the weights of vehicles, whether laden or unladen, or the weights transmitted to the road surface by all or any of the wheels is not complied with, or, where a combination of vehicles is used, if any of the said requirements as to any or all of the vehicles in the combination is not complied with—

(i) save in so far as the highway authority for any road or the bridge authority for any bridge on which it is proposed that the vehicle or, as the case may be, the vehicles will be used dispenses, as respects the use of the vehicle or vehicles on that road or, as the case may be, on that bridge, with the requirements contained in this sub-paragraph as to length of notice or as to the form of notice or the particulars to be given, the [user] of the vehicle or, as the case may be, of the vehicles, before using the vehicle or vehicles on that road or that bridge, shall give to the highway authority for the road and the bridge authority for the bridge at least two clear days' notice in the form and containing the particulars specified in Part I of Schedule 2, and the provisions of Article 26(6) and (7) shall apply as respects any such notice, and

(ii) before using the vehicle or, as the case may be, the vehicles on any road or bridge the [user] of the vehicle or vehicles shall give to the highway authority for the road and to the bridge authority for the bridge an indemnity in the form specified in Part II of Schedule 2, and the provisions of Article 26(6) and (7) shall apply as respects any such indemnity,

and for the purposes of this sub-paragraph references to a combination of vehicles shall be construed in the same manner as is provided in Regulation 139(g) of the Construction and Use Regulations [and references to the highway authority for any road and to the bridge authority for any bridge shall be read as including references to any other person responsible for the maintenance and repair of the road or bridge in question pursuant to an agreement with the authority]; and

(n) in a case specified in an item in column 2 of the Table below, all the Construction and Use Regulations shall apply with the exception of the Regulations which are specified opposite to that item in column 3 of that table and, in relation to items 2 and 3, save as provided in paragraph (f) above.

TABLE

1	2	3
Item	Case	Construction and Use Regulations not applicable
1.	A heavy motor car not forming part of an articulated vehicle.	Regulations 12, 13(2)(b)(ii), 42, 44, 57, 59(5), (6) and (7), 61, 85, 89, 92, 93, 94 and 101 (except paragraph (1)(a)).
2.	A trailer not forming part of an articulated vehicle.	Regulations 12, 42, 73, 74, 79, and 101 (except paragraph (1)(a)).

1	2	3
Item	Case	Construction and Use Regulations not applicable
3.	An articulated vehicle.	Regulations 9(1), 12, 13(2)(b)(ii), 42, 44, 57, 59(5), (6) and (7), 61, 74, 79, 85, 86, 88, 90 to 94 (inclusive) and 101 (except paragraph (1)(a)).

[1162]

NOTES

Commencement: 1 November 1979.

Paras (d), (h), (k): words in square brackets substituted by SI 1987 No 1327, arts 4, 5, 6.

Para (m): first and second words in square brackets substituted by SI 1987 No 1327, art 6; final amendment in square brackets made by SI 1986 No 313, art 4.

16. Motor vehicles and trailers constructed for use outside the United Kingdom or which are new or improved types constructed for tests or trials or are equipped with new or improved equipment or types of equipment

(1) This Article applies to wheeled motor vehicles and trailers not falling within any description of motor vehicle or trailer specified in Article 18 or 19 and references in this Article to motor vehicles and trailers shall be construed accordingly.

(2) The Minister authorises the use on roads—

(A) of motor vehicles and trailers, or types of motor vehicles and trailers, constructed for use outside the United Kingdom and of new or improved types of motor vehicles and trailers constructed for tests or trials notwithstanding that such vehicles do not comply in all respects with the requirements of the Construction and Use Regulations, and

(B) of motor vehicles and trailers equipped with new or improved equipment or types of equipment notwithstanding that such vehicles do not comply in all respects with such of the requirements of the Construction and Use Regulations as cannot, by reason only of the said equipment, be complied with,

subject, in all cases, to the following conditions:—

(a) the vehicle shall not be used otherwise than—

(i) for or in connection with the testing or demonstration of the vehicle, or

(ii) in the course of delivery on sale, or

(iii) for proceeding to or returning from a manufacturer or repairer for the purpose of construction, repair or overhaul;

(b) the vehicle shall comply with Regulations 8, 13, 22, 27, 29, [47], 80A, 81, 97, 100, 101(1)(a), 102, 103, and 107 to 113 (inclusive) of the Construction and Use Regulations, and Regulations 114 to 125 (inclusive), 127 to 131 (inclusive), 133, 137 and [139 to 144C (inclusive)] of the said Regulations shall apply thereto;

(c) the vehicle shall not be used for the carriage of any load other than its necessary gear or equipment or such apparatus or ballast as may be necessary for the purpose of carrying out a test or trial of the vehicle;

(d) save in so far as the chief officer of police of any police area in which it is proposed that the vehicle will be used dispenses, as respects the use of the vehicle in that area, with any of the requirements contained in this sub-paragraph as to length of notice or particulars to be given, the [user] of the vehicle, if its overall width exceeds 2.9 metres or if its overall length exceeds that specified by any provision in Regulation 9 or 73 of the Construction and Use Regulations, before using it on a road, shall give at least two clear days' notice to the chief officer of police of any such area and such notice shall contain particulars of the vehicle concerned, of its overall width and overall length, and of the width and length of any load proposed to be carried, and of the time, date and route of the proposed journey;

(e) subject to any variation in the time, date or route of the journey which may be directed by any such chief officer of police, the vehicle shall be used only in circumstances which accord with the particulars given in compliance with the foregoing sub-paragraph as to the time, date and route of the journey and only if the overall width and overall length of the vehicle and the width and length of any load carried thereon do not exceed the width and length of which particulars have been given as aforesaid;

(f) in the case of the use of a vehicle in respect of which any of the Construction and Use Regulations as to the weights of vehicles, whether laden or unladen, or the weights transmitted to the road surface by all or any of the wheels is not complied with, or, where a combination of vehicles is used, if any of the said requirements as to any or all of the vehicles in the combination is not complied with—

    (i) save in so far as the highway authority for any road or the bridge authority for any bridge on which it is proposed that the vehicle or, as the case may be, the vehicles will be used dispenses, as respects the use of the vehicle or vehicles on that road or, as the case may be, on that bridge, with the requirements contained in this sub-paragraph as to length of notice or to the form of notice or the particulars to be given, the [user] of the vehicle or, as the case may be, of the vehicles, before using the vehicle or the vehicles on that road or that bridge shall give to the highway authority for the road and to the bridge authority for the bridge at least two clear days' notice in the form and containing the particulars specified in Part I of Schedule 2, and the provisions of Article 26(6) and (7) shall apply as respects any such notice, and

    (ii) before using the vehicle or, as the case may be, the vehicles on any road or bridge the [user] of the vehicle or vehicles shall give to the highway authority for the road and to the bridge authority for the bridge an indemnity in the form specified in Part II of Schedule 2, and the provisions of Article 26(6) and (7) shall apply as respects any such indemnity.

and for the purposes of this sub-paragraph references to a combination of vehicles shall be construed in the same manner as is provided in Regulation 139(g) of the Construction and Use Regulations [and references to the highway authority for any road and to the bridge authority for any bridge shall be read as including references to any other person responsible for the maintenance and repair of the road or bridge in question pursuant to an agreement with the authority]. **[1163]**

NOTES
Commencement: 1 November 1979.
Para 2: sub-para (b) amended by SI 1981 No 1664, art 3; in sub-para (d) words in square brackets substituted by SI 1987 No 1327, art 6; in sub-para (f) first and second words in square brackets substituted by SI 1987 No 1327, art 6, final amendment in square brackets made by SI 1986 No 313, art 5.

17. Vehicles fitted with moveable platforms

(1) The Minister authorises the use on roads of a vehicle fitted with a moveable platform notwithstanding that the vehicle does not comply in all respects with the requirements of Regulations 8, 9, 11, 48, 53, 54, 57, 58, 62, 63 or 140 of the Construction and Use Regulations subject to the following conditions:—

   (a) all the relevant requirements of the Construction and Use Regulations other than those specified above shall be complied with;

   (b) the vehicle shall not be used on a road unless its special equipment is fully retracted except when the vehicle is at a place where it is being used to facilitate overhead working;

   (c) any jacks with which the vehicle is fitted for stabilising it while the moveable platform is in use and which project from the sides of the vehicle shall be clearly visible to persons using the road within a reasonable distance of the vehicle; and

   (d) the vehicle, except in respect of its special equipment when the vehicle is at a place where it is being used to facilitate overhead working, shall—

      (i) as respects its overall length, comply with Regulation 9 of the said Regulation,

     (ii) as respects its overall width, comply with Regulations 48, 53, 57 or 62 (as the case may be) of the said Regulations,

    (iii) in the case of a vehicle other than a locomotive, as respects its overhang, comply with Regulations 54, 58 or 63 (as the case may be) of the said Regulations.

(2) In this Article—

   "moveable platform" means a platform which is attached to, and may be moved by means of, an extensible boom, and

   "special equipment" means a moveable platform, the apparatus for moving the platform and any jacks fitted to the vehicle for stabilising it while the moveable platform is in use.   **[1164]**

NOTES
Commencement: 1 November 1979.

PART III

ABNORMAL INDIVISIBLE LOADS, ENGINEERING PLANT AND OTHER VEHICLES CARRYING WIDE LOADS

18. Vehicles for carrying or drawing abnormal indivisible loads

(1) The Minister authorises the use on roads of heavy motor cars and trailers specially designed and constructed for the carriage of abnormal indivisible loads and of locomotives and tractors specially designed and constructed to draw trailers specially so designed and constructed notwithstanding that such vehicles do not comply in all respects with the requirements of the Construction and Use Regulations, subject—

(a) in a case where Article 22, 23, 25 or 26 applies to the conditions contained in such of those Articles as are applicable to that case;

(b) in a case where the overall width of the vehicle or of the vehicle together with the width of any lateral projection or projections of its load exceeds metres [5 metres], to the conditions contained in Article 24; and

(c) in all cases to the further conditions specified in paragraph (2) below.

[(1A) (a) In this article, "the Construction and Use Regulations" means the Road Vehicles (Construction and Use) Regulations 1986.

(b) For the purposes of paragraph (2) below;

(i) "Category 1" shall consist of any vehicle or combination of vehicles where the total weight of the vehicle or vehicles carrying the load is not more than 46,000 kilograms;

"Category 2" shall consist of any motor vehicle or combination of vehicles where the total weight of the vehicle or vehicles carrying the load is not more than 80,000 kilograms;

"Category 3" shall consist of any motor vehicle or combination of vehicles where the total weight of the vehicle or vehicles carrying the load is not more than 150,000 kilograms;

(ii) a vehicle shall comply with the conditions of an appropriate category, and the category under the conditions of which a vehicle is being used shall be that indicated on the sign mentioned in paragraph (2)(t) below.]

(2) The conditions referred to in paragraph 1(c) above are as follows:—

(a) a heavy motor car or trailer which does not comply with Part II of the Construction and Use Regulations shall be used only, save as provided in paragraphs (i) and (m) of this Article, for or in connection with the carriage of an abnormal indivisible load;

(b) a locomotive or tractor which does not comply with Part II of the Construction and Use Regulations shall be used only for or in connection with the drawing of trailers the use of which on roads is authorised by this Article;

(c) the overall width of a heavy motor car [or a trailer] shall not exceed 2.9 metres unless it is used for or in connection with the carriage of a load which can only safely be carried on a heavy motor car [or a trailer] which exceeds that overall width;

(d) the overall width of a locomotive or tractor shall not exceed 2.9 metres unless it is used for or in connection with the carriage of a load on a trailer which exceeds that overall width, being a load which can only be safely carried on such a trailer;

(e) . . .

(f) notwithstanding anything in sub-paragraphs (c), (d) . . . above, the overall width of a heavy motor car, locomotive, tractor or trailer shall not exceed 6.1 metres;

(g) where, in relation to the load carried by a vehicle, there is a lateral projection on one or both sides of the vehicle the overall width of the vehicle together with the width of the projection, or, as the case may be, of both projections shall not exceed 6.1 metres;

(h) where a load is carried in such a manner that its weight rests—

(i) on one vehicle being a heavy motor car or a trailer, the overall length of the heavy motor car or, as the case may be, of the trailer

together with the length of any forward and of any rearward projection of its load shall not exceed 27.4 metres; or
(ii) on more than one vehicle and the vehicles consist of—

(*a*) a motor vehicle drawing one trailer whether constituting an articulated vehicle or not, or
(*b*) any other combination of vehicles,

then, in the case at (a) above, the overall length of the trailer together with the length of any forward projection of the load extending beyond the foremost point of the trailer and of any rearward projection of the load shall not exceed 27.4 metres and, in the case at (b) above, the overall length of the vehicles together with the distance between vehicles and the length of any forward and of any rearward projection of the load shall not exceed 27.4 metres;

(i) the vehicle shall be so constructed that it is a wheeled vehicle;
(j) every wheel of the vehicle shall be equipped with a pneumatic tyre or a tyre of soft or elastic material;
[(*k*) the following restrictions on weight shall apply:

(i) for any vehicle or combination of vehicles carrying the load in Category 1:

(*a*) regulations [75, 76 and 78] of the Construction and Use Regulations shall apply, and in respect of an articulated vehicle, regulation 77 shall apply save for a vehicle to which (b) below is applicable;
[(*aa*) regulation 79 of the Construction and Use Regulations shall apply in the case of a vehicle with two or three closely spaced axles within the meaning of the Construction and Use Regulations;]
(*b*) for an articulated vehicle with a total of 5 or more axles and with a relevant axle spacing specified in column 2 of the Table below, the total weight shall not exceed the weight specified for that item in column 3 of the Table.
[(*c*) in the case of a semi-trailer within the meaning of the Construction and Use Regulations of which the outermost axles of a group of four axles are spaced at a distance apart of 3.25m or less and the smallest distance between any two adjoining axles in the group is at least 0.87 m, the weight transmitted to the road surface by all the wheels of any one of those axles shall not exceed 6,000 kilograms;]

1	*2*	*3*
Item	*Relevant axle spacing (in metres)*	*Weight (in kilograms)*
1	at least 6·5	40,000
2	at least 7·0	42,000
3	at least 7·5	44,000
4	at least 8·0	46,000

(ii) [save as provided in sub-paragraph (iia) below] for any vehicle or combination of vehicles carrying the load in Category 2;

(*a*) the total weight shall be transmitted to the road through at least 5 axles;

(b) the total weight imposed on the road by all the wheels of any one axle shall not exceed 12,500 kilograms, and by any one wheel, 6,250 kilograms;

(c) if the distance between any two adjacent axles is at least 1.1 metres but less than 1.35 metres, the total weight imposed on the road by all the wheels of any one of those axles shall not exceed 12,000 kilograms, and by any one wheel, 6,000 kilograms;

(d) the distance between any two adjacent axles shall not be less than 1.1 metres;

(e) where the distance between the foremost and rearmost axles of the vehicle or vehicles carrying the load is at least as specified in an item in column 2 of the Table below, the total weight of the vehicle or combination of vehicles shall not exceed the weight given for that item in column 3 of the Table:

1	2	3
Item	Distance between foremost and rearmost axles (in metres)	Weight (in kilograms)
1	5·07	38,000
2	5·33	40,000
3	6·0	45,000
4	6·67	50,000
5	7·33	55,000
6	8·0	60,000
7	8·67	65,000
8	9·33	70,000
9	10·0	75,000
10	10·67	80,000

(f) where the axles are in two or more groups (so that adjacent axles in each group are less than 2 metres apart and adjacent axles of different groups are more than 2 metres apart), then the total weight imposed on the road by all the wheels of any one group of axles shall not exceed 50,000 kilograms;

[(iia) until 1st October 1989 an articulated vehicle in Category 2 need not meet the requirements of sub-paragraph (ii) above, but—

(a) the total weight shall be transmitted to the road through at least 4 axles;

(b) the total weight imposed on the road by all the wheels of any one axle shall not exceed 13,500 kilograms, and by any one wheel 6,750 kilograms;

(c) if the total number of axles does not exceed 4, the total weight of the vehicle shall not exceed 46,000 kilograms;]

(iii) [save as provided in sub-paragraph (iiia) below] for any [vehicle] or combination of vehicles carrying the load in Category 3:

(a) the total weight shall be transmitted to the road through at least 6 axles;

(b) the total weight imposed on the road by all the wheels of any one axle shall not exceed 16,500 kilograms, and by any one wheel, 8,250 kilograms;

(c) if the distance between any two adjacent axles is at least 1.1 metres but less than 1.35 metres, the total weight imposed on the road by all the wheels of any one of those axles shall not exceed 15,000 kilograms, and by any one wheel 7,500 kilograms;

(d) the distance between any two adjacent axles shall not be less than 1.1 metres;

(e) where the distance between the foremost and rearmost axles of the vehicle or vehicles carrying the load is at least as specified in an item in column 2 of the Table below the total weight of the vehicle or combination of vehicles shall not exceed the weight given for that item in column 3 of the Table:

1	2	3
Item	Distance between foremost and rearmost axles (in metres)	Weight (in kilograms)
1	5·77	80,000
2	6·23	85,000
3	6·68	90,000
4	7·14	95,000
5	7·59	100,000
6	8·05	105,000
7	8·50	110,000
8	8·95	115,000
9	9·41	120,000
10	9·86	125,000
11	10·32	130,000
12	10·77	135,000
13	11·23	140,000
14	11·68	145,000
15	12·14	150,000

(f) where the axles are in two or more groups (so that adjacent axles in each group are less than 1.5 metres apart and adjacent axles of different groups are more than 1.5 metres apart) then the total weight imposed on the road by all the wheels of any one group of axles shall not exceed 100,000 kilograms, or 90,000 kilograms for a group where the distance betweeen any two adjacent axles of that group is less than 1.35 metres;

[(iiia) until 1st October 1989 a vehicle or combination of vehicles carrying the load in Category 3 need not meet the requirements of sub-paragraphs (c) to (f) of sub-paragraph (iii) above;];

(iv) for the purpose of this sub-paragraph (k):

"axle" shall mean any number of wheels in line transversely;

"relevant axle spacing" shall have the same meaning as in regulation 77(1) of the Construction and Use Regulations;

(v) regulation 3(7) and (8) of the Construction and Use Regulations shall apply to determine the number of wheels and axles for the purpose of this sub-paragraph and regulation 3(10) to determine the distance between axles.]

(l) the vehicle or combination of vehicles shall not carry more than one abnormal indivisible load at any one time:

Provided that—

(i) subject to compliance with all the requirements of the Construction and Use Regulations with respect to the laden weights of vehicles and the weights transmitted to the road surface by all or any of the wheels, it shall be permissible for a vehicle or any vehicles comprised in a combination of vehicles to carry more than one abnormal indivisible load of the same character and, where any abnormal indivisible load is carried, to carry any articles of a similar character;

(ii) in the case of vehicles not falling within the foregoing proviso, it shall be permissible for a vehicle or any vehicles comprised in a combination of vehicles to carry more than one abnormal indivisible load each of the same character if—

[(a) the vehicle or combination of vehicles is in Category 1 or Category 2;]

(b) the overall length in relation to the vehicle or vehicles carrying the loads is such that the provisions of sub-paragraph (i) or (ii) of paragraph (h) above would be complied with were "18.3 metres" substituted for "27.4 metres" except that, where such compliance would be impossible by reason of the length of one of the loads if that were the only one carried, the aforesaid distance of 18.3 metres may be increased to such greater distance not exceeding 27.4 metres as may be necessary to permit the carriage of that load;

(c) the overall width of any vehicle together with the width of any lateral projection of its load does not exceed 2.9 metres or, where it would be impossible for the aforesaid distance to be complied with by reason of the width of one of the loads if that were the only one carried, such greater distance not exceeding 6.1 metres as may be necessary to permit the carriage of that load; and

(d) all the loads carried are loaded at the same place and conveyed to the same destination;

(m) where an abnormal indivisible load consists of engineering plant from which one or more constituent parts have been detached, such abnormal indivisible load and such constituent parts may be carried:

Provided that—

(i) no dimension of such constituent parts protrudes beyond any dimension of the vehicle or combination of vehicles on which such abnormal indivisible load and such constituent parts are being carried to an extent greater than such abnormal indivisible load would protrude if it were being carried without such constituent parts;

(ii) such abnormal indivisible load and such constituent parts are loaded at the same place and have the same destination; and

[(iii) the vehicle or combination of vehicles is in Category 1 or Category 2;]

(n) in the case of a trailer whether manufactured before 1st January 1968 or on or after that date, [regulation 16] of the Construction and Use Regulations shall apply as it applies to trailers manufactured before 1st January 1968;

(o) the conditions specified in Articles 21(1) and 27; and

(p) [for vehicles manufactured before 1st October 1989 and] in a case specified in column 2 of the Table below, all the Construction and Use Regulations shall apply with the exception of the Regulations which are specified opposite to that item in column 3 of that table, and, in relation to [item 3], save as provided in paragraph (n) above.

TABLE

1	2	3
Item	Case	Regulations that do not apply
1	A heavy motor car	8, 16 in so far as it relates to the requirement in item 18(c) of Schedule 3 to the Regulations, 15, 18 (except paragraph (1)), 22, 24, 25, 45, 63, 75–80, 82 and 83(1).
2	A locomotive or tractor	8, 22, 25, 45, 75(3) and 76.
3	A trailer	7, 8, 16 in so far as it relates to the requirements in items 4, 11, 15 and 18 of Schedule 3 to the Regulations, 15, 18 (except paragraph (1)), 21, 22, 24, 25, 63, 64, 75–80, 82 and 83(1).

[(q) in relation to any vehicle or combination of vehicles in a Category specified in column 2 of the Table below and manufactured [on or after 1st October 1989] and any vehicle in Category 1 whenever manufactured, all the Construction and Use Regulations shall apply with the exception of the Regulations which are specified opposite to that item in column 3 of the Table:

1	2	3
Item	Category	Regulations that do not apply
1	1	7, 8, 80 and 82.
2	2 and 3	7, 8, 15, 16, 18 (except paragraph (1)), [25], 45, 64, 65, [75 in so far as it relates to items 1–4, 6–11, 15 and 16 of the Table, 76–80], 82 and 83(1).

[(r) a vehicle or combination of vehicles in Category 2 or Category 3, if manufactured on or after 1st October 1989, shall have a braking system complying with the construction, fitting and performance requirements set out in relation to category N3 motor vehicles and O4 trailers in Annexes I, II and VII to Council Directive 71/320/EEC as amended by Council Directive 74/132/EEC, 75/524/EEC, 79/489/ EEC, 85/647/EEC and 88/194/EEC ("the amended Directive") and, if appropriate, Annexes III, IV, V, VI and X to the amended Directive, modified as follows—

(i) for the purposes of each Type O test conducted in accordance with Annex II—

(*a*) a laden vehicle shall be a vehicle laden with the maximum technically permissible mass specified by the manufacturer for the vehicle speed specified for the test;

(*b*) for a trailer which is designed and constructed for use in a combination of vehicles in Category 3 and for which X (which is stated in the amended Directive as being a percentage of the force corresponding to the maximum mass borne by the wheels of the stationary vehicle) is specified in paragraph 2.2.1.2.1. of Annex II as having the values of 45 or 50, X shall have the value of 30;

(*c*) for a trailer mentioned in (b) above and for which the test speed is specified in paragraph 2.2.1.2.1. of Annex II as 60 km/h, the test speed shall be 48 km/h;

(*d*) for a drawing vehicle in category N3 which is designed and constructed for use with a semi-trailer within the meaning of the Construction and Use Regulations in a combination of vehicles in Category 3, if the performance of a service braking device is determined by measuring the stopping distance in relation to the initial speed, the stopping distance in paragraph 2.1.1.1.1. of Annex II shall be $0.15v + v^2/77.5$, or, if the performance of the device is determined by measuring the reaction time and the mean deceleration, the mean braking deceleration at normal engine speed in paragraph 2.1.1.1.1. of Annex II shall be at least 3 m/s^2;

(*e*) for a drawing vehicle in category N3 mentioned in (d) above, if the performance of a secondary braking device is determined by measuring the stopping distance in relation to the initial speed, the stopping distance in paragraph 2.1.2.1. of Annex II shall be $0.15v + v^2/37.5$ or, if the performance of the device is determined by measuring the reaction time and the mean deceleration, the mean braking deceleration in paragraph 2.1.2.1. of Annex II shall be at least 1.45 m/s^2;

(ii) the requirements of paragraphs 2.2.1.22 and 2.2.2.13 of Annex I and 1.1.4.2 and 1.4 of Annex II shall not apply;

(iii) in Annex I, in paragraph 2.2.1.23 the words "not mentioned in item 2.2.1.22 above" and in paragraph 2.2.2.14 the words "not mentioned in item 2.2.2.13 above" shall not apply;

(iv) for the purposes of Type I tests conducted in accordance with paragraph 1.3 of Annex II on a vehicle which is designed and constructed for use in a combination of vehicles in Category 3, a laden vehicle shall be a vehicle laden with the heaviest weight possible without the total weight imposed on the road by all the wheels of any one axle exceeding 12,500 kilograms; and

(v) if suitable and sufficient wheel chocks are provided in readily accessible positions and capable, when used in conjunction with any parking brakes fitted to the vehicle, of holding the vehicle stationary when loaded to its maximum mass on a gradient of 12%, the requirements of paragraph 2.1.3.2 of Annex II shall not apply;]

(*s*) (i) a vehicle in Category 2 or Category 3, if manufactured [on or after 1st October 1988], shall have a plate complying with the specification prescribed in the Road Vehicles (Marking of Special Weights)

Regulations 1983 except that there need be no indication of any
weight in respect of a speed not exceeding 12 miles per hour;

(ii) the plate fitted in accordance with paragraph (i) above shall be
marked clearly with the words:

"SPECIAL TYPES USE";

(iii) if a vehicle is made up of several modules, each module may be
fitted individually with a plate in accordance with paragraph (i)
above, provided that the information required from the plate in
relation to the vehicle as a whole can be readily determined from
those individual plates;

(iv) a vehicle fitted with any plate in accordance with paragraph (i)
above shall not be used at a weight in excess of any weight
specified on that place in relation to the speed at which the
vehicle is travelling;

(v) a vehicle in Category 1 shall not be used at a weight in excess of
any weight specified on a place fitted in accordance with
regulation 66 of the Construction and Use Regulations in relation
to items 6, 7 and 8 in Part I or items 4, 5, and 6 in Part II of
Schedule 8 to those Regulations;

(t) the vehicle or the drawing vehicle in a combination of vehicles shall
be fitted with a sign indicating the relevant category and complying
with the requirements specified in Schedule 6;

(u) notwithstanding sub-paragraph (*p*) above, regulation 7 of the
Construction and Use Regulations shall not apply in the case of:

(i) an articulated vehicle, or a motor vehicle and a trailer, where the
semi trailer or the trailer is constructed such that the major part
of the load platform does not extend over or between the wheels
and is at a height that is below the height of the top most point of
the tyres of those wheels, measured on level ground and with any
adjustable suspension at the normal travelling height, and where
the height or stability of the load being carried necessitates the
use of such a trailer;

(ii) a vehicle or combination of vehicles unable to comply with that
regulation because of the requirements of sub-paragraphs
(k)(ii)(e) or (k)(iii)(e) above;

(v) notwithstanding sub-paragraph (a) above, a vehicle consisting of two
or more modules may, when being used in connection with the
carriage of but not at the time carrying an abnormal indivisible load,
be disassembled into two or more parts and arranged such that one
part carries the others.]   **[1165]**

NOTES

Commencement: 1 January 1988 (para (1A)); 1 November 1979 (remainder).
Para (1): words in square brackets substituted by SI 1987 No 1327, art 4.
Para (1A): added by SI 1987 No 1327, art 7.
Para (2): in sub-para (c) words in square brackets added by SI 1987 No 1327, art 8; sub-para (e)
revoked and words omitted in sub-para (f) revoked by SI 1987 No 1327, art 8; sub-para (k)
substituted by SI 1987 No 1327, art 9, words in square brackets in sub-sub-para (i) substituted or
added by SI 1989 No 1662, art 3, other words in square brackets added or substituted by SI 1987 No
2161, art 4; sub-paras (l), (m), (n) words in square brackets substituted by SI 1987 No 1327, arts 10-
12; in sub-para (p) first and second words in square brackets substituted by SI 1987 No 2161, art 4,
Table substituted by SI 1987 No 1327, art 13, first, second and final figures in square brackets
therein added by SI 1987 No 2161, art 4, third figures in square brackets substituted by SI 1989 No

1662, art 3; sub-paras (q), (s) added by SI 1987 No 1327, art 14, amended by SI 1987 No 2161, art 4; sub-para (r) added by SI 1987 No 1327, art 14, further substituted by SI 1989 No 1662, art 3; sub-paras (t)-(v) added by SI 1987 No 1327, art 14.

19. Engineering plant

The Minister authorises the use on roads of engineering plant notwithstanding that such vehicles do not comply in all respects with the requirements of the Construction and Use Regulations or the Track Laying Regulations, subject to—

(1) the restriction specified in Article 21(2) [save as provided in paragraph (2A) below].

(2) in a case where Article 22, 23, 25 or 26 applies, the conditions specified in such of those Articles as are applicable, [save as provided in paragraph (2A) below].

[(2A) In a case where a vehicle or combination of vehicles disregarding the date of its manufacture complies with the conditions specified in article 18(2)(k), (q), (r), (s) and (t), the conditions specified in article 21(1) shall apply as if the use of the vehicle or combination of vehicles was authorised by article 18.]

(3) in a case where the overall width of the vehicle, or of the vehicle together with the width of any lateral projection or projections of its load exceeds [5 metres] the conditions specified in Article 24, and

(4) in any case, the following conditions:—

[(a) engineering plant shall be used on a road only;

    (i) for testing or demonstration purposes or delivery on sale;

    (ii) for proceeding to or returning from a manufacturer or repairer for repair or maintenance;

    (iii) for proceeding to or from the site of engineering operations or when actually engaged in such operations;

(b) engineering plant may carry its own necessary gear and equipment but no other load except;

    (i) engineering plant other than a mobile crane when actually engaged on the construction, maintenance or repair of roads may carry materials which it is specifically designed to treat while being carried on the vehicle or materials which have been excavated and raised from the ground by apparatus on the motor vehicle or trailer, and

    (ii) a mobile crane when actually engaged in engineering operations may lift or transport a load.]

(b) a mobile crane shall not be used on a road to lift or transport goods or burden except when actually engaged in engineering operations;

(c) engineering plant other than a mobile crane shall only draw a trailer which is engineering plant or a living van or office hut used in connection with the construction, maintenance and repair of roads;

(d) no mobile crane shall draw a trailer;

(e) the vehicle shall be so constructed that it is either a wheeled vehicle or a track laying vehicle;

(f) in the case of a wheeled motor vehicle Regulations 4, 11, 21, 22, 25 to 38 (inclusive), 47, 80A, 97, 100, 101(1)(a), 102 to 107 (inclusive), 109, 114 to 125 (inclusive), 127, [122, 137, 144A, 144B and 144C] of the Construction and Use Regulations shall apply:

Provided that—

(i) ...

(ii) in the case of a machine designed for use and used solely for the purpose of laying materials for the repair or construction of road surfaces, if the weight transmitted to the road surface by any two wheels in line transversely does not exceed 11,180 kilograms, the said Regulation 11 shall not apply;

(iii) in the case of a motor vehicle designed for use in work of construction or repair of road surfaces, the wheels of which are equipped with pneumatic tyres specially provided with smooth treads for such use and which is incapable by reason of its construction of exceeding a speed of 20 miles per hour on the level under its own power, Regulation 107(1)(f) of the said Regulations shall not apply;

(g) in the case of a wheeled trailer, Regulations 4, 11, 80A, 81, 97, 101(1)(a), 102, 103, 107, 114, [122, 127, 144B and 144C] of the Construction and Use Regulations shall apply:

Provided that in the case of a trailer designed for use in work of construction or repair of road surfaces and the wheels of which are equipped with pneumatic tyres specially provided with smooth treads for such use, Regulation 107(1)(b) of the said Regulations shall not apply;

(h) in the case of a track laying motor vehicle Regulations 4, 6, 9, 13, 14, 16 to 24 (inclusive), 51, 53 to 69 (inclusive), 71, 72 and 78 of the Track Laying Regulations shall apply:

Provided that—

(i) in the case of a motor vehicle registered on or before 31st December 1951 Regulations 16 and 17 of the said Regulations shall not apply, and

(ii) in the case of a motor vehicle which is a road roller the said Regulation 9 shall not apply;

(i) in the case of a track laying trailer Regulations 4, 6, 9, 22, 23, 44, 51, 54, 56, 57, 59, 67 and 71 of the Track Laying Regulations shall apply:

Provided that in the case of a trailer which is a road roller the said Regulation 9 shall not apply;

(j) all the wheels of a vehicle which are not equipped with pneumatic tyres or tyres of soft or elastic material shall be equipped with smooth tyres and have the edges rounded to a radius of not less than 12 millimetres and not more than 25 millimetres:

Provided that in the case of gritting machines designed for use and used for gritting frosted and icebound roads all or any of the tyres may be shod with diagonal cross bars of equal width of not less than 25 millimetres, extending the full breadth of the tyre and so arranged that the distance between adjacent cross bars is not greater than the width of the cross bars;

(k) in the case of any vehicle the weight transmitted to the road surface by any one wheel not equipped with pneumatic tyres where no other wheel is in the same line transversely or by all the wheels not equipped with pneumatic tyres in line transversely shall be such that the average weight per 25 millimetres width of tyre in contact with such surface does not exceed 765 kilograms;

(l) a motor vehicle shall be equipped with an efficient brake:

Provided that—

(i) in the case of a motor vehicle propelled by steam the engine shall be deemed to be an efficient brake if the engine is capable of being reversed, and

(ii) in the case of a motor vehicle registered on or after 1st January 1952 any brake required by this paragraph shall be capable of being set so as to hold the vehicle when stationary unless another brake fitted to the vehicle is capable of being so set;

(m) a trailer shall be equipped with an efficient brake or with suitable scotches or other similar devices to hold the vehicle stationary when necessary;

(n) no motor vehicle which exceeds 7.93 metres in overall length shall draw a trailer:

Provided that this paragraph shall not apply to a motor vehicle which is drawing a broken down vehicle in consequence of the breakdown;

(o) the sum of the weights transmitted to the road surface by all the wheels and tracks of a vehicle shall not exceed 152,400 kilograms;

(p) the overall length of a vehicle shall not exceed 27.4 metres;

(q) the overall width of a vehicle shall not exceed 6.1 metres;

(r) as respects weight—

(i) the weight transmitted to the road surface by any one wheel of a vehicle, other than a heavy motor car registered on or before 31st December 1951 or a trailer manufactured before 1st January 1952, shall not exceed 11,430 kilograms, and for the purposes of this part of this sub-paragraph any two wheels shall be treated as one wheel if the distance between the centres of the areas of contact between such wheels and the road surface is less than 610 millimetres,

(ii) the weight transmitted to any strip of road surface upon which the wheels of a vehicle rest contained between any two parallel lines drawn on that surface at right angles to the longitudinal axis of the vehicle shall not exceed, if the parallel lines are not more than 610 millimetres apart, 45,720 kilograms and, thereafter, additional weight shall be permitted, for any distance apart of the parallel lines in excess of 610 millimetres but not exceeding a total distance apart of 2.13 metres, at a rate of 30,000 kilograms per metre and, thereafter, additional weight shall be permitted, for any distance apart of the parallel lines in excess of 2.13 metres, at a rate of 10,000 kilograms per metre.

(iii) the total weight transmitted to the road surface by any wheels of a vehicle in line transversely not fitted with pneumatic tyres shall be such that the average weight per 25 millimetre width of tyre in contact with the road surface shall not exceed 765 kilograms, and

(iv) in the case of a track laying vehicle, in addition to the foregoing restrictions, the weight transmitted by each track thereof to any strip of road surface contained between any two parallel lines drawn on that surface at right angles to the longitudinal axis of the vehicle shall not exceed, if the parallel lines are not more than 610 millimetres apart, 11,430 kilograms, and, thereafter, additional weight shall be permitted, for any distance apart of the parallel lines in excess of 610 millimetres but not exceeding a total distance apart of 2.13 metres, at a rate of 7,500 kilograms per metre and, thereafter, additional weight shall be permitted, for any distance apart of the parallel lines in excess of 2.13 metres, at a rate of 2,500 kilograms per metre.　　　　**[1166]**

NOTES

Commencement: 1 January 1988 (para (2A)); 1 November 1979 (remainder).
Paras (1), (2): words in square brackets added by SI 1987 No 1327, art 15(a).
Para (2A): added by SI 1987 No 1327, art 15(b).
Para (3): figure in square brackets substituted by SI 1987 No 1327, art 4.
Para (4): sub-para (a) substituted by SI 1987 No 1327, art 16(a); in sub-para (f) first amendment in square brackets made by SI 1981 No 1664, art 4(a), proviso (i) revoked by SI 1987 No 1327, art 16(b); sub-para (g) amended by SI 1981 No 1664, art 4(b).

20. Other vehicles carrying loads exceeding 4.3 metres in width

The Minister authorises the use on roads of motor vehicles and trailers carrying loads where the overall width of the vehicle on which the load is carried together with the width of any lateral projection or projections of the load exceeds 4.3 metres but does not exceed 6.1 metres, subject to the restrictions and conditions contained in [articles 21(1)], 22, 24 and 25 and also to the condition that the vehicle complies in all respects with the requirements of the Construction and Use Regulations (other than Regulation 140(1) and (2)).　　　　**[1167]**

NOTES

Commencement: 1 November 1979.
Words in square brackets substituted by SI 1987 No 1327, art 17.

21. Speed limits imposed for vehicles authorised by Article 18, 19 or 20

[(1) A vehicle or combination of vehicles the use of which on roads is authorised by article 18, if of Category 2 or Category 3 as defined in that article, or by article 20, as indicated by an item in column 2 of the Table below, shall not travel at a speed exceeding that specified in column 3 for that item in relation to the type of road used:

1	2	3		
Item	Authorisation	Speed (mph) Motorway	Dual Carriageway	Other road
1	Article 18 Category 2	40	35	30
2	Article 18 Category 3	30	25	20
3	Article 20	30	25	20

(2) A vehicle the use of which on roads is authorised by Article 19 shall not travel on any road other than a [motorway] at a speed exceeding 12 miles per hour.

(3) ...　　　　**[1168]**

NOTES

Commencement: 1 January 1988 (para (1)); 1 November 1979 (remainder).
Para (1): substituted by SI 1987 No 1327, art 18(a).
Para (2): word in square brackets substituted by SI 1987 No 1327, art 5.
Para (3): revoked by SI 1987 No 1327, art 18(b).

22. Attendants

(1) This Article applies in the case of a vehicle the use of which on roads is authorised by Article 20 and in a case where—

(a) the overall width of the vehicle the use of which on roads is authorised by Article 18 or 19 or of the vehicle together with the width of any lateral projection or projections of its load exceeds 3.5 metres, or

(b) the overall length of the vehicle the use of which on roads is authorised by Article 18 or 19 or of the vehicle together with the length of any forward projection and of any rearward projection of its load exceeds 18.3 metres, or

(c) as respects a motor vehicle (whether or not its use is authorised by Article 18 or 19) which is drawing a trailer or trailers the use of which is so authorised, a load is carried in such a manner that its weight rests on more than one of the vehicles being—

(i) the motor vehicle and one trailer whether forming part of an articulated vehicle or not, or

(ii) any other combination of vehicles,

and, in the case of (i) above, the overall length of the trailer together with the length of any forward projection of the load extending beyond the foremost point of the trailer and of any rearward projection of the load exceeds 18.3 metres and, in the case at (ii) above the overall length of the vehicles together with the distance between vehicles and the length of any forward and of any rearward projection of the load exceeds 18.3 metres, or

(d) a motor vehicle (whether or not its use is authorised by Article 18 or 19) is drawing a trailer or trailers the use of which is so authorised and the overall length of the combination of vehicles together with the length of any forward projection of any load extending beyond the foremost point of the drawing vehicle comprised in the combination and the length of any rearward projection of any load extending beyond the rearmost point of the rearmost vehicle comprised therein exceeds 25.9 metres, or

(e) a vehicle the use of which is authorised by Article 18 or 19 is carrying a load having a forward projection exceeding 1.83 metres in length or a rearward projection exceeding 3.05 metres in length or is fitted with any special appliance or apparatus having such a projection.

(2) As respects a vehicle to which this Article applies at least one person, in addition to the person or persons employed in driving any motor vehicle to which this Article applies, shall be employed—

(a) to warn such driver or drivers, and any other person, of any danger likely to be caused to such other person by the presence of such vehicle, and any vehicle or vehicles being drawn by such vehicle on the road, and

(b) to attend to—

(i) such vehicle and its load,

(ii) any vehicle or vehicles drawn by such vehicle, and

(iii) the load carried on any vehicle or vehicles so drawn.

(3) For the purposes of paragraph (2) above—

(a) in a case where a motor vehicle is drawing a trailer or trailers any person employed in pursuance of section 34 of the Road Traffic Act 1972 in attending that vehicle or any such trailer shall be treated as being an attendant required by that paragraph so long as he is also employed to discharge the duties mentioned in that paragraph,

(b) in a case where a motor vehicle is drawing a trailer or trailers and another motor vehicle is used for the purpose of assisting in their propulsion on the road, the person or persons employed in driving that other motor vehicle shall not be treated as a person or persons employed in attending to the first-mentioned vehicle or any vehicle or vehicles drawn thereby, and

(c) in a case where three or more vehicles to which that paragraph applies are travelling together in convoy, it shall be a sufficient compliance with the requirements of that paragraph if only the first and the last vehicles in the convoy are attended in the manner specified in that paragraph.   **[1169]**

NOTES
Commencement: 1 November 1979.

23. Marking of projecting loads and fixed appliances on apparatus which project

(1) This Article applies in a case where a vehicle the use of which is authorised by Article 18 or 19—

(a) carries a load which—

(i) has a forward or a rearward projection exceeding 1.83 metres in length, or

(ii) has a rearward projection exceeding 1.07 metres in length but not exceeding 1.83 metres in length, or

(b) is fitted with a special appliance or apparatus which—

(i) has a forward or a rearward projection exceeding 1.83 metres in length, or

(ii) has a rearward projection exceeding 1.07 metres in length but not exceeding 1.83 metres in length.

(2) Subject to the provisions of paragraphs (3), (4) and (5) of this Article—

(a) as respects a projection mentioned in sub-paragraph (a)(i) or in sub-paragraph (b)(i) of the foregoing paragraph the conditions specified in paragraph 3 of Schedule 8 to the Construction and Use Regulations shall be complied with, and accordingly the provisions of the said paragraph 3 shall apply in relation to that projection as they apply in relation to a relevant projection as mentioned in that paragraph, and

(b) as respects a projection mentioned in sub-paragraph (a)(ii) or in sub-paragraph (b)(ii) of the foregoing paragraph the conditions specified in paragraph 4 of the said Schedule 8 shall be complied with, and accordingly the provisions of the said paragraph 4 shall apply in relation to that projection as they apply in relation to a relevant projection as mentioned in that paragraph.

(3) Where, in any of the cases mentioned in paragraph (1) of this Article, a vehicle is carrying a load or is fitted with a special appliance or apparatus and the load or the appliance or apparatus has, in relation to the vehicle, a forward

projection or a rearward projection, and another vehicle is attached to that end of the vehicle from which the load or, as the case may be, the appliance or apparatus projects and is attached to that vehicle in such a manner that—

(a) in the case where there is a forward projection, the foremost point of that other vehicle extends beyond the foremost part of the projection or, in the case where there is a rearward projection, the rearmost point of that other vehicle extends beyond the rearmost part of the projection, or

(b) in the case where there is a forward projection, the foremost part of the projection extends beyond the foremost point of that other vehicle or, in the case where there is a rearward projection, the rearmost part of the projection extends beyond the rearmost point of that other vehicle, then—

(i) in either of the cases mentioned in sub-paragraph (a) of this paragraph, the provisions of paragraph (2) of this Article shall not apply as respects any such projection, and

(ii) in either of the cases mentioned in sub-paragraph (b) of this paragraph, the provisions of the said paragraph (2) shall apply as if each of the references in paragraph (1) of this Article to a rearward projection were treated as a reference to so much of a rearward projection as extends beyond the rearmost point of that other vehicle and as if the reference in the said paragraph (1) to a forward projection were treated as a reference to so much of a forward projection as extends beyond the foremost point of that other vehicle measured, in either case, when the longitudinal axis of each vehicle lies in the same vertical plane between vertical planes at right angles to the said longitudinal axis and passing, in the case of a rearward projection, through the rearmost point of the said other vehicle and that part of the projection furthest from that point or, in the case of a forward projection, through the foremost point of the said other vehicle and that part of the projection furthest from that point.

(4) This Article shall not apply to any motor vehicle or trailer being used—

(a) for fire brigade, ambulance or police purposes or for defence purposes (including civil defence purposes), or

(b) in connection with the removal of any obstruction to traffic

if, in any such case, compliance with any provision of this Article would hinder or be likely to hinder the use of the vehicle for the purpose for which it is being used on that occasion.

(5) Notwithstanding that paragraph (2)(a) provides for the conditions specified in paragraph 3 of Schedule 8 to the Construction and Use Regulations to be complied with as respects a load which has a projection to which sub-paragraph (a)(i) of paragraph (1) of this Article applies, those conditions in relation to the exhibition of the end projection surface on that projection need not be complied with in the case of such a load which carries a rear marking in accordance with the Motor Vehicles (Rear Markings) Regulations 1970. **[1170]**

NOTES
Commencement: 1 November 1979.

24. Approval of the Minister as to the time, date and route of a journey by a vehicle or a vehicle and its load exceeding 4.3 metres in width

[(1) This article applies in the case of a vehicle the use of which on roads otherwise would be authorised by article 15, 18, 19 or 20 where the overall width of the vehicle or, if it is used for carrying a load, where the overall width of the vehicle together with the width of any lateral projection of its load, exceeds 5 metres.]

(2) Subject to the provisions of paragraph (3) of this Article, a vehicle mentioned in the foregoing paragraph shall be used only—

   (a) for the purpose of making such a journey between specified places as the Minister may have approved by notice in writing given to the owner of the vehicle and only at such times (if any), on such a date or dates (if any) and on such a route (if any) as the Minister may have specified in the said notice, or as the chief officer of police of any police area in which it is proposed that the vehicle shall be used may have specified, in relation to the use of the vehicle in that area, in a direction given to the [user] of the vehicle, and

   (b) if the notice referred to in the foregoing sub-paragraph is carried on the vehicle at all times while it is being used for the purpose of making the journey for which the Minister's approval has been given.

(3) Where the effect of any such direction as is mentioned in sub-paragraph (a) of the foregoing paragraph is to vary, in relation to a time, a date or a route of the journey approved by the Minister under that sub-paragraph, the time, the date or dates or the route of the said journey, the vehicle shall not be used in accordance with that direction unless the Minister has given his further approval that the vehicle shall be so used.   **[1171]**

NOTES
   Commencement: 1 January 1988 (para (1)); 1 November 1979 (remainder).
   Para (1): substituted by SI 1987 No 1327, art 19.
   Para (2): in sub-para (a) word in square brackets substituted by SI 1987 No 1327, art 6.

25. Notice to police

(1) This Article applies in a case where:—

   (a) the overall width of a vehicle the use of which on roads is authorised by Article 18 or 19 or of the vehicle together with the width of any lateral projection or projections of its load exceeds 2.9 metres, or

   (b) the overall length of a vehicle the use of which on roads is authorised by Article 18 or 19 or of the vehicle together with the length of any forward projection and of any rearward projection of its load exceeds 18.3 metres, or

   (c) as respects a motor vehicle (whether or not its use is authorised by Article 18 or 19) which is drawing a trailer or trailers the use of which is so authorised, a load is carried in such a manner that its weight rests on more than one of the vehicles being—

      (i) the motor vehicle and one trailer whether constituting an articulated vehicle or not, or

      (ii) any other combination of vehicles,

   and, in the case at (i) above, the overall length of the trailer together with the length of any forward projection of the load extending beyond the foremost point of the trailer and of any rearward projection of the load exceeds 18.3 metres and, in the case at (ii) above the overall length of the vehicles together with the distance between vehicles and the length of any forward and of any rearward projection of the load exceeds 18.3 metres, or

(d) a motor vehicle (whether or not its use on roads is authorised by Article 18 or 19) is drawing a trailer or trailers the use of which is so authorised and the overall length of the combination of vehicles together with the length of any forward projection of any load extending beyond the foremost point of the drawing vehicle comprised in the combination and the length of any rearward projection of any load extending beyond the rearmost point of the rearmost vehicle comprised therein exceeds 25.9 metres, or

(e) a vehicle the use of which on roads is authorised by Article 18 or 19 is carrying a load having a forward projection or a rearward projection exceeding 3.05 metres in length or is fitted with any special appliance or apparatus having such a projection as aforesaid, or

(f) the total weight of a vehicle the use of which on roads is authorised by Article 18 or 19 or of such a vehicle and its load or, in a case where a motor vehicle (whether or not its use is so authorised), is drawing a trailer or trailers the use of which is so authorised, the total weight of the combination of vehicles or of the said combination and of any load carried by any vehicle or vehicles comprised therein exceeds [80,000 kilograms], or

(g) the use of a vehicle on roads is authorised by Article 20.

(2) Save in so far as the chief officer of police of any police area in which it is proposed that the vehicle or, as the case may be, the vehicles, will be used dispenses, as respects the use of the vehicle or vehicles in that area, with the requirements contained in this paragraph as to the length or the form of notice or the particulars to be given, the [user] of the vehicle, or, as the case may be, of the vehicles, before using the vehicle or vehicles on a road, shall give at least two clear days' notice to the chief officer of police of any such area and such notice shall, subject to any necessary modification, be in the form and contain the particulars specified in Part I of Schedule 2.

(3) Subject to any variation in the time, date or route of the journey which may be directed by any such chief officer of police, and subject to any delay which may be occasioned by reason of a direction given by a police constable, in the interests of road safety or to avoid undue traffic congestion, to the driver of a vehicle to halt it in a place on or adjacent to the road on which the vehicle is travelling, the vehicle or vehicles shall be used only in circumstances which accord with the particulars given in compliance with paragraph (2) above as to the time, date and route of the journey and only if any dimension or measurement relating to the vehicle or the vehicles (including one relating to a combination of vehicles) or to a special appliance or apparatus or to a load to be carried, being a dimension or measurement of which particulars have been given as aforesaid, is not exceeded.   **[1172]**

NOTES
Commencement: 1 November 1979.
Paras (1), (2): words in square brackets substituted by SI 1987 No 1327, arts 6, 20.

26. Notice and indemnity to highway and bridge authorities

(1) This Article applies to—

(a) a vehicle the use of which on roads is authorised by Article 18 or 19, whether such vehicle is laden or unladen, or

(b) a combination of a motor vehicle (whether or not its use on roads is authorised under Article 18 or 19) and any trailer or trailers the use of which on roads is authorised under the said Articles, whether all or any part of such combination is laden or unladen,

and which, in either case, either—

(i) has a total weight exceeding [80,000 kilograms] or
(ii) does not comply in all respects with the requirements of the Construction and Use Regulations or of the Track Laying Regulations with respect to

(*a*) the weights of vehicles, whether laden or unladen;
(*b*) the weights transmitted to the surface of the road by all or any of the wheels or tracks.

(2) In any case where this Article applies, the [user] of the vehicle or, as the case may be, of the combination of vehicles, shall give to the highway authority for any road and the bridge authority for any bridge on which it is proposed that the vehicle or, as the case may be, the combination of vehicles shall be used—

(a) at any time before such use an indemnity in the form specified in Part II of Schedule 2; and
(b) in any case to which sub-paragraph (i) of paragraph (1) above applies, at least [five clear days] (or such less period as the said highway authority or the said bridge authority, as the case may be, may agree) before such use, and in a case to which sub-paragraph (ii) of paragraph (1) above applies at least two clear days (or such less period as the said highway authority or the said bridge authority, as the case may be, may agree) before such use, a notice in the form and containing the particulars specified in Part I of Schedule 2.

[(2A) In any case where a London council or a metropolitan district council which is a highway authority or a bridge authority has—

(a) delegated all or any of its functions with respect to a road or bridge to another London council or (in the case of a metropolitan district council) another metropolitan district council; or
(b) entered into an agreement for the discharge of all or any of its functions with respect to a road or bridge by some other person,

the notice and indemnity which are required by the provisions of paragraph (2) above shall be treated as given in accordance with that paragraph if they are given to the other council or (as the case may be) to the other person.

(2B) In paragraph (2A) above "London council" means the council of a London borough or the Common Council of the City of London.]

(3) Where, in accordance with requirements specified in paragraph (2) above, notice is required to be given at least [five clear days] before a journey is proposed to be made by a combination of vehicles which include a trailer the use of which on roads is authorised by Article 18 and it is found impracticable to use any vehicle specified in the said notice (not being a vehicle the use of which on roads is authorised by Article 18 or 19) as a vehicle intended to draw the trailer, then any other vehicle of a similar type may be substituted therefor if at least two clear days' notice of the substitution is given to every authority to whom the notice was given, and thereupon the said notice shall have effect as if the substituted vehicle had always been specified therein as the vehicle intended to draw the trailer.

(4) If, by virtue of Article 18, a vehicle is to be used on roads to carry a vehicle specified in either item 1 or item 2 in column 1 of Schedule 1, being the property of, or for the time being under the control of, the persons respectively specified opposite thereto in column 3 of that Schedule, the requirement specified in paragraph (2) above that before such use an indemnity and at least [five clear days'] notice or at least two clear days' notice, as the case may be, shall be given to the authorities specified in that paragraph shall not apply provided that before the vehicle is used on a road—

(a) the notice and indemnity which are required by the provisions of paragraph (2) above are received by or posted to all the said authorities,

(b) the [user] of the carrying vehicle has consulted the Minister on the route proposed to be followed, and

(c) the proper naval, military or air force authority has certified in writing that the journey is urgent and in the national interest.

(5) The provisions of this Article shall not apply to the use on roads of any vehicle which is the property of, or for the time being under the control of, the Secretary of State for Defence.

(6) In the case of a trunk road—

(i) where by virtue of the provisions of section 10 of the Highways Act 1959, the functions of the Minister with respect to maintenance are exercised in England by the council of a county [or of a metropolitan district] or of a London Borough [or by any other person acting pursuant to an agreement with the Minister] or the functions of the Secretary of State with respect to maintenance are exercised in Wales by the council of a county or where, by virtue of the provisions of section 5 of the Trunk Roads Act 1936, as amended or modified by the Trunk Roads Act 1946, the functions of the Secretary of State with respect to maintenance and repair are exercised in Scotland by a regional council, or

(ii) where by virtue of an agreement between, or having effect under paragraph 2 of Schedule 6 to the Transport Act 1962 as if between, the Secretary of State or, as the case may be, the Minister, and either the British Railways Board, the London Transport Executive, the British Transport Docks Board, or the British Waterways Board, the maintenance or, as the case may be, the maintenance and repair of that part are carried out by such Executive or by any such Board, the notice and indemnity required to be given to the Minister by paragraph (2) of this Article shall be treated as given in accordance with that paragraph only if addressed to, or included in any notice and indemnity given to, such council, Executive or Board [or person] as the case may be.

(7) Any notice and indemnity in respect of any part of a trunk road required by the foregoing paragraph to be addressed to, or included in any notice and indemnity given to, the British Railways Board shall be addressed to, or included in a notice and indemnity given to, the Board at the Headquarters of the Regional Railways Board responsible for the part of the railway system which is affected by any such agreement as is mentioned in that paragraph by virtue of the agreement applying to that part of the trunk road. **[1173]**

NOTES
   Commencement: 1 April 1986 (paras (2A), (2B)); 1 November 1979 (remainder).
   Paras (1), (2), (3), (4): words in square brackets substituted by SI 1987 No 1327, arts 6, 21.
   Paras (2A), (2B): added by SI 1986 No 313, art 6(a).
   Para (6): amended by SI 1986 No 313, art 6(b).

27. Restriction on the passage over bridges of vehicles carrying abnormal indivisible loads

Where a motor vehicle the use of which on roads is authorised by Article 18 is so used or where a motor vehicle (whether or not its use is so authorised) is drawing a trailer or trailers the use of which is so authorised and an abnormal indivisible load is being carried by any such vehicle, the driver of the motor vehicle shall not cause or permit either that vehicle or, in the case of a combination of vehicles, any vehicle comprised in the combination—

   (a) to enter on any bridge whilst there is on that bridge any other vehicle which is either carrying an abnormal indivisible load or is being used to draw a trailer carrying such a load the presence of which is known to or could reasonably be ascertained by him, or
   (b) to remain stationary on any bridge except in circumstances beyond his control.   **[1174]**

NOTES
   Commencement: 1 November 1979.

28. Breakdown on bridges of vehicles of excessive weight or carrying excessive loads

(1) This Article applies where—

   [(a) a vehicle (including an articulated vehicle) laden or unladen has a gross weight of more than:
      (i) prior to [1st October 1989], 32,520 kilograms;
      (ii) on or after [1st October 1989], 38,000 kilograms, and]
   (b) the use on roads of a vehicle or of a trailer forming part of an articulated vehicle is authorised by Article 5(2), 6, 11, 15, 16, 18 or 19.

(2) Subject to the provisions of paragraph (3) below, where a vehicle or trailer is caused to stop for any reason while it is on a bridge, it shall, as soon as practicable, be moved clear of the bridge by appropriate action by the person in charge of the vehicle, without applying any concentrated load to the surface of that part of the road carried by the bridge.

(3) If the action described in paragraph (2) above is not practicable and it becomes necessary to apply any concentrated load to the said surface by means of jacks, rollers or other similar means, then the person in charge of the vehicle shall—

   (a) before any such load is applied to that surface, seek the advice of the bridge authority for that bridge [or any other person responsible for the maintenance and repair of the bridge pursuant to an agreement with that authority] about the use of spreader plates to reduce the possibility of any damage caused by the application of such a load, and
   (b) arrange that no such load shall be applied without using such spreader plates as the bridge authority [or such other person] may have advised.   **[1175]**

NOTES
Commencement: 1 November 1979.
Para (1): sub-para (a) substituted by SI 1987 No 1327, art 22, further amended by SI 1987 No 2161, art 5.
Para (3): amended by SI 1986 No 313, art 7.

SCHEDULES

SCHEDULE 1

Order 6

SERVICE AND AVIATION VEHICLES

Column 1	Column 2	Column 3
1. Motor vehicles or trailers constructed either for actual combative purposes or for naval, military or air force training in connection therewith or for use with, or for the carriage or drawing of, instruments of war, including guns and machine guns.	Construction and Use Regulations—All. Track Laying Regulations—All.	The Secretary of State for Defence or the Secretary of State for Industry, or any contractor making such vehicles for the said Secretaries of State or any subcontractor of such contractor.
2. Track laying motor vehicles or track laying trailers constructed either for actual combative purposes or for use with, or for the carriage or drawing of, instruments of war, including guns and machine guns, ammunition, equipment or stores in connection therewith.	Construction and Use Regulations—All. Track Laying Regulations—All.	The Secretary of State for Defence or the Secretary of State for Industry, or any contractor making such vehicles for the said Secretaries of State, or any subcontractor of such contractor.
3. Motor vehicles or trailers constructed for the carriage of tanks.	Construction and Use Regulations—All. Track Laying Regulations—All.	The Secretary of State for Defence or the Secretary of State for Industry, or any contractor making such vehicles for the said Secretaries of State, or any subcontractor of such contractor.
4. Motor vehicles or trailers constructed for the carriage of searchlights or the necessary equipment therefor.	Construction and Use Regulation 12. Track Laying Regulation 7.	The Secretary of State for Defence or the Secretary of State for Industry, or any contractor making such vehicles for the said Secretaries of State, or any subcontractor of such contractor.
5. Motor vehicles or trailers constructed for the carriage of aircraft or aircraft parts.	Construction and Use Regulations 9, 57, 58, 74 and 140. Track Laying Regulations 5, 30 and 75.	The Secretary of State for Defence or the Secretary of State for Industry, or any contractor making such vehicles for the said Secretaries of State, or any subcontractor of such contractor.

Column 1	Column 2	Column 3
6. Motor tractors, heavy motor cars and trailers constructed for naval, military, air force or aviation purposes before 1st January 1949.	Construction and Use Regulations 53, 57, 58, 74, 75 and 76.	The Secretary of State for Defence or the Secretary of State for Industry.
7. Heavy motor cars or trailers constructed for use and used only in connection with flying operations where the additional width is made necessary by the design of the equipment or its installation on the vehicle.	Construction and Use Regulations 57 and 74.	The Secretary of State for Defence or the Secretary of State for Industry, or any contractor making such vehicles for the said Secretaries of State, or any subcontractor of such contractor.
8. Aircraft drawn by motor vehicles.	Construction and Use Regulations 12, 73, 74, 75 and 76.	The Secretary of State for Defence.
9. Motor vehicles or trailers used for the carriage of generating equipment, being equipment used for naval, military or air force purposes.	Construction and Use Regulations 48, 73, 74, 82, 83, 86, 94 and 150.	The Minister of Transport.

[1176]

NOTES
Commencement: 1 November 1979.

SCHEDULE 2
PART I

FORM OF NOTICE TO POLICE AND TO HIGHWAY AND BRIDGE AUTHORITIES (ARTS 15, 16, 25 AND 26)

(Subject to the prior agreement of each of the authorities to which this notice is sent, it may be used to give notice of additional journeys, different vehicles, routes and destinations.)

List of all Police Forces, Highway and Bridge Authorities to which this form is sent.

Operator	....	Telephone No. ....
Address	....	Telex No. ....
	....	Operator's Licence No. ....
	....	Operator's Reference No. ....

In pursuance of Article(s)   of the above mentioned Order, I/we being the operator of the undermentioned vehicle(s) to which the Order applies, hereby give notice that it is my/our intention to use the said vehicle(s) on the roads specified below. The route and Department of Transport Classification numbers proposed to be used are:

PARTICULARS OF JOURNEY

FROM (full address)	TIME AND DATE	via ....

TO (full address)	TIME AND DATE

Registration No. of vehicle (or substitute)	Type of vehicle

PARTICULARS OF LOAD

LOAD PROFILE (rough sketch showing outline of laden vehicle from front or rear. This to be omitted if sent by telex).

DESCRIPTION OF LOAD

PARTICULARS OF VEHICLE

Overall length of vehicle		Projection —front		Projection —rear		Total length	
Overall width		Maximum height		Gross weight or Gross train weight			
No. of wheels per axle							
Axle weight							
Axle spacing							

[1177]

NOTES

Commencement: 1 November 1979.

PART II
FORM OF INDEMNITY (ARTS 15, 16 AND 26)

I/We hereby agree to indemnify you and each and every highway or bridge authority [or other person] responsible for the maintenance and repair of any road or bridge on the journey to which the above notice relates in respect of any damage which may be caused to any such road or bridge—

    (a) by [any of] the above mentioned vehicle[s]—

        (i) by reason of the construction of or weight transmitted to the road surface by [any of] the said vehicle[s], or
        (ii) by reason of the dimensions, distribution or adjustment of the load carried by [any of] the said vehicle[s]; or

    (b) by any other vehicle by reason of the use of [any of] the above-mentioned vehicle[s] on the road or, as the case may be, the bridge except to the extent that the damage was caused or contributed to by the negligence of the driver of the other vehicle:

Provided that any claim in respect of damage so caused by any vehicle shall be made in writing within twelve months from the date on which the vehicle is last used on the journey to which the above notice relates, stating the occasion and place of the damage.

Date .... Signed ....

Note:—Paragraph (a)(ii) above only applies where vehicles are carrying an abnormal indivisible load and in other cases should be omitted.   **[1178]**

NOTES
Commencement: 1 November 1979.
Amended by SI 1986 No 313, art 8.

SCHEDULE 4
Orders 13, 13A

CONDITIONS RELATING TO THE WIDTH OF AGRICULTURAL VEHICLES

[1. If the overall width of the vehicle, or in the case of a combination of vehicles mentioned in Article 13A(1), the overall width of the combination exceeds the width specified in an item in column 2 of the Table below, the vehicle, or in the case of a combination of vehicles, the drawing vehicle, shall not be driven at a speed exceeding that specified in column 3 of that item.

TABLE

1 Item No	2 Overall width	3 Maximum speed
1	3·5 metres	12 miles per hour
2	2·5 metres	20 miles per hour

2. If—

    (a) the overall width of—

        (i) an agricultural motor vehicle,
        (ii) an agricultural trailer,
        (iii) an agricultural trailed appliance, or

    (b) the width specified in Article 13A(2) of a combination of vehicles—

exceeds 3 metres and the whole or part of the journey to be made by the vehicle or combination will be on a road on which there is a speed limit of 40 miles per hour or less or will cover a distance exceeding 5 miles, the operator of the vehicle shall—

(A) before using the vehicle or combination on a road, give at least 24 hours notice of the intended use to the chief officer of police for any police area in which the operator proposes to use the vehicle or combination of vehicles and the notice shall contain the following particulars:—

    (i) the time, date and route of the proposed journey,
    (ii) information about the vehicle or combination of vehicles including the overall width; and

(B) use the vehicle or combination only in accordance with the particulars given in the notice mentioned above, subject to any variation in the time, date or route as may be directed by any chief officer of police as regards his police area,

so, however that a chief officer of police may dispense, within his area, with the said requirements as to length of notice and information about the vehicle or combination.

3. In a case where—

(a) the width of an agricultural motor vehicle exceeds 3 metres, or
(b) an agricultural motor vehicle is towing an agricultural trailer or agricultural trailed appliance in the manner described in Article 13A(1) and the width specified in Article 13A(2) exceeds 3 metres, or
(c) an agricultural motor vehicle is towing an agricultural trailer or an agricultural trailed appliance in a manner not described in Article 13A(1) and the overall width of either the motor vehicle or the trailer or trailed appliance, or both, exceeds 3 metres,

the vehicle or the combination of vehicles shall not draw any trailer or, as the case may be, any other trailer, except

    (i) a two-wheeled trailer used solely for the carriage of equipment for use on the drawing vehicle,
    (ii) an agricultural trailed appliance, or
    (iii) an unladen trailer specially designed for use with the drawing vehicle when it is harvesting.

4. If the overall width of an agricultural motor vehicle, an agricultural trailer on which an implement is mounted as mentioned in Article 13B, or an agricultural trailed appliance, or the width specified in Article 13A(2) of a combination of vehicles, exceeds 3.5 metres—

(a) at least one person, other than the driver of the vehicle or, in the case of a combination of vehicles, the driver of the drawing vehicle, shall be employed to warn any other person (including the driver of the vehicle or the drawing vehicle) of any danger likely to be caused to that other person by the presence of the vehicle or the combination of vehicles on the road; and
(b) the extremities of the vehicle or implement (including any blade or spike) shall be clearly visible at a reasonable distance to any person on the road (other than the driver of the vehicle or, in the case of a combination of vehicles, the driver of the drawing vehicle) and during the hours of darkness or in seriously reduced visibility this condition shall be satisfied by such means as may be required by the Road Vehicles Lighting Regulations 1984.

5. The overall width of a vehicle, or the width specified in Article 13A(2) of a combination of vehicles, shall not exceed 4.3 metres.] **[1179]**

NOTES
    Commencement: 1 March 1985.
    Added by SI 1984 No 1810, art 8.

SCHEDULE 5
Order 13C

PART I

1 Item No	2 Distance of rearward or forward projection	3 Conditions to be complied with
1.	1 metre	A
2.	2 metres	B
3.	4 metres	B C
4.	6 metres	B C D

[1180]

NOTES
Commencement: 1 March 1985.
Added by SI 1984 No 1810, art 8.

PART II

[1. In this Schedule:—

"Condition A" is the condition that the end of each projection is clearly visible at a reasonable distance to any person using the road other than the driver of the vehicle, or in the case of a combination of vehicles, the driver of the drawing vehicle, and during the hours of darkness or in seriously reduced visibility this condition shall be satisfied by such means as may be required by the Road Vehicles Lighting Regulations 1984.

"Condition B" is the condition that—

    (a) the end of each projection is marked with a projection marker of a kind specified in relation to an end projection surface in Part II of Schedule 8 to the Construction and Use Regulations and in respect of which the provisions specified, for the purposes of those Regulations, in paragraph 3(c) of Part I of that Schedule are complied with,

    (b) each side of each projection is marked with a projection marker of a kind specified in relation to a side projection surface in Part II of that Schedule and in respect of which the provisions specified, for the purposes of the said Regulations, in paragraph 3(d) of Part I of that Schedule are complied with, and

    (c) during the hours of darkness or in seriously reduced visibility the markers referred to in paragraphs (a) and (b) shall be illuminated in the manner described, in relation to the extremities of an appliance, in paragraph 3(g) of Schedule 8 to the Construction and Use Regulations, and kept clean and unobstructed.

"Condition C" is the same condition as is specified, in relation to Articles 13 and 13A, in paragraph 2 of Schedule 4; and

"Condition D" is the same condition as is specified, in relation to Articles 13 and 13A, in paragraph 4(a) of Schedule 4.]   **[1181]**

NOTES
Commencement: 1 March 1985.
Added by SI 1984 No 1810, art 8.

Order 18(2)(t)

SCHEDULE 6

FORM OF IDENTIFICATION SIGN

PART I

[1. The sign shall be mounted in a clearly visible position on the front of the vehicle, facing forwards, and as near to the vertical plane as practicable.

2. The sign shall be kept clean and unobscured at all times.

3. The sign shall consist of white letters on a black background.

4. The sign shall take the form shown in Part II. Any variation in a dimension specified in Part II shall be treated as permitted for the purposes of this Order if the variation does not exceed 5 per cent of that dimension.]   **[1182]**

NOTES
    Commencement: 1 January 1988.
    Added by SI 1987 No 1327, art 23.

PART II

400mm

250mm   105mm

70mm

NOTE: THE CATEGORY NUMBER 3 IS SHOWN AS AN EXAMPLE; THE NUMBER COULD BE 1, 2 OR 3 DEPENDING UPON THE CATEGORY OF THE VEHICLE OR COMBINATION OF VEHICLES.]   **[1183]**

NOTES
    COMMENCEMENT: 1 JANUARY 1988.
    ADDED BY SI 1987 NO 1327, ART 23.

MOTOR CYCLES (PROTECTIVE HELMETS) REGULATIONS 1980
(SI 1980 NO 1279)

NOTES
    Made: 22 August 1980
    Authority: Road Traffic Act 1988, ss 16, 17

ARRANGEMENT OF REGULATIONS

1. These Regulations shall come into operation on 20th September 1980 and
may be cited as the Motor Cycles (Protective Helmets) Regulations 1980.**[1184]**

NOTES
   Commencement: 20 September 1980.

3. In these Regulations a reference to a numbered Regulation or Schedule is a
reference to the Regulation or Schedule bearing that number in these
Regulations.   **[1185]**

NOTES
   Commencement: 20 September 1980.

4. (1) Save as provided in paragraph (2) below, every person driving or riding
(otherwise than in a side-car) on a motor bicycle when on a road shall wear
protective headgear.

   (2) Nothing in paragraph (1) above shall apply to any person driving or
riding on a motor bicycle if—

     (a) it is a mowing machine;

     (b) it is for the time being propelled by a person on foot; or

     (c) he is a follower of the Sikh religion while he is wearing a turban.

   (3) In this Regulation:—

     "motor bicycle" means a two wheeled motor cycle, whether having a side-
     car attached thereto or not, and for the purposes of this definition any
     wheels of a motor cycle shall, if the distance between the centres of the
     areas of contact between such wheels and the road surface is less than
     460 millimetres, be counted as one wheel; and
     "protective headgear" means headgear which—

       (a) is either—

         (i) a helmet bearing a marking applied by its manufacturer
         indicating compliance with the specifications contained in
         one of the British Standards mentioned in Schedule 2
         (whether or not as modified by any amendment), or

        (ii) a helmet of a type manufactured for use by persons on motor
         cycles which by virtue of its shape, material and construction
         could reasonably be expected to afford to persons on motor
         bicycles a degree of protection from injury in the event of an
         accident similar to or greater than that provided by a helmet
         of a type prescribed by Regulation 5; and

       (b) if worn with a chin cup attached to or held in position by a strap
        or other fastening provided on the helmet, is provided with an
        additional strap or other fastening (to be fastened under the
        wearer's jaw) for securing the helmet firmly to the head of the
        wearer; and

(c) is securely fastened to the head of the wearer by means of the straps or other fastening provided on the headgear for that purpose. **[1186]**

NOTES
Commencement: 20 September 1980.

5. [(1) The types of helmet hereby prescribed as types of helmet recommended as affording protection to persons on or in motor cycles from injury in the event of an accident are helmets which as regards their shape, construction and other qualities conform—

(a) until 1st September 1986, with any one of the British Standards mentioned in items 5, 6, 7, 8, 9, 10 and 11 in Schedule 2;
(b) on and after 1st September 1986 until 1st April 1989, with any one of the British Standards mentioned in items 9, 10 and 11 in Schedule 2;
(c) on and after 1st April 1989, with the British Standard mentioned in item 11 in Schedule 2;

and which in the case of any helmet is marked with the number of the British Standard with which it conforms and the certification mark of the British Standards Institution (whether or not it is required to be so marked by the British Standard in point).]

(2) A reference in paragraph (1) above to a helmet which, as respects its shape, construction and other qualities, conforms with one of the British Standards mentioned in an item in Schedule 2 is a reference to a helmet which so conforms with one of those British Standards subject to such (if any) of the amendments to the relevant Standard mentioned in the relevant item as had effect at the time of the manufacture of the helmet. **[1187]**

NOTES
Commencement: 11 April 1986 (para (1)); 20 September 1980 (remainder).
Para (1): substituted by SI 1986 No 472, reg 3.

6. Nothing in Regulation 5(1) shall be taken to authorise any person to apply any number or mark referred to therein in contravention of the Trade Descriptions Act 1968. **[1188]**

NOTES
Commencement: 20 September 1980.

SCHEDULES
SCHEDULE 2
BRITISH STANDARDS

1. British Standard 2001: 1956 as amended by the following Amendment Slips:—

Number	Date of Publication
1	11th January 1957.
2	23rd November 1959.
3	27th February 1962.
4	11th June 1964.
5	13th March 1968.
6	18th February 1972.

2. British Standard 1869: 1960 as amended by the following Amendment Slips:—

Number	Date of Publication
1	29th May 1963.

Number	Date of Publication
4	3rd December 1965.
5	13th March 1968.
6	10th August 1971.
7	3rd January 1972.
8	15th May 1973.
9	1st February 1974.
10	2nd September 1974.

3. British Standard 2495: 1960 as amended by the following Amendment Slips:—

Number	Date of Publication
1	29th May 1963.
2	22nd February 1965.
3	7th December 1965.
4	22nd July 1966.
5	10th August 1971.
6	3rd January 1972.
7	1st February 1974.
8	1st March 1975.

4. British Standard 2001: 1972 as amended by the following Amendment Slips:—

Number	Date of Publication
1	12th December 1972.
2	26th January 1973.
3	1st February 1974.
4	2nd September 1974.
5	1st March 1975.

5. British Standard 5361: 1976

6. British Standard 2495: 1977

7. British Standard 5361: 1976 as amended by the following Amendment Slips:—

Number	Date of Publication
1	30th September 1977.
2	31st August 1978.
3	31st August 1979.
4	29th February 1980.

8. British Standard 2495: 1977 as amended by the following Amendment Slips:—

Number	Date of Publication
1	30th September 1977.
2	31st August 1978.
3	31st August 1979.
4	29th February 1980.

[9. British Standard 5361: 1976 as amended by the following Amendment Slips:—

Number	Date of Publication
1	30th September 1977.
2	31st August 1978.
3	31st August 1979.
4	29th February 1980.
5	27th February 1981.

10. British Standard 2495: 1977 as amended by the following Amendment Slips:—

Number	Date of Publication
1	30th September 1977.
2	31st August 1978.
3	31st August 1979.
4	29th February 1980.
5	27th February 1981.

[11. British Standard 6658/1985 as amended by the following Amendment Slip:—

         Number   *Date of Publication*
            1   28th February 1986.

[1189]

NOTES
     Commencement: 11 April 1986 (item 11); 1 April 1981 (items 9, 10); 20 September 1980 (remainder).
     Items 9, 10: added by SI 1981 No 374.
     Item 11: added by SI 1986 No 472, reg 4.

TRAFFIC SIGNS REGULATIONS AND GENERAL DIRECTIONS 1981
(SI 1981 No 859)

NOTES
     Made: 10 June 1981
     Authority: Road Traffic Act 1988, s 36(5); Road Traffic Regulation Act 1984, ss 28, 64, 65

ARRANGEMENT OF REGULATIONS

PART I
TRAFFIC SIGNS REGULATIONS

Section I, Preliminary

Direction   Para

PART II

GENERAL DIRECTIONS

PART I

TRAFFIC SIGNS REGULATIONS

Section I, Preliminary

1. Citation

These Regulations may be cited as the Traffic Signs Regulations 1981.   **[1190]**

NOTES
  Commencement: 13 August 1981.

2. Revocation

The Traffic Signs Regulations 1975 are hereby revoked, and the said Regulations of 1975 are hereinafter in these Regulations referred to as "the Regulations of 1975". **[1191]**

NOTES
  Commencement: 13 August 1981.

3. Savings

(1) Any traffic sign, which immediately before the coming into operation of these Regulations is in being, if it is a sign shown in any of the diagrams Nos. 564.2 to 564.4 in Schedule 1 to the Regulations of 1975 or is a sign for which there is provision in Regulation 27(1)(a)(iv) of those Regulations and if it then complies with the provisions relating thereto by virtue of those Regulations, shall so long as it continues to comply with the said provisions as though the same had not been revoked be treated as if prescribed by these Regulations until 31st December 1985.

(2) Any traffic sign, which immediately before the coming into operation of these Regulations is situated on or near any road, if it is a sign prescribed, or to be treated as if prescribed by the Regulations of 1975 and if it then complies with the provisions relating thereto by virtue of those Regulations, shall so long as it continues to comply with the said provisions as though the same had not been revoked, be treated as if prescribed by these Regulations, any provisions thereof to the contrary notwithstanding;

Provided that this paragraph shall cease to have any effect—

> (i) on and after 1st January 1983 in relation to any sign shown in diagram No. 601 in Schedule 1 to the Traffic Signs Regulations 1964 (hereinafter in these Regulations referred to as "the Regulations of 1964") and to any sign shown in diagram No. 1035 in Schedule 2 to the Regulations of 1975 as varied by the substitution of the words "turn left", "ahead" or "turn right",
> (ii) on and after 1st January 1984 in relation to any sign shown in diagram No. 1002, in Schedule 2 to the Regulations of 1975, and
> [(iia) on and after 1st January 1985 in relation to any sign shown in diagram 649 in Schedule 1 to the Regulations of 1975;]
> (iii) on and after 1st January 1990 in relation to any sign shown in any of the diagrams Nos. 662.1, 626, 628, 639.1, 640.2, ... , 719.3, 806.2, 808.2 and 819 in Schedule 1 to the Regulations of 1975
> [(iv) on and after 1st January 1985 in relation to any sign shown in diagram 649.1 in Schedule 1 to these Regulations].

[(3) Any traffic sign shown in diagram 577 and 651 which immediately before 10th February 1983 is in being and which complied with the provisions in these Regulations relating to the sign in force immediately before that date shall, so long as it continues to comply with those provisions, be treated as prescribed by these Regulations until 31st December 1992.] **[1192]**

NOTES
Commencement: 10 February 1983 (para (3)); 13 August 1981 (remainder).
Para (2): amended by SI 1984 No 966, Part I.
Para (3): added by SI 1982 No 1879, reg 3.
Regulations of 1975: Traffic Signs Regulations 1975; SI 1975 No 1536.

4. Interpretation

(1) In these Regulations the following expressions have the meanings hereby respectively assigned to them:—

"the Act" means the Road Traffic Regulation Act 1967;

["articulated vehicle" means a motor vehicle with a trailer so attached to it as to be partially superimposed upon it;]

"chief officer of police", in relation to England and Wales, has the same meaning as in the Police Act 1964, and, in relation to Scotland, the same meaning as in the Police (Scotland) Act 1967,

["cycle lane" means part of the carriageway of a road which—
(a) starts with the marking shown in diagram 1009, and
(b) is separated from the rest of the carriageway by—

   (i) if it may not be used by vehicles other than pedal cycles, the marking shown in diagram 1049, or
   (ii) if it may be used by vehicles other than pedal cycles, the marking shown in diagram 1004;]

"enactment" includes any instrument made under an Act;

"goods vehicle" means a motor vehicle constructed or adapted for use for the carriage of goods or a trailer so constructed or adapted;

"hours of darkness" means the time between half-an-hour after sunset and half-an-hour before sunrise;

["maximum gross weight" means—
(a) in the case of a motor vehicle not drawing a trailer or in the case of a trailer, its maximum laden weight;
(b) in the case of an articulated vehicle, its maximum laden weight (if it has one) and otherwise the aggregate maximum laden weight of all the individual vehicles forming part of that articulated vehicle; and
(c) in the case of a motor vehicle (other than an articulated vehicle) drawing one or more trailers, the aggregate maximum laden weight of the motor vehicle and the trailer or trailers attached to it,

and the foregoing references to the maximum laden weight of a vehicle are references to the total laden weight which must not be exceeded in the case of that vehicle if it is to be used in Great Britain without contravening any regulations for the time being in force under section 40 of the Road Traffic Act 1972;]

"motorway" means a special road—
(a) which in England or Wales (save as otherwise provided by or under regulations made under, or having effect as if made under section 13 of the Act) can only be used by traffic of Class I or II of the classes of traffic set out in Schedule 4 to the Highways Act 1980, or
(b) which in Scotland can only be used by traffic of Class I or Class II of the classes of traffic set out in Schedule 2 to the Special Roads Act 1949;

["pedal cycle" means a bicycle, tricycle, or cycle having four or more wheels, not being in any case mechanically propelled unless it is an

electrically assisted pedal cycle of such class as is for the purposes of the
Act to be treated as not being a motor vehicle;]

"primary route" means a route, not being a route formed by any part of a
motorway, formed—

    (a) by a length of trunk road,

    (b) by a length of trunk road together with another road, not being a
          trunk road, or

    (c) by a length of road, not being a trunk road,

being a route as respects which the Secretary of State—

> in the case at (a) is of the opinion, and in the cases at (b) and (c)
> after consultation with the highway authority for the road, not
> being a trunk road, is of the opinion that it provides the most
> satisfactory route for through traffic between two or more places
> of traffic importance;

"non-primary route" means a route, not being a primary route or a
motorway or part of a primary route or a motorway;

"scheduled express carriage" means an express carriage operated in
accordance with a time-table, and includes a vehicle operating a service
in accordance with a time-table contained in an authorisation issued
under Council Regulation (EEC) No. 516/72 (shuttle services by means
of coach and bus between Member States) or under Council Regulation
(EEC) No. 517/72 (regular and special regular services by the said
means) both of 28th February 1972;

"school bus" means a vehicle constructed or adapted to carry 12 or more
passengers and being used to carry persons to or from school as defined
by section 114(1) of the Education Act 1944 and, in Scotland, as defined
by section 145 of the Education (Scotland) Act 1962;

"stud" means a prefabricated device fixed or embedded as a mark in the
carriageway;

"temporary statutory provision" means a provision having effect under
section 12 of the Act (temporary prohibition or restriction of traffic on
roads) or section 9 of the Act (which relates to experimental traffic
schemes) as those sections are amended by Part IX of the Transport Act
1968 or contained in sections 57 (traffic signs for giving effect to local
traffic regulations), 58 (emergency traffic signs) or 60 (traffic signs in
connection with experimental traffic schemes in London) of the Act;

"Wales" and "England" have the meanings respectively assigned to them
by section 269 of the Local Government Act 1972;

"works bus" means a vehicle constructed or adapted to carry 12 or more
passengers which has been provided by an employer for the purpose of
carrying persons employed by him or on his behalf to or from their place
of employment and being used for such a purpose.

    (2) Nothing in these Regulations shall have effect so as to authorise any
persons not otherwise authorised to do so to place on or near the road any object
or device for warning traffic of a temporary obstruction.   **[1193]**

NOTES
    Commencement: 13 August 1981.
    Para (1): amended by SI 1982 No 1879, reg 4.

5. Interpretation

(1) References in these Regulations to a numbered Regulation or Schedule
shall, unless the reference is to a regulation of, or a schedule to, specified

regulations, be construed as references to the Regulation or Schedule bearing that number in these Regulations.

(2) References in any of these Regulations to a numbered paragraph shall, unless the reference is to a paragraph of a specified Regulation, be construed as references to the paragraph bearing that number in the first mentioned Regulation.

(3) Any reference in these Regulations to a diagram by a number is a reference to the diagram of that number in any of the Schedules to these Regulations.

(4) Any reference in these Regulations to any sign shown in a diagram being a diagram in Schedule 1, Schedule 2, Schedule 5 or Schedule 6 shall be construed as including a reference to any such sign varied in accordance with the provisions of these Regulations except where otherwise expressly provided.

[(5) Any reference in these Regulations to a numbered direction is a reference to the paragraph bearing that number in the Traffic Signs General Directions 1981.]   **[1194]**

NOTES
   Commencement: 13 April 1990 (para (5)); 13 August 1981 (remainder).
   Para (5): added by SI 1990 No 704, Part I, reg 3.

TRAFFIC SIGN REGULATIONS

Section II, Miscellaneous General Provisions

6. Authorisations by the Secretary of State

Nothing in these Regulations shall be taken to limit the powers of the Secretary of State under section 54 of the Act to authorise the erection or retention of traffic signs of a character not prescribed by these Regulations.   **[1195]**

NOTES
   Commencement: 13 August 1981.
   The Act: Road Traffic Regulation Act 1967.

---

7. Application of [section 36 of the Road Traffic Act 1988] to signs and disqualification for offences

(1) [Section 36 of the Road Traffic Act 1988] shall apply—

   (a) to signs of the type shown in any of the diagrams 601.1, 602, 603, 606, 610, 616 [, 629.2] and [649.2] and to the sign of the type shown in diagram 602 when used in combination with that shown in diagram 602.1,

   (b) to the red signal when shown by the light signals prescribed by Regulation 31, by Regulation 31 as varied by Regulation 32, or by Regulation 33,

   (c) to the road marking shown in diagram 1013.1 insofar as that marking conveys the requirements specified in Regulation 23(2),

   (d) . . .

   [(e) until the 1st January 1985 to any sign of the type shown in diagram 649 in Schedule 1 to the 1975 Regulations or in diagram 649.1 in Schedule 1 to these Regulations, and]

   (f) to any sign which in accordance with Regulation 3(2) is treated as if prescribed by these Regulations, if it is a road marking of the type shown in the diagram numbered 1013 in Schedule 2 to the Regulations of 1964 insofar as that marking conveys the requirements specified in Regulation 23(2) thereof.

(2) The signs specified hereby for the purposes of the paragraph appearing in [column 5 of the entry in Schedule 2 to the Road Traffic Offenders Act 1988 relating to offences under section 36 of the Road Traffic Act 1988] are:—

    (a) the sign shown in the diagram numbered 601.1,

    (b) the sign shown in the diagram numbered [649.2],

    (c) the red signal when shown by light signals prescribed by Regulation 31, by Regulation 31 as varied by Regulation 32, or by Regulation 33,

    (d) the road marking shown in the diagram numbered 1013.1 insofar as that marking conveys the requirements specified in Regulation 23(2),

    (e) ...

    [(*f*) until 1st January 1985 any sign of the type shown in diagram 649 in schedule 1 to the Regulations of 1975 or in diagram 649.1 in Schedule 1 to these Regulations, ...]

    (g) the road marking shown in the diagram numbered 1013 in Schedule 2 to the Regulations of 1964 insofar as it conveys the requirements specified in Regulation 23(2) thereof which marking is in accordance with Regulation 3(2) treated as if prescribed by these Regulations [; and

    (h) the sign shown in the diagram numbered 629.2.] **[1196]**

NOTES

    Commencement: 13 August 1981.

    Heading: words in square brackets substituted by SI 1989 No 2139, Part I, reg 3.

    Para (1): first words in square brackets substituted, and first figure in square brackets added by SI 1989 No 2139, Part I, reg 3; second words and second figure in square brackets substituted, and words omitted revoked by SI 1984 No 966, Part I.

    Para (2): first words in square brackets substituted, final words in square brackets added, and second word omitted revoked, by SI 1989 No 2139, Part I, reg 3; second and third amendments in square brackets made, and first words omitted revoked, by SI 1984 No 966, Part I.

8. Variations in dimensions

(1) Any variation in a dimension (other than a dimension as to the height of a letter or expressed as being the maximum or, as the case may be, minimum) specified in any of the diagrams in Schedule 1 or Schedules 3 to 6 shall be treated as permitted by these Regulations if the variation—

    (a) in the case of a dimension so specified as 300 millimetres or as over 300 millimetres, does not exceed 5 per cent of that dimension,

    (b) in the case of a dimension so specified as 50 millimetres or as over 50 millimetres but as under 300 millimetres, does not exceed 7.5 per cent of that dimension, or

    (c) in the case of a dimension so specified as under 50 millimetres, does not exceed 10 per cent of that dimension.

(2) Any variation in a dimension as to the height of a letter specified in any of the diagram in schedule 1 shall be treated as permitted by these Regulations if the variation—

    (a) in the case of a dimension so specified as 100 millimetres or as over 100 millimetres does not exceed 5 per cent of that dimension, or

    (b) in the case of a dimension so specified as under 100 millimetres, does not exceed 7.5 per cent of that dimension.

(3) Without prejudice to the next following paragraph, any variation in a dimension (other than a dimension expressed in diagrams 1003.4, 1013.1,

1027.1, 1040 to 1045 or 1055 as being the maximum, or as the case may be, minimum) specified in any of the diagrams in Schedule 2 shall be treated as permitted by these Regulations if the variation—

    (a) in the case of a dimension so specified as 3 metres or as over 3 metres, does not exceed 15 per cent of that dimension,

    (b) in the case of a dimension so specified as 300 millimetres or as over 300 millimetres but as under 3 metres, does not exceed 20 per cent of that dimension, or

    (c) in the case of a dimension so specified as under 300 millimetres, does not exceed 30 per cent of the dimension so specified, and is not less than 20 per cent of the dimension so specified.

    (4) Any variation in a dimension as to the angle of hatching specified in any of the diagrams in Schedule 2 except diagrams 1043 to 1045 shall be treated as permitted by these Regulations if the variation does not exceed 5 degrees.

[1197]

NOTES
Commencement: 13 August 1981.

Section III, Traffic Signs shown in Schedule 1

9. Signs to be of the sizes, colours and types shown in diagrams

Subject to the provisions of these Regulations, a traffic sign for conveying—

    (a) to vehicular traffic on roads a warning of the description specified in or under a diagram in Part I of Schedule 1 shall be of the size, colour and type shown in the diagram relating to that warning;

    (b) to vehicular traffic on roads a requirement, prohibition or restriction specified in or under a diagram in Part II of Schedule 1 (other than a requirement shown in diagram 601.1, 602, 602.1, 610 [, 649.1 or 649.2]) shall be of the size, colour and type shown in the diagram relating to that requirement, prohibition or restriction;

    (c) to traffic on a road other than a motorway information of a directional nature of the description specified in or under a diagram in Part III of Schedule 1 shall be of the size, colour and type shown in the diagram relating to that information;

    (d) to traffic on roads information of the description specified in or under a diagram in Part IV of Schedule 1 shall be of the size, colour and type shown in the diagram relating to that information:

          Provided that until 1st January 1992 a traffic sign indicating a stopping place for stage or scheduled express carriages may, notwithstanding that it is not of the size, colour and type shown in any of the diagrams 845 to 852, be of a circular or rectangular shape of not less than 30 square centimetres on which the lettering shall be shown coloured black, dark brown, dark blue or dark red on a white or yellow background, or white or yellow on a red, blue, green, brown or black background if such sign so indicating is situated on or near any road immediately after the coming into operation of these Regulations;

    (e) to traffic on a motorway information of a directional or other nature specified in or under a diagram in Part V of Schedule 1 shall be of the size, colour and type shown in the diagram relating to that information. **[1198]**

NOTES
Commencement: 13 August 1981.
Amended by SI 1984 No 966, Part I.

9A. Sign shown in diagram 610 and its significance

(1) Subject to the provisions of these Regulations, a traffic sign for conveying to vehicular traffic on roads the requirement specified in paragraph (2) or (3) shall be of the size, colour and type shown in diagram 610.

(2) Except as provided in paragraph (3) the requirement conveyed by the sign shown in diagram 610 shall be that vehicular traffic passing the sign must keep to the left of the sign where the arrow is pointed downwards to the left, or to the right of the sign where the arrow is pointed downwards to the right.

(3) On an occasion when a vehicle is being used for fire brigade, ambulance or police purposes and the observance of the requirement specified in paragraph (2) would be likely to hinder the use of that vehicle for the purpose for which it is being used on that occasion, then, instead of that requirement, the requirement conveyed by the traffic sign in question shall be that the vehicle shall not proceed beyond that sign in such a manner or at such a time—

> (i) as is likely to cause danger to the driver of any other vehicle proceeding on or from another road or on or from another part of the same road; or
>
> (ii) as is likely to cause danger to non-vehicular traffic proceeding on or from another road or on or from another part of the same road.   **[1199]**

NOTES
Commencement: 13 August 1981.

11. Signs shown in diagrams 601.1, 602, 602.1 and 649.1 and their significance

[(1) The requirements conveyed by a sign of the size, colour and type shown in a diagram of a type specified in an item in column 2 of the Table below are specified in that item in column 3 of that Table.

TABLE

1 Item No	2 Type of diagram of sign	3 Requirements of sign
1.	601.1	(i) Every vehicle shall stop before crossing the transverse line shown in diagram 1002.1 or, if that line is not clearly visible, before entering the major road in respect of which the sign shown in diagram No 601.1 has been provided; (ii) no vehicle shall proceed past the transverse line shown in diagram 1002.1 or, if that line is not clearly visible, enter the major road in respect of which the sign shown in diagram No 601.1 has been provided, so as to be likely to cause danger to the driver of any other vehicle on the major road or to cause that driver to change the speed or course of his vehicle so as to avoid an accident.

1 Item No	2 Type of diagram of sign	3 Requirements of sign
2.	602	No vehicle shall cross the transverse line shown in diagram 1003 nearest to the major road at the side of which that line is drawn, or if that line is not clearly visible, enter that major road, so as to be likely to cause danger to the driver of any other vehicle or to cause that driver to change the speed or course of his vehicle so as to avoid an accident.
3.	602 when used with 602.1	No vehicle shall cross the transverse line shown in diagram 1003 nearest to the level crossing at the side of which that line is drawn or, if that line is not clearly visible, enter that level crossing, so as to be likely to cause danger to the driver of any railway vehicle or to cause the driver to change the speed or course of his vehicle so as to avoid an accident.
4.	649.1 and 649.2	No abnormal transport unit or, in relation to sign 649.1, no motor vehicle or vehicle combination which would be an abnormal transport unit if in sub-paragraph (a)(iii) of the definition of that expression in paragraph (2) below the reference to 38 tonnes were a reference to 32·5 tonnes, shall proceed onto or over an automatic half-barrier level crossing or an automatic open crossing (R) unless— (a) the driver of the unit has used a telephone provided at or near the crossing for the purpose of obtaining from a person, authorised in that behalf by the railway authority, permission for the unit to proceed; (b) that permission has been obtained before the unit proceeds; and (c) the unit proceeds in accordance with any terms attached to that permission. Provided that sub-paragraphs (b) and (c) above shall not apply if— (i) on the use by the driver of the telephone placed at or near the crossing he receives an indication for not less than two minutes that the telephone at the other end of the telephone line is being called, but no duly authorised person answers it or he receives no indication at all due to a fault or malfunction of the telephone; and (ii) the driver then drives the unit on to the crossing with the reasonable expectation of crossing it within times specified in a railway notice at that telephone as being times between which trains do not normally travel over that crossing.

(2) In this Regulation—

"abnormal transport unit" means—

    (a) a motor vehicle or a vehicle combination—

        (i) the overall length of which, inclusive of the load (if any) on the vehicle or the combination, exceeds 55 feet;

        (ii) the overall width of which, inclusive of the load (if any) on the vehicle or the combination, exceeds 9 feet 6 inches; or

        (iii) the maximum gross weight of which exceeds 38 tonnes; or

    (b) a motor vehicle, or a vehicle combination, which in either case is incapable of proceeding, or is unlikely to proceed, over an automatic half-barrier level crossing or an automatic open crossing (R) at a speed exceeding 5 miles per hour;

"automatic half-barrier level-crossing" means a level crossing where a road is crossed by a railway and where barriers are installed to descend automatically across part of the road when a train approaches;

"automatic open crossing (R)" means a level crossing without automatic barriers where a road is crossed by a railway and where light signals are so installed as to be operated automatically by the trains approaching the crossing and the operation of the signals is monitored remotely from the crossing;

"driver", in relation to an abnormal transport unit, means where that unit is a single motor vehicle the driver of that vehicle and, where that unit is a vehicle combination, the driver of the only or the foremost motor vehicle forming part of that combination;

"major road" means the road at a road junction into which road there emerges vehicular traffic from a minor road;

"minor road" means a road at a road junction on which road there is placed the sign shown in diagram 601.1 or 602; and

"vehicle combination" means a combination of vehicles made up of one or more motor vehicles and one or more trailers all of which are linked together when travelling.]   **[1200]**

NOTES
    Commencement: 13 August 1984.
    Substituted by SI 1984 No 966, Part I.

12. Permitted variants

(1) Where the circumstances so require, the indications given by the signs shown in the diagrams in Schedule 1 shall or may be varied as hereinafter provided in this paragraph—

    (a) any indication given by such a sign may be varied in the respect (if any) in which it is shown below the diagram relating to that sign that the indication may be varied;

    [Wherever an indication in metric units may be substituted for one in imperial units under this sub-paragraph and the sign in which the substitution is permitted is incorporated as a symbol in another sign, the indication given by the symbol so incorporated may be varied in the same manner as the variation permitted for the sign which it symbolises;]

(b) in the signs shown in diagrams 502, 503, 523.1, 524.1, 530, 532.1, 534.1 to 535.1, 556.4, 626.1, 628.1 to 629.2, 712.1, 719.3A and 729.2 the numerals shall be varied to accord with the circumstances except that no fractions of a number shall be used;

(c) in the signs shown in diagrams 527, 565.4, 571, 715, 724, 724.2, [728.1, 728.2, 729,] 730 to [733, 742.5, 742.6], 838.2, 911, 915 and 916, the numerals shall be varied to accord with the circumstances, distances being expressed in miles to the nearest mile except that in the case of any of the signs so shown other than a sign shown in diagram 715, 724.2, 732.2 or 911 the fractions 3/4, 1/2 and 1/4 may be used for distances of less than 3 miles;

(d) in the sign shown in diagram 572 the numerals shall be varied to accord with the circumstances, distances being expressed in yards to the nearest 50 yards;

(e) in the signs shown in diagrams 534.2, 547.3, 556.4, [557.2, 557.3] 569.2, 570, 573, [734.8, 735.1], 746.2, to 753.1, 759, 818.1, 818.2, and 841 to 842.4, the numerals indicating distance shall be varied to accord with the circumstances, distances of less than 1/2 mile being expressed in yards to the nearest 50 yards, distances of 1/2 mile or more but less than 3 miles being expressed in miles so long as no fractions other than 3/4, 1/2 or 1/4 are used, and distances of 3 miles or more being expressed in miles to the nearest mile;

(f) in the sign shown in any diagram in Schedule 1, any numerals which indicate route numbers shall be so varied as to indicate the route number for the time being appropriate to the route to which the indication refers and when a route number has been superseded by a new route number, any such numerals indicating the old route number may be retained in the said sign so long as those numerals so indicating are cancelled by a red bar to indicate that that route number has been superseded;

(g) in the signs shown in diagrams 618, 638 to 641, [646, 656.1] 660.2, 662, 801.5, 805, 806.1, 806.3, [807 and 812.4] the legend shall be varied, so far as respects any reference to a period of time, time of day or day of the week, and may be supplemented by a reference to days of the month or months of the year, so as to accord with the prohibition or restriction imposed in relation to vehicular traffic;

(h) in the signs shown in diagrams 515, 534.2, 553, 556.4, [557.2, 557.3] 567.1, 567.2, 569, 573, 580, 606 (through either 90 degrees or 180 degrees above horizontal), 639, 640, 640.2A, 644, 703.1, 703.2, 705, 714, 718.1, 718.2, 720, 721.1, 723, 724.1, 727, 727.2, 728.1, [730, 730.1, 732.1, 732.5,] 733.1, 734.2, 734.4, 734.9, [734.10, 735.2,] 741.1, [742.4, 742.5] 742.4, 754, 755, 756, 757, 810, 842.2, 844, 855, 910.1 and 912, the direction of any arrow or chevron shown therein shall be varied to accord with the circumstances, so however that no chevron shown in diagrams 515 or 569 and no arrow shown in diagram 553 [557.3, 557.4], 639, 640, 640.2A, 644, 810, 842.2, 855 or 912 shall point otherwise than horizontally either to the left or to the right, and so that from the signs shown in [diagrams 557.4, 639], [640, 742.5, 757] and 842.2, the arrows may be omitted;

(i) in any of the signs shown in diagrams 637, 641, 651, 662, 758, 805, 818.2, 841 and 842.4, an arrow pointing in the appropriate direction horizontally left or right may be included;

(j) in the signs shown in diagrams 713, 714, 724.1, [729.1 to 729.3] and [741 to 742.4] an indication of distance may be expressed to the nearest mile, in the signs shown in diagrams 734.1 to 734.4, 734.6, 736, 736.1, 739 to [739.5] and 756 such an indication as aforesaid may be expressed to the nearest mile for a distance greater than 3 miles, to the nearest 1/4 mile for a distance less than 3 miles but greater than 1/2 mile, and to the nearest 50 yards for a distance of 800 yards or less, and in the signs shown in diagrams 724, 728.1, 728.2, 729, 730 to 732.1, 733, [734.8, 742.5, 742.6,] 749, 759, 841, 842.2 and 842.4 the distance may be omitted;

(k) in the signs shown in diagrams 713, 724, 728, 728.2, 728.3, 732, 732.4, 733, 734.1, 734.3, 734.5 to [734.8, 735.1,] 736, 736.1, 737.1, [739 to 739.5,] 741, 742.1, [742.3, 742.6] 749, 751, 753, 753.1, 755.1, 756.1, 759, 841.1, 842.1, 842.3, 903.1 and 904.1 the direction in which they point shall be reversed;

(l) in the signs shown in diagrams 703.1 to 705, 708 to 711.1, 712.1, 718, 723 and 728.1, where a junction with a motorway is to be indicated, the appropriate panel or panels shall be blue with a white legend and the route number of the motorway shown in characters of the proportion and form shown in Parts I, II and III of Schedule 7; in the signs shown in diagrams 718 to 723 and 728.1 where a non-primary route joins a primary route the primary route number shall be shown in yellow on a green panel; and without prejudice to the foregoing provisions of this sub-paragraph, whenever a motorway route number is indicated on a sign shown in any of the diagrams 701 to 715, 718 to 724.2 and 728, that number shall be shown in white on a blue panel;

(m) in the signs shown in diagrams 701 to 716, 718 to 725, 727 to 733.1, [734.8, 735.1,] 737.1, [739, 739.4,] 741 to 744.1, 747 to [761,] 818.1, 818.2, 838.1, 841 to 842.4, 903.1 to 911 and 915 to 916.1 the route numbers, place names, route symbols, junction numbers and distances (other than the mileages in diagrams 702, [702.1, 703.2, 718.2] 905, 906, 906.2, 908.1 and 908.2) shall, subject to the preceding provisions of this paragraph, be varied, where appropriate and the words "Other routes" or as the case may be, "Ring road" may be substituted for the place name, having regard to the place where any such sign is erected;

(n) in the signs shown in diagrams [727, 728, 728.1, 728.2 and 729 to 732.1,] there may be substituted for, or added to the place name the words "Tourist information", "Toilets", "Ladies toilet", "Mens toilet", "Airport", "Station", "Bus Station", "Coach Station", "Country park" or "Public Telephone", or any of the following symbols, that is to say, the aircraft shown in diagram 733, the white on red symbol indicating British Railways and shown in diagram 734.1, the red circle and bar on white indicating London Transport and shown in diagram 734.4, the parking symbol shown in diagram 734.8, the telephone handset shown in diagram 734.6, the disabled person symbol shown in diagram [736.1, the red rose symbol shown in diagram 742.5 or the variant symbol permitted by that sign,] the building shown in diagram 747, the building shown in diagram 748, the tent and caravan symbol shown in diagram 750, the youth hostel symbol shown in diagram 752, the picnic site symbol shown in diagram 752.1, the black on white letter "i" shown in diagram 758, or the white on blue letter "H" shown in diagram 827;

(o) without prejudice to the next following paragraph, the white lorry symbol shown in diagram 727.2 may be incorporated on a black panel in the signs shown in diagrams 718 to 724.1, 728.1, 728.2 and 729 to 732.1 when those signs are placed on or near a road ... to indicate

that the route with which the symbol is associated on the sign is a route suitable for goods vehicles;
  (p) the aircraft symbol shown in diagram 733 either with or without the name of an airport may be substituted for, or added to, a place name shown on any of the signs shown in diagrams 701 to 714, 718 to 724.1 and 903.1 to 910.1 to indicate the site of an airport.

(2) Where overall dimensions are shown in Schedule 1 for any such sign as is mentioned in the preceding paragraph and where the legend on that sign may be varied and the sign is varied in accordance with that paragraph, the overall dimensions or the number of lines filled by the legend or both may be varied in so far as is necessary to give effect to that variation.

[(2A) Where the sign shown in diagram 812 in Schedule 1 is varied in accordance with the indication given below that diagram the overall dimensions of the sign may be varied so far as is necessary to give effect to the variation.]

(3) In the sign shown in diagram 536 the number of bells shall be increased or decreased according to the width of the road over which it is placed, and in each of the signs shown in diagrams 534.1 to 535. 1 the safe height shown on the sign shall be varied where necessary so that it is between 1 foot 6 inches and 2 feet less than the height of the lowest part of the overhead wire, of which it gives warning, over the highest part of the surface of the carriageway beneath the said wire.

(4) The signs shown in diagrams 732, 733, 734.8, [735,1] 736 to 737.1, 739, [739.4] 741 to 742.4, 743.1, 744.1, 805 (except when varied to convey a condition), 814, 820 to 822, 833 to 836 and 916.1, when erected in Wales may show the information contained on the sign in both the English and Welsh languages:

Provided that—
  (a) except in the case of the signs shown in diagrams 743.1 and 744.1 names indicating the location of a place shall be those in common usage in the English language;
  (b) all information shown on any such sign as is mentioned in this paragraph shall be shown in both the English and Welsh languages;
  (c) one language version of each item of information shall be placed immediately above the other language version of that item; and
  (d) the same size lettering shall be used for each language version of each item of information.

(5) Where a sign shown in diagrams 743.1, 744.1, 805, 814, 820 to 822 and 833 to 836 is varied in accordance with the last preceding paragraph, the overall dimensions as shown in the said diagrams may be varied in so far as is necessary to give effect to that variation.

(6) Where a sign shown in any diagram in Part III of Schedule 1 other than any of the diagrams 742.1 to 759 indicates a road or a route, and that road or route is temporarily closed, there may be affixed to the sign or to that part of the sign where that road or route is indicated, so as to cancel temporarily the indication, a board coloured red and on which are inscribed in white characters the words "road temporarily closed" or "route temporarily closed".　　**[1201]**

NOTES
  Commencement: 10 February 1983 (para (2A)); 13 August 1981 (remainder).
  Para (1): amended by SI 1982 No 1879, reg 5, SI 1983 No 1088, reg 3, SI 1986 No 1859, reg 2.
  Para (2A): added by SI 1982 No 1879, reg 5.
  Para (4): amended by SI 1982 No 1879, reg 5, SI 1983 No 1088, reg 3.

13. Dimensions

(1) Where as respects any diagram in Schedule 1 a dimension for the sign shown in the diagram is indicated in one or more sets of brackets against a dimension not indicated in brackets, any dimension indicated in a set of brackets may be treated as an alternative to the dimension not so indicated.

(2) Where a sign shown in any of the diagrams 606 to 614, 616 or 637 to 645 is placed temporarily on a road by a constable or a person acting under the instructions (whether general or specific) of the chief officer of police for the purposes of a temporary statutory provision any dimension specified for the sign in such a diagram may be reduced so long as any dimension shown in the diagram for measurement horizontally is not reduced to less than 200 millimetres.

(3) A sign shown in a diagram in Part III of Schedule 1 other than in diagrams 717, 726, 734.7 and 754 and a sign shown in a diagram in Part V of that Schedule other than in any of the diagrams 901.1, 910, 912 to 915, and 916.1 to 920 shall be of such dimensions having regard to the character of the road and the speed of the vehicular traffic generally using it as are necessary to accommodate any place name, route symbol, route number, arrow, any indication of distance, or any other indication which in accordance with these Regulations may be shown therein and it is appropriate to show for the purpose for which the sign is placed on a road.

[(4) In any diagram in Schedule 1 and, subject to Regulation 20(2), in Schedule 2, any alternative dimension adopted for a sign shall be so selected that that alternative is matched by the selection of the alternative for every other dimension for which an indication is given in the said diagrams and which corresponds in numerical ascending or descending order with that alternative so adopted.]   **[1202]**

NOTES

    Commencement: 10 February 1983 (para (4)); 13 August 1981 (remainder).
    Para (4): added by SI 1982 No 1879, reg 6.

14. Proportions and form of letters and numerals

(1) Subject to the provisions of paragraphs (2) to (4) of this Regulation, and without prejudice to Regulation 12(1)(l) (variant requirements to signs there specified), all letters incorporated in the signs shown in the diagrams in Schedule 1 other than in diagrams 742.1 to 742.4, 828.1 and 849 to 852 shall have the proportions and form shown in either Part I, Part II, Part V or Part VI of Schedule 7, all numerals incorporated in the signs shown in the diagrams in Schedule 1 shall have the proportions and form shown in Part III or Part VII of Schedule 7 and all other characters incorporated in the signs shown in the diagrams in Schedule 1 shall have the proportions and form shown in Part IV or Part VIII of Schedule 7.

(2) Letters and numerals used for the purposes of indicating a route number on the sign shown in diagram 757 and on any sign shown in a diagram in Part V of Schedule 1 shall have the proportions and form shown in Part IX of Schedule 7.

(3) Any arrow to be used in any of the signs shown in diagrams 703.3, 718.3 or 908.2 when those signs are erected over the carriageway on structures on which there is also mounted equipment for displaying the signs shown in diagram 6021 in Schedule 6 shall have the proportion and form of the arrow shown in the last diagram in Part IV of Schedule 7 and any such arrow to be

used in any of the signs first above-mentioned when those signs are erected over the carriageway on structures on which no such equipment is also mounted shall have the proportion and form of the arrow shown in the penultimate diagram in the said Part IV.

(4) Subject to and within the limits of any dimension specified as maximum or minimum in diagrams 743.1 and 744.1, any letters, numerals or other characters incorporated in those diagrams may have proportions and form other than the proportions and form shown in any Part of Schedule 7.   **[1203]**

NOTES
Commencement: 13 August 1981.

15. Illumination of signs by steady lighting

(1) In this Regulation (except in paragraph (6) as respects the sign shown in diagram 828.1) and in Regulations 16 and 17 the references to lighting shall be construed as references to steady lighting.

(2) Subject to the provisions of paragraph (7), this paragraph applies to the signs shown in diagrams 606, 609 to 616, 617 (except when used with the sign shown in diagram 618), 619, 619.1, 621 to 622.2 [622.4 and 625] in construing the following sub-paragraphs—

  (a) when the signs shown in diagrams 606 and 612 to 614 are fixed to light signals prescribed by Regulation 31, or by Regulation 31 as varied by Regulation 32, they shall be illuminated by a means of internal lighting at all times except when the light signals to which they are fixed are being maintained or repaired;

  (b) when the signs shown in diagrams 606, 609 to 611 [616 and 625] are mounted in a bollard fitted with a means of lighting them internally, they shall be illuminated throughout the hours of darkness by that means of internal lighting;

  (c) without prejudice to the next following sub-paragraph, if a sign specified in sub-paragraph (a) above when not so fixed, or a sign specified in sub-paragraph (b) above when not so mounted, or any other sign to which this paragraph applies is erected on a road within 50 metres of any lamp lit by electricity which forms part of a system of street-lighting furnished by means of at least three such lamps placed not more than 183 metres apart, that sign shall be illuminated by a means of internal or external lighting either for so long as the said system is illuminated, or throughout the hours of darkness, unless it is erected temporarily for any of the following reasons—

   (i) for the purpose of a temporary statutory provision,

   (ii) by reason of some emergency, or,

   (iii) if that road is a road subject to a speed limit of 30 m.p.h. or under, by reason of the execution of works, or of any obstruction on the road;

  (d) any sign to which this paragraph applies and is either not so fixed as provided in sub-paragraph (a) or is erected in such a manner that it is not illuminated regularly throughout the hours of darkness by a means of internal or external lighting, shall be illuminated by the use of reflecting material in accordance with the provisions of Regulation 18(3) and (4).

(3) Subject to the provisions of paragraph (7), this paragraph applies to any sign shown in diagrams 501, 504.1 to 510, 512, 513, 516, 517, 520 to 524.1, 528

to 532.1, 533, 537, 538, 543, 544 to [544.3,] 555, 556, 564, 564.5 to 566, 567.2, 569.2, 569.3, 601.1, 602, 626.1, 628.1 to 632, 642 (if the diameter of that sign is more than 450 millimetres), 649.1, [649.2,] 652 to [654.1,] 701 to 712.1, 714, 718.2, 718.3, 727.2, 818 to 819.2, 837.1 to 838.2, 858 to 858.2, 901.1 to 911, 915 to 916.1, 918.1 and 919.1 in construing the following sub-paragraphs—

    (a) without prejudice to the next following sub-paragraph, if a sign to which this paragraph applies is erected on a road within 50 metres of any such lamp as is described in sub-paragraph (c) of paragraph (2) that sign shall be illuminated by a means of internal or external lighting as is therein provided unless it is erected temporarily for such a reason as is therein specified;

    (b) any sign to which this paragraph applies which is erected in such a manner that it is not illuminated regularly throughout the hours of darkness by a means of internal or external lighting, shall be illuminated by the use of reflecting material as provided by paragraph (2)(d).

(4) Any sign shown in diagrams 515, 539 to 542.2, 545, 548 to 552, 554, 554.1, 557 to 559, 562, 569, 569.1, 569.4, 574, 577, 578, 580, 633 to 635, 642 (if the diameter of that sign is 450 millimetres or less), 646, 647, 655, 713, 715 to 718.1, 719 to 727, 728 to 737.1, 746.2, 754 to 757, 760, 761, 801, 806 to 806.3, 808.1, 808.3, 811 to [812.2, 812.5, 812.6] to 825, 827, 828.2, 830 to 832.2, 838.3, 838.4, 854 to 856, 861 to 863, 912, 917, 920 and 925 may be illuminated by a means of internal or external lighting, but if not so illuminated throughout the hours of darkness, shall be illuminated by the use of reflecting material in accordance with the provisions of Regulation 18(3) and (4).

(5) The signs shown in diagrams [537.1], 603, 604 and 814, shall be illuminated throughout the hours of darkness by a means of internal or external lighting.

(6) The sign shown in diagram 828.1 shall be illuminated by an intermittent light flashing at a rate of not less than 54 nor more than 90 flashes per minute during such times only as it is necessary that the sign shall be illuminated for the purpose of indicating the information shown in diagram 828.1.

(7) Where a sign to which any of the foregoing paragraphs applies is placed on or near a road for the purpose of conveying a warning or information from time to time to vehicular traffic, or in connection with a statutory prohibition, restriction or requirement which relates to such traffic but does not apply at all times, that sign shall be illuminated in accordance with such of the foregoing provisions of this Regulation as apply to it but only during such times as, for the said purpose or in the said connection, it is necessary that the sign shall be visible from a reasonable distance to drivers of approaching motor vehicles, any other provision of this Regulation to the contrary notwithstanding.

(8) Subject to the foregoing paragraphs of this Regulation and to Regulation 19, any sign shown in a diagram in Schedule 1 may be illuminated by a means of internal or external lighting and where, subject as aforesaid, the means of lighting any such sign is external, then that means of lighting shall be either fitted to the sign or to the structure on which it is mounted or otherwise specially provided.   **[1204]**

NOTES
    Commencement: 13 August 1981.
    Paras (2), (4): amended by SI 1982 No 1879, reg 7.
    Para (3): first and third amendments made by SI 1982 No 1879, reg 7; second amendment made by SI 1984 No 966, Part I.

Para (5): amended by SI 1983 No 1088, reg 4.

16. Illumination of signs by steady lighting

Where a sign shown in a diagram in Schedule 1 (not being a sign consisting of a plate) is illuminated by a means of lighting in accordance with the provisions of Regulation 15 and a plate shown in a diagram in that Schedule is used in conjunction with that sign, the said plate shall, unless the means of lighting provided for the illumination of the sign adequately illuminates the plate, be illuminated, during such times as the sign is illuminated, by a means of lighting and that means of lighting shall accord with that one of the methods of lighting, namely, internal or external adopted for the illumination of the sign.   **[1205]**

NOTES
Commencement: 13 August 1981.

17. Illumination of signs shown in diagrams 560 and 561 by reflectors etc

(1) The signs shown in diagrams 560 and 561 shall not be illuminated by the fitting of a means of internal or external lighting.

(2)(a) If the sign shown in diagram 560 has a diameter of 150 millimetres, that sign shall be illuminated by either of the methods prescribed at (i) and (ii) of sub-paragraph (c) below and not otherwise.

    (b) If the said sign has a diameter of 75 millimetres or more but less than 150 millimetres, that sign shall be illuminated by either of the methods prescribed at (iii) and (iv) of sub-paragraph (c) below and not otherwise.

    (c) The methods referred to in sub-paragraphs (a) and (b) above are:—

        (i) by the use of 14 circular reflectors of the corner cube type, each reflector having a diameter of 22 millimetres,

        (ii) by the use of reflecting material extending over the whole surface of the sign,

        (iii) by the use of a single circular reflector of the corner cube type extending over the whole surface of the sign,

        (iv) by the use of reflectors consisting of bi-convex lenses extending over the whole surface of the sign.

    (d) If the sign shown in diagram 561 has an area of 180 square centimetres, that sign shall be illuminated by the method prescribed at sub-paragraph (c) (ii) above and not otherwise; but if that sign so shown has an area of less than 180 square centimetres and no less than 45 square centimetres, then it shall be illuminated either by the use of a single rectangular reflector of the corner cube type extending over the whole surface of the sign or by the method prescribed at sub-paragraph (c)(iv) above but by no other method.

(3) The colour reflected by the sign shown either in diagram 560 or in 561 shall be red when the sign indicates the edge of the left-hand side of the carriageway or an obstruction near that edge and shall be white when the sign indicates the edge of the right-hand side of the carriageway or an obstruction near that edge, unless the sign indicates the edge of the right-hand side of the carriageway of a dual-carriageway road or an obstruction near that edge when the said colour so reflected shall be amber.   **[1206]**

NOTES
Commencement: 13 August 1981.

18. Illumination of signs by reflecting material

(1) Nothing in this Regulation shall apply to the signs shown in diagrams 536, 560, 561 and 828.1.

(2) Subject to the provisions of Regulation 15 and paragraph (1) above, any sign shown in a diagram in Schedule 1 may be illuminated by the use of reflecting material in accordance with the following provisions of this Regulation.

(3) Subject to paragraph (4) where reflecting material is used on any sign shown in a diagram in Schedule 1 it shall be of the same colour as that of, and extend throughout, that part of the sign to which it is applied:

Provided that no reflecting material shall be applied to—

(a) any part of a sign coloured black, or

(b) any part of the sign shown in diagram 605.1 which is coloured fluorescent yellow unless the reflecting material is applied to that part in horizontal strips each such strip being 3 millimetres wide, spaced at intervals of 6 millimetres from each other, the centre of the sign being located at a point in one such interval equidistant from the strips so spaced.

In this paragraph the word "part", in relation to a sign, means any part of the surface of that sign uniformly coloured and bounded by parts of a different colour.

(4)(a) Where in accordance with the last paragraph, different colours of reflecting material are used next to one another on the same sign being a traffic sign to which this paragraph applies in accordance with the next following sub-paragraph, a gap of not more than 20 millimetres in width may be left between the different colours of reflecting material.

(b) This paragraph applies only to traffic signs which being circular in shape have a diameter of at least 1.2 metres, being triangular in shape have a height of at least 1.2 metres along the perpendicular from apex to base, or being rectangular in shape have a side which is at least 1.2 metres in length. **[1207]**

NOTES
  Commencement: 13 August 1981.

19. Illumination of signs by reflecting material

Where a sign shown in a diagram in Schedule 1 (not being a sign consisting of a plate) is illuminated by the use of reflecting material in accordance with the provisions of Regulation 15 and 18 and a plate shown in a diagram in that Schedule, other than a plate shown in diagram 662, is used in conjunction with that sign, the said plate shall be illuminated by the use of reflecting material in accordance with the provisions of Regulation 18(3). **[1208]**

NOTES
  Commencement: 13 August 1981.

20. Road markings

(1) Subject to the provisions of these Regulations, a traffic sign consisting of a line or mark on a road (in these Regulations referred to as a "road marking") for conveying to traffic on roads a warning, a requirement or information of the description specified under a diagram (other than diagrams 1003 and 1013.1) in

Schedule 2 shall be of the size and type shown in the diagram relating to that warning, requirement or information.

(2) In any diagram in Schedule 2, the dimensions indicated in brackets against dimensions not so indicated may be treated as an alternative to the last mentioned dimensions.

(3) Where the circumstances so require, the indication given by any of the signs shown in the diagrams in Schedule 2 shall or may be varied as hereinafter provided in this paragraph:—

(a) any indication given by such a sign may be varied in the respect (if any) in which it is shown below the diagram relating to that sign that the indication may be varied;

(b) in the sign shown in diagram 1035 route numbers place names and the direction in which any arrow-head points shall be varied and interchangeable to accord with the circumstances but the words "turn left", "ahead" or "turn right" shall not appear as a part of the said sign. **[1209]**

NOTES
Commencement: 13 August 1981.

Section IV, Traffic Signs shown in Schedule 2

21. Particular road markings

A road marking for conveying to vehicular traffic the requirement specified in paragraph (2) of the next succeeding Regulation shall be of the size and type shown in diagram 1003. **[1210]**

NOTES
Commencement: 13 August 1981.

22. Particular road markings

(1) For the purposes of this Regulation—

"minor road" means a road at a road junction on which road there are placed the transverse lines shown in diagram 1003;

"major road" means the road at a road junction into which road there emerges vehicular traffic from a minor road.

(2) Except as provided by the next following paragraph, the requirement conveyed by the said transverse lines, whether or not they are used in conjunction with the sign shown in diagram 602, shall be that no vehicle shall proceed past such one of those lines as is nearest to the major road into that road in such a manner or at such a time as is likely to cause danger to the driver of any other vehicle on the major road or as to necessitate the driver of any such other vehicle to change its speed or course in order to avoid an accident with the first-mentioned vehicle.

(3) Whenever the said transverse lines are used in conjunction with the sign shown in diagram 602 and that sign is at the same time used in combination with the sign shown in diagram 602.1 at a level crossing where a road is crossed by a railway then the said requirement shall be that no vehicle shall proceed past such one of those lines as is nearest to the said level crossing in such a

manner or at such a time as is likely to cause the driver of any railway vehicle to change its speed to avoid collision with the vehicle first above-mentioned in this paragraph.   **[1211]**

NOTES
Commencement: 13 August 1981.

23. Particular road markings

(1) A road marking for conveying the requirements specified in the next succeeding paragraph and the warning specified in paragraph (5) shall be of the size and type shown in diagram 1013.1.

(2) The requirements conveyed by the road marking mentioned in the last preceding paragraph shall be that—

    (a) subject to the provisions of paragraph (3), no vehicle shall stop on any length of road along which the marking has been placed at any point between the two ends of the marking; and

    (b) subject to the provisions of paragraph (4), every vehicle proceeding on any length of road along which the marking has been so placed that, as viewed in the direction of travel of the vehicle, a continuous line is on the left of a dotted line or of another continuous line, shall be so driven as to keep the first-mentioned continuous line on the right hand or off side of the vehicle.

(3) Nothing in sub-paragraph (a) of the last preceding paragraph shall apply—

    (a) so as to prevent a vehicle stopping on any length of road so long as may be necessary—

        (i) to enable a person to board or alight from the vehicle,

       (ii) to enable goods to be loaded on to or to be unloaded from the vehicle, or

      (iii) to enable the vehicle, if it cannot be used for such purpose without stopping on that length of road, to be used in connection with any building operation or demolition, the removal of any obstruction to traffic, the maintenance, improvement or reconstruction of that length of road, or the laying, erection, alteration or repair in or near to that length of road of any sewer or of any main, pipe or apparatus for the supply of gas, water or electricity, or of any telegraphic line as defined in the Telegraph Act 1878,

so, however, that no vehicle shall be enabled by virtue of this sub-paragraph to stop for any of the purposes at (i), (ii) or (iii) above on a part of that length of road, not being a lay-by or a road verge, if it is reasonably practicable to stop the vehicle for that purpose on a part of that length of road, being a lay-by or a road verge;

    (b) to a vehicle used for fire brigade, ambulance or police purposes;

    (c) to a pedal bicycle not having a sidecar attached thereto, whether additional means of propulsion by mechanical power are attached to the bicycle or not;

    (d) to a vehicle stopping in any case where the person in control of the vehicle is required by law to stop, or is obliged to do so in order to avoid an accident, or is prevented from proceeding by circumstances outside his control; or

    (e) to anything done with the permission of a police constable in uniform or in accordance with the direction of a traffic warden.

(4) Nothing in sub-paragraph (b) of paragraph (2) shall apply so as to prevent a vehicle crossing or straddling the continuous line first mentioned in that sub-paragraph for the purpose of obtaining access to any other road joining the length of road along which the line is placed or to land or premises situated on or adjacent to the said length of road or if it is necessary to do so—

    (a) in order to pass a stationary vehicle, or owing to circumstances outside the control of the driver or in order to avoid an accident, or

    (b) for the purposes of complying with any direction of a police constable in uniform or a traffic warden.

(5) The warning conveyed by the road marking mentioned in paragraph (1) shall be that no vehicle while travelling next to a dotted line placed on the left, as viewed in the direction of travel of the vehicle, of a continuous line should cross or straddle the first mentioned line unless it is seen by the driver of the vehicle to be safe to do so. **[1212]**

NOTES
Commencement: 13 August 1981.

24. Colour of road markings

(1) Except as otherwise provided by this Regulation, the road markings shown in the diagrams in Schedule 2 shall be white.

(2) Road markings shown in diagrams 1016.1 to 1021, 1027.1 and 1043 to 1045 shall be yellow.

(3) In the road markings shown in the diagrams 1025.1 and 1025.3 the line shown therein as coloured yellow and having a width of 200 or 300 millimetres shall be yellow.

(4) The road markings shown in diagrams 1025 and 1025.2 and when displaying the word "Taxis" in diagram 1028.1 shall be yellow in the following but in no other circumstances, that is to say, where those markings are placed in a part of the carriageway which is subject to restrictions on waiting or on waiting, loading and unloading for at least 8 hours during the period from 7 a.m. to 7 p.m. on at least 4 days, none of them being a Sunday, in any week by all vehicles, other than stage and express carriages in the case of the markings shown in diagrams 1025 or 1025.2 and other than hackney carriages in the case of the marking shown in diagram 1028.1.

(5) Road markings shown in diagram 1055 consisting of marks arranged in transverse lines may be either white or silver or light grey in colour.

(6) In this Regulation, "hackney carriage" has the same meaning as in the Vehicles (Excise) Act 1971. **[1213]**

NOTES
Commencement: 13 August 1981.

25. Use on road markings of reflecting material and studs with reflectors

(1)(a) The road markings shown in diagrams 1011 to 1014 shall be illuminated with reflecting material, and

    (b) studs incorporating reflectors and spaced so as to form a single line of studs at intervals of not less than 3.6 nor more than 4.4 metres apart shall be fitted between the two lines constituting the marking shown in diagram 1013.1 unless that marking—

(i) is placed on any automatic railway level crossing, or

(ii) is placed on a length of the road falling within a distance of 90 metres measured from the transverse stop line provided in association with any such crossing and in conformity with diagram 1001, or

(iii) is so placed that the continuous lines shown in diagram 1013.1 are more than 175 millimetres apart and are separated by an area of cross-hatching so shown.

(c) Where the marking shown in diagram 1013.1 is placed as described in any of the cases in sub-paragraph (b) (i) to (iii) above, then such studs as aforesaid and so spaced as aforesaid shall be fitted either within the width of each of the said two lines or between them.

In this paragraph the expression "automatic railway level crossing" means an automatic half-barrier level crossing, and an automatic open crossing (R) as both those crossings are defined for the purposes of Regulation 11(2) and includes a level crossing which is the same as an automatic open crossing (R) except that the operation of the light signals is monitored at or near the crossing by the driver of the train instead of remotely from the crossing.

(2) Subject to the foregoing provisions of this Regulation, any road marking may be illuminated with reflecting material and studs incorporating reflectors may be fitted to the markings shown in diagrams 1003.4 to 1012.1, 1025.2, 1025.3 and 1040 to 1042 in such a manner that any such stud shall not be fitted to any mark coloured white and forming part of any of the markings so shown as aforesaid but shall be applied to the surface of the carriageway in the gap between any two such marks:

Provided that in the case of the markings shown in diagram 1011 or 1012.1 the said studs shall, if fitted, be applied to the surface of the carriageway at the side of and adjacent to the line shown in the diagram.

[(2A) The road markings shown in [diagrams 1060, 1060.1, 1061 and 1061.1] including the permitted variants shall be illuminated with reflecting material.]

(3) Reflectors incorporated in studs shall be white except that in the case of reflectors fitted to the markings shown in diagrams 1009 to 1012.1, 1025.2, 1025.3, 1041 and 1042 they may be—

(a) red where the near side edge of a carriageway is indicated to drivers of approaching motor vehicles, or when fitted to the markings shown in diagrams 1041 and 1042 to indicate the offside edge of a carriageway.

(b) amber to indicate the offside edge of a carriageway which is contiguous to a central reservation or which carries traffic in one direction only, and

(c) green when fitted to the markings shown in diagrams 1009, 1010, 1025.2 and 1025.3 where the edge of any part of the carriageway available for through traffic at a road junction, a lay-by or a parking place is so indicated as aforesaid.

In this Regulation "central reservation" means any provision made in a road (not being the provision of a street refuge) for dividing the road for the safety or guidance of vehicular traffic.   **[1214]**

NOTES

Commencement: 25 August 1983 (para (2A)); 13 August 1981 (remainder).

Para (2A): added by SI 1983 No 1088, reg 5; words in square brackets therein substituted by SI 1990 No 704, Part I, reg 4.

26. Height of road markings and size of studs

(1) Non-depressible studs incorporating reflectors and fitted as a part of a road marking shall either be in the shape of a circle having a diameter of not more than 20 millimetres in excess of the width of the road marking to which the studs are fitted or of a rectangle having a length of not more than 250 millimetres and a width of not more than 20 millimetres in excess of the width of the road marking to which the studs are fitted.

(2) Subject to paragraph (3), no road marking shall project above the surface of the carriageway in the immediate vicinity more than 6 millimetres at any point unless it is a road marking fitted with non-depressible studs when those studs shall not project above the said surface more than 18 millimetres at the highest point nor more than 6 millimetres at their edges, or unless it is the road marking shown in diagram 1003.4 when that marking shall not project above the said surface more than 125 millimetres at the highest point nor more than 6 millimetres at its edge.

(3) Depressible studs fitted in road markings and incorporating reflectors shall not project above the surface of the carriageway in the immediate vicinity more than 6 millimetres at their edges, nor at their highest points more than 25 millimetres, when not depressed or 20 millimetres when depressed by a force of 300 newtons and "newton" means the unit of force specified in paragraph 1.2.3 of Chapter A of the Annex to Council Directive 71/354 EEC as amended by Council Directive 76/770/EEC.

In this Regulation, the expression "depressible studs", in relation to studs fitted in road markings, means studs so fitted that the height by which they project above the surface of the carriageway in the immediate vicinity is apt to be reduced when pressure is applied to those studs from above; and "non-depressible studs" and "depressed" shall be construed accordingly. **[1215]**

NOTES
Commencement: 13 August 1981.

Section V, Miscellaneous Traffic Signs

27. Certain temporary signs

(1) Notwithstanding the provisions of Regulation 9 and subject to the succeeding paragraphs of this Regulation, signs placed temporarily on or near a road—

    (a) for conveying to traffic—

        (i) information as respects deviations of, or alternative traffic routes,

        (ii) information as respects the route which may conveniently be followed on the occasion of a sports meeting, exhibition or other public gathering, in each case attracting a considerable volume of traffic,

        (iii) information as to the date from which works are to be executed on or near a road, or

        [(iv) information or warnings as to the avoidance of any temporary hazards occasioned by works being executed on or near a road, by adverse weather conditions or other natural causes, by the failure of street lighting or by malfunction of or damage to any apparatus, equipment, or facility used in connection with the road or any thing situated on near or under it or by damage to the road itself;]

(b) for conveying to vehicular traffic any prohibition, restriction or requirement of a description required for the purposes of a temporary statutory provision; or

(c) pending the erection of any permanent sign prescribed by these Regulations, for conveying to traffic the indication which such a permanent sign indicates,

may be of such size, colour and type as is specified in the following provisions of this Regulation.

(2) Every such sign placed as aforesaid (hereinafter referred to as a "temporary sign") shall be of a shape which—

(a) is rectangular;

(b) is rectangular, but with the corners rounded; or

(c) is rectangular, but with one end pointed.

(3) Every temporary sign shall be of such size as is necessary to accommodate the wording, numerals, arrows or chevrons and any symbol taken from any diagram shown in Schedule 1 appropriate to the purpose for which the sign is placed as aforesaid and to accommodate any arms, badge, device, words or letters incorporated in the sign in accordance with the provisions of paragraph (6).

(4) Every letter and numeral incorporated in a temporary sign other than any letter incorporated in the sign in accordance with the provisions of paragraph (6) shall be not less than 40 nor more than 250 millimetres in height, and every arrow so incorporated shall be not less than 250 nor more than 500 millimetres in length except that where an arrow is incorporated in the index part of a sign with a pointed end such arrow shall be not less than 100 nor more than 200 millimetres in length.

(5) Every letter, numeral, arrow, chevron or symbol incorporated in a temporary sign shall be—

(a) black on a background of white, or yellow; or

(b) white on a blue background [; or

(c) if the sign conveys information or warnings as to the avoidance of any temporary hazards such as are mentioned in paragraph (1)(a)(iv) above, white on a red background.]

(6) There may be incorporated in, or attached to, a temporary sign the arms, badge or other device of a highway authority, police authority or an organisation representative of road users, or words or letters indicating the highway authority, or that the sign is a police sign.

(7) No sign shall by virtue of this Regulation convey to traffic any information, warning, requirement, restriction or prohibition of a description which can be so conveyed either by a sign shown in a diagram in Part I, Part II or Part IV of Schedule 1 or by a sign so shown used in combination with or in conjunction with another sign shown in such a diagram.   **[1216]**

NOTES
    Commencement: 13 August 1981.
    Paras (1), (5): amended by SI 1982 No 1879, reg 8.

28. Flashing beacons and flags

(1) Beacons showing an intermittent amber light for conveying the warning that drivers of vehicles should take special care may be used in combination

with any of the signs specified in the last preceding Regulation or with any of the signs shown in diagrams 562 to 569.1, 569.3, [569.4] or 610 subject to the following conditions:—

    (i) the light emitted by the lens or lenses of each such beacon shall be of peak intensity of not less than 100 candelas on the principal axis of the relevant lens;

    (ii) the part of that beacon through which light is emitted shall be of such a shape and size that the perimeter of the area projected horizontally thereby on to any vertical plane shall be capable of lying wholly inside a square having sides of 200 millimetres in length and wholly outside a square having sides of 100 millimetres in length;

    (iii) the height of the centre of the lenses from the surface of the carriageway in the immediate vicinity shall be not less than 800 nor more than 1500 millimetres; and

    (iv) the rate of flashing shall be not less than 120 nor more than 150 flashes per minute and the period between flashes shall not exceed 1/4 of a second.

(2) Beacons showing an intermittent blue light for conveying the warning that drivers of vehicles should take special care may be used by a constable, or a person acting under the instructions (whether general or specific) of the chief officer of police, in combination with any of the signs shown in diagrams 606, 609, 610 and 633 to 635 subject to the same conditions specified in paragraph (1) (iii) and (iv).

(3) Flags of an area of not less than 0.2 square metres and coloured red for conveying the warning that it would be dangerous for drivers to cause their vehicles to proceed may be used in an emergency at or in the vicinity of works being executed, or of an obstruction situated on or near a road.   **[1217]**

NOTES
    Commencement: 13 August 1981.
    Para (1): amended by SI 1982 No 1879, reg 9.

29. Cones and cylinders

(1) A device constructed of rubber or flexible plastic material and [being of the shape, dimension and colours indicated in diagram 577] for conveying the warning that drivers of vehicles should follow a certain route around an obstruction or road works in a road may be placed temporarily on the carriageway thereof [and that part of the device coloured white shall be illuminated with white reflecting material and that part of the device coloured red may be illuminated with red reflecting material.]

(2) A device constructed of rubber or flexible plastic material and [being of the shape, dimensions and colours indicated in diagram 578] for indicating to drivers of vehicles a temporary division of the carriageway made so as to separate traffic moving in one direction from traffic moving in the opposite direction [to delineate the edge of a route for vehicular traffic through or past a temporary obstruction] or for so indicating a part of a dual-carriageway road where vehicles other than those used for fire brigade, ambulance or police purposes, are prohibited from proceeding from one carriageway to the other may be placed temporarily on the carriageway of the road [and that part of the

device coloured white shall be illuminated with white reflecting material and that part of the device colured red may be illuminated with red reflecting material.]   **[1218]**

NOTES
    Commencement: 13 August 1981.
    Amended by SI 1982 No 1879, reg 10.

30. Refuge indicator lamps

A lamp in the form of an illuminated spherical globe for conveying the warning that drivers of vehicles are approaching a street refuge may be used subject to the following conditions:—

(a) the globe shall be white;
(b) the globe shall have a diameter of not less than 290 nor more than 310 millimetres; and
(c) the height of the centre of the globe from the surface of the carriageway in the immediate vicinity shall be not less than 3.8 nor more than 5 metres.   **[1219]**

NOTES
    Commencement: 10 February 1983 (para 2);13 August 1981 (remainder).

31. Light signals for control of vehicular traffic

(1) Light signals may be used for the control of vehicular traffic and shall be of the size, colour and type prescribed by paragraph (2), by paragraph (3) or by paragraph (4).

(2) The size, colour and type of light signals prescribed by this paragraph shall be as follows:—

(a) three lights shall be used, one red, one amber and one green;
(b) the lamps showing the coloured lights aforesaid shall be arranged vertically, the lamp showing a red light being the uppermost and that showing a green light the lowermost;
(c) each lamp shall be separately illuminated and the effective diameter of the lens thereof shall be not less than 195 nor more than 220 millimetres unless the lens is a lens of the kind shown in diagram 3001 when instead the said diameter may be not less than 290 nor more than 310 millimetres;
(d) the height of the centre of the amber lens from the surface of the carriageway in the immediate vicinity shall be in the case of signals placed at the side of the carriageway or on a street refuge not less than 2.4 nor more than 4 metres and in the case of signals placed elsewhere and over the carriageway not less than 6.1 nor more than 9 metres;
(e) the centres of adjacent lenses shall be not less than 305 nor more than 360 millimetres apart;
(f) no lettering shall be used upon the lenses or in connection with a light signal;
(g) the sequence of the lights shown for the purpose of controlling vehicular traffic shall be as follows:—

(i) red,
(ii) amber and red together,
(iii) green,

(iv) amber.

(3) The size, colour and type of light signals prescribed by this paragraph shall be as follows:—

(a) Four lamps each showing an intermittent red light shall be used.

(b) The lamps shall be so fitted as to enclose a rectangular area bounded by the one pair of sides extending horizontally and terminating as to each side in the centres of each pair of lenses (in these Regulations called "the horizontal pairs") and by the other pair of sides extending vertically in relation to the ground and terminating as to each side in the centres of each pair of lenses (in these Regulations called "the vertical pairs").

(c) When the four lamps are erected beside the carriageway, the distance between the centres of the lenses for each of the horizontal pairs shall be not less than 945 nor more than 955 millimetres and for each of the vertical pairs shall be not less than 695 nor more than 705 millimetres in accordance with the arrangement shown in diagram 6032.

(d) When the four lamps are erected over the carriageway, the distance between the said centres for each of the horizontal pairs shall be not less than 1395 nor more than 1405 millimetres and for each of the vertical pairs not less than 545 nor more than 555 millimetres in accordance with the arrangement shown in diagram 6031.

(e) Subject to the provisions of the next following sub-paragraph, each lamp shall be separately illuminated and the effective diameter of the lens thereof shall be not less than 120 nor more than 130 millimetres.

(f) When the signal is operated, each lamp shall show its intermittent red light at a rate of flashing of not less than 60 nor more than 90 flashes per minute, and in such a manner that the lights of one of the vertical pairs are always shown when the lights of the other vertical pair are not shown.

(g) The height of the centres of the lenses comprising the lower of the horizontal pairs from the surface of the carriageway in the immediate vicinity shall be in the case of signals placed at the side of the carriageway not less than 1.8 nor more than 3.2 metres and in the case of signals placed over the carriageway not less than 5.8 nor more than 6.8 metres.

(h) No lettering of any kind shall be used upon any of the lenses.

(4) The size, colour and type of light signals prescribed by this paragraph shall be as follows:—

(a) two lamps each showing an intermittent red light and one lamp showing a steady amber light shall be used;

(b) the lamps showing an intermittent red light shall be arranged horizontally so that there is a distance of not less than 585 nor more than 665 millimetres between the centres of the lenses of the lamps;

(c) the lamp showing the amber light shall be placed below the red lenses in such a position that a vertical line passing through the centre of that lamp is horizontally equidistant from the vertical lines passing through the centre of each red lens and that the vertical distance between a horizontal line passing through the centres of the red lenses is not less than 235 nor more than 345 millimetres;

(d) each lamp shall be separately illuminated and the effective diameter of the lens thereof shall be not less than 195 nor more than 220 millimetres;

(e) when the lamps showing an intermittent red light are operated, each such lamp shall show a red light at a rate of flashing of not less than 60 nor more than 90 flashes per minute, and in such a manner that the light of one lamp is always shown at a time when the light of the other lamp is not shown;

(f) the height of the centre of the amber lens from the surface of the carriageway in the immediate vicinity shall be in the case of signals placed at the side of the carriageway or on a street refuge not less than 2.4 nor more than 4 metres and in the case of signals placed elsewhere and over the carriageway not less than 6.1 nor more than 9 metres;

(g) the lenses shall be provided with a rectangular backing board having an overall width of not less than 1.3 metres and extending not less than 300 millimetres above the centre of each of the red lenses and not less than 300 millimetres below the centre of the amber lens, which board shall be coloured black, save for a white border having a width of not less than 80 nor more than 100 millimetres on the side from which the lamps show;

(h) the sequence of the signal lights under this paragraph shown for the purpose of controlling vehicular traffic shall be amber followed by red;

(i) no lettering of any kind shall appear on any of the lenses.

(5) Light signals prescribed by paragraph (4) may be surmounted by a cross of the size, colour and type shown in diagrams 542 and 542.1.   **[1220]**

NOTES
Commencement: 13 August 1981.

32. Light signals for control of vehicular traffic

(1) Subject to the next following paragraph, a lens or lenses of the size and colour shown in diagram 3001 in Schedule 3, which, when illuminated, shows a green arrow—

(a) may be substituted for the lens showing the green light in the light signals referred to in Regulation 31(2) in any of the methods shown in diagrams 3003, 3005, 3006 and 3011 in the said Schedule;

(b) may be affixed to the light signals referred to in Regulation 31(2) or to those signals as altered in accordance with the preceding sub-paragraph in any of the methods shown in diagram 3002 and diagrams 3004 to 3011 in the said Schedule.

In this paragraph, the substitution authorised in sub-paragraph (a) thereof in the method shown in the said diagram 3011 shall be treated as having been effected by means of the upper arrow shown in that diagram, the lower arrow shown therein being treated as affixed in accordance with sub-paragraph (b) thereof.

(2) When a lens is, or lenses are, so affixed as provided in paragraph (1)(b) and any one lens so affixed is of the larger of the two sizes specified in diagram 3001 in the said Schedule, the distance between the centre of that lens and the centre of any other lens affixed next in position immediately above, below or to the side of that first mentioned lens shall be not less than 415 nor more than 440 millimetres.

(3) The direction in which the arrow shown in diagram 3003 in the said Schedule points may be varied so as to be—

(a) a direction which lies straight upright, or

(b) a direction which lies at any angle between 90 degrees either to the left or to the right of the said upright direction.

(4) The direction in which any arrow shown in any of the diagrams 3002, 3004 to 3006, 3009 and 3010 in the said Schedule points may be varied so as to be—

(a) a direction which lies straight upright, or
(b) a direction which lies between the direction shown in the diagram showing that arrow and the said upright direction.

(5) The direction in which the upper arrow shown in diagram 3007 of the said Schedule points may be varied so as to be a direction which lies at any angle from the upright position shown to an angle of 45 degrees to the left and the direction in which the upper arrow shown in diagram 3008 in that Schedule points may be so varied as aforesaid to an angle of 45 degrees to the right.

(6) The direction in which the lower arrow shown in each of the said diagrams 3007 and 3008 points may be varied so as to be a direction which lies at any angle from the position shown in each such diagram respectively to an angle of 45 degrees towards the upright position as shown for the upper arrow in each such diagram.

(7) When both arrows shown in diagram 3011 of the said Schedule are illuminated and extinguished simultaneously the direction in which the upper arrow shown in that diagram points may be varied so as to be a direction which lies at any angle from the position so shown for that arrow to an angle of 45 degrees to the right passing through an arc of 135 degrees and the direction in which the lower arrow so shown points may be varied so as to be a direction which lies at any angle from the position so shown for that arrow to an angle of 45 degrees towards the upright position or alternatively so as to be a direction lying at any angle from a position in which that arrow faces in the opposite direction from that so shown to an angle 45 degrees towards the upright position.

(8) When both arrows shown in the said diagram 3011 are illuminated and extinguished independently of each other, the direction of each such arrow may be varied so as to be a direction which lies at any angle between 90 degrees either to the left or to the right of the upright position.   **[1221]**

NOTES
Commencement: 13 August 1981.

33. Portable light signals for control of vehicular traffic

(1) Portable light signals may be used for the control of vehicular traffic in the circumstances specified at (a) to (c) of this paragraph—

[(a) on a length of road having no junction along its length with any other road carrying vehicular traffic to or from it and where the width of the carriageway of that length of road is temporarily restricted so that it will carry only one line of traffic.]
(b) at a level crossing where a road is crossed by a railway when work in relation to that crossing is being carried out, or
(c) during the progress of temporary schemes of traffic control, if the signals are being operated and maintained by, and under the regular supervision of, the police or have been erected at a site approved in writing by the highway authority.

[(2) Such light signals shall comply with—

(*a*) the provisions of Regulation 31(2)(a), (b), (c), (f) and (g), or if appropriate, those provisions as varied by Regulation 32(1), and

(*b*) the provisions of Regulation 31(2)(e), or if appropriate, those provisions as varied by Regulation 32(2) as if for "305" there appeared "270".]   **[1222]**

NOTES

Commencement: 10 February 1983 (para 2); 13 August 1981 (remainder).
Amended by SI 1982 No 1879, reg 11.

34. Significance of light signals

(1) The significance of the light signals prescribed by Regulation 31(2) or by Regulation 33 shall be as follows:—

(a) except as provided in the next following sub-paragraph, the red signal shall convey the prohibition that vehicular traffic shall not proceed beyond the stop line on the carriageway provided in conjunction with the signals or, if that line is not for the time being visible or there is no stop line, beyond the post or other structure on or in which the primary signals are mounted;

(b) on an occasion when a vehicle is being used for fire brigade, ambulance or police purposes and the observance of the prohibition conveyed by the red signal as provided by the last preceding sub-paragraph would be likely to hinder the use of that vehicle for the purpose for which it is being used on that occasion, then the said sub-paragraph shall not apply to that vehicle; but instead the prohibition conveyed to that vehicle by the red signal shall be that that vehicle shall not proceed beyond the stop line, or as the case may be as provided by the said sub-paragraph, beyond the said post or other structure in such a manner or at such a time—

(i) as is likely to cause danger to the driver of any other vehicle proceeding on or from another road or on or from another part of the same road in accordance with the indications of the light signals operating there in association with the said red signal or as to necessitate the driver of any other such vehicle to change its speed or course in order to avoid an accident, or

(ii) in the case of any traffic which is not vehicular, as is likely to cause danger to that traffic proceeding on or from another road or on or from another part of the same road;

(c) the amber-with-red signal shall be taken to denote an impending change in the indication given by the signals from red to green but shall not alter the prohibition conveyed by the red signal;

(d) the green signal shall indicate that vehicular traffic may pass the signals and proceed straight on or to the left or to the right;

(e) the amber signal shall, when shown alone, convey the prohibition that vehicular traffic shall not proceed beyond the stop line or, if that line is not for the time being visible or there is no stop line, beyond the said post or other structure, except in the case of any vehicle which when the signal first appears is so close to the said line, post or structure that it cannot safely be stopped before passing the line, post or structure.

(2) The significance of the light signals prescribed by Regulation 31(2) as varied in accordance with the provisions of Regulation 32, shall be as follows:—

(a) subject as provided in sub-paragraph (d) of this paragraph, the red signal shall convey the prohibition that vehicular traffic shall not proceed beyond the stop line on the carriageway provided in conjunction with the signals or if the stop line is not for the time being visible or there is no stop line, beyond the post or other structure on or in which the primary signals are mounted, except that when a vehicle is being used on such an occasion as is specified in paragraph (1)(b), the foregoing prohibition prescribed by this sub-paragraph shall not then apply to that vehicle but instead the prohibition conveyed to it on that occasion by the red signal shall be the same as that provided by paragraph (1)(b) in relation to the vehicle mentioned in that paragraph;

(b) subject as provided in sub-paragraph (d) of this paragraph, the amber-with-red signal shall denote an impending change in the indication given by the signals from red to green (where a green signal is provided) or from red to a green arrow or arrows but shall not alter the prohibition conveyed by the red signal;

(c) the green signal (where a green signal is provided) shall indicate that vehicular traffic may pass the signals and proceed straight on or to the left or to the right;

(d) any green arrow during such time as it is illuminated shall indicate that vehicular traffic may pass the signals and proceed in the direction indicated by the arrow notwithstanding any other indication given by the signals;

(e) the amber signal shall, when shown alone, convey the prohibition that vehicular traffic shall not proceed beyond the stop line, or if the stop line is not for the time being visible or there is no stop line, beyond the said post or other structure, except in the case of any vehicle which when the signal first appears is so close to the said line, post or structure that it cannot safely be stopped before passing the line, post or structure.

(3) Vehicular traffic passing any light signals in accordance with the foregoing provisions of this Regulation shall proceed with due regard to the safety of other users of the road and subject to the direction of any police constable in uniform or other duly authorised person who may be engaged in the regulation of traffic.

(4) The significance of the light signals prescribed by Regulation 31(3) shall be that the intermittent red lights when displayed at the side of the carriageway convey the prohibition that vehicular traffic shall not proceed beyond those lights and when displayed over the carriageway so as to operate in relation to vehicular traffic proceeding in the traffic lane (as defined by Regulation 36(1)) situated immediately beneath them, the said lights convey the prohibition that such vehicular traffic as aforesaid shall not proceed beyond those lights:

Provided that this paragraph shall not apply to a vehicle when it is being used on such an occasion as is specified in Regulation 34(1)(b); and for that vehicle when it is being so used, the intermittent red lights whether so displayed at the side of or over the carriageway shall have no significance.

(5) The significance of the light signals prescribed by Regulation 31(4) shall be as follows:—

(a) the amber signal shall convey the prohibition that vehicular traffic shall not proceed beyond the stop line on the carriageway provided in conjunction with the signal or, if that line is not for the time being visible or there is no stop line, beyond the post or other structure on or in which the primary signals are mounted, except in the case of any vehicle which when the signal first appears is so close to the said post or structure, that it cannot safely be stopped before passing the line post or structure; and

(b) the intermittent red signals shall convey the prohibition that vehicular traffic shall not proceed beyond the stop line on the carriageway provided in conjunction with the signals or, if that line is not for the time being visible or there is no stop line, beyond the said post or structure.

(6) In this Regulation,

(a) the expression "Stop line" means the road marking shown in diagram 1001 placed on the carriageway in conjunction with light signals being either primary signals alone, or secondary signals alone or both primary and secondary signals;

(b) any reference to light signals, to the signals or to a signal of a particular colour, is, where secondary signals have been erected as well as primary signals, a reference to the light signals, signals or particular signal displayed by both the primary signals and the secondary signals or by either the primary signals operating without the secondary signals, or by the secondary signals operating without the primary signals;

(c) the expression "primary signals" means light signals erected on or near the carriageway of a road and sited in the vicinity of either one end or both ends of the stop line or, if there is no stop line, sited at either or both edges of the carriageway or part of that carriageway which is in use by the traffic approaching and controlled by the signals; and

(d) the expression "secondary signals" means light signals erected on or near the carriageway facing approaching traffic in the same direction as the primary signals but sited beyond those signals as viewed from the direction of travel of such traffic.   **[1223]**

NOTES

Commencement: 13 August 1981.

35. Light signals for pedestrians

(1) Light signals for conveying to pedestrians the information mentioned in paragraph (4) may be used facing across the carriageway in conjunction with the light signals prescribed by Regulation 31(2) or those light signals as varied in accordance with the provisions of Regulation 32 and, if so used, shall be of the size, colour and type shown in diagram 4001 or 4002 in Schedule 4:

Provided that the light signals for conveying to pedestrians such information as aforesaid and which are associated as parts of the same electrical circuit shall be all of them of the same size, colour and type, that is to say, as shown either in the said diagram 4001 or alternatively in the said diagram 4002.

(2) The height of the lower edge of the container enclosing the light signals from the surface of the carriageway in the immediate vicinity shall be not less than 2.1 nor more than 2.6 metres.

(3) The said signals shall be so designed that—

(a) the red figure shown in the said Schedule (hereinafter referred to as "the red signal") can be internally illuminated by a steady light;

   (b) the green figure shown in the said Schedule (hereinafter referred to as "the green signal") can be internally illuminated by a steady light;
      . . .

   (c) when one signal is illuminated the other signal is not illuminated [and

   (d) the green signal is and remains illuminated only for so long as there is conveyed to vehicular traffic a requirement, prohibition or restriction against entering that part of the carriageway across which the light signals for pedestrians are facing, being a requirement, prohibition or restriction indicated by the light signals prescribed by Regulation 31(2), by that Regulation as varied in accordance with Regulation 32 as respects the direction of the green arrow, or by the traffic signs shown in diagrams 606, 612, 613 or 616].

(4) (a) The period during which in the interests of safety pedestrians should not cross the carriageway shall be shown by the red signal during such time as it is illuminated;

   (b) the period during which in the interests of safety pedestrians should cross the carriageway shall be shown by the green signal during such time as it is illuminated by the steady light.

(5) A traffic sign of the size, colour and type shown in diagram 4003 may be erected for use in conjunction with either the sign shown in diagram 4001 or that shown in diagram 4002 for the purpose of conveying to pedestrians the indication specified above that diagram. **[1224]**

NOTES
    Commencement: 13 August 1981.
    Para (3): amended by SI 1982 No 1879, reg 12.

36. Light signals for lane control of vehicular traffic

(1) In this Regulation the expression "traffic lane" means, in relation to a road, a part of the carriageway having as a boundary which separates it from another such part, a road marking of the type shown either in diagram 1004, 1005, 1007 or 1013.1.

(2) Light signals placed above the carriageway and facing the direction of the on-coming vehicular traffic may be used for the control of that traffic proceeding along the traffic lane over and in relation to which those signals have been so placed and, subject to the provisions of this Regulation, shall be of the size, colour and type shown in diagrams [5001 to 5004].

(3) The height of the centre of each such signal from the surface of the carriageway in the immediate vicinity shall be not less than 5.5 metres nor more than 9 metres.

(4) The said signals shall be so designed that—

   (a) the red cross shown in diagrams 5003 and 5004 (hereinafter referred to as "the red cross") can be internally illuminated in such manner as to show a steady red light.

   (b) the white arrow shown in diagrams 5001 and 5002 (hereinafter referred to as "the white downward arrow") can be internally illuminated by a steady white light, and

   (c) whenever the red cross is illuminated above a traffic lane, the white downward arrow above that traffic lane is not also then illuminated and whenever the white downward arrow is illuminated above that same lane, the red cross is not also then illuminated.

(5) The significance of the light signals prescribed by this Regulation shall be—

(a) the red cross conveys to vehicular traffic proceeding in the traffic lane above and in relation to which it is displayed the prohibition that such traffic shall not proceed beneath or beyond the red cross in the said traffic lane in the direction opposite to that in which the red cross faces until that prohibition is cancelled by a display over that traffic lane of the white downward arrow or by the display over that traffic lane or beside the carriageway of the traffic sign shown in diagram 6001 or of a traffic sign bearing the legend "End of lane control"; and

(b) the white downward arrow conveys to such traffic proceeding in the traffic lane above and in relation to which it is displayed the information that that traffic may proceed or continue so to do in the said lane beneath or beyond the said arrow and in the direction opposite to that in which that arrow faces.   **[1225]**

NOTES
Commencement: 13 August 1981.
Para (2): amended by SI 1982 No 1879, reg 13.

37. School crossing patrol signs and warning lights

(1) Except where the Secretary of State authorises the use of traffic signs of another description, every traffic sign which is exhibited by a school crossing patrol for the purpose of stopping any vehicle or vehicles in accordance with section 25 of the Act shall be of the size, colour and type shown in diagram 605.1.

(2)(a) A traffic sign for conveying the warning specified in the next following sub-paragraph to vehicular traffic which is approaching a place in a road where children on their way to or from school or on their way from one part of a school to another cross or seek to cross that road may be erected on or near a part of that road in advance, in relation to oncoming traffic, of the said place;

(b) the warning conveyed by the traffic sign mentioned in the preceding sub-paragraph shall be that such a place as aforesaid lies ahead and is either being patrolled by a school crossing patrol or is otherwise in use by children under the supervision of a teacher or other school officer, a traffic warden or a constable in uniform;

(c) the said sign shall be of the following size, colour and type, that is to say—

(i) 2 lamps mounted vertically one above the other, facing in the same direction and each showing an intermittent amber light shall be used;

(ii) each lamp shall be separately illuminated and the effective diameter of the lens thereof shall be not less than 135 nor more than 155 millimetres;

(iii) each lamp shall be so fitted that the centre of the light source which illuminates its lens is located on the axis of that lens; and

(iv) each lamp shall show an intermittent amber light at a rate of flashing of not less than 60 nor more than 90 flashes per minute and in such a manner that the light of one lamp is always shown at a time when the light of the other lamp is not shown.   **[1226]**

NOTES
Commencement: 13 August 1981.

38. Light signals for motorways

A traffic sign for conveying to the driver of a motor vehicle on a motorway the warning that, owing to the existence of a hazard thereon, he should drive at a speed which does not exceed 30 miles per hour shall consist of 2 beacons showing light signals of the following size, colour and type, that is to say—

(1) 2 lamps each showing an intermittent amber light shall be used;

(2) the lamps shall be arranged vertically so that there is a distance of not less than 825 millimetres nor more than 1 metre between the centres of the lenses of the lamps;

(3) each lamp shall be separately illuminated and the effective diameter of the lens thereof shall be not less than 115 nor more than 175 millimetres;

(4) each lamp shall show the said light at a rate of flashing of not less than 60 nor more than 90 flashes per minute, and in such a manner that the light of one lamp is always shown at a time when the light of the other lamp is not shown.   **[1227]**

NOTES
  Commencement: 13 August 1981.

39. Light signals for motorways

(1) Subject to the provisions of these Regulations, a traffic sign for conveying to vehicular traffic on motorways a warning or information of the description specified in or under a diagram in Part I of Schedule 6 shall be of the size, colour and type shown in the diagram relating to that warning or that information.

In this paragraph, the reference to vehicular traffic, where the traffic sign is erected beside the carriageway, is a reference to all vehicular traffic facing that sign and proceeding along the carriageway beside which the sign is so erected, and where the traffic sign is erected over the carriageway so as to operate in relation to vehicular traffic facing that sign and proceeding in the traffic lane (as defined by Regulation 36(1)) situated immediately beneath it, is a reference only to such traffic so facing and proceeding in that lane.

(2) Each of the signs shown in any diagram in Part I of Schedule 6 shall, when displaying the pattern of circles indicated by the diagram relative to that sign, be illuminated by internal white or off-white lights so arranged as to form the said pattern and may be accompanied by four lamps each showing an intermittent amber light as provided in the next following paragraph.

(3) Where the said four lamps accompany any of the signs mentioned in the last preceding paragraph, those lamps shall be of the size, colour and type prescribed by this paragraph, that is to say—

    (a) the lamps shall, in relation to the said pattern of circles, be so arranged as shown in diagram 6022 in Part II of Schedule 6 when erected beside the carriageway or as shown in diagram 6021 in the said Part II when erected over the carriageway;

    (b) each lamp shall show an intermittent amber light and, subject to the provisions of sub-paragraph (f) of this paragraph, be separately illuminated; and the effective diameter of the lens thereof shall be not less than 120 nor more than 130 millimetres;

    (c) the lamps shall be so fitted as to enclose a rectangular area bounded by the one pair of sides extending horizontally in relation to the ground and terminating as to each side in the centres of each pair of lenses (in these Regulations called "the horizontal pairs") and by the other pair of sides extending vertically in relation to the ground and terminating as to each side in the centres of each pair of lenses (in these Regulations called "the vertical pairs");

(d) when the four lamps are erected beside the carriageway, the distance between the centres of the lenses for each of the horizontal pairs shall be not less than 695 nor more than 705 millimetres and for each of the vertical pairs shall be not less than 945 nor more than 955 millimetres;

(e) when the four lamps are erected over the carriageway, the distance between the said centres for each of the horizontal pairs shall be not less than 1045 nor more than 1055 millimetres and for each of the vertical pairs not less than 545 nor more than 555 millimetres;

(f) when the sign is operated, each lamp shall show the said light at a rate of flashing of not less than 60 nor more than 90 flashes per minute, and in such a manner that the lights of one of the horizontal pairs are always shown when the lights of the other horizontal pair are not shown;

(g) the height of the centres of the lenses comprising the lower of the horizontal pairs from the surface of the carriageway in the immediate vicinity shall be in the case of signs placed beside the carriageway not less than 1.8 nor more than 3.2 metres and in the case of signs placed over the carriageway not less than 5.8 nor more than 6.8 metres;

(h) no lettering of any kind shall be used upon any of the lenses.

(4) The light signals prescribed by paragraph (3) shall convey to traffic the warning that the display of a traffic sign shown in a diagram in Part I of Schedule 6 is due to the existence of temporary hazardous conditions on or near the motorway.

(5) Where the circumstances so require, the indications given by the signs shown in Part I of Schedule 6 may be varied as in this paragraph provided, that is to say—

(a) any indication given by such a sign may be varied in the respect (if any) in which it is shown below the diagram relating to that sign that the indication may be varied;

(b) in the sign shown in diagram 6001, the numerals may be varied to accord with the circumstances.   **[1228]**

NOTES
Commencement: 13 August 1981.

Section IV, Traffic Signs shown in Schedule 2

40. Road danger lamps

(1) Subject to the provisions of these Regulations, a lamp showing either a steady or an intermittent light may be used to indicate to traffic the limits of a temporary obstruction of a road and shall be of the size, colour and type prescribed by paragraph 2.

(2)(a) The colour of the light shown by the said lamp whether steady or intermittent shall be amber.

(b) Each lens of the lamp shall be—

(i) if the light so shown is emitted from the lamp in only one, two or three horizontal directions, of such a shape and size that the perimeter of its horizontally projected area on to any vertical plane shall be capable of lying wholly inside a circle having a diameter of 150 millimetres and wholly outside a circle having a diameter of 100 millimetres, and

(ii) if the light so shown is emitted from the lamp in every horizontal direction, of such a shape and size that the perimeter of its horizontally projected area on to any vertical plane shall be capable of lying wholly within a square having sides of 125 millimetres in length and wholly outside a square having sides of 40 millimetres in length.

(c) Each such lamp shall be illuminated separately and by a single source of light.

(d) The height of the centre of any such lens from the surface of the road in the immediate vicinity shall not exceed 1.2 metres.

(e) There shall be displayed in association with that lens a device having an area of not less than 50 square centimetres and fitted with amber reflectors or amber reflecting material.

(f) Where a lamp is used which shows a steady light, then the luminous intensity of that light shall not be less than 0.5 candela measured within 5 degrees above and below and 10 degrees left and right of the principal axis if the light so shown is emitted from the lamp in only one, two or three directions, and measured within 5 degrees above and below the horizontal plane around the vertical axis of symmetry if the said light is so emitted in every direction.

(g) Where a lamp which shows an intermittent light is used, then that lamp shall be of such a size and type that the rate of flashing shall be not less than 900 flashes per minute and the peak luminous intensity measured in accordance with the last preceding sub-paragraph not less than 1 candela; except that where such a lamp is erected within 50 metres of a street lamp lit by electricity on a road subject to a speed limit of 40 miles per hour or less, that lamp may, as an alternative to the size and type last mentioned, be of such a size and type that the said rate shall be not less than 120 nor more than 150 flashes per minute and the said intensity so measured shall be not less than 1.5 candela. **[1229]**

NOTES
Commencement: 13 August 1981.

SCHEDULES
SCHEDULE 1
(REG 9–19)

[For the diagrams in Schedules 1–7, reference should be made to the Queen's Printer's copy of this statutory instrument, which can be obtained from HMSO.]

PART I
WARNING SIGNS

This part of Schedule 1 sets out detailed diagrams of traffic warning signs with requirements as to size and permitted variations of symbols and legends. **[1230]**

NOTES
Commencement: 13 August 1981.
Amended by SI 1982 No 1879, reg 14; SI 1983 No 1088, reg 6; SI 1986 No 1859, reg 2; SI 1990 No 704, Part I, reg 5, Sch 1.

PART II
REGULATORY SIGNS

This part of Schedule 1 sets out detailed diagrams of traffic regulatory signs with requirements as to size and permitted variations of symbols and legends. **[1231]**

NOTES
Commencement: 13 August 1981.
Amended by SI 1982 No 1879, reg 15, and SI 1984 No 966, Part I.

PART III
DIRECTIONAL INFORMATORY SIGNS

This part of Schedule 1 sets out detailed diagrams of directional informatory signs with requirements as to dimensions of the signs and permitted variations of symbols and legends. **[1232]**

NOTES
Commencement: 13 August 1981.
Amended by SI 1982 No 1879, reg 16.

PART IV
OTHER INFORMATORY SIGNS

This part of Schedule 1 sets out detailed diagrams of informatory signs (other than those set out in Parts I–III of this Schedule) with requirements as to dimensions of the signs and permitted variations of symbols and legends. **[1233]**

NOTES
Commencement: 13 August 1981.
Amended by SI 1982 No 1879, reg 17.

PART V
DIRECTIONAL AND OTHER INFORMATORY SIGNS ON MOTORWAYS

This part of Schedule 1 sets out detailed diagrams of directional and informatory signs on motorways with requirements as to dimensions of the signs and permitted variations of symbols and legends. **[1234]**

NOTES
Commencement: 13 August 1981.

SCHEDULE 2
MARKINGS ON THE ROAD (REGS 20–26, DIRECTION 31)

This Schedule sets out markings on the road with requirements as to dimensions and alternative methods of marking and permitted variations of legend. **[1235]**

NOTES
Commencement: 13 August 1981.
Amended by SI 1982 No 1879, reg 18, SI 1983 No 1088, reg 7.
Amended with savings by SI 1990 No 704, Part I, regs 6, 7, Sch 2.

SCHEDULE 3
SIZE AND COLOUR OF ARROW IN LIGHT SIGNALS FOR CONTROL OF VEHICULAR TRAFFIC AND METHODS OF INCORPORATION OF THE ARROW IN THOSE SIGNALS (REG 32, DIRECTION 34)

[1236]

NOTES
Commencement: 13 August 1981.

SCHEDULE 4
SIZE, COLOUR AND TYPE OF LIGHT SIGNALS FOR PEDESTRIANS (REG 35)

[1237]

NOTES
Commencement: 13 August 1981.

SCHEDULE 5
SIZE, COLOUR AND TYPE OF LIGHT SIGNALS FOR LANE CONTROL OF VEHICULAR TRAFFIC (REG 36)

[1238]

NOTES
Commencement: 13 August 1981.

SCHEDULE 6
(REGS 31, 39)

PART I
SIZE, COLOUR AND TYPE OF TEMPORARY INDICATIONS ON MOTOR-WAYS

This part of Schedule 6 sets out detailed diagrams of temporary indications on motorways with requirements as to dimensions and permitted variations of symbols and legends. **[1239]**

NOTES
Commencement: 13 August 1981.

PART II
DIAGRAMS SHOWING THE RELATIONSHIP BETWEEN FLASHING AMBER LIGHTS PRESCRIBED IN REGULATION 39(3) AND MATRIX CAPABLE OF DISPLAYING SIGNS SHOWN IN PART I OF THIS SCHEDULE

[1240]

NOTES
Commencement: 13 August 1981.

PART III
THE RELATIVE POSITIONS OF THE LAMPS COMPRISING THE LIGHT SIGNALS PRESCRIBED BY REGULATION 31(3)

[1241]

NOTES
Commencement: 13 August 1981.

PART IV
NUMERALS FOR USE IN THE SIGN SHOWN AT DIAGRAM 6001

[1242]

NOTES
Commencement: 13 August 1981.

SCHEDULE 7
PROPORTION AND FORM OF LETTERS, NUMERALS AND OTHER CHARACTERS (REG 14)

PART I

TRANSPORT MEDIUM CAPITAL ALPHABET FOR USE ON SIGNS WITH A RED, BLUE OR GREEN BACKGROUND

[1243]

NOTES
Commencement: 13 August 1981.

PART II

TRANSPORT MEDIUM LOWER-CASE ALPHABET FOR USE ON SIGNS WITH A RED, BLUE OR GREEN BACKGROUND

[1244]

NOTES
Commencement: 13 August 1981.

PART III

TRANSPORT MEDIUM NUMERALS FOR USE ON SIGNS WITH A RED, BLUE OR GREEN BACKGROUND

[1245]

NOTES
Commencement: 13 August 1981.

PART IV

TRANSPORT MEDIUM OTHER CHARACTERS FOR USE ON SIGNS WITH A RED, BLUE OR GREEN BACKGROUND, ALSO ON THE GREY OR BLACK BACKGROUND OF A GANTRY

[1246]

NOTES
Commencement: 13 August 1981.

PART V

TRANSPORT HEAVY CAPITAL ALPHABET FOR USE ON SIGNS WITH A WHITE OR YELLOW BACKGROUND

[1247]

NOTES
Commencement: 13 August 1981.

PART VI

TRANSPORT HEAVY LOWER-CASE ALPHABET FOR USE ON SIGNS WITH A WHITE OR YELLOW BACKGROUND

[1248]

NOTES
Commencement: 13 August 1981.

PART VII

TRANSPORT HEAVY NUMERALS FOR USE ON SIGNS WITH A WHITE OR YELLOW BACKGROUND

[1249]

NOTES

Commencement: 13 August 1981.

PART VIII

TRANSPORT HEAVY OTHER CHARACTERS FOR USE ON SIGNS WITH A WHITE OR YELLOW BACKGROUND

[1250]

NOTES

Commencement: 13 August 1981.

PART IX

LETTERS AND NUMERALS FOR USE IN ROUTE NUMBERS ON THE SIGNS SHOWN IN DIAGRAM 757 AND ON ANY SIGN SHOWN IN SCHEDULE 1 PART V

[1251]

NOTES

Commencement: 13 August 1981.

PART X

ROAD MARKING ALPHABET AND NUMERALS WITH A HEIGHT OF 1.6 METRES COLOUR TO BE WHITE

[1252]

NOTES

Commencement: 13 August 1981.

PART XI

ROAD MARKING ALPHABET AND NUMERALS WITH A HEIGHT OF 2.8 METRES COLOUR TO BE WHITE

[1253]

NOTES

Commencement: 13 August 1981.

PART XII

ROAD MARKING ALPHABET FOR USE IN THE MARKINGS SHOWN IN DIAGRAMS 027.1 AND 1028.1 COLOUR OF THE ALPHABET TO BE WHITE OR YELLOW APPROPRIATE TO THE COLOURS PRESCRIBED FOR THE ROAD MARKINGS BY REGULATION 24

[1254]

NOTES

Commencement: 13 August 1981.

SCHEDULE 8
EXERCISE OF POWERS

(1) The power conferred by section 25 of the Road Traffic Regulation Act 1967 is exercised by the Secretary of State for Transport as respects England, by the Secretary of State for Scotland as respects Scotland and the Secretary of State for Wales as respects

Wales (see the definition of 'the appropriate Minister' in section 104(1) as read subject to section 108 of that Act).

(2) The powers conferred by sections 54(1) and 55(1) of the said Act of 1967, as amended by paragraph 24(b) of Schedule 3 to the Secretary of State for the Environment Order 1970 and also the powers conferred by the provision relating to section 22 of the Road Traffic Act 1972 in column 5 of Part I of Schedule 4 to that Act, as that provision is amended by paragraph 9 of Schedule 3 to the Secretary of State for Transport Order 1976 are exercised by those three Secretaries of State acting jointly. **[1255]**

NOTES
Commencement: 13 August 1981.

PART II

GENERAL DIRECTIONS

1. These Directions may be cited as "The Traffic Signs General Directions 1981". **[1256]**

NOTES
Commencement: 13 August 1981.

3. In these Directions the expressions ["cycle lane", "hours of darkness", "motorway", "pedal cycle",] "primary route", "non-primary route", "road marking", "stud", "the Regulations of 1964" and "temporary statutory provision" have the same meanings as they have in the Traffic Signs Regulations 1981 (hereinafter in these Directions referred to as "the Regulations") and the expression "principal road" has the meaning assigned to it by section 84B(8) of the Road Traffic Regulation Act 1967. **[1257]**

NOTES
Commencement: 13 August 1981.
Amended by SI 1982 No 1880, dir 3, Schedule.

4. (1) Any reference in these Directions to a diagram by a number is a reference to the diagram of that number in any of the Schedules to the Regulations.

(2) Any reference in these Directions to any sign shown in a diagram being a diagram in any of the Schedules to the Regulations shall be construed as including a reference to any such sign varied in accordance with the provisions of the Regulations. **[1258]**

NOTES
Commencement: 13 August 1981.

5. Without prejudice to section 64 of the Road Traffic Regulation Act 1967—

(1) whenever a sign shown in diagram 734.7 or in any of the diagrams 837.1 to 838.2 is to be placed for the first time at any given site on or near a primary route, that sign shall not be so placed unless the site shall have first been approved in writing by or on behalf of the Secretary of State; and

(2) whenever the sign shown in diagram 601.1 is to be placed for the first time at any given site on or near any road whatsoever, that sign shall not be so placed unless the site shall have first been so approved as aforesaid, except that if the said site shall already have been duly so approved for placing the sign shown in diagram 601 in Schedule 1 to the Regulations of 1964, its replacement by the sign shown in diagram 601.1 shall be treated as a placing otherwise than for the first time for the purposes of this sub-paragraph. **[1259]**

NOTES
Commencement: 13 August 1981.

6. (1) Except as provided by the next following sub-paragraph, signs shown in diagrams 606, 607, 609, 612 to 614, 616, 617 to 622.2, 622.4 to [625.1, 625.3,] 626.1 to 632, 636 to 640, 640.2A, 640.3 to 640.5, 641 to 644, 646, 647, 650 to 656.1, 660 to 662, 712, 712.1, 719.2, 719.3A, 729.1, 729.2, 760, 761, 801.3 to 801.5, 806 to 808.3, [810, 810.2,] 812.1 to [812.6,] 818.2 to 819.3, 1016.1 to 1021, 1025.1, 1025.3, 1028.1, 1032, 1033, 1036.1, 1036.2, 1037.1, 1043 to 1050, 5001 to 5004 may be placed on or near a road only to indicate the effect of an Act of Parliament, Order, Regulation, Bye-law or Notice which prohibits or restricts the use of the road by traffic.

[(2) The sign shown in a diagram specified in an item in column 2 of the Table may be placed on or near a road in the circumstances specified in that item in column 3 of the Table notwithstanding that it does not in those circumstances indicate the effect mentioned in paragraph (1).

TABLE

Column 1 Item	Column 2 Diagram	Column 3 Circumstances
1	606	On the central island of a roundabout or in combination with a plate of the type shown in diagram 608.
2	609	On a road approaching its junction with a dual-carriageway road or in combination with a plate of the type shown in diagram 608.
3	616, 1046 or 1047	At a site which has been approved in writing by or on behalf of the Secretary of State.
4	629.2	On— (a) the approach to a bridge, tunnel or similar structure which limits the height of vehicles using the road under the bridge, through the tunnel or under or through the similar structure; or (b) any such bridge, tunnel or similar structure.
5	712.1, 719.3A or 729.2	When including a symbol represented in— (a) any diagram in Part I of Schedule 1 to the Regulations; or (b) diagram 629.2 in Part II of that Schedule in the circumstances specified in item 4 above.
6	818.2	When placed to indicate that the prohibition indicated by the sign shown in diagram 629.2 is ahead, provided that that sign has been placed in the circumstances specified in item 4 above.

(3) In this direction, "dual-carriageway road" means a length of road on which one part of the carriageway is separated from another part by a central reservation, and "central reservation" means any provision made in a road (not

being the provision of a street refuge) for separating one part of the carriageway
from another part for the safety and guidance of vehicular traffic using that
road.]   **[1260]**

NOTES
   Commencement: 15 December 1989 (paras (2), (3)); 13 August 1981 (remainder).
   Paras (2), (3): substituted, for para (2) as originally enacted, by SI 1989 No 2139, Part II, dir 4.

7. The signs shown in diagrams 701 to 717 may be placed only on or near a
primary route and the signs shown in diagrams 718 to 726 may be placed only
on or near a non-primary route, except that the signs shown in diagrams 718.2
and 718.3 may be placed on or near any road when varied to include a blue
border.   **[1261]**

NOTES
   Commencement: 13 August 1981.

8. The signs shown in diagrams 823 to 825 when the colour of the background
is blue may be placed only on or near a motorway, when the colour of the
background is green may be placed only on or near a primary route and when
the colour of the background is white may be placed only on or near a non-
primary route; and the signs shown in diagrams 837.1 to 838.2 may be placed
only on or near a primary route or a motorway.   **[1262]**

NOTES
   Commencement: 13 August 1981.

9. The signs shown in diagrams 901.1 to 925 may be placed only on or near a
motorway.   **[1263]**

NOTES
   Commencement: 13 August 1981.

10. The traffic signs shown in the diagrams whose numbers appear in column 1
of the table set out in this paragraph shall not be used on a road unless so used
in conjunction with the road markings shown in the diagrams whose numbers
appear in column 2 of that table opposite to the number in column 1 to which
they relate:

   Provided that the provisions of this paragraph requiring the use of the signs
shown in diagrams 601.1, 602, 611.1 and 650 in conjunction with a road marking
shall not apply during the execution of works on a road in the vicinity of the
place where any of those signs is erected, if those works necessitate the
temporary removal of that marking, and shall not apply if any of those signs is
erected only temporarily in connection with the execution of works on a road.

TABLE

Column 1 Sign diagram number	Column 2 Road marking diagram number
601.1	both 1002.1 and 1022
602	both 1003 and 1023
611.1	both 1003.3 and 1003.4
650	either 1025.1 or 1025.3
653	both 1048 and 1049
654	both 1048 and 1049

Any reference in this paragraph and in the next following paragraph to a traffic sign shown in diagram 601.1 and to the number of that diagram in the said table shall be treated as a reference until the [31st December 1982] inclusive of that date to any sign which can be treated as if prescribed by the Regulations until that date if it is a sign of the type shown in the diagram numbered 601 in Schedule 1 to the Traffic Signs Regulations 1964.

References in this paragraph to the road marking shown in diagram number 1002.1 specified in column 2 of the table above include, until the 31st December 1983 inclusive of that date, references to any road marking which can be treated until that date as if prescribed by the Regulations if it is a sign of the type shown in diagram 1002 in Schedule 2 to the Regulations of 1975.   **[1264]**

NOTES
Commencement: 13 August 1981.
Amended by SI 1982 No 1880, dir 3, 4, Schedule.

11. (1) The sign shown in diagram 501 shall not be used unless used either in combination with a plate of the type shown in diagram 502 and in conjunction with the sign shown in diagram 601.1 or in combination with a plate of the type shown in diagram 503 and in conjunction with the sign shown in diagram 602.

(2) The sign shown in diagram 545 shall not be used unless used in combination with any one of the following, that is to say, with a plate of the type shown in diagram 546 to 547.3 or the traffic sign (warning lights) prescribed by Regulation 37(2) of the Regulations.

(3) The traffic signs shown in the diagrams whose numbers appear in column 1 of the table set out at the end of this paragraph shall not be used unless used in combination with a plate of the type shown in the diagrams whose numbers appear in column 2 of that table opposite to the number in column 1 to which they relate.

(4) Where the indications given by any of the signs shown in diagrams 530, 532.1 and 629 to 629.2 are varied in accordance with Regulation 12(1)(a) of the Regulations, the sign whose indications shall have been so varied shall not be used displaying the permitted variant unless used in combination with another sign of the same type whose indications have not been so varied as aforesaid and which gives the indications prescribed in the relevant diagram without the permitted variant.

[When the signs shown in the diagrams specified in this paragraph are incorporated as symbols displayed by other signs incorporating them and the indications given by those symbols are so varied, this paragraph shall apply to those other signs incorporating the varied symbols in the same way as it applied to the said signs so symbolized.]

TABLE

Column 1 Sign diagram number	*Column 2* Plate diagram number
533	either 534.1 or 534.2 or 535.1
544.2	547.4
562	either 537.3 or 563
617	either 618 or 618.1
632	either 570 or 645
[557.1	557.2, 557.3 or 557.4]

[1265]

NOTES
Commencement: 13 August 1981.
Para (4): amended by SI 1982 No 1880, dir 5.
Table amended by SI 1983 No 1086, dir 2.

12. A plate of the type shown in diagrams 502, 503, 511, 518, 519, 519.1, 525 to 527, 534.1, 534.2, 535.1, 537.1 to 537.4, 546, [547.1 to 547.6], 553, 556.3, 556.4, [,557.2, 557.3, 557.4,], 563, 564.1, 570 to 573, 575, 579, 602.1, 607, 608, 618, 618.1, 619.3, 619.4, 620, 620.1, 622.3, 625.2, 627, 636.1, 642.1, 643 to 645, 656, 656.1, 660.2, 662, 802.1 to 805, 807, 812.3, 812.4 and 817.1 shall not be used unless used in combination with the signs which are specified beneath the diagrams showing the plate.　　　　　　　　　　　　　　　　　　　**[1266]**

NOTES
Commencement: 13 August 1981.
First figures in square brackets substituted by SI 1990 No 704, Part II, dir 2; second figures in square brackets added by SI 1983 No 1086, dir 2(b).

13. A plate of the type shown in diagrams 637, 639, 640, 641 or 646 may be placed on or near the side of a road only if there is placed in conjunction with that plate and on the same side of the road a road marking shown in diagrams 1016.1, 1017 or 1018, except that this paragraph shall not apply where any such plate is so placed for the purposes of a temporary statutory provision.　　**[1267]**

NOTES
Commencement: 13 August 1981.

14. A plate of the type shown in [diagram 638, 640 or 646] may be placed on or near the side of a road only if there is placed in conjunction with that plate and on the same side of the road a road marking shown in diagram 1019, 1020 and 1021, except that this paragraph shall not apply where any such plate is so placed for the purpose of a temporary statutory provision. **[1268]**

NOTES
  Commencement: 13 August 1981.
  Amended by SI 1987 No 1706, dir 3, Schedule.

15. The sign shown in diagram 545 when used in combination with the plate shown in diagram 547.1 or with the sign (amber flashing lights) prescribed by Regulation 37(2) of the Regulations may be placed only on a road on which, in the vicinity of the site of the sign, there is a place patrolled from time to time by a school crossing patrol or otherwise in use by children under supervision as provided by Regulation 37(2)(b). **[1269]**

NOTES
  Commencement: 13 August 1981.

16. The traffic sign shown in diagram 574 may be placed on a site on or near a road only where that site lies either in a place or area which is an infected place or area or part thereof for the purposes of the Diseases of Animals Act 1950, as extended by the Rabies Act 1974, or outside but near the boundaries of such a place or area, and shall not be retained there after that place or area or part thereof ceases to be or to be in such an infected place or area or part thereof.
[1270]

NOTES
  Commencement: 13 August 1981.

17. The signs shown in diagrams 564, 564.1, 564.5 to 569.1, 754 to 756.1 and the signs shown in diagrams 858 to 858.2 when those last-mentioned signs are displayed on the yellow but not on the blue permitted backgrounds may be placed on or near a road only in connection with the execution of works thereon, or a temporary obstruction thereon, and any such sign so placed and any other sign shown in a diagram in Schedule 1 to the Regulations so placed as aforesaid shall not be retained on or near the road after the completion of the works or the removal of the obstruction, as the case may be, unless—

  (i) it is a sign of the type shown in diagram 565.1 and if so, that sign may be retained on or near a road after the completion of the works for so long as the highway authority concerned sees fit, or
  (ii) it is a sign of the type shown in diagram 565.2 bearing the words "Give way markings erased", or "stop markings erased" and if so, that sign shall have been removed as soon as the road markings have been replaced and in any event not later than 28 days from the date of completion of the works. **[1271]**

NOTES
  Commencement: 13 August 1981.

18. (1) Signs shown in diagrams 603 and 604 may be used only where one-way working is necessary owing to a temporary closure to vehicular traffic of a width of the carriageway of a road.

(2) The signs shown in diagrams 615 and 811 shall not be used unless used in conjunction with one another and shall not be used at all in conjunction with the signs shown in diagrams 603 or 604.

(3) The signs shown in diagrams 634 and 635 may be used only by a constable in uniform or a person acting under the instructions or authority of the chief officer of police for the police area in which the signs are to be placed.
[1272]

NOTES
Commencement: 13 August 1981.

19. The sign shown in diagram 569.2 or 569.3 may be placed on or near a road only in connection with works involving an alteration in the layout of the carriageway or involving the removal of or change in the road markings or other traffic signs placed on or near a road at cross roads or other junctions (including in the case of the sign shown in the diagram 569.3 an automatic railway level crossing within the meaning of Regulation 25(1) of the Regulations), and shall be retained for not more than 3 months from the date of the completion of those works. **[1273]**

NOTES
Commencement: 13 August 1981.

20. Signs shown in diagrams 830, 830.1, 831 and 832 (except when varied to contain the words "weight check") may be used only in connection with a traffic census the taking of which on a road has been approved by the highway authority for that road, by the chief officer of police of the police area in which the road is situate, and by or on behalf of the Secretary of State. **[1274]**

NOTES
Commencement: 13 August 1981.

21. The signs shown in diagrams 833 to 836 may be used only to regulate the movement of vehicular traffic into and out of premises with more than one access to a road. **[1275]**

NOTES
Commencement: 13 August 1981.

22. The sign shown in diagram 536 shall be mounted on two posts and so much of each post as extends above ground level shall be coloured black and white in alternate horizontal bands, each band being not less than 250 nor more than 335 millimetres in depth. **[1276]**

NOTES
Commencement: 13 August 1981.

23. (1) The sign shown in diagram 560 or diagram 561 shall be so placed that the top of the sign is not less than 550 millimetres nor more than one metre above the surface of the carriageway in the immediate vicinity.

(2) Where the sign shown in diagram 560 or diagram 561 is mounted on a post specially provided for the purpose, that part of the post which extends above ground level shall be coloured black and white in alternate horizontal bands, each band being not less than 225 nor more than 350 millimetres in depth.

(3) The signs shown in diagrams 560 and 561 shall be so erected as to display the colour red on the left-hand edge of the carriageway viewed by the drivers of approaching vehicles and the colour white on the right-hand edge of that carriageway so viewed as aforesaid unless the said right-hand edge is the edge of the central reservation of a dual carriageway when the said signs shall be so erected as to display the colour amber on the said right-hand edge viewed by those drivers instead of the colour white. **[1277]**

NOTES
    Commencement: 13 August 1981.

23A. [The sign shown in diagram 625.3 shall not be erected on or near a road except when the road has been divided into a part reserved for the use of pedal cycles and a part reserved for use by pedestrians by either—

   (a) the road marking shown in diagram 1049 (when that marking is varied to be 150 millimetres wide), or
   (b) by the presence on the road of works such as distinctive colouring of the surface of each part, a kerb or other device.] **[1278]**

NOTES
    Commencement: 10 February 1983.
    Added by SI 1982 No 1880, dir 6.

PART I
GENERAL DIRECTIONS

24. (1) The road marking shown in diagram 1001 shall not be placed on a road unless it is so placed for use in conjunction with the light signals prescribed by paragraph (2) or paragraph (4) of Regulation 31 of the Regulations or with the light signals prescribed by the said paragraph (2) as varied in accordance with Regulation 32 of the Regulations or unless it is so placed at a site where vehicular traffic is from time to time controlled by the police.

(2) Where both primary and secondary signals within the meaning of Regulation 34(6) of the Regulations have been erected, the reference in sub-paragraph (1) above to light signals prescribed by the said paragraph (2) or paragraph (4) of Regulation 31 or by the said paragraph 2 as so varied as

aforesaid shall be construed as a reference to both the primary and the secondary signals or if either the primary or secondary signals are not operating, to the primary signals operating alone or to the secondary signals operating alone as the case may be.   **[1279]**

NOTES
Commencement: 13 August 1981.

PART II
GENERAL DIRECTIONS

25. The road markings shown in diagrams 1002.1 and 1022 shall not be placed on a road unless they are so placed for use in conjunction with the sign shown in diagram 601.1 or until the [31st December 1982] inclusive of that date, with any sign which can be treated as if prescribed by the Regulations until that date if it is a sign of the type shown in the diagram numbered 601 in Schedule 1 to the Traffic Signs Regulations 1964; and the road marking shown in diagram 1003.4 shall not be so placed as aforesaid unless it is placed for use in conjunction with the sign shown in diagram 611.1.   **[1280]**

NOTES
Commencement: 13 August 1981.
Amended by SI 1982 No 1880, dir 3, Schedule.

26. (1) Subject to sub-paragraph (4) of this paragraph, the road marking shown in diagram 1017 may be placed on a side of a road only for the purpose of indicating a statutory prohibition or restriction on the waiting of vehicles which applies on that side for at least eight hours during the period from 7 a.m. to 7 p.m. on at least four days other than a Sunday in any week.

(2) Subject as aforesaid, the road marking shown in diagram 1018 may be placed on a side of a road only for the purpose of indicating a statutory prohibition or restriction on the waiting of vehicles which applies on that side for at least eight hours during the period from 7 a.m. to 7 p.m. on at least four days other than a Sunday in any week and at some other times other than those during the period from 7 a.m. to 7 p.m.

(3) Subject to sub-paragraph (5) of this paragraph, the road marking shown in diagram 1016.1 may be placed on a side of a road only for the purpose of indicating a statutory prohibition or restriction on the waiting of vehicles which does not fall to be indicated by the road markings mentioned in sub-paragraphs (1) and (2) of this paragraph.

(4) In sub-paragraphs (1) and (2) of this paragraph the references to a statutory prohibition or restriction on the waiting of vehicles shall be construed as excluding references to any such prohibition or restriction as aforesaid imposed—

    (a) on waiting for the purpose of loading or unloading a vehicle,

    (b) so as expressly to limit the duration of waiting of vehicles within a particular period,

    (c) on waiting where the provisions of such prohibition or restriction exempt the waiting of a vehicle in respect of which a certificate of such exemption has been granted to the owner thereof as being one of a class of persons who qualify for the grant of such a certificate solely on the ground that they are all persons whose usual place of abode is at premises situated beside a road specified in relation to the prohibition or restriction, or

    (d) on waiting of a goods vehicle (as defined by section 196(1) of the Road Traffic Act 1972) but of no other vehicle.

(5) In sub-paragraph (3) of this paragraph the reference to a statutory prohibition or restriction on the waiting of vehicles shall be construed as excluding references to any such prohibition or restriction imposed on waiting such as is described in sub-paragraph (4)(a), (c) or (d) of this paragraph. **[1281]**

NOTES
    Commencement: 13 August 1981.

27. (1) The road marking shown in diagram 1020 may be placed on a side of a road only for the purpose of indicating a statutory prohibition or restriction on the waiting of vehicles for the purpose of their being loaded or unloaded (but not for indicating a statutory prohibition or restriction which expressly limits the duration of waiting by vehicles within a particular period for the purpose of their being loaded or unloaded) which applies on that side for at least eight hours during the period from 7 a.m. to 7 p.m. on at least four days other than a Sunday in any week.

(2) The road marking shown in diagram 1021 may be placed on a side of a road only for the purpose of indicating a statutory prohibition or restriction on the waiting of vehicles for the purpose of their being loaded or unloaded (but not for indicating a statutory prohibition or restriction which expressly limits the duration of waiting by vehicles within a particular period for the purpose of their being loaded or unloaded) which applies on that side for at least eight hours during the period from 7 a.m. to 7 p.m. on at least four days other than a Sunday in any week and at some other times other than those during the period from 7 a.m. to 7 p.m.

(3) The road marking shown in diagram 1019 may be placed on a side of a road only for the purpose of indicating a statutory prohibition or restriction on the waiting of vehicles for the purpose of their being loaded or unloaded (but not for indicating a statutory prohibition or restriction which expressly limits the duration of waiting by vehicles within a particular period for the purpose of their being loaded or unloaded) which applies otherwise than is specified in sub-paragraphs (1) and (2) of this paragraph. **[1282]**

NOTES
    Commencement: 13 August 1981.

28. A road marking shown in diagrams 1016.1, 1017 or 1018 shall not be used unless used in conjunction with at least one plate of the type shown in diagrams 637, 639, 640, 641, [642.1 (used as directed in paragraph 12 of these Directions) or 646] which plate shall be placed on the same side of the road as that on which is placed that marking, except that this paragraph shall not apply where any such marking is placed within a controlled parking zone.

In this and the next succeeding paragraph the expression "controlled parking zone" means an area in which all roads have been marked, except where parking places have been designated, with one or more of the road markings shown in diagrams 1016.1 to 1021, the entrances for vehicular traffic into the area being indicated by a sign shown in diagram 806 or 806.1.   **[1283]**

NOTES
  Commencement: 13 August 1981.
  Amended by SI 1982 No 1880, dir 3, Schedule.

29. A road marking shown in diagrams 1019, 1020 or 1021 shall not be used unless used in conjunction with at least one plate of the type shown in diagrams 638, [640, 642.1 or 646] which plate shall be placed on the same side of the road as that on which is placed that marking and such a marking shall be placed on the footway as near as practicable to the edge of the carriageway or, if there is no footway, on the carriageway as near as is practicable to its edge, except that nothing in this paragraph shall require the provision of a plate in conjunction with any such marking if the marking is placed within a controlled parking zone.   **[1284]**

NOTES
  Commencement: 13 August 1981.
  Amended by SI 1982 No 1880, dir 3, Schedule.

30. (1) The road markings shown in diagram 1023 shall not be placed on a road unless so placed for use in conjunction with the road marking shown in diagram 1003.

(2) The road markings shown in diagrams 1025.1 and 1025.3 shall not be placed on a road unless so placed for use in conjunction with at least one sign of the type shown in diagram 650 which shall have been erected on or near the same side of the road as that on which the marking is placed.

(3) The road marking shown in diagram 1048 shall not be placed on a road unless so placed for use in conjunction with the marking shown in diagram 1049 and either the traffic sign shown in diagram 653 or that shown in diagram 654; and the marking shown in diagram 1049 shall not be placed on a road unless so placed for use in conjunction with the marking shown in diagram 1048 and either the sign shown in diagram 653 or that shown in diagram 654.

[(4) No road marking of a kind shown in diagrams 1003, 1023 or 1049 when varied in size to conform with any of the smaller alternative dimensions prescribed for it shall be placed on the carriageway except for use in conjunction with the marking shown in diagram 1057 and also with one or more of the signs shown in diagrams 625, 625.3, 654.1 or 815.

(5) No roadmarking of the kind shown in diagram 1009 when varied in size to conform with the smallest alternative dimensions prescribed for it shall be placed on the carriageway except to mark the junction of a cycle track and another road, in conjunction with road markings of the smallest alternative dimensions prescribed for diagrams 1003 and 1023.

(6) No roadmarking of a kind shown in diagram 1057 shall be placed on a road except in conjunction with at least one of the signs shown in diagrams 625, 625.3, 654.1 or 815 erected along that road.

(7) The road markings shown in diagrams 1058 or 1059 shall not be placed on a road unless so placed for use in conjunction with at least one road marking of the kind shown in diagram 1057.] **[1285]**

NOTES
Commencement: 10 February 1983 (paras (4)-(7)); 13 August 1981 (remainder).
Paras (4)-(7): added by SI 1982 No 1880, dir 7.

31. Studs incorporating reflectors may be placed on a road only if such studs are of a type which has first been approved in writing by or on behalf of the Secretary of State. **[1286]**

NOTES
Commencement: 13 August 1981.

32. No sign, used in accordance with the provisions of Regulation 27 of the Regulations may be retained at any place on or near a principal road after the expiration of six months from the date on which the sign was erected at that place, or such longer time as may be approved in writing by or on behalf of the Secretary of State, or be retained in any case after the termination of the need for such a sign. **[1287]**

NOTES
Commencement: 13 August 1981.

33. Where the lamp mentioned in Regulation 30 of the Regulations is mounted on a post specially provided for the purpose—

(1) if that post is a post placed on a street refuge or central reservation on a zebra crossing and yellow globes also are attached to, or mounted on that post, then the provisions of paragraph 2(4) of Part II of Schedule 2 to the 'Zebra' Pedestrian Crossings Regulations 1971 shall have effect and apply to the colouring of that post in so far as it extends above ground level up to the point where the yellow globes are mounted or attached and beyond that point any remaining part of the post shall be coloured in accordance with sub-paragraph (2) of this paragraph; and

(2) if that post is a post so placed as aforesaid but yellow globes are not also attached to, or mounted on it or if the post is placed elsewhere than on a zebra crossing, then that post shall be coloured grey but with two white bands, each band being not less than 275 nor more than 335 millimetres in depth, being so

arranged that at least 275 but not more than 335 millimetres extend between the nearest edges of the two bands, and the upper edge of the uppermost band being at least 275 but not more than 335 millimetres below the lowest part of the lamp:

Provided that where such a post is constructed of concrete if shall not be coloured in either manner as aforesaid but shall remain in its natural colour.

In this paragraph "zebra crossing" has the same meaning as in the said Regulations of 1971 and "yellow globes" means globes in relation to which the provisions of Part II of Schedule 2 to the said Regulations of 1971 are complied with.   **[1288]**

NOTES
  Commencement: 13 August 1981.

34. (1) Light signals such as are prescribed in Regulations 31 to 33, 35, 36, 37(2), 38 and 39 of the Regulations may be placed on or near a road only if the following conditions are satisfied, that is to say—

    (a) the said signals are so placed that they face the stream of traffic to which they are intended to convey respectively the warning, information, requirements, restrictions or prohibitions prescribed by the Regulations;

    (b) the apparatus (including the content of all instructions stored in, or executable by it) used in connection with the said signals is of a type which has been approved in writing by or on behalf of the Secretary of State; and

    (c) if the light signals are light signals prescribed by Regulation 31(4) of the Regulations and are to be erected at or near a level crossing (where a road is crossed by a railway) otherwise than in pursuance of an Order made by the Secretary of State under section 66 of the British Transport Commission Act 1957 (which empowers the Secretary of State to authorise special arrangements at public level crossings) or, Order so made under section 124 of the Transport Act 1968 (British Railways Board's obligations at level crossings with roads other than public carriage roads) [or of an order under section 1 of the Level Crossings Act 1983 (which empowers the Secretary of State to provide for the protection of those using the level crossing)], the site for, and the number and disposition of, those signals shall first have been approved in writing by or on behalf of the Secretary of State after consideration of such plans for the site and such other information as he may require for the purposes of his function in this condition.

    (2) If, after any light signals such as are mentioned in sub-paragraph (1) of this paragraph have been placed on or near a road, the apparatus used in connection with the said signals is altered so as to enable any further instructions to be stored in, or made executable by, the apparatus, the said signals shall not be further used unless that alteration is of a type which has been approved in writing by or on behalf of the Secretary of State.

(3) The light signals prescribed by Regulation 31(2) and (4) of the Regulations or those light signals as varied in accordance with Regulation 32 thereof shall not be used unless used in conjunction with the road marking shown in diagram 1001, except that this sub-paragraph shall not apply while works which necessitate the temporary removal of that road marking are being executed on a road in the vicinity of the place where the said light signals are erected.

(4) The containers enclosing the lamps of each of the kinds of light signals mentioned in sub-paragraph (1) of this paragraph shall be coloured black, except that if those containers enclose lamps of the light signals prescribed by Regulation 31(3), 36, 37(2) or 39 of the Regulations, they may be coloured grey instead of black.

(5) Any of the kinds of light signals mentioned in sub-paragraph (1) of this paragraph other than the signals prescribed by Regulation 35 of the Regulations may be mounted with a backing board and if so mounted, the backing board shall be coloured black and may have a white border not less than 85 nor more than 95 millimetres in width in the case of signals prescribed by Regulation 31(4) of the Regulations and not less than 45 nor more than 55 millimetres in width in the case of the other kinds of light signals which may be so mounted.

(6) Without prejudice to the next following sub-paragraph, where light signals prescribed by any of the Regulations specified in sub-paragraph (1) of this paragraph are mounted on a post specially provided for the purpose, that part of the post which extends above ground level shall be coloured [grey or black] and may have one white band not less than 140 nor more than 160 millimetres in depth, the lower edge of the band being not less than 1.5 nor more than 1.7 metres above the level of the surface of the ground in the immediate vicinity.

(7) In the case of light signals prescribed by Regulation 33 of the Regulations, instead of being mounted on a post coloured in accordance with the provisions of the last preceding sub-paragraph, they may be mounted on either a post coloured yellow (but having no such white band as therein specified) or alternatively on a tripod coloured yellow.   **[1289]**

NOTES
  Commencement: 13 August 1981.
  Para (1): amended by SI 1984 No 966, Part II.
  Para (6): amended by SI 1987 No 1706, dir 3, Schedule.

---

35. Where a sign shown in a diagram in Schedule 1 other than a sign shown in diagram 569, 569.1, 603 to 605.1, 651, or 845 to 852 is mounted on a post specially provided for the purpose, that part of the post which extends above ground level shall be coloured [grey or black] except to the extent provided in sub-paragraphs (a) to (d) below—

(a) in a case where different provision as to the colouring of the post is made in the foregoing provisions of these Directions;

(b) in a case where the post is constructed of concrete, or is supporting a sign placed temporarily on the road in connection with the execution of works or any obstruction thereon and is constructed of timber, then the concrete post shall remain in its natural colour and the timber post supporting such a sign so placed may remain in its natural colour;

(c) in a case where the post is not likely to be readily visible to pedestrians, then one white band of not less than 140 nor more than 160 millimetres in depth may be provided, the lower edge of the band being between 1.5 and 1.7 metres above the level of the surface of the ground in the immediate vicinity; and

(d) the structure, if any, on which the beacons or the lamp respectively prescribed by Regulations 28(1), and 40 of the Regulations are supported shall be coloured either grey or yellow or in alternate bands of red and white or of black and white; and such a structure for supporting the beacons prescribed by Regulation 28(2) of the Regulations shall be coloured black and white in alternate bands.

[1290]

NOTES
Commencement: 13 August 1981.
Amended by SI 1987 No 1706, dir 3, Schedule.

36. (1) The back of any sign shown in a diagram in Schedule 1, other than a sign shown in diagram 569.1, of any backing board or other fitting provided for the assembly of such a sign, including any container enclosing apparatus for the illumination of that sign, shall be coloured—

(a) black, if the sign is mounted on the same post as that on which light signals prescribed by Regulation 31(2) of the Regulations or those signals as varied by Regulation 32 thereof, or prescribed by Regulation 33 of the Regulations are mounted, and

(b) [grey or black] in any other case except that information about sites for placing the sign may be indicated on the back of the sign in characters not exceeding 15 millimetres in height.

(2) The back of a sign of the type shown in diagram 569.1 in Schedule 1 shall be coloured either grey or white.

[(3) The containers enclosing the road danger lamps prescribed by Regulation 40 shall be coloured yellow.]

[(4) The front of any backing board for a sign mounted otherwise than as described in sub-paragraph (a) of paragraph (1) shall be coloured either grey or yellow.] **[1291]**

NOTES
Commencement: 15 October 1987 (para (4)); 10 February 1983 (para (3)); 13 August 1981 (remainder).
Para (1): sub-para (b) amended by SI 1987 No 1706, dir 3, Schedule.
Para (3): added by SI 1982 No 1880, dir 8.
Para (4): added by SI 1987 No 1706, dir 4.

37. The traffic signs shown in diagrams 806, 806.1, 807 and 808.1 may only be placed on or near a road if every road contained within the controlled parking zone indicated by the said signs so shown has been marked with a road marking of a kind shown in one of the diagrams 1016.1 to 1021 appropriate to the nature of the restriction in force except in so far as the parking places for vehicles have been designated and provided on that road.

In this paragraph the expression "controlled parking zone" has the same meaning as in paragraph 28 of these Directions. **[1292]**

NOTES
Commencement: 13 August 1981.

38. The light signals prescribed by Regulations 31(3) and 38 of the Regulations and the light signals shown in any diagram in Parts I and II of Schedule 6 may be displayed only on or near a motorway.　　　　　**[1293]**

NOTES
　　Commencement: 13 August 1981.

39. The light signals prescribed by Regulation 31(3) of the Regulations shall not be displayed over or in relation to a traffic lane (as defined by Regulation 36(1) of the Regulations) at the same time as any sign shown in any of the diagrams 6001 to 6005 is also being displayed over or in relation to that same traffic lane and at the same place on that lane.　　　　　**[1294]**

NOTES
　　Commencement: 13 August 1981.

40. The traffic signs shown in diagrams 6002 and 6004 may be displayed only over a traffic lane as so defined and the signs shown in diagrams 6006, 6007 and 6008 may be displayed only at the side of the carriageway to which the indications given by those signs relate.　　　　　**[1295]**

NOTES
　　Commencement: 13 August 1981.

41. (1) Without prejudice to the provisions of paragraph 34 of these Directions, this paragraph applies to all traffic signs which are not continuously in use over a period of 24 hours and are capable of being brought into and taken out of use for the time being by the operation of any electrical or other apparatus.

(2) The said electrical or other apparatus by which the traffic signs to which this paragraph applies are brought into and taken out of use and any other apparatus (including the content of all instructions stored in, or executable by it) used to secure that the said traffic signs comply with the relevant provisions of the Regulations shall be of a type which has been approved in writing by or on behalf of the Secretary of State before the said traffic signs are placed on or near any road.

(3) If, after any traffic sign to which this paragraph applies has been placed on or near any road, the said electrical or other apparatus by which the sign is brought into and taken out of use, or which is used to secure that the sign complies with the relevant provisions of the Regulations, is altered so as to enable any further instruction to be stored in, or made executable by, the apparatus, the said sign shall not be further used unless that alteration is of a type which has been approved in writing by or on behalf of the Secretary of State.

[(4) When a traffic sign to which this paragraph applies is not in use, it shall display a plain grey or black face.] **[1296]**

NOTES
  Commencement: 15 October 1987 (para (4)); 13 August 1981 (remainder).
  Para (4): added by SI 1987 No 1706, dir 5.

42. At least one road marking of the kind shown in diagram 1014 shall be placed for use in conjunction with a road marking of the kind shown in diagram 1013.1 on the length of carriageway which extends backwards from the commencement of any continuous line marked on the carriageway as a part of the last mentioned road marking so shown, such commencement being viewed in the direction of travel of a vehicle driven so as to have and keep that continuous line on the right hand or offside thereof in accordance with Regulation 23(2)(b) of the Regulations, and if more than one road marking of the kind first above-mentioned is placed on the said length of carriageway then those road markings shall be so spaced apart that one follows on in line in front of the other. **[1297]**

NOTES
  Commencement: 13 August 1981.

43. Nothing in these Directions shall be taken to limit the power of the Secretary of State acting as the appropriate Minister by any special Direction to dispense with, add to or modify any of the requirements of these Directions in their application to any particular case. **[1298]**

NOTES
  Commencement: 13 August 1981.

PART III

GENERAL CITATION AND COMMENCEMENT

Part III

This Instrument may be cited as the Traffic Signs Regulations and General Directions 1981, and shall come into operation on 13th August 1981. **[1299]**

NOTES
  Commencement: 13 August 1981.

MOTORWAYS TRAFFIC (ENGLAND AND WALES) REGULATIONS 1982
(SI 1982 No 1163)

NOTES
  Made: 11 August 1982
  Authority: Road Traffic Regulation Act 1984, s 17(2), (3)

1. Commencement and citation

These Regulations shall come into operation on 15th September 1982 and may be cited as the Motorways Traffic (England and Wales) Regulations 1982.

[1300]

NOTES
Commencement: 15 September 1982.

2. Revocation

. . .

[1301]

NOTES
Commencement: 15 September 1982.
This regulation revokes SI 1959 No 1147 and 1971 No 1087.

3. Interpretation

(1) In these Regulations, the following expressions have the meanings hereby respectively assigned to them:-

[(a) "the 1984 Act" means the Road Traffic Regulation Act 1984;]
(b) ["carriageway" means that part of a motorway which—

(i) is provided for the regular passage of vehicular motor traffic along the motorway; and
(ii) where a hard shoulder is provided, left-hand or near-side edge has the approximate position of its edges marked with a traffic sign of the type shown in diagram 1012.1 in Schedule 2 to the Traffic Signs Regulations and General Directions 1981];

(c) "central reservation" means that part of a motorway which separates the carriageway to be used by vehicles travelling in one direction from the carriageway to be used by vehicles travelling in the opposite direction;

(d) "excluded traffic" means traffic which is not traffic of Classes I or II;
(e) "hard shoulder" means a part of the motorway which is adjacent to and situated on the left hand or near side of the carriageway when facing in the direction in which vehicles may be driven in accordance with Regulation 6, and which is designed to take the weight of a vehicle;
(f) "motorway" means any road or part of a road to which these Regulations apply by virtue of Regulation 4;
(g) "verge" means any part of a motorway which is not a carriageway, a hard shoulder, or a central reservation.

(2) A vehicle shall be treated for the purposes of any provision of these Regulations as being on any part of a motorway specified in that provision if any part of the vehicle (whether it is at rest or not) is on the part of the motorway so specified.

(3) Any provision of these Regulations containing any prohibition or restriction relating to the driving, moving or stopping of a vehicle, or to its remaining at rest, shall be construed as a provision that no person shall use a motorway by driving, moving or stopping the vehicle or by causing or permitting it to be driven or moved, or to stop or remain at rest, in contravention of that prohibition or restriction.

(4) In these Regulations references to numbered classes of traffic are references to the classes of traffic set out in Schedule 4 to the Highways Act 1980.   **[1302]**

NOTES
    Commencement: 15 September 1982.
    Para (1): sub-para (a) substituted by SI 1992 No 1364, reg 6(1); definition "carriageway" substituted by SI 1984 No 1479.

[4.

Subject to section 17(5) of the 1984 Act, these Regulations apply to every special road or part of a special road which can be used only by traffic of Class I or II.]
          [1303]

NOTES
    Commencement: 1 July 1992
    Substituted by SI 1992 No 1364, reg 6(2).
    1984 Act: Road Traffic Regulation Act 1984.

5. Vehicles to be driven on the carriageway only

Subject to the following provisions of these Regulations, no vehicle shall be driven on any part of a motorway which is not a carriageway.   **[1304]**

NOTES
    Commencement: 15 September 1982.

6. Direction of driving

(1) Where there is a traffic sign indicating that there is no entry to a carriageway at a particular place, no vehicle shall be driven or moved onto that carriageway at that place.

(2) Where there is a traffic sign indicating that there is no left or right turn into a carriageway at a particular place, no vehicle shall be so driven or moved as to cause it to turn to the left or (as the case may be) to the right into that carriageway at that place.

(3) Every vehicle on a length of carriageway which is contiguous to a central reservation, shall be driven in such a direction that the central reservation is at all times on the right hand or off side of the vehicle

(4) Where traffic signs are so placed that there is a length of carriageway (being a length which is not contiguous to a central reservation) which can be entered at one end only by vehicles driven in conformity with paragraph (1) of this Regulation, every vehicle on that length of carriageway shall be driven in such a direction only as to cause it to proceed away from the end of that length of carriageway towards the other end thereof.

(5) Without prejudice to the foregoing provisions of this Regulation, no vehicle which—

(a) is on a length of carriageway on which vehicles are required by any of the foregoing provisions of this Regulation to be driven in one direction only and is proceeding in or facing that direction, or
(b) is on any other length of carriageway and is proceeding in or facing one direction,

shall be driven or moved so as to cause it to turn and proceed in or face the opposite direction **[1305]**

NOTES
Commencement: 15 September 1982.

7. Restriction on stopping

(1) Subject to the following provisions of this Regulation, no vehicle shall stop or remain at rest on a carriageway.

(2) Where it is necessary for a vehicle which is being driven on a carriageway to be stopped while it is on a motorway—

(a) by reason of a breakdown or mechanical defect or lack of fuel, oil or water, required for the vehicle; or
(b) by reason of any accident, illness or other emergency; or
(c) to permit any person carried in or on the vehicle to recover or move any object which has fallen onto a motorway; or
(d) to permit any person carried in or on the vehicle to give help which is required by any other person in any of the circumstances specified in the foregoing provisions of this paragraph,

the vehicle shall, as soon and in so far as is reasonably practicable, be driven or moved off the carriageway onto, and may stop and remain at rest on, any hard shoulder which is contiguous to that carriageway.

(3) (a) A vehicle which is at rest on a hard shoulder shall so far as is reasonably practicable be allowed to remain at rest on that hard shoulder in such a position only that no part of it or of the load carried thereby shall obstruct or be a cause of danger to vehicles using the carriageway.

(b) A vehicle shall not remain at rest on a hard shoulder for longer than is necessary in the circumstances or for the purposes specified in paragraph 2 of this Regulation.

(4) Nothing in the foregoing provisions of this Regulation shall preclude a vehicle from stopping or remaining at rest on a carriageway while it is prevented from proceeding along the carriageway by the presence of any other vehicle or any person or object. **[1306]**

NOTES
Commencement: 15 September 1982.

8. Restriction on reversing

No vehicle on a motorway shall be driven or moved backwards except in so far as it is necessary to back the vehicle to enable it to proceed forwards or to be connected to any other vehicle. **[1307]**

NOTES
Commencement: 15 September 1982.

9. Restriction on the use of hard shoulders

No vehicle shall be driven or stop or remain at rest on any hard shoulder except in accordance with paragraphs (2) and (3) of Regulation 7. **[1308]**

NOTES
Commencement: 15 September 1982.

10. Vehicles not to use the central reservation or verge

No vehicle shall be driven or moved or stop or remain at rest on a central reservation or verge. **[1309]**

NOTES
Commencement: 15 September 1982.

11. Vehicles not to be driven by learner drivers

[(1)] No motor vehicle shall be driven on a motorway by a person who is authorised to drive that vehicle only by virtue of his being the holder of a provisional licence under [section 97(2) of the Road Traffic Act 1988], unless, since the date of coming into force of the said provisional licence that person has passed a test prescribed under [section 89 of that Act] sufficient to entitle him under that Act to be granted a licence, other than a provisional licence, authorising him to drive that vehicle on a road.

[(2) Paragraph (1) above does not apply to a large goods vehicle or to a passenger-carrying vehicle.

(3) In this regulation, "large goods vehicle" and "passenger-carrying vehicle" have the meanings given by section 121 of the Road Traffic Act 1988.]

[1310]

NOTES
Commencement: 15 September 1982 (para (1)); 1 July 1992 (paras (2), (3)).
Amended by SI 1992 No 1364, regs 3, 6(3).
1984 Act: Road Traffic Regulation Act 1984.

12. Restriction on use of right hand or off side lane

[(1) This Regulation applies to—

[(a) a goods vehicle having a maximum laden weight exceeding 7·5 tonnes,];
(b) a motor vehicle constructed solely for the carriage of passengers and their effects the overall length of which exceeds 12 metres;
(c) a motor vehicle drawing a trailer, and
[(d) a vehicle which is a motor tractor, a light locomotive or a heavy locomotive.]

(2) Subject to the provisions of paragraph (3) below, no vehicle to which this Regulation applies shall be driven or moved or stop or remain at rest on the right hand or offside lane of a length of carriageway which has three or more traffic lanes at any place where all the lanes are open for use by traffic proceeding in the same direction.

(3) The prohibition contained in paragraph (2) above shall not apply to a vehicle while it is being driven on any right hand or offside lane such as is mentioned in that paragraph in so far as it is necessary for the vehicle to be driven to enable it to pass another vehicle which is carrying or drawing a load of exceptional width.

[(4) Nothing in this regulation shall have effect so as to require a vehicle to change lane during a period when it would not be reasonably practicable for it to do so without involving danger of injury to any person or inconvenience to other traffic.

(5) In this Regulation—

"goods vehicle" and "maximum laden weight" have the same meanings as in Schedule 6 to the 1984 Act, and

"overall length" has the same meaning given by regulation 3(2) of the Road Vehicles (Construction and Use) Regulations 1986.]] **[1311–1312]**

NOTES
Commencement: 16 April 1983 (paras (1)–(3)); 1 July 1992 (paras (4), (5)).
Substituted by SI 1983 No 374, reg 3.
Para (1): sub-paras (a), (d) substituted by SI 1992 No 1364, reg 4(1), (2).
Paras (4), (5): substituted by SI 1992 No 1364, reg 4(1), (3).

13. (*Revoked by SI 1992 No 1364, reg 5.*)

14. Restrictions affecting animals carried in vehicles

The person in charge of any animal which is carried by a vehicle using a motorway shall, so far as is practicable, secure that—

    (a) the animal shall not be removed from or permitted to leave the vehicle while the vehicle is on a motorway, and

    (b) if it escapes from, or it is necessary for it to be removed from, or permitted to leave, the vehicle—

        (i) it shall not go or remain on any part of the motorway other than a hard shoulder, and

        (ii) it shall whilst it is not on or in the vehicle be held on a lead or otherwise kept under proper control. **[1313]**

NOTES

Commencement: 15 September 1982.

15. Use of motorway by excluded traffic

(1) Excluded traffic is hereby authorised to use a motorway on the occasions or in the emergencies and to the extent specified in the following provisions of this paragraph, that is to say—

    (a) traffic of Classes III or IV may use a motorway for the maintenance, repair, cleaning or clearance of any part of a motorway or for the erection, laying, placing, maintenance, testing, alteration, repair or removal of any structure, works or apparatus in, on, under or over any part of a motorway;

    (b) pedestrians may use a motorway—

        (i) when it is necessary for them to do so as a result of an accident or emergency or of a vehicle being at rest on a motorway in any of the circumstances specified in paragraph (2) of Regulation 7, or

        (ii) in any of the circumstances specified in sub-paragraphs (b), (d), (e) or (f) of paragraph (1) of Regulation 16.

(2) The Secretary of State may authorise the use of a motorway by any excluded traffic on occasion or in emergency or for the purpose of enabling such traffic to cross a motorway or to secure access to premises abutting on or adjacent to a motorway.

(3) Where by reason of any emergency the use of any road (not being a motorway) by any excluded traffic is rendered impossible or unsuitable the Chief Officer of Police of the police area in which a motorway or any part of a motorway is situated, or any officer of or above the rank of superintendent authorised in that behalf by that Chief Officer, may—

    (a) authorise any excluded traffic to use that motorway or that part of a motorway as an alternative road for the period during which the use of the other road by such traffic continues to be impossible or unsuitable, and

    (b) relax any prohibition or restriction imposed by these Regulations in so far as he considers it necessary to do so in connection with the use of that motorway or that part of a motorway by excluded traffic in pursuance of any such authorisation as aforesaid. **[1314]**

NOTES

Commencement: 15 September 1982.

16. Exceptions and relaxations

(1) Nothing in the foregoing provisions of these Regulations shall preclude any person from using a motorway otherwise than in accordance with the provisions in any of the following circumstances, that is to say—

(a) where he does so in accordance with any direction or permission given by a constable in uniform or with the indication given by a traffic sign;

(b) where, in accordance with any permission given by a constable, he does so for the purpose of investigating any accident which has occurred on or near a motorway;

(c) where it is necessary for him to do so to avoid or prevent an accident or to obtain or give help required as the result of an accidnet or emergency, and he does so in such manner as to cause as little danger or inconvenience as possible to other traffic on a motorway;

(d) where he does so in the exercise of his duty as a constable or as a member of a fire brigade or of an ambulance service;

(e) where it is necessary for him to do so to carry out in an efficient manner—

   (i) the maintenance, repair, cleaning, clearance, alteration or improvement of any part of a motorway, or

   (ii) the removal of any vehicle from any part of a motorway, or

   (iii) the erection, laying, placing, maintenance, testing, alteration, repair or removal of any structure, works or apparatus in, on, under or over any part of a motorway; or

(f) where it is necessary for him to do so in connection with any inspection, survey, investigation or census which is carried out in accordance with any general or special authority granted by the Secretary of State.

(2) Without prejudice to the foregoing provisions of these Regulations, the Secretary of State may relax any prohibition or restriction imposed by these Regulations.   **[1315]**

NOTES
Commencement: 15 September 1982.

MOTOR VEHICLES (WEARING OF SEAT BELTS) REGULATIONS 1982
(SI 1982 NO 1203)

NOTES
Made: 23 August 1982
Authority: Road Traffic Act 1988, s 14

ARRANGEMENT OF REGULATIONS

Preamble

Whereas—

(1) the Secretary of State for Transport has, in accordance with section 199(2) of the Road Traffic Act 1972, consulted with representative organisations;

(2) the Secretary of State for Transport has, in accordance with the provisions of section 199(2A) of the Road Traffic Act 1972, laid before each House of Parliament a statement explaining proposals to which these Regulations relate; and

(3) the period of three months has expired since the day on which such statement was so laid:

NOTES

Commencement: 31 January 1983.

1. These Regulations shall come into operation on the twenty-third Monday after these Regulations are made.   **[1316]**

NOTES

Commencement: 31 January 1983.

2. These Regulations may be cited as the Motor Vehicles (Wearing of Seat Belts) Regulations 1982.   **[1317]**

NOTES

Commencement: 31 January 1983.

3. (1) In these Regulations—

"the Construction and Use Regulations" means the Motor Vehicles (Construction and Use) Regulations 1978;

"the Driving Licences Regulations" means the Motor Vehicles (Driving Licences) Regulations 1982;

"disabled person's seat belt" has the same meaning as in Regulation 17(12) of the Construction and Use Regulations;

"disabled person's vehicle" means a vehicle which has been specially designed and constructed, or specially adapted, for the use of a person suffering from some physical defect or disability;

"private hire vehicle" means a motor vehicle constructed or adapted to seat fewer than 9 passengers, other than a taxi or a public service vehicle, which is provided for hire with the services of a driver for the purpose of carrying passengers and which displays a sign pursuant to either section 21 of the Vehicles (Excise) Act 1971 or section 48(2) of the Local Government (Miscellaneous Provisions) Act 1976 or any similar enactment;

"public service vehicle" has the same meaning as in section 1 of the Public Passenger Vehicles Act 1981;

"specified passenger's seat" has the same meaning as in Regulation 17(12) of the Construction and Use Regulations;

"taxi" has the same meaning as in section 64(3) of the Transport Act 1980;

"trade licence" has the same meaning as in section 38(1) of the Vehicles (Excise) Act 1971.

(2) In these Regulations a reference to any Act or subordinate legislation (as defined in section 21(1) of the Interpretation Act 1978) includes a reference to that Act or subordinate legislation as from time to time extended, amended, re-enacted or applied.

(3) In these Regulations, unless the context otherwise requires, any references to a numbered Regulation is a reference to the Regulation bearing that number in these Regulations. **[1318]**

NOTES
Commencement: 31 January 1983.

4. Save as provided in Regulation 5, every person shall wear a seat belt of a description specified in Regulation 7 if he is—

(1) driving a motor vehicle of a class specified in Regulation 6; or

(2) riding in a motor vehicle of that class in—
  (a) the specified passenger's seat, or
  (b) a forward facing seat alongside the driver's seat which is not the specified passenger's seat and the specified passenger's seat is not occupied by another person (whether or not that person is over the age of 14 years). **[1319]**

NOTES
Commencement: 31 January 1983.

5. The requirement specified in Regulation 4 does not apply to a person who is—

  (a) using a vehicle constructed or adapted for the delivery or collection of goods or mail to consumers or addressees, as the case may be, whilst engaged in making local rounds of deliveries or collections;
  (b) driving the vehicle whilst performing a manoeuvre which includes reversing;
  (c) a qualified driver (as defined in Regulation 8(5) of the Driving Licences Regulations) and is supervising the holder of a provisional Licence (as defined in Regulation 3(1) of those Regulations) while that holder is performing a manoeuvre which includes reversing;
  (d) the holder of a valid certificate in a form supplied by the Secretary of State, containing the information required by it, and signed by a registered medical practitioner to the effect that it is inadvisable on medical grounds for him to wear a seat belt;
  (e) a constable protecting or escorting another person;
  (f) not a constable but is protecting or escorting another person by virtue of powers the same as or similar to those of a constable for that purpose;
  (g) in the service of a fire brigade and is donning operational clothing or equipment;
  (h) the driver of—
    (i) a taxi which is being used for seeking hire, or answering a call for hire, or carrying a passenger for hire, or
    (ii) a private hire vehicle which is being used to carry a passenger for hire;

    (i) a person by whom, as provided in the Driving Licences Regulations, a test of competence to drive is being conducted and his wearing a seat belt would endanger himself or any other person;

    (j) occupying a seat for which the seat belt either—

        (i) does not comply with the requirements of Regulation 102A of the Construction and Use Regulations, or

        (ii) has an inertia reel mechanism which is locked as a result of the vehicle being, or having been, on a steep incline; or

    (k) riding in a vehicle, being used under a trade licence, for the purpose of investigating or remedying a mechanical fault in the vehicle.**[1320]**

NOTES
Commencement: 31 January 1983.

6. The classes of vehicle mentioned in Regulation 4 are—

    (a) a vehicle to which Regulation 17 of the Construction and Use Regulations applies; and

    (b) a vehicle which is equipped with anchorage points and seat belts and to which that Regulation would apply if it were not for the circumstances that the vehicle—

        (i) is proceeding to a port for export;

        (ii) has been brought temporarily into Great Britain by a person resident abroad;

      (iii) is within the provisions of Regulation 4(8) of the Contruction and Use Regulations (which relates to vehicles subject to certain tax exemptions by virtue of their impending export);

      (iv) is in the service of a visiting force or headquarters (as defined in Article 8(6) of the Visiting Forces and International Headquarters (Application of Law) Order 1965;

       (v) is within the provisions of Regulation 4(10) of the Construction and Use Regulations (which relates to vehicles subject to certain exemptions relating to tests of satisfactory conditions);

      (vi) is being used under a trade licence; or

    (vii) is not a vehicle to which the Motor Vehicles (Type Approval) (Great Britain) Regulations 1979 applies but which is being driven from premises of the manufacturer by whom it was made, or of a distributor of vehicles or dealer in vehicles

            —to premises of a distributor of or dealer in vehicles of the purchaser of the vehicle, or

            —to premises of a person obtaining possession of the vehicle under a hiring agreement or hire-purchase agreement.

[1321]

NOTES
Commencement: 31 January 1983.

7. The descriptions of seat belt referred to in Regulation 4 are—

    (a) as regards a driver's seat or a specified passenger's seat in respect of which a seat belt is required to be fitted by Regulation 17 of the Construction and Use Regulations—

        (i) in the case of a disabled person's vehicle, a disabled person's seat belt;

(ii) in the case of any other vehicle to which that Regulation applies, a seat belt which complies with the requirements specified in paragraphs (5), (7), (8) and (10) of that Regulation;

(b) as regards a driver's seat or a specified passenger's seat in respect of which a seat belt is not required to be fitted by that Regulation, the seat belt fitted to the vehicle in respect of that seat;

(c) as regards a seat mentioned in Regulation 4(2)(b), the seat belt fitted to the vehicle in respect of that seat.   **[1322]**

NOTES
Commencement: 31 January 1983.

PEDAL CYCLES (CONSTRUCTION AND USE) REGULATIONS 1983
(SI 1983 NO 1176)

NOTES
Made: 1 August 1983
Authority: Road Traffic Act 1988, s 81.

ARRANGEMENT OF REGULATIONS

REQUIREMENTS AS TO SALE OR SUPPLY ETC OF PEDAL CYCLES

12   [1334]

COMMENCEMENT AND CITATION

1. These Regulations shall come into operation on 1st September 1983, and may be cited as the Pedal Cycles (Construction and Use) Regulations 1983.

[1323]

NOTES

Commencement: 1 September 1983.

REVOCATION

2. ...   **[1324]**

NOTES

Commencement: 1 September 1983.

This regulation revokes SI 1954 No 966.

INTERPRETATION

3. (1) In these Regulations:—

  (a) a reference to the manufacturer of a vehicle means, in the case of a vehicle which has been altered so as to become an electrically assisted pedal cycle, the person who made that alteration;

  (b) "pedal cycle" means a pedal cycle which is either—

    (i) not propelled by mechanical power, or

    (ii) an electrically assisted pedal cycle prescribed for the purposes of section 103 of the Road Traffic Regulation Act 1967 and section 193 of the Road Traffic Act 1972 by virtue of the Electrically Assisted Pedal Cycles Regulations 1983;

  (c) "the 1971 British Standard" has the same meaning as in the Electrically Assisted Pedal Cycles Regulations 1983; and

  (d) "the 1981 British Standard" means the Specification for safety requirements for bicycles published by the British Standards Institution under the reference BS 6102: Part I: 1981.

  (2) In these Regulations, unless the context otherwise requires, a reference to a numbered Regulation is to the Regulation bearing that number in these Regulations, and a reference to a numbered paragraph is to the paragraph bearing that number in the Regulation in which the reference occurs. **[1325]**

NOTES

Commencement: 1 September 1983.

REQUIREMENTS AS TO A PEDAL CYCLE TO WHICH THE ELECTRICALLY ASSISTED
PEDAL CYCLES REGULATIONS 1983 APPLY

4. No person shall ride, or cause or permit to be ridden, on a road a pedal cycle
to which the Electrically Assisted Pedal Cycles Regulations 1983 apply unless it
is fitted with—

 (a) a place securely fixed in a conspicuous and readily accessible position
 showing—

  (i) the name of the manufacturer of the vehicle,
  (ii) the nominal voltage of the battery (as defined in the 1971 British
  Standard) of the vehicle, and
  (iii) the continuous rated output (as defined in the 1971 British
  Standard) of the motor of the vehicle;

 (b) braking systems which are so designed and constructed that—

  (i) in the case of a bicycle they comply with the standards specified
  in clause 6 of the 1981 British Standard, and
  (ii) in the case of a tricycle they comply with standards no less than
  the standards of braking systems fitted to a bicycle which comply
  with clause 6 of the 1981 British Standard;

 (c) a battery which does not leak so as to be a source of danger; and
 (d) a device biased to the off position which allows power to come from
 the motor only when the device is operated so as to achieve that
 result. **[1326]**

NOTES
Commencement: 1 September 1983.

5. No person shall ride, or cause or permit to be ridden, on a road a pedal cycle
to which the Electrically Assisted Pedal Cycles Regulations 1983 apply unless
the parts of the vehicle mentioned in—

 (a) Regulation 4(b) and (c) of those Regulations, and
 (b) Regulation 4(b), (c) and (d) of these Regulations,

are in efficient working order. **[1327]**

NOTES
Commencement: 1 September 1983.

REQUIREMENTS AS TO A PEDAL CYCLE TO WHICH THE ELECTRICALLY ASSISTED
PEDAL CYCLES REGULATIONS 1983 DO NOT APPLY

6. No person shall ride, or cause or permit to be ridden, on a road a pedal cycle
to which the Electrically Assisted Pedal Cycles Regulations 1983 do not apply
unless it complies with such of the requirements specified in Regulation 7 or 8
as apply to it. **[1328]**

NOTES
Commencement: 1 September 1983.

7. (1) Save as provided in Regulations 8 and 9—

 (a) every pedal cycle shall be equipped with at least one braking system;
 (b) every bicycle or tricycle the height of the saddle of which is 635
 millimetres or more and every cycle with four or more wheels shall—

(i) if it is so constructed that one or more of the wheels is incapable of rotating independently of the pedals, be equipped with a braking system operating on the front wheel or, if it has more than one front wheel, on at least two front wheels;

(ii) if it is not so constructed that one or more of the wheels is incapable of rotating independently of the pedals, be equipped with two independent braking systems one of which operates on the front wheel, or if it has more than one front wheel, on at least two front wheels, and the other of which operates on the rear wheel, or if it has more than one rear wheel, on at least two rear wheels.

(2) The reference in paragraph (1)(b) to the height of the saddle is a reference to the height above the ground of the part of the seating area of the saddle which is furthest from the ground when the cycle to which the saddle is attached is vertical and the saddle is raised to the fullest extent compatible with safety and the tyres on the wheels of the cycle are fully inflated. **[1329]**

NOTES
Commencement: 1 September 1983.

8. (1) The requirements of Regulation 7 do not apply to a pedal cycle manufactured before 1st August 1984 if, save as provided in Regulation 9 in the case where the cycle has any wheel of which the outside diameter (including any tyre when fully inflated) exceeds 460 millimetres—

(i) the cycle is so constructed that one or more of the wheels is incapable of rotating independently of the pedals, it is equipped with a braking system operating on the front wheel or both the front wheels if it has two front wheels;

(ii) the cycle is not so constructed, it is equipped with two independent braking systems one of which operates on the front wheel or both the front wheels if it has two front wheels, and the other of which operates on the rear wheel or one of the rear wheels if it has two rear wheels. **[1330]**

NOTES
Commencement: 1 September 1983.

9. (1) Nothing in Regulation 7 or 8 applies to—

(a) any pedal cycle so constructed that the pedals act on any wheel or on the axle of any wheel without the interposition of any gearing or chain; or

(b) any pedal cycle brought temporarily into Great Britain by a person resident abroad and intending to make only a temporary stay in Great Britain, while the cycle is being ridden by that person, provided that its brakes comply with the requirements of Article 26 of the International Convention on Road Traffic signed at Geneva on 19th September 1949 as amended.

(2) In the case of a tricycle not constructed or adapted for the carriage of goods it shall be a sufficient compliance with the requirements specified in Regulation 7(1)(b)(ii) and 8(1)(a)(ii) if the tricycle is equipped with two independent braking systems operating on the front wheel if it has two rear wheels, or on the rear wheel if it has two front wheels. **[1331]**

NOTES
Commencement: 1 September 1983.

10. (1) No person shall ride, or cause or permit to be ridden, on a road a pedal cycle to which Regulation 6 applies unless the braking system or systems with which it is required to be fitted in accordance with Regulation 7 or, as the case may be, Regulation 8 are in efficient working order.

(2) For the purpose of this Regulation, except in the case of a cycle having four or more wheels, none of which has a diameter exceeding 250 millimetres (including any tyre when fully inflated), a braking system shall be deemed not to be in efficient working order if any brake operates directly on a pneumatic tyre on any wheel. **[1332]**

NOTES
Commencement: 1 September 1983.

TESTING AND INSPECTION

11. Any constable in uniform is hereby empowered to test and inspect a pedal cycle for the purpose of ascertaining whether any of the requirements specified in Regulation 4(b), or Regulation 7 or, as the case may be, Regulation 8, are satisfied provided he does so either—

   (a) on any premises where the cycle is if the cycle has been involved in an accident, and the test and inspection are carried out within 48 hours of the accident and the owner of the premises consents; or
   (b) on a road. **[1333]**

NOTES
Commencement: 1 September 1983.

REQUIREMENTS AS TO SALE OR SUPPLY ETC OF PEDAL CYCLES

12. No person shall sell or supply, or offer to sell or supply for delivery—

   (a) a pedal cycle to which the Electrically Assisted Pedal Cycles Regulations 1983 apply unless it is equipped with braking systems as specified in Regulation 4(b); or
   (b) on and after 1st August 1984, a pedal cycle to which those Regulations do not apply unless it is

      (i) equipped with braking systems as specified in Regulation 7 or, as the case may be, Regulation 8; or
      (ii) a pedal cycle which has no braking system and is specifically designed for off-road racing on enclosed tracks. **[1334]**

NOTES
Commencement: 1 September 1983.

MOTOR CYCLES (EYE PROTECTORS) REGULATIONS 1985
(SI 1985 NO 1593)

NOTES
Made: 18 October 1985
Authority: Road Traffic Act 1988, s 18

ARRANGEMENT OF REGULATIONS

1. These Regulations may be cited as the Motor Cycles (Eye Protectors) Regulations 1985 and shall come into operation on 1st July 1987.　　**[1335]**

NOTES
　Commencement: 1 July 1987.

2. In these Regulations:—

　　"motor bicycle" means a two wheeled motor cycle, whether having a side-car attached thereto or not, and for the purposes of this definition any wheels of a motor cycle shall, if the distance between the centres of the areas of contact between such wheels and the road surface is less than 460 millimetres, be counted as one wheel;

　　"eye protector" means an appliance designed or adapted for use with any headgear or by being attached to or placed upon the head by a person driving or riding on a motor bicycle and intended for the protection of the eyes.　　**[1336]**

NOTES
　Commencement: 1 July 1987.

3. [The types of eye protector hereby prescribed as authorised for use by persons driving or riding (otherwise than in a side-car) on a motor bicycle are—

　　(a) those which conform to either—

　　　　(i) the requirements relating to Grade X in British Standard BS 4110: 1979, or

　　　　(ii) the requirements relating to Grades XA, YA or ZA in British Standard BS 4110: 1979 as amended by Amendment No. 1 (AMD 3368), Amendment No. 2 (AMD 4060) and Amendment No. 3 (AMD 4630),

　　and in either case are marked with the number of the said British Standard, the Grade and the certification mark of the British Standards Institution (whether or not they are required to be so marked by the said British Standard); and

　　(b) until 1st April 1989, those which fulfil both of the following requirements, that is to say—

　　　　(i) they are fitted with lenses that are designed to correct a defect in sight and that do not fly into fragments if fractured, and

　　　　(ii) they transmit 50 per cent or more of the light with those lenses fitted; and

　　(c) on or after 1st April 1989, those which were first used before that date and fulfill the two requirements mentioned in sub-paragraph (b) above.]　　**[1337]**

NOTES
　Commencement: 11 July 1988.
　Substituted by SI 1988 No 1031, reg 2.

4. Nothing in Regulation 3 above shall apply to any person driving or riding on a motor bicycle if:

> (a) it is a mowing machine;
> (b) it is for the time being propelled by a person on foot; ...
> (c) it is a vehicle brought temporarily into Great Britain by a person resident outside the United Kingdom which has not remained in the United Kingdom for a period of more than one year from the date it was last brought into the United Kingdom [or
> (d) he is in the armed forces of the Crown, on duty and wearing an eye protector supplied to him as part of his service equipment.]   **[1338]**

NOTES
  Commencement: 1 July 1987.
  Word omitted revoked and words in square brackets added by SI 1987 No 675, reg 3.

ROAD VEHICLES (CONSTRUCTION AND USE) REGULATIONS 1986
(SI 1986 No 1078)

NOTES
  Made: 25 June 1986
  Authority: Road Traffic Act 1988, s 41

ARRANGEMENT OF REGULATIONS

PART I
PRELIMINARY

PART II

REGULATIONS GOVERNING THE CONSTRUCTION, EQUIPMENT AND MAINTENANCE OF VEHICLES

A - Dimensions and Manoeuvrability

PART I

PRELIMINARY

1. Commencement and citation

These Regulations shall come into operation on 11th August 1986, and may be cited as the Road Vehicles (Construction and Use) Regulations 1986. **[1339]**

NOTES
  Commencement: 11 August 1986.
  This regulation derived from SI 1955 No 990, reg 1 and SI 1978 No 1017, reg 1.

2. Revocation

The Regulations specified in Schedule 1 are hereby revoked. **[1340]**

NOTES
  Commencement: 11 August 1986.
  This regulation derived from SI 1955 No 990, reg 2, and SI 1978 No 1017, reg 2.

3. Interpretation

(1) In these Regulations, unless the context otherwise requires—

    (a) any reference to a numbered regulation or a numbered Schedule is a reference to the regulation or Schedule bearing that number in these Regulations,

    (b) any reference to a numbered or lettered paragraph or sub-paragraph is a reference to the paragraph or sub-paragraph bearing that number or letter in the regulation or Schedule or (in the case of a sub-paragraph) paragraph in which the reference occurs, and

    (c) any reference to a Table, or to a numbered Table, is a reference to the Table, or to the Table bearing that number, in the regulation or Schedule in which that reference occurs.

(2) In these Regulations, unless the context otherwise requires, the expressions specified in column 1 of the Table have the meaning, or are to be interpreted in accordance with the provisions, specified for them in column 2 of the Table.

1	2
Expression	Meaning
The 1971 Act	The Vehicles (Excise) Act 1971.
The 1972 Act	The Road Traffic Act 1972
The 1981 Act	The Public Passenger Vehicles Act 1981.

1	2
Expression	Meaning
The 1984 Act	The Road Traffic Regulation Act 1984.
The Approval Marks Regulations	The Motor Vehicles (Designation of Approval Marks) Regulations 1979.
The Lighting Regulations	The Road Vehicles Lighting Regulations 1984.
The Plating and Testing Regulations	The Goods Vehicles (Plating and Testing) Regulations 1982.
The Type Approval Regulations	The Motor Vehicles (Type Approval) Regulations 1980.
The Type Approval (Great Britain) Regulations	The Motor Vehicles (Type Approval) (Great Britain) Regulations 1984.
The Type Approval for Goods Vehicles Regulations	The Motor Vehicles (Type Approval for Goods Vehicles) (Great Britain) Regulations 1982.
The Type Approval for Agricultural Vehicles Regulations	The Agricultural or Forestry Tractors and Tractor Components (Type Approval) Regulations 1979.
The Act of Accession	the Treaty concerning the Accession of the Kingdom of Denmark, Ireland, the Kingdom of Norway and the United Kingdom of Great Britain and Northern Ireland to the European Economic Community and the European Atomic Energy Community.
agricultural motor vehicle	a motor vehicle which is constructed or adapted for use off roads for the purpose of agriculture, horticulture or forestry and which is primarily used for one or more of those purposes, not being a dual-purpose vehicle.
agricultural trailer	a trailer which is constructed or adapted for the purpose of agriculture, horticulture or forestry and which is only used for one or more of those purposes, not being an agricultural trailed appliance.
agricultural trailed appliance	a trailer— (a) which is an implement constructed or adapted— (i) for use off roads for the purpose of agriculture, horticulture or forestry and which is only used for one or more of those purposes, and (ii) so that, save in the case of an appliance manufactured before 1st December 1985, or a towed roller, its maximum gross weight is not more than twice its unladen weight; but (b) which is not— (i) a vehicle which is used primarily as living accommodation by one or more persons, and which carries no goods or burden

1	2
Expression	Meaning
	except those needed by such one or more persons for the purpose of their residence in the vehicle; or
	(ii) an agricultural, horticultural or forestry implement rigidly but not permanently mounted on any vehicle whether or not supported by one or more of its own wheels; so however that such an implement is an agricultural trailed appliance if —part of the weight of the implement is supported by one or more of its own wheels, and —the longitudinal axis of the greater part of the implement is capable of articulating in the horizontal plane in relation to the longitudinal axis of the rear portion of the vehicle on which it is mounted.
agricultural trailed appliance conveyor	an agricultural trailer which— (a) has an unladen weight which does not exceed 510 kg; (b) is clearly and indelibly marked with its unladen weight; (c) has a pneumatic tyre fitted to each one of its wheels; (d) is designed and constructed for the purpose of conveying one agricultural trailed appliance or one agricultural, horticultural or forestry implement
articulated bus	a bus so constructed that— (a) it can be divided into two parts, both of which are vehicles and one of which is a motor vehicle, but cannot be so divided without the use of facilities normally available only at a workshop; and (b) passengers carried by it can at all times pass from either part to the other.
articulated vehicle	a heavy motor car or motor car, not being an articulated bus, with a trailer so attached that part of the trailer is superimposed on the drawing vehicle and, when the trailer is uniformly loaded, not less than 20% of the weight of its load is borne by the drawing vehicle.
axle	any reference to the number of axles of a vehicle is to be interpreted in accordance with paragraph (8)
axle weight	in relation to each axle of a vehicle, the sum of the weights transmitted to the road surface by all the wheels of that axle, having regard to the provisions of paragraph (8).
braking efficiency	the maximum braking force capable of being developed by the brakes of a vehicle, expressed as a percentage of the weight of the vehicle including any persons or load carried in the vehicle.

1	2
Expression	Meaning
braking system	is to be interpreted in accordance with paragraph (6)
bus	a motor vehicle which is constructed or adapted to carry more than eight seated passengers in addition to the driver.
[car transporter	a trailer which is constructed and normally used for the purpose of carrying at least two other wheeled vehicles.]
cc	cubic centimetre(s).
close-coupled	in relation to wheels on the same side of a trailer, fitted so that at all times while the trailer is in motion they remain parallel to the longitudinal axis of the trailer, and that the distance between the centres of their respective areas of contact with the road surface does not exceed 1 m.
. . . . .	. . . . .
cm	centimetre(s)
cm^2	square centimetre(s).
[coach	a large bus with a maximum gross weight of more than 7·5 tonnes and with a maximum speed exceeding 60 m.p.h.]
Community Directive, followed by a number	the Directive adopted by the Council or the Commission of the European Communities of which identifying particulars are given in the item in column 3 of Table I in Schedule 2 in which that number appears in column 2; where such a Directive amends a previous Directive mentioned in column 3(d) of the Table [the reference to the amending Directive includes a reference to] that previous Directive as so amended. Any reference to a Directive which has been amended by the Act of Accession is a reference to the Directive as so amended
the Community Recording Equipment Regulation	[Council Regulation (EEC) 3821/85 of 20th December 1985 on recording equipment in road transport, as read with the Community Drivers' Hours and Recording Equipment (Exemptions and Supplementary Provisions) Regulations 1986.]
composite trailer	a combination of a converter dolly and a semi-trailer.
container	an article of equipment, not being a motor vehicle or trailer, having a volume of at least 8 cubic metres, constructed wholly or mostly of metal and intended for repeated use for the carriage of goods or burden.
converter dolly	[(a) a trailer which is—
	(i) equipped with 2 or more wheels,
	(ii) designed to be used in combination with a semi-trailer without any part of the weight of the semi-trailer being borne by the drawing vehicle, and
	(iii) not itself a part either of the semi-trailer or the drawing vehicle when being so used; or

1	2
Expression	Meaning

	(b) a trailer which is—
	    (i) equipped with 2 or more wheels;
	    (ii) designed to be used in combination with a semi-trailer with part of the weight of the semi-trailer being borne by the drawing vehicle;
	    (iii) not itself a part either of the semi-trailer or the drawing vehicle when being so used; and
	    (iv) used solely for the purposes of agriculture, horticulture or forestry, or for any two or for all of those purposes.]

Council Regulation (EEC), followed by a number	the Regulation adopted by the Council of the European Communities.
deck	a floor or platform on which seats are provided for the accommodation of passengers.
design weight	in relation to the gross weight, each axle weight or the train weight of a motor vehicle or trailer, the weight at or below which in the opinion of the Secretary of State or of a person authorised in that behalf by the Secretary of State the vehicle could safely be driven on roads.
double-decked vehicle	a vehicle having two decks one of which is wholly or partly above the other and each of which is provided with a gangway serving seats on that deck only.

dual-purpose vehicle	a vehicle constructed or adapted for the carriage both of passengers and of goods or burden of any description, being a vehicle of which the unladen weight does not exceed 2040 kg, and which either—
	    (i) is so constructed or adapted that the driving power of the engine is, or by the appropriate use of the controls of the vehicle can be, transmitted to all the wheels of the vehicle; or
	    (ii) satisfies the following conditions as to construction, namely—
	        (a) the vehicle must be permanently fitted with a rigid roof, with or without a sliding panel;
	        (b) the area of the vehicle to the rear of the driver's seat must—
	            (i) be permanently fitted with at least one row of transverse seats (fixed or folding) for two or more passengers and those seats must be properly sprung or cushioned and provided with upholstered back-rests, attached either to the seats or to a side or the floor of the vehicle; and

1	2
Expression	Meaning
	(ii) be lit on each side and at the rear by a window or windows of glass or other transparent material having an area or aggregate area of not less than 1850 square centimetres on each side and not less than 770 square centimetres at the rear; and
	(c) the distance between the rearmost part of the steering wheel and the back-rests of the row of transverse seats satisfying the requirements specified in head (i) of sub-paragraph (b) (or, if there is more than one such row of seats, the distance between the rearmost part of the steering wheel and the back-rests of the rearmost such row) must, when the seats are ready for use, be not less than one-third of the distance between the rearmost part of the steering wheel and the rearmost part of the floor of the vehicle.
ECE Regulation followed by a number	the Regulation, annexed to the Agreement concerning the adoption of uniform conditions of approval for Motor Vehicles Equipment and Parts and reciprocal recognition thereof concluded at Geneva on 20th March 1958 as amended to which the United Kingdom is a party, of which identifying particulars are given in the item in column (3)(a), (b) and (c) of Table II in Schedule 2 in which that number appears in column (2); and where that number contains more than two digits, it refers to that Regulation with the amendments in force at the date specified in column (3)(*d*) in that item.
engine power in kilowatts (kW)	the maximum net power ascertained in accordance with Community Directive 80/1269.
[engineering equipment	engineering plant and any other plant or equipment designed and constructed for the purpose of engineering operations.]
engineering plant	(a) movable plant or equipment being a motor vehicle or trailer specially designed and constructed for the special purposes of engineering operations, and which cannot, owing to the requirements of those purposes, comply with all the requirements of these Regulations and which is not constructed primarily to carry a load other than a load being either excavated materials raised from the ground by apparatus on the motor vehicle or trailer or materials which the vehicle or trailer is specially designed to treat while carried thereon; or
	(b) a mobile crane which does not comply in all respects with the requirements of these Regulations.

1	2
Expression	Meaning
exhaust system	a complete set of components through which the exhaust gases escape from the engine unit of a motor vehicle including those which are necessary to limit the noise caused by the escape of those gases.
first used	is to be interpreted in accordance with paragraph (3).
gangway	the space provided for obtaining access from any entrance to the passengers' seats or from any such seat to an exit other than an emergency exit, but excluding a staircase and any space in front of a seat which is required only for the use of passengers occupying that seat or a seat in the same row of seats.
gas	any fuel which is wholly gaseous at 17·5°C under a pressure of 1·013 bar absolute.
gas-fired appliance	a device carried on a motor vehicle or trailer when in use on a road, which consumes gas and which is neither— (a) a device owned or operated by or with the authority of the British Gas Corporation for the purpose of detecting gas, nor (b) an engine for the propulsion of a motor vehicle, nor (c) a lamp which consumes acetylene gas.
goods vehicle	a motor vehicle or trailer constructed or adapted for use for the carriage or haulage of goods or burden of any description.
gritting trailer	a trailer which is used on a road for the purpose of spreading grit or other matter so as to avoid or reduce the effect of ice or snow on the road.
gross weight	(a) in relation to a motor vehicle, the sum of the weights transmitted to the road surface by all the wheels of the vehicle. (b) in relation to a trailer, the sum of the weights transmitted to the road surface by all the wheels of the trailer and of any weight of the trailer imposed on the drawing vehicle.
heavy motor car	a mechanically propelled vehicle, not being a locomotive, a motor tractor, or a motor car, which is constructed itself to carry a load or passengers and the weight of which unladen exceeds 2540 kg.
indivisible load	a load which cannot without undue expense or risk of damage be divided into two or more loads for the purpose of conveyance on a road.
industrial tractor	a tractor, not being an agricultural motor vehicle, which— (a) has an unladen weight not exceeding 7370 kg, (b) is designed and used primarily for work off roads, or for work on roads in connection only with road construction or maintenance (in-

1	2
Expression	Meaning
	cluding any such tractor when fitted with an implement or implements designed primarily for use in connection with such work, whether or not any such implement is of itself designed to carry a load), and
	(c) has a maximum speed not exceeding 20 mph.
invalid carriage	a mechanically propelled vehicle the weight of which unladen does not exceed 254 kg and which is specially designed and constructed, and not merely adapted, for the use of a person suffering from some physical defect or disability and is solely used by such a person.
kerbside weight	the weight of a vehicle when it carries—
	(a) in the case of a motor vehicle,
	(i) no person; and
	(ii) a full supply of fuel in its tank, an adequate supply of other liquids incidental to its propulsion and no load other than the loose tools and equipment with which it is normally equipped;
	(b) in the case of a trailer, no person and is otherwise unladen.
kg	kilogram(s).
km/h	kilometre(s) per hour.
kW	kilowatt(s)
[large bus	a vehicle constructed or adapted to carry more than 16 seated passengers in addition to the driver.]
[light trailer	a trailer with a maximum gross weight which does not exceed 3500 kg.]
living van	a vehicle used primarily as living accommodation by one or more persons, and which is not also used for the carriage of goods or burden which are not needed by such one or more persons for the purpose of their residence in the vehicle.
locomotive	a mechanically propelled vehicle which is not constructed itself to carry a load other than the following articles, that is to say, water, fuel, accumulators and other equipment used for the purpose of propulsion, loose tools and loose equipment, and the weight of which unladen exceeds 7370 kg.
longitudinal plane	a vertical plane parallel to the longitudinal axis of a vehicle.
[low platform trailer	a trailer fitted with tyres with a rim diameter size code of less than 20 and displaying a rectangular plate which—
	(a) is at least 225 mm wide and at least 175 mm high; and
	(b) bears two black letters "L" on a white ground each at least 125 mm high and 90 mm wide with a stroke width of 12 mm.]

1	2
Expression	Meaning
[low loader	a semi-trailer which is constructed and normally used for the carriage of engineering equipment so constructed that the major part of the load platform does not extend over or between the wheels and the upper surface of which is below the height of the top most point of the tyres of those wheels, measured on level ground and when— (a) any adjustable suspension is at the normal travelling height, (b) all pneumatic tyres are suitably inflated for use when the vehicle is fully laden, and (c) the semi-trailer is unladen, (see also the definition of stepframe low loader).]
m	metre(s)
m^2	square metre(s).
m^3	cubic metre(s).
[maximum permitted axle weight	in relation to an axle— (a) in the case of a vehicle which is equipped with a Ministry plate in accordance with regulation 70, the axle weight shown in column (2) of that plate (where the plate is in the form required by Schedule 10) or in column (2) of that plate (where the plate is in the form required by Schedule 10A) in relation to that axle; (b) in the case of a vehicle which is not equipped with a Ministry plate but which is equipped with a plate in accordance with regulation 66, the maximum axle weight shown for that axle on the plate in respect of item 9 of Part I of Schedule 8 in the case of a motor vehicle and item 7 of Part II of Schedule 8 in the case of a trailer; and (c) in any other case, the weight which the axle is designed or adapted not to exceed when the vehicle is travelling on a road.]
maximum gross weight	(a) in the case of a vehicle equipped with a Ministry plate in accordance with regulation 70, the design gross weight shown in column (3) of that plate [(where the plate is in the form required by Schedule 10) or in column (4) of that plate (where the plate is in the form required by Schedule 10A)] or, if no such weight is shown, the gross weight shown in column (2) of that plate; (b) in the case of a vehicle not equipped with a Ministry plate, but which is equipped with a plate in accordance with regulation 66, the maximum gross weight shown on the plate in respect of item 7 of Part 1 of Schedule 8 in the case of a motor vehicle and item 6 of Part II of Schedule 8 in the case of a trailer;

1	2
Expression	Meaning
	(c) in any other case, the weight which the vehicle is designed or adapted not to exceed when the vehicle is travelling on a road.
maximum speed	the speed which a vehicle is incapable, by reason of its construction, of exceeding on the level under its own power when fully laden.
[maximum total design axle weight (an expression used only in relation to trailers)	(a) in the case of a trailer equipped with a Ministry plate in accordance with regulation 70, the sum of the relevant axle weights; (b) in the case of a trailer which is not equipped with a Ministry plate, but which is equipped with a plate in accordance with regulation 66, the sum of the maximum axle weights shown on the plate in respect of item 4 of Part II of Schedule 8; or (c) in the case of any other trailer, the sum of the axle weights which the trailer is designed or adapted not to exceed when the vehicle is travelling on a road; and for the purposes of sub-paragraph (a) the relevant axle weight, in respect to an axle, is the design axle weight shown in column (3) of the Ministry plate (where the plate is in the form required by Schedule 10) or in column (4) of that plate (where the plate is in the form required by Schedule 10A) in relation to that axle or if no such weight is shown, the axle weight shown in column (2) of that plate in relation to that axle;]
minibus	a motor vehicle which is constructed or adapted to carry more than 8 but not more than 16 seated passengers in addition to the driver.
Ministry plate	a plate issued by the Secretary of State for a goods vehicle following the issue or amendment of a plating certificate and in the form in, and containing the particulars required by, Schedule 10 [or Schedule 10A]. the said particular being those shown in the plating certificate for the vehicle.
mm	millimetre(s).
motor ambulance	a motor vehicle which is specially designed and constructed (and not merely adapted) for carrying, as equipment permanently fixed to the vehicle, equipment used for medical, dental, or other health purposes and is used primarily for the carriage of persons suffering from illness, injury or disability.
motor car	a mechanically propelled vehicle, not being a motor tractor, a motor cycle or an invalid carriage, which is constructed itself to carry a load or passengers and the weight of which unladen—

1	2
Expression	Meaning
	(a) if it is constructed solely for the carriage of passengers and their effects and is adapted to carry not more than seven passengers exclusive of the driver does not exceed 3050 kg;
	(b) if it is constructed for use for the conveyance of goods or burden of any description, does not exceed 3050 kg;
	(c) does not exceed 2540 kg in a case falling within neither of the foregoing paragraphs.
[motor caravan	a motor vehicle which is constructed or adapted for the carriage of passengers and their effects and which contains, as permanently installed equipment, the facilities which are reasonably necessary for enabling the vehicle to provide mobile living accommodation for its users.]
motor cycle	a mechanically propelled vehicle, not being an invalid carriage, having less than four wheels and the weight of which unladen does not exceed 410 kg.
motor tractor	a mechanically propelled vehicle which is not constructed itself to carry a load, other than the following articles, that is to say, water, fuel, accumulators and other equipment used for the purpose of propulsion, loose tools and loose equipment, and the weight of which unladen does not exceed 7370 kg.
motor vehicle	a mechanically propelled vehicle intended or adapted for use on roads.
mph	mile(s) per hour.
N/mm^2	newton(s) per square millimetre.
[off-road vehicle	an off-road vehicle as defined in Annex I to Council Directive 70/156/EEC of 6th February 1970 as read with Council Directive 87/403/EEC of 25th June 1987.]
overall height	the vertical distance between the ground and the point on the vehicle which is furthest from the ground, calculated when—
	(a) the tyres of the vehicle are suitably inflated for the use to which it is being put;
	(b) the vehicle is at its unladen weight; and
	(c) the surface of the ground under the vehicle is reasonably flat;
	but, in the case of a trolley bus, exclusive of the power collection equipment mounted on the roof of the vehicle.
overall length	in relation to a vehicle, the distance between transverse planes passing through the extreme forward and rearward projecting points of the vehicle inclusive of all parts of the vehicle, of any receptacle which is of a permanent character and accordingly strong enough for repeated use, and any fitting on, or attached to, the vehicle except—

1	2
Expression	Meaning

	(i) for all purposes—
	  (a) any driving mirror,
	  (b) any expanding or extensible contrivance forming part of a turntable fire escape fixed to a vehicle;
	  (c) any snow-plough fixed in front of a vehicle;
	  (d) any receptacle specially designed to hold and keep secure a seal issued for the purposes of customs clearance;
	  (e) any tailboard which is let down while the vehicle is stationary in order to facilitate its loading or unloading;
	  (f) any tailboard which is let down in order to facilitate the carriage of, but which is not essential for the support of, loads which are in themselves so long as to extend at least as far as the tailboard when upright;
	  (g) any fitting attached to a part of, or to a receptacle on, a vehicle which does not increase the carrying capacity of the part or receptacle but which enables it to be
	    —transferred from a road vehicle to a railway vehicle or from a railway vehicle to a road vehicle,
	    —secured to a railway vehicle by a locking device, and
	    —carried on a railway vehicle by the use of stanchions:
	  (h) any plate, whether rigid or movable, fitted to a trailer constructed for the purpose of carrying other vehicles and designed to bridge the gap between that trailer and a motor vehicle constructed for that purpose and to which the trailer is attached so that, while the trailer is attached to the motor vehicle, vehicles which are to be carried by the motor vehicle may be vehicle before a journey begins, and vehicles which have been carried on the motor vehicle may be moved from it to the trailer after a journey ends;
	  (i) any sheeting or other readily flexible means of covering or securing a load;
	  (j) any receptacle with an external length, measured parallel to the longitudinal axis of the vehicle, not exceeding 2·5 m;
	  (k) any empty receptacle which itself forms a load;
	  (l) any receptacle which contains an indivisible load of exceptional length;

1	2
Expression	Meaning
	(m) any receptacle manufactured before 30th October 1985, not being a maritime container (namely a container designed primarily for carriage on sea transport without an accompanying road vehicle); . . .
	(n) any special appliance or apparatus as described in regulation 81(c) which does not itself increase the carrying capacity of the vehicle; [or
	(o) any rearward projecting buffer made of rubber or other resilient material.]
	(ii) for the purposes of [regulations 7 and 13A]—
	(a) any part of a trailer (not being in the case of an agricultural trailed appliance a drawbar or other thing with which it is equipped for the purpose of being towed) designed primarily for use as a means of attaching it to another vehicle and any fitting designed for use in connection with any such part;
	(b) the thickness of any front or rear wall on a semi-trailer and of any part forward of such front wall or rearward of such rear wall which does not increase the vehicle's load-carrying space.
overall width	the distance between longitudinal planes passing through the extreme lateral projecting points of the vehicle inclusive of all parts of the vehicle, of any receptacle which is of permanent character and accordingly strong enough for repeated use, and any fitting on, or attached to, the vehicle except—
	(a) any driving mirror;
	(b) any snow-plough fixed in front of the vehicle;
	(c) so much of the distortion of any tyre as is caused by the weight of the vehicle;
	(d) any receptacle specially designed to hold and keep secure a seal issued for the purposes of customs clearance;
	(e) any lamp or reflector fitted to the vehicle in accordance with the Lighting Regulations;
	(f) any sideboard which is let down while the vehicle is stationary in order to facilitate its loading or unloading;
	(g) any fitting attached to part of, or to a receptacle on, a vehicle which does not increase the carrying capacity of the part or receptacle but which enables it to be —transferred from a road vehicle to a railway vehicle or from a railway vehicle to a road vehicle;

1	2
Expression	Meaning
	—secured to a railway vehicle by a locking device; and —carried on a railway vehicle by the use of stanchions; (h) any sheeting or other readily flexible means of covering or securing a load; (i) any receptacle with an external width, measured at right angles to the longitudinal axis of the vehicle, which does not exceed 2·5 m; (*j*) any empty receptacle which itself forms a load; (k) any receptacle which contains an indivisible load of exceptional width; (l) any receptacle manufactured before 30th October 1985, not being a maritime container (namely a container designed primarily for carriage on sea transport without an accompanying road vehicle); or (m) any special appliance or apparatus as described in regulation 81(c) which does not itself increase the carrying capacity of the vehicle.

overhang	the distance measured horizontally and parallel to the longitudinal axis of a vehicle between two transverse planes passing through the following two points—
	(a) the rearmost point of the vehicle exclusive of—
	   (i) any expanding or extensible contrivance forming part of a turntable fire escape fixed to a vehicle;
	   (ii) in the case of a motor car constructed solely for the carriage of passengers and their effects and adapted to carry not more than eight passengers exclusive of the driver, any luggage carrier fitted to the vehicle; and
	(b) (i) in the case of a motor vehicle having not more than three axles of which only one is not a steering axle, the centre point of that axle;
	   (ii) in the case of a motor vehicle having three axles of which the front axle is the only steering axle and of a motor vehicle having four axles of which the two foremost are the only steering axles, a point 110 mm behind the centre of a straight line joining the centre points of the two rearmost axles; and
	   (iii) in any other case a point situated on the longitudinal axis of the vehicle and such

1	2
Expression	Meaning
	that a line drawn from it at right angles to that axis will pass through the centre of the minimum turning circle of the vehicle.
passenger vehicle	a vehicle constructed solely for the carriage of passengers and their effects.
pedestrian-con- trolled vehicle	a motor vehicle which is controlled by a pedestrian and not constructed or adapted for use or used for the carriage of a driver or passenger.
pneumatic tyre	a tyre which—
	(a) is provided with, or together with the wheel upon which it is mounted forms, a continuous closed chamber inflated to a pressure substantially exceeding atmospheric pressure when the tyre is in the condition in which it is normally used, but is not subjected to any load;
	(b) is capable of being inflated and deflated without removal from the wheel or vehicle; and
	(c) is such that, when it is deflated and is subjected to a normal load, the sides of the tyre collapse.
public works vehicle	[a mechanically propelled vehicle which is used on a road by or on behalf of—
	(a) the Central Scotland Water Development Board;
	(b) a ferry undertaking;
	(c) a highway or roads authority;
	(d) a local authority;
	(e) a market undertaking;
	(f) the National Rivers Authority;
	(g) an operator of a telecommunications code system within the meaning of paragraph 1(1) of Schedule 4 to the Telecommunications Act 1984;
	(h) a police authority;
	(i) the Post Office;
	(j) a public electricity supplier within the meaning of Part I of the Electricity Act 1989;
	(k) a public gas supplier within the meaning of the Gas Act 1986;
	(l) a statutory undertaker within the meaning of section 329(1) of the Highways Act 1980;
	(m) an undertaking for the supply of district heating;
	(n) a water authority within the meaning of the Water (Scotland) Act 1980; or
	(o) a water or sewerage undertaker within the meaning of the Water Act 1989;
	for the purpose of works which such a body has a duty or power to carry out, and which is used only for the carriage of—

1	2
Expression	Meaning
	(i) the crew, and
	(ii) goods which are needed for works in respect of which the vehicle is used.]
recut pneumatic tyre	a pneumatic tyre in which all or part of its original tread pattern has been cut deeper or burnt deeper or a different tread pattern has been cut deeper or burnt deeper than the original tread pattern.
refuse vehicle	a vehicle designed for use and used solely in connection with street cleansing, the collection or disposal of refuse, or the collection or disposal of the contents of gullies or cesspools.
registered	registered under any of the following enactments— (a) the Roads Act 1920, (b) the Vehicles (Excise) Act 1949, (c) the Vehicles (Excise) Act 1962, or (*d*) the 1971 Act and, in relation to the date on which a vehicle was registered, the date on which it was first registered under any of those enactments.
relevant braking requirement	a requirement that the brakes of a motor vehicle (as assisted, where a trailer is being drawn, by the brakes on the trailer) comply— (i) in a case to which item 1 in Table 1 in regulation 18 applies, with the requirements specified in regulation 18(3) for vehicles falling in that item; (ii) in any other case, with the requirements specified in regulation 18(3) for vehicle classes (a) and (b) in item 2 of that Table (whatever the date of first use of the motor vehicle and the date of manufacture of any trailer drawn by it may be).
resilient tyre	a tyre, not being a pneumatic tyre, which is of soft or elastic material, having regard to paragraph (5).
[restricted speed vehicle	a vehicle displaying at its rear a "50" plate in accordance with the requirements of Schedule 13].
[retreaded tyre	a tyre which has been reconditioned to extend its useful life by replacement of the tread rubber or by replacement of the tread rubber and renovation of the sidewall rubber.]
rigid vehicle	a motor vehicle which is not constructed or adapted to form part of an articulated vehicle or articulated bus.
[rim diameter	is to be interpreted in accordance with the British Standard BS AU 50: Part 2: Section 1: 1980 entitled "British Standard Automobile Series: Specification for Tyres and Wheels Part 2. Wheels and rims Section 1. Rim profiles and dimensions (including openings for valves)" which came into effect on 28th November 1980.]

1	2
Expression	Meaning
[rim diameter size code	is to be interpreted in accordance with the British Standard referred to in the meaning given in this Table to "rim diameter".]
secondary braking system	a braking system of a vehicle applied by a secondary means of operation independent of the service braking system or by one of the sections comprised in a split braking system.
service braking system	the braking system of a vehicle which is designed and constructed to have the highest braking efficiency of any of the braking systems with which the vehicle is equipped.
semi-trailer	a trailer which is constructed or adapted to form part of an articulated vehicle [including (without prejudice to the generality of that) a vehicle which is not itself a motor vehicle but which has some or all of its wheels driven by the drawing vehicle].
silencer	a contrivance suitable and sufficient for reducing as far as may be reasonable the noise caused by the escape of exhaust gases from the engine of a motor vehicle.
single-decked vehicle	a vehicle upon which no part of a deck or gangway is vertically above another deck or gangway.
split braking system	in relation to a motor vehicle, a braking system so designed and constructed that— (a) it comprises two independent sections of mechanism capable of developing braking force such that, excluding the means of operation, a failure of any part (other than a fixed member or a brake shoe anchor pin) of one of the said sections will not cause a decrease in the braking force capable of being developed by the other section; (b) the said two sections are operated by a means of operation which is common to both sections; (c) the braking efficiency of either of the said two sections can be readily checked.
[staircase	a staircase by means of which passengers on a double-decked vehicle may pass to and from the upper deck of the vehicle.]
[stepframe low loader	a semi-trailer (not being a low loader) which is constructed and normally used for the carriage of engineering equipment and is so constructed that the upper surface of the major part of the load platform is at a height of less than 1 m above the ground when measured on level ground and when— (a) any adjustable suspension is at the normal travelling height, (b) all pneumatic tyres are suitably inflated for use when the vehicle is fully laden; and (c) the semi-trailer is unladen.]

1	2
Expression	Meaning
stored energy	in relation to a braking system of a vehicle, energy (other than the muscular energy of the driver or the mechanical energy of a spring) stored in a reservoir for the purpose of applying the brakes under the control of the driver, either directly or as a supplement to his muscular energy.
straddle carrier	a motor vehicle constructed to straddle and lift its load for the purpose of transportation.
statutory power of removal	a power conferred by or under any enactment to remove or move a vehicle from any road or from any part of a road.
temporary use spare tyre	a pneumatic tyre which is designed for use on a motor vehicle only— (a) in the event of the failure of one of the tyres normally fitted to a wheel of the vehicle, and (b) at a speed lower than that for which such normally fitted tyres are designed.
three-wheeled motor cycle	a motor cycle having three wheels, not including a two wheeled motor cycle with a sidecar attached.
towing implement	a device on wheels designed for the purpose of enabling a motor vehicle to draw another vehicle by the attachment of that device to that other vehicle in such a manner that part of that other vehicle is secured to and either rests on or is suspended from the device and some but not all of the wheels on which that other vehicle normally runs are raised off the ground.
track-laying	in relation to a vehicle, so designed and constructed that the weight thereof is transmitted to the road surface either by means of continuous tracks or by a combination of wheels and continuous tracks in such circumstances that the weight transmitted to the road surface by the tracks is not less than half the weight of the vehicle.
trailer	means a vehicle drawn by a motor vehicle and is to be interpreted in accordance with paragraphs (9) and (11).
train weight	in relation to a motor vehicle which may draw a trailer, the maximum laden weight for the motor vehicle together with any trailer which may be drawn by it.
transverse plane	a vertical plane at right angles to the longitudinal axis of a vehicle.
trolley bus	a bus adapted for use on roads without rails and moved by power transmitted thereto from some external source.
unbraked trailer	any trailer other than one which, whether or not regulation 15 or 16 applies to it, is equipped with a braking system in accordance with one of those regulations.

1	2
Expression	Meaning
unladen weight	the weight of a vehicle or trailer inclusive of the body and all parts (the heavier being taken where alternative bodies or parts are used) which are necessary to or ordinarily used with the vehicle or trailer when working on a road, but exclusive of the weight of water, fuel or accumulators used for the purpose of the supply of power for the propulsion of the vehicle or, as the case may be, of any vehicle by which the trailer is drawn, and of loose tools and loose equipment.
vehicle in the service of a visiting force or of a headquarters	a vehicle so described in Article 8(6) of the Visiting Forces and International Headquarters (Application of Law) Order 1965.
wheel	a wheel the tyre or rim of which when the vehicle is in motion on a road is in contact with the ground; two wheels are to be regarded as one wheel in the circumstances specified in paragraph (7).
wheeled	in relation to a vehicle, so constructed that the whole weight of the vehicle is transmitted to the road surface by means of wheels.
wide tyre	a pneumatic tyre of which the area of contact with the road surface is not less than 300 mm in width when measured at right angles to the longitudinal axis of the vehicle.
works trailer	a trailer designed for use in private premises and used on a road only in delivering goods from or to such premises to or from a vehicle on a road in the immediate neighbourhood, or in passing from one part of any such premises to another or to other private premises in the immediate neighbourhood or in connection with road works while at or in the immediate neighbourhood of the site of such works.
works truck	a motor vehicle (other than a straddle carrier) designed for use in private premises and used on a road only in delivering goods from or to such premises to or from a vehicle on a road in the immediate neighbourhood, or in passing from one part of any such premises to another or to other private premises in the immediate neighbourhood or in connection with road works while at or in the immediate neighbourhood of the site of such works.

(3) For the purpose of these Regulations, the date on which a motor vehicle is first used is—

    (a) in the case of a vehicle not falling within sub-paragraph (b) and which is registered, the date on which it was registered;

    (b) in each of the following cases—

   (i) a vehicle which is being or has been used under a trade licence as
        defined in section 16 of the 1971 Act (otherwise than for the
        purposes of demonstration or testing or of being delivered from
        premises of the manufacturer by whom it was made or of a
        distributor of vehicles, or dealer in vehicles, to premises of a
        distributor of vehicles, dealer in vehicles or purchaser thereof or
        to premises of a person obtaining possession thereof under a
        hiring agreement or hire purchase agreement);
  (ii) a vehicle belonging, or which has belonged, to the Crown and
        which is or was used or appropriated for use for naval, military
        or air force purposes;
 (iii) a vehicle belonging, or which has belonged, to a visiting force or
        a headquarters or defence organisation to which in each case the
        Visiting Forces and International Headquarters (Application of
        Law) Order 1965 applies;
 (iv) a vehicle which has been used on roads outside Great Britain
        before being imported into Great Britain; and
  (v) a vehicle which has been used otherwise than on roads after
        being sold or supplied by retail and before being registered;
   the date of manufacture of the vehicle.

In sub-paragraph (b)(v) of this paragraph "sold or supplied by retail" means
sold or supplied otherwise than to a person acquiring it solely for the purpose of
resale or re-supply for a valuable consideration.

(4) The date of manufacture of a vehicle to which the Type Approval for
Goods Vehicles Regulations apply shall be the date of manufacture described
in regulation 2(4)(a) of those Regulations.

(5) Save where otherwise provided in these Regulations a tyre shall not be
deemed to be of soft or elastic material unless the said material is either—

  (a) continuous round the circumference of the wheel; or
  (b) fitted in sections so that so far as reasonably practicable no space is
        left between the ends thereof,

and is of such thickness and design as to minimise, so far as reasonably possible,
vibration when the vehicle is in motion and so constructed as to be free from
any defect which might in any way cause damage to the surface of a road.

(6) For the purpose of these Regulations a brake drum and a brake disc
shall be deemed to form part of the wheel and not of the braking system.

(7) For the purpose of these Regulations other than regulations 26 and 27
any two wheels of a motor vehicle or trailer shall be regarded as one wheel if the
distance between the centres of the areas of contact between such wheels and
the road surface is less than 460 mm.

(8) For the purpose of these Regulations other than regulations 26 and 27 in
counting the number of axles, and in determining the sum of the weights
transmitted to the road surface by any one axle of, a vehicle, all the wheels of
which the centres of the areas of contact with the road surface can be included
between any two transverse planes less than [0.5] m apart shall be treated as
constituting one axle.

[(8A) For the purposes of these Regulations, a reference to axles being closely-spaced is a reference to—

    (a) two axles (not being part of a group of axles falling within sub-paragraph (b) or (c)) which are spaced at a distance apart of not more than 2.5 m;

    (b) three axles (not being part of a group of axles falling within sub-paragraph (c)) the outermost of which are spaced at a distance apart of not more than 3.25 m; or

    (c) four or more axles the outermost of which are spaced at a distance apart of not more than 4.6 m;

the number of axles for the purposes of these paragraphs being determined in accordance with paragraph (8); and a reference to any particular number of closely-spaced axles shall be construed accordingly.]

(9) The provisions of these Regulations relating to trailers do not apply to any part of an articulated bus.

(10) For the purpose of [paragraph (8A) above,] regulations 51, [76, 77 and 79] and Schedule 11 . . ., the distance between any two axles shall be obtained by measuring the shortest distance between the line joining the centres of the areas of contact with the road surface of the wheels of one axle and the line joining the centres of the areas of contact with the road surface of the wheels of the other axle.

(11) For the purpose of the following provisions only, a composite trailer shall be treated as one trailer (not being a semi-trailer or a converter dolly)—

    (a) regulations 7, 76 and 83;

    (b) paragraph (2) of, and items 3 and 10 in the Table in, regulation 75;

    (c) item 2 in the Table in regulation 78. **[1341]**

NOTES

Commencement: 11 August 1986 (except para (8A)); 1 January 1993 (para (8A)).
This regulation derived from SI 1955 No 990, reg 3, and SI 1978 No 1017, reg 3.
Sub-s (2): definition "Ministry Plate" amended by SI 1987 No 676, reg 3; definition "semi-trailer" amended by SI 1987 No 676, reg 5; definitions "coach", "large bus", "motor caravan" and "staircase" added by SI 1987 No 1133, reg 3; definitions "Community Directive followed by a number" and "the Community Recording Equipment Regulation" amended by SI 1989 No 1865, reg 3; definitions "car transporter", "engineering equipment", "low loader" and "stepframe low loader" added by SI 1990 No 317, reg 3; definition "off-road vehicle" added by SI 1990 No 1131, reg 3; definitions of "light trailer", "low platform trailer", "maximum permitted axle weight", "maximum total design axle weight", "restricted speed vehicle", "retreaded tyre", "rim diameter" and "rim diameter size code" inserted by SI 1990 No 1981, reg 3; words in square brackets within definitions "maximum gross weight" inserted by SI 1990 No 1981, reg 3; definition of "public works vehicle" substituted by SI 1990 No 1981, reg 3; definition "converter dolly" substituted by SI 1991 No 1526, reg 3; in definition "overall length", word omitted following sub-para (m) repealed, and, sub-para (o) and word preceding it added, by SI 1991 No 2125, reg 3; remaining amendments in that definition made by SI 1990 No 317, reg 3; definition "closely-spaced" repealed by SI 1992 No 2016, reg 3(1), (2).
Para (8): figure in square brackets substituted by SI 1992 No 2016, reg 3(1), (3).
Para (8A): inserted by SI 1992 No 2016, reg 3(1), (4).
Para (10): first words in square brackets inserted, and words omitted repealed, by SI 1992 No 2016, reg 3(1), (5); second words in square brackets substituted by SI 1988 No 1287, reg 3.
Act of Accession: Cmnd 5179-1.
Council Directive 70/156/EEC: OJ No L42, 23.2.70, p1.
Council Regulation (EEC) 1463/70: OJ L 164, 27.7.70, p1.
Council Regulation (EEC) 1787/73: OJ L 181, 4.7.73, p1.
Council Regulation (EEC) 2828/77: OJ L 334, 24.12.77, p5.
Council Directive 87/403/EEC: OJ No L220, 8.8.87, p44.
Agreement concerning the adoption of uniform conditions of approval for Motor Vehicles Equipment and Parts and reciprocal recognition thereof concluded at Geneva on 20 March 1958 as amended: see Cmnd 2535, Cmnd 3562.

4. Application and exemptions

(1) Save where the context otherwise requires, these Regulations apply to both wheeled vehicles and track-laying vehicles.

(2) Where a provision is applied by these Regulations to a motor vehicle first used on or after a specified date it does not apply to that vehicle if it was manufactured at least six months before that date.

(3) Where an exemption from, or relaxation of, a provision is applied by these Regulations to a motor vehicle first used before a specified date it shall also apply to a motor vehicle first used on or after that date if it was manufactured at least six months before that date.

(4) The regulations specified in an item in column 3 of the Table do not apply in respect of a vehicle of a class specified in that item in column 2.

TABLE

(regulation 4(4))

1 Item	2 Class of Vehicle	3 Regulations which do not apply
1	A vehicle proceeding to a port for export.	The regulations in Part II insofar as they relate to construction and equipment, except regulations 16 (insofar as it concerns parking brakes) 20, 30, 34, 37, 53 and 57(3) and (4). Regulations 66 to 69 and 71.
2	A vehicle brought temporarily into Great Britain by a person resident abroad, provided that the vehicle complies in every respect with the requirements relating to motor vehicles or trailers contained in— (a) article 21 and paragraph (1) of article 22 of the Convention on Road Traffic concluded at Geneva on 19th September 1949 and [Part I,] Part II (so far as it relates to direction indicators and stop lights) and Part III of Annex 6 to that Convention; or (b) paragraphs I, III and VIII of article 3 of the International Convention relative to Motor Traffic concluded at Paris on 24th April 1926.	The regulations in Part II insofar as they relate to construction and equipment except regulations 7, 8, 9(2), 10, 40, 53 and 57(3) and (4). Regulations 66 to 69 and 71.

1 Item	2 Class of Vehicle	3 Regulations which do not apply
3	A vehicle manufactured in Great Britain which complies with the requirements referred to in item 2 above and contained in the Convention of 1949, or, as the case may be, 1926 referred to in that item as if the vehicle had been brought temporarily into Great Britain, and either— (a) is exempt from car tax by virtue of section 7(1), (2) and (3) of the Car Tax Act 1983 (b) has been zero rated under regulation 56 or 57 of the Value Added Tax (General) Regulations 1985.	The regulations in Part II insofar as they relate to construction and equipment, except regulations 7, 8, 9(2), 10, 40, 53 and 57(3) and (4). Regulations 66 to 69 and 71.
4	A vehicle in the service of a visiting force or of a headquarters.	The regulations in Part II insofar as they relate to construction and equipment, except regulations 9(2), 16 (insofar as it concerns parking brakes), 21, 53, 57(3) and (4) and 61. Regulations 66 to 69, 71 and 75 to 79.
5	A vehicle which has been submitted for an examination under section 43 or [section 45] of the 1972 Act while it is being used on a road in connection with the carrying out of that examination and is being so used by a person who is empowered under that section to carry out that examination, or by a person acting under the direction of a person so empowered.	The regulations in Part II except regulations 57(3) and (4). Regulations 75 to 79 and 100.
6	A motor car or a motor cycle in respect of which a certificate has been issued by the Officer in Charge of the National Collections of Road Transport, the Science Museum, London, SW7, that it was designed before 1st January 1905 and constructed before 31st December 1905.	Regulation 16 (except insofar as it applies requirements 3 and 6 in Schedule 3), 21, 37(4), 63 and 99(4).

1 Item	2 Class of Vehicle	3 Regulations which do not apply
7	(a) A towing implement which is being drawn by a motor vehicle while it is not attached to any vehicle except the one drawing it if— (i) the towing implement is not being so drawn during the hours of darkness and (ii) the vehicle by which it is being so drawn is not driven at a speed exceeding 20 mph; or (b) a vehicle which is being drawn by a motor vehicle in the exercise of a statutory power of removal.	The regulations in Part II insofar as they relate to the construction and equipment of trailers, except regulation 20.
[8	Tramcars	The regulations in Parts II, III and IV]

(5) Any reference to a broken down vehicle shall include a reference to any towing implement which is being used for the drawing of any such vehicle.

(6) The Secretary of State is satisfied that it is requisite that the provisions of regulation 40(2) should apply, as from the date on which these Regulations come into operation, to track-laying vehicles registered before the expiration of one year from the making of these Regulations; and that, notwithstanding that those provisions will then apply to these vehicles, no undue hardship or inconvenience will be caused thereby.   **[1342]**

NOTES
   Commencement: 11 August 1986.
   This regulation derived from SI 1955 No 990, reg 4, and SI 1978 No 1017, reg 4.
   Item 8 in Table added by SI 1992 No 1217, reg 13; regulation otherwise amended by SI 1988 No 271, reg 3.
   Convention on Road Traffic concluded at Geneva on 19 September 1949: Cmnd 7997.
   International Convention relative to Motor Traffic concluded at Paris on 24 April 1926: Treaty Series No 11(1930).

5. Trade Descriptions Act 1968

Nothing in any provision of these Regulations whereby any vehicle or any of its parts or equipment is required to be marked with a specification number or the registered certification trade mark of the British Standards Institution or with an approval mark, or whereby such a marking is treated as evidence of compliance with a standard to which the marking relates, shall be taken to authorise any person to apply any such marking to the vehicle, part or equipment in contravention of the Trade Descriptions Act 1968.   **[1343]**

NOTES
   Commencement: 11 August 1986.
   This regulation derived from SI 1978 No 1017, reg 7.

6. Compliance with Community Directives and ECE Regulations

(1) For the purposes of any regulation which requires or permits a vehicle to comply with the requirements of a Community Directive or an ECE Regulation, a vehicle shall be deemed so to have complied at the date of its first use only if—

    (a) one of the certificates referred to in paragraph (2) has been issued in relation to it; or

    (b) the marking referred to in paragraph (3) has been applied; or

    (c) it was, before it was used on a road, subject to a relevant type approval requirement as specified in paragraph (4).

(2) The certificates mentioned in paragraph (1) are—

    (a) a type approval certificate issued by the Secretary of State under regulation 5 of the Type Approval Regulations or of the Type Approval for Agricultural Vehicles Regulations;

    (b) a certificate of conformity issued by the manufacturer of the vehicle under regulation 6 of either of those Regulations; . . .

    (c) a certificate issued under a provision of the law of any member state of the European Economic Community which corresponds to the said regulations 5 or 6[; or

    (d) a sound level measurement certificate issued by the Secretary of State under regulation 4 of the Motorcycles (Sound Level Measurement Certificates) Regulations 1980;]

being in each case a certificate issued by reason of the vehicle's conforming to the requirements of the Community Directive in question.

(3) The marking mentioned in paragraph (1) is a marking designated as an approval mark by regulation 4 of the Approval Marks Regulations, being in each case a mark shown in column 2 of an item in Schedule 2 to those Regulations which refers, in column 5, to the ECE Regulation in question, applied as indicated in column 4 in that item.

(4) A relevant type approval requirement is a requirement of the Type Approval (Great Britain) Regulations or the Type Approval for Goods Vehicles Regulations which appears—

    (a) in column 4 of Table 1 in Schedule 2 in the item in which the Community Directive in question appears in column 3, or

    (b) in column 4 of Table II in Schedule 2 in the item in which the ECE Regulation in question appears in column 3.   **[1344]**

NOTES

    Commencement: 11 August 1986.

    Para (2): word omitted revoked, and words in square brackets added, by SI 1989 No 1865, reg 4.

    See further: the Road Vehicles (Construction and Use) (Amendment) (No 3) Regulations 1989, SI 1989 No 1865, reg 2.

    The Type Approval Regulations: SI 1980 No 1182.

    The Type Approval for Agricultural Vehicles Regulations: SI 1979 No 221 (revoked; see now SI 1988 No 1567, as amended).

    The Approval Marks Regulations: SI 1979 No 1088.

    The Type Approval (Great Britain) Regulations: SI 1984 No 981.

    The Type Approval for Goods Vehicles Regulations: SI 1982 No 1271.

PART II

REGULATIONS GOVERNING THE CONSTRUCTION, EQUIPMENT AND MAINTENANCE OF VEHICLES

A - Dimensions and Manoeuvrability

[7. Length

(1) Subject to paragraphs (2) to (6), the overall length of a vehicle or combination of vehicles of a class specified in an item in column 2 of the Table shall not exceed the maximum length specified in that item in column 3 of the Table, the overall length in the case of a combination of vehicles being calculated in accordance with regulation 81(g) and (h).

TABLE
(regulation 7(1))

1	2	3
Item	Class of vehicle	Maximum length (metres)
	Vehicle Combinations	
1	A motor vehicle drawing one trailer, where the combination of vehicles does not meet the requirements of paragraph (5A) and the trailer is not a semi-trailer.	18
1A	A motor vehicle drawing one trailer where the combination meets the requirements of paragraph (5A) and the trailer is not a semi-trailer.	18·35
2	An articulated bus.	18
3	An articulated vehicle the semi-trailer of which does not meet the requirements of paragraph (6) and is not a low loader.	15·5
3A	An articulated vehicle, the semi-trailer of which meets the requirements of paragraph (6) and is not a low loader.	16·5
3B	An articulated vehicle, the semi-trailer of which is a low loader.	18
	Motor vehicles	
4	A wheeled motor vehicle.	12
5	A track-laying motor vehicle.	9·2
	Trailers	
6	An agricultural trailed appliance manufactured on or after 1st December 1985.	15
7	A semi-trailer manufactured on or after 1st May 1983 which does not meet the requirements of paragraph (6) and is not a low loader.	12·2

1	2	3
Item	Class of vehicle	Maximum length (metres)
7A	A composite trailer drawn by— (a) a goods vehicle being a motor vehicle having a maximum gross weight exceeding 3500 kg; or (b) an agricultural motor vehcile.	14·04
8	A trailer (not being a semi-trailer or composite trailer) with at least 4 wheels which is— (a) drawn by a goods vehicle being a motor vehicle having a maximum gross weight exceeding 3500 kg; or (b) an agricultural trailer.	12
9	Any other trailer not being an agricultural trailed appliance or a semi-trailer	7

(2) In the case of a motor vehicle drawing one trailer where—

(a) the motor vehicle is a showman's vehicle as defined in paragraph 7 of Schedule 3 to the 1971 Act; and
(b) the trailer is used primarily as living accommodation by one or more persons and is not also used for the carriage of goods or burden which are not needed for the purpose of such residence in the vehicle,

item 1 in the Table applies with the substitution of 22 m for 18 m and item 1A in the Table does not apply.

(3) Items 1, 1A, 3, 3A and 3B of the Table do not apply to—

(a) a vehicle combination which includes a trailer which is constructed and normally used for the conveyance of indivisible loads of exceptional length, or
(b) a vehicle combination consisting of a broken down vehicle (including an articulated vehicle) being drawn by a motor vehicle in consequence of a breakdown, or
(c) an articulated vehicle, the semi-trailer of which is a low loader manufactured before 1st April 1991.

(3A) Items 6, 7, 7A, 8 and 9 of the Table do not apply to—

(a) a trailer which is constructed and normally used for the conveyance of indivisible loads of exceptional length,
(b) a broken down vehicle (including an articulated vehicle) which is being drawn by a motor vehicle in consequence of a breakdown, or
(c) a trailer being a drying or mixing plant designed for the production of asphalt or of bituminous or tar macadam and used mainly for the construction, repair or maintenance of roads, or a road planing machine so used.

(3B) Furthermore item 7 does not apply to—

(a) a semi-trailer which is a car transporter,
(b) a semi-trailer which is normally used on international journeys any part of which takes place outside the United Kingdom.]

(4) Where a motor vehicle is drawing—

    (a) two trailers, then only one of those trailers may exceed an overall length of 7 m;

    (b) three trailers, then none of those trailers shall exceed an overall length of 7 m.

(5) Where a motor vehicle is drawing—

    (a) two or more trailers; or

    (b) one trailer constructed and normally used for the conveyance of indivisible loads of exceptional length—

then—

    (i) the overall length of that motor vehicle shall not exceed 9.2 m; and

    (ii) the overall length of the combination of vehicles, calculated in accordance with regulation 81(g) and (h), shall not exceed 25.9m, unless the conditions specified in paragraphs 1 and 2 of Schedule 12 have been complied with.

(5A) The requirements of this paragraph, in relation to a combination of vehicles, are that at least one of the vehicles in the combination is not a goods vehicle or, if both vehicles in the combination are goods vehicles that—

    (a) the maximum distance measured parallel to the longitudinal axis of the combination of vehicles from the foremost point of the loading area behind the driver's cab to the rear of the trailer, less the distance between the rear of the motor vehicle and the front of the trailer, does not exceed 15.65 m; and

    (b) the maximum distance measured parallel to the longitudinal axis of the combination of vehicles from the foremost point of the loading area behind the driver's cab to the rear of the trailer does not exceed 16 m;

but sub-paragraph (a) shall not apply if both vehicles in the combination are car transporters.

(6) The requirements of this paragraph, in relation to a semi-trailer, are that—

    (a) the longitudinal distance from the axis of the king pin to the rear of the semi-trailer does not exceed—

        (i) 12.5 m in the case of a car transporter, or

        (ii) 12 m in any other case; and

    (b) no point in the semi-trailer forward of the transverse plane passing through the axis of the king pin is more than—

        (i) 4.19 m from the axis of the king pin, in the case of a car transporter, or

        (ii) 2.04 m from the axis of the king pin, in any other case.

(6A) For the purposes of paragraph (5A)—

    (a) where the forward end of the loading area of a motor vehicle is bounded by a wall, the thickness of the wall shall be regarded as part of the loading area; and

    (b) any part of a vehicle designed primarily for use as a means of attaching another vehicle to it and any fitting designed for use in connection with any such part shall be disregarded in determining the distance between the rear of a motor vehicle and the front of a trailer being drawn by it.

(7) For the purpose of paragraph (6) the longitudinal distance from the axis of the king pin to the rear of a semi-trailer is the distance between a transverse plane passing through the axis of the king pin and the rear of the semi-trailer.

(7A) Where a semi-trailer has more than one king-pin or is constructed so that it can be used with a king-pin in different positions, references in this regulation to a distance from the king-pin shall be construed as the distance from the rearmost king-pin or, as the case may be, the rearmost king-pin position.

(7B) For the purposes of paragraphs (5A), (6) and (7)—

   (a) a reference to the front of a vehicle is a reference to the transverse plane passing through the extreme forward projecting points of the vehicle; and

   (b) a reference to the rear of a vehicle is a reference to the transverse plane passing through the extreme rearward projecting points of the vehicle,

inclusive (in each case) of all parts of the vehicle, of any receptacle which is of a permanent character and accordingly strong enough for repeated use, and any fitting on, or attached to the vehicle but exclusive of—

   (i) the things set out in sub-paragraph (i) of the definition of "overall length" in the Table in regulation 3(2), and

   (ii) in the case of a semi-trailer, the things set out in sub-paragraph (ii)(a) of that definition.

(8) Where a broken down articulated vehicle is being towed by a motor vehicle in consequence of a breakdown—

   (a) paragraph (5) shall have effect in relation to the combination of vehicles as if sub-paragraph (b) were omitted, and

   (b) for the purposes of paragraph (4) and of paragraph (5) as so modified, the articulated vehicle shall be regarded as a single trailer.

(9) No person shall use or cause or permit to be used on a road, a trailer with an overall length exceeding 18.65 m unless the requirements of paragraphs 1 and 2 of Schedule 12 are complied with.]   **[1345]**

NOTES
   Commencement: 17 October 1991 (paras (5A), (6A), (7B), (9)); 29 June 1990 (para (7A)); 19 March 1990 (paras (3)-(3B), (6), (7), (8)); 11 August 1986 (remainder).
   This regulation derived from SI 1955 No 990, regs 5, 34, and SI 1978 No 1017, reg 9.
   Set out as in SI 1991 No 2125, Schedule.
   The 1971 Act: Vehicles (Excise) Act 1971.

8. Width

(1) Save as provided in paragraph (2), the overall width of a vehicle of a class specified in an item in column 2 of the Table shall not exceed the maximum width specified in column 3 in that item.

TABLE
(regulation 8(1))

1	2	3
Item	Class of vehicle	Maximum width (metres)
1	A locomotive, other than an agricultural motor vehicle.	2·75
2	A refrigerated vehicle.	2·58
3	Any other motor vehicle.	2·5

1	2	3
Item	Class of vehicle	Maximum width (metres)
4	A trailer drawn by a motor vehicle having a maximum gross weight (determined as provided in Part I of Schedule 8 to these Regulations) exceeding 3500 kg.	2·5
5	An agricultural trailer.	2·5
6	An agricultural trailed appliance.	2·5
7	Any other trailer drawn by a vehicle other than a motor cycle.	2·3
8	A trailer drawn by a motor cycle.	1·5

(2) Paragraph (1) does not apply to a broken down vehicle which is being drawn in consequence of the breakdown.

(3) No person shall use or cause or permit to be used on a road a wheeled agricultural motor vehicle drawing a wheeled trailer if, when the longitudinal axes of the vehicles are parallel but in different vertical planes, the overall width of the two vehicles, measured as if they were one vehicle, exceeds 2.5 metres.

(4) In this regulation "refrigerated vehicle" means any vehicle which is specially designed for the carriage of goods at low temperature and of which the thickness of each of the side walls, inclusive of insulation, is at least 45 mm.

[1346]

NOTES
Commencement: 11 August 1986.
This regulation derived from SI 1955 No 990, regs 25, 30, 35 and SI 1978 No 1017, regs 48, 53, 57, 62, 70, 74, 79A, 80 (part).
Words in square brackets substituted by SI 1988 No 1871, reg 3.

9. Height

(1) The overall height of a bus shall not exceed 4.57 m.

(2) Save as provided in paragraph (3), no person shall use or cause or permit to be used on a road any semi-trailer if—

(a) any part of the structure of the vehicle is more than 4.2 m from the ground when the vehicle is on level ground; and
(b) the total laden weight of the semi-trailer and the vehicle by which it is drawn exceeds 32,520 kg.

(3) For the purpose of paragraph (2) the structure of a vehicle includes any detachable structure attached to the vehicle for the purpose of containing any load, but does not include any load which is not a detachable structure or any sheeting or other readily flexible means of covering or securing a load.

The provisions of paragraph (2) do not apply in respect of any vehicle while it is being loaded or unloaded.   **[1347]**

NOTES
Commencement: 11 August 1986.
This regulation derived from SI 1978 No 1017, regs 10, 95A.

10. Indication of overall travelling height

(1) This regulation applies to every motor vehicle which is—

    (a) constructed or adapted so as to be capable of hoisting and carrying a skip;

    (b) carrying a container;

    (c) drawing a trailer or semi-trailer carrying a container;

    (d) engineering plant;

    (e) carrying engineering equipment; or

    (f) drawing a trailer or semi-trailer carrying engineering equipment.

(2) No person shall use or cause or permit to be used on a road a vehicle to which this regulation applies if the overall travelling height exceeds 3.66 m unless there is carried in the vehicle in the manner specified in paragraph (3) a notice clearly indicating in feet and inches and in figures not less than 40 mm tall, the overall travelling height.

(3) The notice referred to in paragraph (2) shall be attached to the vehicle in such a manner that it can be read by the driver when in the driving position.

(4) In this regulation—

    . . .

"overall travelling height" means not less than and not above 25 mm more than the distance between the ground and the point on the motor vehicle, or on any trailer drawn by it, or on any load which is being carried by or any equipment which is fitted to the said motor vehicle or trailer, which is farthest from the ground, and for the purpose of determining the overall travelling height—

    (a) the tyres of the motor vehicle and of any trailer which it is drawing shall be suitably inflated for the use to which the vehicle or combination of vehicles is being put; and

    (b) the surface under the motor vehicle and any trailer which it is drawing and any load which is being carried on and any equipment which is fitted to any part of the said vehicle or combination of vehicles and which projects beyond any part of the said vehicle or combination of vehicles shall be reasonably flat; and

    (c) any equipment which is fitted to the motor vehicle or any trailer which it is drawing shall be stowed in the position in which it is to proceed on the road;

"skip" means an article of equipment designed and constructed to be carried on a road vehicle and to be placed on a road or other land for the storage of materials, or for the removal and disposal of rubble, waste, household or other rubbish or earth. **[1348]**

NOTES

Commencement: 11 August 1986.

This regulation derived from SI 1978 No 1017, reg 80A.

Para (4): words omitted revoked by SI 1990 No 317, reg 6.

11. Overhang

(1) The overhang of a wheeled vehicle of a class specified in an item in column 2 of the Table shall not, subject to any exemption specified in that item in column 4, exceed the distance specified in that item in column 3.

TABLE
(regulation 11(1))

1 Item	2 Class of vehicle	3 Maximum overhang	4 Exemptions
1	Motor tractor	1·83 m.	(a) a track-laying vehicle (b) an agricultural motor vehicle

2	Heavy motor car and motor car	60% of the distance between the transverse plane which passes through the centre or centres of the foremost wheel or wheels and the transverse plane which passes through the foremost point from which the overhang is to be measured as provided in regulation 3(2).	(a) a bus
			(b) a refuse vehicle
			(c) a works truck
			(d) a track-laying vehicle
			(e) an agricultural motor vehicle
			(f) a motor car which is an ambulance
			(g) a vehicle designed to dispose of its load to the rear, if the overhang does not exceed 1·15 m
			(h) a vehicle first used before 2nd January 1933
			(i) a vehicle first used before 1st January 1966 if—
			  (i) the distance between the centres of the rearmost and foremost axles does not exceed 2·29 m and
			  (ii) the distance specified in column 3 is not exceeded by more than 76 mm
			(j) heating plant on a vehicle designed and mainly used to heat the surface of a road or other similar surface in the process of construction, repair or main-tenance shall be disregarded.

(2) In the case of an agricultural motor vehicle the distance measured horizontally and parallel to the longitudinal axis of the rear portion of the vehicle between the transverse planes passing through the rearmost point of the vehicle and through the centre of the rear or the rearmost axle shall not exceed 3 m.   **[1349]**

NOTES
Commencement: 11 August 1986.
This regulation derived from SI 1978 No 1017, regs 54, 58, 63, 79B.

12. Minimum ground clearance

(1) Save as provided in paragraph (2), a wheeled trailer which is—

    (a) a goods vehicle; and
    (b) manufactured on or after 1st April 1984,

shall have a minimum ground clearance of not less than 160 mm if the trailer has an axle interspace of more than 6 m but less than 11.5 m, and a minimum ground clearance of not less than 190 mm if the trailer has an axle interspace of 11.5 m or more.

(2) Paragraph (1) shall not apply in the case of a trailer—

    (a) which is fitted with a suspension system with which, by the operation of a control, the trailer may be lowered or raised, while that system is being operated to enable the trailer to pass under a bridge or other obstruction over a road provided that at such times the system is operated so that no part of the trailer (excluding any wheel) touches the ground or is likely to do so; or
    (b) while it is being loaded or unloaded.

(3) In this regulation—

"axle interspace" means—

    (*a*) in the case of a semi-trailer, the distance between the point of support of the semi-trailer at its forward end and, if it has only one axle, the centre of that axle or, if it has more than one axle, the point halfway between the centres of the foremost and rearmost of those axles; and
    (*b*) in the case of any other trailer, the distance between the centre of its front axle or, if it has more than one axle at the front, the point halfway between the centres of the foremost and rearmost of those axles, and the centre of its rear axle or, if it has more than one axle at the rear, the point halfway between the centre of the foremost and rearmost of those axles; and

"ground clearance" means the shortest distance between the ground and the lowest part of that portion of the trailer (excluding any part of a suspension, steering or braking system attached to any axle, any wheel and trailer and the middle 70% of the axle interspace, such distance being ascertained when the trailer—

    (a) is fitted with suitable tyres which are inflated to a pressure recommended by the manufacturer, and

(b) is reasonably horizontal and standing on ground which is reasonably flat.   **[1350]**

NOTES
Commencement: 11 August 1986.
This regulation derived from SI 1978 No 1017, reg 74A.

13. [Turning circle - buses]

(1) This regulation applies to a bus first used on or after 1st April 1982.

(2) Every vehicle to which this regulation applies shall be able to move on either lock so that no part of it projects outside the area contained between concentric circles with radii of 12 m and 5.3 m.

(3) When a vehicle to which this regulation applies moves forward from rest, on either lock, so that its outermost point describes a circle of 12 m radius, no part of the vehicle shall project beyond the longitudinal plane which, at the beginning of the manoeuvre, defines the overall width of the vehicle on the side opposite to the direction in which it is turning by more than—

(a) 0.8 m if it is a rigid vehicle; or
(b) 1.2 m if it is an articulated bus.

(4) For the purpose of paragraph (3) the two rigid portions of an articulated bus shall be in line at the beginning of the manoeuvre.   **[1351]**

NOTES
Commencement: 11 August 1986.
This regulation derived from SI 1978 no 1017, reg 9A.
Heading: substituted by SI 1990 No 317, reg 5(1).

13A. Turning circle - articulated vehicles other than those incorporating a car transporter

[(1) Subject to paragraphs (2) and (3), this regulation applies to an articulated vehicle having an overall length exceeding 15.5 m.

(2) This regulation does not apply to an articlated vehicle, the semi-trailer of which—

(a) was manufactured before the 1st April 1990, [and]
(b) . . .
(c) has an overall length that does not exceed the overall length it had on that date.

(3) This regulation does not apply to an articulated vehicle the semi-trailer of which is—

(a) a car transporter,
(b) a low loader,
(c) a stepframe low loader, or
(d) constructed and normally used for the conveyance of indivisible loads of exceptional length.

(4) Every vehicle to which this regulation applies shall be able to move on either lock so that, disregarding the things set out in paragraph (i)(a) to (m) in the definition of "overall width" in the Table in regulation 3(2), no part of it projects outside the area contained between concentric circles with radii of 12.5 m and 5.3 m.]   **[1352]**

NOTES
Commencement: 19 March 1990.
Added by SI 1990 No 317, reg 5(2).
Para (2): word in square brackets added and sub-para (b) revoked by SI 1990 No 1163, reg 4.

13B. Turning circle - articulated vehicles incorporating a car transporter

[(1) Subject to paragraphs (2) and (3) this regulation applies to an articulated vehicle having an overall length exceeding 15.5 m the semi-trailer of which is a car transporter.

(2) This regulation does not apply to an articulated vehicle, the semi-trailer of which satisfied the following conditions—

(a) it was manufactured before the 1st April 1990, and
(b) the distance from the front of the trailer to the rearmost axle is no greater than it was on that date.

(3) This regulation does not apply to an articulated vehicle the semi-trailer of which is—

(a) a low loader, or
(b) a stepframe low loader.

(4) Every articulated vehicle to which this regulation applies shall be able to move on either lock so that, disregarding the things set out in paragraph (i)(a) to (m) in the definition of "overall width" in the Table in regulation 3(2), no part of—

(a) the motor vehicle drawing the car transporter, or
(b) the car transporter to the rear of the transverse plane passing through the king pin,

projects outside the area between concentric circles with radii of 12.5 m and 5.3 m]. **[1353]**

NOTES
Commencement: 19 March 1990.
Added by SI 1990 No 317, reg 5(2).

14. Connecting sections and direction - holding of articulated buses

(1) This regulation applies to every articulated bus first used on or after 1st April 1982.

(2) The connecting section of the two parts of every articulated bus to which this regulation applies shall be constructed so as comply with the provisions relating to such a section specified in paragraph 5.9 in ECE Regulation 36 as regards vehicles within the scope of that Regulation.

(3) Every articulated bus to which this regulation applies shall be constructed so that when the vehicle is moving in a straight line the longitudinal median planes of its two parts coincide and form a continuous plane without any deflection. **[1354]**

NOTES
Commencement: 11 August 1986.
This regulation derived from SI 1978 No 1017, reg 9B.
ECE Regulation 36: See reg 3, Sch 2.

B - Brakes

15. Braking systems of certain vehicles first used on or after 1st April 1983

(1) Save as provided in paragraph (2), (3) [except sub-paragraph (b)(ii)] and (4), the braking system of every wheeled vehicle of a class specified in an item in column 2 of the Table which [in the case of a motor vehicle] is first used on or after 1st April 1983 [or which, in the case of a trailer, is manufactured on or after 1st October 1982,] shall comply with the construction, fitting, and performance requirements specified in Annexes I, II and VII to Community Directive 79/489, and if relevant, Annexes III, IV, V, VI and VIII to that Directive, in relation to the category of vehicles specified in that item in column 3.

Provided that it shall be lawful for any vehicle of such a class which, in the case of a motor vehicle, was first used before 1st April 1983 or, in the case of a trailer, was manufactured before 1st October 1982 to comply with the said requirements instead of complying with regulations 16 and 17.

TABLE

(regulation 15(1))

1	2	3
Item	Class of Vehicle	Vehicle Category in the Community Directive
1	Passenger vehicles and dual-purpose vehicles which have 3 or more wheels except— (a) dual-purpose vehicles constructed and adapted to carry not more than 2 passengers exclusive of the driver; (b) motor-cycles with side-car attached; [(c) vehicles with three wheels, an unladen weight not exceeding 410 kg, a maximum design speed not exceeding 50 km/h and an engine capacity not exceeding 50 cc;] (d) buses.	M1
2	Buses having a maximum gross weight which does not exceed 5000 kg.	M2
3	Buses having a maximum gross weight which exceeds 5000 kg.	M3
4	Dual-purpose vehicles not within item 1; and goods vehicles, having a maximum gross weight which does not exceed 3500 kg, and not being motorcycles with a sidecar attached.	N1

1	2	3
Item	Class of Vehicle	Vehicle Category in the Community Directive
5 6	Goods vehicles with a maximum gross weight which— exceeds 3500 kg but does not exceed 12,000 kg. exceeds 12,000 kg.	N2 N3
7 8 9 10	[Trailers with a maximum total design axle weight which—] does not exceed 750 kg. exceeds 750 kg but does not exceed 3500 kg. exceeds 3500 kg but does not exceed 10,000 kg. exceeds 10,000 kg.	O1 O2 O3 O4

[(1A) Save as provided in paragraphs (2), (3)(b) and (c), (3A) and (5), the braking system of every wheeled vehicle of a class specified in an item in column 2 of the Table which [in the case of a motor vehicle] is first used on or after the relevant date [or which, in the case of a trailer, is manufactured on or after the relevant date] shall comply with the construction, fitting and performance requirements specified in Annexes I, II and VII to Community Directive 85/647, and if relevant, Annexes III, IV, V, VI, VIII, X, XI and XII to that Directive, in relation to the category of vehicles specified in that item in column 3.

Provided that it shall be lawful for any vehicle of such a class which, in the case of a motor vehicle, was first used before the relevant date or which, in the case of a trailer, was manufactured before the relevant date, to comply with the said requirements instead of complying with paragraph (1), or with regulations 16 and 17.

(1B) In paragraph (1A), the relevant date in relation to a vehicle of a class specified in item 1 or 2 of the Table is 1st April 1990, in relation to a vehicle specified in item 4 of that Table is 1st April 1992, in relation to a vehicle in items 7, 8, 9 or 10 of that Table is 1st October 1988 and in relation to a vehicle of any other class is 1st April 1989.

(1C) Save as provided in paragraphs (2), (3)(b) and (c), (3A) and (5), the braking system of every wheeled vehicle of a class specified in an item in column 2 of the Table which in the case of a motor vehicle is first used on or after 1st April 1992 or in the case of a trailer is manufactured on or after 1st October 1991 shall comply with the construction, fitting and performance requirements specified in Annexes I, II and VII to Community Directive 88/194, and if relevant, Annexes III, IV, V, VI, VII, X, XI, and XII to that Directive, in relation to the category of vehicles specified in that item in column 3.

Provided that it shall be lawful for any vehicle of such a class which, in the case of a motor vehicle was first used before 1st April 1992 or which, in the case of a trailer, was manufactured before 1st October 1991, to comply with the said requirements instead of complying with paragraph (1) or (1A), or with regulations 16 and 17.]

(2) The requirements specified in [paragraphs (1), (1A) and (1C)] do not apply to—

(a) an agricultural trailer or agricultural trailed appliance that is not, in either case, drawn at a speed exceeding 20 mph;
(b) a locomotive;
(c) a motor tractor;
(d) an agricultural motor vehicle unless it is first used after 1st June 1986 and is driven at more than 20 mph;
(e) a vehicle which has a maximum speed not exceeding 25 km/h;
(f) a works trailer;
(g) a works truck;
(h) a public works vehicle;
(i) a trailer designed and constructed, or adapted, to be drawn exclusively by a vehicle to which sub-paragraph (b), (c), (e), (g), or (h) of this paragraph applies;
(j) a trailer mentioned in regulation 16(3)(b), (d), (e), (f) and (g); or
(k) a vehicle manufactured by Leyland Vehicles Limited and known as the Atlantean Bus, if first used before 1st October 1984.

(3) The requirements specified in [paragraphs (1), (1A) and (1C)] shall apply to the classes of vehicles specified in the Table so that—

(a) in item 3, the testing requirement specified in paragraph 1.5.1 and 1.5.2 of Annex II to Community Directives 79/489, 85/647 and 88/194 shall apply to every vehicle specified in that item other than—

(i) a double-decked vehicle first used before 1st October 1983; or
(ii) a vehicle of a type in respect of which a member state of the European Economic Community has issued a type approval certificate in accordance with Community Directive 79/489, 85/647 or 88/194.

[(b) in items 2 and 3—

(i) the requirements specified in paragraph 1.1.4.2 of Annex II to Community Directive 79/489; and
(ii) sub-note (2) to paragraph 1.17.2 of Annex I to Community Directive 85/647 [or 88/194],

shall not apply:]

(c) in items 1, 2, 3, 4, 5 and 6, in the case of vehicles constructed or adapted for use by physically handicapped drivers, the requirement in paragraph 2.1.2.1 of Annex I to [Community Directive 79/489] that the driver must be able to achieve the braking action mentioned in that paragraph from his driving seat without removing his hands from the steering control shall be modified so as to require that the driver is able to achieve that action while [continuing to steer the vehicle]; and

(d) in items 1, 4, 5, 6, 7, 8, 9 and 10 the requirement specified in paragraph 1.1.4.2 of Annex II to [Community Directive 79/489] shall not apply to a vehicle [first used (in the case of a motor vehicle) or manufactured (in the case of a trailer) before the relevant date as defined in paragraph (1B)] if either—

(i) following a test in respect of which the fee numbered [26024/26250 to 26257, prescribed in Schedule 1 to the Motor Vehicles (Type Approval and Approval Marks) (Fees) Regulations 1990 is payable], a document is issued by the Secretary of State indicating that, at the date of manufacture of the vehicle, the type to which it belongs complies with the requirements specified in Annex 13 to ECE Regulation 13.03, 13.04[, 13.05 or 13.06]; or

(ii) as a result of a notifiable alteration to the vehicle, within the meaning of regulation 3 of the Plating and Testing Regulations, a fitment has been approved as complying with the requirements mentioned in sub-paragraph (i).

(3A) The requirements specified in paragraph (1A) shall apply to a road tanker subject to the exclusion of paragraph 4.3 of Annex X to Community Directive 85/647.]

[(4) Instead of complying with paragraph (1) of this regulation, a vehicle to which this regulation applies may comply with ECE Regulation 13.03, 13.04[, 13.05 or 13.06].

[(5) Instead of complying with paragraph (1A) of this regulation, a vehicle to which this regulation applies may comply with ECE Regulation 13.05 or 13.06.

(5A) Instead of complying with paragraph (1C) of this regulation, a vehicle to which this regulation applies may comply—

(a) in the case of a trailer manufactured before the 1st April 1992, with ECE Regulation 13.05 or 13.06; or

(b) in the case of any vehicle not falling within sub-paragraph (a), with ECE Regulation 13.06.]]

(6) In paragraph (3A) the expression "road tanker" means any vehicle or trailer which carries liquid fuel in a tank forming part of the vehicle or trailer other than that containing the fuel which is used to propel the vehicle, and also includes any tank with a capacity exceeding 3m³ carried on a vehicle.

(7) In this regulation, and in relation to the application to any vehicle of any provision of Community Directive 85/647 [or 88/194], the definitions of "semi-trailer", "full trailer" and "centre-axle trailer" set out in that Directive shall apply and the meaning of "semi-trailer" in column 2 of the Table in regulation 3(2) shall not apply.]   **[1355]**

NOTES

Commencement: 1 April 1992 (paras (5), (5A): 2 November 1990 (paras 1B, 1C, 4); 6 May 1987 (paras (1A), (1B), (3A), (6), (7)); 11 August 1986 (remainder).

This regulation derived from SI 1978 No 1017, reg 14A.

Paras (1A), (3A), (6)-(7): added by SI 1987 No 676, reg 7. Paras (1B) and (1C) were added by SI 1990 No 1981, reg 4.

Paras (1), (2), (3), (4) and Table: words in square brackets substituted or added by SI 1987 No 676, reg 7, SI 1990 No 1981, reg 4, and SI 1992 No 352, reg 3(1)–(3).

Paras (4) and (5) were substituted by SI 1990 No 1981, reg 4. Paras (5), (5A) substituted for para (5) (as substituted as noted ante) by SI 1992 No 352, reg 3(1), (4).

Community Directive 79/489: see reg 3, Sch 2.

ECE Regulation 13: see reg 3, Sch 2.

The Plating and Testing Regulations: SI 1982 No 1478 (revoked: see now SI 1988 No 1478 post).

16. Braking systems of vehicles to which regulation 15 does not apply

(1) Save as provided in paragraphs (2) and (3), this regulation applies to every vehicle to which regulation 15 does not apply.

(2) Paragraph (4) of this regulation does not apply to a vehicle which

complies with regulation 15 by virtue of the proviso to [regulation 15(1), (1A) or (1C), or which complies with Community Directive 79/489, 85/647 or 88/194 or ECE Regulation 13.03, 13.04, 13.05 or 13.06].

(3) This regulation does not apply to the following vehicles, except in the case of a vehicle referred to in (a) insofar as the regulation concerns parking brakes (requirements 16 to 18 in Schedule 3)—

(a) a locomotive first used before 2nd January 1933, propelled by steam, and with an engine which is capable of being reversed;
(b) a trailer which—

    (i) is designed for use and used for street cleansing and does not carry any load other than its necessary gear and equipment;
    (ii) [has a maximum total design axle weight that does not exceed 750 kg];
    (iii) is an agricultural trailer manufactured before 1st July 1947 drawn by a motor tractor or an agricultural motor vehicle if the trailer—

        (*A*) has a laden weight not exceeding 4070 kg; and
        (B) is the only trailer being drawn; and
        (C) is drawn at a speed not exceeding 10 mph; or

    (iv) is drawn by a motor cycle in accordance with regulation 84;

(c) an agricultural trailed appliance;
(d) an agricultural trailed appliance conveyor;
(e) a broken down vehicle;
(f) before 1st October 1986—

    (i) a trailer with an unladen weight not exceeding 102 kg which was manufactured before 1st October 1982; and
    (ii) a gritting trailer; or

(g) on or after 1st October 1986, a gritting trailer with a maximum gross weight not exceeding 2000 kg.

(4) Save as provided in paragraph (7), a vehicle of a class specified in an item in column 2 of the Table shall comply with the requirements shown in column 3 in that item, subject to any exemptions or modifications shown in column 4 in that item, reference to numbers in column 3 being references to the requirements so numbered in Schedule 3.

TABLE

(regulation 16(4))

1	2	3	4
Item	Class of vehicle	Requirements in Schedule 3	Exemptions or modifications
1	*Motor cars* First used before 1st January 1915.	3, 6, 7, 13, 16	Requirements 13 and 16 do not apply to a motor car with less than 4 wheels.

1	2	3	4
Item	Class of vehicle	Requirements in Schedule 3	Exemptions or modifications
2	First used on or after 1st January 1915 but before 1st April 1938.	1, 4, 6, 7, 9, 16	A works truck within items 1 to 11 is not subject to requirements 1, 2, 3 or 4 if it is equipped with one braking system with one means of operation.
3	First used on or after 1st April 1938 and being either a track-laying vehicle or a vehicle first used before 1st January 1968.	1, 4, 6, 7, 8, 9, 16	
4	Wheeled vehicles first used on or after 1st January 1968.	1, 4, 6, 7, 8, 9, [15], 18	
5	*Heavy motor cars* First used before 15th August 1928.	1, 6, 16	
6	First used on or after 15th August 1928 but before 1st April 1938.	1, 4, 6, 7, 8, 16	
7	First used on or after 1st April 1938 and being either a track-laying vehicle or a vehicle first used before 1st January 1968.	1, 4, 6, 7, 8, 9, 16	
8	Wheeled vehicles first used on or after 1st January 1968.	1, 4, 6, 7, 8, 9, [15], 18	
9	*Motor cycles* First used before 1st January 1927.	3, and, in the case of three-wheeled vehicles, 16	
10	First used on or after 1st January 1927 but before 1st January 1968.	2, 7, and, in the case of three-wheeled vehicles, 16	
11	First used on or after 1st January 1968 and not being a motor cycle to which paragraph (5) applies.	2, 7, and, in the case of three-wheeled vehicles, 18	
12	*Locomotives* Wheeled vehicles first used before 1st June 1955.	3, 6, 12, 16	

1	2	3	4
Item	Class of vehicle	Requirements in Schedule 3	Exemptions or modifications
13	Wheeled vehicles first used on or after 1st June 1955 but before 1st January 1968.	3, 4, 6, 7, 8, 9, 18	
14	Wheeled vehicles first used on or after 1st January 1968.	3, 4, 6, 7, 8, 9, 18	
15	Track-laying vehicles.	3, 6, 16	
16	*Motor tractors* Wheeled vehicles first used before 14th January 1931 and track-laying vehicles first used before 1st April 1938.	3, 4, 6, 7, 16	Industrial tractors within items 16 to 19 are subject to requirement 5 instead of requirement 4.
17	Wheeled vehicles first used on or after 14th January 1931 but before 1st April 1938.	3, 4, 6, 7, 9, 16	
18	Wheeled vehicles first used on or after 1st April 1938 but before 1st January 1968.	3, 4, 6, 7, 8, 9, 16	
19	Wheeled vehicles first used on or after 1st January 1968.	3, 4, 6, 7, 8, 9, 18	
20	Track-laying vehicles first used on or after 1st April 1938.	3, 4, 6, 7, 8, 16	
21	*Wheeled agricultural motor vehicles not driven at more than 20 mph* First used before 1st January 1968.	3, 4, 6, 7, 8, 16	
22	First used on or after 1st January 1968 but before 9th February 1980.	3, 4, 6, 7, 8, 18	
23	First used on or after 9th February 1980.	3, 5, 6, 7, 8, 18	
24	*Invalid carriages* Whenever first used	3, 13	
25	*Trailers* Manufactured before 1st April 1938	3, 10, 14, 17	
26	Manufactured on or after 1st April 1938 and being either a track-laying vehicle, an agricultural trailer or a vehicle manufactured before 1st January 1968.	3, 8, 10, 14, 17	Agricultural trailers are not subject to requirement 8.

1	2	3	4
Item	Class of vehicle	Requirements in Schedule 3	Exemptions or modifications
27	Wheeled vehicles manufactured on or after 1st January 1968, not being an agricultural trailer.	3, 4, 8, 11, 15, 18	Trailers equipped with brakes which come into operation on the overrun of the vehicle are not subject to requirement 15.

Provided that wheeled agricultural motor vehicles not driven at more than 20 mph are excluded from all items other than items 21 to 23.

[(5) Subject to paragraphs (5B) and (6), the braking system of a motor cycle to which this regulation applies and which is–

    (a) of a class specified in an item in column 2 of the Table below; and
    (b) first used on or after 1st April 1987 and before 22nd May 1995;

shall comply with ECE Regulation 13.05, 78 or 78.01 in relation to the category of vehicles specified in that item in column 3.

(5A) Subject to paragraph (6), the braking system of a motor cycle to which this regulation applies and which is—

    (a) of a class specified in an item in column 2 of the Table below; and
    (b) first used on or after 22nd May 1995;

shall comply with ECE Regulation 78.01 in relation to the category of vehicles specified in that item in column 3.

TABLE

(Regulation 16(5) and (5A))

1 *Item*	2 *Class of Vehicle*	3 *Vehicle Category in ECE Regulations*
1	Vehicles (without a sidecar attached) with two wheels, an engine capacity not exceeding 50 cc and a maximum design speed not exceeding 50 km/h.	L1
2	Vehicles with three wheels (including two-wheeled vehicles with a sidecar attached) and with an engine capacity not exceeding 50 cc and a maximum design speed not exceeding 50 km/h.	L2

1 *Item*	2 *Class of Vehicle*	3 *Vehicle Category in ECE Regulations*
3	Vehicles with two wheels (without a sidecar attached) and with–	L3
	(a) an engine capacity exceeding 50 cc, or (b) a maximum design speed exceeding 50 km/h.	
4	Vehicles with two wheels, a sidecar attached and—	L4]
	(a) an engine capacity exceeding 50 cc, or (b) a maximum design speed exceeding 50 km/h.	

[[(5B)] In relation to a motor cycle with two wheels manufactured by Piaggio Veicoli Europei Societa per Azione and known as the Cosa 125, the Cosa 125E, the Cosa L125, the Cosa LX125, the Cosa 200, the Cosa 200E, the Cosa L200 or the Cosa LX200, paragraph (5) shall have effect as if ECE Regulation 13.05 were modified by—

(a) the omission of paragraph 4.4 (approval marks), and
(b) in paragraph 5.3.1.1 (independent braking devices and controls), the omission of the word "independent" in the first place where it appears,

but this paragraph shall not apply to a motor cycle first used on or after 1st July 1991.]

(6) Paragraph (5) does not apply to a works truck or to a vehicle constructed or assembled by a person not ordinarily engaged in the business of manufacturing vehicles of that description.

(7) Instead of complying with the provisions of paragraph (4) of this Regulation an agricultural motor vehicle may comply with Community Directive 76/432.   **[1356]**

NOTES
Commencement: 1 April 1992 (paras (5), (5A)); 2 November 1990 (para (5B)); 11 August 1986 (remainder).
This regulation with Sch 3 derived from SI 1955 No 990, regs 8, 28, 29, 30, and SI 1978 No 1017, regs 13, 50, 51, 55, 59, 64, 67, 71, 75, 76, 79C, Sch 4A.
Para (2): words in square brackets substituted by SI 1992 No 352, reg 4(1), (2).
Para (3) and Table to para (4): amended by SI 1990 No 1981, reg 5.
Paras (5), (5A) and Table thereto: substituted for original para (5) by SI 1992 No 352, reg 4(1), (3).
Para (5B) inserted as para (5A) by SI 1990 No 1981, reg 5, and renumbered as para (5B) by SI 1992 No 352, reg (4).
Community Directives 76/432, 79/489, 85/647, 88/194: see reg 3, Sch 2.
ECE Regulations 13, 78: see reg 3, Sch 2.

17. Vacuum or pressure brake warning devices

(1) Save as provided in paragraph (2), every motor vehicle which is equipped with a braking system which embodies a vacuum or pressure reservoir or reservoirs shall be equipped with a device so placed as to be readily visible to the driver of the vehicle and which is capable of indicating any impending failure of, or deficiency in, the vacuum or pressure system.

(2) The requirement specified in paragraph (1) does not apply in respect of—

    (a) a vehicle to which [paragraph (1), (1A) or (1C)] of] regulation 15 applies, or which complies with the requirements of that regulation, of [Community Directive 79/489, 85/647 or 88/194] or of ECE Regulation 13.03, 13.04 or[, 13.05 or 13.06];

    (b) an agricultural motor vehicle which complies with Community Directive 76/432;

    (c) a vehicle with an unladen weight not exceeding 3050 kg propelled by an internal combustion engine, if the vacuum in the reservoir or reservoirs is derived directly from the induction system of the engine, and if, in the event of a failure of, or deficiency in, the vacuum system, the brakes of that braking system are sufficient under the most adverse conditions to bring the vehicle to rest within a reasonable distance; or

    (d) a vehicle first used before 1st October 1937.   **[1357]**

NOTES
    Commencement: 11 August 1986.
    This regulation derived from SI 1955 No 990, reg 10, and SI 1978 No 1017, reg 14.
    Para (2): amended by SI 1990 No 1981, reg 6, and SI 1992 No 352, reg 5.
    Community Directives 76/432, 79/489: see reg 3.
    ECE Regulation 13: see reg 3, Sch 2.

18. Maintenance and efficiency of brakes

(1) Every part of every braking system and of the means of operation thereof fitted to a vehicle shall be maintained in good and efficient working order and be properly adjusted.

[(1A) Without prejudice to paragraph (3), where a vehicle is fitted with an anti-lock braking system ("the ABS"), then while the condition specified in paragraph (1B) is fulfilled, any fault in the ABS shall be disregarded for the purposes of paragraph (1).

(1B) The condition is fulfilled while then vehicle is completing a journey at the beginning of which the ABS was operating correctly or is being driven to a place where the ABS is to undergo repairs.]

(2) Paragraph (3) applies to every wheeled motor vehicle except—

    (a) an agricultural motor vehicle which is not driven at more than 20 mph;

    (b) a works truck; and

    (c) a pedestrian-controlled vehicle.

(3) Every vehicle to which this paragraph applies and which is of a class specified in an item in column 2 of Table I shall, subject to any exemption shown for that item in column 4, be so maintained that—

    (a) its service braking system has a total braking efficiency not less than that shown in column 3(a) for that item; and

    (b) if the vehicle is a heavy motor car, a motor car first used on or after 1st January 1915 or a motor-cycle first used on or after 1st January 1927, its secondary braking system has a total braking efficiency not less than that shown in column 3(b) for those items.

Provided that a reference in Table I to a trailer is a reference to a trailer required by regulation 15 or 16 to be equipped with brakes.

TABLE I

(regulation 18(3))

1	2	3		4
Item	Class of vehicle	Efficiencies (%) (a)	(b)	Exemptions
1	A vehicle to which regulation 15 applies or which complies in all respects other than its braking efficiency with the requirements of that regulation or with [Community Directive 79/489, 85/647 or 88/194] or with ECE Regulation 13.03, 13.04[, 13.05 or 13.06] (a) when not drawing a trailer; (b) when drawing a trailer	50 45	25 25	A motor cycle
2	A vehicle not included in item 1 and not being a motor cycle, which is first used on or after 1st January 1968— (a) when not drawing a trailer; (b) when drawing a trailer manufactured on or after 1st January 1968; (c) when drawing a trailer manufactured before 1st January 1968	50 50 40	25 25 15	
3	Goods vehicles first used on or after 15th August 1928 but before 1st January 1968 having an unladen weight exceeding 1525 kg being— (a) rigid vehicles with 2 axles not constructed to form part of an articulated vehicle— (i) when not drawing a trailer (ii) when drawing a trailer (b) other vehicles, including vehicles constructed to form part of an articulated vehicle, whether or not drawing a trailer.	45 40 40	20 15 15	

1	2	3		4
Item	Class of vehicle	Efficiencies (%) (a)	(b)	Exemptions
4	Vehicles not included in items 1 to 3—			(a) a bus;
	(a) having at least one means of operation applying to at least 4 wheels;	50	25	(b) an articulated vehicle;
	(b) having 3 wheels and at least one means of operation applying to all 3 wheels and not being a motor cycle with sidecar attached—			(c) a vehicle constructed or adapted to form part of an articulated vehicle;
	(i) when not drawing a trailer	40	25	(d) a heavy motor car which is a
	(ii) in the case of a motor cycle when drawing a trailer	40	25	goods vehicle first used before 15th August 1928.
	(c) other			
	(i) when not drawing a trailer	30	25	
	(ii) in the case of a motor cycle when drawing a trailer.	30	25	

(4) A goods vehicle shall not be deemed to comply with the requirements of paragraph (3) unless it is capable of complying with those requirements both at the laden weight at which it is operating at any time and when its laden weight is equal to—

(a) if a plating certificate has been issued and is in force for the vehicle, the design gross weight shown in column (3) of that certificate or, if no such weight is so shown, the gross weight shown in column (2) of that certificate; and

(b) in any other case, the design gross weight of the vehicle.

Provided that in the case of a goods vehicle drawing a trailer, references in this paragraph to laden weight refer to the combined laden weight of the drawing vehicle and the trailer and references to gross weight and design gross weight are to be taken as references to train weight and design train weight respectively.

(5) The brakes of every agricultural motor vehicle which is first used on or after 1st June 1986 and is not driven at more than 20 mph, and of every agricultural trailer manufactured on or after 1st December 1985 shall be capable of achieving a braking efficiency of not less than 25% when the weight of the vehicle is equal to the total maximum axle weights which the vehicle is designed to have.

(6) Every vehicle or combination of vehicles specified in an item in column 2 of Table II shall be so maintained that its brakes are capable, without the

assistance of stored energy, of holding it stationary on a gradient of at least the percentage specified in column 3 in that item.

TABLE II

(regulation 18(6))

1	2	3
Item	Class of vehicle or combination	Percentage gradient
1	A vehicle specified in item 1 of Table I— (a) when not drawing a trailer (b) when drawing a trailer	16 12
2	A vehicle to which requirement 18 in Schedule 3 applies by virtue of regulation 16.	16
3	A vehicle, not included in item 1, drawing a trailer manufactured on or after 1st January 1968 and required, by regulation 15 or 16, to be fitted with brakes.	16

(7) For the purpose of this regulation the date of manufacture of a trailer which is a composite trailer shall be deemed to be the same as the date of manufacture of the semi-trailer which forms part of the composite trailer.

(8) A vehicle which is subject to, and which complies with the requirements in, item 1 in Tables I and II shall not be treated as failing, by reason of its braking efficiency, to comply with regulation 15 or with [Community Directive 79/489, 85/647 or 88/194] or ECE Regulation 13.03, 13.04[, 13.05 or 13.06].

[1358]

NOTES
   Commencement: 1 April 1992 (paras (1A), (1B)); 11 August 1986 (remainder).
   This regulation derived from SI 1955 No 990, reg 54, and SI 1978 No 1017, regs 59(4)-(7), 64(4)-(7), 67(3), 75(4A), 79C(2), 101, 101A, 152, 153, Sch 4.
   Paras (1A), (1B) inserted by SI 1992 No 352, reg 6(1), (2).
   Table I and para (8): amended by SI 1990 No 1981, reg 6, and SI 1992 No 352, reg 6(1), (3).
   Community Directives 79/489, 85/647, 88/194: see reg 3, Sch 2.
   ECE Regulation 13: see reg 3, Sch 2.

19. Application of brakes of trailers

Where a trailer is drawn by a motor vehicle the driver (or in the case of a locomotive one of the persons employed in driving or tending the locomotive) shall be in a position readily to operate any brakes required by these Regulations to be fitted to the trailer as well as the brakes of the motor vehicle unless a person other than the driver [(or in the case of a locomotive a person other than one of the persons employed in driving or tending the locomotive)] is in a position and competent efficiently to apply the brakes of the trailer.

Provided that this regulation shall not apply to a trailer which—

(a) in compliance with these Regulations, is fitted with brakes which automatically come into operation on the overrun of the trailer; or
(b) is a broken down vehicle being drawn, whether or not in consequence of a breakdown, in such a manner that it cannot be steered by its own steering gear.   **[1359]**

NOTES
Commencement: 11 August 1986.
This regulation derived from SI 1955 No 990, reg 70, and SI 1978 No 1017, reg 126.
Amended by SI 1990 No 1981, reg 12.

C - Wheels, Springs, Tyres and Tracks

20. General requirement as to wheels and tracks

Every motor cycle and invalid carriage shall be a wheeled vehicle, and every other motor vehicle and every trailer shall be either a wheeled vehicle or a track-laying vehicle. **[1360]**

NOTES
Commencement: 11 August 1986.
This regulation derived from SI 1978 No 1017, reg 8.

21. Diameter of wheels

All wheels of a wheeled vehicle which are fitted with tyres other than pneumatic tyres shall have a rim diameter of not less than 670 mm.

Provided that this regulation does not apply to—
- (a) a motor vehicle first used on or before 2nd January 1933;
- (b) a trailer manufactured before 1st January 1933;
- (c) a wheel fitted to a motor car first used on or before 1st July 1936, if the diameter of the wheel inclusive of the tyre is not less than 670 mm;
- (d) a works truck or works trailer;
- (e) a refuse vehicle;
- (f) a pedestrian-controlled vehicle;
- (g) a mobile crane;
- (h) an agricultural trailed appliance;
- (i) a broken down vehicle which is being drawn by a motor vehicle in consequence of the breakdown; or
- (j) an electrically propelled goods vehicle the unladen weight of which does not exceed 1270 kg. **[1361]**

NOTES
Commencement: 11 August 1986.
This regulation derived from SI 1978 No 1017, reg 20.

22. Springs and resilient material

(1) Save as provided in paragraphs (3) and (4), every motor vehicle and every trailer shall be equipped with suitable and sufficient springs between each wheel and the frame of the vehicle.

(2) Save as provided in paragraphs (3) and (4), in the case of a track-laying vehicle—
- (a) resilient material shall be interposed between the rims of the weight-carrying rollers and the road surface so that the weight of the vehicle, other than that borne by any wheel, is supported by the resilient material; and
- (b) where the vehicle is a heavy motor car, motor car, or trailer it shall have suitable springs between the frame of the vehicle and the weight-carrying rollers.

(3) This regulation does not apply to—

    (a) a wheeled vehicle with an unladen weight not exceeding 4070 kg and which is—

        (i) a motor tractor any unsprung wheel of which is fitted with a pneumatic tyre;

       (ii) a motor tractor used in connection with railway shunting and which is used on a road only when passing from one railway track to another in connection with such use;

      (iii) a vehicle specially designed, and mainly used, for work on rough ground or unmade roads and every wheel of which is fitted with a pneumatic tyre and which is not driven at more than 20 mph;

      (iv) a vehicle constructed or adapted for, and being used for, road sweeping and every wheel of which is fitted with either a pneumatic tyre or a resilient tyre and which is not driven at more than 20 mph;

    (b) an agricultural motor vehicle which is not driven at more than 20 mph;

    (c) an agricultural trailer, or an agricultural trailed appliance;

    (d) a trailer used solely for the haulage of felled trees;

    (e) a motor cycle;

    (f) a mobile crane;

    (g) a pedestrian-controlled vehicle all the wheels of which are equipped with pneumatic tyres;

    (h) a road roller;

    (i) a broken down vehicle; or

    (j) a vehicle first used on or before 1st January 1932.

    (4) Paragraphs (1) and (2)(b) do not apply to a works truck or a works trailer. **[1362]**

NOTES
Commencement: 11 August 1986.
This regulation derived from SI 1955 No 990, reg 7, and SI 1978 No 1017, reg 12.

23. Wheel loads

(1) Subject to paragraph (2) this regulation applies to—

    (a) a semi-trailer with more than 2 wheels;

    (b) a track-laying vehicle with more than 2 wheels; and

    (c) any other vehicle with more than 4 wheels.

    (2) This regulation does not apply to a road roller.

    (3) Save as provided in paragraphs (4) and (5), every vehicle to which this regulation applies shall be fitted with a compensating arrangement which will ensure that under the most adverse conditions every wheel will remain in contact with the road and will not be subject to abnormal variations of load.

    (4) Paragraph (3) does not apply in respect of a steerable wheel on which the load does not exceed—

    (a) if it is a wheeled vehicle, 3560 kg; and

    (b) if it is a track-laying vehicle, 2540 kg.

    (5) In the application of paragraph (3) to an agricultural motor vehicle, wheels which are in line transversely on one side of the longitudinal axis of the vehicle shall be regarded as one wheel. **[1363]**

NOTES
Commencement: 11 August 1986.
This regulation derived from SI 1955 No 990, reg 6, and SI 1978 No 1017, reg 11.

24. Tyres

(1) Save as provided in paragraph (2), every wheel of a vehicle of a class specified in an item in column 2 of the Table shall be fitted with a tyre of a type specified in that item in column 3 which complies with any conditions specified in that item in column 4.

(2) The requirements referred to in paragraph (1) do not apply to a road roller and are subject, in the case of any item in the Table, to the exemptions specified in that item in column 5.

TABLE

(regulation 24(1))

1	2	3	4	5
Item	Class of vehicle	Type of tyre	Conditions	Exemptions
1	Locomotives not falling in item 6	Pneumatic or resilient		
2	Motor tractors not falling in item 6	Pneumatic or resilient	No re-cut pneumatic tyre shall be fitted to any wheel of a vehicle with an unladen weight of less than 2540 kg unless the diameter of the rim of the wheel is at least 405 mm	
3	Heavy motor cars not falling in item 6	Pneumatic		The following, if every wheel not fitted with a pneumatic tyre is fitted with a resilient tyre— (a) a vehicle mainly used for work on rough ground; (b) a tower wagon; (c) a vehicle fitted with a turntable fire escape; (d) a refuse vehicle; (e) a works truck; (f) a vehicle first used before 3rd January 1933.
4	Motor cars not falling in item 6	Pneumatic	No re-cut tyre shall be fitted to any wheel of a vehicle unless it is— (a) an electrically propelled goods vehicle or,	The following, if every wheel not fitted with a pneumatic tyre is fitted with a resilient tyre— (a) a vehicle mainly used for work on rough ground;

1	2	3	4	5
Item	Class of vehicle	Type of tyre	Conditions	Exemptions
			(b) a goods vehicle with an unladen weight of at least 2540 kg and the diameter of the rim of the wheel is at least 405 mm	(b) a refuse vehicle; (c) a works truck; (d) a vehicle with an unladen weight not exeeding— (i) 1270 kg if electrically propelled; (ii) 1020 kg in any other case; (e) a tower wagon; (f) a vehicle fitted with a turntable fire escape; (g) a vehicle first used before 3rd January 1933.
5	Motor cycles	Pneumatic	No re-cut tyre shall be fitted	The following, if every wheel not fitted with a pneumatic tyre is fitted with a resilient tyre— (a) a works truck; (b) a pedestrian-controlled vehicle
6	Agricultural motor vehicles which are not driven at more than 20 mph	Pneumatic or resilient	The same as for item 2	The requirement in column 3 does not apply to a vehicle of which— (a) every steering wheel is fitted with a smooth-soled tyre which is not less than 60 mm wide where it touches the road; and (b) in the case of a wheeled vehicle, every driving wheel is fitted with a smooth-soled tyre which— (i) is not less than 150 mm wide if the unladen weight of the vehicle exceeds 3050 kg, or 76 mm wide in any other case, and either (ii) is shod with diagonal crossbars not less than 76 mm wide or more than 20 mm thick extending the full breadth of the tyre and so arranged that the space between adjacent bars is not more than 76 mm; or (iii) is shod with diagonal cross-bars of resilient material not less than 60 mm wide extending the full breadth of the tyre and so arranged that the space between adjacent bars is not more than 76 mm

1	2	3	4	5
Item	Class of vehicle	Type of tyre	Conditions	Exemptions
7	Trailers	Pneumatic	Except in the case of a trailer mentioned in paragraph (*d*) of column 5, no recut tyre shall be fitted to any wheel of a trailer drawn by a heavy motor car or a motor car if the trailer— (a) has an unladen weight not exceeding— (i) if it is a living van, 2040 kg; or (ii) in any other case, 1020 kg; or (b) is not constructed or adapted to carry any load, other than plant or other special appliance which is a permanent or essentially permanent fixture and has a gross weight not exceeding 2290 kg	(a) an agricultural trailer manufactured before 1st December 1985; (b) an agricultural trailed appliance; (c) a trailer used to carry water for a road roller being used in connection with road works; (*d*) the following if every wheel which is pneumatic tyre is fitted with a resilient tyre— (i) a works trailer; (ii) a refuse vehicle; (iii) a trailer drawn by a heavy motor car every wheel of which is not required to be fitted with a pneumatic tyre; (iv) a broken down vehicle; or (v) a trailer drawn by a vehicle which is not a heavy motor car or a motor car.

(3) Save as provided in paragraph (4) a wheel of a vehicle may not be fitted with a temporary use spare tyre unless either—

   (a) the vehicle is a passenger vehicle (not being a bus) first used before 1st April 1987; or
   (b) the vehicle complies at the time of its first use with ECE Regulation 64 [or Community Directive 92/23].

(4) Paragraph (3) does not apply to a vehicle constructed or assembled by a person not ordinarily engaged in the trade or business of manufacturing vehicles of that description.   **[1364]**

NOTES
   Commencement: 11 August 1986.
   This regulation derived from SI 1955 No 990, regs 27, 31, 32, 37, 38, and SI 1978 No 1017, regs 52, 56, 60, 65, 68, 77, 78, 79D.
   Para (3): words in square brackets in sub-para (b) inserted by SI 1992/3088, reg 3.
   ECE Regulation 64: see reg 3, Sch 2.

[25. Tyre loads and speed ratings

(1) Save as provided in [paragraphs (3), (4) and (7A)] any tyre fitted to the axle of a vehicle—

   (a) which is a class of vehicle specified in an item in column 2 of Table I; and

(b) in relation to which the date of first use is as specified in that item in column 3 of that Table;

shall comply with the requirements specified in that item in column 4 of that Table.

[TABLE I

(regulation 25(1))

1 Item	2 Class of vehicle	3 Date of first use	4 Requirements
1	Vehicles which are of one or more of the following descriptions, namely— (a) goods vehicles, (b) trailers, (c) buses, (d) vehicles of a class mentioned in column 2 in Table III	Before 1st April 1991	The requirements of paragraphs (5) and (6)
2	Vehicles which are of one or more of the following descriptions— (a) goods vehicles, (b) trailers, (c) buses, (d) vehicles of a class mentioned in column 2 in Table III, and do not fall within item 3 below	On or after 1st April 1991	The requirements of paragraphs (5), (6) and (7)
3	Vehicles of a class mentioned in paragraph (2)	On or after 1st April 1991	The requirements of paragraphs (5)]

[(2) The classes of vehicle referred to in item 3 in column 2 of Table I are—

(a) engineering plant;
(b) track-laying vehicles;
(c) vehicles equipped with tyres of speed category Q;
(d) works trucks; and
(e) motor vehicles with a maximum speed not exceeding 30 mph, not being vehicles of a class specified in—

(i) items 2 and 3 of Table II; or;
(ii) paragraph (7A) or sub-paragraphs (a) to (d) of this paragraph;

or trailers while being drawn by such vehicles.]

(3) Paragraph (1) shall not apply to any tyre fitted to the axle of a vehicle if the vehicle is—

(a) broken down or proceeding to a place where it is to be broken up; and
(b) being drawn by a motor vehicle at a speed not exceeding 20 mph.

(4) Where in relation to any vehicle first used on or after 1st April 1991 a tyre supplied by a manufacturer for the purposes of tests or trials of that tyre is fitted to an axle of that vehicle, [paragraph (7) shall not apply to that tyre while it is being used for those purposes.]

(5) The requirements of this paragraph are that the tyre, as respects strength, shall be designed and manufactured adequately to support the maximum permitted axle weight for the axle.

(6) The requirements of this paragraph are that the tyre shall be designed and [manufactered] adequately to support the maximum permitted axle weight for the axle when the vehicle is driven at the speed shown in column 3 in Table II in the item in which the vehicle is described in column 2 (the lowest relevant speed being applicable to a vehicle which is described in more than one item).

TABLE II
(regulation 25(6))

1	2	3	4	
Item	Class of vehicle	Speed (mph)	Variation to the [load-capacity index] expressed as a percentage	
			[Tyres marked in accordance with ECE Regulation 30, 30.01 or 30.02] [and relevant car tyres]	Tyres marked in accordance with ECE Regulation 54 [and relevant commercial vehicle tyres]
1	A vehicle of a class for which maximum speeds are prescribed by Schedule 6 to the 1984 Act [other than an agricultural motor vehicle]	The highest speed so prescribed	Single wheels: none Dual wheels: 95.5%	None
2	An electrically propelled vehicle used as a multi-stop local collection and delivery vehicle and having a maximum speed of not more than 25 mph	[The maximum speed of the vehicle]	None	150%
3	An electrically propelled vehicle used as a multi-stop local collection and delivery vehicle and having a maximum speed of more than 25 mph and not more than 40 mph	[The maximum speed of the vehicle]	None	130%
4	An electrically propelled vehicle used only within a radius of 25 miles from the permanent base at which it is normally kept and having a maximum speed of more than 40 mph and not more than 50 mph	[The maximum speed of the vehicle]	None	115%
5	A local service bus	50	None Tyres marked in acccordance with ECE Regulations 30.02	110% Tyres marked in accordance with ECE Regulation 54
6	A restricted speed vehicle	50	None	The relevant % variation specified in Annex 8 to ECE Regulation 54 [or Appendix 8 to Annex II to Community Directive 92/23]

1	2	3	4	
Item	Class of vehicle	Speed (mph)	Variation to the [load-capacity index] expressed as a percentage	
7	A low platform trailer[, an agricultural motor vehicle, an agricultural trailer, an agricultural trailed appliance or an agricultural trailed appliance conveyor]	40	None	The relevant % variation specified in Annex 8 to ECE Regulation 54 [or Appendix 8 to Annex II to Community Directive 92/23]
8	A municipal vehicle	40	None	115%
9	A multi-stop local collection and delivery vehicle if not falling within the class of vehicle described in items 2 or 3 above	40	None	115%
10	A light trailer or any trailer equipped with tyres of speed category F or G	60	Single wheels: 110% Dual wheels: 105%	The relevant variation specified in Annex 8 to ECE Regulation 54 [or Appendix 8 to Annex II to Community Directive 92/23]
11	A trailer not falling in items 6–10	60	Single wheels: none Dual wheels: 95.5%	None
12	A [motor] vehicle not falling in items 1–11	70	Single wheels: none Dual wheels: 95.5%	None

(7) The requirement of this paragraph is that the tyre when first fitted to the vehicle [was marked with a designated approval mark or] complied with the requirements of [ECE Regulation 30, 30.01, 30.02] or 54, but this requirement shall not apply to a retreaded tyre.

[(7A) The requirements of paragraphs (6) and (7) shall not apply to a vehicle of a class specified in an item in column 2 of Table III while it is being driven or drawn at a speed not exceeding that specified in that item in column 3 of that Table.

TABLE III

(regulation 25(7A))

1 Item	2 Class of vehicle	3 Speed (mph)
1	Agricultural motor vehicles	20
2	Agricultural trailers	20

1 Item	2 Class of vehicle	3 Speed (mph)
3	Agricultural trailed appliances	20
4	Agricultural trailed appliance conveyors	20
5	Works trailers	18

(8) A vehicle of a class described in column 2 in Table II first used on or after 1st April 1991 shall not be used on a road—

    (a) in the case where there is no entry in column 4 specifying a variation to the [load-capacity index] expressed as a percentage, if the load applied to any tyre fitted to the axle of the vehicle exceeds that indicated by the [load-capacity index]; or

    (b) in the case where there is such an entry in column 4, if the load applied to any tyre fitted to the axle of the vehicle exceeds the variation to the [load-capacity index] expressed as a percentage.

(9) In this regulation—

["designated approval mark" means the marking designated as an approval mark by regulation 5 of the Approval Marks Regulations and shown at item 33 in Schedule 4 to those Regulations (that item being a marking relating to Community Directive 92/23);]

"dual wheels" means two or more wheels which are to be regarded as one wheel by virtue of paragraph 7 of regulation 3 in the circumstances specified in that paragraph;

"load-capacity index" has the same meaning as in [paragraph 2.28 of Annex II to Community Directive 92/23 or] paragraph 2.29 of ECE Regulation 30.02 or [paragraph 2.27] of ECE Regulation 54;

"local service bus" means a bus being used in the provision of a local service as defined in section 2 of the Transport Act 1985;

"municipal vehicle" means a motor vehicle or trailer limited at all times to use by a local authority, or a person acting in pursuance of a contract with a local authority, for road cleansing, road watering or the collection and disposal of refuse, night soil or the contents of cesspools, or the purposes of the enactments relating to weights and measures or the sale of food and drugs;

"multi-stop local collection and delivery vehicle" means a motor vehicle or trailer used for multi-stop collection and delivery services to be used only within a radius of 25 miles from the permanent base at which it is normally kept;

"single wheels" means wheels which are not dual wheels; and

"speed category" has the same meaning as in [paragraph 2.29 of Annex II to Community Directive 92/23 or] [paragraph 2.28] of ECE Regulation 54.

[(9A) For the purposes of this regulation, a tyre is a "relevant car tyre" if—

    (a) it has been marked with a designated approval mark, and

    (b) the first two digits of the approval number comprised is the mark are "02".

(9B) For the purposes of this regulation, a tyre is a "relevant commercial vehicle tyre" if—

    (a) it has been marked with a designated approval mark, and

(b) the first two digits of the approval number comprised in the mark are "00".]

(10) In this regulation any reference to the first use shall, in relation to a trailer, be construed as a reference to the date which is 6 months after the date of manufacture of the trailer.]   **[1365]**

NOTES

Commencement: 1 January 1992 (paras (2), (7A)); 2 November 1990 (remainder).
This regulation substituted by SI 1990 No 1981, reg 7.
Para (1): amended by SI 1991 No 2710, reg 3.
Para (2): amended by SI 1991 No 2710, reg 3.
Para (4): amended by SI 1991 No 2710, reg 3.
Para (6): amended by SI 1991 No 2710, reg 3; words "and relevant car tyres" and "and relevant commercial vehicle tyres" in column 4, words in square brackets in column 4 of items 6, 7, 10, and words in square brackets in column 2 of item 12, inserted by SI 1992 No 3088, reg 4(1), (2).
Para (7): first words in square brackets inserted by SI 1992 No 3088, reg 4(1), (3), second amendment made by SI 1991 No 2710, reg 3.
Para (7A): amended by SI 1991 No 2710, reg 3.
Para (8): amended by SI 1991 No 2710, reg 3.
Para (9): definition "designated approved mark", and words in first pairs of square brackets in definitions "load-capacity index" and "speed category" inserted by SI 1992 No 3088, reg 4(1), (4).
Paras (9A), (9B): inserted by SI 1992 No 3088, reg 4(1), (5).
ECE Regulations 30, 54: see reg 3, Sch 2.

26. Mixing of tyres

(1) Save as provided in paragraph (5) pneumatic tyres of different types of structure shall not be fitted to the same axle of a wheeled vehicle.

(2) Save as provided in paragraphs (3) or (5), a wheeled motor vehicle having only two axles each of which is equipped with one or two single wheels shall not be fitted with—

(a) a diagonal-ply tyre or a bias-belted tyre on its rear axle if a radial-ply tyre is fitted on its front axle; or on its rear axle if a bias-belted tyre is fitted on the front axle.

(b) a diagonal-ply tyre

(3) Paragraph (2) does not apply to a vehicle to an axle of which there are fitted wide tyres not specially constructed for use on engineering plant or to a vehicle which has a maximum speed not exceeding 30 mph.

(4) Save as provided in paragraph (5) pneumatic tyres fitted to—

(a) the steerable axles of a wheeled vehicle; [or]

(b) the driven axles of a wheeled vehicle, not being steerable axles,

shall all be of the same type of structure.

(5) Paragraphs (1), (2), and (4) do not prohibit the fitting of a temporary use spare tyre to a wheel of a passenger vehicle (not being a bus) unless it is driven at a speed exceeding 50 mph.

(6) In this regulation—

"axle" includes—

(i) two or more stub axles which are fitted on opposite sides of the longitudinal axis of the vehicle so as to form—

(a) a pair in the case of two stub axles; and

(b) pairs in the case of more than two stub axles; and

(ii) a single stub axle which is not one of a pair;

"a bias-belted tyre" means a pneumatic tyre, the structure of which is such that the ply cords extend to the bead so as to be laid at alternate angles of substantially less than 90 degrees to the peripheral line of the tread, and are constrained by a circumferential belt comprising two or more layers of substantially inextensible cord material laid at alternate angles smaller than those of the ply cord structure;

"a diagonal-ply tyre" means a pneumatic tyre, the structure of which is such that the ply cords extend to the bead so as to be laid at alternate angles of substantially less than 90 degrees to the peripheral line of the tread, but not being a bias-belted tyre;

"a driven axle" means an axle through which power is transmitted from the engine of a vehicle to the wheels on that axle;

"a radial-ply tyre" means a pneumatic tyre, the structure of which is such that the ply cords extend to the bead so as to be laid at an angle of substantially 90 degrees to the peripheral line of the tread, the ply cord structure being stabilised by a substantially inextensible circumferential belt;

"stub axle" means an axle on which only one wheel is mounted; and

"type of structure", in relation to a tyre, means a type of structure of a tyre of a kind defined in the foregoing provisions of this paragraph. **[1366]**

NOTES

Commencement: 11 August 1986.

This regulation derived from SI 1978 No 1017, reg 108.

Para 4: amended by SI 1990 No 1981, reg 8.

27. Condition and maintenance of tyres

(1) Save as provided in paragraphs (2), (3) and (4), a wheeled motor vehicle or trailer a wheel of which is fitted with a pneumatic tyre shall not be used on a road, if—

    (a) the tyre is unsuitable having regard to the use to which the motor vehicle or trailer is being put or to the types of tyres fitted to its other wheels;

    (b) the tyre is not so inflated as to make it fit for the use to which the motor vehicle or trailer is being put;

    (c) the tyre has a cut in excess of 25 mm or 10% of the section width of the tyre, whichever is the greater, measured in any direction on the outside of the tyre and deep enough to reach the ply or cord;

    (d) the tyre has any lump, bulge or tear caused by separation or partial failure of its structure;

    (e) the tyre has any of the ply or cord exposed;

    (f) the base of any groove which showed in the original tread pattern of the tyre is not clearly visible;

    (g) either—

        (i) the grooves of the tread pattern of the tyre do not have a depth of at least 1 mm throughout a continuous band measuring at least three-quarters of the breadth of the tread and round the entire outer circumference of the tyre; or

        (ii) if the grooves of the original tread pattern of the tyre did not extend beyond three-quarters of the breadth of the tread, any groove which showed in the original tread pattern does not have a depth of at least 1 mm; or

    (h) the tyre is not maintained in such condition as to be fit for the use to which the vehicle or trailer is being put or has a defect which might in any way cause damage to the surface of the road or damage to persons on or in the vehicle or to other persons using the road.

(2) Paragraph (1) does not prohibit the use on a road of a motor vehicle or trailer by reason only of the fact that a wheel of the vehicle or trailer is fitted with a tyre which is deflated or not fully inflated and which has any of the defects described in sub-paragraph (c), (d) or (e) of paragraph (1), if the tyre and the wheel to which it is fitted are so constructed as to make the tyre in that condition fit for the use to which the motor vehicle or trailer is being put and the outer sides of the wall of the tyre are so marked as to enable the tyre to be identified as having been constructed to comply with the requirements of this paragraph.

(3) Paragraph (1)(a) does not prohibit the use on a road of a passenger vehicle (not being a bus) by reason only of the fact that a wheel of the vehicle is fitted with a temporary use spare tyre, unless the vehicle is driven at a speed exceeding 50 mph.

(4)(a) Nothing in paragraph (1)(a) to (g) applies to—

> (i) an agricultural motor vehicle that is not driven at more than 20 mph;
> (ii) an agricultural trailer;
> (iii) an agricultural trailed appliance; or
> (iv) a broken down vehicle or a vehicle proceeding to a place where it is to be broken up, being drawn, in either case, by a motor vehicle at a speed not exceeding 20 mph.

(b) Nothing in paragraph (1)(f) and (g) applies to—

> (i) a three-wheeled motor cycle the unladen weight of which does not exceed 102 kg and which has a maximum speed of 12 mph; or
> (ii) a pedestrian-controlled works truck.

(c) Nothing in paragraph (1)(g) applies to a motorcycle with an engine capacity which does not exceed 50 cc.

[(d) With effect from 1st January 1992, paragraph 1(f) and (g) shall not apply to the vehicles specified in sub-paragraph (e) of this paragraph but such vehicles shall comply with the requirements specified in sub-paragraph (f) of this paragraph.

(e) The vehicles mentioned in sub-paragraph (d) are—

> (i) passenger vehicles other than motor cycles constructed or adapted to carry no more than 8 seated passengers in addition to the driver;
> (ii) goods vehicles with a maximum gross weight which [does] not exceed 3500 kg; and
> (iii) light trailers not falling within sub-paragraph (ii);

first used on or after 3rd January 1933.

(f) The requirements referred to in sub-paragraph (d) are that the grooves of the tread pattern of every tyre fitted to the wheels of a vehicle mentioned in sub-paragraph (e) shall be of a depth of at least 1.6 mm throughout the continuous band [comprising] the central three-quarters of the breadth of tread and round the entire outer circumference of the tyre.]

(5) A recut pneumatic tyre shall not be fitted to any wheel of a motor vehicle or trailer if—

(a) its ply or cord has been cut or exposed by the recutting process; or

(b) it has been wholly or partially recut in a pattern other than the manufacturer's recut tread pattern.

(6)(a) In this regulation—

"breadth of tread" means the breadth of that part of the tyre which can contact the road under normal conditions of use measured at 90 degrees to the peripheral line of the tread;

"original tread pattern" means in the case of—

a re-treaded tyre, the tread pattern of the tyre immediately after the tyre was re-treaded;

a wholly recut tyre, the manufacturer's recut tread pattern;

a partially recut tyre, on that part of the tyre which has been recut, the manufacturer's recut tread pattern, and on the other part, the tread pattern of the tyre when new, and

any other tyre, the tread pattern of the tyre when the tyre was new.

"tie-bar" means any part of a tyre moulded in the tread pattern of the tyre for the purpose of bracing two or more features of such tread pattern;

"tread pattern" means the combination of plain surfaces and grooves extending across the breadth of the tread and round the entire outer circumference of the tyre but excludes any—

(i) tie bars or tread wear indicators;

(ii) features which are designed to wear out substantially before the rest of the pattern under normal conditions of use; and

(iii) other minor features; and

"tread wear indicator" means any bar, not being a tie-bar, projecting from the base of a groove of the tread pattern of a tyre and moulded between two or more features of the tread pattern of a tyre for the purpose of indicating the extent of the wear of such tread pattern.

(b) The references in [this regulation] to grooves are references—

if a tyre has been recut, to the grooves of the manufacturer's recut tread pattern; and

if a tyre has not been recut, to the grooves which showed when the tyre was new.

[(c) A reference in this regulation to first use shall, in relation to a trailer, be construed as a reference to the date which is 6 months after the date of manufacture of the trailer.] **[1367]**

NOTES

Commencement: 11 August 1986.

This regulation derived from SI 1955 No 990, reg 57, and SI 1978 No 1017, reg 107.

Para (4): sub-paras (d)–(f) added by SI 1990 No 1981, reg 9; remaining words in square brackets substituted by SI 1991 No 2710, reg 4.

Para (6): amended by SI 1990 No 1981, reg 9.

28. Tracks

(1) Every part of every track of a track-laying vehicle which comes into contact with the road shall be flat and have a width of not less than 12.5 mm.

(2) The area of the track which is in contact with the road shall not at any time be less than 225 cm² in respect of every 1000 kg of the total weight which is transferred to the road by the tracks.

(3) The tracks of a vehicle shall not have any defect which might damage

the road or cause danger to any person on or in the vehicle or using the road, and shall be properly adjusted and maintained in good and efficient working order.   **[1368]**

NOTES
Commencement: 11 August 1986.
This regulation derived from SI 1955 No 990, regs 9, 56.

D - Steering

29. Maintenance of steering gear

All steering gear fitted to a motor vehicle shall at all times while the vehicle is used on a road be maintained in good and efficient working order and be properly adjusted.   **[1369]**

NOTES
Commencement: 11 August 1986.
This regulation derived from SI 1955 No 990, reg 54, and SI 1978 No 1017, reg 102.

E - Vision

30. View to the front

(1) Every motor vehicle shall be so designed and constructed that the driver thereof while controlling the vehicle can at all times have a full view of the road and traffic ahead of the motor vehicle.

(2) Instead of complying with the requirement of paragraph (1) a vehicle may comply with Community Directive 77/649, 81/643[, 88/366, 90/630] or, in the case of an agricultural motor vehicle, 79/1073.

(3) All glass or other transparent material fitted to a motor vehicle shall be maintained in such condition that it does not obscure the vision of the driver while the vehicle is being driven on a road.   **[1370]**

NOTES
Commencement: 11 August 1986.
This regulation derived from SI 1955 No 990, regs 14, 53, and SI 1978 No 1017, regs 22, 100.
Para 2: figures in square brackets inserted by SI 1991 No 2003, reg 3.
Community Directives 77/649, 79/1073, 81/643, 88/366, 90/630: see reg 3, Sch 2.

31. Glass

(1) This regulation applies to a motor vehicle which is—

    (a) a wheeled vehicle, not being a caravan, first used before 1st June 1978;

    (b) a caravan first used before 1st September 1978; or

    (c) a track-laying vehicle.

(2) The glass fitted to any window specified in an item in column 3 of the Table of a vehicle of a class specified in that item in column 2 shall be safety glass.

TABLE
(regulation 31(2))

1	2	3
Item	Class of vehicle	Windows
1	Wheeled vehicles first used on or after 1st January 1959, being passenger vehicles or dual-purpose vehicles.	Windscreens and all outside windows.
2	Wheeled vehicles first used on or after 1st January 1959, being goods vehicles (other than dual-purpose vehicles), locomotives or motor tractors.	Windscreens and all windows in front of and on either side of the driver's seat.
3	Wheeled vehicles not mentioned in item 1 or 2.	Windscreens and windows facing to the front on the outside, except glass fitted to the upper decks of a double-decked vehicle.
4	Track-laying vehicles.	Windscreens and windows facing to the front.

(3) For the purposes of this regulation any windscreen or window at the front of the vehicle the inner surface of which is at an angle exceeding 30 degrees to the longitudinal axis of the vehicle shall be deemed to face to the front.

[(4) In this regulation and in regulation 32—

"caravan" means a trailer which is constructed (and not merely adapted) for human habitation; and

["designated approval mark" means the marking designated as an approval mark by Regulation 5 of the Approval Marks Regulations and shown at item 31 or 32 in Schedule 4 to those Regulations (those items being markings relating to Community Directive 92/22); and]

"safety glass" means glass so constructed or treated that if fractured it does not fly into fragments likely to cause severe cuts.]

[(5) Paragraph (2) does not apply to glass which is legibly and permanently marked with a designated approval mark.] **[1371]**

NOTES

Commencement: 6 May 1987 (para (4)); 11 August 1986 (remainder).

This regulation derived from SI 1955 No 990, reg 16, and SI 1978 No 1017, reg 25.

Para (4): substituted by SI 1987 No 676, reg 15(1); definition "designated apprval mark" inserted by SI 1992 No 3088, reg 5(1), (2).

Para (5): added by SI 1992 No 3088, reg 5(1), (3).

32. Glass

(1) This regulation applies to—

(a) a caravan first used on or after 1st September 1978, and

(b) a wheeled motor vehicle and a wheeled trailer, not being a caravan, first used on or after 1st June 1978.

(2) Save as provided in paragraphs (3) to (9) the windows specified in column 2 of Table I in relation to a vehicle of a class specified in that column shall be constructed of the material specified in column 3 of that Table.

TABLE I (regulation 32(2))

1	2	3
Item	Window	Material
1	Windscreens and other windows wholly or partly on either side of the driver's seat fitted to motor vehicles first used on or after 1st April 1985.	Specified safety glass (1980).
2	Windscreens and other windows wholly or partly on either side of the driver's seat fitted to a motor vehicle first used before 1st April 1985.	Specified safety glass or specified safety glass (1980).
3	All other windows.	Specified safety glass, specified safety glass (1980), or safety glazing.

(3) The windscreens and all other windows of security vehicles or vehicles being used for police purposes shall not be subject to the requirements specified in paragraph (2), but shall be constructed of either safety glass or safety glazing.

(4) The windscreen of motorcycles not equipped with an enclosed compartment for the driver or for a passenger shall not be subject to the requirements specified in paragraph (2), but shall be constructed of safety glazing.

(5) Any windscreens or other windows which are wholly or partly in front of or on either side of the driver's seat, and which are temporarily fitted to motor vehicles to replace any windscreens or other window which have broken shall—

(a) be constructed of safety glazing; and
(b) be fitted only while the vehicles are being driven or towed either to premises where new windscreens or other windows are to be permanently fitted to replace the windscreens or other windows which have broken, or to complete the journey in the course of which the breakage occurred.

(6) Windows forming all or part of a screen or door in the interior of a bus first used on or after 1st April 1988, shall be constructed either of safety glazing or of specified safety glass (1980).

(7) Windows being—

(a) windows (other than windscreens) of motor vehicles being engineering plant, industrial tractors, agricultural motor vehicles (other than agricultural motor vehicles first used on or after 1st June 1986 and driven at more than 20 mph) which are wholly or partly in front of or on either side of the driver's seat;
(b) windows of the upper deck of a double-decked bus; or
(c) windows in the roof of a vehicle,

shall be constructed of either specified safety glass, specified safety glass (1980) or safety glazing.

(8) In the case of motor vehicles and trailers which have not at any time been fitted with permanent windows and which are being driven or towed to a

place where permanent windows are to be fitted, any temporary windscreens and any other temporary windows shall be constructed of either specified safety glass, specified safety glass (1980) or safety glazing.

(9) No requirement in this regulation that a windscreen or other window shall be constructed of specified safety glass or of specified safety glass (1980) shall apply to a windscreen or other window which is—

(a) manufactured in France;
(b) marked with a marking consisting of the letters "TP GS" or "TP GS E"; and
(c) fitted to a vehicle first used before 1st October 1986.

(10) Save as provided in paragraph (11), the windscreens or other windows constructed in accordance with the foregoing provisions of this regulation of specified safety glass, specified safety glass (1980) or safety glazing and specified in column 3 of Table II in relation to a vehicle of a class specified in column 2 of that Table shall have a visual transmission for light of not less than the percentage specified in relation to those windows in column 4 when measured perpendicular to the surface in accordance with the procedure specified in a document specified in relation to those windows in column 5.

TABLE II (regulation 32(10))

1	2	3	4	5
Item	Class of Vehicles	Windows	Percentage	Documents specifying procedure
1	Motor vehicles first used before 1st April 1985	All windows	70	British Standard Specification No 857 or No 5282
2	Motor vehicles first used on or after 1st April 1985 and trailers	(a) Windscreens	75	The documents mentioned in sub-paragraph (i), (ii) or (iii) of the definition in paragraph (13) of "specified safety glass (1980)."
		(b) All other windows	70	

(11) Paragraph (10) does not apply to—

(a) any part of any windscreen which is outside the vision reference zone;
(b) windows through which the driver when in the driver's seat is unable at any time to see any part of the road on which the vehicle is waiting or proceeding;
(c) windows in any motor ambulance which are not wholly or partly in front of or on either side of any part of the driver's seat; or
(d) windows in any bus, goods vehicle, locomotive, or motor tractor other than windows which—

  (i) are wholly or partly in front of or on either side of any part of the driver's seat;

  (ii) face the rear of the vehicle; or

  (iii) form the whole or part of a door giving access to or from the exterior of the vehicle.

(12) For the purposes of this regulation any window at the rear of the vehicle is deemed to face the rear of the vehicle if the inner surface of such window is at an angle exceeding 30 degrees to the longitudinal axis of the vehicle.

[(12A) Paragraphs (2), (6), (7) and (8) do not apply to a window which is legibly and permanently marked with a designated approval mark.

(12B) Paragraph (10) does not apply to a window if—

  (a) it is a window to which paragraph 12C (applies and is legibly and permanently marked with a designated approval mark which does not comprise the Roman numeral "V" (other than as part of the combination "VI"); or

  (b) it is not a window to which paragraph 12C applies and is legibly and permanently marked with a designated approval mark.

(12C) This paragraph applies to a side or rear window if—

  (a) any part of it is on either side of or forward of the driver's seat; or

  (b) any part of it is within the driver's indirect field of view obtained by means of the mirror or mirrors which are required to be fitted by regulation 33 when such mirrors are properly adjusted;

and for the purposes of this paragraph a mirror shall not be regarded as being required to be fitted by regulation 33 if, were it to be removed, the vehicle would nevertheless meet the requirements of regulation 33.]

(13) In this regulation, unless the context otherwise requires—

  "British Standard Specification No. 857" means the British Standard Specification for Safety Glass for Land Transport published on 30th June 1967 under the number BS 857 as amended by Amendment Slip No. 1 published on 15th January 1973 under the number AMD 1088;

  "British Standard Specification No. 5282" means the British Standard Specification for Road Vehicle Safety Glass published in December 1975 under the number BS 5282 as amended by Amendment Slip No. 1 published on 31st March 1976 under the number AMD 1927, and as amended by Amendment Slip No. 2 published on 31st January 1977 under the number AMD 2185;

  "British Standard Specifications BS AU 178" means the British Standard Specification for Road Vehicle Safety Glass published on 28th November 1980 under the number BS AU 178;

. . .

  ["designated approval mark" means—

  (a) in relation to a windscreen, the marking designated as an approval mark by regulation 5 of the Approval Marks Regulations and shown at item 31 in Schedule 4 to those Regulations, and

  (b) in relation to a window other than a windscreen, the markings designated as approval marks by regulation 5 of those Regulations and shown at item 32 in Schedule 4 to those Regulations.]

  "safety glazing" means material (other than glass) which is so constructed or treated that if fractured it does not fly into fragments likely to cause severe cuts;

"security vehicle" means a motor vehicle which is constructed (and not merely adapted) for the carriage of either—

(i) persons who are likely to require protection from any criminal offence involving violence; or

(ii) dangerous substances, bullion, money, jewellery, documents or other goods or burden which, by reason of their nature or value, are likely to require protection from any criminal offence;

"specified safety glass" means glass complying with the requirements of either—

(i) British Standard Specification No. 857 (including the requirements as to marking); or

(ii) British Standard Specification No. 5282 (including the requirements as to marking);

"specified safety glass (1980)" means glass complying with the requirements of either—

(i) the British Standard Specification for Safety Glass for Land Transport published on 30th June 1967 under the number BS 857 as amended by Amendment Slip No. 1 published on 15th January 1973 under the number AMD 1088, Amendment Slip No. 2 published on 30th September 1980 under the number AMD 3402, and Amendment Slip No. 4 published on 15th February 1981 under the number AMD 3548 (including the requirements as to marking); or

(ii) British Standard Specification BS AU 178 (including the requirements as to marking); or

(iii) ECE Regulation 43 (including the requirements as to marking).

"vision reference zone" means either—

(i) the primary vision area as defined in British Standard Specification No. 857;

(ii) Zone 1, as defined in British Standard Specification No. 5282;

(iii) Zone B (as regards passenger vehicles other than buses) and Zone 1 (as regards all other vehicles) as defined in British Standard Specification BS AU 178 and in ECE Regulation 43; and

"windscreen" includes a windshield;   **[1372]**

NOTES
Commencement: 11 August 1986.
This regulation derived from SI 1978 No 1017, reg 26.
Paras (12A)–(12C): inserted by SI 1992 No 3088, reg 6.
Para (13): definitions "caravan" and "safety glass" revoked by SI 1987 No 676, reg 15(2); definitions "designated approval mark" inserted by SI 1992 No 3088, reg 7.
ECE Regulation 43: see reg 3, Sch 2.

33. Mirrors

(1) Save as provided in paragraphs (5) and (6), a motor vehicle (not being a road roller) which is of a class specified in an item in column 2 of the Table shall be fitted with such mirror or mirrors, if any, as are specified in that item in column 3; and any mirror which is fitted to such a vehicle shall, whether or not it is required to be fitted, comply with the requirements, if any, specified in that item in column 4.

(2) Save as provided in paragraph (5), each exterior mirror with which a vehicle is required to be fitted in accordance with item 2 or 6 of the Table shall,

if the vehicle has a technically permissible maximum weight (as mentioned in Annex 1 to Community Directive 71/127) exceeding 3500 kg, be a Class II mirror (as described in that Annex) and shall in any other case be a Class II or a Class III mirror (as described in that Annex).

(3) Save as provided in paragraph (5), in the case of a wheeled motor vehicle described in item 1, 2, 7 or 8 of the Table which is first used on or after 1st April 1969 the edges of any mirror fitted internally shall be surrounded by some material such as will render it unlikely that severe cuts would be caused if the mirror or that material were struck by any occupant of the vehicle.

(4) Save as provided in paragraph (5), in the case of a motor vehicle falling within paragraph (a) in column 4 of items 1 and 5, or within item 6, of the Table—

(a) each mirror shall be fixed to the vehicle in such a way that it remains steady under normal driving conditions;

(b) each exterior mirror on a vehicle fitted with windows and a windscreen shall be visible to the driver, when in his driving position, through a side window or through the portion of the windscreen which is swept by the windscreen wiper;

(c) where the bottom edge of an exterior mirror is less than 2 m above the road surface when the vehicle is laden, that mirror shall not project more than 20 cm beyond the overall width of the vehicle or, in a case where the vehicle is drawing a trailer which has an overall width greater than that of the drawing vehicle, more than 20 cm beyond the overall width of the trailer;

(d) each interior mirror shall be capable of being adjusted by the driver when in his driving position; and

(e) except in the case of a mirror which, if knocked out of its alignment, can be returned to its former position without needing to be adjusted, each exterior mirror on the driver's side of the vehicle shall be capable of being adjusted by the driver when in his driving position, but this requirement shall not prevent such a mirror from being locked into position from the outside of the vehicle.

TABLE (regulation 33(1))

1	2	3	4
Item	Class of vehicle	Mirrors to be fitted	Requirements to be complied with by any mirrors fitted
1	A motor vehicle which is— (a) drawing a trailer, if a person is carried on the trailer so that he has an uninterrupted view to the rear and has an efficient means of communicating to the driver the effect of signals given by the drivers of other vehicles to the rear, (b)　(i) a works truck; 　　(ii) a track-laying agricultural motor vehicle; and 　　(iii) a wheeled agricultural motor vehicle first used before 1st June 1978.	No requirement	(a) If the vehicle is a wheeled vehicle first used on or after 1st June 1978, Item 2 of Annex I to Community Directive 71/127 or 79/795 or Annex II to Community Directive 86/562 [or 88/321 or paragraphs 4 to 8 of ECE Regulations 46.01] and paragraph (4) of this regulation. (b) In other cases, none, except as specified in paragraph (3).

1	2	3	4
Item	Class of vehicle	Mirrors to be fitted	Requirements to be complied with by any mirrors fitted
	if, in each case, the driver can easily obtain a view to the rear; (c) a pedestrian-controlled vehicle; (d) a chassis being driven from the place where it has been manufactured to the place where it is to receive a vehicle body; or (e) an agricultural motor vehicle which has an unladen weight exceeding 7370 kg and which— (i) is a track-laying vehicle or (ii) is a wheeled vehicle first used before 1st June 1978		
2	A motor vehicle, not included in Item 1, which is— (a) a wheeled locomotive or a wheeled motor tractor first used in either case on or after 1st June 1978; (b) an agricultural motor vehicle, not being a track-laying vehicle with an unladen weight not exceeding 7370 kg (which falls in item 8) or a wheeled agricultural motor vehicle first used after 1st June 1986 which is driven at more than 20 mph (which falls in item (6)); or (c) a works truck.	At least one mirror fitted externally on the offside	None except as specified in paragraphs (2) and (3).
3	A wheeled motor vehicle not included in item 1 first used on or after 1st April 1983 which is— (a) a bus; or (b) a goods vehicle with a maximum gross weight exceeding 3500 kg (not being an agricultural motor vehicle or one which is not driven at more than 20 mph) other than a vehicle described in item 4.	Mirrors complying with item 3 of Annex I to Community Directive 79/795 or with paragraph 2.1 of Annex III to Community Directive 86/562 [or 88/321 or paragraph 16.2.1 of ECE Regulation 46.01] or, except in the case of a goods vehicle first used on or after 1st April 1985, mirrors as required in the entry in this column in item 6	Item 2 of Annex I to Community Directive 71/127 or 79/795 or Annex II to Community Directive 86/562 [or 88/321 or paragraphs 4 to 8 of ECE Regulation 46.01].
4	A goods vehicle not being an agricultural motor vehicle with a maximum gross weight exceeding 12,000 kg which is first used on or after 1st October 1988	Mirrors complying with paragraph 2.1 of Annex III to Community Directive 85/205.	Annex II to Community Directive 86/562 [or 88/321 or paragraph 4 to 8 of ECE Regulation 46.01].

1	2	3	4
Item	Class of vehicle	Mirrors to be fitted	Requirements to be complied with by any mirrors fitted
5	A two-wheeled motor cycle with or without a sidecar attached	No requirement	(a) If the vehicle is first used on or after 1st October 1978, Item 2 of Annex I to Community Directive 71/127, 79/795 or 80/780 or Annex II to Community Directive 86/562 [or 88/321 or paragraphs 4 to 8 of ECE Regulation 46.01] and paragraph (4) of this regulation. (b) In other cases, none.
6	A wheeled motor vehicle not in items 1 to 5, which is first used on or after 1st June 1978 (or, in the case of a Ford Transit motor car, 10th July 1978)	(i) At least one mirror fitted externally on the offside of the vehicle; and (ii) at least one mirror fitted internally, unless a mirror so fitted would give the driver no view to the rear of the vehicle; and (iii) at least one mirror fitted externally on the nearside of the vehicle unless a mirror which gives the driver an adequate view to the rear is fitted internally	Item 2 of Annex I to Community Directive 71/127 or 79/795 or Annex II to Community Directive 86/562 [or 88/321 of paragraphs 4 to 8 of ECE Regulations 46.01] and paragraphs (2) and (4) of this regulation.
7	A wheeled motor vehicle, not in items 1 to 5, first used before 1st June 1978 (or in the case of a Ford Transit motor car, 10th July 1978) and a track-laying motor vehicle which is not an agricultural motor vehicle first used on or after 1st January 1958, which is either case is— (a) a bus; (b) a dual-purpose; or (c) a goods vehicle.	At least one mirror fitted externally on the offside of the vehicle and at least one mirror fitted either internally or externally on the near-side of the vehicle	None, except as specified in paragraph (3).
8	A motor vehicle, whether wheeled or track-laying, not in items 1 to 7	At least one mirror fitted either internally or externally	None, except as specified in paragraph (3).

[(5) Instead of complying with paragraphs (1) to (4) a vehicle may comply—

    (a) if it is a goods vehicle with a maximum gross weight exceeding 3500 kg first used on or after 1st April 1985, and before 1st August 1989, with Community Directive 79/795, 82/205[, 86/562 or 88/321 of ECE Regulation 46.01];

    (b) if it is a goods vehicle first used on or after 1st August 1989—

        (i) in the case of a vehicle with a maximum gross weight exceeding 3500 kg but not exceeding 12,000 kg with Community Directive 79/795, 85/205[, 86/562 or 88/321 of ECE Regulation 46.01]; and

        (ii) in the case of a vehicle with a maximum gross weight exceeding 12,000 kg with Community Directive 85/205[, 86/562 or 88/321 of ECE Regulation 46.01];

(c) if it is an agricultural motor vehicle with Community Directive 71/ 127, 74/346, 79/795, 85/205[, 86/562 or 88/321 of ECE Regulation 46.01];

(d) if it is a two-wheeled motor cycle with or without a side-car with Community Directive 71/127, 79/795, 80/780, 85/205[, 86/562 or 88/ 321 or ECE Regulation 46.01]; and

(e) if it is any other vehicle with Community Directive 71/127, 79/795, 85/205[, 86/562 or 88/321 or ECE Regulation 46.01].]

(6) Instead of complying with the provisions of column 4 in items 3, 5 or 6 of the Table a mirror may comply with the requirements as to construction and testing set out either in Annex I to Community Directive 71/127, excluding paragraphs 2.3.4 and 2.6, or in Annex I to Community Directive 79/795, excluding paragraphs 2.3.3 and 2.6.

(7) In this regulation "mirror" means a mirror to assist the driver of a vehicle to become aware of traffic—

(i) if it is an internal mirror, to the rear of the vehicle; and

(ii) if it is an external mirror fitted on one side of the vehicle, rearwards on that side of the vehicle.

In the case of an agricultural motor vehicle or a vehicle described in items 2 or 6 in the Table when drawing a trailer, the references to a vehicle in sub-paragraphs (i) and (ii) include references to the trailer so drawn. **[1373]**

NOTES

Commencement: 25 July 1988 (para (5)); 11 August 1986 (remainder).
This regulation derived from SI 1955 No 990, reg 15, and SI 1978 No 1017, regs 23, 24, 24A.
Table: amended by SI 1988 No 1178, reg 3, SI 1992 No 3088, reg 8(1), (2).
Para (5): substituted by SI 1988 No 1178, reg 3; amended by SI 1992 No 3088, reg 8(1), (3).
Community Directives 71/127, 74/346, 79/795, 80/780, 85/205, 86/562: see reg 3, Sch 2.

34. Windscreen wipers and washers

(1) Subject to paragraphs (4) and (5), every vehicle fitted with a windscreen shall, unless the driver can obtain an adequate view to the front of the vehicle without looking through the windscreen, be fitted with one or more efficient automatic windscreen wipers capable of clearing the windscreen so that the driver has an adequate view of the road in front of both sides of the vehicle and to the front of the vehicle.

(2) Save as provided in paragraphs (3), (4) and (5), every wheeled vehicle required by paragraph (1) to be fitted with a wiper or wipers shall also be fitted with a windscreen washer capable of cleaning, in conjunction with the windscreen wiper, the area of the windscreen swept by the wiper of mud or similar deposit.

(3) The requirement specified in paragraph (2) does not apply in respect of—

(a) an agricultural motor vehicle (other than a vehicle first used on or after 1st June 1986 which is driven at more than 20 mph);

(b) a track-laying vehicle;

(c) a vehicle having a maximum speed not exceeding 20 mph; or

(d) a vehicle being used to provide a local service, as defined in the Transport Act 1985.

(4) Instead of complying with paragraphs (1) and (2), a vehicle may comply with Community Directive 78/318.

(b) taking the vehicle to a place where the speed limiter is to be repaired or replaced.

(5) In this regulation—

["authorised sealer" has the meaning given in Schedule 3B to these Regulations;]

"Part I of the British Standard" means the British Standard for Maximum Road Speed Limiters for Motor Vehicles which was published by the British Standards Institution under the number BSAU 217: Part I: 1987 and which came into effect on 29th May 1987 [as amended by Amendment Slip No 1 under the number AMD 5969 which was published and came into effect on 30th June 1988];

"set speed" has the same meaning as in clause 2.2 of Part I of the British Standard;

"speed limiter" means a device designed to limit the maximum speed of a motor vehicle by controlling the engine power of the vehicle.]   **[1377]**

NOTES

Commencement: 1 August 1992 (para (3A)); 18 March 1988 (remainder).
Added by SI 1988 No 271, reg 4(1).
Para (3): words in square brackets inserted by SI 1992 No 422, reg 3(1), (2).
Para (3A): inserted by SI 1992 No 422, reg 3(1), (3).
Para (5): definition "authorised sealer" inserted by SI 1992 No 422, reg 3(1), (4); remaining words in square brackets added by SI 1988 No 1524, reg 3.

[**36B.**—(1) Subject to paragraph (6), this regulation applies to every motor vehicle which—

(a) is a goods vehicle;
(b) has a maximum gross weight exceeding 7500 kg;
(c) is first used on or after 1st August 1992; and
(d) has, or if a speed limiter were not fitted to it would have, a relevant speed exceeding 60 mph.

[(1A) Subject to paragraph (6), this regulation also applies to every motor vehicle which—

(a) is a goods vehicle;
(b) has a maximum gross weight exceeding 16,000 kg;
(c) is either—

(i) a vehicle that is constructed or adapted to form part of an articulated vehicle, or
(ii) a rigid vehicle that is constructed or adapted to draw a trailer and has a maximum gross trailer weight which exceeds 5,000 kg;

(d) is first used on or after 1st January 1988; and
(e) has, or if a speed limiter were not fitted to it would have, a relevant speed exceeding 60 mph.]

(2) A vehicle to which this regulation applies shall not have used on a road unless it has been fitted with a speed limiter.

(3) Every speed limiter fitted in accordance with paragraph (2) shall—

(a) comply with Part I of the British Standard;
(b) be calibrated to a set speed not exceeding 60 mph;
(c) be sealed [by an authorised sealer] in such a manner as to protect the limiter against any improper interference or adjustment and against any interruption of its power supply; and

(d) be maintained in good and efficient working order.

[(3A) Paragraph (3)(c) shall have effect in relation to—

(a) a speed limiter fitted before 1st August 1992 to a vehicle first used before that date,

(b) a speed limiter sealed outside the United Kingdom,

as if the words "by an authorised sealer" were omitted.]

(4) Sub-paragraphs (a) and (b) of paragraph (3) shall not apply to a speed limiter which complies with a standard or a technical regulation of another Member State or an international standard recognised in another Member State, which offers equivalent guarantees of safety, suitability and fitness for the purpose, and which is calibrated to a speed not exceeding 60 mph.

(5) A vehicle to which a speed limiter has been fitted shall not be driven on a road unless a speed limiter is functioning except for the purpose of—

(a) completing a journey in the course of which the speed limiter has accidentally ceased to function; or

(b) taking the vehicle to a place where the speed limiter is to be repaired or replaced.

(6) This regulation does not apply to a vehicle—

(a) which is being taken to a place where a speed limiter is to be installed or calibrated;

(b) owned by the Secretary of State for Defence and used for naval, military or air force purposes;

(c) used for naval, military or air force purposes while being driven by a person for the time being subject to the orders of a member of the armed forces of the Crown;

(d) while it is being used for fire brigade, ambulance or police purposes; or

(e) if and so long as it is exempt from vehicle excise duty by section 7(1) of the Vehicles (Excise) Act 1971.

(7) In this regulation—

"Member State" shall be construed in accordance with Schedule I to the European Communites Act 1972;

["authorised sealer"], "Part I of the British Standard", "set speed" and "speed limiter" have the same meanings respectively as in regulation 36A; and

"relevant speed" means the speed which a vehicle is incapable, by reason of its construction, of exceeding on the level under its own power when unladen.]

[(8) For the purposes of this regulation, a motor vehicle has a maximum gross trailer weight exceeding 5,000 kg if—

(a) in the case of a vehicle equipped with a Ministry plate in accordance with regulation 70, the difference between its maximum gross weight and the relevant train weight exceeds 5,000 kg;

(b) in the case of a vehicle not equipped with a Ministry plate, but which is equipped with a place in accordance with regulation 66, the difference between its maximum gross weight and the weight shown on the plate in respect of item 8 of Part I of Schedule 8 exceeds 5,000 kg; and

(c) in the case of any other vehicle, the vehicle is designed or adapted to be capable of drawing a trailer with a laden weight exceeding 5,000 kg when travelling on a road;

and in sub-paragraph (a) "the relevant train weight" is the train weight shown in column (3) of the plate or, if no such weight is shown, the train weight shown in column (2) of the plate (where the plate is in the form required by Schedule 10) or in column (4) of the plate (where the plate is in the form required by Schedule 10A).]   **[1377A]**

NOTES
   Commencement: 1 August 1993 (paras (1A), (8)). 1 August 1992 (para (3A)); 1 August 1991 (remainder).
   Inserted by SI 1991 No 1527, reg 3(1).
   Paras (1A), (8): prospectively inserted or added by SI 1992 No 422, reg 8, as from 1 August 1993.
   Paras (3), (7): words in square brackets inserted by SI 1992 No 422, reg 4(1), (2), (4).
   Para (3A): inserted by SI 1992 No 422, reg 4(3).

[36C. Speed limiters—authorised sealers

Schedule 3B (authorised sealers) shall have effect.]   **[1377B]**

NOTES
   Commencement: 1 August 1992.
   Inserted by SI 1992 No 422, reg 5.

37. Audible warning instruments

(1)(a) Subject to sub-paragraph (b), every motor vehicle which has a maximum speed of more than 20 mph shall be fitted with a horn, not being a reversing alarm or a two-tone horn.

   (b) Sub-paragraph (a) shall not apply to an agricultural motor vehicle, unless it is being driven at more than 20 mph.

(2) Subject to paragraph (6), the sound emitted by any horn, other than a reversing alarm or a two-tone horn, fitted to a wheeled vehicle first used on or after 1st August 1973 shall be continuous and uniform and not strident.

(3) A reversing alarm fitted to a wheeled vehicle shall not be strident.

(4) Subject to paragraphs (5), (6) and (7) no motor vehicle shall be fitted with a bell, gong, siren or two-tone horn.

(5) The provisions of paragraph (4) shall not apply to motor vehicles—

   (a) used for fire brigade, ambulance or police purposes;
   (b) owned by a body formed primarily for the purposes of fire salvage and used for those or similar purposes;
   (c) owned by the Forestry Commission or by local authorities and used from time to time for the purposes of fighting fires;
   (d) owned by the Secretary of State for Defence and used for the purposes of the disposal of bombs or explosives;
   (e) used for the purposes of the Blood Transfusion Service provided under the National Health Service Act 1977 or under the National Health Service (Scotland) Act 1947;
   (f) used by Her Majesty's Coastguard or the Coastguard Auxiliary Service to aid persons in danger or vessels in distress on or near the coast;
   (g) owned by the National Coal Board and used for the purposes of rescue operations at mines;

(h) owned by the Secretary of State for Defence and used by the Royal Air Force Mountain Rescue Service for the purposes of rescue operations in connection with crashed aircraft or any other emergencies; or

(i) owned by the Royal National Lifeboat Institution and used for the purposes of launching lifeboats.

(6) The provisions of paragraphs (2) and (4) shall not apply so as to make it unlawful for a motor vehicle to be fitted with an instrument or apparatus (not being a two-tone horn) designed to emit a sound for the purpose of informing members of the public that goods are on the vehicle for sale.

(7) Subject to paragraph (8), the provisions of paragraph (4) shall not apply so as to make it unlawful for a vehicle to be fitted with a bell, gong or siren—

(a) if the purpose thereof is to prevent theft or attempted theft of the vehicle or its contents; or

(b) in the case of a bus, if the purpose thereof is to summon help for the driver, the conductor or an inspector.

(8) Every bell, gong or siren fitted to a vehicle by virtue of paragraph (7)(a), and every device fitted to a motor vehicle first used on or after 1st October 1982 so as to cause a horn to sound for the purpose mentioned in paragraph (7)(a), shall be fitted with a device designed to stop the bell, gong, siren or horn emitting noise for a continuous period of more than five minutes; and every such device shall at all times be maintained in good working order.

(9) Instead of complying with paragraphs (1), (2) and (4) to (8), a vehicle may comply with Community Directive 70/388 or ECE Regulation 28 or, if the vehicle is an agricultural motor vehicle, with Community Directive 74/151.

(10) In this regulation and in regulation 99—

(*a*) "horn" means an instrument, not being a bell, gong or siren, capable of giving audible and sufficient warning of the approach or position of the vehicle to which it is fitted;

(b) references to a bell, gong or siren include references to any instrument or apparatus capable of emitting a sound similar to that emitted by a bell, gong or siren;

(c) "reversing alarm" means a device fitted to a motor vehicle and designed to warn persons that the vehicle is reversing or is about to reverse; and

(d) "two-tone horn" means an instrument which, when operated, automatically produces a sound which alternates at regular intervals between two fixed notes. **[1378]**

NOTES
Commencement: 11 August 1986.
This regulation derived from SI 1955 No 990, reg 18, and SI 1978 No 1017, reg 29.
Community Directives: 70/388, 74/151: see reg 3, Sch 2.
ECE Regulation 28: see reg 3, Sch 2.

38. Motor cycle sidestands

(1) No motor cycle first used on or after 1st April 1986 shall be fitted with any sidestand which is capable of—

(a) disturbing the stability or direction of the motor cycle when it is in motion under its own power; or

    (b) closing automatically if the angle of the inclination of the motor cycle is inadvertently altered when it is stationary.

    (2) In this regulation "sidestand" means a device fitted to a motor cycle which, when fully extended or pivoted to its open position, supports the vehicle from one side only and so that both the wheels of the motor cycle are on the ground.   **[1379]**

NOTES

    Commencement: 11 August 1986.

G— *Fuel*

39. Fuel tanks

[(1) This regulation applies to every fuel tank which is fitted to a wheeled vehicle for the purpose of supplying fuel to the propulsion unit or to an ancillary engine or to any other equipment forming part of the vehicle.

    (2) Subject to paragraphs (3) and (4), every fuel tank to which this regulation applies—

    (a) shall be constructed and maintained so that the leakage of any liquid from the tank is adequately prevented;

    (b) shall be constructed and maintained so that the leakage of vapour from the tank is adequately prevented; and

    (c) if it contains petroleum spirit (as defined in section 23 of the Petroleum (Consolidation) Act 1928) and is fitted to a vehicle first used on or after 1st July 1973, shall be—

        (i) made only of metal; and

        (ii) fixed in such a position and so maintained as to be reasonably secure from damage.

    (3) Notwithstanding the requirement of paragraph (2)(b), the fuel tank may be fitted with a device which, by the intake of air or the emission of vapour, relieves changes of pressure in the tank.]

    ([4]) Instead of complying with the requirements of [paragraphs (2) and (3)] as to construction, a vehicle may comply with the requirements of Community Directive 70/221 (insofar as they relate to fuel tanks) or ECE Regulation 34 or 34.01 or, if the vehicle is an agricultural motor vehicle, of Community Directive 74/151.   **[1380]**

NOTES

    Commencement: 11 August 1986.
    This regulation derived from SI 1978 No 1017, reg 19.
    Community Directives 70/221, 74/151: see reg 3, Sch 2.
    ECE Regulation 34, 34.01: see reg 3, Sch 2.
    Paras (1) to (3): substituted by SI 1990 No 2212, reg 4.

39A. [(1) Every vehicle to which this regulation applies shall be designed and constructed for running on unleaded petrol.

    (2) No person shall use or cause or permit to be used a vehicle to which this regulation applies on a road if it—

    (a) has been deliberately altered or adjusted for running on leaded petrol, and

(b) as a direct result of such alteration or adjustment it is incapable of running on unleaded petrol.

(3) Subject to paragraph (4) this regulation applies to every motor vehicle which is—

(a) propelled by a spark ignition engine which is capable of running on petrol, and
(b) is first used on or after the 1st April 1991.

(4) Part I of Schedule 3A shall have effect for the purpose of excluding certain vehicles first used before specified dates from the application of this regulation.

(5) In this regulation "petrol", "leaded petrol" and "unleaded petrol" have the same meaning as in Community Directive 85/210.

(6) A vehicle shall be regarded for the purposes of this regulation as incapable of running on unleaded petrol at any particular time if and only if in its state of adjustment at that time prolonged continuous running on such petrol would damage the engine.] **[1381]**

NOTES
Commencement: 1 October 1988.
Added by SI 1988 No 1524, reg 5.

39B. [(1) Subject to paragraph (2), every fuel tank fitted to a vehicle to which regulation 39A applies shall be so constructed and fitted that it cannot readily be filled from a petrol pump delivery nozzle which has an external diameter of 23.6 mm or greater without the aid of a device (such as a funnel) not fitted to the vehicle.

(2) Paragraph (1) does not apply to a vehicle in respect of which both of the following conditions are satisfied, that is to say—

(a) that at the time of its first use the vehicle is so designed and constructed that prolonged continuous running on leaded petrol would not cause any device designed to control the emission of carbon monoxide, hydrocarbons or nitrogen oxides to malfunction, and
(b) that it is conspicuously and legibly marked in a position immediately visible to a person filling the fuel tank with—

(i) the word "UNLEADED", or
(ii) the symbol shown in Part II of Schedule 3A.

(3) In this regulation "fuel tank", in relation to a vehicle, means a fuel tank used in connection with the propulsion of the vehicle.] **[1382]**

NOTES
Commencement: 1 October 1988.
Added by SI 1988 No 1524, reg 5.

40. Gas propulsion systems and gas-fired appliances

(1) A vehicle which is—

(a) a motor vehicle which first used gas as a fuel for its propulsion before 19th November 1982; or
(b) a trailer manufactured before 19th November 1982 to which there is fitted a gas container,

shall be so constructed that it complies either with the provisions of Schedule 4 or with the provisions of Schedule 5.

(2) A vehicle which is—

    (a) a motor vehicle which first used gas as a fuel for its propulsion on or after 19th November 1982; or

    (b) a motor vehicle first used on or after 1st May 1984 or a trailer manufactured on or after 19th November 1982 which is in either case equipped with a gas container or a gas-fired appliance,

shall comply with the provisions of Schedule 5.

(3) The requirements of this regulation are in addition to, and not in derogation from, the requirements of any regulations made under powers conferred by the Petroleum (Consolidation) Act 1928, the Health and Safety at Work etc. Act 1974, the Control of Pollution Act 1974 or any other Act or of any codes of practice issued under the Health and Safety at Work etc. Act 1974.

(4) In this regulation "gas container" has the meaning given in Schedule 4 where compliance with the provisions of that Schedule is concerned and otherwise has the meaning given in Schedule 5. **[1383]**

NOTES
Commencement: 11 August 1986.
This regulation derived from SI 1955 No 990, reg 24, and SI 1978 No 1017, reg 47.

H— Mini-buses

41. Construction

The requirements specified in Schedule 6 shall apply to every minibus first used on or after 1st April 1988 except a vehicle—

    (a) manufactured by Land Rover U.K. Limited and known as the Land Rover; or

    (b) constructed or adapted for the secure transport of prisoners. **[1384]**

NOTES
Commencement: 11 August 1986.

42. Fire extinguishing apparatus

(1) No person shall use, or cause or permit to be used, on a road a minibus first used on or after 1st April 1988 unless it carries suitable and efficient apparatus for extinguishing fire which is of a type specified in Part I of Schedule 7.

(2) The apparatus referred to in paragraph (1) above shall be—

    (a) readily available for use;

    (b) clearly marked with the appropriate British Standards Institution specification number; and

    (c) maintained in good and efficient working order.

(3) This regulation does not apply to a vehicle manufactured by Land Rover U.K. Limited and known as the Land Rover. **[1385]**

NOTES
Commencement: 11 August 1986.

43. First aid equipment

(1) No person shall use, or cause or permit to be used, on a road a minibus first used on or after 1st April 1988 unless it carries a receptacle which contains the items specified in Part II of Schedule 7.

(2) The receptacle referred to in paragraph (1) above shall be—

(a) maintained in a good condition;

(b) suitable for the purpose of keeping the items referred to in the said paragraph in good condition;

(c) readily available for use; and

(d) prominently marked as a first aid receptacle.

(3) The items referred to in paragraph (1) above shall be maintained in good condition and shall be of a good and reliable quality and of a suitable design.

(4) This regulation does not apply to a vehicle manufactured by Land Rover U.K. Limited and known as the Land Rover. **[1386]**

NOTES

Commencement: 11 August 1986.

44. Carriage of dangerous substances

(1) Save as provided in paragraph (2), no person shall use or cause or permit to be used on a road a minibus by which any highly inflammable or otherwise dangerous substance is carried unless that substance is carried in containers so designed and constructed, and unless the substance is so packed, that, notwithstanding an accident to the vehicle, it is unlikely that damage to the vehicle or injury to passengers in the vehicle will be caused by the substance.

(2) Paragraph (1) shall not apply in relation to the electrolyte of a battery installed in an electric wheelchair provided that the wheelchair is securely fixed to the vehicle.

(3) This regulation does not apply to a vehicle manufactured by Land Rover U.K. Limited and known as the Land Rover. **[1387]**

NOTES

Commencement: 11 August 1986.

I— Power to Weight Ratio

45. Power to weight ratio

(1) Save as provided in paragraph (2), every wheeled vehicle which is propelled by a compression ignition engine and which is required to be equipped with a plate by regulation 66(1) shall be so constructed that the power of its engine, calculated in accordance with paragraph 1 of Part III of Schedule 8, is at least 4.4 kW for every 1000 kg of the relevant weight.

(2) Paragraph (1) does not apply to—

(a) a heavy motor car or motor car first used before 1st April 1973;

(b) a vehicle manufactured before 1st April 1973 and powered by a Perkins 6.354 engine; or

(c) a bus.

(3) Every vehicle to which this regulation applies shall—

(a) if it is equipped with machinery or apparatus forming part of the vehicle or mounted on it and used for purposes not connected with the driving of the vehicle;

(b) if that machinery or apparatus is designed for use, or is likely to be used, when the vehicle is in motion on a road at a speed exceeding 5 mph; and

(c) if the power absorbed by that use is provided by the engine propelling the vehicle,

be so constructed that, when that machinery or apparatus is being used, the power of the engine remaining available to drive the vehicle is at least 4.4 kW for every 1000 kg of the relevant weight.

(4) In this regulation "relevant weight" means—

(a) if the vehicle is equipped with a plate in accordance with regulation 66(2)(a), the maximum train weight shown at item 8 on that plate or, if no such weight is shown, the maximum gross weight in Great Britain shown at item 10 on that plate; or

(b) if the vehicle is equipped with a plate in accordance with regulation 66(2)(b) and—

(i) is constructed to draw a trailer, the higher of the weights referred to in column 3 in item 2.1.5 in the Table in regulation 66; or

(ii) is not constructed to draw a trailer, the higher of the weights for motor vehicles referred to in columns 3 and 4 in item 2.1.4 in the Table in regulation 66.   **[1388]**

NOTES

Commencement: 11 August 1986.

This regulation derived from SI 1978 No 1017, regs 44, 45.

J— Protective Systems

46. Seat belt anchorage points

[(1) Save as provided by paragraph (2), this regulation applies to—

(a) every wheeled motor car first used on or after 1st January 1965;

(b) every three-wheeled motor cycle the unladen weight of which exceeds 255 kg and which was first used on or after 1st September 1970; and

(c) every heavy motor car first used on or after 1st October 1988.

(2) This regulation does not apply to—

(a) a goods vehicle (other than a dual-purpose vehicle) which was first used—

(i) before 1st April 1967; or

(ii) on or after 1st April 1980 and before 1st October 1988 and has a maximum gross weight exceeding 3500 kg; or

(iii) before 1st April 1980 or, if the vehicle is of a model manufactured before 1st October 1979, was first used before 1st April 1982 and in either case, has an unladen weight exceeding 1525 kg;

(b) a bus, being—

(i) a minibus—

(A) if first used before 1st October 1988, constructed or adapted to carry more than twelve passengers; or

(B) if first used on or after 1st October 1988, having a maximum gross weight exceeding 3500 kg; or

(ii) a large bus (other than a coach first used on or after 1st October 1988);

(c) an agricultural motor vehicle;
(d) a motor tractor;
(e) a works truck;
(f) an electrically-propelled goods vehicle first used before 1st October 1988;
(g) a pedestrian-controlled vehicle;
(h) a vehicle which has been used on roads outside Great Britain and has been imported into Great Britain, whilst it is being driven from the place where it has arrived in Great Britain to a place of residence of the owner or driver of the vehicle, or from any such place to a place where, by previous arrangement, it will be provided with such anchorage points as are required by this regulation and such seat belts as are required by regulation 47;
(i) a vehicle having a maximum speed not exceeding 16 mph;
(j) a motor cycle equipped with a driver's seat of a type requiring the driver to sit astride it, and which is constructed or assembled by a person not ordinarily engaged in the trade or business of manufacturing vehicles of that description; or
(k) a locomotive.

(3) A vehicle which was first used before 1st April 1982 shall be equipped with anchorage points which are designed to hold securely in position on the vehicle seat belts for the driver's seat and specified passenger's seat (if any).

(4) Save as provided in paragraph (4A) or (4B) a vehicle which is first used on or after 1st April 1982 shall be equipped with anchorage points which—

(a) are designed to hold securely in position on the vehicle seat belts for—

(i) in the case of a minibus, motor ambulance or a motor caravan—

(A) if first used before 1st October 1988, the driver's seat and the specified passenger's seat (if any); or
(B) if first used on or after 1st October 1988, the driver's seat and any forward-facing front seat; and

(ii) in the case of any other passenger or dual-purpose vehicle, every forward-facing seat constructed or adapted to accommodate one adult;

(iii) in every other case, every forward-facing front seat and every non-protected seat, and

(b) comply with the technical and installation requirements of Community Directive 76/115 or 81/575 or 82/318 [or 90/629] or ECE Regulation 14 [or 14.01 or 14.02] whether or not those instruments apply to the vehicle, so however, that the requirements in those instruments which relate to testing shall not apply.

(4A) The requirements specified in paragraph (4) shall not apply to—

(a) a goods vehicle first used on or after 1st October 1988 and having a maximum gross weight exceeding 3500 kg, but any such vehicle shall be equipped with two belt anchorages designed to hold securely in position on the vehicle lap belts for the driver's seat and each forward-facing front seat; or

(b) a coach equipped with anchorage points which are designed to hold securely in position on the vehicle seat belts for all exposed forward-facing seats and which—

    (i) comply with the requirements in paragraph (4)(b); or

    (ii) in any case where the anchorage points form part of a seat, do not when a forward horizontal force is applied to them become detached from the seat of which they form part before that seat becomes detached from the vehicle.

(4B) Instead of complying with the requirements in paragraph (4), a vehicle may comply [with—

    (a) Community Directive 76/115 or 81/575 or 82/318 [or 90/629]; or

    (b) ECE Regulation 14 or 14.01 or 14.02.]

(5) Save as provided in paragraph (5A), a vehicle of a type mentioned in paragraphs (4), (4A) and (4B) which is fitted with anchorage points other than those required by those paragraphs shall comply with the requirements in paragraph (4)(b), or in the case of a coach the requirements in paragraph (4A)(b)(ii), in respect of any additional anchorage points as well as in respect of the anchorage points required by paragraph (4), (4A) or (4B) to be provided.

(5A) The requirements in paragraph (5) shall not apply in respect of any additional anchorage points first fitted before 1st April 1986 in the case of a vehicle of a type mentioned in paragraph (4)(a)(i)(A), or before 1st October 1988 in the case of a vehicle of any other type.

(6) In this regulation—

    (a) the expressions "exposed forward-facing seat", "forward-facing seat", "forward-facing front seat", "lap belt", "seat belt" and "specified passenger's seat" have the same meaning as in regulation 47(8); . . .

    [(b) a seat is a "non protected seat" if it is not a front seat and the screen zones within the protected area have a combined surface area of less than 800 cm^2; and

    (c) "screen zone" and "protected area" in relation to a seat, shall be construed in accordance with paragraph 4.3.3 of Annex 1 to Community Directive 81/575.]] **[1389]**

NOTES

Commencement: 11 August 1986.

This regulation derived from SI 1978 No 1017, reg 17 (part).

Set out as amended by SI 1987 No 1133, regs 5, 8, Schedule.

Para (4)(b): words in square brackets inserted by SI 1991 No 2003, reg 4(1), (2).

Para (4B): first words in (outer) square brackets substituted by SI 1989 No 1478, reg 3; second words in (inner) square brackets inserted by SI 1991 No 2003, reg 4(1), (3).

Para (6): words omitted repealed and words in square brackets substituted by SI 1991 No 2003, reg 4(1), (4).

Community Directives 76/115, 81/575, 82/318, 90/629: see reg 3, Sch 2.

ECE Regulations 14, 14.01, 14.02: see reg 3, Sch 2.

Type Approval (Great Britain) Regulations: SI 1984 No 981.

47. Seat belts

[(1) This regulation applies to every vehicle to which regulation 46 applies.

(2) Save as provided in paragraph (4) a vehicle to which—

    (a) this regulation applies which was first used before 1st April 1981 shall be provided with—

       (i) a body-restraining belt, designed for use by an adult, for the driver's seat; and

       (ii) a body-restraining seat belt for the specified passenger's seat (if any);

(b) this regulation applies which is first used on or after 1st April 1981 shall be provided with three-point seat belts for the driver's seat and for the specified passenger's seat (if any);

(c) regulation 46(4)(a)(ii) applies which is first used on or after 1st April 1987 shall be fitted with seat belts additional to those required by sub-paragraph (b) as follows—

    (i) for any forward-facing front seat alongside the driver's seat, not being a specified passenger's seat, a seat belt which is a three-point belt, or a lap belt installed in accordance with paragraph 3.1.2.1 of Annex 1 to Community Directive 77/541 or a disabled person's belt;

    (ii) in the case of a passenger or dual-purpose vehicle having not more than two forward-facing seats behind the driver's seat with either—

        (A) an inertia reel belt for at least one of those seats, or

        (B) a three-point belt, a lap belt, a disabled person's belt or a child restraint for each of those seats;

    (iii) in the case of a passenger or dual-purpose vehicle having more than two forward-facing seats behind the driver's seat, with either—

        (A) an inertia reel belt for one of those seats being an outboard seat and a three-point belt, a lap belt, a disabled person's belt or a child restraint for at least one other of those seats;

        (B) a three-point belt for one of those seats and either a child restraint or a disabled person's belt for at least one other of those seats; or

        (C) a three-point belt, a lap belt, a disabled person's belt or a child restraint for each of those seats.

(d) regulation 46(4)(a)(i)(B) applies shall be fitted with seat belts as follows—

    (i) for the driver's seat and the specified passenger's seat (if any) a three-point belt; and

    (ii) for any forward-facing front seat which is not a specified passenger's seat, a three-point belt or a lap belt installed in accordance with the provisions of sub-paragraph (c)(i);

(e) regulation 46(4A)(b) applies shall be equipped with seat belts which shall be three-point belts, lap belts or disabled person's belts.

Where a lap belt is fitted to a forward-facing front seat of a minibus, a motor ambulance or a motor caravan, or to an exposed forward-facing seat [(other than the driver's seat or any crew seat) of a coach either—

    (i) there shall be provided padding to a depth of not less than 50 mm, on that part of the surface or edge of any bar, or the top or edge of any screen or partition, which would be likely to be struck by the head of a passenger wearing the lap belt in the event of accident; or

    (ii) the technical and installation requirements of Annex 4 to ECE Regulation 21 shall be met, in respect of any such bar, screen or partition,

but nothing in sub-paragraph (i) above shall require padding to be provided on any surface more than 1 m from the centre of the line of intersection of the seat cushion and the back rest or more than 150 mm on either side of the longitudinal vertical plane which passes through the centre of that line, nor shall it require padding to be provided on any instrument panel of a minibus.]

(3) Every seat belt for an adult, other than a disabled person's belt, provided for a vehicle in accordance with paragraph (2)(b), (c), (d) or (e) shall, except as provided in paragraph (6), comply with the installation requirements specified in paragraph 3.2.2 to 3.3.4 of Annex I to Community Directive 77/541 [or 82/319 or 90/628] whether or not [those Directives apply] to the vehicle.

(4) The requirements specified in paragraph (2) do not apply—

(a) to a vehicle while it is being used under a trade licence within the meaning of section 16 of the 1971 Act;

(b) to a vehicle, not being a vehicle to which the Type Approval (Great Britain) Regulations apply, while it is being driven from premises of the manufacturer by whom it was made, or of a distributor of vehicles or dealer in vehicles—

(i) to premises of a distributor of or dealer in vehicles or of the purchaser of the vehicle, or

(ii) to premises of a person obtaining possession of the vehicle under a hiring agreement or hire-purchase agreement;

(c) in relation to any seat for which there is provided—

(i) a seat belt which bears a mark including the specification number of the British Standard for Passive Belt Systems, namely BS AU 183:1983 and including the registered certification trade mark of the British Standards Institution; or

(ii) a seat belt designed for use by an adult which is a harness belt comprising a lap belt and shoulder straps which bears a British Standard mark or a mark including the specification number for the British Standard for Seat Belt Assemblies for Motor Vehicles, namely BS 3254:1960 or [BS 3254: Part 1: 1988] and including the registered certification trade mark of the British Standards Institution, or the marking designated in item 16 in Schedule 2 to the Approval Marks Regulations;

(d) in relation to the driver's seat or the specified passenger's seat (if any) of a vehicle which has been specially designed and constructed, or specially adapted, for the use of a person suffering from some physical defect or disability, in a case where a disabled person's belt for an adult person is provided for use for that seat;

(e) to a vehicle to which regulation 46(4A)(a) applies.

(5) Every seat belt provided in pursuance of paragraph (2) shall be properly secured to the anchorage points provided for it in accordance with regulation 46; or, in the case of a child restraint, to anchorages specially provided for it or, in the case of a disabled person's belt, secured to the vehicle or to the seat which is being occupied by the person wearing the belt.

(6) Paragraph (3), in so far as it relates to the second paragraph of paragraph 3.3.2 of the Annex there mentioned (which concerns the locking or releasing of a seat belt by a single movement) does not apply in respect of a seat belt fitted for—

(a) a seat which is treated as a specified passenger's seat by virtue of the provisions of sub-paragraph (ii) in the definition of "specified passenger's seat" in paragraph (8); or

(b) any forward-facing seat for a passenger alongside the driver's seat of a goods vehicle which has an unladen weight of more than 915 kg and has more than one such seat, any such seats for passengers being joined together in a single structure; or

(c) any seat (other than the driver's seat) fitted to a coach.

(7) Every seat belt, other than a disabled person's belt or a seat belt of a kind mentioned in paragraph 4(c)(i) or (ii) above, provided for any person in a vehicle to which this regulation applies shall be legibly and permanently marked—

(a) if the vehicle was first used before 1st April 1981 or if the belt is a child restraint, with a British Standard mark or a designated approval mark; or

(b) in any other case, with a designated approval mark.

Provided this paragraph shall not operate so as to invalidate the exception permitted in paragraph (6).

(8) In this regulation—

"body-restraining seat belt" means a seat belt designed to provide restraint for both the upper and lower parts of the trunk of the wearer in the event of an accident to the vehicle;

"British Standard mark" means a mark consisting of—

(i) the specification number of one of the following British Standards for Seat Belts Assemblies for Motor Vehicles, namely—

(a) if it is a seat belt for an adult, BS 3254:1960 [or BS 3254: Part 1: 1988]; or

(b) if it is a child restraint, BS 3254:1960, or BS 3254: 1960 as amended by Amendment No 16 published on 31st July 1986 under the number AMD 5210, [BS 3254: Part 2: 1988], BS AU 185, BS AU 186 or 186a, BS AU 202 [or BS AU 202a]; and, in either case,

(ii) the registered certification trade mark of the British Standards Institution;

"child restraint" means a seat belt for the use of a young person which is designed either to be fitted directly to a suitable anchorage or to be used in conjunction with a seat belt for an adult and held in place by the restraining action of that belt:

Provided that for the purposes of paragraph (2)(c)(ii)(B) and (2)(c)(iii) it means only such seat belts fitted directly to a suitable anchorage and excludes belts marked with the specification numbers BS AU 185 and BS AU 186 or 186a.

"crew seat" has the same meaning as in regulation 3(1) of the Public Service Vehicles (Conditions of Fitness Equipment, Use and Certification) Regulations 1981;

"designated approval mark" means

(a) if it is a seat belt other than a child restraint, the marking designated as an approval mark by regulation 4 of the Approval Marks Regulations and shown at [items 16 and 16A] of Schedule 2 to those Regulations or the marking designated as an approval mark by regulation 5 of those Regulations and shown at item 23[, 23A and 23B] in Schedule 4 to those Regulations, and

(b) if it is a child restraint, [any] of the markings designated as approval marks by regulation 4 of those Regulations and shown at [items 44, 44A and 44B] in Schedule 2 to those Regulations.

"disabled person's belt" means a seat belt which has been specially designed or adapted for use by an adult or young person suffering from some physical defect or disability and which is intended for use solely by such a person;

"exposed forward-facing seat" means—

(i) a forward-facing seat (including any crew seat) and the driver's seat; and

(ii) any other forward-facing seat which is not immediately behind and on the same horizontal plane as a forward-facing high-backed seat;

"forward-facing seat" means a seat which is attached to a vehicle so that it faces towards the front of the vehicle in such a manner that a line passing through the centre of both the front and the back of the seat is at an angle of 30° or less to the longitudinal axis of the vehicle;

"forward-facing front seat" means—

(i) any forward-facing seat alongside the driver's seat; or

(ii) if the vehicle normally has no seat which is a forward-facing front seat under sub-paragraph (i) of this definition, each forward-facing seat for a passenger which is foremost in the vehicle;

"forward-facing high-backed seat" means a forward-facing seat which is also a high-backed seat;

"high-backed seat" means a seat the highest part of which is at least 1 metre above the deck of the vehicle;

"inertia reel belt" means a three-point belt of either of the types required for a front outboard seating position by paragraph 3.1.1. of Annex 1 to Community Directive 77/541;

"lap belt" means a seat belt which passes across the front of the wearer's pelvic region and which is designed for use by an adult;

"seat" includes any part designed for the accommodation of one adult of a continuous seat designed for the accommodation of more than one adult;

"seat belt" means a belt intended to be worn by a person in a vehicle and designed to prevent or lessen injury to its wearer in the event of an accident to the vehicle and includes, in the case restraint, any special chair to which the belt is attached;

"specified passenger's seat" means—

(i) in the case of a vehicle which has one forward-facing front seat alongside the driver's seat, that seat, and in the case of a vehicle which has more than one such seat, the one furthest from the driver's seat; or

(ii) if the vehicle normally has no seat which is the specified passenger's seat under sub-paragraph (i) of this definition the forward-facing front seat for a passenger which is foremost in the vehicle and furthest from the driver's seat, unless there is a fixed partition separating that seat from the space in front of it alongside the driver's seat; and

"three-point belt" means a seat belt which—

(i) restrains the upper and lower parts of the torso;

(ii) includes a lap belt;

(iii) is anchored at not less than three points; and

(iv) is designed for use by an adult.]   **[1390]**

NOTES
    Commencement: 11 August 1986.
    This regulation derived from SI 1978 No 1017, reg 17 (part).
    Set out as amended by SI 1987 No 1133, regs 5, 8, Schedule.
    Paras (2), (4): words and figures in square brackets substituted by SI 1989 No 1478, reg 4.
    Para (3): words in square brackets substituted or inserted by SI 1991 No 2003, reg 5(1), (2).
    Para (8): second words in square brackets in definition "designated approval mark" substituted
by SI 1991 No 2003, reg 5(1), (3); remaining words and figures in that para substituted by SI 1989
No 1478, reg 4.
    Community Directives 77/541, 82/319, 90/628: see reg 3, Sch 2.
    The 1971 Act: Vehicles (Excise) Act 1971.
    Type Approval (Great Britain) Regulations: SI 1984 No 981.
    Approval Marks Regulations: SI 1979 No 1088.

48. Maintenance of seat belts and anchorage points

(1) This regulation applies to every seat belt with which a motor vehicle is required to be provided in accordance with regulation 47 and to the anchorages, fastenings, adjusting device and retracting mechanism (if any) of every such seat belt [and also to every anchorage with which a goods vehicle is required to be provided in accordance with regulation 46(4A)(a)].

(2) For the purposes of this regulation the anchorages and anchorage points of a seat belt shall, in the case of a seat which incorporates integral seat belt anchorages, include the system by which the seat assembly itself is secured to the vehicle structure.

(3) The anchorage points provided for seat belts shall be used only as anchorages for the seat belts for which they are intended to be used or capable of being used.

(4) Save as provided in paragraph (5) below—

   (a) all load-bearing members of the vehicle structure or panelling within 30 cm of each anchorage point shall be maintained in a sound condition and free from serious corrosion, distortion or fracture;

   (b) the adjusting device and (if fitted) the retracting mechanism of the seat belt shall be so maintained that the belt may be readily adjusted to the body of the wearer, either automatically or manually, according to the design of the device and (if fitted) the retracting mechanism;

   (c) the seat belt and its anchorages, fastenings and adjusting device shall be maintained free from any obvious defect which would be likely to affect adversely the performance by the seat belt of the function of restraining the body of the wearer in the event of an accident to the vehicle;

   (d) the buckle or other fastening of the seat belt shall—

      (i) be so maintained that the belt can be readily fastened or unfastened;

      (ii) be kept free from any temporary or permanent obstruction; and

      (iii) except in the case of a disabled person's seat belt, be readily accessible to a person sitting in the seat for which the seat belt is provided;

   (e) the webbing or other material which forms the seat belt shall be maintained free from cuts or other visible faults (as, for example, extensive fraying) which would be likely to affect adversely the performance of the belt when under stress;

(f) the ends of every seat belt, other than a disabled person's seat belt, shall be securely fastened to the anchorage points provided for them; and

(g) the ends of every disabled person's seat belt shall, when the seat belt is being used for the purpose for which it was designed and constructed, be securely fastened either to some part of the structure of the vehicle or to the seat which is being occupied by the person wearing the belt so that the body of the person wearing the belt would be restrained in the event of an accident to the vehicle.

(5) No requirement specified in paragraph (4) above applies if the vehicle is being used—

(a) on a journey after the start of which the requirement ceased to be complied with; or

(b) after the requirement ceased to be complied with and steps have been taken for such compliance to be restored with all reasonable expedition.

(6) Expressions which are used in this regulation and are defined in regulation 47 have the same meaning in this regulation as they have in regulation 47.   **[1391]**

NOTES
   Commencement: 11 August 1986.
   This regulation derived from SI 1978 No 1017, reg 102A.
   Sub-s (1): amended by SI 1987 No 1133, reg 7.

49. Rear under-run protection

(1) Save as provided in paragraph (2), the regulation applies to a wheeled goods vehicle being either—

(a) a motor vehicle with a maximum gross weight which exceeds 3500 kg and which was first used on or after 1st April 1984; or

(b) a trailer manufactured on or after 1st May 1983 with an unladen weight which exceeds 1020 kg.

(2) This regulation does not apply to—

(a) a motor vehicle which has a maximum speed not exceeding 15 mph;

(b) a motor car or a heavy motor car constructed or adapted to form part of an articulated vehicle;

(c) an agricultural trailer;

(d) engineering plant;

(e) a fire engine;

(f) an agricultural motor vehicle;

(g) a vehicle fitted at the rear with apparatus specially designed for spreading material on a road;

(h) a vehicle so constructed that it can be unloaded by part of the vehicle being tipped rearwards;

(i) a vehicle owned by the Secretary of State for Defence and used for naval, military or air force purposes;

(j) a vehicle to which no bodywork has been fitted and which is being driven or towed—

   (i) for the purpose of a quality or safety check by its manufacturer or a dealer in, or distributor of, such vehicles; or

(ii) to a place where, by previous arrangement, bodywork is to be fitted or work preparatory to the fitting of bodywork is to be carried out; or

(iii) by previous arrangement to premises of a dealer in, or distributor of, such vehicles;

(k) a vehicle which is being driven or towed to a place where by previous arrangement a device is to be fitted so that it complies with this regulation;

(l) a vehicle specially designed and constructed, and not merely adapted, to carry other vehicles loaded onto it from the rear;

(m) a trailer specially designed and constructed, and not merely adapted, to carry round timber, beams or girders, being items of exceptional length;

(n) a vehicle fitted with a tail lift so constructed that the lift platform forms part of the floor of the vehicle and this part has a length of at least 1 m measured parallel to the longitudinal axis of the vehicle;

(o) a trailer having a base or centre in a country outside Great Britain from which it normally starts its journeys, provided that a period of not more than 12 months has elapsed since the vehicle was last brought into Great Britain;

(p) a vehicle specially designed, and not merely adapted, for the carriage and mixing of liquid concrete;

(q) a vehicle designed and used solely for the delivery of coal by means of a special conveyor which is carried on the vehicle and when in use is fitted to the rear of the vehicle so as to render its being equipped with a rear under-run protective device impracticable; or

(r) an agricultural trailed appliance.

(3) Subject to the provisions of paragraphs (4), (5) and (6), every vehicle to which this regulation applies shall be equipped with a rear under-run protective device.

(4) A vehicle to which this regulation applies and which is fitted with a tail lift, bodywork or other part which renders its being equipped with a rear under-run protective device impracticable shall instead be equipped with one or more devices which do not protrude beyond the overall width of the vehicle (excluding any part of the device or the devices) and which comply with the following requirements—

(a) where more than one device is fitted, not more than 50 cm shall lie between one device and the device next to it;

(b) not more than 30 cm shall lie between the outermost end of a device nearest to the outermost part of the vehicle to which it is fitted and a longitudinal plane passing through the outer end of the rear axle of the vehicle on the same side of the vehicle or, in a case where the vehicle is fitted with more than one rear axle, through the outer end of the widest rear axle on the same side of the vehicle, and paragraph II.5.4.2 in the Annex to Community Directive 79/490 shall not have effect in a case where this requirement is met; and

(c) the device or, where more than one device is fitted, all the devices together, shall have the characteristics specified in paragraphs [II.5.4.1] to II.5.4.5.5.2 in the Annex to the said Directive save—

(i) as provided in sub-paragraphs (a) and (b) above;

(ii) that for the reference in paragraph II.5.4.5.1 in that Annex to 30 cm there is substituted a reference to 35 cm; and

(iii) that the distance of 40 cm specified in paragraph II.5.4.5 in that Annex may be measured exclusive of the said tail-lift, bodywork or other part.

(5) The provisions of paragraph (3) shall have effect so that in the case of—

(a) a vehicle which is fitted with a demountable body, the characteristics specified in paragraph II.5.4.2 in the Annex to the said Directive have effect as if the reference to 10 cm were a reference to 30 cm and as if in paragraph II.5.4.5.1 the reference to 30 cm were a reference to 35 cm; and

(b) a trailer with a single axle or two close-coupled axles, the height of 55 cm referred to in paragraph II.5.4.1 in that Annex is measured when the coupling of the trailer to the vehicle by which it is drawn is at the height recommended by the manufacturer of the trailer.

(6) Instead of complying with paragraphs (3) to (5) a vehicle may comply with Community Directive 79/490.

(7) In this regulation—

"rear under-run protective device" means a device within the description given in paragraph II.5.4 in the Annex to Community Directive 79/490.
[1392]

NOTES
Commencement: 11 August 1986.
This regulation derived from SI 1978 No 1017, reg 46B.
Para (4): in sub-para (c) amendment in square brackets made by SI 1987 No 676, reg 15(3).
Community Directive 79/490: see reg 3, Sch 2.

50. Maintenance of rear under-run protective device

Every device fitted to a vehicle in compliance with the requirements of regulation 49 shall at all times when the vehicle is on a road be maintained free from any obvious defect which would be likely to affect adversely the performance of the device in the function of giving resistance in the event of an impact from the rear.   **[1393]**

NOTES
Commencement: 11 August 1986.
This regulation derived from SI 1978 No 1017, reg 105A.

51. Sideguards

(1) Save as provided in paragraph (2), this regulation applies to a wheeled goods vehicle being—

(a) a motor vehicle first used on or after 1st April 1984 with a maximum gross weight which exceeds 3500 kg; or

(b) a trailer manufactured on or after 1st May 1983 with an unladen weight which exceeds 1020 kg; or

(c) a semi-trailer manufactured before 1st May 1983 which has a relevant plate showing a gross weight exceeding 26,000 kg and which forms part of an articulated vehicle with a relevant train weight exceeding 32,520 kg.

(2) This regulation does not apply to—

(a) a motor vehicle which has a maximum speed not exceeding 15 mph;

(b) an agricultural trailer;

(c) engineering plant;

(d) a fire engine;

(e) an agricultural motor vehicle;

(f) a vehicle so constructed that it can be unloaded by part of the vehicle being tipped sideways or rearwards;

(g) a vehicle owned by the Secretary of State for Defence and used for naval, military or air force purposes;

(h) a vehicle to which no bodywork has been fitted and which is being driven or towed—

    (i) for the purpose of a quality or safety check by its manufacturer or a dealer in, or distributor of, such vehicles;

    (ii) to a place where, by previous arrangement, bodywork is to be fitted or work preparatory to the fitting of bodywork is to be carried out; or

    (iii) by previous arrangement to premises of a dealer in, or distributor of, such vehicles;

(i) a vehicle which is being driven or towed to a place where by previous arrangement a sideguard is to be fitted so that it complies with this regulation;

(j) a refuse vehicle;

(k) a trailer specially designed and constructed, and not merely adapted, to carry round timber, beams or girders, being items of exceptional length;

(l) a motor car or a heavy motor car constructed or adapted to form part of an articulated vehicle;

(m) a vehicle specially designed and constructed, and not merely adapted, to carry other vehicles loaded onto it from the front or the rear;

(n) a trailer with a load platform—

    (i) no part of any edge of which is more than 60 mm inboard from the tangential plane; and

    (ii) the upper surface of which is not more than 750 mm from the ground throughout that part of its length under which a sideguard would have to be fitted in accordance with paragraph (5)(d) to (g) if this exemption did not apply to it;

(o) a trailer having a base or centre in a country outside Great Britain from which it normally starts its journeys, provided that a period of not more than 12 months has elapsed since the vehicle was last brought into Great Britain; or

(p) an agricultural trailed appliance.

[(2A) This regulation also applies to a wheeled goods vehicle, whether of a description falling within paragraph (2) or not, which is a semi-trailer some or all of the wheels of which are driven by the drawing vehicle.]

(3) Every vehicle to which this regulation applies shall be securely fitted with a sideguard to give protection on any side of the vehicle where—

(a) if it is a semi-trailer, the distance between the transverse planes passing through the centre of its foremost axle and through the centre of its king pin or, in the case of a vehicle having more than one king pin, the rearmost one, exceeds 4.5 m; or

(b) if it is any other vehicle, the distance between the centres of any two consecutive axles exceeds 3 m.

(4) Save as provided in paragraphs (6) and (7), a sideguard with which a vehicle is by this regulation required to be fitted shall comply with all the specifications listed in paragraph (5).

(5) Those specifications are—

(a) the outermost surface of every sideguard shall be smooth, essentially rigid and either flat or horizontally corrugated, save that—

    (i) any part of the surface may overlap another provided that the overlapping edges face rearwards or downwards;

    (ii) a gap not exceeding 25 mm measured longtidinally may exist between any two adjacent parts of the surface provided that the foremost edge of the rearward part does not protrude outboard of the rearmost edge of the forward part; and

    (iii) domed heads of bolts or rivets may protrude beyond the surface to a distance not exceeding 10 mm;

(b) no part of the lowest edge of a sideguard shall be more than 550 mm above the ground when the vehicle to which it is fitted is on level ground and, in the case of a semi-trailer, when its load platform is horizontal;

(c) in a case specified in an item in column 2 of the Table the highest edge of a sideguard shall be as specified in that item in column 3;

(d) the distance between the rearmost edge of a sideguard and the transverse plane passing through the foremost part of the tyre fitted to the wheel of the vehicle nearest to it shall not exceed 300 mm;

(e) the distance between the foremost edge of a sideguard fitted to a semi-trailer and a transverse plane passing through the centre of the vehicle's king pin or, if the vehicle has more than one king pin, the rearmost one, shall not exceed 3 m;

(f) the foremost edge of a sideguard fitted to a semi-trailer with landing legs shall, as well as complying with sub-paragraph (e), not be more than 250 mm to the rear of a transverse plane passing through the centre of the leg nearest to that edge;

(g) the distance between the foremost edge of a sideguard fitted to a vehicle other than a semi-trailer and a transverse plane passing through the rearmost part of the tyre fitted to the wheel of the vehicle nearest to it shall not exceed 300 mm if the vehicle is a motor vehicle and 500 mm if the vehicle is a trailer;

(h) the external edges of a sideguard shall be rounded at a radius of at least 2.5 mm;

(i) no sideguard shall be more than 30 mm inboard from the tangential plane;

(j) no sideguard shall project beyond the longitudinal plane from which, in the absence of a sideguard, the vehicle's overall width would fall to be measured;

(k) every sideguard shall cover an area extending to at least 100 mm upwards from its lowest edge 100 mm downwards from its highest edge, and 100 mm rearwards and inwards from its foremost edge, and no sideguard shall have a vertical gap measuring more than 300 mm nor any vertical surface measuring less than 100 mm; and

(l) except in the case of a vehicle described in paragraph (1)(c) every sideguard shall be capable of withstanding a force of 2 kilonewtons applied perpendicularly to any part of its surface by the centre of a ram the face of which is circular and not more than 220 mm in diameter, and during such application—

    (i) no part of the sideguard shall be deflected by more than 150 mm, and

    (ii) no part of the sideguard which is less than 250 mm from its rearmost part shall be deflected by more than 30 mm.

TABLE (regulation 51(5))

1	2	3
Item	Case	Requirement about highest edge of sideguard
1	Where the floor of the vehicle to which the sideguard is fitted— (i) extends laterally outside the tangential plane; (ii) is not more than 1·85 m from the ground; (iii) extends laterally over the whole of the length of the sideguard with which the vehicle is required by this regulation to be fitted; and (iv) is wholly covered at its edge by a side-rave the lower edge of which is not more than 150 mm below the underside of the floor.	Not more than 350 mm below the lower edge of the side-rave.
2	Where the floor of the vehicle to which the sideguard is fitted— (i) extends laterally outside the tangential plane; and (ii) does not comply with all of the provisions specified in sub-paragraphs (ii), (iii) and (iv) in item 1 above, and any part of the structure of the vehicle is cut within 1·85 m of the ground by the tangential plane.	Not more than 350 mm below the structure of the vehicle where it is cut by the tangential plane.
3	Where— (i) no part of the structure of the vehicle is cut within 1·85 m of the ground by the tangential plane; and (ii) the upper surface of the load carrying structure of the vehicle is less than 1·5 m from the ground.	Not less than the height of the upper surface of the load carrying structure of the vehicle.
4	A vehicle specially designed, and not merely adapted, for the carriage and mixing of liquid concrete.	Not less than 1 m from the ground.
5	Any other case.	Not less than 1·5 m from the ground.

(6) The provisions of paragraph (4) apply—

(a) in the case of an extendible trailer when it is, by virtue of the extending mechanism, extended to a length greater than its minimum, so as not to require, in respect of any additional distance solely attributable to the extension, compliance with the specifications mentioned in paragraph (5)(d) to (g);

(b) in the case of a vehicle designed and constructed, and not merely adapted, to be fitted with a demountable body or to carry a container, when it is not fitted with a demountable body or carrying such a container as if it were fitted with such a body or carrying such a container; and

(c) only so far as it is practicable in the case of—

(i) a vehicle designed solely for the carriage of a fluid substance in a closed tank which is permanently fitted to the vehicle and provided with valves and hose or pipe connections for loading or unloading; and

(ii) a vehicle which requires additional stability during loading or unloading or while being used for operations for which it is designed or adapted and is fitted on one or both sides with an extendible device to provide such stability.

(7) In the case of a motor vehicle to which this regulation applies and which is of a type which was required to be approved by the Type Approval for Goods Vehicles Regulations before 1st October 1983—

(a) if the bodywork of the vehicle covers the whole of the area specified as regards a sideguard in paragraph (5)(b), (c), (d) and (g) above the other provisions of that paragraph do not apply to that vehicle; and

(b) if the bodywork of the vehicle covers only part of that area the part of that area which is not so covered shall be fitted with a sideguard which complies with the provisions of paragraph (5) above save that there shall not be a gap between—

(i) the rearmost edge of the sideguard or the rearmost part of the bodywork (whichever is furthest to the rear) and the transverse plane mentioned in paragraph 5(d) of more than 300 mm;

(ii) the foremost edge of the sideguard or the foremost part of the bodywork (whichever is furthest to the front) and the transverse plane mentioned in paragraph (5)(g) of more than 300 mm; or

(iii) any vertical or sloping edge of any part of the bodywork in question and the edge of the sideguard immediately forwards or rearwards thereof of more than 25 mm measured horizontally.

(8) In this regulation

"relevant plate" means a Ministry plate, where fitted, and in other cases a plate fitted in accordance with regulation 66;

"relevant train weight" means the train weight shown in column 2 of the Ministry plate, where fitted, and in other cases the maximum train weight shown at item 8 of the plate fitted in accordance with regulation 66; and

"tangential plane", in relation to sideguard, means the vertical plane tangential to the external face of the outermost part of the tyre (excluding any distortion caused by the weight of the vehicle) fitted to the outermost wheel at the rear and on the same side of the vehicle.

[(9) Instead of complying with the foregoing provisions of this regulation a vehicle may comply with Community Directive 89/297.]   **[1394]**

NOTES

Commencement: 30 October 1989 (para (9)); 6 May 1987 (para (2A)); 11 August 1986 (remainder).

This regulation derived from SI 1978 No 1017, regs 46C, 46D.

Para (2A): added by SI 1987 No 676, reg 6.
Para (9): added by SI 1989 No 1695, reg 3.
Type Approval for Goods Vehicles Regulations: SI 1982 No 1271.
Community Directive 89/297: OJ No L124, 5.5.89, p.1.

52. Maintenance of sideguards

Every sideguard fitted to a vehicle in compliance with the requirements of
regulation 51 shall at all times when the vehicle is on a road be maintained free
from any obvious defect which would be likely to affect adversely its
effectiveness.   **[1395]**

NOTES
Commencement: 11 August 1986.
This regulation derived from SI 1978 No 1017, reg 105B.

53. Mascots

(1) Subject to paragraph (2), no mascot, emblem or other ornamental object
shall be carried by a motor vehicle first used on or after 1st October 1937 in any
position where it is likely to strike any person with whom the vehicle may
collide unless the mascot is not liable to cause injury to such person by reason of
any projection thereon.

(2) Instead of complying with the requirements of paragraph (1) a vehicle
may comply with Community Directive 74/483 or 79/488 or ECE Regulation
26.01.   **[1396]**

NOTES
Commencement: 11 August 1986.
This regulation derived from SI 1955 No 990, reg 76, and SI 1978 No 1017, reg 142.
Community Directives 74/483, 79/488: see reg 3, Sch 2.
ECE Regulation 26.01: see reg 3, Sch 2.

53A. Strength of superstructure

[(1) This regulation applies to every coach which is—

    (a) a single decked vehicle;
    (b) equipped with a compartment below the deck for the luggage of
        passengers; and
    (c) first used on or after [1st April 1993].

(2) Every vehicle to which this regulation applies shall comply with the
requirements of ECE Regulation 66.]   **[1397]**

NOTES
Commencement: 31 July 1987.
Added by SI 1987 No 1133, reg 4.
Para 1: date in square brackets substituted by SI 1989 No 2360, reg 3.

53B. Additional exits from double-decked coaches

[(1) This regulation applies to every coach which is—

    (a) a double-decked vehicle; and
    (b) first used on or after 1st April 1990.

(2) Subject to the following provisions of this regulation, every vehicle to
which this regulation applies shall be equipped with two staircases, one of
which shall be located in one half of the vehicle and the other in the other half
of the vehicle.

(3) Instead of being equipped with two staircases in accordance with paragraph (2), a vehicle to which this regulation applies may be equipped in accordance with the following provisions of this regulation with a hammer or other similar device with which in case of emergency any side window of the vehicle may be broken.

(4) Where a vehicle is equipped with—

(a) a staircase located in one half of the vehicle; and
(b) an emergency exit complying with regulation 21(8) of the Public Service Vehicles (Conditions of Fitness, Equipment, Use and Certification) Regulations 1981 located in the same half of the upper deck of the vehicle;

the hammer or the similar device shall be located in the other half of that deck.

(5) Any hammer or other similar device with which a vehicle is equipped pursuant to this regulation shall be located in a conspicuous readily accessible position in the upper deck of the vehicle.

(6) There shall be displayed, in a conspicuous position in close proximity to the hammer or other similar device, a notice which shall contain in clear and indelible lettering—

(a) in letters not less than 25 mm high, the heading "IN EMERGENCY"; and
(b) in letters not less than 10 mm high, instructions that in case of emergency the hammer or device is to be used first to break any side window by striking the glass near the edge of the window and then to clear any remaining glass from the window aperture.

(7) For the purposes of this regulation a staircase, emergency exit, hammer or other similar device (as the case may be) shall be considered to be located in the other half of the vehicle if the shortest distance between any part of that staircase, exit, hammer or device (as the case may be) and any part of any other staircase, emergency exit, hammer or device is not less than one half of the overall length of the vehicle.] **[1398]**

NOTES

Commencement: 31 July 1987.
Added by SI 1987 No 1133, reg 4.

K— Control of Emissions

54. Silencers

(1) Every vehicle propelled by an internal combustion engine shall be fitted with an exhaust system including a silencer and the exhaust gases from the engine shall not escape into the atmosphere without first passing through the silencer.

(2) Every exhaust system and silencer shall be maintained in good and efficient working order and shall not be altered so as to increase the noise made by the escape of exhaust gases.

(3) Instead of complying with paragraph (1) a vehicle may comply with Community Directive 77/212, 81/334, 84/372 or 84/424 or, in the case of a motor cycle other than a moped, 78/1015.

(4) In this regulation "moped" has the meaning given to it in paragraph (5) of Schedule 9. **[1399]**

NOTES
Commencement: 11 August 1986.
This regulation derived from SI 1955 No 990, regs 19, 55, and SI 1978 No 1017, reg 116A.
Community Directives 77/212, 78/1015, 81/334, 84/372, 84/424: see reg 3, Sch 2.

55. Noise limits-general

(1) Save as provided in paragraph (2) and regulation 59, this regulation applies to every wheeled motor vehicle having at least three wheels and first used on or after 1st October 1983 which is—

    (a) a vehicle, not falling within sub-paragraph (b) or (c), with or without bodywork;

    (b) a vehicle not falling within sub-paragraph (c) which is—

        (i) engineering plant;
        (ii) a locomotive other than an agricultural motor vehicle;
        (iii) a motor tractor other than an industrial tractor or an agricultural motor vehicle;
        (iv) a public works vehicle;
        (v) a works truck; or
        (vi) a refuse vehicle; or

    (c) a vehicle which—

        (i) has a compression ignition engine;
        (ii) is so constructed or adapted that the driving power of the engine is, or by appropriate use of the controls can be, transmitted to all wheels of the vehicle; and
        (iii) falls within category I.1.1., I.1.2, or I.1.3 specified in Article 1 of Community Directive 77/212.

(2) This regulation does not apply to—

    (a) a motorcycle with a sidecar attached;

    (b) an agricultural motor vehicle which is first used before 1st June 1986 or which is not driven at more than 20 mph;

    (c) an industrial tractor;

    (d) a road roller;

    (e) a vehicle specially constructed, and not merely adapted, for the purpose of fighting fires or salvage from fires at or in the vicinity of airports, and having an engine power exceeding 220 kW;

    (f) a vehicle which runs on rails; or

    (g) a vehicle manufactured by Leyland Vehicles Ltd. and known as the Atlantean Bus, if first used before 1st October 1984.

(3) Save as provided in paragraphs (4) and (5), every vehicle to which this regulation applies shall be so constructed that it complies with the requirements set out in item 1, 2, 3 or 4 of the Table; a vehicle complies with those requirements if—

    (a) its sound level does not exceed the relevant limit specified in column 2(a), (b) or (c), as the case may be, in the relevant item when measured under the conditions specified in column 3 in that item and by the method specified in column 4 in that item using the apparatus prescribed in paragraph (6); and

    (b) in the case of a vehicle referred to in paragraph 1(a) (other than one having less than four wheels or a maximum speed not exceeding 25 km/h) or 1(c), the device designed to reduce the exhaust noise meets the requirements specified in column 5 in that item.

TABLE (regulation 55(3))

Item	Limits of sound level			Conditions of measurement	Method of measurement	Requirements for exhaust device
	(a) Vehicle referred to in paragraph (1)(a)	(b) Vehicle referred to in paragraph (1)(b)	(c) Vehicle referred to in paragraph (1)(c)			
1	Limits specified in paragraph 1.1 of the Annex to Community Directive 77/212.	89dB(A)	82dB(A)	Conditions specified in paragraph 1.3 of the Annex to Community directive 77/212	Method specified in paragraph 1.4.1 of the Annex to Community Directive 77/212	Requirements specified in heading II of the Annex to Community Directive 77/212 (except paragraphs II.2 and II.5).
2	Limits specified in paragraph 5.2.2.1 of Annex I to Community Directive 81/334.	89dB(A)	82dB(A)	Conditions specified in paragraph 5.2.2.3 of Annex I to Community Directive 81/334.	Method specified in paragraph 5.2.2.4 of Annex I to Community Directive 81/334. Interpretation of results as specified in paragraph 5.2.2.5 of that Annex.	Requirements specified in section 3 and paragraphs 5.1 and 5.3.1 of Annex I to Community Directive 81/334.
3	Limits specified in paragraph 5.2.2.1 of Annex I to Community Directive 84/372	89dB(A)	82dB(A)	Conditions specified in paragraph 5.2.2.3 of Annex I to Community Directive 84/372	Method specified in paragraphs 5.2.2.4 of Annex I to Community Directive 84/372, except that vehicles with 5 or more forward gears and a maximum power to maximum gross weight ratio not less than 75 kW per 1000 kg may be tested in 3rd gear only. Interpretation of results as specified in paragraph 5.2.2.5 of that Annex.	Requirements specified in section 3 and paragraphs 5.1 and 5.3.1 of Annex I to Community Directive 84/372.
4	Limits specified in paragraph 5.2.2.1 of Annex I to Community Directive 84/424	Vehicles with engine power— less than 75 kW —84dB(A) not less than 75 kW —86dB(A)	Limits specified in paragraph 5.2.1 of Annex I to Community Directive 84/424	Conditions specified in paragraph 5.2.2.3 of Annex I to Community Directive 84/424	Method specified in paragraph 5.2.2.4 of Annex I to Community Directive 84/424, except that vehicles with 5 or more forward gears and a maximum power to maximum gross weight ratio not less than 75 kW per 1000 kg may be tested in 3rd gear only. Interpretation of results as specified in paragraph 5.2.2.5 of that Annex	Requirements specified in section 3 and paragraphs 5.1 and 5.3.1 of Annex I to Community Directive 84/424.

(4) Save as provided in paragraph (5), paragraph (3) applies to every vehicle to which this regulation applies and which is first used on or after 1st April 1990, unless it is equipped with 5 or more forward gears and has a maximum power to maximum gross weight ratio not less than 75 kW per 1000 kg, and is of a type in respect of which a type approval certificate has been issued under the Type Approval (Great Britain) Regulations as if, for the reference to items 1, 2, 3 or 4 of the Table there were substituted a reference to item 4 of the Table.

(5) Paragraph (4) does not apply to a vehicle in category 5.2.2.1.3 as defined in Annex I to Directive 84/424 and equipped with a compression ignition engine, a vehicle in category 5.2.2.1.4 as defined in that Annex, or a vehicle referred to in paragraph 1(b) unless it is first used on or after 1st April 1991.

(6) The apparatus prescribed for the purposes of paragraph 3(a) and regulations 56(2)(a) and [57(1A)(a)] is a sound level meter of the type described in Publication No. 179 of the International Electrotechnical Commission, in either its first or second edition, a sound level meter complying with the specification for Type 0 or Type 1 in Publication No. 651 (1979) "Sound Level Meters" of the International Electrotechnical Commission, or a sound level meter complying with the specifications of the British Standard Number BS 5969:1981 which came into effect on 29th May 1981.

(7) Instead of complying with the preceding provisions of this regulation a vehicle may comply at the time of its first use with Community Directive 77/212, 81/334, 84/372 or 84/424. **[1400]**

NOTES
Commencement: 11 August 1986.
This regulation derived from SI 1978 No 1017, reg 31A.
Para (6): figures in square brackets substituted by SI 1989 No 1865, reg 5.
See further: the Road Vehicles (Construction and Use) (Amendment) (No 3) Regulations 1989, SI 1989 No 1865, reg 2.
Community Directives 77/212, 81/334, 84/372, 84/424: see reg 3, Sch 2.
Type Approval (Great Britain) Regulations: SI 1984 No 981.

56. Noise limits— agricultural motor vehicles and industrial tractors

(1) Save as provided in regulation 59, this regulation applies to every wheeled vehicle first used on or after 1st April 1983 being an agricultural motor vehicle or an industrial tractor, other than—

(a) an agricultural motor vehicle which is first used on or after 1st June 1986 and which is driven at more than 20 mph; or
(b) a road roller.

(2) Every vehicle to which this regulation applies shall be so constructed—

(a) that its sound level does not exceed—

(i) if it is a vehicle with engine power of less than 65kW, 89 dB(A);
(ii) if it is a vehicle with engine power of 65kW or more, and first used before 1st October 1991, 92dB(A); or
(iii) if it is a vehicle with engine power of 65kW or more, and first used on or after 1st October 1991, 89 dB(A),

when measured under the conditions specified in paragraph I.3 of Annex VI of Community Directive 74/151 by the method specified in paragraph I.4.1 of that Annex using the apparatus prescribed in regulation 55(6); and

(b) that the device designed to reduce the exhaust noise meets the requirements specified in paragraph II.1 of that Annex and, if fibrous absorbent material is used, the requirements specified in paragraphs II.4.1 to II.4.3 of that Annex.　　　**[1401]**

NOTES
Commencement: 11 August 1986.
This regulation derived from SI 1978 No 1017, reg 31C.
Community Directive 74/151: see reg 3, Sch 2.

57. Noise limits - motor cycles

[(1) Save as provided in regulation 59, the requirements specified in paragraph (1A) apply to every motor vehicle first used on or after 1st April 1983 but not later than 31st March 1991 which is—

(a) a moped; or
(b) a two-wheeled motor cycle, whether or not with sidecar attached, which is not a moped.

(1A) The requirements referred to in paragraph (1) are that—

(a) the vehicle shall be so constructed that its sound level does not exceed the relevant limit specified in column 2 of item 1 or 2 of the Table when measured under the conditions specified in column 3 in that item by the method specified in column 4 in that item using the apparatus prescribed in regulation 55(6); and
(b) the device designed to reduce the exhaust noise meets the requirements specified in column 5.

TABLE

1	2		3	4	5
Item	Limits of sound level		Conditions of measurement	Methods of measurement	Requirements for exhaust device
	Vehicle referred to in paragraph (1)(a) or 2(a)	Vehicle referred to in paragraph (1)(b) or (2)(b)			
1	73dB(A)	Limits specified in paragraph 2.1.1 of Annex I to Community Directive 78/1015	Conditions specified in paragraph 2.1.3 of Annex 4 to Community Directive 78/1015	Method specified in paragraph 2.1.4 of Annex I to Community Directive 78/1015. Interpretation of results as in paragraphs 2.1.5.2, 2.1.5.3 and 2.1.5.4 of that Annex	Requirements as specified in paragraph 3 of Annex I to Community Directive 78/1015 except for sub-paragraph 3.2.
2	73dB(A)	First stage limits specified in paragraph 2.1.1 of Annex I to Community Directive 87/56	Conditions specified in paragraph 2.1.3 of Annex I to Community Directive 87/56	Method specified in paragraph 2.1.4 of Annex I to Community Directive 87/56. Interpretation of results as in paragraphs 2.1.5.2, 2.1.5.3 and 2.1.5.4 of that Annex	Requirements as specified in paragraph 3 of Annex I to Community Directive 87/56 except for sub-paragraph 3.2.

(1B) Instead of complying with paragraph (1), a vehicle referred to in paragraph (1)(b) may comply at the time of its first use with Community Directive 78/1015 or 87/56.

(2) Save as provided in regulation 59, the requirements specified in paragraph (2A) apply to every motor vehicle first used on or after 1st April 1991 which is—

(a) a moped; or
(b) a two-wheeled motor cycle, whether or not with sidecar attached, which is not a moped.

(2A) The requirements referred to in paragraph (2) are those mentioned in paragraph (1A) save that for the reference to item 1 or 2 of the Table there is substituted a reference to item 2 of the Table.

(2B) Instead of complying with paragraph (2), a vehicle referred to in paragraph (2)(b) may comply at the time of its first use with Community Directive 87/56.]

(3) The silencer which forms part of the exhaust system of a motorcycle first used on or after 1st January 1985 shall be either—

(a) that with which the vehicle was fitted when it was manufactured; or
(b) clearly and indelibly marked with either—

  (i) the British Standard marking indicating that it has been tested in accordance with test 2; or
  (ii) a reference to its make and type specified by the manufacturer of the vehicle.

(4) A motor cycle shall not be used on a road if it is fitted with an exhaust system any part of which is marked with the words "NOT FOR ROAD USE" or words to the like effect.

(5) ...

(6) In this regulation—

  "British Standard marking" means a marking specified in paragraph 6.1 of the British Standard Specification for replacement motorcycle and moped exhaust systems, which came into effect on 30th September 1983, issued by the British Standards Institution under reference number BS AU 193:1983, and "test 2" means the test so described in that Specification and therein specified; and

  "moped" has the meaning given to it in paragraph 5 of Schedule 9. **[1402]**

NOTES
Commencement: 8 November 1989 (Paras (1)-(2B), Table); 11 August 1986 (remainder).
This regulation derived from SI 1978 No 1017, regs 31B, 116C.
Paras (1), (1A), Table, (1B)-(2B): substituted, for paras (1), (2), Table as originally enacted, by SI 1989 No 1865, reg 6(a).
Para (5): revoked by SI 1989 No 1865, reg 6(b).
See further: the Road Vehicles (Construction and Use) (Amendment) (No 3) Regulations 1989, SI 1989 No 1865, reg 2.
Community Directive 78/1015: see reg 3, Sch 2.

58. Noise limits - vehicles not subject to regulations 55 to 57, first used on or after 1st April 1970

(1) Save as provided in paragraph (2) and in regulation 59, every wheeled motor vehicle which was first used on or after 1st April 1970 and which is not subject to regulations 55, 56 or 57 shall be so constructed that the sound level (A weighting) in decibels does not exceed the maximum permitted level shown in column 2 of the Table for the relevant class of vehicle shown in column 1, when

the noise emitted by it is measured under the specified conditions using the prescribed apparatus.

(2) A vehicle to which this regulation applies is not required to comply with paragraph (1) if at the time of its first use it complied with Community Directive 70/157, 73/350 or 77/212 or, in the case of an agricultural motor vehicle, 74/151, or if it is—

(a) a road roller;

(b) a vehicle specially constructed, and not merely adapted, for the purposes of fighting fires or salvage from fires at or in the vicinity of airports, and having an engine power exceeding 220 kW;

(c) a vehicle propelled by a compression ignition engine and which is of a type in respect of which a type approval certificate has been issued under the Type Approval (Great Britain) Regulations;

(d) a motorcycle first used on or after 1st October 1980, with an engine capacity not exceeding 50 cc which complies with the requirements specified in [regulation 57(1A) and (2A)]; or

(e) an agricultural motor vehicle manufactured on or after 7th February 1975 which complies with the requirements specified in regulation 56(2).

(3) The definition of sound level (A weighting) in decibels contained in clause 2 of the British Standard Specification for Sound Level Meters published by the British Standards Institution on 7th September 1962 under the number BS 3539: 1962, as amended by Amendment Slip No. 1, numbered AMD22 and published on 1st July 1968, applies for the purposes of this regulation.

(4) In this regulation, "the specified conditions" means the method described by the British Standard Method for the Measurement of Noise Emitted by Motor Vehicles published on 24th June 1986 under the number BS 3425:1966.

(5) In this regulation "the prescribed apparatus" means a noise meter—

(a) which is in good working order and complies with the requirements laid down for vehicle noise meters in Part I of the said British Standard Specification numbered BS 3539: 1962, as amended by the said Amendment Slip No. 1;

(b) which has, not more than 12 months before the date of the measurement made in accordance with paragraph (1), undergone all the tests for checking calibration applicable in accordance with the Appendix to the said British Standard Specification; and

(c) in respect of which there has been issued by the National Physical Laboratory, the British Standards Institution or the Secretary of State a certificate recording the date on which as a result of those tests the meter was found to comply with the requirements of clauses 8 and 9 of the said British Standard Specification.

Table (regulation 58(1))

1	2	3
Item	Class of vehicle	Maximum permitted sound level in dB(A)
1	Motor cycle of which the cylinder capacity of the engine does not exceed 50 cc	77

1	2	3
Item	Class of vehicle	Maximum permitted sound level in dB(A)
2	Motor cycle of which the cylinder capacity of the engine exceeds 50 cc but does not exceed 125 cc	82
3	Motor cycle of which the cylinder capacity of the engine exceeds 125 cc	86
4	Goods vehicle to which regulation 66 applies and which is equipped with a plate complying with the requirements of regulation 66 and showing particulars of a maximum gross weight of more than 3560 kg	89
5	Motor car not being a goods vehicle of the kind described in item 4 above	85
6	Motor tractor	89
7	Locomotive	89
8	Agricultural motor vehicle	89
9	Works truck	89
10	Engineering plant	89
11	Passenger vehicle constructed for the carriage of more than 12 passengers exclusive of the driver	89
12	Any other passenger vehicle	84
13	Any other vehicle	85

[1403]

NOTES
Commencement: 11 August 1986.
This regulation derived from SI 1978 No 1017, reg 31.
Para (2): words in square brackets substituted by SI 1989 No 1865, reg 7.
See further: the Road Vehicles (Construction and Use) (Amendment) (No 3) Regulations, SI 1989 No 1865, reg 2.
Community Directives 70/157, 73/350, 74/151, 77/212: see reg 3, Sch 2.
Type Approval (Great Britain) Regulations: SI 1984 No 981.

59. Exceptions to regulations 55 to 58

Regulations 55, 56, [57(1A) and (2A)] and 58 do not apply to a motor vehicle which is—

    (a) proceeding to a place where, by previous arrangement—

        (i) noise emitted by it is about to be measured for the purpose of ascertaining whether or not the vehicle complies with such of those provisions as apply to it; or

        (ii) the vehicle is about to be mechanically adjusted, modified or equipped for the purpose of securing that it so complies; or

  (b) returning from such a place immediately after the noise has been so
  measured.   **[1404]**

NOTES
 Commencement: 11 August 1986.
 This regulation derived from SI 1978 No 1017, reg 31D.
 Words in square brackets substituted by SI 1989 No 1865, reg 8.
 See further: the Road Vehicles (Construction and Use) (Amendment) (No 3) Regulations 1989,
SI 1989 No 1865, reg 2.

60. Radio interference suppression

(1) Save as provided in paragraph (2), every wheeled motor vehicle first used
on or after 1st April 1974 which is propelled by a spark ignition engine shall
comply at the time of its first use with Community Directive 72/245 or ECE
Regulation 10 or 10.01 or, in the case of an agricultural motor vehicle,
Community Directive 75/322.

 (2) This regulation does not apply to a vehicle constructed or assembled by
a person not ordinarily engaged in the trade or business of manufacturing
vehicles of that description, but nothing in this paragraph affects the application
to such vehicles of the Wireless Telegraphy (Control of Interference from
Ignition Apparatus) Regulations 1973.   **[1405]**

NOTES
 Commencement: 11 August 1986.
 This regulation derived from SI 1978 No 1017, reg 32.
 Community Directives 72/245, 75/322: see reg 3, Sch 2.
 ECE Regulations 10, 10.01: see reg 3, Sch 2.

61. Emission of smoke, vapour, gases, oily substances etc

(1) Subject to paragraph (4), every vehicle shall be constructed [and maintained]
so as not to emit any avoidable smoke or avoidable visible vapour.

 (2) Every motor vehicle using solid fuel shall be fitted with—

  (a) a tray or shield to prevent ashes and cinders from falling onto the
  road; and
  (b) an efficient appliance to prevent any emission of sparks or grit.

 (3) Subject to paragraph (4) and to the exemptions specified in an item in
column 4 of [Table I], every wheeled vehicle of a class specified in that item in
column 2 shall be constructed so as to comply with the requirements specified
in that item in column 3.

 [(3A) A motor vehicle to which an item in Table II applies shall be so
constructed as to comply with the requirements relating to conformity of
production models set out in the provisions specified in that item in column (4)
of that Table.]

 [(3B) Instead of complying with paragraph (1) a vehicle may comply with a
relevant instrument.

 (3C) Instead of complying with such provisions of items 1, 2 and 3 in Table
I as apply to it, a vehicle may at the time of its first use comply with a relevant
instrument.]

 (4) [For the purposes of paragraphs (3B) and (3C), a reference to a vehicle
complying with a relevant instrument is a reference to a vehicle complying]—

(a) if it is propelled by a compression ignition engine, with Community Directive 72/306 (or, in the case of an agricultural vehicle, 77/537) or ECE Regulation 24.01, 24.02 or 24.03; or

[(b) if it is propelled by a spark ignition engine—

    (i) in a case where the first use is before 1 April 1991, with Community Directive 78/665, 83/351[, 88/76 or 91/441], or ECE Regulation 15.03 or 15.04; . . .

    [(ii) in a case where the first use is on or after 1st April 1991 but before 31st December 1992,[, or, in a case where the vehicle is a vehicle to which Part III of Schedule 1B of the Type Approval (Great Britain) Regulations applies,] with Community Directive 83/351, 88/76 or 91/441, or ECE Regulation 5.04; or.

    (iii) in any other case, with Community directive 91/441.]]

(5) No person shall use, or cause or permit to be used, on a road any motor vehicle—

(a) from which any smoke, visible vapour, grit, sparks, ashes, cinders or oily substance is emitted if that emission causes, or is likely to cause, damage to any property or injury or danger to any person who is, or who may reasonably be expected to be, on the road;

(b) which is subject to the requirement in item 2 of [Table I] (whether or not it is deemed to comply with that requirement by virtue of paragraph (4)), if the fuel injection equipment, the engine speed governor or any other parts of the engine by which it is propelled have been altered or adjusted so as to increase the emission of smoke; or

(c) which is subject to the requirement in item 1 of [Table I] if the device mentioned in column 2 in that item is used while the vehicle is in motion.

(6) No person shall use, or cause or permit to be used, on a road a motor vehicle to which item 3 of [Table I] applies unless it is so maintained that the means specified in column 3 of that item are in good working order.

[(7) Subject to paragraphs [(7A)] (8), (9) and (10), no person shall use, or cause or permit to be used, on a road a motor vehicle to which an item in Table II applies if, in relation to the emission of the substances specified in column (6) of the item, the vehicle does not comply with the requirements relating to conformity of production models specified in column (4) unless the following conditions are satisfied in respect to it—

(a) the failure to meet those requirements in relation to the emission of those substances does not result from an alteration to the propulsion unit or exhaust system of the vehicle,

(b) [neither would those requirements] be met in relation to the emission of those substances nor would such emissions be materially reduced if maintenance work of a kind which would fall within the scope of a normal periodic service of the vehicle were to be carried out on the vehicle, and

(c) the failure to meet those requirements in relation to such emissions does not result from any device designed to control the emission of carbon monoxide, hydrocarbons, oxides of nitrogen or particulates fitted to the vehicle being other than in good and efficient working order.

[(7A) In relation to a vehicle to which Part III of Schedule 1B of the Type Approval (Great Britain) Regulations applies, item 8 of Table III shall have effect as if for the entry in column (3) there were substituted "31st December 1993".]

(8) Paragraph (7) shall not apply to a vehicle first used before 26th June 1990.

(9) Where—

    (a) a vehicle is fitted with a device of the kind referred to in sub-paragraph (c) of paragraph (7),

    (b) the vehicle does not comply with the requirements specified in that paragraph in respect to it, and

    (c) the conditions specified in sub-paragraphs (a) and (b) of that paragraph are satisfied in respect to the vehicle,

nothing in paragraph (7) shall prevent the vehicle being driven to a place where the device is to be repaired or replaced.

[(10) Where a vehicle is constructed or assembled by a person not ordinarily engaged in the business of manufacturing motor vehicles of that description, the date on which it is first used shall, for the purposes of paragraphs (3A), (7), (8) and (9), be regarded as being 1st January immediately preceding the date of manufacture of the engine by which it is propelled.

However, the date on which a vehicle is first used shall not, by virtue of the foregoing provisions of this paragraph, be regarded in any circumstances as being later than the date on which it would otherwise have been regarded as being first used had those provisions been omitted.]

[(10A) Without prejudice to paragraphs (1) and (7) no person shall use, or cause or permit to be used on a road, a vehicle first used on or after the 1 August 1975 and propelled by a four-stroke spark ignition engine, unless the vehicle is in such a condition that, when the engine is idling—

    (a) the carbon monoxide content of the exhaust emissions from the engine does not exceed—

        (i) in the case of a vehicle first used on or after 1 August 1983, 4.5%; or

        (ii) in any other case, 6%;

    of the total exhaust emissions from the engine by volume; and

    (b) the hydrocarbon content of those emissions does not exceed 0.12% of the total exhaust emisions form the engine by volume.

(10B) Paragraph (10A) does not apply to—

(a) a vehicle if at the date that the engine was manufactured, that engine was incapable of meeting the requirements specified in that paragraph;

(b) a vehicle being driven to a place where it is to undergo repairs;

(c) a vehicle which was constructed or assembled by a person not ordinarily engaged in the business of manufacturing motor vehicles of that description;

(d) an exempt vehicle within the meaning given by paragraph (12)(a) above;

(e) a goods vehicle with a maximum gross weight exceeding 3,500 kg;

(f) engineering plant, an industrial tractor, or a works truck; ...

(g) a Class V or Class VI vehicle within the meaning of the Motor Vehicles (Tests) Regulations 1981.] [or

(h) a vehicle first used before 1st August 1987 if the engine is a rotary piston engine;

and for the purposes of this paragraph "the engine", in relation to a vehicle, means the engine by which it is propelled.]

[(10C) For the purposes of this regulation—

(a) any rotary piston engine shall be deemed to be a four-stroke engine; and

(b) "rotary piston engine" means an engine in which the torque is provided by means of one or more rotary pistons and not by any reciprocating piston.]

(11) In this regulation, a reference to a vehicle to which an item in Table II applies is a reference to a vehicle which—

(a) is of a class specified in that item in column (2) of that Table,

(b) is first used on or after the date specified in that item in column (3) of that Table, and

(c) is not exempted by the entry in that item in column (5) of that Table [and for the purposes of determining whether a vehicle is a vehicle to which item 8, 9 or 10 in that Table applies, regulation 4(2) shall be disregarded].

(12) In Table II—

(a) "exempt vehicle" means—

(i) a vehicle with less than 4 wheels,

(ii) a vehicle with a maximum gross weight of less than 400 kg,

(iii) a vehicle with a maximum speed of less than 25 km/h, or

(iv) an agricultural motor vehicle;

(b) "direct injection" means a fuel injection system in which the injector communicates with an open combustion chamber or the main part of a divided combustion chamber.

(c) "indirect injection" means a fuel injection system in which the injector communicates with the subsidiary part of a divided combustion chamber.

(d) a reference in column (5) to a vehicle complying with an item is a reference to a vehicle that complies with the provisions specified in that item in column (4) whether the vehicle is or is not within the class of vehicles to which that item applies and any instrument mentioned in that item shall for the purposes of the reference have effect as if it applied to the vehicle in question (whether it would otherwise have done so or not).]

Table I (regulation 61(3))

1	2	3	4
Item	Class of vehicle	Requirements	Exemptions
1	Vehicles propelled by a compression ignition engine and equipped with a device designed to facilitate starting the engine by causing it to be supplied with excess fuel.	Provision shall be made to ensure the device cannot readily be operated by a person inside the vehicle.	(a) a works truck: (b) a vehicle on which the device is so designed and maintained that— (i) its use after the engine has started cannot cause the engine to be supplied with excess fuel, or (ii) it does not cause any increase in the smoke or visible vapour emitted from the vehicle.
2	Vehicles first used on or after 1st April 1973 and propelled by a compression ignition engine.	The engine of the vehicle shall be of a type for which there has been issued by a person authorised by the Secretary of State a type test certificate in accordance with the British Standard Specification for the Performance of Diesel Engines for Road Vehicles published on 19th May 1971 under number BS AU 141a 1971. In the case of an agricultural motor vehicle (other than one which is first used after 1st June 1986 and is driven at more than 20 mph), an industrial tractor, a works truck or engineering plant, for the purposes of that Specification as to the exhaust gas opacity, measurements shall be made with the engine running at 80% of its full load over the speed range from maximum speed down to the speed at which maximum torque occurs as declared by the manufacturer of the vehicle for those purposes.	(a) a vehicle manufactured before 1st April 1973 and propelled by an engine known as the Perkins 6-354 engine; (b) a vehicle propelled by an engine having not more than 2 cylinders and being an agricultural motor vehicle (other than one which is first used on or after 1st June 1986 and which is driven at more than 20 mph), an industrial tractor, a works truck or engineering plant.

1	2	3	4
Item	Class of vehicle	Requirements	Exemptions
3	Vehicles first used on or after 1st January 1972 and propelled by a spark ignition engine other than a 2-stroke engine.	The engine shall be equipped with means sufficient to ensure that, while the engine is running, any vapours or gases in the engine crank case, or in any other part of the engine to which vapours or gases may pass from that case, are prevented, so far as is reasonably practicable, from escaping into the atmosphere otherwise than through the combustion chamber of the engine.	(a) a two-wheeled motor cycle with or without a sidecar attached; (b) a vehicle to which item 4 below applies.
4	Vehicles first used on or after 1st October 1982 and propelled by a spark ignition engine.	The vehicle shall comply at the time of its first use with Community Directive 78/665 or 83/351 or ECE Regulation 15.03 or 15.04.	(a) a vehicle with a maximum gross weight exceeding 3500 kg; (b) a vehicle which has only two wheels; (c) a vehicle with an unladen weight of less than 400 kg; (d) a vehicle with less than 4 wheels and having a maximum speed not exceeding 30 mph

Table II (regulation 61(3A) and (7))

(1) Item	(2) Class of Vehicle	(3) Date of First Use	(4) Design, construction and equipment requirements		(5) Vehicles exempted from requirements	(6) Emitted Substances
			(a) Instrument	(b) Place in instrument where requirements are stated		
1	Vehicles propelled by a spark ignition engine.	1st October 1982.	Community Directive 78/665, or ECE Regulation 15.03.	Annex I, paragraphs 3 and 5. Paragraphs 5, 8 and 11.	(a) A vehicle whose maximum gross weight exceeds 3500 kg; (b) A vehicle which complies with the requirements of item 2, 4, 5 or 8; (c) A vehicle whose maximum speed is less than 50 km/h; (d) An exempt vehicle.	Carbon monoxide, hydrocarbons and oxides of nitrogen.
2	All vehicles.	1st April 1991.	Community Directive 83/351, or ECE Regulation 15.04.	Annex I, paragraphs 5, 7 and 8. Paragraphs 5, 8 and 12.	(a) A vehicle propelled by a compression ignition engine and whose maximum gross weight exceeds 3500 kg; (b) A vehicle which complies with the requirement of item 4, 5 or 8; (c) A vehicle within the meaning given by Article 1 of Community Directive 88/77 and which complies with the requirements of item 6, 9 or 10; (d) An industrial tractor, works truck or engineering plant; (e) A vehicle whose maximum speed is less than 50 km/h; (f) An exempt vehicle.	Carbon monoxide, hydrocarbons and oxides of nitrogen.
3	Industrial tractors, works trucks and engineering plant propelled in each case by a compression ignition engine.	1st April 1993.	ECE Regulation 49.	Paragraphs 5 and 7.	A vehicle which complies with the requirements of item 6, 9 or 10.	Carbon monoxide, hydrocarbons and oxides of nitrogen.

(1) Item	(2) Class of Vehicle	(3) Date of First Use	(4) Design, construction and equipment requirements		(5) Vehicles exempted from requirement	(6) Emitted Substances
			(a) Instrument	(b) Place in instrument where requirements are stated		
4	Passenger vehicles which— (a) are constructed or adapted to carry not more than 5 passengers excluding the driver, and (b) have a maximum gross weight of not more than 2500 kg, not being off-road vehicles	1st April 1991.	Community Directive 88/76. or Community Directive 89/458 or ECE Regulation 83.	Annex I, paragraphs 5, 7 and 8. Annex I, paragraphs 5, 7 and 8. Paragraphs 5, 8 and 13.	(a) A vehicle which complies with the requirements of item 2 or 8; (b) A vehicle whose maximum speed is less than 50 km/h; (c) An exempt vehicle.	Carbon monoxide, hydrocarbons and oxides of nitrogen.
5	Vehicles which are not of a description specified in this column in item 4 but which— (a) are propelled by a spark ignition engine, and have a maximum gross weight of not more than 2000 kg, or (b) are propelled by a compression ignition engine and have a maximum gross weight of more than 3500 kg.	1st April 1992. 1st April 1991.	Community Directive 88/76. or ECE Regulation 83.	Annex I, paragraphs 5, 7 and 8. Paragraphs 5, 8 and 13.	(a) A vehicle within the meaning given by Article 1 of Community Directive 88/77 and which complies with the requirements of item 6, 9 or 10; (b) An industrial tractor, works truck or engineering plant; (c) A vehicle whose maximum speed is less than 50 km/h; (d) A vehicle which complies with the requirements of item 8; (e) An exempt vehicle.	Carbon monoxide, hydrocarbons and oxides of nitrogen.
6	All vehicles propelled by compression ignition engines.	1st April 1991.	Community Directive 88/77. or ECE Regulation 49.01	Annex I, paragraphs 6, 7 and 8. Paragraphs 5, 6 and 7.	(a) A vehicle whose maximum gross weight is less than 3500 kg and which complies with the requirements of item 2; (b) A vehicle which complies with the requirements of item 4, 5, 8, 9 or 10;	Carbon monoxide, hydrocarbons and oxides of nitrogen.

(1) Item	(2) Class of Vehicle	(3) Date of First Use	(4) Design, construction and equipment requirements		(5) Vehicles exempted from requirement	(6) Emitted Substances
			(a) Instrument	(b) Place in instrument where requirements are stated		
					(c) A fire appliance which is first used before 1 October 1992; (d) An industrial tractor, works truck or engineering plant; (e) An exempt vehicle.	
7	Passenger vehicles which— (a) are constructed or adapted to carry not more than 5 passengers excluding the driver, and (b) have a maximum gross weight of not more than 2500 kg, and (c) are propelled by a compression ignition engine of the indirect injection type.	1st April 1991.	Community Directive 88/436.	Annex I, paragraphs 5, 7 and 8, as far as they relate to particulate emissions.	(a) A vehicle which complies with the requirements of item 8; (b) A vehicle whose maximum speed is less than 50 km/h; (c) An off-road vehicle; (d) An exempt vehicle.	Particulates.
8	All vehicles.	31st December 1992.	Community Directive 91/441	Annex I, paragraphs 5, 7 and 8.	(a) A vehicle within the meaning given by Article 1 of Community Directive 88/77 and which complies with the requirements of item 6 and is first used before 1st October 1993 or which complies with the requirements of item 9 or 10; (b) An industrial tractor, works truck or engineering plant; (c) A vehicle whose maximum speed is less than 50 km/h; (d) An exempt vehicle.	Carbon monoxide, hydrocarbons, oxides of nitrogen, and particulates.
9	All vehicles propelled by compression ignition engines.	1st October 1993.	Community Directive 91/542.	Annex I, paragraphs 6, 7 and 8 (excluding line B in the Tables in sub-paragraphs 6.2.1 and 8.3.1.1).	(a) A vehicle which complies with the requirements of item 8 or 10; (b) An industrial tractor, works truck or engineering plant; (c) An exempt vehicle.	Carbon monoxide, hydrocarbons, oxides of nitrogen, and particulates.

(1) Item	(2) Class of Vehicle	(3) Date of First Use	(4) Design, construction and equipment requirements		(5) Vehicles exempted from requirement	(6) Emitted Substances
			(a) Instrument	(b) Place in instrument where requirements are stated		
10	All vehicles propelled by compression ignition engines.	1st October 1996.	Community Directive 91/542.	Annex I, paragraphs 6, 7 and 8 (excluding line A in the Tables in sub-paragraphs 6.2.1 and 8.3.1.1).	(a) A vehicle which complies with the requirements of item 8; (b) An industrial tractor, works truck or engineering plant; (c) An exempt vehicle.	Carbon monoxide, hydrocarbons, oxides of nitrogen and particulates.

[1406]

NOTES
Commencement: 31 December 1992 (paras (7A), (10), (10C)); 1 November 1991 (paras (3B), (3C), (10A), (10B); 26 June 1990 (paras (3A), (7)-(12)); 11 August 1986 (remainder).
This regulation derived from SI 1955 No 990, regs 20, 21, 28, and SI 1978 No 1017, regs 33, 38, 109, 110, 111, 112.
Paras (1): words in square brackets inserted by SI 1991 No 1526, reg 5(1), (2).
Paras (3), (5), (6): words in square brackets substituted by SI 1990 No 1131, regs 2, 4(2).
Paras (3A), (7)-(9), (12): added by SI 1990 No 1131, regs 2, 4.
Paras (3B), (3C): inserted by SI 1991 No 1526, reg 5(1), (3).
Para (4): first words in square brackets substituted by SI 1991 No 1526, reg 5(1), (4); sub-para (b) substituted by SI 1988 No 1524, reg 7, and amended by SI 1992 No 2137, reg 3(1), (2), and SI 1992 No 2909, reg 3(1), (2).
Para (7): figure in square brackets inserted by SI 1992 No 2909, reg 3(1), (3) and words in square brackets in sub-para (b) substituted by SI 1992 No 2137, reg 3(1), (3).
Para (7A): inserted by SI 1992 No 2909, reg 3(1), (4).
Para (10): added by SI 1990 No 1131, reg 4, and substituted by SI 1992 No 2137, reg 3(1), (4).
Paras (10A), (10B): inserted by SI 1991 No 1526, reg 5(1), (5), and amended, in the case of para (10B), by SI 1992 No 2137, reg 3(1), (5).
Para (10C): inserted by SI 1992 No 2137, reg 3(1), (6).
Para 11: added by SI 1990 No 1131, reg 4, and amended by SI 1992 No 2137, reg 3(1), (7).
Table I: renumbered as such, and words in square brackets added, and item 4 revoked, by SI 1990 No 1131, regs 2, 4(5).
Table II: added by SI 1990 No 1131, regs 2, 4(6), and substituted by SI 1992 No 2137, reg 3(1), (8).
Type Approval (Great Britain) Regulations: SI 1984 No 981.
Community Directives 70/157, 72/306, 73/350, 74/151, 77/212, 77/537, 78/665, 83/351, 88/76, 91/441: see reg 3, Sch 2.
ECE Regulation 15.03, 15.04, 24.01, 24.02, 24.03: see reg 3, Sch 2.
Motor Vehicles (Tests) Regulations 1981: SI 1981 No 1694, as amended.
Type Approval (Great Britain) Regulations: SI 1984 No 981, as amended.

[1406]

62. Closets etc

(1) No wheeled vehicle first used after 15th January 1931 shall be equipped with any closet or urinal which can discharge directly on to a road.

(2) Every tank into which a closet or urinal with which a vehicle is equipped empties, and every closet or urinal which does not empty into a tank, shall contain chemicals which are non-inflammable and non-irritant and provide an efficient germicide. **[1407]**

NOTES
Commencement: 11 August 1986.
This regulation derived from SI 1978 No 1017, regs 39, 113.

63. Wings

(1) Save as provided in paragraph (4), this regulation applies to—

    (a) invalid carriages;
    (b) heavy motor cars, motor cars and motor cycles, not being agricultural motor vehicles or pedestrian-controlled vehicles;
    (c) agricultural motor vehicles driven at more than 20 mph; and
    (d) trailers.

(2) Subject to paragraphs (3) and (5), every vehicle to which this regulation applies shall be equipped with wings or other similar fittings to catch, so far as practicable, mud or water thrown up by the rotation of its wheels or tracks.

(3) The requirements specified in paragraph (2) apply, in the case of a trailer with more than two wheels, only in respect of the rearmost two wheels.

(4) Those requirements do not apply in respect of—

    (a) a works truck;
    (b) a living van;
    (c) a water cart;
    (d) an agricultural trailer drawn by a motor vehicle which is not driven at a speed in excess of 20 mph;
    (e) an agricultural trailed appliance;
    (f) an agricultural trailed appliance conveyor;
    (g) a broken down vehicle;
    (h) a heavy motor car, motor car or trailer in an unfinished condition which is proceeding to a workshop for completion;
    (i) a trailer used for or in connection with the carriage of round timber and the rear wheels of any heavy motor car or motor car drawing a semi-trailer so used; or
    (j) a trailer drawn by a motor vehicle the maximum speed of which is restricted to 20 mph or less under Schedule 6 to the 1984 Act.

(5) Instead of complying with paragraph (2) a vehicle may comply with Community Directive 78/549.   **[1408]**

NOTES
    Commencement: 11 August 1986.
    This regulation derived from SI 1955 No 990, regs 33, 39, and SI 1978 No 1017, regs 61, 66, 69, 72, 79.
    The 1984 Act: Road Traffic Regulation Act 1984.
    Community Directive 78/549: see reg 3, Sch 2.

64. Spray suppression devices

(1) Save as provided in paragraph (2), this regulation applies to every wheeled goods vehicle which is—

    (a) a motor vehicle first used on or after 1st April 1986 having a maximum gross weight exceeding 12,000 kg;
    (b) a trailer manufactured on or after 1st May 1985 having a maximum gross weight exceeding 3500 kg; or
    (c) a trailer, whenever manufactured, having a maximum gross weight exceeding 16,000 kg and 2 or more axles.

(2) This regulation does not apply to—

    (a) a motor vehicle so constructed that the driving power of its engine is, or can by use of its controls be, transmitted to all the wheels on at least one front axle and on at least one rear axle;
    (b) a motor vehicle of which no part which lies within the specified area is less than 400 mm vertically above the ground when the vehicle is standing on reasonably flat ground;

(c) a works truck;

(d) a works trailer;

(e) a broken down vehicle;

(f) a motor vehicle which has a maximum speed not exceeding 30 mph;

(g) a vehicle of a kind specified in sub-paragraphs (b), (c), (d), (e), (f), (g), (h), (j), (k), (o) or (p) of regulation 51(2);

(h) a vehicle specially designed, and not merely adapted, for the carriage and mixing of liquid concrete; or

(i) a vehicle which is being driven or towed to a place where by previous arrangement a device is to be fitted so that it complies with the requirements specified in paragraph (3).

[(2A) This regulation shall not apply to a vehicle fitted with a spray-suppression system in accordance with the requirements of Annex III of Community Directive 91/226 if the spray suppression devices with which the vehicle is equipped are legibly and permanently marked with a designated approval mark.]

(3) A vehicle to which this regulation applies and which is of a class specified in an item in column 2 of the Table shall not be used on a road on or after the date specified in column 3 in that item, unless it is fitted in relation to the wheels on each of its axles, with such containment devices as satisfy the technical requirements and other provisions about containment devices specified in the British Standard Specification, provided that in the case of a containment device fitted before 1st January 1985 the said requirements shall be deemed to be complied with if that containment device substantially conforms to those requirements.

TABLE (regulation 64(3))

1	2	3
Item	Class of vehicle	Date
1	A trailer manufactured before 1st January 1975	1st October 1987
2	A trailer manufactured on or after 1st January 1975 but before 1st May 1985	1st October 1986
3	A trailer manufactured on or after 1st May 1985	1st May 1985
4	A motor vehicle	1st April 1986

(4) In this regulation—

["the British Standard Specification" means—

(a) in relation to a containment device fitted before 1st May 1987, Part 1a of the amended Specification and Part 2 of the original Specification; and

(b) in relation to a containment device fitted on or after 1st May 1987, Part 1a and Part 2a of the amended Specification;

["designated approval mark" means the marking designated as an approval mark by regulation 5 of the Approval Marks Regulations and shown at item 30 in Schedule 4 to those Regulations;]

"the original Specification" means the British Standard Specification for Spray Reducing Devices for Heavy Goods Vehicles published under the reference BS AU 200: Part 1: 1984 and BS AU 200: Part 2: 1984;

"the amended Specification" means the original Specification as amended and published under the reference BS AU 200: Part 1a: 1986 and BS AU 200: Part 2a: 1986;

"containment device" means any device so described in the original Specification or the amended Specification;]

"the specified area" means the area formed by the overall length of the vehicle and the middle 80% of the shortest distance between the inner edges of any two wheels on opposite sides of the vehicle (such distance being ascertained when the vehicle is fitted with suitable tyres inflated to a pressure recommended by the manufacturer, but excluding any bulging of the tyres near the ground).

(5) Nothing in this regulation derogates from any requirement specified in regulation 63.   **[1409]**

NOTES
Commencement: 1 April 1992 (para (2A)); 11 August 1986 (remainder).
This regulation derived from SI 1978 No 1017, reg 46E.
Para (2A): inserted by SI 1992 No 646, reg 2(1), (2).
Para (4): definition "designated approval mark" inserted by SI 1992 No 646, reg 2(1), (3); remaining amendments made by SI 1986 No 1597, reg 4.
Community Directive 91/226: see reg 3, Sch 2.
Approval Marks Regulations: SI 1979 No 1088.

65. Maintenance of spray suppression devices

Every part of every containment device with which a vehicle is required to be fitted by the provisions of regulation 64 shall at all times when the vehicle is on a road be maintained free from any obvious defect which would be likely to affect adversely the effectiveness of the device.   **[1410]**

NOTES
Commencement: 11 August 1986.
This regulation derived from SI 1978 No 1017, reg 105C.

PART III
PLATES, MARKINGS, TESTING AND INSPECTION

66. Plates for goods vehicles and buses

(1) This regulation applies to—

(a) a wheeled heavy motor car or motor car first used on or after 1st January 1968 not being—

    (i) a dual-purpose vehicle;
    (ii) an agricultural motor vehicle;
    (iii) a works truck;
    (iv) a pedestrian-controlled vehicle; or
    (v) save as provided in sub-paragraph (b) below, a passenger vehicle;

(b) a bus (whether or not it is an articulated bus) first used on or after 1st April 1982;

(c) a wheeled locomotive or motor tractor first used on or after 1st April 1973 not being—

    (i) an agricultural motor vehicle;
    (ii) an industrial tractor;
    (iii) a works truck;
    (iv) engineering plant; or
    (v) a pedestrian-controlled vehicle;

(d) a wheeled trailer manufactured on or after 1st January 1968 which exceeds 1020 kg in weight unladen not being—

    (i) a trailer not constructed or adapted to carry any load, other than plant or special appliances or apparatus which is a permanent or essentially permanent fixture, and not exceeding 2290 kg in total weight;
    (ii) a living van not exceeding 2040 kg in weight unladen and fitted with pneumatic tyres;
    (iii) a works trailer;
    (iv) a trailer mentioned in regulation 16(3)(b) to (g); or
    (v) a trailer which was manufactured and used outside Great Britain before it was first used in Great Britain; and

(e) a converter dolly manufactured on or after 1st January 1979.

(2) Every vehicle to which this regulation applies shall be equipped with a plate securely attached to the vehicle in a conspicuous and readily accessible position which either—

(a) contains the particulars required, in the case of a motor vehicle by Part I of Schedule 8 or, in the case of a trailer, by Part II of that Schedule, and complies with the provisions of Part III of that Schedule; or

(b) complies with the requirements specified in the Annex to Community Directive 78/507 or, in the case of a vehicle first used before 1st October 1982, in the Annex to Community Directive 76/114, such requirements being in any case modified as provided in paragraph (3).

(3) Instead of the particulars required by items 2.1.4 to 2.1.7 of that Annex, the plate required by paragraph (2)(b) shall show, for a vehicle of a class specified in column 2 of the Table against an item of that Annex so specified in column 1, the following particulars—

(a) the maximum permitted weight for that class, if any, shown in column 3 of the Table;

(b) where the maximum weight shown in column 4 of the Table exceeds the maximum permitted weight, the maximum weight in a column on the plate to the right of the maximum permitted weight; and

(c) if no weight is shown in column 3 of the Table, the maximum weight shown in column 4 of the Table, in the right hand column of the plate.

TABLE (regulation 66(3))

1	2	3	4
Item in Annex to Directive	Class of vehicle	Maximum permitted weight	Maximum weight
2.1.4 (Laden weight of vehicle)	(i) Motor vehicles	The maximum gross weight in Great Britain referred to in item 10 in Part I of Schedule 8.	The maximum gross weight referred to in item 7 in Part I of Schedule 8.
	(ii) Trailers, other than semi-trailers	The maximum gross weight in Great Britain referred to in item 8 in Part II of Schedule 8.	The maximum gross weight referred to in item 6 in Part II of Schedule 8.
	(iii) Semi-trailers		The maximum gross weight referred to in item 6 in Part II of Schedule 8.
2.1.5 (Train weight of motor vehicle)	Motor vehicles constructed to draw a trailer	The lower of— (a) the maximum train weight referred to in item 8 in Part I of Schedule 8; and (b) the maximum laden weight specified, in the case of vehicles constructed to form part of an articulated vehicle, in regulation 77, and, in other cases, in regulation 76.	The maximum train weight referred to in item 8 in Part I of Schedule 8.
2.1.6 (Axle weight of vehicle)	(i) Motor vehicles	The maximum weight in Great Britain for each axle referred to in item 9 in Part I of Schedule 8.	The maximum weight for each axle referred to in item 6 in Part I of Schedule 8.

1	2	3	4
Item in Annex to Directive	Class of vehicle	Maximum permitted weight	Maximum weight
	(ii) Trailers	The maximum weight in Great Britain for each axle referred to in item 7 in Part II of Schedule 8.	The maximum weight for each axle referred to in item 4 in Part II of Schedule 8.
2.1.7 (Load imposed by semi-trailer)	Semi-trailers		The maximum load imposed on the drawing vehicle referred to in item 5 in Part II of Schedule 8.

(4) Part III of Schedule 8 applies for determining the relevant weights to be shown on a plate in accordance with this regulation. **[1411]**

NOTES
Commencement: 11 August 1986.
This regulation derived from SI 1978 No 1017, reg 42.
Community Directives 76/114, 78/507: see reg 3, Sch 2.

67. Vehicle identification numbers

(1) This regulation applies to a wheeled vehicle which is first used on or after 1st April 1980 and to which the Type Approval (Great Britain) Regulations apply.

(2) A vehicle to which this regulation applies shall be equipped with a plate which is in a conspicuous and readily accessible position, is affixed to a vehicle part which is not normally subject to replacement and shows clearly and indelibly—

    (a) the vehicle identification number in accordance with the requirements specified—

        (i) in the case of a vehicle first used before 1st April 1987, in paragraphs 3.1.1 and 3.1.2 of the Annex to Community Directive 76/114/EEC; or

        (ii) in any case, in sections 3 and 4 of the Annex to Community Directive 78/507/EEC;

    (b) the name of the manufacturer; and

    (c) the approval reference number of either—

        (i) the type approval certificate which relates to the vehicle model or the model variant of the vehicle model, as the case may be, issued in accordance with the provisions of regulation 9(1) of, and Part I of Schedule 3 to, the Type Approval (Great Britain) Regulations; or

    (ii) the Minister's approval certificate which relates to the vehicle issued in accordance with the provisions of regulation 9(2) of, and Part 1A of Schedule 4 to, the said Regulations.

Provided that the information required under sub-paragraph (c) above may be shown clearly and indelibly on an additional plate which is fitted in a conspicuous and readily accessible position and which is affixed to a vehicle part which is not normally subject to replacement.

    (3) The vehicle identification number of every vehicle to which this regulation applies shall be marked on the chassis, frame or other similar structure, on the off side of the vehicle, in a clearly visible and accessible position, and by a method such as hammering or stamping, in such a way that it cannot be obliterated or deteriorate.   **[1412]**

NOTES
    Commencement: 11 August 1986.
    This regulation derived from SI 1978 No 1017, reg 43.
    Type Approval (Great Britain) Regulations: SI 1984 No 981.
    Community Directives 76/114/EEC, 78/507/EEC: see reg 3, Sch 2.

---

68. Plates - agricultural trailed appliances

(1) Save as provided in paragraph (3) below, every wheeled agricultural trailed appliance manufactured on or after 1st December 1985 shall be equipped with a plate affixed to the vehicle in a conspicuous and readily accessible position and which is clearly and indelibly marked with the particulars specified in paragraph (2) below.

    (2) Those particulars are—

    (a) the name of the manufacturer of the appliance;
    (b) the year in which the appliance was manufactured;
    (c) the maximum gross weight;
    (d) the unladen weight; and
    (e) the maximum load which would be imposed by the appliance on the drawing vehicle.

    (3) In the case of a towed roller consisting of several separate rollers used in combination, a single plate shall satisfy the requirement specified in paragraph (2) above.   **[1413]**

NOTES
    Commencement: 11 August 1986.
    This regulation derived from SI 1978 No 1017, reg 42A.

---

69. Plates - motor cycles

(1) This regulation applies to every motor cycle first used on or after 1st August 1977 which is not—

    (a) propelled by an internal combustion engine with a cylinder capacity exceeding 150 cc if the vehicle was first used before 1st January 1982 or 125 cc if it was first used on or after 1st January 1982;
    (b) a mowing machine; or

(c) a pedestrian-controlled vehicle.

(2) Every vehicle to which this regulation applies shall be equipped with a plate which is securely affixed to the vehicle in a conspicuous and readily accessible position and which complies with the requirements of Schedule 9.

[1414]

NOTES
Commencement: 11 August 1986.
This regulation derived from SI 1978 No 1017, reg 46.

70. Ministry plates

(1) Every goods vehicle to which the Plating and Testing Regulations apply and in respect of which a plating certificate has been issued shall, from the date specified in paragraph (2), be equipped with a Ministry plate securely affixed, so as to be legible at all times, in a conspicuous and readily accessible position, and in the cab of the vehicle if it has one.

(2) That date is in the case of—

(a) a vehicle to which the Type Approval for Goods Vehicles Regulations apply, the date of the fourteenth day after the plate was issued; or

(b) any other vehicle, the date by which it is required, by the said Regulations, to be submitted for examination for plating. **[1415]**

NOTES
Commencement: 11 August 1986.
This regulation derived from SI 1978 No 1017, reg 148.
Plating and Testing Regulations: SI 1982 No 1478 (repealed; see now SI 1988 No 1478 post).
Type Approval for Goods Vehicles Regulations: SI 1982 No 1271.

[70A. Speed limiters - plates

(1) Paragraph (2) applies to every vehicle to which regulation 36A (speed limiters) applies and which is fitted with a speed limiter which complies with Part I of the British Standard.

(2) Every vehicle to which this paragraph applies shall be equipped with a plate [which has been supplied by the authorised sealer who sealed the speed limiter and] which is in a conspicuous and readily accessible position within the driving compartment and which shows clearly and indelibly the particulars specified in clause 10 of Part I of the British Standard.

(3) Paragraph (4) applies to every vehicle to which regulation 36(A) applies and which is fitted with a speed limiter which does not comply with Part I of the British Standard.

(4) Every vehicle to which this paragraph applies shall be equipped with a plate [which has been supplied by the authorised sealer who sealed the speed limiter and] which is in a conspicuous and readily accessible position within the driving compartment and which shows clearly and indelibly—

(a) the words "SPEED LIMITER FITTED";
(b) the set speed in mph to which the limiter is calibrated; and
(c) the name or trade mark of the [limiter calibrator].

[(4A) Paragraphs (2) and (4) shall have effect, in relation to a vehicle which is not required to be fitted with a speed limiter which has been sealed by an authorised sealer, as if the words "which has been supplied by the authorised sealer who sealed the speed limiter and" had been omitted.]

(5) In this regulation—

    (a) "Part I of the British Standard" and "speed limiter" have the same meanings respectively as in regulation 36A;

    (b) [limiter calibrator] and "set speed" have the same meanings respectively as in Part I of the British Standard; and

    (c) "trade mark" has the same meaning as in the Trade Marks Act 1938.]   **[1416]**

NOTES

  Commencement: 1 August 1992 (para (4A)); 18 March 1988 (remainder).
  Added by SI 1988 No 271, reg 4(2).
  Para (2): words in square brackets inserted by SI 1992 No 422, para 6(1), (2).
  Para (4): first words in square brackets inserted by SI 1992 No 422, para 6(1), (2); remaining words in square brackets substituted by SI 1988 No 1524, reg 4.
  Para (4A): inserted by SI 1992 No 422, para 6(1), (3).
  Para (5): words in square brackets substituted by SI 1988 No 1524, reg 4.

[**70B.**—(1) Paragraph (2) applies to every vehicle to which regulation 36B applies and which is fitted with a speed limiter . . .

(2) Every vehicle to which this paragraph applies shall be equipped with a plate [which has been supplied by the authorised sealer who sealed the speed limiter and] which is in a conspicuous and readily accessible position within the driving compartment and which—

    (a) if the speed limiter fitted to the vehicle complies with Part I of the British Standard, satisfies the requirements of paragraph (3), or

    (b) whether that speed limiter complies with Part I of the British Standard or not, satisfies the requirements of paragraph (4),

in relation to that speed limiter.

(3) In order to satisfy the requirements of this paragraph, a plate must show clearly and indelibly the particulars specified in clause 10 of Part I of the British Standard and the words "SPEED LIMITER FITTED".

(4) In order to satisfy the requirements of this paragraph, a plate must show clearly and indelibly—

    (a) details of a relevant standard with which the speed limiter complies,

    (b) the name or trade mark of the calibrator,

    (c) the speed at which the speed limiter has been set, and

    (d) the words "SPEED LIMITER FITTED".

[(4A) Paragraph (2) shall have effect, in relation to a vehicle which is not required to be fitted with a speed limiter which has been sealed by an authorised sealer, as if the words "which has been supplied by the authorised sealer who sealed the speed limiter and" had been omitted.]

(5) In this regulation—

"calibrator", in relation to a speed limiter fitted to a vehicle means—

    (a) if the person who carried out the final check of the installation and calibration of the speed limiter was employed to do so by another person, his employer; or

    (b) in any other case, the person who carried out that final check.

"Member State" shall be construed in accordance with Schedule I to the European Communities Act 1972;

"Part I of the British Standard" and "speed limiter" have the same meaning respectively as in regulation 36A;

"relevant standard" means a standard or a technical regulation of another Member State or an international standard recognised in another Member State, which offers equivalent guarantees of safety, suitability and fitness for the purpose; and

"trade mark" has the same meaning as in Regulation 70A.]   **[1416A]**

NOTES
Commencement: 1 August 1993 (para (4A)); 1 August 1991 (remainder).
Inserted by SI 1991 No 1527, reg 3(2).
Amended by SI 1992 No 422, reg 7.

71. Marking of weights on certain vehicles

(1) This regulation applies to a vehicle (other than an agricultural motor vehicle which is either a track-laying vehicle not exceeding 3050 kg in unladen weight or a wheeled vehicle) which is—

    (a) a locomotive;
    (b) a motor tractor;
    (c) a heavy motor car which is registered under the 1971 Act (or any enactment repealed thereby) if the unladen weight of the vehicle is not shown on its Ministry plate; or
    (d) an unbraked wheeled trailer, other than one mentioned in regulation 16(3)(b)(i), (iii), [or (iv)] or (c) to (g).

(2) There shall be plainly marked in a conspicuous place on the outside of a vehicle to which this regulation applies, on its near side—

    (a) if it is a vehicle falling in paragraph (1)(a), (b) or (c), its unladen weight; and
    (b) if it is a vehicle falling in paragraph (1)(d), its maximum gross weight.   **[1417]**

NOTES
Commencement: 11 August 1986.
This regulation derived from SI 1955 No 990, reg 40, and SI 1978 No 1017, regs 46A, 80.
Community Directives 70/157, 73/350, 74/151, 77/212: see reg 3, Sch 2.
Type Approval (Great Britain) Regulations: SI 1984 No 981.
The 1971 Act: Vehicles (Excise) Act 1971.
Para (1): amended by SI 1990 No 1981, reg 12.

72. Additional markings

(1) This regulation applies to every goods vehicle to which the Plating and Testing Regulations apply and for which a plating certificate has been issued.

(2) Without prejudice to the provisions of regulation 70, any weight which by virtue of regulation 80 may not be exceeded in the case of a goods vehicle to which this regulation applies may be marked on either side, or on both sides, of the vehicle.

(3) Where at any time by virtue of any provision contained in regulation 75 a goods vehicle to which this regulation applies may not be used in excess of a weight which is less than the gross weight which may not be exceeded by that vehicle by virtue of regulation 80, the first mentioned weight may be marked on either side, or on both sides, of the vehicle.

(4) Where at any time by virtue of any provision contained in regulation 76 and 77 a goods vehicle to which this regulation applies is drawing, or being drawn by, another vehicle and those vehicles may not be used together in excess

of a laden weight applicable to those vehicles by virtue of any such provision, that weight may be marked on either side, or on both sides, of that goods vehicle.　　　　　　　　　　　　　　　　　　**[1418]**

NOTES
　　Commencement: 11 August 1986.
　　This regulation derived from SI 1978 No 1017, reg 151.
　　Plating and Testing Regulations: SI 1982 No 1478 (revoked: see now SI 1988 No 1478 post).

73. Test date discs

(1) Every Ministry test date disc which is issued, following the issue of a goods vehicle test certificate, in respect of a trailer to which the Plating and Testing Regulations apply and for which a plating certificate has been issued shall be carried on the trailer in a legible condition and in a conspicuous and readily accessible position in which it is clearly visible by daylight from the near side of the road, from the date of its issue until but not beyond the date of expiry of that test certificate or the date of issue of a further test certificate for that trailer, whichever date is the earlier.

(2) In this regulation "Ministry test date disc" means a plate issued by the Secretary of State for a goods vehicle, being a trailer, following the issue of a goods vehicle test certificate for that trailer under the Plating and Testing Regulations and containing the following particulars—

　　(a) the identification mark allotted to that trailer and shown in that certificate;

　　(b) the date until which that certificate is valid; and

　　(c) the number of the vehicle testing station shown in that certificate.

　　　　　　　　　　　　　　　　　　[1419]

NOTES
　　Commencement: 11 August 1986.
　　This regulation derived from SI 1978 No 1017, reg 149.
　　Plating and Testing Regulations: SI 1982 No 1478 (revoked: see now SI 1988 No 1478 post).

74. Testing and Inspection

(1) Subject to the conditions specified in paragraph (2), the following persons are hereby empowered to test and inspect the brakes, silencers, steering gear and tyres of any vehicle, on any premises where that vehicle is located—

　　(a) a police constable in uniform;

　　(b) a person appointed by the Commissioner of Police of the Metropolis to inspect public carriages for the purpose of the Metropolitan Public Carriage Act 1869;

　　(c) a person appointed by the police authority for a police area to act for the purposes of section 53 of the 1972 Act;

　　(d) a goods vehicle examiner as defined in section 56 of the 1972 Act;

　　(e) a certifying officer as defined in section 7(1) of the 1981 Act; and

　　(f) a public service vehicle examiner appointed as mentioned in section 7(2) of the 1981 Act.

(2) Those conditions are—

　　(a) any person empowered as there mentioned shall produce his authorisation if required to do so;

　　(b) no such person shall enter any premises unless the consent of the owner of those premises has first been obtained;

(c) no such person shall test or inspect any vehicle on any premises unless—

    (i) the owner of the vehicle consents thereto;

    (ii) notice has been given to that owner personally or left at his address not less than 48 hours before the time of the proposed test or inspection, or has been sent to him at least 72 hours before that time by the recorded delivery service to his address last known to the person giving the notice; or

    (iii) the test or inspection is made within 48 hours of an accident to which section 25 of the 1972 Act applies and in which the vehicle was involved.

(3) For the purposes of this regulation, the owner of the vehicle shall be deemed to be in the case of a vehicle—

(a) which is for the time being registered under the 1971 Act, and is not being used under a trade licence under that Act the person appearing as the owner of the vehicle in the register kept by the Secretary of State under that Act;

(b) used under a trade licence, the holder of the licence; or

(c) exempt from excise duty by virtue of the Motor Vehicles (International Circulation) Order 1975, the person resident outside the United Kingdom who has brought the vehicle into Great Britain;

and in cases (a) and (b) the address of the owner as shown on the said register or, as the case may be, on the licence may be treated as his address. **[1420]**

NOTES
    Commencement: 11 August 1986.
    This regulation derived from SI 1955 No 990, reg 79, and SI 1978 No 1017, reg 145.
    Para (1): modified by virtue of the Road Traffic Act 1991, s 9(2).
    See further: the Road Vehicles Lighting Regulations 1989, SI 1989 No 1796, reg 28 post.
    The 1972 Act: Road Traffic Act 1972.
    The 1981 Act: Public Passenger Vehicles Act 1981.
    The 1971 Act: Vehicles (Excise) Act 1971.

PART IV

CONDITIONS RELATING TO USE

A - Laden Weight

75. Maximum permitted laden weight of a vehicle

(1) Save as provided in paragraph (2), the laden weight of a vehicle of a class specified in an item in column 2 of the Table shall not exceed the maximum permitted laden weight specified in that item in column 3.

(3) The maximum permitted laden weight of a vehicle first used before 1st June 1973 which falls in item 1 or 2 shall not be less than would be the case if the vehicle fell in item 9.

TABLE (regulation 75(1))

1	2	3
Item	Class of vehicle	Maximum permitted laden weight (kg)
1	A wheeled heavy motor car or motor car which is not described in items [1A, 2,] 4 or 5 and which complies with the relevant braking requirement [(see regulation 78(3) to (6) in relation to buses)]	[The weight determined in accordance with Part I of Schedule 11]
[1A	A wheeled heavy motor car or motor car which is not described in item 2, 4 or 5, which complies with the relevant braking requirement and in which— (a) every driving axle not being a steering axle is fitted with twin tyres; and (b) either every driving axle is fitted with road friendly suspension or no axle has an axle weight exceeding 9,500 kg.	The weight determined in accordance with Part IA of Schedule 11]
2	A wheeled heavy motor car or motor car (not being an agricultural motor vehicle) which forms part of an articulated vehicle and which complies with the relevant braking requirement	The weight specified in column (5) in Part II of Schedule 11 in the item which is appropriate having regard to columns (2), (3) and (4) in that Part
3	A wheeled trailer, including a composite trailer, but not including a semi-trailer, which is drawn by a motor tractor, heavy motor car or motor car which complies with the relevant braking requirement, other than a trailer described in items 6, 7, 8 or 11	As for item 1
[4	An articulated bus (see regulation 78(3) to (5))	27,000]
5	A wheeled agricultural motor vehicle	As for item 1, but subject to a maximum of 24,390
6	A balanced agricultural trailer, as defined in paragraph (4), which is not described in items 8, 11 or 16	As for item 1, but subject to a maximum of 18,290

1	2	3
Item	Class of vehicle	Maximum permitted laden weight (kg)
7	An unbalanced agricultural trailer, as defined in paragraph (4) which is not described in items 8, 11 or 16	18,290 inclusive of the weight imposed by the trailer on the drawing vehicle
8	A wheeled trailer manufactured on or after 27th February 1977 and fitted with brakes which automatically come into operation on the over-run of the trailer (whether or not it is fitted with any other brake), except an agricultural trailer which is being drawn by an agricultural motor vehicle, which complies with the requirements specified in items 3, 14 and 17 of Schedule 3 and of which the brakes can be applied either by the driver of the drawing vehicle or by some other person on that vehicle or on the trailer	3,500
9	A wheeled heavy motor car or motor car not described in items 1, 2, 4 or 5— (a) with not more than 4 wheels (b) with more than 4 but not more than 6 wheels (c) with more than 6 wheels	14,230 20,330 24,390
10	A wheeled trailer not described in items 3, 6, 7, 8 or 11 having less than 6 wheels, and not forming part of an articulated vehicle; and an agricultural trailed appliance	14,230
11	A trailer manufactured before 27th February 1977 and having no brakes other than— (i) a parking brake and (ii) brakes which come into operation on the overrun of the trailer	3,560
12	A wheeled locomotive, not described in item 5, which is equipped with suitable and	

1	2	3
Item	Class of vehicle	Maximum permitted laden weight (kg)
	sufficient springs between each wheel and the vehicle's frame and with a pneumatic tyre or a tyre of soft or elastic material fitted to each wheel— (a) if having less than 6 wheels (b) if having 6 wheels (c) if having more than 6 wheels	 22,360 26,420 30,490
13	A track-laying locomotive with resilient material interposed between the rims of the weight-carrying rollers and the road so that the weight of the vehicle (other than that borne by any wheels and the portion of the track in contact with the road) is supported by the resilient material	22,360
14	A locomotive not described in items 5, 12 or 13	20,830
15	A track-laying heavy motor car or motor car	22,360
16	A track-laying trailer	13,210

(3) The maximum total weight of all trailers, whether laden or unladen, drawn at any one time by a locomotive shall not exceed 40,650 kg.

[(3A) Nothing in item 1 or 1A of the Table shall prevent a vehicle being used on a road if—

(a) a plating certificate in respect of the vehicle was in force immediately before the 1st January 1993; and

(b) the laden weight of the vehicle does not exceed the weight shown in that certificate as being the weight not to be exceeded in Great Britain.]

(4) [In this Part of the Regulations and in Schedule 11—]

["air spring" means a spring operated by means of air or other compressible fluid under pressure;

"air suspension" means a suspension system in which at least 75 per cent of the spring effect is caused by an air spring.]

"balanced agricultural trailer" means an agricultural trailer the whole of the weight of which is borne by its own wheels; and

"unbalanced agricultural trailer" means an agricultural trailer of which some, but not more than 35%, of the weight is borne by the drawing vehicle and the rest of the weight is borne by its own wheels.

[(5) For the purposes of this Part of these Regulations and Schedule 11, an axle shall be regarded as fitted with a road friendly suspension if its suspension is—

    (a) an air suspension, or
    (b) a suspension, not being an air suspension, which is regarded as being equivalent to an air suspension for the purposes of Community Directive 92/7.

(6) For the purposes of this Part of these Regulations and Schedule 11, an axle shall be regarded as fitted with twin tyres if it would be regarded as fitted with twin tyres for the purposes of Community Directive 92/7.]   **[1421]**

NOTES
    Commencement: 1 January 1993 (paras (3A), (5), (6)); 11 August 1986 (remainder).
    This regulation derived from SI 1955 No 990, regs 45, 48, and SI 1978 No 1017, regs 82, 85, 89A, 89B, 94, 95.
    Amended by SI 1992 No 2016, reg 4.
    Community Directive 92/7: see reg 3, Sch 2.

76. Maximum permitted laden weight of a vehicle and trailer, other than an articulated vehicle

(1) The total laden weight of a motor vehicle and the trailer or trailers (other than semi-trailers) drawn by it shall not, in a case specified in an item in column 2 of the Table, exceed the maximum permitted train weight specified in that item in column 3.

[(2) In this regulation the expression "road friendly suspension", "twin tyres" and "unbalanced agricultural trailer" shall be construed in accordance with regulation 75(4), (5) and (6).]

Table (regulation 76(1))

1	2	3
Item	Vehicle combination	Maximum permitted train weight (kg)
[1	A wheeled trailer which is drawn by a wheeled motor tractor, heavy motor car or motor car (not being in any case an agricultural motor vehicle), the drawing vehicle being a vehicle which— (a) was first used on or after 1st April 1973; (b) complies with the relevant braking requirement; and (c) is part of a combination which is being used for international transport	35,000

1	2	3
Item	Vehicle combination	Maximum permitted train weight (kg)
1A	A wheeled trailer which is drawn by a wheeled motor tractor, heavy motor car or motor car (not being in any case an agricultural motor vehicle), in respect of which the following conditions are satisfied in relation to the drawing vehicle, namely— (a) it was first used on or after 1st April 1973; (b) it complies with the relevant braking requirement; (c) every driving axle not being a steering axle is fitted with twin tyres; and (d) every driving axle is fitted with road friendly suspension	35,000
1B	A wheeled trailer, not being part of a combination of vehicles described in items 1 or 1A, which is drawn by a wheeled motor tractor, heavy motor car or motor car, (not being in any case an agricultural motor vehicle), the drawing vehicle of which— (a) is fitted with power-assisted brakes which can be operated by the driver of the drawing vehicle and are not rendered ineffective by the non-rotation of its engine; and (b) is equipped with a warning device so placed as to be readily visible to the driver when in the driving seat in order to indicate an impending deficiency or failure in the vacuum or pressure system	32,520 32,520

1	2	3
Item	Vehicle combination	Maximum permitted train weight (kg)
1C	A wheeled trailer which is of a description specified in item 8 in the Table of regulation 75 drawn by a wheeled motor tractor, heavy motor car or motor car (not being in any case an agricultural motor vehicle), the drawing vehicle being a vehicle which— (a) was first used on or after 1st April 1973; and (b) complies with the relevant braking requirement	29,500]
2	A wheeled agricultural motor vehicle drawing a wheeled unbalanced agricultural trailer, if the distance between the rearmost axle of the trailer and the rearmost axle of the drawing vehicle does not exceed 2·9 m	20,000
3	A wheeled trailer or trailers drawn by a wheeled motor tractor, heavy motor car, motor car or agricultural motor vehicle, not being a combination of vehicles mentioned in items 1[, 1A, 1B, 1C] or 2	24,390
4	A track-laying trailer drawn by a motor tractor, heavy motor car or motor car, whether wheeled or tracklaying and a wheeled trailer, drawn by a track-laying vehicle being a motor tractor, heavy motor car or motor car	22,360

[1422]

NOTES

Commencement: 1 January 1993 (para 2); 11 August 1986 (remainder).
This regulation derived from SI 1955 No 990, regs 45, 46, 47, 49, and SI 1978 No 1017, regs 83, 86, 87, 89, 90, 94, 95, 96A.
Amended by SI 1992 No 2016, reg 5.

77. Maximum permitted laden weight of an articulated vehicle

(1) Except as provided in paragraph (2), the laden weight of an articulated vehicle of a class specified in an item in column 2 of the Table shall not exceed the weight specified in column 3 in that item.

Table (Regulation 77(1))

1	2	3
Item	Class of vehicle	Maximum permitted laden weight (kg)
1	An articulated vehicle which complies with the relevant braking requirement.	Whichever is the lower of— (a) the weight specified in column (3) of Part III of Schedule 11 in the item in which the spacing between the rearmost axles of the motor vehicle and the semi-trailer is specified in column (2), provided that the weights in items 13 to 18 shall not apply unless the overall length of the articulated vehicle is at least that specified in column (4) in those items; and (b) If the vehicle is of a description specified in an item in column (2) of Part IV of Schedule 11, the weight specified in column (3) of that item
2	An articulated vehicle which does not comply with the relevant braking requirement if the trailer has— (a) less than 4 wheels (b) 4 wheels or more	 20,330 24,390

(2) This regulation does not apply to an agricultural motor vehicle, an agricultural trailer or an agricultural trailed appliance.

[(3) In Part IV of Schedule 11, "road friendly suspension" and "twin tyres" shall be construed in accordance with regulation 75(5) and (6)].   **[1423]**

NOTES

Commencement: 1 January 1993 (para (3)); 11 August 1986 (remainder).
This regulation derived from SI 1955 No 990, reg 45, and SI 1978 No 1017, regs 88, 91, 94, 95.
Para 3: inserted by SI 1992 No 2016, reg 6.

78. Maximum permitted wheel and axle weights

(1) The weight transmitted to the road by one or more wheels of a vehicle as mentioned in an item in column 2 of the Table shall not exceed the maximum permitted weight specified in that item in column 3.

(2) The Parts of the Table have the following application—

(a) Part I applies to wheeled heavy motor cars, motor cars and trailers which comply with the relevant braking requirement and to wheeled agricultural motor vehicles, agricultural trailers and agricultural trailed appliances; items 1(b) and 2 also apply to buses;

(b) Part II applies to wheeled heavy motor cars, motor cars and trailers which do not fall in Part I;

(c) Part III applies to wheeled locomotives; and

(d) Part IV applies to track-laying vehicles.

TABLE (regulation 78(1))

PART I

(wheeled heavy motor cars, motor cars and trailers which comply with the relevant braking requirement and wheeled agricultural motor vehicles, agricultural trailers and agricultural trailed appliances; and, in respect of items 1(b) and 2, buses)

1	2	3
Item	Wheel criteria	Maximum permitted weight (kg)
1	Two wheels in line transversely each of which is fitted with a wide tyre or with two pneumatic tyres having the centres of their areas of contact with the road not less than 300 mm apart, measured at right angles to the longitudinal axis of the vehicle—	
	(a) if the wheels are on the sole driving axle of a motor vehicle [not being a bus],	10,500
	(b) if the vehicle is a bus which has 2 axles and of which the weight transmitted to the road surface by its wheels is calculated in accordance with regulation 78(5),	10,500
	(c) in any other case	10,170
2	Two wheels in line transversely otherwise than as mentioned in item 1	9,200
3	More than two wheels in line transversely—	
	(a) in the case of a vehicle manufactured before 1st May 1983 [where] the wheels are on one axle of a group of . . . closely spaced axles . . .,	10,170
	(b) in the case of a vehicle manufactured on or after 1st May 1983,	10,170
	(c) in any other case	11,180
4	One wheel not transversely in line with any other wheel—	

1	2	3
Item	Wheel criteria	Maximum permitted weight (kg)
	(a) if the wheel is fitted as described in item 1, (b) in any other case	5,090 4,600

PART II

(wheeled heavy motor cars, motor cars and trailers not falling in Part I)

1	2	3
Item	Wheel criteria	Maximum permitted weight (kg)
5	More than two wheels transmitting weight to a strip of the road surface on which the vehicle rests contained between two parallel lines at right angles to the longitudinal axis of the vehicle— (a) less than 1·02 m apart, (b) 1·02 m or more apart but less than 1·22 m apart, (c) 1·22 m or more apart but less than 2·13 m apart	 11,180 16,260 18,300
6	Two wheels in line transversely	9,200
7	One wheel, where no other wheel is in the same line transversely.	4,600

PART III (wheeled locomotives)

1	2	3
Item	Wheel criteria	Maximum permitted weight (kg)
8	Two wheels in line transversely (except in the case of a road roller, or a vehicle with not more than four wheels first used before 1st June 1955)	11,180
9	Any two wheels in the case of a wheeled locomotive having not more than four wheels first used before 1st June 1955 (not being a road roller or an agricultural motor vehicle which is not driven at more than 20 mph)	Three quarters of the total weight of the locomotive.

PART IV
(track-laying vehicles)

1	2	3
Item	Wheel criteria	Maximum permitted weight (kg)
10	The weight of a heavy motor car, motor car or trailer transmitted to any strip of the road surface on which the vehicle rests contained between two parallel lines 0·6 m apart at right angles to the longitudinal axis of the vehicle	10,170
11	Two wheels in line— (a) heavy motor cars or motor cars with 2 wheels, (b) heavy motor cars or motor cars with more than 2 wheels	8,130 7,630
12	One wheel, where no other wheel is in the same line transversely, on a heavy motor car or a motor car	4,070

(3) In the case of an articulated bus, or, subject to paragraph (4), of a bus first used before 1st April 1988, the laden weight, for the purposes of ... regulation 75, and the weight transmitted to the road surface by wheels of the vehicle, for the purposes of items 1 and 2 of the Table in this regulation, shall be calculated with reference to the vehicle when it is complete and fully equipped for service with—

(a) a full supply of water, oil and fuel; and
(b) weights of 63.5 kg for each person (including crew)—

    (i) for whom a seat is provided in the position in which he may be seated; and
    (ii) who may by or under any enactment be carried standing, the total of such weights being reasonably distributed in the space in which such persons may be carried, save that in the case of a bus (not being an articulated bus) only the number of such persons exceeding 8 shall be taken into account.

(4) The weights for the purposes referred to in paragraph (3) may, in the case of a bus to which that paragraph applies, be calculated in accordance with paragraph (5) instead of paragraph (3).

(5) In the case of a bus first used on or after 1st April 1988, the weights for the purposes referred to in paragraph (3) shall be calculated with reference to the vehicle when it is complete and fully equipped for service with—

(a) a full supply of water, oil and fuel;

(b) a weight of 65 kg for each person (including crew)—

    (i) for whom a seat is provided, in the position in which he may be seated; and

    (ii) who may by or under any enactment be carried standing, the total of such weights being reasonably distributed in the space in which such persons may be so carried, save that in the case of a bus (not being an articulated bus) only the number of such persons exceeding 4 shall be taken into account;

(c) all luggage space within the vehicle but not within the passenger compartment loaded at the rate of 100 kg per m^3 or 10 kg per person mentioned in sub-paragraph (b) above, whichever is the less; and

(d) any area of the roof of the vehicle constructed or adapted for the storage of luggage loaded with a uniformly distributed load at the rate of 75 kg per m^2.

[(6) Regulation 75 shall not apply to a two axle bus if—

(a) its laden weight as calculated in accordance with paragraph (5) does not exceed 17,000 kg; and

(b) the distance between the two axles is at least 3.0 m.]   **[1424]**

NOTES

Commencement: 1 January 1993 (para (6)); 11 August 1986 (remainder).

This regulation derived from SI 1955 No 990, reg 45, and SI 1978 No 1017, regs 93, 94, 95.

Para (1): in Part I of the Table, first words in square brackets substituted by SI 1987 No 676, reg 13(1); remaining words in square brackets substituted and words omitted repealed, by SI 1992 No 2016, reg 7(a).

Para (3): words omitted repealed by SI 1992 No 2016, reg 7(b).

Para (6): added by SI 1992 No 2016, para 7(c).

79. Maximum permitted weights for certain closely-spaced axles etc

(1) This regulation applies to—

(a) a wheeled motor vehicle which complies with the relevant braking requirement;

(b) a wheeled trailer which is drawn by such a motor vehicle; and

(c) an agricultural motor vehicle, an agricultural trailer and an agricultural trailed appliance.

[(2) Save as provided in paragraph (5), where a vehicle to which this regulation applies is of a description specified in an item in column 2 of Part V of Schedule 11 and has two closely-spaced axles, the total weight transmitted to the road surface by all the wheels of those axles shall not exceed the maximum permitted weight specified in column 3 of that item.

(3) Save as provided in paragraph (5), where a vehicle to which this regulation applies is of a description specified in an item in column 2 of Part VI of Schedule 11 and has three closely-spaced axles, the total weight transmitted to the road surface by all the wheels of those axles shall not exceed the weight specified in column 3.

(4) Save as provided by paragraph (5), where a vehicle is fitted with four or more closely-spaced axles, the weight transmitted to the road surface by all the wheels of those axles shall not exceed 24,000 kg.]

(5) Nothing in paragraphs (2), (3) or (4) of this regulation shall apply so as to prevent a vehicle first used before 1st June 1973 from being used on a road at a weight as respects those axles at which it could be used if it fell within item 5 in the Table in regulation 78 [and nothing in those paragraphs shall prevent a vehicle being used on a road if—

(a) a plating certificate in respect of the vehicle was in force immediately before the 1st January 1993; and
(b) no axle has an axle weight exceeding the weight shown in that certificate as being the weight not to be exceeded in Great Britain for that axle.]

[(6) In Parts V and VI of Schedule 11, "air-suspension", "road friendly suspension" and "twin tyres" shall be construed in accordance with regulation 75(4), (5) and (6).]   **[1425]**

NOTES
   Commencement: 1 January 1993 (paras (2)–(4), (6)); 11 August 1986 (remainder).
   This regulation derived from SI 1955 No 990, reg 45, and SI 1978 No 1017, regs 92, 94, 95.
   Paras (2)–(4): substituted by SI 1992 No 2016, reg 8(1), (2).
   Para (5): words in square brackets substituted by SI 1992 No 2016, reg 8(1), (3).
   Para (6): substituted for paras (6)–(8) (as added by SI 1988 No 1287, reg 4) by SI 1992 No 2016, reg 8(1), (4).

80. Over-riding weight restrictions

(1) Subject to paragraph (2), no person shall use, or cause or permit to be used, on a road a vehicle—

(a) fitted with a plate in accordance with regulation 66, but for which no plating certificate has been issued, if any of the weights shown on the plate is exceeded;
(b) for which a plating certificate has been issued, if any of the weights shown in column (2) of the plating certificate is exceeded; or
(c) required by regulation 68 to be fitted with a plate, if the maximum gross weight referred to in paragraph (2)(c) of that regulation is exceeded.

(2) Where any two or more axles are fitted with a compensating arrangement in accordance with regulation 23 the sum of the weights shown for them in the plating certificate shall not be exceeded. In a case where a plating certificate has not been issued the sum of the weights referred to shall be that shown for the said axles in the plate fitted in accordance with regulation 66.

(3) Nothing in regulations 75 to 79 shall permit any such weight as is mentioned in the preceding provisions of this regulation to be exceeded and nothing in this regulation shall permit any weight prescribed by regulations 75 to 79 in relation to the vehicle in question to be exceeded.   **[1426]**

NOTES
   Commencement: 11 August 1986.
   This regulation derived from SI 1955 No 990, reg 45, and SI 1978 No 1017, regs 94, 95.

B - Dimensions of Laden Vehicles

81. Restrictions on use of vehicles carrying wide or long loads or having fixed appliances or apparatus

For the purposes of this regulation, regulation 82 and Schedule 12—

(a) "lateral projection", in relation to a load carried by a vehicle, means that part of the load which extends beyond a side of the vehicle;

(b) the width of any lateral projection shall be measured between longitudinal planes passing through the extreme projecting point of the vehicle on that side on which the projection lies and that part of the projection furthest from that point;

(c) references to a special appliance or apparatus, in relation to a vehicle, are references to any crane or other special appliance or apparatus fitted to the vehicle which is a permanent or essentially permanent fixture;

(d) "forward projection" and "rearward projection"—

   (i) in relation to a load carried in such a manner that its weight [is borne by] only one vehicle, mean respectively that part of the load which extends beyond the foremost point of the vehicle and that part which extends beyond the rearmost point of the vehicle;

   (ii) in relation to a load carried in such a manner that part of its weight [is borne by] more than one vehicle, mean respectively that part of the load which extends beyond the foremost point of the foremost vehicle by which the load is carried except where the context otherwise requires and that part of the load which extends beyond the rearmost point of the rearmost vehicle by which the load is carried; and

   (iii) in relation to any special appliance or apparatus, mean respectively that part of the appliance or apparatus which, if it were deemed to be a load carried by the vehicle, would be a part of a load extending beyond the foremost point of the vehicle and that part which would be a part of a load extending beyond the rearmost point of the vehicle,

   and references in regulation 82 and Schedule 12 to a forward projection or to a rearward projection in relation to a vehicle shall be construed accordingly;

(e) the length of any forward projection or of any rearward projection shall be measured between transverse planes passing—

   (i) in the case of a forward projection, through the foremost point of the vehicle and that part of the projection furthest from that point; and

   (ii) in the case of a rearward projection, through the rearmost point of the vehicle and that part of the projection furthest from that point.

   In this and the foregoing sub-paragraph "vehicle" does not include any special appliance or apparatus or any part thereof which is a forward projection or a rearward projection;

(f) references to the distance between vehicles, in relation to vehicles carrying a load, are references to the distance between the nearest points of any two adjacent vehicles by which the load is carried, measured when the longitudinal axis of each vehicle lies in the same vertical plane.

   For the purposes of this sub-paragraph, in determining the nearest point of two vehicles any part of either vehicle designed primarily for use as a means of attaching the one vehicle to the other and any fitting designed for use in connection with any such part shall be disregarded;

(g) references to a combination of vehicles, in relation to a motor vehicle which is drawing one or more trailers, are references to the motor vehicle and the trailer or trailers drawn thereby, including any other motor vehicle which is used for the purpose of assisting in the propulsion of the trailer or the trailers on the road;

(h) the overall length of a combination of vehicles shall be taken as the distance between the foremost point of the drawing vehicle comprised in the combination and the rearmost point of the rearmost vehicle comprised therein, measured when the longitudinal axis of each vehicle comprised in the combination lies in the same vertical plane;

(i) the extreme projecting point of a vehicle is the point from which the overall width of the vehicle is calculated in accordance with the definition of overall width contained in regulation 3(2);

(j) without prejudice to sub-paragraph (e) the foremost or, as the case may be, the rearmost point of a vehicle is the foremost or rearmost point from which the overall length of the vehicle is calculated in accordance with the definition of overall length contained in regulation 3(2); and

(k) an agricultural, horticultural or forestry implement rigidly but not permanently mounted on an agricultural motor vehicle, agricultural trailer or agricultural trailed appliance, whether or not part of its weight is supported by one or more of its own wheels, shall not be treated as a load, or special appliance, on that vehicle.   **[1427]**

NOTES
Commencement: 11 August 1986.
This regulation derived from SI 1955 No 990, reg 75, and SI 1978 No 1017, regs 139, 140.
Words in square brackets substituted by SI 1991 No 2125, reg 7.

82. Restrictions on use of vehicles carrying wide or long loads or having fixed appliances or apparatus

(1) No load shall be carried on a vehicle so that the overall width of the vehicle together with the width of any lateral projection or projections of its load exceeds 4.3m.

(2) Subject to the following provisions of this regulation, no load shall be carried on a vehicle so that—

(a) the load has a lateral projection or projections on either side exceeding 305mm; or

(b) the overall width of the vehicle and of any lateral projection or projections of its load exceeds 2.9m.

Provided that this paragraph does not apply to the carriage of—

(i) loose agricultural produce not baled or crated; or
(ii) an indivisible load if—
(A) it is not reasonably practicable to comply with this paragraph and the conditions specified in [paragraphs 1 and 5] of Schedule 12 are complied with; and
(B) where the overall width of the vehicle together with the width of any lateral projection or projections of its load exceeds 3.5m, the conditions specified in paragraph 2 of Schedule 12 are complied with.

(3) Where a load is carried so that its weight rests on a vehicle or vehicles, the length specified in paragraph (5) shall not exceed 27.4m.

[(4) A load shall not be carried so that its weight is borne by a vehicle or vehicles if either—

(a) the length specified in paragraph (5) exceeds 18.65 m; or

(b) the load is borne by a trailer or trailers and the length specified in paragraph (6) exceeds 25.9 m,

unless the conditions specified in paragraphs 1 and 2 of Part I of Schedule 12 are complied with.]

(5) The length referred to in paragraphs (3) and (4)(a) is—

(a) where the [weight of the load is borne by] a single vehicle, the overall length of the vehicle together with the length of any forward and rearward projection of the load;

(b) where the [weight of the load is borne by] a motor vehicle and one trailer, whether or not forming an articulated vehicle, the overall length of the trailer together with the length of any projection of the load in front of the foremost point of the trailer and of any rearward projection of the load; and

(c) in any other case, the overall length of all the vehicles [which bear the weight of the load], together with the length of any distance between them and of any forward or rearward projection of the load.

(6) The length referred to in paragraph (4)(b) is the overall length of the combination of vehicles, together with the length of any forward or rearward projection of the load.

(7) Subject to the following provisions of this regulation no person shall use, or cause or permit to be used, on a road a vehicle, not being a straddle carrier, carrying a load or fitted with a special appliance or apparatus if the load, appliance or apparatus has a forward projection of a length specified in an item in column 2 of the Table, or rearward projection of a length specified in an item in column 3, unless the conditions specified in that item in column 4 are complied with.

TABLE (regulation 82(7))

1	2	3	4	
Item	Length of forward projection	Length of rear-ward projection	Conditions to be complied with	
			(a) if the load consists of a racing boat propelled solely by oars	(b) in any other case
1	Exceeding 1 m but not exceeding 2 m	—	Para 4 of Schedule 12	—
2	Exceeding 2 m but not exceeding 3·05 m	—	Para 4 of Schedule 12	Paras 2 and 3 of Schedule 12
3	Exceeding 3·05 m	—	Paras 1 and 4 of Schedule 12	Paras 1, 2 and 3 of Schedule 12
4	—	Exceeding 1 m but not exceeding 2 m	Para 4 of Schedule 12	Para 4 of Schedule 12
5	—	Exceeding 2 m but not exceeding 3·05 m	Para 4 of Schedule 12	Para 3 of Schedule 12

1	2	3	4	
Item	Length of forward projection	Length of rear-ward projection	Conditions to be complied with	
			(a) if the load consists of a racing boat propelled solely by oars	(b) in any other case
6	—	Exceeding 3·05 m	Paras 1 and 4 of Schedule 12	Paras 1, 2 and 3 of Schedule 12

(8) Subject to the following provisions of this regulation, no person shall use, or cause or permit to be used, on a road a straddle carrier carrying a load if—

(a) the load has a rearward projection exceeding 1m unless the conditions specified in paragraph 4 of Schedule 12 are met;

(b) the load has a forward projection exceeding 2m or a rearward projection exceeding 3m; or

(c) the overall length of the vehicle together with the length of any forward projection and of any rearward projection of its load exceeds 12.2m

Provided that—

(i) sub-paragraph (a) does not apply to a vehicle being used in passing from one part of private premises to another part thereof or to other private premises in the immediate neighbourhood;

(ii) sub-paragraphs (b) and (c) do not apply to a vehicle being used as in proviso (i) above if—

(A) the vehicle is not being driven at a speed exceeding 12mph; and

(B) where the overall length of the vehicle together with the length of any forward projection and of any rearward projection of its load exceeds 12.2m, the conditions specified in paragraphs 1 and 2 of Schedule 12 are complied with.

(9) Where another vehicle is attached to that end of a vehicle from which a projection extends, then for the purposes of any requirement in this regulation to comply with paragraph 3 or 4 of Schedule 12, that projection shall be treated as a forward or rearward projection only if, and to the extent that it extends beyond the foremost point or, as the case may be, the rearmost point, of that other vehicle, measured when the longitudinal axis of each vehicle lies in the same vertical plane.

(10) In the case of a vehicle being used—

(a) for fire brigade, ambulance or police purposes or for defence purposes (including civil defence purposes); or

(b) in connection with the removal of any obstruction to traffic,

if compliance with any provision of this regulation would hinder or be likely to hinder the use of the vehicle for the purpose for which it is being used, that provision does not apply to that vehicle while it is being so used.

(11) No person shall use, or cause or permit to be used, on a road an agricultural, horticultural or forestry implement rigidly, but not permanently, mounted on a wheeled agricultural motor vehicle, agricultural trailer, or

agricultural trailed appliance, whether or not part of its weight is supported by one or more of its own wheels if—

    (a) the overall width of the vehicle together with the lateral projection of the implement exceeds 2.5m; or

    (b) the implement projects more than 1m forwards or rearwards of the vehicle,

so however, that this restriction shall not apply in a case where—

        (i) part of the weight of the implement is supported by one or more of its own wheels; and

        (ii) the longitudinal axis of the greater part of the implement is capable of articulating in the horizontal plane in relation to the longitudinal axis of the rear portion of the vehicle. **[1428]**

NOTES
Commencement: 11 August 1986.
This regulation derived from SI 1955 No 990, reg 75, and SI 1978 No 1017, regs 139, 140.
Paras (2), (4), (5): amended by SI 1991 No 2125, reg 8.
See further: the Road Vehicles Lighting Regulations 1989, SI 1989 No 1796, reg 22 post.

C - Trailers and Sidecars

83. Number of trailers

(1) No person shall use, or cause or permit to be used, on a road a wheeled vehicle of a class specified in an item in column 2 of the Table drawing a trailer, subject to any exceptions which may be specified in that item in column 3.

TABLE (regulation 83(1))

1	2	3
Item	Class of vehicles	Exceptions
1	A straddle carrier	—
2	An invalid carriage	—
3	An articulated bus	—
4	A bus not being an articulated bus or a minibus	(a) 1 broken down bus where no person other than the driver is carried in either vehicle or (b) 1 trailer having an overall length, including the draw-bar, not exceeding 5 m provided that the overall length of the combination does not exceed 15 m
5	A locomotive	3 trailers
6	A motor tractor	1 trailer if laden, 2 trailers if neither is laden
7	A heavy motor car or a motor car not described in item 1, 3 or 4	2 trailers if one of them is a towing implement and part of the other is secured to and either rests on or is suspended from that implement 1 trailer in any other case

1	2	3
Item	Class of vehicles	Exceptions
8	An agricultural motor vehicle	(a) in respect of trailers other than agricultural trailers and agricultural trailed appliances, such trailers as are permitted under items 5, 6 or 7 above, as the case may be; or (b) in respect of agricultural trailers and agricultural trailed appliances— (i) 2 unladen agricultural trailers, or (ii) 1 agricultural trailer and 1 agricultural trailed appliance, or (iii) 2 agricultural trailed appliances

(2) For the purposes of items 5, 6 and 7 of the Table—

(a) an unladen articulated vehicle, when being drawn by another motor vehicle because it has broken down, shall be treated as a single trailer; and

(b) a towed roller used for the purposes of agriculture, horticulture or forestry and consisting of several separate rollers shall be treated as one agricultural trailed appliance.

(3) No track-laying motor vehicle which exceeds 8 m in overall length shall draw a trailer other than a broken down vehicle which is being drawn in consequence of the breakdown.

[(4) For the purpose of this regulation, the word "trailer" does not include a vehicle which is drawn by a steam powered vehicle and which is used solely for carrying water for the purpose of the drawing vehicle.]   **[1429]**

NOTES

Commencement: 6 May 1987 (para (4)); 11 August 1986 (remainder).

This regulation derived from SI 1955 No 990, reg 73, and SI 1978 No 1017, regs 132, 135, 137.

Para (1): words in square brackets in items 4 and 6 in the Table substituted by SI 1989 No 2360, reg 4.

Para (4): added by SI 1987 No 676, reg 14.

84. Trailers drawn by motor cycles

(1) Save as provided in paragraph (2), no person shall use, or cause or permit to be used, on a road a motor cycle—

(a) drawing behind it more than one trailer;

(b) drawing behind it any trailer carrying a passenger;

(c) drawing behind it a trailer with an unladen weight exceeding 254 kg;

(d) with not more than 2 wheels, without a sidecar, and with an engine capacity which does not exceed 125 cc, drawing behind it any trailer; or

(e) with not more than 2 wheels, without a sidecar and with an engine capacity exceeding 125 cc, drawing behind it any trailer unless—

(i) the trailer has an overall width not exceeding 1 m;

(ii) the distance between the rear axle of the motor cycle and the rearmost part of the trailer does not exceed 2.5 m;

(iii) the motor cycle is clearly and indelibly marked in a conspicuous and readily accessible position with its kerbside weight;

(iv) the trailer is clearly and indelibly marked in a conspicuous and readily accessible position with its unladen weight; and

(v) the laden weight of the trailer does not exceed 150 kg or two thirds of the kerbside weight of the motor cycle, whichever is the less.

(2) The provisions of paragraph (1)(b), (d) and (e) do not apply if the trailer is a broken down motorcycle and one passenger is riding it.   **[1430]**

NOTES
Commencement: 11 August 1986.
This regulation derived from SI 1978 No 1017, reg 130.

85. Trailers drawn by agricultural motor vehicles

(1) No person shall use, or cause or permit to be used, on a road a wheeled agricultural motor vehicle drawing one or more wheeled trailers if the weight of the drawing vehicle is less than a quarter of the weight of the trailer or trailers, unless the brakes fitted to each trailer in compliance with regulation 15 or 16 are operated directly by the service braking system fitted to the motor vehicle.

(2) No person shall use, or cause or permit to be used, on a road, any motor vehicle drawing an agricultural trailer of which—

(a) more than 35% of the weight is borne by the drawing vehicle; or

(b) the gross weight exceeds 14,230 kg, unless it is fitted with brakes as mentioned in paragraph (1).

(3) No person shall use, or cause or permit to be used, on a road an agricultural trailer manufactured on or after 1st December 1985 which is drawn by a motor vehicle first used on or after 1st June 1986 unless the brakes fitted to the trailer—

(a) in accordance with regulation 15 can be applied progressively by the driver of the drawing vehicle, from his normal driving position and while keeping proper control of that vehicle, using a means of operation mounted on the drawing vehicle; or

(b) automatically come into operation on the over-run of the trailer.

[1431]

NOTES
Commencement: 11 August 1986.
This regulation derived from SI 1978 No 1017, reg 137A.

86. Distance between motor vehicles and trailers

(1) Where a trailer is attached to the vehicle immediately in front of it solely by means of a rope or chain, the distance between the trailer and that vehicle shall not in any case exceed 4.5 m, and shall not exceed 1.5 m unless the rope or chain is made clearly visible to any other person using the road within a reasonable distance from either side.

(2) For the purpose of determining the said distance any part of either vehicle designed primarily for use as a means of attaching the one vehicle to the other and any fitting designed for use in connection with any such part shall be disregarded.   **[1432]**

NOTES
Commencement: 11 August 1986.
This regulation derived from SI 1955 No 990, reg 72 and SI 1978 No 1017, reg 128.

87. Unbraked trailers

(1) Save as provided in paragraph (2), no person shall use, or cause or permit to be used, on a road an unbraked wheeled trailer if—

(a) its laden weight exceeds its maximum gross weight; or

(b) it is drawn by a vehicle of which the kerbside weight is less than twice the sum of the unladen weight of the trailer and the weight of any load which the trailer is carrying.

(2) This regulation does not apply to—

(a) an agricultural trailer; or

(b) a trailer mentioned in [paragraphs (b) (excluding subparagraph (ii)) to (g) of regulation 16(3)].   **[1433]**

NOTES
Commencement: 11 August 1986.
This regulation derived from SI 1978 No 1017, reg 136A.
Para (2): amended by SI 1987 No 676, reg 15(4).

88. Use of bridging plates between motor vehicles and trailers

(1) Save as provided in paragraph (2), no person shall use or cause or permit to be used on a road a motor vehicle constructed for the purpose of carrying other vehicles or any trailer constructed for that purpose so that while such vehicle or trailer is on a road any part of the weight of any vehicle which is being carried rests on a plate of a kind mentioned in paragraph (h) in the definition in regulation 3(2) of "overall length".

(2) The provisions of paragraph (1) do not apply—

(a) while the motor vehicle or trailer constructed for the purpose of carrying other vehicles is being loaded or unloaded; or

(b) if the plate is folded or withdrawn so that it does not bridge the gap between the motor vehicle and the trailer.   **[1434]**

NOTES
Commencement: 11 August 1986.
This regulation derived from SI 1978 No 1017, reg 128A.

89. Leaving trailers at rest

No person in charge of a motor vehicle, or trailer drawn thereby, shall cause or permit such trailer to stand on a road when detached from the drawing vehicle unless one at least of the wheels of the trailer is (or, in the case of a track-laying trailer, its tracks are) prevented from revolving by the setting of the brake or the use of a chain, chock or other efficient device.   **[1435]**

NOTES
Commencement: 11 August 1986.
This regulation derived from SI 1955 No 990, reg 71, and SI 1978 No 1017, reg 127.

90. Passengers in trailers

(1) Save as provided in paragraph (2), no person shall use, or cause or permit to be used, on a road any trailer for the carriage of passengers for hire or reward.

(2) The provisions of paragraph (1) do not apply in respect of a wheeled trailer which is, or is carrying, a broken down motor vehicle if—

    (a) the trailer is drawn at a speed not exceeding 30mph; and

    (b) where the trailer is, or is carrying, a broken down bus, it is attached to the drawing vehicle by a rigid draw bar.

(3) Save as provided in paragraph (4), no person shall use, or cause or permit to be used, on a road a wheeled trailer in which any person is carried and which is a living van having either—

    (a) less than 4 wheels; or

    (b) 4 wheels consisting of two close-coupled wheels on each side.

(4) The provisions of paragraph (3) do not apply in respect of a trailer which is being tested by—

    (a) its manufacturer;

    (b) a person by whom it has been, or is being, repaired; or

    (c) a distributor of, or dealer in, trailers.   **[1436]**

NOTES
    Commencement: 11 August 1986.
    This regulation derived from SI 1955 No 990, reg 74, and SI 1978 No 1017, regs 133, 134.

91. (*Revoked by the Road Traffic (Consequential Provisions) Act 1988, s 3, Sch 1, Pt II.*)

92. Attachment of sidecars

Every sidecar fitted to a motor cycle shall be so attached that the wheel thereof is not wholly outside the space between transverse planes passing through the extreme projecting points at the front and at the rear of the motor cycle. **[1437]**

NOTES
    Commencement: 11 August 1986.
    This regulation derived from SI 1978 No 1017, reg 129.

93. Use of sidecars

No person shall use or cause or permit to be used on a road any two-wheeled motor cycle registered on or after 1st August 1981, not being a motor cycle brought temporarily into Great Britain by a person resident abroad, if there is a sidecar attached to the right (or off) side of the motor cycle.   **[1438]**

NOTES
    Commencement: 11 August 1986.
    This regulation derived from SI 1978 No 1017, reg 141A.

D - Use of Gas Propulsion Systems and Gas-Fired Appliances

94. Use of gas propulsion systems

(1) No person shall use, or cause or permit to be used, on a road a vehicle with a gas propulsion system unless the whole of such system is in a safe condition.

(2) No person shall use, or cause or permit to be used, in any gas supply system for the propulsion of a vehicle when the vehicle is on a road any fuel except liquefied petroleum gas.

(3) No person shall use, or cause or permit to be used, on a road a vehicle

which is propelled by gas unless the gas container in which such fuel is stored is on the motor vehicle, and not on any trailer, and in the case of an articulated vehicle on the portion of the vehicle to which the engine is fitted.

(4) In this regulation and in regulation 95 "liquefied petroleum gas" means—

(a) butane gas in any phase which meets the requirements contained in the specification of commercial butane and propane issued by the British Standards Institution under the number BS4250: 1975 and published on 29th August 1975; or

(b) propane gas in any phase which meets the requirements contained in the said specification; or

(c) any mixture of such butane gas and such propane gas.   **[1439]**

NOTES

Commencement: 11 August 1986.
This regulation derived from SI 1978 No 1017, reg 144A.

95. Use of gas-fired appliances - general

(1) No person shall use, or cause or permit to be used, in or on a vehicle on a road any gas-fired appliance unless the whole of such appliance and the gas system attached thereto is in an efficient and safe condition.

(2) No person shall use, or cause or permit to be used, in any gas-fired appliance in or on a vehicle on a road any fuel except liquefied petroleum gas as defined in regulation 94(4).

(3) No person shall use, or cause or permit to be used, in or on a vehicle on a road any gas-fired appliance unless the vehicle is so ventilated that—

(a) an ample supply of air is available for the operation of the appliance;

(b) the use of the appliance does not adversely affect the health or comfort of any person using the vehicle; and

(c) any unburnt gas is safely disposed of to the outside of the vehicle.

(4) No person shall use, or cause or permit to be used, on a road a vehicle in or on which there is—

(a) one gas-fired appliance unless the gas-supply for such appliance is shut off at the point where it leaves the container or containers at all times when the appliance is not in use;

(b) more than one gas-fired appliance each of which has the same supply of gas unless the gas supply for such appliances is shut off at the point where it leaves the container or containers at all times when none of such appliances is in use; or

(c) more than one gas-fired appliance each of which does not have the same supply of gas unless each gas supply for such appliances is shut off at the point where it leaves the container or containers at all times when none of such appliances which it supplies is in use.   **[1440]**

NOTES

Commencement: 11 August 1986.
This regulation derived from SI 1978 No 1017, reg 144B.

96. Use of gas-fired appliances when a vehicle is in motion

(1) Subject to paragraph (2), this regulation applies to every motor vehicle and trailer.

(2) Paragraphs (3) and (4) do not apply to a vehicle constructed or adapted for the conveyance of goods under controlled temperatures.

(3) No person shall use, or cause or permit to be used, in any vehicle to which this paragraph applies, while the vehicle is in motion on a road, any gas-fired appliance except—

    (a) a gas-fired appliance which is fitted to engineering plant while the plant is being used for the purposes of the engineering operations for which it was designed;

    (b) a gas-fired appliance which is permanently attached to a bus, provided that any appliance for heating or cooling the interior of the bus for the comfort of the driver and any passengers does not expose a naked flame on the outside of the appliance; or

    (c) in any other vehicle, a refrigerating appliance or an appliance which does not expose a naked flame on the outside of the appliance and which is permanently attached to the vehicle and designed for the purpose of heating any part of the interior of the vehicle for the comfort of the driver and any passengers.

(4) No person shall use, or cause or permit to be used, in any vehicle to which this paragraph applies, while the vehicle is in motion on a road, any gas-fired appliance to which—

    (a) sub-paragraph (3)(a) refers, unless the appliance complies with the requirements specified in paragraphs 12 and 13 of Schedule 5 and the gas system to which it is attached complies with the requirements specified in paragraphs 2 to 9 and 15 of Schedule 5; or

    (b) sub-paragraph (3)(b) refers, unless the appliance complies with the requirements specified in paragraphs 12, 13 and 14 of Schedule 5 and the gas system to which it is attached complies with the requirements specified in paragraphs 2 to 9, 11 and 15 of Schedule 5; or

    (c) sub-paragraph (3)(c) refers, unless the appliance complies—

        (i) if it is fitted to a motor vehicle, with the requirements specified in paragraphs 12, 13 and 14 of Schedule 5; and

        (ii) in any other case, with the requirements specified in paragraphs 12 and 13 of Schedule 5;

    and the gas system to which the appliance is attached complies with the requirements specified in paragraphs 2 to 9 and 15 of Schedule 5.

(5) No person shall use, or cause or permit to be used, in a vehicle to which this regulation applies which is in motion on a road any gas-fired appliance unless it is fitted with a valve which stops the supply of gas to the appliance if the appliance fails to perform its function and causes gas to be emitted. **[1441]**

NOTES
    Commencement: 11 August 1986.
    This regulation derived from SI 1978 No 1017, reg 144C.

E - Control of Noise

97. Avoidance of excessive noise

No motor vehicle shall be used on a road in such manner as to cause any excessive noise which could have been avoided by the exercise of reasonable care on the part of the driver. **[1442]**

NOTES
    Commencement: 11 August 1986.

This regulation derived from SI 1978 No 1017, reg 115.

98. Stopping of engine when stationary

(1) Save as provided in paragraph (2), the driver of a vehicle shall, when the vehicle is stationary, stop the action of any machinery attached to or forming part of the vehicle so far as may be necessary for the prevention of noise.

(2) The provisions of paragraph (1) do not apply—

    (a) when the vehicle is stationary owing to the necessities of traffic;

    (b) so as to prevent the examination or working of the machinery where the examination is necessitated by any failure or derangement of the machinery or where the machinery is required to be worked for a purpose other than driving the vehicle; or

    (c) in respect of a vehicle propelled by gas produced in plant carried on the vehicle, to such plant.   **[1443]**

NOTES

Commencement: 11 August 1986.

This regulation derived from SI 1955 No 990, reg 61, and SI 1978 No 1017, reg 117.

99. Use of audible warning instruments

(1) Subject to the following paragraphs, no person shall sound, or cause or permit to be sounded, any horn, gong, bell or siren fitted to or carried on a vehicle which is—

    (a) stationary on a road, at any time, other than at times of danger due to another moving vehicle on or near the road; or

    (b) in motion on a restricted road, between 23.30 hours and 07.00 hours in the following morning.

(2) The provisions of paragraph (1)(a) do not apply in respect of the sounding of a reversing alarm when the vehicle to which it is fitted is about to move backwards and its engine is running.

(3) No person shall sound, or cause or permit to be sounded, on a road any reversing alarm fitted to a vehicle—

    (a) unless the vehicle is a goods vehicle which has a maximum gross weight not less than 2000 kg, a bus, engineering plant, [a refuse vehicle,] or a works truck; or

    (b) if the sound of the alarm is likely to be confused with a sound emitted in the operation of a pedestrian crossing established, or having effect as if established, under Part III of the 1984 Act.

(4) Subject to the provisions of the following paragraphs, no person shall sound, or cause or permit to be sounded a gong, bell, siren or two-tone horn, fitted to or otherwise carried on a vehicle (whether it is stationary or not).

(5) Nothing in paragraph (1) or (4) shall prevent the sounding of—

    (a) an instrument or apparatus fitted to, or otherwise carried on, a vehicle at a time when the vehicle is being used for one of the purposes specified in regulation 37(5) and it is necessary or desirable to do so either to indicate to other road users the urgency of the purposes for which the vehicle is being used, or to warn other road users of the presence of the vehicle on the road; or

    (b) a horn (not being a two-tone horn), bell, gong or siren—

(i) to raise alarm as to the theft or attempted theft of the vehicle or its contents; or

(ii) in the case of a bus, to summon help for the driver, the conductor or an inspector.

(6) Subject to the provisions of section 62 of the Control of Pollution Act 1974 and notwithstanding the provisions of paragraphs (1) and (4) above, a person may, between 12.00 hours and 19.00 hours, sound or cause or permit to be sounded an instrument or apparatus, other than a two-tone horn, fitted to or otherwise carried on a vehicle, being an instrument or apparatus designed to emit a sound for the purpose of informing members of the public that the vehicle is conveying goods for sale, if, when the apparatus or instrument is sounded, it is sounded only for that purpose.

(7) For the purposes of this regulation the expressions which are referred to in regulation 37(10) have the meanings there given to them and the expression "restricted road" in paragraph (1) means a road which is a restricted road for the purpose of section 81 of the 1984 Act.   **[1444]**

NOTES
    Commencement: 11 August 1986.
    This regulation derived from SI 1955 No 990, regs 62, 63, and SI 1978 No 1017, reg 118.
    Para (3): amended by SI 1987 No 676, reg 15(5).
    1984 Act: Road Traffic Regulation Act 1984.

F - Avoidance of Danger

100. Maintenance and use of vehicle so as not to be a danger, etc

(1) A motor vehicle, every trailer drawn thereby and all parts and accessories of such vehicle and trailer shall at all times be in such condition, and the number of passengers carried by such vehicle or trailer, the manner in which any passengers are carried in or on such vehicle or trailer, and the weight, distribution, packing and adjustment of the load of such vehicle or trailer shall at all times be such, that no danger is caused or is likely to be caused to any person in or on the vehicle or trailer or on a road.

Provided that the provisions of this regulation with regard to the number of passengers carried shall not apply to a vehicle to which the Public Service Vehicles (Carrying Capacity) Regulations 1984 apply.

(2) The load carried by a motor vehicle or trailer shall at all times be so secured, if necessary by physical restraint other than its own weight, and be in such a position, that neither danger nor nuisance is likely to be caused to any person or property by reason of the load or any part thereof falling or being blown from the vehicle or by reason of any other movement of the load or any part thereof in relation to the vehicle.

(3) No motor vehicle or trailer shall be used for any purpose for which it is so unsuitable as to cause or be likely to cause danger or nuisance to any person in or on the vehicle or trailer or on a road.   **[1445]**

NOTES
    Commencement: 11 August 1986.
    This regulation derived from SI 1955 No 990, reg 51, and SI 1978 No 1017, reg 97.

[100A. (1) No person shall use, or cause or permit to be used, on a road a vehicle displaying the rectangular plate described in the definition of "low platform trailer" in the Table in regulation 3(2) or anything resembling such a plate at a speed exceeding 40 mph.

(2) No person shall use, or cause or permit to be used on a road a vehicle displaying the rectangular plate described in Schedule 13 (Plate for restricted speed vehicle) or anything resembling such a plate at a speed exceeding 50 mph.] **[1445A]**

NOTES
Commencement: 2 November 1990.
This regulation was added by SI 1990 No 1981, reg 10.

101. Parking in darkness

(1) Save as provided in paragraph (2) no person shall, except with the permission of a police officer in a uniform, cause or permit any motor vehicle to stand on a road at any time between . . . sunset and . . . sunrise unless the near side of the vehicle is as close as may be to the edge of the carriageway.

(2) The provisions of paragraph (1) do not apply in respect of any motor vehicle—

(a) being used for fire brigade, ambulance or police purposes or for defence purposes (including civil defence purposes) if compliance with those provisions would hinder or be likely to hinder the use of the vehicle for the purpose for which it is being used on that occasion;

(b) being used in connection with—

   (i) any building operation or demolition;
   (ii) the repair of any other vehicle;
   (iii) the removal of any obstruction to traffic;
   (iv) the maintenance, repair or reconstruction of any road; or
   (v) the laying, erection, alteration or repair in or near to any road of any sewer, main, pipe or apparatus for the supply of gas, water or electricity, of any telecommunication apparatus as defined in Schedule 2 to the Telecommunication Act 1984 or of the apparatus of any electric transport undertaking,

   if, in any such case, compliance with those provisions would hinder or be likely to hinder the use of the vehicle for the purpose for which it is being used on that occasion;

(c) on any road in which vehicles are allowed to proceed in one direction only;

(d) standing on a part of a road set aside for the parking of vehicles or as a stand for hackney carriages or as a stand for buses or as a place at which such vehicles may stop for a longer time than is necessary for the taking up and setting down of passengers where compliance with those provisions would conflict with the provisions of any order, regulations or byelaws governing the use of such part of a road for that purpose; or

(e) waiting to set down or pick up passengers in accordance with regulations made or directions given by a chief officer of police in regard to such setting down or picking up. **[1446]**

NOTES
Commencement: 11 August 1986.
This regulation derived from SI 1955 No 990, reg 66, and SI 1978 No 1017, reg 123.

Para (1): words omitted repealed by SI 1991 No 2125, reg 10.

102. Passengers on motor cycles

If any person in addition to the driver is carried astride a two-wheeled motor cycle on a road (whether a sidecar is attached to it or not) suitable supports or rests for the feet shall be available on the motor cycle for that person.   **[1447]**

NOTES
> Commencement: 11 August 1986.
> This regulation derived from SI 1978 No 1017, reg 141.

103. Obstruction

No person in charge of a motor vehicle or trailer shall cause or permit the vehicle to stand on a road so as to cause any unnecessary obstruction of the road.   **[1448]**

NOTES
> Commencement: 11 August 1986.
> This regulation derived from SI 1955 No 990, reg 67, and SI 1978 No 1017, reg 122.

104. Driver's control

No person shall drive or cause or permit any other person to drive, a motor vehicle on a road if he is in such a position that he cannot have proper control of the vehicle or have a full view of the road and traffic ahead.   **[1449]**

NOTES
> Commencement: 11 August 1986.
> This regulation derived from SI 1955 No 990, reg 64 and SI 1978 No 1017, reg 119.

105. Opening of doors

No person shall open, or cause or permit to be opened, any door of a vehicle on a road so as to injure or endanger any person.   **[1450]**

NOTES
> Commencement: 11 August 1986.
> This regulation derived from SI 1978 No 1017, reg 125.

106. Reversing

No person shall drive, or cause or permit to be driven, a motor vehicle backwards on a road further than may be requisite for the safety or reasonable convenience of the occupants of the vehicle or other traffic, unless it is a road roller or is engaged in the construction, maintenance or repair of the road.

[1451]

NOTES
> Commencement: 11 August 1986.
> This regulation derived from SI 1955 No 990, reg 65, and SI 1978 No 1017, reg 120.

107. Leaving motor vehicles unattended

(1) Save as provided in paragraph (2), no person shall leave, or cause or permit to be left, on a road a motor vehicle which is not attended by a person licensed to drive it unless the engine is stopped and any parking brake with which the vehicle is required to be equipped is effectively set.

(2) The requirement specified in paragaph (1) as to the stopping of the engine shall not apply in respect of a vehicle—

(a) being used for ambulance, fire brigade or police purposes; or
(b) in such a position and condition as not to be likely to endanger any person or property and engaged in an operation which requires its engine to be used to—

   (i) drive machinery forming part of, or mounted on, the vehicle and used for purposes other than driving the vehicle; or
   (ii) maintain the electrical power of the batteries of the vehicle at a level required for driving that machinery or apparatus.

(3) In this regulation "parking brake" means a brake fitted to a vehicle in accordance with requirement 16 or 18 in Schedule 3. **[1452]**

NOTES
   Commencement: 11 August 1986.
   This regulation derived from SI 1955 No 990, reg 69, and SI 1978 No 1017, reg 124.

108. Securing of suspended implements

Where a vehicle is fitted with any apparatus or appliance designed for lifting and part of the apparatus or appliance consists of a suspended implement, the implement shall at all times while the vehicle is in motion on a road and when the implement is not attached to any load supported by the appliance or apparatus be so secured either to the appliance or apparatus or to some part of the vehicle that no danger is caused or is likely to be caused to any person on the vehicle or on the road. **[1453]**

NOTES
   Commencement: 11 August 1986.
   This regulation derived from SI 1978 No 1017, reg 144.

109. Television sets

(1) No person shall drive, or cause or permit to be driven, a motor vehicle on a road, if the driver is in such a position as to be able to see, whether directly or by reflection, a television receiving apparatus or other cinematographic apparatus used to display anything other than information—

(a) about the state of the vehicle or its equipment;
(b) about the location of the vehicle and the road on which it is located;
(c) to assist the driver to see the road adjacent to the vehicle; or
(d) to assist the driver to reach his destination.

(2) In this regulation "television receiving apparatus" means any cathode ray tube carried on a vehicle and on which there can be displayed an image derived from a television broadcast, a recording or a camera or computer.
[1454]

NOTES
   Commencement: 11 August 1986.
   This regulation derived from SI 1978 No 1017, reg 143.

SCHEDULES
SCHEDULE 1
REGULATIONS REVOKED BY REGULATION 2

. . .

NOTES
  Commencement: 11 August 1986.
  This Schedule lists the regulations revoked by reg 2 ante.

Regulation 3

SCHEDULE 2

COMMUNITY DIRECTIVES AND ECE REGULATIONS

TABLE I COMMUNITY DIRECTIVES

Item	2 Reference No.	3 Community Directives				4 Item No. in Schedule 1 to—	
		(a) Date	(b) Official Journal Reference	(c) Subject matter	(d) Previous Directives included	(a) The Type Approval (Great Britain) Regulations	(b) The Type Approval for Goods Vehicles Regulations
1	70/157	6.2.70	L42, 23.2.70, p 16	The permissible sound level and the exhaust system of motor vehicles			
2	70/220	20.3.70	L76, 6.4.70, p 1	Measures to be take against air pollution by gases from spark ignition engines of motor vehicles			
3	70/221	20.3.70	L76, 6.4.70, p 23	Liquid fuel tanks and rear protective devices for motor vehicles and their trailers			
4	70/388	27.7.70	L176, 10.8.70, p 12	Audible warning devices for motor vehicles			
5	71/127	1.3.71	L68, 22.3.71, p 1	The rear-view mirrors of motor vehicles		10	

Item	2 Reference No.	3 Community Directives				4 Item No. in Schedule 1 to—	
		(a) Date	(b) Official Journal Reference	(c) Subject matter	(d) Previous Directives included	(a) The Type Approval (Great Britain) Regulations	(b) The Type Approval for Goods Vehicles Regulations
6	71/320	[26.7.71]	L202, 6.9.71, p 37	The braking devices of certain categories of motor vehicles and their trailers			
7	72/245	20.6.72	L152, 6.7.72, p 15	The suppression of radio interference produced by spark ignition engines fitted to motor vehicles		2A	5A
8	72/306	2.8.72	L190, 20.8.72, p 1	The emission of pollutants from diesel engines for use in vehicles		5	3
9	73/350	7.11.73	L321, 22.11.73, p 33	The permissible sound level and the exhaust system of motor vehicles	70/157		4A
10	74/132	11.2.74	L74, 19.3.74, p 7	The braking devices of certain categories of motor vehicles and their trailers	71/320		
11	74/151	4.3.74	L84, 28.3.74, p 25	Parts and characteristics of agricultural motor vehicles (see Note 1)			

Item	2 Reference No.	3 Community Directives				4 Item No. in Schedule 1 to—	
		(a) Date	(b) Official Journal Reference	(c) Subject matter	(d) Previous Directives included	(a) The Type Approval (Great Britain) Regulations	(b) The Type Approval for Goods Vehicles Regulations
12	74/290	28.5.74	L159, 15.6.74, p 61	Measures to be taken against air pollution by gases from spark ignition engines for motor vehicles	70/220		
13	74/346	25.6.74	L191, 15.7.74, p 1	Rear view mirrors for agricultural motor vehicles (see Note 1)			
14	74/347	25.6.74	L191, 15.7.74, p 5	Field of vision and windscreen wipers for agricultural motor vehicles (see Note 1)			
15	74/483	17.9.74	L266, 2.10.74, p 4	External projections of motor vehicles		19	
16	75/322	20.5.75	L147, 9.6.75, p 28	Suppression of radio interference from spark ignition engines of agricultural motor vehicles (see Note 1)			
17	75/443	26.6.75	L196, 26.7.75, p 1	Reverse and speedometer equipment of motor vehicles		20	

Item	2 Reference No.	3 Community Directives				4 Item No. in Schedule 1 to—	
		(a) Date	(b) Official Journal Reference	(c) Subject matter	(d) Previous Directives included	(a) The Type Approval (Great Britain) Regulations	(b) The Type Approval for Goods Vehicles Regulations
18	75/524	25.7.75	L236, 8.9.75, p 3	The braking devices of certain categories of motor vehicles and their trailers	71/320 as amended by 74/132	13A	
19	76/114	18.12.75	L24, 30.1.76, p 1	Statutory plates and inscriptions for motor vehicles and trailers			
20	76/115	18.12.75	L24, 30.1.76, p 6	Anchorages for motor vehicle seat belts		12A	
21	76/432	6.4.76	L122, 8.5.76, p 1	Braking devices of agricultural vehicles (see Note 1)			
22	77/102	30.11.76	L32, 3.2.77, p 32	Measures to be taken against air pollution by gases from spark ignition engines of motor vehicles	70/220 as amended by 74/290		
23	77/212	8.3.77	L66, 12.3.77, p 33	The permissible sound level and the exhaust system of motor vehicles	70/157 as amended by 73/350	14B	4B, 4C, 4D
24	77/537	28.6.77	L220, 29.8.77, p 38	Emission of pollution from diesel engines for agricultural motor vehicles (see Note 1)			

	2	3				4	
		Community Directives				Item No. in Schedule 1 to—	
Item	Reference No.	(a) Date	(b) Official Journal Reference	(c) Subject matter	(d) Previous Directives included	(a) The Type Approval (Great Britain) Regulations	(b) The Type Approval for Goods Vehicles Regulations
25	77/541	28.6.77	L220, 29.8.77, p 95	Seat belts and restraint systems for motor vehicles		12A	
26	77/649	27.9.77	L267, 19.10.77, p 1	Field of vision of motor vehicle drivers		22	
27	78/318	21.12.77	L81, 28.3.78, p 49	Wiper and washer systems of motor vehicles			
28	78/507	19.5.78	L155, 13.6.78, p 31	Statutory plates and inscriptions for motor vehicles and trailers	76/114		
29	78/549	12.6.78	L168, 26.6.78, p 45	Wheel guards of motor vehicles			
30	78/665	14.7.78	L223, 14.8.78, p 48	Measures to be taken against air pollution by gases from spark ignition engines of motor vehicles	70/220 as amended by 74/290 and 77/102	4B, 4C	2
31	78/1015	23.11.78	L349, 13.12.78, p 21	The permissible sound level and exhaust system of motorcycles			
32	79/488	18.4.79	L128, 26.5.79, p 1	External projections of motor vehicles	74/483	19A	
33	79/489	18.4.79	L128, 26.5.79, p 12	The braking devices of certain categories of motor vehicles and their trailers	71/320 as amended by 74/132 and 75/524	13B	6, 6C

Item	2 Reference No.	3 Community Directives				4 Item No. in Schedule 1 to—	
		(a) Date	(b) Official Journal Reference	(c) Subject matter	(d) Previous Directives included	(a) The Type Approval (Great Britain) Regulations	(b) The Type Approval for Goods Vehicles Regulations
34	79/490	18.4.79	L128, 26.5.79, p 22	Liquid fuel tanks and rear under-run protection	70/221		
35	79/795	20.7.79	L239, 22.9.79, p 1	The rear-view mirrors of motor vehicles	71/127	10A	
36	79/1073	22.11.79	L331, 27.12.79, p 20	Field of vision and windscreen wipers for agriculutral motor vehicles	74/347		
37	80/780	22.7.80	L229, 30.8.80, p 49	Rear view mirrors for motor cycles			
38	80/1269	16.12.80	L375, 31.12.80, p 46	The engine power of motor vehicles			
39	81/334		L131, 18.5.81, p 6	The permissible sound level and exhaust system of motor vehicles	70/157 as amended by 73/350 and 77/212	14C	4B, 4C, 4D
40	81/575	29.7.81	L209, 29.7.81, p 30	Anchorages for motor vehicle seat belts	76/115	12A	
41	81/576	29.8.81	L209, 29.7.81, p 32	Seat belts and restraint systems for motor vehicles	77/541	12A	
42	81/643	29.7.81	L231, 15.8.81, p 41	Field of vision of motor vehicle drivers	77/649		

Item	2 Reference No.	3 Community Directives				4 Item No. in Schedule 1 to—	
		(a) Date	(b) Official Journal Reference	(c) Subject matter	(d) Previous Directives included	(a) The Type Approval (Great Britain) Regulations	(b) The Type Approval for Goods Vehicles Regulations
43	82/318	2.4.82	L139, 19.5.82, p 9	Anchorages for motor vehicle seat belts	76/115 as amended by 81/575	12A	
44	82/319	2.4.82	L139, 19.5.82, p 17	Seat belts and restraint systems for motor vehicles	77/541 as amended by 81/576	12A	
45	82/890	17.12.82	L378, 31.12.82, p 45	Agricultural motor vehicles			
46	83/351	16.6.83	L197, 20.7.83, p 1	Air pollution by gases from positive ignition engines of motor vehicles	70/220 as amended by 74/290, 77/102 and 78/665	4C	
47	84/372	3.7.84	L196, 26.7.84, p 47	The permissible sound level and exhaust system of motor vehicles	70/157 as amended by 73/350, 77/212 and 81/334		
48	84/424	3.9.84	L238, 6.9.84, p 31	The permissible sound level and exhaust system of motor vehicles	70/157 as amended by 73/350, 77/212, 81/334 and 84/372		

Item	2 Reference No.	3 Community Directives (a) Date	(b) Official Journal Reference	(c) Subject matter	(d) Previous Directives included	4 Item No. in Schedule 1 to— (a) The Type Approval (Great Britain) Regulations	(b) The Type Approval for Goods Vehicles Regulations
[48A	85/3	19.12.84	L2, 3.1.85, p 14	The weights dimensions and other technical characteristics of certain road vehicles			]
49	85/205	18.2.85	L90, 29.3.85, p 1	Mirrors	71/127 as amended by 79/795	10B	
[49A	85/210	20.3.85	L96, 3.4.85, p 25	The lead content of petrol			
50	85/647	23.12.85	L380, 31.12.85, p 1	The braking devices of certain motor vehicles and their trailers	71/320 as amended by 74/132, 75/524 and 79/489		
[50A	86/360	24.7.86	L217, 5.8.86, p 19	The weights dimensions and other technical characteristics of certain road vehicles	85/3		
51	86/562	6.11.86	L327, 27.11.86, p 49	Mirrors	71/127 as amended by 79/795 and 185/205		
51A	87/56	18.12.86	L24, 27.1.87, p 42	The permissible sound level and exhaust system of motorcycles	78/1015		]

Item	2 Reference No.	3 Community Directives				4 Item No. in Schedule 1 to—	
		(a) Date	(b) Official Journal Reference	(c) Subject matter	(d) Previous Directives included	(a) The Type Approval (Great Britain) Regulations	(b) The Type Approval for Goods Vehicles Regulations
52	88/76	3.12.87	L36, 9.2.88, p 1	Measures to be taken against air pollution by gases from the engines of motor vehicles	70/220 as amended by 74/290, 77/102, 78/665 and 83/351	40	2B
53	89/297	13.4.89	L124, 5.5.89, p 1	Lateral protection (side guards) of certain motor vehicles and their trailers			
54	88/77	3.12.87	L36, 9.2.88, p 33	Measures to be taken against the emission of gaseous pollutants from diesel engines for use in vehicles		4E	2D
54A	88/194	24.3.88	L92, 9.4.88, p 47	The braking devices of certain categories of motor vehicles and their trailers	71/320 as amended by 74/132, 75/524, 79/489 and 85/647		
[54B	88/321	16.5.88	L147, 14.6.88, p 77	Mirrors	75/127 as amended by 79/795, 85/205 and 86/562	—	—]
55	88/195	24.3.88	L92, 9.4.88, p 50	Engine power of motor vehicles	80/1269		

Item	2 Reference No.	3 Community Directives				4 Item No. in Schedule 1 to—	
		(a) Date	(b) Official Journal Reference	(c) Subject matter	(d) Previous Directives included	(a) The Type Approval (Great Britain) Regulations	(b) The Type Approval for Goods Vehicles Regulations
[55A	88/366	17.5.88	L181, 12.7.88, p 40	Field of vision of motor vehicle drivers	77/649 as amended by 81/643]		]
[55A	88/218	11.4.88	L98, 15.4.88, p 48	The weights dimensions and other technical characteristics of certain road vehicles	85/3 as amended by 86/360		
56	88/436	16.6.88	L214, 6.8.88, p 1	Measures to be taken against air pollution by gases from engines of motor vehicles (restriction of particulate pollutant emissions from diesel engines)	70/220 as amended by 74/290, 77/102, 78/665, 83/351 and 88/76	27	
[56A	89/338	27.4.89	L142, 25.5.89, p 3	The weights dimensions and other technical characteristics of certain road vehicles	85/3 as amended by 86/360 and 88/218		
57	89/458	18.7.89	L226, 3.8.89, p 1	Measures to be taken against air pollution by emissions from motor vehicles	70/220 as amended by 74/290, 77/102, 78/665, 83/351, 88/76 and 88/436		]

Item	2 Reference No.	3 Community Directives				4 Item No. in Schedule 1 to—	
		(a) Date	(b) Official Journal Reference	(c) Subject matter	(d) Previous Directives included	(a) The Type Approval (Great Britain) Regulations	(b) The Type Approval for Goods Vehicles Regulations
[57A	89/460	18.7.89	L226, 3.8.89, p 5	The weights dimensions and other technical characteristics of certain road vehicles	85/3 as amended by 86/360, 88/218 and 89/338		
57B	89/461	18.7.89	L226, 3.8.89, p 7	The weights dimensions and other technical characteristics of certain road vehicles	85/3 as amended by 86/360, 88/218, 89/338 and 89/460		
[58	90/628	30.10.90	L341, 6.12.90, p 1	Safety belts and restraint systems of mnotor vehicles	77/541 as amended by 81/576 and 82/319	12A	
59	90/269	30.10.90	L341, 6.12.90, p 14	Anchorages for motor vehicles safety belts	76/115 as amended by 81/575 and 82/318	12A	
60	90/630	30.10.90	L341, 6.12.90, p 20	Field of vision of motor vehicle drivers	77/649 as amended by 81/643 and 88/366]		

| 2 | | 3 | | | | 4 | |
| Item | Reference No. | Community Directives | | | | Item No. in Schedule 1 to— | |
		(a) Date	(b) Official Journal Reference	(c) Subject matter	(d) Previous Directives included	(a) The Type Approval (Great Britain) Regulations	(b) The Type Approval for Goods Vehicles Regulations
[60A	91/60	4.2.91	L37, 9.2.91, p 37	The weights dimensions and other technical characteristics of certain vehicles	85/3 as amended by 86/360, 88/218, 89/338, 89/460 and 89/641		]
[61	91/226	27.3.91	L103, 23.4.91, p 5	Spray-supression systems of certain categories of motor vehicles and their trailers]			
[62	92/7	10.2.91	L57, 2.3.92, p 29	The weights dimensions and other technical characteristics of certain road vehicles	85/3 as amended by 86/360, 88/218, 89/338, 89/460 and 89/641		]
[63	91/441	26.6.91	L242, 30.8.91, p 1	Measures to be taken against air pollution by emissions from motor vehicles	70/220 as amended by 74/290, 77/102, 78/665, 83/351, 88/76, 88/436 and 89/458	4G	2F

Item	Reference No.	Community Directives				Item No. in Schedule 1 to—	
		(a) Date	(b) Official Journal Reference	(c) Subject matter	(d) Previous Directives included	(a) The Type Approval (Great Britain) Regulations	(b) The Type Approval for Goods Vehicles Regulations
64	91/542	1.10.91	L295, 25.10.91, p 1	Measures to be taken against the emission of gaseous pollutants from diesel engines for use in vehicles	88/77	4H	2G]
[65	92/22	31.3.92	L129, 14.5.92, p 11	Safety glazing and glazing materials on motor vehicles and their trailers	—	—	—
66	92/23	31.3.92	L129, 14.5.92, p 95	Tyres of motor vehicles and their trailers and their fitting	—	—	—

NOTE 1. This item is to be interpreted as including reference to the amendments made by Community Directive 82/890 (item 45).   **[1456]**

NOTES

Commencement: 11 August 1986.

Items 48A, 50A, 55A (second printed above), 56A, 57A, 57B, 60A, 62: inserted or added by SI 1992 No 2016, reg 9(1).

Items 49A, 52: added by SI 1988 No 1524, reg 8.

Item 50: added by SI 1987 No 676, reg 11.

Item 51: added by SI 1988 No 1178, reg 4.

Item 51A: added by SI 1989 No 1865, reg 9.

Item 53: added by SI 1989 No 1695, reg 4.

Item 54A: added by SI 1990 No 1981, reg 12.

Items 54B, 65, 66: inserted by SI 1992 No 3088, reg 9(1)–(3).

Items 54, 55, 56, 57: added by SI 1990 No 1131, reg 6(1).

Items 55A (first printed above), 58–60: added by SI 1991 No 2003, reg 6.

Item 61: added by SI 1992 no 646, reg 3.

Items 63, 64 added by SI 1992 No 2137, reg 4(1).

See further: the Road Vehicles (Construction and Use) (Amendment) (No 3) Regulations 1989, SI 1989 No 1865, reg 2.

TABLE II ECE REGULATIONS

Item	Reference No.	ECE Regulations				Item No. in Schedule 1 to—	
		(a) Number	(b) Date	(c) Subject matter	(d) Date of amendment	(a) The Type Approval (Great Britain) Regulations	(b) The Type Approval for Goods Vehicles Regulations
1	10	10	17.12.68	Radio interference suppression	—	2	5
2	10.01	10	17.12.68	Radio interference suppression	19.3.78	2A	5A
3	13.03	13	29.5.69	Brakes	4.1.79	13C, 13D	6A, 6B, 6D
4	13.04	13	29.5.69	Brakes	11.8.81	13C, 13D	6A, 6B, 6D
4A	13.05	13	29.5.69	Brakes	26.11.84	—	⌐
[4B	13.06	13	29.5.69	Brakes	22.11.90	—	
5A	14	14	30.1.70	Anchorages for seat belts	—	12A	—
6	14.01	14	30.1.70	Anchorages for seat belts	28.4.76	12A	—
6A	14.02	14	30.1.70	Anchorages for seat belts	22.11.84	4B	2
7	15.03	15	11.3.70	Emission of gaseous pollutants	6.3.78	4C	2
8	15.04	15	11.3.70	Emission of gaseous pollutants	20.10.81	12A	—
9	16.03	16	14.8.70	Seat belts and restraint systems	9.12.79	5	3
10	24.01	24	23.8.71	Emission of pollutants by a diesel engine	11.9.73	5A	3A
11	24.02	24	23.8.71	Emission of pollutants by a diesel engine	11.2.80	—	—
12	24.03	24	23.8.71	Emission of pollutants by a diesel engine	20.4.86	—	—
13	26.01	26	28.4.72	External projections	11.9.73	19	—
[13A	30	30	1.4.75	Pneumatic tyres for motor vehicles and their trailers	—	17,17A	⌐
13B	30.01	30	1.4.75	Pneumatic tyres for motor vehicles and their trailers	25.9.77	17,17A	
13C	30.02	30	1.4.75	Pneumatic tyres for motor vehicles and their trailers	5.10.87	17	17A
14	34	34	25.7.75	Prevention of fire risks	—	—	—
15	34.01	34	25.7.75	Prevention of fire risks	18.1.79	—	—
16	36	36	12.11.75	Construction of public service vehicles	—	—	—
17	39	39	11.7.78	Speedometers	—	20	—
18	43	43	15.9.80	Safety glass and glazing materials	—	15B	—
19	43.01	43	15.9.80	Safety glass and glazing materials	12.11.82	15B	—
20	44	44	1.2.81	Child restraints	—	—	—
21	44.01	44	1.2.81	Child restraints	1.2.84	—	—
[21A	46.01	46	21.10.84	Mirrors	30.5.88	—	⌐
21B	49	49	15.4.82	Emissions of gaseous pollutants	—	—	
[21AA	49.01	49	14.5.90	Emissions of gaseous pollutants	—	—	

Item	Reference No.	ECE Regulations				Item No. in Schedule 1 to—	
		(a) Number	(b) Date	(c) Subject matter	(d) Date of amendment	(a) The Type Approval (Great Britain) Regulations	(b) The Type Approval for Goods Vehicles Regulations
21C.	54	54	1.3.83	Pneumatic tyres for commercial vehicles and their trailers	—	—	17A
22	64	64	1.8.85	Vehicles with temporary-use spare wheels/tyres		—	—
[23]	78	78	15.10.88	Brakes	—	—	—
[24]	78.01	78	15.10.88	Brakes	22.11.90	—	—

[1457]

NOTES

Commencement: 11 August 1986.

Items 4A, 4B: item 4A renumbered (from item 5 to item 4A) and item 4B inserted by SI 1992 No 352, reg 8.

Items 5A, 6A: added by SI 1989 No 1478, reg 5.

Items 13A, 13B: inserted by SI 1991 No 2710, reg 5.

Item 13C: inserted as item, 13A by SI 1990 No 1981, reg 12, and renumbered as item 13C by SI 1991 No 2710, reg 5.

Item 21A: inserted by SI 1992 No 3088, reg 9(1), (4).

Item 21B: added by SI 1990 No 1131, reg 6(2), and renumbered from item 21A to item 21B by SI 1992 No 3088, reg 9(1), (4).

Item 21AA: inserted by SI 1992 No 2137, reg 4(2).

Item 21C: inserted by SI 1990 No 1981, reg 12, and renumbered (from item 21B to 21C) by SI 1992 No 3088, reg 9(1), (4).

Items 23, 24: inserted as items 9A, 9B by SI 1992 No 352, reg 8, and renumbered as items 23, 24 by SI 1992 No 2016, reg 9(2).

SCHEDULE 3

Regulation 16

BRAKING REQUIREMENTS

1. The braking requirements referred to in regulation 16(4) are set out in the Table and are to be interpreted in accordance with paragraphs 2 to 5 of this Schedule.

TABLE
(Schedule 3)

Number	Requirement
1	The vehicle shall be equipped with— (a) one efficient braking system having two means of operation; (b) one efficient split braking system having one means of operation; or (c) two efficient braking systems each having a separate means of operation, and in the case of a vehicle first used on or after 1st January 1968, no account shall be taken of a multi-pull means of operation unless, at first application, it operates a hydraulic, electric or pneumatic device which causes the application of brakes with total braking efficiency not less than 25%.
2	The vehicle shall be equipped with— (a) one efficient braking system having two means of operation; or (b) two efficient braking systems each having a separate means of operation.
3	The vehicle shall be equipped with an efficient braking system.
4	The braking system shall be so designed that in the event of failure of any part (other than a fixed member or a brake shoe anchor pin) through or by means of which the force necessary to apply the brakes is transmitted, there shall still be available for application by the driver brakes sufficient under the most adverse conditions to bring the vehicle to rest within a reasonable distance. The brakes so available shall be applied to— (a) in the case of a track-laying vehicle, one track on each side of the vehicle; (b) in the case of a wheeled motor vehicle, one wheel if the vehicle has 3 wheels and otherwise to at least half the wheels; and (c) in the case of a wheeled trailer, at least one wheel if it has only 2 wheels and otherwise at least 2 wheels. This requirement applies to the braking systems of both a trailer and the vehicle by which it is being drawn except that if the drawing vehicle complies with regulation 15, [Community Directive 79/489, 85/647 or 88/194] or ECE Regulation 13.03, 13.04 or 13.05, the requirement applies only to the braking system of the drawing vehicle. It does not apply to vehicles having split braking systems (which are subject to regulation 18(3)(b)) or to road rollers. (The expressions "part" and "half the wheels" are to be interpreted in accordance with paragraphs (3) and (4) respectively).
5	The braking system shall be so designed and constructed that, in the event of the failure of any part thereof, there shall still be available for application by the driver a brake sufficient under the most adverse conditions to bring the vehicle to rest within a reasonable distance.

Number	Requirement
6	The braking system of a vehicle, when drawing a trailer which complies with regulation 15, [Community Directive 79/489, 85/647 or 88/194] or ECE Regulation 13.03, 13.04 or 13.05, shall be so constructed that, in the event of a failure of any part (other than a fixed member or brake shoe anchor pin) of the service braking system of the drawing vehicle (excluding the means of operation of a split braking system) the driver can still apply brakes to at least one wheel of the trailer, if it has only 2 wheels, and otherwise to at least 2 wheels, by using the secondary braking system of the drawing vehicle. (The expression "part" is to be interpreted in accordance with paragraph 3).
7	The application of any means of operation of a braking system shall not affect or operate the pedal or hand lever of any other means of operation.
8	The braking system shall not be rendered ineffective by the non-rotation of the engine of the vehicle or, in the case of a trailer, the engine of the drawing vehicle (steam-propelled vehicles, other than locomotives and buses, are excluded from this requirement).
9	At least one means of operation shall be capable of causing brakes to be applied directly, and not through the transmission gear, to at least half the wheels of the vehicle. This requirement does not apply to a works truck with an unladen weight not exceeding 7370 kg, or to an industrial tractor; and it does not apply to a vehicle with more than 4 wheels if— (a) the drive is transmitted to all wheels other than the steering wheels without the interposition of a differential driving gear or similar mechanism between the axles carrying the driving wheels; and (b) the brakes applied by one means of operation apply directly to 2 driving wheels on opposite sides of the vehicle; and (c) the brakes applied by another means of operation act directly on all the other driving wheels. (The expression "half the wheels" is to be interpreted in accordance with paragraph (4)).
10	The brakes of a trailer shall come into operation automatically on its overrun or, in the case of a track-laying trailer drawn by a vehicle having steerable wheels at the front or a wheeled trailer, the driver of, or some other person on, the drawing vehicle or on the trailer shall be able to apply the brakes on the trailer.
11	The brakes of a trailer shall come into operation automatically on its overrun or the driver of the drawing vehicle shall be able to apply brakes to all the wheels of the trailer, using the means of operation which applies the service brakes of the drawing vehicle.
12	The brakes of the vehicle shall apply to all wheels other than the steering wheels.
13	The brakes of the vehicle shall apply to at least 2 wheels.
14	The brakes of the vehicle shall apply in the case of a wheeled vehicle to at least 2 wheels if the vehicle has no more than 4 wheels and to at least half the wheels if the vehicle has more than 4 wheels; and in the case of a track-laying vehicle to all the tracks.
15	The brakes shall apply to all the wheels.

Number	Requirement
16	The parking brake shall be so designed and constructed that— (a) in the case of a wheeled heavy motor car or motor car, its means of operation is independent of the means of operation of any split braking system with which the vehicle is fitted; (b) in the case of a motor vehicle other than a motor cycle or an invalid carriage, either— (i) it is capable of being applied by direct mechanical action without the intervention of any hydraulic, electric or pneumatic device; or (ii) the vehicle complies with requirement 15; and (c) it can at all times when the vehicle is not being driven or is left unattended be set so as— (i) in the case of a track-laying vehicle, to lock the tracks; and (ii) in the case of a wheeled vehicle, to prevent the rotation of at least one wheel in the case of a three wheeled vehicle and at least two wheels in the case of a vehicle with more than three wheels.
17	The parking brake shall be capable of being set so as effectively to prevent two at least of the wheels from revolving when the trailer is not being drawn.
18	The parking brake shall be so designed and constructed that— (a) in the case of a motor vehicle, its means of operation (whether multi-pull or not) is independent of the means of operation of any braking system required by regulation 18 to have a total braking efficiency of not less than 50%; and (b) in the case of a trailer, its brakes can be applied and released by a person standing on the ground by a means of operation fitted to the trailer; and (c) in either case, its braking force, when the vehicle is not being driven or is left unattended (and in the case of a trailer, whether the braking force is applied by the driver using the service brakes of the drawing vehicle or by a person standing on the ground in the manner indicated in sub-paragraph (b)) can at all times be maintained in operation by direct mechanical action without the intervention of any hydraulic, electric or pneumatic device and, when so maintained, can hold the vehicle stationary on a gradient of at least 16% without the assistance of stored energy.

2. For the purposes of requirement 3 in the Table, in the case of a motor car or heavy motor car propelled by steam and not used as a bus, the engine shall be deemed to be an efficient braking system with one means of operation if the engine is capable of being reversed and, in the case of a vehicle first used on or after 1st January 1927, is incapable of being disconnected from any of the driving wheels of the vehicle except by the sustained effort of the driver.

3. For the purpose of requirements 4 and 6 in the Table, in the case of a wheeled motor car and of a vehicle first used on or after 1st October 1938 which is a locomotive, a motor tractor, a heavy motor car or a track-laying motor car, every moving shaft which is connected to or supports any part of a braking system shall be deemed to be part of the system.

4. For the purpose of [requirements 4, 9 and 14] in the Table, in determining whether brakes apply to at least half the wheels of a vehicle, not more than one front wheel shall be treated as a wheel to which brakes apply unless the vehicle is—

(a) a locomotive or motor tractor with more than 4 wheels;
(b) a heavy motor car or motor car first used before 1st October 1938;
(c) a motor car with an unladen weight not exceeding 1020 kg;
(d) a motor car which is a passenger vehicle but is not a bus;
(e) a works truck;
(f) a heavy motor car or motor car with more than 3 wheels which is equipped in respect of all its wheels with brakes which are operated by one means of operation; or
(g) a track-laying vehicle.

5. In this Schedule a "multi-pull means of operation" means a device forming part of a braking system which causes the muscular energy of the driver to apply the brakes of that system progressively as a result of successive applications of that device by the driver.   **[1458]**

NOTES
Commencement: 11 August 1986.
Para 1: in sub-paras 4 and 6, amendments in square brackets made by SI 1987 No 676, reg 12.
Table: directives amended by SI 1990 No 1981, reg 6.
Para 4: amended by SI 1987 No 676, reg 15(6).
Community Directive 79/489: see reg 3, Sch 2.
ECE Regulation 13.03, 13.04, 13.05: see reg 3, Sch 2.

SCHEDULE 3A
(SEE REGS 39A AND 39B) EXCLUSION OF CERTAIN VEHICLES FROM THE APPLICATION OF REGULATION 39A

PART I

[1.—(1) In this Part—

"EEC type approval certificate" means a certificate issued by a member state of the European Economic Community in accordance with Community Directive 70/220 as originally made or with any amendments which have from time to time been made before 5th September 1988;

"engine capacity" means in the case of a reciprocating engine, the nominal swept volume and, in the case of a rotary engine, double the nominal swept volume;

. . .

"relevant authority" means—

(a) in relation to an EEC type approval certificate issued by the United Kingdom, the Secretary of State, and
(b) in relation to an EEC type approval certificate issued by any other member state of the European Economic Community, the authority having power under the law of that state to issue that certificate.

(2) The references in this Schedule to a M1 category vehicle is a reference to a vehicle described as M1 in Council Directive 70/156/EEC of 6th February 1970 as amended at 5th September 1988.

[2]. A vehicle of a description specified in column 2 of the Table below is excluded from the application of regulation 39A if it is first used before the date specified in column 3 and the conditions specified in paragraph 3 are satisfied in respect to it on that date.

[3]. The conditions referred to in paragraph 2 are—

(a) that the vehicle is a model in relation to which there is in force an EEC type approval certificate issued before 1st October 1989;

(b) that the manufacturer of the vehicle has supplied to the relevant authority which issued the EEC type approval certificate, a certificate stating that adapting vehicles of that model to the fuel requirements specified in the Annexes to Community Directive 88/76 would entail a change in material specification of the inlet or exhaust valve seats or a reduction in the compression ratio or an increase in the engine capacity to compensate for loss of power; and

(c) that the relevant authority has accepted the certificate referred to in sub-paragraph (b).

Table

Item	Description of vehicle	Date before which vehicle must be first used
(1)	(2)	(3)
1	Vehicles with an engine capacity of less than 1400cc	1.4.92
2	Vehicles with an engine capacity of not less than 1400c and not more than 2000cc	1.4.94
3	M1 category vehicles with an engine capacity of more than 2000cc and which— (a) are constructed or adapted to carry not more than 5 passengers excluding the driver, or (b) have a maximum gross weight of not more than 2500 kg. not being in either case, an off-road vehicle.	1.4.93

[1459]

NOTES
Commencement: 1 October 1988.
Added by SI 1988 No 1524, reg 6, Schedule.
Paras 2, 3: renumbered as such by SI 1990 No 1131, reg 6(3).
Council Directive 70/156/EEC: OJ L 42, 23.2.70, p 1.

PART II

SYMBOL INDICATING THAT VEHICLE CAN RUN ON UNLEADED PETROL

[1460]

NOTES
Commencement: 1 October 1988.

Regulation 36C

[SCHEDULE 3B

Authorised Sealers

PART I

GENERAL

1. The Secretary of State may authorise—

    (a) an individual proposing to seal speed limiters other than on behalf of another person;

    (b) a firm; or

    (c) a corporation;

to seal speed limiters for the purposes of regulation 36A or 36B and a person or body so authorised is referred to in this Schedule as an "authorised sealer".

2. An authorised sealer shall comply with the conditions set out in Part II of this Schedule and with such other conditions as may from time to time be imposed by the Secretary of State.

3. An authorised sealer may charge for sealing a speed limiter.

4. The Secretary of State may at any time withdraw an authorisation granted under this Schedule.

5.—(1) An authorisation under this Schedule in respect of an individual shall terminate if—

    (a) he dies;

    (b) is adjudged bankrupt or, in Scotland, has his estate sequestrated; or

    (c) becomes a patient within the meaning of Part VII of the Mental Health Act 1983 or, in Scotland, becomes incapable of managing his own affairs.

(2) An authorisation under this Schedule in respect of a firm shall terminate if the firm is dissolved or if all the partners are adjudged bankrupt.

(3) An authorisation under this Schedule in respect of a company shall terminate if—

    (a) the company goes into liquidation or an administration order is made in relation to it;

    (b) a receiver or manager of the trade or business of the company is appointed; or

    (c) possession is taken by or on behalf of the holders of any debenture secured by a floating charge, or any property of the company comprised in or subject to the charge, occurs.]   **[1460A]**

NOTES
Commencement: 1 August 1992.
Inserted by SI 1992 No 422, reg 5(2), Schedule.

[PART II

THE CONDITIONS

6. An authorised sealer shall not—

    (a) seal a speed limiter fitted to a vehicle to which regulation 36A applies unless he is satisfied that the speed limiter fulfils the requirements of paragraph (3)(a), (b) and (d) of that regulation, or

(b) seal a speed limiter fitted to a vehicle to which regulation 36B applies unless he is satisfied that the speed limiter fulfils the requirements of paragraph (3)(a), (b) and (d) of tht regulation.

7. When sealing a speed limiter fitted to a vehicle to which regulation 36A applies, an authorised sealer shall do so in such manner that the speed limiter fulfils the requirements of paragraph (3)(c) of that regulation.

8. When sealing a speed limiter fitted to a vehicle to which regulation 36B applies, an authorised sealer shall do so in such a manner that the speed limiter fulfils the requirements of paragraph (3)(c) of that regulation.

9. When an authorised sealer has sealed a speed limiter fitted to a vehicle to which section 36A applies he shall supply the owner with a plate which fulfils the requirements of regulation 70A.

10. When an authorised sealer has sealed a speed limiter fitted to a vehicle to which section 36B applies he shall supply the owner with a plate which fulfils the requirements of regulation 70B.]   **[1460B]**

NOTES
   Commencement: 1 August 1992.
   Inserted by SI 1992 No 422, reg 5(2), Schedule.

SCHEDULE 4

Regulation 40

GAS CONTAINERS

PART I

Definitions relating to gas containers

1. In this Schedule, unless the context otherwise requires, the following expressions have the meanings hereby assigned to them respectively, that is to say—

   "gas container" means a container fitted to a motor vehicle or a trailer and intended for the storage of gaseous fuel for the purpose of the propulsion of the vehicle or the drawing vehicle as the case may be;
   "gas cylinder" means a container fitted to a motor vehicle or a trailer and intended for the storage of compressed gas for the purpose of the propulsion of the vehicle or the drawing vehicle as the case may be;
   "compressed gas" means gaseous fuel under a pressure exceeding 1.0325 bar above atmospheric pressure;
   "pipe line" means all pipes connecting a gas container or containers—
   (a) to the engine or the mixing device for the supply of a mixture of gas and air to the engine; and
   (b) to the filling point on the vehicle;
   "pressure pipe line" means any part of a pipe line intended for the conveyance of compressed gas; and
   "reducing valve" means an apparatus which automatically reduces the pressure of the gas passing through it.

Gas containers

2. Every gas container shall—

   (a) be securely attached to the vehicle in such manner as not to be liable to displacement or damage due to vibration or other cause; and

(b) be so placed or insulated as not to be adversely affected by the heat from the exhaust system.

Pipe lines

3.—(1) Every pipe line shall be supported in such manner as to be protected from excessive vibration and strain.

(2) No part of a pipe line shall be in such a position that it may be subjected to undue heat from the exhaust system.

(3) Every pressure pipe line shall be made of steel solid drawn.

(4) The maximum unsupported length of a pressure pipe line shall not exceed 920 mm.

Unions

4.—(1) Every union shall be so constructed and fitted that it will—

(a) not be liable to work loose or develop leakage when in use; and
(b) be readily accessible for inspection and adjustment.

(2) No union on a pressure pipe line or on a gas cylinder shall contain a joint other than a metal to metal joint.

Reducing valves

5. Every reducing valve shall be—

(a) so fitted as to be readily accessible; and
(b) so constructed that there can be no escape of gas when the engine is not running.

Valves and cocks

6.—(1) Every valve or cock intended to be subjected to a pressure exceeding 6.8948 bar shall be of forged steel or of brass or bronze complying with the specification contained in Part II of this Schedule.

(2) A valve or cock shall be fitted to the pipe line to enable the supply of gas from the container or containers to the mixing device to be shut off.

(3)(a) In the case of a pressure pipe line the valve or cock shall be placed between the reducing valve and the container or containers and shall be readily visible and accessible from the outside of the vehicle and a notice indicating its position and method of operation shall be affixed in a conspicuous position on the outside of the vehicle carrying the gas container or containers.

(b) In other cases, if the valve or cock is not so visible and accessible as aforesaid, a notice indicating its position shall be affixed in a conspicuous position on the outside of the vehicle carrying the container or containers.

Pressure gauges

7. Every pressure gauge connected to a pressure pipe line shall be so constructed as not to be liable to deterioration under the action of the particular gases employed and shall be so constructed and fitted that—

(a) in the event of failure of such pressure gauge no gas can escape into any part of the vehicle;
(b) it is not possible owing to leakage of gas into the casing of the pressure gauge for pressure to increase therein to such extent as to be liable to cause a breakage of the glass thereof; and

(c) in the event of failure of such pressure gauge the supply of gas thereto may be readily cut off.

Charging connections

8.—(1) Every connection for charging a gas container shall be outside the vehicle and in the case of a public service no such connection shall be within 610 mm of any entrance or exit.

(2) An efficient shut-off valve shall be fitted as near as practicable to the filling point.

Provided that in cases where compressed gas is not used a cock or an efficient non-return valve may be fitted in lieu thereof.

(3) Where compressed gas is used an additional emergency shut-off valve shall be fitted adjacent to the valve referred to in sub-paragraph (2) of this paragraph.

(4) A cap shall be fitted to the gas filling point on the vehicle and where compressed gas is used this cap shall be made of steel with a metal to metal joint.

Trailers

9.—(1) Where a trailer is used for the carriage of a gas cylinder, a reducing valve shall be fitted on the trailer.

(2) No pipe used for conveying gas from a trailer to the engine of a vehicle shall contain compressed gas.

Construction, etc., of system

10. Every part of a gas container propulsion system shall be—

(a) so placed or protected as not to be exposed to accidental damage and shall be soundly and properly constructed of suitable and well-finished materials capable of withstanding the loads and stresses likely to be met with in operation and shall be maintained in an efficient, safe and clean condition; and

(b) so designed and constructed that leakage of gas is not likely to occur under normal working conditions, whether or not the engine is running. **[1461]**

NOTES

Commencement: 11 August 1986.

This Part derived from SI 1955 No 990, Sch 3, Part I, and SI 1978 No 1017, Sch 3, Part I.

PART II

SPECIFICATION FOR BRASS OR BRONZE VALVES

Manufacture of valves

1. The stamping or pressing from which each valve is manufactured shall be made from bars produced by (a) extrusion, (b) rolling, (c) forging, (d) extrusion and drawing, or (e) rolling and drawing.

Heat treatment

2. Each stamping or pressing shall be heat treated so as to produce an equiaxed microstructure in the material.

Freedom from defects

3. All stampings or pressings and the bars from which they are made shall be free from cracks, laminations, hard spots, segregated materials and variations in composition.

Tensile test

4. Tensile tests shall be made on samples of stampings or pressings taken at random from any consignment. The result of the tensile test shall conform to the following conditions—

Yield Stress.—Not less than 231.6 N/mm^2.
Ultimate Tensile Stress.—Not less than 463.3 N/mm^2.

Elongation on 50 mm gauge length.—Not less than 25%.

Note.—When the gauge length is less than 50 mm the required elongation shall be proportionately reduced.

The fractured test piece shall be free from piping and other defects (see paragraph 3 of this Part of this Schedule).   **[1462]**

NOTES
Commencement: 11 August 1986.
This Part derived from SI 1955 No 990, Sch 3, Part II, and SI 1978 No 1017, Sch 3, Part II.

SCHEDULE 5

Regulations 40, 96

GAS SYSTEMS

Definitions

1. In this Schedule—

"check valve" means a device which permits the flow of gas in one direction and prevents the flow of gas in the opposite direction;

"design pressure" means the pressure which a part of a gas system has been designed and constructed safely to withstand;

"double-check valve" means a device which consists of two check valves in series and which permits the flow of gas in one direction and prevents the flow of gas in the opposite direction;

"excess flow valve" means a device which automatically and instantaneously reduces to a minimum the flow of gas through the valve when the flow rate exceeds a set value;

"fixed gas container" means a gas container which is attached to a vehicle permanently and in such a manner that the container can be filled without being moved;

"gas container" means any container, not being a container for the carriage of gas as goods, which is fitted to or carried on a motor vehicle or trailer and is intended for the storage of gas for either—

(a) the propulsion of the motor vehicle, or
(b) the operation of a gas-fired appliance;

"high pressure" means a pressure exceeding 1.0325 bar absolute;

"high pressure pipeline" means a pipeline intended to contain gas at high pressure;

"pipeline" means any pipe or passage connecting any two parts of a gas propulsion system of a vehicle or of a gas-fired appliance supply system on a vehicle or any two points on the same part of any such system;

"portable gas container" means a gas container which may be attached to a vehicle but which can readily be removed;

"pressure relief valve" means a device which opens automatically when the pressure in the part of the gas system to which it is fitted exceeds a set value, reaches its maximum flow capacity when the set value is exceeded by 10% and closes automatically when the pressure falls below a set value; and

"reducing valve" means a device which automatically reduces the pressure of the gas passing through it, and includes regulator devices.

Gas containers

2.—(1) Every gas container shall—

(a) be capable of withstanding the pressure of the gas which may be stored in the container at the highest temperature which the gas is likely to reach,

(b) if fitted inside the vehicle be so arranged as to prevent so far as is practicable the possibility of gas entering the engine, passenger or living compartments due to leaks or venting from the container or valves, connections and gauges immediately adjacent to it, and the space containing these components shall be so ventilated and drained as to prevent the accumulation of gas,

(c) be securely attached to the vehicle in such a manner as not to be liable to displacement or damage due to vibration or other cause, and

(d) be so placed and so insulated or shielded as not to suffer any adverse effect from the heat of the exhaust system of any engine or any other source of heat.

(2) Every portable gas container shall be either—

(a) hermetically sealed, or

(b) fitted with a valve or cock to enable the flow of gas from the container to be stopped.

(3) Every fixed gas container shall—

(a) be fitted with—

(i) at least one pressure relief valve, and

(ii) at least one manually operated valve which may be extended by an internal dip tube inside the gas container so as to indicate when the container has been filled to the level corresponding to the filling ratio specified in the British Standards Institution Specification for Filling Ratios and Developed Pressure for Liquefiable and Permanent Gases (as defined, respectively, in paragraphs 3.2 and 3.5 of the said Specification) published in May 1976 under the number BS 5355, and

(b) be conspicuously and permanently marked with its design pressure.

(4) If any fixed gas container is required to be fitted in a particular attitude or location, or if any device referred to in sub-paragraph (3) above requires the container to be fitted in such a manner, then it shall be conspicuously and permanently marked to indicate that requirement.

(5) If the operation of any pressure relief valve or other device referred to in sub-paragraph (3) above may cause gas to be released from the gas container, an outlet shall be provided to lead such gas to the outside of the vehicle so as not to suffer any adverse effect from the heat of the exhaust system of any engine or any other source of heat, and that outlet from the pressure relief valve shall not be fitted with any other valve or cock.

Filling systems for fixed gas containers

3.—(1) Every connection for filling a fixed gas container shall be on the outside of the vehicle.

(2) There shall be fitted to every fixed gas container either—

(a) a manually operated shut-off valve and an excess flow valve, or

(b) a manually operated shut-off valve and a single check valve, or

(c) a double-check valve.

and all parts of these valves in contact with gas shall be made entirely of suitable metal except that they may contain non-metal washers and seals provided that such washers and seals are supported and constrained by metal components.

(3) In every case where a pipe is attached to a gas container for the purpose of filling the gas container there shall be fitted to the end of the pipe furthest from the gas container a check valve or a double-check valve.

(4) There shall be fitted over every gas filling point on a vehicle a cap which shall—

(a) prevent any leakage of gas from the gas filling point,

(b) be secured to the vehicle by a chain or some other suitable means,

(c) be made of suitable material, and

(d) be fastened to the gas filling point by either a screw thread or other suitable means.

Pipelines

4.—(1) Every pipeline shall be fixed in such a manner and position that—

(a) it will not be adversely affected by the heat of the exhaust system of any engine or any other source of heat,

(b) it is protected from vibration and strain in excess of that which it can reasonably be expected to withstand, and

(c) in the case of a high pressure pipeline it is so far as is practicable accessible for inspection.

(2) Save as provided in sub-paragraph (4) below, every high pressure pipeline shall be—

    (a) a rigid line of steel, copper or copper alloy of high pressure hydraulic grade, suitable for service on road vehicles and designed for a minimum service pressure rating of not less than 75 bar absolute, and

    (b) effectively protected against, or shielded from, or treated so as to be resistant to, external corrosion throughout its length unless it is made from material which is corrosion resistant under the conditions which it is likely to encounter in service.

(3) No unsupported length of any high pressure pipeline shall exceed 600 mm.

(4) Flexible hose may be used in a high pressure pipeline if—

    (a) it is reinforced either by stainless steel wire braid or by textile braid,

    (b) its length does not exceed 500 mm, and

    (c) save in the case of a pipeline attached to a gas container for the purpose of filling that container the flexibility which it provides is necessary for the construction or operation of the gas system of which it forms a part.

(5) If a high pressure pipeline or part of such a pipeline is so constructed or located that it may, in the course of its normal use (excluding the supply of fuel from a gas container), contain liquid which is prevented from flowing, a relief valve shall be incorporated in that pipeline.

Unions and joints

5.—(1) Every union and joint on a pipeline or gas container shall be so constructed and fitted that it will—

    (a) not be liable to work loose or leak when in use, and

    (b) be readily accessible for inspection and maintenance.

(2) Every union on a high pressure pipeline or on a gas container shall be made of suitable metal but such a union may contain non-metal washers and seals provided that such washers and seals are supported and constrained by metal components.

Reducing valves

6. Every reducing valve shall be made of suitable materials and be so fitted as to be readily accessible for inspection and maintenance.

Pressure relief valves

7.—(1) Every pressure relief valve which is fitted to any part of a gas system (including a gas container) shall—

    (a) be made entirely of suitable metal and so constructed and fitted as to ensure that the cooling effect of the gas during discharge shall not prevent its effective operation,

    (b) be capable, under the most extreme temperatures likely to be met (including exposure to fire), of a discharge rate which prevents the pressure of the contents of the gas system from exceeding its design pressure,

    (c) have a maximum discharge pressure not greater than the design pressure of the gas container;

    (d) be so designed and constructed as to prevent unauthorised interference with the relief pressure setting during service, and

    (e) have outlets which are—

        (i) so sited that so far as is reasonably practicable in the event of an accident the valve and its outlets are protected from damage and the free discharge from such outlets is not impaired, and

        (ii) so designed and constructed as to prevent the collection of moisture and other foreign matter which could adversely affect their performance.

(2) The pressure at which a pressure relief valve is designed to start lifting shall be clearly and permanently marked on every such valve.

(3) Every pressure relief valve which is fitted to a gas container shall communicate with the vapour space in the gas container and not with any liquefied gas.

Valves and cocks

8.—(1) A valve or cock shall be fitted to every supply pipeline as near as practicable to every fixed gas container and such valve or cock shall by manual operation enable the supply of gas from the gas container to the gas system to be stopped, and save as provided in sub-paragraph (2) below, shall—

    (a) if fitted on the outside of the vehicle, be readily visible and accessible from the outside of the vehicle, or

    (b) if fitted inside the vehicle be readily accessible for operation and be so arranged as to prevent so far as is practicable the possibility of gas entering the engine, passenger or living compartments due to leaks, and the space containing the valve or cock shall be so ventilated and drained as to prevent the accumulation of gas in that space.

(2) Where a fixed gas container supplies no gas system other than a gas propulsion system and the gas container is so located that it is not practicable to make the valve or cock referred to in sub-paragraph (1) above readily accessible there shall be fitted an electrically-operated valve which shall either be incorporated in the valve or cock referred to in sub-paragraph (1) above or be fitted immediately downstream from it and shall—

    (a) be constructed so as to open when the electric power is applied and to close when the electric power is cut off,

    (b) be so fitted as to shut off the supply of gas from the gas container to the gas system when the engine is not running, and

    (c) if fitted inside the vehicle be so arranged as to prevent as far as is practicable the possibility of gas entering the engine, passenger or living compartments due to leaks, and the space containing the valve shall be so ventilated and drained as to prevent the accumulation of gas in that space.

(3) A notice clearly indicating the position, purpose and method of operating every valve or cock referred to in sub-paragraphs (1) and (2) above shall be fitted—

    (a) in all cases, in a conspicuous position on the outside of the vehicle, and

    (b) in every case where the valve or cock is located inside the vehicle in a conspicuous position adjacent to the gas container.

(4) In the case of a high pressure pipeline for the conveyance of gas from the gas container an excess flow valve shall be fitted as near as practicable to the gas container and such valve shall operate in the event of a fracture of the pipeline or other similar failure.

(5) All parts of every valve or cock referred to in this paragraph which are in contact with gas shall be made of suitable metal, save that they may contain non-metal washers and seals provided that such washers and seals are supported and constrained by metal components.

Gauges

9. Every gauge connected to a gas container or to a pipeline shall be so constructed as to be unlikely to deteriorate under the action of the gas used or to be used and shall be so constructed and fitted that—

    (a) no gas can escape into any part of the vehicle as a result of any failure of the gauge, and

    (b) in the event of any failure of the gauge the supply of gas to the gauge can be readily stopped.

Provided that the requirement specified in sub-paragraph (b) above shall not apply in respect of a gauge fitted as an integral part of a gas container.

Propulsion systems

10.—(1) Every gas propulsion system shall be so designed and constructed that—

(a) the supply of gas to the engine is automatically stopped by the operation of a valve when the engine is not running at all or is not running on the supply of gas, and

(b) where the reducing valve is relied on to comply with sub-paragraph (a) above, the supply of gas to the engine is automatically stopped by the operation of an additional valve when the engine is switched off.

(2) Where the engine of a vehicle is constructed or adapted to run on one or more fuels as alternative to gas, the safety and efficiency of the engine and any fuel system shall not be impaired by the presence of any other fuel system.

Special requirements for buses

11. In the case of a bus there shall be fitted as near as practicable to the gas container a valve which shall stop the flow of gas into the gas supply pipeline in the event of—

(a) the angle of tilt of the vehicle exceeding that referred to in regulation 6 of the Public Service Vehicles (Conditions of Fitness, Equipment, Use and Certification) Regulations 1981, and

(b) the deceleration of the vehicle exceeding 5g.

Gas-fired appliances

12. Every part of a gas-fired appliance shall be—

(a) so designed and constructed that leakage of gas is unlikely to occur, and

(b) constructed of materials which are compatible both with each other and with the gas used.

13. Every gas-fired appliance shall be—

(a) so located as to be easily inspected and maintained,

(b) so located and either insulated or shielded that its use shall not cause or be likely to cause danger due to the presence of any flammable material,

(c) so constructed and located as not to impose undue stress on any pipe or fitting, and

(d) so fastened or located as not to work loose or move in relation to the vehicle.

14. With the exception of catalytic heating appliances, every appliance of the kind described in regulation 96(3)(b) or (c) which is fitted to a motor vehicle shall be fitted with a flue which shall be—

(a) connected to an outlet which is on the outside of the vehicle,

(b) constructed and located so as to prevent any expelled matter from entering the vehicle, and

(c) located so that it will not cause any adverse effect to, or suffer any adverse effect from, the exhaust outlet of any engine or any other source of heat.

General requirements

15. Every part of a gas propulsion system or a gas-fired appliance system, excluding the appliance itself, shall be—

(a) so far as is practicable so located or protected as not to be exposed to accidental damage,

(b) soundly and properly constructed of materials which are compatible with one another and with the gas used or to be used and which are capable of withstanding the loads and stresses likely to be met in operation, and

(c) so designed and constructed that leakage of gas is unlikely to occur.   [1463]

NOTES

Commencement: 11 August 1986.

This Schedule derived from SI 1978 No 1017, Sch 3A.

SCHEDULE 6

Regulation 41

CONSTRUCTION OF MINIBUSES

The requirements referred to in regulation 41 are as follows—

Exhaust pipes

1. The outlet of every exhaust pipe fitted to a minibus shall be either at the rear or on the off side of the vehicle.

Doors-number and position

2.—(1) Every minibus shall be fitted with at least—

    (a) one service door on the near side of the vehicle; and

    (b) one emergency door either at the rear or on the side of the vehicle so, however, that any emergency door fitted on the off side of the vehicle shall be in addition to the driver's door and there shall be no requirement for an emergency door on a minibus if it has a service door at the rear in addition to the service door on the near side.

(2) No minibus shall be fitted with any door on its off side other than a driver's door and an emergency door.

Emergency Doors

3. Every emergency door fitted to a minibus, whether or not required pursuant to these Regulations, shall—

    (a) be clearly marked, in letters not less than 25 mm high, on both the inside and the outside, "EMERGENCY DOOR" or "FOR EMERGENCY USE ONLY", and the means of its operation shall be clearly indicated on or near the door.

    (b) if hinged, open outwards;

    (c) be capable of being operated manually; and

    (d) when fully opened, give an aperture in the body of the vehicle not less than 1210 mm high nor less than 530 mm wide.

Power-operated doors

4.—(1) Every power-operated door fitted to a mini-bus shall—

    (a) incorporate transparent panels so as to enable a person immediately inside the door to see any person immediately outside the door;

    (b) be capable of being operated by a mechanism controlled by the driver of the vehicle when in the driving seat;

    (c) be capable, in the event of an emergency or a failure of the supply of power for the operation of the door, of being opened from both inside and outside the vehicle by controls which—

        (i) over-ride all other controls,

        (ii) are placed on, or adjacent to, the door, and

        (iii) are accompanied by markings which clearly indicate their position and method of operation and state that they may not be used by passengers except in an emergency;

    (d) have a soft edge so that a trapped finger is unlikely to be injured; and

    (e) be controlled by a mechanism by virtue of which if the door, when closing, meets a resistance exceeding 150 Newtons, either

        —the door will cease to close and begin to open, or

        —the closing force will cease and the door will become capable of being opened manually.

(2) No minibus shall be equipped with a system for the storage or transmission of energy in respect of the opening or closing of any door which, either in normal operation or if the system fails, is capable of adversely affecting the operation of the vehicle's braking system.

Locks, handles and hinges of doors

5. No minibus shall be fitted with—

    (a) a door which can be locked from the outside unless, when so locked, it is capable of being opened from inside the vehicle when stationary;

    (b) a handle or other device for opening any door, other than the driver's door, from inside the vehicle unless the handle or other device is designed so as to prevent, so far as is reasonably practicable, the accidental opening of the door, and is fitted with a guard or transparent cover or so designed that it must be raised to open the door;

(c) a door which is not capable of being opened, when not locked, from inside and outside the vehicle by a single movement of the handle or other device for opening the door;

(d) a door in respect of which there is not a device capable of holding the door closed so as to prevent any passenger falling through the doorway;

(e) a side door which opens outwards and is hinged at the edge nearest the rear of the vehicle except in the case of a door having more than one rigid panel;

(f) a door, other than a power-operated door, in respect of which there is not either—

   (i) a slam lock of the two-stage type; or

   (ii) a device by means of which the driver, when occupying the driver's seat, is informed if the door is not securely closed, such device being operated by movement of the handle or other device for opening the door or, in the case of a handle or other device with a spring-return mechanism, by movement of the door as well as of the handle or other device.

Provided that the provisions of sub-paragraphs (a), (c), (d) and (f) of this paragraph shall not apply in respect of a near side rear door forming part of a pair of doors fitted at the rear of a vehicle if that door is capable of being held securely closed by the other door of that pair.

View of doors

6.—(1) Save as provided in sub-paragraph (2), every minibus shall be fitted with mirrors or other means so that the driver, when occupying the driver's seat, can see clearly the area immediately inside and outside every service door of the vehicle.

(2) The provisions of sub-paragraph (1) shall be deemed to be satisfied in respect of a rear service door if a person 1.3 metres tall standing 1 metre behind the vehicle is visible to the driver when occupying the driver's seat.

Access to doors

7.—(1) Save as provided in sub-paragraph (2), there shall be unobstructed access from every passenger seat in a minibus to at least two doors one of which must be on the nearside of the vehicle and one of which must be either at the rear or on the offside of the vehicle.

(2) Access to one only of the doors referred to in sub-paragraph (1) may be obstructed by either or both of—

(a) a seat which when tilted or folded does not obstruct access to that door; and

(b) a lifting platform or ramp which—

   (i) does not obstruct the handle or other device on the inside for opening the door with which the platform or ramp is associated, and

   (ii) when the door is open, can be pushed or pulled out of the way from the inside so as to leave the doorway clear for use in an emergency.

Grab handles and hand rails

8. Every minibus shall be fitted as respects every side service door with a grab handle or a hand rail to assist passengers to get on or off the vehicle.

Seats

9.—(1) No seat shall be fitted to any door of a minibus.

(2) Every seat and every wheelchair anchorage fitted to a minibus shall be fixed to the vehicle.

(3) No seat, other than a wheelchair, fitted to a minibus shall be less than 400 mm wide, and in ascertaining the width of a seat no account shall be taken of any arm-rests, whether or not they are folded back or otherwise put out of use.

(4) No minibus shall be fitted with an anchorage for a wheelchair in such a manner that a wheelchair secured to the anchorage would face either side of the vehicle.

(5) No minibus shall be fitted with a seat—

(a) facing either side of the vehicle and immediately forward of a rear door unless the seat is fitted with an arm-rest or similar device to guard against a passenger on that seat falling through the doorway; or

(b) so placed that a passenger on it would, without protection, be liable to be thrown through any doorway which is provided with a power-operated door or down any steps, unless the vehicle is fitted with a screen or guard which affords adequate protection against that occurrence.

Electrical equipment and wiring

10.—(1) Save as provided in sub-paragraph (2) no minibus shall be fitted with any—

(a) electrical circuit which is liable to carry a current exceeding that for which it was designed;

(b) cable for the conduct of electricity unless it is suitably insulated and protected from damage;

(c) electrical circuit, other than a charging circuit, which includes any equipment other than—

(i) a starter motor,

(ii) a glow plug,

(iii) an ignition circuit, and

(iv) a device to stop the vehicle's engine,

unless it includes a fuse or circuit breaker so, however, that one fuse or circuit breaker may serve more than one circuit; or

(d) electrical circuit with a voltage exceeding 100 volts unless there is connected in each pole of the main supply of electricity which is not connected to earth a manually-operated switch which is—

(i) capable of disconnecting the circuit, or, if there is more than one, every circuit, from the main supply,

(ii) not capable of disconnecting any circuit supplying any lamp with which the vehicle is required to be fitted, and

(iii) located inside the vehicle in a position readily accessible to the driver.

(2) The provisions of sub-paragraph (1) do not apply in respect of a high tension ignition circuit or a circuit within a unit of equipment.

Fuel tanks

11. No minibus shall be fitted with a fuel tank or any apparatus for the supply of fuel which is in the compartments or other spaces provided for the accommodation of the driver or passengers.

Lighting of steps

12. Every minibus shall be provided with lamps to illuminate every step at a passenger exit or in a gangway.

General construction and maintenance

13. Every minibus, including all bodywork and fittings, shall be soundly and properly constructed of suitable materials and maintained in good and serviceable condition, and shall be of such design as to be capable of withstanding the loads and stresses likely to be met in the normal operation of the vehicle.

Definitions

14. In this Schedule—

"driver's door" means a door fitted to a minibus for use by the driver;

"emergency door" means a door fitted to a minibus for use by passengers in an emergency; and "service door" means a door fitted to a minibus for use by passengers in normal circumstances. **[1464]**

NOTES
Commencement: 11 August 1986.

SCHEDULE 7
FIRE EXTINGUISHING APPARATUS AND FIRST AID EQUIPMENT FOR MINIBUSES

PART I
FIRE EXTINGUISHING APPARATUS (REG 42)

[A fire extinguisher which complies in all respects with the specification for portable fire extinguishers issued by the British Standards Institution numbered BS 5423: 1977 or BS 5423: 1980 or BS 5423: 1987 and which—

    (a) has a minimum test fire rating of 8A or 21B, and
    (b) contains water or foam or contains, and is marked to indicate that it contains, halon 1211 or halon 1301.] **[1465]**

NOTES
Commencement: 11 January 1990.
Substituted by SI 1989 No 2360, reg 5.

PART II
FIRST AID EQUIPMENT (REG 43)

    (i) Ten antiseptic wipes, foil packed;
    (ii) One conforming disposable bandage (not less than 7.5 cm wide);
    (iii) Two triangular bandages;
    (iv) One packet of 24 assorted adhesive dressings;
    (v) Three large sterile unmedicated ambulance dressings (not less than 15.0 cm × 20.0 cm);
    (vi) Two sterile eye pads, with attachments;
    (vii) Twelve assorted safety pins; and
    (viii) One pair of rustless blunt-ended scissors. **[1466]**

NOTES
Commencement: 11 August 1986.

SCHEDULE 8
Regulation 66

PLATES FOR CERTAIN VEHICLES

PART I

Particulars to be shown on plate for motor vehicles (including motor vehicles forming part of articulated vehicles)

1. Manufacturer's name.

2. Vehicle type.

3. Engine type and power (a).

4. Chassis or serial number.

5. Number of axles.

6. Maximum axle weight for each axle (b).

7. Maximum gross weight (c).

8. Maximum train weight (d).

9. Maximum weight in Great Britain for each axle (b) (e).

10. Maximum gross weight in Great Britain (c) (e).

(a) The power need not be shown in the case of a motor vehicle manufactured before 1st October 1972 (hereinafter in this Schedule referred to as "an excepted vehicle") and shall not be shown in the case of any motor vehicle which is propelled otherwise than by a compression ignition engine.

(b) This weight as respects each axle is the sum of the weights to be transmitted to the road surface by all the wheels of that axle.

(c) This weight is the sum of the weights to be transmitted to the road surface by all the wheels of the motor vehicle (including any load imposed by a trailer, whether forming part of an articulated vehicle or not, on the motor vehicle).

(d) This weight is the sum of the weights to be transmitted to the road surface by all the wheels of the motor vehicle and of any trailer drawn, but this item need not be completed where the motor vehicle is not constructed to draw a trailer.

(b), (c), (d) References to the weights to be transmitted to the road surface by all or any of the wheels of the vehicle or of any trailer drawn are references to the weights so to be transmitted both of the vehicle or trailer and of any load or persons carried by it.

(e) This item need not be completed in the case of an excepted vehicle or in the case of a vehicle which is a locomotive or motor tractor.   **[1467]**

NOTES
  Commencement: 11 August 1986.
  This Part derived from SI 1978 No 1017, Sch 2, Part I.

PART II

Particulars to be shown on plate for trailers (including trailers forming part of articulated vehicles)

1. Manufacturer's name.

2. Chassis or serial number.

3. Number of axles.

4. Maximum of weight for each axle (a).

5. Maximum load imposed on drawing vehicle [manufactured before 1st February 1992] (b).

6. Maximum gross weight (c).

7. Maximum weight in Great Britain for each axle (a) (e).

8. Maximum gross weight in Great Britain (c) (f).

9. Year of manufacture (d).

(a) This weight as respects each axle is the sum of the weights to be transmitted to the road surface by all the wheels of that axle.

(b) Only for trailers forming part of articulated vehicles or where some of the weight of the trailer or its load is to be imposed on the drawing vehicle. This item need not be completed in the case of a converter dolly.

(c) This weight is the sum of the weights to be transmitted to the road surface by all the wheels of the trailer, including any weight of the trailer to be imposed on the drawing vehicle.

(a), (b), (c) References to the weights to be transmitted to the road surface by all or any of the wheels of the trailer are references to the weight so to be transmitted both of the trailer and of any load or persons carried by it and references to the weights to be imposed on the drawing vehicle are references to the weights so to be imposed both of the trailer and of any load or persons carried by it except where only the load of the trailer is imposed on the drawing vehicle.

(d) This item need not be completed in the case of a trailer manufactured before 1st April 1970.

(e) This item need not be completed in the case of a trailer manufactured before 1st October 1972.

(f) This item need not be completed in the case of a trailer manufactured before 1st October 1972 or which forms part of an articulated vehicle. **[1468]**

NOTES
Commencement: 11 August 1986.
This Part derived from SI 1978 No 1017, Sch 2, Part II.
Words in square brackets added by SI 1991 No 1526, reg 4.

PART III

1. The power of an engine, which is to be shown only in the case of a compression ignition engine on the plate in respect of item 3 in Part I of this Schedule, shall be the amount in kilowatts equivalent to the installed power output shown in a type test certificate issued—

    (a) by a person authorised by the Secretary of State for the type of engine to which the engine conforms; and

    (b) in accordance with either—

        (i) the provisions relating to the installed brake power output specified in the British Standard Specification for the Performance of Diesel Engines for Road Vehicles published on 19th May 1971 under the number BS AU 141a: 1971;

        (ii) the provisions relating to the net power specified in Community Directive 80/1269 but after allowance has been made for the power absorbed by such equipment, at its minimum power setting, driven by the engine of the vehicle as is fitted for the operation of the vehicle (other than its propulsion) such power being measured at the speed corresponding to the engine speed at which maximum engine power is developed; or

        (iii) the provisions of Annex 10 of ECE Regulation 24.02 as further amended with effect from 15th February 1984 [or Annex 10 of ECE Regulation 24.03 or Community Directive 88/195] relating to the method of measuring internal combustion engine net power, but after allowance has been made for the power absorbed by any disconnectable or progressive cooling fan, at its maximum setting, and by any other such equipment, at its minimum power setting, driven by the engine of the vehicle as is fitted for the operation of the vehicle (other than its propulsion), such power being measured at the speed corresponding to the engine speed at which maximum engine power is developed.

2.—(1) The weights to be shown on the plate in relation to items 6, 7 and 8 in Part I and in relation to items 4, 5 and 6 in Part II shall be the weight limits at or below which the vehicle is considered fit for use, having regard to its design, construction and equipment and the stresses to which it is likely to be subject in use, by the Secretary of State if the vehicle is one to which the Type A Approval for Goods Vehicles Regulations apply, and by the manufacturer if the vehicle is one to which those Regulations do not apply.

Provided that, where alterations are made to a vehicle which may render the vehicle fit for use at weights which exceed those referred to above in this paragraph and shown on the plate—

    (a) there may be shown on the plate, in place of any of those weights, such new weights as the manufacturer of the vehicle or any person carrying on business as a manufacturer of motor vehicles or trailers (or a person duly authorised on behalf of that manufacturer or any such person) or a person authorised by the Secretary of State considers to represent the weight limits at or below which the vehicle will then be fit for use, having regard to its design, construction and equipment and to those alterations and to the stresses to which it is likely to be subject in use; and

    (b) the name of the person who has determined the new weights shall be shown on the plate as having made that determination and, where he is a person authorised by the Secretary of State, his appointment shall be so shown.

(2) In relation to a vehicle manufactured on or after 1st October 1972, in the foregoing paragraph—

(a) the references to equipment shall not be treated as including a reference to the type of tyres with which the vehicle is equipped; and

(b) for the words "weight limits at or below" in both places where they occur there shall be subsituted the words "maximum weights at".

3. The weights to be shown on the plate in respect of—

(a) item 9 in Part I of this Schedule shall be the weights shown at item 6 in that Part and in respect of item 7 in Part II of this Schedule shall be the weights shown at item 4 in that Part, in each case reduced so far as necessary to indicate the maximum weight applicable to each axle of the vehicle, if the vehicle is not to be used in contravention of regulations 23, 75, 78 or 79, and if the tyres with which the vehicle is equipped are not, as respects strength, to be inadequate to support the weights to be so shown at item 9 and item 7.

(b) item 10 in the said Part I shall be the weight shown at item 7 in that Part and in respect of item 8 in the said Part II shall be the weight shown at item 6 in that Part, in each case reduced so far as necessary to indicate the maximum permissible weight applicable if the vehicle is not to be used in contravention of regulation 75 if the tyres with which the vehicle is equipped are not, as respects strength, to be inadequate to support the weights to be shown at item 10 and item 8.

4.—(1) Subject to sub-paragraph (2) of this paragraph weights on plates first affixed to a vehicle on or after 1st October 1972 shall be shown in kilograms and weights on plates first so affixed before that date shall be shown in tons and decimals thereof.

(2) Where a new weight is first shown on a plate by virtue of the proviso to paragraph 2(1) the weight shall be shown as if it was on a plate first affixed to a vehicle on the date it was first shown.

5. All letters and figures shown on the plate shall be not less than 6mm in height.

6. In this Schedule references to the manufacturer of a motor vehicle or trailer are in relation to—

(a) a vehicle constructed with a chassis which has not previously formed part of another vehicle, references to the person by whom that chassis was made;

(b) any other vehicle, references to the person by whom that vehicle was constructed.   **[1469]**

NOTES
Commencement: 11 August 1986.
This Part derived from SI 1978 No 1017, Sch 2, Part III.
Para 1: in sub-para (b) words in square brackets substituted by SI 1990 No 1131, reg 5.
Community Directive 80/1269: see reg 3, Sch 2.
Community Directive 88/195: OJ No L92, 9.4.88, p.50.
ECE Regulations 24.02, 24.03: see reg 3, Sch 2.
Type Approval for Goods Vehicles Regulations: SI 1982 No 1271.

SCHEDULE 9

Regulation 69

PLATES FOR MOTOR CYCLES

1. The plate required by regulation 69 shall be firmly attached to a part of the motor cycle which is not normally subject to replacement during the life of the motor cycle.

2. The plate shall be in the form shown in the diagram in this paragraph, shall have dimensions not less than those shown in that diagram and shall show the information provided for in that diagram and detailed in the Notes below.

Diagram of Plate

←——30 mm——→

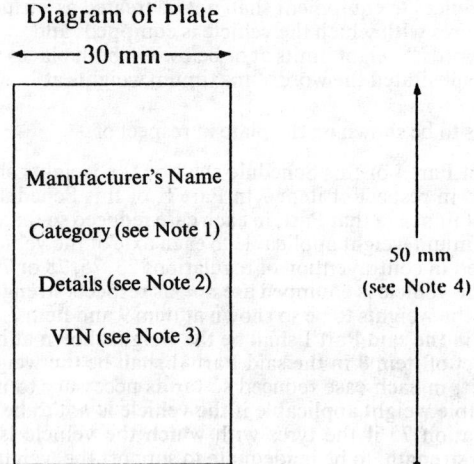

Manufacturer's Name

Category (see Note 1)

Details (see Note 2)

VIN (see Note 3)

50 mm
(see Note 4)

Notes:

1. The categories are "standard motor cycle" and "moped".
2. The details are—
(a) for standard motor cycles-

(i) the engine capacity,
(ii) the maximum engine power, and
(iii) the power to weight ratio,
provided that the details under (ii) and (iii) need not be shown for a vehicle first used before 1st January 1982;

(b) for mopeds—

(i) the engine capacity,
(ii) the kerbside weight, and
(iii) the maximum speed.

3. The vehicle identification number (VIN) shall be marked in the form used by the manufacturer to identify any one individual vehicle.
4. In the case of a plate fitted to a vehicle first used before 1st January 1982 or to a moped this dimension shall be 40 mm.

3. The information on the plate shall be shown in characters not less than 4 mm in height and in the positions on the plate indicated in the diagram above.

4. No information, other than that provided for in the diagram above, shall be marked within the rectangle which is shown in that diagram.

5. In this Schedule and, in respect of the definition of "moped", in regulations 54 and 57—

"maximum engine power" means the maximum net power the motor cycle engine will develop, in kilowatts, when measured in accordance with the test conditions specified in the International Standard number ISO 4106 developed by the technical committee of the International Organisation for Standardisation, and approved by member bodies, including the United Kingdom, and published under the reference ISO 1978 4106-09-01;

"moped" means a motor cycle which—

(a) has a kerbside weight not exceeding 250 kg, and

(b) if propelled by an internal combustion engine, has an engine with a cylinder capacity which does not exceed 50 cc, and

(c) is designed to have a maximum speed not exceeding 30 mph when driven under the conditions set out in paragraph 6.

"power to weight ratio" means the ratio of the maximum engine power to the kerbside weight of the vehicle measured, as regards the maximum engine power, in kilowatts and, as regards the kerbside weight, in 1000 kg;

"standard motor cycle" means a motor cycle which is not a moped.

6. A motor cycle shall be regarded as complying with paragraph (c) of the definition of "moped" in paragraph 5 if it cannot exceed 35 mph when tested under the following conditions—

(a) the surface on which it is tested shall be dry asphalt or concrete;

(b) the rider shall be a person not exceeding 75 kg in weight;

(c) no passenger or load shall be carried;

(d) the test route shall be so located that acceleration to, and deceleration from, maximum speed can take place elsewhere than on the test route itself;

(e) the test route shall not have a gradient exceeding 5%;

(f) the motor cycle shall be ridden in opposite directions along the test route and the speed recorded for the purpose of the test shall (in order to minimise the effect of wind resistance and gradient) be the average of speeds shown for each direction;

(g) when being driven along the test route, the motor cycle shall be driven in such manner and in such gear as to achieve the maximum speed of which it is capable; and

(h) if the motor cycle is fitted with a device which can, without the use of specialist tools or equipment, be readily modified or removed so as to increase its maximum speed, the test shall be carried out with the device in the modified condition or, as the case may be, without the device.   **[1470]**

NOTES
Commencement: 11 August 1986.
This Schedule derived from SI 1978 No 1017, Schs 12, 12A.

Regulation 70

SCHEDULE 10
MINISTRY PLATE

DEPARTMENT OF TRANSPORT

Road Traffic Act 1972, Sections 40 and 47
Examination of Goods Vehicles

PLATE			Serial No.
REGISTRATION/IDENTIFICATION MARK	YEAR ORIGINAL REGISTRATION	YEAR OF MANUFACTURE	DTp REF. NO.
CHASSIS/SERIAL No.		UNLADEN WEIGHT	MAKE AND MODEL

(1) DESCRIPTION OF WEIGHTS APPLICABLE TO VEHICLE		(2) WEIGHTS NOT TO BE EXCEEDED IN GREAT BRITAIN	(3) DESIGN WEIGHTS (if higher than shown in col (2))	FUNCTION
		KILOGRAMS	KILOGRAMS	
AXLE WEIGHT (axles numbered from front to rear)	AXLE 1			
	AXLE 2			
	AXLE 3			
	AXLE 4			
GROSS WEIGHT (see warning opposite)				
TRAIN WEIGHT (see warning opposite)				DATE OF ISSUE

WARNING

1. A reduced gross weight may apply in certain cases to a vehicle towing or being towed by another.
2. A reduced train weight may apply depending on the type of trailer drawn.
3. All weights shown are subject to fitting of correct tyres.

Notes: 1. A Ministry plate may contain the words "MINISTRY OF TRANSPORT" or "DEPARTMENT OF THE ENVIRONMENT" instead of the words "DEPARTMENT OF TRANSPORT", and may contain the words "Road Safety Act 1967, Sections 8 and 9" or or of the words "Road Traffic Act 1972, Sections 40 and 45". (In a case where the Type Approval For Goods Vehicles Regulations do not apply). It may also contain additional columns in Columns (2) and (3) showing the weights in tons.

2. Entries in respect of train weight are required in the case of—(a) a motor vehicle constructed or adapted to form part of an articulated vehicle; and (b) a rigid vehicle which is constructed or adapted to draw a trailer and is first used on or after 1st April 1983.

3. A Ministry plate shows the unladen weight and function of the vehicle in a case where the Type Approval for Goods Vehicles Regulations apply.

4. A Ministry plate may have separate spaces for the "make" and "model" of the vehicle.

5. A Ministry plate may have no "Reference Number" or may refer to the "Department of the Environment Reference No."

NOTES

Commencement: 11 August 1986.

This Schedule derived from SI 1978 No 1017, Sch 11.

[1471]

SCHEDULE 10A
Ministry Plate (see reg 70)

SCHEDULE

Regulation 4

SCHEDULE 10A (see regulation 70)
MINISTRY PLATE

PLATE VTG 6A	DEPARTMENT OF TRANSPORT Road Traffic Act 1972. Sections 40, 45 and 47 Examination of Goods Vehicles			SERIAL NUMBER		
				UNLADEN WEIGHT		DTp REF No
				5. VEHICLE DIMENSIONS		
REGISTRATION/ IDENTIFICATION MARK	YEAR OF ORIGINAL REG	YEAR OF MANUFACTURE	FUNCTION	LENGTH (L)		
				WIDTH (W)		
MANUFACTURER/MODEL				a. (See Note 1) COUPLING CENTRE TO VEHICLE FOREMOST PART	MAXIMUM	MINIMUM
TYPE APPROVAL VARIANT No						
VEHICLE IDENTIFICATION No						
(1) DESCRIPTION OF WEIGHTS APPLICABLE TO VEHICLE	(2) WEIGHT NOT TO BE EXCEEDED IN Gt. BRITAIN	(3) EEC MAXIMUM PERMITTED WEIGHTS (See Note 4)	(4) DESIGN WEIGHTS (if higher than shown in column 2)	b. (See Note 2) COUPLING CENTRE TO VEHICLE REARMOST PART	MAXIMUM	MINIMUM
GROSS WEIGHT (See warning below)						
TRAIN WEIGHT (See warning below)						
MAXIMUM TRAIN WEIGHT (See Note 3)						
AXLE WEIGHTS (Axles numbered from front to rear) Axle 1						
Axle 2						
Axle 3						
Axle 4						
MAXIMUM KINGPIN LOAD (Semi-trailers only)				DATE OF ISSUE		

N.B. ALL WEIGHTS IN KILOGRAMS/ALL DIMENSIONS IN MILLIMETRES.

WARNING

a. A reduced gross weight may apply in certain cases to a vehicle towing or being towed by another.
b. A reduced train weight may apply depending on the type of trailer drawn.
c. All weights shown are subject to the fitting of correct tyres.

NOTES

1. This dimension only applies to drawing vehicles of trailers and semi-trailers.
2. This dimension only applies to trailers and semi-trailers.
3. This weight only applies to a 3 axle tractor with a 2 or 3 axle semi-trailer carrying a 40 foot ISO container as a combined transport operation.
4. Where there is no weight shown in the EEC maximum permitted weights column this is because there is no EEC standard relating to that weight.

NOTES

1. Entries in respect of train weight are required in the case of – (a) a motor vehicle constructed or adapted to form an articulated vehicle; and (b) a rigid vehicle which is constructed or adapted to draw a trailer and is first used on or after 1st April 1983.
2. A Ministry plate shows the unladen weight and function of the vehicle in a case where the Type Approval for Goods Vehicles Regulations apply.
3. A Ministry plate may have no 'Reference Number'.

[1472]

NOTES
    Commencement: 6 May 1987.
    Added by SI 1987 No 676, reg 4, Schedule.

SCHEDULE 11

Regulations 75, 77, 79

MAXIMUM PERMITTED WEIGHTS, ETC

PART I (see regulation 75)

MAXIMUM PERMITTED LADEN WEIGHTS OF (1) TRAILERS AND (2) HEAVY MOTOR CARS AND MOTOR CARS NOT FITTED WITH ROAD FRIENDLY SUSPENSION; IN EACH CASE NOT FORMING PART OF AN ARTICULATED VEHICLE

1. The maximum permitted laden weight of a two or three axle vehicle to which this Part applies of a description specified in column 2 of Table I below shall, for the purposes of regulation 75, be the weight specified in column 3 of that item.

2. In the case of a vehicle to which this Part applies and which is not of a description specified in an item in column 2 of Table I below, the maximum permitted laden weight shall, for the purposes of regulation 75, be the weight specified in column 4 of Table II below in the item which is appropriate having regard to columns 2 and 3 of that Table.

TABLE I

MAXIMUM PERMITTED LADEN WEIGHTS OR CERTAIN TWO AND THREE AXLE VEHICLES

(1) Item	(2) Description of Vehicle	(3) Maximum permitted laden weight (kg)
1	A two axle trailer in which— (a) the two axles are closely spaced, and (b) the distance between the foremost axle of the trailer and the rearmost axle of the drawing vehicle is at least 4.2 m	18,000
2	A three axle trailer in which– (a)) the three axles are closely spaced, and (b) the distance between the foremost axle of the trailer and the rearmost axle of the drawing vehicle is at least 4.2 m	24,000
3	A two axle motor vehicle which is a goods vehicle in which the distance between the foremost and rearmost axles is at least 3.0 m	17,000
4	A two axle trailer in which the distance between the foremost axle and the rearmost axle is at least 3.0 m	18,000

TABLE II

MAXIMUM PERMITTED LADEN WEIGHTS OF VEHICLES NOT FALLING WITHIN TABLE I

(1) Item	(2) No. of axles	(3) Distance between foremost and rearmost axles (metres)	(4) Maximum permitted laden weight (kg)
1	2	Less than 2.65	14,230
2	2	At least 2.65	16,260
3	3 or more	Less than 3.0	16,260
4	3 or more	At least 3.0 but less than 3.2	18,290
5	3 or more	At least 3.2 but less than 3.9	20,330
6	3 or more	At least 3.9 but less than 4.9	22,360
7	3	At least 4.9	25,000
8	4 or more	At least 4.9 but less than 5.6	25,000

(1) Item	(2) No. of axles	(3) Distance between foremost and rearmost axles (metres)	(4) Maximum permitted laden weight (kg)
9	4 or more	At least 5.6 but less than 5.9	26,420
10	4 or more	at least 5.9 but less than 6.3	28,450
11	4 or more	At least 6.3	30,000

[1473]

NOTES
  Commencement: 1 January 1993.
  Substituted by SI 1992 No 2016, reg 10(a), Sch 2, Part I.

PART IA (see regulation 75)

MAXIMUM PERMITTED GROSS WEIGHTS FOR HEAVY CARS AND MOTOR CARS IF THE DRIVING AXLES ARE FITTED WITH ROAD FRIENDLY SUSPENSION ETC AND IN EACH CASE NOT FORMING PART OF AN ARTICULATED VEHICLE

1. Subject to paragraph 2, the maximum permitted gross weight of a vehicle to which this Part applies shall, for the purposes of regulation 75, be the weight shown in column 4 of the Table below in the item which is appropriate, having regard to columns 2 and 3 in that Table.

2. In the case of a vehicle to which this Part applies being a two axle goods vehicle which has a distance between its axles of at least 3.0 m, the maximum permitted laden weight for the purposes of regulation 75 shall be 17,000 kg.

TABLE
MAXIMUM PERMITTED LADEN WEIGHT

(1) Item	(2) No. of axles	(3) Distance between foremost and rearmost axles (metres)	(4) Maximum permitted laden weight (kg)
1	2	Less than 2.65	14,230
2	2	At least 2.65	16,260
3	3 or more	Less than 3.0	16,260
4	3 or more	At least 3.0 but less than 3.2	18,290
5	3 or more	At least 3.2 but less than 3.9	20,330
6	3 or more	At least 3.9 but less than 4.9	22,360
7	3 or more	At least 4.9 but less than 5.2	25,000
8	3	At least 5.2	26,000
9	4 or more	At least 5.2 but less than 6.4	The distance in metres between the foremost and rearmost axles multiplied by 5,000, rounded up to the next 10 kg
10	4 or more	At least 6.4	32,000

[1473A]

NOTES
  Commencement: 1 January 1993.
  Inserted by SI 1992 No 2016, reg 10(b), Sch 2, Part II.

PART II

MAXIMUM PERMITTED LADEN WEIGHTS FOR HEAVY MOTOR CARS AND MOTOR CARS FORMING PART OF ARTICULATED VEHICLES (REG 75)

Section

1	2	3	4	5
Item	No of axles	Distance between foremost and rearmost axles (**a**) (metres)	Weight not exceeded by any axle not being the foremost or rearmost (kg)	Maximum permitted laden weight (kg)
1	2	At least 2·0	—	14,230
2	2	At least 2·4	—	16,260
3	2	At least 2·7	—	17,000
4	3 or more	At least 3·0	8,390	20,330
5	3 or more	At least 3·8	8,640	22,360
6	3 or more	At least 4·0	10,500	22,500
7	3 or more	At least 4·3	9,150	24,390
8	3 or more	At least 4·9	10,500	24,390

[1474]

NOTES
   Commencement: 11 August 1986.
   This Part derived from SI 1978 No 1017, Sch 7, Part II.
   Item 3: words in italics prospectively revoked by SI 1987 No 676, reg 13(2), as from 1 April 1988.

PART III

MAXIMUM PERMITTED LADEN WEIGHT OF ARTICULATED VEHICLES (REG 77)

1	2	3	4	5
Item	Relevant axle spacing (**a**) (metres)		Maximum weight (kg)	Minimum overall length (metres)
	(a) Where motor vehicle has 2 axles	(b) Where motor vehicle has more than 2 axles		
1	At least 2·0	At least 2·0	20,330	—
2	At least 2·2	At least 2·2	22,360	—
3	At least 2·6	At least 2·6	23,370	—
4	At least 2·9	At least 2·9	24,390	—
5	At least 3·2	At least 3·2	25,410	—
6	At least 3·5	At least 3·5	26,420	—
7	At least 3·8	At least 3·8	27,440	—
8	At least 4·1	At least 4·1	28,450	—
9	At least 4·4	At least 4·4	29,470	—
10	At least 4·7	At least 4·7	30,490	—
11	At least 5·0	At least 5·0	31,500	—
12	At least 5·3	At least 5·3	32,520	—
13	At least 5·5	At least 5·4	33,000	10·0
14	At least 5·8	At least 5·6	34,000	10·3
15	At least 6·2	At least 5·8	35,000	10·5
16	At least 6·5	At least 6·0	36,000	11·0
17	At least 6·7	At least 6·2	37,000	11·5
18	At least 6·9	At least 6·3	38,000	12·0

[1475]

NOTES
   Commencement: 11 August 1986.
   This Part derived from SI 1978 No 1017, Sch 7, Part III.

[PART IV (see regulation 77)

MAXIMUM PERMITTED LADEN WEIGHT OF ARTICULATED VEHICLES

(1) Item	(2) Type of articulated vehicle	(3) Maximum permitted laden weight (kg)
1	Motor vehicle first used on or after 1st April 1973 and semi-trailer having a total of 5 or more axles	38,000
2	Motor vehicle with 2 axles first used on or after 1st April 1973 and semi-trailer with 2 axles while being used for international transport	35,000
3	Motor vehicle with 2 axles first used on or after 1st April 1973 in which— (a) every driving axle not being a steering axle is fitted with twin tyres; and (b) every driving axle is fitted with road friendly suspension; and a semi-trailer with 2 axles	35,000
4	Motor vehicle and semi-trailer having a total of 4 axles and not described in item 2 or 3	32,520
5	Motor vehicle with 2 axles first used on or after 1st April 1973 in which— (a) every driving axle not being a steering axle is fitted with twin tyres; and (b) every driving axle is fitted with road friendly suspension; and a semi-trailer with 1 axle	
6	Motor vehicle with 2 axles and a semi-trailer with 1 axle being a combination not described in item 5	25,000]

[1476]

NOTES
   Commencement: 1 January 1993.
   Substituted by SI 1992 No 2016, reg 10(c), Sch 2, Part III.

[PART V Regulation 79(2)

VEHICLES WITH TWO CLOSELY-SPACED AXLES

(1) Item	(2) Description of vehicle	(3) Maximum permitted weight of the two closely-spaced axles (kg)
1	A motor vehicle or trailer in which (in either case) the distance between the two closely-spaced axles is less than 1.3 metres	16,000
2	A vehicle being— (a) a motor vehicle in which the distance between the two closely-spaced axles is at least 1.3 m, or (b) a trailer in which that distance is at least 1.3 m and less than 1.5 m, not being a vehicle described in item 3 or 4	18,000

(1) *Item*	(2) *Description of vehicle*	(3) *Maximum permitted weight of the two closely-spaced axles (kg)*
3	A motor vehicle in which the distance between the two closely-spaced axles is at least 1.3 m and—	19,000
	(a) every driving axle not being a steering axle is fitted with twin tyres; and	
	(b) either every driving axle is fitted with road friendly suspension or neither of the two closely-spaced axles has an axle weight exceeding 9,500 kg	
4	A trailer in which—	19,000
	(a) the two closely-spaced axles are driven from the motor vehicle drawing the trailer and are fitted with twin tyres; and	
	(b) either those axles are fitted with road friendly suspension or neither of them has an axle weight exceeding 9,500 kg	
5	A trailer in which the distance between the two closely-spaced axles is at least 1.5 m and less than 1.8 m	19,320
6	A trailer in which the distance between the two closely-spaced axles is at least 1.8 m	20,000]

[1477]

NOTES
    Commencement: 1 January 1993.
    Substituted by SI 1992 No 2016, reg 10(d), Sch 2, Part IV.

[PART VI Regulation 79(3)

VEHICLES WITH THREE CLOSELY-SPACED AXLES

(1) *Item*	(2) *Description of vehicle*	(3) *Maximum permitted weight of the three closely-spaced axles (kg)*
1	A vehicle in which the smallest distance between any two of the three closely-spaced axles is less than 1.3 m	21,000
2	A vehicle in which the smallest distance between any two of the three closely-spaced axles is at least 1.3 m and at least one of those axles does not have air suspension	22,500
3	A vehicle in which the smallest distance between any two of the three closely-spaced axles is at least 1.3 m and all three axles are fitted with air suspension	24,000]

[1478–1479]

NOTES
    Commencement: 1 January 1993.
    Substituted by SI 1992 No 2016, reg 10(e), Sch 2, Part V.

(Part VII repealed by SI 1992 No 2016, reg 10(f).)

SCHEDULE 12

Regulations 81, 82

CONDITIONS TO BE COMPLIED WITH IN RELATION TO THE USE OF VEHICLES CARRYING WIDE OR LONG LOADS OR VEHICLES CARRYING LOADS OR HAVING FIXED APPLIANCES OR APPARATUS WHICH PROJECT

PART I

Advance notice to Police

1. (a) Before using on a road a vehicle or vehicles to which this paragraph applies, the owner shall give notice of the intended use to the Chief Officer of Police for any area in which he proposes to use the vehicle or vehicles. The notice shall be given so that it is received by the date after which there are at least two working days before the date on which the use of the vehicle or vehicles is to begin, and shall include the following details—

    (i) time, date and route of the proposed journey, and

    [(ia) in a case to which regulation 7(9) applies, the overall length of the trailer,]

    (ii) in a case to which regulation 82(2) applies, the overall length and width of the vehicle by which the load is carried and the width of the lateral projection or projections of its load,

    (iii) in a case to which regulation 82(4)(a) applies, the overall length and width of each vehicle by which the load is carried, the length of any forward or rearward projection and, where the load rests on more than one vehicle, the distance between the vehicles,

    (iv) in a case to which regulation 82(4)(b) applies, the overall length of the combination of vehicles and the length of any forward or rearward projection of the load, and

    (v) in a case to which regulation 82(7) and (8) applies, the overall length of the vehicle and the length of any forward or rearward projection of the load or special appliance or apparatus.

The Chief Officer of Police for any police area may, at his discretion, accept a shorter period of notice or fewer details.

(b) The vehicle or vehicles shall be used only in accordance with the details at (a) subject to any variation in the time, date or route which may be directed by—

    (i) any such Chief Officer of Police to the owner of the vehicle or vehicles, or

    (ii) a police constable to the driver in the interests of road safety or in order to avoid undue traffic congestion by halting the vehicle or vehicles in a place on or adjacent to the road on which the vehicle or vehicles are travelling.

(c) In this paragraph—

    (i) "Chief Officer of Police" has, in relation to England and Wales, the same meaning as in the Police Act 1964, and in relation to Scotland, the same meaning as in the Police (Scotland) Act 1967,

    (ii) "working day" means a day which is not a Sunday, a bank holiday, Christmas Day or Good Friday, and

    (iii) "bank holiday" means a day which is a bank holiday by or under the Banking and Financial Dealings Act 1971, either generally or in the locality in which the road is situated.

Attendants

2. At least one person in addition to the person or persons employed in driving a motor vehicle to which this paragraph applies shall be employed—

(a) in attending to that vehicle and its load and any other vehicle or vehicles drawn by that vehicle and the load or loads carried on the vehicle or vehicles so drawn, and

(b) to give warning to the driver of the said motor vehicle and to any person of any danger likely to be caused to any such other person by reason of the presence of the said vehicle or vehicles on the road.

Provided that, where three or more vehicles as respects which the conditions in this paragraph are applicable are travelling together in convoy, it shall be a sufficient compliance with this paragraph if only the foremost and rearmost vehicles in the convoy are attended in the manner prescribed in this paragraph.

For the purpose of this paragraph when a motor vehicle is drawing a trailer or trailers—

(i) any person employed in pursuance of section 34 of the 1972 Act in attending that vehicle or any such trailer shall be treated as being an attendant required by this paragraph so long as he is also employed to discharge the duties mentioned in this paragraph; and

(ii) when another motor vehicle is used for the purpose of assisting in their propulsion on the road, the person or persons employed in driving that other motor vehicle shall not be treated as a person or persons employed in attending to the first-mentioned vehicle or any vehicle or vehicles drawn thereby.

Marking of longer projections

3. (a) Every forward and rearward projection to which this paragraph applies shall be fitted with—

(i) an end marker, except in the case of a rearward projection which is fitted with a rear marking in accordance with the Lighting Regulations, and

(ii) where required by sub-paragraphs (c) and (d) of this paragraph, two or more side markers;

which shall be of the size, shape and colour described in Part II of this Schedule.

(b) the end marker shall be so fitted that—

(i) it is as near as is practicable in a transverse plane,

(ii) it is not more than 0.5 m from the extreme end of the projection,

(iii) the vertical distance between the lowest point of the marker and the road surface is not more than 2.5 m,

(iv) it, and any means by which it is fitted to the projection, impedes the view of the driver as little as possible, and

(v) it is clearly visible within a reasonable distance to a person using the road at the end of the vehicle from which the projection extends;

(c) where the forward projection exceeds 2 m or the rearward projection exceeds 3 m, one side marker shall be fitted on the right hand side and one on the left hand side of the projection so that—

(i) each marker is as near as is practicable in a longitudinal plane,

(ii) no part extends beyond the end of the projection,

(iii) the vertical distance between the lowest part of each marker and the surface of the road is not more than 2.5 m,

(iv) the horizontal distance between each marker and the end marker or, as the case may be, the rear marking carried in accordance with the Lighting Regulations does not exceed 1m, and

(v) each marker is clearly visible within a reasonable distance to a person using the road on that side of the projection;

(d) where—

(i) a forward projection exceeds 4.5 m, or

(ii) a rearward projection exceeds 5 m

extra side markers shall be fitted on either side of the projection so that the horizontal distance between the extreme projecting point of the vehicle from which the projection extends and the nearest point on any side marker from that point, and between the nearest points of any adjacent side markers on the same side does not exceed—

2.5 m in the case of a forward projection, or

3.5 m in the case of a rearward projection.

For the purposes of this sub-paragraph the expression "the vehicle" shall not include any special appliance or apparatus or any part thereof which is a forward projection or a rearward projection within the meaning of regulation 81;

(e) the extra side markers required by this sub-paragraph shall also meet the requirements of (i), (iii) and (v) of sub-paragraph (c);

(f) every marker fitted in accordance with this paragraph shall be kept clean and unobscured and [between sunset and sunrise] be illuminated by a lamp which renders it readily visible from a reasonable distance and which is so shielded that its light, except as reflected from the marker, is not visible to other persons using the road.

Marking of shorter projections

4. A projection to which this paragraph applies shall be rendered clearly visible to other persons using the road within a reasonable distance, in the case of a forward projection, from the front thereof or, in the case of a rearward projection, from the rear thereof and, in either case, from either side thereof.

[*Marking of wide loads*

5. (a) Subject to sub-paragraph (d), every load carried on a vehicle in circumstances where this paragraph applies shall be fitted on each side and in the prescribed manner, with—

    (i) a prescribed marker in such a position that it is visible from the front of the vehicle, and

    (ii) a prescribed marker in such a position that it is visible from the rear of the vehicle,

(b) For the purposes of sub-paragraph (a)—

    (i) a marker on a side of the load is fitted in the prescribed manner if at least part of it is within 50 mm of a longitudinal plane passing through the point on that side of the load which is furthest from the axis of the vehicle; and

    (ii) a prescribed marker is a marker of the size, shape and colour described in Part II of this Schedule.

(c) Every marker fitted pursuant to this paragraph shall be kept clean and between sunset and sunrise be illuminated by a lamp which renders it readily visible from a reasonable distance and which is so shielded that its light, except as reflected from the marker, is not visible to other persons using the road.

(d) If the load does not extend beyond the longitudinal plane passing through the extreme projecting point on one side of the vehicle, it shall not be necessary for a marker to be fitted to the load on that side.]   **[1480]**

NOTES

Commencement: 17 October 1991 (para 5); 11 August 1986 (remainder).
This Part derived from SI 1978 No 1017, Sch 8, Part I.
Para 1(a): sub-para (ia) inserted by SI 1991 No 2125, reg 6.
Para 3(f): words in square brackets substituted by SI 1991 No 2125, reg 9(2).
Para 5: inserted by SI 1991 No 2125, reg 9(1).
The 1972 Act: Road Traffic Act 1972.
Lighting Regulations: SI 1984 No 812 (revoked; see now SI 1989 No 1796 post).

PART II
PROJECTION MARKERS

[(see paragraph 3(a) and 5(b) of this Schedule)]

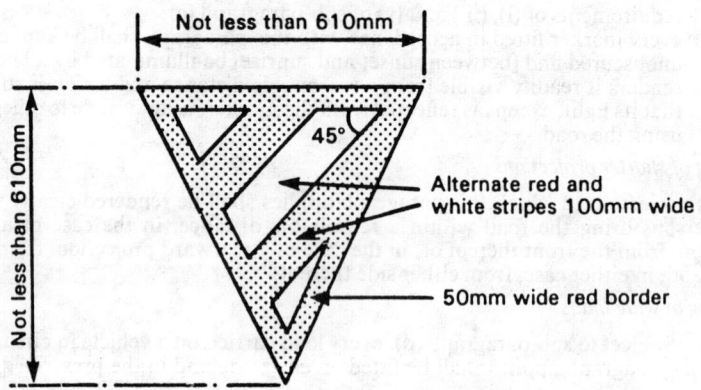

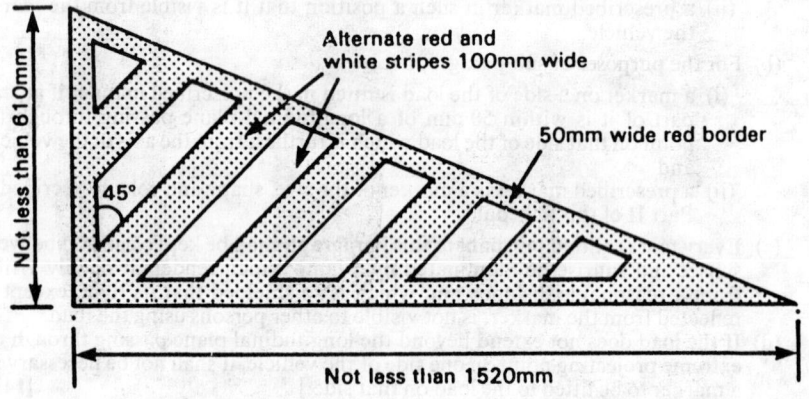

[1481]

NOTES
    Commencement: 11 August 1986.
    Words in square brackets substituted by SI 1991 No 2125, reg 9(3).

[SCHEDULE 13

(see regulation 3(2))

PLATE FOR RESTRICTED SPEED VEHICLE

1. A vehicle displays a plate in accordance with the requirements of this Schedule if a plate in respect of which the following conditions are satisfied is displayed on the vehicle in a prominent position.

(2) The conditions are—

(a) the plate must be in the form shown in the diagram below;
(b) the plate must be at least 150 mm wide and at least 120 mm high;
(c) the figures "5" and "0" must be at least 100 mm high and 50 mm wide with a stroke width of at least 12 mm, the figures being black on a white background; and
(d) the border must be black and between 3 mm and 5 mm wide.

. . .]

[1481A]

NOTES
Commencement: 2 November 1990.
This Schedule was added by SI 1990 No 1981, reg 11, Sch.

COMMUNITY DRIVERS' HOURS AND RECORDING EQUIPMENT (EXEMPTIONS AND SUPPLEMENTARY PROVISIONS) REGULATIONS 1986
(SI 1986 NO 1456)

NOTES
Made: 22 August 1986
Authority: European Communities Act 1972, s 2(2)

ARRANGEMENT OF REGULATIONS

1. Citation, commencement, interpretation and revocation

(1) These Regulations may be cited as the Community Drivers' Hours and Recording Equipment (Exemptions and Supplementary Provisions) Regulations 1986 and shall come into operation on 29th September 1986.

(2) In these Regulations—

"the Community Drivers' Hours Regulation" means council Regulation (EEC) No. 3820/85 of 20th December 1985 on the harmonisation of certain social legislation relating to road transport;

"the Community Recording Equipment Regulation" means Council Regulation (EEC) No. 3821/85 of 20th December 1985 on recording equipment in road transport;

"permissible maximum weight" has the same meaning as in section 110 of the Road Transport Act 1972.

(3) Subject to paragraph (2) above, any expression used in these Regulations which is used in the Community Drivers' Hours Regulation has the same meaning as in that Regulation.

(4) ... **[1482]**

NOTES
Commencement: 29 September 1986.
Para (4): revokes SI 1978 No 1158, SI 1980 No 266, SI 1980 No 2018, SI 1981 No 1855, SI 1985 No 615.
Council Regulation (EEC) No 3820/85; OJ L 370/1, 31.12.85.
Council Regulation (EEC) No 3821/85; OJ L 370/8, 31.12.85.

2. Exemption from the Community Drivers' Hours Regulation

[(1) Pursuant to Article 13(1) of the Community Drivers' Hours Regulation, exemption is granted from all the provisions of that Regulation, except Article

5 (minimum ages for drivers), in respect of any vehicle falling within a description specified in the Schedule to these Regulations.

(2) Pursuant to Article 13(2) of the Community Drivers' Hours Regulation, exemption is granted from all the provision of that Regulation, except Article 5, in respect of any vehicle falling within a description specified in Part II of the Schedule to these Regulations.] **[1483]**

NOTES
Commencement: 1 June 1987.
Substituted by SI 1987 No 805, reg 3.

3. Supplementary provisions relating to the Community Drivers' Hours Regulation

(1) Pursuant to Article 6(1) of the Community Drivers' Hours Regulation, the application of the fourth sub-paragraph of that Article shall be extended to national passenger services other than regular passenger services.

(2) Pursuant to Article 7(3) of the Community Drivers' Hours Regulation, if—

    (a) the driver of a vehicle which is engaged in the national carriage of passengers on a regular service observes in a relevant area, immediately after any period of driving not exceeding four hours, a break of at least 30 minutes; and

    (b) it was not possible for him to observe, at any time during that period of driving, a break of at least 15 minutes,

that period of driving shall be disregarded for the purposes of Article 7(1) of that Regulation.

(3) In paragraph (2) above "relevant area", in relation to the driver of a vehicle which is engaged in the national carriage of passengers on a regular service, means any of the following areas, namely—

    (a) The London Borough of Camden;

    (b) the Royal Borough of Kensington and Chelsea;

    (c) the London Borough of Islington; ...

    (d) the City of Westminster,

    [(e) in the City of Birmingham, an area comprising Digbeth Coach Station, Rea Street, Bradford Street, Barford Street, Cheapside and Birchall Street;

    (f) in the City of Bristol an area comprising Marlborough Street Coach Station, Marlborough Street, Maudlin Street, Lower Maudlin Street, Earl Street and Whitson Street;

    (g) in the City of Leeds an area comprising Wellington Street Coach Station, Wellington Street, York Place, Queen Street, Little Queen Street and King Street;

    (h) in the City of Leicester, an area comprising St Margaret's Bus Station, Abbey Street, Gravel Street, Church Gate, Mansfield Street, Sandacre Street, New Road, Burleys Ways and St. Margaret's Way;

    (i) in the City of Nottingham, an area comprising Victoria Bus Station, Glasshouse Street, Huntingdon Street, York Street, Cairns Street, Woodborough Road, Mansfield Road, Milton Street, Lower Parliament Street and Union Road; and

    (j) in the City of Oxford an area comprising Oxpens Coach Park, Oxpens Road, Thames Street and Holybush Hill,] in which passengers are taken up or set down in the course of the service. **[1484]**

NOTES
   Commencement: 29 September 1986.
   Para (3): amended by SI 1986 No 1669, reg 3.

4. Exemption from the Community Recording Equipment Regulation

[(1) Pursuant to Article 3(2) of the Community Recording Equipment Regulation, exemption is granted from the provisions of that Regulation in respect of any vehicle falling within a description specified in the Schedule to these Regulations.

(2) Pursuant to Article 3(3) of the Community Recording Equipment Regulations, exemption is granted from the provisions of that Regulation in respect of:

   (a) any vehicle falling within a description specified in Part II of the Schedule to these Regulations; and
   (b) any vehicle which is being used for collecting sea coal.]   **[1485]**

NOTES
   Commencement: 1 June 1987.
   Substituted by SI 1987 No 805, reg 4.

5. Application of the Community Recording Equipment Regulation

(1) Pursuant to Article 3(4) of the Community Recording Equipment Regulation, that Regulation shall apply (notwithstanding the exemption in Article 3(1)) to vehicles used for the carriage of postal articles on national transport operations except—

   (a) vehicles which have a permissible maximum weight which does not exceed 3.5 tonnes; and
   (b) vehicles which are being used by the Post Office in connection with the carriage of letters.

(2) In paragraph (1) above "letter" has the same meaning as in in the Post Office Inland Post Scheme 1979.

(3) This Regulation shall not have effect—

   (a) before 1st April 1988 in relation to vehicles which have a pemissible maximum weight of 7.5 tonnes or more; or
   (b) before 1st January 1990 in relation to vehicles which have a permissible maximum weight which exceeds 3.5 tonnes but which is less than 7.5 tonnes.   **[1486]**

NOTES
   Commencement: 29 September 1986.

SCHEDULE
EXEMPTED VEHICLES

[PART I—VEHICLES EXEMPTED BY REGULATIONS 2(1) AND 4(1)]

1. Any vehicle used for the carriage of passengers which is by virtue of its construction and equipment suitable for carrying not more than 17 persons including the driver and is intended for that purpose.

2.—(1) Any vehicle which, on or after 1st January 1990, is being used by a public authority to provide public services otherwise than in competition with professional road hauliers.

(2) A vehicle does not fall within the description specified in this paragraph unless the vehicle—

    (a) is being used by a health authority in England and Wales or a Health Board in Scotland or the Common Services Agency for the Scottish Health Service—

        (i) to provide ambulance services in pursuance of its duty under the National Health Service Act 1977 of the National Health Service (Scotland) Act 1978; or

        (ii) to carry staff, patients, medical supplies or equipment in pursuance of its general duties under that Act;

    (b) is being used by a local authority for the purposes of the Local Authority Social Services Act 1970 or the Social Work (Scotland) Act 1968 to provide, in the exercise of social services functions—

        (i) services for old persons; or

        (ii) services for persons to whom section 29 of the National Assistance Act 1948 (welfare arrangements for physically and mentally handicapped persons) applies;

    (c) is being used by Her Majesty's Coastguard, a general lighthouse authority or a local lighthouse authority;

    (d) is being used by a harbour authority within the limits of a harbour for the improvement, maintenance or management of which the authority is responsible;

    (e) is being used for an airports authority within the perimeter of an airport owned or managed by the authority;

    (f) is being used by the British Railways Board, London Regional Transport, any wholly owned subsidiary of London Regional Transport, a Passenger Transport Executive or a local authority for the purpose of maintaining railways; or

    (g) is being used by the British Waterways Board for the purpose of maintaining navigable waterways.

(3) In this paragraph—

"airport" means an aerodrome within the meaning given by section 105(1) of the Civil Aviation Act 1982;

"airports authority" means the British Airports Authority or a local authority which owns or manages an airport;

"general lighthouse authority" and "local lighthouse authority" have the meanings given by section 634 of the Merchant Shipping Act 1894;

"harbour" and "harbour authority" have the meanings given by section 57(1) of the Harbours Act 1964;

"local authority", unless the contrary intention appears, means—

    (a) in relation to England and Wales, a county or district council, a London borough council or the Common Council of the City of London; and

    (b) in relation to Scotland, a regional, islands or district council;

"social services functions"—

    (a) in relation to England and Wales, has the meaning given by section 3(1) of the Local Authority Social Services Act 1970; and

    (b) in relation to Scotland, means functions under the enactments referred to in section 2(2) of the Social Work (Scotland) Act 1968;

"wholly owned subsidiary", in relation to London Regional Transport, has the meaning given by section 68 of the London Regional Transport Act 1984.

3.—(1) Any vehicle which is being used by an agricultural, horticultural, forestry or fishery undertaking to carry goods within a 50 kilometre radius of the place where the vehicle is normally based, including local administrative areas the centres of which are situated within that radius.

(2) A vehicle which is being used by a fishery undertaking does not fall within the description specified in this paragraph unless the vehicle is being used—

(a) to carry live fish; or
(b) to carry a catch of fish from the place of landing to a place where it is to be processed.

4. Any vehicle which is being used to carry animal waste or carcases which are not intended for human consumption.

5. Any vehicle which is being used to carry live animals between a farm and a local market or from a market to a local slaughterhouse.

6. Any vehicle which is being used—

(a) as a shop at a local market;
(b) for door-to-door selling;
(c) for mobile banking, exchange or saving transactions;
(d) for worship;
(e) for the lending of books, records of cassettes; or
(f) for cultural events or exhibitions,

and is specially fitted for that use.

7.—(1) Any vehicle used for the carriage of goods which has a permissible maximum weight not exceeding 7.5 tonnes and is carrying material or equipment for the driver's use in the course of his work within a 50 kilometre radius of the place where the vehicle is normally based.

(2) A vehicle does not fall within the description specified in this paragraph if, driving the vehicle constitutes the driver's main activity.

8. Any vehicle which operates exclusively on an island which does not exceed 2300 square kilometres in area and is not linked to the rest of Great Britain by a bridge, ford or tunnel open for use by motor vehicles.

9. Any vehicle used for the carriage of goods which has a permissible maximum weight not exceeding 7.5 tonnes and is propelled by means of gas produced on the vehicle or by means of electricity.

10.—(1) Any vehicle which is being used for driving instruction with a view to obtaining a driving licence.

(2) A vehicle does not fall within the description specified in this paragraph if the vehicle or any trailer or semi-trailer drawn by it is being used for the carriage of goods—

(a) for hire or reward; or
(b) for or in connection with any trade or business.

11. Any tractor which, on or after 1st January 1990, is used exclusively for agricultural and forestry work. **[1487]**

NOTES

Commencement: 29 September 1986.
Renumbered by SI 1987 No 805, reg 5.

PART II

VEHICLES EXEMPTED BY REGULATIONS 2(2) AND 4(2)

[12. Any vehicle which is being used by the Royal National Lifeboat Institution for the purpose of hauling lifeboats.

13. Any vehicle which was manufactured before 1st January 1987.

14. Any vehicle which is propelled by steam.]

[15.—(1) Any vehicle which is by virtue of its construction and equipment suitable for carrying passengers and which on the occasion on which it is being driven—

    (a) is a vintage vehicle;

    (b) is not carrying more than 9 persons including the driver;

    (c) is not used for carrying passengers with a view to profit; and

    (d) is being driven—

        (i) in a vintage vehicle rally or to or from such a rally, or

        (ii) to or from a museum, or other place where the vehicle is to be or has been displayed to members of the public, or

        (iii) to or from a place where the vehice is to be or has been repaired, maintained or tested.

(2) For the purposes of this paragraph:—

    (a) a vehicle is a vintage vehicle on any occasion on which it is being driven if it was manufactured more than 25 years before that occasion; and

    (b) "vintage vehicle rally" means an event in which a collection of historic vehicles are driven on a road open to the public along a pre-determined route.]   **[1488]**

NOTES

    Commencement: 20 May 1988 (para 15); 1 June 1987 (remainder).
    Added by SI 1987 No 805, reg 5.
    Para 15: added by SI 1988 No 760, reg 2.

"PELICAN" PEDESTRIAN CROSSINGS REGULATIONS AND GENERAL DIRECTIONS 1987
(SI 1987 NO 16)

NOTES

    Made: 12 January 1987
    Authority: Road Traffic Regulation Act 1984, ss 25, 64, 65(1)

ARRANGEMENT OF REGULATIONS

PART I

GENERAL

PART I

GENERAL

1. Citation and commencement

This instrument may be cited as the "Pelican" Pedestrian Crossings Regulations
and General Directions 1987 and shall come into force on 18th February 1987.

[1489]

NOTES
   Commencement: 18 February 1987.

2. Revocation

. . .

[1490]

NOTES
   Commencement: 18 February 1987.
   This regulation revokes SI 1969 No 888 and SI 1979 No 401.
   See further SI 1987 No 16, Pt II, reg 3.

3. Interpretation

(1) In this Instrument—

   (a) any reference to a numbered regulation is a reference to the regulation
       bearing that number in the Regulations contained in Part II of this
       Instrument; and
   (b) except where otherwise stated, any reference to a numbered Schedule
       is a reference to the Schedule to the Regulations contained in Part II
       of this Instrument bearing that number.

(2) In this Instrument the following expressions have the meanings hereby respectively assigned to them—

"the 1984 Act" means the Road Traffic Regulation Act 1984;

"the 1969 Regulations" means the "Pelican" Pedestrian Crossing Regulations 1969;

"appropriate authority" means, in relation to a trunk road, the appropriate Secretary of State and, in relation to any other road, the local authority who established the crossing;

"appropriate Secretary of State" means, in relation to a crossing established or to be established on a road in—

(a) England, the Secretary of State for Transport;

(b) Scotland, the Secretary of State for Scotland; or

(c) Wales, the Secretary of State for Wales;

"carriageway" means—

(a) where it is in a highway, a way constituting or comprised in the highway being a way over which the public have a right of way for the passage of vehicles; and

(b) where it is in any other road to which the public has access, that part of the road to which vehicles have access,

but does not, in either case, include any central reservation (whether within the limits of a crossing or not);

"central reservation" means any provision which separates one part of a carriageway from another part of that carriageway, and includes a refuge for pedestrians;

"crossing" means a crossing for pedestrians established either:

(a) in the case of any road other than a trunk road, by a local authority under the provisions of section 23 of the 1984 Act; or

(b) in the case of a trunk road, by the appropriate Secretary of State in discharge of the duty imposed on him by section 24 of the 1984 Act;

"indicator for pedestrians" means the traffic sign of that description prescribed by regulation 2(1) and Schedule 1;

"one-way street" means any road on which the driving of vehicles otherwise than in one direction is prohibited at all times;

"pedestrian" means a foot passenger;

"pedestrian light signals" means the traffic signs of that description prescribed by regulation 2(1) and Schedule 1;

"Pelican crossing" means a crossing—

(a) at which there are traffic signs of the size, colour and type prescribed, or treated as if prescribed, by regulation 2(1) and Schedule 1; and

(b) the presence and limits of which are indicated, or are treated as indicated, in accordance with regulation 2(2) and Schedule 2;

"Pelican controlled area" means, in relation to a "Pelican" crossing, the area of the carriageway in the vicinity of the crossing and lying on both sides of the crossing or only one side of the crossing, the presence and limits of which are indicated, or are treated as indicated, in accordance with regulation 3 and Schedule 2;

"primary signal" means the traffic sign prescribed as a vehicular light signal by regulation 2(1) and Schedule 1 erected on or near the carriageway facing traffic approaching the "Pelican" crossing and sited between the stop line and the line of studs indicating the limits of the crossing in accordance with Schedule 2 nearest to the stop line;

"refuge for pedestrians" means an area of a carriageway to which vehicles do not have access and on which pedestrians may wait after crossing one part of that carriageway and before crossing the other part;

"secondary signal" means the traffic sign prescribed as a vehicular light signal by regulation 2(1) and Schedule 1 erected on or near the carriageway facing traffic approaching the "Pelican" crossing but sited beyond the furthest edge of the "Pelican" crossing as viewed from the direction of travel of such traffic;

"stop line" means, in relation to the driver of a vehicle approaching a "Pelican" crossing, the transverse white line which is parallel to the limits of the crossing as indicated in accordance with Schedule 2 and on the same side of the crossing as the driver;

"stud" means any mark or device on the carriageway, whether or not projecting above the surface thereof;

"a system of staggered crossings" means two "Pelican" crossings provided on a road where there is a central reservation in the road, each separately constituted as a "Pelican" crossing, one such crossing being on one side of the central reservation and the other such crossing being on the other side and which together do not form a straight line across the road.

(3) Any reference in this Instrument to a vehicular light signal is—

    (a) where a primary signal has been erected without a secondary signal, a reference to the light signal displayed by the primary signal; and

    (b) where a secondary signal has been erected as well as a primary signal, a reference to the light signal displayed by both the primary signal and the secondary signal or by either the primary signal operating without the secondary signal or by the secondary signal operating without the primary signal.   **[1491]**

NOTES
Commencement: 18 February 1987.

PART II

REGULATIONS

1. Citation

The Regulations contained in this Part of this Instrument may be cited as the "Pelican" Pedestrian Crossings Regulations 1987.   **[1492]**

NOTES
Commencement: 18 February 1987.

2. "Pelican" crossings

(1) The provisions of Schedule 1 shall have effect as respects the size, colour and type of the traffic signs which are to be placed at or near a crossing for the purpose of constituting it a "Pelican" crossing.

(2) The provisions of Schedule 2 shall have effect for regulating the manner in which the presence and limits of a crossing are to be indicated for the purpose of constituting it a "Pelican" crossing.

(3) Any crossing which, immediately before the coming into operation of these Regulations, was constituted as a "Pelican" crossing in accordance with the 1969 Regulations shall, notwithstanding the revocation of those Regulations,

be treated as constituted in accordance with these Regulations for so long as the traffic signs situated at or near it and the manner in which its presence and limits are indicated comply with the 1969 Regulations.   **[1493]**

NOTES
Commencement: 18 February 1987.
1969 Regulations: "Pelican" Pedestrian Crossings Regulations 1969.

3. "Pelican" controlled areas

(1) The provisions of Schedule 2 shall have effect as respects the size, colour and type of the traffic signs which shall be placed in the vicinity of a "Pelican" crossing for the purpose of constituting a "Pelican" controlled area in relation to that crossing and of indicating the presence and limits of that area.

(2) A stop line shall indicate to vehicular traffic proceeding towards a "Pelican" crossing the position at which a driver of a vehicle shall stop it for the purpose of complying with regulations 16 and 17.

(3) Where the appropriate authority is satisfied in relation to a particular area of carriageway in the vicinity of the "Pelican" crossing that, by reason of the layout or character of the roads in the vicinity of the crossing, the application of such a prohibition as is mentioned in any of regulations 12, 13, 14, 19 and 20 to that particular area or the constitution of that particular area as a "Pelican" controlled area by the placing of traffic signs in accordance with Schedule 2 would be impracticable, it shall not be necessary for that area to be constituted a "Pelican" controlled area but if, by virtue of this paragraph, it is proposed that no area, on either side of the limits of a "Pelican" crossing (not on a trunk road), is to be constituted a "Pelican" controlled area by 18th February 1989, a notice in writing shall be sent by the appropriate authority to the appropriate Secretary of State stating the reasons why it is proposed that no such area should be constituted.

(4) Where immediately before the coming into operation of these Regulations, the approach for vehicular traffic to a "Pelican" crossing has been indicated by a pattern of studs placed and white lines marked on the carriageway in accordance with the provisions of paragraph 3 of Schedule 2 to the 1969 Regulations, then, notwithstanding the revocation effected by article 2 of Part I of this Instrument, that approach may until 18th February 1989 continue to be so indicated for so long as the said pattern of studs and white lines does not lie within a "Pelican" controlled area or in the vicinity of such an area on the same side of the crossing as that pattern.   **[1494]**

NOTES
Commencement: 18 February 1987.
1969 Regulations: "Pelican" Pedestrian Crossings Regulations 1969.

4. Variations in dimensions

(1) Any variation in—

        (i) a dimension (other than as to the height of a letter) specified in any of the diagrams in Parts II and III of Schedule 1; or

        (ii) a dimension as to the height of a letter specified in the diagram in Part III of that Schedule,

shall be treated as permitted by these Regulations if the variation—

        (a) in the case of a dimension of less than 10 millimetres, does not exceed 1 millimetre;

(b) in the case of a dimension of 10 millimetres or more but less than 50 millimetres, does not exceed 10% of that dimension;

(c) in the case of a dimension of 50 millimetres or more but less than 300 millimetres, does not exceed 7 1/2% of that dimension; or

(d) in the case of a dimension of 300 millimetres or more, does not exceed 5% of that dimension.

(2) Any variation in a dimension specified in any of the diagrams in Schedule 2 shall be treated as permitted by these Regulations if the variation—

(a) in the case of a dimension of 300 millimetres or more, does not exceed 20% of that dimension; or

(b) in the case of a dimension of less than 300 millimetres, where the actual dimension exceeds the dimension so specified, does not exceed 30% of the dimension so specified, does not exceed 10% of the dimension so specified. **[1495]**

NOTES

Commencement: 18 February 1987.

5. Box for housing equipment

Apparatus designed to control or to monitor, or to control and monitor, the operation of the vehicular light signals and pedestrian light signals may be housed in one or more boxes attached to the post or other structure on which such signals are mounted. **[1496]**

NOTES

Commencement: 18 February 1987.

6. Additional traffic signs

In addition to the traffic signs prescribed in regulation 2(1) and Schedule 1, the traffic signs specified in diagrams 610, 611, 612, 613 and 616 in Schedule 1 to the Traffic Signs Regulations 1981 may be placed at or near a "Pelican" crossing. **[1497]**

NOTES

Commencement: 18 February 1987.

7. Significance of traffic signs

Regulations 8 to 10 are made under section 64 of the 1984 Act and shall have effect for the purpose of prescribing the warnings, information, requirements and prohibitions which are to be conveyed to traffic by the traffic signs of the size, colour and type prescribed by regulations 2(1) and 6 and Schedule 1. **[1498]**

NOTES

Commencement: 18 February 1987.
1984 Act: Road Traffic Regulation Act 1984.

8. Significance of vehicular light signals

(1) The vehicular light signal at a "Pelican" crossing shall convey the following information, requirements and prohibitions—

(a) the steady green light shall convey the information that vehicular traffic may proceed across the crossing;

(b) except as provided in sub-paragraph (d) below, the steady amber light shall convey the prohibition that vehicular traffic shall not proceed beyond the stop line, or, if the stop line for the time being visible, beyond the post or other structure on which is mounted the primary signal facing such traffic on the side of the carriageway on which vehicles approach the crossing except in the case of any vehicle which when the steady amber light is first shown is so close to the stop line, post or structure that it cannot safely be stopped before passing the line, post or structure;

(c) except as provided in sub-paragraph (d) below, the red light shall convey the prohibition that vehicular traffic shall not proceed beyond the stop line, or, if the stop line is not for the time being visible, beyond the post or other structure on which is mounted the primary signal facing such traffic on the side of the carriageway on which vehicles approach the crossing;

(d) on any occasion when a vehicle is being used for fire brigade, ambulance or police purposes and the observance of the prohibitions conveyed by the steady amber and red lights (as specified in sub-paragraphs (b) and (c) above respectively) would be likely to hinder the use of the vehicle for the purpose in question, then sub-paragraphs (b) and (c) above shall not apply to that vehicle. In the circumstances described in the preceding part of this sub-paragraph, the steady amber light and the red light shall each convey the information that the vehicle may only proceed beyond the stop line or (as the case may be) the post or other structure if the driver—

　(i) accords precedence to any pedestrian who is on that part of the carriageway which lies within the limits of the crossing or on a central reservation which lies between two crossings which do not form a system of staggered crossings; and

　(ii) subject to sub-paragraph (i) above, does not proceed in such a manner or at such a time as is likely to cause danger to any other vehicle approaching or waiting at the crossing, or in such a manner as to compel the driver of any such vehicle to change its speed or course in order to avoid an accident; and

(e) the flashing amber light shall convey the information that vehicular traffic may proceed across the crossing but that every pedestrian if he is on the carriageway or a central reservation within the limits of that crossing (but not if he is on a central reservation which lies between two crossings which form a system of staggered crossings) before any part of a vehicle has entered those limits, has the right of precedence within those limits over that vehicle, and the requirement that the driver of a vehicle shall accord such precedence to any such pedestrian.

(2) Vehicular traffic passing the vehicular light signal in accordance with the foregoing provisions of this regulation shall proceed with due regard to the safety of other users of the road and subject to the direction of any police constable in uniform or traffic warden who may be engaged in the regulation of traffic.   **[1499]**

NOTES

Commencement: 18 February 1987.

---

9. Significance of pedestrian traffic signals

(1) The pedestrian traffic signal at a "Pelican" crossing shall convey to pedestrians the warnings and information specified in the following paragraphs of this regulation.

(2) The pedestrian light signal shall convey to pedestrians the following warnings and information—

    (a) the red light shall convey to a pedestrian the warning that he should not in the interests of safety use the crossing;

    (b) the steady green light shall convey to a pedestrian the information that he may use the crossing and drivers of vehicles may not cause their vehicles to enter the limits of the crossing; and

    (c) the flashing green light shall convey—

        (i) to a pedestrian who is already on the crossing when the flashing green light is first shown the information that he may continue to use the crossing, and that if he is on the carriageway or on a central reservation within the limits of that crossing (but not if he is on a central reservation which lies between two crossings which form part of a system of staggered crossings) before any part of a vehicle has entered those limits he has the right of precedence within those limits over that vehicle; and

        (ii) to a pedestrian who is not already on the crossing when the flashing green light is first shown the warning that he should not in the interests of safety start to cross the carriageway.

(3) When the word "WAIT" shown by the indicator for pedestrians is illuminated it shall convey to a pedestrian the same warning as that conveyed by the red light shown by the pedestrian light signal, that is to say, the he should not in the interests of safety use the crossing.

(4) Any audible signal emitted by any device for emitting audible signals provided in conjunction with the steady green light for pedestrians, and any tactile signal made by any device for making tactile signals similarly provided, shall convey to a pedestrian the same information as that conveyed by the steady green light, that is to say, that he may use the crossing and drivers of vehicles may not cause their vehicle to enter the limits of the crossing.　　**[1500]**

NOTES
    Commencement: 18 February 1987.

10. Significance of additional traffic signs

The traffic signs referred to in regulation 6 shall convey the information, prohibitions or requirements mentioned in relation thereto in the captions to the diagrams in Schedule 1 to the Traffic Sign Regulations 1981 mentioned in that regulation.　　**[1501]**

NOTES
    Commencement: 18 February 1987.
    Traffic Signs Regulations 1981: SI 1981 No 859.

11. Movement of traffic and precedence of pedestrians

Regulations 12 to 20 are made under section 25 of the 1984 Act and shall have effect with respect to the movement of traffic (including pedestrians) and the precedence of pedestrians over vehicles at and in the vicinity of a "Pelican" crossing.　　**[1502]**

NOTES
    Commencement: 18 February 1987.
    1984 Act: Road Traffic Regulation Act 1984.

Prohibition on stopping in areas adjacent to "Pelican" crossings

12. (1) For the purposes of this regulation and the next two following regulations, the expression "vehicle" shall not include a pedal bicycle not having a sidecar attached thereto, whether additional means of propulsion by mechanical power are attached to the bicycle or not.

(2) Save as provided in regulations 13 and 14, and subject to regulation 15, the driver of a vehicle shall not cause the vehicle or any part thereof to stop in a "Pelican" controlled area. **[1503]**

NOTES
    Commencement: 18 February 1987.

13. A vehicle shall not by regulation 12 be prevented from stopping in any length of road on any side thereof—

    (a) if the driver has stopped for the purpose of complying with regulation 16, 17 or 19;

    (b) if the driver is prevented from proceeding by circumstances beyond his control or it is necessary for him to stop in order to avoid an accident; or

    (c) for so long as may be necessary to enable the vehicle, if it cannot be used for such purpose without stopping in that length of road, to be used for fire brigade, ambulance or police purposes or in connection with any building operation, demolition or excavation, the removal of any obstruction to traffic, the maintenance, improvement or reconstruction of that length of road, or the laying, erection, alteration, repair or cleaning in or near to that length of road of any sewer or of any main, pipe or apparatus for the supply of gas, water or electricity, or of any telecommunications apparatus kept installed for the purposes of a telecommunications code system or of any other telecommunications apparatus lawfully kept installed in any position. **[1504]**

NOTES
    Commencement: 18 February 1987.

14. (1) A vehicle shall not by regulation 12 be prevented from stopping in a "Pelican" controlled area—

    (a) if the vehicle is stopped for the purpose of making a left or right turn; or

    (b) if the vehicle is a public service vehicle being used—

        (i) in the provision of a service which is a local service within the meaning of the Transport Act 1985; or

        (ii) to carry passengers for hire or reward at separate fare otherwise than in the provision of a local service,

but excluding in each case any such vehicle being used on an excursion or tour, and the vehicle is waiting, after having proceeded past the "Pelican" crossing in relation to which the "Pelican" controlled area is indicated, in order to take up or set down passengers.

(2) In sub-paragraph (b) of paragraph (1) of this regulation "local service" and "excursion or tour" have respectively the same meanings as in the Transport Act 1985. **[1505]**

NOTES
Commencement: 18 February 1987.

15. Saving for crossings constituted in accordance with 1969 Regulations

In relation to any crossing which, immediately before the coming into operation of these Regulations, was constituted as a "Pelican" crossing in accordance with the 1969 Regulations, for a period of two years commencing on the date these Regulations come into operation regulations 12, 13 and 14 shall not apply and regulation 9 of the 1969 Regulations shall, notwithstanding the repeal of those Regulations, continue to have effect but only for so long during that period as the crossing remains so constituted. **[1506]**

NOTES
Commencement: 18 February 1987.
1969 Regulations: "Pelican" Pedestrian Crossings Regulations 1969.

16. Prohibition against the proceeding of vehicles across a "Pelican" crossing

When the vehicular traffic light signal is showing a red light, the driver of a vehicle shall not cause the vehicle or any part thereof to proceed beyond the stop line, or, if that line is not for the time being visible, beyond the post or other structure on which is mounted the primary signal facing the driver on the side of the carriageway on which vehicles approach the crossing. **[1507]**

NOTES
Commencement: 18 February 1987.

17. Precedence of pedestrians over vehicles on a "Pelican" crossing

When the vehicular traffic light signal at a "Pelican" crossing is showing a flashing amber light, every pedestrian, if he is on the carriageway, or a central reservation within the limits of that crossing (but not if he is on a central reservation which lies between two crossings which form part of a system of staggered crossings) before any part of the vehicle has entered those limits, shall have precedence within those limits over that vehicle and the driver of a vehicle shall accord such precedence to any such pedestrian. **[1508]**

NOTES
Commencement: 18 February 1987.

18. Prohibition against the waiting of vehicles and pedestrians on a "Pelican" crossing

(1) The driver of a vehicle shall not cause the vehicle or any part thereof to stop within the limits of a "Pelican" crossing unless either he is prevented from proceeding by circumstances beyond his control or it is necessary for him to stop in order to avoid an accident.

(2) No pedestrian shall remain on the carriageway within the limits of a "Pelican" crossing longer than is necessary for the purpose of passing over the crossing with reasonable despatch. **[1509]**

NOTES
Commencement: 18 February 1987.

Prohibition against overtaking at a "Pelican" crossing

19. The driver of a vehicle while it or any part of it is in a "Pelican" controlled area and it is proceeding towards the limits of a "Pelican" crossing in relation to which the area is indicated (hereinafter referred to as "the approaching vehicle") shall not cause that vehicle, or any part of it—

    (a) to pass ahead of the foremost part of another moving motor vehicle being a vehicle proceeding in the same direction wholly or partly within that area; or

    (b) subject to the next succeeding regulation, to pass ahead of the foremost part of a stationary vehicle on the same side of the crossing as the approaching vehicle, which stationary vehicle is stopped for the purpose of complying with regulation 16 or 17.

For the purposes of this regulation—

    (i) the reference to another moving motor vehicle is, in a case where only one other motor vehicle is proceeding in the same direction in a "Pelican" controlled area, a reference to that vehicle, and, in a case where more than one other motor vehicle is so proceeding, a reference to such one of those vehicles as is nearest to the limits of the crossing; and

    (ii) the reference to a stationary vehicle is, in a case where only one other vehicle is stopped for the purpose of complying with regulation 16 or 17, a reference to that vehicle, and, in a case where more than one other vehicle is stopped for that purpose, a reference to such one of those vehicles as is nearest to the limits of the crossing.   **[1510]**

NOTES
Commencement: 18 February 1987.

20. Nothing in paragraph (b) of regulation 19 shall apply so as to prevent the approaching vehicle from passing ahead of the foremost part of a stationary vehicle within the meaning of that paragraph, if the stationary vehicle is stopped for the purpose of complying with regulation 16 or 17 in relation to a "Pelican" crossing which is a separate crossing from the "Pelican" crossing towards the limits of which the approaching vehicle is proceeding.   **[1511]**

NOTES
Commencement: 18 February 1987.

SCHEDULE 1   REG 2(1))

THE SIZE, COLOUR AND TYPE OF TRAFFIC SIGNS AT A "PELICAN" CROSSING

PART I

TRAFFIC SIGNS

1. The traffic signs which are to be placed at or near a crossing for the purpose of constituting it a "Pelican" crossing shall consist of a combination of—

    (a) vehicular light signals;
    (b) pedestrian light signals; and
    (c) indicators for pedestrians,

of the size, colour and type prescribed by the following provisions of this Schedule, together with any additional traffic signs placed at or near the crossing pursuant to regulation 6.

Vehicular traffic signals

2. The vehicular light signals shall be as follows—

(a) three lights shall be used, one red, one amber, and one green;

(b) the lamps showing the aforesaid lights shall be arranged vertically, the lamp showing the red light being the uppermost and that showing the green light the lowermost;

(c) each lamp shall be separately illuminated and the effective diameter of the lens thereof shall be not less than 195 millimetres nor more than 220 millimetres;

(d) the height of the centre of the amber lens from the surface of the carriageway in the immediate vicinity shall, in the case of signals placed at the side of the carriageway or on a central reservation, be not less than 2.4 metres nor more than 4 metres and, in the case of signals placed elsewhere and over the carriageway, not less than 6.1 metres nor more than 9 metres;

(e) the centres of the lenses of adjacent lamps shall be not less than 305 millimetres nor more than 360 millimetres apart;

(f) the lamp showing the amber light shall be capable of showing a steady light or a flashing light such that it flashes at a rate of not less than 70 nor more than 90 flashes per minute; and

(g) no lettering or symbols shall be used upon the lens.

Pedestrian light signals

3.—(1) The pedestrian light signals shall be of the size, colour and type shown in the diagrams in Part II of this Schedule.

(2) The height of the lower edge of the container enclosing the light signals from the surface of the carriageway in the immediate vicinity shall be not less than 2.1 metres nor more than 2.6 metres.

(3) The said signals shall be so designed that—

(a) the red figure shown in the said diagrams can be internally illuminated by a steady light;

(b) the green figure shown in the said diagrams can be internally illuminated by a steady light or by a flashing light at a rate of not less than 70 nor more than 90 flashes per minute; and

(c) when one signal is illuminated the other signal is not illuminated.

(4) A device for emitting audible signals may be provided for use when the green figure is illuminated by a steady light.

Indicator for pedestrians

4.—(1) The indicator for pedestrians shall be of the size, colour and type shown in the diagram in Part III of this Schedule.

(2) The indicator for pedestrians shall be so designed and constructed that "WAIT" as shown on the diagram can be illuminated and that there is incorporated in the indicator a device, which may be a push button or pressure pad and which is hereinafter in this Schedule referred to as "a push button", which can be used by pedestrians with the effect hereinafter described.

(3) The instruction for pedestrians shown in the diagram may be internally illuminated.

(4) A device for making tactile signals may be provided for use when the green figure shown in the diagram is illuminated by a steady light.

Sequence of signals

5.—(1) The vehicular light signals and pedestrian light signals and the indicators for pedestrians when they are placed at or near any crossing shall be so designed and constructed that—

(a) before the signals and indicators are operated by the pressing of a push button or as described in paragraph 6 of this Schedule the vehicular light signal shows a steady green light, the pedestrian light signal shows a red light, the word "WAIT" in the indicator for pedestrians is not illuminated, any device for making tactile signals is inactive, and any device for emitting audible signals is silent;

(b) when a push button is pressed—

   (i) after the expiration of the vehicle period but before the vehicular light signals are showing a steady amber light, the signals and indicators, unless they are working as described in paragraph 6 of this Schedule, are caused to show lights in the sequences specified in descending order in column 1 in the case of vehicular light signals, in column 2 in the case of pedestrian light signals and in column 3 in the case of the indicators for pedestrians, of either Part IV or Part V of this Schedule;

   (ii) when the vehicular light signals are showing a steady amber light or a red light when the signal to pedestrians shows a red or steady green light, there is no effect;

   (iii) when the pedestrian light signals are showing a flashing green light, the word "WAIT" in each of the indicators for pedestrians is illuminated immediately and the signals and indicators are caused to show lights in the sequence specified in sub-paragraph (i) of this paragraph at the end of the next vehicle period; and

   (iv) after the pedestrian light signals have ceased to show a flashing green light and before the end of the next vehicle period, the word "WAIT" in each of the indicators for pedestrians is illuminated immediately and the signals and indicators are caused to show lights in the sequence specified in sub-paragraph (i) of this paragraph at the end of the vehicle period;

(c) the periods during which lights are shown by the signals and the indicators, commence and terminate in relation to each other as shown in either Part IV or Part V of this Schedule as if each horizontal line therein represented one moment in time, subsequent moments occurring in descending order, but the distances between the horizontal lines do not represent the lengths of the periods during which the lights shown by the signals and the indicator are, or are not, lit.

(2) Where a device for emitting audible signals has been provided pursuant to paragraph 3(4) of this Schedule, it shall be so designed and constructed that a pulsed sound is emitted throughout every period when the pedestrian light signals are showing a steady green light, and at the same time the vehicular light signals are showing a red light, but only during such periods and at no other times, save that such a device need not operate during the hours of darkness.

(3) Where a device for making tactile signals has been provided pursuant to paragraph 4(4) of this Schedule, it shall be so designed and constructed that a regular movement perceptible to touch by pedestrians is made throughout every period when the pedestrian light signals are showing a steady green light, and at the same time the vehicular light signals are showing a red light, but only during such periods and at no other times.

(4) In this paragraph "vehicle period" means such period as may be fixed from time to time in relation to a "Pelican" crossing, which commences when the vehicular light signals cease to show a flashing amber light and during which the vehicular traffic light signals show a green light.

Operation by remote control

6. The vehicular light signals, pedestrian light signals, indicators for pedestrians, any device or making tactile signals, and any device for emitting audible signals, when they are placed at or near any crossing may also be so designed and constructed that they can by remote control be made to operate—

(a) as if a push button has been pressed; and

(b) so that the pressing of a push button has no effect, other than causing the word "WAIT" in each of the indicators for the pedestrians to be illuminated, until normal operation is resumed. **[1512]**

NOTES
Commencement: 18 February 1987.

THE SIZE, COLOUR AND TYPE OF TRAFFIC SIGNS AT A "PELICAN" CROSSING (REG 2(1))
PART II
[*For diagram, reference should be made to the Queen's Printer's copy of this statutory instrument, which can be obtained from HMSO.*] **[1513]**

NOTES
Commencement: 18 February 1987.

PART III
[*For diagram, reference should be made to the Queen's Printer's copy of this statutory instrument, which can be obtained from HMSO.*] **[1514]**

NOTES
Commencement: 18 February 1987.

PART IV
SEQUENCE OF OPERATION OF VEHICULAR AND PEDESTRIAN LIGHT SIGNALS AND INDICATOR FOR PEDESTRIANS (BUT NOT THE AUDIBLE SIGNALS)

Sequence of vehicular traffic light signals	Sequence of pedestrian signals	
	Pedestrian light signals	Indicator for pedestrians
(1)	(2)	(3)
Green light	Red light	The word "WAIT" is illuminated
Amber light		
Red light		
	Green light	The word "WAIT" is not illuminated
Flashing amber light	Flashing green light	The word "WAIT" is illuminated
	Red light	
Green light		

[1515]

NOTES
Commencement: 18 February 1987.

PART V

ALTERNATIVE SEQUENCE OF OPERATION OF VEHICULAR AND
PEDESTRIAN LIGHT SIGNALS AND INDICATOR FOR PEDESTRIANS
(BUT NOT THE AUDIBLE SIGNALS)

Sequence of vehicular traffic light signals	*Sequence of pedestrian signals*	
	Pedestrian light signals	*Indicator for pedestrians*
(1)	(2)	(3)
Green light	Red light	The word "WAIT" is illuminated
Amber light		
Red light		
	Green light	The word "WAIT" is not illuminated
Flashing amber light	Flashing green light	The word "WAIT" is illuminated
	Red light	
Green light		

[1516]

NOTES
    Commencement: 18 February 1987.

SCHEDULE 2   (REG 2(2))

THE MANNER OF INDICATING THE PRESENCE AND LIMITS OF A "PELICAN" CROSSING AND
"PELICAN" CONTROLLED AREA

General

1. In this Schedule, and except where otherwise stated, any reference to a numbered
diagram is a reference to the diagram bearing that number in this Schedule.

2.—(1) Every crossing which is a "Pelican" crossing on a road which is not a one-
way street shall have its limits indicated, subject to the following provisions of this
Schedule, by the pattern of studs on or in and lines on the carriageway in the manner
shown—

    (a) in diagram 1 where there is no central reservation;
    (b) in diagram 2 where there is a central reservation, but the crossing does not
        form part of a system of staggered crossings; and
    (c) in diagram 3 where the crossing forms part of a system of staggered crossings.

(2) Every crossing which is a "Pelican" crossing on a road which is a one-way street
shall have its limits indicated, subject to the following provisions of this Schedule, by the
pattern of studs on or in and lines on the carriageway in the manner shown—

    (a) in diagram 4 where there is no central reservation;
    (b) in diagram 5 where there is a central reservation but the crossing does not form
        part of a system of staggered crossings; and
    (c) in diagram 6 where the crossing forms part of a system of staggered crossings.

Manner of indicating the limits of the crossing

3. The limits of a "Pelican" crossing shall be indicated by two lines of studs in the
positions shown, and in accordance with the measurements in, the diagram corresponding
to the type of crossing.

4. The two lines of studs indicating the limits of the crossing need not be at right angles to the edge of the carriageway, but shall form straight lines and shall as near as is reasonably practicable be parallel to each other.

Manner of indicating a "Pelican" controlled area and provision as to placing the stop line

5. Subject to paragraph 8 of this Schedule, the presence and limits of a "Pelican" controlled area shall be indicated by the pattern of lines placed in the positions shown, and in accordance with the measurements, in the diagram corresponding to the type of crossing, and in accordance with the provisions of paragraphs 6 and 7 of this Schedule.

6. Where the crossing is on a road which is not a one-way street the pattern of lines shall consist of—

(1) a stop line placed on the carriageway parallel to the nearer row of studs indicating the limits of the crossing and extending, in the manner indicated in the appropriate diagram, across the part of the carriageway used by vehicles approaching the crossing from the side on which the stop line is placed;

(2) two or more longitudinal white broken lines (hereinafter referred to as "zig-zag lines") placed on the carriageway or, where the road is a dual-carriageway road, on each part of the carriageway, each zig-zag line containing not less than 8 nor more than 18 marks and extending away from the crossing in the manner indicated in the appropriate diagram;

(3) subject to sub-paragraph (4) of this paragraph, where a central reservation is provided the road marking shown in diagram 1040.1 in Schedule 2 to the Traffic Signs Regulations 1981 may be placed on the carriageway between the zig-zag lines on the approaches to the central reservation;

(4) where a central reservation is provided connecting crossings which form part of a system of staggered crossings, the road markings mentioned in sub-pararaph (3) of this paragraph shall be placed on the carriageway in the manner indicated in diagram 3.

7. Where the crossing is on a road which is a one-way street the pattern of lines shall consist of:

(1) a stop line placed parallel to the nearer row of studs indicating the limits of the crossing and extending—

    (a) in the case of a crossing of the type shown in diagram 4 or 5, from one edge of the carriageway to the other; and

    (b) in the case of a crossing of the type shown in diagram 6, from the edge of the carriageway to the central reservation;

(2) two or more zig-zag lines placed on the carriageway, each containing not less than 8 and not more than 18 marks, and extending away from the crossing;

(3) subject to sub-paragraph (4) of this paragraph, where a central reservation is provided the road marking shown in diagram 1041 in Schedule 2 to the Traffic Signs Regulations 1981 may be placed on the carriageway between the zig-zag lines on the approaches to the central reservation; and

(4) where a central reservation is provided connecting crossings which form part of a system of staggered crossings, the road markings mentioned in sub-paragraph (3) of this paragraph shall be placed on the carriageway in the manner indicated in diagram 6.

8.—(1) Where the appropriate authority is satisfied in relation to a particular area of carriageway in the vicinity of a "Pelican" crossing that by reason of the layout of, or character of, the roads in the vicinity of the crossing it would be impracticable to lay the pattern of lines as shown in the diagrams in, and in accordance with paragraphs 5 to 7 of, this Schedule any of the following variations as respects the pattern shall be permitted—

    (a) the number of marks contained in each zig-zag line may be reduced from 8 to not less than 2; and

    (b) a mark contained in a zig-zag line may be varied in length so as to extend for a distance not less than 1 metre and less than 2 metres, but where such a variation is made as respects a mark each other mark in each zig-zag line shall be of the same or substantially the same length as that mark, so however that the number of marks in each zig-zag line shall not be more than 8 nor less than 2.

(2) The angle of the stop line in relation to the nearer line of studs indicating the limits of a crossing may be varied, if the appropriate authority is satisfied that such variation is necessary having regard to the angle of the crossing in relation to the edge of the carriageway at the place where the crossing is situated.

(3) The maximum distance of 3 metres between the stop line and the nearer line of studs indicating the limits of the crossing shown in the diagrams in this Schedule may be increased to such greater distance, not in any case exceeding 10 metres, as the appropriate authority may decide.

(4) Where by reason of regulation 3(3) an area of carriageway in the vicinity of a "Pelican" crossing is not constituted a "Pelican" controlled area by the placing of a pattern of lines as provided in the foregoing provisions of this Schedule, a stop line shall nevertheless be placed on the carriageway as previously provided in this Schedule.

Colour and dimensions of road markings and studs

9. The road markings shown in the diagrams in this Schedule shall be white in colour, and may be illuminated by reflecting material.

10.—(1) The studs shown in the diagrams shall be either white, silver or light grey in colour and shall not be fitted with reflective lenses.

(2) The said studs shall be either circular in shape with a diameter of not more than 110 millimetres or less than 95 millimetres or square in shape with each side being not more than 110 millimetres or less than 95 millimetres.

(3) Any stud which is fixed or embedded in the carriageway shall not project more than 18 millimetres above the carriageway at its highest point nor more than 6 millimetres at its edges.

11. Where in any diagram in this Schedule a dimension or measurement is indicated in brackets against a dimension or measurement not indicated in brackets any dimension or measurement indicated in brackets may be treated as an alternative to the dimension or measurement not so indicated.

Supplementary

12. The foregoing provisions of this Schedule shall be regarded as having been complied with in the case of any pattern of studs or white lines if most of the studs or lengths of white lines comply notwithstanding that one or more studs or some of the lengths of white lines may not comply with those provisions by reason of discoloration, temporary removal, displacement or for some other reason so long as the general appearance of the pattern of studs or white lines is not thereby materially impaired.

Schedule 2 Diagram 1

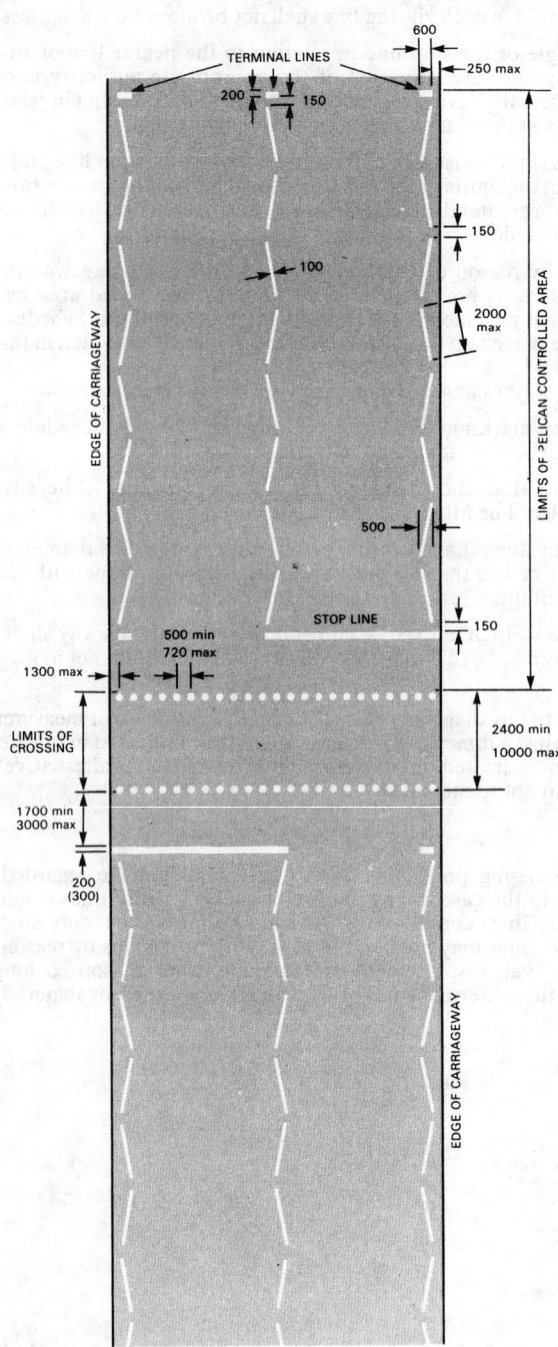

NOTE:- Each zigzag line need not contain the same number of marks.

ALL DIMENSIONS IN MILLIMETRES

Schedule 2 Diagram 2

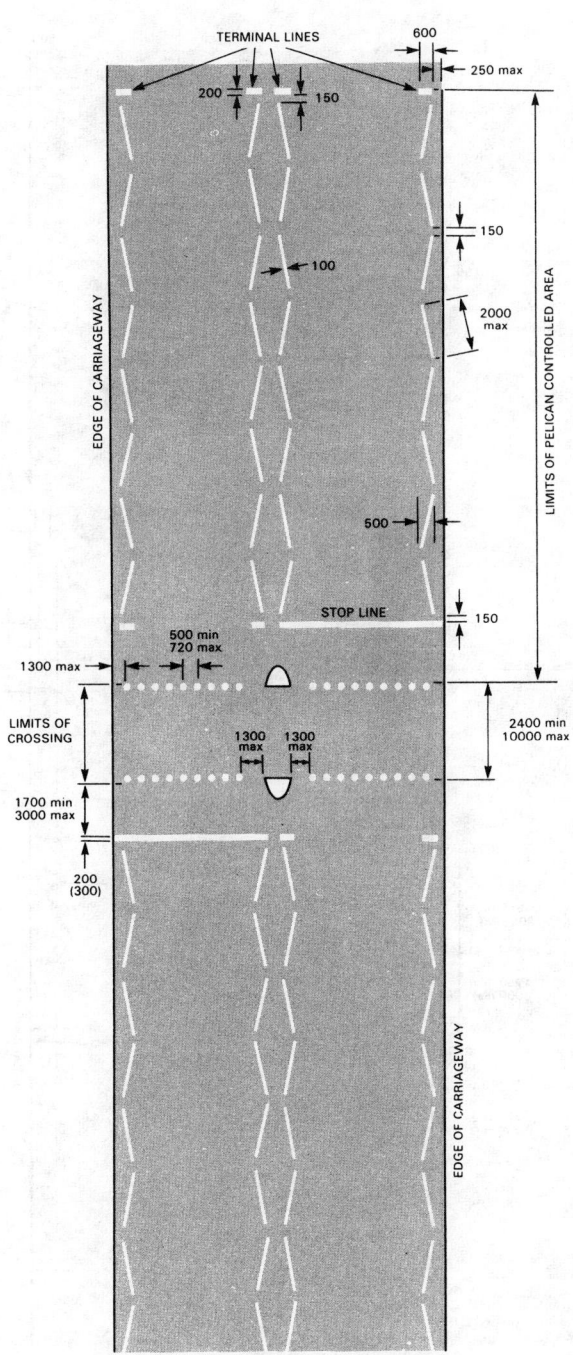

NOTE:- Each zigzag line need not contain the same number of marks.

ALL DIMENSIONS IN MILLIMETRES

Schedule 2   Diagram 3

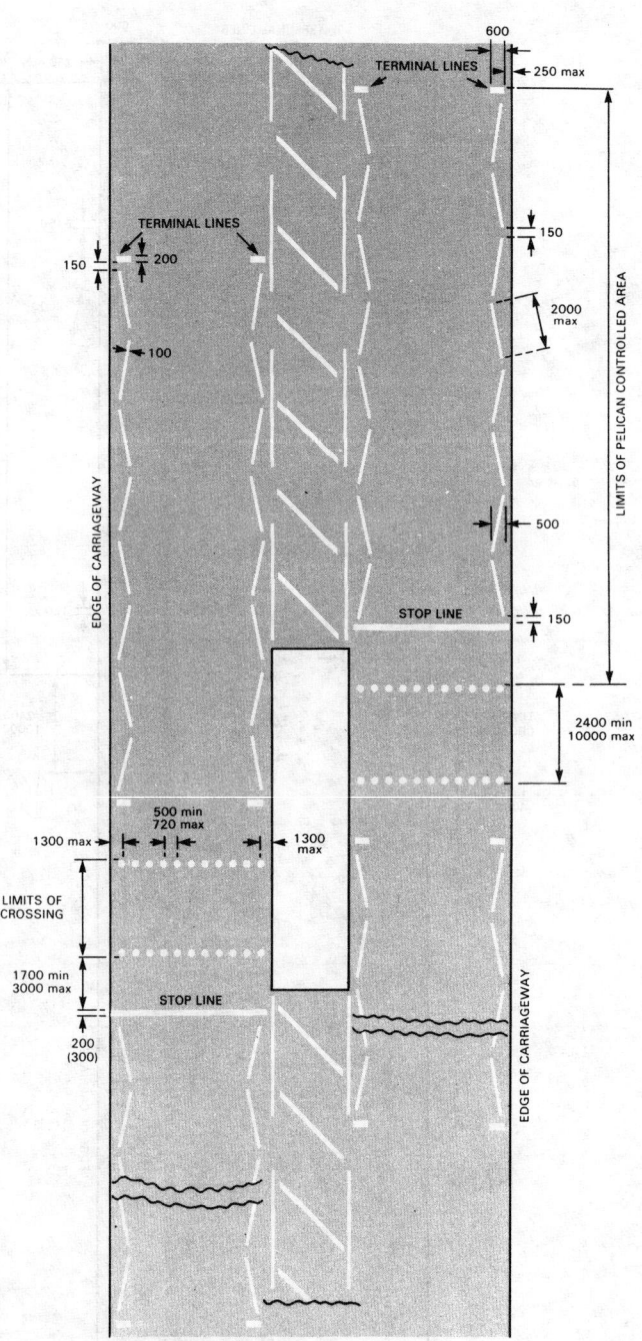

NOTE:- Each zigzag line need not contain the same number of marks.
      The stagger may be reversed as required

ALL DIMENSIONS IN MILLIMETRES

Schedule 2   Diagram 4

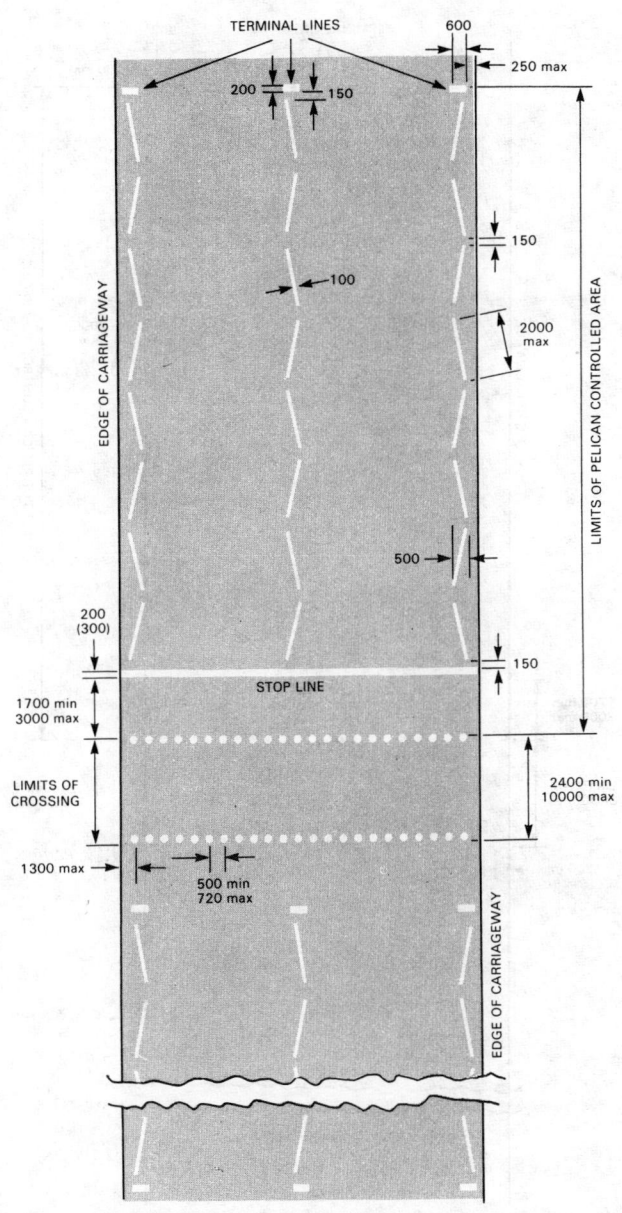

NOTE:- Each zigzag line need not contain the same number of marks.

ALL DIMENSIONS IN MILLIMETRES

Schedule 2   Diagram 5

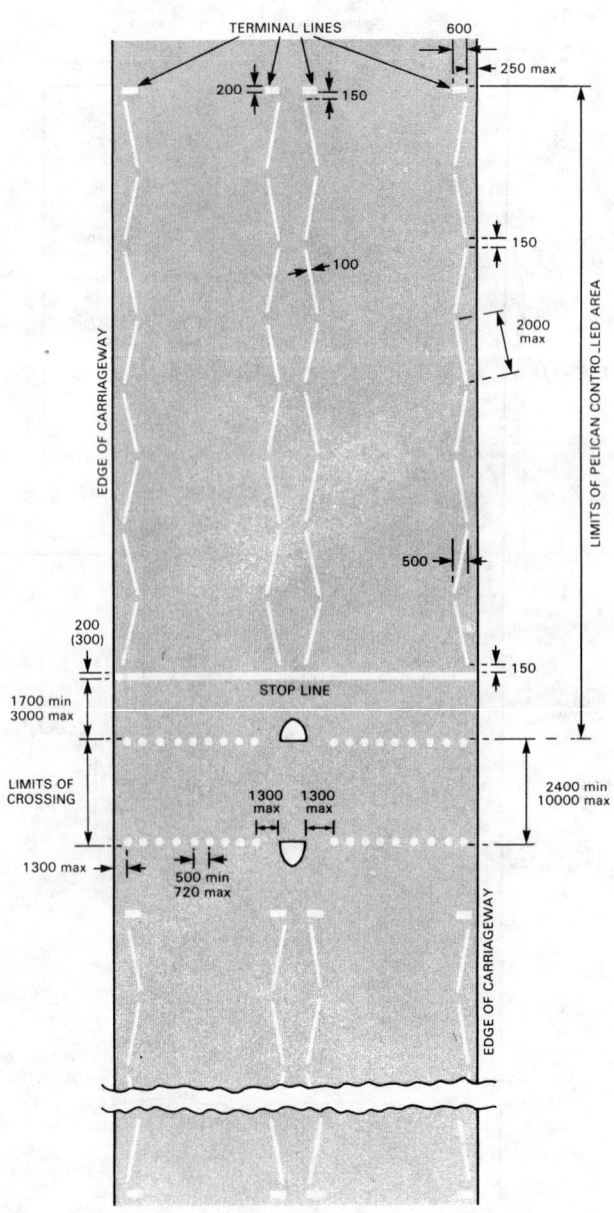

NOTE:- Each zigzag line need not contain the same number of marks.

ALL DIMENSIONS IN MILLIMETRES

Schedule 2   Diagram 6

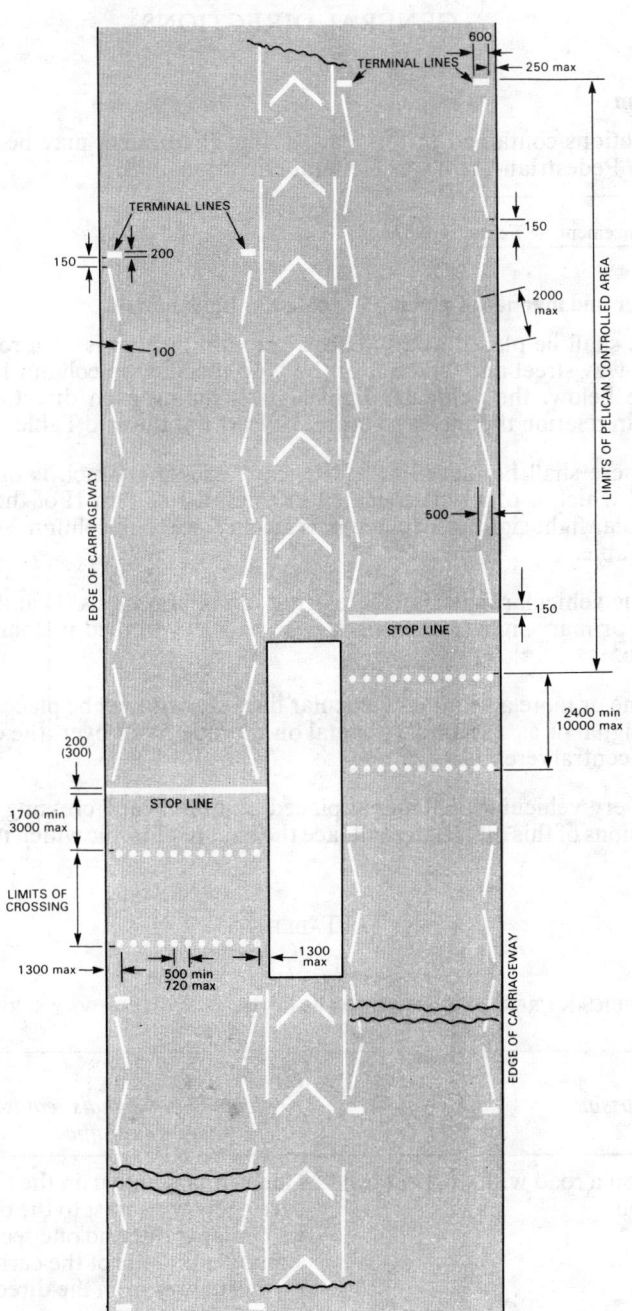

NOTE:- Each zigzag line need not contain the same number of marks. The stagger may be reversed as required
ALL DIMENSIONS IN MILLIMETRES

[1517]

NOTES
Commencement: 18 February 1987.

PART III
GENERAL DIRECTIONS

1. Citation

The Directions contained in this Part of this Instrument may be cited as the "Pelican" Pedestrian Crossings General Directions 1987.   **[1518]**

NOTES
  Commencement: 18 February 1987.

2. Number and manner of placing of vehicular light signals

(1) There shall be placed at a "Pelican" crossing which is on a road which is not a one-way street and which is of the type specified in column 1 of Part I of the Table below, the vehicular light signals facing each direction of traffic specified in relation thereto in column 2 of Part I of the said Table.

(2) There shall be placed at a "Pelican" crossing which is on a one-way street and which is of a type specified in column 1 of Part II of the said Table the vehicular light signals specified in relation thereto in column 2 of Part II of the said Table.

(3) The vehicular light signals referred to in paragraphs (1) and (2) shall be placed as primary signals or secondary signals as specified in column 2 of the said Table.

(4) One or more additional vehicular light signals may be placed either as a primary signal or as a secondary signal on the side of, or over, the carriageway or on any central reservation.

(5) Every vehicular light signal placed at a "Pelican" crossing pursuant to the provisions of this direction shall face the stream of traffic which it is intended to control.

TABLE

PART I

PELICAN CROSSINGS ON ROADS WHICH ARE NOT ONE-WAY STREETS

(1) *Type of crossing*	(2) *Vehicular light signals required facing each direction of traffic*
Crossing on a road without a central reservation.	One primary signal on the side of the carriageway nearest to the direction of vehicular traffic and one secondary signal on the side of the carriageway furthest away from the direction of vehicular traffic.
Crossing on a road with a central reservation which does not form part of a system of staggered crossings.	One primary signal on the side of the carriageway nearest to the direction of vehicular traffic and one secondary signal on the central reservation.

(1) *Type of crossing*	(2) *Vehicular light signals required facing each direction of traffic*
Crossing which forms part of a system of staggered crossings.	One primary signal on the side of the carriageway nearest to the direction of vehicular traffic and one primary signal on the central reservation.

PART II

PELICAN CROSSINGS ON ROADS WHICH ARE ONE-WAY STREETS

(1) *Type of crossing*	(2) *Vehicular light signals required*
Crossing on a road without a central reservation.	One primary signal on each side of the carriageway.
Crossing on a road with a central reservation which does not form part of a system of staggered crossings.	One primary signal on each side of the carriageway and one secondary signal on the central reservation.
Crossing which forms part of a system of staggered crossings.	One primary signal on the side of the carriageway and one primary signal on the central reservation.

[1519]

NOTES
Commencement: 18 February 1987.

3. Number and manner of placing of pedestrian light signals and indicators for pedestrians

(1) At least one pedestrian light signal and at least one indicator for pedestrians shall be placed at each end of a "Pelican" crossing.

(2) Where there is a central reservation in a crossing, one or more additional indicators for pedestrians shall be placed on the central reservation.

(3) Each pedestrian light signal at either end of the crossing shall be so placed as to be clearly visible to any person who is about to use the crossing at the other end of the crossing.

(4) Each indicator for pedestrians shall be so placed that the push button in the indicator is readily accessible to pedestrians who wish to press it.   **[1520]**

NOTES
Commencement: 18 February 1987.

4. Additional traffic signs

The traffic signs specified in diagrams 610 and 611 in Schedule 1 to the Traffic Signs Regulations 1981 shall be placed only on a central reservation in a crossing, or on a central reservation which lies between two crossings which form part of a system of staggered crossings.   **[1521]**

NOTES
Commencement: 18 February 1987.

5. Colouring of containers and posts

(1) The containers of the vehicular light signals and of the pedestrian light signals shall be coloured black and may be mounted with a backing board and if so mounted the backing board shall be coloured black and may have a white border not less than 45 millimetres nor more than 55 millimeteres in width which may be of a reflective material.

(2) Where a vehicular light signal, a pedestrian light signal or an indicator for pedestrians is mounted on a post specially provided for the purpose, that part of the post which extends above ground level shall be coloured grey and may have one white band not less than 140 millimetres nor more than 160 millimetres in depth, the lower edge of the band being not less than 1.5 metres nor more than 1.7 metres above the level of the surface of the ground in the immediate vicinity.

(3) Any box attached to a post or other structure on which pedestrian light signals or vehicular light signals are mounted and housing apparatus designed to control, or to monitor, or to control and monitor, the operation of such signals shall be coloured grey, yellow or black, or a combination of any of those colours. **[1522]**

NOTES
Commencement: 18 February 1987.

6. Approval for mechanisms and sequence adjustments

(1) Vehicular light signals, pedestrian light signals and indicators for pedestrians may be placed at or near any "Pelican" crossing only if the apparatus (including the content of all instructions stored in, or executable by, it) used to secure that the signals and indicators comply with the relevant provisions of the Regulations is of a type approved in writing by or on behalf of the Secretary of State.

(2) Such signals may be retained in place notwithstanding the subsequent withdrawal of any approval relating to any such apparatus. **[1523]**

NOTES
Commencement: 18 February 1987.

7. Special Cases

Nothing in these Directions shall be taken to limit the power of the Secretary of State by any special direction to dispense with, add to or modify any of the requirements of the Directions in relation to any particular case. **[1524]**

NOTES
Commencement: 18 February 1987.

MOTOR VEHICLES (DRIVING LICENCES) REGULATIONS 1987
(SI 1987 NO 1378)

NOTES
Made: 31 July 1987
Authority: Road Traffic Act 1988, ss 88(5), 89, 91(b), 92, 94(5), 96, 97, 98(4), 99(2), 101, 105, 106(2), 164(2), 186(4).

ARRANGEMENT OF REGULATIONS

PART I
PRELIMINARY

PART II
LICENCES

PART III
TESTS OF COMPETENCE TO DRIVE

Persons by whom tests may be conducted

PART IIIA
APPROVED TRAINING COURSES FOR MOTOR CYCLES

PART IV

SUPPLEMENTARY

SCHEDULES

PART I

PRELIMINARY

1. Citation and commencement

These Regulations may be cited as the Motor Vehicles (Driving Licences) Regulations 1987 and shall come into force on 3rd September 1987.　　**[1525]**

NOTES
   Commencement: 3 September 1987.

2. Revocation and saving

The Regulations specified in Schedule 1 are hereby revoked but, subject as hereinafter provided, any reference in any application or appointment made, notice or approval given, licence, certificate or other document granted or issued or other thing done under the said Regulations to any provision of the Regulations revoked by these Regulations, whether specifically or by means of a general description, shall, unless the context otherwise requires, be construed as a reference to the corresponding provision of these Regulations.　　**[1526]**

NOTES
   Commencement: 3 September 1987.

3. Interpretation

(1) In these Regulations, unless the context otherwise requires, the following expressions have the meanings hereby respectively assigned to them, that is to say:—

"1972 Act" means the Road Traffic Act 1972;

"1981 Act" means the Public Passenger Vehicles Act 1981;

"1985 Act" means the Transport Act 1985;

["appropriate driving test" and "extended driving test" have the same meaning as in section 36 of the Road Traffic Offenders Act 1988;"]

["category" in relation to a class of motor vehicles means a category of motor vehicles of the classes specified in the second column of Schedule 3, and a category identified by a letter means the category corresponding to the letter in the first column of that Schedule;]

. . .

"controlled by a pedestrian" in relation to a vehicle means that the vehicle either—
   (a) is constructed or adapted for use under such control; or
   (b) is constructed or adapted for use either under such control or under the control of a person carried on it but is not for the time being in use under, or proceeding under, the control of a person carried on it;

"disability" includes disease;

"full licence" means a licence other than a provisional licence;

. . .

"kerbside weight" means the weight of a vehicle when it carries—
   (a) in the case of a motor vehicle—
      (i) no person; and
      (ii) a full supply of fuel in its tank, an adequate supply of other liquids incidental to its propulsion and no load other than the tools and equipment with which it is normally equipped; or
   (b) in the case of a trailer, no person and is otherwise unladen;

"licence" means a licence to drive a motor vehicle granted under Part III of the 1972 Act [other than a large goods vehicle or passenger-carrying vehicle driver's licence as defined in section 110(2) of the Road Traffic Act 1988];

"licensing authority" means the Secretary of State;

["maximum authorised mass" has the same meaning—
   (a) in relation to goods vehicles as "permissible maximum weight" in section 108(1) of the Road Traffic Act 1988, and
   (b) in relation to any other vehicle or trailer as "maximum gross weight" in regulation 3(2) of the Road Vehicles (Construction and Use) Regulations 1986;]

"maximum speed" means the speed which a vehicle is incapable, by reason of its construction, of exceeding on the level under its own power when fully laden;

"moped" means—

(a) in the case only of motor cycles which are first used on or after 1st August 1977, a motor cycle (not being a motor vehicle of [category K]) which has a maximum speed which does not exceed 30 miles per hour, a kerbside weight which does not exceed 250 kilograms, and, if propelled by an internal combustion engine, an engine the cylinder capacity of which does not exceed 50 cubic centimetres, or

(b) in the case only of motor cycles which are first used before 1st August 1977, a motor cycle which has an engine with a cylinder capacity not exceeding 50 cubic centimetres and is equipped with pedals by means of which the cycle is capable of being propelled;

. . .

"provisional licence" means a licence granted by virtue of secton 88(2) of the 1972 Act;

"test" means a test of competence to drive conducted under section 85 of the 1972 Act [and includes an extended driving test.] . . .;

"vehicle propelled by electrical power" means a vehicle of which the motive power is solely derived from any electrical storage battery carried on the vehicle and not connected to any source of power when the vehicle is in motion;

"vehicle with automatic transmission" means a vehicle in which the driver is not provided with any means whereby he may, independently of the use of the accelerator or the brakes, vary gradually the proportion of the power being produced by the engine which is transmitted to the road wheels of the vehicle.

(2) In determining for the purpose of these Regulations when a motor cycle is first used, the date of such first use shall be taken to be such date as is the earliest of the undermentioned relevant dates applicable to that cycle—

(a) in the case of a motor cycle registered under the Roads Act 1920, the Vehicles (Excise) Act 1949, the Vehicles (Excise) Act 1962 or the Vehicles (Excise) Act 1971, the relevant date is the date on which it was first so registered; and

(b) in each of the following cases:—

(i) in the case of a motor cycle which is being or has been used under a trade licence as defined in section 16 of the Vehicles (Excise) Act 1971 (otherwise than for the purposes of demonstration or testing or of being delivered from premises of the manufacturer by whom it was made, or of a distributor of vehicles or dealer in vehicles to premises of a distributor of vehicles, dealer in vehicles or purchaser thereof, or to premises of a person obtaining possession thereof under a hiring agreement or hire purchase agreement);

(ii) in the case of a motor cycle which belongs or has belonged to the Crown and which is or was used or appropriated for use for naval, military or air force purposes;

(iii) in the case of a motor cycle which belongs or has belonged to a visiting force or a headquarters or defence organisation to which in each the Visiting Forces and International Headquarters (Application of Law) Order 1965 applies;

(iv) in the case of a motor cycle which has been used on roads outside Great Britain and has been imported into Great Britain; and

(v) in the case of a motor cycle which has been used otherwise than on roads after being sold or supplied by retail and before being registered,

the relevant date is the date of manufacture of the cycle.

In this paragraph "sold or supplied by retail" means sold or supplied otherwise than to a person acquiring solely for the purpose of re-sale or re-supply for a valuable consideration.

(3) The provisions of paragraph 6 of Schedule 9 to the Road Vehicles (Construction and Use) Regulations 1986 shall apply for determining, for the purposes of the definition of "moped" in paragraph (1), whether the maximum speed of a motor cycle does not exceed 30 mph.

(4) Except where otherwise expressly provided, any reference in these Regulations to a numbered regulation or Schedule is a reference to the regulation or Schedule bearing that number in these Regulations, and any reference to a numbered paragraph is a reference to the paragraph bearing that number in the regulation in which the reference occurs.   **[1527]**

NOTES
   Commencement: 3 September 1987.
   Para (1): definitions "category" and "maximum authorised mass" added, definition "group" revoked, and words in square brackets in definition "moped" substituted, by SI 1990 No 842, regs 2, 3, Sch 1; definition "clerk to the traffic Commissioner" revoked by SI 1990 No 1115, reg 2(2); words in square brackets in definition "licence" added by SI 1990 No 2385, reg 3(a); definition "part of a test" and words omitted from definition "test" revoked by SI 1990 No 2334, reg 5(2); definition "appropriate driving test" and words in square brackets in definition "test" inserted by SI 1992 No 1318, reg 3.

PART II
LICENCES

4. Minimum ages for holding or obtaining licences

(1) Subsection (1) of section 96 of the 1972 Act (which specifies the minimum age for holding or obtaining a licence to drive certain classes of motor vehicles) shall have effect as if in the Table in that subsection—

(a) in item 2, the age of 17 were substituted for the age of 16 in relation to all motor cycles other than—

(i) mopeds;
(ii) motor cycles which are mowing machines; or
(iii) motor cycles which are vehicles controlled by a pedestrian;

(b) in item 3, the age of 16 were substituted for the age of 17 in the case of a person to whom an award of a mobility allowance has been made in pursuance of section 37A of the Social Security Act 1975 provided that where the award was made before he attained the age of 16 it is in force when he attains that age;

(c) in item 4, in relation to an agricultural tractor which—

(i) is so constructed that the whole of its weight is transmitted to the road surface by means of wheels;
(ii) has an overall width not exceeding 2.45 metres;
(iii) is chargeable with duty under section 1 of the Vehicles (Excise) Act 1971 by reference to paragraph 1 of Schedule 3 to that Act as being an agricultural machine or, by virtue of the provisions of section 7(1) of that Act, is not chargeable with duty thereunder; and

(iv) is driven without a trailer attached to it, other than a trailer which has an overall width not exceeding 2.45 metres and which is either a two-wheeled or close-coupled four-wheeled trailer,

the age of 16 were substituted for the age of 17, but in the case of a person who has not passed the test of competence prescribed under section 85(2) of the 1972 Act to drive such a tractor, only while taking, proceeding to or returning from, such a test;

(d) in item 6, the age of 17 were substituted for the age of 21 in relation to a road roller falling within that item if the roller—

(i) is propelled otherwise than by steam;
(ii) has an unladen weight not exceeding 11,690 kilograms; and
(iii) is not constructed or adapted for the conveyance of a load other than the following articles, that is to say, water, fuel, accumulators and other equipment used for the purpose of propulsion, loose tools, loose equipment and objects such as are mentioned in paragraph (3) below,

and if no wheel of the roller is fitted with a pneumatic, soft or elastic tyre;

(e) in item 6, the age of 18 were substituted for the age of 21 in the case of a person employed by a Health Authority or, in Scotland, the Common Services Agency when driving a vehicle for the purposes of an ambulance service of such an Authority or of that Agency;

(f) in item 6, the age of 18 were substituted for the age of 21 in the case of a person who fulfils the conditions—

(i) that he is employed by a registered employer; and
(ii) that he is a registered employee of such an employer,

in relation to any vehicle (other than a road roller) which is a heavy goods vehicle (hgv) of a class [or a large goods vehicle (lgv) of a category] to which his training agreement applies and is owned [or operated] by his employer or by a registered hgv [or lgv] driver training establishment;

(g) in item 6, the age of 18 were substituted for the age of 21 in relation to a large passenger vehicle where—

(i) the driver of the vehicle is not engaged in the carriage of passengers and either holds a licence to drive a public service vehicle granted under section 22 of the 1981 Act [or a passenger-carrying vehicle driver's licence], is undergoing [a test of his ability to drive a passenger-carrying vehicle in pursuance of regulations for the time being in force under section 89 of the Road Traffic Act 1988] or is acting under the supervision of a person who holds such a licence; or
(ii) the driver is engaged in the carriage of passengers—

(a) on a regular service over a route which does not exceed 50 kilometres; or
(b) on a national transport operation when the vehicle used is constructed and equipped to carry not more than 17 persons including the driver,

and the vehicle is operated under a PSV operator's licence granted under section 12 of the 1981 Act, a permit granted under section 19 of the 1985 Act or a community bus permit granted under section 22 of that Act, and in each case the driver holds a licence to drive the vehicle granted under section 22 of the 1981 Act [or a passenger-carrying vehicle driver's licence];

(h) in items 5 and 6, the age of 17 were substituted for the ages of 18 and 21 respectively in the case of members of the armed forces of the Crown in relation to any vehicle when being used in the course of urgent work of national importance in accordance with an order of the Defence Council in pursuance of the Defence (Armed Forces) Regulations 1939 which were contained permanently in force in the form set out in Part C of Schedule 2 to the Emergency Laws (Repeal) Act 1959 by section 2 of the Emergency Powers Act 1964;

(i) in items 5 and 6, the age of 17 were substituted for the ages of 18 and 21 respectively in the case of a member of the armed forces of the Crown when receiving instruction in the driving of [large goods vehicles of any category in preparation for a test of competence under section 89 of the Road Traffic Act 1988 to drive vehicles of that category], or when taking, proceeding to, or returning from any such test.

(2) For the purposes of paragraph (1)(c) any implement fitted to a tractor shall be deemed to form part of the tractor notwithstanding that it is not a permanent or essentially permanent fixture, and in that paragraph—

(i) "overall width", in relation to a vehicle, means the width of the vehicle measured between vertical planes parallel to the longitudinal axis of the vehicle and passing through the extreme projecting points thereof exclusive of any driving mirror and so much of the distortion of any tyre as is caused by the weight of the vehicle; and

(ii) "close-coupled", in relation to wheels on the same side of a trailer, means fitted so that at all times while the trailer is in motion they remain parallel to the longitudinal axis of the trailer and that the distance between the centres of their respective areas of contact with the road surface does not exceed 840 millimetres.

(3) For the purposes of paragraph 1(d) the unladen weight of a vehicle shall be treated as including the weight of any object for the time being attached to the vehicle, being an object specially designed to be so attached for the purpose of temporarily increasing the vehicle's gross weight.

(4) In paragraph 1(f) and in this paragraph—

["heavy goods vehicle" has the same meaning as in Part I of Schedule 1 to the Road Traffic (Driver Licensing and Information Systems) Act 1989;

"large goods vehicle", "passenger-carrying vehicle" and "passenger-carrying vehicle driver's licence" have the same meaning as in Part IV of the Road Traffic Act 1988;]

"registered" means registered for the time being by the Training Committee in accordance with the relevant provisions of the training scheme;

"the Training Committee" means the committee which has been established by the employers' associations and the trade unions in the road goods transport industry with a constitution approved by the Secretary of State and which is known as the National Joint Training Committee for Young HGV Drivers in the Road Goods Transport Industry [or the National Joint Training Committee for Young LGV Drivers in the Road Goods Transport Industry];

"the training scheme" means the scheme which has been established by the

Training Committee with the approval of the Secretary of State for training young drivers of hgvs [or lgvs] and which provides for—

    (a) the registration by the Training Committee of employers who are willing and able to provide hgv [or lgv] driver training for persons employed by them;

    (b) the registration by the Training Committee of persons operating establishments for providing hgv [or lgv] driver training;

    (c) a syllabus for hgv [or lgv] driver training; and

    (d) the registration by the Training Committee of individual employees who are undergoing, or are to undergo, hgv [or lgv] driver training in the service of a registered employer in accordance with a form of agreement approved by the Training Committee;

    and "training agreement", in relation to an individual who is undergoing, or is to undergo, such training as aforesaid, means his agreement therefor with his registered employer in pursuance of the training scheme.

(5) In paragraph (1)(g), "large passenger vehicle" means a motor vehicle which is constructed solely to carry passengers and their effects and is adapted to carry more than nine persons inclusive of the driver and expressions used which are also used in the Community Drivers' Ages and Hours of Work Regulation have the same meaning as in that instrument.

(6) In paragraph (5), "the Community Drivers' Ages and Hours of Work Regulation" means Council Regulation (EEC) 3820/85 as read with regulation 4 of the Community Drivers Hours and Recording Equipment (Exemptions and Supplementary Provisions) Regulations 1986. **[1528]**

NOTES
    Commencement: 3 September 1987.
    Paras (1), (4): words in square brackets substituted, inserted or added by SI 1991 No 485, reg 3.
    The 1972 Act: Road Traffic Act 1972.
    The 1981 Act: Public Passenger Vehicles Act 1981.
    The 1985 Act: Transport Act 1985.

[5. Applications for the grant of licences

(1) Applications for the grant of a licence may be received and dealt with at any time within two months before the date on which the grant of the licence is to take effect.

(2) For the purposes of section 89(1)(f) of the Road Traffic Act 1988 the period of normal residence in Great Britain or, as the case may be, the United Kingdom, during which the holder of an exchangeable licence shall be eligible for the grant of a licence is one year.] **[1529]**

NOTES
    Commencement: 1 April 1991.
    Substituted by SI 1991 No 485, reg 4.

6. Refusal of a provisional licence for group D

(1) Notwithstanding anything in section 88 of the 1972 Act and subject to paragraph (2), the licensing authority shall refuse to grant a provisional licence authorising the driving of a motor cycle of a class included in [category A] if the applicant has held such a licence and the licence applied for would come into force—

(a) except in the circumstances specified in sub-paragraph (b) of this paragraph, within the period of one year beginning at the end of the period for which the previous licence authorised (or would, if not surrendered or revoked, have authorised) the driving of such a motor cycle; or

(b) where the licence would be for a period of less than two years and the previous licence was surrendered or revoked, within the period of two months beginning on the date of such surrender or revocation.

(2) Paragraph (1) shall not apply—

(a) where the previous licence was granted before 1st October 1982;

(b) where the applicant appears to the Secretary of State to be a person suffering from a relevant or prospective disability within the meaning of section 87 of the 1972 Act; or

(c) where the previous licence was surrendered or revoked in pursuance of section 89(2) or (3) of the 1972 Act.   **[1530]**

NOTES

Commencement: 3 September 1987.
Para (1): words in square brackets substituted by SI 1990 No 842, reg 2, Sch 1.
The 1972 Act: Road Traffic Act 1972.

[7. Fees for licences

The fee payable for a licence granted on or after [1st February 1992] shall be, in the case of a licence of a description, and in certain instances granted in particular circumstances, specified in column (1) of the Table in this regulation, the fee specified in relation to that licence in column (2) of that Table.

(1) *Description of Licence*	(2) *Fee*
(1) A licence (except a licence falling in paragraph (2) below) granted to a person—	
(a) who has not held a licence before, or	
(b) whose last licence was a full licence granted before 1st January 1976, or	
(c) whose last licence was a full licence which expired before 31st December 1978, or	
(d) whose last licence was a provisional licence granted before 1st October 1982.	£21
(2) A full licence granted in exchange for a full Northern Ireland licence or to a person who has held a full Northern Ireland licence which was granted on or after 1st January 1976.	£6
(3) A full or provisional licence granted in exchange for a subsisting licence or in place of a licence revoked pursuant to section 99(3) of the Road Traffic Act 1988 except—	
(a) where the licence granted is a first full licence granted in exchange for a provisional licence, or	
(b) where the licence is issued pursuant to section 118(4) of the Road Traffic Act 1988, or	
(c) where the subsisting or revoking licence is surrendered pursuant to section 99(3) or (4) of the Road Traffic Act 1988 and the Secretary of State is required to grant a new licence free of charge.	£6

(1)	(2)
Description of Licence	*Fee*

(4) A provisional licence (except a licence falling in paragraph (1) above or (7) or (9) below) which authorises the driving of vehicles of any class in category A save where such a licence is granted in place of a licence which was revoked pursuant to section 93 or 94 of the Road Traffic Act 1988. £6

(5) A full or provisional licence (except a licence falling in paragraph (1)(a) above) granted to a person on or after that person's 70th birthday except where that person has been granted a licence falling within this paragraph within the previous 3 years and, on the grant of that licence, paid the prescribed fee for it. £6

(6) The first licence (except a licence falling in paragraph (1) above or (7) or (8) below) granted to a person after the expiration of a period of disqualification imposed on him by an order of the court—

    (a) in the circumstances prescribed under section 94(4) of the Road Traffic Act 1988 but irrespective of the date when the order of the court was made; £20

    (b) otherwise than in the circumstances prescribed under section 94(4) of that Act. £12

(7) The first provisional licence (except a licence falling in paragraph (1) above) granted to a person after he has been disqualified by an order of the court made pursuant to section 36 of the Road Traffic Offenders Act 1988 whether or not the court also made an order pursuant to section 34 or 35 of that Act—

    (a) in the circumstances prescribed under section 94(4) of the Road Traffic Act 1988 but irrespective of the date when the order of the court was made; £20

    (b) otherwise than in the circumstances prescribed under section 94(4) of that Act. £12

(8) The first full licence granted to a person after he has passed a driving test which he was required to take by an order of the court made pursuant to section 36 of the Road Traffic Offenders Act 1988 except where the person has never held a full licence. £6

(9) A duplicate licence. £6]

[1531]

NOTES

Commencement: 1 November 1988.
Substituted by SI 1988 No 1062, reg 2.
Words in square brackets and whole of table substituted by SI 1991 No 2493, reg 2.

8. Duration of provisional licences

(1) Subject to paragraph (2), for the purposes of subsection (1A) of section 89 of the 1972 Act there is hereby prescribed—

    (a) a motor cycle of a class falling within group [category A];
    (b) a period of two years; and
    (c) in relation to a licence granted to the holder of a previous licence which was surrendered, revoked or treated as being revoked, the circumstances—

(i) that the licence would come into force within the period of one year beginning on the date the previous licence was surrendered, revoked, or treated as being revoked; and

(ii) that the licence when granted would be for a period of one month or more.

(2) Paragraph (1) shall not apply in the case of a licence granted in pursuance of section 89(1)(*aa*) or (4) of the 1972 Act.   **[1532]**

NOTES
   Commencement: 3 September 1987.
   Para (1): words in square brackets substituted by SI 1990 No 842, reg 2, Sch 1.
   The 1972 Act: Road Traffic Act 1972.

9. Conditions attached to provisional licences

(1) Subject to paragraphs (2), (3), (4) and (5), the holder of a provisional licence shall comply with the following conditions in relation to motor vehicles of a class which he is authorised to drive by virtue of the provisional licence, that is to say he shall not drive or ride such a motor vehicle—

(a) otherwise than under the supervision of a qualified driver who is present with him in or on the vehicle;

(b) unless a distinguishing mark in the form set out in Schedule 2 is displayed on the vehicle in such manner as to be clearly visible to other persons using the road from within a reasonable distance from the front and from the back of the vehicle;

(c) while it is being used to draw a trailer; and

(d) in the case of a motor bicycle not having attached thereto a side-car, while carrying on it [another person]:

Provided that where the holder of a provisional licence has passed a test which authorises him to be granted a full licence to drive or ride a particular class of vehicles the above-mentioned conditions shall cease to apply in relation to the driving or riding (as the case may be) by him of motor vehicles of that class.

(2) The condition specified in paragraph (1)(a) shall not apply when the holder of the provisional licence—

(a) is undergoing a test . . .;

(b) is driving a vehicle (not being a motor car) constructed to carry only one person and not adapted to carry more than one person;

(c) is driving a vehicle the unladen weight of which does not exceed 815 kilograms, being a vehicle propelled by electrical power, constructed or adapted to carry only one person and constructed or adapted for the carriage of goods or burden of any description;

(d) is driving a road roller the unladen weight of which does not exceed 3050 kilograms, being a vehicle constructed or adapted for the carriage of goods or burden of any description;

(e) is riding a motor bicycle, whether or not having attached thereto a side-car; or

(f) is driving a motor vehicle on a road in an exempted island.

(3) The condition specified in paragraph (1)(c) shall not apply when the holder of the provisional licence is driving an agricultural tractor, nor shall it prevent the holder of a provisional licence from driving an articulated vehicle.

(4) The condition specified in paragraph (1)(d) shall not apply when the

holder of the provisional licence is riding a pedal cycle of the tandem type to which additional means of propulsion by mechanical power are attached.

(5) Any holder of a provisional licence need not comply with this regulation during any period in which—

(a) he is treated, by virtue of regulation 25, for the purposes of section 84(1) and (2) of the 1972 Act as the holder of a licence; or

(b) he is entitled, by virtue of article 2(1) of the Motor Vehicles (International Circulation) Order 1975,

to drive motor vehicles of a class which he is authorised by virtue of the provisional licence.

(6) In this regulation—

"exempted island" means any island outside the mainland of Great Britain from which motor vehicles, unless constructed for special purposes, can at no time be conveniently driven to a road in any other part of Great Britain by reason of the absence of any bridge, tunnel, ford or other way suitable for the passage of such motor vehicles but this expression "exempted island" does not include any of the following islands, namely, the Isle of Wight, St. Mary's (Isles of Scilly), the islands of Arran, Barra, Bute, Great Cumbrae, Islay, the island which comprises Lewis and Harris, Mainland (Orkney), Mainland (Shetland), Mull, the island which comprises North Uist, Benbecula and South Uist, Skye and Tiree;

"leg disability" means a disability which consists solely of any one or more of the following—

(a) the absence of a leg or legs;

(b) the deformity of a leg or legs; or

(c) the loss of use of a leg or legs,

and references to a leg include references to a foot or part of a leg or foot, and the reference to loss of use, in relation to a leg, includes a reference to a deficiency of movement or power in the leg;

"qualified driver" means a person who holds—

(i) a full licence authorising him to drive as a full licence holder a motor vehicle of the same class as the vehicle being driven by the holder of the provisional licence; or

(ii) in the case only of the supervision of the driver of a motor car by a person whose licence is limited, in pursuance of an application in that behalf by him or under section 87(4)(ii) of the 1972 Act solely on account of a leg disability to motor vehicles of a particular construction or design [or class], a full licence authorising him so to drive motor cars of a class falling within the same [category] as the motor car being driven by the holder of the provisional licence [and who, in either such case except in the case of a member of the armed forces of the Crown acting in the course of his duties, is at least 21 years of age and has held the licence referred to above for at least 3 years].   **[1533]**

NOTES

Commencement: 3 September 1987.

Para (1): words in square brackets substituted by SI 1990 No 842, reg 5.

Para (2): words revoked by SI 1990 No 2385, reg 3(b).

Para (6): in definition "qualified driver" first words in square brackets added, and second word in square brackets substituted, by SI 1990 No 842, reg 5; words in final set of square brackets inserted by SI 1990 No 1396, reg 3.

The 1972 Act: Road Traffic Act 1972.

10. Restricted provisional licences

A provisional licence shall be restricted so as to authorise only the driving of
motor vehicles of a class included in [category K] in any case where the applicant
is unable to read in good daylight at a distance of 20.5 metres (with the aid of
glasses or contact lenses if worn) a registration mark which is fixed to a motor
vehicle and comprises letters and figures 79.4 millimetres high. **[1534]**

NOTES
Commencement: 3 September 1987.
Words in square brackets substituted by SI 1990 No 842, reg 2, Sch 1.

11. Full licences not carrying provisional entitlement

(1) Section 88(4) of the 1972 Act shall not apply in the case of a licence which—

    (a) is limited to vehicles of a particular construction or design whether
pursuant to an application in that behalf by the holder of the licence
or pursuant to section 87(4)(ii) of the 1972 Act; or

    (b) authorises its holder to drive vehicles of a class included in [category
K] only.

(2) Section 88(4) of the 1972 Act in its application to a full licence granted
on or after 1st October 1982 which does not authorise the driving of a vehicle of
a class included in [category B, B plus E, B1, C1, C1 plus E, D1, D1 plus E or P]
shall have effect subject to the limitation that it shall not authorise the holder of
such a licence to drive any motor cycle of a class included in [category A] subject
to the same conditions as if he were authorised by a provisional licence to drive
the last mentioned vehicles. **[1535]**

NOTES
Commencement: 3 September 1987.
Words in square brackets substituted by SI 1990 No 842, reg 2, Sch 1.
The 1972 Act: Road Traffic Act 1972.

12. Signature of licences

Every person to whom a licence is granted shall forthwith sign it in ink with his
usual signature. **[1536]**

NOTES
Commencement: 3 September 1987.

13. Lost or defaced licences

(1) If the holder of a licence—

    (a) satisfies the licensing authority that—

        (i) the licence [or its counterpart] has been lost or defaced; and
        (ii) the holder is entitled to continue to hold the licence; and

    (b) pays the fee prescribed by regulation 7,

the licensing authority shall [, on surrender of any licence or counterpart that
has not been lost, issue to him a duplicate licence and counterpart and shall
endorse upon the counterpart any particulars endorsed upon the original licence
or counterpart as the case may be and the duplicates so issued shall have the
same effect as the originals.]

(2) If at any time while a duplicate licence is in force the original licence is found, the person to whom the original licence was issued, if it is in his possession, shall return it to the licensing authority, or if it is not in his possession, but he becomes aware that it is found, shall take all reasonable steps to obtain possession of it and if successful shall return it as soon as may be to the licensing authority.

[(3) The obligation in paragraph (2) shall apply in respect of the counterpart of a licence as if for the words "original licence" in each place where they occur there were substituted the words "original counterpart".]   **[1537]**

NOTES

Commencement: 30 April 1990 (para (3)); 3 September 1987 (remainder).

Para (1): first words in square brackets added, and final words in square brackets substituted, by SI 1990 No 842, reg 6.

Para (3): added by SI 1990 No 842, reg 6.

PART III

TESTS OF COMPETENCE TO DRIVE

Persons by whom tests may be conducted

14. (1) Subject to paragraph (2) tests may be conducted—

(a) by examiners appointed by the licensing authority;

(b) by the Secretary of State for Defence, in so far as concerns the testing of persons in the service of the Crown under his department;

(c) in England and Wales, by the chief officer of any fire brigade maintained in pursuance of the Fire Services Act 1947, or, in Scotland, by the firemaster of such a brigade, in so far as concerns the testing of members of any such brigade or of persons employed in the driving of motor vehicles for the purposes of any such brigade;

(d) by any chief officer of police in so far as concerns the testing:—

(i) of members of a police force; or

(ii) of persons employed in the driving of motor vehicles for police purposes by a police authority or by the Receiver for the Metropolitan Police District;

(e) by the Commissioner of Police of the Metropolis in so far as concerns the testing of any person who is the holder of or is an applicant for a licence to drive a motor cab by virtue of the Metropolitan Public Carriage Act 1869; and

(f) by any person appointed for the purpose by the licensing authority under the provisions of regulation 15.

[(2) Where a person is disqualified until he passes the appropriate driving test, that test shall be conducted either by—

(a) an examiner appointed by the licensing authority; or

(b) the Secretary of State for Defence if the person who has been disqualified is in the service of the Crown under the Ministry of Defence and agrees to be tested by the Secretary of State for Defence.]   **[1538]**

NOTES

Commencement: 3 September 1987 (para (1)); 1 July 1992 (para (2)).

Para (2): substituted by SI 1992 No 1318, reg 4.

15. (1) Any person may apply to the licensing authority to be appointed to conduct tests of persons [(other than persons who have been disqualified until they pass the appropriate driving test)] employed or proposed to be employed by him as drivers, and the licensing authority may, if he is satisfied that—

    (a) the number of drivers of motor vehicles ordinarily employed by the applicant exceeds 250;

    (b) proper arrangements will be made by the applicant for the conduct of such tests in accordance with these Regulations; and

    (c) proper records of such tests and the results thereof will be kept by the applicant,

grant the application subject to any special conditions, which he may think fit to impose.

    (2) The licensing authority may at any time revoke an appointment made by him under this regulation and the authority to conduct tests shall thereupon cease.   **[1539–1540]**

NOTES
Commencement: 3 September 1987.
Para (1): words in square brackets inserted by SI 1992 No 1318, reg 5.

16. (*Revoked by SI 1990 No 2334, reg 5(1), Sch 1.*)

17. Any person appointed by sub-paragraph (b), (c), (d), (e) or (f) of paragraph (1) [or (b) of paragraph (2)] of regulation 14 to conduct tests may, subject to the approval of the licensing authority, authorise suitable persons to act as examiners of those who submit themselves for a test.   **[1541]**

NOTES
Commencement: 3 September 1987.
Words in square brackets inserted by SI 1992 No 1318, reg 6.

18. Appointment for tests and notice of cancellation thereof

(1) A person who desires to take a test to be conducted by an examiner appointed under paragraph (1)(a) [or (2)(a) (as the case may be)] of regulation 14 shall apply for an appointment for such a test to [the licensing authority],

    (2) An applicant for such an appointment as aforesaid shall, when making the application, pay to [the licensing authority] such fee in respect of the test as is [prescribed] and [the licensing authority] shall make any arrangements necessary for the taking of the test.

    (3) For the purposes of paragraph (b) of section 86 of the 1972 Act (which section specifies the only circumstances in which a fee paid on application for an appointment for a test may be repaid) notice cancelling an appointment for such a test as is mentioned in paragraph (1) shall be given to [the licensing authority] not less than [ten] clear days (excluding Saturdays, Sundays, any bank holiday, Christmas Day or Good Friday) before the date of the appointment.

    (4) In paragraph (3) "bank holiday" means a day which is, or is to be, observed as a bank holiday under the Banking and Financial Dealings Act 1971, either generally or in the locality in which [the applicant is due to take his test].   **[1542]**

NOTES

Commencement: 3 September 1987.

Para (1): words in the first pair of square brackets inserted by SI 1992 No 1318, reg 7(a), words in the second pair of square brackets substituted by SI 1990 No 1115, reg 2(3).

Para (2): words in the first and third pairs of square brackets substituted by SI 1990 No 1115, reg 2(3): words in the second pair of square brackets inserted by SI 1992 No 1318 reg 7(b).

Para (3): first words in square brackets substituted, by SI 1990 No 1115, reg 2(3); final word in square brackets substituted by SI 1988 No 965, regs 3, 5.

Para (4): words in square brackets substituted by SI 1990 No 115, reg 2(3).

The 1972 Act: Road Traffic Act 1972.

19. Fees in respect of tests

(1) The following provisions of this regulation shall apply in the case of a person who submits himself for a test [other than an extended driving test] or applies for an appointment for a test [other than an extended driving test].

(2) No fee shall be payable—

    (a) in respect of a test conducted by a person appointed under paragraph (1)(b), (c), (d) or (f) of regulation 14; . . .

    (b) . . .

[(3) The fee payable in respect of a test to be conducted on a day other than a Saturday by an examiner appointed under paragraph 1(a) of regulation 14 is–

    (a) in the case of a test to drive a motor vehicle in category A or category P—

        [(i) £34 if the test is to commence before half past four in the afternoon, and

        (ii) £44 if the test is to commence at or after that time,]

    (b) in the case of any other test—

        [(i) £23.50 if the test is to commence before half past four in the afternoon, and

        (ii) £35 if the test is to commence at or after that time,]

    save that no fee is payable in respect of a test to be taken in an invalid carriage.

(3A) The fee payable in respect of a test to be conducted on a Saturday by an examiner appointed under paragraph 1(a) of regulation 14 is—

    (a) in the case of a test to drive a motor vehicle is category A or category P—

        (i) £26 if the application for the test is made before 3rd June 1991; and

        (ii) £44 if that application is made on or after that date; and

    (b) in the case of any other test—

        (i) £19.50 if the application for the test is made before 3rd June 1991; and

        (ii) £35 if that application is made on or after that date,

    save that no fee is payable in respect of a test to be taken in an invalid carriage.]

(4) . . .

(5) The fee payable in respect of a test to be conducted by a person appointed by paragraph (1)(e) of regulation 14 is [£23.50] and that fee shall be paid to that person to be retained by him as remuneration. **[1543]**

[**19A.** (1) The following provisions of this regulation shall apply in the case of a person who submits himself for an extended driving test or applies for an appointment for such a test.

(2) No fee shall be payable in respect of a test to be conducted by the Secretary of State for Defence.

(3) The fee payable in respect of a test to be conducted on a day other than a Saturday by an examiner appointed under paragraph (2)(a) of regulation 14 is—

(a) in the case of a test to drive a motor vehicle in category A or category P, £57; and

(b) in the case of any other test, £47,

save that no fee is payable in respect of a test to be taken in an invalid carriage.

(4) The fee payable in respect of a test to be conducted on a Saturday by an examiner appointed under paragraph (2)(a) of regulation 14 is—

(a) in the case of a test to drive a motor vehicle in category A or category P, £90; and

(b) in the case of any other test, £75,

save that no fee is payable in respect of a test to be taken in an invalid carriage.]   **[1543A]**

20. Nature of tests

(1) Subject to [paragraph (5), except where a person is disqualified until he passes an extended driving test] the test which a person is required to pass before a licence can be granted to him authorising him to drive a motor vehicle of a class included in any particular [category] shall be a test carried out on a vehicle [(other than a vehicle of a class included in category B plus E, C1 plus E or D1 plus E)] of that class which satisfies the person conducting the test—

(a) that the person taking the test is fully conversant with the contents of the Highway Code;

(b) generally that the person taking the test is competent to drive, without danger to and with due consideration for other users of the road, the vehicle on which he is tested; and

(c) that the person taking the test is able to comply with such of the additional requirements specified in Schedule 4 as are referred to in the third column of Schedule 3 in relation to the [category] which includes the class of vehicle on which he is tested[.]

(d) . . .

. . . . .

[(2) Subject to paragraphs (3) to (5), the extended driving test which a person disqualified under section 36 of the Road Traffic Offenders Act 1988 following conviction of an offence involving obligatory disqualification or following disqualification under section 35 of that Act is required to pass before a licence can be granted to him authorising him to drive a motor vehicle of a class included in any particular category shall be a test—

(a) carried out on a vehicle (other than a vehicle of a class included in category B plus E, C1 plus E or D1 plus E) of that class which satisfies the person conducting the test as to the matters set out in sub-paragraphs (a)–(c) of paragraph (1); and

(b) during which the person being tested is required to drive for a minimum of 60 minutes.

(3) Where a person who is disqualified until he passes the appropriate driving test passes such a test on a vehicle of a class included in any particular category the disqualification shall be deemed to have expired in relation to—

(a) all classes of vehicle included in that particular category unless—

(i) the test is passed on a vehicle with automatic transmission and that particular category is B, C1 or D1, in which case the disqualification shall be deemed to have expired only in relation to such classes of vehicle included in that particular category with automatic transmission, or

(ii) the test is passed on an invalid carriage, in which case the disqualification shall be deemed to have expired only in relation to such classes of vehicle included in that particular category as are invalid carriages, or

(iii) the test is passed on a vehicle which is adapted to meet the particular needs of the person tested, in which case the disqualification shall be deemed to have expired only in relation to such cases of vehicle included in that particular category as are so adapted; and

(b) all classes of vehicle included in any other category which is referred to in the fourth column of Schedule 3 as being an additional category in relation to that particular category unless—

(i) the test is passed on a vehicle with automatic transmission and the additional category is B, C1, D1, B plus E, C1 plus E or D1 plus E, in which case the disqualification shall be deemed to have expired only in relation to such classes of vehicle included in the additional category with automatic transmission, or

(ii) the test is passed on an invalid carriage, or

(iii) the test is passed on a vehicle which is adapted to meet the particular needs of the person tested, in which case the disqualification shall be deemed to have expired only in relation to such classes of vehicle included in the additional category as are so adapted.

(4) Where a person who is disqualified until he passes the appropriate driving test passes such a test on a vehicle of a class included in category B, C1 or D1 the disqualification shall be deemed to have expired in relation to all classes of vehicle included in category C, C plus E, D, and D plus E.

(5) Where a person passes a test on a vehicle of a class included in any particular category he shall be deemed for the purposes of the Road Traffic Act 1988 and of these Regulations competent to drive—

(a) all classes of vehicle included in that particular category unless—

    (i) the test is passed on a vehicle with automatic transmission and that particular category is B, C1 or D1, in which case he shall be deemed for those purposes competent to drive only such classes of vehicle included in that particular category with automatic transmission, or

    (ii) the test is passed on an invalid carriage, in which case he shall be deemed for those purposes competent to drive only such classes of vehicle included in that particular category as are invalid carriages, or

    (iii) the test is passed on a vehicle which is adapted to meet the particular needs of the person tested, in which case he shall be deemed for those purposes competent to drive only such classes of vehicle included in that particular category as are so adapted; and

(b) all classes of vehicle included in any other category which is referred to in the fourth column of Schedule 3 as being an additional category in relation to that particular category unless—

    (i) the test is passed on a vehicle with automatic transmission and the additional category is B, C1, D1, B plus E, C1 plus E or D1 plus E, in which case he shall be deemed for those purposes competent to drive only such classes of vehicle included in the additional category with automatic transmission, or

    (ii) the test is passed on an invalid carriage, or

    (iii) the test is passed on a vehicle which is adapted to meet the particular needs of the person tested, in which case he shall be deemed for those purposes competent to drive only such classes of vehicle included in the additional category as are so adapted.]

(6) . . .

[Provided that where the test was passed on a vehicle with automatic transmission of a class included in category B, C1 or D1 he shall, as regards those categories when listed as additional categories as above, be deemed for those purposes competent to drive only vehicles of a class included in any of those categories with automatic transmission and where the test was passed on an invalid carriage he shall be deemed for those purposes competent to drive only invalid carriages included in any additional category.]

(7) . . .

NOTES

    Commencement: 3 September 1987 (except paras (2)–(5)); 1 July 1992 (paras (2)–(5)).

    Para (1): words in the first and third pairs of square brackets substituted or inserted, and the proviso was revoked, by SI 1992 No 1318, reg 10(1) the words in the second and fourth pairs of square brackets substituted by SI 1990 No 842, regs 2, 7, Sch 1; full stop in square brackets substituted, and words omitted revoked, by SI 1990 No 2334, reg 5(1), (3), Sch 1.

    Paras (2)–(5): substituted by SI 1992 No 1318, reg 10(3).

    Para (6): revoked by SI 1992 No 1318, reg 10(2).

    Para (7): revoked by SI 1990 No 2334, reg 5(1), Sch 1.

21. Production of vehicle for test etc

(1) A person submitting himself for a test shall—

(a) provide for the purposes of the test a motor vehicle [(not being a motor vehicle of a class included in category B plus E, C1 plus E or D1 plus E)], which—

(i) is suitable for the purposes of the test; and

(ii) is not fitted with a device designed to permit a person other than the driver to operate the accelerator, unless any pedal or lever by which the device is operated and any other parts which it may be necessary to remove to make the device inoperable by such a person during the test have been removed;

(b) sign the examiner's attendance record;

[(bb) produce evidence of his identity to the satisfaction of the examiner in the form of—

(i) a licence to drive a motor vehicle granted under Part III or IV of the Road Traffic Act 1988 or under the 1981 Act [bearing his signature],

(ii) a Northern Ireland licence [bearing his signature],

(iii) a British external licence [bearing his signature],

(iv) a British Forces licence [bearing his signature],

(v) a driving permit issued by the service authorities of a visiting force specified in Article 3 of the Motor Vehicles (International Circulation) Order 1975 [bearing his signature],

(vi) a Convention driving permit as defined in Article 2(7) of that Order [bearing his signature],

(vii) an exchangeable licence [bearing his signature],

(viii) any other document falling within the definition of "domestic driving permit" in that Article which bears the holder's name in the roman alphabet, his photograph and his signature,

(ix) a passport [bearing his signature], or

(x) an identity card issued by his employer which bears the holder's name in the roman alphabet, his photograph and his signature;]

(c) except when the test is for a motor bicycle, allow to travel in the vehicle mentioned in paragraph (1)(a) during the test—

(i) the person authorised to conduct the test; and

(ii) any person authorised by the licensing authority to attend the test for the purpose of supervising it or otherwise; and

(d) when the test is for a motor bicycle, allow the attendance of—

(i) the person authorised to conduct the test; and

(ii) any person authorised by the licensing authority for the purpose of supervising the test or otherwise.

(2) Where a person submitting himself for a test fails—

(a) to produce a vehicle which complies with sub-paragraph (a) of paragraph (1); or

(b) to comply with any of the provisions of sub-paragraphs (b), [(bb)], (c) and (d) of that paragraph,

the examiner may refuse to conduct the test. **[1545]**

NOTES

Commencement: 3 September 1987.

Para (1); words in square brackets in para (1)(a) inserted by SI 1992 No 1318, reg 11: para (1)(bb) inserted by SI 1990 No 1396, reg 4, and amended by SI 1991 No 485, reg 5.

Para (2): words in square brackets added by SI 1990 No 1396, reg 4.

22. Evidence of results of tests

(1) A person who passes a test shall be furnished with a certificate to that effect in the form (adapted as the case may require) set out in Part I of Schedule 6.

(2) A person who fails to pass a test shall be furnished with a statement to that effect in the form (adapted as the case may require) set out in Part II of Schedule 6.

(3) . . .

(4) An applicant for a licence who before the licence is granted is required to satisfy the licensing authority that he has passed a test shall at the time when he applies for the licence deliver the certificate furnished to him under paragraph (1) to the licensing authority for retention.

(5) . . . **[1546]**

NOTES
 Commencement: 3 September 1987.
 Paras (3), (5): revoked by SI 1990 No 2334, reg 5(1), Sch 1.

23. Period of ineligibility for a subsequent test

(1) Subject to the provisions of section 85(3) of the 1972 Act the period during which a person who has submitted himself for a test and failed to pass that test shall be ineligible to submit himself for another test on a vehicle of a class included in the same [category] shall be one month.

(2) . . . **[1547]**

NOTES
 Commencement: 3 September 1987.
 Para (1): word in square brackets substituted by SI 1990 No 842, reg 2, Sch 1.
 Para (2): revoked by SI 1990 No 2334, reg 5(1), Sch 1.
 The 1972 Act: Road Traffic Act 1972.

[PART IIIA

APPROVED TRAINING COURSES FOR MOTOR CYCLISTS

23A. Persons by whom approved training courses may be provided.

(1) Approved training courses for motor cyclists may be provided—

    (a) by the Secretary of State for Defence, in so far as concerns the training of persons in the service of the Crown under his department;

    (b) in England and Wales, by the chief officer of any fire brigade maintained in pursuance of the Fire Services Act 1947 or, in Scotland, by the firemaster of such a brigade, in so far as concerns the training of members of any such brigade or of persons employed in the driving of motor vehicles for the purposes of any such brigade;

    (c) by any chief officer of police, in so far as concerns the training of members of a police force or of persons employed in the driving of motor vehicles for police purposes by a police authority; and

    (d) by any person approved for the purpose by the licensing authority.

(2) Any person may apply to the licensing authority to be approved to provide an approved training course for motor cyclists under sub-paragraph (d) of paragraph (1) above, and the licensing authority may, if satisfied that—

(a) proper arrangements will be made by the applicant for the conduct of the course in accordance with these Regulations; and

(b) proper records of the course and results thereof will be kept by the applicant, grant the application subject to any conditions which it thinks fit to impose.

(3) Subject to paragraphs (4) to (10) below, a person who provides an approved training course for motor cyclists in pursuance of paragraph (1) above may authorise motor cycle instructors to conduct the motor cycle training on his behalf.

(4) A motor cycle instructor may be authorised under paragraph (3) above if and only if—

(a) he satisfies the conditions set out in sub-paragraphs (a), (b) and (c) of paragraph (5) below, in which case, on being authorised, he shall be known as a certified instructor; or

(b) he satisfies the conditions set out in sub-paragraphs (a) and (c) of paragraph (5) below, in which case, on being authorised, he shall be known as an assistant instructor.

(5) The conditions referred to in paragraph (4) above are that—

(a) he holds a full licence to drive vehicles in category A; and

(b) he has held that licence for a period of, or for periods amounting to, at least 2 years; and

(c) either—

(i) he has completed successfully the licensing authority's assessment course for motor cycle instructors, or

(ii) he has been trained by a motor cycle instructor who has completed such a course successfully.

(6) Subject, in the case of a certified instructor, to paragraphs (7) to (9) below, and in the case of an assistant instructor, to paragraphs (7) and (8) below—

(a) a certified instructor shall be entitled to conduct the training of motor cyclists and, provided he has completed successfully the licensing authority's assessment course for motor cycle instructors, to train other motor cycle instructors to conduct the training of motor cyclists; and

(b) an assistant instructor shall be entitled to conduct the training of motor cyclists save that he shall not be entitled to conduct the training of motor cyclists in practical on-road riding skills.

(7) Certified and assistant instructors shall not be entitled to conduct any training until—

(a) the person giving the authorisation under paragraph (3) above has notified the licensing authority of the authorisation in writing; and

(b) the licensing authority has approved the authorisation in writing.

(8) Where the licensing authority does not approve an authorisation given under paragraph (3) above that authorisation shall be of no effect.

(9) A certified instructor shall not be entitled to conduct training as a certified instructor unless there is in force in respect of him a certificate, which shall be renewable every four years, issued by the licensing authority and obtained by the person who has authorised him under paragraph (3) above, in the form set out in Schedule 7.

(10) An assistant instructor who, subsequent to his authorisation under paragraph (3) above, satisfies the condition set out in sub-paragraph (b) of paragraph (5) above, shall become a certified instructor on satisfying the condition, but he shall not be entitled to conduct training as a certified instructor unless paragraph (9) above is satisfied.

(11) When conducting motor cycle training a certified instructor shall carry with him the certificate issued in respect of him by the licensing authority.

(12) A person who is approved to provide an approved training course for motor cyclists in pursuance of sub-paragraph (d) of paragraph (1) above and who satisfies the conditions set out in sub-paragraphs (a), (b) and (c) of paragraph (5) above shall, in relation to training conducted by himself, be deemed for the purposes of this Part of these Regulations to be a certified instructor, and shall be entitled to conduct training as a certified instructor provided there is in force in respect of him a certificate, renewable every four years and issued to him by the licensing authority, in the form set out in Schedule 7, and he complies with paragraph (11) above.

(13) A person who is approved to provide an approved training course for motor cyclists in pursuance of sub-paragraph (d) of paragraph (1) above and who satisfies the conditions set out in sub-paragraphs (a) and (c) of paragraph (5) above shall, in relation to training conducted by himself, be deemed for the purposes of this Part of these Regulations to be an assistant instructor and shall be entitled to conduct the training of motor cyclists save that he shall not be entitled to conduct the training of motor cyclists in practical on-road riding skills.

(14) The licensing authority may at any time by notice in writing—

(a) withdraw an approval made under sub-paragraph (d) of paragraph (1) above; or
(b) revoke an authorisation given under paragraph (3) above.

(15) Where the licensing authority withdraws an approval made under sub-paragraph (d) of paragraph (1) above, the approval and the authority of any

person to act as a certified or assistant instructor on behalf of the person whose approval has been withdrawn shall cease forthwith; and where the licensing authority revokes an authorisation given under paragraph (3) above, the authority of the person whose authorisation is revoked to act as a certified or assistant instructor, as the case may be, shall cease forthwith.

(16) Where the licensing authority withdraws an approval made under sub-paragraph (d) of paragraph (1) above, the person whose approval is withdrawn shall, within 28 days from the date of that withdrawal, return to the licensing authority all certificates which were supplied to him under paragraphs (9) and (12) above and all forms for certificates which were supplied to him under regulation 23B(5) below.

(17) Where the licensing authority revokes an authorisation given under paragraph (3) above in respect of a certified instructor, or where a certified instructor authorised under paragraph (3) above ceases to conduct training on behalf of the person who authorised him, the certified instructor shall return to the person who authorised him the certificate he was required to carry under paragraph (11) above as soon as is reasonably practicable; and, on receiving it, the person who authorised him shall return that certificate to the licensing authority immediately.]   **[1547A]**

NOTES
Commencement: 1 December 1990.
Part IIIA (regs 23A–23H) inserted by SI 1990 No 2334, reg 4.

[23B. Nature and approval of training courses

(1) A training course for motor cyclists shall comprise the elements A to E set out in Schedule 8 and shall be approved by the licensing authority.

(2) Before any practical training is given to motor cyclists on an approved training course the requirements of paragraphs 1 and 2 of Schedule 8 must be fulfilled.

(3) To complete an approved training course successfully, a motor cyclist must satisfy the person who provides the course of each of the following in sequence, commencing with sub-paragraph (a)—

(a) that he has fulfilled the requirements set out in paragraph 3 of Schedule 8; and
(b) that he can execute the manoeuvres set out in paragraph 4 of Schedule 8; and
(c) that the requirements of paragraph 5 of Schedule 8 are fulfilled; and

(d) that he rides safely on roads in a variety of road traffic situations, including as many as practicable of those set out in paragraph 6 of Schedule 8.

(4) On the successful completion of an approved training course a motor cyclist shall be issued with a certificate of completion signed on behalf of the person providing the course by a certified instructor, who may be the person providing the course, on a form supplied supplied by the licensing authority as prescribed in Schedule 9.

(5) Forms for certificates evidencing the successful completion of an

approved training course shall be supplied by the licensing authority to those authorised to provide approved training courses pursuant to paragraph (1) of regulation 23A above at a charge of [£5.00] per form.]   **[1547B]**

NOTES
Commencement: 1 December 1990.
See the note to reg 23A ante.
Para (5): figure in square brackets substituted by SI 1992 No 1757, reg 5.

[**23C.** When, during an approved training course, motor cyclists are receiving practical on site training or are undertaking practical on site riding there shall be no more than 4 motor cyclists in the charge of any one certified or assistant instructor at any one time; and when, during such a course, motor cyclists are undertaking practical on-road riding there shall be no more than 2 motor cyclists in the charge of any one certified instructor at any one time.]   **[1547C]**

NOTES
Commencement: 1 December 1990.
See the note to reg 23A ante.

[23D. Exemptions and Transitional and Supplementary Provisions

(1) For the purposes of regulations 23E, 23F, 23G and 23H below—

"provisional licence holder" means a person who holds a valid provisional licence under which he drives and which, subject to section 97(3) of the Road Traffic Act 1988, authorises him to drive a vehicle of a class included in category A or category P; and
"provisional entitlement holder" means a person who holds and drives under a valid licence which, not being a provisional or full licence to drive a vehicle of a class included in category A or category P, authorises him (by virtue of Section 98(2) of the Road Traffic Act 1988) to drive a class of vehicle in one of those categories as if he were a provisional licence holder.

(2) For the purposes of regulation 23G below "exempted island" means an island outside the mainland of Great Britain other than—

(a) the Isle of Wight, Lewis and Harris, North Uist, Benbecula and South Uist, Mainland Orkney, Mainland Shetland and Skye; and
(b) an island from which motor vehicles, not constructed for special purposes, can at some time be conveniently driven to a road in any part of the mainland of Great Britain because of the presence of a bridge, tunnel, ford, or other way suitable for the passage of such motor vehicles.]   **[1547D]**

NOTES
Commencement: 1 December 1990.
See the note to reg 23A ante.

[**23E.**—(1) A person who was a provisional licence holder immediately before 1st December 1990 shall be exempt from the restriction imposed by section 97(3)(e) of the Road Traffic Act 1988 during the validity of that licence [and if that licence has been exchanged for a full licence entitling him to drive a vehicle of a class included in category B and he has not, after that exchange, been disqualified until he passes the appropriate driving test, section 98(3)(c) of the Road Traffic Act 1988 shall not apply to him].

(2) A provisional licence holder who has passed Part I of the test for motor bicycles shall be exempt from the restriction imposed by section 97(3)(e) and from the requirement imposed by section 89(2A) of the Road Traffic Act 1988 for the period during which the certificate furnished to him under regulation 22(1) is valid.

(3) Section 98(3)(c) of the Road Traffic Act 1988 shall not apply to a person who was a provisional entitlement holder immediately before 1st December 1990 [unless he has been disqualified until he passes the appropriate driving test] or to a provisional entitlement holder who has passed Part I of the test for motor bicycles for the period during which the certificate furnished to him under regulation 22(1) is valid.

(4) A provisional entitlement holder who has passed Part I of the test for motor bicycles shall be exempt from the requirement imposed by section 89(2A) of the Road Traffic Act 1988 for the period during which the certificate furnished to him under regulation 22(1) is valid.

(5) A person who is disqualified until he passes the appropriate driving test shall be exempt from the restriction imposed by section 97(3)(e) and the requirement imposed by section 89(2A) of the Road Traffic Act 1988 if, before the date on which he is disqualified, he has passed a test to drive a vehicle of a class included in category A or on a vehicle of a class included in category P].

[1547E]

NOTES
Commencement: 1 December 1990 (except para (5)); 1 July 1992 (para (5)).
See the note to reg 23A ante.
Paras (1), (3): words in square brackets inserted by SI 1992 No 1318, reg 12(a), (b).
Para (5): added by SI 1992 No 1318 reg 12(c).

[**23F.** A person who was a provisional licence or provisional entitlement holder immediately before 1st December 1990 and who applies to take and takes a test of competence to drive a vehicle of a class included in category P or a motor bicycle fitted with a side-car on or before 31st May 1991 shall be exempt from the requirement imposed by section 89 (2A) of the Road Traffic Act 1988.]

[1547F]

NOTES
Commencement: 1 December 1990.
See the note to reg 23A ante.

[**23G.**—(1) A provisional licence or provisional entitlement holder who is resident on an exempted island shall be exempt from the requirement imposed by section 89(2A) of the Road Traffic Act 1988 in respect of a test of competence to drive a vehicle of a class included in category A or category P taken, or to be taken, on an island, whether or not that island is an exempted island.

(2) A provisional licence holder who is resident on an exempted island shall be exempt from the restriction imposed by section 97(3)(e) of the Road Traffic Act 1988 when he satisfies either of the conditions set out in paragraph (4) below.

(3) Section 98(3)(c) of the Road Traffic Act 1988 shall not apply to a provisional entitlement holder who is resident on an exempted island when he satisfies either of the conditions set in paragraph (4) below.

(4) The conditions referred to in paragraphs (2) and (3) above are—

    (a) that the holder is driving on an exempted island, whether or not he is also resident on that island; or

    (b) that the holder is driving on a non-exempted island for the purpose of getting to or from an approved training course or to a place where he is to take, or from a place where he has taken, a test of competence to drive a vehicle of a class included in category A or category P.]

[1547G]

NOTES
Commencement: 1 December 1990.
See the note to reg 23A ante.

[**23H.** Without prejudice to regulations 23F and 23G(1) above a person who, immediately before 1st December 1990, is a provisional licence or provisional entitlement holder may take Part I of the test for motor bicycles instead of an approved training course if, but for this provision, he would be required to take an approved training course, provided he takes Part I of the test for motor bicycles on or before 31st May 1991.] **[1547H]**

NOTES
Commencement: 1 December 1990.
See the note to reg 23A ante.

PART IV
SUPPLEMENTARY

24. Disabilities

(1) The following disabilities are prescribed for the purposes of section 87(1) of the 1972 Act—

    (a) epilepsy;

    (b) severe mental handicap;

    (c) liability to sudden attacks of disabling giddiness or fainting, other than such attacks falling within paragraph (1)(d);

    (d) liability to sudden attacks of disabling giddiness or fainting which are caused by any disorder or defect of the heart as a result of which the applicant for the licence or, as the case may be, the holder of the licence has a device implanted in his body, being a device which, by operating on the heart so as to regulate its action, is designed to correct the disorder or defect; and

(e) inability to read in good daylight (with the aid of glasses or contact lenses if worn) a registration mark fixed to a motor vehicle and containing letters and figures 79.4 millimetres high at a distance of—

    (i) 20.5 metres, in any case except that mentioned below; or

    (ii) 12.3 metres, in the case of an applicant for a licence authorising the driving of vehicles of a class included in [category K] only.

(2) Epilepsy is prescribed for the purposes of section 87(3)(b) of the 1972 Act and an applicant for a licence suffering from epilepsy shall satisfy the conditions that—

    (a) he shall have been free from any epileptic attack during the period of two years immediately preceding the date when the licence is [granted]; or

    [(b) in the case of an applicant who has had an epileptic attack or attacks only whilst asleep during that period—

        (i) he shall have had an epileptic attack whilst asleep more than three years before the date the licence is granted; and

        (ii) he shall have had no epileptic attack or attacks whilst awake but only whilst asleep since he had that attack; and]

    (c) the driving of a vehicle by him in pursuance of the licence is not likely to be a source of danger to the public.

(3) The disability prescribed in paragraph (1)(d) is prescribed for the purpose of section 87(3)(b) of the 1972 Act and an applicant for a licence suffering from that disability shall satisfy the conditions that—

    (a) the driving of a vehicle by him in pursuance of the licence is not likely to be a source of danger to the public; and

    (b) he has made adequate arrangements to receive regular medical supervision by a cardiologist (being a supervision to be continued throughout the period of the licence) and is conforming to those arrangements.

(4) The following disability is prescribed for the purposes of paragraphs (a) and (c) of section 87(3) of the 1972 Act namely a disability which is not progressive in nature and which consists solely of any one or more of the following:—

    (a) the absence of one or more limbs;

    (b) the deformity of one or more limbs; and

    (c) the loss of use of one or more limbs.

(5) The disability prescribed in paragraph (1)(e) is prescribed for the purposes of section 87A(2)(b) of the 1972 Act.

(6)(a) In paragraph (1)(b), the expression "severe mental handicap" means a state of arrested or incomplete development of mind which includes severe impairment of intelligence and social functioning.

    (b) In paragraph (3)(b), the expression "cardiologist" means a registered medical practitioner who specialises in disorders or defects of the heart and who, in that connection, holds a hospital appointment.

    (c) In paragraph (4), references to a limb include references to a part of a limb, and the reference to loss of use, in relation to a limb, includes a reference to a deficiency of limb movement or power.

[(7) Subject to paragraph (8), the circumstances prescribed for the purposes of subsection (5) of section 94 of the Road Traffic Act 1988, under subsection

(4) of that section, are that the person who is an applicant for, or holder of, a licence—

    (a) has been disqualified by an order of a court by reason that the proportion of alcohol in his breath, blood or urine exceeded the limit prescribed by virtue of section 5 of the Road Traffic Act 1988 by at least two and a half times or that he failed, without reasonable excuse, to provide a specimen when required to do so pursuant to section 7 of that Act; or

    (b) has been disqualified by an order of a court on two or more occasions within any period of 10 years by reason that the proportion of alcohol in his breath, blood or urine exceeded the limit prescribed by virtue of section 5 of the Road Traffic Act 1988 or that he was unfit to drive through drink contrary to section 4 of that Act.

    (8) In paragraph (7)(a) the order of the court shall have been made on or after 1st June 1990 and in paragraph (7)(b) at least the last such order shall have been made on or after 1st June 1990.] **[1548]**

NOTES
> Commencement: 1 June 1990 (paras (7), (8)); 3 September 1987 (remainder).
> Para (1): words in square brackets substituted by SI 1990 No 842, reg 2, Sch 1.
> Para 2: words in square brackets substituted by SI 1989 No 373, reg 2.
> Paras (7), (8): added by SI 1990 No 842, reg 8.
> The 1972 Act: Road Traffic Act 1972.

25. Persons who become resident in Great Britain

(1) A person who becomes resident in Great Britain shall during the period of one year after he becomes so resident be treated for the purposes of section 84(1) and (2) of the 1972 Act as the holder of a licence authorising him to drive motor vehicles of the classes which he is authorised to drive by any permit of which he is a holder, if he satisfies the conditions specified in paragraph (2).

    (2) The conditions mentioned in paragraph (1) are that—

    (a) the person who becomes resident shall be the holder of a permit which is for the time being valid; and

    (b) he is not disqualified for holding or obtaining a licence in Great Britain.

    (3) The following enactments relating to licences or licence holders shall apply in relation to permits or the holders of permits (as the case may be) subject to modifications in accordance with the following provisions:—

    [(a) section 47(2) of the Road Traffic Offenders Act 1988 (which relates to the powers and duties of a court when it orders a disqualification or an endorsement) shall apply in relation to the holder of a permit, only where the court has ordered him to be disqualified and as if for the words "send the licence" onwards there were substituted the words "send the permit", on its being produced to the court, to the Secretary of State who shall keep the permit until the disqualification has expired or been removed or the person entitled to the permit leaves Great Britain and in any case has made a demand in writing for its return to him;

    (b) section 7 of the Road Traffic Offenders Act 1988 (production of licence and counterpart to court) shall apply as if the references to a licence were references to a permit and as if the words after paragraph (c) thereof were omitted;

(c) section 27(1), (2) and (3) of the Road Traffic Offenders Act 1988 (production of licence and counterpart) shall apply as if the references to a licence were references to a permit, but with the omission—

    (i) of any reference to the counterpart of a licence,

    (ii) in subsection (1) of the words ", before making any order under section 44 of this Act,", and

    (iii) in subsection (3) of the words ", unless he satisfies the Court that he has applied for a new licence and has not received it";

(d) section 42(5) of the Road Traffic Offenders Act 1988 (which relates to the duty of a court when it orders a disqualification to be removed) shall apply in relation to the holder of a permit as if for the words "endorsed on the counterpart of the licence" onwards there were substituted the words "notified to the Secretary of State";

(e) section 164(1), (6) and (8) of the Road Traffic Act 1988 (which authorise a police constable to require the production of a licence and its counterpart) shall apply as if the references to a licence were references to a permit and any reference to a counterpart of a licence were omitted; and

(f) section 173 of the Road Traffic Act 1988 (forgery of documents, etc) shall apply as if the reference in paragraph (a) of subsection (2) of that section to any licence under any Part of that Act were a reference to a permit and the reference, in the case of a licence to drive, to any counterpart were omitted.]

(4) In this regulation "permit" means a "domestic driving permit" a "Convention driving permit" or a "British Forces (BFG) driving licence" as defined in article 2(6) of the Motor Vehicles (International Circulation) Order 1975 not being a domestic driving permit or a British Forces (BFG) driving licence in the case of which any order made, or having effect as if made, by the Secretary of State is for the time being in force under article 2(5) of that Order.

[1549]

NOTES
Commencement: 3 September 1987.
Para (3): sub-paras (a)-(f) substituted by SI 1990 No 842, reg 9.
The 1972 Act: Road Traffic Act 1972.

26. Statement of date of birth

The circumstances in which a person specified in section 161(1) of the 1972 Act shall, on being required by a police constable, state his date of birth are as follows:—

(1) where that person fails to produce forthwith for examination his licence on being required to do so by a police constable under that section; or

(2) where, on being so required, that person produces a licence—

    (a) which the police constable in question has reason to suspect—

        (i) was not granted to that person;

        (ii) was granted to that person in error; or

        (iii) contains an alteration in the particulars entered on the licence (other than as described in paragraph (b) below) made with intent to deceive; or

    (b) in which the driver number has been altered, removed or defaced [; or

(2A) where that person is a person specified in subsection (1)(d) of that section and the police constable has reason to suspect that he is under 21 years of age.]

(3) In paragraph (2), "driver number" means the number described as the driver number in the licence.   **[1550]**

NOTES
    Commencement: 3 September 1987.
    The 1972 Act: Road Traffic Act 1972.
    The words in square brackets were inserted by SI 1990 No 1396, reg 5.

27. Learner motor cycles

For the purposes of section 88(2)(c) of the 1972 Act (provisional licence not to authorise the driving of certain motor cycles) the first use of a motor cycle shall be taken to have occurred on the date of first use as determined in accordance with paragraph (2) of regulation 3.   **[1551]**

NOTES
    Commencement: 3 September 1987.
    The 1972 Act: Road Traffic Act 1972.

28. Invalid carriages

For the purposes of Part III of the 1972 Act and all regulations made thereunder the maximum weight specified in section 190(5) of that Act (which defines the expression "invalid carriage" for the purposes of the Act) shall be varied from 254 kilograms to 510 kilograms.   **[1552]**

NOTES
    Commencement: 3 September 1987.
    The 1972 Act: Road Traffic Act 1972.

29. Entitlement to groups

[(1) Subject to paragraphs (2) and (3), the categories of vehicles specified in the second column of the table in Schedule 3 are hereby designated as groups for the purposes of section 89(1)(a) and (b) of the Road Traffic Act 1988.

(2) In the case of a person who has passed a test in a vehicle with automatic transmission of a class included in category B, C1 or D1 or who has held a licence restricted to vehicles with automatic transmission of any such class, the categories of vehicles designated as groups by paragraph (1) are, in the case of categories B, C1 and D1, restricted to vehicles of any class with automatic transmission.

(3) In the case of a person who has passed a test in an invalid carriage, the categories of vehicles designated as groups by paragraph (1) are restricted to invalid carriages in such categories.]   **[1553]**

NOTES
    Commencement: 1 June 1990.
    Substituted by SI 1990 No 842, reg 10.

30. Effect of changes in classification of vehicles by reason of changed definition of "moped"

(1) In licences (whether full or provisional) issued before 1st August 1977—

(a) any reference to motor vehicles of group E shall be construed as a reference to motor vehicles of new group E;

(b) any reference to motor vehicles of group L shall be construed as reference to motor vehicles of new group L;

(c) any reference to motor vehicles of any other group the constitution of which was affected by the amendments made by the Motor Vehicles (Driving Licences) (Amendment) Regulations 1976 shall be construed as references to motor vehicles of the group in question as so amended in constitution; and

(d) any reference to a moped shall be construed by reference to the revised definition of "moped".

(2) In relation to an application for the grant of a licence by a person who—

(a) before 1st August 1977 held a licence granted under Part III of the 1972 Act, or under any enactment which that Part replaced, or under a relevant external law (as defined in section 85(1) of the 1972 Act) to drive motor vehicles of a class included in old group E; or

(b) before that date passed a test to drive motor vehicles of a class included in old group E or a test which by virtue of regulation 20(6) is regarded as a test to drive such motor vehicles,

and in relation to any licence issued in pursuance of such applications, the licence which he held, or the test which he passed, before that date shall for the purposes of section 85(1) and (4) of the 1972 Act (restrictions on grant of licences etc.) be regarded as a licence or test (as the case may be) to drive vehicles of a class included in new group E.

(3) A person whose entitlement to the grant of a licence to drive vehicles of new group E is preserved by this regulation may, not withstanding anything in section 84(1) and (2) of the 1972 Act (drivers of motor vehicles to have driving licences), at any time pending the grant of such a licence to him drive, and be employed in driving, such vehicles if—

(a) his application in accordance with section 88(1)(a) of the 1972 Act (provisions as to grant of licences), together with the fee prescribed under that section, for the grant of such a licence has been received by the Secretary of State;

(b) he satisfies the requirements of subsection (1)(b) and (c) of that section;

(c) he is not disqualified by reason of age or otherwise for obtaining the licence;

(d) he is not a person to whom the Secretary of State is required by section 87(2) of the 1972 Act (requirement as to physical fitness of drivers) to refuse to grant the licence;

(e) in the case of a person on whom notice under subsection (4) of that section, or any enactment which that provision replaced, has been served, the vehicles are of the particular construction and design [or class] specified in the notice; and

(f) he complies, in relation to that driving, with such of the conditions specified in regulation 8(1) as will apply to the driving of those vehicles by him under the authority of that licence, when granted.

(4) In this regulation, references to "old group" and "new group" followed by a letter are references respectively to the group in question as constituted before and after the coming into operation of the Motor Vehicles (Driving Licences) (Amendment) Regulations 1976, and the reference to the revised

definition of "moped" is a reference to the definition of that word in regulation 3(1), which was inserted in regulation 3(1) of the Motor Vehicles (Driving Licences) Regulations 1976 by the said amendment Regulations. **[1554]**

NOTES
Commencement: 3 September 1987.
Para (3): words in square brackets added by SI 1990 No 842, reg 2, Sch 1.
The 1972 Act: Road Traffic Act 1972.

31. Effect of changes in classification of vehicles by reason of changed weight limit for motor tricycles

(1) In licences (whether full or provisional) issued before the date of re-classification any reference to motor vehicles of a group identified by a letter shall be construed for all purposes on and after that date as a reference to motor vehicles of the new group as well as the old group identified by that letter.

(2) In relation to an application for the grant of a licence coming into force on or after the date of re-classification by a person who—

    (a) before that date held a licence granted under Part III of the 1972 Act, or under any enactment which that Part III replaced, or under a relevant external law (as defined in section 85(1) of the 1972 Act) to drive motor vehicles of a class included in an old group; or

    (b) before that date passed a test to drive motor vehicles of a class included in an old group or a test which by virtue of regulation 20(6) is regarded as a test to drive such vehicles,

and in relation to any licence issued in pursuance of such an application, the licence which he held, or the test which he passed, before that date shall, for the purposes of section 85(1) and (4) of the 1972 Act (restrictions on the grant of licences etc.), be regarded as a licence or test, as the case may be, to drive vehicles of a class included in the new group as well as the old group identified by the same letter.

(3) In this regulation references to "old group" and "new group" are references respectively to the group in question as constituted before and after the date of re-classification and "the date of re-classification" refers respectively to 12th August 1981 when the weight limit for motor tricycles in group C was increased to 425 kilograms unladen and 2nd September 1985 when that weight limit was increased to 450 kilograms unladen. **[1555]**

NOTES
Commencement: 3 September 1987.
The 1972 Act: Road Traffic Act 1972.

32. Effect of changes in classification of vehicles by reason of deletion of group M

(1) The deletion of group M in Schedule 3 by regulation 9(e) of the Motor Vehicles (Driving Licences) (Amendment) (No. 4) Regulations 1982 shall not affect—

    (a) any entitlement of a holder of a licence for vehicles of a class included in that group granted before the date of coming into operation of the said regulation 9(e) to drive vehicles of that class, and vehicles of any other class included in that group, in pursuance of the licence; or

    (b) any such licence ceasing to be in force whether before or after that date, or any right that the person who held the licence would have had to the grant of a further licence on or after that date authorising him to drive such vehicles.

(2) In licences (whether full or provisional) issued before the date of coming into operation of regulation 9(e) of the Motor Vehicles (Driving Licences) (Amendment) (No. 4) Regulations 1982 any reference to groups A or B shall be construed for all purposes on and after that date as a reference to the groups as prescribed in these Regulations on and after that date.   **[1556]**

NOTES

Commencement: 3 September 1987.

[33. Effect of change in classification from groups to categories

(1) [Subject to paragraph (4) below,] In licences (whether full or provisional) issued before 1st June 1990 any reference (including a reference construed in accordance with regulations 30, 31 and 32) to motor vehicles of a group specified in column (1) of the table in this regulation shall be construed as a reference to motor vehicles of the category specified opposite thereto in column (2) of that table and licences to drive vehicles of a class included in such a group shall authorise the holder to drive motor vehicles of a class included in that category in addition to motor vehicles of a class included in that group.

(2) A person who before 1st June 1990 has passed or is regarded as having passed a test to drive motor vehicles of a class included in a group specified in column (1) of the table in this regulation shall also be regarded as having passed a test to drive motor vehicles of a class included in the category specified opposite thereto in column (2) of that table.

(3) In this regulation "group" has the same meaning as it had in these Regulations before they were amended by the Motor Vehicles (Driving Licences) (Amendment) Regulations 1990.

Table

(1) *Group*	(2) *Category*
A	B
B	B, limited to vehicles with automatic transmission
C	B1
D	A
E	P
F	F
G	G
H	H
J	B1, limited to invalid carriages
K	K
L	L
M	Trolley vehicles used for the carriage of passengers, with more than 16 seats in addition to the driver's seat
N	N.

[(4) Paragraph (1) above shall not authorise a person to drive motor vehicles used for the carriage of passengers with more than 16 seats in addition to the driver's seat on or after 1st April 1992.]   **[1557]**

NOTES

Commencement: 1 June 1990.
Added by SI 1990 No 842, reg 11.
Para (1): amended by SI 1991 No 485, reg 6.

Para (4): added by SI 1991 No 485, reg 6.

[34. Effect of change in classification on entitlement to drive large buses

(1)–(3) . . .

(4) The provisions of section 98(2) of the Road Traffic Act 1988 shall not apply so far as to confer on a person who holds a full licence to drive motor vehicles of certain classes only, entitlement to drive a motor vehicle used for the carriage of passengers, with more than 16 seats in addition to the driver's seat.

(5) A person may not drive a vehicle by virtue of this regulation if he could not, by reason of the provisions of section 101 of the Road Traffic Act 1988, lawfully hold a licence to drive such a vehicle.

[(6) Paragraph (2) above shall cease to have effect on [1st October 1992].]]

[1558]

NOTES
Commencement: 1 June 1990.
Added by SI 1990 No 842, reg 11.
Para (1): revoked by SI 1991 No 485, reg 7(a).
Para (2): revoked by virtue of para (6) above.
Para (3): revoked by SI 1991 No 485, reg 7(a).
Para (6): substituted by SI 1991 No 485, reg 7(b), and words in square brackets substituted by SI 1992 No 539.
The 1981 Act: Public Passenger Vehicles Act 1981.

35. Effect of change in classification on entitlement to drive heavy goods vehicles to which Part IV of the Road Traffic Act 1988 does not apply

[The holder of a licence to drive vehicles in categories B and C1 may also drive a heavy goods vehicle of any of the classes listed in regulation 29 of the Heavy Goods Vehicles (Drivers' Licences) Regulations 1977.]   **[1559]**

NOTES
Commencement: 1 June 1990.
Added by SI 1990 No 842, reg 11.

SCHEDULES
SCHEDULE 1
Regulation 2

REGULATIONS REVOKED

. . .

[1560]

NOTES
Commencement: 3 September 1987.
This Schedule lists the regulations revoked by reg 2.

SCHEDULE 2
Regulation 9(1)

DIAGRAM OF DISTINGUISHING MARK TO BE DISPLAYED ON A MOTOR VEHICLE BEING DRIVEN UNDER A PROVISIONAL LICENCE

[1561]

NOTES
Commencement: 3 September 1987.

SCHEDULE 3

Regulations 20, 29

[Categories of Motor Vehicles for Driving Test Purposes]

(1) Category	(2) Class of Vehicle included in the Category	(3) Additional Requirements	(4) Additional Categories Covered
A	Motor bicycle (with or without side-car) but excluding any vehicle included in category K or P.	1, 2, 3, 4, 5, 6, 9, 10, 12 and 13	B1 and P
B	Motor vehicle with a maximum authorised mass not exceeding 3·5 tonnes and not more than 8 seats in addition to the driver's seat, not included in any other category and including such a vehicle drawing a trailer with a maximum authorised mass not exceeding 750 kg.	1, 2, 3, 4, 5, 6, 7, . . . 9 and 10	B plus E, B1, C1, C1 plus E, D1, D1 plus E, F, K, L, N and P
B1	Motor tricycle [with an unladen mass not exceeding 500 kg and with a maximum design speed exceeding 50 km per hour] but excluding any vehicle included in category K, L or P.	1, 2, 3, 4, 5, 6, 9 and 10 and, if fitted with a means for reversing, 7 and 8	K, L and P
C1	Motor vehicle used for the carriage of goods with a maximum authorised mass exceeding 3·5 tonnes but not exceeding 7·5 tonnes and including such a vehicle drawing a trailer with a maximum authorised mass not exceeding 750 kg.	1, 2, 3, 4, 5, 6, 7, . . . 9 and 10	B, B plus E, B1, C1 plus E, D1, D1 plus E, F, K, L, N and P
D1	Motor vehicle used for the carriage of passengers (but not for hire or reward) with more than 8 seats, but not more than 16 seats, in addition to the driver's seat, and including such a vehicle drawing a trailer with a maximum authorised mass not exceeding 750 kg.	1, 2, 3, 4, 5, 6, 7, . . . 9 and 10	B, B plus E, B1, C1, C1 plus E, D1 plus E, F, K, L, N and P
B plus E	Combination of a motor vehicle in category B and a trailer with a maximum authorised mass exceeding 750 kg.		
C1 plus E	Combination of a motor vehicle in category C1 and a trailer with a maximum authorised mass exceeding 750 kg [where the		

(1) Category	(2) Class of Vehicle included in the Category	(3) Additional Requirements	(4) Additional Categories Covered
	maximum authorised mass of the combination does not exceed 8·25 tonnes].		
D1 plus E	Combination of a motor vehicle in category D1 and a trailer with a maximum authorised mass exceeding 750 kg.		
F	Agricultural tractor, but excluding any vehicle included in category H.	1, 2, 3, 4, 5, 6, 7, 9 and 10	K
G	Road Roller.	1, 2, 3, 4, 5, 6, 7, 9 and 10	
H	Track-laying vehicle steered by its tracks.	1, 2, 3, 4, 5, 6, 9, 10 and 11	
K	Mowing machine or pedestrian controlled vehicle.	1, 2, 3, 4, 5 and 6	
L	Vehicle propelled by electrical power but excluding any vehicle included in category A, K or P.	1, 2, 3, 4, 5, 6, 9 and 10 and, if fitted with a means for reversing, 7 . . .	K
N	Vehicle exempted from duty under section 7(1) of the Vehicles (Excise) Act 1971.	1, 2, 3, 4, 5 and 6	
P	Moped.	1, 2, 3, 4, 5, 6, 9, 10, 12 and 13	

[1562]

NOTES
    Commencement: 1 June 1990.
    Substituted by SI 1990 No 842, reg 12, Sch 2.
    Words in first and second pairs of square brackets substituted by SI 1990 No 1396, reg 6; words in third pair of square brackets inserted by SI 1992 No 3090.
    Words omitted repealed by SI 1991 No 485, reg 8.

SCHEDULE 4

Regulation 20(1)(c)

ADDITIONAL REQUIREMENTS FOR DRIVING TESTS

The additional requirements as to certain of which a candidate for a test must satisfy the person conducting the test in accordance with regulation 20 and the preceding Schedule are his ability to do the following:—

    1. Read in good daylight (with the aid of glasses or contact lenses if worn) a registration mark fixed to a motor vehicle and containing letters and figures 79.4 millimetres high at a distance of—

        (a) 20.5 metres, in any case except that mentioned below; and
        (b) 12.3 metres, in the case of a driving test carried out on a vehicle of a class included in [category K] only.

    2. Start the engine of the vehicle;

    3. Move away straight ahead or at an angle;

    4. Overtake, meet or cross the path of other vehicles and take an appropriate course; ·

    5. Turn right-hand and left-hand corners correctly;

6. Stop the vehicle in an emergency and normally, and in the latter case bring it to rest at an appropriate part of the road;

[7. Carry out manoeuvres involving the use of reverse gear.]

9. Indicate his intended actions at appropriate times by giving appropriate signals in a clear and unmistakeable manner:

Provided that, in the case of a vehicle with a left-hand drive or of a disabled driver for whom it is impracticable or undesirable to give signals by arm, there shall be no requirement to give signals which cannot be given by mechanical means;

10. Act correctly and promptly on all signals given by traffic signs and traffic controllers and take appropriate action on signs given by other road users;

11. Drive the vehicle backwards and cause it to face in the opposite direction by means of its tracks.

[12. Drive the vehicle slowly, while keeping it under control.

13. Cause the vehicle to face in the opposite direction by driving it foward ("U" turn).]   **[1563–1564]**

NOTES
  Commencement: 2 October 1989 (paras 12, 13); 3 September 1987 (remainder).
  Para 1: words in square brackets substituted by SI 1990 No 842, reg 2, Sch 1.
  Para 7: substituted for original paras 7, 8 by SI 1991 No 485, reg 9.
  Paras 12, 13: added by SI 1989 No 1612, reg 5.

SCHEDULE 5
(Revoked by SI 1990 No 2334, reg 5(1)).

[SCHEDULE 6
Regulation 22(1) (and 2)

FORM OF CERTIFICATE AND STATEMENT OF DRIVING TEST RESULT

PART I

ROAD TRAFFIC ACT 1988

Certificate of passing of a test of competence to drive *other than an extended driving test**
....

has, on a vehicle of a class included in category   , passed the test of competence to drive prescribed *for the purposes of section 36 of the Road Traffic Offenders Act 1988** by virtue of section 89(3) of the Road Traffic Act 1988.

Dated

* delete the words in italics if they are inapplicable.   **[1565]**

PART II

ROAD TRAFFIC ACT 1988

Statement of failure to pass a test of competence to drive *which was an extended driving test**
....

has failed to pass the test of competence to drive prescribed *for the purposes of section 36 of the Road Traffic Act 1988** by virtue of section 89(3) of the Road Traffic Act 1988.

Dated

* delete the words in italics if they are inapplicable.]   **[1566]**

NOTES
  Commencement: 1 July 1992.

Substituted by SI 1992 No 1318, reg 13, Sch 1.

[SCHEDULE 7

Regulation 23A(9)

Road Traffic Act 1988   **Certified Motorcycle Instructor**
                                           Certificate of Authorisation

                                           Name of certificate holder

[Photograph of
certificate
holder]   Instructor No.

                                           Name and address of training
                                           establishment for which the
                                           certificate is valid

Date of expiry

———————————————————]   **[1566A]**

NOTES
    Commencement: 1 December 1990.
    Inserted by SI 1990 No 2334, reg 6, Sch 2.

[SCHEDULE 8

Regulation 23B(1)

ELEMENTS OF AN APPROVED TRAINING COURSE

(A) INTRODUCTION

    1. Trainees must be told and must understand:—

        —the aims of the approved training course;
        —the importance of having the right equipment and clothing;
        —the need to be clearly visible to other road users (the use of conspicuity aids);
        —the legal requirements for riding on the road;
        —why motor cyclists are more vulnerable than most road users;
        —the need to drive at the correct speed according to road and traffic conditions;
        —the importance of reading and understanding the Highway Code.

    2. Trainees eyesight must be tested. Trainees must be able to read, in good daylight, a vehicle registration mark containing letters and figures 79·4 mm high at a distance of 20·5 metres (with the aid of glasses or contact lenses if worn).

(B) PRACTICAL ON SITE TRAINING

    3. Trainees must receive practical on site training at the conclusion of which they must fulfil the following requirements, that is to say they must—

        —be familiar with the motor cycle, its controls and how it works;
        —be able to cary out basic machine checks to a satisfactory standard and be able to take the bike on and off the stand satisfactorily;
        —be able to wheel the machine around to the left and right showing proper balance and bring the motorcycle to a controlled halt by braking;
        —be able to start and stop the engine satisfactorily.

(C) **PRACTICAL ON SITE RIDING**

4. Trainees must undertake practical on site riding at the conclusion of which they must be able to execute the following manoeuvres, that is to say they must be able to:—

—ride the machine under control in a straight line and bring the machine to a controlled halt;
—ride the machine round a figure of eight circuit under control;
—ride the machine slowly under control;
—bring the machine to a stop under full control as in an emergency;
—carry out controlled braking using both brakes;
—change gear satisfactorily;
—carry out rear observation correctly;
—carry out simulated left and right hand turns correctly using the Observation-Signal-Manoeuvre (OSM) and Position-Speed-Look (PSL) routines.

(D) **PRACTICAL ON ROAD TRAINING**

5. Before undertaking practical on road riding trainees must be told and must understand the need to:—

—ride defensively and anticipate the actions of other road users;
—use rear observation at appropriate times;
—assume the correct road position when riding;
—leave sufficient space when following another vehicle;
—pay due regard to the effect of varying weather conditions when riding;
—be aware of the various types of road surface that can be encountered.

(E) **PRACTICAL ON ROAD RIDING**

6. Trainees must undertake on road riding. They must ride safely in a variety of situations including as many of the following as practicable:—

—roundabouts
—junctions
—pedestrian crossings
—traffic lights
—gradients
—bends
—obstructions.]   **[1566B]**

NOTES
    Commencement: 1 December 1990.
    Inserted by SI 1990 No 2334, reg 6, Sch 2.

[SCHEDULE 9

Regulation 23B(4)

ROAD TRAFFIC ACT 1988

**Certificate of Completion of an Approved Training
Course for Motor Vehicles in Categories A and P**

Driver number
of Candidate

Date and time of course completion

Current name

Current address

                                                        Postcode

has successfully completed an approved training course for motor vehicles in categories
A and P, prescribed for the purpose of Section 97 of the Road Traffic Act 1988 as
amended by Section 6 of the Road Traffic (Driver Licensing and Information Systems)
Act 1989.]   **[1566C]**

NOTES
    Commencement: 1 December 1990.
    Inserted by SI 1990 No 2334, reg 6, Sch 2.

DRIVERS' HOURS (GOODS VEHICLES) (KEEPING OF RECORDS) REGULATIONS 1987
(SI 1987 NO 1421)

NOTES
    Made: 5 August 1987
    Authority: Transport Act 1968, ss 98, 101(2)

ARRANGEMENT OF REGULATIONS

1. Commencement and citation

These Regulations may be cited as the Drivers' Hours (Goods Vehicles)
(Keeping of Records) Regulations 1987 and shall come into force on 2nd
November 1987.   **[1567]**

NOTES
    Commencement: 2 November 1987.

2. Revocation

    . . .   **[1568]**

NOTES
    Commencement: 2 November 1987.
    This regulation revokes SI 1976 No 1447 and SI 1986 No 1493.

3. Interpretation

In these Regulations, unless the context otherwise requires—

    "the Act" means the Transport Act 1968;

"driver's record book" means a book which complies with regulation 5, and any reference in relation to a driver's record book to a front sheet, instructions to drivers for completion of sheets, and weekly record sheets is a reference to those components of a driver's record book in regulation 5.

"operator's licence" has the same meaning as in section 60(1) of the Act; and

"passenger vehicles" and "goods vehicles" have the same meaning as in section 95(2) of the Act.   **[1569]**

NOTES
Commencement: 2 November 1987.

4. Application of Regulations

Subject to the provisions of regulations 12 and 13 these Regulations apply to drivers of goods vehicles and to employers of employee-drivers of such vehicles but they do not so apply in relation to a journey made or work done by a driver in a case where the journey or, as the case may be, the work to which the applicable Community rules apply.   **[1570]**

NOTES
Commencement: 2 November 1987.

5. Form of Driver's Record Book

A driver's record book shall contain—

    (a) a front sheet;
    (b) instructions to drivers for completion of sheets;
    (c) notes for guidance on use of the book; and
    (d) weekly record sheets divided up into boxes for entry of information relating to each day of the week and a duplicate of each weekly record sheet together with one sheet of carbon paper or other means whereby an entry on a weekly record sheet may be simultaneously reproduced on the duplicate of that sheet

each of which shall conform to the model in the Schedule to these Regulations and shall have the standard A6 format (105 x 148mm) or a larger format. **[1571]**

NOTES
Commencement: 2 November 1987.

6. Issue of Driver's Record Books

(1) Where an employee-driver is required by these Regulations to enter information in a driver's record book the employer shall issue to him and from time to time as may be necessary while the employee-driver remains in the employment of that employer supply him with a new driver's record book.

(2) If on the date of the coming into operation of these Regulations or at any time thereafter an employee-driver has more than one employer in relation to whom he is an employee-driver of a vehicle, the employer who is to issue a new driver's record book to him shall be the employer for whom the employee-driver first acts in the course of his employment on or after the said date or time.

(3) Where during the currency of a driver's record book an employee-driver ceases to be employed by an employer who has issued that book to him he shall return that book, (including all unused weekly record sheets), to that employer

and, if he is at that time employed by some other person or persons in relation to whom he is an employee-driver of a vehicle, that other or person, if there is more than one such other person, that one of them for whom he first acts in the course of his employment after ceasing to be so employed as aforesaid, shall issue a new driver's record book to him in accordance with the provisions of paragraph (1) above.   **[1572]**

NOTES
Commencement: 2 November 1987.

7. Entries in driver's record books

(1) An employer of an employee-driver or an owner-driver shall enter or secure that there is entered on the front sheet the information specified in items 4 and 6 of that sheet.

(2) The entries referred to in paragraph (1) shall be made—

    (a) in the case of an employer, before the driver's record book is issued to the driver pursuant to regulation 6, and

    (b) in the case of an owner-driver before the book is used.

(3)(a) For the purpose of entering the information specified in item 4, the address shall, in the case of an owner-driver, be the address of the driver's place of business.

    (b) For the purpose of entering the information specified in item 6 the Operator's Licence No. shall be the serial number of the operator's licence granted under Part V of the Act by virtue of which each goods vehicle used by the driver during the currency of the record book is an authorised vehicle for the purposes of the said Part V.

(4) A driver shall enter, and where he is an employee-driver, his employer shall cause him to enter, in accordance with the instructions to drivers for the completion of sheets—

    (a) on the front sheet the information specified in relation to the front sheet in these instructions; and

    (b) in the appropriate boxes in the weekly record sheet the information specified in relation to weekly record sheets in those instructions.

(5) A driver when making an entry in a weekly record sheet (including signing such a sheet) shall ensure by the use of carbon paper or otherwise, that the entry is simultaneously reproduced on the duplicate of that sheet.   **[1573]**

NOTES
Commencement: 2 November 1987.
The Act: Transport Act 1968.

8. Manner of keeping driver's record books - supplementary

(1) Where a weekly record sheet has been completed by an employee-driver he shall deliver the driver's record book (including the duplicate of the weekly record sheet which has been completed) to the employer who issued or should have issued the record book to him within a period of seven days from the date when the weekly record sheet was completed or earlier if so required by the employer.

(2) An employer to whom a driver's record book has been delivered pursuant to paragraph 1 above shall—

(a) examine the weekly record sheet which has been completed and sign it and its duplicate;

(b) detach the duplicate sheet; and

(c) return the book to the driver before he is next on duty.

(3) When all the weekly record sheets in a driver's record book have been used, the driver shall retain the book for a period of fourteen days from the date on which the book was last returned to him pursuant to paragraph (2)(c) above and shall then return the book to the employer as soon as is reasonably practicable.

(4) When a weekly record sheet has been completed by an owner-dirver he shall, within a period of seven days from the date of its being completed, detach the duplicate sheet and deliver it to the address which is required to be entered in item 4 on the front sheet.

(5) An employee-driver or an owner-driver shall not be treated as having failed to comply with any of the requirements of pararaphs (1) and (4) above with respect to the period within which the duplicate of a weekly record sheet shall be delivered if he can show that it was not reasonably practicable to comply with that requirement and that the duplicate of the weekly record sheet was delivered as soon as it was reasonably practicable to do so.

(6) A driver who is in possession of a driver's record book in which he has made any entry pursuant to regulation 7 shall not, until all the weekly record sheets in that book have been completed, make any entry in any other record book.

(7) An employee-driver shall not make any entry in a driver's record book pursuant to regulation 7 if the book was not supplied to him by his employer unless a driver's record book so supplied was not available to him.

(8) No person shall erase or obliterate any entry once made in a driver's record book, and if a correction is required it shall be made by striking the original entry through in such a way that it may still be read and by writing the appropriate correction near to the entry so struck through, and any person making such a correction shall initial it. **[1574]**

NOTES

Commencement: 2 November 1987.

---

9. Production of driver's record books by employee-drivers

(1) Where an employee-driver has or has had during any period more than one employer in relation to whom he is an employee-driver each employer, who is not the employer who is required by these Regulations to issue a driver's record book to that employee-driver, shall require that driver to produce his current driver's record book and shall enter on the front sheet the information contained in item 5.

(2) An employee-driver shall produce his current driver's record book for inspection by the employer who issued it to him, or by any other person in relation to whom he is at any time during the period of the currency of that book an employee-driver, whenever required to do so by that employer or that other person. **[1575]**

NOTES

Commencement: 2 November 1987.

10. Driver's record books to be carried by drivers

A driver shall have his current driver's record book (including all unused record sheets) in his possession at all times when he is on duty.   **[1576]**

NOTES
    Commencement: 2 November 1987.

11. Preservation of driver's record books

(1) An owner-driver shall preserve his driver's record book intact when it has been completed or he has ceased to use it, and the employer of an employee-driver to whom any driver's record book relating to that employee-driver has been returned shall preserve that book intact, for the period specified in paragraph (3) below.

(2) An employer of an employee-driver or an owner-driver who has detached duplicates of weekly sheets pursuant to regulation 8(2)(b) or as the case may be regulation 8(4) shall preserve those sheets for the period specified in paragraph (3) below.

(3) The period for which driver's record books and duplicates of weekly record sheets must be preserved as required by this regulation shall be one year reckoned, in the case of an owner-driver, from the day on which that book was completed or ceased to be used by him, or in the case of an employee-driver, from the day on which that book was returned to his employer pursuant to regulation 8(3).   **[1577]**

NOTES
    Commencement: 2 November 1987.

12. Exemptions

(1) Where a driver does not during any working day drive any goods vehicle other than a vehicle the use of which is exempted from any requirement to have an operator's licence or, in the public service of the Crown, would be so exempted by virtue of section 60(2) of the Act, were it not such a vehicle, that driver and, if he is an employee-driver, his employer, shall be exempted for that period from the specified requirements.

(2)(a) Where in any working day a driver does not drive a goods vehicle for more than four hours and does not drive any such vehicle outside a radius of 50 kilometres from the operating centre of the vehicle, then he and, if he is an employee-driver, his employer, shall be exempted for that period from the specified requirements.

    (b) For the purposes of computing the period of four hours mentioned in sub-paragraph (a) above no account shall be taken of any time spent in driving a vehicle elsewhere than on a road if the vehicle is being so driven in the course of operations of agriculture, forestry or quarrying or in the course of carrying out work in the construction, reconstruction, alteration or extension or maintenance of, or of a part of, a building, or of any other fixed works of construction of civil engineering (including works for the construction, improvement or maintenance of a road) and, for the purposes of this sub-paragraph, where the vehicle is being driven on, or on a part of, a road in the course of carrying out of any work for the improvement or maintenance of, or of that part of, that road, it shall be treated as being driven elsewhere than on a road.

(3) Where during any working day a driver does not spend all or the greater part of the time when he is driving vehicles to which Part VI of the Act applies in driving goods vehicles, then he and, if he is an employee-driver, his employer, shall be exempted for that working day from the specified requirements.

(4) Where a vehicle is used in such circumstances that by virtue of regulation 5 of the Community Drivers' Hours and Recording Equipment (Exemptions and Supplementary Provisions) Regulations 1986 Council Regulation (EEC) No. 3821/85 of 20th December 1985 on recording equipment in road transport applies to the vehicle, the driver of the vehicle and, if he is an employee-driver, his employer, shall be exempted from the specified requirements in relation to the use of the vehicle in those circumstances.

(5)(a) In this regulation "the specified requirements" means the provisions of regulations 7 and 10.

    (b) In paragraph (2)(a) above "operating centre" has the same meaning as in section 92 of the Act. **[1578]**

NOTES
    Commencement: 2 November 1987.
    The Act: Transport Act 1968.
    Council Regulation (EEC) No 3821/85, OJ L 370, 31.12.85, p 8.

13. Drivers of goods vehicles and passenger vehicles

(1) Subject to the provisions of regulation 12(3), regulations 7 and 10 apply to a driver who in any working week drives goods and passenger vehicles as they apply to a driver who only drives a goods vehicles and the information to be entered in the driver's record book pursuant to regulation 7 shall be information in relation to his employments in connection with both goods and passenger vehicles.

(2) If a driver of both goods vehicles and passenger vehicles has a different employer in relation to his employment in connection with goods vehicles from his employer in relation to his employment in connection with passenger vehicles his employer for the purpose of regulation 6 shall be his employer in relation to his employment in connection with goods vehicles notwithstanding the provisions of regulation 6(2). **[1579]**

NOTES
    Commencement: 2 November 1987.

SCHEDULE
MODEL FOR DRIVER'S RECORD BOOK

(a) Front Sheet

RECORD BOOK FOR DRIVERS IN ROAD TRANSPORT

1. Date book first used .. ..

2. Date book last used .. ..

3. Surname, first name(s), and address of holder of book .. ..
.. ..

4. Name, address, telephone number and stamp (if any) of employer/undertaking ..
.. ..

5. Name, address, telephone number and stamp (if any) of any other employer(s) .. ..
.. ..

6. Operator's Licence No. (Nos.) ... ...

(b) Instructions to drivers for completion of sheets

INSTRUCTIONS TO DRIVERS FOR COMPLETION OF SHEETS

FRONT SHEET

1. Enter your surname, first name(s) and address (item 3). Owner-drivers need not make any entry in item 3 unless their personal address is different from the address of their place of business.

2. Enter the date on which you first use the book (item 1).

3. Immediately after you have completed all the weekly sheets enter in item 2 the date on which you last made an entry in a weekly sheet. If you cease to be employed by the employer who issued you with a record book enter the last date on which you were employed in item 2.

WEEKLY RECORD SHEET

4. Use a new sheet each week. A week runs from midnight on Sunday/Monday to midnight the next Sunday/Monday.

5. Complete boxes 1 and 2 at the beginning of each week in which you work as a driver.

6. Each day on which you do work as a driver complete boxes 3-9 in accordance with the instructions below.

7. Enter in box 3 for the day in question the registration number of any vehicle used during that day.

8. Complete boxes 4 and 5 at the beginning of each day on which you do work as a driver.

9. Complete boxes 6, 7 and 8 and 9 at the end of the day's work.

(c) Notes for guidance on the use of the book

NOTES FOR GUIDANCE ON THE USE OF RECORD BOOKS

FOR EMPLOYERS

1. After completing items 4 and 6 on the front sheet, issue a record book to the drivers employed by you.

2. Give the holder the necessary instructions for correct use of the book.

3. When the record book is handed in to you by the drivers employed by you within seven days of the end of each week of driving, examine and sign the weekly record sheet (including the duplicate sheet) for the week to which it relates. Tear out and keep the duplicate sheets, leaving the top sheets in the book and return the book to the driver before he is next on duty.

4. When the used books have been handed back to you by the drivers employed by you preserve them together with the duplicate sheets for not less than one year.

FOR EMPLOYEE-DRIVERS

5. Ensure that items 1 and 3 on the front sheet are completed before you use the book.

6. This record book is personal. Carry it with you when on duty and produce it to any authorised inspecting officer on request. Hand it over to your employer when you leave the undertaking.

7. Produce this record book to your employer within 7 days of the end of each week of driving, so that he can check and countersign your entries. Keep the top sheets in the book.

8. When the book is completed, complete item 2 on the front sheet and keep the book for 2 weeks so that it can be produced at any time to an authorised inspecting officer and then hand it to your employer.

FOR OWNER-DRIVERS

9. Ensure that items 1, 3 (if applicable) 4 and 6 on the front sheet are completed before you use the record book. Enter your business address in item 4.

10. This record book is personal. Carry it with you when on duty and produce it to any authorised inspecting officer on request.

11. Tear out and keep the duplicate of each weekly record sheet at the end of the week to which it relates.

12. When the book is completed, complete item 2 on the front sheet. Preserve the used books and the duplicate sheets for not less than a year.

GENERAL

13. All entries must be made in ink or with a ball-point pen.

14. If you have to correct an entry, strike the incorrect entry through, write the correct entry near it and initial the correction.

(These notes are for guidance only and reference should be made to Part VI of the Transport Act 1968 and, the Drivers' Hours (Keeping of Records) Regulations 1987 for particulars of the statutory provisions).

(d) Weekly record sheets

WEEKLY SHEET

1. DRIVER'S NAME

2. PERIOD COVERED BY SHEET
WEEK COMMENCING (DATE) ....
TO WEEK ENDING (DATE) ....

DAY ON WHICH DUTY COMMENCED	REGISTRATION NO. OF VEHICLE(S) 3	PLACE WHERE VEHICLE(S) BASED 4	TIME OF GOING ON DUTY 5	TIME OF GOING OFF DUTY 6	TIME SPENT DRIVING 7	TIME SPENT ON DUTY 8	SIGNATURE OF DRIVER 9
MONDAY							
TUESDAY							
WEDNESDAY							
THURSDAY							
FRIDAY							
SATURDAY							
SUNDAY							

10. CERTIFICATION BY EMPLOYER

I HAVE EXAMINED THE ENTRIES IN THIS SHEET
SIGNATURE ....
POSITION HELD ....

[1580]

NOTES

Commencement: 2 November 1987.

GOODS VEHICLES (PLATING AND TESTING) REGULATIONS 1988
(SI 1988 NO 1478)

NOTES
   Made: 22 August 1988
   Authority: Road Traffic Act 1988, ss 49, 53(5), 63(5)

ARRANGEMENT OF REGULATIONS

PART I
GENERAL

PART II
TIMING AND METHOD OF APPLICATION FOR EXAMINATIONS AND TESTS

PART III
REGULATIONS GOVERNING FIRST EXAMINATIONS

Examination for plating

PART IV
REGULATIONS GOVERNING PERIODICAL TESTS

PART V

REGULATIONS GOVERNING NOTIFIABLE ALTERATIONS, AMENDMENTS OF PLATING CERTIFICATES AND RE-EXAMINATIONS IN CONNECTION THEREWITH

Secretary of State to be informed of notifiable alterations

PART VI

MISCELLANEOUS MATTERS

PART VII

CROWN VEHICLES

PART VIII

EXEMPTIONS

SCHEDULES

PART I

GENERAL

1. Citation and commencement

These Regulations may be cited as the Goods Vehicles (Plating and Testing) Regulations 1988 and shall come into force on 23rd September 1988.   **[1581]**

NOTES

Commencement: 23 September 1988.

2. Revocation

The Regulations specified in Schedule 4 are hereby revoked. **[1582]**

NOTES
Commencement: 23 September 1988.

3. Interpretation

(1) In these Regulations, except where the context otherwise requires, the following expressions have the meanings hereby respectively assigned to them:—

"the 1971 Act" means the Vehicles (Excise) Act 1971;

["the 1988 Act" means the Road Traffic Act 1988];

"the Construction and Use Regulations" means the Road Vehicles (Construction and Use) Regulations 1986;

"the National Type Approval for Goods Vehicles Regulations" means the Motor Vehicles (Type Approval for Goods Vehicles) (Great Britain) Regulations 1982;

"agricultural motor vehicle", "agricultural trailer", "agricultural trailed appliance", "agricultural trailed appliance conveyor", "articulated vehicle", "converter dolly", "dual-purpose vehicle", "engineering plant", "Ministry plate", "registered", "semi-trailer", "straddle carrier", "track-laying", "works trailer", and "works truck" have the same meanings respectively as in the Construction and Use Regulations;

"appeal officer" means the person appointed by the Secretary of State for the purposes of appeals to the Secretary of State;

"area engineer" means the area mechanical engineer appointed by the Secretary of State for the purposes of appeals other than appeals to the Secretary of State;

"auxiliary station" means a vehicle testing station which is regularly not open for the carrying out of re-tests on certain normal working days;

"break-down vehicle" means a motor vehicle—

(a) on which is permanently mounted apparatus designed for raising one disabled vehicle partly from the ground and for drawing that vehicle when so raised; and

(b) which is not equipped to carry any load other than articles required for the operation of, or in connection with, that apparatus or for repairing disabled vehicles;

["design gross weight" means—

(a) in the case of a vehicle equipped with a Ministry plate, the weight shown thereon as the design weight or, if no weight is so shown thereon, the weight shown thereon as the weight not to be exceeded in Great Britain;

(b) in the case of a vehicle which is not equipped with a Ministry plate, but which is equipped with a plate in accordance with regulation 66 of the Construction and Use Regulations, the maximum gross weight shown on the plate in respect of item 7 of Part I of Schedule 8 to those Regulations; and

(c) in any other case, the weight which the vehicle is designed or adapted not to exceed when in normal use and travelling on a road laden;]

"examination" means any operation being—

(a) a first examination;
(b) a re-test;
(c) a periodical test;
(d) a re-examination under regulation 33; or
(e) a re-examination on an appeal under regulation 25, 29 or 37;

"first examination", in relation to a vehicle, means an examination being both an examination for plating and a first goods vehicles test;

"Goods Vehicle Centre" means the Goods Vehicle Centre at Welcombe House, 91-92 The Strand, Swansea, SA1 2DH.

"living van" means a vehicle whether mechanically propelled or not which is used as living accommodation by one or more persons, and which is also used for the carriage of goods or burden which are not needed by such one or more persons for the purpose of their residence in the vehicle;

"Ministry test date disc" means a plate issued by the Secretary of State for a goods vehicle being a trailer, following the issue of a goods vehicle test certificate for that trailer under these Regulations and containing—

(a) the identification mark allotted to that trailer and shown in that certificate;
(b) the date until which that certificate is valid; and
(c) the number of the vehicle testing station shown in the said certificate;

"notifiable alteration", in relation to a vehicle, means—

(a) an alteration made in the structure or fixed equipment of the vehicle which varies the carrying capacity or towing capacity of the vehicle;
(b) an alteration, affecting any part of a braking system or the steering system with which the vehicle is equipped or of the means of operation of either of those systems; or
(c) any other alteration made in the structure or fixed equipment of the vehicle which renders or is likely to render the vehicle unsafe to travel on roads at any weight equal to any plated weight shown in the plating certificate for that vehicle.

"periodical test", in relation to a vehicle, means a goods vehicle test carried out under Part IV of these Regulations on a vehicle in respect of which a goods vehicle test certificate has been issued on a first examination of it or as a result of a re-test following that examination or as a result of an appeal under any provision in these Regulations;

"plated particulars" means those particulars which are required to be shown in a Ministry plate under Schedule 10 to the Construction and Use Regulations;

"plated weights" means such of the plated particulars related to gross weight, axle weight for each axle and train weight as are required to be shown in column (2) on the Ministry plate;

"play bus" means a motor vehicle which was originally constructed to carry more than 12 passengers but which has been adapted primarily for the carriage of play things for children (including articles required in connection with the use of those things);

"the prescribed construction and use requirements", in relation to a vehicle, means those of the requirements specified in Schedule 3 which apply to the vehicle;

"re-test", in relation to a vehicle, means an examination which is

(a) an examination for plating and a goods vehicle test carried out on a vehicle under Part III of these Regulations subsequent to a first examination of that vehicle as a result of which a notice of refusal was issued; or

(b) a goods vehicle test carried out on a vehicle under Part IV of these Regulations subsequent to a periodical test of that vehicle as a result of which a notice of refusal was issued;

"Secretary of State" means the Secretary of State for Transport;

"sender" means a person who informs the Secretary of State of a notifiable alteration under regulation 30;

"sold or supplied by retail", in relation to a trailer, means sold or supplied otherwise than to a person acquiring solely for the purpose of resale or of resupply for a valuable consideration;

"the standard lists" means lists—

(a) prepared by the Secretary of State after consultation with representative organisations of the motor manufacturing and road transport industries and other connected organisations and published by the Goods Vehicle Centre; and

(b) showing, as respects goods vehicles of a make, model and type specified in the lists and complying in the case of motor vehicles with certain particulars relating to the engine, transmission, brakes and dimensions so specified and in the case of trailers with certain particulars relating to type of coupling, dimensions, brakes and tyres so specified (hereinafter referred to as "the constructional particulars") the gross weight for, and the axle weight for each axle of, vehicles of that make, model and type and, in the case of motor vehicles, the train weight for vehicles of that make, model and type, the said weights being weights at or below which the Secretary of State considers vehicles of that make, model and type could safely be driven on roads having regard to—

(i) the weights at which vehicles of that make, model and type were originally designed to operate;

(ii) in the case of motor vehicles, the requirements as to brakes of regulations 15, 16 and 18 of the Construction and Use Regulations;

(iii) in the case of trailers, the requirements of regulations 15 and 16 of the Construction and Use Regulations and the provisions of Schedule 1 as respects braking force; and

"vehicle testing station" means a station provided by the Secretary of State under [section 52(2) of the 1988 Act].

(2) Any reference in these Regulations to—

(a) an examination for plating includes, in relation to a vehicle to which regulation 18 applies, an examination provided for in that regulation; and

(b) a vehicle of a make, model and type shall in relation to a trailer, include a reference to a vehicle of a make and bearing a serial number.

(3) For the purpose of these Regulations, in counting the number of axles of a vehicle, where the centres of the areas of contact between all the wheels and the road surface can be included between any two vertical planes at right angles to the longitudinal axis of the vehicle less than 1.02 metres apart, those wheels shall be treated as constituting one axle.

(4) For the purpose of these Regulations, in determining when a trailer is first sold or supplied by retail the date of such first sale or supply by retail shall in the case of a trailer which is constructed with a chassis be taken to be the date on which the chassis (with or without a body mounted on it) is first sold or supplied by retail and in the case of any other trailer be taken to be the date the trailer is first sold or supplied by retail.

(5) Unless the context otherwise requires, any reference in these Regulations to—

(a) a numbered regulation or Schedule is a reference to the regulation or Schedule bearing that number in these Regulations;
(b) a numbered paragraph is a reference to the paragraph bearing that number in the regulation or Schedule in which the reference appears;
(c) a vehicle is a reference to a vehicle to which these Regulations apply.

[1583]

NOTES
Commencement: 23 September 1988.
Para (1): definition "1988 Act" and words in square brackets in definition "vehicle testing station" substituted by SI 1990 No 448, reg 3; definition "design gross weight" inserted by SI 1991 No 252, reg 3.

4. Application

(1) Subject to paragraph (2), these Regulations apply to goods vehicles being—

(a) heavy motor cars and motor cars constructed or adapted for the purpose of forming part of an articulated vehicle;
(b) other heavy motor cars;
[(c) other motor cars, the design gross weight of which exceeds 3500 kilograms;]
(d) semi-trailers;
(e) converter dollies of any unladen weight manufactured on or after 1st January 1979; or
(f) trailers, not being converter dollies or semi-trailers, the unladen weight of which exceeds 1020 kilograms.

(2) Nothing in these Regulations applies to goods vehicles of any of the classes of vehicle specified in Schedule 2. **[1584]**

NOTES
Commencement: 23 September 1988 (except sub-s (1)(c)); 18 March 1991 (sub-s (1)(c)).
Sub-s (1): para (c) substituted by SI 1991 No 252, reg 4.

5. Prescribed requirements for tests

(1) Subject to these Regulations, every vehicle submitted for a goods vehicle test in accordance with these Regulations shall be examined for the purpose of ascertaining whether the prescribed construction and use requirements are complied with.

(2) For the purposes of these Regulations the applicability of any of the prescribed construction and use requirements to a vehicle is not affected by Item 5 in the Table in regulation 4(4) of the Construction and Use Regulations (which exempts vehicles being used in the course of a goods vehicle test from certain construction and use requirements). **[1585]**

NOTES
Commencement: 23 September 1988.

6. Supervision of tests

Subject to these Regulations, every examination for plating and every goods vehicle test shall be carried out by or under the direction of a goods vehicle examiner. **[1586]**

NOTES
Commencement: 23 September 1988.

7. Authority to drive and duties of driver

(1) The person who drove the vehicle to an examination shall, except so far as he is permitted to be absent by the person who is carrying out the examination, be present throughout the whole of the examination, and shall drive the vehicle and operate its controls when and in such a manner as he may be directed by the person who is carrying out the examination to do so.

(2) The person who is carrying out an examination is authorised to drive the vehicle on a road or elsewhere.

(3) A contravention of this regulation is hereby declared to be an offence.

[1587]

NOTES
Commencement: 23 September 1988.

8. Conditions of acceptance of vehicle

(1) In this regulation, "examiner" means—

    (a) in relation to an examination other than one under [section 50(2) or (4) of the 1988 Act], a goods vehicle examiner;

    (b) in relation to an examination under [section 50(2) of the 1988 Act], the area engineer; and

    (c) in relation to an examination under [section 50(4) of the 1988 Act], the appeal officer.

(2) An examiner shall not be under an obligation to accept a vehicle for examination or to proceed with an examination in any case where—

    (a) the vehicle is not submitted for examination at the time fixed under these Regulations for the examination;

    (b) the applicant for the examination does not, after being requested to do so, produce the notice of appointment (if any) relating to the examination and—

        (i) in the case of a motor vehicle, either the registration document relating to the vehicle or other evidence of the date of its first registration or, in the case of a motor vehicle not registered before the date of the examination, evidence of the date of its manufacture; or

(ii) in the case of a trailer, evidence of the date of its manufacture;

(c) the fee in respect of that examination has not been paid and is not tendered in cash;

(d) the particulars relating to the vehicle and shown in any application form relevant to that examination are found to be substantially incorrect;

(e) the vehicle is one as respects which it has been stated in the application form that it is to be used on roads to draw a trailer and in the last notice of appointment preceding the examination it was required that the vehicle should be accompanied by a trailer which is to be so drawn, and the vehicle is not accompanied by such a trailer;

(f) the vehicle is a trailer and is not accompanied by a motor vehicle suitable for drawing that trailer and capable of operating any braking system with which the trailer is equipped;

(g) there is not permanently affixed to the chassis or main structure of the vehicle in a conspicuous and easily accessible position so as to be readily legible either—

(i) the chassis or serial number shown in the registration document relating to the vehicle; or

(ii) if no such number is shown or exists, the identification mark allotted to the vehicle by the Secretary of State;

(h) the vehicle, or any motor vehicle by which it is accompanied, or any part of or any equipment of the vehicle is so dirty or dangerous as to make it unreasonable for the examination to be carried out in accordance with these Regulations or [with any directions] given under [section 52(1) of the 1988 Act], or the applicant for the examination does not produce any certificate required in the last notice of appointment preceding the examination, that a vehicle used for carrying toxic, corrosive or inflammable loads has been properly cleaned or otherwise made safe;

(i) an examiner is not able to complete the examination without the vehicle or, in the case of a trailer the motor vehicle by which it is accompanied being driven and such vehicle or, as the case may be, accompanying vehicle is not provided with fuel and oil to enable it to be driven to such extent as may be necessary for the purpose of the examination;

(j) an examiner is not able to complete the examination of a trailer unless the motor vehicle by which it is accompanied is driven on a road, and that motor vehicle cannot be so driven in compliance with section 8 of the 1971 Act because no licence under that Act is in force for such vehicle;

(k) the vehicle or any trailer by which it is accompanied is not loaded or unloaded in the manner (if any) specified for the purposes of the examination ... in the last notice of appointment preceding the examination ... ;

(l) an examiner is not able to complete the examination due to the failure of a part of the vehicle, or of any vehicle by which it is drawn or intended to be drawn, which renders the vehicle, or any such accompanying vehicle incapable of being moved in safety under the power of the vehicle or, as the case may be, the accompanying vehicle;

(m) on the submission of a vehicle for a periodical test, or a re-test following a periodical test the driver of the vehicle or, in the case of a trailer, the driver of the vehicle which accompanies it, does not produce to an examiner the last plating certificate (or a photocopy of it) and the last goods vehicle test certificate (or a photocopy of it) which have been issued in respect of the vehicle submitted; ...

(n) on the submission of a vehicle to which regulation 18 applies for a first examination, or for a re-test under regulation 15 following a first examination, the driver of the vehicle does not produce to the examiner the certificate mentioned in regulation 18(2).

[or;

(o) on the submission of the vehicle for a periodical test or a re-test following a periodical test, the Ministry plate issued in respect of the vehicle—

(i) is not affixed in accordance with regulation 70(1) of the Construction and Use Regulations; or

(ii) contains particulars which do not correspond to the vehicle to which it is affixed.] **[1588]**

NOTES
Commencement: 23 September 1988 (except sub-s (2)(o)); 18 March 1991 (sub-s (2)(o)).
Para (1): words in square brackets substituted by SI 1990 No 448, reg 4(a).
Para (2): in sub-para (h), words in first pair of square brackets substituted by SI 1991 No 252, reg 5(a); words in second pair of square brackets substituted by SI 1990 No 448, reg 4(b); in sub-para (k), words omitted revoked by SI 1989 No 1693, reg 3; sub-para (o) and the word "or" immediately preceding it inserted by SI 1991 No 252, reg 5(b).
1971 Act: Vehicles (Excise) Act 1971.
1988 Act: Road Traffic Act 1988.

PART II
TIMING AND METHOD OF APPLICATION FOR EXAMINATIONS AND TESTS

9. Dates by which vehicles are to be submitted for first examinations

(1) Every motor vehicle shall be submitted for a first examination no later than the end of the calendar month in which falls the first anniversary of the date on which it was registered.

(2) Every trailer shall be submitted for a first examination not later than the end of the calendar month in which falls the first anniversary of the date on which it was first sold or supplied by retail.

(3) Paragraphs (1) and (2) shall not prevent the Secretary of State authorising the submission of a vehicle for a first examination after the date by which the vehicle is required by those paragraphs to be submitted for a first examination. **[1589]**

NOTES
Commencement: 23 September 1988.

10. Dates by which vehicles are to be submitted for periodical tests

(1) Every vehicle shall, in each calendar year subsequent to the issue of a first goods vehicle test certificate, be submitted for a periodical test either—

(a) not later than each anniversary of the date on which the vehicle was required under regulation 9 to be submitted for a first examination; or

(b) if there is in force for the vehicle a goods vehicle test certificate with an expiry date other than that anniversary, not later than that expiry date.

(2) Paragraph (1) and regulation 11 shall not prevent the Secretary of State authorising a vehicle being submitted for a periodical test after the date by which the vehicle is required by those provisions to be submitted for a periodical test.   **[1590]**

NOTES
Commencement: 23 September 1988.

11. Period of validity of goods vehicle test certificate

(1) A goods vehicle test certificate issued as a result of a first examination, or a re-test following a first examination, or an appeal by a person aggrieved by a determination on a first examination or a re-test following a first examiation, shall be valid from the date of its issue until the day of the same month in the following year.

(2) A goods vehicle test certificate issued in the circumstances described in column (2) of an item in the Table below as a result of a periodical test, or a re-test following a periodical test, or an appeal by a person aggrieved by a determination on a periodical test or a re-test following a periodical test, shall be valid for the period described in column (3) of that item.

Table (regulation 11(2))

(1) Item	(2) Circumstances	(3) Period of validity
1	Vehicle submitted for periodical test more than two months before the expiry date of the current test certificate	From the date of issue of the certificate until the last day of the same month in the next following year.
2	Vehicle submitted for periodical test two months or less before the expiry date of the current test certificate.	From the date of issue of the certificate until the last day of the month in which falls the first anniversary of that expiry date.
3	Vehicle submitted for periodical test after the expiry date of the most recent test certificate for the vehicle (except in the circumstances described in column (2) of item 4).	From the date of issue of the certificate until the last day of the month in which falls the first anniversary of that expiry date save that, if this would result in a period of validity of two months or less, the certificate shall be valid from the date of issue until the last day of the month in which falls the second anniversary of the expiry date.
4	Motor vehicle submitted for periodical test after the expiry date of the most recent test certificate for the vehicle and after the most recent licence for the vehicle under the 1971 Act has expired or been surrendered.	From the date of issue of the certificate until the last day of the same month in the next following year.

(3) In this regulation any reference to a period ending on a day includes that day. **[1591]**

NOTES
Commencement: 23 September 1988.
1971 Act: Vehicles (Excise) Act 1971.

12. Manner of making application for first examinations or periodical tests, and fees

(1) Any person wishing to have a first examination or periodical test carried out on a vehicle shall make an application for that purpose [to the Secretary of State].

(2) ...

(3) Every application made under paragraph (1) shall be on a form approved by the Secretary of State, and shall contain the particulars required by that form and shall be accompanied by a fee of [£34.70] in the case of a motor vehicle and of [£17.90] in the case of a trailer.

[(4) Where the date appointed for a first examination or periodical test fixed at the applicant's request is a Saturday, the fee in respect of the examination or test shall be increased by [£19.50] in the case of a motor vehicle and [£12.30] in the case of trailer.

(5) Any sum payable by virtue of paragraph (4) shall be paid to the Secretary of State on or before the date reserved by him or on his behalf for the examination or test.] **[1592]**

NOTES
Commencement: 31 October 1989 (paras (4), (5)); 23 September 1988 (remainder).
Para (1): words in square brackets substituted by SI 1989 No 1693, reg 4(2).
Para (2): revoked by SI 1989 No 1693, reg 4(3).
Para (3): figures in square brackets substituted by SI 1992 No 2447.
Paras (4), (5): added by SI 1989 No 1693, reg 4(4); figures in square brackets substituted by SI 1992 No 564.

13. Time of application for first examinations and periodical tests

(1) Except as provided in paragraph (2), every application for a first examination or periodical test of a vehicle shall be made—

    (a) at least one calendar month before the date on which the applicant desires to submit the vehicle for the examination or test, and

    (b) not more than three calendar months before the last day by which the vehicle is required by these Regulations to be submitted for the examination or test.

(2) If the Secretary of State is satisfied that there are reasonable grounds for an application for a first examination or periodical test of a vehicle not being made within the period specified in paragraph (1) he may permit the application to be accepted and dealt with as if it had been made within that period. **[1593]**

NOTES
Commencement: 23 September 1988.

14. Notice of place and time of first examinations or periodical tests

(1) As soon as reasonably practicable after the date of the receipt of an application for a first examination or periodical test of a vehicle under regulation 12(1)(a) the Secretary of State shall send to the applicant notice of the vehicle testing station at which the examination or test is to take place, and the date and time reserved by the Secretary of State for that examination [or test].

(2) On receipt of an application under regulation 12(1)(b) the person in charge of the vehicle testing station shall send to the applicant notice of the date and time at which the examination or test will be carried out.   **[1594]**

NOTES
Commencement: 23 September 1988.
Para (1): words in square brackets added by SI 1989 No 1693, reg 5.

15. Application for re-tests following first examinations or periodical tests

(1) Where, under regulation 23(1) or 26, a notification of the refusal of a goods vehicle test certificate in respect of a vehicle is issued the vehicle may be submitted, if need be on more than one occasion, at a vehicle testing station for a re-test in accordance with the following provisions of this regulation.

(2) Where an applicant desires to submit a vehicle for a re-test, within 14 days after the date on which it was submitted for its first examination or periodical test, at the vehicle testing station at which its first examination or periodical test was carried out or, where that station was an auxiliary station, at that or another testing station, such applicant shall make arrangements as to the date and time at which the vehicle is to be submitted for the re-test with the person in charge of the station at which the vehicle is to be submitted.

(3) Where an applicant desires to submit a vehicle for a further re-test, within 14 days after the date on which it was submitted for a re-test in accordance with the provisions of paragraph (4), at the vehicle testing station at which such re-test was carried out or, where that station was an auxiliary station, at that or another testing station, such applicant shall make arrangements as to the date and time at which the vehicle is to be submitted for the further re-test with the person in charge of the station at which the vehicle is to be submitted.

(4) Where an applicant desires to submit a vehicle for a re-test in circumstances other than those to which paragraph (2) or (3) applies, he shall apply in writing to the person in charge of such vehicle testing station as he shall select for a date and time at which the vehicle may be submitted for the re-test, and every such application shall be made not later than 7 days before the date on which the re-test is required on a form approved by the Secretary of State and shall contain the particulars required by that form, and upon receipt of the application the Secretary of State shall send to the applicant a notice stating where the re-test is to take place.   **[1595]**

NOTES
Commencement: 23 September 1988.

16. Fees for re-tests

(1) Save as provided in [paragraphs (2A) and (3)], the fee for a re-test of a vehicle carried out under regulation 15(2) or (3) is [£17.60] in the case of a motor vehicle and [£9.70] in the case of a trailer and such fee shall be paid to the Secretary of State on the submission of the vehicle for the re-test ....

(2) [Save as provided in paragraph (2B)] the fee for a re-test of a vehicle carried out under regulation 15(4) is [£34.70] in the case of a motor vehicle and [£17.90] in the case of a trailer, and such fee shall be paid to the Secretary of State at the same time as the application for the re-test under regulation 15(4) is made.

[(2A) Where the date arranged for a re-test under regulation 15(2) or (3) is, at the applicant's request, a Saturday, the fee in respect of the re-test shall be increased by [£9.80] in the case of a motor vehicle and [£6.10] in the case of a trailer.

(2B) Where the date appointed for a re-test under regulation 15(4) is, at the applicant's request, a Saturday, the fee in respect of the re-test shall be increased by [£19.50] in the case of a motor vehicle and [£12.30] in the case of a trailer.

(2C) Any sum payable by virtue of paragraph (2A) or (2B) shall be paid to the Secretary of State on or before the date appointed for the examination or test.]

(3) [The fees prescribed in paragraphs (1) and (2A)] shall not be payable if—

(a) the vehicle is submitted for a re-test on the same day as the day on which the first examination or periodical test, as the case may be, was carried out, or the next following day on which the vehicle testing station at which arrangements have been made to carry out the re-test is open;

(b) the fee for the first examination, periodical test or last preceding re-test, as the case may be, has been paid; and

(c) the re-test is due only to one or more defects in the vehicle as a result of which any of the following prescribed construction and use requirements are not complied with, namely those contained in—

(i) the following items in paragraphs 1 and 2 of Schedule 3, namely 8, 9, 11, 12, 14, 15, 18 (so far as the regulation there mentioned relates to the emission of an oily substance), . . . 21 (so far as that item relates to the spare wheel carrier, fuel tanks and system, bumpers and the cab), 22 to 33 and 36 to 41; and

(ii) paragraph 3 in Schedule 3.　　　　　　　　　　**[1596]**

NOTES

Commencement: 31 October 1989 (paras (2A)-(2C)); 23 September 1988 (remainder).

Para (1): words in square brackets substituted, and words omitted revoked, by SI 1989 No 1693, reg 6(2); figures in square brackets substituted by SI 1992 No 2447.

Para (2): words in square brackets added by SI 1989 No 1693, reg 6(3); figures in square brackets substituted by SI 1992 No 2447.

Paras (2A)-(2C): added by SI 1989 No 1693, reg 6(4); figures in square brackets substituted by SI 1992 No 564.

Para (3): words in square brackets substituted by SI 1989 No 1693, reg 6(5); word omitted repealed by SI 1991 No 252, reg 6.

PART III

REGULATIONS GOVERNING FIRST EXAMINATIONS

Examination for plating

17. (1) In a case where a vehicle is submitted for an examination for plating, a goods vehicle examiner shall cause the vehicle to be examined for the purpose of determining whether—

(a) the vehicle is of a make, model and type to which the standard lists apply;

(b) the constructional particulars relating to that make, model and type are substantially complied with by the vehicle; and

(c) the weights shown in the standard lists are applicable to the vehicle.

(2) For the purpose mentioned in paragraph (1) the goods vehicles examiner shall have regard to—

(a) the particulars as respects the vehicle shown in the application mentioned in regulation 12 relating to the vehicle; and

(b) any information which may have been supplied by the Secretary of State subsequent to the publication of the standard lists as to the applicability of any of the weights shown in those lists.   **[1597]**

NOTES
Commencement: 23 September 1988.

18. (1) This regulation applies to every vehicle to which these Regulations apply and for which there has been issued a certificate of conformity or a Minister's approval certificate as required under the National Type Approval for Goods Vehicles Regulations.

(2) On the submission for a first examination under these Regulations of a vehicle to which this regulation applies, the driver of the vehicle shall produce to the examiner the certificate or a substitute, issued by the Secretary of State, for it which, by virtue of [section 59(4) of the 1988 Act], is treated as the plating certificate of the vehicle.

(3) The examiner shall examine a vehicle so submitted to ascertain whether or not—

(a) particulars on the certificate or substitute mentioned in paragraph (2) are appropriate for the vehicle having regard to the standard lists and the condition of the vehicle; and

(b) the vehicle has been subject to any notifiable alteration which has not been notified.

(4) In the case of a vehicle where the examiner is satisfied that—

(a) no notifiable alteration which has not been notified has occurred; and

(b) the particulars on the certificate or substitute mentioned in paragraph (2) are appropriate as mentioned in paragraph (3),

the certificate or substitute shall be deemed to have been issued as a result of the examination under the above paragraphs of this regulation as well as in consequence of the certificate of conformity or Minister's approval certificate.

(5) In the case of a vehicle where the examiner is not satisfied as mentioned in paragraph (4)—

(a) the vehicle shall be subject to a first examination as if no certificate of conformity or Minister's approval certificate had been issued in respect of it;

(b) if any notifiable alteration has been made but not reported to the Secretary of State in accordance with regulation 30 the fee prescribed by regulation 34 shall be paid before the said first examination is started; and

(c) any certificate or substitute mentioned in paragraph (2) issued before the vehicle was submitted for its first examiation shall, as from the date of submission, be of no effect. **[1598]**

NOTES
Commencement: 23 September 1988.
Para (2): words in square brackets substituted by SI 1990 No 448, reg 5.
1988 Act: Road Traffic Act 1988.

19. In the event of a goods vehicle examiner determining that the vehicle (not being a vehicle to which regulation 18(4) applies) submitted for an examination for plating is of a make, model and type or otherwise one to which the weights shown in the standard lists apply there shall be determined—

(a) as the plated weights of the vehicle, weights relating to the gross weight and axle weight for each axle being the equivalent weights shown as the design weights in the standard lists for vehicles of that make, model and type:
Provided that if the use on roads of the vehicle at any such equivalent weight would contravene any of the provisions of regulation 25, 75, 78 or 79 of the Construction and Use Regulations, then any such equivalent weight shall for the purpose of determination of a plated weight under this regulation be reduced to such extent as is necessary to avoid such contravention;

(b) if the vehicle is a motor vehicle, as its plated weight relating to train weight, the equivalent weight shown as a design weight in the standard lists for vehicles of that make, model and type:
Provided that if any such equivalent weight exceeds the maximum weight at which the vehicle can lawfully be used on a road in Great Britain by virtue of the Construction and Use Regulations, then such equivalent weight shall be reduced to that maximum weight. **[1599]**

NOTES
Commencement: 23 September 1988.

20. In the event of a goods vehicle examiner determining that the vehicle submitted for an examination for plating is not of a make, model and type or otherwise one to which the weights shown in the standard lists apply he shall determine the plated weights of the vehicle having regard—

(a) to any information which may have been supplied by the Secretary of State as to the plated weights which have been determined for similar vehicles under these Regulations;

(b) to the design, construction and equipment of the vehicle, and the stresses to which it is likely to be subject when in use on roads;

(c) to any information which may be available about the weights at which the vehicle was originally designed to be driven on roads;

(d) if the vehicle or its equipment has, or appears to have, been altered since the date of its manufacture, to the likely effect of any such alteration in making the vehicle fit to be driven safely on roads at weights different from those at which it appears to the examiner the vehicle was originally designed to be so driven;

(e) if the vehicle is a motor vehicle, to the requirements as to brakes specified in the definition of "the standard lists" in regulation 3(1);

(f) if the vehicle is a trailer, to—

(i) the requirements of regulations 15 and 16 of the Construction and Use Regulations; and

(ii) the provisions of Schedule 1; and

(g) to the need to comply with regulations 25, 75, 78 and 79 of the Construction and Use Regulations, and with the requirement that no plated weight relating to the train weight of a motor vehicle shall exceed the maximum train weight at which the vehicle can lawfully be used on a road in Great Britain by virtue of the Construction and Use Regulations.   **[1600]**

NOTES
Commencement: 23 September 1988.

21. Issue of plating certificates and particulars to be contained therein

(1) Save as provided in paragraph (2), after the determination of the plated weights of a vehicle submitted for an examination for plating there shall, unless there is a refusal to issue a goods vehicle test certificate in respect of that vehicle, be issued a plating certificate in respect of that vehicle.

(2) Paragraph (1) does not apply in a case to which regulation 18(4) applies.

(3) Every plating certificate issued in relation to a vehicle shall—

(a) be signed either by the goods vehicle examiner who carried out, or under whose direction the examination for plating was carried out, or by a person authorised in that behalf by the Secretary of State; and

(b) contain—

(i) the date on which it was issued;

(ii) the number allotted by the Secretary of State to the vehicle testing station at which it was issued or the letters GVC if it was issued at the Goods Vehicle Centre;

(iii) the plated weights determined for that vehicle under regulation 19, 20 or 24;

(iv) where any such plated weight determined under regulation 19 is less than the equivalent weight shown as a design weight in the standard lists, that equivalent weight;

(v) where any such plated weight determined under regulation 20 is less than the weight which would have been determined but for paragraph (g) of that regulation the weight which would have been determined but for that paragraph shall be shown as a design weight;

(vi) the other plated particulars ascertained from the application mentioned in regulation 12 and an inspection of the vehicle;

(vii) any alteration in the vehicle or its equipment which is required by these Regulations to be notified to the Secretary of State; and

(viii) the sizes of the tyres fitted to the wheels of the vehicle at the time of the issue of the certificate, and the particular conditions, if any, in which a vehicle should be used on roads at or below its plated weights when fitted with those tyres properly maintained.

(4) A plating certificate issued in relation to a vehicle under the provisions of these Regulations may contain (in addition to the particulars mentioned in paragraph (3))—

(a) the DOE (Department of the Environment) or DTp (Department of Transport) reference number for the particular type of vehicle, and

(b) the maximum authorised weights and dimensions in accordance with article 2 of Council Directive 85/3/EEC.   **[1601]**

NOTES
Commencement: 23 September 1988.
Council Directive 85/3/EEC: OJ L2, 3.1.1985, p 14.

22. Goods vehicle test

After there has been carried out on a vehicle either an examination for plating or an examination as mentioned in regulation 18(3) a goods vehicle examiner shall arrange for the vehicle to undergo a goods vehicle test. **[1602]**

NOTES
Commencement: 23 September 1988.

23. Issue of goods vehicle test certificates (or of notices of refusal) and particulars to be contained therein

(1) Where as a result of a goods vehicle test a vehicle is found not to comply with the prescribed construction and use requirements there shall be issued a notice of the refusal of a goods vehicle test certificate, and such notice shall state the grounds of such refusal.

(2) Where as a result of a goods vehicle test a vehicle is found to comply with the prescribed construction and use requirements a goods vehicle test certificate shall be issued as respects that vehicle and such certificate shall state the period of the validity of the certificate and that the vehicle was found to comply with the prescribed construction and use requirements.

(3) Every notice issued under paragraph (1) and every certificate issued under paragraph (2) shall—

    (a) be signed by either the goods vehicle examiner who carried out, or under whose direction the goods vehicle test was carried out, or by a person authorised in that behalf by the Secretary of State; and

    (b) contain—

        (i) the date on which it was issued;

       (ii) the number allotted by the Secretary of State to the vehicle testing station at which it was issued;

      (iii) in the case of a certificate or notice issued for a motor vehicle, the registration mark (if any) exhibited on the vehicle or, if no such mark is so exhibited, the chassis or serial number marked on the vehicle or, if no such number is so marked, the identification mark which shall have been allotted to the vehicle by the Secretary of State in the notice of appointment relating to the first examination of the vehicle; and

      (iv) in the case of a certificate or notice issued for a trailer, the identification mark which shall have been allotted to the trailer by the Secretary of State in the notice of appointment (if any) relating to the first examination of the trailer or shall have otherwise been allotted to the trailer by the Secretary of State under these Regulations. **[1603]**

NOTES
Commencement: 23 September 1988.

24. Re-test procedure, and issue of plating and test certificates (or notices of refusal)

(1) Where on a first examination of a vehicle no plating certificate has been issued in respect of that vehicle and it is submitted for a re-test under regulation

15 a goods vehicle examiner shall determine as the plated weights of the vehicle—

    (a) if after examination of the vehicle he is satisfied that no alteration has been made to the vehicle or its equipment which would render inapplicable the plated weights determined for the vehicle on its first examination, the weights so determined; or

    (b) if he is not so satisfied, weights consistent with regulation 19 or, as the case may be, regulation 20.

(2) A goods vehicle examiner in carrying out an examination pursuant to regulation 15(2) and (3) shall be under an obligation only to examine the vehicle for the purpose of ascertaining whether it complies with the particular items of the prescribed construction and use requirements with which it was shown in the last notice of a refusal of a test certificate not to comply.

(3) Where a goods vehicle examiner finds that the vehicle complies with the particular items of the prescribed construction and use requirements mentioned in paragraph (2) and has no reason to believe that the other prescribed construction and use requirements are not complied with in relation to the vehicle, there shall be issued a goods vehicle test certificate and also a plating certificate for the vehicle.

(4) Where a goods vehicle examiner finds that the vehicle does not comply with the particular items of the prescribed construction and use requirements mentioned in paragraph (2) or that any other prescribed construction and use requirement is not complied with in relation to the vehicle, there shall be issued a notice of the refusal of a goods vehicle test certificate and in that event no plating certificate shall be issued for the vehicle.

(5) On completion of an examination of a vehicle pursuant to regulation 15(4) a goods vehicle examiner shall arrange for the vehicle to undergo a goods vehicle test, and when that test has been completed there shall be issued—

    (a) where the vehicle is found to comply with the prescribed construction and use requirements, a goods vehicle test certificate and also a plating certificate for that vehicle; or

    (b) where the vehicle is found not to comply with the prescribed construction and use requirements, a notice of the refusal of a goods vehicle test certificate, and in that event no plating certificate shall be issued for the vehicle. **[1604]**

NOTES
  Commencement: 23 September 1988.

25. Appeals

(1) Any person aggrieved by a determination made on a first examination, or on a consequent re-test of a vehicle, may appeal to the area engineer for the traffic area in which that determination was made, and any person aggrieved by the determination of the area engineer under this regulation may appeal to the Secretary of State.

(2) Any appeal to the area engineer shall be lodged at the office of the relevant traffic area not later than 10 days from the date of the determination, and any appeal to the Secretary of State shall be lodged at the Goods Vehicle Centre, not later than 14 days from the date of the determination.

(3) Every appeal shall be made on a form approved by the Secretary of State and shall contain the particulars required by that form.

(4) An appeal to the area engineer shall be accompanied by a fee of £15 and an appeal to the Secretary of State shall be accompanied by a fee of £25.

(5) As soon as reasonably practicable after the date of the receipt of the appeal, the area engineer or, as the case may be, the appeal officer shall send a notice, addressed to the appellant at the address of the appellant stated in the form of appeal, stating where and when a re-examination for the purpose of determining the issues raised on the appeal is to take place.

(6) The place to be selected by the area engineer or, as the case may be, the appeal officer, for the re-examination for the purposes of the appeal may be either a vehicle testing station or such other place as he may consider convenient for the purposes of carrying out that re-examination.

(7) The vehicle shall be submitted for the re-examination (which will be carried out by the area engineer or, as the case may be, the appeal officer) at the place and time specified in the notice sent to the appellant under paragraph (5) unless arrangements are made with the agreement of the area engineer or, as the case may be, the appeal officer, for the carrying out of the examination at some other place or time.

(8) On the submission of a vehicle for a re-examination for the purpose of an appeal the person submitting the vehicle for the re-examination shall, if requested to do so by the area engineer or the appeal officer,

    (a) produce—

        (i) if the appeal relates to a determination made on an examination for plating, or on a re-examination by an area engineer, and as a result of which a plating certificate was issued, that certificate; or

        (ii) if the appeal relates to a determination made on a goods vehicle test, or on a re-examination by an area engineer, the notice of refusal of a goods vehicle test certificate issued as a result of that test or re-examination; and

    (b) give such information as may reasonably be required relating to any alteration made or repairs carried out, or any accident or other event occurring since the date of the determination appealed against, which may have affected the vehicle or its equipment.

(9) The area engineer or, as the case may be, the appeal officer shall not be required to proceed with the re-examination unless the person submitting the vehicle for the re-examination complies with paragraph (8) and nothing in this paragraph shall be taken to derogate from regulation 8.

(10) On completion of the re-examination the area engineer or, as the case may be, the Secretary of State shall make such determination as he thinks fit, and may—

    (a) where the appeal relates to a determination made on or in connection with an examination for plating as respects which a plating certificate was issued, either determine that such certificate was properly issued or issue a different plating certificate upon surrender of the first mentioned certificate; or

    (b) where the appeal relates to a determination made on a goods vehicle test, or by an area engineer in connection with a notice of refusal of a goods vehicle test certificate, issue either a goods vehicle test certificate and plating certificate for the vehicle or a notice of refusal of a goods vehicle test certificate stating the grounds thereof and in that event no plating certificate shall be issued for the vehicle.

(11) Plating certificates, goods vehicle test certificates and notices of refusal of a goods vehicle test certificate issued under the foregoing provisions of this regulation shall be signed by the area engineer or, as the case may be, the appeal officer and shall contain—

(a) the same particulars as are appropriate in the case of plating certificates, goods vehicle test certificates and notices of refusal of a goods vehicle test certificate mentioned in regulation 21 or 23, subject nevertheless to such modifications as may be appropriate and subject in the case of a plating certificate to that certificate showing particulars of the plated weights determined for that vehicle by the area engineer or by the Secretary of State;

(b) in the case of a plating certificate—

(i) where the vehicle is one of a make, model and type and otherwise one to which the standard lists apply and any plated weight so determined is less than the equivalent weight shown as a design weight in such lists, particulars of that equivalent weight; and

(ii) where any plated weight so determined is less than the weight that would have been otherwise determined under regulation 20 but for paragraph (g) of that regulation, particulars of the last mentioned weight (which shall be shown as a design weight).

[1605]

NOTES
Commencement: 23 September 1988.

PART IV

REGULATIONS GOVERNING PERIODICAL TESTS

26. Periodical tests, and issue of test certificates (or notices of refusal)

On the submission of a vehicle for a periodical test a goods vehicle examiner shall arrange for a vehicle to undergo that test, and when that test has been completed there shall be issued—

(a) where the vehicle is found to comply with the prescribed construction and use requirements, a goods vehicle test certificate; or

(b) were the vehicle is found not to comply with the prescribed construction and use requirements, a notice of the refusal of a goods vehicle test certificate.   **[1606]**

NOTES
Commencement: 23 September 1988.

27. Re-test procedure, and issue of test certificates (or notices of refusal)

(1) Where a vehicle is submitted for a re-test at a vehicle testing station under regulation 15(2) or (3), a goods vehicle examiner shall in carrying out the test be under an obligation only to examine the vehicle for the purpose of ascertaining whether it complies with the particular items of the prescribed construction and use requirements with which it was shown in the last notice of a refusal of a test certificate not to comply.

(2) Where a goods vehicle examiner finds that the vehicle complies with the particular items of the prescribed construction and use requirements mentioned in paragraph (1) and has no reason to believe that the other prescribed construction and use requirements are not complied with in relation to the vehicle, there shall be issued a goods vehicle test certificate.

(3) Where a goods vehicle examiner does not find that the vehicle complies with the particular items of the prescribed construction and use requirements mentioned in paragraph (1) or finds that any other prescribed construction and use requirement is not complied with in relation to the vehicle, there shall be issued a notice of the refusal of a test certificate.

(4) Where a vehicle is submitted for a re-test at a vehicle testing station under regulation 15(4), a goods vehicle examiner shall arrange for the vehicle to undergo a goods vehicle test, and when that test has been completed there shall be issued—

    (a) where the vehicle is found to comply with the prescribed construction and use requirements, a goods vehicle test certificate;

    (b) where the vehicle is found not to comply with the prescribed construction and use requirements, a notice of the refusal of a goods vehicle test certificate. **[1607]**

NOTES
Commencement: 23 September 1988.

28. Form of test certificates and notices of refusal

Goods vehicle test certificates and notices of the refusal of a goods vehicle test certificate issued under regulation 24, 26 or 27 shall contain the same particulars as are appropriate in the case of goods vehicle test certificates and notices of the refusal of a goods vehicle test certificate mentioned in regulation 23 and shall be signed in the same manner as is provided in regulation 23. **[1608]**

NOTES
Commencement: 23 September 1988.

29. Appeals

(1) Any person aggrieved by a determination made on a periodical test of a vehicle, or on a consequent re-test of a vehicle, by the person in charge of that test may appeal to the area engineer for the traffic area in which that determination was made, and any person aggrieved by the determination of the area engineer under this regulation may appeal to the Secretary of State.

(2) Paragraphs (2) to (11) of regulation 25 apply in relation to any appeal under paragraph (1) as they apply in relation to an appeal under regulation 25 relating to a determination made on a goods vehicles test, but for the purposes of such application each reference in regulation 25 to a plating certificate shall be treated as being omitted. **[1609]**

NOTES
Commencement: 23 September 1988.

PART V

REGULATIONS GOVERNING NOTIFIABLE ALTERATIONS, AMENDMENTS OF PLATING CERTIFICATES AND RE-EXAMINATIONS IN CONNECTION THEREWITH

Secretary of State to be informed of notifiable alterations

30. In the event of a notifiable alteration being made to a vehicle in respect of which a plating certificate has been issued, and before the vehicle to which the alteration has been made is used on roads, particulars of that alteration on a form approved by the Secretary of State shall be sent to him at the Goods Vehicles Centre, and any such form may contain a request by the sender for an amendment to be made as respects a plated weight shown on the plating certificate for the vehicle.   **[1610]**

NOTES
Commencement: 23 September 1988.

31. In this Part of these Regulations, any reference to the re-examination of a vehicle shall, as regards a vehicle for which there has been issued a certificate of conformity or a Minister's approval certificate and which has not been submitted for an examination as provided in regulation 18, be construed as a reference to an examination of the vehicle.   **[1611]**

NOTES
Commencement: 23 September 1988.

32. Other amendments to the plating certificate

Where, otherwise than by reason of a notifiable alteration, any particular (with reference to a plated weight or any other matter) contained in a plating certificate for a vehicle becomes or may have become no longer applicable to that vehicle, an application on a form approved by the Secretary of State may be sent to him ... , for the purpose of having the vehicle re-examined with a view to that particular being amended.   **[1612]**

NOTES
Commencement: 23 September 1988.
Words omitted revoked by SI 1989 No 1693, reg 7.

33. Provision as to re-examination

(1) Where, under regulation 33, particulars of a notifiable alteration are sent to the Secretary of State and the form contains a request as provided in that regulation the Secretary of State shall by notice to the sender require him to submit the vehicle for re-examination.

(2) Where, under regulation 30, particulars of a notifiable alteration are sent to the Secretary of State and the form does not contain a request as provided in that regulation the Secretary of State shall determine whether to require a re-examination of the vehicle. If the Secretary of State determines that no re-examination is required he shall by notice inform the sender accordingly, and if the Secretary of State determines that a re-examination is required he shall by notice require the sender to submit the vehicle for re-examination.

(3) Where, under regulation 32, an application to have a vehicle re-examined is received by the Secretary of State he shall by notice require the sender to submit the vehicle for re-examination.

(4) Any notice by which the Secretary of State requires a vehicle to be submitted for re-examination under paragraph (1), (2) or (3) shall specify the vehicle testing station, date and time appointed by the Secretary of State for that re-examination. **[1613]**

NOTES
Commencement: 23 September 1988.

34. Fee for re-examination

[(1)] Where such a request as is mentioned in regulation 30 is contained in the form mentioned in that regulation or where an application mentioned in regulation 32 is made, a fee of [£13.90] shall be sent to the Secretary of State with that form or, as the case may be, with that application.

[(2) Where the date appointed for a re-examination under regulation 33 is, at the request of the person required to submit the vehicle for re-examination, a Saturday, the fee in respect of the re-examination shall be increased by [£8.40].

(3) Any sum payable by virtue of paragraph (2) shall be paid to the Secretary of State on or before the date appointed for the re-examination.] **[1614]**

NOTES
Commencement: 31 October 1989 (paras (2), (3)); 23 September 1988 (remainder).
Para (1): numbered by SI 1989 No 1693, reg 8; amount in square brackets substituted by SI 1992 No 2447.
Paras (2), (3): added by SI 1989 No 1693, reg 8; figure in square brackets in sub-s (2) substituted by SI 1992 No 564.

35. Condition of acceptance of vehicle

A goods vehicle examiner shall not be under an obligation to proceed with a re-examination of a vehicle under this Part of these Regulations where on the submission of a vehicle for the re-examination the sender does not, after being required to do so, produce to the examiner the plating certificate relating to the vehicle, and nothing in this paragraph shall be taken to [derogate from regulation 8]. **[1615]**

NOTES
Commencement: 23 September 1988.
Words in square brackets substituted by SI 1991 No 252, reg 7.

36. Re-examination procedure, and issue or amendment of plating certificates (or notices of refusal)

(1) Where a vehicle is submitted for a re-examination under this Part of these Regulations a goods vehicle examiner shall—

  (a) in a case where the re-examination is carried out by reason of a notifiable alteration examine the vehicle for the purpose of determining to what extent that notifiable alteration has rendered the plated weights shown in the plating certificate relating to that vehicle no longer appropriate; or

  (b) in any other case examine the vehicle for the purpose of determining to what extent any particular contained in the said plating certificate is no longer applicable.

(2) On completion of the re-examination the goods vehicle examiner shall either—

  (a) by notice inform the sender that—

    (i) the notifiable alteratation has not rendered any of the plated weights shown in the plating certificate no longer appropriate;
    (ii) the particular is still applicable; or

(b) amend the plating certificate to show any new plated weights or any new particulars which the examiner has determined for the vehicle; or

(c) issue a new plating certificate in place of the certificate required to be produced under regulation 35 and mark as cancelled the certificate so produced.

(3) Any goods vehicle examiner amending or cancelling a plating certificate shall authenticate the amendment or cancellation by showing on the certificate or on a document securely attached to it his name, the address of the place at which the examination as a result of which the amendment or cancellation occurs, and the date on which the amendment or cancellation takes effect.

(4) Where a new plating certificate is issued for a vehicle it shall contain—

(a) particulars of any plated weights determined for the vehicle under this regulation;

(b) where the vehicle is one of a make, model and type and otherwise one to which the standard lists apply and any such plated weight so determined is less than the equivalent weight shown as a design weight in such lists, particulars of that equivalent weight;

(c) where any such plated weight so determined is less than the weight that would have been otherwise determined under regulation 20 but for paragraph (g) of that regulation, particulars of the last mentioned weight which shall be shown as a design weight;

(d) any other new particular determined for the vehicle under this regulation; and

(e) subject to sub-paragraphs (a) to (d) above, the same particulars as are appropriate in the case of the plating certificate mentioned in regulation 21.

(5) A new plating certificate shall be signed by the goods vehicle examiner who carried out, or under whose direction the re-examination was carried out, or shall be signed on behalf of that examiner by a person authorised in that behalf by the Secretary of State. **[1616]**

NOTES
Commencement: 23 September 1988.

37. Appeals

(1) Any person aggrieved by a determination made on a re-examination of a vehicle under this Part of these Regulations may appeal to the area engineer for the traffic area in which that determination was made, and any person aggrieved by the determination of the area engineer under this regulation may appeal to the Secretary of State.

(2) Paragraphs (2) to (9) of regulation 25 shall apply in relation to an appeal under paragraph (1) as they apply to an appeal under regulation 25, but for the purposes of such application paragraph (8) of that regulation shall have effect as if the references therein to a plating certificate were references to any plating certificate relevant to the appeal under this regulation.

(3) On completion of the re-examination of the vehicle for the purpose of the appeal, the area engineer or, as the case may be, the Secretary of State, shall

make such determination in the matter as he thinks fit and may issue a different plating certificate upon the surrender of any plating certificate previously issued for the vehicle.

(4) Any different plating certificate issued under paragraph (3) shall—

(a) be signed by the area engineer who carried out the re-examination or, as the case may be, on behalf of the Secretary of State by an officer appointed by him for the purpose; and

(b) contain—

(i) the same particulars as are appropriate in the case of a plating certificate issued under regulation 21 subject to such modifications as may be appropriate and subject to the certificate showing particulars of the plated weights determined for that vehicle by the area engineer who carried out the re-examination or, as the case may be, by the Secretary of State in a case where such plated weight is so determined;

(ii) where the vehicle is one of a make, model and type and otherwise one to which the standard lists apply and any such plated weight so determined is less than the equivalent weight shown as a design weight in such lists, particulars of that equivalent weight; and

(iii) where any such plated weight so determined is less than the weight that would have been otherwise determined under regulation 20 but for paragraph (g) of that regulation, particulars of the last mentioned weight which shall be shown as a design weight. **[1617]**

NOTES
Commencement: 23 September 1988.

PART VI

MISCELLANEOUS MATTERS

39. General provisions as to fees

(1) In this regulation "exceptional circumstances" means an accident, a fire, an epidemic, severe weather, a failure in the supply of essential services or other unexpected happening (excluding a breakdown or mechanical defect in a vehicle or non-delivery of spare parts therefor).

(2) Where any fee under these Regulations in respect of an examination has been paid that fee shall, subject to paragraph (3), be payable notwithstanding that the vehicle is not submitted for an examination on the day at the time fixed under these Regulations for that examination and notwithstanding that the examination is not carried out by reason of any provision of regulation 8.

(3) If the applicant for an examination—

(a) has not less than 7 days before the day fixed under these Regulations for the carrying out of the examination given the Secretary of State notice (whether in writing or otherwise) at the vehicle testing station at which the examination has been arranged that he does not propose to submit the vehicle for examination on that day; or

(b) satisfies the Secretary of State that the vehicle cannot, or as the case may be, could not be submitted for the examination on the day or at the time fixed for the examination because of exceptional circumstances occurring not more than 7 days before the said time and of which the applicant gives notice to the Secretary of State (whether in writing or otherwise) within 3 days of the occurrence of those circumstances,

then the applicant may either—

(i) make an application in writing to the Secretary of State at the vehicle testing station at which the examination has been arranged either at the time of the notice given under paragraph (3)(a) or (b) or within 28 days of the date thereof, for another examination of the same kind for that vehicle or another vehicle to be carried out within three months of the date of the application, and in that event the said fee shall be treated as having been paid in respect of that application unless the fee in respect of that application is greater, in which case the fee already paid shall be treated as having been paid towards the fee payable in respect of that application; or

(ii) give notice to the Secretary of State at the place mentioned in sub-paragraph (i) above and at the time of the notice given under paragraph (3)(a) or (b) or within 28 days of the date thereof, that no other examination of the same kind is required for that vehicle or another vehicle, and in that event [the fee shall be reduced to £1.50 (the balance of any sum already paid in respect of the fee being refundable)]. **[1618]**

NOTES
Commencement: 23 September 1988.
Para (3): words in square brackets substituted by SI 1989 No 1693, reg 10.

40. Provisions as to fees on appeal

(1) After the completion of a re-examination for the purposes of an appeal under [section 50(1) or (3) of the 1988 Act] the Secretary of State may repay to the appellant, as he thinks fit, either the whole or part of the fee paid on the appeal, where it appears to him there were substantial grounds for contesting the whole or part of the determination against which the appeal was made.

(2) A fee payable on an appeal in accordance with these Regulations shall be payable notwithstanding that the vehicle is not submitted for re-examination in accordance with regulation 25(8) or in accordance with that regulation as applied by any other regulation contained in these Regulations;

Provided that, if the appellant has before the time fixed under regulation 25, or under that regulation as so applied, for the carrying out of the re-examination given the Secretary of State not less than two clear days' notice (whether in writing or otherwise) at the office at which his appeal was lodged that the appellant does not propose to submit the vehicle for re-examination at that time, the appeal shall be treated for the purposes of this regulation as one in respect of which no fee is payable and any amount previously paid in respect of such a fee shall be repaid by the Secretary of State to the appellant unless another time is arranged for carrying out of the re-examination. **[1619]**

NOTES
Commencement: 23 September 1988.
Para (1): words in square brackets substituted by SI 1990 No 448, reg 6.
1988 Act: Road Traffic Act 1988.

41. Replacements of plates and certificates

(1) If a Ministry plate, a plating certificate (whether issued under these Regulations or being treated as a plating certificate by virtue of [section 59(4) of the 1988 Act]), a goods vehicle test certificate or a Ministry test date disc has been lost or defaced, an application for the issue of a replacement for the plate, certificate or disc lost or defaced may be made in writing to the Goods Vehicle Centre, and every such application shall be accompanied by the payment of the fee of [£[9.50]].

(2) On the receipt of an application and fee mentioned in paragraph (1) the Secretary of State shall determine whether the vehicle shall be re-examined, and if he determines—

(a) that no re-examination of the vehicle is required he shall issue to the applicant a replacement for the plate, certificate or disc to which the application relates and any such replacement shall have the same effect as the plate, certificate or disc which it replaces and shall be marked "replacement";

(b) that a re-examination of the vehicle is required, he shall by notice to the sender require the vehicle to be submitted for re-examination at a vehicle testing station specified in the notice and appoint a date and time for the examination.

(3) A re-examination under paragraph (2)(b) shall be carried out as if it were a first examination under regulations 17 to 23, the appropriate fee shall be paid as if the examination were a first examination, and the appropriate documents shall be issued in accordance with regulations 21 and 23.   **[1620]**

NOTES
Commencement: 23 September 1988.
Para (1): words and figures in square brackets substituted by SI 1992 No 2447.
1988 Act: Road Traffic Act 1988.

42. Provisions as to notices

(1) Except as otherwise provided in these Regulations, every notice under these Regulations shall be in writing and may be given by post.

(2) For the purposes of calculating the period of any notice given in accordance with the provisions of these Regulations a Saturday, Sunday, Good Friday, Christmas Day or a bank holiday (as defined in the Banking and Financial Dealings Act 1971) shall be excluded from the period.

(3) When giving any notice referred to in regulation 14(1), 15(4) or 33 the Secretary of State shall have regard, so far as is reasonably practicable, to any preference expressed by the person to whom the notice is addressed as to the vehicle testing station and the date and time at which the examination shall take place.   **[1621]**

NOTES
Commencement: 23 September 1988.

PART VII
CROWN VEHICLES

43. Provision as to Crown vehicles

(1) Except as provided in paragraphs (2) and (3), these Regulations apply to goods vehicles which are of a class specified in regulation 4 and which are—

(a) goods vehicles in the public service of the Crown which are registered or liable to be registered under the 1971 Act; or

(b) trailers in the public service of the Crown while drawn by goods vehicles (whether or not in the public service of the Crown) which are registered or liable to be registered under the 1971 Act.

(2) A first examination of a vehicle, a periodical test or a re-examiation of a vehicle under Part V of these Regulations may be made by or under the direction of an examiner (in this regulation referred to as an "authorised examiner") authorised for the purpose by the Secretary of State instead of by or under the direction of a goods vehicle examiner, and in relation to any such examination made by an authorised examiner these Regulations shall apply as if—

(a) regulations 6, 8, 12, 13, 14, 15, 25, 29 and 37 were omitted;

(b) any reference to a goods vehicle examiner included a reference to an authorised examiner, and any reference to a vehicle testing station included a reference to premises approved by the Secretary of State for the carrying out of examinations under these Regulations by an authorised examiner;

(c) in regulations 17(2)(a) and 21(3)(b)(vi) the reference to the application included a reference to a form approved by the Secretary of State for the purpose of an application for an examination under these Regulations by an authorised examiner; and

(d) in regulation 23(3)(b)(iii) and (iv) the reference to the identification mark included a reference to an identification mark allotted by the Secretary of State for the purpose of an examination under these Regulations by an authorised examiner.

(3) Any person aggrieved by a determination of an authorised examiner on a first examination of a vehicle, a periodical test or a re-examination of a vehicle under Part V of these Regulations may appeal to the Secretary of State and on the appeal the Secretary of State shall cause the vehicle to be re-examined by an officer appointed by him for the purpose and may make such determination on the basis of the re-examination as he thinks fit and, where appropriate, may issue a plating certificate, a goods vehicle test certificate or a notice of the refusal of a goods vehicle test certificate. **[1622]**

NOTES

Commencement: 23 September 1988.
1971 Act: Vehicles (Excise) Act 1971.

PART VIII

EXEMPTIONS

44. [Exemptions from section 53(1) and (2) of the 1988 Act]

(1) The provisions of [section 53(1) and (2) of the 1988 Act] do not apply to the use of a vehicle for any of the following purposes—

(a) the purpose of submitting it by previous arrangement for, or of bringing it away from, or being used in the course of or in connection with any examination;

(b) where a goods vehicle test certificate is refused on an examination—

(i) the purpose of delivering it by previous arrangement at, or bringing it away from, a place where work is to be or has been done on it to remedy the defects on the grounds of which the certificate was refused; or

(ii) the purpose of delivering it, by towing it, to a place where it is to be broken up;

(c) when unladen, the purpose of being driven or drawn by a vehicle driven under a trade licence issued under section 16 of the 1971 Act;

(d) the purpose of being driven or drawn where it has been imported into Great Britain after arrival in Great Britain on the journey from the place where it has arrived in Great Britain to a place where it is to be kept by the person importing the vehicle or by any other person on whose behalf the vehicle has been imported, and in this sub-paragraph the reference to a vehicle being imported into Great Britain is a reference, in the case of a vehicle which has been so imported more than once, to the first such importation, and in determining for the purposes of this sub-paragraph when a vehicle was first so imported any such importation as is referred to in paragraph 24 of Schedule 2 shall be disregarded;

(e) any purpose for which it is authorised to be used on roads by an order under [section 44 of the 1988 Act];

(f) any purpose connected with its seizure or detention by [a constable];

(g) any purpose connected with its removal, detention, seizure, condemnation or forfeiture under any provision in the Customs and Excise Management Act 1979; and

(h) the purpose of removing it under section 3 of the Refuse Disposal (Amenity) Act 1978, or under section 99 of the Road Traffic Regulation Act 1984 or of removing it from a parking place in pursuance of an order under section 35(1) of the Road Traffic Regulation Act 1984, an order relating to a parking place designated under section 45 thereof, or a provision of a designation order having effect by virtue of section 53(3) thereof.

(2) The provisions of [section 53(1) and (2) of the 1988 Act] shall not apply to the use of a vehicle in so far as such use occurs in any place (excluding the Isle of Wight, the islands of Lewis, Mainland (Orkney), Mainland (Shetland) and Skye) being an island or to any area mainly surrounded by water, being an island or area from which motor vehicles not constructed for special purposes can at no time be conveniently driven to a road in any other part of Great Britain by reason of the absence of any bridge, tunnel, ford or other way suitable for the passage of such motor vehicles.   **[1623]**

NOTES
Commencement: 23 September 1988.
Heading: words in square brackets substituted by SI 1990 No 448, reg 8.
Paras (1), (2): words in square brackets substituted by SI 1990 No 448, reg 9.
1971 Act: Vehicle (Excise) Act 1971.
1988 Act: Road Traffic Act 1988.

45. [Exemption from section 63(2) of the 1988 Act]

Motor vehicles other than those manufactured on or after 1st October 1982 and first used on or after 1st April 1983, not constructed or adapted to form part of an articulated vehicle are hereby exempted from the provisions of [section 63(2) of the 1988 Act].   **[1624]**

NOTES
Commencement: 23 September 1988.
Heading: words in square brackets substituted by SI 1990 No 448, reg 10.
Words in square brackets substituted by SI 1990 No 448, reg 11.
1988 Act: Road Traffic Act 1988.

46. Certificates of temporary exemption

(1) The person in charge of the Goods Vehicle Centre or a vehicle testing station may issue in respect of a vehicle a certificate of temporary exemption, by virtue of which that vehicle shall not, during the period specified in paragraph (2)(d), be subject to the provisions of [section 53(1) or (2) of the 1988 Act], where—

(a) he is satisfied that by reason of exceptional circumstances, as defined in regulation 39(1) affecting either a vehicle testing station or the vehicle, an examination cannot be completed by a date fixed under these Regulations for carrying out the examination; and

(b) the use of the vehicle on or after that date would be unlawful by virtue of the said provisions.

(2) Every certificate of temporary exemption shall be on a form approved by the Secretary of State and shall be signed by a person duly authorised on his behalf and shall contain—

(a) in the case of a certificate issued for a motor vehicle, the registration mark (if any) exhibited on the vehicle or, if no such mark is so exhibited, the chassis or serial number marked on the vehicle or, if no such number is so marked, the identification mark which shall have been allotted to the vehicle by the Secretary of State in the notice of appointment relating to the first examination of the vehicle;

(b) in the case of a certificate issued for a trailer, the identification mark which shall have been allotted to the trailer by the Secretary of State in the notice of appointment (if any) relating to the first examination of the trailer or shall have otherwise been allotted to the trailer by the Secretary of State under these Regulations;

(c) the date on which the certificate is issued; and

(d) the period during which the vehicle is exempted from the provisions of [section 53(1) or (2) of the 1988 Act] so, however, that no such period shall exceed three months in duration.   **[1625]**

NOTES

Commencement: 23 September 1988.
Paras (1), (2): words in square brackets substituted by SI 1990 No 448, reg 12.
1988 Act: Road Traffic Act 1988.

SCHEDULES
SCHEDULE 1

Regulations 3(1), 20

PROVISIONS AS TO BRAKING FORCE OF TRAILERS

1. In this Schedule—

the letter "W" represents—

(a) in the case of a trailer so designed that part of the weight of the trailer is imposed on the drawing vehicle, the axle weight, or, as the case may be, the sum of the axle weights which is or are to be determined for the trailer on an examination for plating;

(b) in any other case the gross weight of the trailer which is to be so determined.

2. The minimum braking force capable of being developed by the brakes of a trailer manufactured before 1st January 1968 should in the case of—

(a) a trailer, not being a semi-trailer, be 0.4 W;

(b) a semi-trailer for which a gross weight of 6100 kilograms or more is to be determined for the vehicle on an examination for plating, be 0.35 W;

(c) a semi-trailer for which a gross weight of less than 6100 kilograms is to be so determined, be 0.32 W.

3. The minimum braking force capable of being developed by the brakes of a trailer manufactured on or after 1st January 1968 but before 1st October 1982 should in the case of—

(a) a trailer, not being a semi-trailer, be 0.5 W;
(b) semi-trailer, be 0.4 W.

4. The minimum braking force capable of being developed by the brakes of a trailer manufactured on or after 1st October 1982 should be 0.45 W. **[1626]**

NOTES
Commencement: 23 September 1988.

SCHEDULE 2
Regulation 4

CLASSES OF VEHICLES TO WHICH THESE REGULATIONS DO NOT APPLY

1. Dual-purpose vehicles not constructed or adapted to form part of an articulated vehicle.

2. Mobile cranes as defined in Schedule 3 to the 1971 Act.

3. Break-down vehicles.

4. Engineering plant and plant, not being engineering plant, which is movable plant or equipment being a motor vehicle or trailer (not constructed primarily to carry a load) especially designed and constructed for the special purposes of engineering operations.

5. Trailers being drying or mixing plant designed for the production of asphalt or of bituminous or tar macadam.

6. Tower wagons as defined in—
(a) section 4(2) of the 1971 Act; or
(b) Schedule 4 to that Act.

7. Road construction vehicles as defined in section 4(2) of the 1971 Act and road rollers.

8. Vehicles designed for fire fighting or fire salvage purposes.

9. Works trucks, straddle carriers used solely as works trucks, and works trailers.

10. Electrically-propelled motor vehicles.

11. Vehicles used solely for one or both of the following purposes—
(a) clearing frost, ice or snow from roads by means of a snow plough or similar contrivance, whether forming part of the vehicle or not, and
(b) spreading material on roads to deal with frost, ice or snow.

12. Motor vehicles used for no other purpose than the haulage of lifeboats and the conveyance of the necessary gear of the lifeboats which are being hauled.

[13. Living vans the design gross weight of which does not exceed 3500 kilograms.]

14. Vehicles constructed or adapted for, and used primarily for the purpose of, carrying equipment permanently fixed to the vehicle which equipment is used for medical, dental, veterinary, health, educational, display, clerical or experimental laboratory purposes, such use—
(a) not directly involving the sale, hire or loan of goods from the vehicle; and
(b) not directly or indirectly involving drain cleaning or sewage or refuse collection.

15. Trailers which have no other brakes than a parking brake and brakes which automatically come into operation on the over-run of the trailer.

16. Vehicles exempted from duty under the 1971 Act by virtue of section 7(1) of that Act and any trailer drawn by such a vehicle.

17. Agricultural motor vehicles and agricultural trailed appliances.

18. Agricultural trailers and agricultural trailed appliance conveyors drawn on roads only by an agricultural motor vehicle.

[18A. Converter dollies used solely for the purposes of agriculture, horticulture and forestry, or for any one or two of those purposes.]

19. Public service vehicles (as defined in section 1 of the Public Passenger Vehicles Act 1981).

20. Licensed taxis (as defined in section 13(3) of the Transport Act 1985).

21. Vehicles used solely for the purposes of funerals.

22. Goods vehicles to which any of the prescribed construction and use requirements do not apply by virtue of either of the following items in the Table in regulation 4(4) of the Construction and Use Regulations namely—

    (a) item 1 (which relates to vehicles proceeding to a port for export);

    (b) item 4 (which relates to vehicles in the service of a visiting force or of a headquarters).

23. Vehicles equipped with a new or improved equipment or types of equipment and used, solely by a manufacturer of vehicles or their equipment or by an importer of vehicles, for or in connection with the test or trial of any such equipment.

24. Motor vehicles brought into Great Britain and displaying a registration mark mentioned in regulation 5 of the Motor Vehicles (International Circulation) Regulations 1971, a period of twelve months not having elapsed since the vehicle in question was last brought into Great Britain.

25. Motor vehicles for the time being licensed under the Vehicles (Excise) Act (Northern Ireland) 1972.

26. Vehicles having a base or centre in any of the following islands, namely, Arran, Bute, Great Cumbrae, Islay, Mull, Tiree or North Uist from which the use of the vehicle on a journey is normally commenced.

27. Trailers brought into Great Britain and having a base or centre in a country outside Great Britain from which the use of the vehicle on a journey is normally commenced, a period of twelve months not having elapsed since the vehicle in question was last brought into Great Britain.

28. Track-laying vehicles.

29. Steam propelled vehicles.

30. Motor vehicles first used before 1st January 1960, used unladen and not drawing a laden trailer, and trailers manufactured before 1st January 1960 and used unladen.

For the purposes of this paragraph any determination as to when a motor vehicle is first used shall be made as provided in regulation 3(3) of the Construction and Use Regulations.

31. Motor vehicles constructed, and not merely adapted, for the purpose of street cleansing, or the collection or disposal of refuse or the collection or disposal of the contents of gullies and which are either—

    (a) three-wheeled vehicles, or

    (b) vehicles which—

        (i) are incapable by reason of their construction of exceeding a speed of 20 miles per hour on the level under their own power, or

        (ii) have an inside track width of less than 810 millimetres.

32. Vehicles designed and used for the purpose of servicing or controlling or loading or unloading aircraft while so used—

(a) on an aerodrome as defined in section 105(1) of the Civil Aviation Act 1982;

(b) on roads outside such an aerodrome if, except when proceeding directly from one part of such an aerodrome to another part thereof, the vehicles are unladen and are not drawing a laden trailer.

33. Vehicles designed for use, and used on an aerodrome mentioned in paragraph 32, solely for the purpose of road cleansing, the collection or disposal of refuse or the collection or disposal of the contents of gullies or cesspools.

34. Vehicles provided for police purposes and maintained in workshops approved by the Secretary of State as suitable for such maintenance, being vehicles provided in England and Wales by a police authority or the Receiver for the metropolitan police district, or, in Scotland, by a police authority or a joint police committee.

35. Heavy motor cars or motor cars constructed or adapted for the purpose of forming part of an articulated vehicle and which are used for drawing only a trailer falling within a class of vehicle specified in paragraph 13, 14 or 15 of this Schedule or a trailer being used for or in connection with any purpose for which it is authorised to be used on roads by an order under [section 44(1) of the 1988 Act], being an order authorising that trailer or any class or description of trailers comprising that trailer to be used on roads.

36. Play buses.   **[1627]**

NOTES
Commencement: 23 September 1988.
Para 13: substituted by SI 1992 No 252, reg 8(a).
Para 18A: inserted by SI 1992 No 252, reg 8(b).
Para 35: words in square brackets substituted by SI 1990 No 448, reg 14.
1971 Act: Vehicle (Excise) Act 1971.
1988 Act: Road Traffic Act 1988.

SCHEDULE 3
Regulations 3, 16

THE PRESCRIBED CONSTRUCTION AND USE REQUIREMENTS

The construction and use requirements which are prescribed for the purposes of a goods vehicle test are as follows:—

1. The requirements contained in the following provisions of the Construction and Use Regulations:—

Item No	Regulation	Affecting	Applicable to	
			Motor vehicles	Trailers
1	15 or 16	Parking brake	Yes	Yes
2	15 or 17	Pressure, Vacuum braking systems	Yes	No
3	15, 16 or 18	Brakes	Yes	Yes
4	24	Recut pneumatic tyres	Yes	Yes
5	25	Strength of tyres	Yes	Yes
6	26 and 27	Mixing and maintenance of tyres	Yes	Yes
7	29	Maintenance of steering gear	Yes	Yes
8	30	View to the front	Yes	No
9	33	Mirrors	Yes	No
10	34	Windscreen Wipers and Washers	Yes	No
11	35	Speedometer	Yes	No
12	37	Audible warnings	Yes	No
13	46, 47 and 48	Seat Belts	Yes	No
14	49 and 50	Rear under-run protection	Yes	Yes
15	51 and 52	Sideguards	Yes	Yes
16	54	Maintenance of silencers	Yes	No

Item No	Regulation	Affecting	Applicable to	
			Motor vehicles	Trailers
		. . . . .		
18	61	Smoke emission, oil etc	Yes	No
19	64 and 65	Spray suppression equipment	Yes	Yes
		. . . . .		
21	100	Safe condition of the vehicle and its accessories and in particular—		
		(a) Spare Wheel carrier	Yes	Yes
		(b) Trailer coupling on vehicle	Yes	Yes
		(c) Coupling on trailer	No	Yes
		(d) The chassis	Yes	Yes
		(e) Electrical wiring and equipment	Yes	Yes
		(f) Landing legs	No	Yes
		(g) Engine mountings	Yes	Yes
		(h) Fuel tanks and system	Yes	Yes
		(i) Transmission shafts and associated equipment	Yes	see note
		(j) Exhaust system	Yes	Yes
		(k) Battery	Yes	No
		(l) Wheels and hubs	Yes	Yes
		(m) Suspension system	Yes	Yes
		(n) Axles and Steering gear	Yes	Yes
		(o) Shock absorbers	Yes	Yes
		(p) Bumpers	Yes	Yes
		(q) Wings	Yes	Yes
		(r) The cab	Yes	No
		(s) Driving seat	Yes	No
		(t) The Body	Yes	Yes
		(u) Driver's controls	Yes	No
		(v) Cab step or step rings	Yes	No
		(w) Glass or other transparent material in windscreen or cab windows	Yes	No

Note: Item 21(i) is applicable to semi-trailers which have some or all of their wheels driven by the drawing vehicle, but not to other trailers.

2. The requirements contained in the following provisions of the Road Vehicles Lighting Regulations 1984.

Item No	Regulation and Schedule	Affecting	Applicable to	
			Motor vehicles	Trailers
22	Regulation 16, Schedule 1, item 1 and Schedule 2, Part I	Obligatory front position lamps	As specified in item 1 of Schedule 1	No
23	Regulation 16, Schedule 1, item 1 and Schedule 4, Part I	Obligatory dipped-beam headlamps	As specified in item 1 of Schedule 1	No
24	Regulation 17 and Schedule 4, Part II	Obligatory dipped-beam headlamps	If fitted, yes	No

Item No	Regulation and Schedule	Affecting	Applicable to	
			Motor vehicles	Trailers
25	Regulation 16, Schedule 1, item 1 and Schedule 5, Part I	Obligatory main-beam headlamps	As specified in item 1 of Schedule 1	No
26	Regulation 17 and Schedule 5, Part II	Optional main-beam headlamps	If fitted, yes	No
27	Regulation 16 and Schedule 1, item 1 or 6 and Schedule 10, Part I	Obligatory rear position lamps	As specified in item 1 of Schedule 1	As specified in item 6 of Schedule 1
28	Regulation 16 and Schedule 1, item 1 or 6 and Schedule 16, Part I	Obligatory side-reflex reflectors	As specified in item 1 of Schedule 1	As specified in item 6 of Schedule 1
29	Regulation 16 and Schedule 1, item 1 or 6 and Schedule 17, Part I	Obligatory rear reflex reflectors	As specified in item 1 of Schedule 1	As specified in item 6 of Schedule 1
30	Regulation 16 and Schedule 1, item 1 or 6 and Schedule 7, Parts I and II	Obligatory direction indicators	As specified in item 1 of Schedule 1	As specified in item 6 of Schedule 1
31	Regulation 17 and Schedule 7, Parts I and II	Optional direction indicators	If fitted, yes	If fitted, yes
32	Regulation 16, Schedule 1 or 6, and Schedule 12, Part I	Obligatory stop lamps	As specified in item 1 of Schedule 1	As specified in item 6 of Schedule 1
33	Regulation 17 and Schedule 12, Part II	Optional stop lamps	If fitted, yes	If fitted, yes
34	Regulation 16, Schedule 1, item 1 or 6 and Schedule 18, Part I	Obligatory rear markings	As specified in item 1 of Schedule 1	As specified in item 6 of Schedule 1
35	Regulation 17 and Schedule 18, Part II	Optional rear markings	If fitted, yes	If fitted, yes
36	Regulation 16 and Schedule 1, item 1 or 6 and Schedule 11, Part I	Obligatory rear fog lamps	As specified in item 1 of Schedule 1	As specified in item 6 of Schedule 1
37	Regulation 17 and Schedule 11, Part II	Optional rear fog lamps	If fitted, yes	If fitted, yes
38	Regulation 20(1) so far as relating to lamps, reflectors or markings mentioned in next column forward	Maintenance of obligatory front position lamp, rear position lamp, headlamp, rear fog lamps, reflex reflectors and rear markings	Yes	Yes
39	Regulation 20(1) so far as relating to lamp or indicator mentioned in next column forward	Maintenance of stop lamps and direction indicators	In case of obligatory lamp or indicator, yes. In case of optional lamp or indicator, yes, if fitted	In case of obligatory lamp, yes. In case of optional lamps, yes if fitted

Item No	Regulation and Schedule	Affecting	Applicable to	
			Motor vehicles	Trailers
40	Regulation 20(3)	Maintenance of dipped-beam headlamp	In case of obligatory lamp, yes. In case of optional lamp, yes if fitted	No
41	Regulation 20(3)	Maintenance of rear fog lamp	In case of obligatory lamp, yes. In case of optional lamp, yes, if fitted	In case of obligatory lamp, yes. In case of optional lamp, yes, if fitted

3. The requirements, in so far as they relate to the installation of recording equipment in Article 3 and the seals to be affixed to such equipment in Article 15 and paragraph 4 of Section V of Annex 1 of the Community Recording Equipment Regulation [(as defined in section 85 of the 1988 Act)].

Item No	Affecting	Applicable to	
		Motor vehicles	Trailers
42	Installation and seals of tachograph	Yes	No

[1628]

NOTES
    Commencement: 23 September 1988.
    Para 3: words in square brackets substituted by SI 1990 No 448, reg 15.
    1988 Act: Road Traffic Act 1988.

SCHEDULE 4

Regulation 2

REGULATIONS REVOKED BY REGULATION 2

. . .   **[1629]**

NOTES
    Commencement: 23 September 1988.
    This schedule lists the regulations revoked by reg 2.

MOTOR VEHICLES (WEARING OF SEAT BELTS BY CHILDREN IN REAR SEATS) REGULATIONS 1989
(SI 1989 NO 1219)

NOTES
    Made: 14 July 1989
    Authority: Road Traffic Act 1988, s 15(3), (5), (6), (9)

ARRANGEMENT OF REGULATIONS

1. Citation and commencement

These Regulations may be cited as the Motor Vehicles (Wearing of Seat Belts by Children in Rear Seats) Regulations 1989 and shall come into force on 1st September 1989.   **[1630]**

NOTES

Commencement: 1 September 1989.

2. General interpretation

(1) In these Regulations—

"the Act" means the Road Traffic Act 1988;

"adult seat belt" means—

(a) a three-point belt, or
(b) a lap belt,

which has been marked in accordance with regulation 47(7) of the Construction and Use Regulations;

"booster cushion" means a cushion designed for a person of small stature to sit on to improve the fit of an adult seat belt (including a cushion that has an integral back above the seating plane);

"child restraint" means a seat belt for the use of a young person—

(a) which is designed either to be fitted directly to a suitable anchorage or to be used in conjunction with an adult seat belt and held in place by the restraining action of that belt; and
(b) which has been marked in accordance with regulation 47(7) of the Construction and Use Regulations;

"Construction and Use Regulations" means the Road Vehicles (Construction and Use) Regulations 1986;

"medical certificate", in relation to a person, means a valid certificate signed by a medical practitioner to the effect that it is inadvisable on medical grounds for that person to wear a seat belt;

"rear seat" in relation to a vehicle means a seat not being the driver's seat, a seat alongside the drivers seat or a specified passenger seat; and

"disabled person's belt", "lap belt", "seat", "specified passenger seat" and "three-point belt" have the meanings given by regulation 47(8) of the Construction and Use Regulations.

(2) Without prejudice to sections 17 and 20 of the Interpretation Act 1978, a reference to a provision of the Construction and Use Regulations is a reference to that provision as from time to time amended or as from time to time re-enacted with or without modification.

(3) For the purposes of these Regulations a seat belt is appropriate—

(a) in relation to a child under the age of 14 years, if it is of a description specified for a child of his class in regulation 3(2), and

(b) in relation to a person aged 14 years or more, if it is an adult seat belt.
[1631]

NOTES
Commencement: 1 September 1989.

3. Descriptions of seat belts and the manner in which they are to be used

(1) A child shall be regarded as wearing a seat belt in conformity with regulations for the purposes of section 15(3) if and only if—

(a) he is wearing a seat belt of a description prescribed by paragraph (2) below for a child of his class, and

(b) where paragraph (3) is applicable, he is using the seat belt in the manner prescribed by that paragraph.

(2) The descriptions of seat belt prescribed by this paragraph are—

(a) for any child, a child restraint appropriate to the weight of the child in accordance with the indication of weight shown on the marking required under regulation 47(7) of the Construction and Use Regulations; and

(b) for any child aged 1 year or more, an adult seat belt.

(3) If a child who has attained the age of 1 year but not the age of 4 years wears an adult seat belt, the manner prescribed by this paragraph is that it must be used in conjunction with a booster cushion.   **[1632]**

NOTES
Commencement: 1 September 1989.
Section 15(3): Road Traffic Act 1988, s 15(3).
Construction and Use Regulations: Construction and Use Regulations 1986, SI 1986 No 1078.

4. Vehicles to which section 15(3) of the Act does not apply

The following classes of vehicles are exempt from the prohibition in section 15(3) of the Act, that is to say—

(a) vehicles which are not motor cars within the meaning of section 185 of the Act, and

(b) licensed taxis and licensed hire cars within the meanings given by section 13 of the Transport Act 1985 in which (in each case) the rear seats are separated from the driver by a fixed partition.   **[1633]**

NOTES
Commencement: 1 September 1989.
The Act: Road Traffic Act 1988.

5. Exemptions

(1) The prohibition in section 15(3) of the Act shall not apply to—

(a) a child for whom there is a medical certificate;

(b) a child aged under 1 year in a carry cot provided that the carry cot is restrained by straps; or

(c) a disabled child who is wearing a disabled person's belt.

(2) The prohibition in section 15(3) of the Act shall not apply to the driving of a vehicle where the condition specified in paragraph (3) below is satisfied as respects every child aged under 14 years who is in the rear of the vehicle and not wearing an appropriate seat belt.

(3) The condition is that no appropriate seat belt is available for the child.

NOTES
> Commencement: 1 September 1989.
> The Act: Road Traffic Act 1988.

6. Intrepretation of reference to availability

(1) An appropriate seat belt shall not be regarded as being available for a child for the purposes of regulation 5(2) unless such a belt is regarded as available to him by virtue of paragraph (2) below.

(2) Subject to paragraph (5) below, if any rear seat in a vehicle is provided with a seat belt which is appropriate for a particular child ("the child in question") that belt ("the relevant belt") shall be regarded as available for that child for the purposes of regulation 5(2) unless—

(a) another person is wearing the relevant belt and it is an appropriate belt for that person;

(b) another person is occupying the seat and wearing some other seat belt, that other belt being an appropriate belt for that person;

(c) another person, being a person for whom there is a medical certificate, is occupying the seat;

(d) the child in question is prevented from occupying the seat by the presence of a carry cot which is restrained as mentioned in regulation 5(1)(b) and in which there is a child aged under 1 year.

(e) the child in question is prevented from occupying the seat by the presence of a correctly secured child restraint which—

    (i) is not appropriate to his weight in accordance with the indication of weight shown on the marking referred to in regulation 47(7) of the Construction and Use Regulations, and

    (ii) could not readily be removed without the aid of tools;

(f) in the case of a seat that is specially designed so that—

    (i) its configuration can be adjusted in order to increase the space in the vehicle available for goods or personal effects, and

    (ii) when it is so adjusted the seat cannot be used as such,
the configuration is adjusted in the manner described in sub-paragraph (i) and it would not be reasonably practicable for the goods and personal effects carried in the vehicle to be so carried were the configuration not so adjusted;

(g) the child in question has attained the age of 1 year but not the age of 4 years, the relevant belt is an adult seat belt and there is no booster cushion in or on the vehicle that is not being used by a child in that age range who is wearing an adult seat belt.

(3) Paragraph (2)(b) above shall not apply unless the presence of the person renders it impracticable for the child in question to wear the relevant belt.

(4) Paragraph (2)(d) above shall not apply if it would be reasonably practicable for the carry cot to be carried in any other part of the vehicle where it could be restrained as mentioned in regulation 5(1)(b) so as to render it practicable for the child in question to wear the relevant belt.

(5) An adult seat belt shall not be regarded as available for any child for the purposes of regulation 5(2) if—

(a) it has an inertia reel mechanism which is locked as a result of the vehicle being, or having been, on a steep incline, or

(b) it does not comply with the requirements of regulation 48 of the Construction and Use Regulations.

(6) A seat belt shall be regarded as provided for a seat for the purposes of this regulation if—

(a) it is fixed in such a position that it can be worn by an occupier of that seat, or

(b) it is elsewhere in or on the vehicle but—

    (i) it could readily be fixed in such a position without the aid of tools, and

    (ii) it is not being worn by a person for whom it is appropriate and who is occupying another seat. **[1635]**

NOTES
Commencement: 1 September 1989.
Construction and Use Regulations: SI 1986 No 1078.

ROAD VEHICLES LIGHTING REGULATIONS 1989
(SI 1989 NO 1796)

NOTES
Made: 28 September 1989
Authority: Road Traffic Act 1988, ss 41, 81

ARRANGEMENT OF REGULATIONS

PART I

PRELIMINARY

PART II

REGULATIONS GOVERNING THE FITTING OF LAMPS, REFLECTORS, REAR MARKINGS AND DEVICES

PART III

REGULATIONS GOVERNING THE MAINTENANCE AND USE OF LAMPS, REFLECTORS, REAR MARKINGS AND DEVICES

PART IV

TESTING AND INSPECTION OF LIGHTING EQUIPMENT AND REFLECTORS

SCHEDULES

Preamble

The Secretary of State for Transport, in exercise of the powers conferred by—

    (a) section 81 of the Road Traffic Act 1988, in so far as these Regulations revoke enactments having effect as if they had been made under that section;

    (b) section 41 as read with section 43 of that Act as regards all other provisions of these Regulations,

and all other enabling powers, and after consultation with representative organisations in accordance with section 195 of that Act, hereby makes the following Regulations

PART I
PRELIMINARY

1. Commencement, citation and revocations

(1) These Regulations may be cited as the Road Vehicles Lighting Regulations 1989 and shall come into force on 1st November 1989.

(2) ...   **[1636]**

NOTES
Commencement: 1 November 1989.
Para (2): revokes SI 1984 No 812 and SI 1987 No 1315.

2. Statement under section 43(3) of the Road Traffic Act 1988

(1) The Secretary of State is satisfied that—

(a) it is requisite that the provisions mentioned in paragraph (2) which vary the requirements about the construction of the vehicles to which those provisions apply, shall apply as from 1st November 1989 to such of those vehicles as are registered under the Vehicles (Excise) Act 1971 before the expiration of one year from the making of these Regulations; and

(b) notwithstanding that these provisions will then apply to those vehicles, no undue hardship or inconvenience will be caused thereby.

(2) The provisions referred to in paragraph (1) are those set out in the Table below—

Number of regulation or Schedule	Nature of requirements
Regulation 3(6)	Interpretation of requirements in relation to British Standard marks.
Schedule 1 Table V	Invalid carriages with a maximum speed exceeding 4 mph to be fitted with direction indicators and hazard warning signal devices.
Schedule 4 Part I paragraph 4	The aim of dipped-beam headlamps.

[1637]

NOTES
Commencement: 1 November 1989.

3. Interpretation

(1) Unless the context otherwise requires, any reference in these Regulations—

(a) to a numbered regulation or Schedule is a reference to the regulation or Schedule bearing that number in these Regulations,

(b) to a numbered paragraph is to the paragraph bearing that number in the regulation or Schedule in which the reference occurs, and

(b) to a numbered or lettered sub-paragraph is to the sub-paragraph bearing that number in the paragraph in which the reference occurs.

(2) In these Regulations, unless the context otherwise requires, any expressions for which there is an entry in column 1 of the Table has the meaning

given against it in column 2 or is to be construed in accordance with directions given against it in that column.

TABLE

(1) *Expression*	(2) *Meaning*
"The Act"	The Road Traffic Act 1988.
"The Construction and Use Regulations"	The Road Vehicles (Construction and Use) Regulations 1986.
"The Designation of Approval Marks Regulations"	The Motor Vehicles (Designation of Approval Marks) Regulations 1979.
"Agricultural vehicle"	A vehicle constructed or adapted for agriculture, grass cutting, forestry, land levelling, dredging or similar operations and primarily used for one or more of these purposes, and includes any trailer drawn by an agricultural vehicle.
"Angles of visibility"	A requirement for a lamp or reflector fitted to a vehicle to have specified horizontal and vertical angles of visibility is a requirement that at least 50 per cent of the apparent surface must be visible from any point within those angles when every door, tailgate, boot lid, engine cover, cab or other movable part of the vehicle is in the closed position.
"Apparent surface"	For any given direction of observation, is the orthogonal projection of a light-emitting surface in a plane perpendicular to the direction of observation and touching that surface.
"Articulated bus"	Has the same meaning as in the Construction and Use Regulations.
"Articulated vehicle"	Has the same meaning as in the Construction and Use Regulations.
"Breakdown vehicle"	A vehicle used to attend an accident or breakdown or to draw a broken down vehicle.
"Bus"	Has the same meaning as in the Construction and Use Regulations.
"Caravan"	A trailer which is constructed (and not merely adapted) for human habitation.
"cc"	Cubic centimetre or centimetres (as the case may be).
"Circuit-closed tell-tale"	A light showing that a device has been switched on.
"cm"	Centimetre or centimetres (as the case may be).
"cm²"	Square centimetre or centimetres (as the case may be).

(1) *Expression*	(2) *Meaning*
"Combat vehicle"	A vehicle of a type described at item 1, 2 or 3 in column 1 of Schedule 1 to the Motor Vehicles (Authorisation of Special Types) General Order 1979.
"Community Directive 76/756/ EEC, as amended"	Council Directive 76/756/EEC of 27.7.76 (OJ L262, 27.9.76, p 1) as amended by Commission Directive 80/233/EEC of 21.11.79 (OJ L51, 25.2.80, p 8). Commission Directive 82/244/EEC of 17.3.82 (OJ L109, 22.4.82, p 31), Council Directive 83/276/EEC of 26.5.83 (OJ L151, 9.6.83, p 47), Commission Directive 84/8/EEC of 14.12.83 (OJ L9, 12.1.84, p 24) and Commission Directive 89/278/ EEC of 23.3.89 (OJ L109, 20.4.89, p 38).
"Daytime hours"	The time between half an hour before sunrise and half an hour after sunset.
"Dim-dip device"	A device which is capable of causing a dipped-beam headlamp to operate at reduced intensity.
"Dipped beam"	A beam of light emitted by a lamp which illuminates the road ahead of the vehicle without causing undue dazzle or discomfort to oncoming drivers or other road users.
"Direction indicator"	A lamp on a vehicle used to indicate to other road users that the driver intends to change direction to the right or to the left.
"Dual-purpose vehicle"	Has the same meaning as in the Construction and Use Regulations.
"Emergency vehicle"	A motor vehicle of any of the following descriptions— (a) a vehicle used for fire brigade, ambulance or police purposes; (b) an ambulance, being a vehicle (other than an invalid carriage) which is constructed or adapted for the purposes of conveying sick, injured or disabled persons and which is used for such purposes; (c) a vehicle owned by a body formed primarily for the purposes of fire salvage and used for those or similar purposes; (d) a vehicle owned by the Forestry Commission or by a local authority and used from time to time for the purposes of fighting fires;

(1)	(2)
Expression	*Meaning*

	(e) a vehicle owned by the Secretary of State for Defence and used—
	(i) for the purposes of the disposal of bombs or explosives,
	(ii) by the Naval Emergency Monitoring Organisation for the purposes of a nuclear accident or an incident involving radioactivity,
	(iii) by the Royal Air Force Mountain Rescue Service for the purposes of rescue operations or any other emergencies, or
	(iv) by the Royal Air Force Armament Support Unit;
	(f) a vehicle primarily used for the purposes of the Blood Transfusion Service provided under the National Health Service Act 1977 or under the National Health Service (Scotland) Act 1978;
	(g) a vehicle used by Her Majesty's Coastguard or Coastguard Auxiliary Service for the purposes of giving aid to persons in danger or vessels in distress on or near the coast;
	(h) a vehicle owned by the British Coal Corporation and used for the purposes of rescue operations at mines;
	(i) a vehicle owned by the Royal National Lifeboat Institution and used for the purposes of launching lifeboats; and
	(j) a vehicle primarily used for the purposes of conveying any human tissue for transplanting or similar purposes.
"End-outline marker lamp"	A lamp fitted near the outer edge of a vehicle in addition to the front and rear position lamps to indicate the presence of a wide vehicle.
"Engineering plant"	Has the same meaning as in the Construction and Use Regulations.
"Extreme outer edge"	In relation to a side of a vehicle, the vertical plane parallel with the longitudinal axis of the vehicle, and coinciding with its lateral outer edge, disregarding the projection of—

(1) Expression	(2) Meaning
	(a) so much of the distortion of any tyre as is caused by the weight of the vehicle.
	(b) any connections for tyre pressure gauges.
	(c) any anti-skid devices which may be mounted on the wheels,
	(d) rear-view mirrors,
	(e) lamps and reflectors,
	(f) customs seals affixed to the vehicle, and devices for securing and protecting such seals, and
	(g) special equipment.
"Front fog lamp"	A lamp used to improve the illumination of the road in front of a motor vehicle in conditions of seriously reduced visibility.
"Front position lamp"	A lamp used to indicate the presence and width of a vehicle when viewed from the front.
"First used"	References to the date of first use of a vehicle shall be construed in accordance with regulation 3(3) of the Construction and Use Regulations.
"Hazard warning signal device"	A device which is capable of causing all the direction indicators with which a vehicle, or a combination of vehicles, is fitted to operate simultaneously.
"Headlamp"	A lamp used to illuminate the road in front of a vehicle and which is not a front fog lamp.
"Headlamp levelling device"	Either—
	(a) an automatic headlamp levelling device by means of which the downward inclination of any dipped-beam headlamp is automatically maintained regardless of the load on the vehicle, or
	(b) a manual headlamp levelling device by means of which the downward inclination of any dipped-beam headlamp may be adjusted by a manual control operable from the driving seat of the vehicle.
"Home forces"	The naval, military or air forces of Her Majesty raised in the United Kingdom.
"Home forces' vehicle"	A vehicle owned by, or in the service of, the home forces and used for naval, military or air force purposes.

(1) *Expression*	(2) *Meaning*
"Horse-drawn"	In relation to a vehicle, means that the vehicle is drawn by a horse or other animal.
"Hours of darkness"	The time between half an hour after sunset and half an hour before sunrise.
"Illuminated area"	The expression, in relation to a headlamp, front fog lamp and reversing lamp, in each case fitted with a reflector, means the orthogonal projection of the full aperture of the reflector on a plane (touching the surface of the lamp) at right angles to the longitudinal axis of the vehicle to which the lamp is fitted. If the light-emitting surface extends over only part of the full aperture of the reflector, then the projection of only that part shall be taken into account. In the case of a dipped-beam headlamp, the illuminated area is limited by the apparent trace of the cut-off on the lens.
	The expression, in relation to any other lamp, means the part of the orthogonal projection of the light-emitting surface on a plane (touching the surface of the lamp) at right angles to the longitudinal axis of the vehicle to which it is fitted, the boundary of which is such that if the straight edge of an opaque screen touches it at any point 98 per cent of the total intensity of the light is shown in the direction parallel to the longitudinal axis of the vehicle. Accordingly, for the purposes of determining the lower, upper and later edges of the lamp, only a screen placed with its straight edge horizontally or vertically needs to be considered.
"Industrial tractor"	Has the same meaning as in the Construction and Use Regulations.
"Installation and performance requirements"	In relation to any lamp, reflector, rear marking or device, the requirements specified in the Schedules to these Regulations relating to that lamp, reflector, rear marking or device.
"Invalid carriage"	A mechanically propelled vehicle constructed or adapted for the carriage of one person, being a person suffering from some physical defect or disability.
"Kerbside weight"	Has the same meaning as in the Construction and Use Regulations.

(1) *Expression*	(2) *Meaning*
"kg"	Kilogram or kilograms (as the case may be).
"Light-emitting surface"	In relation to a lamp, that part of the exterior surface of the lens through which light is emitted when the lamp is lit, and in relation to a retro reflector that part of the exterior surface of the retro reflector from which light can be reflected.
"m"	Metre or metres (as the case may be).
"Main beam"	A beam of light emitted by a headlamp which illuminates the road over a long distance ahead of the vehicle.
"Matched pair"	In relation to lamps, a pair of lamps in respect of which— (a) both lamps emit light of substantially the same colour and intensity, and (b) both lamps are of the same size and of such a shape that they are symmetrical to one another.
"Maximum distance from the side of the vehicle"	The expression means— (a) in relation to a lamp fitted to a vehicle, the shortest distance from the boundary of the illuminated area to an extreme outer edge of the vehicle, and (b) in relation to a retro reflector fitted to a vehicle, the shortest distance from the boundary of the reflecting area to an extreme outer edge of the vehicle.
"Maximum gross weight"	Has the same meaning as in the Construction and Use Regulations.
"Maximum height above the ground"	The height above which no part of the illuminated area in the case of a lamp, or the reflecting area in the case of a retro reflector, extends when the vehicle is at its kerbside weight and when each tyre with which the vehicle is fitted is inflated to the pressure recommended by the manufacturer of the vehicle.
"Maximum speed"	Has the same meaning as in the Construction and Use Regulations.

(1) *Expression*	(2) *Meaning*
"Minimum height above the ground"	The height below which no part of the illuminated area in the case of a lamp, or the reflecting area in the case of a retro reflector, extends when the vehicle is at its kerbside weight and when each tyre with which the vehicle is fitted is inflated to the pressure recommended by the manufacturer of the vehicle.
"mm"	Millimetre or millimetres (as the case may be).
"Motor bicycle combination"	A combination of a solo motor bicycle and a sidecar.
"Motor tractor"	Has the same meaning as in the Construction and Use Regulations.
"Motorway"	Has the same meaning as in Schedule 6 of the Road Traffic Regulation Act 1984.
"Movable platform"	A platform which is attached to, and may be moved by means of, an extendible boom.
"mph"	Mile per hour or miles per hour (as the case may be).
"Obligatory"	In relation to a lamp, reflector, rear marking or device, means a lamp, reflector, rear marking or device with which a vehicle, its load or equipment is required by these Regulations to be fitted.
"Operational tell-tale"	A warning device readily visible or audible to the driver and showing whether a device that has been switched on is operating correctly or not.
"Optional"	In relation to a lamp, reflector, rear marking or device, means a lamp, reflector, rear marking or device with which a vehicle, its load or equipment is not required by these Regulations to be fitted.
"Overall length"	Has the same meaning as in the Construction and Use Regulations.
"Overall width"	Has the same meaning as in the Construction and Use Regulations.
"Pair"	In relation to lamps, reflectors or rear markings means a pair of lamps, reflectors or rear markings, including a matched pair, one on each side of the vehicle, in respect of which the following conditions are met—
	(a) each lamp, reflector or rear marking is at the same height above the ground, and

(1) *Expression*	(2) *Meaning*
	(b) each lamp, reflector or rear marking is at the same distance from the extreme outer edge of the vehicle. In the case of an asymmetric vehicle, those conditions shall be deemed to be met if they are as near as practicable to being met.
"Passenger vehicle"	Has the same meaning as in the Construction and Use Regulations.
"Pedal cycle"	A vehicle which is not constructed or adapted to be propelled by mechanical power and which is equipped with pedals, including an electrically-assisted pedal cycle prescribed for the purposes of section 189 of the Act and section 140 of the Road Traffic Regulation Act 1984.
"Pedal retro reflector"	A retro reflector attached to or incorporated in the pedals of a pedal cycle or motor bicycle.
"Pedestrian-controlled vehicle"	Has the same meaning as in the Construction and Use Regulations.
"Rear fog lamp"	A lamp used to render a vehicle more readily visible from the rear in conditions of seriously reduced visibility.
"Rear position lamp"	A lamp used to indicate the presence and width of a vehicle when viewed from the rear.
"Rear retro reflector"	A retro reflector used to indicate the presence and width of a vehicle when viewed from the rear.
"Rear registration plate lamp"	A lamp used to illuminate the rear registration plate.
"Reflecting area"	In relation to a retro reflector fitted to a vehicle, the area of the orthogonal projection on a vertical plane (touching the surface of the reflector)— (a) at right angles to the longitudinal axis of the vehicle of that part of the reflector designed to reflect light in the case of a front or a rear retro reflector, and (b) parallel to the longitudinal axis of the vehicle of that part of the reflector designed to reflect light in the case of a side retro reflector.
"Reversing lamp"	A lamp used to illuminate the road to the rear of a vehicle for the purpose of reversing and to warn other road users that the vehicle is reversing or about to reverse.

(1) *Expression*	(2) *Meaning*
"Road clearance vehicle"	A mechanically propelled vehicle used for dealing with frost, ice or snow on roads.
"Running lamp"	A lamp (not being a front position lamp, an end-outline marker lamp, headlamp or front fog lamp) used to make the presence of a moving motor vehicle readily visible from the front.
"Separation distance"	In relation to two lamps or two retro reflectors the expression means, except where otherwise specified, the shortest distance between the orthogonal projections in a plane perpendicular to the longitudinal axis of the vehicle of the illuminated areas of the two lamps or the reflecting areas of the two reflectors.
"Service braking system"	Has the same meaning as in the Construction and Use Regulations.
"Side marker lamp"	A lamp fitted to the side of a vehicle or its load and used to render the vehicle more visible to other road users.
"Side retro reflector"	A reflector fitted to the side of a vehicle or its load and used to render the vehicle more visible from the side.
"Solo motor bicycle"	A motor bicycle without a sidecar.
"Special equipment"	A movable platform fitted to a vehicle, the apparatus for moving the platform and any jacks fitted to the vehicle for stabilising it while the movable platform is in use.
"Special warning lamp"	A lamp, fitted to the front or rear of a vehicle, capable of emitting a blue flashing light and not any other kind of light.
"Stop lamp"	A lamp used to indicate to road users that the brakes of a vehicle or combination of vehicles are being applied.
"Traffic sign"	Has the same meaning given by section 64(1) of the Act.
"Trailer"	A vehicle constructed or adapted to be drawn by another vehicle.
"Unrestricted dual-carriageway road"	A dual-carriageway within the meaning given by paragraph 2 of Schedule 6 to the Road Traffic Regulation Act 1984 on which a motor vehicle may lawfully be driven at a speed exceeding 50 mph.

(1) Expression	(2) Meaning
"Unladen weight"	Has the same meaning as in the Construction and Use Regulations.
"Vehicle in the service of a visiting force or of a headquarters"	Has the same meaning as in the Construction and Use Regulations.
"Visiting vehicle"	Has the meaning given by regulation 3(1) of the Motor Vehicles (International Circulation) Regulations 1971.
"Warning beacon"	A lamp that is capable of emitting a flashing or rotating beam of light throughout 360° in the horizontal plane.
"Wheel"	Has the same meaning as in the Construction and Use Regulations (see also paragraph (7)).
"Wheeled"	Has the same meaning as in the Construction and Use Regulations.
"Work lamp"	A lamp used to illuminate a working area or the scene of an accident, breakdown or roadworks in the vicinity of the vehicle to which it is fitted.
"Works trailer"	Has the same meaning as in the Construction and Use Regulations.
"Works truck"	Has the same meaning as in the Construction and Use Regulations.

(3) Material designed primarily to reflect light is, when reflecting light, to be treated for the purposes of these Regulations as showing a light, and material capable of reflecting an image is not, when reflecting the image of a light, to be so treated.

(4) In these Regulations a reference to one lamp, except in the case of a dipped-beam headlamp, a main-beam headlamp and a front fog lamp, includes any combination of two or more lamps, whether identical or not, having the same function and emitting light of the same colour, if it comprises devices the aggregate illuminated area of which occupies 60 per cent or more of the area of the smallest rectangle circumscribing those illuminated areas.

(5) In these Regulations a reference to two lamps includes—

(a) a single illuminated area which—

(i) is placed symmetrically in relation to the longitudinal axis of the vehicle,

(ii) extends on both sides to within 400 mm of the extreme outer edge of the vehicle,

(iii) is not less than 800 mm long, and

    (iv) is illuminated by not less than two sources of light, and

  (b) any number of illuminated areas which—

    (i) are juxtaposed,

    (ii) if on the same transverse plane have illuminated areas which occupy not less than 60 per cent of the area of the smallest rectangle circumscribing their illuminated areas,

    (iii) are placed symmetrically in relation to the median longitudinal plane of the vehicle,

    (iv) extend on both sides to within 400 mm of the extreme outer edge of the vehicle,

    (v) do not have a total length of less than 800 mm, and

    (vi) are illuminated by not less than two sources of light.

(6) Where a part fitted to a vehicle is required by these Regulations to be marked with a British Standard mark, the requirements shall not be regarded as met unless, in addition to being marked as required, the part complied with the relevant British Standard at the time when the part was first fitted to the vehicle.

(7) A reference in these Regulations to the number of wheels of a vehicle shall be construed in accordance with regulation 3 of the Construction and Use Regulations.

(8) A reference in a Schedule to there being no requirement in relation to a lamp, reflector, rear marking or device is without prejudice to any other provision in these Regulations affecting same.   **[1638]**

NOTES
Commencement: 1 November 1989.

4. Exemptions - General

(1) Where a provision is applied by these Regulations to a motor vehicle first used on or after a specified date it does not apply to any vehicle manufactured at least six months before that date.

(2) Where an exemption from, or a relaxation of, a provision is applied by these Regulations to a motor vehicle first used before a specified date it shall also apply to a motor vehicle first used on or after that date if it was manufactured at least six months before that date.

(3) Nothing in these Regulations shall require any lamp or reflector to be fitted between sunrise and sunset to—

  (a) a vehicle not fitted with any front or rear position lamp,

  (b) an incomplete vehicle proceeding to a works for completion,

  (c) a pedal cycle,

  (d) a pedestrian-controlled vehicle,

  (e) a horse-drawn vehicle,

  (f) a vehicle drawn or propelled by hand, or

  (g) a combat vehicle.

(4) Without prejudice to regulation 16, for the purposes of these Regulations a lamp shall not be treated as being a lamp if it is—

  (a) so painted over or masked that it is not capable of being immediately used or readily put to use; or

(b) an electric lamp which is not provided with any system of wiring by means of which that lamp is, or can readily be, connected with a source of electricity. **[1639]**

NOTES
Commencement: 1 November 1989.

5. Exemptions - Temporarily imported vehicles and vehicles proceeding to a port for export

Part II of these Regulations does not apply to—

(a) any vehicle having a base or centre in a country outside Great Britain from which it normally starts its journeys, provided that a period of not more than 12 months has elapsed since the vehicle was last brought into Great Britain;
(b) a visiting vehicle;
(c) any combination of two or more vehicles, one of which is drawing the other or others, if the combination includes any vehicle of the type mentioned in sub-paragraph (a) or (b); or
(d) a vehicle proceeding to a port for export,

if in each case the vehicle or combination of vehicles complies in every respect with the requirements about lighting equipment and reflectors relating thereto contained in the Convention on Road Traffic concluded at Geneva on 19th September 1949 or the International Convention relating to Motor Traffic concluded at Paris on 24th April 1926. **[1640]**

NOTES
Commencement: 1 November 1989.

6. Exemptions - Vehicles towing or being towed

(1) No motor vehicle first used before 1st April 1986 and no pedal cycle or trailer manufactured before 1st October 1985 is required by regulation 18 to be fitted with any rear position lamp, stop lamp, rear direction indicator, rear fog lamp or rear reflector whilst a trailer fitted with any such lamp or reflector is attached to its rear.

(2) No trailer manufactured before 1st October 1985 is required by regulation 18 to be fitted with any front position lamp whilst being drawn by a passenger vehicle.

(3) No trailer is required by regulation 18 to be fitted with any stop lamp whilst being drawn by a vehicle which is not required by regulation 18 to be fitted with any such lamp.

(4) Paragraph (3) shall apply respectively to rear fog lamps and direction indicators as it applies to stop lamps.

(5) No trailer manufactured before 1st October 1990 is required by regulation 18 to be fitted with any stop lamp or direction indicator whilst being drawn by a motor vehicle fitted with one or two stop lamps and two or more direction indicators if the dimensions of the trailer are such that when the longitudinal axis of the drawing vehicle and the trailer lie in the same vertical plane such stop lamps and at last one direction indicator on each side of the vehicle are visible to an observer in that vertical plane from a point 6 m behind the rear of the trailer whether it is loaded or not.

(6) No rear marking is required to be fitted to any vehicle by regulation 18

if another vehicle in a combination of which it forms part would obscure any such marking.

(7) Where a broken-down vehicle is being drawn by another vehicle—

(a) regulations 18 and 23 shall not apply to the broken-down vehicle between sunrise and sunset, and

(b) between sunset and sunrise those regulations shall apply to the broken-down vehicle only in respect of rear position lamps and reflectors.

(8) The references in paragraphs (3) and (4) to a vehicle which is required to be fitted with a lamp shall be construed as if paragraph (1) did not have effect.   **[1641]**

NOTES

Commencement: 1 November 1989.

7. Exemptions - Military vehicles

(1) Regulation 18 does not apply to a home forces' vehicle or to a vehicle in the service of a visiting force or of a headquarters whilst being used—

(a) in connection with training which is certified in writing for the purposes of this regulation by a person duly authorised in that behalf to be training on a special occasion and of which not less than 48 hours' notice has been given by that person to the chief officer of police of every police area in which the place selected for the training is wholly or partly situate; or

(b) on manoeuvres within such limits and during such period as may from time to time be specified by Order in Council under the Manoeuvres Act 1958.

(2) Where not less than 6 nor more than 12 vehicles being home forces' vehicles or vehicles of a visiting force or of a headquarters are proceeding together in a convoy on tactical or driving exercises which are authorised in writing by a person duly authorised in that behalf, and of which not less than 48 hours' notice in writing has been given by that person to the chief officer of police of every police area through which it is intended that the convoy shall pass and the interval between any two vehicles in such convoy does not exceed 20 m—

(a) front position lamps shall be required only on the vehicle leading the convoy; and

(b) rear position lamps shall be required only on the rearmost vehicle provided that every other vehicle in the convoy carries a bright light under the vehicle illuminating either a part of the vehicle or anything attached to the vehicle or the road surface beneath the vehicle, in such a manner that the presence of the vehicle can be detected from the rear.

(3) No lamp is required to be fitted to any home forces' vehicle or any vehicle in the service of a visiting force or of a headquarters if the vehicle is constructed or adapted for combat and is such that compliance with these provisions is impracticable and it is fitted with two red rear position lamps and two red rear retro reflectors when on a road between sunset and sunrise. Such lamps and reflectors need not meet any of the requirements specified in Schedules 10 and 18.

(4) Part II of these Regulations does not apply to a vehicle in the service of

a visiting force or of a headquarters if the vehicle complies in every respect with the requirements as to lighting equipment and reflectors relating thereto contained in a Convention referred to in regulation 5. **[1642]**

NOTES
Commencement: 1 November 1989.

8. Exemptions - Invalid carriages

An invalid carriage having a maximum speed not exceeding 4 mph is required by these Regulations to be fitted with lamps and reflectors only when it is used on the carriageway of a road between sunset and sunrise otherwise than for the sole purpose of crossing it. **[1643]**

NOTES
Commencement: 1 November 1989.

9. Exemptions - Vehicles drawn or propelled by hand

A vehicle drawn or propelled by hand which has an overall width, including any load, not exceeding 800 mm is required by these Regulations to be fitted with lamps and reflectors only when it is used on the carriageway of a road between sunset and sunrise other than—

    (a) close to the near side or left-hand edge of the carriageway, or

    (b) to cross the carriageway. **[1644]**

NOTES
Commencement: 1 November 1989.

9A. Exemptions—Tramcars

Parts II to IV of these Regulations do not apply to tramcars. **[1644A]**

NOTES
Commencement: 1 July 1992.
Inserted by SI 1992 No 1217, reg 14.

10. Provision as respects the Trade Descriptions Act 1968

Where by any provision in these Regulations any vehicle or any of its parts or equipment is required to be marked with a specification number or a registered certification trade mark of the British Standards Institution or with any approval mark, nothing in that provision shall be taken to authorise any person to apply any such number or mark to the vehicle, part or equipment in contravention of the Trade Descriptions Act 1968. **[1645]**

NOTES
Commencement: 1 November 1989.

PART II

REGULATIONS GOVERNING THE FITTING OF LAMPS, REFLECTORS, REAR MARKINGS AND DEVICES

11. Colour of light shown by lamps and reflectors

(1) No vehicle shall be fitted with a lamp which is capable of showing a red light to the front, except—

(a) a red and white chequered domed lamp, or a red and white segmented mast-mounted warning beacon, fitted to a fire service control vehicle and intended for use at the scene of an emergency;

(b) a side marker lamp or a side retro reflector;

(c) retro reflective material or a retro reflector designed primarily to reflect light to one or both sides of the vehicle and attached to or incorporated in any wheel or tyre of—

  (i) a pedal cycle and any sidecar attached to it;
  (ii) a solo motor bicycle or a motor bicycle combination; or
  (iii) an invalid carriage; or

(d) a traffic sign.

(2) No vehicle shall be fitted with a lamp which is capable of showing any light to the rear, other than a red light, except—

(a) amber light from a direction indicator or side marker lamp;

(b) white light from a reversing lamp;

(c) white light from a work lamp;

(d) light to illuminate the interior of a vehicle;

(e) light from an illuminated rear registration plate;

(f) light for the purposes of illuminating a taxi meter;

(g) in the case of a bus, light for the purposes of illuminating a route indicator;

(h) blue light and white light from a chequered domed lamp fitted to a police control vehicle and intended for use at the scene of an emergency;

(i) white light from a red and white chequered domed lamp, or a red and white segmented mast-mounted warning beacon, fitted to a fire service control vehicle and intended for use at the scene of an emergency;

(j) green light and white light from a chequered domed lamp fitted to an ambulance control vehicle and intended for use at the scene of an emergency;

(k) blue light from a warning beacon or rear special warning lamp fitted to an emergency vehicle, or from any device fitted to a vehicle used for police purposes;

(l) amber light from a warning beacon fitted to—

  (i) a road clearance vehicle;
  (ii) a vehicle constructed or adapted for the purpose of collecting refuse;
  (iii) a breakdown vehicle;
  (iv) a vehicle having a maximum speed not exceeding 25 mph or any trailer drawn by such a vehicle;
  (v) a vehicle having an overall width (including any load) exceeding 2.9 m;
  (vi) a vehicle used for the purposes of testing, maintaining, improving, cleansing or watering roads or for any purpose incidental to any such use;
  (vii) a vehicle used for the purpose of inspecting, cleansing, maintaining, adjusting, renewing or installing any apparatus which is in, on, under or over a road, or for any purpose incidental to any such use;
  (viii) a vehicle used for or in connection with any purpose for which it is authorised to be used on roads by an order under section 44 of the Act;

(ix) a vehicle used for escort purposes when travelling at a speed not exceeding 25 mph;

(x) a vehicle used by the Commissioners of Customs and Excise for the purpose of testing fuels;

(xi) a vehicle used for the purpose of surveying;

(xii) a vehicle used for the removal or immobilisation of vehicles in exercise of a statutory power or duty;

(m) green light from a warning beacon fitted to a vehicle used by a medical practitioner registered by the General Medical Council (whether with full, provisional or limited registration);

(n) yellow light from a warning beacon fitted to a vehicle for use at airports;

(o) light of any colour from a traffic sign which is attached to a vehicle;

(p) reflected light from amber pedal retro reflectors;

(q) reflected light of any colour from retro reflective material or a retro reflector designed primarily to reflect light to one or both sides of the vehicle and attached to or incorporated in any wheel or tyre of—

(i) a pedal cycle and any sidecar attached to it;

(ii) a solo motor bicycle or motor bicycle combination; or

(iii) an invalid carriage;

(r) reflected light from amber retro reflective material on a road clearance vehicle;

(s) reflected light from yellow retro reflective registration plates;

(t) reflected light from yellow retro reflective material incorporated in a rear marking of a type specified in Part I Section B of Schedule 19 and fitted to—

(i) a motor vehicle having a maximum gross weight exceeding 7500 kg;

(ii) a motor vehicle first used before 1st August 1982 having an unladen weight exceeding 3000 kg;

(iii) a trailer having a maximum gross weight exceeding 3500 kg;

(iv) a trailer manufactured before 1st August 1982 having an unladen weight exceeding 1000 kg;

(v) a trailer which forms part of a combination of vehicles one of which is of a type mentioned in a previous item of this sub-paragraph;

(vi) a load carried by any vehicle; or

(u) reflected light from orange retro reflective material incorporated in a sign fitted to the rear of a vehicle carrying a dangerous substance within the meaning of the Dangerous Substances (Conveyance by Road in Road Tankers and Tank Containers) Regulations 1981 or the Road Traffic (Carriage of Dangerous Substances in Packages etc) Regulations 1986.   **[1646]**

NOTES

Commencement: 1 November 1989.

12. Movement of lamps and reflectors

(1) Save as provided in paragraph (2), no person shall use, or cause or permit to be used, on a road any vehicle to which, or to any load or equipment of which, there is fitted a lamp, reflector or marking which is capable of being moved by swivelling, deflecting or otherwise while the vehicle is in motion.

(2) Paragraph (1) does not apply in respect of—

(a) a headlamp which can be dipped only by the movement of the headlamp or its reflector;

(b) a headlamp which is capable of adjustment so as to compensate for the effect of the load carried by the vehicle;

(c) a lamp or reflector which can be deflected to the side by the movement of, although not necessarily through the same angle as, the front wheel or wheels of the vehicle when turned for the purpose of steering the vehicle;

(d) a headlamp or front fog lamp which can be wholly or partially retracted or concealed;

(e) a direction indicator fitted to a motor vehicle first used before 1st April 1986;

(f) a work lamp;

(g) a warning beacon;

(h) an amber pedal retro reflector; or

(i) retro reflective material or a retro reflector of any colour which is fitted so as to reflect light primarily to one or both sides of the vehicle and is attached to or incorporated in any wheel or tyre of—

(i) a pedal cycle and any sidecar attached to;

(ii) a solo motor bicycle or motor bicycle combination; or

(iii) an invalid carriage.   **[1647]**

NOTES
Commencement: 1 November 1989.

13. Lamps to show a steady light

(1) Save as provided in paragraph (2), no vehicle shall be fitted with a lamp which automatically emits a flashing light.

(2) Paragraph (1) does not apply in respect of—

(a) a direction indicator;

(b) a headlamp fitted to an emergency vehicle;

(c) a warning beacon or special warning lamp;

(d) a lamp or illuminated sign fitted to a vehicle used for police purposes;

(e) a green warning lamp used as an anti-lock brake indicator; or

(f) lamps forming part of a traffic sign.   **[1648]**

NOTES
Commencement: 1 November 1989.

14. Filament lamps

(1) Where a motor vehicle first used on or after 1st April 1986 or any trailer manufactured on or after 1st October 1985 is equipped with any lamp of a type that is required by any Schedule to these Regulations to be marked with an approval mark, no filament lamp other than a filament lamp referred to in the Designation of Approval Marks Regulations in—

(a) regulation 4 and Schedule 2, items 2 or 2A, 8, 20, 37 or 37A; or

(b) regulation 5 and Schedule 4, item 18,

shall be fitted to any such lamp.

(2) Where any pedal cycle manufactured on or after 1st October 1990 is equipped with any lamp that is required by any Schedule to these Regulations to be marked with a British Standard mark, no filament lamp other than a

filament lamp marked with the marking indicated in the British Standard specification for Filament Lamps for Cycles published by the British Standards Institution under the reference 6873: 1988 namely "B.S. 6873" shall be fitted to any such lamp. **[1649]**

NOTES
Commencement: 1 November 1989.

15. General requirements for electrical connections

(1) Every motor vehicle first used on or after 1st April 1991 shall be so constructed that every position lamp, side marker lamp, end-outline marker lamp and rear registration plate lamp with which the vehicle is fitted is capable of being switched on and off by the operation of one switch and, save as provided in paragraph (2), not otherwise.

(2) Sub-paragraph (a) of paragraph (1) shall not prevent one or more position lamps from being capable of being switched on and off independently of any other lamp referred to in that sub-paragraph. **[1650]**

NOTES
Commencement: 1 November 1989.

16. Restrictions on fitting blue warning beacons, special warning lamps and similar devices

No vehicle, other than an emergency vehicle, shall be fitted with—

    (a) a blue warning beacon or special warning lamp, or
    (b) a device which resembles a blue warning beacon or a special warning lamp, whether the same is in working order or not. **[1651]**

NOTES
Commencement: 1 November 1989.

17. Obligatory warning beacons

(1) Subject to paragraph (2), no person shall use, or cause or permit to be used, on an unrestricted dual-carriageway road any motor vehicle with four or more wheels having a maximum speed not exceeding 25 mph unless it or any trailer drawn by it is fitted with at least one warning beacon which—

    (a) complies with Schedule 16, and
    (b) is showing an amber light.

(2) Paragraph (1) shall not apply in relation to—

    (a) any motor vehicle first used before 1st January 1947; and
    (b) any motor vehicle, or any trailer being drawn by it, to which paragraph (1) would otherwise apply, when that vehicle or trailer is on any carriageway of an unrestricted dual-carriageway road for the purpose only of crossing that carriageway in the quickest manner practicable in the circumstances. **[1652]**

NOTES
Commencement: 1 November 1989.

18. Obligatory lamps, reflectors, rear markings and devices

(1) Save as provided in the foregoing provisions of these Regulations and in paragraph (2), every vehicle of a class specified in a Table in Schedule 1 shall be fitted with lamps, reflectors, rear markings and devices which—

    (a) are of a type specified in column 1 of that Table, and

    (b) comply with the relevant installation, alignment and performance requirements set out in the Schedule or Part of a Schedule shown against that type in column 2 of that Table.

(2) The requirements specified in paragraph (1) do not apply in respect of a lamp, reflector, rear marking or device of a type specified in column 1 of a Table in the case of a vehicle shown against it in column 3 of that Table.

(3) The requirements specified in paragraph (1) apply without prejudice to any additional requirements specified in regulations 20 and 21.

(4) The Schedules referred to in the Tables in Schedule 1 are Schedules 2 to 21.　　　　　　**[1653]**

NOTES
    Commencement: 1 November 1989.

19. Restrictions on the obscuration of certain lamps and reflectors

Every vehicle shall be so constructed that at least part of the apparent surface of any—

    (a) front and rear position lamp,

    (b) front and rear direction indicator, and

    (c) rear retro reflector,

which is required by these Regulations to be fitted to a vehicle is visible when the vehicle is viewed from any point directly in front of or behind the lamp or reflector, as appropriate, when every door, tailgate, boot lid, engine cover, cab or other movable part of the vehicle is in a fixed open position.　　　　　　**[1654]**

NOTES
    Commencement: 1 November 1989.

20. Optional lamps, reflectors, rear markings and devices

Every optional lamp, reflector, rear marking or device fitted to a vehicle, being of a type specified in an item in column 2 of the Table below, shall comply with the provisions shown in column 3 of that Table.

TABLE

(1) Item No	(2) Type of lamp, reflector, rear marking or device	(3) Provisions with which compliance is required	
1	Front position lamp	Schedule 2, Part II	⎫
2	Dim-dip device and running lamp	Schedule 3, Part II	
3	Dipped-beam headlamp	Schedule 4, Part II	
4	Main-beam headlamp	Schedule 5, Part II	and Parts I of
5	Front fog lamp	Schedule 6	Schedules 2 to
7	Direction indicator	Schedule 7, Part II	5, 7, 9 to 13 and

(1) Item No	(2) Type of lamp, reflector, rear marking or device	(3) Provisions with which compliance is required	
8	Hazard warning signal device	Schedule 8	⎫ 17 to 21 to the ⎪ extent specified
9	Side marker lamp	Schedule 9, Part II	⎪ in parts II of
10	Rear position lamp	Schedule 10, Part II	⎪ those Schedules.
11	Rear fog lamp	Schedule 11, Part II	⎬
12	Stop lamp	Schedule 12, Part II	⎪
13	End-outline marker lamp	Schedule 13, Part II	⎪
14	Reversing lamp	Schedule 14	⎪
15	Warning beacon	Schedule 16	⎪
16	Side retro reflector	Schedule 17, Part II	⎪
17	Rear retro reflector	Schedule 18, Part II	⎪
18	Rear marking	Schedule 19, Part II	⎪
19	Pedal retro reflector	Schedule 20, Part II	⎪
20	Front retro reflector	Schedule 21, Part II	⎭

[1655]

NOTES
Commencement: 1 November 1989.

21. Projecting trailers and vehicles carrying overhanging or projecting loads or equipment

(1) No person shall use, or cause or permit to be used, on a road in the circumstances mentioned in paragraph (2)—

(a) any trailer which forms part of a combination of vehicles which projects laterally beyond any preceding vehicle in the combination; or

(b) any vehicle or combination of vehicles which carries a load or equipment

in either case under the conditions specified in an item in column 2 of the Table below, unless the vehicle or combination of vehicles complies with the requirements specified in that item in column 3 of that Table.

TABLE

(1) Item No	(2) Conditions	(3) Requirements
1	A trailer which is not fitted with front position lamps and which projects laterally on any side so that the distance from the outermost part of the projection to the outermost part of the illuminated area of the obligatory front position lamp on that side fitted to any preceding vehicle in the combination exceeds 400 mm.	A lamp showing white light to the front shall be fitted to the trailer so that the outermost part of the illuminated area is not more than 400 mm from the outermost projection of the trailer. The installation and performance requirements relating to front position lamps do not apply to any such lamp.

(1) Item No	(2) Conditions	(3) Requirements
2	A trailer which is not fitted with front position lamps and which carries a load or equipment which projects laterally on any side of the trailer so that the distance from the outermost projection of the load or equipment to the outermost part of the illuminated area of the obligatory front position lamp on that side fitted to any preceding vehicle in the combination exceeds 400 mm.	A lamp showing white light to the front shall be fitted to the trailer or the load or equipment so that the outermost part of the illuminated area is not more than 400 mm from the outermost projection of the load or equipment. The installation and performance requirements relating to front position lamps do not apply to any such lamp.
3	A vehicle which carries a load or equipment which projects laterally on any side of the vehicle so that the distance from the outermost part of the load or equipment to the outermost part of the illuminated area of the obligatory front or rear position lamp on that side exceeds 400 mm.	Either— (a) the obligatory front or rear position lamp shall be transferred from the vehicle to the load or equipment to which must also be attached a white front or a red rear reflecting device; or (b) an additional front or rear position lamp and a white front or a red rear reflecting device shall be fitted to the vehicle, load or equipment. All the installation, performance and maintenance requirements relating to front or rear position lamps shall in either case be complied with except that for the purpose of determining the lateral position of such lamps and reflecting devices any reference to the vehicle shall be taken to include the load or equipment except special equipment on a vehicle fitted with a moveable platform or the jib of any crane.
4	A vehicle which carries a load or equipment which projects beyond the rear of the vehicle or, in the case of a combination of vehicles, beyond the rear of the rearmost vehicle in the combination, more than— (a) 2 m in the case of an agricultural vehicle or a vehicle carrying a fire escape; or	An additional rear lamp capable of showing red light to the rear and a red reflecting device, both of which are visible from a reasonable distance, shall be fitted to the vehicle or the load in such a position that the distance between the lamp and the reflecting device, and the rearmost projection of the load

(1) Item No	(2) Conditions	(3) Requirements
	(b) 1 m in the case of any vehicle.	or equipment does not exceed 2 m in the case mentioned in sub-paragraph (a) in column 2 of this item or 1 m in any other case. The installation and performance requirements relating to rear position lamps do not apply to any such additional lamp.
5	A vehicle which carries a load or equipment which projects beyond the front of the vehicle more than— (a) 2 m in the case of an agricultural vehicle or a vehicle carrying a fire escape; or	An additional front lamp capable of showing white light to the front and a white reflecting device, both visible from a reasonable distance, shall be fitted to the vehicle or the load in such a position that the distance between the lamp and the reflecting device, and the foremost projection of the load or equipment, does not exceed 2 m in the case mentioned in sub-paragraph (a) in column 2 of this item or 1 m in any other case. The installation and performance requirements relating to front position lamps and front retro reflectors do not apply to any such additional lamp and reflecting device.
6	A vehicle which carries a load or equipment which obscures any obligatory lamp, reflector or rear marking.	Either— (a) the obligatory lamp, reflector or rear marking shall be transferred to a position on the vehicle, load or equipment where it is not obscured; or (b) an additional lamp, reflector or rear marking shall be fitted to the vehicle, load or equipment. All the installation, performance and maintenance requirements relating to obligatory lamps, reflectors or rear markings shall in either case be complied with.

(2) The circumstances referred to in paragraph (1) are—

    (a) as regards item 6 in the Table, in so far as it relates to obligatory stop lamps and direction indicators, all circumstances; and

    (b) as regards items 1 to 5 in the Table and item 6 in the Table, except in so far as it relates to obligatory stop lamps and direction indicators, the time between sunset and sunrise or, except in so far as it relates to obligatory reflectors, when visibility is seriously reduced between sunrise and sunset.   **[1656]**

NOTES
Commencement: 1 November 1989.

22. Additional side marker lamps

(1) Save as provided in paragraph (2), no person shall use, or cause or permit to be used, on a road between sunset and sunrise, or in seriously reduced visibility between sunrise and sunset, any vehicle or combination of vehicles of a type specified in an item in column 2 of the Table below unless each side of the vehicle or combination of vehicles is fitted with the side marker lamps specified in that item in column 3 and those lamps are kept lit.

TABLE

(1) Item No	(2) Vehicle or combination of vehicles	(3) Side marker lamps
1	A vehicle or a combination of vehicles the overall length of which (including any load) exceeds 18·3 m.	There shall be fitted— (a) one lamp no part of the light-emitting surface of which is more than 9·15 m from the foremost part of the vehicle or vehicles (in either case inclusive of any load); (b) one lamp no part of the light-emitting surface of which is more than 3·05 m from the rearmost part of the vehicle or vehicles (in either case inclusive of any load); and (c) such other lamps as are required to ensure that not more than 3·05 m separates any part of the light-emitting surface of one lamp and any part of the light-emitting surface of the next lamp.
2	A combination of vehicles the overall length of which (including any load) exceeds 12·2 m but does not exceed 18·3 m and carrying a load supported by any two of the vehicles but not including a load carried by an articulated vehicle.	There shall be fitted— (a) one lamp no part of the light-emitting surface of which is forward of, or more than 1530 mm rearward of the rearmost part of the drawing vehicle; and (b) if the supported load extends more than 9·15 m rearward of the rearmost part of the drawing vehicle, one lamp no part of the light-emitting surface of which is forward of, or more than 1530 mm rearward of, the centre of the length of the load.

(2) The requirements specified in paragraph (1) do not apply to—

    (a) a combination of vehicles where any vehicle being drawn in that combination has broken down; or

    (b) a vehicle (not being a combination of vehicles) having an appliance or apparatus or carrying a load of a kind specified in the Table to regulation 82(7) or in regulation 82(8) of the Construction and Use Regulations, if the conditions specified in paragraphs 3 and 4 (which provide for the special marking of projections from vehicles) of Schedule 12 to those Regulations are complied with in relation to the special appliance or apparatus or load as if the said conditions had been expressed in the said regulation 82 to apply in the case of every special appliance or apparatus or load of a kind specified in that regulation.

(3) Every side marker lamp fitted in accordance with this regulation shall comply with Part I of Schedule 9. **[1657]**

NOTES

Commencement: 1 November 1989.

PART III

REGULATIONS GOVERNING THE MAINTENANCE AND USE OF LAMPS, REFLECTORS, REAR MARKINGS AND DEVICES

23. Maintenance of lamps, reflectors, rear markings and devices

(1) No person shall use, or cause or permit to be used, on a road a vehicle unless every lamp, reflector, rear marking and device to which this paragraph applies is in good working order and, in the case of a lamp, clean.

    (2) Save as provided in paragraph (3), paragraph (1) applies to—

    (a) every—

        (i) front position lamp,
        (ii) rear position lamp,
        (iii) headlamp,
        (iv) rear registration plate lamp,
        (v) side marker lamp,
        (vi) end-outline marker lamp,
        (vii) rear fog lamp,
        (viii) retro reflector, and
        (ix) rear marking of a type specified in Part I of Section B of Schedule 19,

with which the vehicle is required by these Regulations to be fitted; and

    (b) every—

        (i) stop lamp,
        (ii) direction indicator,
        (iii) running lamp,
        (iv) dim-dip device,
        (v) headlamp levelling device, and
        (vi) hazard warning signal device,

with which it is fitted.

    (3) Paragraph (2) does not apply to—

(a) a rear fog lamp on a vehicle which is part of a combination of vehicles any part of which is not required by these Regulations to be fitted with a rear fog lamp;

(b) a rear fog lamp on a motor vehicle drawing a trailer;

(c) a defective lamp, reflector, dim-dip device or headlamp levelling device on a vehicle in use on a road between sunrise and sunset, if any such lamp, reflector or device became defective during the journey which is in progress or if arrangements have been made to remedy the defect with all reasonable expedition; or

(d) a lamp, reflector, dim-dip device, headlamp levelling device or rear marking on a combat vehicle in use on a road between sunrise and sunset.   **[1658]**

NOTES
Commencement: 1 November 1989.

24. Requirements about the use of front and rear position lamps, rear registration plate lamps, side marker lamps and end-outline marker lamps

(1) Save as provided in paragraphs (5) and (9), no person shall—

(a) use, or cause or permit to be used, on a road any vehicle which is in motion—

(i) between sunset and sunrise, or

(ii) in seriously reduced visibility between sunrise and sunset; or

(b) allow to remain at rest, or cause or permit to be allowed to remain at rest, on a road any vehicle between sunset and sunrise

unless every front position lamp, rear position lamp, rear registration plate lamp, side marker lamp and end-outline marker lamp with which the vehicle is required by these Regulations to be fitted is kept lit and unobscured.

(2) Save as provided in paragraphs (5) and (9), where a solo motor bicycle is not fitted with a front position lamp, no person shall use it, or cause or permit it to be used, on a road (other than when it is parked) between sunset and sunrise or in seriously reduced visibility between sunrise and sunset, unless a headlamp is kept lit and unobscured.

(3) Save as provided in paragraphs (5) and (9), no person shall allow to remain parked, or cause or permit to be allowed to remain parked between sunset and sunrise—

(a) a motor bicycle combination which is required to be fitted only with a front position lamp on the sidecar; or

(b) a trailer to the front of which no other vehicle is attached and which is not required to be fitted with front position lamps,

unless a pair of front position lamps is fitted and kept lit and unobscured.

(4) Save as provided in paragraphs (5) and (9), no person shall allow to remain parked, or cause or permit to be allowed to remain parked between sunset and sunrise a solo motor bicycle which is not required to be fitted with a front position lamp, unless a front position lamp is fitted and kept lit and unobscured.

(5) Paragraphs (1), (2), (3) and (4) shall not apply in respect of a vehicle of a class specified in paragraph (7) which is parked on a road on which a speed limit of 30 mph or less is in force and the vehicle is parked—

(a) in a parking place for which provision is made under section 6, or which is authorised under section 32 or designated under section 45 of the Road Traffic Regulation Act 1984, or which is set apart as a parking place under some other enactment or instrument and the vehicle is parked in a manner which does not contravene the provision of any enactment or instrument relating to the parking place; or

(b) in a lay-by—

    (i) the limits of which are indicated by a traffic sign consisting of the road marking shown in diagram 1010 in Schedule 2 of the Traffic Signs Regulations and General Directions 1981; or

    (ii) the surface of which is of a colour or texture which is different from that of the part of the carriageway of the road used primarily by through traffic; or

    (iii) the limits of which are indicated by a continuous strip of surface of a different colour or texture from that of the surface of the remainder of the carriageway of the road; or

(c) elsewhere than in such a parking place or lay-by if—

    (i) the vehicle is parked in one of the circumstances described in paragraph (8); and

    (ii) no part of the vehicle is less than 10 m from the junction of any part of the carriageway of any road with the carriageway of the road on which it is parked whether that junction is on the same side of the road as that on which the vehicle is parked or not.

(6) Sub-paragraph (5)(c)(ii) shall be construed in accordance with the diagram in Schedule 22.

(7) The classes of vehicle referred to in paragraph (5) are—

(a) a motor vehicle being a goods vehicle the unladen weight of which does not exceed 1525 kg.

(b) a passenger vehicle other than a bus;

(c) an invalid carriage; and

(d) a motor cycle or a pedal cycle in either case with or without a sidecar;

not being—

    (i) a vehicle to which a trailer is attached;

    (ii) a vehicle which is required to be fitted with lamps by regulation 21; or

    (iii) a vehicle carrying a load, if the load is required to be fitted with lamps by regulation 21.

(8) The circumstances referred to in paragraph (5)(c) are that—

(a) the vehicle is parked on a road on which the driving of vehicles otherwise than in one direction is prohibited at all times and its left or near side is as close as may be and parallel to the left-hand edge of the carriageway or its right or off side is as close as may be and parallel to the right-hand edge of the carriageway; or

(b) the vehicle is parked on a road on which such a prohibition does not exist and its left or near side is as close as may be and parallel to the edge of the carriageway.

(9) Paragraphs (1), (2), (3) and (4) do not apply in respect of—

(a) a solo motor bicycle or a pedal cycle being pushed along the left-hand edge of a carriageway;

    (b) a pedal cycle waiting to proceed provided it is kept to the left-hand or near side edge of a carriageway; or

    (c) a vehicle which is parked in an area on part of a highway on which roadworks are being carried out and which is bounded by amber lamps and other traffic signs so as to prevent the presence of the vehicle, its load or equipment being a danger to persons using the road.	**[1659]**

NOTES
Commencement: 1 November 1989.

25. Requirements about the use of headlamps and front fog lamps

(1) Save as provided in paragraph (2), no person shall use, or cause or permit to be used, on a road a vehicle which is fitted with obligatory dipped-beam headlamps unless every such lamp is kept lit—

    (a) during the hours of darkness, except on a road which is a restricted road for the purposes of section 81 of the Road Traffic Regulation Act 1984 by virtue of a system of street lighting when it is lit; and

    (b) in seriously reduced visibility.

(2) The provisions of paragraph (1) do not apply—

    (a) in the case of a motor vehicle fitted with one obligatory dipped-beam headlamp or a solo motor bicycle or motor bicycle combination fitted with a pair of obligatory dipped-beam headlamps, if a main-beam headlamp or a front fog lamp is kept lit;

    (b) in the case of a motor vehicle, other than a solo motor bicycle or motor bicycle combination, fitted with a pair of obligatory dipped-beam headlamps, if—

        (i) a pair of main-beam headlamps is kept lit; or

        (ii) in seriously reduced visibility, a pair of front fog lamps which is so fitted that the outermost part of the illuminated area of each lamp in the pair is not more than 400 mm from the outer edge of the vehicle is kept lit;

    (c) to a vehicle being drawn by another vehicle;

    (d) to a vehicle while being used to propel a snow plough; or

    (e) to a vehicle which is parked.

(3) For the purposes of this regulation a headlamp shall not be regarded as lit if its intensity is reduced by a dim-dip device.	**[1660]**

NOTES
Commencement: 1 November 1989.

26. Requirements about the use of warning beacons

No person shall use, or cause or permit to be used, on an unrestricted dual-carriageway road a vehicle which is required to be fitted with at least one warning beacon by regulation 17 unless every such beacon is kept lit.	**[1661]**

NOTES
Commencement: 1 November 1989.

27. Restrictions on the use of lamps other than those to which regulation 24 refers

No person shall use, or cause or permit to be used, on a road any vehicle on which any lamp, hazard warning signal device or warning beacon of a type

specified in an item in column 2 of the Table below is used in a manner specified
in that item in column 3.

TABLE

(1) Item No	(2) *Type of lamp, hazard warning signal device or warning beacon*	(3) *Manner of use prohibited*
1	Headlamp	(a) Used so as to cause undue dazzle or discomfort to other persons using the road. (b) Used so as to be lit when a vehicle is parked.
2	Front fog lamp	(a) Used so as to cause undue dazzle or discomfort to other persons using the road. (b) Used so as to be lit at any time other than in conditions of seriously reduced visibility. (c) Used so as to be lit when a vehicle is parked.
3	Rear fog lamp	(a) Used so as to cause undue dazzle or discomfort to the driver of a following vehicle. (b) Used so as to be lit at any time other than in conditions of seriously reduced visibility. (c) Save in the case of an emergency vehicle, used so as to be lit when a vehicle is parked.
4	Reversing lamp	Used so as to be lit except for the purpose of reversing the vehicle.
5	Hazard warning signal device	Used other than— (i) to warn persons using the road of a temporary obstruction when the vehicle is at rest; or (ii) on a motorway or unrestricted dual-carriageway, to warn following drivers of a need to slow down due to a temporary obstruction ahead; or (iii) in the case of a bus, to summon assistance for the driver or any person acting as a conductor or inspector on the vehicle.
6	Warning beacon emitting blue light and special warning lamp	Used so as to be lit except— (i) at the scene of an emergency; or

(1) Item No	(2) Type of lamp, hazard warning signal device or warning beacon	(3) Manner of use prohibited
		(ii) when it is necessary or desirable either to indicate to persons using the road the urgency of the purpose for which the vehicle is being used, or to warn persons of the presence of the vehicle or a hazard on the road.
7	Warning beacon emitting amber light	Used so as to be lit except— (i) at the scene of an emergency; (ii) when it is necessary or desirable to warn persons of the presence of the vehicle; and (iii) in the case of a breakdown vehicle, while it is being used in connection with, and in the immediate vicinity of, an accident or breakdown, or while it is being used to draw a broken-down vehicle.
8	Warning beacon emitting green light	Used so as to be lit except whilst occupied by a medical practitioner registered by the General Medical Council (whether with full, provisional or limited registration) and used for the purposes of an emergency.
9	Warning beacon emitting yellow light	Used so as to be lit on a road.
10	Work Lamp	(a) Used so as to cause undue dazzle or discomfort to the driver of any vehicle. (b) Used so as to be lit except for the purpose of illuminating a working area, accident, breakdown or works in the vicinity of the vehicle.
11	Any other lamp	Used so as to cause undue dazzle or discomfort to other persons using the road.

[1662]

NOTES
    Commencement: 1 November 1989.

PART IV

TESTING AND INSPECTION OF LIGHTING EQUIPMENT AND REFLECTORS

28. Testing and inspection of lighting equipment and reflectors

The provisions of regulation 74 of the Construction and Use Regulations apply in respect of lighting equipment and reflectors with which a vehicle is required by these Regulations to be fitted in the same way as they apply in respect of brakes, silencers, steering gear and tyres. **[1663]**

NOTES
Commencement: 1 November 1989.

SCHEDULES

SCHEDULE 1

Regulation 18

OBLIGATORY LAMPS, REFLECTORS, REAR MARKINGS AND DEVICES

TABLE I MOTOR VEHICLE HAVING THREE OR MORE WHEELS NOT BEING
A VEHICLE TO WHICH ANY OTHER TABLE IN THIS SCHEDULE APPLIES

(1) *Type of lamp, reflector, rear marking or device*	(2) *Schedule in which relevant installation and performance requirements are specified*	(3) *Exceptions*
Front position lamp	Schedule 2: part I	None.
Dim-dip device or running lamp	Schedule 3: Part I	A vehicle having a maximum speed not exceeding 40 mph; A vehicle first used before 1st April 1987; A home forces' vehicle; A vehicle in respect of which the following conditions are satisfied— (a) there is fitted to the vehicle all the lighting and light-signalling devices listed in items 1.5.7 to 1.5.20 of Annex I of Community Directive 76/756/EEC, as amended, which are required to be fitted under that Annex; and (b) all those devices are so installed that they comply with the requirements set out in items 3 and 4 of that Annex including, in particular, item 4.2.6 (Alignment of dipped-beam headlamps).
Dipped-beam headlamp	Schedule 4: Part I	A vehicle having a maximum speed not exceeding 15 mph; A vehicle first used before 1st April 1986 being an agricultural vehicle or a works truck; A vehicle first used before 1st January 1931.

(1) *Type of lamp, reflector, rear marking or device*	(2) *Schedule in which relevant installation and performance requirements are specified*	(3) *Exceptions*
Main-beam headlamp	Schedule 5: Part I	A vehicle having a maximum speed not exceeding 25 mph; A vehicle first used before 1st April 1986 being an agricultural vehicle or a works truck; A vehicle first used before 1st January 1931.
Direction indicator	Schedule 7: Part I	An invalid carriage having a maximum speed not exceeding 4 mph and any other vehicle having a maximum speed not exceeding 15 mph; An agricultural vehicle having an unladen weight not exceeding 255 kg; A vehicle first used before 1st April 1986 being an agricultural vehicle, an industrial tractor or a works truck; A vehicle first used before 1st January 1936.
Hazard warning signal device	Schedule 8: Part I	A vehicle not required to be fitted with direction indicators; A vehicle first used before 1st April 1986.
Side marker lamp	Schedule 9: Part I	A vehicle having a maximum speed not exceeding 25 mph; A passenger vehicle; An incomplete vehicle proceeding to a works for completion or to a place where it is to be stored or displayed for sale; A vehicle the overall length of which does not exceed 6 m; A vehicle first used before 1st April 1991; A vehicle in respect of which the following conditions are satisfied— (a) there is fitted to the vehicle all the lighting and light-signalling devices listed in items 1.5.7 to 1.5.20 of Annex I of Community Directive 76/756/EEC, as amended, which are required to be fitted under that Annex; and (b) all those devices are so installed that they comply with the requirements set out in items 3 and 4 of that Annex including, in particular, item 4.2.6 (Alignment of dipped-beam headlamps).
Rear position lamp	Schedule 10: Part I	None.
Rear fog lamp	Schedule 11: Part I	A vehicle having a maximum speed not exceeding 25 mph; A vehicle first used before 1st April 1986 being an agricultural vehicle or a works truck; A vehicle first used before 1st April 1980; A vehicle having an overall width which does not exceed 1300 mm.

(1) Type of lamp, reflector, rear marking or device	(2) Schedule in which relevant installation and performance requirements are specified	(3) Exceptions
Stop lamp	Schedule 12: Part I	A vehicle having a maximum speed not exceeding 25 mph; A vehicle first used before 1st April 1986 being an agricultural vehicle or a works truck; A vehicle first used before 1st January 1936.
End-outline marker lamp	Schedule 13: Part I	A vehicle having a maximum speed not exceeding 25 mph; A motor vehicle having an overall width not exceeding 2100 mm; An incomplete vehicle proceeding to a works for completion or to a place where it is to be stored or displayed for sale; A motor vehicle first used before 1st April 1991.
Rear registration plate lamp	Schedule 15.	A vehicle not required to be fitted with a rear registration plate; A works truck.
Side retro reflector	Schedule 17: Part I	A vehicle having a maximum speed not exceeding 25 mph; A goods vehicle— (a) first used on or after 1st April 1986, the overall length of which does not exceed 6 m; or (b) first used before 1st April 1986, the overall length of which does not exceed 8 m; A passenger vehicle; An incomplete vehicle proceeding to a works for completion or to a place where it is to be stored or displayed for sale; A vehicle primarily constructed for moving excavated material and being used by virtue of an Order under section 44 of the Act; A mobile crane or engineering plant.
Rear retro reflector	Schedule 18: Part I	None.
Rear marking	Schedule 19: Part I	A vehicle having a maximum speed not exceeding 25 mph; A vehicle first used before 1st August 1982 the unladen weight of which does not exceed 3050 kg; A vehicle the maximum gross weight of which does not exceed 7500 kg; A passenger vehicle not being an articulated bus; A tractive unit for an articulated vehicle; An incomplete vehicle proceeding to a works for completion or to a place where it is to be stored or displayed for sale;

(1) *Type of lamp, reflector, rear marking or device*	(2) *Schedule in which relevant installation and performance requirements are specified*	(3) *Exceptions*
		A vehicle first used before 1st April 1986 being an agricultural vehicle, a works truck or engineering plant; A vehicle first used before 1st January 1940; A home forces' vehicle; A vehicle constructed or adapted for— (a) fire fighting or fire salvage; (b) servicing or controlling aircraft; (c) heating and dispensing tar or other material for the construction or maintenance of roads; or (d) transporting two or more vehicles or vehicle bodies or two or more boats.

[1664]

NOTES
    Commencement: 1 November 1989.

TABLE II SOLE MOTOR BICYCLE AND MOTOR BICYCLE COMBINATION

(1) *Type of lamp or reflector*	(2) *Schedule in which relevant installation and performance requirements are specified*	(3) *Exceptions*
Front position lamp	Schedule 2: Part I	A solo motor bicycle fitted with a headlamp.
Dipped-beam headlamp	Schedule 4: part I	A vehicle first used before 1st January 1931.
Main-beam headlamp	Schedule 5: Part I	A vehicle having a maximum speed not exceeding 25 mph; A vehicle first used before 1st January 1972 and having an engine with a capacity of less than 50 cc; A vehicle first used before 1st January 1931.
Direction indicator	Schedule 7: Part I	A vehicle having a maximum speed not exceeding 25 mph; A vehicle first used before 1st April 1986; A vehicle which is constructed or adapted primarily for use off roads (whether by reason of its tyres, suspension, ground clearance or otherwise) and which can carry only one person or which, in the case of a motor bicycle combination, can carry only the rider and one passenger in the sidecar.
Rear position lamp	Schedule 10: Part I	None.

(1) Type of lamp or reflector	(2) Schedule in which relevant installation and performance requirements are specified	(3) Exceptions
Stop lamp	Schedule 12: Part I	A vehicle having a maximum speed not exceeding 25 mph; A vehicle first used before 1st April 1986 and having an engine with a capacity of less than 50 cc; A vehicle first used before 1st January 1936.
Rear registration plate lamp	Schedule 15	A vehicle not required to be fitted with a rear registration plate.
Rear retro reflector	Schedule 18: Part I	None.

[1665]

NOTES
Commencement: 1 November 1989.

TABLE III PEDAL CYCLE

(1) Type of lamp or reflector	(2) Schedule in which relevant installation and performance requirements are specified	(3) Exceptions
Front position lamp	Schedule 2: Part I	None.
Rear position lamp	Schedule 10: Part I	None.
Rear retro reflector	Schedule 18: Part I	None.
Pedal retro reflector	Schedule 20: Part I	A pedal cycle manufactured before 1st October 1985.

[1666]

NOTES
Commencement: 1 November 1989.

TABLE IV PEDESTRIAN-CONTROLLED VEHICLE, HORSE-DRAWN VEHICLE AND TRACK-LAYING VEHICLE

(1) Type of lamp or reflector	(2) Schedule in which relevant installation and performance requirements are specified	(3) Exceptions
Front position lamp	Schedule 2: Part I	None.
Rear position lamp	Schedule 10: Part I	None.
Rear retro reflector	Schedule 18: Part I	None.

[1667]

NOTES
Commencement: 1 November 1989.

TABLE V VEHICLE DRAWN OR PROPELLED BY HAND

(1) *Type of lamp or reflector*	(2) *Schedule in which relevant installation and performance requirements are specified*	(3) *Exceptions*
Front position lamp	Schedule 2: Part I	None.
Rear position lamp	Schedule 10: Part I	A vehicle fitted with a rear retro reflector.
Rear retro reflector	Schedule 18: Part I	A vehicle fitted with a rear position lamp.

[1668]

NOTES
   Commencement: 1 November 1989.

TABLE VI TRAILER DRAWN BY A MOTOR VEHICLE

(1) *Type of lamp, reflector or rear marking*	(2) *Schedule in which relevant installation and performance requirements are specified*	(3) *Exceptions*
Front position lamp	Schedule 2: Part I	A trailer with an overall width not exceeding 1600 mm; A trailer manufactured before 1st October 1985 the overall length of which, excluding any drawbar and any fitting for its attachment, does not exceed 2300 mm; A trailer constructed or adapted for the carriage and launching of a boat.
Direction indicator	Schedule 7: Part I	A trailer manufactured before 1st September 1965; An agricultural vehicle or a works trailer in either case manufactured before 1st October 1990.
Side marker lamp	Schedule 9: Part I	A trailer the overall length of which, excluding any drawbar and any fitting for its attachment, does not exceed— (a) 6 m, (b) 9.15 m in the case of a trailer manufactured before 1st October 1990; An incomplete trailer proceeding to a works for completion or to a place where it is to be stored or displayed for sale; An agricultural vehicle or a works trailer; A caravan; A trailer constructed or adapted for the carriage and launching of a boat; A trailer in respect of which the following conditions are satisfied—

(1) *Type of lamp, reflector or rear marking*	(2) *Schedule in which relevant installation and performance requirements are specified*	(3) *Exceptions*
		(a) there is fitted to the trailer all the lighting and light-signalling devices listed in items 1.5.7 to 1.5.20 of Annex I of Community Directive 76/756/EEC, as amended, which are required to be fitted under that Annex; and (b) all those devices are so installed and maintained that they comply with the requirements set out in items 3 and 4 of that Annex.
Rear position lamp	Schedule 10: Part I	None.
Rear fog lamp	Schedule 11: Part I	A trailer manufactured before 1st April 1980; A trailer the overall width of which does not exceed 1300 mm; An agricultural vehicle or a works trailer.
Stop lamp	Schedule 12: Part I	An agricultural vehicle or a works trailer.
End-outline marker lamp	Schedule 13: Part I	A trailer having an overall width not exceeding 2100 mm; An incomplete trailer proceeding to a works for completion or to a place where it is to be stored or displayed for sale; An agricultural vehicle or a works trailer; A trailer manufactured before 1st October 1990.
Rear registration plate lamp	Schedule 15	A trailer not required to be fitted with a rear registration plate.
Side retro reflector	Schedule 17: Part I	A trailer the overall length of which, excluding any drawbar, does not exceed 5 m; An incomplete trailer proceeding to a works for completion or to a place where it is to be stored or displayed for sale; Engineering plant; A trailer primarily constructed for moving excavated material and which is being used by virtue of an Order under section 44 of the Act.
Front retro reflector	Schedule 21: Part I	A trailer manufactured before 1st October 1990; An agricultural vehicle or a works trailer.
Rear retro reflector	Schedule 18: Part I	None.
Rear marking	Schedule 19: Part I	A trailer manufactured before 1st August 1982 the unladen weight of which does not exceed 1020 kg; A trailer the maximum gross weight of which does not exceed 3500 kg; An incomplete trailer proceeding to a works for completion or to a place where it is to be stored or displayed for sale;

(1) *Type of lamp, reflector or rear marking*	(2) *Schedule in which relevant installation and performance requirements are specified*	(3) *Exceptions*
		An agricultural vehicle, a works trailer or engineering plant; A trailer drawn by a bus; A home forces' vehicle; A trailer constructed or adapted for— (a) fire fighting or fire salvage; (b) servicing or controlling aircraft; (c) heating and dispensing tar or other material for the construction or maintenance of roads; (d) carrying asphalt or macadam, in each case being mixing or drying plant; or (e) transporting two or more vehicles or vehicle bodies or two or more boats.

[1669]

NOTES
  Commencement: 1 November 1989.

TABLE VII TRAILER DRAWN BY A PEDAL CYCLE

(1) *Type of lamp, reflector or rear marking*	(2) *Schedule in which relevant installation and performance requirements are specified*	(3) *Exceptions*
Rear position lamp	Schedule 10: Part I	None.
Rear retro reflector	Schedule 18: Part I	None.

[1670]

NOTES
  Commencement: 1 November 1989.

SCHEDULE 2
Regulations 18, 20

PART I

REQUIREMENTS RELATING TO OBLIGATORY FRONT POSITION LAMPS AND TO FRONT POSITION LAMPS TO THE EXTENT SPECIFIED IN PART II

1. Number—
   (a) Any vehicle not covered by sub-paragraph (b), (c), (d), (e) or (f):   Two
   (b) A pedal cycle with less than four wheels and without a sidecar: One
   (c) A solo motor bicycle: One
   (d) A motor bicycle combination with a headlamp on the motor bicycle: One, on the sidecar

(e) An invalid carriage: One
(f) A vehicle drawn or propelled by hand: One

2. Position—
  (a) Longitudinal: No requirement
  (b) Lateral—
    (i) Where two front position lamps are required to
      be fitted—
      (A) Maximum distance from the side of the
         vehicle—
         (1) A motor vehicle first used on or after   400 mm
             1st April 1986:
         (2) A trailer manufactured on or after 1st   150 mm
             October 1985;
         (3) Any other vehicle manufactured on or   400 mm
             after 1st October 1985:
         (4) A motor vehicle first used before 1st   510 mm
             April 1986 and any other vehicle
             manufactured before 1st October 1985:
      (B) Minimum separation distance between   No requirement
         front position lamps:
    (ii) Where one front position lamp is required to be
      fitted—
      (A) A sidecar forming part of a motor bicycle   On the centre-line of the
         combination: sidecar or on the side of
                              the sidecar furthest
                              from the motor bicycle
      (B) Any other vehicle: On the centre-line or
                                   off-side of the vehicle

  (c) Vertical
    (i) Maximum height above the ground—
      (A) Any vehicle not covered by sub-paragraph   1500 mm or, if the struc-
         (B), (C) or (D):   ture of the vehicle
                                makes this impractica-
                                ble, 2100 mm
      (B) A motor vehicle first used before 1st April 2300 mm
         1986 and a trailer manufactured before 1st
         October 1985:
      (C) A motor vehicle, first used on or after 1st 2100 mm
         April 1986, having a maximum speed not
         exceeding 25 mph:
      (D) A large passenger-carrying vehicle and a   No requirement
         road clearance vehicle:
    (ii) Minimum height above the ground   No requirement

3. Angles of visibility—
  (a) A motor vehicle (not being a motor bicycle
    combination or an agricultural vehicle) first used on
    or after 1st April 1986 and a trailer manufactured
    on or after 1st October 1985—
    (i) Horizontal—
      (A) Where one lamp is required to be fitted: 80° to the left and to the
                                   right
      (B) Where two lamps are required to be fitted: 80° outwards and 45°
                                   inwards (5° inwards in
                                   the case of a trailer)
    (ii) Vertical—
      (A) Any case not covered by sub-paragraph   15° above and below the
         (B):   horizontal

(B) Where the highest part of the illuminated area of the lamp is less than 750 mm above the ground:	15° above and 5° below the horizontal
(b) Any other vehicle:	Visible to the front
4. Alignment:	To the front

5. Markings—

(a) A motor vehicle (other than a solo motor bicycle or a motor bicycle combination) first used on or after 1st January 1972 and a trailer manufactured on or after 1st October 1985:	An approval mark
(b) A solo motor bicycle and a motor bicycle combination in either case first used on or after 1st April 1986;	An approval mark
(c) Any other vehicle manufactured or first used on or after 1st October 1990:	An approval mark or a British Standard mark
(d) Any other vehicle:	No requirement
6. Size of illuminated area:	No requirement
7. Colour:	White or, if incorporated in a headlamp which is capable of emitting only a yellow light, yellow
8. Wattage:	No requirement

9. Intensity—

(a) A front position lamp bearing any of the markings mentioned in paragraph 5:	No requirement
(b) Any other front position lamp:	Visible from a reasonable distance
10. Electrical connections:	No individual requirement
11. Tell-tale:	No requirement

12. Other requirements—

(a) Except in the case of a vehicle covered by sub-paragraph (b), where two front position lamps are required to be fitted they shall form a pair.

(b) In the case of a trailer manufactured before 1st October 1985 and a motor bicycle combination, where two front position lamps are required to be fitted they shall be fitted on each side of the longitudinal axis of the vehicle.

13. Definitions—

In this Schedule—
"approval mark" means—
(a) in relation to a solo motor bicycle or a motor bicycle combination, a marking designated as an approval mark by regulation 4 of the Designation of Approval Marks Regulations and shown at item 50A of Schedule 2 to those Regulations, and

(b) in relation to any other motor vehicle or any trailer, either—

    (i) a marking designated as an approval mark by regulation 5 of the Designation of Approval Marks Regulations and shown at item 5 of Schedule 4 to those Regulations, or

    (ii) a marking designated as an approval mark by regulation 4 of the Designation of Approval Marks Regulations and shown at item 7 of Schedule 2 to those Regulations;

"British Standard mark" means the mark indicated in the specifications for photometric and physical requirements for lighting equipment published by the British Standards Institution under the reference BS 6102: Part 3: 1986, namely "BS 6102/3". **[1671]**

NOTES
Commencement: 1 November 1989.

PART II

REQUIREMENTS RELATING TO OPTIONAL FRONT POSITION LAMPS

1. In the case of a solo motor bicycle first used on or after 1st April 1991 which is not fitted with any obligatory front position lamp, not more than two may be fitted which must comply with the requirement specified in pararaph 7 of Part I. Where two are fitted these shall be situated as close together as possible.

2. In the case of a solo motor bicycle first used on or after 1st April 1991 which is fitted with one obligatory front position lamp, not more than one additional lamp may be fitted which must comply with the requirement specified in paragraph 7 of Part I and shall be situated as close as possible to the obligatory front position lamp.

3. In the case of any other vehicle the only requirement prescribed by these Regulations in respect of any which are fitted is that in paragraph 7 of Part I. **[1672]**

NOTES
Commencement: 1 November 1989.

SCHEDULE 3
Regulations 18, 20

PART I

REQUIREMENTS RELATING TO OBLIGATORY DIM-DIP DEVICES AND RUNNING LAMPS

1. A dim-dip device fitted to satisfy regulation 18 shall cause light to be emitted from the dipped-beam filament of each obligatory dipped-beam headlamp, each such light having, so far as is practicable, an intensity of between 10 and 20 per cent of the intensity of the normal dipped beam.

2. Running lamps fitted to satisfy regulation 18 shall be in the form of a matched pair of front lamps, each of which—

    (a) is fitted in a position in which an obligatory front position lamp may lawfully be fitted, and

    (b) is capable of emitting white light to the front having an intensity of not less than 200 candelas, measured from directly in front of the centre of the lamp in a direction parallel to the longitudinal axis of the vehicle, and of not more than 800 candelas in any direction.

3. The electrical connections to the obligatory dim-dip device or running lamps, as the case may be, shall be such that the light output specified in paragraph 1 or 2 above is emitted automatically whenever—

    (a) the engine of the vehicle is running, or the key or devices which control the starting or stopping of the engine are in the normal position for driving the vehicle, and

        (i) the obligatory position lamps, but not the headlamps, of the vehicle are switched on, or

        (ii) the obligatory position lamps are switched off. **[1673]**

NOTES
Commencement: 1 November 1989.

PART II

REQUIREMENTS RELATING TO OPTIONAL DIM-DIP DEVICES AND RUNNING LAMPS

There is no requirement relating to an optional dim-dip device or an optional running lamp.   **[1674]**

NOTES
  Commencement: 1 November 1989.

SCHEDULE 4

Regulations 18, 20

PART I

REQUIREMENTS RELATING TO OBLIGATORY DIPPED-BEAM HEADLAMPS AND TO OPTIONAL DIPPED-BEAM HEADLAMPS TO THE EXTENT SPECIFIED IN PART II

1. Number—

   (a) Any vehicle not covered by sub-paragraph (b), (c), (*d*) or (e):   Two

   (b) A solo motor bicycle and a motor bicycle combination: One

   (c) A motor vehicle with three wheels, other than a motor bicycle combination, first used before 1st January 1972:   One

   (*d*) A motor vehicle with three wheels, other than a motor bicycle combination, first used on or after 1st January 1972 and which has an unladen weight of not more than 400 kg and an overall width of not more than 1300 mm: One

   (e) A bus first used before 1st October 1969:   One

2. Position—

   (a) Longitudinal: No requirement

   (b) Lateral—

     (i) Where two dipped-beam headlamps are required to be fitted—

       (A) Maximum distance from the side of the vehicle

         (1) Any vehicle not covered by sub-paragraph (2) or (3):   400 mm

         (2) A vehicle first used before 1st January 1972:   No requirement

         (3) An agricultural vehicle, engineering plant and an industrial tractor: No requirement

       (B) Minimum separation distance between a pair of dipped-beam headlamps: No requirement

     (ii) Where one dipped-beam headlamp is required to be fitted—

       (A) Any vehicle not covered by sub-paragraph (B):   (i) On the centre-line of the motor vehicle (disregarding any sidecar forming part of a motor bicycle combination), or

(ii) At any distance from the side of the motor vehicle (disregarding any sidecar forming part of a motor bicycle combination) provided that a duplicate lamp is fitted on the other side so that together they form a matched pair. In such a case, both lamps shall be regarded as obligatory lamps.

(B) A bus first used before 1st October 1969:   No requirement

(c) Vertical—

    (i) Maximum height above the ground—

        (A) Any vehicle not covered by sub-paragraph (B):   1200 mm

        (B) A vehicle first used before 1st January 1952, an agricultural vehicle, a road clearance vehicle, an aerodrome fire tender, an aerodrome runway sweeper, an industrial tractor, engineering plant and a home forces' vehicle: No requirement

    (ii) Minimum height above the ground—

        (A) Any vehicle not covered by sub-paragraph (B):   500 mm

        (B) A vehicle first used before 1st January 1956:   No requirement

3. Angles of visibility: No requirement

4. Alignment—

When a vehicle is at its kerbside weight and has a weight of 75 kg on the driver's seat, and any manual headlamp levelling device control is set to the stop position, the alignment of every dipped-beam headlamp shall, as near as practicable, be as follows:

(a) In the case of a vehicle having a maximum speed exceeding 25 mph—

    (i) If the dipped-beam headlamp bears an approval mark its aim shall be set so that the horizontal part of the cut-off of the beam pattern is inclined downwards as indicated by the vehicle manufacturer in a marking on the vehicle, as mentioned in sub-paragraph 12(b) or, where no such marking is provided—

(A) 1.3 per cent if the height of the centre of the headlamp is not more than 850 mm above the ground, or

(B) 2 per cent if the height of the centre of the headlamp is more than 850 mm above the ground;

    (ii) If the dipped-beam headlamp does not bear an approval mark and the headlamp can also be used as a main-beam headlamp its aim shall be set so that the centre of the main-beam pattern is horizontal or inclined slightly below the horizontal;

    (iii) If the dipped-beam headlamp does not bear an approval mark and the headlamp cannot also be used as a main-beam headlamp its aim shall be set so as not to cause undue dazzle or discomfort to other persons using the road;

(b) In the case of a vehicle having a maximum speed not exceeding 25 mph—

    (i) If the dipped-beam headlamp bears an approval mark or not and the headlamp can also be used as a main-beam headlamp its aim shall be set so that the centre of the mean-beam pattern is horizontal or inclined slightly below the horizontal;

    (ii) If the dipped-beam headlamp bears an approval mark or not and the headlamp cannot also be used as a main-beam its aim shall be set so as not to cause undue dazzle or discomfort to other persons using the road.

5. Markings—	
(a) Any vehicle not covered by sub-paragraph (b), (c) or (d):	An approval mark or a British Standard mark
(b) a motor vehicle first used before 1st April 1986:	No requirement
(c) A three-wheeled motor vehicle, not being a motor bicycle combination, first used on or after 1st April 1986 and having a maximum speed not exceeding 50 mph:	No requirement
(d) A solo motor bicycle and a motor bicycle combination:	No requirement
6. Size of illuminated area:	No requirement
7. Colour:	White or yellow
8. Wattage—	
(a) A motor vehicle with four or more wheels first used on or after 1st April 1986:	No requirement
(b) A three-wheeled motor vehicle, not being a motor bicycle combination, first used on or after 1st April 1986—	
(i) having a maximum speed not exceeding 50 mph:	15 watts minimum
(ii) having a maximum speed exceeding 50 mph:	No requirement
(c) A motor vehicle with four or more wheels first used before 1st April 1986:	30 watts minimum
(d) A three-wheeled motor vehicle, not being a motor bicycle combination, first used before 1st April 1986:	24 watts minimum
(e) A solo motor bicycle and a motor bicycle combination—	
(i) having an engine not exceeding 250 cc and a maximum speed not exceeding 25 mph:	10 watts minimum
(ii) having an engine not exceeding 250 cc and a maximum speed exceeding 25 mph:	15 watts minimum
(iii) having an engine exceeding 250 cc:	24 watts minimum
9. Intensity:	No requirement

10. Electrical connections—

Where a matched pair of dipped-beam headlamps is fitted they shall be capable of being switched on and off simultaneously and not otherwise.

11. Tell-tale:	No requirement

12. Other requirements—

  (a) Every dipped-beam headlamp shall be so constructed that the direction of the beam of light emitted therefrom can be adjusted whilst the vehicle is stationary.

  (b) Every vehicle which—

    (i) is fitted with dipped-beam headlamps bearing an approval mark,

    (ii) has a maximum speed exceeding 25 mph, and

    (iii) is first used on or after 1st April 1991 shall be marked with a clearly legible and indelible marking, as illustrated in Schedule 23, close to either the headlamps or the manufacturer's plate showing the setting recommended by the manufacturer for the downward inclination of the horizontal part of the cut-off of the beam pattern of the dipped-beam headlamps when the vehicle is at its kerbside weight and has a weight of 75 kg on the driver's seat. That setting shall be a single figure—

(A) between 1 and 1.5 per cent if the height of the centre of the headlamp is not more than 850 mm above the ground, and

(B) between 1 and 2 per cent if the height of the centre of the headlamp is more than 850 mm above the ground.

(c) Every dipped-beam headlamp fitted to a vehicle first used on or after 1st April 1986 in accordance with this part of this Schedule shall be designed for a vehicle which is intended to be driven on the left-hand side of the road.

(d) Where two dipped-beam headlamps are required to be fitted they shall form a matched pair.

13. Definitions—

In this Schedule—

"approval mark" means either—

(a) a marking designated as an approval mark by regulation 5 of the Designation of Approval Marks Regulations and shown at item 12 or 13 or 14 or 16 or, in the case of a vehicle having a maximum speed not exceeding 25 mph, 27 or 28 of Schedule 4 to those Regulations, or

(b) a marking designated as an approval mark by regulation 4 of the Designation of Approval Marks Regulations and shown at item 1A or 1B or 1C or 1E or 5A or 5B or 5C or 5E or 8C or 8D or 8E or 8F or 8G or 8H or 8K or 8L or 20C or 20D or 20E or 20F or 20G or 20H or 20K or 20L or 31A or 31C or, in the case of a vehicle having a maximum speed not exceeding 25 mph, 1H or 1I or 5H or 5I of Schedule 2 to those Regulations; and

"British Standard mark" means the specification for sealed beam headlamps published by the British Standards Institution under the reference BS AU 40: Part 4a: 1966 as amended by Amendment AMD 2188 published in December 1976, namely "B.S. AU40". **[1675]**

NOTES
Commencement: 1 November 1989.

PART II

REQUIREMENTS RELATING TO OPTIONAL DIPPED-BEAM HEADLAMPS

1. In the case of a vehicle with three or more wheels having a maximum speed exceeding 25 mph first used on or after 1st April 1991, two and not more than two may be fitted and the only requirements prescribed by these Regulations in respect of any which are fitted are—

(a) those specified in paragraphs 2(c), 4, 7, 10 and 12(a) of Part I,

(b) that they are designed for a vehicle which is intended to be driven on the right-hand side of the road,

(c) that they form a matched pair, and

(d) that their electrical connections are such that not more than one pair of dipped-beam headlamps is capable of being illuminated at a time.

2. In the case of any other vehicle, any number may be fitted and the only requirements prescribed by these Regulations in respect of any which are fitted are those specified in paragraphs 2(c), 4, 7 and 12(a) of Part I. **[1676]**

NOTES
Commencement: 1 November 1989.

SCHEDULE 5

Regulations 18, 20

PART I

REQUIREMENTS RELATING TO OBLIGATORY MAIN-BEAM HEADLAMPS AND TO OPTIONAL MAIN-BEAM HEADLAMPS TO THE EXTENT SPECIFIED IN PART II

1. Number—

(a) Any vehicle not covered by sub-paragraph (b), (c) or (d):	Two
(b) A solo motor bicycle and motor bicycle combination:	One
(c) A motor vehicle with three wheels, other than a motor bicycle combination, first used before 1st January 1972:	One
(d) A motor vehicle with three wheels, other than a motor bicycle combination, first used on or after 1st January 1972 and which has an unladen weight of not more than 400 kg and an overall width of not more than 1300 mm:	One

2. Position—

(a) Longitudinal:	No requirement
(b) Lateral—	
(i) Where two main-beam headlamps are required to be fitted—	
(A) Maximum distance from the side of the vehicle:	The outer edges of the illuminated areas must in no case be closer to the side of the vehicle than the outer edges of the illuminated areas of the obligatory dipped-beam headlamps.
(B) Maximum separation distance between a pair of main-beam headlamps:	No requirement
(ii) Where one main-beam headlamp is required to be fitted:	(i) On the centre-line of the motor vehicle (disregarding any sidecar forming part of a motor bicycle combination), or
	(ii) At any distance from the side of the vehicle (disregarding any sidecar forming part of a motor bicycle combination) provided that a duplicate lamp is fitted on the other side so that together they form a matched pair. In such a case, both lamps shall be treated as obligatory lamps.
(c) Vertical:	No requirement

3. Angles of visibility: No requirement

4. Alignment: To the front

5. Markings—

    (a) Any vehicle not covered by sub-paragraph (b), (c)   An approval mark or a
        or (d):   British Standard mark

    (b) A motor vehicle first used before 1st April 1986:   No requirement

    (c) A three-wheeled motor vehicle, not being a motor   No requirement
        bicycle combination, first used on or after 1st April
        1986 and having a maximum speed not exceeding
        50 mph:

    (d) A solo motor bicycle and a motor bicycle combina-   No requirement
        tion:

6. Size of illuminated area: No requirement

7. Colour: White or yellow

8. Wattage—

    (a) A motor vehicle, other than a solo motor bicycle or   No requirement
        motor bicycle combination, first used on or after 1st
        April 1986:

    (b) A motor vehicle, other than a solo motor bicycle or   30 watts minimum
        a motor bicycle combination, first used before 1st
        April 1986:

    (c) A solo motor bicycle and a motor bicycle combi-
        nation—

          (i) having an engine not exceeding 250 cc: 15 watts minimum
          (ii) having an engine exceeding 250 cc: 30 watts minimum

9. Intensity: No requirement

10. Electrical connections—

(a) Every main-beam headlamp shall be so constructed that the light emitted
    therefrom—

    (i) can be deflected at the will of the driver to become a dipped beam, or

    (ii) can be extinguished by the operation of a device which at the same time
       either—

          (A) causes the lamp to emit a dipped beam, or
          (B) causes another lamp to emit a dipped beam.

(b) Where a matched pair of main-beam headlamps is fitted they shall be capable of
    being switched on and off simultaneously and not otherwise.

11. Tell-tale—

    (a) Any vehicle not covered by sub-paragraph (b):   A circuit-closed tell-tale
                                                   shall be fitted

    (b) A motor vehicle first used before 1st April 1986:   No requirement

12. Other requirements—

    (a) Every main-beam headlamp shall be so constructed that the direction of the
        beam of light emitted therefrom can be adjusted whilst the vehicle is stationary.

    (b) Except in the case of a bus first used before 1st October 1969, where two main-
        beam headlamps are required to be fitted they shall form a matched pair.

13. Definitions—

In this Schedule—

"approval mark" means—

    (a) a marking designated as an approval mark by regulation 5 of the Designation
        of Approval Marks Regulations and shown at item 12 or 13 or 17 of Schedule
        4 to those Regulations; or

    (b) a marking designated as an approval mark by regulation 4 of the Designation
        of Approval Marks Regulations and shown at item 1A or 1B or 1F or 5A or 5B

or 5F or 8C or 8D or 8E or 8F or 8M or 8N or 20C or 20D or 20E or 20F or 20M or 20N or 31A or 31D of Schedule 2 to those Regulations; and

"British Standard mark" means the specification for sealed beam headlamps published by the British Standards Institution under the reference BS AU 40: Part 4a: 1966 as amended by Amendment AMD 2188 published in December 1976, namely "B.S. AU40". **[1677]**

NOTES
Commencement: 1 November 1989.

PART II

REQUIREMENTS RELATING TO OPTIONAL MAIN-BEAM HEADLAMPS

Any number may be fitted and the only requirements prescribed by these Regulations in respect of any which are fitted are those specified in paragraphs 7, 10 and 12(a) of Part I and, in the case of a motor vehicle first used on or after 1st April 1991, paragraph 5 of Part I. **[1678]**

NOTES
Commencement: 1 November 1989.

SCHEDULE 6

Regulation 20

REQUIREMENTS RELATING TO OPTIONAL FRONT FOG LAMPS

1. Number—
   (a) Any vehicle not covered by sub-paragraph (b):   No requirement
   (b) A motor vehicle, other than a motor bicycle or   Not more than two
       motor bicycle combination, first used on or after 1st
       April 1991:

2. Position—
   (a) Longitudinal: No requirement
   (b) Lateral—
       (i) Where a pair of front fog lamps is used in
           conditions of seriously reduced visibility in
           place of the obligatory dipped beam head-
           lamps—
           Maximum distance from side of vehicle: 400 mm
       (ii) in all other cases: No requirement
   (c) Vertical—
       (i) Maximum height above the ground—
           (A) Any vehicle not covered by sub-paragraph   1200 mm
               (b):
           (B) An agricultural vehicle, a road clearance   No requirement
               vehicle, an aerodrome fire tender, an
               aerodrome runway sweeper, an industrial
               tractor, engineering plant and home
               forces' vehicle:
       (ii) Minimum height above the ground: No requirement

3. Angles of visibility: No requirement

4. Alignment: To the front and so
                 aimed that the upper
                 edge of the beam is, as
                 near as practicable, 3
                 per cent below the hor-
                 izontal when the vehicle
                 is at its kerbside weight
                 and has a weight of 75
                 kg on the driver's seat.

5. Markings—
    (a) A vehicle first used on or after 1st April 1986:   An approval mark
    (b) A vehicle first used before 1st April 1986:   No requirement

6. Size of illuminated area: No requirement

7. Colour: White or Yellow

8. Wattage: No requirement

9. Intensity: No requirement

10. Electrical connections: No individual requirement

11. Tell-tale: No requirement

12. Other requirements—
Every front fog lamp shall be so constructed that the direction of the beam of light emitted therefrom can be adjusted whilst the vehicle is stationary.

13. Definitions—
In this Schedule "approval mark" means either—
    (a) a marking designated as an approval mark by regulation 5 of the Designation of Approval Marks Regulations and shown at item 19 of Schedule 4 to those Regulations; or
    (b) a marking designated as an approval mark by regulation 4 of the Designation of Approval Marks Regulations and shown at item 19 or 19A of Schedule 2 of those Regulations.

[1679]

NOTES
Commencement: 1 November 1989.

SCHEDULE 7
Regulations 18, 20

PART I

REQUIREMENTS RELATING TO OBLIGATORY DIRECTION INDICATORS AND TO OPTIONAL DIRECTION INDICATORS TO THE EXTENT SPECIFIED IN PART II

1. Number (on each side of a vehicle)—
    (a) A motor vehicle with three or more wheels, not being a motor bicycle combination, first used on or after 1st April 1986:   One front indicator (Category 1, 1a or 1b), one rear indicator (Category 2, 2a or 2b) and one side repeater indicator (Category 5) or, in the case of a motor vehicle having a maximum speed not exceeding 25 mph, one front indicator (Category 1, 1a or 1b) and one rear indicator (Category 2, 2a or 2b).

(b) A trailer manufactured on or after 1st October 1985 drawn by a motor vehicle: — One rear indicator (Category 2, 2a or 2b) or, in the case of a trailer towed by a solo motor bicycle or a motor bicycle combination, one rear indicator (Category 12).

(c) A solo motor bicycle and a motor bicycle combination, in each case first used on or after 1st April 1986: — One front indicator (Category 1, 1a, 1b or 11) and one rear indicator (Category 2, 2a, 2b or 12).

(d) A motor vehicle first used on or after 1st January 1936 and before 1st April 1986, a trailer manufactured on or after 1st January 1936 and before 1st October 1985, a pedal cycle with or without a sidecar or a trailer, a horse-drawn vehicle and a vehicle drawn or propelled by hand: — Any arrangement of indicators so as to satisfy the requirements for angles of visibility in paragraph 3.

(e) A motor vehicle first used before 1st April 1936 and any trailer manufactured before that date: — Any arrangement of indicators so as to make the intention of the driver clear to other road users.

2. Position—

(a) Longitudinal—

(i) A side repeater indicator which is required to be fitted in accordance with paragraph 1(a): — Within 2600 mm of the front of the vehicle

(ii) Any other indicator: — No requirement

(b) Lateral—

(i) Maximum distance from the side of the vehicle—

(A) Any vehicle not covered by sub-paragraph (B): — 400 mm

(B) A motor vehicle first used before 1st April 1986, a trailer manufactured before 1st October 1985, a solo motor bicycle, a pedal cycle, a horse-drawn vehicle and a vehicle drawn or propelled by hand: — No requirement

(ii) Minimum separation distance between indicators on opposite sides of a vehicle—

(A) A motor vehicle (other than a solo motor bicycle or a motor bicycle combination or an invalid carriage having a maximum speed not exceeding 8 mph) first used on or after 1st April 1986, a trailer manufactured on or after 1st October 1985, a horse-drawn vehicle, a pedestrian-controlled vehicle and a vehicle drawn or propelled by hand: — 500 mm or, if the overall width of the vehicle is less than 1400 mm, 400 mm

(B) A solo motor bicycle having an engine exceeding 50 cc and first used on or after 1st April 1986—

(1) Front indicators: — 300 mm
(2) Rear indicators: — 240 mm

(C) A solo motor bicycle having an engine not exceeding 50 cc and first used on or after 1st April 1986 and a pedal cycle—

(1) Front indicators:	240 mm
(2) Rear indicators:	180 mm
(D) A motor bicycle combination first used on or after 1st April 1986:	400 mm
(E) An invalid carriage having a maximum speed not exceeding 8 mph—	
(1) Front indicators:	240 mm
(2) Rear indicators:	300 mm
(F) A motor vehicle first used before 1st April 1986 and a trailer manufactured before 1st October 1985:	No requirement
(iii) Minimum separation distance between a front indicator and any dipped-beam headlamp or front fog lamp—	
(A) Fitted to a motor vehicle, other than a solo motor bicycle or a motor bicycle combination, first used on or after 1st April 1991:	(a) in the case of a Category 1 indicator, 40 mm; (b) in the case of a Category 1a indicator, 20 mm; (c) in the case of a Category 1b indicator, no requirement
(B) Fitted to a solo motor bicycle or a motor bicycle combination in either case first used on or after 1st April 1986:	100 mm
(C) Fitted to any other vehicle:	No requirement
(c) Vertical—	
(i) Maximum height above the ground—	
(A) Any vehicle not covered by sub-paragraph (B) or (C):	1500 mm or, if the structure of the vehicle makes this impracticable, 2300 mm.
(B) A motor vehicle first used before 1st April 1986 and a trailer manufactured before 1st October 1985:	No requirement
(C) A motor vehicle having a maximum speed not exceeding 25 mph:	No requirement
(ii) Minimum height above the ground:	350 mm
3. Angles of visibility—	
(a) A motor vehicle first used on or after 1st April 1986 and a trailer manufactured on or after 1st October 1985—	
(i) Horizontal (see diagrams in Part III of this Schedule)—	
(A) A front or rear indicator fitted to a motor vehicle, other than a solo motor bicycle or a motor bicycle combination, having a maximum speed exceeding 25 mph and every rear indicator fitted to a trailer:	80° outwards and 45° inwards
(B) A front or rear indicator fitted to a solo motor bicycle or a motor bicycle combination:	80° outwards and 20° inwards
(C) A front or rear indicator fitted to a motor vehicle, other than a solo motor bicycle or a motor bicycle combination, having a maximum speed not exceeding 25 mph:	80° outwards and 3° inwards

(D) A side repeater indicator fitted to a motor vehicle or a trailer:	Between rearward angles of 5° outboard and 60° outboard or, in the case of a motor vehicle having a maximum speed not exceeding 25 mph where it is impracticable to comply with the 5° angle, this may be replaced by 10°.

(ii) Vertical—

(A) Except as provided by sub-paragraph (B) or (C):	15° above and below the horizontal
(B) Where the highest part of the illuminated area of the lamp is less than 1900 mm above the ground and the vehicle is a motor vehicle having a maximum speed not exceeding 25 mph:	15° above and 10° below the horizontal
(C) Where the highest part of the illuminated area of the lamp is less than 750 mm above the ground:	15° above and 5° below the horizontal

(b) A motor vehicle first used before 1st April 1986, a trailer manufactured before 1st October 1985, a pedal cycle, a horse-drawn vehicle and a vehicle drawn or propelled by hand:	Such that at least one (but not necessarily the same) indicator on each side is plainly visible to the rear in the case of a trailer and both to the front and rear in the case of any other vehicle.

4. Alignment—

(a) A front indicator:	To the front
(b) A rear indicator:	To the rear
(c) A side repeater indicator (Category 5):	As shown in the first sketch in Part III of this Schedule

5. Markings—

(a) a motor vehicle, other than a solo motor bicycle or a motor bicycle combination, first used on or after 1st April 1986 and a trailer, other than a trailer drawn by a solo motor bicycle or a motor bicycle combination, manufactured on or after 1st October 1985:	An approval mark and, above such mark, the following numbers— (a) in the case of a front indicator, "1", "1a" or "1b"; (b) in the case of a rear indicator, "2", "2a" or "2b"; (c) in the case of a side repeater indicator, "5".

(b) A solo motor bicycle and a motor bicycle combination in either case first used on or after 1st April 1986, a trailer, manufactured on or after 1st October 1985, drawn by such a solo motor bicycle or a motor bicycle combination, a pedal cycle, a horse-drawn vehicle and a vehicle drawn or propelled by hand:

An approval mark and, above such mark, the following numbers—
(a) in the case of a front indicator, "1", "1a", "1b" or "11";
(b) in the case of a rear indicator, "2", "2a", "2b" or "12";
(c) in the case of a side repeater indicator, "5"

(c) A motor vehicle first used before 1st April 1986 and a trailer manufactured before 1st October 1985:

No requirement

6. Size of illuminated area:

No requirement

7. Colour—
(a) Any vehicle not covered by sub-paragraph (b):

Amber

(b) An indicator fitted to a motor vehicle first used before 1st September 1965 and any trailer drawn thereby—
(i) if it shows only the front:

White or amber

(ii) if it shows only the rear:

Red or amber

(iii) if it shows both to the front and to the rear:

Amber

8. Wattage—
(a) Any front or rear indicator which emits a flashing light and does not bear an approval mark:

15 to 36 watts

(b) Any other indicator:

No requirement

9. Intensity—
(a) An indicator bearing an approval mark:

No requirement

(b) An indicator not bearing an approval mark:

Such that the light is plainly visible from a reasonable distance

10. Electrical connections—

(a) All indicators on one side of a vehicle together with all indicators on that side of any trailer drawn by the vehicle, while so drawn, shall be operated by one switch.

(b) All indicators on one side of a vehicle or combination of vehicles showing a flashing light shall flash in phase, except that in the case of a solo motor bicycle, a motor bicycle combination and a pedal cycle, the front and rear direction indicators on one side of the vehicle may flash alternately.

11. Tell-tale—

(a) One or more indicators on each side of a vehicle to which indicators are fitted shall be so designed and fitted that the driver when in his seat can readily be aware when it is in operation; or

(b) The vehicle shall be equipped with an operational tell-tale for front and rear indicators (including any rear indicator on the rearmost of any trailers drawn by the vehicle).

12. Other requirements—

(a) Every indicator (other than a semaphore arm, that is an indicator in the form of an illuminated sign which when in operation temporarily alters the outline of the vehicle to the extent of at least 150 mm measured horizontally and is visible from both the front and rear of the vehicle) shall when in operation show a light which flashes constantly at the rate of not less than 60 nor more than 120 flashes per minute. However, in the event of a failure, other than a short-circuit of an indicator, any other indicator on the same side of the vehicle or combination of vehicles may continue to flash, but the rate may be less than 60 or more than 120 flashes per minute. Every indicator shall when in operation perform efficiently regardless of the speed of the vehicle.

(b) Where two front or rear direction indicators are fitted to a motor vehicle first used on or after 1st April 1986, and two rear direction indicators are fitted to a trailer manufactured on or after 1st October 1985, in each case, they shall be fitted so as to form a pair.

(c) A rear direction indicator on each side of a vehicle shall not be fitted on a boot lid or other movable part of the vehicle.

13. Definitions—

In this Schedule "approval mark" means either—

(a) a marking designated as an approval mark by regulation 5 of the Designation of Approval Marks Regulations and shown at item 9 of Schedule 4 to those Regulations; or

(b) a marking designated as an approval mark by regulation 4 of the Designation of Approval Marks Regulations and shown at item 6 or, in the case of a solo motor bicycle or a motor bicycle combination, a pedal cycle, a horse-drawn vehicle or a vehicle drawn or propelled by hand, at item 50 of Schedule 2 to those Regulations.   **[1680]**

NOTES

Commencement: 1 November 1989.

PART II

REQUIREMENTS RELATING TO OPTIONAL DIRECTION INDICATORS

1. No vehicle shall be fitted with a total of more than one front indicator nor more than two rear indicators, on each side.

2. Any number of side indicators may be fitted to the side (excluding the front and rear) of a vehicle.

3. The only other requirements prescribed by these Regulations in respect of any which are fitted are those specified in paragraphs 5, 7, 8, 9, 10, 11, 12(a) and 12(b) of Part I.   **[1681]**

NOTES

Commencement: 1 November 1989.

PART III

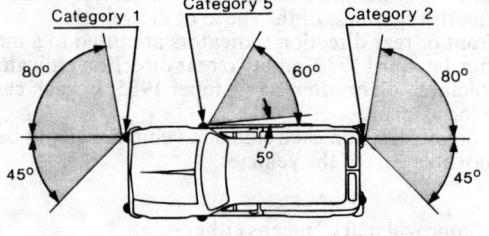

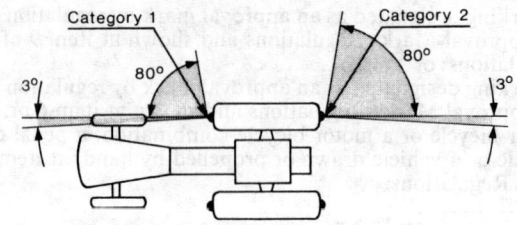

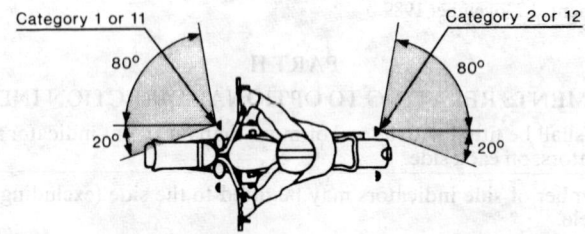

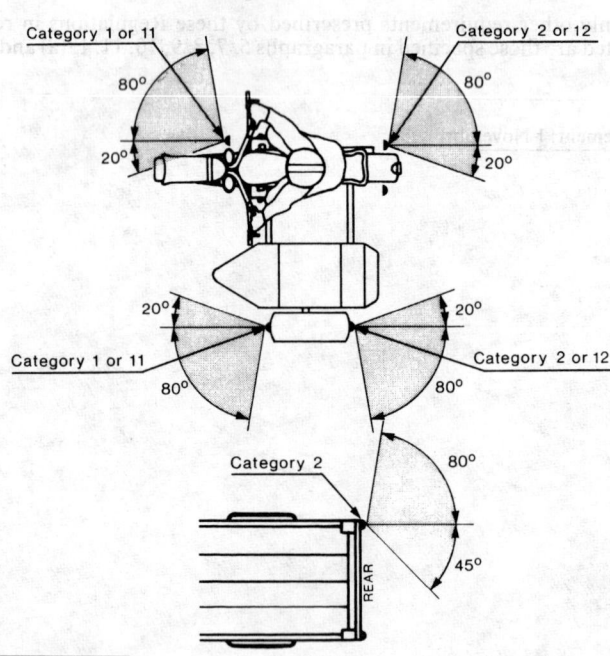

NOTES

Commencement: 1 November 1989.

SCHEDULE 8

Regulations 18, 20

REQUIREMENTS RELATING TO OBLIGATORY AND OPTIONAL HAZARD WARNING SIGNAL
DEVICES

Every hazard warning signal device shall—

    (a) be operated by one switch;

    (b) cause all the direction indicators with which a vehicle or a combination of
vehicles is equipped to flash in phase;

    (c) be provided with a circuit-closed tell-tale in the form of a flashing light which
may operate in conjunction with any direction indicator tell-tale; and

    (d) be able to function even if the device which controls the starting and stopping
of the engine is in a position which makes it impossible to start the engine.

[1683]

NOTES

Commencement: 1 November 1989.

SCHEDULE 9

Regulations 18, 20, 22

PART I

REQUIREMENTS RELATING TO OBLIGATORY SIDE MARKER LAMPS AND
TO OPTIONAL SIDE MARKER LAMPS TO THE EXTENT SPECIFIED IN PART
II

1. Number—

    (a) A vehicle not covered by sub-paragraph (b) which
is—

(i) a motor vehicle first used on or after 1st April 1991 or a trailer manufactured on or after 1st October 1990:	On each side: two and as many more as are sufficient to satisfy the requirements of paragraph 2(a)
(ii) a trailer manufactured before 1st October 1990:	One on each side
(b) Long vehicles and vehicle combinations to which regulation 22 applies:	The numbers required by regulation 22

2. Position—

    (a) Longitudinal—

        (i) A vehicle of a type mentioned in sub-paragraph
1(a)(i)—

(A) Maximum distance from the front of the vehicle, including any drawbar, in respect of the foremost side marker lamp on each side:	4 m
(B) Maximum distance from the rear of the vehicle in respect of the rearmost side marker lamp on each side:	1 m
(C) Maximum separation distance between the light-emitting surfaces of adjacent side marker lamps on the same side of the vehicle:	3 m or, if this is not practicable, 4 m

(ii) A vehicle of a type mentioned in sub-paragraph 1(a)(ii):	Such that no part of the light-emitting surface is forward of, or more than 1530 mm to the rear of, the centre point of the overall length of the trailer
(iii) Long vehicles and vehicle combinations, including any loads, to which regulation 22 applies:	As specified in regulation 22
(b) Lateral:	No requirement
(c) Vertical—	
(i) Maximum height above the ground:	2300 mm
(ii) Minimum height above the ground:	No requirement
3. Angles of visibility—	
(a) Horizontal:	45° to the left and to the right when viewed in a direction at right angles to the longitudinal axis of the vehicle
(b) Vertical:	No requirement
4. Alignment:	To the side
5. Markings:	No requirement
6. Size of illuminated area:	No requirement
7. Colour:	Amber or, if within 1 m of the rear of the vehicle it may be red or, if the vehicle is a trailer manufactured before 1st October 1990, it may be white when viewed from the front and red when viewed from the rear
8. Wattage:	No requirement
9. Intensity:	Visible from a reasonable distance
10. Electrical connections:	No individual requirement
11. Tell-tale:	No requirement

[1684]

NOTES
Commencement: 1 November 1989.

PART II

REQUIREMENTS RELATING TO OPTIONAL SIDE MARKER LAMPS

Any number may be fitted and the only requirement prescribed by these Regulations in respect of any which are fitted is that specified in paragraph 7 of Part I. **[1685]**

NOTES
Commencement: 1 November 1989.

SCHEDULE 10

Regulations 18, 20

PART I

REQUIREMENTS RELATING TO OBLIGATORY REAR POSITION LAMPS AND TO OPTIONAL REAR POSITION LAMPS TO THE EXTENT SPECIFIED IN PART II

1. Number—

(a)	Any vehicle not covered by sub-paragraph (b), (c), (d), (e), (f), (g) or (h):	Two
(b)	A bus first used before 1st April 1955:	One
(c)	A solo motor bicycle:	One
(d)	A pedal cycle with less than four wheels and without a sidecar:	One
(e)	A trailer drawn by a pedal cycle and a trailer, the overall width of which does not exceed 800 mm, drawn by a solo motor bicycle or by a motor bicycle combination:	One
(f)	An invalid carriage having a maximum speed not exceeding 4 mph:	One
(g)	A vehicle drawn or propelled by hand:	One
(h)	A motor vehicle having three or more wheels and a maximum speed not exceeding 25 mph and a trailer drawn by any such vehicle if, in either case, the structure of the vehicle makes it impracticable to meet all of the relevant requirements of paragraphs 2 and 3 below with two lamps:	Four

2. Position—

(a)	Longitudinal:	At or near the rear
(b)	Lateral—	

　　(i) Where two lamps are required to be fitted—

　　　　(A) Maximum distance from the side of the vehicle—

	(1) Any vehicle not covered by sub-paragraph (2):	400 mm
	(2) A motor vehicle first used before 1st April 1986 and any other vehicle manufactured before 1st October 1985:	800 mm

　　　　(B) Minimum separation distance between a pair of rear position lamps—

	(1) Any vehicle not covered by sub-paragraph (2):	500 mm. If the overall width of the vehicle is less than 1400 mm, 400 mm or if less than 800 mm, 300 mm
	(2) A motor vehicle first used before 1st April 1986 and any other vehicle manufactured before 1st October 1985:	No requirement

　　(ii) Where one lamp is required to be fitted: — On the centre-line or off side of the vehicle

　　(iii) Where four lamps are required to be fitted—

　　　　(A) Maximum distance from the side of the vehicle—

(1) One pair of lamps:	Such that they satisfy the relevant requirements in sub-paragraph 2(b)(i)(A)
(2) The other pair of lamps:	No requirement

(B) Minimum separation distance between rear position lamps—

(1) One pair of lamps:	Such that they satisfy the relevant requirements in sub-paragraph 2(b)(i)(B)
(2) The other pair of lamps:	No requirement

(c) Vertical—

  (i) Maximum height above the ground where one or two rear position lamps are required to be fitted—

(A) Any vehicle not covered by sub-paragraph (B) or (C):	1500 mm or, if the structure of the vehicle makes this impracticable, 2100 mm
(B) A bus first used before 1st April 1986:	No requirement
(C) A motor vehicle first used before 1st April 1986 not being a bus, a trailer manufactured before 1st October 1985, an agricultural vehicle, a horse-drawn vehicle, an industrial tractor and engineering plant:	2100 mm

  (ii) Maximum height above the ground where four rear position lamps are required to be fitted—

(A) One pair of lamps:	Such that they satisfy the relevant requirements in paragraph 2(c)(i)
(B) The other pair of lamps:	No requirement

  (iii) Minimum height above the ground—

(A) A vehicle not covered by sub-paragraph (B):	350 mm
(B) A motor vehicle first used before 1st April 1986 and any other vehicle manufactured before 1st October 1985	No requirement

3. Angles of visibility—

(a) A motor vehicle, other than a motor bicycle combination, first used on or after 1st April 1986 and a trailer manufactured on or after 1st October 1985—

  (i) Horizontal—

(A) Where two lamps are required to be fitted:	45° inwards and 80° outwards
(B) Where one lamp is required to be fitted:	80° to the left and to the right
(C) Where four lamps are required to be fitted—	
(1) The outer pair of lamps:	0° inwards and 80° outwards
(2) The inner pair of lamps:	45° inwards and 80° outwards

  (ii) Vertical—

(A) Where one or two rear position lamps are required to be fitted—

(1) Any vehicle not covered by sub-paragraph (2) or (3):	15° above and below the horizontal
(2) Where the highest part of the illuminated area of the lamp is less than 1500 mm above the ground:	15° above and 10° below the horizontal
(3) Where the highest part of the illuminated area of the lamp is less than 750 mm above the ground:	15° above and 5° below the horizontal
(B) Where four rear position lamps are required to be fitted—	
(1) One pair of lamps:	Such that they satisfy the relevant requirements in paragraph 3(a)(ii)(A)
(2) The other pair of lamps:	Visible to the rear
(b) A motor vehicle, other than a motor bicycle combination, first used before 1st April 1986 and any other vehicle manufactured before 1st October 1985:	Visible to the rear
(c) A vehicle drawn or propelled by hand, a pedal cycle, a horse-drawn vehicle and a motor bicycle combination:	Visible to the rear
4. Alignment:	To the rear
5. Markings—	
(a) A motor vehicle or a trailer not covered by sub-paragraph (b), (c) or (*d*):	An approval mark
(b) A motor vehicle first used before 1st January 1974 and a trailer, other than a trailer drawn by a pedal cycle, manufactured before that date:	No requirement
(c) A solo motor bicycle and a motor bicycle combination, in each case first used before 1st April 1986, and a trailer manufactured before 1st October 1985 and drawn by a solo motor bicycle or a motor bicycle combination:	No requirement
(*d*) A pedal cycle, a trailer drawn by a pedal cycle, an invalid carriage having a maximum speed not exceeding 4 mph, a horse-drawn vehicle and a vehicle drawn or propelled by hand:	An approval mark or a British Standard mark
6. Size of illuminated area:	No requirement
7. Colour:	Red
8. Wattage:	No requirement
9. Intensity—	
(a) A rear position lamp bearing any of the markings mentioned in paragraph 4:	No requirement
(b) Any other rear position lamp:	Visible from a reasonable distance
10. Electrical connections:	No individual requirement
11. Tell-tale:	No requirement

12. Other requirements—

    (a) Except in the case of a motor vehicle first used before 1st April 1986, any other vehicle manufactured before 1st October 1985 and a motor bicycle combination, where two rear position lamps are required to be fitted they shall form a matched pair and where four rear position lamps are required to be fitted they shall form two matched pairs.

(b) A rear position lamp shall not be fitted on a boot lid or other moveable part of the vehicle.

13. Definitions—

In this Schedule—
"approval mark" means—
(a) in relation to a solo motor bicycle, a motor bicycle combination and a trailer drawn by a solo motor bicycle or a motor bicycle combination, a marking designated as an approval mark by regulation 4 of the Designation of Approval Marks Regulations and shown at item 50A of Schedule 2 to those Regulations, and
(b) in relation to any other motor vehicle or any other trailer, either—

   (i) a marking designated as an approval mark by regulation 5 of the Designation of Approval Marks Regulations and shown at item 6 or, if combined with a stop lamp, at item 8 of Schedule 4 to those Regulations, or
   (ii) a marking designated as an approval mark by regulation 4 of the Designation of Approval Marks Regulations and shown at item 7A or, if combined with a stop lamp, at item 7C of Schedule 2 to those Regulations; and

"British Standard mark" means—
(a) the mark indicated in the specification for cycle rear lamps published by the British Standards Institution under the reference 3648:1963 as amended by Amendment PD 6137 published in May 1967 and by AMD 4753 published in July 1985, or
(b) the mark indicated in the specification for photometric and physical requirements for lighting equipment published by the British Standards Institution under the reference BS 6102: Part 3: 1986, namely "BS 6102/3".

[1686]

NOTES
Commencement: 1 November 1989.

PART II
REQUIREMENTS RELATING TO OPTIONAL REAR POSITION LAMPS

Any number may be fitted and the only requirement prescribed by these Regulations in respect of any which are fitted is that specified in paragraph 7 of Part I.   **[1687]**

NOTES
Commencement: 1 November 1989.

SCHEDULE 11
Regulations 18, 20

PART I
REQUIREMENTS RELATING TO OBLIGATORY REAR FOG LAMPS AND TO OPTIONAL REAR FOG LAMPS TO THE EXTENT SPECIFIED IN PART II

1. Number: One

2. Position—

  (a) Longitudinal: At or near the rear of
                                      the vehicle

  (b) Lateral—

(i) Where one rear fog lamp is fitted:	On the centre-line or off side of the vehicle (disregarding any sidecar forming part of a motor bicycle combination)
(ii) Where two lamps are fitted:	No requirement

(c) Vertical—
    (i) Maximum height above the ground—

(A) Any vehicle not covered by sub-paragraph (B):	1000 mm
(B) An agricultural vehicle, engineering plant and a motor tractor:	2100 mm
(ii) Minimum height above the ground:	250 mm

(*d*) Minimum separation distance between a rear fog lamp and a stop lamp—

(i) In the case of a rear fog lamp which does not share a common lamp body with a stop lamp:	A distance of 100 mm between the light-emitting surfaces of the lamps when viewed in a direction parallel to the longitudinal axis of the vehicle
(ii) In the case of a rear fog lamp which shares a common lamp body with a stop lamp:	100 mm

3. Angles of visibility—

(a) Horizontal:	25° inwards and outwards. However, where two rear fog lamps are fitted it shall suffice if throughout the sector so defined at least one lamp (but not necessarily the same lamp) is visible
(b) Vertical:	5° above and below the horizontal
4. Alignment:	To the rear
5. Markings:	An approval mark
6. Size of illuminated area:	No requirement
7. Colour:	Red
8. Wattage:	No requirement
9. Intensity:	No requirement
10. Electrical connections:	No rear fog lamp shall be fitted to any vehicle so that it can be illuminated by the application of any braking system on the vehicle
11. Tell-tale:	A circuit-closed tell-tale shall be fitted

12. Other requirements—
Where two rear fog lamps are fitted to a motor vehicle first used on or after 1st April 1986 or to a trailer manufactured on or after 1st October 1985 they shall form a matched pair.

13. Definitions—

In this Schedule "approval mark" means either—
  (a) a marking designated as an approval mark by regulation 5 of the Designation of Approval Marks Regulations and shown at item 20 of Schedule 4 to those Regulations; or
  (b) a marking designated as an approval mark by regulation 4 of the Designation of Approval Marks Regulations and shown at item 38 of Schedule 2 to those Regulations. **[1688]**

NOTES
Commencement: 1 November 1989.

PART II
REQUIREMENTS RELATING TO OPTIONAL REAR FOG LAMPS

1. In the case of a motor vehicle first used before 1st April 1980 and any other vehicle manufactured before 1st October 1979, any number may be fitted and the only requirements prescribed by these Regulations in respect of any which are fitted are those specified in paragraphs 2(d), 7 and 10 of Part I.

2. In the case of a motor vehicle first used on or after 1st April 1980 and any other vehicle manufactured on or after 1st October 1979, not more than two may be fitted and the requirements prescribed by these Regulations in respect of any which are fitted are all those specified in this Schedule. **[1689]**

NOTES
Commencement: 1 November 1989.

SCHEDULE 12
Regulations 18, 20

PART I
REQUIREMENTS RELATING TO OBLIGATORY STOP LAMPS AND TO OPTIONAL STOP LAMPS TO THE EXTENT SPECIFIED IN PART II

1. Number—
  (a) Any vehicle not covered by sub-paragraph (b) or (c)   Two
  (b) A solo motor bicycle, a motor bicycle combination,   One
     an invalid carriage and a trailer drawn by a solo
     motor bicycle or a motor bicycle combination:
  (c) Any other motor vehicle first used before 1st   One
     January 1971 and any other trailer manufactured
     before that date:

2. Position—
  (a) Longitudinal: No requirement
  (b) Lateral—
     (i) Maximum distance from the side of the vehi-
        cle—
        (A) Where two stop lamps are fitted: One on each side of the longitudinal axis of the vehicle
        (B) Where only one stop lamp is fitted: On the centre-line or off side of the vehicle (disregarding any sidecar forming part of a motor bicycle combination)

(ii) Minimum separation distance between two obligatory stop lamps: — 400 mm

(c) Vertical—

  (i) Maximum height above the ground—

    (A) Any vehicle not covered by sub-paragraph (B): — 1500 mm or, if the structure of the vehicle makes this impracticable, 2100 mm

    (B) A motor vehicle first used before 1st January 1971, a trailer manufactured before that date and a motor vehicle having a maximum speed not exceeding 25 mph: — No requirement

  (ii) Minimum height above the ground—

    (A) Any vehicle not covered by sub-paragraph (B): — 350 mm

    (B) A motor vehicle first used before 1st January 1971 and a trailer manufactured before that date: — No requirement

3. Angles of visibility—

(a) A motor vehicle first used on or after 1st January 1971 and a trailer manufactured on or after that date—

  (i) Horizontal: — 45° to the left and to the right

  (ii) Vertical—

    (A) Except in a case specified in sub-paragraph (B) or (C): — 15° above and below the horizontal

    (B) Where the highest part of the illuminated area of the lamp is less than 150 mm above the ground: — 15° above and 10° below the horizontal

    (C) Where the highest part of the illuminated area of the lamp is less than 750 mm above the gound: — 15° above and 5° below the horizontal

(b) A motor vehicle first used before 1st January 1971 and a trailer manufactured before that date: — Visible to the rear

4. Alignment: — to the rear

5. Markings—

(a) Any vehicle not covered by sub-paragraph (b) or (c): — An approval mark

(b) A motor vehicle first used before 1st February 1974 and a trailer manufactured before that date: — No requirement

(c) A solo motor bicycle and a motor bicycle combination, in each case first used before 1st April 1986, and a trailer manufactured before 1st October 1985 drawn by a solo motor bicycle or a motor bicycle combination: — No requirement

6. Size of illuminated area: — No requirement

7. Colour: — Red

8. Wattage—

(a) A stop lamp fitted to a motor vehicle first used before 1st January 1971 or a trailer manufactured before that date and a stop lamp bearing an approval mark: — No requirement

(b) Any other stop lamp: — 15 to 36 watts

9. Intensity: — No requirement

10. Electrical connections—
    (a) Every stop lamp fitted to—

        (i) a solo motor bicycle or a motor bicycle combination first used on or after 1st April 1986 shall be operated by the application of every service brake control provided for the use of the rider;

        (ii) any other motor vehicle, shall be operated by the application of the service braking system.

    (b) Every stop lamp fitted to a trailer drawn by a motor vehicle shall be operated by the application of the service braking system of that motor vehicle.

11. Tell-tale: No requirement

12. Other requirements—
    Where two stop lamps are required to be fitted, they shall form a pair.

13. Definitions—

In this Schedule "approval mark" means—
    (a) in relation to a solo motor bicycle, a motor bicycle combination or a trailer drawn by a solo motor bicycle or a motor bicycle combination, a marking designated as an approval mark by regulation 4 of the Designation of Approval Marks Regulations and shown at item 50A of Schedule 2 to those Regulations; and

    (b) in relation to any other vehicle, either—

        (i) a marking designated as an approval mark by regulation 5 of the Designation of Approval Marks Regulations and shown at item 7 or, if combined with a rear position lamp, at item 8 of Schedule 4 to those Regulations; or

        (ii) a marking designated as an approval mark by regulation 4 of the Designation of Approval Marks Regulations and shown at item 7B or, if combined with a rear position lamp, at item 7C of Schedule 2 to those Regulations.   **[1690]**

NOTES
Commencement: 1 November 1989.

PART II

REQUIREMENTS RELATING TO OPTIONAL STOP LAMPS

Any number may be fitted, and the requirements prescribed by these Regulations in respect of any which are fitted are all those specified in Part I except—

    (a) those specified in paragraphs 1, 2 and 3; and

    (b) in the case of a stop lamp fitted to a pedal cycle, those specified in paragraphs 5 and 8; and

    (c) in the case of a stop lamp fitted to a motor vehicle not being a motor bicycle, first used on or after 1st April 1991 either centrally or in such a manner as to project light through the rear window the intensity of the light emitted to the rear of the vehicle shall be not less than 20 candelas and not more than 60 candelas when measured from directly behind the centre of the lamp in a direction parallel to the longitudinal axis of the vehicle.   **[1691]**

NOTES
Commencement: 1 November 1989.

SCHEDULE 13

Regulations 18, 20

PART I

REQUIREMENTS RELATING TO OBLIGATORY END-OUTLINE MARKER LAMPS AND TO OPTIONAL END-OUTLINE MARKER LAMPS TO THE EXTENT SPECIFIED IN PART II

1. Number:	Two visible from the front and two visible from the rear
2. Position—	
(a) Longitudinal:	No requirement
(b) Lateral—	
(i) Maximum distance from the side of the vehicle:	400 mm
(ii) Minimum separation distance between a pair of end-outline marker lamps:	No requirement
(c) Vertical—	
(i) At the front of a motor vehicle:	The horizontal plane tangential to the upper edge of the illuminated area of the lamp shall not be lower than the horizontal plane tangential to the upper edge of the transparent zone of the windscreen
(ii) At the front of a trailer and at the rear of any vehicle:	At the maximum height compatible with:
	(a) the requirements relating to the lateral position and to being a pair, and
	(b) the use for which the vehicle is constructed
3. Angles of visibility—	
(a) Horizontal:	0° inwards and 80° outwards
(b) Vertical:	5° above and 20° below the horizontal
4. Alignment	Such that white light is shown towards the front and red light is shown towards the rear
5. Markings:	An approval mark
6. Size of illuminated area:	No requirement
7. Colour:	White towards the front and red towards the rear
8. Wattage:	No requirement
9. Intensity:	No requirement
10. Electrical connections:	No individual requirement
11. Tell-tale:	No requirement

12. Other requirements—
    The two lamps which emit white light towards the front, and the two lamps which emit red light towards the rear, shall in each case form a matched pair. The white front lamp and red rear lamp on one side of a vehicle may be combined into a single lamp with a single light source.

13. Definitions—
    In this Schedule, "approval mark" means the approval mark for a front or rear position lamp, as the case may be.   **[1692]**

NOTES
Commencement: 1 November 1989.

PART II
REQUIREMENTS RELATING TO OPTIONAL END-OUTLINE MARKER LAMPS

Any number may be fitted, and the only requirement prescribed by these Regulations in respect of any which are fitted is that specified in paragraph 7 of Part I.   **[1693]**

NOTES
Commencement: 1 November 1989.

SCHEDULE 14
Regulation 20

REQUIREMENTS RELATING TO OPTIONAL REVERSING LAMPS

1. Number:	Not more than two
2. Position:	No requirement
3. Angles of visibility:	No requirement
4. Alignment:	To the rear
5. Markings—	
(a) A motor vehicle first used on or after 1st April 1986 and a trailer manufactured on or after 1st October 1985:	An approval mark
(b) A motor vehicle first used before 1st April 1986 and a trailer manufactured before 1st October 1985:	No requirement
6. Size of illuminated area:	No requirement
7. Colour:	White
8. Wattage—	
(a) A reversing lamp bearing an approval mark:	No requirement
(b) A reversing lamp not bearing an approval mark:	The total wattage of any one reversing lamp shall not exceed 24 watts
9. Intensity:	No requirement
10. Electrical connections:	No requirement
11. Tell-tale—	
(a) A motor vehicle first used on or after 1st July 1954, provided that the electrical connections are such that the reversing lamp or lamps cannot be illuminated other than automatically by the selection of the reverse gear of the vehicle:	No requirement
(b) Any other motor vehicle first used on or after 1st July 1954:	A circuit-closed tell-tale shall be fitted
(c) A motor vehicle first used before 1st July 1954:	No requirement
(d) Any vehicle which is not a motor vehicle:	No requirement

12. Definitions—

In this Schedule "approval mark" means either—

(a) a marking designated as an approval mark by regulation 5 of the Designation of Approval Marks Regulations and shown at item 21 of Schedule 4 to those Regulations; or

(b) a marking designated as an approval mark by regulation 4 of the Designation of Approval Marks Regulations and shown at item 23 or 23A of Schedule 2 to those Regulations.   **[1694]**

NOTES
Commencement: 1 November 1989.

SCHEDULE 15
Regulation 18

REQUIREMENTS RELATING TO OBLIGATORY REAR REGISTRATION PLATE LAMPS

1. Number:	Such that the lamp or
2. Position:	lamps are capable of
	adequately illuminat-
3. Angles of visibility:	ing the rear registration
4. Alignment:	plate

5. Markings—

(a) A motor vehicle first used on or after 1st April 1986 and a trailer manufactured on or after 1st October 1985:	An approval mark
(b) A motor vehicle first used before 1st April 1986 and a trailer manufactured before 1st October 1985:	No requirement
6. Size of illuminated area:	No requirement
7. Colour:	White
8. Wattage:	No requirement
9. Intensity:	No requirement
10. Electrical connections:	No individual requirement
11. Tell-tale:	No requirement

12. Definitions—

In this Schedule "approval mark" means—
(a) in relation to a solo motor bicycle, a motor bicycle combination and a trailer drawn by a solo motor bicycle or a motor bicycle combination, a marking designated as an approval mark by regulation 4 of the Designation of Approval Marks Regulations and shown at item 50A of Schedule 2 to those Regulations; and
(b) in relation to any other motor vehicle and any other trailer, either—

(i) a marking designated as an approval mark by regulation 5 of the Designation of Approval Marks Regulations and shown at item 10 of Schedule 4 to those Regulations; or
(ii) a marking designated as an approval mark by regulation 4 of the Designation of Approval Marks Regulations and shown at item 4 of Schedule 2 to those Regulations.   **[1695]**

NOTES
Commencement: 1 November 1989.

SCHEDULE 16

Regulations 17, 20

REQUIREMENT RELATING TO OBLIGATORY AND OPTIONAL WARNING BEACONS

1. Number:
   Sufficient to satisfy the requirements of paragraph 3

2. Position—
   Every warning beacon shall be so mounted on the vehicle that the centre of the lamp is at a height not less than 1200 mm above the ground.

3. Angles of visibility—
   The light shown from at least one beacon (but not necessarily the same beacon) shall be visible from any point at a reasonable distance from the vehicle or any trailer being drawn by it.

4. Markings:
   No requirement

5. Size of illuminated area:
   No requirement

6. Colour:
   Blue, amber, green or yellow in accordance with Regulation 11

7. Wattage:
   No requirement

8. Intensity:
   No requirement

9. Electrical connections:
   No requirement

10. Tell-tale:
    No requirement

11. Other requirements—
    The light shown by any one warning beacon shall be displayed not less than 60 nor more than 240 equal times per minute and the intervals between each display of light shall be constant.

[1696]

NOTES
Commencement: 1 November 1989.

SCHEDULE 17

Regulations 18, 20

PART I

REQUIREMENTS RELATING TO OBLIGATORY SIDE RETRO REFLECTORS AND OPTIONAL SIDE RETRO REFLECTORS TO THE EXTENT SPECIFIED IN PART II

1. Number—
   (a) A motor vehicle first used on or after 1st April 1986 and a trailer manufactured on or after 1st October 1985:
   On each side: two and as many more as are sufficient to satisfy the requirements of paragraph 2(a)

   (b) A motor vehicle first used before 1st April 1986 and a trailer manufactured before 1st October 1985:
   On each side: Two

2.
   Position—
   (a) Longitudinal—
      (i) A motor vehicle first used on or after 1st April 1986 and a trailer manufactured on or after 1st October 1985—
      (A) Maximum distance from the front of the vehicle, including any drawbar, in respect of the foremost reflector on each side:
      4 m

(B) Maximum distance from the rear of the vehicle in respect of the rearmost reflector on each side:	1 m
(C) Maximum separation distance between the reflecting areas of adjacent reflectors on the same side of the vehicle:	3 m or, if this is not practicable, 4 m

(ii) A motor vehicle first used before 1st April 1986 and a trailer manufactured before 1st October 1985—

(A) Maximum distance from the rear of the vehicle in respect of the rearmost reflector on each side:	1 m
(B) The other reflector on each side of the vehicle:	Towards the centre of the vehicle
(b) Lateral:	No requirement

(c) Vertical—

(i) Maximum height above the ground:	1500 mm
(ii) Minimum height above the ground:	350 mm

3. Angles of visibility—

(a) A motor vehicle first used on or after 1st April 1986 and a trailer manufactured on or after 1st October 1985—

(i) Horizontal:	45° to the left and to the right when viewed in a direction at right angles to the longitudinal axis of the vehicle

(ii) Vertical—

(A) Except in a case specified in sub-paragraph (B):	15° above and below the horizontal
(B) Where the highest part of the reflecting area is less than 750 mm above the ground:	15° above and 5° below the horizontal
(b) A motor vehicle first used before 1st April 1986 and a trailer manufactured before 1st October 1985:	Plainly visible to the side
4. Alignment:	To the side
5. Markings:	An approval mark
6. Size of reflecting area:	No requirement

7. Colour—

(a) Any vehicle not covered by sub-paragraph (b):	Amber or if within 1 m of the rear of the vehicle it may be red
(b) A solo motor bicycle, a motor bicycle combination, a pedal cycle with or without a sidecar or an invalid carriage:	No requirement
8. Other requirements:	No side retro reflector shall be triangular

9. Definitions—

(a) In this Schedule "approval mark" means either—

(i) a marking designated as an approval mark by regulation 4 of the Designation of Approval Marks Regulations and shown at item 3 or 3B of Schedule 2 to those Regulations and which includes the marking 1 or 1A; or

(ii) a marking designated as an approval mark by regulation 5 of the Designation of Approval Marks Regulations and shown at item 4 of Schedule 4 to those Regulations and which includes the marking I; and

(b) In this Schedule references to "maximum distance from the front of the vehicle" and "maximum distance from the rear of the vehicle" are references to the maximum distance from that end of the vehicle (as determined by reference to the overall length of the vehicle exclusive of any special equipment) beyond which no part of the reflecting area of the side retro reflector extends.

[1697]

NOTES
Commencement: 1 November 1989.

(REGS 18, 20)

PART II

REQUIREMENTS RELATING TO OPTIONAL SIDE RETRO REFLECTORS

Any number may be fitted, and the only requirements prescribed by these Regulations in respect of any which are fitted are those specified in paragraphs 7 and 8 of Part I. **[1698]**

NOTES
Commencement: 1 November 1989.

SCHEDULE 18

Regulations 18, 20

PART I

REQUIREMENTS RELATING TO OBLIGATORY REAR RETRO REFLECTORS AND OPTIONAL REAR RETRO REFLECTORS TO THE EXTENT SPECIFIED IN PART II

1. Number—

   (a) Any vehicle not covered by sub-paragraph (b) or (c):   Two

   (b) A solo motor bicycle, a pedal cycle with less than four wheels and with or without a sidecar, a trailer drawn by a pedal cycle, a trailer the overall width of which does not exceed 800 mm drawn by a solo motor bicycle or a motor bicycle combination, an invalid carriage having a maximum speed not exceeding 4 mph and a vehicle drawn or propelled by hand: One

   (c) A motor vehicle having three or more wheels and a maximum speed not exceeding 25 mph and a trailer drawn by any such vehicle if, in either case, the structure of the vehicle makes it impracticable to meet all of the requirements of paragraphs 2 and 3 below with two reflectors: Four

2. Position—

   (a) Longitudinal: At or near the rear

   (b) Lateral—

   (i) Where two rear reflectors are required to be fitted—

   (A) Maximum distance from the side of the vehicle—

   (1) Any vehicle not covered by sub-paragraph (2), (3) or (4):   400 mm

(2) A bus first used before 1st October 1964 and a horse-drawn vehicle manufactured before 1st October 1985:	No requirement
(2) A vehicle constructed or adapted for the carriage of round timber:	765 mm
(4) Any other motor vehicle first used before 1st April 1986 and any other vehicle manufactured before 1st October 1985:	610 mm
(B) Minimum separation distance between a pair of rear reflectors—	
(1) Any vehicle not covered by sub-paragraph (2):	600 mm. If the overall width of the vehicle is less than 1300 mm, 400 mm or if less than 800 mm, 300 mm
(2) A motor vehicle first used before 1st April 1986 and any other vehicle manufactured before 1st October 1985:	No requirement
(ii) Where one rear reflector is required to be fitted:	On the centre-line or off side of the vehicle
(iii) Where four rear reflectors are required to be fitted—	
(A) Maximum distance from the side of the vehicle—	
(1) One pair of reflectors:	Such that they satisfy the relevant requirements in sub-paragraph 2(b)(i)(B)
(2) The other pair of reflectors:	No requirement
(B) Minimum separation distance between rear reflectors—	
(1) One pair of reflectors:	Such that they satisfy the relevant requirements in sub-paragraph 2(b)(i)(B)
(2) The other pair of reflectors:	No requirement
(c) Vertical—	
(i) Maximum height above the ground where one or two rear reflectors are required to be fitted—	
(A) Any vehicle not covered by sub-paragraph (B):	900 mm or, if the structure of the vehicle makes this impracticable, 1200 mm
(B) A motor vehicle first used before 1st April 1986 and any other vehicle manufactured before 1st October 1985:	1525 mm
(ii) Maximum height above the ground where four rear reflectors are required to be fitted—	
(A) One pair of reflectors:	Such that they satisfy the relevant requirements in paragraph (2)(c)(i)
(B) The other pair of reflectors	2100 mm
(iii) Minimum height above the ground—	
(A) Any vehicle not covered by sub-paragraph (B):	350 mm

(B) A motor vehicle first used before 1st April 1986 and any other vehicle manufactured before 1st October 1985:

No requirement

3. Angles of visibility—

(a) A motor vehicle (not being a motor bicycle combination) first used on or after 1st April 1986 and a trailer manufactured on or after 1st October 1985—

   (i) Where one or two rear reflectors are required to be fitted—

       (A) Horizontal—

           (1) Where two rear reflectors are required to be fitted:

30° inwards and outwards

           (2) Where one rear reflector is required to be fitted:

30° to the left and to the right

       (B) Vertical—

           (1) Except in a case specified in subparagraph (2):

15° above and below the horizontal

           (2) Where the highest part of the reflecting area is less than 750 mm above the ground:

15° above and 5° below the horizontal

   (ii) Where four rear reflectors are required to be fitted—

       (A) One pair of reflectors:

Such that they satisfy the relevant requirements in paragraph 3(a)(i)

       (B) The other pair of reflectors:

Plainly visible to the rear

(b) A motor vehicle (not being a motor bicycle combination) first used before 1st April 1986 and a trailer manufactured before 1st October 1985:

Plainly visible to the rear

(c) A motor bicycle combination, a pedal cycle, a sidecar attached to a pedal cycle, a horse-drawn vehicle and a vehicle drawn or propelled by hand:

Plainly visible to the rear

4. Alignment:

To the rear

5. Markings—

(a) A motor vehicle first used—

   (i) On or after 1st April 1991:

An approval mark incorporating "I" or "IA"

   (ii) On or after 1st July 1970 and before 1st April 1991:

(A) An approval mark incorporating "I" or "IA", or
(B) A British Standard mark which is specified in sub-paragraph (i) of the definition of "British Standard mark" below followed by "LI" or "LIA" or
(C) In the case of a vehicle manufactured in Italy, an Italian approved marking

   (iii) Before 1st July 1970:

No requirement

(b) A trailer (other than a broken-down motor vehicle) manufactured—

(i) On or after 1st October 1989:	An approval mark incorporating "III" or "IIIA"
(ii) On or after 1st July 1970 and before 1st October 1989:	(A) An approval mark incorporating "III" or "IIIA"; or (B) A British Standard mark which is specified in sub-paragraph (i) of the definition of "British Standard mark" below followed by "LIII" or "LIIIA", or (C) In the case of a trailer manufactured in Italy, an Italian approved marking
(iii) Before 1st July 1970:	No requirement

(c) A pedal cycle, an invalid carriage having a maximum speed not exceeding 4 mph, a horse-drawn vehicle and a vehicle drawn or propelled by hand, in each case manufactured—

(i) On or after 1st October 1989:	(A) An approval mark incorporating "I" or "IA": or (B) A British Standard mark which is specified in sub-paragraph (ii) of the definition of "British Standard mark" below
(ii) On or after 1st July 1970 and before 1st October 1989:	(A) Any of the markings mentioned in sub-paragraph (c)(i) above; or (B) A British Standard mark which is specified in sub-paragraph (i) of the definition of "British Standard mark" below followed by "LI" or "LIA"
(iii) Before 1st July 1970:	No requirement

6. Size of reflecting area:	No requirement
7. Colour:	Red

8. Other requirements—

(a) Except in the case of a motor vehicle first used before 1st April 1986, any other vehicle manufactured before 1st October 1985 and a motor bicycle combination, where two rear reflectors are required to be fitted they shall form a pair. Where four rear reflectors are required to be fitted they shall form two pairs.

(b) No vehicle, other than a trailer or a broken-down motor vehicle being towed, may be fitted with triangular-shaped rear reflectors.

(c) A rear reflector shall not be fitted on a boot lid or other movable part of the vehicle.

9. Definitions—

In this Schedule—

(a) "approval mark" means either—

> (i) a marking designated as an approval mark by regulation 4 of the Designation of Approval Marks Regulations and shown at item 3 or 3A or 3B of Schedule 2 to those Regulations; or
>
> (ii) a marking designated as an approval mark by regulation 5 of the Designation of Approval Marks Regulation and shown at item 4 of Schedule 4 to those Regulations;

(b) "British Standard mark" means either—

> (i) the mark indicated in the specification for retro reflectors for vehicles, including cycles, published by the British Standards Institution under the reference B.S. AU 40: Part 2: 1965, namely "AU 40"; or
>
> (ii) the mark indicated in the specification for photometric and physical requirements of reflective devices published by the British Standards Institution under the reference BS 6102: Part 2: 1982, namely "BS 6102/2"; and

(c) "Italian approved marking" means—
a mark approved by the Italian Ministry of Transport, namely, one including two separate groups of symbols consisting of "IGM" or "DGM" and "C.1." or "C.2.". **[1699]**

NOTES
Commencement: 1 November 1989.

PART II

REQUIREMENTS RELATING TO OPTIONAL REAR RETRO REFLECTORS

Any number may be fitted and the only requirements prescribed by these Regulations in respect of any which are fitted are those specified in paragraphs 7 and 8(b) of Part I.
[1700]

NOTES
Commencement: 1 November 1989.

SCHEDULE 19

Regulations 18, 20

PART I

REQUIREMENTS RELATING TO OBLIGATORY REAR MARKINGS AND OPTIONAL REAR MARKINGS TO THE EXTENT SPECIFIED IN PART II

SECTION A

GENERAL REQUIREMENTS

1. Number—
   (a) A motor vehicles the overall length of which—

(i) does not exceed 13 m:	A rear marking shown in diagram 1, 2 or 3 in Section B of this Schedule
(ii) exceeds 13 m:	A rear marking shown in diagram 4 or 5 in Section B of this Schedule

   (b) A trailer if it forms part of a combination of vehicles the overall length of which—

(i) does not exceed 11 m:	A rear marking shown in diagram 1, 2 or 3 in Section B of this Schedule
(ii) exceeds 11 m but does not exceed 13 m:	A rear marking shown in diagram 1, 2, 3, 4 or 5 in Section B of this Schedule
(iii) exceeds 13 m:	A rear marking shown in diagram 4 or 5 in Section B of this Schedule

2. Position—

(a) Longitudinal:	At or near the rear of the vehicle
(b) Lateral—	
(i) A rear marking shown in diagram 2, 3 or 5 in Section B of this Schedule:	Each part shall be fitted as near as practicable to the outermost edge of the vehicle on the side thereof on which it is fitted so that no part of the marking projects beyond the outermost part of the vehicle on either side
(ii) A rear marking shown in diagram 1 or 4 in Section B of this Schedule:	The marking shall be fitted so that the vertical centreline of the marking lies on the vertical plane through the longitudinal axis of the vehicle and no part of the marking projects beyond the outermost part of the vehicle on either side
(c) Vertical:	The lower edge of every rear marking shall be at a height of not more than 1700 mm nor less than 400 mm above the ground whether the vehicle is laden or unladen

3. Angles of visibility: Plainly visible to the rear, except while the vehicle is being loaded or unloaded

4. Alignment: The lower edge of every rear marking shall be fitted horizontally. Every part of a rear marking shall lie within 20° of a transverse vertical plane at right angles to the longitudinal axis of the vehicle and shall face to the rear

5. Markings:	A British Standard mark
6. Size:	In accordance with Sections B and C of this Schedule
7. Colour:	Red fluorescent material in the stippled areas shown in any of the diagrams in Section B of this Schedule and yellow retro reflecting material in any of the areas so shown, being areas not stippled and not constituting a letter. All letters shall be coloured black

8. Other requirements—
The two parts of every rear marking shown in diagrams 2, 3 or 5 in Section B of this Schedule shall form a pair.

9. Definitions—
In this Schedule "British Standard mark" means the specification for rear marking plates for vehicles published by the British Standards Instititution under the references BS AU 152: 1970, namely "BS AU 152".

SECTION B

SIZE, COLOUR AND TYPE OF REAR MARKINGS

Left　　　　　　　　　　　　　　　　　　　　　　　　　　　　　　　**Right**

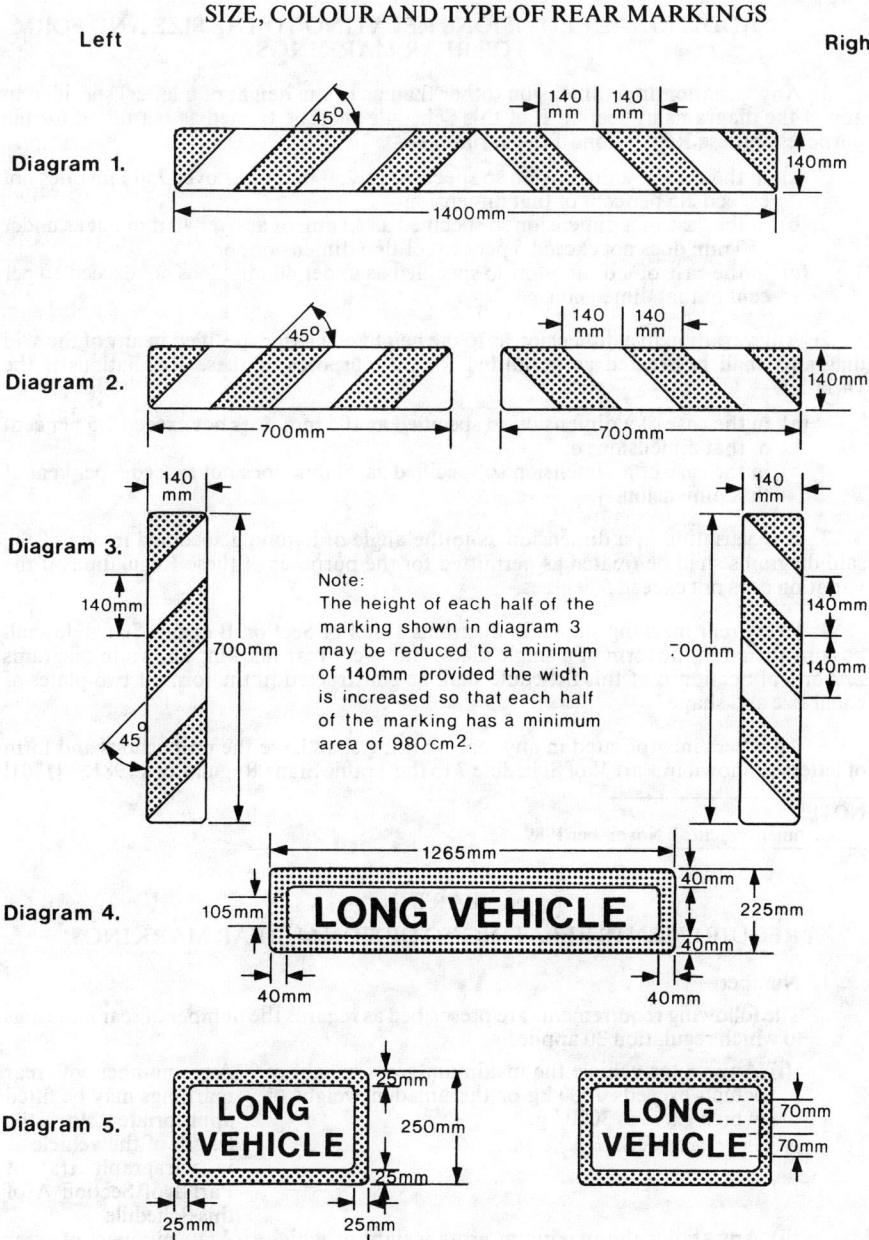

Diagram 1.

Diagram 2.

Diagram 3.

Note:
The height of each half of the marking shown in diagram 3 may be reduced to a minimum of 140mm provided the width is increased so that each half of the marking has a minimum area of 980cm².

Diagram 4.

LONG VEHICLE

Diagram 5.

LONG VEHICLE

SECTION C

ADDITIONAL PROVISIONS RELATING TO THE SIZE AND FORM OF REAR MARKINGS

1. Any variation in a dimension (other than as to the height of a letter) specified in any of the diagrams in Section B of this Schedule shall be treated as permitted for the purposes of these Regulations if the variation—

   (a) in the case of a dimension so specified as 250 mm or as over 250 mm does not exceed 2.5 per cent of that dimension;
   (b) in the case of a dimension so specified as 40 mm or as over 40 mm but as under 250 mm does not exceed 5 per cent of that dimension; or
   (c) in the case of a dimension so specified as under 40 mm does not exceed 10 per cent of that dimension.

2. Any variation in a dimension as to the height of a letter specified in any of the said diagrams shall be treated as permitted for the purposes of these Regulations if the variation—

   (a) in the case of a dimension so specified as 105 mm does not exceed 2.5 per cent of that dimension; or
   (b) in the case of a dimension so specified as 70 mm does not exceed 5 per cent of that dimension.

3. Any variation in a dimension as to the angle of hatching specified in any of the said diagrams shall be treated as permitted for the purposes of these Regulations if the variation does not exceed 5 degrees.

4. Every rear marking shown in diagrams 1 or 4 of Section B of this Schedule shall be constructed in the form of a single plate, and every rear marking shown in diagrams 2, 3 or 5 of Section B of this Schedule shall be constructed in the form of two plates of equal size and shape.

5. All letters incorporated in any rear marking shall have the proportions and form of letters as shown in Part V of Schedule 7 to the Traffic Signs Regulations 1981.   **[1701]**

NOTES
Commencement: 1 November 1989.

PART II

REQUIREMENTS RELATING TO OPTIONAL REAR MARKINGS

1. Number—

   The following requirements are prescribed as regards the number of rear markings to which regulation 20 applies—

   (i) Any motor vehicle the maximum gross weight of which exceeds 7500 kg or the unladen weight of which exceeds 3000 kg:

   Any number of rear markings may be fitted appropriate to the length of the vehicle as in paragraph 1(a) of Part I of Section A of this Schedule

   (ii) Any trailer the maximum gross weight of which exceeds 3500 kg or the unladen weight of which exceeds 1000 kg:

   Any number of rear markings may be fitted appropriate of the length of the combination of vehicles as in paragraph 1(b) of Section A of Part I of this Schedule

(iii) Any trailer which is being drawn by a vehicle which is itself required or permitted to be fitted with a rear marking:

Any number of rear markings may be fitted appropriate to the length of the combination of vehicles as in paragraph 1(b) of Section A of Part I of this Schedule

(iv) Any other vehicle:

No rear marking may be fitted

2. Other provisions—
    The requirements specified in paragraphs 2 to 8 of Section A of Part I of this Schedule and in Sections B and C of that Part are also prescribed for optional rear markings.   **[1702]**

NOTES
    Commencement: 1 November 1989.

SCHEDULE 20
Regulations 18, 20

PART I

REQUIREMENTS RELATING TO OBLIGATORY PEDAL RETRO REFLECTORS AND OPTIONAL PEDAL RETRO REFLECTORS TO THE EXTENT SPECIFIED IN PART II

1. Number:

Two reflectors on each pedal

2. Position—
    (a) Longitudinal:

On the leading edge and the trailing edge of each pedal

    (b) Lateral:

No requirement

    (c) Vertical:

No requirement

3. Angles of visibility:

Such that the reflector on the leading edge of each pedal is plainly visible to the front and the reflector on the trailing edge of each pedal is plainly visible to the rear

4. Markings:

A British Standard mark

5. Size of reflecting area:

No requirement

6. Colour:

Amber

7. Definitions—
    In this Schedule "British Standard mark" means the specification for photometric and physical requirements of reflective devices published by the British Standards Institution under the references BS 6102: Part 2: 1982, namely "BS 6102/2".   **[1703]**

NOTES
    Commencement: 1 November 1989.

PART II

REQUIREMENTS RELATING TO OPTIONAL PEDAL RETRO REFLECTORS

Any number may be fitted and the only requirement prescribed by these Regulations in respect of any which are fitted is that specified in paragraph 6 of Part I. **[1704]**

NOTES
Commencement: 1 November 1989.

SCHEDULE 21
Regulations 18, 20

PART I

REQUIREMENTS RELATING TO OBLIGATORY FRONT RETRO REFLECTORS AND TO OPTIONAL FRONT RETRO REFLECTORS TO THE EXTENT SPECIFIED IN PART II

1. Number: Two

2. Position—
   (a) Longitudinal: No requirement
   (b) Lateral—
       (i) Maximum distance from the side of the trailer: 150 mm
       (ii) Minimum separation distance between a pair of front reflectors: 600 mm or, if the overall width of the trailer is less than 1400 mm 400 mm
   (c) Vertical—
       (i) Maximum height above the ground: 900 mm or, if the structure of the trailer makes this impracticable, 1500 mm
       (ii) Minimum height above the ground: 350 mm

3. Angles of visibility—
   (a) Horizontal: 30° outwards and 5° inwards
   (b) Vertical—
       (i) Any case not covered by sub-paragraph (ii): 15° above and below the horizontal
       (ii) Where the highest point of the reflecting area is less than 750 mm above the ground: 15° above and 5° below the horizontal

4. Alignment: To the front

5. Markings: An approval mark

6. Size of reflecting area: No requirement

7. Colour: White

8. Other requirements—
   (a) Where two front reflectors are required to be fitted they shall form a pair.
   (b) Triangular shaped retro reflectors shall not be fitted to the front of any trailer.

9. Definitions—

In this Schedule—
"approval mark" means either—
(a) a marking designated as an approval mark by regulation 4 of the Designation of Approval Marks Regulations and shown at item 3 or 3A or 3B of Schedule 2 to those Regulations; or

(b) a marking designated as an approval mark by regulation 5 of the Designation of Approval Marks Regulation and shown at item 4 of Schedule 4 to those Regulations   **[1705]**

NOTES
    Commencement: 1 November 1989.

PART II

REQUIREMENTS RELATING TO OPTIONAL FRONT RETRO REFLECTORS

Any number may be fitted and the only requirements prescribed by these regulations in respect of any which are fitted are that specified in paragraph 8(b) of Part I and that the colour shall not be red.   **[1706]**

NOTES
    Commencement: 1 November 1989.

SCHEDULE 22

Regulation 24(3)

DIAGRAM SHOWING WHERE UNLIT PARKING IS NOT PERMITTED NEAR A JUNCTION

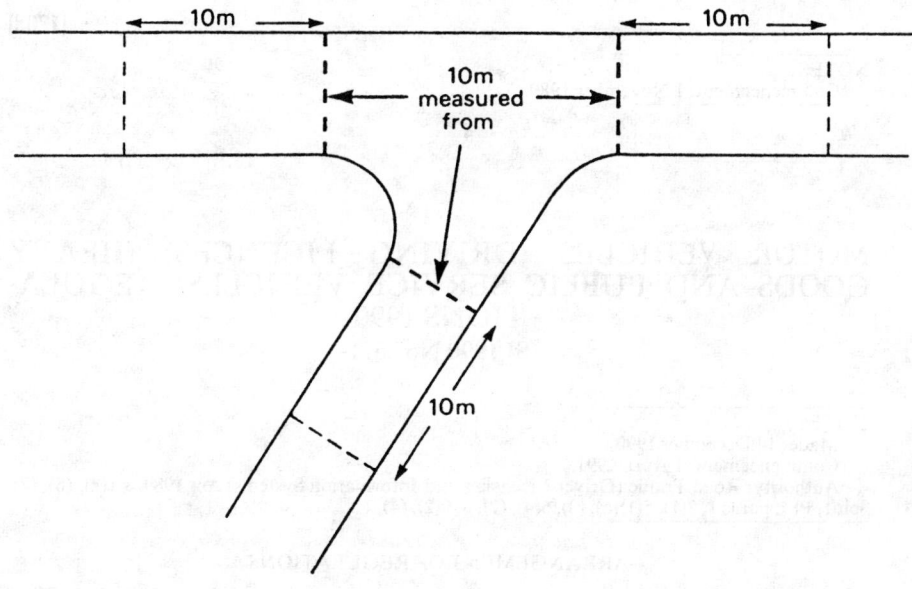

[1707]

NOTES
    Commencement: 1 November 1989.

SCHEDULE 23
(Sch 4, Part I, paras 4, 12)

Example of marking showing the vertical downwards inclination of the dipped-beam headlamps when the vehicle is at its kerbside weight and has a weight of 75 kg on the driver's seat

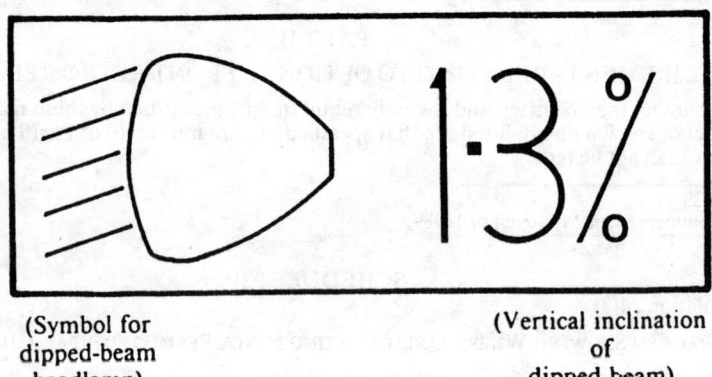

(Symbol for
dipped-beam
headlamp)

(Vertical inclination
of
dipped beam)

[1708]

NOTES
Commencement: 1 November 1989.

MOTOR VEHICLES (DRIVING LICENCES) (HEAVY GOODS AND PUBLIC SERVICE VEHICLES) REGULATIONS 1990
(SI 1990 No 2611)

NOTES
Made: 14 December 1990.
Commencement: 1 April 1991.
Authority: Road Traffic (Driver Licensing and Information Systems) Act 1989, s 1(2), (6), (7), Sch 1, Pt I, paras 1, 3(1), 5(1)(a), (3), 6(4), (7), 8, 9(2), (4), 12.

ARRANGEMENT OF REGULATIONS

PART I

Preliminary

PART II

Licences

PART III

Provisional and Trainee HGV Licence Holders

PART IV

Supplementary

SCHEDULES

PART I

PRELIMINARY

1. Citation, commencement and application

(1) These Regulations may be cited as the Motor Vehicles (Driving Licences) (Heavy Goods and Public Service Vehicles) Regulations 1990 and shall come into force on 1st April 1991.

(2) These Regulations apply in respect of existing heavy goods vehicle and public service vehicle licences.　　　　　　　　　　　　　**[1709]**

NOTE
　　Commencement: 1 April 1991.

2. Interpretation

(1) In these Regulations, unless the context otherwise requires—

"the 1989 Act" means the Road Traffic (Driver Licensing and Information Systems) Act 1989;

"articulated goods vehicle combination" has the same meaning as in section 108(1) of the 1988 Act;

"full" in relation to an existing heavy goods vehicle licence or a large goods vehicle driver's licence means such a licence which is not a provisional heavy goods vehicle licence or a provisional large goods vehicle driver's licence as the case may be;

"holder", in relation to a licence, means the person to whom the licence was granted;

"hgv trainee driver's licence" means an existing heavy goods vehicle licence which—

    (i) is a licence to drive heavy goods vehicles of class 1, 1A, 2, 2A, 3 or 3A,

    (ii) was applied for by a person under the age of 21 on the date of the application, and

    (iii) has effect for a period during the whole or part of which the holder is under the age of 21;

"large goods vehicle" and "large goods vehicle driver's licence" have the same meaning as in Part IV of the 1988 Act;

"lgv trainee driver's licence" has the same meaning as in the Motor Vehicles (Driving Licences) (Large Goods and Passenger-Carrying Vehicles) Regulations 1990;

"licence" means an existing licence;

"Northern Ireland ordinary driving licence" means a licence to drive a motor vehicle granted under the law for the time being in force in Northern Ireland equivalent to Part III of the 1988 Act but does not include such a licence in so far as it authorises a person to drive large goods vehicles or passenger-carrying vehicles of any category;

"ordinary driving licence" means a licence to drive a motor vehicle granted under Part III of the 1988 Act other than a large goods vehicle driver's licence or a passenger-carrying vehicle driver's licence;

"passenger-carrying vehicle driver's licence" has the same meaning as in Part IV of the 1988 Act;

"penalty points" means penalty points endorsed on an ordinary driving licence or the counterpart of such a licence pursuant to sections 28 and 29 of the Road Traffic Offenders Act 1988 or counted as having been so endorsed pursuant to paragraph 7(3) of Schedule 4 to the Road Traffic (Consequential Provisions) Act 1988;

"relevant endorsement" means an endorsement on a Northern Ireland ordinary driving licence of particulars of a conviction in pursuance of those provisions for the time being in force in Northern Ireland that correspond to sections 44 and 45 of the Road Traffic Offenders Act 1988;

"standard" in relation to an existing heavy goods vehicle licence or a large goods vehicle driving licence means such a licence which is not an hgv or an lgv trainee driver's licence as the case may be;

"traffic commissioner" means in relation to the holder of a licence the traffic commissioner in whose area the holder of the licence resides except in relation to service personnel to whom regulation 14 applies.

(2) In these Regulations, unless the context otherwise requires, any reference to a class of heavy goods or public service vehicle is a reference to a class specified in column (2) of Part I or II, as the case may be, of Schedule 1, and in the case of a class identified by a number in relation to that number, and reference to a category of vehicle is a reference to a category specified in column (2) of Schedule 1 to the Motor Vehicles (Driving Licences) (Large Goods and Passenger-Carrying Vehicles) Regulations 1990 or in column (2) of Schedule 3 to the Motor Vehicles (Driving Licences) Regulations 1987, and in the case of a category identified by a letter in relation to that letter.

(3) In these Regulations, unless the context otherwise requires, a reference to a regulation or Schedule followed by a number is a reference to the regulation or Schedule bearing that number in these Regulations, and a reference to a

paragraph followed by a number is a reference to the paragraph bearing that number in the regulation in which it appears. **[1710]**

NOTE
Commencement: 1 April 1991.

PART II
LICENCES

3. Notification of change of name or address

If, during the currency of a licence, the holder changes his name or address he shall, forthwith notify the Secretary of State of the new name or address, as the case may be, and surrender his licence for replacement by a licence to drive large goods vehicles or passenger-carrying vehicles as the case may be. **[1711]**

NOTE
Commencement: 1 April 1991.

4. Withdrawal of ordinary driving licence or Northern Ireland ordinary driving licence

If the holder of a licence is disqualified for holding or obtaining an ordinary driving licence under section 34, 35 or 36 of the Road Traffic Offenders Act 1988 or under the law for the time being in force in Northern Ireland which corresponds to any of those sections for holding or obtaining a Northern Ireland ordinary driving licence, or if such a licence is refused, under section 92 of the 1988 Act or any provision of that law that corresponds to that section, he shall surrender his first mentioned licence to the traffic commissioner. **[1712]**

NOTE
Commencement: 1 April 1991.

5. Duplicate licences

(1) If a licence has been lost, the holder shall forthwith notify the traffic commissioner and the traffic commissioner, if satisfied that the licence has been lost and on payment of the fee specified in paragraph (5), shall issue a copy of it marked as a duplicate.

(2) If a licence referred to in paragraph (1) is subsequently recovered by the holder he shall forthwith return it to the traffic commissioner.

(3) If a licence becomes defaced, the holder shall forthwith return it to the traffic commissioner and on such return the traffic commissioner shall, on payment of the fee specified in paragraph (5), issue a copy of the licence marked as a duplicate.

(4) A copy of a licence issued and marked as a duplicate in accordance with paragraph (1) or (3) shall have the same effect as the licence which it duplicates.

(5) The fee for the issue of a duplicate licence shall be [£6].

(6) Upon the issue of a duplicate licence to him the holder shall sign it in ink with his usual signature. **[1713]**

NOTES
Commencement: 1 April 1991.
Para (5): figure in square brackets substituted by SI 1991 No 2491, reg 2.

6. Custody and production

(1) Save as provided in paragraph (2), on being required to do so by any certifying officer, vehicle examiner or person authorised by any traffic commissioner on production, in any such case, if so required, of his authority, or by any constable, the holder of a licence shall forthwith produce his licence for examination by such officer, examiner, person or constable, as the case may be.

(2) If any person is unable to produce his licence when required to do so in accordance with paragraph (1) it shall be a sufficient compliance with that paragraph if—

(a) in a case where the licence was required by a constable to be produced, within 7 days after the production of the licence was so required, it is produced in person by the holder for examination at such police station as may have been specified by him at the time its production was required; or

(b) in any other case, within 10 days after the production of the licence was so required it is made available for examination at such office as the person requiring its production may have specified at the time its production was required.

(3) Where a licence has been suspended or revoked, then if the holder of the licence fails to deliver it for endorsement, cancellation or transmission as required by regulation 8, a constable or a vehicle examiner may require him to produce it, and upon its being produced may seize it and deliver it for endorsement, cancellation, or transmission in accordance with that regulation.

(4) In this regulation—

(a) "certifying officer" means an officer appointed under section 7(1) of the 1981 Act;

(b) "vehicle examiner" means a person appointed as such in accordance with section 7(2) of the 1981 Act or under section 68(1) of the 1988 Act; and

(c) "licence" includes an existing Northern Ireland licence. **[1714]**

NOTE
Commencement: 1 April 1991.

7. Revocation of licences

(1) For the purposes of paragraph 5(1)(a)(i) of Part I of Schedule 1 to the 1989 Act (obligatory revocation of licence), the following physical disabilities are prescribed:—

(a) [liability to epileptic seizures];

(b) abnormal sight in one or both eyes where—

(i) in the case of a person who held a licence on 1 January 1983 and who holds such a licence on 1 April 1991, the visual acuity is worse than 6/12 with the better eye and worse than 6/36 with the other eye and, if corrective lenses are worn, the uncorrected acuity in each eye is worse than 3/60, or

(ii) in any other case, the visual acuity is worse than 6/9 in the better eye and worse than 6/12 in the other eye and, if corrective lenses are worn, the uncorrected acuity in each eye is worse than 3/60;

(c) sign in only one eye unless—

(i) in the case of a person who held a licence on 1 January 1983 and who holds such a licence on 1 April 1991 the traffic commissioner in whose area he resides or the traffic commissioner who granted the last-mentioned licence knew of the disability before 1 January 1991 and the visual acuity in that eye is no worse than 6/12, or

(ii) in the case of a person who did not hold a licence on 1 January 1983 but who holds such a licence on 1 April 1991 the traffic commissioner in whose area he resides or the traffic commissioner who granted the last-mentioned licence knew of the disability before 1 January 1991 and the visual acuity in that eye is no worse than 6/9;

(d) diabetes subject to insulin treatment unless the person in question held on 1 April 1991 a licence and the traffic commissioner in whose area he resides or the traffic commissioner who granted the licence knew of the disability before 1 January 1991.

(2) The following circumstances relating to conduct are prescribed for the purposes of paragraph 5(1)(a)(ii) of Part I of Schedule 1 to the 1989 Act (obligatory revocation of licence) namely, in the case of the holder of an existing heavy goods vehicle licence who is under the age of 21,—

(a) that his ordinary driving licence, or in the case of such a licence which came into force on or after 1 June 1990 the counterpart of that licence, has more than three penalty points endorsed on it; or

(b) that his Northern Ireland ordinary driving licence, or in the case of such a licence which came into force on or after 1 January 1991 the counterpart of that licence, bears more than one relevant endorsement.

(3) In this regulation references to measurements of visual acuity are references to visual acuity measured on the Snellen Scale.   **[1715]**

NOTE
Commencement: 1 April 1991.
Amended by SI 1992 No 3085.

---

8. Surrender of licences

The holder of an existing licence, or an existing Northern Ireland licence, which has been suspended or revoked shall within 7 days of receipt of notice, either delivered to him personally or sent by post, of the decision to suspend or revoke the licence, send or deliver such licence, in the case of the holder of an existing licence, to the traffic commissioner, in whose area he resides and, in the case of the holder of a Northern Ireland licence, to the traffic commissioner for the North Western traffic area, for endorsement and return to the holder, or for cancellation, or transmission to the licensing authority in Northern Ireland, as the case may require.   **[1716]**

NOTE
Commencement: 1 April 1991.

---

9. Disqualification

(1) Where in pursuance of paragraph 5(1)(a)(i) of Part I of Schedule 1 to the 1989 Act the Secretary of State has revoked a person's licence the Secretary of State shall order that person to be disqualified indefinitely.

(2) Where in pursuance of paragraph 5(1)(a)(ii) of Part I of Schedule 1 to the 1989 Act the Secretary of State has revoked a person's licence the Secretary

of State shall order that person to be disqualified until he reaches 21 years of age or for such longer period as the Secretary of State may determine.

(3) For the purposes of paragraph 6(7) of Part I of Schedule 1 to the 1989 Act, the prescribed classes of large goods vehicles are categories C and C plus E and the prescribed classes of passenger-carrying vehicles are categories D and D plus E.   **[1717]**

NOTE
Commencement: 1 April 1991.

10. Removal of disqualification

(1) Subject to paragraph (2) and (3) below, the Secretary of State may, under paragraph 6(4) of Part I of Schedule 1 to the 1989 Act, remove a disqualification imposed under paragraph 6(2)(a) of that Schedule if the application for the removal of the disqualification is made after the expiration of whichever is relevant of the following periods from the commencement of the disqualification, that is to say—

    (a) two years, if the disqualification is for less than four years;

    (b) one half of the period of the disqualification, if it is for less than ten years, but not less than four years;

    (c) five years in any other case, including disqualification for an indefinite period.

(2) The applicant must have incurred no further penalty points or relevant endorsements.

(3) Where an application under paragraph (1) above for the removal, under paragraph 6(4) of Part I of Schedule 1 to the 1989 Act, of a disqualification is refused, a further such application shall not be entertained if made within three months after the date of refusal.   **[1718]**

NOTE
Commencement: 1 April 1991.

PART III

PROVISIONAL AND TRAINEE HGV LICENCE HOLDERS

11. Provisional standard licences for heavy goods vehicles

(1) A full standard existing licence to drive heavy goods vehicles of class 2, 2A, 3 or 3A shall also be treated (in so far as it does not by virtue of regulation 16 operate as a full licence to drive such vehicles) as a provisional standard licence to drive heavy goods vehicles of a class in respect of which the holder is not by reason of his age disqualified under section 101(1) of the 1988 Act for holding or obtaining a large goods vehicle driver's licence.

(2) Subject to paragraph (3) below, a provisional standard existing heavy goods vehicle licence, including a full standard licence which is treated as a provisional standard licence under paragraph (1) above, shall be subject to the following conditions, which are prescribed conditions for the purposes of paragraph 3(1) of Part I of Schedule 1 to the 1989 Act, that is to say, the holder shall not drive a heavy goods vehicle of any class which he may drive by virtue of the licence or a large goods vehicle of any category which he is entitled to drive by virtue of regulation 16—

(a) otherwise than under the supervision of a person who is present with him in the vehicle and who holds a full standard heavy goods vehicle licence or a full standard large goods vehicle driver's licence to drive the vehicle; and

(b) unless there is clearly displayed in a conspicuous manner on the front and on the back of the vehicle a distinguishing mark—

    (i) before the expiry of 5 years after these Regulations come into force, in either form A or B set out in Schedule 2; or

    (ii) after the expiry of that period in form B set out in that Schedule.

(3) The condition specified in paragraph (2)(a) shall not apply whilst the holder of the licence is undergoing a test of competence to drive large goods vehicles of any category, being a test for which provision is made under section 89 of the 1988 Act, and the conditions specified in paragraph (2)(a) and (b) shall not apply in relation to the driving of a large goods vehicle of any category where the holder of the licence has passed such a test for a vehicle of that category. **[1719]**

NOTE
    Commencement: 1 April 1991.

12. HGV trainee drivers' licences

(1) Every hgv trainee driver's licence shall be subject to the following conditions, which are prescribed conditions for the purposes of paragraph 3(1) of Part I of Schedule 1 to the 1989 Act—

(a) that the holder shall not drive a heavy goods vehicle of any class for which the licence is issued or for which the licence is treated as a provisional licence unless the holder is the registered employee of a registered employer named in the licence and either—

    (i) the vehicle is a heavy goods vehicle of a class to which the holder's training agreement applies and which is stated in the licence, and the vehicle is owned or operated by that registered employer or by a registered hgv driver training establishment named in the licence; or

    (ii) the holder is a part-time member of the armed forces of the Crown and the vehicle is owned by the Secretary of State for Defence and used for naval, military or air force purposes, and

(b) in the case of a holder of an hgv trainee driver's full licence, that he shall not drive a heavy goods vehicle of any class for which the licence is issued, if the vehicle is being used to draw a trailer, otherwise than under the supervision of a person who is present with him in the vehicle and who holds a full standard existing heavy goods vehicle licence or a full standard large goods vehicle driver's licence to drive the vehicle.

(2) Subject to paragraphs (3) and (4), an hgv driver's provisional licence, including an hgv trainee driver's full licence which is treated as an hgv trainee driver's provisional licence, shall be subject to the following conditions (additional to that prescribed by paragraph (1) above), which are prescribed conditions for the purposes of paragraph 3(1) of Part I of Schedule 1 to the 1989 Act, that is to say, that the holder shall not drive a heavy goods vehicle of any class which he may drive by virtue of the licence—

(a) otherwise than under the supervision of a person who is present with him in the vehicle and who holds a full standard existing heavy goods vehicle licence or a full standard large goods vehicle driver's licence to drive the vehicle;

(b) unless there is clearly displayed in a conspicuous manner on the front and on the back of the vehicle a distinguishing mark—

(i) before the expiry of 5 years after these Regulations come into force in either form A or B set out in Schedule 2;

(ii) after the expiry of that period, in form B set out in that Schedule;

(c) if the vehicle is being used to draw a trailer, unless the combination of the vehicle and trailer falls within category C plus E.

(3) The condition specified in paragraph (2)(a) shall not apply while the holder of an hgv trainee driver's provisional licence (including a full licence which is treated as a provisional licence) is undergoing a test of competence to drive large goods vehicles of any category, being a test for which provision is made under section 89 of the 1988 Act.

(4) Where the holder of an hgv trainee driver's provisional licence (including a full licence which is treated as a provisional licence) has passed a test for a large goods vehicle of a category for which the licence is, or is treated as, a provisional licence, the conditions specified in paragraph (2) (except (a) where the vehicle is in category C and is being used to draw a trailer or is in category C plus E) shall not apply so far as regards the driving of a vehicle in that category.

(5) In this regulation, unless the context otherwise requires—

"registered" means registered for the time being by the Training Committee in accordance with the relevant provisions of the training scheme;

"training agreement", in relation to an individual who is undergoing, or is to undergo, hgv driver training, means his agreement therefore with his registered employer in pursuance of the training scheme;

"the Training Committee" means the Committee which has been established by the employers' associations and the trade unions in the road goods transport industry with a constitution approved by the Secretary of State and which is known as the National Joint Training Committee for Young HGV Drivers in the Road Goods Transport Industry;

"the training scheme" means the scheme which has been established by the Training Committee with the approval of the Secretary of State (given for the purpose of regulations under section 101 of the 1988 Act before the date of coming into force of these Regulations) for training young drivers of heavy goods vehicles and which provides for—

(i) the registration by the Training Committee of employers who are willing and able to provide hgv driver training for persons employed by them,

(ii) the registration by the Training Committee of persons operating establishments for providing hgv driver training,

(iii) a syllabus for hgv driver training, and

(iv) the registration by the Training Committee of individual employees who are undergoing, or are to undergo, hgv driver training in the service of a registered employer in accordance with a form of agreement approved by the Training Committee.

[1720]

NOTE
Commencement: 1 April 1991.

PART IV
SUPPLEMENTARY

13. Issue of existing licence after reconsideration or appeal

Where a heavy goods vehicle or public service vehicle licence is issued as a result of any reconsideration by, or appeal from, a licensing authority under section 116 of the 1988 Act or section 23 of the 1981 Act, which was continued under section 1(3) of the 1989 Act, that licence shall be issued in the form of an existing licence and the person to whom it is issued shall sign it in ink with his usual signature.   **[1721]**

NOTE
Commencement: 1 April 1991.

14. Service personnel

The functions of the traffic commissioners under these Regulations shall, except where the context otherwise requires, be exercisable in relation to holders of licences subject to the Naval Discipline Act 1957, to military law or to air force law who are not resident in Great Britain by the traffic commissioner for the South-Eastern and Metropolitan Traffic Area.   **[1722]**

NOTE
Commencement: 1 April 1991.

15. Northern Ireland licences

(1) For the purposes of paragraph 9(2) of Part I of Schedule 1 to the 1989 Act the prescribed traffic commissioner is the traffic commissioner for the North Western Traffic Area.

(2) For the purposes of paragraph 9(4) of Part I of Schedule 1 to the 1989 Act the prescribed magistrates' court or prescribed sheriff to whom the holder of an existing Northern Ireland licence who is not resident in Great Britain and who is aggrieved may appeal are—

   (i) such a magistrates' court or sheriff as he may nominate at the time he puts down his appeal, or

   (ii) in the absence of a nomination of a particular court under sub-paragraph (i) above, the magistrates' court in whose area the office of the traffic commissioner for the North Western Traffic Area is situated.   **[1723]**

NOTE
Commencement: 1 April 1991.

16. Entitlement to drive large goods and passenger-carrying vehicles

The holder of a licence other than an hgv trainee driver's licence conferring entitlement to drive vehicles of a class specified in an entry in column (1) of Part I or Part II, as the case may be, of the table in Schedule 3 (including a licence conferring such entitlement by virtue of regulation 11(1)) shall also be entitled during the currency of that licence to drive large goods and passenger-carrying vehicles of a category specified in the entry opposite thereto in column (2) of

Part I or II, as the case may be, of that table, and in respect of a licence for vehicles in class 3 or 3A which is restricted to vehicles having a permissible maximum weight not exceeding 10 tonnes by virtue of—

(a) paragraph 3(3) and (5) of Schedule 2 to the Road Traffic (Drivers' Ages and Hours of Work) Act 1976; or

(b) paragraph (1) or (2) of regulation 31 of the Heavy Goods Vehicles (Drivers' Licences) Regulations 1977 before they ceased to have effect with the repeal of Part IV of the 1988 Act by section 1 of the 1989 Act,

without any such restriction.   **[1724]**

NOTE
Commencement: 1 April 1991.

17. Offences

The holder of a licence who contravenes, or fails to comply without reasonable excuse, with, any provision of regulation 3, 4, 5, 6(1) and (2), 8 or 13 shall be guilty of an offence.   **[1725]**

NOTE
Commencement: 1 April 1991.

SCHEDULE 1

Regulation 2(2)

PART I
CLASSES OF HEAVY GOODS VEHICLES

(1) Class	(2) Definition
1	An articulated goods vehicle combination without automatic transmission.
1A	An articulated goods vehicle combination with automatic transmission.
2	A heavy goods vehicle without automatic transmission, other than an articulated goods vehicle combination, designed and constructed to have more than four wheels in contact with the road surface.
2A	A heavy goods vehicle with automatic transmission, other than an articulated goods vehicle combination, designed and constructed to have more than four wheels in contact with the road surface.
3	A heavy goods vehicle without automatic transmission, other than an articulated goods vehicle combination, designed and constructed to have not more than four wheels in contact with the road surface.
3A	A heavy goods vehicle with automatic transmission, other than an articulated goods vehicle combination, designed and constructed to have not more than four wheels in contact with the road surface.

For the purposes of the above definitions where a vehicle is fitted with two wheels in line transversely and the distance between the centres of their respective areas of contact with the road is less than 457 mm they shall be regarded as only one wheel.

PART II

CLASSES OF PUBLIC SERVICE VEHICLES

(1) Class	(2) Definition
1	A double-decked vehicle without automatic transmission.
1A	A double-decked vehicle with automatic transmission.
2	A single-decked vehicle without automatic transmission or a half-decked vehicle without automatic transmission being in either case a vehicle the overall length of which exceeds 8.5 metres.
2A	A singled-decked vehicle with automatic transmission or a half-decked vehicle with automatic transmission being in either case a vehicle the overall length of which exceeds 8.5 metres.
3	A single-decked vehicle without automatic transmission or a half-decked vehicle without automatic transmission being in either case a vehicle the overall length of which does not exceed 8.5 metres but which does exceed 5.5 metres.
3A	A single-decked vehicle with automatic transmission or a half-decked vehicle with automatic transmission being in either case a vehicle the overall length of which does not exceed 8.5 metres but which does exceed 5.5 metres.
4	A single-decked vehicle without automatic transmission or a half-decked vehicle without automatic transmission being in either case a vehicle the overall length of which does not exceed 5.5 metres.
4A	A single-decked vehicle with automatic transmission or a half-decked vehicle with automatic transmission being in either case a vehicle the overall length of which does not exceed 5.5 metres.
4B	A vehicle specified in item 4 or 4A above but restricted to uses specified in the licence.

[1726]

NOTE
Commencement: 1 April 1991.

SCHEDULE 2

Regulations 11(2)(b), 12(2)(b)

DIAGRAM OF DISTINGUISHING MARKS TO BE DISPLAYED ON A VEHICLE DRIVEN UNDER A PROVISIONAL LICENCE

(This Schedule contains diagrams of distinguishing marks to be displayed on vehicles driven under a provisional licence.)   **[1727]**

NOTE
Commencement: 1 April 1991.

SCHEDULE 3

Regulation 16

ENTITLEMENT TO DRIVE CORRESPONDING CATEGORIES OF LARGE GOODS AND PASSENGER-CARRYING VEHICLES

PART I

(1) Class of heavy goods vehicle	(2) Category of large goods vehicle
1	C, C plus E.
1A	As in 1 but limited to vehicles with automatic transmission.

(1) Class of heavy goods vehicle	(2) Category of large goods vehicle
2	C, C plus E but limited to drawbar trailer combinations only.
2A	As in 2 but limited to vehicles with automatic transmission.
3	As in 2.
3A	As in 2A.

PART II

(1) Class of public service vehicle	(2) Category of passenger-carrying vehicle
1	D, D plus E.
1A	As for 1 but limited to vehicles with automatic transmission.
2	As for 1.
2A	As for 1 but limited to vehicles with automatic transmission.
3	D.
3A	As for 3 but limited to vehicles with automatic transmission.
4	D limited to vehicles of not more than 5.5 metres in length.
4A	As for 4 but limited to vehicles with automatic transmission.
4B	B.

[1728]

NOTE
    Commencement: 1 April 1991.

MOTOR VEHICLES (DRIVING LICENCES) (LARGE GOODS AND PASSENGER-CARRYING VEHICLES) REGULATIONS 1990
(SI 1990 No 2612)

NOTES
    Made: 19 December 1990
    Commencement: 1 April 1991
    Authority: Public Passenger Vehicles Act 1981, s 60(1)(g), the Road Traffic Act 1988, ss 88(5), (6), 89(3), (4), (6), (7), 89A(3), (5), 91, 92(2), 97(1), (3), 98(4), 99(1), (1A), 101, 105, 108(1), 114(1), 115(1), (3), 117(4), (7), 118(4), 120, 121, 122(2), (4), 183(6), 192(1)(b), (3).

ARRANGEMENT OF REGULATIONS

PART I

Preliminary

PART I

PRELIMINARY

1. Citation, commencement and revocation

(1) These Regulations may be cited as the Motor Vehicles (Driving Licences)
(Large Goods and Passenger-Carrying Vehicles) Regulations 1990 and shall
come into force on 1st April 1991.

     (2) ...   **[1729]**

NOTES
Commencement: 1 April 1991.
Para (2): revokes SI 1977 No 1309, reg 26, SI 1985 No 214, regs 17–20.

2. Interpretation

(1) In these Regulations, unless the context otherwise requires—

"the 1981 Act" means the Public Passenger Vehicles Act 1981;

"the 1988 Act" means the Road Traffic Act 1988;

"the 1989 Act" means the Road Traffic (Driver Licensing and Information Systems) Act 1989;

["appropriate driving test" has the same meaning as in section 36 of the Road Traffic Offenders Act 1988;]

"existing licence", "existing heavy goods vehicle licence" and "existing public service vehicle licence" have the same meaning as in Part I of Schedule 1 to the 1989 Act;

"full" with reference to an ordinary driving licence or a large goods vehicle or passenger-carrying vehicle driver's licence or an existing heavy goods vehicle licence means such a licence other than a provisional licence;

"heavy goods vehicle" has the same meaning as it had for the purposes of Part IV of the 1988 Act before its repeal by section 1 of the 1989 Act;

"holder", in relation to a licence, means the person to whom the licence was granted;

"hgv trainee driver's licence" means an existing heavy goods vehicle licence which—

(i) is a licence to drive heavy goods vehicles of class 1, 1A, 2, 2A, 3 or 3A or any combination thereof,

(ii) was applied for by a person under the age of 21 on the date of the application, and

(iii) has effect for a period during the whole or part of which the holder is under the age of 21;

"licence" means a large goods vehicle driver's licence or a passenger-carrying vehicle driver's licence;

"lgv trainee driver's licence" means a large goods vehicle driver's licence which—

(i) is a licence to drive large goods vehicles of category C or C plus E or both,

(ii) was applied for by a person under the age of 21 on the date of the application, and

(iii) has effect for a period during the whole or part of which the holder is under the age of 21;

"maximum authorised mass" has the same meaning—

(i) in relation to goods vehicles as "permissible maximum weight" in section 108(1) of the 1988 Act, and

(ii) in relation to any other vehicle or trailer as "maximum gross weight" in regulation 3(2) of the Road Vehicles (Construction and Use) Regulations 1986

"Northern Ireland ordinary driving licence" means a licence to drive a motor vehicle granted under the law for the time being in force in Northern Ireland equivalent to Part III of the 1988 Act but does not include such a licence in so far as it authorises a person to drive large goods vehicles or passenger-carrying vehicles of any category;

"ordinary driving licence" means a licence to drive a motor vehicle granted under Part III of the 1988 Act other than a large goods vehicle or passenger-carrying vehicle driver's licence;

"penalty points" mean penalty points endorsed on an ordinary driving licence or the counterpart of an ordinary driving licence pursuant to sections 28 and 29 of the Road Traffic Offenders Act 1988 or counted as having been so endorsed pursuant to paragraph 7(3) of Schedule 4 to the Road Traffic (Consequential Provisions) Act 1988;

"PSV operator's licence" and "public service vehicle" have the meanings given by section 82(1) of the 1981 Act;

"registered" means registered for the time being by the Training Committee in accordance with the relevant provisions of the training scheme;

"relevant endorsement" means an endorsement on a Northern Ireland ordinary driving licence or its counterpart of particulars of a conviction in pursuance of those provisions for the time being in force in Northern Ireland that correspond to sections 44 and 45 of the Road Traffic Offenders Act 1988;

"standard" in relation to an existing heavy goods vehicle licence or a large goods vehicle driver's licence means such a licence which is not an hgv trainee driver's licence or an lgv trainee driver's licence as the case may be;

"test" means a test of competence to drive large goods vehicles or passenger-carrying vehicles, as the case may be, of any category, being a test for which provision is made under section 89(3) of the 1988 Act;

"traffic commissioner" means in relation to an applicant for or the holder of a licence the traffic commissioner in whose area the applicant or holder resides except in relation to service personnel to whom section 183(6) of the 1988 Act and regulation 23 applies;

"training agreement" in relation to an individual who is undergoing, or is to undergo, lgv driver training, means his agreement therefor with his registered employer in pursuance of the training scheme;

"the Training Committee" means the Committee which has been established by the employers' associations and the trade unions in the road goods transport industry with a constitution approved by the Secretary of State and which is known as the National Joint Training Committee for Young LGV Drivers in the Road Goods Transport Industry;

"the training scheme" means the scheme which has been established by the Training Committee with the approval of the Secretary of State (given for the purpose of regulations under section 120 of the 1988 Act) for training young drivers of large goods vehicles and which provides for—

(i) the registration by the Training Committee of employers who are willing and able to provide lgv driver training for persons employed by them;

(ii) the registration by the Training Committee of persons operating establishments for providing lgv driver training;

(iii) a syllabus for lgv driver training; and

(iv) the registration by the Training Committee of individual employees who are undergoing, or are to undergo, lgv driver training in the service of a registered employer in accordance with a form of agreement approved by the Training Committee;

"vehicle with automatic transmission" means a vehicle in which the driver is not provided with any means whereby he may, independently of the use of the accelerator or the brakes, vary gradually the proportion of the power being produced by the engine which is transmitted to the road wheels of the vehicle.

(2) In these Regulations, unless the context otherwise requires, any reference to a class of heavy goods or public service vehicle is a reference to a class defined in column (2) in Part I or II, as the case may be, of Schedule 1 to the Motor Vehicles (Driving Licences) (Heavy Goods and Public Service Vehicles) Regulations 1990, and in the case of a class identified by a number in relation to that number and any reference to a category of vehicle is a reference to a category specified in column (2) of Schedule 1 or column (2) of Schedule 3 to the Motor Vehicles (Driving Licences) Regulations 1987, and in the case of a category identified by a letter in relation to that letter.

(3) In these Regulations, unless the context otherwise requires, a reference to a regulation or Schedule followed by a number is a reference to the regulation or Schedule bearing that number in these Regulations, and a reference to a paragraph followed by a number is a reference to the paragraph bearing that number in the regulation in which it appears. **[1730]**

NOTE
  Commencement: 1 April 1991 (except definition "appropriate driving test"); 1 July 1992 (remainder).
  Para (1): definition "appropriate driving test" inserted by SI 1992 No 1356, regs 2, 3.

3. Application

(1) These Regulations apply in respect of large goods or passenger-carrying vehicle drivers' licences and tests of competence to drive large goods or passenger-carrying vehicles except those falling within categories C1 and D1.

(2) The Motor Vehicles (Driving Licences) Regulations 1987, except regulations 4, [5(2)], 7 (in so far as it applies to exchange and duplicate licences), 11(1)(a), 12, 13, 24[(1)(b) to (e), (3), (4), (5), (6), (7) and (8)], 25 and 26 and the other provisions of the 1987 Regulations, in so far as applicable to those regulations, shall not apply in respect of large goods or passenger-carrying vehicle drivers' licences or tests of competence to drive large goods or passenger-carrying vehicles in respect of which these Regulations apply. **[1731]**

NOTES
  Commencement: 1 April 1991.
  Para (2): words in first square brackets inserted by SI 1991 No 515, reg 3; words in second pair of square brackets inserted by SI 1992 No 3089, reg 3.

PART II

LICENCES

4. Applications for the grant of licences

A person who desires to obtain the grant of a licence shall—

  (a) submit his application not more than three months before the date on which the licence is to take effect; and
  (b) send with his application—
    (i) if required by the Secretary of State, a certificate, in such form as the Secretary of State may require, that has been signed by a registered medical practitioner not more than four months prior to the date on which the licence is to take effect,

      (ii) if required by the Secretary of State, any ordinary driving licence, Northern Ireland driving licence or existing licence held by him,

      (iii) a pass certificate showing that he has passed the test within the relevant period for the category of vehicles which the licence applied for will authorise him to drive, except in the case of an application for a provisional licence or where he is entitled to the grant of a licence by having held a previous licence as set out in sections 89 and 89A of the 1988 Act, and

      (iv) in the case of an application for a licence to drive the vehicles in category D specified in regulation 28(1) by an applicant who relies upon that regulation, a certificate, in such form as the Secretary of State may require to the effect that he has been regularly driving vehicles in category D with more than 16 seats in addition to the driver's seat during the period of three years immediately preceding his application for such a licence. **[1732]**

NOTE

Commencement: 1 April 1991.

---

5. Qualifications of applicants

(1) An applicant for a licence shall when the licence is granted have the following qualifications—

    (a) he must not be a person who—

      (i) subject to paragraph (3), holds a licence which has been suspended or a Northern Ireland large goods or passenger-carrying vehicle driver's licence which has been suspended, whether (in either case) the suspension has effect under section 115 of the 1988 Act or under the provision of the law for the time being in force in Northern Ireland that corresponds to that section;

      (ii) subject to paragraph (3), is disqualified for holding or obtaining a licence or a Northern Ireland large goods or passenger-carrying vehicle driver's licence, whether (in either case) the disqualification has effect under section 117 of the 1988 Act or under the provision of the law for the time being in force in Northern Ireland that corresponds to that section;

      (iii) is disqualified by a court for holding or obtaining an ordinary driving licence or by a court in Northern Ireland for holding or obtaining a Northern Ireland ordinary driving licence;

      (iv) is disqualified by reason of his age for holding or obtaining a licence to drive any of the vehicles in the category of vehicles to which the licence is to relate; or

      (v) would hold more than one large goods vehicle driver's licence or such a licence and a Northern Ireland licence, British external licence, British Forces licence, exchangeable licence or existing licence authorising him to drive large goods vehicles of any category or would hold more than one passenger-carrying vehicle driver's licence or such a licence and a Northern Ireland licence, British external licence, British Forces licence, exchangeable licence or existing licence authorising him to drive passenger-carrying vehicles of any category;

    (b) he shall hold a full ordinary driving licence or a full Northern Ireland ordinary driving licence authorising him to drive motor vehicles in category B or he shall be authorised to drive motor vehicles in category

B as a full licence holder by virtue of section 88 of the 1988 Act (licence applied for or surrendered for correction of particulars, etc.), or any corresponding Northern Ireland provision or by having passed a test for that category; and

(c) in the case of an applicant for an lgv trainee driver's licence—

   (i) the licence referred to in sub-paragraph (b) above or its counterpart shall be free from any penalty points or relevant endorsements,

   (ii) he shall be a person who is a registered employee of a registered employer.

(2) Paragraph (1)(b) above shall not apply in the case of an applicant who is a full-time member of the armed forces of the Crown.

(3) A person is qualified to apply for a large goods vehicle driver's licence notwithstanding that when the licence is granted has passenger-carrying vehicle driver's licence is suspended or he is disqualified for holding or obtaining such a licence if such suspension or disqualification relates to his conduct other than as a driver of a motor vehicle. **[1733]**

NOTE
Commencement: 1 April 1991.

6. Disabilities

(1) The following disabilities are prescribed as relevant disabilities for the purpose of section 92(2) of the 1988 Act in relation to large goods vehicle or passenger-carrying vehicle drivers' licences (in addition to the disabilities prescribed by regulation 24[(1)(b) to (e)] of the Motor Vehicles (Driving Licences) Regulations 1987)—

(a) [liability to epileptic seizures];
(b) abnormal sight in one or both eyes where—

   (i) in the case of a person who held an existing licence on 1st January 1983 and who holds such a licence on 1st April 1991, the visual acuity is worse than 6/12 with the better eye and worse than 6/36 with the other eye and, if corrective lenses are worn, the uncorrected acuity in each eye is worse than 3/60, or

   [(ii) [in the case of a person not falling within paragraph (1)(b)(i) above] who held a licence or an existing licence on 1st March 1992, the visual acuity is worse than 6/9 in the better eye and worse than 6/12 in the other eye and, if corrective lenses are worn, the uncorrected acuity in each eye is worse than 3/60, or

   (iii) in any other case, the visual acuity is worse than 6/9 in the better eye or worse than 6/12 in the other eye or, if corrective lenses have to be worn to ensure that the visual acuity in one eye or both eyes is no worse than 6/9 in the better eye and 6/12 in the other eye, the uncorrected acuity in each eye is worse than 3/60;]

(c) sight in only one eye unless—

   (i) in the case of a person who held an existing licence on 1st January 1983 and who holds such a licence on 1st April 1991 the traffic commissioner in whose area he resides or the traffic commissioner who granted the last-mentioned licence knew of the disability before 1st January 1991 and the visual acuity in that eye is no worse than 6/12, or

(ii) in the case of a person who did not hold an existing licence on 1st January 1983 but who holds an existing licence on 1st April 1991 the traffic commissioner in whose area he resides or the traffic commissioner who granted the last-mentioned licence knew of the disability before 1st January 1991 and the visual acuity in that eye is no worse than 6/9;

(d) diabetes subject to insulin treatment unless the person in question held, on 1st April 1991, an existing licence and the traffic commissioner in whose area he resides or the traffic commissioner who granted the licence knew of the disability before 1st January 1991.

(2) In this regulation references to measurements of visual acuity are references to visual acuity measured on the Snellen Scale.   **[1734]**

NOTES
    Commencement: 1 April 1991 (except para (1)(b)(ii), (iii); 1 March 1992 (para (1)(b)(ii), (iii)).
    Para (1): words in first pair of square brackets inserted, words in second pair of square brackets substituted, by SI 1992 No 3089, reg 4(a), (b); sub-para (b)(ii), (iii) substituted for the original sub-para (b)(ii) by SI 1992 No 166, and words in second (inner) pair of square brackets substituted by SI 1992 No 3089, reg 4(c).

7. Grant of licences subject to a limitation

Where an applicant for a provisional licence—

(a) holds an ordinary driving licence which contains a provision under section 92(7) or 97(3) of the 1988 Act limiting the applicant to the driving of vehicles of a particular construction or design or class only; or

(b) holds a Northern Ireland ordinary driving licence which contains a similar provision under the law for the time being in force in Northern Ireland that corresponds to the said section 92(7) or 97(3);

any such licence granted to the applicant to drive large goods vehicles or passenger-carrying vehicles of any category shall contain a corresponding limitation.   **[1735]**

NOTE
    Commencement: 1 April 1991.

8. Correspondences

For the purposes of section 89A of the 1988 Act, a class of heavy goods vehicle or public service or a test of competence to drive heavy goods vehicles or public service vehicles of a class specified in column (1) of Part I or Part II, as the case may be, of the table in Schedule 2 corresponds to a category of large goods vehicle or passenger-carrying vehicle or a test of competence to drive a category of large goods vehicle or passenger-carrying vehicle, as the case may be, specified in column (2) of Part I or Part II of that table, and in respect of an existing heavy goods vehicle licence for vehicles in class 3 or 3A which is restricted to vehicles having a permissible maximum weight not exceeding 10 tonnes by virtue of—

(a) paragraph 3(3) and (5) of Schedule 2 to the Road Traffic (Drivers' Ages and Hours of Work) Act 1976; or

(b) paragraph (1) or (2) of regulation 31 of the Heavy Goods Vehicles (Drivers' Licences) Regulations 1977 before they ceased to have effect with the repeal of Part IV of the 1988 Act by section 1 of the 1989 Act,

without any such restriction.   **[1736]**

NOTE
Commencement: 1 April 1991.

9. Fees for licences

(1) Subject to paragraph (2) below, the fees for the grant of licences shall be as set out in Schedule 3.

(2) When an application for more than one licence is made at the same time only the highest fee prescribed by paragraph (1) above shall be payable on the grant of the licences and when an application for a licence and for an ordinary driving licence is made at the same time only the highest fee prescribed by that paragraph or by regulation 7 of the Motor Vehicles (Driving Licences) Regulations 1987 shall be so payable. **[1737]**

NOTE
Commencement: 1 April 1991.

10. Provisional licences and provisional entitlement

(1) The entitlement to drive vehicles in category C, D, C plus E or D plus E subject to the same conditions as a provisional licence holder conferred by section 98(2) and (3) of the 1988 Act shall not apply in the case of the holder of a full licence to drive vehicles of category B.

(2) The entitlement to drive vehicles in category C or C plus E subject to the same conditions as a provisional licence holder conferred by section 98(2) and (3) of the 1988 Act shall not apply in the case of the holder of a full licence to drive vehicles of category D or D plus E, and the entitlement to drive vehicles in category D or D plus E subject to those conditions shall not apply in the case of the holder of a full licence to drive vehicles of category C or C plus E.

(3) Subject to paragraph (5), a large goods vehicle or passenger-carrying vehicle driver's licence issued as a provisional licence, including a full licence which is treated as a provisional licence under section 98(2) or (3), shall be subject to the following conditions prescribed for the purposes of section 114(1) of the 1988 Act, that is to say, the holder shall not drive a vehicle of any category which he may drive by virtue of the licence—

    (a) otherwise than under the supervision of a person who is present with him in the vehicle and who holds a full licence or a full existing licence to drive the vehicle; and

    (b) unless there is clearly displayed in a conspicuous manner on the front and on the back of the vehicle a distinguishing mark—

        (i) before a date 5 years after these Regulations come into force, in either form A or B set out in Schedule 4, or

        (ii) on or after that date, in form B only.

[(4) A passenger-carrying vehicle driver's licence issued as a provisional licence, including a licence which is treated as a provisional licence under section 98(2) and (3), shall be subject to the condition prescribed for the purposes of section 114(1) of the 1988 Act, that the holder shall not drive a passenger-carrying vehicle which he may drive by virtue of the licence while carrying any passenger in the vehicle other than—

    (a) the person specified in paragraph (3)(a);

    (b) a person specified in regulation 18(5); or

    (c) a person who holds a passenger-carrying vehicle driver's licence or an existing public service vehicle licence and is giving or receiving instruction in the driving of passenger-carrying vehicles or who has given or received, or is to give or receive, such instruction.

(5) The condition specified in paragraph (3)(a) shall not apply whilst the holder of a provisional licence is undergoing a test; neither of the conditions specified in paragraph (3) nor the condition in paragraph (4) shall apply in relation to the driving of a vehicle of any category when the holder of the licence has passed a test for a vehicle of that category or whilst the holder of the licence is driving a vehicle he is entitled to drive by virtue of regulation 33(1) or 34(2) of the Motor Vehicles (Driving Licences) Regulations 1987.]

(6) This regulation shall not apply to lgv trainee drivers and lgv trainee drivers' licences.   **[1738]**

NOTES
Commencement: 1 April 1991.
Paras (4), (5): substituted for the original paras (4), (5), by SI 1991 No 515, reg 4.

11. Large goods vehicles drivers' licences issued to persons under the age of 21

(1) A large goods vehicle driver's licence issued to a person under the age of 21 shall be subject to the following conditions prescribed for the purposes of section 114(1) of the 1988 Act—

 (a) in the case of a full-time member of the armed forces of the Crown, that he shall not drive a large goods vehicle of any category otherwise than for naval, military or air force purposes; and

 (b) in the case of the holder of an lgv trainee driver's licence, that he shall not drive a large goods vehicle of any category for which the licence is issued or for which by virtue of subsections (2) and (3) of section 98 of the 1988 Act (which authorise holders of full licences for certain classes of vehicles to drive all other classes subject to provisional licence conditions) the licence is treated as provisional licence, unless the holder is the registered employee of a registered employer and either—

  (i) the vehicle is a large goods vehicle of a category to which his training agreement applies and is owned or operated by that registered employer or by a registered lgv driver training establishment, or

  (ii) the holder is a part-time member of the armed forces of the Crown and the vehicle is owned by the Secretary of State for Defence and used for naval, military or air force purposes, and

 (c) in the case of the holder of an lgv trainee driver's full licence, that he shall not drive a vehicle of any category for which the licence is issued if the vehicle is being used to draw a trailer, otherwise than under the supervision of a person who is present with him in the vehicle and who holds a full standard licence or a full standard existing licence to drive the vehicle.

(2) In the case of an lgv trainee driver's full licence to drive large goods vehicles of category C, the provisions of subsections (2) and (3) of section 98 of the 1988 Act shall apply in respect of category C plus E after the expiration of the period of two years from the date on which he passed the test to drive large goods vehicles of category C.

(3) The holder of an hgv trainee driver's full licence to drive heavy goods vehicles of class 2 or 3 may, on surrendering that licence and paying the fee

prescribed in Schedule 3, apply for an lgv trainee driver's licence which will be a full lgv trainee driver's licence to drive large goods vehicles of category C and which, two years from the date on which he passed the test to drive heavy goods vehicles of class 3, will also act as an lgv trainee driver's provisional licence to drive vehicles of category C plus E.

(4) Subject to paragraphs (5), (6) and (7), an lgv trainee driver's provisional licence, including an lgv trainee driver's full licence which is treated as an lgv trainee driver's provisional licence by virtue of subsections (2) and (3) of section 98 of the 1988 Act, shall be subject to the following conditions (additional to that required by paragraph (1)), that is to say, that the holder shall not drive a large goods vehicle of any category which he may drive by virtue of the licence—

(a) otherwise than under the supervision of a person who is present with him in the vehicle and who holds a full standard licence or a full standard existing licence to drive the vehicle; and

(b) unless there is clearly displayed in a conspicuous manner on the front and on the back of the vehicle a distinguishing mark—

(i) before a date 5 years after these Regulations come into force, in either form A or B set out in Schedule 4, or

(ii) on or after that date, in form B; and

(c) if the vehicle is being used to draw a trailer, unless the licence is for category C plus E and the combination of vehicle and trailer would fall within that category.

(5) The condition specified in paragraph (4)(a) shall not apply while the holder of the licence is undergoing a test.

(6) Where the holder of an lgv trainee driver's provisional licence (including a full licence which is treated as a provisional licence as mentioned above) has passed a test for a category of large goods vehicle for which the licence is, or is treated as, a provisional licence the conditions specified in paragraph (4) (except (a) where the vehicle is in category C and is being used to tow a trailer or is in category C plus E) shall not apply so far as regards the driving of a vehicle in that category. **[1739]**

NOTE

Commencement: 1 April 1991.

12. Obligatory revocation of large goods vehicle drivers' licences and disqualification on revocation

(1) The prescribed circumstances for the purposes of section 115(1)(a) of the 1988 Act (obligatory revocation of licence) are that, in the case of the holder of a large goods vehicle driver's licence who is under the age of 21, the counterpart of his ordinary driving licence bears more than three penalty points.

(2) Where a large goods vehicle driver's licence is revoked under section 115((1)(a) the cases in which the person whose licence has been revoked must be disqualified indefinitely or for a period, shall be determined by the Secretary of State.

(3) Where the Secretary of State determines that a person whose licence has been revoked under section 115(1)(a) is to be disqualified for a period he shall be disqualified until he reaches 21 years of age or for such longer period as the Secretary of State may determine. **[1740]**

NOTE
    Commencement: 1 April 1991.

[12A. Applicants for and holders of a licence who are disqualified by order of the court

(1) Where a person who is disqualified by order of a court until he passes the appropriate driving test passes such a test on a vehicle included in category B, C1 or D1 the disqualification shall be deemed to have expired in relation to all vehicles included in category C, C plus E, D and D plus E.

(2) Subject to paragraphs (3) to (5), where a person's licence is treated as revoked by virtue of section 37(1) of the Road Traffic Offenders Act 1988 (Effect of disqualification by order of a court) the Secretary of State may—

    (a) order that person to be disqualified indefinitely or for such period as the Secretary of State thinks fit under section 117(2)(a) of the 1988 Act; or

    (b) except where the licence treated as revoked by virtue of section 37(1) of the Road Traffic Offenders Act 1988 is a provisional licence, if it appears to the Secretary of State that, owing to the conduct of the person, it is expedient to require him to comply with the prescribed conditions applicable to provisional licences until he passes the test prescribed under regulation 17 for large goods vehicles or passenger-carrying vehicles of any class, order him to be disqualified for holding or obtaining a full licence until he passes such a test under section 117(2)(b) of the 1988 Act.

(3) Where a person's licence is treated as revoked by virtue of section 37(1) of the Road Traffic Offenders Act 1988 and the Secretary of State would have been required to revoke that person's licence under section 115(1)(a) of the 1988 Act had he not been disqualified by order of a court, the Secretary of State must order that person to be disqualified indefinitely or for a period under section 117(1) of the 1988 Act.

(4) The cases in which a person to whom paragraph (3) applies must be disqualified indefinitely or for a period shall be determined by the Secretary of State.

(5) Where the Secretary of State determines that a person to whom paragraph (3) applies is to be disqualified for a period that person shall be disqualified until he reaches 21 years of age or for such longer period as the Secretary of State may determine.]   **[1740A]**

NOTES
    Commencement: 1 July 1992.
    Inserted by SI 1992 No 1356, regs 2, 4.

13. Removal of disqualification

(1) Subject to paragraph (2) and (3), the Secretary of State may remove a disqualification under section 117(4) of the 1988 Act, after consultation with the traffic commissioner in cases which had been referred to him, if the application for the removal of the disqualification is made after the expiration of whichever is relevant of the following periods from the commencement of the disqualification, that is to say—

    (a) two years, if the disqualification is for less than four years;

(b) one half of the period of the disqualification, if it is for less than ten years, but not less than four years;

(c) five years in any other case, including disqualification for an indefinite period.

(2) The applicant must have incurred no further penalty points or relevant endorsements.

(3) Where an application under paragraph (1) for the removal, under section 117(4) of the 1988 Act, of a disqualification is refused, a further such application shall not be entertained if made within three months after the date of refusal.

[1741]

NOTE
Commencement: 1 April 1991.

14. Prescribed classes of goods and passenger-carrying vehicles

For the purposes of sections 89A(3) and (5), 99(1) and (1A) and 117(7) of the 1988 Act, the prescribed classes of goods vehicles or large goods vehicles are those in categories C and C plus E and the prescribed classes of passenger-carrying vehicles are those in categories D and D plus E. **[1742]**

NOTE
Commencement: 1 April 1991.

PART III

TESTS OF COMPETENCE

15. Applications for tests

(1) A person who desires to take a test to be conducted by an examiner appointed under regulation 19(1)(a) shall apply for an appointment for a test to the Secretary of State at any office of the Driving Standards Agency.

[(2) An applicant for such an appointment shall, when making the application, specify the category of vehicle in respect of which he desires to take the test and pay—]

[(a) in respect of a test to be conducted on a day other than a Saturday—

(i) £48 if the application for the test is made before 14th August 1992, and

(ii) £55.50 if the application is made on or after that date;

(b) in respect of a test to be conducted on a Saturday, £75.] **[1743]**

NOTES
Commencement: 1 April 1991 (para (1)); 3 June 1991 (para (2) (except sub-paras (a), (b))); 14 August 1992 (remainder).
Para (2): substituted by SI 1991 No 1122; sub-paras (a), (b) further substituted for sub-paras (a)–(c) by SI 1992 No 1761.

16. Qualifications of applicants for tests

An applicant for a test shall be a person who is the holder of a provisional large goods vehicle or passenger-carrying vehicle driver's licence or a provisional heavy goods vehicle licence, or a full licence which is treated as such a provisional licence, entitling him to drive a vehicle or vehicles in the category of vehicles in respect of which he desires to take the test. **[1744]**

NOTE

Commencement: 1 April 1991.

17. Nature of tests

The test which a person is required to pass before a full licence can be granted to him authorising him to drive a large goods vehicle or passenger-carrying vehicle of a particular category shall be a test carried out on a vehicle of that category, being a test which satisfies the examiner—

    (a) that the candidate is fully conversant with the contents of the Highway Code;

    (b) that he has sufficient knowledge of the mechanical operation of the vehicle on which he is tested, including, at the discretion of the examiner, the effect of distribution of load on the performance of the vehicle, to enable him to drive it safely;

    (c) that he is competent to drive without danger to, and with due consideration for, other users of the road, the vehicle on which he is tested; and

    (d) that he is able to perform safely and competently the operations specified in Schedule 5.   **[1745]**

NOTE

Commencement: 1 April 1991.

18. Requirements for tests

(1) A person submitting himself for a test shall—

    (a) provide for the purposes of the test a vehicle which is suitable for the purposes of the test and which, in particular, is suitable for the purposes of the test under paragraph (3) [or paragraph (3A), whichever is appropriate,] and—

        (i) is not carrying passengers or goods or burden of any description,

        (ii) is fitted with a seat which is firmly secured to the vehicle and in such a position that the examiner is able properly to conduct the test from it and is afforded adequate protection from bad weather when conducting the test,

        (iii) is not fitted with a device designed to permit a person other than the driver to operate the accelerator, unless any pedal or lever by which the device is operated and any other parts which it may be necessary to remove to make the device inoperable by such a person during the test have been removed, and

        (iv) in the case of a test of competence to drive passenger-carrying vehicles, save as provided in paragraph (2), is so constructed that the examiner can, from the deck of the vehicle on which the driver is seated, get a clear view of the road to the rear of the vehicle without the use of any optical device; and

    (b) sign the examiner's attendance record; and

    (c) produce evidence of identity to the satisfaction of the examiner in the form of—

        (i) a licence to drive a motor vehicle granted under Part III of the 1988 Act or an existing licence bearing his signature,

        (ii) a Northern Ireland licence bearing his signature,

        (iii) a British external licence bearing his signature,

        (iv) a British Forces licence bearing his signature,

    (v) a driving permit issued by the service authorities of a visiting force specified in Article 3 of the Motor Vehicles (International Circulation) Order 1975 bearing his signature,

    (vi) a Convention driving permit as defined in Article 2(7) of that Order bearing his signature,

    (vii) an exchangeable licence bearing his signature,

    (viii) any other document falling within the definition of "domestic driving permit" in Article 2(7) of that Order which bears his name in the roman alphabet, his photograph and his signature,

    (ix) a passport bearing his signature, or

    (x) an identity card issued by his employer which bears his name in the roman alphabet, his photograph and his signature.

(2) The requirement specified in paragraph (1)(a)(iv) does not apply in a case where—

    (a) the construction of the vehicle makes fulfilment of that requirement impracticable, and

    (b) the examiner consents to that requirement not being complied with in consequence of arrangements to conduct part or all of the test not on a road.

(3) [A passenger-carrying vehicle shall not be suitable for the purposes of the test unless]—

    (a) if the test is taken before the 1st April 1994—

      (i) ...

      (ii) in the case of a test for category D not limited as in sub-paragraph (iii) below, it has an overall length of at least 8.5 metres;

      (iii) in the case of a test for category D limited under regulation 29 to vehicles with not more than 16 seats, in addition to the driver's seat, it has an overall length of less than 8.5 metres;

      (iv) ...

      (v) in the case of a test for category D plus E, it is a combination of vehicles comprising a vehicle which is suitable for a test for category D under paragraph (ii) above and a trailer with a permissible maximum weight of at least 1.25 tonnes; and

    (b) if the test is taken on or after that date, it is capable of a speed of at least 80 kilometres per hour and—

      (i) ...

      (ii) in the case of a test for category D not limited as in sub-paragraph (iii) below, it has an overall length of at least 9 metres;

      (iii) in the case of a test for category D limited under regulation 29 to vehicles with not more than 16 seats, in addition to the driver's seat, it has an overall length of less than 9 metres;

      (iv) ...

      (v) in the case of a test for category D plus E, it is a combination of vehicles comprising a vehicle which is suitable for a test for category D under sub-paragraph (ii) above and a trailer with a permissible maximum weight of at least 1.25 tonnes.

[(3A) A large goods vehicle shall not be suitable for the purpose of a test unless—

    (a) if the test is taken before 1st July 1996—

      (i) in the case of a test for category C, it has a maximum authorised mass which exceeds 7.5 tonnes;

    (ii) in the case of a test for Category C plus E, it is either—

        (a) an articulated goods vehicle combination, or

        (b) a combination of vehicles comprising a vehicle in category C and a trailer with at least two axles with a permissible maximum weight in relation to the combination of at least 15 tonnes; and

  (b) if the test is taken on or after that date, it is capable of a speed of at least 80 kilometres per hour and—

    (i) in the case of a test for category C, it has a maximum authorised mass of at least 10 tonnes and an overall length of at least 7 metres;

    (ii) in the case of a test for category C plus E, it is either—

        (a) an articulated goods vehicle with a maximum authorised mass of at least 18 tonnes and an overall length of at least 12 metres, or

        (b) a combination of vehicles with a maximum authorised mass of at least 18 tonnes and an overall length of at least 12 metres comprising a vehicle in category C with a maximum authorised mass of at least 10 tonnes and an overall length of at least 7 metres and a trailer with an overall length of at least 4 metres.]

(4) Where a person submitting himself for a test provides a vehicle which does not comply with paragraph (1) or otherwise refuses or fails to comply with that paragraph the examiner may refuse to conduct the test.

(5) A person submitting himself for a test shall allow to travel in the vehicle—

  (a) the examiner; and

  (b) any person authorised by the Secretary of State to attend the test for the purpose of supervising it or otherwise. **[1746]**

NOTE

    Commencement: 1 April 1991.

    Para (1): words in square brackets inserted by SI 1992 No 3089, reg 5(a).

    Para (3): words in square brackets substituted by SI 1992 No 3089, reg 5(b); sub-paras (a)(i), (iv), (b)(i), (iv) revoked by SI 1992 No 3089, reg 5(c).

    Para (3A): inserted by SI 1992 No 3089, reg 5(d).

19. Persons who may conduct tests

(1) Tests may be conducted-

  (a) by examiners appointed for that purpose by the Secretary of State;

  (b) by examiners appointed for that purpose by the Secretary of State for Defence, insofar as concerns the testing of persons subject to the Naval Discipline Act 1957, to military law or to air force law, or of persons employed in the driving of motor vehicles for naval, military or air force purposes;

  (c) in England and Wales, by the chief officer of any fire brigade maintained in pursuance of the Fire Services Act 1947 or, in Scotland, by the fire-master of such a brigade, insofar as concerns the testing of members of any such brigade or of persons employed in the driving of motor vehicles for the purposes of any such brigade;

  (d) by any chief officer of police in so far as concerns the testing—

    (i) of members of a police force, or

> > (ii) of persons employed in the driving of motor vehicles for police purposes by a police authority, or by the Receiver for the Metropolitan Police District or by the Commissioner of Police for the Metropolis; and

> [(e) in the case of tests of competence to drive passenger-carrying vehicles, by an examiner—

> > (i) who is, or is employed by, the holder of a PSV operator's licence, and

> > (ii) who is authorised by the Secretary of State to conduct tests of persons employed or proposed to be employed in the course of the business conducted by virtue of that licence.]

(2) Any person authorised by virtue of paragraph 1(c) or (d) to conduct tests may, subject to the approval of the Secretary of State, authorise suitable persons to act as examiners of those who submit themselves for a test.

(3) ... **[1747]**

NOTES

Commencement: 1 April 1991 (except para (1)(e)), 5 August 1991 (para (1)(e)).
Para (1): sub-para (e) substituted by SI 1991 No 1541, reg 2.
Para (3): revoked by SI 1991 No 1541, reg 2.

20. Evidence of results of tests

(1) A person who passes a test shall be furnished with a certificate to that effect in the form (adapted as the case may require) set out in Part I of Schedule 6.

(2) A person who fails to pass a test shall be furnished with a statement to that effect in the form (adapted as the case may require) set out in Part II of Schedule 6. **[1748]**

NOTE

Commencement: 1 April 1991.

21. Repayment of fees

(1) The period of notice prescribed for the purposes of section 91(b) of the 1988 Act (repayment of test fee on giving prescribed period of notice) in respect of the fee for a test is notice of not less than five clear days (excluding Saturdays, Sundays, any bank holidays, Christmas Day or Good Friday) before the date of the appointment to the office of the Driving Standards Agency with whom the appointment was made.

(2) For the purposes of this regulation "bank holiday" means a day which is a bank holiday by or under the Banking and Financial Dealings Act 1971 either generally or in the locality in which is situated the office of the Driving Standards Agency to whom notice cancelling an appointment for a test falls to be given. **[1749]**

NOTE

Commencement: 1 April 1991.

22. Additional qualification

A person who has passed tests to drive vehicles of a class included in category

C plus E and a class included in category D shall be deemed for the purposes of the 1988 Act and of these Regulations competent to drive, in addition to vehicles of those classes also vehicles of the class included in category D plus E which corresponds to the said class included in category D.   **[1750]**

NOTE
    Commencement: 1 April 1991.

PART IV

SUPPLEMENTARY

23. Service personnel

The traffic commissioner for the South-Eastern and Metropolitan Traffic Area is hereby prescribed for the purposes of section 183(6) of the 1988 Act (discharge of Part IV functions in relation to HM Forces).   **[1751]**

NOTE
    Commencement: 1 April 1991.

24. Northern Ireland licences

(1) The traffic commissioner for the North Western Traffic Area is hereby prescribed for the purposes of section 122(2) of the 1988 Act (suspension, revocation and disqualification in respect of Northern Ireland licences as respects Great Britain).

(2) For the purposes of section 122(4) of the 1988 Act, the magistrates' court or sheriff to whom an appeal shall lie by the holder of a Northern Ireland licence, being a person who is not resident in Great Britain and who is aggrieved by the suspension or revocation of the licence or by the ordering of disqualification for holding or obtaining licence, shall be—

    (i) such a magistrates' court or sheriff as he may nominate at the time he puts down his appeal; or

    (ii) in the absence of a nomination of a particular court under sub-paragraph (i) above, the magistrates' court in whose area the office of the traffic commissioner for the North Western Traffic Area is situated.   **[1752]**

NOTE
    Commencement: 1 April 1991.

25. Entitlement to groups

The categories of vehicles specified in column (2) of the table in Schedule 1 are hereby designated as groups for the purposes of paragraphs (a) and (b) of section 89(1) of the 1988 Act.   **[1753]**

NOTE
    Commencement: 1 April 1991.

26. Transitional provisions

(1) If an application for the grant of a licence in respect of any of the classes of vehicle in column (1) of the table below is made and the licence has not been

granted or refused before the date that these Regulations come into force, the application shall be taken on and after that date to be an application in respect of the categories of vehicles in column (2) of the table below.

TABLE

(1) Class of Heavy Goods Vehicle	(2) Corresponding Category of Large Goods Vehicle
2, 3	C and C plus E limited to drawbar trailer combinations only
2A, 3A	C and C plus E limited to drawbar trailer combinations only and in both cases limited to vehicles with automatic transmission
1	C plus E
1A	C plus E limited to vehicles with automatic transmission

(1) Class of Public Service Vehicle	(2) Corresponding Category of Passenger-Carrying Vehicle
4	D limited to vehicles not more than 5.5 metres in length
4A	D limited to vehicles not more than 5.5 metres in length and with automatic transmission
4B	B
3	D
3A	D limited to vehicles with automatic transmission
1,2	D plus E
1A, 2A	D plus E limited to vehicles with automatic transmission

(2) If an application for a test in respect of any of the classes of vehicles in column (1) of the table below is made and the test has not been taken before the date that these Regulations come into force, the application shall be taken on and after that date to be an application in respect of the categories of vehicles in column (2) of the table below—

TABLE

(1) Class of Heavy Goods Vehicle	(2) Corresponding Category of Large Goods Vehicle
2, 3	C
2A, 3A	C limited to vehicles with automatic transmission
1	C plus E
1A	C plus E limited to vehicles with automatic transmission

(1)	(2)
Class of Public Service Vehicle	**Corresponding Category of Passenger-Carrying Vehicle**
4	D limited to vehicles with no more than sixteen seats
4A	As for 4 but limited to vehicles with automatic transmission
3, 2, 1	D
3A, 2A, 1A	As for 3, 2, 1 but limited to vehicles with automatic transmission

[1754]

NOTE
    Commencement: 1 April 1991.

27. Exemptions

(1) Part IV of the 1988 Act and these Regulations shall not apply to large goods vehicles of any of the following classes, that is to say—

    (a) track laying vehicles;

    (b) vehicles propelled by steam;

    (c) road rollers;

    (d) road construction vehicles used or kept on the road solely for the conveyance of built-in road construction machinery (with or without articles or materials used for the purpose of that machinery);

    (e) engineering plant;

    (f) works trucks;

    (g) industrial tractors;

    (h) agricultural motor vehicles;

    (i) digging machines;

    (j) vehicles exempted from excise duty by virtue of section 7(1) of the Vehicles (Excise) Act 1971 (vehicles used for less than a certain distance on public roads);

    (k) any motor car as defined in section 185(1) of the 1988 Act which is so constructed that a trailer designed to carry goods may by partial superimposition be attached thereto in such a manner as to cause a substantial part of the weight of the trailer to be borne thereby, but to which no trailer is attached;

    (l) vehicles used for no other purpose than the haulage of lifeboats and the conveyance of the necessary gear of the lifeboats which are being hauled;

    (m) vehicles manufactured before 1st January 1960 used unladen and not drawing a laden trailer;

    (n) vehicles in the service of a visiting force or headquarters as defined in the Visiting Forces and International Headquarters (Application of Law) Order 1965;

    (o) wheeled armoured vehicles being the property of, or for the time being under the control of, the Secretary of State for Defence;

    (p) any vehicle driven by a constable for the purpose of removing or avoiding obstruction to other road users or other members of the public, for the purpose of protecting life or property (including the large goods vehicle and its load) or for other similar purposes;

    (q) any articulated goods vehicle combination which has a maximum authorised mass not exceeding 7.5 tonnes, or the tractive unit of which does not exceed 2.05 tonnes unladen weight;

(r) any vehicle having a relevant maximum weight not exceeding 3.5 tonnes to which a trailer is attached, not being an articulated goods vehicle combination;

(s) any vehicle (not being an articulated goods vehicle combination) which—

    (i) has an unladen weight not exceeding 10.2 tonnes,

    (ii) is being operated by the holder of a PSV operator's licence,

    (iii) is being driven by a person who holds an existing public service vehicle licence or a passenger-carrying vehicle driver's licence, and

    (iv) is being used for the purpose of—

        (a) proceeding to, or returning from, a place where assistance is to be, or has been, given to a disabled passenger-carrying vehicle; or

        (b) giving assistance to or moving a disabled passenger-carrying vehicle or moving a wreck which, immediately before it became a wreck, was a passenger-carrying vehicle;

(t) any vehicle fitted with apparatus designed for raising a disabled vehicle partly from the ground and for drawing a disabled vehicle when so raised (whether by partial superimposition or otherwise) being a vehicle which—

    (i) is used solely for dealing with disabled vehicles;

    (ii) is not used for the conveyance of any load other than a disabled vehicle when so raised, water, fuel and accumulators and articles required for the operation of, or in connection with, such apparatus as aforesaid or otherwise for dealing with disabled vehicles; and

    (iii) has an unladen weight not exceeding 3.05 tonnes;

(u) any vehicle which was originally constructed to carry passengers but has been adapted to carry goods or burden of any description—

    (i) when driven for the carriage of—

        (a) play equipment for children, or such equipment and not more than 8 passengers, to or from the place where the equipment is to be, or has been, made available for such use, or

        (b) articles required for the purposes of the display or of an exhibition, or such articles and not more than 8 passengers, to or from the place where the display or exhibition is to be mounted, or

    (ii) being a vehicle used for the carriage of such equipment or articles as specified in sub-paragraph (i) above, when driven—

        (a) to or from the place where a mechanical defect in the vehicle is to be, or has been remedied, or

        (b) in such circumstances that by virtue of section 5 of the Vehicles (Excise) Act 1971 the vehicle is not chargeable with duty in respect of of its use on public roads;

(v) vehicles which are designed for fire fighting or fire salvage purposes and which are the property of, or for the time being under the control of, the Secretary of State for Defence, when being driven by a member of the armed forces of the Crown; and

(w) any vehicle when being driven by a member of the armed forces of the Crown in the course of urgent work of national importance with an order of the Defence Council in pursuance of the Defence (Armed Forces) Regulations 1939 which were continued permanently in force, in the form set out in Part C of Schedule 2 to the Emergency Laws (Repeal) Act, 1959, by section 2 of the Emergency Powers Act 1964.

(2) Part IV of the 1988 Act and these Regulations shall not apply to passenger-carrying vehicles of any of the following classes, that is to say—

    (a) vehicles manufactured more than 30 years ago and not used for hire or reward or for the carriage of more than 8 passengers;

    (b) any vehicle driven by a constable for the purpose of removing or avoiding obstruction to other road users or other members of the public, for the purpose of protecting life or property (including the passenger-carrying vehicle and its passengers) or for other similar purposes.

(3) A person may drive a large goods vehicle specified in paragraph (1) if he is the holder of a full licence to drive vehicles in category B and C1, and a passenger-carrying vehicle specified in paragraph (2) if he is the holder of a full licence to drive vehicles in category B and D1.

(4) Except in the case of a vehicle mentioned in paragraph (5), Part IV of the 1988 Act and these Regulations, in their application to large goods vehicles, shall not apply to vehicles which are passenger-carrying vehicles as well as large goods vehicles.

(5) Part IV of the 1988 Act and these Regulations, in their application to passenger-carrying vehicles, shall not apply to large goods vehicles in category C driven by members of the armed forces of the Crown and used for the carriage of passengers for naval, military or air force purposes which are adapted to carry up to 24 passengers.

(6) In this Regulation—

    "digging machine" has the same meaning as in Schedule 3 to the Vehicles (Excise) Act 1971;

    "agricultural motor vehicle", "engineering plant", "industrial tractor", "track laying" and "works truck" have the same meaning as in regulation 3(2) of the Motor Vehicles (Construction and Use) Regulations 1986;

    "play equipment for children" includes articles required in connection with the use of such equipment by children; and

    "road construction vehicle" and "road construction machinery" have the same meanings as in section 4(2) of the Vehicles (Excise) Act 1971.

[1755]

NOTE

    Commencement: 1 April 1991.

---

28. Effect of the change in classification on entitlement to drive large buses

(1) A person who held a full licence to drive vehicles in category B and D1 on 31st May 1990, who satisfies the Secretary of State that he has been regularly driving a vehicle or vehicles in Category D with more than 16 seats in addition to the driver's seat during the period of three years immediately preceding his application for a licence to drive such vehicles and who makes such application before [1st October 1992] shall, notwithstanding anything in regulation 17 as it applies to section 89 of the 1988 Act, be entitled, on satisfying the other requirements of the 1988 Act and these Regulations, to the grant of a full licence

to drive vehicles in that category subject to the limitation that the vehicles are not used for hire or reward.

(2) A person who holds a full hgv driver's licence or a full licence to drive vehicles in category C, may also drive motor vehicles used for the carriage of passengers with more than 16 seats, in addition to the driver's seat which are not being used for hire or reward or for the carriage of more than 8 passengers.

[1756]

NOTES
Commencement: 1 April 1991.
Para (1): words in square brackets substituted by SI 1992 No 538.

29. Effect of the change in classification on the granting of licences to drive minibuses

A person who has taken the test prescribed by these Regulations for vehicles in category D (which includes vehicles with not more than 16 seats, in addition to the driver's seat, used for hire or reward) in a vehicle in that category of which the overall length—

    (a) in the case of a test taken before 1st April 1994 is less than 8.5 metres and

    (b) in the case of a test taken on or after that date is less than 9 metres,

shall be granted a licence limited to the driving of vehicles in that category with not more than 16 seats, in addition to the driver's seat.   **[1757]**

NOTE
Commencement: 1 April 1991.

SCHEDULE 1
Regulations 2(2), 25

CATEGORIES OF VEHICLES

(1)	(2)
C	Motor vehicles used for the carriage of goods and whose maximum authorised mass exceeds 3.5 tonnes including such a vehicle drawing a trailer with a maximum authorised mass not exceeding [, in the case of a trailer with a single axle, 5 tonnes or, in the case of any other trailer, 750 kg] but not including any vehicle in category C1.
D	Motor vehicles used for the carriage of passengers with more than eight seats in addition to the driver's seat including such a vehicle drawing a trailer with a maximum authorised mass not exceeding [, in the case of a trailer with a single axle, 5 tonnes or, in the case of any other trailer, 750 kg] but not including any vehicle in category D1.
C plus E	Combinations of motor vehicles in category C and a trailer with a maximum authorised mass exceeding [, in the case of a trailer with a single axle, 5 tonnes or, in the case of any other trailer, 750 kg].
D plus E	Combinations of motor vehicles in category D and a trailer with a maximum authorised mass exceeding [, in the case of a trailer with a single axle, 5 tonnes or, in the case of any other trailer, 750 kg].

[1758]

NOTE
Commencement: 1 April 1991.
Amended by SI 1992 No 3089, reg 6.

SCHEDULE 2

Regulation 8

TABLE OF CORRESPONDENCES

PART I

(1) **Class of heavy goods vehicle**	(2) **Category of large goods vehicle**
1	C, C plus E
1A	As for 1 but limited to vehicles with automatic transmission
2	C, C plus E limited to drawbar trailer combinations only
2A	As for 2 but limited to vehicles with automatic transmission
3	As for 2
3A	As for 2A

PART II

(1) **Class of public service vehicle vehicle**	(2) **Category of passenger-carrying vehicle**
1	D, D plus E
1A	As for 1 but limited to vehicles with automatic transmission
2	As for 1
2A	As for 1 but limited to vehicles with automatic transmission
3	D
3A	As for 3 but limited to vehicles with automatic transmission
4	D limited to vehicles of not more than 5.5 metres in length
4A	As for 4 but limited to vehicles with automatic transmission
4B	B

[1759]

NOTE
    Commencement: 1 April 1991.

[SCHEDULE 3

Regulations 9, 11(3)

FEES FOR LICENCES

Description of Licence	*Fee*
(1) A full licence for any category not being a licence falling in paragraph (2) or (3) below or a licence granted in exchange for a provisional licence (including a licence which is so treated under section 98 of the 1988 Act).	£21
(2) The first full licence for any category, not being a licence falling in paragraph (3) below, granted to a person following the expiration of a period of disqualification imposed on him for holding or obtaining a full licence except where his previous such licence was revoked and, but for	£12

Description of Licence	Fee

its revocation, would have expired before or within 3 months after the date of his current application for a licence.

(3) The first full licence for any category granted to a person after he has passed a driving test which he was ordered to take under section 117 of the 1988 Act except where his previous full licence was revoked and, but for its revocation, would have expired before or within 3 months after the date of his current application for a licence. — £6

(4) A provisional licence not being a licence falling in paragraph (5) below. — £21

(5) The first provisional licence granted to a person after he has been ordered to take a driving test under section 117 of the 1988 Act. — £12

(6) A full lgv trainee driver's licence for category C or an lgv trainee driver's provisional licence for category C plus E granted to the holder of an hgv trainee driver's full licence to drive heavy goods vehicles of class 2 or 3. — £6]

[1760]

NOTE
Commencement: 1 February 1992.
This Schedule was substituted by SI 1991 No 2492.

SCHEDULE 4

Regulations 10(3)(b), 11(4)(b)

FORMS A AND B

(This Schedule contains diagrams of distinguishing marks to be displayed on vehicles driven under a provisional licence.) **[1760A]**

NOTE
Commencement: 1 April 1991.

SCHEDULE 5

Regulation 17

NATURE OF TESTS - OPERATIONS

A. Start the engine of the vehicle.

B. Move off straight ahead and at an angle.

C. Maintain a proper position in relation to a vehicle immediately in front.

D. Overtake and take an appropriate course in relation to other vehicles.

E. Turn right and left.

F. Make an emergency stop.

G. (1) In the case of a test conducted off the highway, drive the vehicle forwards and backwards and whilst driving the vehicle backwards steer the vehicle along a predetermined course to make it enter a narrow opening and to bring it to rest in a predetermined position; or

(2) In the case of a test conducted on the highway, drive the vehicle backwards and whilst doing so cause it to enter a narrow opening to the left or to the right and then bring it to rest in a predetermined position.

H. Indicate his intended actions by appropriate signals at appropriate times in a clear and unmistakeable manner.

I. Act correctly and promptly in response to all signals given by any traffic sign and by any person lawfully directing traffic and any other person using the road.

[1761]

NOTE
  Commencement: 1 April 1991.

SCHEDULE 6

Regulation 20

EVIDENCE OF RESULTS OF TESTS

PART I

FORM OF CERTIFICATE OF PASSING A TEST OF COMPETENCE TO DRIVE
A LARGE GOODS VEHICLE OR PASSENGER-CARRYING VEHICLE

ROAD TRAFFIC ACT 1988
MOTOR VEHICLES (DRIVING LICENCES) (LARGE GOODS AND PASSEN-
GER-CARRYING VEHICLES) REGULATIONS 1990

Pass Certificate

I certify that (name of person passing the test) ....
address etc ....
....
has been examined and has passed the test of competence to drive a vehicle of category
.... with/without automatic transmission/whilst drawing a trailer (Delete if
inapplicable) as prescribed for the purposes of section 89 of the Road Traffic Act 1988
on (date) ....

Signed ....
Examiner conducting the test pursuant to Regulation 19(1) of the above mentioned Regulations.

Signed ....

Applicant (who is to sign here immediately after the examiner has signed and in his
presence).

If the test has been conducted by an examiner referred to in regulation 19(1)(e) the
name of the holder of the PSV operator's licence by whom the applicant is employed or
proposed to be employed should be stated below.

[PART II

FORM OF STATEMENT OF FAILURE TO PASS A TEST OF COMPETENCE TO DRIVE A LARGE GOODS VEHICLE OR PASSENGER-CARRYING VEHICLE

ROAD TRAFFIC ACT 1988
MOTOR VEHICLES (DRIVING LICENCES) (LARGE GOODS AND PASSEN-GER-CARRYING VEHICLES) REGULATIONS 1990

Statement of Failure

Name ....

has been examined on a vehicle of category .... with/without automatic transmission/whilst drawing a trailer* and has failed to pass the test of competence to drive prescribed for the purposes of section 89 of the Road Traffic Act 1988 on (date) ....

Signed ....

Examiner conducting the test pursuant to Regulation 19(1) of the above mentioned Regulations.

If the test has been conducted by an examiner referred to in regulation 19(1)(e) the name of the holder of the PSV operator's licence by whom the applicant is employed or proposed to be employed should be stated below. **[1762]**

* Delete if inapplicable]

NOTE
    Commencement: 1 April 1991.
    Part II: substituted by SI 1992 No 3089, reg 7, Sch 7.

MOTOR VEHICLES (WEARING OF SEAT BELTS IN REAR SEATS BY ADULTS) REGULATIONS 1991
(SI 1991 No 1255)

NOTES
    Made: 23 May 1991.
    Commencement: 1 July 1991.
    Authority: Road Traffic Act 1988, s 14(1), (2).

1. Citation and commencement

These Regulations may be cited as the Motor Vehicles (Wearing of Seat Belts in Rear Seats by Adults) Regulations 1991 and shall come into force on 1st July 1991. **[1763]**

NOTE
Commencement: 1 July 1991.

2. General interpretation

(1) In these Regulations—

"adult seat belt" means—

(a) a three-point belt, or
(b) a lap belt,

which has been marked in accordance with regulation 47(7) of the Construction and Use Regulations;

"child restraint" means a seat belt or any other description of restraining device for the use of a young person—

(a) which is designed either to be fitted directly to a suitable anchorage or to be used in conjunction with an adult seat belt and held in place by the restraining action of that belt; and
(b) which has been marked in accordance with regulation 47(7) of the Construction and Use Regulations;

and any reference to wearing a child restraint is to be construed accordingly;

"Construction and Use Regulations" means the Road Vehicles (Construction and Use) Regulations 1986;

"medical certificate", in relation to a person, means a valid certificate signed by a medical practitioner to the effect that it is inadvisable on medical grounds for that person to wear a seat belt;

"rear seat" in relation to a vehicle means a seat not being the driver's seat, a seat alongside the driver's seat or a specified passenger seat;

"trade licence" has the same meaning as in section 38(1) of the Vehicles (Excise) Act 1971;

"disabled person's belt", "lap belt", "seat", "specified passenger seat" and "three point belt" have the meanings given by regulation 47(8) of the Construction and Use Regulations.

(2) Without prejudice to section 17 of the Interpretation Act 1978, a reference to a provision of the Construction and Use Regulations is a reference to that provision as from time to time amended or as from time to time re-enacted with or without modification.

(3) For the purposes of these Regulations, a child restraint is appropriate, in relation to a child under the age of 14 years, if it is a child restraint appropriate to the weight of the child in accordance with the indication of weight shown on the marking required under regulation 47(7) of the Construction and Use Regulations.   **[1764]**

NOTE
Commencement: 1 July 1991.

3. Application

These Regulations apply to every motor car which is not constructed or adapted to carry more than 8 passengers in addition to the driver.   **[1765]**

NOTE
Commencement: 1 July 1991.

4. Requirement for adults to wear seat belts

Subject to the following provisions of these Regulations, every person shall wear an adult seat belt if he is aged 14 years or more and riding in the rear of a motor car to which these Regulations apply. **[1766]**

NOTE
 Commencement: 1 July 1991.

5. Exemptions

(1) The requirements of regulation 4 shall not apply to—
  (a) a person holding a medical certificate;
  (b) a person using a vehicle constructed or adapted for the delivery of goods or mail to consumers or addressees, as the case may be, while engaged in making local rounds of deliveries or collections;
  (c) a constable protecting or escorting another person;
  (d) a person who is not a constable but is protecting or escorting another person by virtue of powers the same as or similar to those of a constable for that purpose;
  (e) a person in the service of a fire brigade and who is donning operational clothing or equipment;
  (f) a person riding in a vehicle, being used under a trade licence, for the purpose of investigating or remedying a mechanical fault in the vehicle;
  (g) a disabled person who is wearing a disabled person's belt; or
  (h) a person riding in a vehicle which is taking part in a procession organised by or on behalf of the Crown.

(2) Without prejudice to paragraph (1)(h) above, the requirements of regulation 4 do not apply to a person riding in a vehicle which is taking part in a procession held to mark or commemorate an event if either—
  (a) the procession is one commonly or customarily held in the police area or areas in which it is being held, or
  (b) notice in respect of the procession was given in accordance with section 11 of the Public Order Act 1986.

(3) The requirements of regulation 4 do not apply to a person riding in a vehicle if no adult seat belt is available for him. **[1767]**

NOTE
 Commencement: 1 July 1991.

6. Interpretation of reference to availability

(1) An adult seat belt shall not be regarded as being available for a person for the purposes of regulation 5(3) unless such a belt is regarded as available to him by virtue of paragraph (2) below.

(2) Subject to paragraph (5) below, if any rear seat in a vehicle is provided with an adult seat belt, that belt ("the relevant belt") shall be regarded as available for a particular person ("the person in question") for the purposes of regulation 5(3) unless—
  (a) another person is wearing the relevant belt;
  (b) a child under the age of 14 is occupying the seat and wearing a child restraint which is an appropriate child restraint for that child;

    (c) another person, being a person holding a medical certificate, is occupying the seat;

    (d) a disabled person (not being the person in question) is occupying the seat and wearing a disabled person's belt;

    (e) by reason of his disability, it would not be practicable for the person in question to wear the relevant belt;

    (f) the person in question is prevented from occupying the seat by the presence of a carry cot which is restrained by straps and in which there is a child aged under 1 year;

    (g) the person in question is prevented from occupying the seat by the presence of a child restraint which could not readily be removed without the aid of tools; or

    (h) in the case of a seat that is specially designed so that—

        (i) its configuration can be adjusted in order to increase the space in the vehicle available for goods or personal effects, and

        (ii) when it is so adjusted the seat cannot be used as such,

    the configuration is adjusted in the manner described in sub-paragraph (i) and it would not be reasonably practicable for the goods and personal effects being carried in the vehicle to be so carried were the configuration not so adjusted.

(3) Paragraph (2)(b) or (d) above shall not apply unless the presence of the other person renders it impracticable for the person in question to wear the relevant belt.

(4) Paragraph (2)(f) above shall not apply if it would be reasonably practicable for the carry cot to be carried in any other part of the vehicle where it could be restrained by straps so as to render it practicable for the person in question to wear the relevant belt.

(5) A seat belt shall not be regarded as available for any person for the purposes of regulation 5(3) if—

    (a) it has an inertia reel mechanism which is locked as a result of the vehicle being, or having been, on a steep incline, or

    (b) it does not comply with the requirements of regulation 48 of the Construction and Use Regulations.

(6) A seat belt shall be regarded as provided for a seat for the purposes of this regulation if it is fixed in such a position that it can be worn by an occupier of that seat. **[1768]**

NOTE
  Commencement: 1 July 1991.

RETENTION OF REGISTRATION MARKS REGULATIONS 1992
(SI 1992 No 510)

NOTES
  Made: 6 March 1992.
  Commencement: 1 April 1992.
  Authority: Finance Act 1989, s 11.

1. Citation, commencement and interpretation

These Regulations may be cited as the Retention of Registration Marks Regulations 1992 and shall come into force on 1st April 1992. **[1769]**

NOTE
Commencement: 1 April 1992.

2.—(1) In these Regulations—

"the 1971 Act" means the Vehicles (Excise) Act 1971;

"the 1988 Act" means the Road Traffic Act 1988;

"duplicate retention document" means a copy of a retention document issued under regulation 8;

"G.B. records" means the records kept under the 1971 Act, on behalf of the Secretary of State, by the Driver and Vehicle Licensing Agency and does not include any records kept under that Act, on behalf of the Secretary of State, by a Northern Ireland department;

"grantee" in relation to a right of retention, means the person to whom the right is granted;

"right of retention" means such a right as is mentioned in regulation 3(1);

"retention document" shall be construed in accordance with regulation 7.

(2) In these Regulations unless the context otherwise requires—

    (a) any reference to a numbered regulation is a reference to the regulation bearing that number in the Regulations; and

    (b) any reference to a numbered paragraph is a reference to paragraph bearing that number in the regulation in which the reference occurs.

[1770]

NOTE
Commencement: 1 April 1992.

3. Rights of retention

(1) Subject to the following provisions of these Regulations, a person in whose name a vehicle is registered may be granted by the Secretary of State a right, exercisable on a single occasion falling within the period mentioned in paragraph (2), to have the registration mark for the time being assigned to the vehicle assigned to some other vehicle, being a vehicle registered—

    (a) in that person's name; or

    (b) in the name of some other person nominated by him in the application for the grant of the right.

(2) The period referred to in paragraph (1) is—

    (a) within one year from the date of the grant of the right; or

    (b) within such further period if the Secretary of State thinks fit in the circumstances of any particular case.

(3) This regulation applies only to vehicles which are recorded as being registered vehicles in the G.B. records. **[1771]**

NOTE
Commencement: 1 April 1992.

4. Application for the grant of a right of retention

An application for the grant of a right of retention shall be made in writing to the Secretary of State and shall be accompanied by—

    (a) the registration document issued under the 1971 Act in respect of the vehicle to which the registration mark is for the time being assigned (in this paragraph referred to as "the vehicle"); and

    (b) a vehicle licence for the time being in force issued in respect of the vehicle under the 1971 Act or a valid application for such a licence.

[1772]

NOTE
Commencement: 1 April 1992.

5. The fee on the making of an application shall be £25 and may be retained by the Secretary of State whether or not the application is granted. **[1773]**

NOTE
Commencement: 1 April 1992.

6. The applicant shall, if required to do so by the Secretary of State, make available the vehicle to which the registration mark is for the time being assigned for inspection at a place designated by the Secretary of State. **[1774]**

NOTE
Commencement: 1 April 1992.

7. Retention document

If the Secretary of State grants a right of retention, he shall issue to the applicant a document ("a retention document") which—

    (a) records the date of the grant;

    (b) records the end of the period during which the right is exercisable by virtue of regulation 3(1);

    (c) records the name of the applicant and where applicable, his nominee;

    (d) records the registration mark in question; and

    (e) identifies the type of vehicle to which the registration mark was assigned at the time of the grant. **[1775]**

NOTE
Commencement: 1 April 1992.

8. Issue of duplicate retention documents

(1) If the grantee notifies the Secretary of State that a retention document has been lost or destroyed, the Secretary of State, upon being satisfied that the retention document has been lost or destroyed, shall issue a copy of the retention document marked as a duplicate.

(2) In any case where a duplicate of a lost retention document has been issued and the lost retention document subsequently comes into the possession of the grantee he shall forthwith return it to the Secretary of State.

(3) If a retention document becomes defaced or illegible, the grantee may return it to the Secretary of State so that the Secretary of State may issue a copy of the retention document marked as a duplicate. **[1776]**

NOTE
    Commencement: 1 April 1992.

9. Refusal of an application for a grant of a right of retention

The Secretary of State may refuse an application for the grant of a right of retention on such grounds as he thinks fit.   **[1777]**

NOTE
    Commencement: 1 April 1992.

10. Exercise of a right of retention

(1) A right of retention shall be exercisable by means of the presentation by the grantee to the Secretary of State of—

    (a) the retention document or a duplicate retention document; and

    (b) the registration document issued under the 1971 Act in respect of the vehicle to which the grantee proposes that the registration mark be assigned, being a vehicle registered in the name of the grantee or his nominee as recorded in the retention document.   **[1778]**

NOTE
    Commencement: 1 April 1992.

11. Non-transferability of right of retention

A right of retention shall be non-transferable but without prejudice to the vesting of any such right in a person by operation of law.   **[1779]**

NOTE
    Commencement: 1 April 1992.

12. Conditions for the assignment of a registration mark

(1) A registration mark may not be assigned to a vehicle in pursuance of a right of retention unless the conditions specified in paragraph (2) are satisfied.

    (2) The conditions are—

    (a) where the registered number in a registration mark contains a single letter of the alphabet, that the assignment of that mark to a vehicle would not give an indication that the vehicle was first registered more recently than is the case;

    (b) that a vehicle licence issued under the 1971 Act is in force for the vehicle;

    (c) that the vehicle is—

        (i) one to which section 47 of the 1988 Act applies, or would apply if the vehicle had been registered under the 1971 Act more than three years earlier; or

        (ii) of a class to which regulations under section 49 of the 1988 Act applies;

    (d) that the Secretary of State is satisfied as to the origins of the vehicle and the date on which it was first used; and

    (e) that the vehicle is recorded as being a registered vehicle in the G.B. records.

    (3) For the purpose of determining whether a vehicle falls within sub-paragraph (2)(c)(i), the Motor Vehicles (Tests) Regulations 1981 shall have

effect as if sub-paragraph (xvi) of regulation 6(1) of those Regulations (which relates amongst other things to test certificates issued in respect of a vehicle under the law of Northern Ireland) were omitted.

(4) In this regulation, "registered number" has the same meaning as in regulation 9 of the Road Vehicles (Registration and Licensing) Regulations 1971. **[1780]**

NOTE
Commencement: 1 April 1992.

13. Revocation of right of retention

The Secretary of State may revoke a right of retention if it appears to him that there are special reasons for doing so. **[1781]**

NOTE
Commencement: 1 April 1992.

14. Payment of charge upon an assignment

In respect of any assignment of a registration mark in pursuance of a right of retention, the charge as is for the time being prescribed by virtue of section 12(1) of the Finance Act 1976 shall be payable. **[1782]**

NOTE
Commencement: 1 April 1992.

LONDON PRIORITY ROUTE ORDER 1992
(SI 1992 No 1372)

NOTES
Made: 10 June 1992
Commencement: 2 July 1992
Authority: Road Traffic Act 1991, s 50(1)

1. This Order may be cited as the London Priority Route Order 1992 and shall come into force on 2nd July 1992. **[1783]**

NOTE
Commencement: 2 July 1992.

2. The following roads are designated as priority routes for the purposes of Part II of the Road Traffic Act 1991—

    (a) the roads specified in the Schedule to this Order; and
    (b) every slip road (not falling within sub-paragraph (a) above) which links a road mentioned in any paragraph of the Schedule to this Order with a road mentioned in any other paragraph of that Schedule in the vicinity of the place where the two roads join or cross. **[1784]**

NOTE
Commencement: 2 July 1992.

3. In the Schedule to this Order the description of a road shall be read as including the area of any intersection between the road and any road which crosses it at the same level.   **[1785]**

NOTE
    Commencement: 2 July 1992.

4. Where a paragraph of the Schedule to this Order contains a description of a road followed by a reference to the inclusion of one or more particular roads (for example paragraph 2) the reference to the inclusion of the one or more particular roads shall be treated as having been inserted for the avoidance of doubt and as being without prejudice to the generality of the preceding description.   **[1786]**

NOTE
    Commencement: 2 July 1992.

THE SCHEDULE

Regulation 2

'A' Roads (in numerical order)

1. A1 from where it crosses the boundary of London to the south-east side of its junction with Wakley Street including the road shown stippled on plan 2 in Part II of the Schedule to the Metropolitan Roads Trunking Order 1986 (which roads comprise the Archway Interchange).

2. A2 from the boundary of London to its junction with Borough High Street (A3) excluding Rochester Way from its junction with Kidbrooke Way to its junction with Riefield Road but including—

    (a) Amersham Road from its junction with New Cross Road to the south side of its junction with Parkfield Road;

    (b) Lewisham Way from its junction with New Cross Road to the south-east side of its junction with Parkfield Road;

    (c) Parkfield Road; and

    (d) Rochester Way Relief Road.

3. A3 Kingston By-Pass from the boundary of London to its junction with St George's Road (A302) and New Kent Road (A201) including—

    (a) Elephant and Castle from its junction with Newington Butts to its junction with Elephant and Castle roundabout; and

    (b) Newington Butts.

4. A3 from the south-west side of its junction with Marshalsea Road (A3201) and Great Dover Street (A2) to its junction with Cannon Street (A4) and Eastcheap (A100).

5. A4 from the boundary of London to the north-east side of its junctions with Park Lane including—

    (a) Duke of Wellington Place;

    (b) Grosvenor Place from its junction with Hyde Park Corner to the south-east side of its junction with Duke of Wellington Place; and

    (c) Hyde Park Corner.

6. A5 from the north-west side of its junction with St John's Wood Road (A5205) to its junction with Marble Arch (A40).

7. A10 from the boundary of London to its junction with Bishopsgate (A1213 section) including—

    (a) Evering Road;

    (b) Manse Road;

(c) Northwold Road from its junction with Stoke Newington High Street and Stamford Hill to its junction with Rectory Road; and

(d) Rectory Road from its junction with Northwold Road to the south side of its junction with Manse Road.

8. A11 from the Green Man Roundabout, Leytonstone to its junction with Middlesex Street (A1210) including—

(a) Braham Street;

(b) Mansell Street from its junction with Aldgate High Street and Whitechapel High Street to the south side of its junction with Braham Street;

(c) Whitechapel High Street; and

(d) the unnamed street from its junction with Whitechapel High Street to its junction with Braham Street and Commercial Road (A13).

9. A12 from the boundary of London to its junction with A11 at Green Man Roundabout, Leytonstone.

10. A13 from the boundary of London a few yards to the south of its junction with Ingrebourne Road to its junction with Braham Street (A11).

11. A20 from the boundary of London to its junctions with Lewisham Way (A2) and Amersham Road (A2) including—

(a) Amersham Road from its junction with Lewisham Way to the south side of its junction with Parkfield Road (A2); and

(b) Lewisham Way from its junction with Loampit Hill to the south-west side of its junction with Parkfield Road (A2).

12. A21 from the boundary of London to its junction with Rushey Green and Sangley Road (A205).

13. A21 from its junction with Rushey Green and Brownhill Road (A205) to its junction with Lewisham High Street (A20 section) and Lee High Road (A20).

14. A23 from the boundary of London to the south-east side of its junction with Kennington Park Road (A3) including—

(a) Banstead Road;

(b) Foxley Lane from the north-west side of its junction with Banstead Road to its junctions with Purley Way;

(c) Purley Road from its junction with Banstead Road to the south-east side of its junction with Russell Hill Parade;

(d) Purley Way; and

(e) Russell Hill Parade.

15. A23 from the north-west side of its junction with Kennington Park Road (A3) to its junction with Kennington Lane (A3204).

16. A24 from the boundary of London to its junction with Long Road and Clapham High Street (A3) including—

(a) Christchurch Road from the south side of its junction with Merantun Way to its junction with Merton High Street;

(b) Crown Lane from the west side of its junction with Crown Road to its junction with London Road;

(c) Crown Road;

(d) Merton High Street from the south-west side of its junction with Priory Road to its junction with Colliers Wood; and

(e) Priory Road.

17. A30 from where it crosses the boundary of London to its junction with Bath Road and Great West Road (A4).

18. A40 from the boundary of London to its junction with Westway (A40(M)).

19. A40 intersection at Marble Arch from the west side of its junction with Bayswater Road (A40) to the east side of its junction with Oxford Street (A40) comprising—

(a) Cumberland Gate;

(b) Marble Arch;

(c) Oxford Street from its junction with Marble Arch to the east side of its junction with Park Lane (A4202); and

(d) Park Lane from its junction with Oxford Street to the south-east side of its junction with Cumberland Gate.

20. A41 from the boundary of London to its junction with Barnet Way and Watford Way (A1).

21. A41 from its junction with Watford Way and Great North Way (A1) to its junctions with Marylebone Road (A501) including—

(a) Baker Street from its junction with Park Road to its junction with Marylebone Road (A501);

(b) Dorset Square (east side only);

(c) Gloucester Place from its junctions with Park Road to the north side of its junction with Dorset Square;

(d) Gloucester Place from the south side of its junction with Dorset Square to its junction with Marylebone Road (A501); and

(e) Park Road.

22. A100 Eastcheap from its junction with King William Street (A3) to the east side of its junction with Gracechurch Street (A1213).

23. A100 from the west side of its junction with Minories (A1211) to its junction with Great Dover Street and Old Kent Road (A2).

24. A101 from its junction with Jamaica Road and Lower Road (A200) to its junction with Branch Road (A1203).

25. A102 from its junction with Lower Clapton Road (A107) to its junction with East Cross Route (A 102(M)).

26. A 102 from its junction with East Cross Route (A102(M)) to its junction with Blackwall Tunnel Southern Approach (A102(M)) including—

(a) Brunswick Road;

(b) Hamelin Street:

(c) Robin Hood Lane;

(d) St Leonard's Road: and

(e) the unnamed slip road south-east of East India Dock Road (A13).

27. A105 from the north-west side of its junction with Westbury Avenue (A1080) to its junction with Seven Sisters Road (A503).

28. A106 from its junction with Leytonstone High Road (A11) to the east side of its junction with East Cross Route (A102(M)) including—

(a) Alexandra Road;

(b) Francis Road from the north-west side of its junction with Warren Road to its junction with Grove Green Road:

(c) Grove Green Road:

(d) Ruckholt Road:

(e) Warren Road: and

(f) York Road from the north-west side of its junction with Ruckholt Road and Warren Road to the south-east side of its junction with Alexandra Road.

29. A107 from its junction with Stamford Hill (A10) to its junction with Urswick Road (A102).

30. A109 from the west side of its junction with Boreham Road (A1080) to the east side of its junction with The Roundway (Al 080) and Downhills Way (B155).

31. A112 from its junction with Stratford High Street and Broadway (A11) to its junction with The Grove (A11).

32. A17 from its junction with Newham Way (A13) to Woolwich Ferry.

33. A126 from its junction with The Highway (A1203) to Commercial Road (A13).

34. A127 from its junction with M25 Motorway to its junction with Eastern Avenue East and Colchester Road (A12).

35. A200 from its junction with Tower Bridge Road (A100) to the south-east side of its junction with Rotherhithe Tunnel Approach (A101).

36. A201 from its junction with Pentonville Road (A501) to the south side of its junction with Acton Street.

37. A201 from its junction with Elephant and Castle and Newington Causeway (A3) to its junction with Great Dover Street and Old Kent Road (A2).

38. A202 from its junctions with New Cross Road (A2) to its junctions with Victoria Street (A302) including—

    (a) Besson Street;
    (b) Kender Street;
    (c) Neathouse Place;
    (d) Queens Road; and
    (e) Wilton Road from its junction with Victoria Street (A302) to the south-east side of its junction with Neathouse Place.

39. A203 from its junctions with Brixton Road (A23) to its junction with A202 at Vauxhall Cross including—

    (a) Stockwell Park Walk; and
    (b) Stockwell Road.

40. A204 from its junction with Brixton Hill and Brixton Road (A23) to the south side of its junction with Matthews Road.

41. A205 Clapham Common West Side from its junction with Battersea Rise and Clapham Common North Side (A3) to its junction with The Avenue (A205).

42. A205 from its junction with Great West Road (A4) to its junction with West Hill (A3).

43. A205 from its junction with Clapham Common North Side (A3) to its junction with Woolwich Church Street and High Street (A206) including—

    (a) Atkins Road from the south side of its junction with Poynders Road to its junction with Streatham Place;
    (b) Brownhill Road;
    (c) Christchurch Road:
    (d) Hardel Rise:
    (e) Norwood Road from the north side of its junction with Tulse Hill to the south side of its junction with Christchurch Road;
    (f) Plassy Road;
    (g) Poynders Road;
    (h) Rushey Green from the south side of its junction with Sangley Road to the north side of its junction with Brownhill Road;
    (i) Sangley Road from its junction with Bromley Road and Rushey Green to the east side of its junction with Plassy Road; and
    (j) Tulse Hill from the north-west side of its junction with Hardel Rise to its junction with Norwood Road.

44. A210 from its junction with Eltham Road and Sidcup Road (A20) to its junction with Westhorne Avenue (A205).

45. A214 from its junction with Huguenot Place and Wandsworth Common North Side (A3) to its junctions with Streatham High Road (A23) including—

    (a) Ambleside Avenue;
    (b) Gleneagle Road from the south-west side of its junction with Ambleside Avenue to its junction with Streatham High Road (A23); and
    (c) Tooting Bec Gardens.

46. A215 from its junction with Elephant and Castle (A3) to the east side of its junction with Newington Butts (A3).

47. A217 from boundary of London to and including its junction with St Helier Avenue (A297).

48. A217 from its junctions with Putney Bridge Road (A3209) and Wandsworth High Street (A3) to its junction with York Road (A3205) including—

    (a) Armoury Way; and

(b) Ram Street.

49. A232 from where it crosses the boundary of London to its junction with Purley Way (A23) including—

(a) Chalk Pit Way;
(b) Grove Road from its south-west junction with Sutton Park Road to its junction with Brighton Road (B2230) and High Street;
(c) Sutton Court Road from its junction with Brighton Road (B2230) and High Street to its junction with Chalk Pit Way; and
(d) Sutton Park Road.

50. A232 from the east side of its junctions with Purley Way (A23) to the west side of its junction with Barclay Road including—

(a) Epsom Road; and
(b) Stafford Road from the east side of its junction with Purley Way (A23) to its junction with Epsom Road.

51. A232 from the north-east side of its junction with Chepstow Road to its junction with Farnborough Common (A21).

52. A297 from its junction with Reigate Avenue and Bishopsford Road (A217) to its junction with London Road and Morden Road (A24).

53. A302 from its junction with Grosvenor Place and Duke of Wellington Place (A4) to the east side of its junction with Bressenden Place (A3217).

54. A306 from its junction with Upper Richmond Road (A205) to its junction with Kingston Road (A3).

55. A312 from its junction with M4 to its junction with Country Way and Great Chertsey Road (A316).

56. A316 from the boundary of London to its junction with A4 at Chiswick Square.

57. A400 from the south-east side of its junctions with Parkway (A4201) and Camden Road (A503) to its junction with Euston Road (A501) including—

(a) Camden High Street from the south-east side of its junction with Parkway (A4201) and Camden Road (A503) to its junction with Eversholt Street (A4200);
(b) Camden Street from the south-east side of its junction with Camden Road (A503) to its junction with Oakley Square:
(c) Hampstead Road;
(d) Harrington Square (south side);
(e) Lidlington Place; and
(f) Oakley Square (south east section) from its junction with Camden Street to its junction with Lidlington Place.

58. A404 from the west side of its junction with Westbourne Road to the east side of its junction with Old Marylebone Road (A501).

59. A406 from its junction with Great West Road (A4) to the south-west side of its junction with Great North Way (A1).

60. A406 from the east side of its junction with Falloden Way (A1) to its junction with Newham Way (A13).

61. A501 from its junction with Westway (A40(M)) to its junction with Old Street (A5201).

62. A501 Old Marylebone Road from its junction with Edgware Road (A5) to its junction with Marylebone Road (A501).

63. A503 from the east side of its junction with High Road (A10) to its junction with The Hale.

64. A503 from the north-east side of its junction with Green Lanes (A105) to its junction with Parkway (A4201) including—

(a) Camden Road;
(b) Isledon Road;
(c) Parkhurst Road;

    (d) Seven Sisters Road from the north-east side of its junction with Parkhurst Road to the north-east side of its junction with Green Lanes (A105); and
    (e) Tollington Road.

65. A1080 from its junction with Great Cambridge Road and The Roundway (A10) to its junction with High Road and Green Lanes (A105) including—

    (a) Boreham Road; and
    (b) Westbury Avenue.

66. A1202 from its junction with Braham Street (A11) to the south side of its junction with Prescot Street.

67. A1202 from its junctions with Old Street (A5201) to its junction with Whitechapel High Street (A11) including—

    (a) Curtain Road from its junction with Old Street (A5201) to its junction with Great Eastern Street (A1202); and
    (b) Great Eastern Street.

68. A1203 from its junction with Tower Hill (A100) to its junction with Commercial Road (A13).

69. A1205 from its junction with Mile End Road (A11) to its junction with Commercial Road and East India Dock Road (A13).

70. A1210 from the south side of its junction with Braham Street and Mansell Street (A11) to its junction with East Smithfield (A1203).

71. A1211 from the north side of its junction with Goodmans Yard to its junction with Tower Hill (A100).

72. A1213 from its junction with Eastcheap (A100) to its junction with Threadneedle Street and Bishopsgate (A10).

73. A1400 from its junction with Chigwell Road (A113) to its junction with Eastern Avenue (A12) at Gants Hill Roundabout.

74. A2198 from its junction with Borough High Street (A3) to the east side of its junction with Tabard Street.

75. A2204 from its junction with Woolwich Church Street and High Street (A206) to Woolwich Ferry.

76. A2207 from its junction with Tower Bridge Road (A100) to the south-east side of its junction with Tanner Street.

77. A2210 from the north-west side of its junction with Jerrard Street to its junction with Loampit Vale (A20).

78. A2213 from its junction with Rochester Way Relief Road (A2) to its junction with Eltham Road (A20).

79. A3036 from its junction with East Hill (A3) to the east side of its junction with Marcilly Road.

80. A3036 from the south side of its junction with Nine Elms Lane and Parry Street (A3205) to its junction with A202 at Vauxhall Cross.

81. A3123 from its junction with Vauxhall Bridge Road (A202) to its junction with Eaton Square (A3217).

82. A3204 from its junction with A202 at Vauxhall Cross to its junction with Kennington Park Road and Newington Butts (A3).

83. A3205 from its junction with Swandon Way (A217) to its junction with South Lambeth Road (A203).

84. A3209 from the north side of its junction with Armoury Way to its junction with Wandsworth High Street (A3).

85. A3212 from its junction with Cheyne Walk (A3220 section) to its junction with Bessborough Gardens and Vauxhall Bridge (A202).

86. A3217 from the south-west side of its junction with Eccleston Street (A3123) to its junction with Victoria Street (A302).

87. A3220 from its junction with West Cross Route (M41) to its junction with Clapham Common North Side (A3) including—

    (a) Addison Crescent from its junction with Holland Road to its junction with Addison Road;

    (b) Addison Road from its junction with Addison Crescent to its junction with Warwick Gardens;

    (c) Ashburnam Road from its junction with Gunter Grove to its junction with Cremorne Road;

    (d) Earls Court Road from the north-east side of its junction with Pembroke Road to its junction with Redcliffe Gardens;

    (e) Edith Grove;

    (f) Finborough Road;

    (g) Gunter Grove;

    (h) Holland Road;

    (i) Pembroke Road from its junction with Warwick Gardens to its junction with Earls Court Road;

    (j) Redcliffe Gardens;

    (k) Warwick Gardens; and

    (l) Warwick Road.

88. A3221 from its junction with Swandon Way (A217) to its junction with Wandsworth High Street and East Hill (A3).

89. A4200 from its junction with Camden High Street (A400) to its junction with Euston Road (A501).

90. A4202 (both sections) from its junctions with Cumberland Gate (A40) to its junction with Hyde Park Corner (A4) including—

    (a) Achilles Way;

    (b) Brook Gate;

    (c) Grosvenor Gate; and

    (d) Stanhope Gate from its junction with Park Lane (Western Section) to its junction with Park Lane (Eastern Section).

91. A5200 from its junction with Euston Road (A501) to the south side of its junction with Acton Street.

92. A5201 from its junction with City Road (A501) to its junction with Kingsland Road and Shoreditch High Street (A10).

93. A5205 from its junction with Maida Vale and Edgware Road (A5) to its junction with Wellington Road and Park Road (A41).   **[1787]**

NOTE

Commencement: 2 July 1992.

'B' Roads (in numerical order)

94. B509 from its junction with Finchley Road (A41) to the east side of its junction with Avenue Road (B525).

95. B519 from its junction with Aylmer Road and Archway Road (A1) to the south-east side of its junction with Bakers Lane.

96. B525 from Swiss Cottage intersection to the south side of its junction with Adelaide Road (B509).

97. B2230 from the south side of its junction with Cheam Road and Carshalton Road (A232) to the south side of its junction with Grove Road and Sutton Court Road (A232).

    [1788]

NOTE

Commencement: 2 July 1992.

Other Roads (in alphabetical order)

98. Acton Street from its junction with Gray's Inn Road (A5200) to its junction with King's Cross Road (A201).

99. Allington Street from the south side of its junction with Allington Street to its junction with Victoria Street (A302).

100. Allington Street from the west side of its junction with Allington Street to its junction with Bressenden Place (A3217).

101. Bakers Lane from its junction with North Hill (B519) to its junction with Archway Road (A1).

102. Barclay Road from the east side of its junction with Park Lane (A232) to its junction with Fairfield Road.

103. Baron Street from the north side of its junction with White Lion Street to its junction with Pentonville Road.

104. Bond Way from the north side of its junction with Parry Street (A3205) to its junction with Wandsworth Road (A3036).

105. Cambridge Road from its junction with Battersea Bridge Road (A3220) to and including its junction with Albert Bridge Road (A3031).

106. Chepstow Road from its junction with Fairfield Road to the south-west side of its junction with Addiscombe Road (A232).

107. Durham Street from its junction with Kennington Lane (A3204) to its junction with Harleyford Road (A202).

108. Fairfield Road from its junction with Barclay Road to its junction with Chepstow Road.

109. Goodmans Yard from its junction with Minories (A1211) to its junction with Mansell Street (A1210).

110. Jerrard Street from its junction with Loampit Hill and Loampit Vale (A20) to its junction with Thurston Road (A2210).

111. Marcilly Road from its junction with East Hill and St John's Hill (A3036) to its junction with Wandsworth Common North Side (A3).

112. Matthews Road from its junction with Brixton Hill (A23) to its junction with Effra Road (A204).

113. Molesworth Street from its junction with Loampit Vale (A20) to its junction with Lewisham High Street (A21).

114. Monument Way from its junction with High Road (A10) to its junction with The Hale.

115. Nebraska Street from its junction with Great Dover Street (A2) to its junction with Tabard Street.

116. Prescot Street from its junction with Mansell Street (A1210) to its junction with Leman Street(A1202).

117. Prince of Wales Drive from its junction with Battersea Bridge Road (A3220) to and including its junction with Albert Bridge Road (A3031).

118. Shorter Street from its junction with Tower Hill (A100) to its junction with Mansell Street (A1210).

119. South Lambeth Place from its junction with South Lambeth Road (A203) to its junction with A202 at Vauxhall Cross.

120. Swinton Street from its junction with Gray's Inn Road (A5200) to its junction with King's Cross Road (A201).

121. Tabard Street from the south side of its junction with Long Lane (A2198) to the southeast side of its junction with Nebraska Street.

122. Tanner Street from its junction with Druid Street (A2207) to its junction with Tooley Street and Jamaica Road (A200).

123. The Hale from its junction with Monument Way to its junction with Broad Lane (A503).

124. Tyburn Way from its junction with Marble Arch (A40) to its junction with Cumberland Gate (A40).

125. Wakley Street from its junction with City Road (A501) to its junction with Goswell Road (A1).

126. Wandsworth Plain from its junction with Wandsworth High Street (A3) to its junction with Armoury Way (A217).

127. White Lion Street from the west side of its junction with Baron Street to its junction with Islington High Street (A1). **[1789]**

NOTE
    Commencement: 2 July 1992.

TRANSPORT (GUIDED SYSTEMS) ORDER 1992
(SI 1992 No 2044)

NOTES
    Made: 27 August 1992
    Commencement: 7 December 1992
    Authority: Transport and Works Act 1992, s 26(3)

1. Citation and commencement

This Order may be cited as the Transport (Guided Systems) Order 1992 and shall come into force on 7th December 1992. **[1790]**

NOTE
    Commencement: 7 December 1992.

2. Specified systems

The Secretary of State hereby specifies for the purposes of Chapter 1 of Part II of the Act the systems which use a mode of guided transport of which particulars are given in the Schedule to this Order. **[1791]**

NOTE
    Commencement: 7 December 1992.

3. Interpretation

(1) In this Order—

"magnetic levitation" means a mode in which the vehicles are supported and guided by means of magnetic force;

"monorail" means a mode in which the vehicles are supported and guided wholly or mainly by means of a single rail or beam; and

"track-based with side guidance" means a mode in which the vehicles are—

(a) supported by means of a track or other structure not being a road; and

(b) guided wholly or mainly by means of horizontally-inclined wheels bearing outwards against fixed apparatus.

(2) In this Order "road" has the same meaning as in the Road Traffic Regulation Act 1984.   **[1792]**

NOTE

Commencement: 7 December 1992.

SCHEDULE

(Article 2)

THE SPECIFIED SYSTEMS

EVIDENCE OF RESULTS OF TESTS

Mode	Location	Terminal points	Operator
Magnetic levitation	Birmingham International Airport Solihull West Midlands	Birmingham International Airport and Birmingham International railway station	Birmingham International Airport plc
Monorail	Merry Hill Centre Brierley Hill Dudley West Midlands	Boulevard station and Waterfront East station	Von Roll Transport Systems (UK) Limited
Track-based with side guidance	Gatwick Airport Crawley West Sussex	South Terminal and North Terminal	Gatwick Airport Limited
Track-based with side guidance	Gatwick Airport Crawley West Sussex	South Terminal and South Terminal satellite/pier 3	Gatwick Airport Limited
Track-based with side guidance	Stanstead Airport Uttlesford Essex	Airport terminal and satellite 1	Stansted Airport Limited

[1793]

ROAD TRAFFIC (COURSES FOR DRINK-DRIVE OFFENDERS) REGULATIONS 1992
(SI 1992 No 3013)

NOTES
Made: 2 December 1992.
Commencement: 24 December 1992.
Authority: Road Traffic Offenders Act 1988, ss 34B(3), (8), 34C(3).

1. Citation and commencement

These Regulations may be cited as The Road Traffic (Courses for Drink-Drive Offenders) Regulations 1992 and shall come into force on 24th December 1992.

[1794]

NOTES
Commencement: 24 December 1992.

2. Interpretation

In these Regulations—

"the Act" means the Road Traffic Offenders Act 1988;
"course" means a course approved by the Secretary of State for the purposes of section 34A of the Act;
"manager", in relation to a course, means the person for the time being nominated as the manager of the course by the Secretary of State.

[1795]

NOTES
Commencement: 24 December 1992.

3. Certificate of completion

The certificate referred to in section 34B(1) of the Act shall be a certificate in such form and contain such particulars as may from time to time be determined by the Secretary of State.   **[1796]**

NOTE
Commencement: 24 December 1992.

4. Course organiser

The person responsible for giving the certificates mentioned in section 34B(1) of the Act in respect of the completion of a course shall be the person for the time being nominated for that purpose by the manager.   **[1797]**

NOTES
Commencement: 24 December 1992.

5. Notice of non-completion

A notice under subsection (5) of section 34B of the Act shall, for the purposes of that subsection, be treated as given a person if it was sent by registered post or recorded delivery service addressed to him at his last known address, notwithstanding that it was returned as undelivered or was for any other reason not received by him. **[1798]**

NOTE
Commencement: 24 December 1992.

COURSES FOR DRINK-DRIVE OFFENDERS (DESIGNA-TION OF AREAS) ORDER 1992
(SI 1992 No 3014)

NOTES
Made: 2 December 1992.
Commencement: 24 December 1992.
Authority: Road Traffic Act 1991, s 31(4), (6).

1. This Order may be cited as the Courses for Drink-Drive Offenders (Designation of Areas) Order 1992 and shall come into force on 24th December 1992. **[1799]**

NOTES
Commencement: 24 December 1992.

2. The following areas and districts are hereby designated for the purposes of section 31 of the Road Traffic Act 1991—

    (a) the petty sessions areas specified in Schedule 1 to this Order;
    (b) the districts and the commission area in Scotland specified in Schedule 2 to this Order. **[1800]**

NOTES
Commencement: 24 December 1992.

SCHEDULE 1
Article 2(a)

PETTY SESSIONS AREAS

Petty sessional divisions of non-metropolitan counties and metropolitan districts

    Birmingham
    Carmarthen South
    Carmarthen North
    Corby
    Exeter
    Exmouth
    Felixstowe
    Hartlepool
    Lincoln District
    Maidenhead
    Maidstone
    Medway
    Newcastle and Ogmore
    Shrewsbury
    Southampton

Stoke-on-Trent
Swindon
Taunton Deane
West Allerdale
Woodbridge

Metropolitan districts not divided into petty sessional divisions

Sheffield
South Tyneside
Wolverhampton

Outer London borough not divided into petty sessional divisions

Bromley

Petty sessional divisions of the inner London area

South Central
South Westminster   [1801]

NOTE

Commencement: 24 December 1992.

SCHEDULE 2
Article 2(b)

DISTRICTS AND COMMISSION AREA IN SCOTLAND
Districts

Glasgow and Strathkelvin Sheriff Court District
Stornoway Sheriff Court District
Commission area City of Glasgow district   [1802]

NOTE

Commencement: 24 December 1992.

MOTOR VEHICLES (COMPULSORY INSURANCE) REGULATIONS 1992
(SI 1992 No 3036)

NOTES

Made: 2 December 1992.
Commencement: 31 December 1992.
Authority: European Communities Act 1992, s 2(2).

1. These Regulations may be cited as the Motor Vehicles (Compulsory Insurance) Regulations 1992 and shall come into force on 31st December 1992.
[1803]

NOTE

Commencement: 31 December 1992.

2—(1). In section 145 of the Road Traffic Act 1988 (requirements in respect of policies of insurance) in subsection (3) after paragraph (a) there shall be inserted the following paragraph—

"(aa) must, in the case of a vehicle normally based in the territory of another member State, insure him or them in respect of any civil liability which may be incurred by him or them as a result of an event related to the use of the vehicle in Great Britain if,—

> (i) according to the law of that territory, he or they would be required to be insured in respect of a civil liability which would arise under that law as a result of that event if the place where the vehicle was used when the event occurred were in that territory, and
>
> (ii) the cover required by that law would be higher than that required by paragraph (a) above, and".

(2) In paragraph (b) of subsection (3) of that section (which requires a policy to provide insurance in respect of certain liabilities in accordance with the law on compulsory motor insurance of the State where the liability may be incurred) after the word "must" there shall be inserted ", in the case of a vehicle normally based in Great Britain," and for the words from "the law" to the end of the paragraph there shall be substituted—

> "(i) the law on compulsory insurance against civil liability in respect of the use of vehicles of the State in whose territory the event giving rise to the liability occurred; or
>
> (ii) if it would give higher cover, the law which would be applicable under this Part of this Act if the place where the vehicle was used when that event occurred were in Great Britain; and".

(3) After subsection (4) of that section there shall be inserted the following subsection—

> "(4A) In the case of a person—
>
> (a) carried in or upon a vehicle, or
> (b) entering or getting on to, or alighting from, a vehicle,

the provisions of paragraph (a) of subsection (4) above do not apply unless cover in respect of the liability referred to in that paragraph is in fact provided pursuant to a requirement of the Employers' Liability (Compulsory Insurance) Act 1969." **[1804]**

NOTE
Commencement: 31 December 1992.

STREET WORKS (NOTICES) ORDER 1992
(SI 1992 No 3053)

NOTES
Made: 3 December 1992.
Commencement: 1 January 1993.
Authority: New Roads and Street Works Act 1991, s 102.

1—(1). This Order may be cited as the Street Works (Notices) Order 1992 and shall come into force on 1st January 1993.

(2) In this Order—

"enactment" means any enactment passed or made before the commence-ment of section 102 of the New Roads and Street Works Act 1991 (not being a special enactment to which section 101(1), (2) or (3) of that Act applies).   **[1805]**

NOTE

Commencement: 1 January 1993.

2. Any notice given in compliance with any of the provisions of the Street Works (Registers, Notices, Directions and Designations) Regulations 1992 shall be deemed to satisfy any requirement made by or under any enactment or any instrument having effect under or by virtue of any enactment to give notice of any matter covered by the Regulations to the person to whom that notice is required to be given by or under such enactment or instrument.   **[1806]**

NOTE

Commencement: 1 January 1993.

GOODS VEHICLES (COMMUNITY AUTHORISATIONS) REGULATIONS 1992
(SI 1992 No 3077)

NOTES

Made: 8 December 1992.
Commencement: 1 January 1993.
Authority: European Communities Act 1992, s 2(2).

1. Citation and commencement

These Regulations may be cited as the Goods Vehicles (Community Authoris-ations) Regulations 1992 and shall come into force on 1st January 1993.   **[1807]**

NOTE

Commencement: 1 January 1993.

2. Purpose and interpretation

(1) These Regulations implement the Council Regulation.

(2) In these Regulations—

"actual holder", in relation to a person established as a haulier in Great Britain, has the meaning which it bears in regulation 32A(1) of the 1984 Regulations;

"Community authorisation" means a Community authorisation issued under the Council Regulation;

"competent authority" has the meaning given by regulation 4 of these Regulations;

"the Council Regulation" means Council Regulation (EEC) No. 881/92 of 26th March 1992 on access to the market in the carriage of goods by road within the Community to or from the territory of a member State or passing across the territory of one or more member States;

"the First Council Directive" means the First Council Directive of 23 July 1962 on the establishment of common rules for certain types of carriage of goods by road;

"operating centre" has the meaning which it bears in section 92(1) of the Transport Act 1968;

"operator's licence" means an operator's licence within the meaning of section 60(1) of the Transport Act 1968 or section 14 of the Transport Act (Northern Ireland) 1967;

"standard operator's licence" means an operator's licence which is a standard licence within the meaning of regulation 3(2) of the 1984 Regulations;

"the 1984 Regulations" means the Goods Vehicles (Operators' Licences, Qualifications and Fees) Regulations 1984; and

"traffic area" means a traffic area constituted for the purposes of the Public Passenger Vehicles Act 1981,

and, subject thereto, expressions used which are also used in the Council Regulation have the meaning which they bear in that Regulation. **[1808]**

NOTE
Commencement: 1 January 1993.

3. Use of goods vehicle without Community authorisation

A person who uses a vehicle in the United Kingdom in contravention of Article 3.1 of the Council Regulations shall be guilty of an offence and liable on summary conviction to a fine not exceeding level 4 on the standard scale. **[1809]**

NOTE
Commencement: 1 January 1993.

4. Competent authorities

The competent authority for the purposes of the Council Regulation and of these Regulations shall be—

(a) in relation to a haulier with an operating centre in a traffic area in Great Britain, the traffic commissioner for that area, and

(b) in relation to a haulier established in Northern Ireland, the Department of the Environment for Northern Ireland. **[1810]**

NOTE
Commencement: 1 January 1993.

5. Entitlement to the issue of Community authorisation

(1) A person shall be entitled to be issued with a Community authorisation under Article 3.2 of the Council Regulation if—

(a) in the case of a person established as a haulier in Great Britain, he holds a standard operator's licence covering international transport operations; or

(b) in the case of a person established as a haulier in Northern Ireland, he holds an operator's licence covering international transport operations.

(2) For the purposes of paragraph (1)(a) above, "international transport operations" has the meaning which it bears in regulation 3(2) of the 1984 Regulations. **[1811]**

NOTE
Commencement: 1 January 1993.

6. Rights of appeal

A person who—

    (a) being entitled to be issued with a Community authorisation under regulation 5 above, is aggrieved by the refusal of the competent authority to issue such authorisation to him, or

    (b) being the holder of a Community authorisation, is aggrieved by the decision of the competent authority who issued it to withdraw it,

may appeal—

    (i) if he is established as a haulier in Great Britain, to the Transport Tribunal; or

    (ii) if he is established as a haulier in Northern Ireland, to the Northern Ireland Operator and Vehicle Licensing Review Body.   **[1812]**

NOTE
Commencement: 1 January 1993.

7. Effect of failure to comply with conditions governing use of Community authorisation

A person who uses a vehicle in the United Kingdom under a Community authorisation and, without reasonable excuse, fails to comply with any of the conditions governing the use of that authorisation under the Council Regulations shall be guilty of an offence and liable on summary conviction to a fine not exceeding level 4 on the standard scale.   **[1813]**

NOTE
Commencement: 1 January 1993.

8. Authorised inspecting officers

Authorised inspecting officers for the purposes of the Council Regulations shall be police constables and—

    (a) in Great Britain, examiners appointed under section 56(1) of the Road Traffic Act 1972 or section 66A(1) of the Road Traffic Act 1988, and

    (b) in Northern Ireland, inspectors appointed under section 37 of the Transport Act (Northern Ireland) 1967 and inspectors of vehicles, as defined in Article 2(2) of the Road Traffic (Northern Ireland) Order 1981.   **[1814]**

NOTE
Commencement: 1 January 1993.

9. Return of documents

(1) The holder of a Community authorisation which is withdrawn by the competent authority in accordance with Article 8.2 of the Council Regulation shall within 7 days of such withdrawal return to the competent authority which issued it the original authorisation and all certified true copies of it.

(2) The holder of a Community authorisation shall return to the competent authority which issued it such certified true copies of the authorisation as the

authority may require pursuant to any reduction in the number of vehicles at the disposal of the holder or any decision of the authority under Article 8.3 of the Council Regulation to suspend certified true copies of that authorisation.

(3) A person who, without reasonable excuse, fails to comply with any provision of paragraphs (1) or (2) above shall be guilty of an offence and liable on summary conviction to a fine not exceeding level 4 on the standard scale.

[1815]

NOTE
Commencement: 1 January 1993.

10. Supply of information

(1) The holder of a Community authorisation shall furnish such information as the competent authority which issued it may reasonably require from time to time to enable the authority to decide whether the holder is entitled to retain that authorisation.

(2) A person who, without reasonable excuse, fails to supply any information required under paragraph (1) above shall be guilty of an offence and liable on summary conviction to a fine not exceeding level 4 on the standard scale. **[1816]**

NOTE
Commencement: 1 January 1993.

11. Death, bankruptcy etc. of holder of Community authorisation

Where a person is treated as the holder of an operator's licence by virtue of a direction under Regulation 32A of the 1984 Regulations or by virtue of regulations made under section 33(2) of the Transport Act (Northern Ireland) 1967, such person shall also be treated as the holder of any Community authorisation held by the actual holder of that operator's licence, for the same period as is specified in that direction or under such regulations. **[1817]**

NOTE
Commencement: 1 January 1993.

12. Bodies corporate

(1) Where an offence under these Regulations has been committed by a body corporate and it is proved to have been committed with the consent or connivance of, or to be attributable to any neglect on the part of, any director, manager, secretary or other similar officer of the body corporate or any person who was purporting to act in any such capacity, he as well as the body corporate shall be guilty of the offence and shall be liable to be proceeded against and punished accordingly.

(2) Where the affairs of a body corporate are managed by its members, paragraph (1) above shall apply in relation to the acts and defaults of a member in connection with his functions of management as if he were a director of the body corporate.

(3) Where an offence under these Regulations has been committed by a Scottish partnership and it is proved to have been committed with the consent or connivance of, or to be attributable to any neglect on the part of, a partner, he as well as the partnership shall be guilty of the offence and shall be liable to be proceeded against and punished accordingly. **[1818]**

NOTE
Commencement: 1 January 1993.

13. Amendment of the Goods Vehicles (International Road Haulage Permits) Regulations 1975

(1) The Goods Vehicles (International Road Haulage Permits) Regulations 1975 shall be amended as follows.

(2) In regulation 2 (interpretation), in paragraph (1), in the definition of "international road haulage permit", the words "a Community instrument relating to the carriage of goods by road between member States or" shall be omitted.

(3) In regulation 4 (journeys to which Regulations apply), in paragraph (2), the words "The Republic of France, The Federal Republic of Germany, The Republic of Italy" shall be omitted.

(4) In regulation 5 (exceptions), in the Table, items 2, 3 and 4 and the entries relating to those items in columns (2), (3) and (9) shall be omitted.   **[1819]**

NOTE
Commencement: 1 January 1993.

14 (*Amends the Transport Act 1968, s 60 ante.*)

15. Amendment of the Goods Vehicles (Operators' Licences) (Temporary Use in Great Britain) Regulations 1980

(1) The Goods Vehicles (Operators' Licences) (Temporary Use in Great Britain) Regulations 1980 shall be amended as follows.

(2) In regulation 3 (interpretation), in paragraph (1)—

(a) after the definition of "Community cabotage authorisation", there shall be inserted—

"'Council Regulation No. 881/92' means Regulations (EEC) No. 881/92 of 26th March 1992 on access to the market in the carriage of goods by road within the Community to or from the territory of a member State or passing across the territory of one or more member States;";

(b) in the definition of "foreign goods vehicle", after paragraph (a), there shall be inserted—

"(aa) which is not being used for international carriage by a haulier established in a member State other than the United Kingdom and not established in the United Kingdom;";

(c) after the definition of "foreign goods vehicle", there shall be inserted—

" 'international carriage' has the meaning which it bears in the Council Regulation; and

(d) in the definition of "Northern Ireland goods vehicle", after paragraph (a), there shall be inserted—

"(aa) which is not being used for international carriage by a haulier established in Northern Ireland and not established in Great Britain;".

(3) For regulation 6 (exemptions for Northern Ireland or foreign goods

vehicles with international authorisations or licences), there shall be substituted—

"*Exemptions for Northern Ireland or foreign goods vehicles with international licences*

6. Notwithstanding anything in Regulations 7 to 33, section 60(1) of the Act shall not apply to the use in Great Britain or a Northern Ireland or foreign goods vehicle for the carriage of goods for hire or reward if the vehicle is being used by virtue of a licence issued pursuant to the scheme adopted by Resolution of the Council of Ministers of Transport on 14th June 1973 and the licence is carried on the vehicle or, if the vehicle is a trailer, on the motor vehicle by which it is drawn,"

(4) Regulations 8, 12, 14, 15, 16, 17, 19, 20, 21, 23, 27 and 29 are hereby revoked. **[1820]**

NOTE
Commencement: 1 January 1993.

APPENDICES

ENDORSABLE OFFENCE CODES AND PENALTY POINTS[1]

Code	Offences	Penalty points
Offences in relation to accidents		
AC10	Failing to stop to give particulars after an accident	5–10
AC20	Failing to give particulars or to report an accident within 24 hours	5–10
AC30	Undefined accident offence	4–9
Offences of driving while disqualified		
BA10	Driving while disqualified by order of court	6
BA20	Driving while disqualified as under age	(*obsolete*)
BA30	Attempting to drive while disqualified by order of court (England/Wales only)	6
Careless driving offences		
CD10	Driving without due care and attention	3–9
CD20	Driving without reasonable consideration for other road users	3–9
CD30	Driving without due care and attention or without reasonable consideration for other road users	3–9
CD40	Causing death by careless driving when unfit through drink	(†)
CD50	Causing death by careless driving when unfit through drugs	(†)
CD60	Causing death by careless driving with alcohol level above the limit	(†)
CD70	Causing death by careless driving then failing to supply specimen for analysis	3–11
Construction and use offences (vehicles or parts dangerous)		
CU10	Using a vehicle with defective brakes	3
CU20	Causing or likely to cause danger by reason of use of unsuitable vehicle or using a vehicle with parts or accessories (excluding brakes, steering or tyres) in dangerous condition	3
CU30	Using a vehicle with defective tyres	3
CU40	Using a vehicle with defective steering	3
CU50	Causing or likely to cause danger by reason of load or passengers	3
CU60	Undefined failure to comply with construction and use regulations	3
Reckless driving offences		
DD30	Reckless driving	10
DD40	Dangerous driving	(†)
DD60	Manslaughter or, in Scotland, culpable homicide while driving a motor vehicle	(†)
DD70	Causing death by reckless driving	(†)
DD80	Causing death by dangerous driving	(†)
Drink or drugs offences		
DR10	Driving or attempting to drive with alcohol concentration above limit	(†)
DR20	Driving or attempting to drive when unfit through drink or drugs	(†)
DR30	Driving or attempting to drive, then refusing to provide a specimen for analysis	(†)
DR40	In charge of a vehicle with alcohol concentration above limit	10
DR50	In charge of a vehicle when unfit through drink or drugs	10
DR60	Failure to provide a specimen for analysis in circumstances other than driving or attempting to drive	10
DR70	Failing to provide a specimen for breath test	4

		Penalty
Code	Offences	points
DR80	Driving or attempting to drive when unfit through drugs	(†)
DR90	In charge of vehicle when unfit through drugs	10

Insurance offences

IN10	Using a vehicle uninsured against third-party risks	6–8

Licence offences

LC10	Driving without a licence	2
LC20	Driving otherwise than in accordance with a licence	3–6
LC30	Driving after making a false declaration about fitness when applying for a licence	3–6
LC40	Driving vehicle having failed to notify a disability	3–6
LC50	Driving after licence has been revoked or refused on medical grounds	3–6

Miscellaneous offences

MS10	Leaving vehicle in a dangerous position	3
MS20	Unlawful pillion riding	1
MS30	Playstreet offence	2
MS40*	Driving with uncorrected defective eyesight or refusing to submit to a test of eyesight	2
MS50	Motor racing on the highway	(†)
MS60	Offences not covered by other codes	as appropriate
MS70	Driving with uncorrected defective eyesight	3
MS80	Refusing to submit to eyesight test	3
MS90	Failing to give information as to identity of driver in certain cases	3

* Following the introduction of MS70 and MS80 the offence code MS40 can no longer be used but will continue to appear on existing licences for some time.

Motorway offence

MW10	Contravention of special roads regulations (excluding speed limits)	3

Non-endorsable offence

NE99	A disqualification under section 24 of the Criminal Justice Act 1972 and section 44 of the Powers of Criminal Courts Act	

Pedestrian crossing offences

PC10	Undefined contravention of pedestrian crossing regulations	3
PC20	Contravention of pedestrian crossing regulations with moving vehicle	3
PC30	Contravention of pedestrian crossing regulations with stationary vehicle	3

Provisional licence offences

PL10	Driving without L-plates	(obsolete)
PL20	Not accompanied by a qualified person	(obsolete)
PL30	Carrying a person not qualified	(obsolete)
PL40	Drawing an unauthorised trailer	(obsolete)
PL50	Undefined failure to comply with the conditions of a provisional licence	(obsolete)

Speed limits offences

SP10	Exceeding goods vehicle speed limit	3
SP20	Exceeding speed limit for type of vehicle (excluding goods/ passenger vehicles)	3

Code	Offences	Penalty points
SP30	Exceeding statutory speed limit on a public road	3
SP40	Exceeding passenger vehicle speed limit	3
SP50	Exceeding speed limit on a motorway	3
SP60	Undefined speed limit offence	3

Traffic directions and signs offences

TS10	Failing to comply with traffic light signals	3
TS20	Failing to comply with double white lines	3
TS30	Failing to comply with a "stop" sign	3
TS40	Failing to comply with a direction of a constable or traffic warden	3
TS50	Failing to comply with a traffic sign (excluding stop signs, traffic lights or double white lines)	3
TS60	Failure to comply with a school crossing patrol sign	3
TS70	Undefined failure to comply with a traffic direction or sign	3

Offences of theft or unauthorised taking

UT10	Taking and driving away a vehicle without consent or an attempt thereat (in England and Wales prior to Theft Act 1968 only). Driving a vehicle knowing it to have been taken without consent. Allowing oneself to be carried in or on a vehicle knowing it to have been taken without consent. (Primarily for use by Scottish Courts.)	*(obsolete)*
UT20	Stealing or attempting to steal a vehicle	*(obsolete)*
UT30	Going equipped for stealing or taking a motor vehicle	*(obsolete)*
UT40	Taking or attempting to take a vehicle without consent. Driving or attempting to drive a vehicle knowing it to have been taken without consent. Allowing oneself to be carried in or on a vehicle knowing it to have been taken without consent.	*(obsolete)*

Special code

TT99   ONLY to be used to indicate a disqualification under the penalty points procedures i.e. where the number of penalty points totals 12 or more—including any penalty points "taken into account", but not endorsed because a driver has been disqualified.
NB When using this code, a date of conviction must always be shown on the licence.

Aiding and/or abetting and/or counselling and/or procuring

Offences as coded above but with zero changed to "2", eg UT10 becomes UT12.

Causing or permitting

Offences coded as above but with zero changed to "4", eg PL10 becomes PL14.

Inciting

Offences as coded above but with zero changed to "6", eg DD30 becomes DD36.

Obsolete special code

XX99   To signify a disqualification under the old "totting-up" procedure

Following the introduction of the penalty points scheme XX99 can no longer be used, but will continue to appear on existing licences for some time.   **[2000]**

NOTES

  [1] Appended to Home Office Circular No 85/1982 and amended by Home Office Circulars Nos 16 and 46 of 1983.

  † This offence carries obligatory disqualification except for special reasons when 3—11 points are imposed.

Sentence Codes[1]

A —Imprisonment
B —Detention in a place specified by the Secretary of State
C —Suspended Prison Sentence
D —Suspended Sentence Supervision Order
E —Conditional Discharge (maximum 3 years)
F —Bound Over
M —Community Service Order (minimum 40 hours, maximum 240)
N —Cumulative Sentence (Scottish Courts only)
P —Youth Custody Sentence
Q —Parent or Guardian Order
R —Borstal (minimum 6 months, maximum 2 years)
S —Compensation Orders (Scottish Courts)

G —Probation (minimum 6 months maximum 3 years)
H —Supervision Order
J —Absolute discharge
K —Attendance Centre (minimum 12 hours, maximum 24 hours)
L —Detention Centre (minimum 3 months, maximum 6 months)
T —Hospital Guardianship Order
U —Admonition (Scottish Courts only)
V —Young Offenders Institution (Scottish Courts only)
W —Care order
X —Total period of partially suspended sentence, ie period sentence served and period sentence suspended

[2001]

NOTE

[1] Appended to Home Office Circular No 85/1982 and amended by Home Office Circulars Nos 16 and 46 of 1983.

HIGHWAY CODE[1]

NOTE

[1] A print purporting to be printed under the superintendence or authority of Her Majesty's Stationery Office is admissible in evidence (Documentary Evidence Act 1882). As to the legal effect of this code, see the Road Traffic Act 1988, s 38, ante.

PEDESTRIANS

General

1. Where there is a pavement or footpath, use it. Where possible, avoid walking next to the kerb with your back to the traffic. If you have to step into the road, watch out for traffic.

2. Where there is no pavement or footpath, walk on the right-hand side of the road so that you can see oncoming traffic. Keep close to the side of the road. Take care at sharp right-hand bends; it may be safer to cross the road well before you reach one so that oncoming traffic has a better chance of seeing you. After the bend cross back to face the oncoming traffic. Walk in single file if possible, especially on narrow roads or in poor light.

3. Wear or carry something that will help you to be seen. Light-coloured, bright or fluorescent items will help in poor visibility. At night use reflective materials (eg reflective armbands and sashes) which can be seen in headlights up to three times as far away as non-reflective materials.

4. Do not let young children out alone on the pavement or road (see Rule 7). When taking children out, walk between them and the traffic and hold their hands firmly. Strap very young children in push-chairs or use reins.

5. A group of people involved in an organised march on the road should keep to the left. There should be look-outs in front and at the back wearing fluorescent clothes in daylight and reflective clothes in the dark. At night, the look-out in front should carry a white light and the one at the back a bright red light which is visible from behind. People on the outside of large groups should also carry lights and were reflective clothing.

6. You **MUST NOT** walk on motorways or their slip roads except in an emergency (see Rule 183). **[2002]**

Crossing the road

The Green Cross Code

7. The Green Cross Code gives advice on crossing the road. It is for all pedestrians. Children should be taught it and should not be allowed out alone until they can understand and use it properly. The age when they can do this is different for each child. Many children under ten cannot judge how fast vehicles are going or how far away they are. Children learn by example, so parents should always use the Code in full when out with children. Parents are responsible for deciding at what age their children can use it safely by themselves.

  a. First find a safe place to cross, then stop.

It is safer to cross at subways, footbridges, islands, Zebra, Pelican and Puffin crossings, traffic lights or where there is a police officer, school crossing patrol or traffic warden. Otherwise choose a place where you can see clearly in all directions. Try to avoid crossing between parked cars (see Rule 23). Move to a space where drivers can see you clearly.

  b. Stand on the pavement near the kerb.

Stop just before you get to the kerb—where you can see if anything is coming, but where you will not be too close to the traffic. If there is no pavement, stand back from the edge of the road but make sure you can still see approaching traffic.

  c. Look all around for traffic and listen.

Traffic could come from any direction, so look along every road. Listen also because you can sometimes hear traffic before you see it.

  d. If traffic is coming, let it pass. Look all round again.

If there is any traffic near, let it go past. Then look around again. Listen to make sure no other traffic is coming.

  e. When there is no traffic near, walk straight across the road.

When there is no traffic near, it is safe to cross. Remember, even if traffic is a long way off, it may be approaching very quickly.

  When it is safe, walk straight across the road—do not run.

  f. Keep looking and listening for traffic while you cross.

When you have started to cross, keep looking and listening in case there is any traffic you did not see—or in case other traffic suddenly appears.

Crossing where there is a central island in the road

8. Use the Green Cross Code to cross to the island. Stop there and use the Code again to cross the second half of the road.

Crossing at a junction

9. When you cross the road at a junction look out for traffic coming round the corner, especially from behind you.

Crossing at a Zebra crossing

10. If there is a Zebra crossing nearby, use it. Do not cross at the side of a crossing on the zig-zag lines—it is very dangerous.

  11. Give traffic plenty of time to see you and to stop before you start to cross. Vehicles need more time to stop when rain or ice have made the road slippery. If necessary put one foot on the crossing; until you have stepped on to a Zebra crossing, the traffic does not have to stop. But do not cross until the traffic has stopped. Do not push a wheelchair or pram on to the crossing until the traffic has stopped.

  12. When the traffic has stopped, walk straight across but keep looking both ways and listening in case a driver or rider has not seen you and attempts to overtake a vehicle that has stopped.

  13. If there is an island in the middle of a crossing, wait on the island and follow Rules 11 and 12 before you cross the second half of the road—it is a separate crossing.

Crossing at a Pelican crossing

14. If there is a Pelican crossing nearby, use it. Do not cross at the side of a crossing on the zig-zag lines—it is very dangerous. At this type of crossing the traffic lights instruct the traffic when to stop and pedestrians when to cross. When the red figure shows, do not cross. Press the button on the box and wait. When the lights change to show a steady green figure check that the traffic has stopped and then cross with care. (At some Pelicans there is also a bleeping sound or voice to tell blind or partially sighted people when the steady green figure is showing.) After a while, the green figure will begin to flash. This means that you should not start to cross. But if you have already started you will have time to finish crossing safely.

15. A "staggered" crossing should be treated as two separate crossings. On reaching the central island you must press the button again to obtain a steady green figure.

Crossing at a Puffin crossing
16. Puffin crossings are similar to Pelican crossings except that the pedestrian signals are on your side of the road. After pressing the button, you should wait where indicated for the green figure to show. Infra-red detectors will vary the length of time of the red light for drivers to ensure that pedestrians have enough time to cross safely.

Crossing at traffic lights
17. Some traffic lights have pedestrian signals similar to those at Pelican crossings. The green figure does not flash but there will be enough time to finish crossing after it goes out. If there are no pedestrian signals, watch carefully and do not cross until the traffic lights are red and the traffic has stopped. Even then, look out for traffic turning the corner. Remember that traffic lights may let traffic move in some lanes while other lanes are stopped.

Crossings controlled by police, traffic wardens or school crossing patrols
18. Where a police officer, traffic warden or school crossing patrol is controlling the traffic, do not cross the road until they signal you to do so. Always cross in front of them.

Guard rails
19. Guard rails are there for your safety. Cross the road only at the gaps provided for pedestrians. Do not climb over the guard rails or walk between them and the road.

Tactile paving
20. Some pedestrian crossing points have textured paving to let blind or partially sighted people know where to stand while waiting to cross the road.

Crossing one-way streets
21. Use the Green Cross Code. Check which way the traffic is moving. Do not cross until it is safe to do so without stopping. In some one-way streets, bus lanes operate in the opposite direction to the rest of the traffic.

Crossing bus and cycle lanes
22. Use the Green Cross Code. Vehicles in bus lanes may be going faster than traffic in other lanes. Watch out for cyclists who may be riding in bus or cycle lanes.

Parked vehicles
23. If you have to cross between parked vehicles, use the outside edge of the vehicles as if it were the kerb. Stop there and make sure you can see all around and that the traffic can see you. Then carry on using the Green Cross Code. Do not stand in front of or behind any vehicle that has its engine running.

Crossing the road at night
24. Use the Green Cross Code. If there is no pedestrian crossing or central island nearby, cross near a street light so that traffic can see you more easily. It is harder for others to see you at night so wear something reflective.   [2003]

Emergency vehicles

25. If you see or hear ambulances, fire engines, police or other emergency vehicles with their blue lights flashing or their sirens sounding, **KEEP OFF THE ROAD**.   [2004]

Getting on or off a bus

26. Only get on or off a bus when it has stopped to allow you to do so. Never cross the road directly behind or in front of a bus. Wait until it has moved off and you can see the road clearly in both directions.   [2005]

Railways and tramways

27. Take extra care at railway level crossings and near tramways (see Rules 225–234 and 241–242).   [2006]

DRIVERS, MOTORCYCLISTS AND CYCLISTS

(More detailed guidance is given in The Driving Standards Agency's publications *The Driving Manual* and *The Motorcycling Manual*.)

General

Vehicle condition
28. You **MUST** ensure your vehicle is roadworthy. Take special care of lights, brakes, steering, tyres (including spare), exhaust system, seat belts, demisters, windscreen wipers and washers. Keep windscreens, windows, lights, indicators, reflectors, mirrors and number plates clean and clear. Ensure your seat, seat belt, head restraint and mirrors are adjusted correctly before you drive.

Loads
29. Any loads carried or towed **MUST** be secure and **MUST NOT** stick out dangerously. You **MUST NOT** overload your vehicle or trailer.

Motorcycles
30. The rider and pillion passenger on a motorcycle, scooter or moped **MUST** wear an approved safety helmet which **MUST** be fastened securely. It is also advisable to wear eye protectors, and strong boots, gloves and clothes that will help protect you if you fall off. Pillion passengers **MUST** sit astride the machine on a proper seat and keep both feet on the footrests. To help you to be seen, wear something light-coloured or bright. Fluorescent material helps in the daylight, as do dipped headlights on larger machines. Reflective material helps in the dark.

Tiredness or illness
31. If you feel tired or ill, **DO NOT DRIVE**.

32. Driving can make you feel sleepy. To help avoid this, make sure there is a supply of fresh air into your vehicle. If you feel tired while driving, find a safe place to stop and rest.

33. You **MUST NOT** drive under the influence of drugs or medicines. When taking prescribed medicines, ask your doctor if it is safe to drive. When taking other medicines, ask the pharmacist.

Vision
34. You **MUST** be able to read a vehicle number plate from a distance of 20.5 metres (67 ft) which is about five car lengths. If you need glasses (or contact lenses) to do this you **MUST** wear them when driving.

35. At night or in poor visibility, do not use tinted glasses, lenses or visors. Do not use spray-on or other tinting materials for windows and windscreens.

Learners
36. Learner drivers in a car **MUST** be supervised by someone at least 21 years old who has held a full British licence for that type of car (automatic or manual) for at least three years and still holds one.

37. If you are learning to ride a motorcycle, scooter or moped you **MUST** take basic training with an approved training body before riding on the road, unless exempt. You **MUST NOT** carry a pillion passenger, pull a trailer or ride a solo motorcycle with an engine capacity in excess of 125 cc.

38. All vehicles under the control of a learner **MUST** display L-plates, which should be removed or covered at all other times (except on driving school vehicles).

Alcohol and the motorist
39. Do not drink and drive. Drinking alcohol seriously affects your driving. It reduces your coordination, slows down your reactions, affects your judgement of speed, distance and risk, and gives you a false sense of confidence. Your driving may be badly affected even if you are below the legal limit.

Remember: you may still be unfit to drive in the evening after drinking at lunchtime or in the morning after drinking the previous evening.

Seat belts
40. Wearing seat belts saves lives and reduces the risk of serious injury in an accident. You **MUST** wear a seat belt if one is available, unless you are exempt.

The following table summarises the main legal requirements for wearing seat belts.*

	Front seat	*Rear seat*	*Whose responsibility*
Driver	Must be worn if fitted	—	Driver
CHILD under 3 YEARS OF AGE	Appropriate child restraint must be worn	Appropriate child restraint must be worn if available	Driver
CHILD AGED 3 to 11 and under 1.5 metres (about 5 feet) in height	Appropriate child restraint must be worn if available. If not, an adult seat belt must be worn	Appropriate child restraint must be worn if available. If not, an adult seat belt must be worn if available	Driver
CHILD AGED 12 or 13 or younger child 1.5 metres or more in height	Adult seat belt must be worn if available	Adult seat belt must be worn if available	Driver
ADULT PASSENGERS	Must be worn if available	Must be worn if available	Passenger

* This table takes account of the requirements of EC Directive 91/671/EEC which applies from January 1993.

41. An appropriate child restraint is a baby carrier, child seat, harness or booster seat appropriate to the child's weight.

Children in cars
42. Do not let children sit behind the rear seats in an estate car or hatchback. Make sure that child safety door locks, where fitted, are used when children are in the car. Keep children under control in the car.

Car telephones and microphones
43. You **MUST** exercise proper control of your vehicle at all times. Do not use a hand-held telephone or microphone while you are driving. Find a safe place to stop first. Do not speak into a hands-free microphone if it will take your mind off the road. You **MUST NOT** stop on the hard shoulder of a motorway to answer or make a call, except in an emergency.

Traffic light signals and traffic signs
44. You **MUST** obey all traffic light signals and traffic signs giving orders. Make sure you also know and act on all other traffic signs and road markings.

Signals
45. Give signals to help and warn other road users, including pedestrians. Give them clearly and in plenty of time. Make sure your indicators are cancelled after use.

46. Watch out for signals given by other road users and take appropriate action.

47. You **MUST** obey signals by police officers and traffic wardens and signs used by school crossing patrols. **[2007]**

Driving your vehicle

Moving off
48. Use your mirrors before you move off. Signal if necessary before moving out. Look round as well for a final check. Only move off when it is safe to do so.

Driving along
49. Keep to the left, except where road signs or markings indicate otherwise or when you want to overtake, turn right or pass parked vehicles or pedestrians in the road. Let others overtake you if they want to.

50. You **MUST NOT** drive on a pavement or footpath except for access to property.

51. Use your mirrors frequently so you always know what is behind and to each side of you. Use them well before you carry out a manoeuvre or change speed; then give the correct signal if you need to. Motorcyclists should always look behind before manoeuvring.

Remember: mirrors–signal–manoeuvre

52. Watch out for cycles and motorcycles. Two-wheelers are far harder to spot than larger vehicles—but their riders have the same rights as other road users and are particularly vulnerable. Give riders plenty of room, especially if you are driving a long vehicle or towing a trailer.

53. Do not hold up a long queue of traffic. If you are driving a large or slow-moving vehicle and the road is narrow or winding, or there is a lot of traffic coming towards you, pull in where you can do so safely so that other vehicles can overtake.

Speed limits
54. You **MUST NOT** exceed the maximum speed limits for the road and for your vehicle. Street lights usually indicate a 30 mph speed limit unless signs show other limits.

55. Drive slowly in residential areas. In some roads there are features such as road humps and narrowings intended to slow you down. A 20 mph maximum speed limit may also be in force.

56. A speed limit does not mean it is safe to drive at that speed. Drive according to the conditions. Slow down if the road is wet or icy and in fog. Drive more slowly at night when it is harder to see pedestrians and cyclists.

Stopping distances
57. Drive at a speed that will allow you to stop well within the distance you can see to be clear. Leave enough space between you and the vehicle in front so that you can pull up safely if it suddenly slows down or stops. The safe rule is never to get closer than the overall stopping distances shown [below]. But in good conditions on roads carrying fast traffic, a two second time gap may be sufficient. The gap should be at least doubled on wet roads and increased further on icy roads. Large vehicles and motorcycles need more time to stop than cars. Drop back if someone overtakes and pulls into the gap in front of you.

SHORTEST STOPPING DISTANCES—IN METRES AND FEET

mph	Thinking distance		Braking distance		Overall stopping distance		On a dry road, a good car with good brakes and tyres and an alert driver will stop in the distances shown. Remember these are shortest stopping distances. Stopping distances increase greatly with wet and slippery roads, poor brakes and tyres, and tired drivers.
20	6	20	6	20	12	40	
30	9	30	14	45	23	75	
40	12	40	24	80	36	120	
50	15	50	38	125	53	175	
60	18	60	55	180	73	240	
70	21	70	75	245	96	315	

Fog code

58. Before driving in fog, consider if your journey is essential. If it is, allow extra time. Make sure your windscreen, windows and lights are clean and that all your lights (including brake lights) are working.

When driving in fog:

- See and be seen. If you cannot see clearly use dipped headlights. Use front or rear fog lights if visibility is seriously reduced (see Rule 133) but switch them off when visibility improves. Use your windscreen wipers and demisters.
- Check your mirrors and slow down. Keep a safe distance behind the vehicle in front. You should always be able to pull up within the distance you can see clearly.
- Do not hang on to the tail lights of the vehicle in front; it gives a false sense of security. In thick fog, if you can see the vehicle in front you are probably too close unless you are travelling very slowly.
- Be aware of your speed; you may be going much faster than you think. Do not accelerate to get away from a vehicle which is too close behind you. When you slow down, use your brakes so that your brake lights warn drivers behind you.
- When the word "Fog" is shown on a roadside signal but the road appears to be clear, be prepared for a bank of fog or drifting smoke ahead. Fog can drift rapidly and is often patchy. Even if it seems to be clearing, you can suddenly find yourself back in thick fog.

Winter driving

59. Prepare your vehicle for winter. Ensure that the battery is well maintained and that there are appropriate anti-freeze agents in the radiator and windscreen washer bottle.

60. In freezing or near freezing conditions, drive with great care even if the roads have been gritted. Roads may be slippery and surface conditions can change abruptly. Take care when overtaking gritting vehicles, particularly if you are riding a motorcycle.

61. Do not drive in snow unless your journey is essential. If it is, drive slowly but keep in as high a gear as possible to help avoid wheel spin. Avoid harsh acceleration, steering and braking. You **MUST** use headlights when visibility is seriously reduced by falling snow (see Rule 131).

62. Watch out for snow-ploughs which may throw out snow on either side. Do not overtake them unless the lane you intend to use has been cleared of snow.

The safety of pedestrians

63. Show consideration to pedestrians. Drive carefully and slowly when there are pedestrians about, especially in crowded shopping streets or residential areas and near bus and tram stops, parked milk floats or mobile shops. Watch out for pedestrians emerging suddenly into the road, especially from behind parked vehicles.

64. Watch out for children and elderly pedestrians who may not be able to judge your speed and could step into the road in front of you. Watch out for blind and partially sighted people who may be carrying white sticks (white with two red reflective bands for deaf and blind people) or using guide dogs and for people with other disabilities. Give them plenty of time to cross the road. Do not assume that a pedestrian can hear your vehicle coming; they may have hearing difficulties.

65. Drive slowly near schools. In some places, there may be a flashing amber signal below the "School" warning sign which tells you that there may be children crossing the road ahead. When these signals are flashing, drive very slowly until you are well clear of the area. Drive carefully when passing a stationary bus showing a "School Bus" sign as children may be getting on or off.

66. You **MUST** stop when a school crossing patrol shows a "STOP—CHILDREN" sign.

67. Be careful near a parked ice-cream van—children are more interested in ice-cream than in traffic.

68. At road junctions, give way to pedestrians who are already crossing the road into which you are turning.

69. Give way to pedestrians on a pavement you need to cross, eg to reach a driveway.

Remember: pavements are for people—not for vehicles

70. Be prepared for pedestrians walking in the road, especially on narrow country roads. Give them plenty of room. Take extra care on left-hand bends and keep your speed down.

Pedestrian crossings

71. As you approach a Zebra crossing, look out for people waiting to cross (especially children, elderly people or people with disabilities). Be ready to slow down or stop to let them cross. When someone has stepped on to a crossing, you **MUST** give way. Allow more time for stopping on wet or icy roads. Do not wave people across; this could be dangerous if another vehicle is approaching.

72. You **MUST NOT** overtake or park on a Zebra or Pelican crossing, including the area marked by zig-zag lines. Even when there are no zig-zags, do not overtake just before the crossing.

73. In a queue of traffic, you **MUST** keep pedestrian crossings clear.

74. At Pelican crossings a flashing amber light will follow the red "STOP" light. When the amber light is flashing, you **MUST** give way to any pedestrians on the crossing. A Pelican crossing which goes straight across the road is one crossing even when there is a central island and you **MUST** wait for pedestrians crossing from the other side of the island. Do not harass pedestrians—for example, by revving your engine.

75. At pedestrian crossings controlled by lights, give way to pedestrians who are still crossing after the signal for vehicles has changed to green.

Emergency vehicles

76. Look and listen for ambulances, fire engines, police or other emergency vehicles with flashing blue lights or sirens. Make room for them to pass (if necessary by pulling to the side of the road and stopping) but do not endanger other road users. A flashing green light on a vehicle indicates a doctor answering an emergency call so give way as soon as possible.

Flashing amber lights on vehicles

77. Drive carefully when you see a flashing amber light as it warns of a slow-moving vehicle (such as a road gritter or tractor) or a vehicle which has broken down.

Police stopping procedures

78. If the police want to stop your vehicle they will, where possible, attract your attention from behind by flashing their headlights or blue light or by sounding their siren or horn. A police officer will direct you to pull over to the side by pointing and using the left indicator. You **MUST** pull over and stop as soon as it is safe to do so and then switch off your engine.

Buses

79. Give way to buses whenever you can do so safely, especially when they signal to pull away from bus stops. Look out for people leaving the bus and crossing the road.

Animals

80. Watch out for animals being led or ridden on the road and take extra care at left-hand bends and on narrow country roads. Drive slowly past animals. Give them plenty of room and be ready to stop. Do not scare animals by sounding your horn or revving your engine.

81. Look out for horse riders' signals and be aware that they may not move to the centre of the road prior to turning right. Riders of horses and ponies are often children—so take extra care.

Single-track roads

82. Some roads (often called single-track roads) are only wide enough for one vehicle. They may have special passing places. Pull into a passing place on your left, or wait opposite a passing place on your right, when you see a vehicle coming towards you, or the driver behind you wants to overtake. Give way to vehicles coming uphill whenever you can. Do not park in passing places. **[2008]**

Lines and lanes along the road

83. A single broken line, with long markings and short gaps, along the centre of the road is a hazard warning line. Do not cross it unless you can see that the road is clear well ahead.

84. Where there are double white lines along the road and the line nearest to you is unbroken, you **MUST NOT** cross or straddle it unless you need to get in or out of property or a side road, or avoid something stationary blocking your lane.

85. Where there are double white lines along the road and the line nearest to you is broken, you may cross the lines to overtake if it is safe, provided you can do so before reaching an unbroken white line on your side.

86. Areas of white diagonal stripes or white chevrons painted on the road are to separate traffic lanes or to protect traffic turning right. Where the marked area is bordered by an unbroken white line, you **MUST NOT** enter it except in an emergency. Where the line is broken, you should not enter the area unless you can see that it is safe to do so.

87. Short broken white lines divide the road into lanes—keep between them. Coloured reflecting road studs may be used with white lines—white studs to mark the lanes or middle of the road, red studs to mark the left edge of the road and amber studs by the central reservation of a dual carriageway. Green studs may be used across lay-bys and side roads.

88. On some hills an extra uphill "crawler" lane may be provided. Use this lane if you are driving a slow moving vehicle or if there are vehicles behind you wishing to overtake.

Lane discipline
89. If you need to change lane, first use your mirrors to make sure you will not force another driver or rider to swerve or slow down. If it is safe to move over, signal before you do so.

Remember: mirrors—signal—manoeuvre

90. At some junctions, lanes may go in different directions. Follow the signs and get into the correct lane in good time.

91. In a traffic hold-up, do not try to "jump the queue" by cutting into another lane or by overtaking the vehicles in front of you.

92. Where a single carriageway has three lanes and the road markings do not give priority to traffic in either direction, use the middle lane only for overtaking or turning right. Remember—you have no more right to use the middle lane than a driver coming from the opposite direction. Do not use the right-hand lane.

93. Where a single carriageway has four or more lanes, do not use the lanes on the right-hand side of the road unless signs and markings indicate that you can.

94. On a two-lane dual carriageway, use the right-hand lane only for overtaking or turning right.

95. On a three-lane dual carriageway, stay in the left-hand lane. If there are slower vehicles than you in that lane, use the middle lane to overtake them but return to the left-hand lane when it is clear. The right-hand lane is for overtaking (or turning right); if you use it for overtaking, move back into the middle lane and then into the left-hand lane as soon as it is safe to do so.

96. In one-way streets, choose the correct lane for your exit as soon as you can. Do not change lanes suddenly. Unless road signs or markings indicate otherwise, choose the left-hand lane when going to the left, the right-hand lane when going to the right and the most appropriate lane when going straight ahead. Remember—traffic could be passing on both sides.

97. Bus and tram lanes are shown by road markings and signs. You **MUST NOT** drive in a tram lane or in a bus lane during its period of operation unless the signs indicate you may do so.

98. Cycle lanes are shown by road markings and signs. You **MUST NOT** drive or park in a cycle lane marked by an unbroken white lane during its period of operation. Do not drive in a cycle lane marked by a broken white line unless if is unavoidable.

[2009]

Overtaking

99. Do not overtake unless you can do so safely. Make sure the road is sufficiently clear ahead and behind. Do not get too close to the vehicle you intend to overtake—it will obscure your view of the road ahead. Use your mirrors. Signal before you start to move out. Take extra care at night and in poor visibility when it is harder to judge speed and distance.

Remember: mirrors—signal—manoeuvre

100. Once you have started to overtake, quickly move past the vehicle you are overtaking, leaving it plenty of room. Then move back to the left as soon as you can but do not cut in.

101. When overtaking motorcyclists, pedal-cyclists or horse riders, give them at least as much room as you would give a car. Remember that cyclists may be unable to ride in a straight line, especially when it is windy or the road surface is uneven.

102. Do not overtake on the left unless:

* the vehicle in front is signalling to turn right, and you can overtake on the left safely;
* traffic is moving slowly in queues and vehicles in a lane on the right are moving more slowly than you are.

103. In slow-moving traffic queues, move to a lane on your left only to turn left. Do not change lanes to the left to overtake. Cyclists and motorcyclists overtaking traffic queues should watch out for pedestrians crossing between vehicles and vehicles emerging from junctions.

104. Do not increase your speed when you are being overtaken. Slow down if necessary to let the overtaking vehicle pass and pull in.

105. On a two-lane single carriageway give way to vehicles coming towards you before passing parked vehicles or other obstructions on your side of the road.

106. a You **MUST NOT** overtake:

* if you would have to cross to straddle double white lines with an unbroken line nearest to you;
* if you are in the zig-zag area at a pedestrian crossing;
* after a "No Overtaking" sign and until you pass a sign cancelling the restriction;

b DO NOT overtake:

i) where you cannot see far enough ahead to be sure it is safe, for example when you are approaching or at:

* a corner or bend;
* a hump bridge;
* the brow of a hill; or

ii) where you might come into conflict with other road users, for example:

* approaching or at a road junction on either side of the road;
* where the road narrows;
* when approaching a school crossing patrol;
* where you would have to drive over an area marked with diagonal stripes or chevrons;
* where you would have to enter a lane reserved for buses, trams or cyclists;
* between a bus or tram and the kerb when it is at a stop;
* where traffic is queuing at junctions or road works;
* when you would force another vehicle to swerve or slow down;
* at a level crossing.

If in doubt—do not overtake **[2010]**

Road junctions

107. Take extra care at junctions. Check your position and speed. Junctions are particularly dangerous for cyclists, motorcyclists and pedestrians, so watch out for them before you turn. Watch out for long vehicles which may be turning at a junction ahead; they may have to use the whole width of the road to make the turn.

108. Give way to pedestrians crossing a road into which you are turning.

109. At a junction with a "STOP" sign and an unbroken white line across the road, you **MUST** stop behind the line. Wait for a safe gap in the traffic before you move off.

110. At a junction with broken white lines across the road (it may also have a "Give Way" sign or a triangle marked on the road), you **MUST** give way to traffic on the other road.

111. When waiting at a junction, do not assume that a vehicle coming from the right and signalling left will do so. Wait and make sure.

112. When going straight across or turning right into a dual carriageway, treat each half as a separate road. Wait in the central reservation until there is a safe gap in the traffic on the second half of the road. If the central reservation is too narrow for the length of your vehicle, wait until you can cross both carriageways in one go.

113. Box junctions have criss-cross yellow lines painted on the road. You **MUST NOT** enter the box until your exit road or lane from it is clear. But you may enter the box when you want to turn right and are only stopped from doing so by oncoming traffic or by vehicles waiting to turn right.

Junctions controlled by traffic lights
114. At junctions controlled by traffic lights, you **MUST** stop behind the white "STOP" line across your side of the road unless the light is green. You **MUST NOT** move forward when the red and amber lights are showing. Do not go forward when the traffic lights are green unless there is room for you to clear the junction safely or you are taking up a position to turn right.

115. Where traffic lights have a green filter arrow indicating a filter only lane, do not enter that lane unless you want to go in the direction of the arrow. Give other traffic, especially cyclists, room to move into the correct lane.

116. If the traffic lights are not working, proceed with caution.

Turning right
117. Well before you turn right, use your mirrors to make sure you know the position and movement of traffic behind you. Give a right-turn signal and, as soon as it is safe for you to do so, take up a position just left of the middle of the road or in the space marked for right-turning traffic. If possible leave room for other vehicles to pass on the left. Wait until there is a safe gap between you and any oncoming vehicle. Watch out for cyclists, motorcyclists and pedestrians; then make the turn, but do not cut the corner. Take great care when turning into a main road; you will need to watch for traffic in both directions and wait for a safe gap.

Remember: mirrors—signal—manoeuvre

118. When turning right at a junction where an oncoming vehicle is also turning right, it is normally safer to keep the other vehicle to your right and turn behind it: ie offside-to-offside. Before you complete the turn, check for other traffic on the road you want to cross.

119. If the lay-out of the junction or the traffic situation makes offside-to-offside passing impracticable, pass nearside-to-nearside, but take care. The other vehicle could obstruct your view of the road so watch carefully for oncoming traffic.

120. When turning right from a dual carriageway, wait in the opening in the central reservation until you are sure it is safe to cross the other carriageway.

Turning left
121. Well before you turn left, use your mirrors and give a left-turn signal. Do not overtake a cyclist, motorcyclist or horse rider immediately before turning left and watch

out for traffic coming up on your left before you make the turn. When turning, keep as close to the left as it is safe to do so.

122. If you want to turn left across a bus lane, cycle lane or tramway, give way to any vehicles using it from either direction. [2011]

Roundabouts

123. On approaching a roundabout, decide as early as possible which exit you need to take and get into the correct lane. Reduce your speed. On reaching the roundabout, give way to traffic on your right unless road markings indicate otherwise. Watch out for traffic already on the roundabout, especially cyclists and motor cyclists. At some junctions there may be more than one roundabout. At each one, use the normal rules for roundabouts.

124. Unless signs or road markings indicate otherwise:
- When turning left:
  - signal left and approach in the left-hand lane;
  - keep to the left on the roundabout and continue signalling left.
- When going straight ahead:
  - do not signal on approach;
  - approach in the left-hand or centre lane on a three-lane road (on a two-lane road you may approach in the right-hand lane if the left-hand lane is blocked);
  - take the same course on the roundabout;
  - signal left after you have passed the exit before the one you want.
- When turning right or going full circle:
  - signal right and approach in the right-hand lane;
  - keep to the right on the roundabout;
  - continue to signal right until you have passed the exit before the one you want, then signal left.

When there are more than three lanes at the entrance to a roundabout, use the most appropriate lane on approach and through the roundabout.

125. Watch out for traffic crossing in front of you on the roundabout, especially vehicles intending to leave by the next exit. Show them consideration.

126. Watch out for motorcyclists, cyclists and horse riders. Give them plenty of room. Cyclists and horse riders will often keep to the left on the roundabout; they may also indicate right to show they are continuing around the roundabout.

127. Long vehicles may have to take a different course, both approaching and on the roundabout. Watch for their signals and give them plenty of room.

128. The same rules apply to mini-roundabouts. If possible, pass around the central marking. Watch out for vehicles making a U-turn and for long vehicles which may have to cross the centre of the mini-roundabout. [2012]

Reversing

129. Before reversing make sure there are no pedestrians—particularly children—or obstructions in the road behind you. Be aware of the "blind spot" behind you—the part of the road you cannot see from the driving seat. Reverse with care. If you cannot see clearly, get someone to guide you. You **MUST NOT** reverse your vehicle for longer than necessary.

130. NEVER reverse from a side-road into a main road. Avoid reversing into the road from a driveway; where possible, reverse in and drive out. [2013]

Vehicle Lights

131. You **MUST**:
- make sure all your lights are clean, that they work and that your headlights are properly adjusted—badly adjusted headlights can dazzle other road users and may cause accidents;
- use sidelights between sunset and sunrise;
- use headlights at night (between half an hour after sunset and half an hour before sunrise) on all roads without street lighting and on roads where the street lights are more than 185 metres (600 ft) apart or are not lit;

- use headlights or front fog lights when visibility is seriously reduced, generally when you cannot see for more than 100 metres (328 ft).

132. You should also:

- use headlights at night on lit motorways and roads with a speed limit in excess of 50 mph;
- use dipped headlights at night in built-up areas unless the road is well lit;
- cut down glare. If your vehicle has dim-dip, use it instead of dipped headlights in dull daytime weather and at night in built-up areas with good street lighting;
- dip your headlights when meeting vehicles or other road users and before you dazzle the driver of a vehicle you are following;
- slow down or stop if you are dazzled by oncoming headlights.

Fog lights
133. Use fog lights when visibility is seriously reduced, generally when you cannot see for more than 100 metres (328 ft). You **MUST NOT** use fog lights at other times. Remember to switch them off when visibility improves.

Hazard warning lights
134. Hazard warning lights may be used when your vehicle is stopped to warn that it is temporarily obstructing traffic. You may only use them whilst driving if you are on a motorway or unrestricted dual carriageway and you need to warn drivers behind you of a hazard or obstruction ahead. Only use them for just long enough to ensure that your warning has been observed. Never use them as an excuse for dangerous or illegal parking.

Flashing headlights
135. Flashing your headlights means only one thing—it lets another road user know you are there. Do not flash your headlights for any other reason and never assume that it is a signal to proceed.

Use of the horn
136. When your vehicle is moving, use your horn only if you need to warn other road users of your presence. Never sound your horn aggressively. You **MUST NOT** use your horn:

- between 11.30 pm and 7.00 am in a built-up area;
- when your vehicle is stationary, unless a moving vehicle poses a danger.   **[2014]**

Waiting and parking

137. Wherever possible, pull off the road on to an area provided for parking. If you have to stop on the road, stop as close as you can to the side. Leave plenty of room when parking next to or behind a vehicle displaying a disabled person's badge. Before you or your passengers open a door, make sure it will not hit anyone passing on the road or pavement or force them to swerve; watch out particularly for pedestrians, cyclists and motorcyclists. It is safer for you and your passengers (especially children) to get out on the side next to the kerb. You **MUST** switch off the engine and headlights. Before leaving the vehicle, ensure that the handbrake is on firmly. Always lock your vehicle.

138. You **MUST NOT** stop or park on:

- the carriageway of a motorway (see Rules 179–180);
- a pedestrian crossing, including the area marked by the zig-zag lines (see Rule 72);
- a Clearway;
- an Urban Clearway within its hours of operation except to pick up or set down passengers;
- a road marked with double white lines even if one of the lines is broken, except to pick up or set down passengers;
- a bus, tram or cycle lane during its period of operation.

139. You **MUST NOT** park where there are parking restrictions shown by yellow lines along the edge of the carriageway, or red lines in the case of specially designated "red routes". The periods when restrictions apply are indicated by signs either adjacent to the kerb or on entry to a controlled parking zone. Use an authorised parking space if one is available.

140. Think before you park. **DO NOT** park your vehicle where it would endanger or inconvenience pedestrians or other road users, for example:

- on a footpath, pavement or cycle track;
- near a school entrance;
- at or near a bus stop or taxi rank;
- on the approach to a level crossing;
- within 10 metres (32 ft) of a junction, except in an authorised parking space;
- near the brow of a hill or hump bridge;
- opposite a traffic island or (if this would cause an obstruction) another parked vehicle;
- where you would force other traffic to enter a tram lane;
- where the kerb has been lowered to help wheelchair users;
- in front of the entrance to a property.

141. You **MUST NOT** park in a parking space reserved for specific users, such as Orange Badge holders or residents, unless entitled to do so.

Parking at night
142. You **MUST NOT** park at night facing against the direction of traffic flow.

143. When parking on the road at night, you **MUST** leave your sidelights on. However cars, goods vehicles not exceeding 1525 kg unladen, invalid carriages and motorcycles may be parked without lights on a road with speed limit of 30 mph or less if they are:

- at least 10 metres (32 ft) away from any junction, close to the kerb and facing in the direction of the traffic flow; or
- in a recognised parking place.

Other vehicles and trailers, and all vehicles with projecting loads, **MUST NOT** be left on a road at night without lights.

Parking in fog
144. It is especially dangerous to park on the road in fog. If it is unavoidable, leave your sidelights on.

Loading and unloading
145. Restrictions on loading and unloading are shown by yellow markings on the kerb. Loading and unloading may be permitted when parking is otherwise restricted.

146. Goods vehicles with a maximum laden weight of over 7.5 tonnes (including any trailer) **MUST NOT** be parked on a central reservation without police permission or on a verge or footway, except where this is essential for loading or unloading (in which case the vehicle **MUST NOT** be left unattended). **[2015]**

Road works

147. Special care is needed at road works. Watch out for and act on all signs on the approach to and at road works. Use your mirrors and get into the correct lane for your vehicle in good time. Do not switch lanes to overtake queuing traffic or drive through an area marked off by traffic cones. Watch out for traffic entering or leaving the works area, but do not be distracted by what is going on there.

148. You **MUST NOT** exceed any temporary maximum speed limit. **[2016]**

Breakdowns and accidents

149. If you have a breakdown, think first of other traffic. Get your vehicle off the road if possible.

150. If your vehicle is causing an obstruction, warn other traffic by using your hazard warning lights. If you carry a red warning triangle, put it on the road at least 50 metres (164 ft) before the obstruction and on the same side of the road (150 metres [492 ft] on the hard shoulder of motorways). At night or in poor visibility, do not stand behind your vehicle or let anyone else do so—you could prevent other drivers seeing your rear lights.

151. If anything falls from your vehicle on to the road, stop and retrieve it as soon as it is safe to do so (for motorways see Rule 178).

152. If you see warning signs or the flashing lights of emergency vehicles or vehicles in the distance moving very slowly or stopped, there could have been an accident. Slow down and be ready to stop. Do not be distracted when passing the accident; you could cause another one.

153. If you are involved in, or stop to give assistance at, an accident:

*   warn other traffic, eg by switching on your hazard warning lights. Ask drivers to switch off their engines and put out any cigarettes;
*   arrange for the emergency services to be called immediately with full details of the accident location and any casualties; on a motorway, use the emergency telephone;
*   do not move injured people from their vehicles unless they are in immediate danger from fire or explosion. Do not remove a motorcyclist's helmet unless it is essential. Be prepared to give first aid;
*   move uninjured people away from the vehicles to safety; on a motorway this should be well away from the traffic, the hard shoulder and the central reservation;
*   stay at the scene until emergency services arrive.

Accidents involving dangerous goods

154. Vehicles carrying dangerous goods in packages will be marked with plain orange reflectorised plates. Road tankers and vehicles carrying tank containers will have hazard warning plates. If an accident involves a vehicle containing dangerous goods, follow the advice in Rule 153 and, in particular:

*   switch off engines and **DO NOT SMOKE**;
*   keep uninjured people well away from the vehicle and where the wind will not blow dangerous substances towards them. Even if you act to save a life, take care that you too are not affected by dangerous substances;
*   give the emergency services as much information as possible about the labels and other markings. **[2017]**

MOTORWAYS

Many other Rules also apply to motorway driving, either wholly or in part: Rules 28–35, 39–49, 51, 52, 54, 56–62, 76–78, 87, 89–91, 94, 95, 131–136, 138, 147–150, 152–154 and 213.

General

155. Motorways **MUST NOT** be used by pedestrians, provisional licence holders, riders of motorcycles under 50 cc, cyclists and horse riders. Slow-moving vehicles, agricultural vehicles and some invalid carriages are also prohibited.

156. Traffic on motorways travels more quickly than on other roads, so you have to think quickly too. It is especially important to use your mirrors earlier and look much further ahead than you would on other roads.

157. Make sure your vehicle is fit to cruise at speed, has correct tyre pressures and enough fuel, oil and water to get you at least to the next service area. See that the windscreen, windows, mirrors, lights and reflectors are clean and that the windscreen washer bottle is topped up. You **MUST** make sure that any load you are carrying or towing is secure. **[2018]**

Joining the motorway

158. When you join the motorway you will normally approach it from a road on the left (a slip-road). You **MUST** give way to traffic already on the motorway. While on the slip-road, check the traffic already on the motorway and adjust your speed so that you join the left-hand lane where there is a safe gap and at the same speed as traffic in that lane.

159. At some junctions the slip-road will continue as an extra lane on the motorway.

Where signs indicate that this will happen, stay in that lane until it becomes part of the motorway.

160. After joining the motorway, stay in the left-hand lane long enough to get used to the speed of traffic before overtaking. **[2019]**

On the motorway

161. When you can see well ahead and the road conditions are good, drive at a steady cruising speed which you and your vehicle can handle easily. You **MUST NOT** exceed the maximum speed limit for your vehicle. Keep a safe distance from the vehicle in front and increase the gap on wet or icy roads, or in fog (see Rules 57–58).

162. Driving can make you feel sleepy. To help prevent this, make sure there is a supply of fresh air into your vehicle, stop at a service area or leave the motorway and find a safe place to stop.

163. You **MUST NOT** reverse, cross the central reservation, or drive against the traffic flow. Even if you have missed your exit, or have taken the wrong route, carry on to the next exit.

Lane discipline

164. Keep in the left-hand lane unless overtaking. You may use the lane to the right of a stream of slower vehicles to overtake them but return to the lane to your left when you have passed them.

165. When approaching a junction make sure you are in the correct lane; at some junctions a lane may lead directly off the motorway.

166. Some vehicles **MUST NOT** use the right-hand lane of a motorway with three or more lanes.

Overtaking

167. Overtake only on the right unless traffic is moving in queues and the queue on your right is moving more slowly than you are. Do not move to a lane on your left to overtake. You **MUST NOT** use the hard shoulder for overtaking.

168. Do not overtake unless you are sure it is safe to do so. Before you start to overtake, make sure that the lane you will be joining is sufficiently clear ahead and behind. Use your mirrors. Remember that traffic may be coming up behind you very quickly. Signal before you move out. Be especially careful at night and in poor visibility when it is harder to judge speed and distance.

169. Always get back to the left-hand lane or, if it is occupied, the middle lane, as soon as you can after overtaking. Signal your intention to change lanes. Do not cut in on the vehicle you have overtaken.

Remember: mirrors—signal—manoeuvre

Motorway signals

170. Motorway signals are used to warn you of a danger ahead, for example an accident or risk of skidding. Usually they are situated on the central reservation where they apply to all lanes. On very busy stretches, they may be overheard with a signal for each lane.

171. Where there is danger, amber lights flash. The signal may also show a temporary maximum speed limit, lanes that are closed or a message (for example, "Fog"). Reduce your speed and look out for the danger until you pass a signal which is not flashing and you are sure it is safe to increase your speed.

172. If red lights on the overhead signals flash above your lane (there may also be a red X), you **MUST NOT** go beyond the signal in that lane. If red lights flash on a signal in the central reservation or a slip-road, you **MUST NOT** go beyond the signal in any lane.

173. All signals are there to protect you. Always do what they say. Remember—danger, such as drifting fog, may be there even if you cannot immediately see the cause.

Road studs and signs
174. To help drivers on motorways at night, there are amber-coloured studs marking the right-hand edge of the road, red studs marking the left-hand edge and green studs separating the slip-road from the motorway. White studs separate the lanes on the motorway.

175. On some motorways, directions signs are placed over the road. If you need to change lanes, do so in good time.

Fog
176. When driving in fog, obey the fog code (see Rule 58).

Road works
177. Take special care at road works (see Rules 147–148). One or more lanes may be closed to traffic and a lower speed limit may apply. Keep a safe distance from the vehicle in front (see Rule 57).

Obstructions
178. If anything that could be dangerous falls from your vehicle or any other vehicle, stop at the next emergency telephone to tell the police. Do not try to remove it yourself.

Stopping and parking
179. You **MUST NOT** stop except:

- in an emergency;
- when told to do so by the police, by an emergency sign or by flashing red light signals.

180. You **MUST NOT** park on:

- the carriageway;
- the slip-road;
- the hard shoulder;
- the central reservation.

181. You **MUST NOT** pick up or set down anyone on a slip-road or on any other part of the motorway.

182. You **MUST NOT** walk on the carriageway except in an emergency.

Breakdowns
183. If your vehicle develops a problem, leave the motorway at the next exit or pull into a service area. If you cannot do so, you should:

- try to stop near an emergency telephone (you will find them at one mile intervals along the hard shoulder);
- pull on to the hard shoulder and stop as far to the left as possible;
- switch on your hazard warning lights;
- keep your sidelights on if it is dark or visibility is poor;
- leave the vehicle by the left-hand door and ensure your passengers do the same (leave any animals inside);
- ensure passengers wait near the vehicle, but well away from the carriageway and hard shoulder, and that children are kept under control;
- walk to an emergency telephone (following the arrows on the posts at the back of the hard shoulder)—it is free to use and connects directly to the police. Give full details to the police—tell them if you are a woman travelling alone—and then return to your vehicle;
- wait near your vehicle but well away from the carriageway and hard shoulder. If you feel at risk, return to your vehicle by a left-hand door and lock all doors. Leave your vehicle again as soon as you feel the danger has passed.

If you cannot get your vehicle on to the hard shoulder:

- switch on your hazard warning lights;
- leave your vehicle only if you are sure you can safely get clear of the carriageway;
- if in doubt, remain in your vehicle wearing a seat belt until the emergency services arrive;
- do not attempt to place a warning triangle on the carriageway.

If you have a disability which prevents you from following the above advice:
- stay in your vehicle with all doors locked;
- switch on your hazard warning lights;
- display a "Help" pennant or, if you have a car telephone, contact the emergency services.

Do not attempt even simple repairs and remember you **MUST NOT** try to cross the motorway.

184. Before rejoining the carriageway, build-up speed on the hard shoulder and watch for a safe gap in the traffic.   [2020]

Leaving the motorway

185. Unless signs indicate that a lane leads directly off the motorway, you will leave the motorway by a slip-road on your left. Watch for the signs letting you know you are getting near your exit. If you are not already in the left-hand lane, move into it well before reaching your exit and stay in it. Signal left in good time and slow down as necessary.

186. When leaving the motorway or using a link road between motorways, your speed may be higher than you think—50 mph may feel like 30 mph. Check your speedometer and adjust your speed accordingly. Some slip-roads and link roads have sharp bends so you will need to slow down.   [2021]

EXTRA RULES FOR CYCLISTS

Choosing and maintaining your cycle

187. Choose the right size of cycle for comfort and safety.

188. Make sure that the:
- lights and reflectors are kept clean and in good working order;
- tyres are in good condition and inflated to the pressure recommended by the cycle manufacturer;
- brakes and gears are working correctly;
- chain is properly adjusted and oiled;
- saddle is adjusted to the correct height.

189. Fit a bell and use it when necessary to warn other road users, particularly blind and partially sighted pedestrians, that you are there.   [2022]

Safety equipment and clothing

190. Wear a cycle helmet which conforms to recognised safety standards. Choose appropriate clothes for cycling. Avoid long coats or other clothes which may get tangled in the chain or a wheel. Light-coloured or fluorescent clothing helps other road users see you in daylight and poor visibility.

191. At night you **MUST** use front and rear lights and a red rear reflector. Reflective material such as belts, arm and ankle bands, wheel reflectors and "spacer" flags will also help you to be seen at night.   [2023]

Cycling

192. You **MUST** obey traffic signs and traffic light signals. You **MUST NOT** cycle on the pavement.

193. Look all around before moving away from the kerb, turning or manoeuvring to make sure it is safe to do so. Then give a clear arm signal to show other road users what you intend to do.

194. Look well ahead for obstructions in the road, such as drains, pot-holes and parked cars so that you do not have to swerve suddenly to avoid them. Leave plenty of room when passing parked cars and watch out for doors being opened into your path.

195. Take care near road humps, narrowings and other traffic calming features. Do not ride along a drainage channel at the edge of the road to avoid such features.

196. Do not leave your cycle where it would endanger or obstruct other road users, for example lying on the pavement. Use cycle parking facilities where provided.

Road junctions
197. Watch out for vehicles turning in front of you from or into a side road. Do not overtake on the left of vehicles slowing down to turn left. Pay particular attention to long vehicles which need a lot of room to manoeuvre at corners and may have to move over to the right before turning left. Wait until they have completed the manoeuvre.

198. When turning right, check the traffic behind you, signal and when it is safe move to the centre of the road. Wait until there is a safe gap in traffic before completing the turn. It may be safer to wait on the left until there is a safe gap or to dismount and walk your cycle across the road.

Signal controlled junctions
199. Traffic signals also apply to cyclists. You **MUST NOT** cross the stop line across the road when the lights are red. Some junctions have advanced stop lines which enable cyclists to position themselves ahead of other traffic. Where these are provided, use them.

Roundabouts
200. Rules 123–128 set out the correct procedures at roundabouts but you may feel safer approaching in the left-hand lane and keeping to the left in the roundabout. If you do keep to the left, take extra care when cycling across exits and signal right to show you are not leaving. Watch out for vehicles crossing your path to leave or join the roundabout.

201. Watch out for long vehicles on the roundabout as they need more space to manoeuvre. It may be safer to wait until they have cleared the roundabout.

202. If you are unsure about using the roundabout, dismount and walk your cycle round on the pavement or verge.

Bus lanes
203. You may only use a bus lane if the signs include a cycle symbol. Be very careful when overtaking a bus or leaving a bus lane as you will be entering a busier traffic flow.

Dual carriageways
204. Take great care when crossing or turning on to a dual carriageway where there are no traffic light signals. Wait for safe gaps and cross each carriageway in turn. Remember that traffic on most dual carriageways travels quickly.

Cycle lanes and tracks
205. Use cycle lanes and tracks wherever possible. They can make your journey safer and quicker.

206. Cycle lanes are marked by either an unbroken or broken white line along the carriageway (see Rule 98). Keep within the lane and watch out for traffic emerging from side turnings.

207. Cycle tracks are located away from the road. Where a cycle track is shared with a footpath, you **MUST** keep to the track intended for cyclists. Watch out for pedestrians, especially elderly people and people with disabilities, using the footpath or crossing the cycle track.

208. Cycle tracks on opposite sides of the road are sometimes linked by signalled crossings. If the crossing is provided for cyclists only, you may ride across but you **MUST NOT** cross until the green cycle symbol is showing. Do not ride across a Pelican crossing.

Safe riding
209. When cycling:

- keep both hands on the handlebars except when signalling or changing gear;
- keep both feet on the pedals;
- do not ride more than two abreast;
- ride in single file on cycle tracks and lanes, and on narrow roads when in traffic;
- do not ride close behind another vehicle;

- do not carry anything which will affect your balance or may get tangled up with your wheels or chain.

210. You **MUST NOT** carry a passenger unless your cycle has been built or adapted to carry one.

211. You **MUST NOT** ride under the influence of drink or drugs. **[2024]**

ANIMALS

General

212. Do not let your dog out on its own. Keep it on a short lead when taking it for a walk on or near a road or on a path shared with cyclists.

213. Keep animals under control in vehicles. Make sure they cannot distract you while you are driving. Do not let a dog out of a vehicle on to the road unless it is on a lead.

214. If you are herding animals, keep to the left of the road; if possible, send another person along the road to warn other road users, for example at bends and the brows of hills.

215. If you have to herd animals after dark, wear reflective clothing and ensure that white lights are carried at the front and red lights at the rear of the herd. **[2025]**

Horse riders

216. Before you take a horse on to a road, make sure you can control it. If you think that your horse will be nervous of traffic, always ride with other, less nervous, horses.

217. Make sure all tack fits well and is in good condition. Never ride a horse without a saddle or bridle.

218. Wear an approved safety helmet and fasten it securely—children under the age of 14 **MUST** do this. You should also wear boots or shoes with hard soles and heels.

219. If you have to ride at night, wear reflective clothing and make sure your horse has reflective bands on its legs above the fetlock joints. Carry lights which show white to the front and red to the rear.

220. Before riding off or turning, look behind you to make sure it is safe and then give a clear arm signal. When riding, keep to the left. If you are leading a horse, keep it to your left. In one-way streets, move in the direction of the traffic flow.

221. Never ride more than two abreast. Ride in single file on narrow roads.

222. You **MUST NOT** take a horse on to a footpath, pavement or cycle track. Use a bridle-path where possible.

223. Avoid roundabouts wherever possible. If you have to use them, keep to the left and watch out for vehicles crossing your path to leave or join the roundabout. Signal right when riding across exits to show you are not leaving. Signal left just before you leave the roundabout.

224. When riding:
- keep both hands on the reins unless you are signalling;
- keep both feet in the stirrups;
- do not carry another person;
- do not carry anything which might affect your balance or get tangled up with the reins;
- wear light-coloured or fluorescent clothing in daylight and reflective materials at night. **[2026]**

RAILWAY LEVEL CROSSINGS

General

225. A level crossing is where a road crosses railway lines. Approach and cross it with care. Never drive on to a crossing until the road is clear on the other side—do not drive "nose to tail" over it. Never stop on or just after a crossing. Never park close to a crossing.

226. Most crossings have full or half barriers, traffic light signals with a steady amber light and twin flashing red stop lights and an audible alarm. You **MUST** stop behind the white line across the road when the lights come on. If you have already crossed the white line when the amber lights or audible alarm start, keep going.

227. If a train goes by and the red lights continue to flash or the audible alarm changes tone, you must wait. Another train will be passing soon. It is only safe to cross when the lights go off and any barriers open.

228. At crossings with half barriers, never zig-zag around the barriers. They are lowered because a train is approaching.

Railway telephones
229. If you are driving a large or slow-moving vehicle, or herding animals, you **MUST** obey any sign instructing you to use the railway telephone to obtain permission to cross. You **MUST** also telephone when clear of the crossing.

Accidents and breakdowns
230. If your vehicle breaks down, or if you have an accident on a crossing:

* get everyone out of the vehicle and clear of the crossing;
* if there is a railway telephone, use it immediately to tell the signal operator and follow the instructions you are given;
* if it is possible, and there is time before a train arrives, move the vehicle clear of the crossing. If the alarm sounds, or the amber light comes on, get clear of the crossing.

Crossings without signals
231. At crossings where there are gates or barriers but no lights, stop when they begin to close. Pedestrians should wait at the barrier or gate.

Unattended crossings with signals
232. Some unattended crossings with gates or barriers have "STOP" signs and small red and green lights. Do not cross when the red light is on as a train is approaching. Only cross if the green light is on. If crossing with a vehicle, open the gates or barriers on both sides of the crossing, then check that the green light is still on and cross quickly. Close the gates or barriers when you are clear of the crossing.

Unattended crossings without signals
233. Some crossings have gates but no attendant or traffic signals. At such crossings, stop, look both ways, listen and make sure no train is approaching. If there is a railway telephone, contact the signal operator to make sure it is safe to cross. If crossing with a vehicle, open the gates on both sides of the crossing, then check that no train is coming and cross quickly. When you have cleared the crossing, close both gates. Remember to inform the signal operator again when you are clear of the crossing.

Open crossings
234. At an open crossing with no gates, barriers, attendant or traffic lights, there will be a "Give Way" sign. Look both ways, listen and make sure there is no train coming before you cross. Always "Give Way" to trains—they cannot stop easily! **[2027]**

TRAMWAYS

General

235. You **MUST NOT** enter a road or lane reserved for trams. Diamond-shaped signs give instructions to tram drivers only.

236. Take extra care where trams (which can be up to 60 metres [196 ft] in length) run along the road. The area taken up by moving trams is often shown by tram lanes which will be marked by white lines or by a different type of road surface.

237. Take extra care where the track crosses from one side of the road to the other and where the road narrows and the tracks come close to the kerb. They will usually be separate traffic light signals giving instructions to tram drivers and to other traffic. Always give way to trams; do not try to race or overtake them.

238. Where tram stops have platforms, either in the middle or at the side of the road, you **MUST** follow the route shown by the road signs and markings. At stops without platforms, you **MUST NOT** drive between a tram and the left-hand kerb. If a tram is approaching a stop, look out for pedestrians, especially children, running to catch it.

239. You **MUST NOT** park your vehicle where it would get in the way of trams or where it would force other drivers to do so.

240. Cyclists and motorcyclists should take extra care when riding close to or crossing the tracks, especially if the rails are wet. **[2028]**

Pedestrians

241. Where trams run through pedestrian areas, their path will be marked out by shallow kerbs, changes in the road surface or white lines. If the track is unfenced, you may cross at any point. Look both ways and when it is clear, walk straight across; do not walk along the track.

242. Use designated crossing places where provided. Some may have flashing amber lights to warn you that a tram is approaching. Do not start to cross the track when the lights are flashing. If you are already crossing when the lights start to flash, it will be safe to continue. Avoid treading on the rails. **[2029]**

INDEX

References are to paragraph numbers

F

FALSE STATEMENTS AND FALSIFICATION, [372]-[375]

FENCES
obstruction of roads, Scotland, [186], [194]

FENCING OF OBSTRUCTIONS, Scotland, [178]

FIRE BRIGADE VEHICLE
drivers' hours, [43]
exemption
from excise duty, [49]
from speed limit, [129]
exemptions, from traffic signs, [1199]
meaning, [49]

FIRE EXTINGUISHER
in minibus, [1385], [1465]

FIRST AID EQUIPMENT
in minibus, [1386], [1466]

FOG
driving, Highway Code provisions, [2015]
lamps *see under* **Lighting**

FOOTPATHS AND FOOTWAYS
meaning, [162], [391]
motor vehicle trials on, [230]
parking on, heavy goods vehicles, [216]
Scotland
access over, [181]
animals, [197D]
meaning, [197D], [197G]
obstruction, [197D]
use of appliances, [182]
vehicular traffic, [197D]

FORESTRY VEHICLES
drivers' hours, [34]

FORGERY, [372]-[375]
licence and registration documents, [72]
registration marks, [72]

FRONTAGER
Scotland, meaning, [197D]

FUEL
regulations, [1380]-[1383]
see also **Gas; Petrol**

G

GAS
containers, valves, etc, [1461]-[1463]
emissions from vehicles, [1406]
gas-fired appliances in vehicles, [1440]-[1441]
gas propulsion
meaning, [84]
regulations, [1383], [1439]

GLASS
specification of, [1371]-[1372]

GONGS AND BELLS, [1378], [1444]

GOODS VEHICLES
certifying officers and examiners powers, [365]
drivers' hours *see under* **Drivers' hours**
driving licences *see under* **Driving licences**
heavy *see* **Heavy goods vehicles**

GOODS VEHICLES—*cont.*
inspection by operator, [272]
large *see* **Large goods vehicles**
licences, excise duty, rebate, [64A]
loading, [266]
maintenance, [266]
meaning, [30], [158], [391]
operating centre *see* **Operating centre**
operators' licence *see* **Operators' licence**
overloaded
offences, [269]
prohibition of use, [268]-[269]
plates *see under* **Plates**
power to weight ratio, [1388]
rear under-run protection, [1392]-[1393]
records of inspection, [272]
sideguards, [1394]-[1395]
speed limiters, [1377A]
speed limits, [163]
tests, [246]-[250]
appeals, [247]
certificates, [250]
falsification, [374]
following plating test, [1602]
maintenance and loading, [267]
of plated weight, [246], [248]
powers, [266]
of satisfactory condition, [246], [248]
testing stations, [249]
vehicles on road, condition of, [266]
under-run protection
rear, [1392]-[1393]
sideguards, [1394]-[1395]
unfit vehicle
offences, [269]
prohibition of use, [267]-[267A], [270]-[271]
weight *see* **Weight of Vehicles**

GRASS CUTTING VEHICLE, [160]
construction and use, [1153]-[1154]

GREEN CROSS CODE, [2003]

GROUND CLEARANCE OF VEHICLES, [1350]

GUIDED TRANSPORT SYSTEMS, [1790]-[1793]

H

HACKNEY CARRIAGE
meaning, [84]
seating capacity, [67], [1083]
signs on, [67]-[68], [1082]
specification of, [1093]

HAND-DRAWN VEHICLE
lighting, [1668]

HEADGEAR *see* **Protective headgear**

HEALTH SERVICE VEHICLE
exemption
from excise duty, [52]
from insurance, [343]
see also **Ambulance**

HEAVY COMMERCIAL VEHICLE
meaning, [158], [217]